books by william hjortsberg

Alp

Gray Matters

Symbiography

Toro! Toro! Toro!

Falling Angel

Tales & Fables

Nevermore

Legend of Darkness (A Screenplay)

Odd Corners
The Slipstream World of William Hjortsberg

jubilee
hitchhiker

**the life
and times
of Richard
Brautigan**

william hjortsberg

COUNTERPOINT

BERKELEY

this book is
for the board
of directors

"Talent does whatever it wants to do: genius only what it can do."

—Eugene Delacroix
(quoted by Kenneth Tynan in a letter to Johnny Carson, April 22, 1979)

"With talent, you do what you like. With genius, you do what you can."

—Jean-Auguste-Dominique Ingres
(quoted by Julien Green in his *Diary 1928–1957*)

"Genius does what it must, and talent does what it can."

—Owen Meredith
(quoted by John Powers in *Vogue*, January 1999)

"GENIUS DOES WHAT IT MUST, AND TALENT DOES WHAT IT CAN."

—Anonymous
(found in a fortune cookie, August 1993)

contents

part one: **flowerburger**

one: **john doe number 9** • 3

two: **honor thy father** • 21

three: **american dust** • 26

four: **tacoma ghosts** • 30

five: **dick porterfield** • 36

six: **midnight driver's ed** • 59

seven: **pounding at the gates of american literature** • 61

eight: **white wooden angel of love** • 65

nine: **the rub of a strange cat** • 82

ten: **family album** • 95

eleven: **reno** • 97

twelve: **frisco** • 102

thirteen: **on the beach** • 111

fourteen: **ginger** • 122

fifteen: **the general** • 131

sixteen: **scorpio rising** • 138

seventeen: **scaling mount parnassus** • 139

eighteen: **gone fishing** • 170

nineteen: **the fastest car on earth** • 183

twenty: **o, tannenbob** • 207

twenty-one: **moosemelon** • 209

twenty-two: **aborted dreams** • 228

twenty-three: **the museum** • 256

twenty-four: **the emperor's new clothes** • 261

twenty-five: **digger daze** • 264

twenty-six: **rx: dr. leary** • 279

twenty-seven: **banzai** • 281

twenty-eight: **bread and circuses** • 283

twenty-nine: **willard** • 309

thirty: **brief encounter** • 313

thirty-one: **summer of love** • 315

part two: bushido gunslinger

thirty-two: **hitching a ride** • 335

thirty three: **ten day barons** • 340

thirty-four: **the great public library publishing caper** • 375

thirty-five: **cover girls** • 377

thirty-six: **satori** • 391

thirty-seven: **fame's feathery crowbar** • 392

thirty-eight: **lit crit** • 448

thirty-nine: **my home's in montana** • 450

forty: **over easy** • 489

forty-one: **the five-year plan** • 491

forty-two: **stockholm** • 510

forty-three: **throwing a hoolihan** • 511

forty-four: **kids** • 557

forty-five: **tokyo throes** • 562

forty-six: **the paradise valley ladies' book club luncheon** • 582

forty-seven: **aki** • 584

forty-eight: **rattrap roulette** • 600

forty-nine: **banned in the boondocks** • 602

fifty: **rashomon** • 624

fifty-one: **trouble and strife** • 626

fifty-two: **r.i.p.** • 652

fifty-three: **midnight express** • 654

fifty-four: **shinola** • 690

fifty-five: **blowing in the wind** • 692

fifty-six: **deathgrowth** • 732

fifty-seven: **the itch** • 777

fifty-eight: **the pitch** • 778

fifty-nine: **the end** • 780

OM
for Richard

O
Venus
Unblinking
Third eye
Watching above
The grinning
Crescent moon
High
In a pale evening
Sky
Buddha
Dreams
Of love

3/11/96

*Written in the Utah desert, somewhere on Route 50
(the loneliest highway in America) on the road to
Fallon, Nevada, for Brautigan research*

part one:

flowerburger

RICHARD BRAUTIGAN NEVER heard his final gunshot. Traveling three times the speed of sound, the Winchester Western Super X .44 Magnum hollow point exploded up through the poet's head, destroying his face, dislodging his wire-rimmed eyeglasses, blasting off the back of his skull. Continuing on, the bullet tore a hole in the molding above a corner window, struck a one-by-four nailed inside, and fell back into the space within the wall. At the same instant, all his dreams, fears, hopes, and ambition were erased forever, his brain disintegrated, the nerves of his spinal cord were disconnected, and Brautigan's knees buckled, his body dropping straight down, as the weapon, a nickel-plated Smith & Wesson Model 28 revolver, flew from his lifeless hand. He was dead before he hit the floor.

It was a beautiful bright Sunday afternoon: September 16, 1984. Clad in tan corduroy trousers, a T-shirt, and socks, Richard Brautigan's body lay on its back in the main living area on the second floor of his house at 6 Terrace Avenue in Bolinas, California, a small seacoast village he referred to as "the freeze-dried sixties." His left front pocket held a crumpled $5 bill and a couple singles. A radio in the kitchen at the back of the house blared at full volume. Richard Brautigan was forty-nine years old when he died.

Next door, in a smaller house sharing the same unpaved semicircular driveway with Brautigan's place, his neighbor, Jim Zeno, watched football (Raiders/Chiefs) on TV with a friend. In the middle of a noisy touchdown, they heard an explosive boom outside. It seemed to come from Richard Brautigan's house. The two men exchanged a glance but said nothing, continuing to watch the game. Zeno's wife, Karly, came upstairs. "Did you hear that noise?" she asked. They discussed the strange sound, "definitely a loud bang," but there was no thought of going over to check on it. Part of being what Brautigan described as "impeccable neighbors" involved not entering his space except when invited, so the Zenos remained at home to watch Los Angeles come from behind and defeat Kansas City, 22–20, with a nineteen-yard field goal in the final minute of play.

Across the way, the acrid smell of cordite hung in the still, hot air. All the windows and doors at 6 Terrace Avenue were tightly shut, the blinds drawn. The shadowy house resonated with a radio's insistent discordant jabber. Four small bedrooms on the third floor were rarely used because Brautigan believed the ghost of a young Chinese woman dwelled in that part of the house. Various stories circulated about her. Some claimed she had drowned in the Bolinas Lagoon during World War I. Others said she'd been a servant, employed by the original owners, who had committed suicide in the house. Richard hung a looking glass on the wall over the stairway, telling his friend Dr. John Doss, "The reason I have a mirror here is because ghosts can't see themselves in mirrors." Brautigan's daughter, Ianthe, believed the mirror kept the ghost from coming downstairs.

Several visitors reported walking through mysterious cold spots, and an Eastern woman journalist claimed to have seen a young female sitting next to Brautigan on the torn black Naugahyde sofa while she interviewed him. When the writer Keith Abbott volunteered his pickup truck in 1973 to move boxes of books out to Bolinas, he was startled to see a momentary apparition in the tiny junk-filled upstairs east bedroom, "almost like a slide being placed in a projector of a girl wearing a white nightgown." He dismissed the unearthly vision as "a mild hallucination." Richard told him three other people had seen an identical specter.

The novelist Don Carpenter believed the ghost was a "twelve-year-old Japanese girl who lives in the house and determines what goes on." He based this assumption on testimony from two people who didn't know each other but had both seen the ghost on separate occasions. After Don's apartment in the city burned to the ground, he was living in his ex-wife's place in Mill Valley. Richard offered him the use of the Bolinas house for $100 a month, "a joke because the heating bill alone was $100 a month."

Keith Abbott and a buddy came over with his truck. They packed up Don's furniture and drove it to 6 Terrace Avenue. Because of a ruptured disc, Carpenter was unable to lift anything heavy, so he went inside to have a look around while Keith and his friend unloaded. "I've never had a more awful, dreadful, terrible, foreboding feeling," Don Carpenter recalled. "Except when I thought I was dying of cancer."

Don went back out to the driveway. All his furniture stood waiting to be moved inside. "Keith," he said, "I can't live here."

Because he had done none of the physical labor, Don felt uncomfortable about this. "These guys who were doing this for free. I didn't want to say, 'We've got to pack up this truck and go back to Mill Valley.' But I did and Keith said, 'I understand perfectly.' We packed up the truck and off we went."

The spacious second level served Brautigan as a combination living quarters and office. A large California state flag hung from the ceiling, functioning as a room divider between the barren fireplace and the kitchen door. The back roof leaked, and the floor boards in the rear had warped and buckled. The flag concealed the damage. Beneath it, the haunted sofa added solidity to the makeshift partition.

Richard Brautigan's six-foot four-inch body stretched full length in the southwest corner of the room. What remained of his head faced an unmade double bed, the tangled blankets suggesting a bachelor's inattentive housekeeping. His feet pointed toward the corner windows, where the .44 Magnum landed, barrel forward, on the seat of a blood-splattered white school desk, the kind with a single wide writing arm. A bloodied eyeglass lens rested upon it.

Brautigan's writing area, a large round table littered with various works in progress, stood to the right of his body, the hard blue chair he favored on the far side. A coffee cup sat among the scattered manuscripts and notebooks. Like some macabre action painting, blood and brains splashed vividly across the table's surface and sprayed the adjacent window. Richard's tan IBM typewriter sat nearby, the plastic cover gray with dust. When writer and performer Bobbie Louise Hawkins saw the shrouded machine she assumed he wasn't working. The ex-wife of poet Robert Creeley thought her friend had been fibbing when he came an hour late for a breakfast invitation, claiming to have written fifteen pages that morning.

Perhaps she didn't know Richard Brautigan did most of his preliminary work in longhand, scribbling away in spiral-bound notebooks and on stray scraps of paper, worrying poems and stories through multiple drafts in his pinched, childlike scrawl. His last efforts bore an ultimate validation: the writer's blood staining nearly every page. Brautigan left no final note rationalizing his suicide. This gory pile of manuscripts said it all.

Altogether, eight notebooks dating from earlier in the year lay, along with many assorted manuscripts, on the blood-soaked work table. For more than thirty years, Richard Brautigan had used his notebooks as a testing ground, beginning certain pieces over and over again. The material on the table contained many such false starts. There were more than two dozen handwritten drafts of poems and stories on the tissue-thin stationery of the Keio Plaza Inter-Continental Hotel, where Brautigan stayed when he was in Tokyo. Some were typewritten. Richard Brautigan had been a very fast typist. Machine-gun speed, blasting out a first draft with little thought for the niceties of spelling or punctuation, two skills he never mastered. "Determination," rendered quickly, became "dtertination." Richard paused only when something felt wrong. He used a repeated virgule (//////) to cross out unwanted material.

All his work went to a professional typist who corrected any orthographic oversights. The idea was to get it all down on paper as fast as possible, straight from the unconscious to the page, first word—best word, a notion Brautigan acquired in San Francisco's North Beach during the early "Renaissance" days of the Beat movement. Breakneck first drafts proved an apt counterpoint to his pensive notebook ruminations.

Six typed transcriptions from earlier handwritten drafts were stacked neatly elsewhere in the room, untouched by Brautigan's blood. These included "The Complete Absence of Twilight" (a brief, haunting piece of fiction, which Brautigan optimistically referred to as a "book" in a letter sent to his agent, Jonathan Dolger, from Tokyo the previous April; three short stories ("Mussels," "The Habitue," and "Sandwalker"); a six-page extract from "The Fate of a West German Model in Tokyo," compressing the manuscript into twin enumerated lists of monologue; and a finished version of "Russell Chatham: Portrait of an Artist in his Time," which had gone through three previous incarnations in the notebooks.

Russell Chatham had lived in downtown Bolinas in the 1960s. The painter rented an apartment and a separate studio upstairs in the old H. Hoirut property, a complex of late-nineteenth-century buildings on Wharf Road. At the time the first floor was the home of a hamburger joint called Scowley's. Chatham and Brautigan did not know one another back then. The impoverished poet lived in San Francisco and would not buy the house on Terrace Avenue until 1972. The painter, yet to sell a single canvas, settled in Bolinas, attracted by the low rents.

For years, the simple, cheap life lured numbers of artists and bohemians north from the city. During Chatham's residency, Bolinas was also home to poets Robert Creeley and Tom Clark (then poetry editor of the *Paris Review*); painter Arthur Okamura; a movie-making outfit called Dome Film Productions; writers Thomas McGuane and William Hjortsberg (both unpublished at the time; Chatham later referred to them as "two guys like me who didn't have jobs"); and Paul Kantner of Jefferson Airplane, who owned a large home on the beach at the far end of Brighton Avenue, once a popular seaside teahouse called The Ship's Lantern.

Bolinas, California, had hardly changed in over a hundred years. Local citizens tore down the highway signs marking a turnoff from Route 1 faster than the California state road crews replaced them. At the time of Brautigan's death, the old blacksmith shop still functioned as an auto repair garage. Smiley's Schooner Saloon, built in the 1850s, had operated as a tavern almost all of that time under various names. Across the street, a false-fronted grocery had been slicing cold meat and cheese at the same location since 1863. It was the town Richard Brautigan called "a hippie Brigadoon."

Set above the street, the three-story house at 6 Terrace Avenue, a dark, brown-shingled Arts and Crafts movement building made of locally milled redwood around 1885, was part of the Grande Vista Tract, Marin County's first subdivision. Screened by several tall redwood trees and a growth of Scotch broom nearly two stories high that blocked a potentially fine view of the ocean, the place remained perpetually in shadow. Overgrown with ivy, the garage resembled a small hill more than a building. Richard refused to have any of it cut, preferring the illusion of privacy provided by the dense foliage.

The house was gloomy inside as well. Raw ceiling beams and dark redwood walls had been unaltered since drying bouquets hung from the rafters when the place had been the summer home of Mary Elizabeth Parsons, who wrote the influential guidebook *The Wildflowers of California: Their Names, Haunts and Habits* (first published in 1897). Brautigan's poet/playwright friend Michael McClure remembered Parsons's "jewel-like descriptions of California wildflowers" as "among the best prose-poetry of the end of the nineteenth century."

On September 16, 1984, the musky smell of congealing blood lingered in the enclosed air, not the sweetness of dried flowers. The loud radio echoing from the kitchen drowned an insistent buzz of gathering flies. As it grew dark, the automatic timer controlling the electric lights switched on. A little later, the phone rang. After four rings, the answering machine picked up and the tape of Richard's voice sounded bland and noncommittal: "This is the recorded voice of Richard Brautigan. He's not in right now. Leave a message when you hear the beep and I may return your call." But there was no beep, only a dull click. Richard had set the machine on "answer only," making it impossible to leave a message.

"Hello, Richard . . . ? Are you there . . . ? It's me."

No answer, just the buzz of disconnection. The caller was painter Marcia Clay, an old friend from San Francisco who had reunited with Brautigan only two days earlier after a four-year estrangement. She'd phoned an hour before midnight the previous night. He said he'd call right back but never did. Marcia waited ten minutes and phoned back, getting Richard's answering machine message. Alone on a hot night in the city, she made a third attempt to reach him, hearing only the noncommittal message.

For the next few days, the old house remained a noisy tomb. No one came around to visit. Brautigan had alienated himself from most of his poet friends in Bolinas and had recently been eighty-sixed from Smiley's for his unpleasant, erratic behavior. Occasionally, the phone rang. Although she wrote in her diary that she didn't "have the energy or interest to play cat and mouse with him," Marcia Clay kept trying to reach Richard. So did Curt Gentry, Don Carpenter, Andy Cole, and Tony Dingman, writing and drinking buddies from the old days in North Beach.

Montana poet Greg Keeler tried to leave a message. Ditto journalist Toby Thompson, calling from Cabin John, Maryland. Richard's attorney in Livingston phoned three times the following week. Jonathan Dolger, his New York literary agent, made several calls. He had good news regarding the possible sale of the film rights to *Dreaming of Babylon* to Warner Brothers. They all got the answering machine with its disconcerting click.

At some point early in October, one of the neighbors came over, annoyed by the blasting radio. Because the stairs to the upper deck had rotted and been removed, whoever it was knocked on the door of the true first floor, a nearly empty spare bedroom and storage area. No answer. Brautigan had departed on one of his lengthy journeys without having the decency to turn off the damned radio. Wanting to silence the round-the-clock radio playing, the irate neighbor found the central power breaker by the meter and switched off all the electricity to the house.

Upstairs, all was quiet now, except for the metallic drone of the flies. There were many, many flies, a nightmare population of blowflies, houseflies, bluetails, and greenbottles swarming everywhere in the melancholy twilight of the shaded main room. They clustered densely about Brautigan's corpse. Thickening blood and the enormous head wound provided powerful attractions for these rapacious insects. The inexorable process of decay began the moment his body hit the floor a couple weeks before.

With the power switched off, the automatic timer failed to trigger the lights that night and the house remained shrouded in darkness. The Zenos next door thought nothing of it. Richard was always coming and going mysteriously. He had his own peculiar reasons for the way he did things. He had mentioned that he might leave for a hunting trip to Montana in early October. Maybe he decided not to leave the light-timer on. When the phone in Brautigan's office/bedroom rang, the answering machine, running now on internal batteries, continued to pick up and deliver the same noncommittal message. It was a perfect vanishing act. The dead poet had managed to completely disappear.

The long, hot California fall days merged into weeks. Heat accelerated the process of decomposition and the eager swarming flies, finding easy access through the massive cranial damage, deposited thousands of their eggs inside Brautigan's body. When they hatched, the cadaver teemed with maggots, the rice-sized larvae writhing in his decaying flesh. At the same time, the batteries in the answering machine began wearing down and the recorded message grew distorted, the words slurred, like a man underwater. Even this final echo of the poet's voice began to die.

If no one in Bolinas seemed to care that Richard Brautigan had disappeared (either they were no longer talking to him and just didn't give a damn or else he had told them he was leaving on an extended journey), others among his closest friends began to grow concerned. At one point, Klyde Young, a housepainter and friend of Brautigan's who had done odd jobs for the writer off and on for the past dozen years, ran into Jim Zeno in Stinson Beach. Young was alarmed to hear that no one had been to Richard's house in more than two weeks.

Soon after, Young talked with Tony Dingman, saying if he got authorization from Ianthe he would get into the house, break a small window, and check things out. Dingman had also been worried. The last time he spoke with Richard on the phone, the day before he died, Brautigan said he'd swallowed an overdose of sleeping pills the previous night but that they'd had no effect. Knowing his buddy once made a similar halfhearted suicide attempt after the breakup of his second marriage, Dingman didn't take this latest pill episode too seriously. But weeks without any word caused concern, and Dingman had several conversations with Richard Breen, another Brautigan crony. They both hoped Richard had gone back to Amsterdam with a Dutch critic who had visited California earlier that summer.

This didn't seem right to Klyde Young. He drove to Bolinas and wandered outside the gloomy house on Terrace Avenue. Nothing looked amiss. No mail had accumulated. Klyde figured if a body was inside he would smell it. There was no odor. The front porch steps were gone, yet, for inexplicable reasons, he couldn't bring himself to attempt the interior entryway stairs. Young looked through the windows. The blinds were drawn all the way around. He couldn't see a thing. No one remembered Brautigan being in town lately. Klyde Young assumed that he had taken off for the start of bird season in Montana, and headed back to Tiburon. Doubts remained, but he didn't want to take any drastic action on his own. How would he explain it to Richard when he returned?

On October 4, Jonathan Dolger sent a Mailgram to Brautigan's address in Bolinas reading: "Have been unable to reach you these past three weeks. Stop. Please call to discuss two new book and movie offers." This was exactly the sort of good news Richard had been waiting for. Receiving the message might not have saved his life but almost certainly would have prolonged it.

Up in Montana, things felt very bad. Where was Richard? He had missed the opening of the upland bird season and wasn't answering his calls. Becky Fonda felt particularly troubled by the garbled message on Brautigan's machine at the Bolinas number. Even when drunk, Richard didn't sound like that. She made several calls and discovered no one, including his agent, had heard from him in over a month. Joseph Swindlehurst, Brautigan's Montana lawyer who handled his accounts in Livingston, told her that Richard hadn't written or cashed a single check in all that time. Joe said mail was being returned unclaimed. He had called Dick Hodge and Joel Shawn, the author's former and current California attorneys, asking them to look into the matter. Something seemed terribly wrong.

Becky and her husband, actor Peter Fonda, talked things over and determined to find out what was going on. On October 23, 1984, they phoned San Francisco private investigator David Fechheimer, protégé of the legendary Hal Lipset and a pal of Brautigan's since the early sixties. The detective had also been worried about his friend. He told Becky Fonda that he'd been over to the Bolinas house before leaving on a business trip about three weeks earlier. He'd found the lights on and the radio playing within. The door downstairs was locked. Fechheimer made no attempt to force an entry after knocking and not getting any answer.

He didn't tell Becky he suspected there might have been a booby trap waiting inside. After twenty years in his peculiar business, Fechheimer figured it would be unwise to go into Richard's empty house in Bolinas under those circumstances without thinking about "Take this, you cock-sucker!" Another thing he didn't tell Becky was that he knew the moment she informed him Brautigan hadn't written any checks in over a month that his friend was dead.

David Fechheimer assured the Fondas he would get to the bottom of things. He told them he'd go out to Bolinas the next day. It had been on his mind to have another look at Richard's house later that week. Fechheimer asked Tony Dingman if he wanted to come along. Dingman declined, fearing it might turn out to be a "horror show," but suggested an acquaintance named Dwain Cox, a big guy who'd once been photographed for *People* magazine hauling Brautigan around San Francisco in a rickshaw. Dwain knew some people in Bolinas. Maybe he could get them to investigate.

Later the same day, twenty-four-year-old Ianthe Swensen called Dingman from her home in Santa Rosa. She had not spoken with her father since the previous June, but people had recently asked about him, and now she wanted to know, "Where's my daddy?" Dingman immediately phoned Curt Gentry and told him about Fechheimer's request. Having coauthored the best seller

Helter Skelter with Vincent Bugliosi, the district attorney who prosecuted Charles Manson, Gentry was well acquainted with the appalling grotesqueries hidden behind locked doors.

The writer had an old friend, a commercial fisherman named Bob Junsch, who lived in Stinson Beach. Curt had known him since the early days when they both worked as bartenders in San Francisco. Junsch also knew Brautigan, having accompanied him on his first adult trip to Montana. Gentry promised Tony Dingman he'd call out to Stinson right away. Bob was a stand-up guy, someone who could be counted on when the chips were down.

Bob Junsch moored his fishing boat, the *Pacific Fin*, in Morro Bay above San Luis Obispo and flew down from Marin County to make his living whenever the albacore or swordfish were running. Things were slow at the time, and Junsch was staying at home between trips when Curt Gentry called him on the evening of October 24. The next morning, Junsch and his deck hand, Jim O'Neill, made the short drive around the lagoon from Stinson Beach to Bolinas, arriving at Terrace Avenue a little after ten o'clock. They climbed out of the car and had a quick look. Everything felt still, mysteriously quiet. A dog barked somewhere in the distance. Some local mongrel with a red bandana tied around his neck. "Probably named 'Siddhartha' or 'Steppenwolf,'" Richard Brautigan once joked.

Before trying the door, Bob Junsch went around back, where the house was built up against the sloping hillside. Shading his eyes, he peered through a small uncurtained kitchen window about a foot square. He barely made out what looked to be liquid on the floor, as if something had been spilled. Junsch also glimpsed a single sneaker, "an Adidas-type shoe," lying alone and forgotten. Somehow, it looked wrong. Junsch felt things "had a bad ring to it." The back kitchen door was locked. He returned to the front of the old shingled house and had Jim O'Neill boost him up the corner onto the second-story deck.

A pair of French doors opened onto the porch, unlocked but tightly closed. Junsch pulled them open with a fierce tug. He was struck by an odor of rot so overpoweringly putrid as to seem almost tangible. Clouds of flies swarmed everywhere inside. Bob Junsch followed his nose hesitantly into the twilight gloom. Hundreds of larval shells crunched underfoot. An anticipatory dread assailed him. Looking around the unmade brass bed, Junsch spotted Brautigan's maggot-infested corpse stretched out in the corner.

He was a shocking sight, most of the head gone and his stomach exploded. The facial features were missing, the ruined skull gaping horribly. All of his remaining skin tissue had turned black. A large quantity of blood and the fluids of decomposition contaminated the floor around the body. For a moment, Bob Junsch stood transfixed by shock. At that same instant, downstairs under the house, Jim O'Neill had been poking around. Discovering the power was turned off, he flipped the main switch back on. The radio in the kitchen blasted full volume into raucous life and the sudden unexpected clamor "scared the shit" out of Junsch. He ran down the inside stairs, unbolting the door and rushing into the clean, fresh morning air.

Junsch blurted out what he had just seen upstairs to O'Neill. They went next door and told Karly Zeno of their grotesque discovery. "He's in there," Bob said, visibly shaken. "He's like totally undescribable. You can't recognize him at all." Mrs. Zeno got him a beer. Junsch didn't want to stick around. He wondered if he would ever wash the morbid taste of death from his throat. After calling Curt Gentry, Bob gave Karly Zeno his home phone number over in Stinson and he and Jim O'Neill took off.

Here the mists of time draw a confused curtain across the memories of the participants. David Fechheimer phoned the Marin County Sheriff's Office to report the discovery of Richard Brautigan's body. He remembers Bob Junsch calling him with the grim news. Junsch recalls it differently. Acting on the behest of Curt Gentry, he didn't have Fechheimer's number. "And Curt didn't call me to say, 'Go check on Richard. If you find him call Fechheimer.'" After leaving Bolinas, Bob Junsch drove straight up to Petaluma and headed for a bar.

Whoever called Fechheimer did so promptly. At about ten thirty, the dispatcher at the sheriff's office contacted Sergeant Weldon Travis and Deputy Joseph Dentoni, directing them to 6 Terrace Avenue in Bolinas, to investigate the report of a dead body discovered at that address. Upon arrival, Deputy Dentoni, the responding officer, was met by Karly Zeno. She told him friends of Richard Brautigan had seen what they thought was his body earlier that morning. Checking the residence, Dentoni found the front door ajar, just as Bob Junsch left it during his hasty departure. After mounting the stairs, the sheriff's deputy came upon "a decomposed male body lying on his back with the top part of his skull missing."

When Sergeant Travis had a look at the scene, he immediately contacted the Marin County Sheriff's Office and requested a response from trained investigators. Due to the condition of the body and a lack of any visible identification, neither of the lawmen could be certain the remains in question were those of Richard Brautigan. The initial report referred to the event as an "unattended death." At 12:40 PM, Deputy Dentoni phoned Bob Junsch's number in Stinson Beach. There was no answer.

Shortly before two o'clock, Sergeant Anthony Russo and Detective Dave Estes arrived from the sheriff's office in San Rafael. While Sergeant Russo began gathering evidence, Detective Estes was assigned the task of photographing the surrounding area. As reporting officer, Estes also prepared a rough sketch (a floor plan) of the second level of Brautigan's house. During Russo's examination of "the crime scene," he came across a pair of wire-rimmed spectacles, the right frame bent and one lens missing, lying on the window ledge near the "victim's" body. The right-hand lens was recovered from the arm of the blood-splattered, white-painted school desk.

Sergeant Russo also discovered the bullet hole in the molding above the southwest corner window. He removed the wood around the hole and subsequently recovered a spent large-caliber slug from within the wall. Russo bagged the evidence: the eyeglasses and missing lens, a tape recorder (containing a tape) found near the body, the nickel-plated .44 caliber Smith & Wesson (serial number N 284972), the spent bullet, and numerous miscellaneous notebooks and papers.

William Thomas, an investigator from the Marin County Coroner's Office, arrived and conducted his investigation after being briefed by the police officers. He had never before witnessed such a gruesome scene. Thomas noted the many fly larvae shells, some found and measured as far as thirty feet away from the cadaver. A set of false teeth turned up in the kitchen and was removed as possible evidence. (It was later determined they did not belong to the victim and had been kept by Brautigan as a novelty gag.) In the bathroom just off the office area, Thomas uncovered a variety of prescription medications: two bottles of Dalmane, 30 mg.; one bottle of Tranxene, 7.5 mg.; a bottle of Halcion, .5 mg.; and tubes of Tridesilon topical ointment and Montistat Derm, 2 percent, along with three packages of Durex condoms.

For most of the afternoon, the police were in and out of the Zenos' house next door, using their telephone. From overheard fragments of conversation, Jim and Karly concluded some question remained as to whether it was indeed a suicide. Perhaps homicide had been committed at 6 Terrace Avenue. When Jim Zeno asked one of the officers, "Well, do you think someone might have killed him or something?" the detective replied that it was possible. Further talk concerned the bullet's entry and exit path. They didn't seem to align in the normal fashion of a suicide. What about the downstairs door, was it locked or unlocked? And if this guy Brautigan was supposed to be some kind of writer, how come he left no note? They had no way yet of knowing if the victim actually was Richard Brautigan. Officially, it was just the ninth unidentified male body found in Marin County so far that year.

Zeno informed them one way to be certain was to look at his cock. Richard had told him that years of herpes had left his penis covered with knobs and ridges. Brautigan joked about his "built-in French tickler."

"Cock, hell," said the cop. "We're scooping him up with a shovel."

Marin County had no central morgue, so the Coroner's Office contracted with individual mortuaries, chosen geographically on a month-to-month rotation. In October 1984, the designated morgue for the area was the Russell and Gooch Funeral Chapel of Mill Valley. The firm's removal van arrived at 6 Terrace Avenue in Bolinas in the afternoon. Bagged and anonymous, the body identified as John Doe number 9 was loaded into the meat wagon and driven away. Soon after, the yellow tape went up and the residence was officially sealed.

By four fifteen, Sergeant Russo, Detective Estes, and Coroner's Investigator Thomas gathered in the preparation room at Russell and Gooch on Miller Avenue for an examination of the body. They cut away and searched the stiffened clothing, finding no personal identification. The wadded currency was all his pockets contained. While Bill Thomas had a closer look at the extensive damage to the cranial area and noted the gold restorations in the victim's molars, the two detectives checked out the handgun. The shiny Smith & Wesson revolver was found to be loaded with five live rounds and one spent shell in the top position of the cylinder under the hammer. The weapon was dusted for latent fingerprints and shipped for further testing, along with the bullets and spent shell, to the Department of Justice Criminalistics Laboratory in Santa Rosa.

Bad news traveled fast. Becky Fonda heard about Richard's death through David Fechheimer and passed the sad word along. John Fryer felt angry upon hearing from her. A Western horseman at heart, Fryer operated the unique store (Sax & Fryer's in Livingston) his grandfather had founded in the 1880s. "Richard finally found a way to hurt all his friends at once," Fryer said.

As it happened, most of the Montana gang was off in New York at the time, staying at different hotels, pursuing various careers, their trajectories randomly intersecting. Tom McGuane was in town to celebrate the reissue of *The Bushwhacked Piano* in the new Vintage Contemporaries series, along with Jim Crumley for *Dancing Bear*. Russell Chatham was there to discuss a future one-man show of his paintings. William "Gatz" Hjortsberg was working on a screenplay outline with Paris-based film director Bob Swaim. Jim Harrison had come in for meetings with his agent, Bob Dattila, and his publisher, Seymour Lawrence, who had also published Brautigan for nearly fifteen years.

Becky called from Montana and word quickly spread, from hotel room to hotel room. Tom McGuane commented that "if Richard committed suicide to punish us he did a good job." That evening, Chatham, Harrison, Hjortsberg, Dattila, Lawrence, and others gathered for a huge Chinese feast at a restaurant on the East Side, raising a sad toast, bidding a departed friend farewell. Sam Lawrence put it best, paraphrasing literary scholar F. O. Matthiessen (his professor at Harvard, who committed suicide by jumping out of a Boston hotel window), when he said Richard "died of the Great American Loneliness."

The following morning (October 26, 1984), pathologist Ervin J. Jindrich, MD, performed an autopsy on what was left of John Doe number 9. Dr. Jindrich repeatedly noted the presence of extensive maggot activity. In the thoracic cavity he found only residual tissue, with a few fragments of identifiable lung and heart within the pericardial region. In the abdominal cavity there was a small amount of dried parchmentlike material appearing to be residual intestine. He uncovered no evidence of internal hemorrhage and no trauma to the ribs, thorax, or vertebral column. What was left of the head was deformed, flattened in a transverse direction, with the superior scalp and calvarium absent. The skull was massively fractured and in numerous small fragments, containing no remaining brain tissue. Contrary to police speculation, the external genitalia revealed an identifiable penis.

Dr. Jindrich finished his work by eleven o'clock. He was unable to detect any powder residue on the victim's head and found it impossible to determine whether a large defect above the right ear was antemortem or caused by insect destruction. His diagnosis revealed only a gunshot wound to the head with marked postmortem decomposition. Before typing up his report, the pathologist completed a couple final tasks. He surgically removed Richard Brautigan's blackened hands for neutron activation studies. These tests would reveal the presence of microscopic gunpowder particles and demonstrate whether the subject had discharged a firearm prior to his death. Dr. Jindrich also retained the lower jaw and excised the upper for odontologic examination. Most of the upper front teeth were missing, avulsed from the impact of the fatal gunshot, yet many molars remained and hopefully surviving dental work would positively identify the victim.

A dentist's bill from Dr. Bennett Dubiner, DDS, who maintained an office on Sutter Street in San Francisco, was among the miscellaneous papers taken as evidence from Richard Brautigan's home. Contacted by the Marin County Sheriff's Department, Dr. Dubiner telephoned the Coroner's Office the same day as the autopsy and reported he had last seen the writer professionally on September 9, 1984. During that office visit he had taken three bilateral bitewings and one periapical X-ray.

The forensic odontologist for the Coroner's Office, Dr. J. Robert Laverine, was notified and immediately called Dr. Dubiner. Subsequent phone conversations compared the September X-rays with the victim's remaining postmortem teeth. There were three full gold crowns, two three-quarter crown bridge abutments, and two onlays in addition to two amalgam-filled molars. A couple of impacted upper third molars were also significant. The gold restorations and their radiographic outlines showing numerous concordant points proved beyond a doubt that the body in question was Richard Brautigan.

A set of x-rays from Dr. James E. Smith, DDS, Brautigan's Montana dentist, were being shipped down from Livingston over the weekend. Although a positive identification had been made, Dr. Laverine would not complete his final report until he had a chance to study this additional material. At the same time, a media bottom-feeding frenzy was well under way. The AP and UPI both put the story out on their wire services on the morning of the twenty-sixth, date line: Bolinas. Although the sheriff's office stated they had not positively identified the body, Seymour Lawrence publicly announced the author's death from his office at Delacorte Press in New York City.

Phones started ringing. Reporters from all over the country called Brautigan's friends, acquaintances, and lovers, past and present. Don Carpenter, among those contacted, remembered the interviews with a certain ironic relish. "It would have destroyed Richard to know how his friends are talking about him," he said. "It would have upset the shit out of him in a wonderful way and I sort of enjoy that. Because he was so secretive and he swore you to secrecy over the most minute details and now he can no longer swear anyone to secrecy. All the secrets, all the little secrets that he bottled up over the years, were being garbaged all over the place."

The quality of the news stories varied widely. One paper printed the AP wire copy, severely truncated, slugging it with the headline Hippie Author Dies. The *Oregonian* went with most of the AP story, running it as an obituary. The staid *New York Times* charted a more prudent course, not without certain inaccuracies, running the piece (October 26, 1984) above the weather map on page 6 of the second section, just before the classified ads. ("A body discovered yesterday by the police in a house in Bolinas, Calif., was believed to be the remains of Richard Brautigan, a quixotic counterculture poet and writer, his publisher said.") The San Francisco papers, the *Chronicle* and the *Examiner*, each carried long stories with the basic AP text sufficiently enhanced by staff writers to justify bylines.

Several newspapers (including the *Times* and the *Chronicle*) reported that Brautigan was born in Spokane, Washington (Tacoma, in fact), and that his first wife was named Virginia Dionne. (Virginia Alder's middle name was Dionne). Norman Melnick, writing in the *Examiner*, proved sufficiently inventive not to rely on the AP for his mistakes. He wrote that Brautigan "apparently did not complete high school" and that *Trout Fishing in America* was "a novel written during the San Francisco flower child era." Nearly every subsequent newspaper article included a quote from Tom McGuane: "When the 1960s ended, [Brautigan] was the baby that was thrown out with the bath water."

Over in his office at the Sheriff's Department Investigations Division in the Frank Lloyd Wright–designed Marin County Civic Center, Sergeant Tony Russo had too much work to spend time reading newspapers. At ten in the morning on October 26, he interviewed Richard Brautigan's daughter, Ianthe, and her husband, Paul Swensen. In her statement, Ianthe mentioned her father's financial difficulties, calling him "cash poor." Recently, he had begun borrowing money against the properties he owned in Montana. Her father had been depressed for quite some time, she told Sgt. Russo, and had been drinking heavily for the past five years. When alone and drinking, he would threaten suicide, most often talking about killing himself with a gun. In any case, he never believed he'd live a long life. Ianthe also said her father loved large-caliber nickel-plated handguns.

"Mrs. Swensen did not have any frequent direct contact with her father," Sgt. Russo observed in his report. He noted some confusion concerning their final conversation. Ianthe mentioned she last spoke to her father at the end of May, when he called her from the neighbors' house, not yet having the phone connected at his place. She also indicated that she had talked with him on Father's Day. In any case, it had been at least three or four months before Richard Brautigan's death since she last heard the sound of his voice.

Just before two, Sgt. Russo spoke with Judge Richard Hodge at the Alameda County Superior Court. Hodge was the executor of Brautigan's will and had been his attorney for a number of years. He remembered that during their last conversation, Richard said that he was writing a screenplay and sounded more "upbeat" than usual. Sgt. Russo asked Judge Hodge if Brautigan had been having problems with anyone.

Thinking it over, the judge replied that Richard had been concerned "about some sort of conspiracy to get him by some woman poet who lived in Bolinas." Rumors had circulated in the community that Brautigan had made "disparaging remarks" about a Vietnam veteran also living there. Judge Hodge had heard a story that the angry vet had come by to see Brautigan with a gun but that he had talked the matter over with him and had "gotten it settled." The judge observed in closing that he had never heard Richard Brautigan ever mention anything about suicide.

At 2:15 PM, Sgt. Russo called Joel Shawn at his law office in San Francisco. Shawn represented Richard Brautigan's legal interests in California but said he not seen his client recently. A lunch date for September 5, 1984, had been broken when Brautigan missed the bus into the city.

Shawn described the writer as being almost "childlike": honest, righteous, a "straightforward guy." Recently, he had seemed like "good old Richard" again, excited by the work he was doing in spite of financial problems. Asked about suicide, Joel Shawn said that Brautigan had never talked about it with him.

Twenty minutes later, the detective telephoned Joe Swindlehurst in Livingston, Montana. The attorney stated that he last spoke with Richard Brautigan on September 13, when his client called to ask about selling his Montana property and to request some tax information for his accountant. Swindlehurst indicated Brautigan was experiencing financial troubles. Cash was not coming in, and he had mortgaged his Pine Creek place to raise money. Brautigan drank too much, Swindlehurst said. He hadn't heard any talk about suicide, but it would not surprise him as Richard had a fascination for large-caliber firearms. Swindlehurst told Sgt. Russo about the times the writer had shot off a handgun inside his ranch house. "Maybe somebody will notice the holes Richard Brautigan put in the floor."

At 3:00 PM, Sgt. Russo made his final phone call for the day, contacting David Fechheimer at his home and office on the corner of Hyde and Lombard. Fechheimer told Russo that, having spoken with Becky Fonda in Montana, he had called Bob Junsch the day before, instructing him to check out Brautigan's Bolinas house. If the sergeant informed him his friend's death had been a suicide, he wouldn't be surprised. Brautigan had long been interested in Japanese culture, he said, and in Japan suicide had "an altogether different meaning than it has in the United States."

Sgt. Russo asked the private detective his routine question, had the victim been having "any problems with anyone." Fechheimer and Judge Hodge had heard the same stories. He replied that Brautigan told him that he'd been involved in a feud over a Vietnam veteran with Joanne Kyger, a poet in Bolinas. Sgt. Russo heard the name wrong. He wrote it down in his report as "Kieter."

Over the weekend, the press coverage continued unabated. Richard Brautigan was back in the headlines one last time. With each subsequent newspaper story, the spread of misinformation widened. Inaccuracies included referring to Brautigan's daughter as "Ianthe Wiston" and stating Richard's body "was found by a private investigator hired by the author's New York agent." Most egregious, an utterly fictitious story reported that a half-empty whiskey bottle, "with sunlight refracting through it," had been discovered standing close beside the corpse.

On Saturday, October 27, Brautigan's obituary ran in the *New York Times*. It referred to him as "a literary idol of the 1960's who eventually fell out of fashion." Another obituary in the *Times* of London appeared the same day, incorrectly giving the author's age as fifty-one and saying that "in later years, feeling that he had been unfairly discarded by public and critics alike, he became depressed and began to drink heavily."

One piece so teemed with malice as to be worthy of Tom McGuane's adroit bon mot: "urinal ism." Warren Hinckle III (whose black eye-patch, Falstaffian manner, and ever-present basset hound, Bentley, made him a local San Francisco celebrity since the days when he edited *Ramparts* in the midsixties), had an eponymous column, "Hinckle's Journal," running in the *Chronicle*. In a piece he called "The Big Sky Fell In on Brautigan," Hinckle spun a vituperative tall tale suggesting the author had been destroyed by "a macho sense of competition" in what he termed "the jet-set enclave in the wilds of Montana."

The source of this dubious information was Ken Kelley, an Oakland-based journalist, acclaimed for his incisive *Playboy* interviews. It was Kelley who brought down Anita Bryant, letting her babble buoyantly about "queers." A recent friend of Brautigan's, Kelley had been invited to Pine Creek in the summer of 1979. Hoist by his own petard, Kelley rambled on and on to Hinckle, Jack Daniel's in hand. "A bunch of artistic weirdos living in rancher country," claimed Kelley. "It was the whole mental macho thing in Montana that I think really got to Richard."

Hyper and excitable, discursively elaborating to the eager note-taking Hinckle, Kelley appeared almost possessed as he furiously paced the deck of his shabby penthouse. "And the artists seemed compelled to compete in macho terms against the cowboys, and then tried to out-macho each other. Every night seemed to be the boy's night out. You had to get drunk and get your gun and shoot off more bullets than the other guy. It was all so competitive and so incestuous. Everybody knew everybody else and was sleeping with everybody else, et cetera."

Hinckle, after the easy score, made no effort to follow up or check on other sources. Ken Kelley found himself caught in the crossfire when the story broke. Two weeks later, he published more reflective feelings ("That's the way I am right now. Richard is dead, and I just feel rotten.") in a piece for *Express*, a free weekly newspaper serving the East Bay. By then it was too late.

Seymour Lawrence, Russell Chatham, and Terry McDonell (assistant managing editor) of *Newsweek* wrote letters to the *Chronicle*, denouncing Hinckle's column. Chatham called Warren Hinckle "a piece of festering tripe," and denounced Kelley. The painter suggested that "The word macho should be sculpted out of used razorblades and rudely rammed up the ass of every insensitive moron like yourself, who misunderstands and misapplies it every time they are called upon to discuss art or artists who are not domesticated or properly shelved and labeled." In a note to Ken Kelley, Hinckle called these letters "Hit mail from the Brautigan Mafia." The *Chronicle* never printed any of their angry words.

The most astonishing Brautigan news story to break on that late October Saturday originated in Tacoma, Washington, the city of the writer's birth. Having seen a report of Richard's presumed death on television in San Francisco the night before, his half brother, David Folston, telephoned their mother, Mary Lou Folston, at her home in Eugene, Oregon, to deliver the sad news. She told the press they had "corresponded frequently," but in truth, Mary Lou had not seen or heard from her first-born son in over twenty-eight years. Still, she proudly followed his career and growing fame since he burst onto the national scene in 1969.

After the call from her surviving son, Mary Lou phoned her sister, Eveline Fjetland, in Tacoma, to share the bad tidings and ask for a favor. This involved making contact with her first husband, a seventy-six-year-old retired laborer named Bernard Brautigan, who still lived in the area. When she left him, five decades earlier, Mary Lou neglected to mention she was pregnant. Now, she wanted him to know the truth. When Eveline phoned the elder Brautigan and told him Richard had been found dead in Bolinas, he replied, "Who's Richard? I don't know nothing about him."

Confused, Bernard Brautigan made a long-distance call from Tacoma. He had not spoken with his ex-wife in fifty years. Their conversation was brief and unpleasant. When Brautigan asked Mary Lou for an explanation, she snapped, "You know I was pregnant when you left."

"The hell I did!" he said and hung up.

Denying ever having had a son to the press, Bernard said, "If I had anything to do with it, how come she waited fifty years to tell me?" In her own telephone interview, Mary Lou was also evasive. "He asked me if Richard was his son, and I said no. I told him I found Richard in the gutter. I just packed my things in a bag and left. Richard never questioned who his father was and never was interested in it." In her opinion, there was no need to dwell further on the matter. "It's a dead issue," she said.

The next day, Sunday, October 28, Richard Brautigan's remains were cremated at the Pleasant Hills crematory in Sebastopol, California. There was no formal service. Mary Lou Folston had not been informed of the funeral plans. Like some perverted metaphor, the writer's hands and his jaws remained sealed in evidence bags, awaiting further tests. What became of them is not known. Brautigan's ashes were placed in a Japanese ceramic funeral urn. When he departed Montana for Europe and Japan the year before, Richard left the mysterious container in the care of Tom McGuane, along with his guns and fishing rods. Contacted following his return from New York, McGuane shipped the urn to California.

Twenty-seven years after Richard Brautigan's death, his ashes remain unburied. The Japanese urn resides, along with a bottle of sake, in the top drawer of a dresser in his daughter's Santa Rosa home. "I won't keep him forever," Ianthe told an interviewer for the *Pacific Sun* on August 29, 2000, "but he's safe now." A slat nailed to the wall prevents the drawer holding the urn from being pulled out more than a couple of inches. "He can't get out," she said, "whenever I think of putting him to rest, so to speak, I just can't. My stomach just churns."

On Monday morning, October 29, 1984, Herb Caen's column in the *Chronicle* led off with a long paragraph about Brautigan. The "Sakamenna Kid" recounted the first time he met the writer (1968) "standing at a Powell St. cable car stop, handing out seed packets on which he had written poems, a different one on each packet." The columnist remembered *Please Plant This Book*. Caen's piece ended incorrectly. Repeating the weekend's erroneous story that his New York literary agent had hired "the S.F. private eye who found Brautigan dead," Caen added a final dramatic irony. "The agent had news that might have saved Brautigan's life: an offer of a two-book contract."

Over in Marin County, Dr. Jim Smith's dental x-rays arrived from Montana. Dr. Laverine took the delivery and completed his odontological presentation. At five minutes after ten, Sgt. Tony Russo was on the phone, conducting his first interview of the day. He contacted James Sakata, proprietor of Cho-Cho, a restaurant on 1020 Kearny Street in North Beach. The .44 caliber Smith & Wesson revolver Richard Brautigan had used to end his life was registered to Mr. Sakata, and his name was engraved on the butt. He stated he had loaned the gun to Brautigan in March or April of 1984, around the time he returned from Japan. Brautigan told him that he didn't have any weapons in his Bolinas residence and "just wanted one around."

Sakata told Sgt. Russo that he lost Richard Brautigan's telephone number and had last seen him in September, when they discussed a long poem Richard wrote about the Los Angeles Olympics. Asked about suicide, Sakata said Brautigan never talked about it in a personal way but they'd once had a discussion about other writers who had taken their own lives. He remembered the focus had been on Ernest Hemingway. Sakata got the impression that Brautigan was "fascinated with his own suicide."

At quarter to three in the afternoon, Russo telephoned Becky Fonda at Indian Hill Ranch, her home in Paradise Valley, south of Livingston. Their conversation was brief. She told the sergeant she'd last spoken with Brautigan on the third of September, when he talked about coming up to Montana for the bird-hunting season. She tried calling him two weeks before but was unable to reach him. Brautigan's answering machine appeared not to be working. Alarmed by this, she contacted David Fechheimer, asking him to look for their friend. Mrs. Fonda mentioned Brautigan's fondness for guns, adding that he was an avid hunter and an excellent shot. Asked about the writer's death, she said that she would suspect suicide before foul play.

Sgt. Russo phoned Marcia Clay in San Francisco at 3:00 PM. It was his last call on this case for the day. There wasn't much to tell. Marcia Clay had seen Richard Brautigan only once in the past four years, when she encountered him somewhat accidentally at Enrico's Sidewalk Café on Friday, September 14, 1984. She described their meeting and a subsequent phone conversation, shortly after eleven o'clock on the night of the fifteenth. Clay said Brautigan wanted to read her a new piece of his writing and asked her to call back in five minutes. When she did, he didn't answer. After that, she tried calling several times but was unable to reach him. Marcia Clay said that during her last conversation with Richard he "seemed to be saying his goodbyes."

Tuesday, October 30, 1984, was the final day Sgt. Russo spent interviewing friends of the late Richard Brautigan. He made only two calls, the first at "1440 hours" to William Brown, a novelist who operated a landscape gardening business from his home on Brighton Avenue in Bolinas. Bill Brown had known Brautigan since the fifties but had not seen him recently. Pressed for particulars, Brown said as far as he could remember he thought he might have encountered Brautigan in Bolinas four or five weeks ago, just before his death.

Bill Brown stated that Brautigan was given to intense depression, especially when drinking. He referred to Richard as "a heavy drinker," adding that his personality "seemed to go downhill when he was drinking." He'd been particularly depressed during the last few months. Money was possibly at the root of the problem. Brown also mentioned Brautigan's admiration for Ernest Hemingway, saying they had talked some about Hemingway's suicide, although the subject of Brautigan actually taking his own life had never come up.

At 3:00 PM, Sgt. Russo made his last call, to Andy Cole, who refused to give his address. Living at the time in Bolinas, Cole said that he first met Brautigan in San Francisco approximately twenty years before. In his opinion, the author appeared industrious recently and happy with his current work. His only problem was that "because Bolinas had a small-town atmosphere, he was not able to cut loose as he could in the big city."

Cole rambled on to Sgt. Russo, relating a secondhand story of a recent unexpected and unpleasant meeting in San Francisco between Brautigan and his ex-wife Akiko. However, he got his dates badly jumbled, talking about both April and October. Cole said Brautigan told him he planned on returning to Montana soon to sell his "ranch," indicating that he was no longer interested in the place. When Cole didn't see him around, he assumed he had gone.

Andy Cole telephoned Richard Brautigan on Sunday, September 16, but only got the answering machine. He said he called three days in a row and became upset on the fourth because he knew that Richard had a beeper and could access his messages even when away from home. Confined to a wheelchair, Cole asked a friend to go over to the house on Terrace Avenue. He claimed his friend knocked on Brautigan's door and got no answer. Cole stated that Brautigan "never used drugs," and "was not constantly drunk as some others portrayed him."

That night, an impromptu wake for Richard Brautigan was held at Enrico's on Broadway in San Francisco. Established in 1959 by Enrico Banducci, a prominent figure in North Beach since the days when he took over the hungry i from its founder, Eric "Big Daddy" Nord, the sidewalk café had been a watering hole for the city's literary scene from the moment it opened. In his newspaper column, Herb Caen compared the place to the Algonquin Round Table. When Ted Koppel, in town earlier in July to cover the Democratic National Convention for ABC News, asked in an interview, "What kind of place are you running?" Enrico replied, "It's where sables and sandals meet." Brautigan had been hanging out there for two decades. Whenever he was in town, he came in every day.

No formal invitations were issued. By word of mouth, news of the event spread over the telephone, one old friend calling another. Curt Gentry was there along with Michael McClure, Don Carpenter, Tony Dingman, Donald Allen, Keith Abbott, David Fechheimer, Jeremy Larner, Judge Richard Hodge, and Peter Berg, one of the original Diggers. The artist Bruce Conner was in attendance, as were film directors Frances Ford Coppola and Phil Kaufman. Many of the more colorful members on the local scene were present, including restaurateur Magnolia Thunderpussy and Margo St. James, founder of COYOTE, the prostitutes' union. Marcia Clay wandered through, feeling that, had such an assembly occurred while Richard was still alive, she "would have been at his side, a closest companion, a mate to his soul as we were once."

The mood was very low-key. Enrico Banducci found it "grim." When someone asked Don Allen, who had first published *Trout Fishing in America* in the sixties, if he expected a suicide, Allen replied, "I wasn't surprised." Many of Brautigan's friends agreed. While Enrico thought Richard's death might have been a drunken accident ("he played Russian roulette with life"), Keith Abbott felt Brautigan "planned his suicide." David Fechheimer was of a like mind. "I think he'd decided to do it [at least a year before]," the detective said. "He was more at peace during the summer, like he'd passed a hurdle."

Everybody sat around, quietly talking, smoking, drinking to Brautigan. Glasses of Calvados, Richard's favorite drink, were raised. He used to call it "jet fuel." Enrico stocked this exotic French apple brandy especially for him. No one else ever ordered it, and when what was left behind the bar was gone, Banducci knew he would not carry it anymore.

Enrico told a story about the time Brautigan poured half a bottle of Calvados into his boot. "I said, 'What are you doing? Killing the bugs in your boot?' And he says, 'No, I'm going to drink it.' I said, 'Oh, okay, go ahead.' And he took the boot and drank it. It was running down his face." Every so often, someone else tried to tell another funny story about Brautigan, but nobody laughed. It was grim.

Jimmy Sakata did not attend the wake at Enrico's. He worried about how Brautigan's daughter and friends might react to his presence. Curt Gentry observed that Jim "was very concerned at how

[Ianthe] might feel." After the gathering dwindled, Curt and Tony Dingman took Ianthe down to Cho-Cho. "Jim was nervous about talking to her," Gentry said. Sakata acted with wonderful grace, telling stories, showing them drawings and Richard's letters from Japan. Ianthe, at her loveliest, "wanted to reassure him that she didn't blame him for anything."

At one point, she excused herself to go to the bathroom. When Ianthe was out of earshot, Sakata leaned over the bar and asked, "I don't suppose this is the time to ask when I can get my gun back?"

On November 2, 1984, Dr. Laverine filed his final Dental Reporting Form with the coroner's office in Marin County. He officially identified John Doe number 9 as the author Richard Brautigan. In the days and weeks that followed, newspaper and magazine stories appeared sporadically. The "Transition" section of *Time* carried the news of Brautigan's death on November 5. William Hamilton, the *New Yorker* cartoonist known for deftly skewering the fatuous small-talk of the filthy rich, had an unsigned lead piece in "The Talk of the Town," saying that his late friend Richard "had a penchant for absurdity akin to the jolly-serious outrages cooked up by the young Dadaists of Paris in the early nineteen-twenties." Even *People* ran a remarkably balanced and sensitive article, wishing Brautigan "So long, *sensei*. *Arigato*, pardner."

Seymour Lawrence issued "An American Original, an official statement," in which he said, "Richard was a joy to publish." Sam concluded: "Richard was a consummate craftsman not only in his use of language but in his choice of typography, design, jacket art, advertising copy. He was deeply involved in every detail and aspect of his books. He had an unerring eye and we gave him autonomy and latitude few authors enjoy. In Hollywood, it's called 'final cut.' He was an American original in the tradition of Mark Twain and he deserved the best. He never let us down except to die."

Longer investigations were yet to come. Lawrence Wright arrived in San Francisco, asking questions for a lengthy article commissioned by *Rolling Stone*, where Richard Brautigan had published his short stories and poetry in the sixties. *Vanity Fair* hired Michael McClure and East Coast writer Peter Manso, who had a book due out on Norman Mailer, to assemble a spoken-word examination of Brautigan's life and death. McClure later wrote, "Perhaps Richard killed himself because he'd made his point and used himself up like a butterfly uses itself up in the process."

McClure had been best friends with Brautigan in the early sixties. They had grown apart in recent years, but he still wished to protect his old white-port-drinking buddy's reputation when Peter Manso arrived from New York, eager to go for the jugular. Manso, a small, intense man, considered Brautigan's work "to be of very dubious significance," his death "the price paid for overnight literary fame in a decade of media hype and narcissistic self-congratulation."

Given Manso's preconceptions, Michael McClure did his best to rein in his new partner's killer instincts. At one point, they drove out to Bolinas to check out Brautigan's house. Approaching 6 Terrace Avenue on foot, Manso wanted to break in and snoop around. McClure dissuaded him. The place was still under seal by the police. They climbed up onto the second-floor deck and had a look in through the window. McClure clearly saw the death shadow of Richard Brautigan's body etched into the floorboards where his corpse had lain undiscovered for many long weeks. Brautigan's body fat had liquefied, what coroners call a "lipid breakdown," and had seeped into the wood, leaving behind a phantom image.

McClure saw just where his friend stood when he raised the revolver to his mouth. Turning, he took in Brautigan's final view. More than a decade later, when McClure recounted this event, slowly lifting his hand with the forefinger extended like a pistol barrel, tears welled in his eyes. Like a photographic ghost, Richard Brautigan's impression might have remained forever to haunt the old shingled house. The new owners tried scrubbing it free, but no solvents or detergent would do the trick. In the end, they had to rent a belt sander to erase the final tangible memory of the poet Ken Kesey called an American Bashō. "Five hundred years from now," Kesey observed, "when the rest of us are forgotten, they'll still be reading Brautigan."

two: honor thy father

A PIRANDELLIAN PARADOX ARISES when an author turns out to be a character in the story he's writing. Aspiring to truth only adds another layer of mystery, a further dimension to the puzzle. This is the tale of Richard Brautigan's life. Gatz Hjortsberg is only a peripheral thread in a rich and complex tapestry. For narrative purposes, I plan on referring to myself in the third person. But, quick as a three-card monte dealer, I've slipped the first-person singular in under the reader's nose even when promising otherwise. Verbal sleight of hand. Nothing is quicker than the I.

Richard Brautigan was my friend, my neighbor for seven years, and a writer whose work I admired long before we met. In small, unexpected ways, my own investigative journey became entwined with Richard's story. While wishing to remain concealed behind a third-person identity, from time to time, I must step out of the shadows and into a personal pronoun.

Richard Brautigan knew nothing of his paternal lineage. A sequence of nearly anonymous stepfathers recycled through his young life. His true father's identity remained a mystery. In researching Brautigan's life, I spent more time with his father than he ever did. Richard rarely spoke of his impoverished childhood in the Pacific Northwest. One memory often retold involved a youthful search through downtown Tacoma for a man he'd been told was his father. His kid odyssey ended in a barber shop, the talc-scented bastion of 1940s masculinity. Richard approached the man he'd been told was his father. When he identified himself, the stranger steered Richard outside, handed him a big shiny silver dollar, and told him to go to the movies.

In her touching memoir, *You Can't Catch Death*, Ianthe Brautigan wrote: "When he was about four, Mary Lou had pushed him into a room with his father. My father watched him shave without saying a word and then his father handed him a dollar." A second meeting occurred when Richard was about seven, outside the restaurant where his mother worked as cashier. His father happened along and stopped where he was playing on the sidewalk. Just enough time to say hello and give the kid fifty cents. Then, he was gone forever, a memory lost in a dream.

Bernard Frederick Brautigan, the man later identified as Richard's father, also knew very little of his own paternal genealogy. He was born on July 29, 1908, in Winlock, Washington, an isolated logging town in rural Lewis County. His father, Frederic "Fritz" Brautigam, born on January 12, 1878, in Hirschberg, Westfalen, Prussia, emigrated to the United States, sailing from Antwerp on the SS *Kensington* and arriving in New York on September 12, 1899, to follow the path of his uncle Ferdinand, who had come over twelve years earlier.

The original spelling of the family name, "Brautigam," so carefully rendered by Fritz in his fine Prussian copperplate hand on numerous courthouse documents, only gradually evolved into

"Brautigan." In the 1910 census and the birth registration of his last child, Fritz spelled his surname with an "m." At that time, his uncle Ferd was already known everywhere as Brautigan.

Fritz quickly learned English and became a naturalized citizen, moving to the state of Washington at the beginning of a brand-new century. On June 14, 1906, Fritz Brautigam married twenty-three-year-old Rebecca Kingston, in a simple Catholic ceremony. Rebecca was born in Oakland, California, to George Kingston and Hanorah Hayes, both Irish immigrants. By 1900, the Kingston family moved to Lewis County and bought a farm. Fritz Brautigam died on July 1, 1910, three weeks before his wife gave birth to their third child. At the time, Bernard was not yet two years old.

Rebecca Brautigan remarried a cook named William Morisette who had also come west from Wisconsin. Bernard Brautigan grew up next to the oldest in a mixed brood of eight kids. According to Mary Lou Folston, two of them died suicides, another drank herself to death at age twenty-four, and one succumbed to an infection from a self-induced abortion. "That was the craziest family," Mary Lou remembered. "They never talked about anything they did. They just did it and forgot it."

When first investigating the life of Richard Brautigan in January of 1991, the story of the missing father who resurfaced only after news reports of his famous son's suicide intrigued me. I found Bernard Brautigan's phone number in Tacoma through information and gave him a call. The voice on the other end of the line sounded gruff and impatient. He clearly had no interest in further questions six years after Richard's death. "Don't want to talk about it!" he grunted brusquely when I brought the matter up.

I mentioned the book I was researching and said I would be happy to present his version of events.

"Not interested," came the curt reply of an old man who didn't want to be bothered.

Feeling uncomfortable, I muttered something about how he'd talked plenty to the newspapers when the story first broke. "Go read the newspapers then," Brautigan snapped, slamming down the receiver.

The following June found me snooping around the Pacific Northwest again. I spent several weeks in Eugene, Oregon, where I interviewed Mary Lou Folston, as well as several of Richard's friends from high school, and unexpectedly stumbled upon a cache of six early Brautigan notebook manuscripts sealed for more than thirty-five years in a safe deposit box belonging to an old woman named Edna Webster. The key was lost, and I hired a locksmith to drill the box open. After Xeroxing this serendipitous literary treasure trove, I headed north to Portland and on to Tacoma, Washington, where I paid $11 for a photocopy of Richard's birth certificate at the Health Department's Bureau of Statistics.

Richard Gary Brautigan was born at the Pierce County hospital. His mother's maiden name was entered as Lula Mary Kehoe, age twenty-three; occupation, housewife. Bernard F. Brautigan, a "common laborer," aged twenty-seven, had been listed as the father, with 813 East Sixty-fifth Street, Tacoma, recorded as their shared address. The baby's birth was declared legitimate.

I looked up Bernard Brautigan in the white pages by a pay phone at the Board of Health. The address listed on Sixty-fifth Street was not that far away. I found the place easily, a modest one-story house on a side street off McKinley Avenue, set well back off the road behind a spacious sloping lawn fringed by fruit trees. A low fence bordered the property, and a sign on the gate read

BEWARE OF THE DOG. Walking to the front steps, I exercised a certain caution, half-expecting huge red-eyed Dobermans to leap savagely for my throat. My fears verged on the preposterous when a lap dog's enthusiastic yapping greeted the doorbell's ring.

A moment later, a small ancient man appeared behind the screen door beside the frantic leaping terrier. Veiled by wire mesh, his shadow-masked features were difficult to discern. I remember thinking it curious that two such tiny people (Mary Lou Folston was a petite woman) might have produced such a towering son. I introduced myself, mentioning my previous phone call seeking an interview. His brusque manner remained the same. He told me through the screen that he had nothing more to say about the matter. I said his son was one of the most famous American writers of the century. "He's not my son!" Brautigan spat venomously. "That woman even said so."

Feeling like a gambler with little to lose, I called his bluff. "I'll pay you $100 an hour to talk with me," I said. Bernard Brautigan shut the door in my face.

The late summer of 1993 found me back in the Pacific Northwest. I attended Richard's fortieth high school reunion in Eugene, an event he would himself have avoided like a dose of the clap. One inebriated woman unfamiliar with Brautigan's work cornered me in a banquet room at the sprawling Valley River Inn. "Why do you want to write about him for?" She waved her plastic cocktail glass and told me she wrote professional verse for greeting card companies, a career she considered more worthy of a biography.

Early in September, I worked my way back up the coast to Tacoma for more interviews. I took advantage of a sun-drenched day and explored Richard Brautigan's childhood neighborhood with a simple aim-and-shoot thirty-five-millimeter camera. Snapshots provide handy visual aids when writing description. I proved such an inept photographer that all of the film came out blank.

Circling the narrow two-story white frame house on East Sixty-fifth Street where Richard had lived as a small child, shooting a roll of film, I thought about Bernard Brautigan's place, only ten blocks away down McKinley Avenue. It made sense to get a couple of photos there. I drove to the little house set back from the road. Everything looked the same, the metal sign on the gate still warning of dangerous dogs. Not a soul in sight. With the aplomb of a spy, I pulled out the camera.

Perhaps never to be in Tacoma again, I decided to give the interview another try. "What can he do, shoot me?" I thought, retracing two-year-old footsteps. I rang the doorbell. A cosmic eraser swept clean the blackboard of the past. Ben Brautigan's mood (Mary Lou Folston said he was called Ben) seemed as sunny as the bright late-summer day. My first question got him talking and he stepped out into the afternoon's warmth, followed by Buff, his surprisingly docile little dog.

I asked if I could turn on my tape recorder. Ben Brautigan agreed. He'd been married to Lula Mary Kehoe for about seven years when they broke up. There was another man. "She was running around," the old man insisted. "Yeah, yeah. Sure, she knew it was Ron Bluett. He lived not very far from us out there on 64th and McKinley. But, we were split up for a long time before we got a divorce. And I got sewered [sic] for divorce and got the divorce."

"And you think this fellow, Bluett, was the actual paternal father?" I asked, as Buff sniffed around our feet.

"Oh, yes, yes, yes, I know. I'd swear to it. Absolutely. She would, too, if she wanted to, you know, make herself clear." Frowning with assumed sagacity, he tried to sum up his thoughts about Richard. "For her to say a thing like that, that's what hurt him. He knew that in his mind all this stuff was going on that he has no way to prove it."

Ben tossed a worn tennis ball across the yard. Buff barked in frantic pursuit. I said Richard's mother obviously never told him anything about this man, Bluett.

"No, no, no. And if she ever told him anything about me being the father, it would seem like he'd come up here."

Somewhat hesitantly, I brought up Richard's claim of seeking him out decades before in a barber shop.

"It's just a story, that's all it is," Ben Brautigan said.

I asked him if he thought Richard had made the story up.

"Yeah. Because if I had a feeling that he was—I'd invite him over so we could talk. For coffee or a glass of beer or something. But, I have no idea, no idea."

I looked carefully at Ben Brautigan. Although he was a short man and eighty-six years old there was something about the sharpness of his long nose and the emphatic candor of his distant blue eyes clearly reminiscent of Richard. "So," I asked, "your marriage with Lula Mary Kehoe had broken up considerably long before the child was born?"

"Oh, yes, yes, yes, yes, yes. Yeah. I was probably single, away from her, for three, four years."

When I mentioned that Mary Lou had listed him as the father on the birth certificate, Ben replied, "Yeah, yeah. But, she comes out now and she says that she got that child alongside the road. Why did she use that figure?"

I said I didn't know. We talked some about Mary Lou's other three children, each by a different father. I mentioned it must have been a terrible shock to learn about Richard only after his suicide.

"Yes, it was." Ben's anger resurfaced. "I said, my god o'mighty! You know, to be a father and don't know nothing about it . . ."

"That's why I really wanted to hear your side of it," I said. "You never met Richard or even saw him and—"

"I don't know none of the family!" Ben Brautigan interjected.

"And when he was born, she never notified you then?"

"No, no, no, no."

I said it seemed highly unlikely that had he been the father she wouldn't have gotten in touch with him.

"Right in the neighborhood even," he snorted. "She's over there and I was here and he was over in the hospital."

I was astonished. "You were living in this house in '35?" I asked. "Right here on Sixty-fifth Street?"

"Yeah. It's in the phone book."

"Right. And she never said a word to you?"

"No, uh-uh, not a word. Why should I hide it?"

"She put your name on the birth certificate but didn't bother to tell you?"

"Yeah, yeah." Old Ben Brautigan stared thoughtfully out over the fruit trees shading his lawn. "I wish I had the opportunity to see him, not even talk to him, but see him. And, too, his mother to lie like that, to hurt everybody. Not only the poor kid had to suffer about it, but that it'll go on for years and years and years, till they find out what in the hell the real truth is. You know, if Lula knew that was mine," he mused, "why didn't she have nerve enough to step over a couple of doors and tell me?"

I asked if his ex-wife had ever requested any child support from him.

"No. It's funny, the hospital didn't come after me to pay for the bill."

"They never did? They never approached you?"

"No, no. It's funny. It isn't a lot of things, you know, that we try to figure out ourself [*sic*] in our own mind, but that's as far as we get, is to try to figure 'em out." Ben Brautigan struggled to express the great eternal conundrum of never knowing the answers to anything. Wrestling with the ineffable seemed to tire him. Something inside sagged a little. His watery eyes lost their focus for a moment as he stared at the endless sky.

A more relentless and diligent investigator might have probed on, but I didn't have the heart for it. Ben and I talked about the trolleys that once ran the length of McKinley Avenue in the thirties and how he had worked as a laborer in a local plywood factory for most of his life. I remarked what a pretty spot he had, saying I understood why he'd happily lived here for nearly sixty years.

"Yeah," the old man murmured, "I lost two wives living here. I was married to one, I was married to her for thirty, about thirty-two years."

"Your second wife?" I asked, patting Buff as he nosed around me.

"Yeah. And my third wife, I was married to her. She died not too long ago, about five years. She died of cancer. She didn't have cancer when I married her, but she got it and picked it up fast."

Not knowing quite how to reply, I told Ben Brautigan that he looked to be in very good health. I said I hoped he continued to have it.

"I do, too. I do, too. There's a lot out here yet to enjoy."

We talked a bit longer but I couldn't think of much more to say. "Any time I can help you, stop in," he called as I headed back to my car. I figured on phoning him once I sorted out my notes. I might as well have been a paving contractor on the highway to hell. When I tried to get in touch with Ben Brautigan again, he was dead.

three: american dust

IN HIS WONDERFUL short story "Revenge of the Lawn," Richard Brautigan combines details from the lives of his grandmother and great-grandmother to create a character who, "in her own way, shines like a beacon down the stormy American past." Brautigan's great-grandmother had a poem for her name. Madora Lenora Ashlock was born on April 20, 1856, in Collin County, Texas, just across the line from the Indian Territory. There had been Ashlocks in North America since 1720.

At sixteen, on January 9, 1873, Madora wed her first cousin, William Ashlock, a tall, charming man six years her senior. The Ashlocks returned to Greene County, Illinois, where William's branch of the family had settled on land made available to veterans of the war of 1812. Altogether, they had nine children. The youngest daughter, Elizabeth Cordelia (called "Bessie"), born in Woodville, Illinois, on September 30, 1881, became Richard Brautigan's grandmother. Mary Lou described her mother as a "big Spaniard woman, six foot two, dark eyes, and dark hair . . . quite a stature about her."

Life on the Ashlock farm found its way into Brautigan's fiction. The episode when Madora plucked a flock of drunken geese reverberated for a hundred years through family legend until it came to rest in "Revenge of the Lawn." Knowing his great-grandfather, William Ashlock, signed up with the Pinkerton National Detective Agency may have inspired Brautigan to write *Dreaming of Babylon: A Private Eye Novel 1942.*

Not much is known about William Ashlock's career as a shamus. Late nights in low-life taverns disguised as somebody else led the dark-haired detective into the company of loose women. It nearly killed Madora Lenora when she discovered her husband's philandering. She sued for divorce, not a common practice in the nineteenth century. Dora Ashlock was the first in her devout Catholic family to take such a drastic step. Like modern single mothers, Madora went off to raise her large brood on her own.

Her daughter Bessie Cordelia Ashlock first married Michael Joseph Kehoe, a Boston Irishman who listed his occupation as "peddler." The couple settled in St. Louis, Missouri. With Kehoe, she had two daughters, Eveline Elaine, born in 1909, and two years later, on April 7, 1911, Lulu (baptized with the middle name Mary), who was called "Tootie" as a child and "Mary Lou" later in life. Beginning a lifelong habit of reinventing herself, Bessie shed a year from her age on the her second daughter's birth certificate.

Things didn't take with Kehoe. Like her mother, Bessie divorced her husband. She soon remarried. Jesse George Dixon was a carpenter from Kentucky. On July 21, 1914, Bessie had a son by Dixon, naming him Jesse Woodrow, known to the family as "Sone." This time, Bessie was three years younger on the certificate. Two years later, the day before her thirty-fifth birthday in September 1916, another son, Edward Martin, followed. Bessie stated her age as thirty-one.

When Mary Lou was six years old, the Dixon family moved to the Pacific Northwest, settling in Tacoma, Washington. By 1920, the Eighteenth Amendment made Prohibition the law of the land. Before the "Jazz Age" was a month old, Congress passed the Volstead Act, and the twenties began to roar. Bootleg booze provided an opportunity for those with ambition and vision. Bessie Dixon, a natural-born business woman, had ample amounts of both. By decade's end, she was known as "Moonshine Bess."

In 1921, Mary Lou's mother worked at Manning's Coffee Shop on Converse Street in Tacoma. A regular customer, an Italian named Frank Campana, spoke broken English and had been a machine gunner during the world war. Mary Lou remembered him as an insulting man, "very crude and insolent." Her mother left Jesse Dixon and after an "ugly divorce battle," began a relationship with Campana that lasted for the rest of her life.

Bessie Dixon never married her bootlegger Italian lover. Frank Campana sold illegal hooch out of a place a couple doors down the street from Manning's. Bessie became his business partner. They opened a restaurant on Pacific Avenue and Twenty-fifth Street, housing a "blind pig" in the rear. In league with several other Italians, Frank and Bessie maintained a still hidden in the woods, cooking moonshine under the towering fir trees. They brought the booze into town in gallon jugs and hid it under the sawdust in a woodshed potato bin behind Bessie's place on 813 East Sixty-fifth Street.

Along with their speakeasy behind the restaurant on Twenty-fifth Street, Moonshine Bess and her Italian cohorts operated another joint known as Ruth's Place above a branch of the Bank of California in downtown Tacoma. Customers slipped furtively up the side stairs to buy hooch while the honest johns down below negotiated short-term loans. The bankers never suspected that bootleggers prospered above their heads.

When Ruth's Place got raided, Johnny Pisanni was upstairs taking a bath as the cops pounded on the door. His brother George thought it was an overeager client. The police stormed in and nabbed him. Hearing the commotion below, Johnny slipped out the bathroom window onto the roof of the bank, clad only in a towel. A neighbor spotted Pisanni prowling around in the rain and called the law, claiming a naked bandit was robbing the bank.

Somehow, towel-wrapped Johnny Pisanni eluded the law. His brother and Robert Columbini went to the slammer but didn't rat out their partners. George Pisanni was deported back to Italy and Columbini sent to McNeil Island Penitentiary for a three-year stretch. Frank Campana and Bessie Dixon got off scot-free. When Columbini was released from prison they paid him off for his silence.

In 1923, Bessie Dixon asked her mother to come live in Tacoma. Over six feet tall and pushing two hundred pounds, Dora Ashlock knew how to whip some sense into her unruly grandkids. With her mother keeping an eye on things, Moonshine Bess moved with Frank Campana to St. Helens, Oregon, a little town north of Portland on the Columbia River. They opened a restaurant there called The Boy's Place.

Tensions ran high in the little house on Sixty-fifth Street. Eveline's rebellious spirit did not take well to Grandmother Dora's restrictions and strict discipline. At sixteen, within two years of Dora Ashlock's arrival, Eveline ran away from home and went to live with Johnny Pisanni, Bessie's old bootlegging partner. They kept house together, as the saying went in those days.

The year before, in the summer of 1924, Mary Lou met Ben Brautigan for the first time. She worked in her mother's Twenty-fifth Street grill for $2 a day, helping out wherever needed. Brautigan worked nearby as a planer in the local plywood factory for the same princely wage: twenty-five cents an hour. He lived in a workingman's hotel above Bessie's restaurant and ate there day and night. She called him Benny. He was sixteen that summer. Mary Lou was thirteen.

Ben Brautigan kept coming around. Mary Lou observed he was a good steady worker, five days a week at the planing mill. He got a raise of ten cents an hour. At sixteen, Mary Lou said yes. Bernard Frederick Brautigan and "Lula Mary Kehoe" were married in the Pierce County courthouse in Tacoma on July 18, 1927, by Judge Frank A. McGill. Asked to designate "Spinster, Widow or Divorced," on the Marriage Return, Mary Lou wrote "spinster." Underage, she lied on the form, stating she was eighteen on her last birthday. The groom's mother and stepfather were the witnesses.

Within a couple years, the marriage was in trouble. So small he could wear Mary Lou's shirt, Ben Brautigan considered himself something of a dandy and a lady's man. A pint-sized sheik with a size 9 shoe, he fancied patent leather footwear and by 1929 was waxing his mustache, wearing his sideburns long, and putting on mascara. Half-inebriated, he'd flirt with the flappers and shebas crowding the speakeasies of Tacoma. "He'd go koochie, koochie, koo, and rolled his eyes around," Mary Lou said, scornfully recalling Ben's gin mill shenanigans. "My god, it was sickening."

When she was nineteen, during one of her numerous separations from Ben Brautigan, Mary Lou drove with Eveline and her now brother-in-law, Johnny Pisanni, down to St. Helens to visit their mother. When not running The Boy's Place with Frank Campana, Bessie Dixon raised canaries in the apartment upstairs above the tavern, and her musical flock numbered around two dozen. Before Mary Lou left, Bessie gave her a canary.

Back in Tacoma, Mary Lou was drinking pop at the New Country Grocery, the business her sister and Pisanni operated across from the Union Pacific depot on Pacific Avenue. Jealous because she didn't also get a gift canary, Eveline stepped up and smacked the bottle into Mary Lou's mouth, knocking out her front teeth.

Eveline ran. Mary Lou nailed her sister between the shoulders with the empty bottle. Eveline gained the safety of her bedroom, locking the door behind her. Furious, Mary Lou got an ax. Johnny Pisanni interceded, dropping to his knees before his sister-in-law as she prepared to chop down the bedroom door. "Please, Tootie," he pleaded, "I just rent this place. I'll be evicted. Don't do it! Don't do it." In the end, Mary Lou relented. She put down the ax, collected her canary, and left.

Nineteen thirty was a bad year for Mary Lou Brautigan. On March 13, she came down with appendicitis and had surgery. A month or so after the appendectomy her grandmother grew sick with cirrhosis of the liver. In May, Ben moved back into the family home on sixty-fifth street to help take care of Mary Lou.

Not long after, the police came by the house looking for Mary Lou's brother Jesse. An older kid in the neighborhood used a pair of handcuffs to restrain younger children and beat them up. He sold the handcuffs to Jesse for fifty cents. When the cops found the cuffs, they arrested Jesse Dixon and took him to jail. He got sick while locked up. Once released, the boy came home and grew worse, lying in his upstairs bedroom, burning with fever.

Dora Ashlock's liver problems developed into cancer. When the doctor came out to treat her, no mention was made of the teenager lying above their heads. Jesse was dying from peritonitis brought on by a ruptured appendix. Mary Lou called an ambulance the next day. She and Edward kept a lonely vigil at their brother's bedside in St. Joseph's Hospital. Bessie Dixon refused to grant permission for an operation until she came up from St. Helens. By the time she arrived, it was too late. "I'll be operating on a dead boy," the physician in charge told her. She insisted they go ahead. Jesse lived less than a day, slipping away on May 8, 1930.

Jesse Woodrow Dixon was buried in the Calvary Cemetery on Mother's Day. At the funeral, Mary Lou and Eveline made a vow over "Sone's" casket. They'd never fight with each other again. Two months later, Madora Ashlock and her daughter Edith (who perished from locked bowels) were also dead. Moonshine Bess lost her son, her mother, and a sister, all within sixty days.

After Jesse's funeral, Bessie took her surviving son, Edward, back to St. Helens, to live with her and Frank Campana. Mary Lou and Ben Brautigan nursed her grandmother until her death on July 17, 1930. Another funeral left the couple alone at 813 East Sixty-fifth Street. Mary Lou slept by herself in a little room off the back porch.

Edward didn't do well at The Boy's Place, barely lasting a year in St. Helens. He couldn't get along with Campana. One night, while studying in his room, a bullet came whistling through the wall, missing Edward's head by inches. The Italian bootlegger claimed it was an accident. "I was just cleaning my gun," Frank Campana said.

Edward didn't wait around for another "accident." He ran away from home the very next day, a departure so swift he barely took anything with him, a teenage rebel clad in blue jeans and a black leather jacket. He left a short note behind under his pillow along with his bank account book and a picture of his dead brother. Bessie Dixon notified the police but they were unable to determine where he might have gone. Edward never finished high school. He disappeared, swallowed up into the vast immensity of America.

four: tacoma ghosts

THE DIXON FAMILY home, recently alive with laughter and raucous teenage pranks, crowded with the polite comings and goings of elderly church ladies, now seemed peopled only by ghosts. Edward and Jesse were gone. Grandmother Ashlock's few possessions had all been packed away. Mary Lou and Ben Brautigan coexisted uneasily in the gloomy silence. She had her private hideaway. He made beer.

Ben turned the kitchen into a brewery. A galvanized washtub burbled with barley malt mash. Rows of empty bottles lined the counters. The sweet stink of fermentation pervaded the house. Ben stored the sealed bottles in the cold cookstove oven, since Mary Lou wasn't in a domestic mood and prepared few meals. Anxious to drink his suds as soon as possible, he capped the bottles before the brew finished working. Many exploded, adding to the alcoholic reek.

At last Mary Lou heard from Edward. He was living in Los Angeles, earning a living doing odd jobs: yard work, gardening, mowing lawns. "He was a kind of handyman for the wealthy rich widows," Mary Lou recalled. On Friday evening, March 10, 1933, Edward was playing cards in Long Beach with a young married couple. At five minutes to six, everything began to shake. A massive 6.4 earthquake struck the area. Edward grabbed his two friends and pulled them into the safety of a door frame. The terrified husband broke away, attempting to run outside. The house collapsed, and he was killed "right in front of their eyes," one of 120 people who died in the quake.

Fearful of losing her surviving brother, Mary Lou persuaded Edward to come back to Tacoma and live with her. Ben Brautigan had moved out. She was pregnant. After Jesse died, an older man named Michael Connelly, who "did a lot of gardening work for people," asked if he could help. He started dropping by on a regular basis, so Mary Lou had some company. She never told her mother of Edward's return, fearful Campana might finish his dirty work if her brother went back to St. Helens.

Edward and Tootie spent the summer of 1934 building a wooden boat in the backyard. The day Mary Lou went into labor, her brother was out on Puget Sound, fishing in their boat. He caught a twenty-five-pound salmon just before a storm blew in. Anxious to show his sister his prize catch, Edward raced the swelling whitecaps back to shore and tied the boat up at the dock, where the storm smashed it to splinters against the pilings. When he got home, Tootie had already left for the hospital.

Richard Brautigan was born at 12:30 AM (under the sign of Aquarius) just as the day began on January 30, 1935. He had big blue eyes and a full head of ethereal white hair. January 30 was also President Franklin Delano Roosevelt's fifty-third birthday. Richard was a well-behaved infant who had no colic and never cried or threw any screaming tantrums. Mary Lou recalled that "he had a kind of beller [*sic*] if something was bothering him."

Richard Gary Brautigan was baptized a Catholic on March 17, 1935, at Holy Rosary Church with Michael Connelly serving as godfather. Connelly spent a lot of time with his godson during that first year. Mary Lou didn't have a stroller (the Depression foreclosed such luxuries) and Michael carried the baby around the neighborhood. When Richard learned to walk (taking his first steps on his first birthday) the old man strolled with him along the sidewalk, holding his tiny hand.

"Richie never liked hardly any solid food." Mary Lou remembered a time when "modern" mothers were instructed to feed their babies pabulum twice a day. Once in a while, she'd slip some mashed potatoes and gravy into his mouth. His favorite snack was apples. He didn't want the fruit peeled, cut up, or mashed but tore into apples whole with his perfect little teeth. Other than a few simple "baby-talk" words, Richard didn't speak until he was four or five. He said "Mama" and called his milk bottle "nummy-nose." Later, he had a code word for his potty so that no one but his mother knew what he meant. "People sometimes asked me, 'Is that kid dumb? He never says anything.'" Mary Lou laughed at the memory. "Well, I knew he wasn't dumb."

Richard was a keenly observant child. His aunt Eveline took him out into the backyard at night to stargaze. She held him in her arms, and he looked fixedly up at the stars and the moon, studying them with an intense curiosity unusual in someone so young. He also stared at people, never saying a word, just watching and listening. It was unnerving. Folks didn't know what to make of this little white-haired kid, staring at them with his big unblinking blue eyes. Was he from another planet?

When Richard was two, Aunt Eveline gave him a beautiful yellow Taylor tricycle. He loved his new velocipede, pedaling around and around the house, refusing to get off, not even for meals. Mary Lou had to feed him on the trike. His little red wagon was another favorite vehicle. Richard pulled it out the back door and across the yard to the alley. A half block further, he cut across a vacant lot, dragging his wagon over to the Bill & Mid Market, a grocery store on McKinley Avenue.

In later years, Brautigan often told of learning to read from looking at canned goods, associating the fruit and vegetables pictured on the colorful paper labels with the printed words. Corn. Peas. Green Beans. Tomatoes. Beets. The corner market became his kindergarten, and time after time, Richard loaded up his little red wagon with cans and jars, piling them like alphabet blocks and hauling the load home down the alley.

"He saw me go in the store and do it, so he was going to do mother's shopping for her," Mary Lou Folston recalled. The store owners watched without comment, enjoying the comedy inherent in this tiny criminal's pilfering. They let Richard haul off his loot, knowing that as soon as he got home, his mother would either send him back or come and pay for what he had taken.

Boats fascinated Richard when he was two years old. He liked floating sticks of stove wood in the sink, launching homemade armadas. One night, sleeping upstairs, Mary Lou was awakened by the sound of running water. She pulled on a robe and went down to the kitchen. Richard had drawn a chair up to the sink, turned on the taps, and floated one of her new shoes in the basin.

Another terrible twos misadventure involved a German shepherd named Mark that Moonshine Bess brought to Tacoma when she came to visit. The animal watched over the toddler playing in the front yard. Once, Richard removed his diaper and pooped on the lawn. Overcome by scatological artistic inclinations, the little boy smeared handfuls of his shit all over the patient dog.

Mary Lou moved out of her family home that same year. She got a job in town and rented a place nine miles in the country. Her brother Edward continued living on Sixty-fifth Street, inviting his friend Ronald Bluett to share the house with him. Bluett, the man Bernard Brautigan accused of having an affair with his wife and Ben believed was Richard's actual father. Bluett was later crushed to death while working for a lumber outfit.

Eveline continued running the New Country Grocery with her husband, selling imported Italian foods. Mary Lou often stopped by to see her sister in the afternoons after work. She caught the bus home right in front of the store. The Pisannis had opened a bar in the same building. The Teamster's Union Hall stood only half a block away and the drivers gathered there, drinking beer while waiting for a call to make a run. A Norwegian trucker named "Big Jack" Fjetland took a shine to Eveline. One afternoon, Fjetland sat drinking and remarked to the proprietor, "You know, Pisanni, I'm in love with your wife."

Not taking him seriously, John Pisanni said, "Who wants her? You can have her."

Jack Fjetland meant business, and Eveline moved out. "She was married to Pisanni for ten years," Mary Lou recalled, "and for ten years she kept her suitcase packed to leave him."

Eveline lived in the country with Mary Lou for a year until her divorce was final and she married Fjetland. In 1937, the year Eveline met Big Jack, he and Arthur Martin Titland, another Norwegian truck driver, became beer-drinking buddies at the New Country Grocery. One afternoon, before catching the bus outside back to the country, Mary Lou met Titland. He was ten years older, a "dark Norwegian" with black hair and a swarthy complexion. "He wasn't any good. He was a drunk," she said later. "He drank up the family house. He drank up everything."

Mary Lou started living with Arthur and on May 1, 1939, at the Tacoma General Hospital, she gave birth to a daughter, Barbara Jo Titland. By then, the couple had already separated. It's doubtful they were ever legally married. No marriage certificate can be found, and Mary Lou's divorce from Bernard Brautigan was not final until January 17, 1940.

Richard Brautigan was four years old when his sister was born. His first memories eventually found their way into his fiction. His mother always said Richard had a "photostatic [sic] memory." In "Revenge of the Lawn," Brautigan wrote that his first memory "occurred in my grandmother's front yard. The year was either 1936 or 1937." He remembered "[Frank Campana] cutting down the pear tree and soaking it with kerosene" at The Boy's Place in St. Helens. Like the character in the story, Campana had a morbid fear of bees.

Brautigan wrote of his adventures with the little red wagon in an unpublished short story called "Cracker Jacks." He was four years old and loaded up his wagon with two hundred boxes of Cracker Jack from a store display. He wanted the prizes, not to keep, but to bury in a small animal cemetery in the backyard where he interred dead birds and insects. Brautigan described his tiny graveyard in part 9 ("My Insect Funeral") of his early pamphlet-length poem, *The Galilee Hitch-hiker*.

Young Richard added the purloined prizes to his miniature necropolis, tamping damp earth onto the tiny toys. In the story, he gets caught red-handed with the ripped-open Cracker Jack boxes and spanked. His mother shelled out eight bucks (a substantial sum in the Depression) in recompense. The family ate Cracker Jacks for breakfast for weeks. Richard never told anyone what he had done with all the prizes.

Brautigan often claimed to have twice flunked the first grade. "I couldn't figure school out," he said. "It didn't make sense to me. I wasn't able to learn the system." Richard transposed this yarn of early failure directly into his fiction. In truth, Mary Lou enrolled him in the first grade at Tacoma's Central Avenue grade school (September 1940) when he was five years old. Brautigan graduated from high school in June of 1953, a normal twelve-year course of study. Richard's sister, Barbara, thought that he'd actually skipped a year. ("He either skipped the fourth or the fifth grade because he was really smart.") Brautigan later concurred, writing: "I was smart and a year ahead in school."

Richard told many stories about learning to read. Along with the can label tale, two other conflicting versions survive. He once confided to his friend Keith Abbott that he kept a World War II Japanese machine gun in his Geary Street apartment because it "reminded him of how he learned to read at age six, when he understood a headline about the Japanese attack on Pearl Harbor ("Japs Bomb Pearl Harbor") and made the connection between letters and reality." In 1980, Brautigan told a reporter from the Tacoma *News Tribune* that he realized he could read in April 1942. Wandering aimlessly around the city, he came across a newspaper spread over a storm sewer grate. "I could read the front page headline," he noted. "It was 'Doolittle Bombs Tokyo.'"

In the last novel published during his lifetime, *So the Wind Won't Blow It All Away*, Brautigan wrote of moving into "an apartment that was annexed to a funeral parlor." This happened when he was five, in the late spring of 1940. Mary Lou had been living an increasingly transient life. That year, she moved five times in two months. "Anytime I didn't like anything, I moved."

One of these moves was to a street crowded with five mortuaries: Lyon's, Buckley-King, Melinger's, Lynn, Cassedy and Allen. Mary Lou occupied an apartment below Lynn. "I moved at night and didn't know that it was a mortuary." They lived below the mortuary only "long enough to find another place." She woke up in the morning with Richard staring out the front room window. "He says, 'Look, Mama, there's a whole lot of people out in front of the house.' I took a look and they were having a funeral. All the mourners were there. I thought, oh my god, no wonder it was so quiet."

Richard wrote of living near the funeral parlor "for a few months." He described getting up early in the morning in his pajamas, while everyone else was still asleep, to watch the funerals through the window, so small he had to climb up on a chair to get a better view. It made a lasting impression. Thirty-nine years later, in his fiction, Brautigan recalled the mortician's blond-haired six-year-old daughter, whose ice-cold hands terrified him. Death remained a recurring image in his fiction and poetry. Like a funeral cortege haunting a sunny spring day, graves, shadows, cemeteries, and other glimpses of mortality add a pervasive melancholy to work so seemingly lighthearted on the surface.

A short while before Mary Lou occupied the apartment below the mortuary, either late 1939 or early in 1940, her brother Edward moved out of the family home. His friend Ron Bluett wanted them to head up to Seattle and find work in an aircraft factory. Instead, Edward Dixon took a job with Simms & Drake Construction Company in San Francisco. Ron Bluett ended up working in the timber industry, where he met his death. Within the year, Edward traveled to Midway Island in the Pacific. Simms & Drake was building an airstrip for the U.S. Navy. He had always written poetry. Many of these poems, composed during his off hours, were printed in the *Gooney Gazette*, the island's military newspaper, which Edward mailed home to his family.

In 1941, when Richard Brautigan was six, he and his mother lived in one of an ongoing sequence of low-rent buildings in Tacoma. A ninety-three-year-old woman occupied another cheap apartment on the same floor. She had been a widow for seventy years and lived by herself. Twice each week, on Monday and Thursday evenings, Richard played Chinese checkers with her. She served him tea and cookies and told stories about a deceased husband who had drawn his last breath during the administration of President Ulysses S. Grant. "I always liked old people," Richard Brautigan wrote forty years later, "so I spent as much time with them as I could. They fascinated me like spiders."

America's sudden entry into World War II had a profound effect on Richard Brautigan. On December 7, 1941, units of the Imperial Japanese Navy attacked Midway as well as the U.S. Naval Base near Honolulu. Uncle Edward heard the incoming planes and hurried outside to help set up a machine gun. He managed to fire off a few rounds before a bomb exploded and everything went black.

Edward Dixon woke up on a hospital ship bound for Hawaii, head swathed in bandages. The doctor studying his chart by the foot of the bed said, "I know you. I used to go to school with you in Tacoma. How's your mother and your two sisters?"

Edward thought he was dying. "I'm not going to make it," he told his old friend. "I want you to tell my mother and sisters goodbye for me."

"You're going to make it, all right," the doctor said. "I won't leave you." He stayed by Edward's side for the remainder of the voyage.

Dixon spent five months recovering in a hospital in Honolulu. He wrote poetry "in the vein of Rudyard Kipling, Robert W. Service, and Omar Khayyam," filling several spiral-bound notebooks. In May 1942, another construction job waited for him in Alaska. After a stopover in San Francisco and a passionate two-week love affair with a divorcee, he went home for a quick visit, arriving in St. Helens in time for Mother's Day. Bessie thought he wasn't well enough to go to work. Edward insisted the doctors gave him a clean bill of health. For a studio photograph taken at the time, the photographer posed Dixon so the patch bandage on the back of his head didn't show.

Mary Lou had just moved again when Edward arrived in Tacoma. He had only a couple days and stayed with his sister Eveline and her husband. No one knew where to find Mary Lou. Jack Fjetland took Edward looking for her, but they mostly made the rounds of local taverns and ended up falling asleep at a movie show. Edward shipped out for Sitka, Alaska, a few days later to work on another airfield. Mary Lou never saw her brother again.

1942 was a disastrous year for Mary Lou and her growing brood. Her daughter, Barbara, had eye surgery. Richard came down with chicken pox, whooping cough, and the mumps in quick succession. All three, mother and both children, had tonsillectomies in 1942. Richard had an allergic reaction to the tonsillitis medication. His head grew monstrously swollen. He raged with fever.

Mary Lou found another doctor. Together they spent the night nursing the boy, too sick to be moved to the hospital. Richard was better by morning, but the episode resonated in his imagination. Decades later in Montana, he told Tom McGuane an amplified tale of lying alone in darkness for a year with his head blown to the size of a watermelon. "I guess his mind became his only toy during that time," McGuane said, recalling this story.

At his construction site in Sitka, on the morning of August 11, 1942, Edward Dixon stepped onto a platform load of lumber, hitching a ride aloft to the third floor of an unfinished building. The crane operator didn't see him. When the load jerked, Edward tumbled off, falling sixteen feet and landing on his head. He died from a cerebral hemorrhage when he was twenty-six years old.

It took almost two weeks to ship Edward's body south through the war zone on the Southland boat to Seattle. The Dixon family mortician drove up from Tacoma to bring him home and came upon a macabre sight in the baggage storeroom. The coffin had splintered into pieces. Edward's corpse, his head crushed sideways, lay in a corner. Mrs. Forkenbrock had her assistants pick up the splinters and place them in the wagon along with Edward's body. They nailed the crude transport coffin back together in the mortuary, but provided a more elaborate casket for the burial.

At the funeral parlor on a rainy night in Tacoma, Richard Brautigan, age seven, stared into the open coffin containing his uncle Edward's grotesquely painted remains, the thick makeup intended to recapture a final illusion of life. The gathered relatives urged the little boy "to kiss the lipstick on his dead mouth." Richard refused and ran screaming up the aisle, past the gathered mourners, out into the comforting rain. In 1949, the family opened the mausoleum and placed Bessie Dixon's ashes inside the casket with Edward's body.

Many years later, when he was twenty-six, the same age as his uncle when he died, Brautigan wrote a three-stanza lyric poem in memory of Edward Dixon. After it was first published in *The Octopus Frontier*, Richard identified "1942" as one of his "favorites."

Piano tree, play
in the dark concert halls
of my uncle,
take his heart
for a lover
and take his death
for a bed,
and send him homeward bound
on a ship from Sitka
to bury him
where I was born.

five: dick porterfield

N 1943, MARY Lou Brautigan worked as a cashier at Laughlin's Café on Pacific Avenue in Tacoma. The restaurant hired Robert Geoffry Porterfield, a fry cook who could also handle dinner specials, in May. Known to his friends as "Tex" (actually born in Deadwood, South Dakota, in 1896), Porterfield was a broad-shouldered man standing about five nine, with a small mustache and a crew cut going gray at the temples. "He was not good-looking, but he thought he was," Mary Lou observed. Tex came from a wealthy oil family but ran away from home at sixteen and joined the navy.

"He was an alcoholic." Mary Lou remembered her ex-husband with considerable distaste. "He was crazy in the head. He had to sustain so much alcohol every day to walk around," she recalled. "[Tex] had a big mouth, a dirty mouth, a filthy mouth. All he could think and talk about was filth. People he didn't even know. It's a wonder he didn't get punched out."

After working together for several months, Mary Lou agreed to go out on a date with Tex Porterfield. "He took me to a tavern, and I didn't drink. Wasn't that a joke?" The place had a small band. Tex Porterfield was a good dancer, one of his redeeming features. He was also something of a barroom conjurer, performing simple legerdemain and small sleights. Mary Lou remembered his act. "He did tricks, like taking a glass of beer and turning it upside down and putting it back on the bar without spilling a drop. All sorts of junk like that. Magician."

Lulu Mary Kehoe Brautigan "Titland" married Robert Geoffry "Tex" Porterfield in Tacoma on September 20, 1943. Pastor Burton W. Smith tied the knot in a Lutheran ceremony. "You don't know what I did or what I give up to marry you," Tex told her. Mary Lou frowned at the unpleasant memory. "That's a nice thing to tell your old lady," she said. "I had to work all the time to support myself." Both Richard and his sister used their stepfather's surname, becoming known as Barbara and Dick Porterfield.

By early 1944, Tex and Mary Lou split up. He headed east to Great Falls, Montana, where he secured a job as a fry cook. Letter-writing was one of Porterfield's accomplishments. When he took a mind, he adroitly turned his thoughts to words of love. After several torrid missives from her estranged husband, Mary Lou bundled up the two kids and boarded the Great Northern "Empire Builder," traveling overnight to Great Falls for a Valentine's Day rendezvous. She brought along the pet canary her mother had given her, but it froze to death in the baggage car.

Mary Lou wasn't impressed with the little city on the Missouri River. "That Great Falls is nothing but old miners and stuff. Cold people. Dirty people. Drunks that go around shaking silver dollars in their pockets. They see a woman, they start shaking their money in their pockets." Any hope of rekindling a hot Valentine romance went up in a blue barroom blur of cigarette smoke. Mary Lou soon tired of watching Tex perform his beer mug sleight of hand.

"He would sit in the tavern with some women that he never even saw. Would tell them the filthiest stories. These were just acquaintances passing through the night." Mary Lou was only another stranger ricocheting in and out of Porterfield's life. Two weeks later, after traveling nearly a thousand miles to be in his arms, she headed back to Tacoma on a train, leaving the kids behind in Montana, alone in a rooming house with filthy Tex.

Looking back through the wonder-struck eyes of a four-year-old, Barbara remembered the winter spent in Great Falls as a magical time. She recalled going down to the railroad depot with Dick day after day to watch the passenger trains come and go. All the energy and commotion provided an intense excitement for the little girl. The big steam locomotives with their exotic smell of grease and hot metal lured them back again and again. "We'd always say, 'Let's go to that smell,'" Barbara reminisced. They stood on the platform, two little raggedy kids waving at the black porters and cooks who threw them pieces of gum and candy.

Other days, Dick and Barbara went skating. Too poor to afford real skates, they slid across the ice on their street shoes. It was extremely cold, and Barbara remembered "just freezing all the time." Having fun made her ignore the subzero weather. There was a pond in a local park where people skated, and Dick took Barbara there, the protective big brother holding her hand, sliding with her across the gleaming frozen surface on the leather soles of their cheap shoes.

In the early spring of 1944, Porterfield brought Dick and Barbara back to Tacoma. His reunion with Mary Lou went better this time, and it wasn't very long before she was pregnant again. Even this didn't hold the couple together. By summer, Mary Lou moved to Salem, Oregon, without Tex. During the fourteen months she lived in the state capital, Mary Lou changed her address three or four times. As her pregnancy progressed, she found the kids were more than she could handle and boarded Richard and Barbara out with another family.

Mary Lou arranged to spend occasional weekends with her children. In March of 1945, they all stayed at the Grand Hotel, a clean, quiet place, sleeping together in a great big bed. One afternoon, the family went to the movies: *To Have and Have Not*, starring Humphrey Bogart and Lauren Bacall. Halfway through the picture, before Betty asked Bogie if he knew how to whistle, Mary Lou went into labor. "We've got to go," she whispered. Dick, a lifelong film fanatic, didn't want to leave. "You've got to go," his mother insisted, "you can come back later and see the show."

They hurried out of the theater, and Mary Lou checked into the Salem General Hospital. Sandra Jean Porterfield was born on April 1, 1945. Mary Lou spent nearly two weeks in the hospital with her new baby. Children were not permitted to visit, so Dick boarded close to Salem General and came every evening and stood outside the window, waving at his mother. Each time, he left a fresh flower on the front steps. The nurses went out after he'd gone and brought the gift blossom in to Mary Lou. "He was very grown-up when he was ten," she said.

The Salem General Hospital played a recurring role in their lives. Less than two months after Sandra's birth, a tough kid at school jumped on Dick's stomach. The next day, he complained of not feeling well and lay around reading comic books. "He'd read and reread them." By evening, he insisted he was not sick and "ate a great big supper." On Sunday morning, Dick slept in late. When Mary Lou checked on him, he was burning with fever, his stomach distended.

The Porterfields had no phone at the time. Mary Lou ran to the office of the motel where they lived. She didn't know anyone in town, and the owners called Dr. Terence King. "Don't touch him or move him," he told Mary Lou. Dr. King got to the motel in no time. The diagnosis was acute appendicitis. Mary Lou loaded Dick into the backseat of the physician's car and noticed that Dr. King had only a thumb and one forefinger on his right hand, something of a handicap for a surgeon. She sat with her son during the slow ride to the hospital, his head hanging down and his feet across her lap as he writhed in pain.

Many years later, when Brautigan told Keith Abbott of this incident, he added fabrications, elevating the story into myth. He said his mother had put him to bed with a fever and left him there until a concerned neighbor telephoned for help five days later. "Richard recalled the doctor driving to the hospital at ten miles an hour," Abbott wrote, describing his friend's version of events, "holding Richard on his lap for fear the swollen appendix would burst. The memory remained of the doctor's tears falling on him, as he wept out of rage and pity for Richard's condition."

During the long operation, Mary Lou paced back and forth along a path between the hospital buildings, chain-smoking cigarettes. A group of men and women sitting outside on benches stared at her with peculiar expressions. The next day, she found out the state mental hospital was part of the medical complex. "It was a nuthouse. And they were out there for air. My god!"

The operation was over by early afternoon. Eleven inches of Dick's lower colon had been removed, along with a quart of poisonous fluid. Mary Lou looked in on him. Filled with Sulfathiazole to fight the infection and hooked up to an IV, Dick had a drain in his side for peritonitis. Dr. King came by in his hospital whites and suggested Mrs. Porterfield go home and get some rest. It wasn't until the next day that he told her Dick was going to live: "I know he's going to make it now." Ten days later, Dick Porterfield ran around the neighborhood climbing cherry trees.

News of the Japanese surrender came on August 14. Young Dick was at the movies, watching a Dennis Morgan film. He later wrote, "I think it was a singing foreign legion desert picture but I cannot be certain." In the middle of the action, a yellowed strip of paper was projected onto the screen with a typewritten message announcing Japan's unconditional capitulation. The audience began laughing and yelling. Dick remembered the ecstatic sound. They all rushed out of the matinee into the heat of a summertime afternoon. Car horns blared. Complete strangers embraced. "Everything was in Pandemonium."

Caught up in the general euphoria, Mary Lou had another abortive reunion with Tex. She rented a house at 2235 Hazel Avenue and he took a night job cooking in a café. Things went badly almost from the start. Dick didn't move fast enough carrying in wood for the heating stove, and Porterfield beat the boy unmercifully. When Tex went to work one evening, Mary Lou gathered together as much as she could pack, roused the kids from bed, and fled into the night. She first went to her mother in St. Helens. Later, she flipped a quarter on a street corner in Portland. Heads, she would move to Eugene. Tails, she'd go the other way. The coin came up heads.

Home of the University of Oregon, the city of Eugene stands at the head of the Willamette Valley near the confluence of the McKenzie and Willamette rivers. Founded in 1846 by Eugene Skinner, an Illinois county sheriff who came west by wagon train, the place was known for years as "Skinner's Mudhole." When Mrs. Porterfield arrived with three young children in tow in the fall of 1945, Eugene was the second largest city in Oregon yet, even with the university, it remained a rural backwater. Mary Lou rented a small white house on the corner of Twenty-third and Agate streets, close by the U of O campus. Tex Porterfield followed and lived there a short while before taking off forever. She never saw him again.

By December, the Porterfield family moved when the owner of the little white house returned from Alaska and needed the place for himself. Mary Lou put all her belongings in storage and found a motel room across the river in Glenwood, a strip town adjoining neighboring Springfield. A week or so after they moved in, torrential rains swept the area. "It was just a davenport rain that never stopped," she remembered. The rain continued for days, and the water began to rise.

On the twenty-ninth of December, Mary Lou stood by the kitchen window bathing Sandra in the sink and saw a bed float down the turbid rain-swollen Willamette River. Dick and his sister, now nicknamed B.J., played outside in the storm with some other children. "Mommy, mommy," they shouted, bursting into the room, "everybody in the court is out there. Even the sheriff." Mary Lou saw them all milling about in the downpour. The sheriff told her it was time to evacuate.

Mary Lou picked up the baby, wrapping her in a blanket. Hearing someone next door, she called out for help. The woman came over, and Mary Lou handed Sandra to her. "Take my baby over to Eugene and tell the police where you have her." Mary Lou rolled up the mattresses and stacked her things on the furniture, setting her little Christmas tree on the bed in the corner. Dick and Barbara kept running up and down outside, yelling in the pouring rain. They were soaking wet, having too much fun to care. Mary Lou and her kids were the last to leave, watching the highway fold up behind them "like scrambled eggs."

Dick and Barbara each went to stay with a different family. Baby Sandra was taken in by another. Several days later, when the floodwaters receded, they reunited, and Mary Lou made one last trip over to Glenwood to retrieve her possessions. She would never return. Barbara remembered wandering the riverbank with her brother. They found jars of salmon eggs washed out of the stores and full bottles of pop. It was like a treasure hunt.

After the flood, Mary Lou rented a place at Seal's Motel at 1600 Sixth Avenue West in Eugene, two rooms with a kitchenette and a shower for $149.50 a month. In *So the Wind Won't Blow It All Away*, Brautigan wrote of when he lived "in a cabin at an auto court, but we didn't have an automobile." He claimed he and his family "were guests of the Welfare Department." The fatherless Porterfield family was extremely poor. Mary Lou had worked as a waitress, never a lucrative job, even in the best of times. Now unemployed, with three kids at home, she often had to rely on public assistance over the next few years.

Dick Porterfield became a lifelong fisherman during his stay in Seal's Motel. At a time when Chambers Street more or less defined the western boundary of Eugene, the little motor court was practically out in the country. A half-dozen sawmills were located in the area, bordering logging ponds alive with bluegills, crappies, perch, and catfish. A steam railroad servicing the mills ran north and south, and the local highway rose on an arching overpass above the tracks. Beyond lay open fields and abandoned fruit orchards. Apples, pears, cherries, and plums grew wild on the edge of town. All waited within an easy walk for an eleven-year-old boy with adventure on his mind.

An old hermit lived in a shack built from packing crates at the edge of one pool. A family of fat people in bib overalls came at night to fish, unloading a roomful of furniture off a pickup, making themselves at home along the bank, fishing poles in one hand, coffee mugs in the other. An air of the fantastic permeates later literary descriptions of this bizarre logging pond world, but Barbara remembered it all to be true. She was afraid of the old bearded man in the shack, but the large couple with their sagging sofa became a treasured memory from her nocturnal angling expeditions with Dick.

Barbara was entrusted to her brother's care when she was a toddler. The two Porterfield children went everywhere together. "The first memories I have, I have of [Dick] and not my mother or a stepdad," Barbara recalled. "I never talked about anything with my mom, but if I had any problems or wanted to know anything, I'd always discuss it with [Dick]. I'd never go to my mother for advice or anything." In his sister's opinion, Dick was given so much responsibility at such an early age, he "grew up very fast. Very fast."

Barbara trusted her big brother completely. Walking to the logging ponds, they never followed Highway 99 because of the heavy traffic. There was only one way in and out of Eugene in those days, and the road was always very busy. The kids cut across abandoned fields and orchards instead, stopping to eat whatever fruit they came upon. During the day, they fished for bluegill, bass, and perch. Neither had proper equipment. Dick cut willow stems for poles, rigging them with string and safety-pin hooks. On a slow day or if they caught so many it grew boring, they jumped on the big logs floating in the ponds. Neither knew how to swim. The water stood over twenty feet deep, but they gave no thought to the danger involved. It was too much fun jumping from log to log, pretending to be lumberjacks.

At night, they returned to the ponds, angling for catfish. They built a big fire on the bank for warmth and because the light attracted fish. They stayed out quite late, past ten or eleven o'clock. If Mary Lou had concerns about her children's whereabouts, she made no mention of it. Dick had the responsibility of caring for his younger sister, and that was that.

Dick Porterfield proudly brought his nocturnal catch back to Seal's Motel. "He would supply nearly everybody with his darn catfish." The little family on welfare ate a lot of fried catfish. Dick and Barbara heard people calling frog legs a gourmet delight and learned how to "jig" for them, dangling a treble hook baited with bits of red flannel in front of squatting bullfrogs.

When they brought the frogs home, Mary Lou refused to have anything to do with them. "They jump around in the pan," she said. The Porterfields lived in the end unit at Seal's, down by the laundry room. On the other side lived "a real nice lady," who shared the kids' gastronomic curiosity. "If you get any, I'll fry them for you," she offered. Richard cut the legs off, and the neighbor lady cooked them. "It was the best food I ever ate," Barbara reminisced.

One morning, Mary Lou answered a knock at the door. A neatly dressed stranger stood outside. "Mrs. Porterfield?" he asked.

"Yes."

"Mrs. Robert Geoffry Porterfield."

Another affirmative. The man asked if he could speak with Mr. Porterfield. Mary Lou told him her husband didn't live there. He inquired if she knew where to find him. "No. I haven't seen him for a long, long time."

The stranger identified himself as an FBI agent. Tex Porterfield was charged with wartime desertion from the navy. Eddie Slovick, a U.S. Army private in France, had recently been executed by firing squad for a similar offense. Mary Lou's hair stood on end. She remembered Tex telling her, "You don't know what I did to get you." The G-man asked a few more questions, but she wasn't much help, having no interest in finding Tex Porterfield. He was ancient history.

Dick Porterfield attended classes at Lincoln Elementary School, an old two-story clapboard building at the corner of West Tenth and Monroe, not far from Seal's Motel. Mary Lou never attended any school functions. When the time came for Barbara to start first grade, Dick brought her with him at the beginning of the fall term and parked her in the proper room. He had already previously enrolled himself so it didn't seem like such a big deal. Barbara remembered that when the teacher got to the end of the roll call, she asked if she'd missed anyone. Barbara Porterfield raised her hand. She didn't have the proper papers. The authorities went to talk with her brother, and things got straightened out.

The two kids did almost everything together. Not having money for real toys, they used their imaginations, improvising six-guns out of wood scraps and cutting tree branches for their fishing poles. They played guns a lot and were always running, pretending to be horses. A long-gone wrecking yard located about ten blocks from where they lived provided an enticing place to play King of the Mountain. They climbed over the wrecks, leaping from one junker to another. Barbara was afraid to jump and recalled her long-legged brother saying, "Come on. You can do it. You can do it.'"

Barbara gave it her best shot, landing half on and half off the adjoining wreck. Dick pulled her across, and she cut her knee. She started crying. "Hey, guess what?" Dick said. "You're King of the Mountain." As if by magic, her knee no longer hurt.

Early in 1947, the Porterfield family moved from Seal's Motel to a rental belonging to Frances Shields, a woman with "a bunch of kids." The Shields house seemed enormous after the confinement of motel life. A two-story home located at 1765 West Thirteenth Avenue between Grant and Hayes out in the country on the edge of town, beyond Chambers Street, where the Amazon Creek flooded the unpaved streets almost every year, turning the area into a vast swamp. People abandoned their cars and rowed around in boats until the spring runoff subsided.

"It was old, and several of the rooms upstairs weren't finished, and everything creaked," Barbara remembered. Her mother worked late at various menial jobs, waitressing or cleaning motel rooms and medical offices downtown. "She'd leave, and we'd be there sometimes until twelve, one, two o'clock in the morning by ourselves. She couldn't afford a babysitter. Richard's job was to take care of me. He would fix my meals and tell me it was time to go to bed and get me up in the morning and get me ready for school. He was a surrogate mother."

The Shields place stood surrounded by a huge yard shaded by old black walnut trees in front and cherry and apple trees out back. A perfect place for kids to play, but the new yard held much less interest for Dick and Barbara than the outlying fields and forgotten orchards or the eternal promise of angling adventure at the logging ponds. In the summer of 1947, the two youngsters began picking fruit to earn much-needed spending money. Dick already gathered discarded beer bottles (worth a penny each) along Highway 99, filling a gunnysack to the bursting point.

Blackberries provided a more accessible yield. In Oregon, the thorny vines grew unrestrained, weedlike, taking over vacant lots and coiling along the roadsides in concertina-wire profusion. "Blackberry Motorist," a Brautigan short story, recalled the past. Near their new house, in "an industrial area that had seen its day," vines engulfed the sides of several abandoned warehouses. Barbara remembered planks laid across the vast snarling thorn-bush, "like bridges." The ripest berries grew toward the center, and much "medieval blackberry engineering" was required to reach their bounty. "I'm too heavy to go up there," Dick told B.J., "so you go up and pick them."

The kids peered into the "deep shadowy dungeon-like places" and discovered the carcass of a Model A sedan lurking within the tangled thorn fortress. Dick Porterfield tunneled his way through the needle-sting of the vines until at last he sat behind the wheel of the Model A, "staring from twilight darkness through the windshield up into green sunny shadows." Barbara remembered the old Ford hidden by vines but had been scared to climb down inside. Dick clambered into the rusting car on every visit.

During blackberry season, the kids picked along the vast bramble "at least once, if not a couple times a week." Some of their yield went home for jam making, but mostly they sold blackberries door-to-door by the quart when they "needed more money than the price of a movie." Once, lacking enough ripe fruit to fill a basket, they packed the center with green ones artfully camouflaged by their best berries and sold it to an unsuspecting neighbor.

"It seemed like we always bought food with our money," Barbara remembered. "Corn was like twelve ears for fifty cents. We would walk to the store, and he'd buy twelve ears. They'd always throw in an extra one. And we'd come home and that would be our lunch. I'd probably eat two ears. He'd eat eleven out of thirteen. Sit down and eat eleven ears of corn without stopping."

Summertime meant commercial picking season. Dick and Barbara bought their own school clothes with earnings from picking on the farms in the Willamette Valley. "We'd have to buy everything for the whole year," Barbara recalled. They weren't the only ones who needed the money. All the neighborhood kids picked beans and strawberries and cherries for two or two and a half cents a pound. Farm trucks collected the youngsters around six in the morning at designated spots downtown and hauled them out to the fields.

The kids worked in teams of two on either side of the bean rows, filling five-gallon metal buckets. Full buckets were emptied into burlap sacks tagged with the picker's name. The sacks held thirty to fifty pounds of beans. Once the sacks filled, they were tied off with twine and loaded onto trucks bound for the cannery. The goal was to pick a hundred pounds. The most industrious picked an additional hundred. The rowdy crowd horsed around instead, starting water fights.

Bean picking was "a miserable job," according to Gary Stewart, who lived on the same hard edge of town as Dick Porterfield. They met in the summer of 1947, out at the big blackberry patch. The two boys became immediate friends, the "odd paths" of their imaginations linking on the outskirts of the fantastic. They wondered how it would be if the vines had actual muscles and could move like a blackberry octopus, coiling and striking with their briars. "Would they take over the world?" Dick and Gary spent all summer and much of the school year together.

They were dissimilar as Mutt and Jeff: a tall kid with white hair from a home broken many times and a short redhead from a big happy family. Gary's father, Milo Stewart, worked for the highway department and had converted to Mormonism five years before. Dick Porterfield attended no church although he read in the Bible every night before bed. Bonded by imagination and a shared poverty, they toiled in the bean fields and fished the logging ponds. Once, finding a nest of baby pigeons high in an unused lumber yard teepee burner, they speculated on how wonderful it would be to fly.

The two boys went camping at Paradise Campground sixty miles up the McKenzie, a swift dangerous river. They fashioned a lean-to from a tarp and length of rope, sleeping wrapped in blankets on the ground. A log had fallen across the main channel. Dick and Gary crossed this bridge many times to a deep pool on the other side where they could look down and see beautiful huge trout holding. They dropped their bait right in front of them, catching "some pretty good fish."

Several other kids remembered Dick Porterfield as a tall loner in overalls like Huckleberry Finn, hitchhiking up the McKenzie with his fishing pole. They called him "Whitey."

Dick bought himself the best equipment as soon as he saved the money. Big commercial tackle suppliers like Eagle Claw manufactured inexpensive split bamboo cane rods. "He had a fly pole that he really, really liked," Barbara recalled. "It broke down in three or four pieces and fit in this little bag with a drawstring." Dick Porterfield enjoyed the freedom of a fatherless household. As if in celebration, his body grew eleven inches during his twelfth year.

"He towered over everybody." Melvin Corbin, another kid living "out in the country," on Eighteenth Street, remembered Dick Porterfield from the fifth grade at Lincoln. "All of a sudden, he was just there. I didn't think he belonged and asked the teacher, 'How come this big kid is in grammar school?' She told me that he was just exceptionally big. That he was a genius. I didn't know what a genius was at the time." Corbin's teacher claimed young Porterfield read at an eleventh-grade level.

"I looked older than I actually was—" Dick described himself at thirteen. "I was tall for my age, so that I could easily be mistaken for fifteen—" Porterfield's rapid growth caused scoliosis, a permanent lateral curvature of the spine. His chest developed asymmetrically and gave his upper back a slight hump, forcing his right shoulder higher than the left. "He could not hold his neck up straight," Mary Lou remembered dispassionately. "He had therapy and everything."

Melvin Corbin recalled a skinny kid with a sunken chest, an undernourished genius allowed to go through the cafeteria lunch line again and again because he was poor and his family received some kind of assistance. Their fifth-grade teacher was much impressed with Dick Porterfield's photographic memory. "Whatever he read, he remembered." Dick's reading consisted mainly of the Reader's Digest Condensed Books his mother kept around the house. Mary Lou said her son could "flash read" any book and, when given the page number, repeat what was printed there. "I checked him out on it, and it was incredible."

Sixth grade marked a period of ambition and enterprise. Dick and Gary went into the worm business. A lot of kids gathered worms, selling them to filling stations for a penny apiece. The retail price for night crawlers was twenty-five cents per dozen. Dick and Gary figured they could make a profit undercutting the competition by a dime. They searched damp lawns at night with flashlights and stored their catch in a box of dirt down in Gary's cool dark basement. "We'd put a sign out in front of my house because I was on a busier street closer to town," Gary said. "When somebody would want some, we'd go down and dig them up and put them in takeout boxes like you get at a Chinese restaurant. We sold them for fifteen cents."

Both Barbara and Sandi remembered their big brother taking them hunting worms at night with a flashlight. They pulled on their rubber boots and went out into the pitch dark around eleven o'clock. Dick taught B.J. to feel in the wet grass of a freshly watered lawn. "When you see a worm you have to be fast," he said. Night crawlers stretched like Plastic Man over six inches through the grass. "They keep one end in the ground," Dick instructed. "If you miss, they snap back inside."

Delivering newspapers became another Horatio Alger enterprise for Dick Porterfield. Melvin Corbin had an *Oregonian* route that went out Chambers Street, down Eighteenth, and up River Road into the hills. He had been assigned a different route and gave the old one to Dick, who was suddenly in need of a bicycle. Melvin just got a new bike and offered to sell his old one. Dick had never owned a bicycle. During the war, they were almost unobtainable. The price was $25.

Dick made a deal with Melvin to pay him back monthly with the proceeds from the paper route and took immediate possession of a bicycle that "always looked shitty." Barbara remembered Dick's "old broken-down bicycle." B.J. never had a bicycle either and was "always taking off" on her brother's. "Seemed like every time he came back to ride it, it had a flat tire. Thanks to me." Barbara never mentioned the flat. Dick often made the unhappy discovery in the early morning, waking up to patch a tire before delivering newspapers.

Dick Porterfield "was a kid who didn't like to do his chores." He lived in a household where cooking and heating required wood and "always hated to chop wood." Dick also disliked working in the big vegetable garden the family depended upon and loathed pushing the hand-powered lawn mower across the vast expanse of surrounding yard.

"He didn't seem to have any ambition as far as physical work went," Melvin Corbin remembered. Fixing flat bike tires at four in the morning provided a special challenge for a kid utterly unfamiliar with tools. "Richard didn't even know what a screwdriver was," his mother claimed, "or a vise." He regarded lightbulbs with trepidation. As an adult, he instructed his teenage daughter never to change a bulb on her own, warning "instant death and dismemberment might result."

Dick Porterfield abandoned his paper route after nine months but did not give Melvin Corbin back the bicycle. Mary Lou recalled the predawn mornings: "He lost money every month. People would order the paper and then they would move out, you know, deadbeats." Melvin remembered it differently: "I think he didn't have the guts to go out and collect afterwards. He probably went once and didn't go follow up."

Eventually, the *Oregonian* route manager made the collection. He asked Melvin Corbin to take Dick Porterfield's route back. Melvin still wasn't getting his monthly bike payment and started going by Dick's place on West Thirteenth, looking for his money. "The house was always clean around it. It was never junky-looking. It was run-down, but never junky." Even with his sharp eye for real estate, Melvin never spotted Dick. "Each time I went there for the money, he would always seem to disappear." B.J. fronted for her brother, telling the strange angry boy that Dick wasn't at home. Melvin finally spotted Porterfield one day, pedaling his battered bike down Chambers Street. "So I turned around and went back after him, and he just threw the bike in the ditch and took off."

Along with Gary Stewart, Dick's other classmates at Lincoln were the Hiebert twins, Donald and Ronald, both prankster outcasts who formed the instant nucleus of any gang. They lived further up Dick's street on the edge of town and spent most of their time, "day and night," hanging out with Porterfield. Melvin Corbin also sometimes "ran with the twins." The Hieberts were part of a large family. Richard's mother thought there were ten children. Melvin Corbin remembered seven.

The Hieberts' old man worked in a slaughterhouse. His violent profession carried over into his personal life. Mary Lou described a strict disciplinarian who beat his kids with a length of garden hose. Mrs. Hiebert had shown Dick Porterfield a large pair of scissors she kept hidden under the pillow on her bed. She had said she would kill her husband if he attempted to have sex with her again. Dick had been deeply affected by this domestic melodrama. "Worried him an awful lot," his mother recalled.

Like Dick Porterfield, the Hiebert twins were wild practical jokers, delighting in playing pranks on everyone. Melvin Corbin remembered Halloween mischief. Eugene had no sewer system yet on the outskirts of town. Dick and the Hieberts tipped over outhouses or moved them back in the night, just far enough so the next customer would "accidentally" step in the hole. Another wild Halloween stunt involved collecting human excrement in newspaper. "They'd all take turns crapping in the paper," Corbin said. Porterfield and the twins placed the night soil bundles on the front porches of the unsuspecting, lit the newspaper on fire, rang the doorbell, and ran, watching from a safe distance as their victims stomped on the flaming shit.

Richard's mother recalled a more malicious prank: "We had a bunch of pullets in the backyard—they were sick—[we] got out the bolo knife and went out there and killed them all and buried them up there in the ground. So, they dug them up on Halloween." After disinterring the rotting chickens, Dick Porterfield and the Hieberts smuggled their stinking corpses into the supermarket at Eleventh and Chambers and put them in the freezer.

Like the Porterfields, the Hieberts were a poor family. The kids earned their own way doing odd jobs and picking beans in the fields around Eugene. Only Johnnie, one of the younger brothers, didn't work in the summertime because he had a hernia, ruptured, as they said in those days. Johnnie Hiebert loved to drink Kool-Aid, never imagining his addiction would be immortalized many years later in *Trout Fishing in America*.

Mary Lou remembered making Kool-Aid for Johnnie Hiebert by the pitcherful. "Put it out there on the shelf, you know, with a glass. Everybody was giving him food and stuff. We called him the Kool-Aid Kid." Neon-colored Kool-Aid reigned supreme as the poor man's soft drink. At a time when a seven-ounce bottle of Coke cost a nickel, a package of Kool-Aid for the same price yielded two quarts. "We drank a lot of Kool-Aid," Barbara remembered.

Watermelon provided another memorable summertime treat. Although cheap by the pound, watermelons weighed a lot, and poor kids had to save their pennies. "Sometimes we'd go around to the stores." Gary Stewart smiled at the memory. "Sometimes they'd drop one. They'd come in big trucks and they'd toss them." Broken watermelons were set outside the back door of the market, and the kids gathered up sweet juicy hunks of scarlet fruit, delighting in the arching trajectory of spit black seeds.

"One time we went and bought a watermelon." Barbara laughed as she told the story. "I was around eight or nine years old. We walked downtown. It was real hot, one summer day, and this store was selling watermelon for like a penny and a half a pound." Dick Porterfield picked out a huge one. Twenty-five pounds. He paid for it with his own money. "He says, 'Okay, we're going to take turns carrying this watermelon back home. I'll carry it a block, and you carry it a block.'"

Barbara was small for her age, and it was a long trudge back to Hayes Street. After about eight blocks, changing off and on with him, Barbara said, "Richard, you've got to help me. I'm going to drop it. My arms won't hold it anymore. And then, *crash!* I dropped it on the grass. Broke into like twenty pieces. And he looked at me, and he said, 'Well, we'd better sit down and eat it. I don't want it to go to waste.' So, right then and there on someone's lawn, we sat down and ate that watermelon. Ate the whole thing."

Gary Stewart also cherished juicy watermelon dreams. One summer afternoon, he and Dick Porterfield were hanging out on the U of O campus. They spent a lot of time roaming the open stacks of the college library. Over a million volumes. "The library was sort of our home. We got full run of the University of Oregon library." In those days, Thirteenth Street traversed the campus and on that particular afternoon a watermelon dropped off a passing truck just as the two kids happened by. "We went out, and we just ate the heart. Something you've always wanted to do. Just eat the heart."

In the fall of 1947, Dick Porterfield, Gary Stewart, and the Hiebert twins began their first year of junior high at Woodrow Wilson school on Jefferson Street. In a bizarre life coincidence seemingly lifted from the pages of Brautigan's fiction, among their classmates in the seventh grade were two other sets of identical twins. The edge-of-town boys soon became fast friends with Charles and Arthur Wical and with Jerry and John Wicks, each pair mirror-image bookends. They all shared a passion for basketball. Dick Porterfield played center for Wilson Junior High during his first year. This didn't last long. By the time they reached high school none of them tried out for the team for fear of spending most of the season warming the bench.

The Hiebert twins were Baptists and attended a church on Ninth and Broadway that had a gym. They'd all go there after school to shoot some hoops. "We'd slip in the back door," Gary Stewart recalled. Art Wical remembered the ceilings in the downstairs gym at First Baptist were less than ten feet high. "It was a shortened court, and we used to have to shoot shorter shots, and we'd try to learn how to slam the ball there because the basket was smaller."

Being tallest, Dick Porterfield played center. The other four starting players were the Hieberts and the Wical brothers. The impromptu clandestine games evolved into an official church team. First Baptist played against Eugene's other denominations in a league organized by the YMCA. The same group of kids also played noon intramural ball at the Wilson school playground. Don Hiebert dubbed this gang of look-alikes the "Vagrant Varlets." They all got in on the gag, taunting their opponents with mock Old English insults in the heat of the action. "Fie on you," they'd shout, whenever a point was scored against them. "A pox on your head; you fouled me!" It drove the other teams crazy. "A pox on you all!"

Along with their pithy archaic epithets, the Varlets had a talent for ball handling. They won the league championship and went on to the regional YMCA finals in Walla Walla, Washington. Here, luck ran out and they got their asses kicked. Not even extravagant extemporaneous wit saved the day.

Nominally a Catholic, young Dick began attending the First Baptist Church about the same time he started sneaking into their basement gym. During his first year at Woodrow Wilson, he received a signed certificate for his attendance at the Junior High Week Day Church School. In grade school, Dick attended Bible class for an hour each day. He took his Bible to bed with him every night until he was twenty, but Dick Porterfield's affiliation with any organized religion was short-lived.

The family never prayed or went to church together. "We never did anything together as a family, let alone pray," Barbara said. Gary Stewart remembered his friend as "sort of a teenage philosopher." Peter Webster, another friend from those years who played for the First Christian Church basketball team against the Varlets, recalled that "Dick claimed to be an atheist. We had long discussions about God, church, and religion. But they consisted mostly of Dick talking and my listening."

Don Hiebert stated that Brautigan seemed "angry" at those whose religious feelings did not coincide with his own. Whatever his spiritual beliefs, Dick Porterfield soon stopped going to church altogether. "He believed in God and in the Bible but he didn't like preachers," Mary Lou commented. "'Because, Mother,' he says, 'It's all graft. You have to donate 20 percent of your income to the preacher.' He said all the preachers in Eugene are millionaires."

Dick Porterfield's true religion was going to the movies, worshipping at the altar of the silver screen. In the period after World War II, there were six movie theaters in Eugene. The McDonald and the Heilig ("holy" in German) featured first-run shows. Boasting plush seats and gilded ornamentation, the Heilig Theater was the finest building in town when it opened in 1903 (as the Eugene), hosting touring vaudeville companies before converting to motion picture use in 1926.

The Heilig had an elaborate electric sign arching across Willamette Street, advertising its odd name in letters large enough to be seen from the Southern Pacific Railroad Station many blocks away on Fourth Avenue. Ken Kesey, born the same year as Brautigan and raised in Springfield, just across the river, described the fabulous sign: "flashing what we all took to be the Norwegian word for 'hello,' . . . 'Heilig, Heilig, Heilig.'"

Of the second-run theaters, the Mayflower and the Lane were both managed by the Heilig, while the McDonald controlled the Rex. The State Theater, a miserable hole-in-the-wall, was not well attended. Run-down and shabby, the Lane showed mainly Westerns. Located on a side street off the lower end of Willamette (at that time Eugene's skid row), the Lane charged only a dime. Hobos and winos frequently went in to sleep off a jag, their muffled snores competing with the thundering hoof beats and *crack* of six-guns. Mary Lou remembered large rats running across the stage in the dark at the Lane. Barbara recalled the rodents coming even closer. "It wasn't unusual if you felt something brush your leg."

Dick and B.J. went to the movies together frequently, walking eighteen blocks downtown to save bus fare. An Arthur Murray Studio was located close by the Lane. "Walk in and dance out," Dick quipped to his sister as they passed the entrance. They never bought any popcorn in the theater, another economy measure. The show was always a double feature, with newsreels, cartoons, a serial episode, and an occasional short subject. On Saturdays, they arrived early, shortly after noon, when the first bill began, and stayed through until closing, around midnight, seeing the films over and over. They didn't ever sit together. Dick enjoyed being up close to the screen. Barbara preferred sitting in the back. After the show was over (and over and over), they'd meet outside and walk home, talking about what they had just seen.

Peter Webster remembered Dick as "a fanatic about movies." In the summer, he would go "every day of the week if he could. When he found one he liked he would watch it again and again." *Shane*, starring Alan Ladd and Jack Palance, was one of Dick Porterfield's particular favorites. "He loved it because the props were so authentic and the costumes were authentic." Dick first saw *Shane* on his only trip to a drive-in. The picture came on during an electrical storm, furious flashes of heat lightning igniting the dark sky behind the screen. "It made *Shane* seem almost like a religion."

Movies haunted Dick Porterfield's imagination. Playing make-believe games with the neighborhood gang, Dick pretended to be Frankenstein's monster, "dragging his foot and waving his arms." Another horror movie had a profound effect on young Dick's psyche. *The Beast with Five Fingers*, starring Peter Lorre, was a Curt Siodmak tale of a murdered pianist whose disembodied hand assumed a life of its own, creeping around spiderlike on its fingertips, taking revenge in the dead of night.

Dick saw the picture with Gary Stewart in the fall of 1947. They walked downtown and when the show was over headed home together. It was late and very dark. There was no traffic, and the two boys walked up the middle of Tenth Street, the film's grim mood enveloping them. Low flights of migrating geese thrashed through the blackness overhead. Filled with dread, they held hands.

Gary looked back over his shoulder and saw a shadowy "hand" scuttling after them down the street. They panicked and ran for their lives. Gripped by utter terror, they fled into the darkness for five or six blocks before reason prevailed. Gasping for breath, the boys agreed they'd seen a large dry maple leaf blown along the macadam by the wind.

Imagination feeds on the irrational. By the time Dick Porterfield arrived home that night, uncontrollable fear gripped him like a fever. "God, he was wild," his mother remembered. "He'd wake up screaming. I laid down on the bed beside him and spent the night with him. All he mentioned was the hand was going to get him. He was so frightened."

The horrors of actual life exact a more profound toll than manufactured fantasies. Donald Husband, Dick Porterfield's ninth-grade classmate at Woodrow Wilson, died on March 29, 1949, in a shooting accident involving a .22 rifle. Donny played first string on the basketball team and had been a member of the Golden Ball Tournament champions the previous year. Wealthy by Eugene standards, the Husband family lived in a big house on Charnelton Street. Dad was a partner in a local law firm. The smiling picture above *The Register-Guard*'s front-page article showed a confident, well-loved kid.

Donald Husband died hunting pheasants among the old apple orchards on Bailey Hill, where Dick Porterfield often shot birds with Barbara. His death struck a powerful chord in the future author. Sudden tragic events take a permanent hold on the youthful imagination. "All of us at school remember," Gary Stewart said of Donny's unexpected death. "He was a popular kid."

Not long after the Porterfields moved into the house on Thirteenth, Mary Lou caught the eye of her neighbor, Bill Folston, who was one-half Nez Percé. Recently discharged from the army, Bill lived with his father in the little house they owned on Hayes Street. He was three years younger than the grass widow next door. However they first met, whether because Sandra toddled over through the fence into the lonely bachelor's yard as she remembered, or if Mary Lou draped herself across the woodpile, feigning a swoon in her ratty fur coat, as Barbara recalled, Mrs. Porterfield was soon pregnant by Folston and suffered a miscarriage in 1949. "We lived together for three years," Mary Lou recalled, "and I said, 'I'm not going to marry you, you big Indian swamp, you.' Oh, god, I was constantly insulting him."

Moonshine Bess died of myocardial infarction at the Good Samaritan Hospital in Portland on April 19, 1950. Around the same time, Mary Lou found herself once again in a family way. "She never, ever showed," Sandra recalled. "I don't ever remember her wearing a maternity outfit when she was pregnant with my younger brother." Though she was "under the shotgun," Mary Lou looked quite trim when she applied for a license and married William Folston in Nevada on June 12, 1950. They tied the knot at the Washoe County Courthouse in Reno, District Judge A. J. Maestretti presiding. She used the name Mary Lou Porterfield. On her marriage license application affidavit, she claimed that her previous husband was deceased.

In fact, Mary Lou's divorce from Robert Geoffry Porterfield did not become final until one month later, on the twelfth of July, but she didn't let legal technicalities get in the way. "I kept telling that man I wasn't going to marry him until we got to the courthouse," she insisted. "It was all assigned like that, you know. Three minutes. 'I now pronounce you husbands and wives. My fee is $10 each and goodbye. I don't want to see you back here for a divorce next month either.' And he said it all in broken English."

That night at the motel, the newlyweds lay in bed watching a pair of rats cavort in the moonlight on the window ledge. Nose to nose, the rodents did something strange with their mouths. It looked like they were kissing. "And this on our wedding day. Oh my god! What a nightmare."

Bill Folston dreamed a different dream. "I don't think there was anybody in the world any better-hearted than him," recalled Barbara's husband, Jim Fitzhugh. Barbara assessed her new stepfather with affection. "I have to admire him for taking on a woman that had three children and then having a fourth and working two jobs and doing the best he could to support this family." A born-again optimist, Bill Folston probably viewed the kissing rats as a good omen, lying in the dark beside his new bride, the son he longed for already growing inside her.

Life changed for the Porterfield clan after their mother's marriage to the man next door. Mary Lou never worked outside the home again. No more waitress jobs or walking downtown to clean a dentist's office. She had found her nest at last. Just before David's birth some deficiency was detected in her blood and her doctor prescribed a pint of beer per day. "It was to build up something in her blood," Barbara said. "She hated beer. For a long time she had a terrible time getting that one beer down."

After a while, the medicine got easier to swallow. One beer led to another, "and then it became more and more and more and more." Most days, by late afternoon Mary Lou was feeling no pain. Even on deer-hunting trips with the boisterous Folston clan, she made sure to bring along a little taste. "I'd always have a couple quarts of beer that I used to put in the creek and get it nice and cold," Mary Lou said. "Sneak it on the side." It got so Dick and Barbara couldn't stand to see their mother chain-smoking, a glass in the other hand, that glazed look clouding her eyes. After one particularly bad afternoon, the two kids promised each other, "We'll never do that. We don't want to end up like her."

William David Folston was born in Eugene on December 19, 1950. For a time after the baby arrived, the family occupied both residences on the corner lot at Hayes and West Thirteenth. "Mom and Bill and Sandi lived in the other house," Barbara recollected. She and Dick remained at the rented Shields place. "By ourselves. Over there." They raised cats in secret, feeding them the heads and innards of the catfish they caught in the logging ponds. Once, they kept a pet mouse in a fish bowl filled with torn-up newspaper. When Mary Lou found out, "it disappeared."

At night, they listened to the radio. They didn't have a phonograph, so this provided their only source for music. Dick liked the pseudo-Peruvian warbling of Yma Sumac and Eartha Kitt's low feline growl. "I Love a Mystery," "The Lone Ranger," "Inner Sanctum," and "The Shadow" were among their favorite dramatic programs.

"He'd make up stories," Barbara remembered fondly. "We'd sit there and he'd tell me these ghost stories." Barbara thought Dick's made-up tales were better than the ones on the radio. "I'd be more scared from the things he'd tell me." The bond between Dick and B.J. grew ever stronger in these shared hours of make-believe. Their isolation reinforced a conviction born two years earlier after being unfairly punished by their mother. "We got to talking," Barbara remembered, "and he asked me: 'Do you think we're adopted?'"

"And I said, 'Well, I probably am because I sure don't look like any of the family.'"

"And he said something to the fact that the way we were punished and everything, that we just didn't fit in with the rest of the family and perhaps we were adopted. And then we couldn't figure it out. If she indeed didn't like us, why would she take us with her? It was obvious to us that she didn't care for us."

There wasn't space enough in the little one-bedroom house at 1287 Hayes for Dick and B.J. This inherent inhospitality manifested itself in various odd ways. When Barbara wandered over one afternoon during canning season, she found a kettle full of fruit jars sterilizing on the stove. All the water had boiled away and the little girl in pigtails was only helping out when she poured a pan of cold water onto the hot glass. The jars exploded in her face. "It's just amazing Barbara was never scarred from that," Sandra observed.

Psychological scars endure long after all trace of physical injury fades. Soon after David's birth, Bill Folston added a bedroom onto his house. Mary Lou moved in the minute it was finished. Not wanting any more children, she dropped a final curtain on sleeping with her husband. Big-hearted Bill wished to bring the family closer, so he moved Dick and Barbara over to live at his place. Cramped quarters grew even tighter. B.J. and Sandi slept on a fold-out davenport in the dining/living area opposite the kitchen. Dick Porterfield bunked on a cot set up in the tiny breakfast nook. Dick was over six foot at fifteen. His legs hung far off the end of the cot, and his mother placed a crate there so he'd have a place to rest his size 12s.

Postwar prosperity bypassed the corner of West Thirteenth and Hayes, where the Kitchen of Tomorrow remained today's impossible dream. Only Depression-era amenities graced the Folston household. Two iron wood-burning stoves, one in the kitchen, the other perching, squat and black, in the living area, provided heat and cooking facilities. Not having electric refrigeration, the family made do with a discarded commercial "Coke" cooler with a sliding top and a recessed opener mounted in the side.

Celebrating Christmas had never been a very big deal for the Porterfields, and the holiday remained a low-key occasion even after they moved in with Bill Folston. Mary Lou baked a turkey and a mince pie, what she called "gourmet cooking." Barbara recalled that it wasn't "like most kids think Christmas is. You've seen the trees like in Snoopy, where there is a tree with five branches . . . ? That was our tree. On a wooden cross stand. One set of bubble lights. Maybe ten or twelve balls. I think we each got one present. And that was it." Barbara and Dick never exchanged Christmas gifts.

The Folston family ate a lot of venison, the pauper's filet. Bill went hunting with his brothers near the family ranch in eastern Oregon every year, filling not only his own tag, but those he bought for his wife and stepson as well. They stored the meat in a Eugene cold locker for use throughout the rest of the year. A good hand in camp, Bill Folston assumed his share of the cooking chores at home as well. Bill made a delicious gravy from deer steak drippings that he called "coyote puke," pouring it over fresh-baked biscuits for breakfast. Dick Porterfield loved it, never passing on seconds.

Coming back a day late from a deer-hunting trip cost Bill Folston his job. He'd been working as a draper at Lyon's Furniture. Depressed after getting canned, he lay "around on the davenport and read the paper about ten days." Simmering with adolescence, Dick Porterfield had a teen-tuned sense of inequality that boiled over one afternoon when he came across his stepfather stretched out on the couch, a spread newspaper over his face. "What're you going to do? Lay around on your butt all the time and have Mama do all the work for you?"

Bill got up and went out the front door without a word. He signed on at Wyatt's, recapping tires, the very same day. Even so, tension remained electric between Dick and Bill. Having a new man around Mom after more than five years undoubtedly added unfamiliar emotional energy to the teenager's awakening sexuality. Even big-hearted Bill didn't want to see that hostile stare every time he came into his pop-stand kitchen. He set immediately to work on further home reconstruction. A built-on garage with a dirt floor sagged against the outside kitchen wall. It was not a big space, the floor area no more than eight feet by ten feet. The Folstons stored stove wood there, as well as in the shed on the other side of the kitchen door. They decided the old garage would make a perfect bedroom for Dick Porterfield.

Bill fixed the place up in a rudimentary way. "It was just tar paper," Barbara remembered. "Tar paper on the outside, tar paper on the inside of the house part, and he kind of finished it up a little bit."

"It was more like a hut than anything else," Chuck Wical recollected. For Dick Porterfield, it promised pure Huck Finn freedom. Having a separate entrance from the main house allowed him to come and go as he pleased. B.J. fretted because he didn't have direct access to a bathroom. When the hour grew late, Dick avoided disturbing the others by not using the inside facilities. "I think that was why he did a lot of walking," Barbara surmised. "He'd walk to a service station or something to go to the bathroom if he had to."

B.J., a vivacious and gregarious girl, didn't comprehend the solitary compulsions of a natural-born loner like her brother. Dick never explained his need to wander the dark streets of Eugene for hours late at night. The seeds of poetry often require nocturnal cultivation. Walking along alone in the shadows also felt kind of cool. His primitive tar paper room became both Dick's refuge and a portal to independence.

"It was very, very messy." Art Wical spent many hours in Dick's hideout room, yet couldn't remember ever meeting any of his family. "I just knew that he had a sister." Young Porterfield began a lifelong habit of compartmentalizing his friendships. He assumed a secret life. By the last year of high school, Dick had a typewriter, a telephone, and a radio out in his room. Certain physical improvements had also been made. A window went in after Bill Folston spotted an advertisement for salvage in the paper. "Grandpa" Charlie Hines, a neighbor, performed the needed carpentry. He also hung the door Dick found somewhere to replace what his mother called "an old shackle-door."

Once he started high school, Dick retreated to the sanctity of his room, spending less time with Barbara. Babysitting continued as a regular chore, but Sandi was now the little girl he hauled along to the logging ponds. More than ever before, fishing consumed Dick Porterfield's life. Adventurous trips meant heading up the McKenzie. Peter Webster said his friend "knew every fishing hole on the river." Dick's favorite stretch ran from Leaburg Dam to the South Fork of the McKenzie. "We fished Gate Creek, Indian Creek, Vida, Leaburg Reservoir, Blue River, Good Pasture Islands, South Fork, Clear Lake, Olala, Paradise."

Dick walked or hitchhiked to his favorite spots on the McKenzie. One afternoon when he was twelve, Dick caught a ride with an affable stranger. After a few minutes, the guy put his hand on Dick's leg. The kid didn't panic. Keeping a straight face, he told the pederast that his father was chief of police of the next little town down the road. The offending hand was immediately withdrawn. The pervert dropped Dick off safely. Years later, when Richard told this story to his daughter, she took the moral to be "it's okay to lie in order to save your ass."

B.J. remained enough of a tomboy at twelve to still want to go fishing. She remembered "getting up early in the morning" and walking twenty miles with her brother if they didn't thumb down a ride. "We'd get home late at night during the summer." Lorna Smith, two years younger than Dick Porterfield, glimpsed him once during this period from a bus window and retained an image all the rest of her life: "He was tall and had overalls on and looked raggedy, and that's how he stuck in my mind. He had a fishing pole, and it reminded me of Tom Sawyer."

The soup bowl haircuts Mary Lou gave her white-blond oldest son only enhanced this archetype, a Mark Twain character hitchhiking up the McKenzie in the rain with a fly rod under his arm and a peanut butter sandwich in his pocket. A number of cherished Folston family tales involved Dick's fishing obsession. In the retelling, they sound like ghost chapters from *Trout Fishing in America*.

A year or so before she died, Bessie Dixon paid her last visit to Eugene, bringing her grandson a brand-new woolen suit. Mary Lou organized a picnic. The family went out to Skinner Butte, a popular city park where bears were kept caged in pits. The Willamette River provided the park's northern boundary. After lunch, Dick went fishing. He'd long admired a snapshot of Moonshine Bess and a twenty-five-pound salmon she'd caught from the cupola-covered sundeck of her riverbank home in St. Helens. Richard returned at dusk, having slipped and fallen in the river. His new wool trousers had shrunk comically high above his ankles, as if he'd swapped clothes with a midget.

Mary Lou thought her son "was kind of afraid" of Bessie. "I don't remember any loving affection between him or her. My mother was businesslike. She'd kiss you hello and goodbye and that was that." Barbara recalled things differently. "Richard and I both liked her. Jovial, easygoing, seemed to me she laughed all the time. Was very warm and loving, I can remember, but we didn't get to see her that much. I have maybe about three or four recollections of visiting with her. My mother wasn't that close to her."

Another time, Dick Porterfield hooked a huge salmon spawning in shallow water far up the McKenzie. After a monumental thrashing fight, he maneuvered the big fish up onto a gravel bank. Barbara remembered that "he called home and asked my stepdad if he could come up there, probably because it was illegal. It must have weighed twenty-five pounds." Mary Lou related how her son failed once to come home from fishing. Having a laissez-faire attitude about Dick's late-night angling, she didn't get worried until the next day and was on the phone with the sheriff when he finally walked in the door just before noon. He'd gotten lost after dark far up the McKenzie, fishing some remote feeder creek, and had taken refuge in a strange mountain cabin.

"Mama, they were really crazy," he said of the people he met there. "They scared me to death." Mary Lou recalled that he spent the night in the cabin but didn't sleep. "He was eyeing them and they were eyeing him. They were really weird." Perhaps this was the "large shack [. . .] with a lot of old cars surrounding it" described in the short story "A Short History of Oregon." There was something spooky about the old place with a "crude makeshift porch," where four shoeless children with hair "unruly like dwarf witches'," watched the narrator pass by in the rain.

For Christmas in 1951, Bill Folston gave his stepson a side-by-side double-barreled sixteen-gauge shotgun, the first firearm Dick ever owned. Later in life, Richard Brautigan told his daughter that his stepfather "taught me how to hunt and bought me a .22 rifle for my thirteenth birthday." According to Mary Lou, Dick Porterfield did not have a .22 rifle when he was a kid. She remembered her husband once giving Dick a fine pearl-handled pocket knife. "He said, 'Put this away for me, Mama.' And I still got that thing. I figured he didn't want it because Papa gave it to him."

Dick Porterfield owned a little dog, a ten-pound brown and white rat terrier named Pluto. Bill Folston brought home a pair of pups given to him by a neighbor. Pluto was the runt of the litter, his sister, "fat and sassy." They kept the little dogs in a cardboard box in the kitchen and fed them milk from a bottle. The bitch was given away. Dick named Pluto after the Disney character. The feisty little dog loved chasing car tires. Potholes cratered the gravel street outside, and traffic passed slowly. Pluto ran out from ambush and bit hold of the tires, whirling round and round, "two or three times," before being hurled free from the jouncing automobiles. Pluto bit automobile tires every day for years until he was killed by a car one night, following Dick to a neighborhood grocery store.

Though he was famed as a watch dog and slayer of rats, Pluto's finest canine attribute was his ability to find birds. "He'd take off running, in wheat fields and tall grass, and he would point." Dick and Barbara hunted pheasants together out West Sixth Street and up among the old orchards on Bailey Hill, where the Husband boy had been killed. "He had no license or nothing," his mother remembered, "but he could bag pheasants." Dick was right-handed but shot left-handed. He was a decent wing-shot.

Hunting together with Pluto became Dick and B.J.'s final shared adventure. The next year she contracted polio. At twelve, she still walked by his side, watching him bring down the birds Pluto flushed out of weed-choked irrigation ditches. Barbara thought her brother might soon need glasses. He couldn't tell the roosters from the hens. "When he killed the hens, I carried them under my coat," B.J. said. "And if it was a rooster, he carried it across his shoulder."

They hunted for food. Mary Lou served fried pheasant whenever Dick brought birds home. Dick went out with Pluto alone after B.J. was ill. Sometimes he was accompanied by Gary Stewart. The two boys hunted together before Bill gave Dick the shotgun. "We used to get my dad's guns," Gary remembered, "sneak those out, and we'd go hunt pheasants out West Eleventh as far as Fern Ridge." They also hunted the sloughs south of Eugene. "Every Sunday morning we'd make a run down through that gully, and there would always be a few ducks that came up."

The Folston family owned a ranch in Halsey, in eastern Oregon. Every fall the brothers hunted deer and elk together up Bridge Creek or Gable Creek in the nearby mountains of the Ochoco National Forest. At fourteen, Dick Porterfield accompanied Bill Folston, not yet married to Mary Lou, and stepuncles (Matt, Andy, Seldon, Jim, and Larry) on his first and only deer-hunting expedition.

Dick never talked about an incident in camp on this trip. Uncle Larry rubbed venison blood all over his face while he lay sleeping and woke the boy by pouring ice-cold creek water into his ear. "Uncle Larry was mean," Mary Lou declared. "And so was his wife." The blood baptism occurred the same year Donald Husband died. "I don't know what happened," Barbara said. "He went once, and he would never go again. He just hated that whole thing."

Dick and B.J. didn't do much together once he was in high school. She was sick a lot. Starting with polio at thirteen, Barbara was hit with life-threatening illnesses on a yearly basis. Mary Lou summed things up: "She had polio and she had spinal meningitis the following year and the year after that she had virus of the spine." Healthy again at sixteen, B.J. gladly took a live-in job away from home, caring for the children of the wealthy Guistina family, who owned a local lumber yard.

Dick Porterfield attended Eugene High School, a three-story factorylike brick building at the corner of Seventeenth and Lincoln. With its many windows, it must have seemed quite progressive when the block-long structure was built in 1915. Termed "commodious" at the time, the school could no longer accommodate its student population. The Class of 1953 (Dick's class), was the last to graduate before a new campus opened across town as South Eugene High.

American high schools in the early 1950s resembled Archie Andrews much more than *Blackboard Jungle.* Everybody sported "I Like Ike" and "I Go Pogo" pins. Rock and roll had not emerged from the black rhythm-and-blues stations at the far ends of the AM band to knock Joni James, Eddie Fisher, Johnnie Ray, and Patti Page off the pop charts forever. Eugene High held noontime hops, and the kids slow-danced to the strains of "How Much Is That Doggie in the Window," "Love Letters in the Sand," and "Ghost Riders in the Sky."

The big clothing fad among the boys demanded garish plaid or checked trousers. Most guys trimmed their hair short in crew cuts, popular since the GIs came home victorious from World War II. The gals looked even worse, sporting short, perky "Which Twin Has the Toni" perms, Peter Pan blouses, bobby socks, saddle shoes, and straight skirts hemmed at midcalf, the most unflattering length of the century.

Dick Porterfield remained impervious to fads and the sartorial demands of the clique fashion police. "He was a loner, you know," his mother explained. Solitary by nature, Dick withdrew more and more into a private realm several dimensions away from high school high jinks. He and Gary Stewart "sort of drifted apart. We were friends, but I had a different group of people that I went around with." Dick still played intramural ball with the Heibert and Wical twins, but he mainly hung out with Stan Oswald and Rex Sorenson, helping them with their homework. Rexford's mother was a schoolteacher, and he needed all the help he could get to live up to her lofty expectations. Rex also aspired to become a writer. He planned on going to college and learning how to write but ended up with a PhD in education instead.

No one expected anything much of Dick Porterfield, who had no plans for college. He continued to be an indifferent scholar at best. Don Hiebert remembered his friend writing "genius level" papers in high school. He felt Dick capable of the honor roll had he cared about grades. The school officials listed Dick's IQ as 105. He probably also goofed off during his intelligence tests. Hiebert thought Porterfield did lesser work to "flaunt it" to his teachers. Barbara recalled her brother being "very good in school—in the subjects that he liked."

Dick Porterfield remained an invisible presence at Eugene High. Roland Medel (editor of the *EHS News,* varsity football player, and National Honor Society member), a BMOC with a wide range of friends and acquaintances, can't recall him at all. Medel became a fan of Brautigan's work twenty years later and was stunned to discover they had once been classmates. He asked many of those from his varied circles if they remembered Richard in school. The best answer he got was, "'Kind of a tall lanky kid—maybe light-colored hair.'"

Dick Porterfield's anonymity arose from his diffidence as much as from his difference. He never attended any school sporting events and was not an easy social mixer. "We used to hold up the wall at the dances," Chuck Wical recalled. "Have our leather jackets on . . ."

"He was very shy around women," remembered Barbara. "He was so good-looking. He had the most gorgeous blue eyes and perfect teeth. I thought he was very handsome. Pure blond hair. He wore his hair longer than the other boys, combing it in a platinum wave across his forehead."

However gorgeous, Dick Porterfield had no girlfriends in high school, nor did he go out on a single date during those hormonally turbulent years. He was a neat boy who liked to look nice. The leather jacket he wore to the dances was tan suede with knit cuffs and collar, styled like a letterman's sweater. Not just something cheap off the rack at Penney's but quality goods from a downtown haberdashery. "Cost him quite a bit of money," B.J. noted.

At home, Dick kept to himself, hanging out in his room when meals and his chores were done. A neighbor had shown him how to tie flies, and he labored over the Thompson vise with his bodkin and beeswax-coated thread, winding fur and feathers and tinsel into tiny exquisite barbed creations as intricate and bright as jewelry. Sandra remembers her brother with the vise in his lap, tying flies on the gold couch in the new addition Bill Folston had built onto the living room.

Work remained the polar opposite of fishing. Dick Porterfield's height allowed him to abandon picking beans, a close-to-the-ground crop, and work the hops harvest instead. Hops orchards, rare in the Willamette Valley today, were quite numerous in the 1950s. The leafy vine grew on wire trellises more than six feet high. Kids with a religious bent, like Peter Webster, wouldn't pick hops because the dried blossoms were used in the manufacture of beer. It was very hard work. The long sacks dragged on the ground, and it took a vast quantity of the feathery flowers to have enough for a paycheck.

Dick Porterfield finally found a dream job after school and on Saturdays, working for Mrs. Manerude, a prosperous old woman who owned a big house in the university district. She hired him for yard work and various odd chores around her place. "Manerude-Huntington" was how Mary Lou remembered her, "very wealthy lumber, fuel people." Mrs. Manerude figures in the chapter from *Trout Fishing* called "Trout Fishing on the Street of Eternity": "She was in her nineties [. . .] The house was four stories high and had at least thirty rooms and the old lady was five-feet high and weighed about eighty-two pounds."

The new employment occasioned a change in the domestic routine at home. Dick and Barbara had long shared the chore of washing dishes. He did the drying. Working for Mrs. Manerude caused him to start slacking off. "He felt it beneath him to do the dishes," B.J. noted. They hassled over the matter continuously until Mary Lou laid down the law. One week Dick washed. The next was Barbara's turn. The system seemed "pretty fair" to the kids. Dick soon started slacking off again, coming up with excuses every time his turn rolled around. He offered to pay his sister twenty-five cents a week for his share of the dish washing.

"That was a lot of money back then," Barbara recalled. She started doing the dishes every night. At first, she collected her two bits like clockwork every Friday. Before long, Dick got behind on his payments. Eventually, his debt totaled over $9. Barbara was furious. Her dark curls framed her anger like a thunder cloud when she demanded her money. Dick said he'd pay her tomorrow. He returned from work the next day carrying a heavy paper sack. "Here's your $9 and change that I owe you," he said without a trace of a smile as he poured nearly two hundred nickels out onto the kitchen table.

Before Sandra was born, Mary Lou bought an old wicker baby carriage for $5. It had wood spoke wheels and a hood. In *So the Wind Won't Blow It All Away*, this "baby buggy" was used to collect beer bottles along the highway. Barbara remembered pushing Sandi as an infant in the wicker carriage. The family wheeled it out once again for baby David. Dick appropriated the buggy for gathering discarded deposit bottles and "pretended that it was a covered wagon for a while and pulled my sisters and other kids around in it." With his mother's permission, he also used it to haul his gardening tools all the way across town to Mrs. Manerude's house.

Mrs. Manerude liked the pale-haired boy and gave him plants culled from her garden. He carted them home to his mother in the wicker baby buggy. Mary Lou was proud of her extensive flower garden and grateful for all the contributions from Mrs. Manerude. Her son was on to a good thing. "She just adored him. He was perfect. And because I was his mother she'd call me on the phone and talk sometimes for an hour or two if she'd get lonely."

During his high school years, Dick Porterfield's babysitting responsibilities assumed a level of vigilance more in keeping with his approaching manhood. When Sandi was a little girl, the mean-spirited sons of an itinerant preacher stripped off all her clothing and sent her home naked, "crying so hard that she had blood spots on her face." The preacher lived nearby on West Twelfth. "Mother, you stay out of this," Dick said when he heard of the outrageous abuse. "I'll handle it."

Dick Porterfield marched straight over to the shabby house on West Twelfth. The preacher and his kids were inside with the door locked. When Dick knocked, they wouldn't let him in. He kicked the front door off its hinges, demanding to know what they had done to his little sister. "They said they didn't do nothing to her," Mary Lou recounted. When her son returned home, "he said, 'Mom, I could have wrung their grizzly necks.'" Shortly thereafter, the preacher and his family packed up their stuff and vanished in the middle of the night.

On another occasion, Sandi came home from school one wet winter day "all covered in green slime." She had been accosted by a neighborhood "half-wit" on a shortcut across Amazon Creek and pushed into the shallow slough. Her pretty new red wool coat had been ruined. The brutal kid ("a big oaf and mean") lived just up the street from the Folstons. Sandi easily identified him. When he heard about it, Dick Porterfield headed over to the oaf's house to settle the score. "He was very firm and very direct when something was wrong," Mary Lou said. "We never saw that kid again."

In the fall of 1952, at the beginning of Dick's senior year, Mary Lou dropped a bombshell on him and B.J. Their last name wasn't really Porterfield. "Richard was getting ready to graduate from high school," Barbara recalled, "and I was getting ready to graduate from junior high, and my mother said to Richard, 'Well, you might as well go by your real name. Better have your real name put on your diploma.' And I looked at him, and he looked at me. 'Real name? That is our name!' Because that's what we thought it was. So, she told him his name was Brautigan and then he started going by that." There was no fuss made about his new identity. It was no big deal. Dick Porterfield slipped out of his old name with as little regret as a snake shedding its skin.

Not long after his eighteenth birthday on January 30, 1953, the young man who reported to his draft board for a preinduction physical registered as Richard Brautigan. A group of draft-age boys were bused together to Portland from Eugene and put up at a hotel close by the Selective Service induction center for three days of testing and medical examination. A rough sergeant harangued the young men for hours, telling them it was time to straighten out, they soon would be pulled from their loving homes and never see their families again. Dick Brautigan seemed changed somehow when he came home that Sunday evening. "Richard was shook up," Mary Lou recounted. "He says, 'Mother, I'll never put a gun in my hands to kill another man.'" Dick at first was classified 1A but that designation changed to 4F because of his scoliosis.

On his permanent high school record, Dick had been listed as "Porterfield, Richard Gary." His new last name, "Brautigan," was typed in just above the previous one. His father remained recorded as "Robert Porterfield," profession: "laborer, cook." Brautigan once boasted to Keith Abbott of getting "straight As" for a semester on a whim and then abandoning the experiment "because he couldn't find any reason to continue." Like many tall tales he told of his youth, this was pure fiction. Richard Brautigan graduated with a grade point average of 2.093, standing number 230 in a class of 287.

As graduation approached, Dick participated in all the usual rites of passage. He had appeared in the 1951 annual as "R. Porterfield," as always towering a head above his classmates in the group photograph. In 1952, he skipped the photo session entirely and was not mentioned in the *Eugenean* under any name at all. He sat for his formal portrait in 1953 (perhaps the only picture ever taken of Richard Brautigan wearing a necktie) and appeared alphabetically, a sly smile on his face, with his classmates in the yearbook. His first prescription for eyeglasses had already been filled, but Dick didn't wear his new cheaters in front of the camera. As he had joined no clubs, participated in no activities, and played no sport other than intramural basketball, his picture does not appear anywhere else in the 162-page volume.

When the annuals were passed out on the last day of school, Dick grabbed Pete Webster's copy, although he knew the varsity letterman only slightly. He scrawled a quick inscription and handed it back with his Cheshire cat grin. Pete read, "To my good friend, Peter Webster, drop dead!" It was signed, "Dick Brautigan."

"What'd you do that for?" Pete asked.

"Well," Dick shrugged, "what are friends for?"

The final issue of the high school paper came out on June 5. In the 1953 Class Will, "Dick Brautigan wills his science fiction books to Marsha Meyers." A certain editorial desperation clings to this entry. What do you say about a guy nobody knows? None of his family members nor his closest friends remembered any science fiction books.

At the last minute, Dick Brautigan announced his plans to skip the graduation ceremony, telling his mother, "I'm not going to graduate with those slobs."

"God, he's sick in the head," Mary Lou thought. "Those are the boys he grew up with, his friends, the Hiebert twins and all of that."

Dick told the authorities to mail his diploma to the house on Hayes. "The principal called me up and he was really upset," Mary Lou remembered. "I said, 'You take that kid in your office and you measure him for a cap and gown!' And he did. And Richard brought home this big old blue gown, and it took me three hours to press the wrinkles out of the thing. And I had a picture taken of him in it, eight by ten in color."

Dick dutifully wore his mortarboard and the flapping blue gown. At 8:00 PM, on June 9, 1953, he marched in with his class for the baccalaureate ceremony at McArthur Court, a large auditorium used for basketball, cultural, and civic activities on the University of Oregon campus. Bill and Mary Lou Folston arrived in their Sunday best. B.J. did not attend. She was already working for Guistina's and living away from home. Mary Lou cried when the high school band played Elgar's *Pomp and Circumstance*.

Mark O. Hatfield, dean of students at Willamette University and not yet embarked on his long political career, delivered the commencement address, choosing an optimistic theme, "The Golden Age," as his subject. The principal of Eugene High School presented the Class of 1953 to the gathered friends, relatives, and dignitaries, and the young men and women filed forward to receive their diplomas. Richard Gary Brautigan marched up in the front ranks, between Nellie Leah Brainard and Ronald Milton Bray. After the new graduates joined in singing their alma mater, a brief benediction followed, and the band played the recessional as they paraded out into the rest of their lives.

Backstage, the mood seemed jubilant. Mary Lou had her arms around Dick and Gary. The kids were off to a party that would last thirty-six hours. All except Dick Brautigan. "He came home," his mother remembered. "He said nuts with it." Dick didn't drink and had no desire to hang out with a bunch of puking drunks for the next day and a half. "He just came home, took off his clothes, and he went to bed or read or something." An apocryphal story circulating after Brautigan's suicide described a high school diploma leaning against the half-empty bottle by his body. Only another myth, cobwebs blown into the moonlight by a ghostly wind.

six: midnight driver's ed

THE FOLSTON FAMILY owned a '38 Chevy with no backseat. More than ten years old when they bought it, the shabby vehicle was all the car they could afford. Mary Lou never liked the original tan color. One summer day, she painted it black, using cans of house paint and a flat three-inch brush. Every Fourth of July, they'd drive north for a picnic at Uncle Larry's in Halsey, Oregon. David, the youngest and smallest, got to ride on the narrow shelf below the rear window. The other three kids rode in the trunk. Mary Lou folded a blanket in back to provide some comfort. Bill propped up the lid so they wouldn't smother to death. This was also how they traveled on family trips up the McKenzie to Fall Creek. Most of the time, the old heap rusted in the curving driveway in front of their home on Hayes Street.

In the early 1950s, public schools in Eugene did not offer driver's education and the more automotively adventurous youngsters improvised their learning experience. Chuck and Art Wical went joy-riding in their parents' car late at night when the old folks were asleep. The twins enlisted Dick Porterfield into their nocturnal driving scheme, not wanting to risk stealing their family auto one more time. They all waited in the darkness until the lights went out in the Folston household, letting another half hour go by "because people usually don't fall asleep that quickly," Art explained. When they thought the coast was clear, Dick sneaked back into the house, returning right away.

"Do you have them?" the twins whispered.

"Yeah." Dick Porterfield held up the keys. "Should I put them in the car?"

"No," they told him, "just unlock the door and roll down the window so we can steer it." Dick helped the brothers push the car toward the street. "There was quite a long driveway," Art recalled. "It was not a paved driveway. There were two tire-recessed areas, where they would drive in." It was sixty or seventy feet to the street and they had a difficult time maneuvering the old junker over an indentation in the drive.

Once they got the car on the street, they pushed it for another block and a half. This was standard operating procedure for the Wical brothers. "We didn't want to take it out where the lights were." At this point, Dick Porterfield climbed in, turned on the ignition, and put it in gear. "It was a stick shift, and we pushed it and had a heck of a time getting it started." As it happened, the battery was low, although they weren't aware of it at the time. When the engine turned over, they all piled in, driving slowly away down Hayes and turning left onto West Eleventh, heading out into the open countryside. None of them really knew how to drive.

After a mile or so, the headlights grew dimmer and dimmer. Worried, the Wicals instructed Dick to slow down and turn around. Dick swung the wheel but it was too late. The engine died, and they couldn't get the car going again. "We tried to push it, and still it wouldn't start," Art remembered. In the end, they had to push the old Chevy back down Eleventh, grunting and sweat-ing for more than a mile as they rolled the heavy car every foot of the way to Dick's house.

This misadventure was not Dick Porterfield's first automotive mishap. Walking home from a recent midnight ramble, he encountered a stranger lugging a five-gallon gas can up by the Moose Lodge. "Can I help you with that?" Dick inquired politely. He assisted the fellow with his heavy load, carrying the can all the way to where his car was parked on Chambers Street. The next morn-ing when Bill Folston got up to drive to work, there wasn't any gas in his tank. The mysterious stranger had stolen every drop.

Their epic endeavor with the Folston car cured the Wical twins of their illicit midnight driv-ing lessons. For Dick Porterfield, the experience led to a lifelong abhorrence of the automobile. Richard Brautigan never really learned how to drive. "I just don't have a love affair with the car," he wrote in *People* magazine in 1981. "I started to learn how to drive when I was a teenager, but I lost interest quickly."

seven: pounding at the gates of american literature

N THE SHORT story "⅓, ⅓, ⅓," Richard Brautigan's narrator "lived in a cardboard-lined shack of my own building." In 1952, Dick Porterfield was seventeen, and the "shack" was his make-shift bedroom in the lean-to garage. Brautigan's description of the neighborhood fits Thirteenth and Hayes. "We lived in a poor part of town where the streets weren't paved. The street was nothing more than a big mud puddle that you had to walk around." Dick Porterfield pounded on his typewriter late into the night, chasing his dreams in the tar paper shack. His fictional counterpart also typed the night away. "I was made a ⅓ partner because I had the typewriter."

Richard Brautigan's portrait of the artist as Dick Porterfield rings true. The teenager began his writing career in the tar paper bedroom on Hayes Street. Crazy comic-book-inspired fantasies and ghost stories improvised to amuse his sisters were warm-up exercises for the all-nighters at the typewriter. "I started writing poetry when I was 17-years old," Brautigan scrawled in a notebook dating from 1955. "At the age of twenty, I'm through writing poetry. Why does a poet stop writing poetry? I guess for the same reason the wind goes down in the evening."

Brautigan never stopped writing poetry. Everything he wrote remained essentially poetic, even when labeled short stories or novels. Dick Porterfield's first written composition achieving any sort of recognition came at the end of his sophomore year, in 1951. He and Gary Stewart were in the same Social Living class "and [Dick] wrote a piece that a stand-up comedian would do." Gary suggested that he read Dick's monologue aloud to the other students on the last day of school. Dick was too shy to face the class on his own.

Gary Stewart received permission from their teacher, Caroline Wood, to read Dick Porterfield's satiric piece on the dubious educational benefits of forcing kids to study such boring literary "classics" as *Silas Marner*. "It got laughs all the way through," Gary remembered, "and applause afterwards." The author, he recalled, "was very pleased." At sixteen, Dick Porterfield had already determined to make writing his life's work.

Like many other teenage boys who dreamed of becoming writers in the early 1950s, Dick's idol was Ernest Hemingway. Papa's rough-and-tumble enthusiasms (his irresistible grin serene amid the carnage of bullrings, African safaris, and Gulf Stream blue-water fishing) had erased any lingering public notion that writers were sissies. Twain, London, and Crane had earlier blazed their own adventurous trails for boys of Hemingway's generation to follow. Peter Webster recalled, "Richard talked about [Hemingway] all the time."

One of the earliest surviving Brautigan typescripts (original title, "A Refugee") dates from 1955 or before. "Somebody from Hemingway Land" is a two-hundred-word short story. It concerned the breakup of an interracial couple, an unusual theme for a young man living in the Pacific Northwest in the midfifties. The quirky humor of having a black woman interrupt hard-boiled dialogue with "Don't start talking like somebody from Hemingway Land," sets this brief vignette apart from other high school Hemingway imitations. In "Argument," an early poem from this same period, Brautigan wrote that he had met Hemingway in a dream and had a "terrible argument" with the older writer because he "thought that he was / a better writer / than I am." His family and friends didn't remember the story or the poem but agreed Ernest Hemingway was Dick's favorite writer.

Young writers need mentors even as they search for heroic models. In the fall of his senior year at Eugene High, Dick Brautigan enrolled in a creative writing class taught by Juliette Claire Gibson, a native New Yorker who had originated the course years before. A remarkable, flamboyant woman, Miss Gibson began teaching at the school in 1926 and had been there long enough to have guided the parents of many of her current students through the mysteries of syntax. In 1930, she wrote "A Tribute," the high school's alma mater. ("Stately she stands, our Alma Mater/Bright with the sunlight of youth . . .") The young writer was drawn to his teacher. Like Brautigan, Miss Gibson was no ordinary individual. Many students considered her to be "weird," the same pejorative they hung on her prize student.

Beneath Juliette Gibson's makeup and lingering perfume, her extravagant scarves and gaudy costume jewelry, beat a heart forged of steel. She had been tempered by the fires of adventure, wounded in action while serving with the Army Nursing Corps in the trenches of the First World War. Rumors abounded that her fiancé had been killed overseas, one of ten million fatalities in the bloody carnage of the European conflict. Juliette Gibson never married, living the rest of her life with Mildred Pearl Snow, another nurse, whom she met in France.

Dick Brautigan always sat by the window in Miss Gibson's classroom, slouching at his desk with his feet propped on the nearest empty chair. When reprimanded about his posture, he straightened up for a time, gradually sliding back into a lanky sprawl. The view out the window comprised an ivy-covered wall, the leaves a vivid scarlet in autumn. Brautigan never participated in class discussion, preferring to daydream. When Juliette Gibson held forth on poetry (she was fond of quoting from *Vagabond's House*, a book of sentimental Hawaiian-themed rhymes by Don Blanding, a friend she met during visits to the islands in the thirties and forties), young Dick appeared not to be listening, engrossed instead sketching outrageous cartoons: grotesque birds, dragons, caricatures. "Fiddle-faddle" was Miss Gibson's dismissive term for such flights of fancy.

Eileen Dawson, a junior enrolled in the creative writing class, remembered Miss Gibson chiding Brautigan for "wasting his time" with these drawings, encouraging him to concentrate on his writing. She recalled the teacher "praising him for his writing, whether it was short stories or poetry. She told him he could become a very good writer." Juliette Gibson had her students stand in front of the class to read their work, but Dick Brautigan was too self-conscious. Eileen Dawson had no memory of him ever reading aloud. "He sat back and didn't comment one way or the other. He did the work. She commented often about the quality of it."

A selection of student writing from Juliette Gibson's fall term was showcased in "Poet's Nook" ("Creative Writers Express Christmas Spirit"), a section of the December 19, 1952, edition of the *EHS News*. Compared with the clumsy rhymed doggerel of the other young writers, the short, sensitive poem signed "Richard Brautigan" deserved its premier position. It was his first published work.

The Light

Into the sorrow of the night
Through the valley of dark dispair [sic]
Across the black sea of iniquity
Where the wind is the cry of the suffering
There came a glorious saving light
The light of eternal peace
Jesus Christ, the King of Kings.

The creative writing class worked on various forms of short fiction as well as poetry. "We wrote plays and skits and everything," Eileen Dawson recalled, remembering many of Brautigan's early stories "tended toward science fiction." E. William Laing, a fellow senior studying with Miss Gibson, had very few memories of his famous classmate ("a tall slender young man with blond hair and a very fair complexion") outside the writing group. The budding writer remained so anonymous in high school that Laing didn't realize Dick Porterfield had changed his name until decades later, when he read *Trout Fishing in America.*

One of Brautigan's earliest tales stayed in Laing's memory throughout the years. "I remember a story Richard wrote about a fly-fishing trip to a remote stream," Bill Laing recollected. "He was all alone several miles from the nearest community and was not having very good luck when he met an old fisherman." Brautigan described the old man in detail, relating how he told him how to fish the stream and gave him several special flies. The old man's advice and flies did the trick. Richard caught lots of fish. On the way home, he stopped at the local community store for a soda. Richard described his encounter with the old fisherman. The owner knew the old man's name and recognized the flies as a special pattern only he had tied. "Then, he informed Richard the old man had died several years ago while fishing his favorite pool on his favorite trout stream, the one Richard had just described to him."

Juliette Gibson's experience and sophistication set her apart from the 1950s provincialism of the Pacific Northwest, and she made it a goal to expose her students to a world larger than the one encompassed by the Willamette Valley. Literature provided the map charting a course to wider horizons. Miss Gibson submitted the best work produced in her class to a competition sponsored by the National High School Poetry Association. The winners were to be published nationally, an award more valuable than prize money for the aspiring young poets.

"Ten Creative Writers Rate in National Anthology Book" headed a brief story in the *EHS News* (1/30/53). All the writers were from Juliette Gibson's class. Richard Brautigan was not mentioned. A follow-up piece ("Poets' Prize Poems Published") on April 10, 1953, listed "Dick Braudigan [sic]" as one of ten Eugene High students to be featured in the anthology. Bill Laing and Eileen Dawson also had poetry included.

Young America Sings: 1953 Anthology of Northwest States High School Poetry (a cheaply produced volume in wraps bound with twine tied through twin punched holes), came out in the late spring with fifteen young writers from Eugene among the contributors. It was Richard Brautigan's first appearance in a book-length publication. His poem, "The Ochoco," shines like a polished gemstone among a mountain of dross, its virtues magnified by proximity to lines like "Our kitchen lab in home ec / While we're cooking is a wreck." Brautigan's poem celebrated the mountain landscape of the Ochoco Range near the Folston family ranch in Eastern Oregon. Dick told Eileen Dawson that it was written after spending a summer vacation there. She remembered "it was a place he especially liked."

Juliette Gibson retired from teaching in 1958. She stayed on in Eugene, remaining active in the American Legion and little theater productions. By the time she died at age eighty-one in 1971, Richard Brautigan had achieved international fame. Dick Brautigan never gave his mentor a second thought once he left Eugene. After the gates of American Literature swung open, he walked through and never looked back. Aside from a brief stopover on a reading tour, he avoided his home town, returning only in imagination to capture the Pacific Northwest within the pages of his enduring art.

eight: white wooden angel of love

DURING HARVEST SEASON the summer after graduation, Dick Brautigan worked out at the packing plant for a buck forty an hour. He also continued his part-time odd jobs for Mrs. Manerude, living at home in his add-on writer's shack. Dick and Stan Oswald worked on the Eugene Fruit Growers Association beet line. Pete Webster's job was on the bean line. Although classmates and intramural basketball opponents, Dick and Peter had not been close friends in school.

Pete Webster played end on the varsity football team, earning the nickname "Moose." The longest time he and Dick ever spent together was during the college entrance exams held over at the U of O. After the tests, Stan, Dick, and Pete headed for the student union building to shoot pool. "The two of them weren't concerned about the tests at all, although they passed them with flying colors. They had no intention of going on to college."

Pete worked the night shift at the cannery, eleven and a half hours, from 6:30 PM to 6:30 AM, with a half hour off for "lunch." Putting in a six-night week, he cleared $100 in his pay envelope. Dick and Stan worked days. Ten-and-a-half-hour shifts, carrying fresh produce in from the carts for cleaning and grading, or at the other end, toting loads of steaming cans as they came sealed from the cooker. Sometimes, the schedules overlapped. One hot afternoon, the line shut down and the three young men decided to go fishing. Pete owned a '37 Ford, so he provided transportation. "It was my first time fishing with Richard and my first time on the McKenzie River."

The two became fast friends after that, fishing together "at every opportunity." Absent stepfathers provided another bond. Having used the name "Webster" all his life, Pete also found out abruptly his senior year that his blood father bore a different last name. Just as school officials asked Dick Porterfield about "Brautigan," they inquired if Peter Webster wanted "McGuire" on his diploma. The two boys made opposing decisions. Pete stuck with Webster.

Many of the Pacific Northwest streams mentioned in *Trout Fishing in America* ("Hayman Creek, Graveyard Creek") were fictitious. Grider Creek and Tom Martin Creek (chapter titles in the novel) actually exist. Both are tributaries of the Klamath, bracketing the tiny streamside town of Seiad Valley in Siskiyou County, California, south of the Oregon line two hundred miles from Eugene. Much too far for a day trip. Brautigan camped several days there when he fished the area.

Richard Brautigan recalled the Long Tom River in two *Revenge of the Lawn* short stories. In "Forgiven," he fished alone: "The Long Tom River was forty miles away. I usually hitch-hiked there late in the afternoon and would leave in the twilight to hitch-hike the forty miles back home." The Long Tom flowed out of Fern Ridge Reservoir. Peter Webster cherished a memory of fishing a quarter-mile stretch with Dick. "It was called a river, but the part we fished was about twelve feet wide and eighteen inches deep." Pete and Dick caught eight little six- to ten-inch cutthroat trout that morning. Dick brought along a frying pan and some spuds, and they fried the fish over a wood fire. Brautigan wrote that the flesh of the humpbacked trout "tasted sweet as the kisses of Esmeralda."

Peter recalled another fishing trip east toward Bend. "If you blinked you would miss Indian Creek." This beautiful little stream boasted numbers of small trout. They fished wet in their Levi's and sneakers, casting Royal Coachmen with eight-and-a-half-foot fiberglass fly rods. Dick wore a fishing vest with a sheepskin pad on which he hooked his extra flies. "We hiked and waded upstream for about two miles and discovered some gorgeous waterfalls. One was fifty feet high. We climbed around it and fished the upper stream. We caught no fish that day but had the time of our lives."

All summer long, Dick Brautigan maintained a cavalier attitude toward his Eugene Fruit Growers Association paychecks. Mrs. Manerude provided his spending money, and he did not foresee a long career in the canning industry. "He'd throw his paycheck," Mary Lou remembered, "wrap it up in a ball and throw it up there." She gestured toward the top of the fridge. "Never cash them. And one day I was sick, and this woman come in to clean the house, and she got up there, and she found a whole sack full of those checks." When the sack was brought to Dick's attention, he took it downtown and opened a bank account.

That summer after graduation, the young writer started sending his stories and poems out to magazines and newspapers. Rejection slips began appearing in the Folston mailbox. "He was trying to sell some of his writings, and they all came back," Barbara remembered. "And how bad he felt when they came back." From time to time, good news arrived. On Monday, August 24, 1953, "A Cigarette Butt," a poem by Richard Brautigan, appeared below the political cartoon on the editorial page of the Eugene *Register-Guard*. No paycheck was involved.

Acceptance by the *Oregonian*, a statewide daily published in Portland, meant climbing a higher rung up the ladder. The newspaper's poetry editor, Ethel Romig Fuller, was a tiny woman weighing under one hundred pounds. Her 1927 poem "Proof" was included in *Bartlett's Familiar Quotations* and read by Arthur Godfrey on his national radio program. Godfrey said the author was unknown. In fact, Mrs. Fuller had published three books of verse and was one of only three Oregonians belonging to the Poetry Society of America.

Governor Paul Paterson declared October 15, 1953, to be Oregon Poetry Day. As part of the program, the *Sunday Oregonian Magazine* (10/11) devoted an entire page to local poetry: ("State Recognizes Oregon Poets.") Nineteen poets appeared, including Richard Brautigan of Eugene. His six-line poem, "Moonlight on a Cemetery," contained images and themes he would return to again and again throughout his long career. The familiar elements (brevity, sentiment, melancholy, mordant wit) of a typical "Brautigan" poem were already in place. It was his first publication to reach an audience wider than the boundaries of his hometown.

A month and a half later, his "Winter Sunset" appeared in the *Sunday Oregonian Magazine*, (11/29/53) in "Oregonian Verse," Ethel Romig Fuller's regular column of "1st Publication Poetry." Brautigan's three-line haiku remained spiritually true to its model and revealed the poet understood the seasonal nuances of this antique Japanese form. "I was seventeen and then eighteen and began to read Japanese haiku poetry from the Seventeenth century," Brautigan wrote two decades later.

"I read Bashō and Issa. I liked the way they used language concentrating emotion, detail and image until they arrived at a form of dew-like steel."

In the fall of 1953, Peter Webster, a deeply religious young man, enrolled as a freshman at Northwest Christian College, whose campus stands adjacent to the University of Oregon. As part of Pete's financial arrangement, NCC assigned him to maintain their grounds during the summer. He mowed the grass and ran the college sprinkler system. Between jobs, he'd head over to the Folston place and hang out. "I remember Pete used to stay until we about run out of groceries," Mary Lou Folston said. "Three weeks at a stretch, you know. It wasn't just potatoes and a piece of meat. I would spend hours and hours cooking, making cakes, pastry, fancy salads, and everything."

Peter Webster remembered things differently. Once, when he was staying with Dick over on Hayes Street, his friend offered him something to eat. "He went to the refrigerator, and the only thing that was there was a half a loaf of bread. So, we each took a piece of bread, no butter, and then he had a little packet of Kool-Aid, and no sugar, and he mixed up the Kool-Aid and served the bread on a plate. And it was like having communion. Here was bread and Kool-Aid representing the wine. And there couldn't have been any more sacred moment than when he offered me everything he had. That was the only thing there was. The refrigerator was bare."

Dick Brautigan didn't regard this simple meal in the same religious light. "He was in love with nature and with all the out of doors," Peter admitted, "but as far as knowing a Christian faith, he claimed to be an atheist."

When he stayed over, Pete camped out in Dick's lean-to bedroom. He had his old jalopy and he and Dick and Barbara drove around together a lot that summer, looking for fun. B.J. never mentioned having a secret crush on Pete. The wet lawns over on campus suggested night crawler hunting. Dick Brautigan was back in the worm business, this time with Pete Webster. All summer long and well into the fall, the two young men gathered night crawlers on the vast combined grounds of NCC and the U of O. They carried one- or two-quart glass jars, dropping in the worms after they pounced on them. One night, working until dawn, Dick and Pete caught over fifteen hundred worms.

They sold the night crawlers for a penny apiece to the Cedar Flats Grocery Store, a little crossroads place about twelve miles up the McKenzie out of Eugene. Brautigan wrote of selling night crawlers in *So the Wind Won't Blow It All Away*, at "the Crossroads Filling Station . . . small, tired, run by an old man who wasn't much interested in selling gas. He sold worms to passing fishermen and pop to thirsty kids during the summer."

Once the school year started, Pete's days were taken up with class work. In the evenings, often long after midnight, he'd drive over to Dick's place with his portable typewriter. Knowing his friend to be a night owl, he counted on finding him awake at any hour. The outside entrance to Dick's add-on bedroom gave his pals easy anonymous access. Pete typed term papers there, while Dick worked on poetry or short stories. Peter Webster remembered often leaving at six in the morning after these all-night sessions.

Other nights, Dick Brautigan wandered the streets of Eugene alone. During the summer, he went to the movies every day off from the packing plant when he wasn't fishing or out catching worms with Pete. Afterward, he might roam about until dawn. Two early stories written during this period deal with voyeurism. A year or so later, Brautigan's nocturnal wanderings caused him to be suspected as a Peeping Tom. "He loved going downtown at night," his sister recalled, "because he was a loner, I guess. The darkness didn't bother him. I was always afraid to go with him when it was that dark."

Recovering from a spinal virus infection all that year, Barbara spent less and less time with her brother, and he roamed the nighttime streets alone. Dick was still a virgin at twenty, yet a Brautigan story from this period ("in god's arms") describes making love in a graveyard. The Peeping Tom stories might also have sprung from fantasy. Some thought otherwise. Donald Hiebert claimed Brautigan used to "spy" on his mother and stepfather while they engaged in sex.

"The Egg Hunter," a first-person narrative written in a faux-naive colloquial style, a dimwit's account of snooping on a young couple making love. "He did somethin I couldnt hardly believe at all I mean they was just like sheep and dogs and cows and things. I watched them do it. It sure made me feel pretty funny all over." Adding a professional touch, Brautigan typed a thirty-dash—journalism's symbol marking the end of a piece of copy—at the conclusion of his seven-hundred-word story.

The other early tale, "The Flower Burner," was submitted to (and rejected by) Margarita G. Smith at *Mademoiselle*. It is an odd faux-Western featuring an eccentric cast of characters who might seamlessly step into any of Brautigan's later fictions. The story begins, "I sure like to hide in the bushes and watch Penny swim naked, because she's just about the prettiest Indian in the whole county." The narrator prefers reading Mickey Spillane to the Bible, throws stones at a rattlesnake, talks to a man who thinks he's a bird, and watches Mrs. Dragoo burn irises in her backyard. At twenty, young Dick Brautigan had found his métier.

A new poem, "The Ageless Ones," appeared in Ethel Romig Fuller's poetry column on February 7, 1954, in what *The Sunday Oregonian* now called the *Northwest Magazine*. He would not publish again until June 22, when another poem ran on the editorial page of the *Register-Guard*. All through that winter and spring, Dick devoted his nights to writing and peregrination. Daylight hours were for sleeping. The add-on bedroom provided a certain measure of illusory independence. Dick had his own typewriter and telephone but was still living at home under his parents' supervision, and his bohemian habits soon began to irritate the Folstons.

In this period of nocturnal wandering, Brautigan began his lifelong habit of carrying a cheap pocket notebook wherever he went. When an idea sprang into his mind on the midnight streets of Eugene, he stopped and jotted it down under the pooled yellow light of a streetlamp. Sometimes in the wee hours, Pete and Dick met at Snappy Service, an all-night restaurant on Olive Street between Eighth and Broadway. Dick favored their hotcakes. Snappy Service served a stack of three and a cup of coffee for thirty-five cents. "They kept the coffee coming and coming," Pete remembered. "We'd stay there for four or five hours." Dick talked about his writing and the artistic economy he learned from reading Hemingway. "Some people like to peel life like an apple," Brautigan said, "but I like to slice it to the core."

Peter Webster recalled his friend's frustration with his early work. He often watched him tear up stories and poetry. "Richard destroyed a lot of his writings [in a] fit of fury. Either they had not been accepted or they weren't up to his standards." In spite of these frequent acts of critical self-destruction, many of Brautigan's first tentative efforts survive today. The young writer was already a dedicated artist, completely focused on his projected life's work.

That fall, Dick Brautigan took Peter Webster pheasant hunting in the fields west of Eugene. It was the first time in his life Pete had ever hunted. He lacked a natural gift for the sport. "I emptied a whole box of shells that day and never hit a thing. Richard was losing his patience with me." The impatient instructor bagged a couple pheasants, but when the boys flushed a covey of quail they both missed every one.

It was bitterly cold (barely fifteen degrees) on a duck-hunting expedition out to Fern Hill Reservoir, and the boys built a crude lean-to, huddling together for warmth, trying to sleep. Eventually, they gave up and retreated to the car, where they kept the heater on and the windows cracked. At dawn, having barely slept, they crouched, shivering with their shotguns in the frozen cattails, waiting for the ducks that never came.

Pete was a frequent visitor at the Folston home, but Dick Brautigan rarely ventured over to the Webster place at 41 Madison Street, a household as dysfunctional as his own. At the time, there were eight Webster children, almost all by different fathers. Their mother was away in California, working for the Shrine Circus in San Francisco. The kids were being raised by their grandmother, Lydia Smith (known as Alice), a short, resolute woman whom they all called "Mom."

Peter Webster and his sister Lorna, the two oldest children, were both born in the little house on Madison Street where their mother, Edna, had lived since the age of ten. She wasn't at home in the summer of 1954, when Dick Brautigan became an infrequent visitor. One time, he and B.J. went over to play cards with Pete and his younger sister Linda. A West Indian pop song played on the phonograph. Pete had given the forty-five to Linda, who favored calypso, rhythm and blues, and other esoteric black music. Dick Brautigan took no notice of Linda Webster on this occasion.

Continued family pressure at home to get a "real job" compelled the young writer to investigate new sources of part-time employment, so Dick and Pete went into the Christmas tree business. They made arrangements with a property owner on West Eleventh Street to sell trees on his unused lot. There was an old empty building, and the boys had the power turned on. Dick brought a small heater from home and they huddled around it for warmth while waiting for customers. Barbara recalled accompanying her brother on one of their harvesting expeditions: "Peter and Dick rented an old broken-down beater truck. It sounded like it was on its last legs. It had panels on the side, and they went up and cut down a whole bunch of Douglas fir."

"During our search for trees, I was overcome by the beauty of the area," Peter Webster remembered, "and fell down in amazement and looked up in the sky at the trees and the hills. Richard came running over to see what was the matter, and when he found out that I wasn't hurt, but rather that I was overwhelmed by the whole scene, he was profoundly touched. We didn't make any money selling Christmas trees, but our friendship from that moment was forever."

On May 29, 1955, "So Many Twilights," a new Brautigan poem describing an old woman rocking on her front porch, appeared in the "Oregonian Verse" column in the recently renamed *Northwest Roto Magazine* of *The Sunday Oregonian*. Around that time, Edna Webster returned home to Eugene from San Francisco with her newborn baby, Tim. There were now nine children in the brood. "Four pairs and a spare," the family quipped. Linda was the spare. Over the past year, she had developed into a lovely young woman, but when Dick Brautigan started dropping by 41 Madison Street that summer, he was mainly interested in talking with her mother.

Mrs. Webster was a fascinating person. An independent, liberated female, she had proven herself adept at surviving in a male-dominated world. During World War II, Edna Webster transported the chassis of unfinished lend-lease trucks from their West Coast factories to ports on the

Eastern Seaboard for shipment to England, where final assembly took place. Later, she drove a bus and became the first female cabbie in Eugene. Along the way, she also worked as a taxi dispatcher and designed a modular home at a time when no one else had ever heard of such a thing.

All of this diverse activity was informed by an active and inquiring mind. "Edna liked to get into deep conversations with people," her daughter Lorna recalled, "talk for hours, deep subjects, all kinds of things, fascinating discussions."

Dick Brautigan thirsted for such conversation; there was no stimulating talk at home or among his friends. Barbara lived with the Guistina family at this time, taking care of their kids after school. She was free once they'd gone to sleep. Dick phoned her from his outside bedroom and discussed his poetry. "He would call me up every night and talk for about a half an hour or an hour at least. Read what he had written that day to me. I didn't appreciate it, because the most important thing to me was what happened at school." A single line of her brother's poetry from this period stayed with her for more than forty years: "'I saw Jesus Christ coming out of a pay toilet.' That one sentence really stuck in my mind."

Before long, Dick Brautigan was riding the rattletrap bicycle he'd acquired after the demise of his paper route over to the little house on Madison Street every single day to talk with Edna Webster. She became his closest friend and confidant. Her daughter Linda listened in, having recently returned from visiting an aunt in Long Beach, California. Although Dick didn't remember her from the card game the previous year, she knew who he was. Linda thought he dressed strangely and had an odd, bowl-shaped haircut. She remembered seeing Dick on his junker bicycle with a fishing rod. "Nobody went around in Eugene riding a bike with a fishing pole."

One summer morning in the Webster kitchen, not long after Linda had come back from California, the conversation turned to "some of the things down there." The fourteen-year-old had brought along several books on the black music she adored. Fascinated by black culture, Linda talked about gangs. Dick started writing little improvisations, making her laugh. "I thought he was funny," Linda recalled. "We became really good friends." A typewriter in the kitchen led to a little game with Dick, typing up Linda's tales of life in Los Angeles as she drew funny pictures to illustrate them. "That was the first time, and then he started coming over all the time."

The typewriter got moved to the open back porch, and soon Dick and Linda spent every day out there, laughing, joking, telling stories, writing poetry and short tales. Sometimes, Linda started a story and Dick picked up where she left off, typing the ending. They wrote reams and reams of copy together. Once, without Linda Webster's knowledge, Dick signed her name to a short story he had written ("The Day That My Aunt Millie Brought Back the Dead") and entered it in a *Seventeen* magazine competition for teenage writers. The story was turned down.

Linda realized Dick "hated his mother" from reading his work. Brautigan bared his soul to her. At twenty, the shy young man who had never gone out on a date or danced with a girl was falling in love for the first time. Linda saw things differently. Just blossoming into a woman, she had no romantic inclinations for Dick Brautigan. "He seemed like a man to me. Too old. Too old."

Even so, Linda Webster enjoyed the young man's attentions. She regarded Dick Brautigan as an older brother. Someone fun with whom to pal around. Peter, engaged in his religious studies, didn't fit the bill. Dick liked to kid and tell jokes. Linda remembered him as "very innocent," but knew "he had to have had knowledge of the world."

Once, drawing pictures out on the back porch, Dick sketched a "self-portrait" in the manner of a "droodle," the popular comic cartoon riddle invented by bow-tied TV comedian Roger Price. Prophetic and self-revelatory, Brautigan's sketch showed only the back of a wide-brimmed hat poking up from behind the slope of a conical mountain. Like the public persona Richard later adopted, the simple iconic drawing concealed the author's true identity while creating an instantly identifiable image.

Dick brought his childhood friend Gary Stewart over to the Webster house and introduced him to Linda. He'd confessed his loved for the girl, enthusing over her beauty. Gary was amazed. A college man now, a sophomore fraternity member, he knew only girls who were grown women. "This can't be," Gary thought. He tried to reason with his friend. "She's too young," he told Brautigan. His advice fell on deaf ears. "He was really in love with her."

Sometime that same summer, the Folstons had their fill of the unemployed poet who wandered the city streets at night and slept in until noon. They suggested Dick get his own place. A room was found on the second floor of 467 West Seventeenth Avenue, a family home between Charnelton and Lincoln converted into apartments. Dick's room was to the right of the stairs and faced the street. From his lone window, he could look across to his old high school, a block away.

"Just a place to crash," a friend recalled. Furnished with a single bed, a two-burner hot plate, and a table and chair, the communal bathroom located down the hall, it possessed the Spartan austerity of a monk's chambers. At home with the monastic, Brautigan had few material needs beyond his portable Royal typewriter and a couple changes of clothing. To facilitate the move, Bill Folston paid his stepson's first month's rent and gave him a little money for food.

Dick Brautigan contemplated adopting a pen name. He thought "Duvall" had a distinguished sound, though nothing ever came of it. He also began using the Webster home as his return address for the manuscripts he submitted with dogged regularity to magazines ranging from *Playboy* to the *New Yorker*. In the rooming house, the tenants' mail accumulated in the downstairs hall. Linda Webster remembered all the rejection slips coming to 41 Madison Street.

While sending his fiction out to commercial magazines, Dick sought a more sophisticated venue for his poetry than the back pages of the *Sunday Oregonian*. The university bookstore sold a variety of poetry journals and literary quarterlies. Brautigan studied these, submitting poems to those that appealed to him. Sometime that summer, a surprise arrived in the mail from Alpine, Texas. *Flame*, a year-old quarterly, had accepted "Someplace in the World a Man Is Screaming in Pain," an eight-line poem about a woman shelling peas. Along with a note from the editor, Lilith Lorraine, was a check for $2. It was the first time Richard Brautigan had ever been paid for his writing. He immediately mailed new poetry off to *Flame*.

Once Peter Webster began his sophomore year at NCC, Dick Brautigan found himself without a steady ride up the McKenzie. He renewed a friendship with Bill Brown, a high school classmate who had been in Dick's homeroom back when he was still known as Porterfield. They'd played a little intramural ball but had been in only one course together. Bill began working as a post office sub at the start of May. As a PTM, he had a flexible schedule providing a fair amount of free time. Best of all, he owned a car. "Every day off, every Sunday, every afternoon that we had a chance, we hit the river," Brown recalled. "We must have gone fishing a hundred times that summer. We fished Gate Creek. We fished the Blue River. We fished Indian Creek, and he calls that 'The Great

American Tragedy.' And we fished Rebel Creek that runs into the South Fork, and French Pete."
Bill enjoyed Dick's company, delighting in his "dry sense of humor."

Once, Dick brought along his iron skillet, salt and pepper, and a lemon. Bill had the grill from
a propane stove. After fishing all morning on the South Fork of the McKenzie, they found a little
island in the middle of the stream. The water was low, and they waded over in their tennis shoes.
"We got firewood and built a fire and fried the fish. Had it for lunch. And they were small, six,
eight inches. I mean, they were legal." Like Peter Webster, Bill Brown got a faraway look in his eyes
remembering the magical meal. "That's the best fish I ever ate in my life."

When he wasn't fishing, Dick Brautigan spent much of his free time at the Webster house. He
talked about Scripture and philosophy with Edna. "We often discussed the Bible," she recalled.
"He wanted it to be a beautiful world. He believed that his writing could help people to see a different world, to see the truth. He wanted to know what truth is. Philosophically he grew away from
what he had learned when he was younger. He didn't understand that it is an ongoing program."
Although young Dick held fast to many strong moral positions, he was no longer influenced by
mere doctrine. "He committed himself to being his own man, and Pete committed himself to being
God's man."

With Peter off studying hard for the ministry, the conversation quite naturally turned at times
to the subject of higher education and whether going to college was worth the time and effort. "He
talked to me about going, and I said, 'Do you want to go? What do you want to train for?' And he
said he thought he knew what he wanted to do already, and I said, "You don't need college to do
that.' He was going to be a writer."

Dick discussed his admiration for Ernest Hemingway with Edna. "He thought if Hemingway
made it as a writer so he would, too. He believed that he had something to say that people needed
to hear, and the way he said it was different. People would want to hear it because it was based on
truth and love." Dick Brautigan's belief in his eventual success approached a level of religious faith.
Even as the rejection slips piled up around him, he never lost hope. "Things are going to change,"
he told Edna Webster. "People will see it differently."

"He *knew* he was going to be a famous author someday." Edna fervently echoed Brautigan's
youthful conviction. At times, he showed new work to Juliette Gibson, his former creative writing
teacher. One evening, Dick brought over a sheaf of recent poems. After reading through them, Miss
Gibson expressed her considered opinion that just maybe young Brautigan might turn out to be a
homosexual.

Furious, Dick stormed straight over to 41 Madison Street, telling Edna Webster all about this
incredible insult. To an innocent virgin, Miss Gibson's comments on his potential sexuality seemed
the most dire of prophesies. "Whenever he had any problems, he came and talked to me. And I was
always willing to talk back." On that troubled night, she advised him, "Ignore it. It's stupid. You
don't pay attention to stupid people. Forget it. That's just ugly."

Edna Webster sculpted ceramic busts as a hobby. Dick Brautigan felt her work deserved a
wider audience. "He wanted to do something for me," she explained. He took one of Edna's heads,
hitchhiking up to the State Fair in Salem, and entered the piece in the fine art competition. Edna
Webster won a second-place ribbon. "He was always doing neat things for people," she said.

A new poem by Brautigan appeared in the *Oregonian*'s *Northwest Roto Magazine* on August 14,
1955. "First Star on the Twilight River" described the poet telling his little brother, David, a story

about "A flower that fell / In love with a star." It spoke of Brautigan's sensitivity that a man in his early twenties would take the time to sit on the steps with a five-year-old, improvising fairy tales in the twilight.

Linda Webster discovered Dick Brautigan's true feelings for her one afternoon when they were out on the back porch together fooling around with the typewriter, making up short stories and poetry like any other afternoon. Linda wore a scooped-neck white blouse, and she happened to bend over, retrieving something she'd dropped. Looking up, she caught Dick staring down inside her blouse. "And his face, his neck, everything turned just bright red." Linda didn't remember ever seeing anyone blush so vividly before. Inexperienced as she was, the burgeoning woman within knew instantly what Dick had on his mind.

Dick Brautigan felt so embarrassed he couldn't talk, stammering and inarticulate as his face reddened and he groped for words to make things right again. He lacked the sophistication to turn it all into a joke. In matters of the heart, Dick was a bumbling novice. A surge of anger burned through Linda. Outwardly, she suppressed her feelings. Deep inside, fury raged, as she realized Dick was interested in a lot more than just being her big brother buddy. All those days of poetry and wordplay seemed like nothing but a ruse. He was no different from the horny boys in junior high.

Dick Brautigan didn't stick around the Webster place much longer on that particular afternoon. He expressed his feelings in the only way he knew how, by writing a poem for Linda. The next day, he brought it by on his bicycle, but Linda was mad and not interested in continuing their back porch poetry games. After that, Dick rode over several times a day to leave his conciliatory poetry offerings. Linda avoided him. She climbed a cherry tree in the Websters' softball-field-sized backyard. The leafy hiding place provided an excellent vantage point to spot Dick's bike approaching. "I didn't want to see him," she remembered.

On the ninth of September, Dick dropped off a one-line note asking Linda if she wanted "to go to the show on May 3, 1959," his offhand joking way of telling her that he was willing to wait for her to come of age. The poems Dick Brautigan wrote during this period were all about Linda Webster. Most were love poems, but many were pieces he knew would make her laugh. "I think he was obsessed with me," she recalled. This was not altogether unpleasant. Even though she didn't want to see him, Linda enjoyed receiving his daily poetic offerings. She'd tell her ninth-grade friends about them, and they'd all giggle. Secretly, she was proud of Dick's devotion.

All the while, Brautigan stewed in utter despair. He called his sister Barbara every night and read her what he'd written that day. "I spent hours writing this poem," he'd said. "What do you think?"

Her standard answer was "I think it's great. That's the best you've written so far."

"Well, she didn't understand it," he complained. "She didn't like it."

"I'm not surprised," Barbara told her brother. "She's just real young. You have to give her time. I'm sure it's not that she doesn't care for you. She's just probably not into poetry."

Barbara thought Dick was satisfied with these answers, but he'd always call again the next evening to read her another new poem. "You're a girl," he insisted, "and you know how girls think."

In truth, B.J. had no idea what Linda Webster was thinking. Dick grew more and more desperate as she continued avoiding him. "He didn't know why," Barbara remembered. "And it really bothered him." She noticed that his writing seemed different, too. "Kind of on the dark side. You could definitely tell he was depressed."

Gary Stewart also detected the change in his friend. Gary owned a car, and "every once in a while," Dick asked him drive them by the house on Madison Street, hoping for a glimpse of the elusive Linda. In spite of such obsessive behavior, Gary believed Dick's condition was caused more by "intense poverty" than the pangs of love. The Folstons paid the rent for Dick's room, but he had to take care of his food and subsisted mainly on canned beans. He spent only $3 a week on food. His weight dropped to 145 pounds. "He was just skin and bones," Gary remembered. "Looked like something that came out of a Nazi war camp." Gary worked full-time during the days that summer. In the evenings, he frequently invited Dick over to his family home for a decent meal, "to fatten him up."

Brautigan had written several new stories. Gary Stewart remembered one in particular. Dick pointed out the short, crisp Hemingway-inspired sentences. The story started with a man in a serious automobile accident. The ER team arrived and loaded the victim into an ambulance. When he got to the hospital, the doctors noticed their patient's eyes were open and had a glimmer of hope. Then, a fly landed on the blank gleaming cornea. Dead men don't blink.

As a devout Mormon, Gary Stewart was required to embark upon a two-and-a-half-year mission once he turned twenty. In September 1955, the Stewart family gathered to bid their departing son farewell. Before leaving, he asked them to continue having Dick Brautigan over for home-cooked meals. "Look after him when I'm gone." There were no planes out of Eugene in those days, nor did the trains go in the direction Gary was headed. Later in the evening, the young missionary, not wanting his mom standing around weeping, said goodbye to the folks and found himself waiting in the art deco Greyhound/Trailways bus depot on Olive Street in the company of Dick and another buddy.

Because the narrow roads did not permit full-sized buses to travel west from Eugene, Gary Stewart took an old three-seat Chrysler limo over the mountains to Bend, where he caught the Greyhound bound for Salt Lake City. Whatever transpired that night so impressed Dick Brautigan that he went home to his furnished room and wrote what he called "the funniest and saddest story that has ever crawled out of my brain."

In a letter to Gary a few days later, he asked his friend's permission to include him by name in his fiction ("i don't believe a writer should write about peoples he knows without tellin em foist") and, knowing the young Mormon would soon be heading to Europe on his long mission, cautioned him, "when you get to holland [sic] and wonder [sic] around speechless for a while, remember the language of love." (Brautigan was wrong about Stewart's destination. He was bound for Belgium.) Dick closed with "this here letter dieth like what dies tomorrow?" The mood of the letter was playful and ebullient. The young writer signed himself "richard broodigan."

On October 2, 1955, Brautigan published a new poem, "Butterfly's Breath," in the Sunday *Oregonian Northwest Roto Magazine*. Wistful and evanescent, with just a tinge of melancholy ("The shadow is as silent / As the birth of a rose"), the poem captured Dick's fragile mood at the time, a young man helplessly lost in the bathos of unrequited love. It was his final work to appear in the *Oregonian*. Feeling he had "goofed completely" with Linda Webster, Dick focused his talents over the next couple weeks on writing a sequence of letters, some long, others very brief, he hoped would catch the attention of his fourteen-year-old dream girl.

Brautigan wrote a short jocular note to Linda on October 3, announcing, "Gee, I'm a schemer," and asking if she'd "ever been kidnaped to a show?" He signed himself "Hitchard

Black Jack" and appended a postscript telling Linda he was going to buy "a roll of adhesive tape and four hundred feet of rope and then, ha, ha, ha, ha, ha . . ." A few days later, on the seventh and the eighth, Dick continued in this vein, penning two more brief missives, both unsigned. The first asked Linda not to open the letter until she went to bed and concluded "Good Night." The second requested that she not open it until she was "halfway through eating dinner," ending with "Please pass the salt."

On October 8, Brautigan wrote a more serious and lyrical letter, a prose poem describing Linda's beauty. It began "I think you are more beautiful than white pigeons cooing in a soft spring rain and the laughter of little children [. . .]" Dick told Linda she was "more beautiful than the dawn gently kissing and hugging the hills of eastern Oregon [. . .] more beautiful than old men lovingly telling about people and days gone forever." Then, mocking his own sensitivity, he signed the letter "Yours, Itchard Brat Again." His PS acknowledged Linda's wish that he not write or bother her, explaining, "I've already made a damn fool out of myself, I might as well try to break the world's record."

True to his word, Dick Brautigan spent the next week or so writing two long letters created for an audience of one, a girl barely in her teens who was not the least interested. "I hope that you understand some of this. by the time i was 14, i understood things no one should ever understand. what things does a genius remember about a girl? what things burn in the forest of his mind?"

Dick remembered the first time he saw Linda wearing a gray sweatshirt and red pedal-pushers and mentioned the song "That Old Black Magic." ("'It really kills me,' I said. 'Meanwhile, back at the ranch.'") Linda laughed and asked Dick to repeat his remark, but he was too shy. His heart beat rapidly when she made a second request. "I said something shy and did not do it," Brautigan wrote. Another time Edna nursed her baby in the kitchen, and Dick felt embarrassed, staring at the stove while Linda kept her eyes fixed on him. "Every time i looked up her eyes were on me. i shall never forget that look as long as i live. linda staring at me." Recalling their afternoon poetry-writing sessions on the back porch: "I wanted very much to take linda in my arms and show her love so gentle that it would turn her into a piece of softness. love so gentle that it would turn her into the first light of dawn. but i didn't do that. i wrote a god damn poem instead."

Sharing a bag of potato chips on their way home from fishing one evening, Bill Brown suggested to Dick that Linda thought of him only as a "big brother." Dick choked on his chip. "Do you think I goofed completely?" he asked.

"Man," Brown replied, "the ways you didn't goof with her haven't been invented yet. I'd give it up if I were you. It's hopeless, man."

Dick typed a final letter to Linda soon afterward. He admitted he wrote "because I wanted very much to show you something about me. I wanted to show you that I'm awfully clever and amusing and nice, but I guess you are too young to appreciate the things which are me." He promised he wouldn't write or try to call her anymore. "It's like trying to catch a bird with my hands." His postscript said, "Life is a very short visit. When you're dead, you're dead for a long time [. . .] I believe in quality over quantity. I believe an inch of truth is more than a mile of lies."

Dick Brautigan never mailed these letters. He typed "For Linda" on the envelopes and brought them over to 41 Madison Street, leaving them with Edna Webster to give to her daughter. For reasons of her own, Edna never did. She hid the letters away, and they remained out of sight for forty years. Eventually, they were sold to the Bancroft Library at the University of California in Berkeley, where curious scholars probed them long before Linda Webster, now a woman in her seventies, read the words a lovesick young poet had written to her so many years ago.

In late October (1955), not long after his desperate letter-writing campaign, Dick asked Edna Webster's permission to take Linda fishing. "I trusted him," Edna said and consented to the angling expedition. Linda recollected that things had more or less been prearranged without consulting her: "I think my mother told me that I was going fishing with Richard." Dick asked Bill Brown, providing the transportation, if it would be okay if Linda went along. "Sure," Brown said. "No problem."

Early on a spectacular fall day, the three headed up the McKenzie under a crystalline blue sky, fall colors tinting the cottonwoods along the river and air crisp as biting into an apple. They drove to Vida, a little town named for Vida Pepiot, a pioneer woman, not much more than a grade school and a post office/general store on the side of the road. Pronounced "V-(eye)-da" (a distinction Brautigan retained a decade later in *The Abortion* when he called his heroine Vida), the town stood close to Gate Creek.

Bill Brown rigged his rod and waded upstream. Dick had no intention of going fishing. He and Linda walked downriver to the Goodpasture Bridge, one of about 140 covered bridges still in daily use in Oregon in 1955. Built by Lane County in 1938, its 165-foot span remained the longest of any surviving covered bridge in the state. A graceful white structure with a peaked shingled roof and ten slatted, Gothic-arched windows along either side, the Goodpasture Bridge seemed to float above the reflected autumnal dazzle of the McKenzie like some improbable airborne sailing ship.

Dick Brautigan led Linda Webster under the curved portal into the dim interior of the bridge. The cathedral windows provided illumination for big logging trucks, and the crepuscular light inside felt cool and inviting, a magical moment of midday twilight. This was a special place for Dick, and he wanted to share it with Linda. Her own feelings were confused, a jumble of apprehension, anger, and a strange joy occasioned by such an unbelievable fall day.

Goodpasture Bridge was hushed and quiet, like being in church. The thick foot-wide wooden planks muffled Dick and Linda's footsteps. The bridge struck Brautigan as a holy temple. He explained to Linda how their presence constituted a form of worship. "The way he told me was very beautiful," she remembered. Dick pointed into the rafters, telling Linda that angels lived up there, spreading their golden wings among the shadows masking the king posts and triangular trusses. He gathered his courage and attempted a kiss, fighting an inherent shyness.

Linda wasn't interested. Slipping away, she ran to one of the Gothic windows, staring through the slanted horizontal slats dividing her view of the river. Linda recalled, "I'd go and look out one window, and he'd come over and stand real close to me, and I'd run clear over to the other side and look out that one. I probably wasn't very nice."

Dick struggled to maintain his composure, keeping cool while bleak darkness closed around him. Years later, in his short story "Forgiven," Brautigan wrote of fishing downstream from a bridge "into a fast shallow run covered over closely with trees like a shadowy knitted tunnel." Fishing there, surrounded by "nothing but darkness," a nameless, uncontrollable fear took hold of him. Panic-stricken, he ran. "Every horror in the world was at my back [. . .] they were all without names and had no shape but perception itself." He ran on and saw "the dim white outline of the bridge standing out against the night, my soul was born again through a vision of rescue and sanctuary [. . .] the bridge bloomed like a white wooden angel in my eyes [. . .]"

For as long as Richard Brautigan lived, Goodpasture Bridge, the graceful covered structure where angels nested, remained a symbol of hope, salvation, and enduring love. On that sad, beautiful October afternoon in 1955, he wasn't feeling quite so poetic. "He was very upset," Linda Webster remembered. Riding home to Eugene, instead of sitting in back with Linda, Dick slouched on the front seat, not saying much, as Bill Brown talked about his time on the stream.

When the boys dropped Linda off, Edna asked her daughter how the day went with Dick. "Linda said that he was boring." She never went "fishing" with Dick Brautigan again. As far as he knew, aside from an accidental meeting at the front door of her home, he never saw her again. It wasn't from want of trying. Soon after, Dick brought a small bowl of goldfish over to the Webster house, accompanied by a poem, as a gift for Linda. The long-lost poem spoke of being happy to know that the fish were swimming around in her room. Although she didn't want to see him, Linda remembered how very sad she felt when the goldfish died.

Discussing the fishing trip later with Edna, Dick said, "I was so embarrassed. I couldn't talk to her. I can't understand why she doesn't want me. I prayed about it. She doesn't respond."

A complimentary copy of the Autumn issue of *Flame* (vol. II, no. 3) arrived in the mail about the same time, the names of contributors printed on the cover beneath an arching red logo blazing like the fiery lettering painted on the hood of a hot rod. Richard Brautigan's short poem was the final piece in the issue, crouching at the bottom of the page on the inside of the back cover.

Another pleasant surprise arrived that fall from *Epos*, an established poetry quarterly located in Lake Como, Florida. Edited by poet Evelyn Thorne, *Epos* championed the work of young unknown poets, Charles Bukowski among them. Thorne published her own work as Will Inman, adopting a masculine pseudonym because she felt the deck was stacked against women. Acceptance came as welcome news. "The Second Kingdom" was a love poem inspired by Linda Webster ("The sound of / your eyes: snow / coming down / the stairs / of the wind). Not even a modest payment was forthcoming. *Epos* sent poets two copies of the quarterly containing their work.

Around this same time, Brautigan submitted a short story to *Playboy* magazine. The first paragraph of "My Name Is Richard Brautigan," consisted of two short sentences announcing the author's name and age ("I'm twenty-years-old.") The second paragraph speculated on "how nice it would be if my name were Ernest Hemingway." That name in the title would grab the editor's attention. He'd want to read the rest of the story instead of tossing it aside because he'd never heard of a writer named Richard Brautigan.

The story came back with a personal letter from the editor. "If this piece was as fresh and clear as its opening, you might have something," the letter began. "As it stands, the opening has no connection with the story, is a gimmick-for-the-sake-of-a-gimmick only, and the story itself is over before it starts, has no discernable point. Thanks, though." Encouraged, Brautigan "hunted up a discernable point lickity-split" and immediately rewrote the story. On a dreary rain-soaked day close to the end of October, suffering from his second bad head cold of the month, Brautigan sat on his bed in the furnished room, handwriting a letter to Gary Stewart while Bill Brown retyped the revised *Playboy* story. Bill volunteered for this task as a mental distraction because he was "having girl trouble" and feeling blue.

Dick had the blues pretty bad himself and for similar reasons. "Linda Webster broke my heart," he wrote. "I've been feeling like hell for over two months. Memories of her haunt the castles of my brain. I never knew I could be hurt so much. I never knew that much hurt existed in the world." Brautigan told about going to visit Gary's folks a couple Sundays before, eating cake, watching TV, and thinking "about killing your little brother." He also mentioned that he had started writing poetry again and included a recent example. "Hi," a brief bit of trivia, exuded a surprising amount of good cheer considering his bleak mood.

Lack of money continued to trouble Dick Brautigan. Bill Brown tried to get him work at the post office. Such regimented employment ran contrary to his nature. "He wasn't really too enthused," Brown remembered. Instead, Dick sold his typewriter for $100. Bill Brown witnessed the transaction. "I was there when the guy paid him for it," he said. "Packed it out the door, guy and his wife." Afterward, the two boys went downtown and Brautigan bought some flannel shirts at Eugene Surplus. Having tended to his limited sartorial needs, Dick went shopping for food.

Without a typewriter, Brautigan began using a pencil, writing longhand in a number of inexpensive spiral-bound notebooks. He joked that he favored this method because "you can write in the most comfortable positions." He had started on a book of short stories he called *These Few Precious Days*. The Folstons had cut off his rent payments, and the typewriter money was soon exhausted. Always desperately short of cash, Dick took a job for a few days picking walnuts, earning over $2 an hour. The work injured his hands, and his fingers grew too sore to hold a pencil. He came home from the job so exhausted he had only enough energy to open a can of cold beans for dinner before collapsing into bed.

On the night of October 28, Dick telephoned Edna Webster. Her mother, Alice Smith, picked up the receiver.

"May I speak to Edna?" Dick asked.

"She isn't here."

Standing in the kitchen, Linda Webster thought the call was for her. "I'm here," she yelled at her grandmother. Dick Brautigan hung up without another word and wept.

Two days later, on another bleak rainy afternoon, Dick sat in a rocking chair in his furnished room and wrote another letter to Gary Stewart. A sore finger pained him enough that he joked about gangrene setting in. "I'm so poor that I'll have to amputate it myself." Hungry but unsure what he'd have for dinner, Dick quipped, "I'll probably eat the big rat who has been staring at me while I've been writing this letter." The overall tone of the letter was bleak. Dick told Gary about the book of stories he had started, adding that he would never try to publish it.

> *Because I know that I don't have any talent. The book has the very best of me in it, and I know it isn't worth a shit.*
>
> *I really wanted to give the world something. When I was young, I used to pray to God to let me give the world something. I have never wanted to take anything from the world. I just wanted to give the world something. It is a sad feeling to know that I will never give the world anything because I don't have any brains or any talent. I'm just a little zero. It makes me sad. I wanted to tell the world so many things. But I will never tell the world anything. At the age of twenty, I've run out of gas and there are no service stations. All of my dreams are cold, wet leaves lying in the gutter of time.*

Grinding poverty and an energy-depleting malnutrition laid the foundation for his acute depression, but the framework remained a broken heart. Brautigan called it the "Linda Webster Blues." She had become an obsession. In the grip of his feelings, Brautigan began losing sight of reality. "I love her, but she hates me. It hurts and hurts and hurts me. I feel like a God-damn fool [. . .] Isn't it ridiculous for a person as ugly as I am to love a person as beautiful [as] Linda. And she's only fourteen-years-old, too. My heart is insane." He hoped "to God" that he would never see her or hear the sound of her voice ever again.

Avoiding the Webster household to spare himself the pain of running into Linda, Dick transferred his need for family over to Gary Stewart's mother and father, "a pair of the nicest people alive." He visited and phoned them regularly. "You are very, very lucky to have such wonderful parents," he wrote Gary, signing himself "a nothing called Brautigan." A pathetic PS observed, "These letters are stupid, horrible things. If you want me to stop writing them, I will."

The next three weeks dragged on in a similar fashion. No money. Not enough to eat. The dreary cold wet weather enhanced the bleakness Brautigan felt inside. Dick was going down fast, his lonely craft all he had left to sustain him. In spite of low self-esteem, this "little zero" continued wielding a pencil, struggling to perfect his prose and poetry in the twenty-five-cent school notebooks he could barely afford.

On Tuesday, November 22, 1955, he flipped open the cover of one and wrote "i love You" in a diagonal descending across the first page. At the bottom of the second sheet, in tiny lowercase letters, he wrote, "by richard brautigan." On the third leaf came the dedication, carefully printed in huge block printing dwarfing all the rest: "for LINDA." The very next day, Dick Brautigan found God.

"The night is over," Dick wrote to Gary Stewart. "Now I will walk in the sun. / Oh, Gary, I am so happy. / It was the longest night." Finding God greatly improved his attitude. "I have so much intelligence and sensitivity and love to communicate to the world," his letter continued. "My writing has improved tremendously during the last month. I believe that God is going to help me to be a literary sensation by summer. God has made me know something about myself. I know that I am [a] genius with creative power beyond description. And I am very humble about it."

The intensity of Brautigan's words vibrate with the psychotic fervor of an extremely troubled young man. "This letter is very, very hard to write. I want my writing to be perfect. I want to say exactly what I want to say." The manic drive for perfection didn't arise out of his admiration for Hemingway's lapidary styling or his newfound godliness. It came from his all-consuming love for Linda Webster. "I love Linda with a love deeper than the river, purer than the river," Dick declared. "I want to build a cage around her. A delicate cage. The cage will be made out of the strangest thing in the world: gentleness. I shall feed her the food of my love, and give her the milk of my love to drink, and I shall grow her up and make her beautiful beyond all things."

Dick believed he would do his "greatest writing" when he finally had Linda. He planned to complete his book of love poetry in three days. He very carefully printed the title, "i love You," emphasizing the capitalization of the second-person pronoun. "It is a very lovely book," Dick declared. "I have created a new form of love poetry." Two examples follow:

kitten

> *for easter*
> *i will give You*
> *a white kitten.*

a cookie

> *i pray to God*
> *for Him to let me*
> *have You.*
>
> *if He will let me*
> *have You,*
> *i will give Him a cookie.*

Brautigan felt he had discovered "a very lovely form." He decided not to publish "because it does not belong to me. It is Linda's book." On the surface, his recent religious conversion appeared to bring some peace. "Oh, I am so happy now that I have found God," he told his friend. Brautigan finished his book of love poetry two days behind his strict schedule and carefully wrote on the next-to-last page: "this is Linda Webster's book. / it is a symbol of my love for Her. / i will not give this book to Linda / until i know that She loves me. / if the world is going to get this book, / Linda will have to give it to the world. / will i give this book to Linda? / will the world get this book? / only God knows. richard brautigan / November 27th, 1955 / eugene, oregon." The final page contained just three words: "love / never / ends."

Everything about Brautigan's "love" book revealed the author's deep instability. The compulsion to finish the book by a certain date, the use of the lowercase for all names and personal pronouns except those referring to (and thus equating) Linda Webster and God, the belief that these spare, slight verses created a new form of love poetry; all pointed to a disturbed mental state. Certainly his critical facilities were compromised. Compared with the intricate beauty of "The Second Kingdom," the poems in "i love You" amounted to little more than innocent fluff.

True to his declaration, Dick Brautigan did not give "i love You" to Linda Webster. Instead, as he had done with his letters, he handed the notebook over to Edna, who, again for reasons of her own, never passed it along to her daughter. Decades went by. Eventually the little spiral-bound volume was sold to rare book dealers, along with the rest of the contents of Edna Webster's safe deposit box. It resides now in the Bancroft Library. Linda Webster has only a Xerox copy (given to her by the author of this book), having never laid eyes upon the original.

Bill Brown didn't see all that much of Dick after the fishing season closed but continued to loan him money from time to time. "He wasn't into me for large amounts," Brown remembered. "Fifty, sixty, seventy bucks. Of course, back in those days that was quite a bit." Dick also borrowed from Pete Webster. "A dollar here, a dollar there, until it amounted to $20."

The young writer's health was not good. The chill rainy weather caused him to be frequently sick that fall. Once, on a visit to Gary Stewart's parents, he found himself down on his knees, praying with the family. Dick thought it was "a lovely experience," one he would never forget. Afterward, alone in his room, he prayed on his knees twice every day.

Through poverty and illness and newfound religious fervor, Dick Brautigan continued to write, his work seemingly all that held him together. He started a new book of poetry, "Behold This Place," considering it half-done by the second week of December. He changed the title of the book of short stories in progress from "These Few Precious Days" to "What a Strange Place This Is" and felt it was "coming along well." By mid-December, he had completed thirty stories, many extremely brief, half a page or less in length. He thought them "awfully good."

A letter to Gary Stewart postmarked 4:30 PM, December 12, 1955, exposed the raw nerves of his emotions. Writing on another rainy evening, Dick declared, "I am sad a mountain. Why? Ohhhh, because. I think. That I will die before I am 23-years-old. That I will never enchant Linda. (Soon my huger than spring love for her will start to destroy me.) If I am not accepted as an American genius this coming year, I will be destroyed." Dick wrote that he needed fame to gain the confidence "to enchant Linda, whom I cannot live without."

Dick told Gary about his recent writing. "All for the beautiful Linda. All for mankind. I crawl around in my puke and tears. Will it be in vain[?]" In an attempt to lighten things up, he expressed his amazement about recently discovering that women found him attractive. It had taken him an hour to reach the middle of the second page, erasing his words over and over. Levity just wasn't in him on this particular night. "I have a strong feeling," he wrote, "that I will never see you again in this life time. [As it turned out, he never did.] I am obsessed with death. I have been ever since I was 11-years-old [. . .] I am afraid of everything in this world except death."

Acknowledging that his letters were "intense experiences," Brautigan summed up his present condition succinctly: "I am out of work and broke and need money like crazy [. . .] Gary, you've never really lived until you're flat broke and starving to death." Dick knew poverty was often an artist's lot in life. In fact, he believed it to be beneficial for the artist. "It increases his capacity for pity." Although his own poverty was fast "reaching the harmful stage," his propensity for optimistic self-delusion remained undiminished, and he included a fair copy of a short story "that will help me become famous." "First Cat in the Rain," was only eight sentences long.

"All for the beautiful Linda," Dick wrote for the second time. "All for mankind. Without Linda I am nothing. I have nothing. I will be nothing. Nothing. Nothing. Nothing." Then, stepping back to honestly assess his situation, he added a succinct single line: "Love will kill me." As the hours passed, his mood swung back and forth, a pendulum ticking between gentle irony and deep despair. "Following my mind is like following an enchanted rabbit though a strange forest," Dick observed.

It was now past midnight. The rain pattered down outside. Dick had been working on his letter for hours. The premonition that he would not see his friend Gary ever again steeped him in melancholy. "Remember duck hunting?" he wrote in conclusion. "Oh, those were the days! Gone forever. So many things gone forever. So many things gone forever. So many things gone forever. A boy with yellow hair. A boy with red hair. Hunting ducks. Gone forever."

nine: the rub of a strange cat

ON WEDNESDAY EVENING, December 14, 1955, the fragile texture of Dick Brautigan's little world (poverty, newfound religious fervor, heartbreak, artistic endeavor) unraveled completely. Feeling panicked because his folks tried convincing him to seek psychiatric help, he walked over to the Northwest Christian College campus. Desperately short of cash, he dropped in on Peter Webster's dorm room and asked for a loan of $5. Pete said only after Dick repaid the twenty bucks he already owed him. Brautigan flew into a rage and stormed out.

Dick wandered the wet streets of Eugene, his emotions boiling over in a frenzy. He was so mad he wanted to kill somebody. A long walk led him to 41 Madison Street. He went in to talk with Edna. Dick spilled out his feelings in a passionate, uncontrollable torrent. The way Linda utterly ignored him drove him almost crazy. Mrs. Webster listened patiently, trying to offer advice, yet nothing she said was of any comfort. She followed Dick outside and prevented him from punching his fist into the garage door. "He was so angry when he left here that he just felt like doing something irrational."

Lost in fury, wanting to destroy somebody, anybody, even himself, Dick Brautigan wandered downtown to the public library, one of his favorite haunts. Across the street, on the corner of Willamette and Eleventh, stood city hall. Originally built as the Eugene High School in 1903, the vine-covered building had been used for municipal purposes since 1915. Above the portico enclosing the front steps, an oblong sign glowed like a beacon of salvation in the night: POLICE. He logically assumed the police would offer him protection from himself.

Officer William Smith manned the desk when Dick Brautigan lurched into the station, distraught and wild-eyed. "I want to go to jail," he demanded. Dick told the policeman he was afraid of what he might do to himself and others, asking to be locked up. Officer Smith attempted to humor the disturbed youth. He said only criminals went to jail.

Dick walked back out onto the street and found a rock. Returning to the police station in city hall, he again faced Officer Smith. "I am a criminal," Brautigan announced. "I am going to break the law." Rearing back, he hurled the rock through a gilt-lettered, pebble-glass panel in the department's front door. This did the trick. Smith arrested Brautigan and booked him on a charge of disorderly conduct. Locked up in the city jail, agitated and distraught, Dick blurted out that he was insane.

Next morning in municipal court, Brautigan pleaded guilty to the charge and his case was continued until Saturday. The judge said he would give him some time to think about it. All anger drained, Dick felt chagrined as he was led back to the crowded communal cell. A little later, a pair of city detectives came by to talk to him. After hearing Dick's story, they told the young man he needed a mistress much more than a psychiatrist.

Thursday's *Register-Guard* contained a small article at the bottom of the front page ("Eugenean's Wish Granted") recapping the story in a few succinct lines. "A Eugene man who said he wanted to go to jail got his wish Wednesday night." Linda Webster read the article later in the day and knew immediately Dick's troubles happened because of her. She clipped the piece and saved it, feeling guilty for years.

As soon as Pete Webster learned his friend was in jail, he drove straight over to visit him. Dick appeared very embarrassed, staring out through the bars of the drunk tank. "Why did you come here?" he demanded. Pete said he was a concerned friend. Dick expressed surprise at seeing him. Glancing around a cell crowded with common prisoners, he asked Pete not to come back again "under those conditions." Peter agreed. He left the jail thinking his friend would soon be a free man.

After Edna Webster found out about Dick's predicament, she telephoned her friend Lois Barton. Lois and her husband, Hal, were Quakers, involved in causes dear to Edna's heart. Hal Barton's social work dealt with mental health issues. Edna hoped he would follow up on Dick's case and see if there was any way he might help. "Dick was facing an appearance before a local magistrate," Hal recalled, "and she was concerned about the approach of that magistrate to cases like his. He had a tendency to want to crack them down."

Hal Barton went straight over to the city jail for a visit with Dick Brautigan. "He wasn't too much of one to talk," Barton remembered. "There was no question of the circumstances. I mean, he just revealed them as they were and that was about it." Mr. Barton left the jail that night with the impression that Dick had been "feeling suicidal and wanted to be put away where he wouldn't be able to do that." When the police refused to arrest him because he hadn't committed a crime, he immediately obliged them "in order to get protection for the night."

On Saturday, December 17, 1955, Richard Gary Brautigan made a second appearance in the municipal courtroom. Just as Edna suspected, the presiding judge, John L. Barber Jr., had a reputation among the young people of Eugene as a hardnose, handing out stiff fines whenever teenagers were caught with alcohol. Police officer William Smith observed "Judge Barber thought a dose of strong medicine was what was needed for anyone who got slightly out of line." The judge accepted Brautigan's guilty plea and continued the case until the following Monday for sentencing.

The young writer spent a long weekend in the slammer. Paranoia and claustrophobia grow palpable in a cell, charting the bleak boundaries of an unfamiliar new reality. He was already steeped in inconsolable misery, and Dick Brautigan's incarceration exaggerated the smallest discomforts. Dick didn't smoke. Cigarettes take on an almost mystical importance in the joint. As jailhouse currency, cigarettes become synonymous with doing time, and tobacco smoke obscured the air in the crowded common cell of the Eugene city jail. For Brautigan, every breath was torture.

The extreme stress of the situation took an immediate toll. Brautigan's fine blond hair started falling out. He lost it in such quantities he feared he would become completely bald and "quite ugly" before he was twenty-two years old. Paper and a pencil provided magic tools to transport him out of despair. He found solace in his work. New poetry flowed freely from his imagination. Even in jail, every poem he wrote was about Linda Webster.

On Monday the nineteenth, Richard Gary Brautigan was back in court as case number 11563. Municipal Judge Barber ruled on a total of nineteen cases that day. Brautigan's ornate vocabulary struck him as particularly annoying. Barber sentenced Dick to ten days and a $25 fine. Court records indicate the fine was never paid. Brautigan paid a much more severe penalty. With credit for time already served, he should have been out of jail by Saturday, in time for Christmas Eve.

Events didn't work out that way. The young man's behavior in the police station struck the stern judge as somewhat peculiar. This episode seemed to be more than just another disorderly conduct prank. The whole business sounded wacky, and Judge Barber ordered a medical evaluation of Dick Brautigan prior to his scheduled release on December 24.

Hal Barton attended Dick Brautigan's Saturday hearing in the Lane County Courthouse with Judge Barber presiding. Two psychiatrists and a medical doctor were in attendance. "It didn't last very long," Hal recalled. "Seemed like we were out of there as soon as we were in almost." The medical men reported their findings to the judge, and he rendered a decision, committing Richard Gary Brautigan to the Oregon State Hospital for a thirty-day observation period. When Barton spoke with the judge about it afterward, he was told the boy "needed a little picture of reality, and the only way he was going to get it was to be given a rather sharp sentencing."

Crying outside the hearing room, Mary Lou approached her son, her lips soundlessly forming his name as if in a dream. His stepfather tried reassuring him that things would work out fine. "Everything is going to be OK." Dick was not so optimistic. He didn't see much hope in being shipped had to the madhouse on Christmas Eve. The bleakness building inside over the past several months had now become manifest, a demon wrapping its black, cold tentacles about his soul.

After the hearing, the officials loaded Dick into a government car for the trip up to Salem. He sat in the front seat between the driver and a guard. Another prisoner, wearing handcuffs, sat in back beside a second guard. A gentle rain fell from the pewter-colored winter sky. Dick stared out the window as the guards made small talk. Above the windshield wipers' steady *swish*, he heard the jingle of handcuffs behind him. He thought about Linda Webster, picturing her face, remembering the sound of her voice. He imagined what she would think of him when she learned he'd been sent to the insane asylum and "tried very hard not to cry."

Ten years before, Dick Brautigan had had his appendix removed at Salem General and had left a rose blossom on the front steps every night after his mother gave birth to his sister Sandra. Feelings of dread erased these memories when the government car transporting him arrived at the state mental hospital. Public health facilities are never designed with aesthetics as a primary concern, and the first grim appearance of the asylum through the drizzle looked as welcoming as a glimpse of Count Dracula's Transylvanian castle in a flash of midnight lightning. *One Flew Over the Cuckoo's Nest*, Milos Forman's motion picture version of Ken Kesey's novel, was filmed at the Oregon State Hospital, an institution as much a prison as a medical facility.

Dick Brautigan walked into the hospital accompanied by a guard who brought along the police report. Dick offered no resistance, cooperative throughout the bureaucratic admissions procedure. "Do I have to spend thirty days here?" he asked. "I'll be driven crazy, or else I'll be bored to death." Referring to the report, Dick told the officials, "You have it all in there, haven't you? There were two psychiatrists and a doctor at the hearing, and they took notes. You'll get them in time." He was not deemed dangerous, posing no threat to himself or the other patients, and was allowed the run of Ward J. The holiday season had never been a big deal for Brautigan, but spending his twentieth Christmas in a mental hospital, provisionally diagnosed as a paranoid schizophrenic ("chronic, severe") expanded the boundaries of the bleak.

Mary Lou Folston remembered driving up to celebrate Christmas with her son in Salem, bring-ing presents and clothing. They visited in a huge recreation room furnished with benches, windows barred, institutional green walls sporting a few stray decorations. "We'd sit and talk and walk around the room," Mary Lou recollected. She and her husband, Bill, tried to visit every Sunday. Unable to fully comprehend what was happening to her son, Mary Lou resorted to desperate measures and phoned Edna Webster, a woman she actively disliked, in hopes of finding out some answers. Dick told her Mrs. Webster had complimented his fine blond hair and ethereal blue eyes. She suspected the older woman might have been her son's lover.

"She used to call me on the phone and talk to me a lot," Edna recalled. "Oh, she was frantic about him. Couldn't understand what made Richard the way he was."

Edna went up to visit Dick "several times; three times, I guess it was." Once, she and her son Pete made the trip with the Folstons. "Father let Pete drive in our car," Mary Lou remembered. Dick was allowed out of the hospital for this unsupervised visit, and they all went to a nearby res-taurant. Mrs. Webster recalled how the Folstons "insisted Pete sit in a booth with them and I sit in a booth with Richard. And Richard was embarrassed, and so was I. She treated us as if I were his girlfriend."

"There's nothing wrong with you," Edna reassured Dick in the booth. "You're okay. Just make other people see that. Conform to their way of acting, because then they will think that you are okay. When you don't say anything, people will think you agree with them. Don't tell them what you feel. Don't tell them anything."

Edna's sage advice came too late. Dick had already told the doctors plenty, and they filled their report with harsh clinical observations. Brautigan said he was a genius, which the interview-ing physicians interpreted as evidence of pompous self-deception. They viewed him as sarcastic, hostile, and suspicious, "a petty and would-be intellectual." Listening to his "long rambling and wordy description of his difficulties," the medical staff at Salem felt he deliberately used all the big words he could muster, "although most of them are poorly selected and out of context." Brautigan showed the psychiatrist an outline "of what he calls a novel" that he had written the day before. "Is there censorship here?" he asked. "Am I deprived of my constitutional rights? Am I a menace to society? Does that work seem to be the product of a mentally ill mind?"

When Dick Brautigan spoke of his writing as being "great literature," the doctors referred to the police report describing his work as "obscene" and having "very little literary merit." Brautigan's commitment papers stated that the patient "had the delusion that he was a writer of great ability. He had various former teachers and other people read some of his writings, and they were without question some of the most weird and lewd material they had ever read." Brautigan himself admitted that much of his work "was variations on sexual themes that would make Erskine Caldwell look like Elsie Dinsmore."

Uncomfortable in an unfamiliar menacing environment, Dick Brautigan attempted to impress his interviewers, not realizing he was under such dispassionate scrutiny. The doctors thought he talked with "an effeminate voice" and noted his "use of gesture" and how he gazed up at the ceil-ing "a good deal of the time," taking off his glasses, sighing, and posturing "in a very dramatic fashion." They noted "considerable giggling, grimacing and laughing."

Dick told the doctors that he had considered suicide at times although he never attempted it. Talking about sex, he said, "I'm a Platonic animal, I don't bask in carnality. I have never masturbated, it seems a rather vulgar practice to me." He also said, "My mind conjures up many weird things," and "I'm obsessed with good and evil."

Brautigan's claim to be "a genius in the literary line" sealed his fate in the mental hospital. How could a lowly cannery worker with only a high school education presume so much? "There is considerable delusory ideation, most of it of a grandiose nature," reasoned the psychobabblers. "The patient appears to be moderately mentally ill," they stated, issuing an ultimate diagnosis of "schizophrenic reaction, paranoid type."

The medical men recommended a severe therapy. On January 3, 1956, Dick Brautigan was transferred to Ward M, where Electroconvulsive therapy (ECT) was administered. By January 9, the authorities at the Oregon State Hospital had given him four electroshock treatments. "I didn't sign any papers, and didn't give them any permission," Mary Lou Folston said, "and when I called again he had had six of those things . . . *Boom, boom, boom, boom!*"

On January 26, Brautigan received his twelfth and final electroshock, completing his course of treatment. The doctors felt they had been successful. Patient number 22877 was now properly socialized. His problematic intellectual pretensions were subdued. Dick Brautigan appeared much more normal to the authorities. He was judged to be in remission from his psychosis.

After decades of snake-pit bad rep shock therapy has regained a certain measure of medical respectability as a treatment for acute depression. Back in the middle 1950s, the procedure was administered without anesthesia or muscle relaxants and often used as a punishment for unruly patients. Today, written consent must first be obtained from either the patient or a court-appointed guardian. No such approval was needed when the electrodes were attached to the head of Richard Gary Brautigan.

The avowed purpose of electroshock was to induce a seizure within the brain of a depressed patient in hope of obtaining a calming effect. Early on, before the procedure was fully understood, shock treatment was more or less experimental, with wide variables in dosage and duration, often inducing painful grand mal seizures, which, in turn, occasionally produced such serious injuries as bone fractures and dislocations.

Dick told his mother he had assisted the staff in administering shock treatment to other patients. "His job was to put them on this gurney and wheel them in there when they put the gizmo on them," Mary Lou remembered. "He was holding them down while they put the thing in the mouth before they turn the juice on. And how they'd spit up foam and stuff like that. He didn't like to hold the men down when they were getting their shocks, see."

Perhaps Dick told his mother these made-up war stories to distance her from his own suffering, his abstract way of describing how he himself bucked against the straps, gnawing the mouth guard that kept him from biting off his tongue when the lightning bolts crashed through his brain. At some point, he informed Edna Webster that shock treatments "were a vicious thing to do to a person." Pete Webster remembered Dick telling him they were "very painful" and that they "blocked out his memory." At first, he maintained a daily journal of ward life during the therapy, trying to measure potential memory loss. In his sister Barbara's recollection, "it was two or three days before he was functioning again after these treatments." Mary Lou maintained a no-nonsense logic, believing Dick's odd story to be true. "See, it was a nuthouse," she said. "They don't care."

Institutional life was not without positive side effects. Three squares a day packed twenty-one pounds on Dick's skeletal frame in a month. Having enough to eat does wonders to improve a man's spirit. Dancing provided another beneficial result. Barbara reported that Dick made a friend in the hospital, a young woman who taught him how to dance during the institution's social hours. "He was very proud of the fact that he had learned to dance."

Mary Lou remembered the second month of her son's stay at the mental hospital as an agreeable time for him. "He acted pleasant and happier than he'd ever been," she said. In her opinion, none of the attendants knew that Richard had been sent to Salem by the court. "They thought he self-committed himself. Here he had the freedom of the grounds and the buildings and everything. Come and went as he pleased, except for bedtime and mealtime." Dick had also resumed his writing, always effective therapy for depression.

Welcome news came in January when Mary Lou sent along Dick's mail. Lilith Lorraine, editor of *Flame*, forwarded a letter (dated December 29, 1955) that had come from her "good friend and fellow-editor, Mr. D. Vincent Smith." Smith was an SP3 in the Seventh Cavalry Regiment (Custer's old outfit) with an APO address in San Francisco. He was also "editor & publisher" of Olivant House, which distributed its publications out of Fitzgerald, Georgia, although the "editorial office" was stationed in Japan along with SP3 Smith. In his letter, Smith informed Brautigan that he had chosen to reprint the poem from *Flame* ("Someplace in the World a Man Is Screaming in Pain") in issue no. 1 of *Olivant*, a revival of *Olivant Quarterly*, scheduled for release in March.

Smith also enclosed an advertisement that he hoped Brautigan might post in a public place. "I look forward to seeing more of your work," he wrote, asking for a "selection" of Brautigan's poetry, proposing to publish the poems in a monthly supplement to *Olivant*. "I hope to pay at least $100.00 for each group of poems selected." Brautigan mailed off a batch of his poetry to D. Vincent Smith in Japan. He suggested the title "Tiger in the Telephone Booth" for the collection. Dick also wrote to Evelyn Thorne in Lake Como, Florida, requesting a revision for his biographical note in the upcoming issue of *Epos*. Stating his age as twenty-one and referring obliquely to his hospital confinement, Dick declared, "I have been writing poetry since I was 17. Olivant will publish my first book of poems, Tiger in the Telephone Booth. Making paper flowers out of love and death is a disease, but how beautiful it is."

Another intriguing piece of mail came separately from Lilith Lorraine, a brief handwritten note in response to a new poem Brautigan had submitted to *Flame*: "Excellent but anybody who can write satire like you should be prohibited from writing anything else. So—Give: L. L." Dick approached his poetry with near-religious sincerity. He desired to make the world a better place through his writing with no satirical intentions. The editor mistook fervor for irony.

There was nothing ironic about a collection of poetry (*Linda*) that Brautigan mailed to The Macmillan Company in New York City. Only three pages long, the manuscript consisted of fourteen short poems and a dedication page "for Linda." All but two of the tortured little poems were untitled. Some of their first lines ("when I was a piece of death," "desire in a bowl of potatoes," "love is where you find it," "I knew a gal who was cold as death") provided a glimpse inside Dick's tormented soul and a sneak preview of the poet he was soon to become.

At some point during his stay in the mental hospital, Dick wrote a longhand letter to Linda. "I hope that you do not think that I am crazy," he began. "I am not crazy. Why did I break that window and make a fool out of myself? I did it because I was too tired and mixed-up inside that my nerves broke and I had a breakdown. Life is such a strange place." He next recounted a night he walked in the beautiful warm spring rain with a friend and commented that "'I will go so high that I will be able to look down on the bottom.' I was right. I went so low that I had to look up with a pair of binoculars to see the bottom." Brautigan had not abandoned hope. "I am going to write and write this coming year," he confided to Linda. "I must know something and I will find it out this coming year. I will find a place in the sun."

With nothing left to lose, Dick laid bare his soul to the girl he loved. "I hope that I can live," he wrote. "I am so sensitive and can put my sensitivity down on paper. I think that I can give the world some new thing if I live. If I live. If I live. Do you wonder why I am telling you all of this? I guess I am telling it to you because I like you. I hope that you are not too embarrassed too much or do not feel too awful knowing that a jailbird likes you." Dick concluded by enclosing three of the poems he wrote while locked in the Eugene jail. Linda Webster never received this letter. Like all the others, it remained in her mother's possession, hidden from view for almost forty years.

By the time he wrote to Linda, Dick Brautigan badly wanted out of Salem. He had turned twenty-one in the insane asylum. His future did not look at all bright, and his past was being erased, shock by shock, memory by memory. The madhouse was no place for poets. "People will listen to what they want to hear." Edna Webster's advice echoed in his tattered subconscious. "You're ingenious enough," she had told him. "You can figure out what they want to hear and tell them that and they'll let you go."

And that's just what he did. He played the part, and the authorities ruled him fit enough for a supervised discharge. On February 19, 1956, Hal Barton drove up to Salem to sign Dick Brautigan out of the loony bin. The hospital designated his release a parole. Once again, Edna played a role in encouraging this move. "She figured this was a nice out of the way place where he wouldn't get into trouble," Lois Barton recalled, "and would we take him on for a little while?" The Bartons' faith as members of the Society of Friends involved being the best of Samaritans. Hal made the trip to the state capital and came home with a very grateful young poet. Not that Dick gushed with gratitude. He was too reticent for that.

The Bartons lived outside Eugene, on a small farm on Harry Taylor Road, up along the ridge above Spencer Butte. Harry Taylor had pioneered the area in the early 1930s, buying land there for fifty cents an acre. Out back behind the Bartons' house stood a one-room unpainted tin-roofed shack Taylor had built for himself when he first settled the area. Over time, the exterior board walls weathered to a driftwood gray, giving the little place a melancholy look, like some faded memento from the distant past. This was where Dick Brautigan lived during his stay with the Bartons. "We were a little leery about having him upstairs with all our kids," Lois Barton recalled.

Neither of the Bartons remembered him ever leaving the place, as he had no means of transportation, but Brautigan was an experienced hitchhiker, and he frequently slipped away and thumbed a ride down to town. He visited with Edna Webster when Linda was off in school, so there'd be no danger of a painful unexpected encounter. Dick helped Edna with the dishes, drying as she washed. A friend stopped by, and Edna quipped, "We've been standing here trying to figure out if Richard's a poetic dish-dryer or a dish-drying poet."

A letter for Brautigan from Lilith Lorraine in Alpine, Texas, postmarked February 29, 1956, had just arrived. In it were four of his poems rejected by *Flame*. While this new work employed his "usual striking imagery," they struck Lorraine as "a little light in thought content" compared with the poem she'd previously accepted, "which contained such exquisite satire and which elicited so many favorable comments." She asked to see more "work of that type."

It snowed that day in Eugene. Sometime after midnight, Dick was snug in the little woodstove-heated cabin on Harry Taylor Road, lying on his bed, starting a letter to Gary Stewart. Brautigan always enjoyed writing late at night. This was the first time he'd written his old friend since before the arrest in December. "So many things have happened upon me since last I wrote to you," the letter began. "So many things covered with nightmare and tears." Dick wrote of returning to Eugene. "Back to the place where all the horror started growing [. . .]" He was trying for a fresh start and told his friend he prayed to God every night, sometimes on his knees. Still searching for something to give the world, Dick was most emphatic in assessing his immediate future: "I do not want anymore trouble."

Brautigan said he'd been thinking about his oldest friend that day and correctly prophesied that Gary would "succeed in life." Dick concluded: "Gary, Maybe by the time you get back to Eugene, I'll be a known writer. Maybe I'll be busy enchanting somebody. Giving her bunches of flowers from the garden of my heart. Maybe by the time you get back to Eugene, I'll have a million dollars, too." The letter ended abruptly here, trailing off like a forlorn shout into the wind. There was no closing, and Brautigan did not sign his name. It was the last time he ever wrote to Gary Stewart.

Dick had recently written two "books": *I Watched the World Glide Effortlessly Bye*, and *The Horse That Had a Flat Tire* (both published only after Brautigan's death), either while in the Salem Hospital or soon after arriving at the Bartons'. Composed in one of the small twenty-five-cent spiral-bound notebooks he favored, the first was dedicated to Edna. In a study in minimalism, Brautigan divided it into "Book One," with twenty-six "chapters," and "Book Two," with fifty-seven, each not longer than a single sentence. Several consisted of only one or two words.

The finished notebook was a fair copy (an earlier draft titled "Poet in a Cage" also survives in notebook form), the title page meticulously hand-printed, each of the tiny "chapters" laid out precisely, as if to guide a typesetter. In 315 words, Brautigan narrated an intense, poetic vision of his trip to the State Mental Hospital. He fictionalized himself as "Tommy." The prisoner wearing handcuffs in the backseat became "Jesus Christ," a favorite recurring character in Brautigan's later poetry.

"The Horse That Had a Flat Tire" also was the title of a poem in Brautigan's 1968 collection, *The Pill versus the Springhill Mining Disaster*, which referred to New Mexico, a state the poet had not yet visited in 1956. It remained one of the few fragments of his early writing he chose to preserve. Dick planned five more "books." He hoped to get them all done. If he failed as a writer it would "be because I am no good."

Part of Dick's arrangement with the Bartons included working for them around the farm. They paid him an hourly rate for these chores. A half day at a time, Brautigan cut thistles with a hoe on the edge of their field. Thistles were a noxious weed needing to be controlled. "He also cut the brush along the fence on the right-of-way from the mailbox," Hal remembered. "For a few days, not long. I don't think he particularly liked to work. He had his mind on other things. He wanted to get out. He wanted to go to California."

In his letter to Gary Stewart, Dick wrote: "I have made a plan for the future of my writing. I think it is a good plan." Out in the little shack behind the Bartons' house during his two- or three-month stay, he finished the five "books" he envisioned. "Seven Rooms Each as Big as God," a poetry collection containing an early version of "The Chinese Checker Players" (a poem based on an early childhood memory eventually published in *The Pill*) began with a mock introductory dedication: "This undernourished volume is for Richard Brautigan without whose help and encouragement I never could have written it." The four other notebooks were all dedicated to Edna.

The undated notebooks were carefully scripted fair copies. The order of composition cannot be determined. The author's penmanship was notoriously awkward, and these efforts demonstrated his careful labor to achieve legibility with an obvious eye focused on layout and design. "A Love Letter from State Insane Asylum" was veiled autobiography divided into ten brief numbered chapters, each a sentence occupying a single page describing episodes from the life of a three-year-old child named Calvin.

"ROCK around the CLOCK" was a collection of eight minuscule short stories. Three dealt with death. Two others involved ghosts and hauntings. The title story concerned a boy in a record shop, staring at a fifteen-year-old girl through the glass wall of a listening booth. These were standard features in record stores, allowing customers to sample the music before making a purchase. She selects a record ("Love Is a Many-Splendored Thing," sung by the Four Aces) and steps into the adjoining booth. He listens to the number one song of the year, "Rock Around the Clock" by Bill Haley and His Comets.

Would You Like to Saddle Up a Couple of Goldfish and Swim to Alaska?, inspired by Dick's gift of a pair of goldfish to Linda Webster, was a love fantasy in which the teenage boy and girl lived happily together, hugging and giggling. Divided into five sections, each page again containing only a single sentence or sentence fragment, the notebook provided an intriguing glimpse into Brautigan's psyche. Grace, the character representing Linda, also has brown hair and blue eyes. The narrator, who described himself as "being the world's greatest unknown writer," likes to lie awake, watching Grace as she sleeps.

"There's Always Somebody Who Is Enchanted" was a collection of nine extremely short stories. "A Trite Story" contained only six sentences. It described the winter Brautigan spent in Montana when he was a child. The first line changed Great Falls to "Butte" but correctly described Tex Porterfield (who the author calls "my father") as a cook. This tiny vignette owned an emotional power far in excess of its brevity. The second sentence remains haunting in its ambivalence: "That was after my mother had run off with a man named Frank, or Jack."

Sometime early in Brautigan's stay at the Bartons', two copies of the poetry quarterly *Epos* arrived in the mail from Lake Como, Florida. The cover announced the names of fourteen of the contributors above the motto "The Work of Outstanding American and British Poets." Lilith Lorraine got a mention. Richard Brautigan was one of those included in small print as "and others." He was in good company. Among the others not listed on the cover were George Garrett, A. R. Ammons, and Clark Ashton Smith, the fantasist and pioneer science fiction writer, whose work influenced a diverse group of writers including Jack London, George Sterling, H. P. Lovecraft, Ray Bradbury, and Harlan Ellison. Largely forgotten today, Smith found literary fame in 1912 at age nineteen, when he published *The Star-Treader and Other Poems*.

Perhaps influenced by the brief nonsense plays written by Ring W. Lardner in the 1920s (*Clemo Uti—"The Water Lilies," I. Gaspiri*, and *Taxidea Americana*), Dick turned his hand to drama, writing three short experimental pieces, each less than a single page and to be performed on a bare stage. "Please Let Me Walk" concerned a young woman who reads a poem about "a very beautiful god" breaking the world's neck, after which she is carried into the wings by four uniformed nurses.

In "Everybody and the Rose" an old woman attempts to sell roses to a large group of people standing immobilized on the stage. When no one reacts, she sits down and cries.

The final piece, "Linda," exposed the young poet's emotions like an open wound. A youth pantomimes taking an "imaginary" pistol from a dresser drawer. He puts it to his head, mutters "Linda" softly, and pulls the trigger. A real gunshot is heard. The young man collapses. A laughing couple crosses the stage holding hands. They stop and kiss, oblivious of the body lying at their feet, and exit. Laughter is heard offstage as the curtain falls. Signing himself R. G. Brautigan, he mailed the three little plays (under the collective title *Experimental Dreams*) to the Drama Department at the University of Oregon.

Dick ate all his meals in the main house with the Barton family. "Just one of the bunch," Hal Barton remembered, "which was the way he was." Lois recalled how "persnickety" Dick acted about food. She baked all the family's bread, a half-dozen loaves at a time, and always used molasses instead of white sugar in the yeast starter because of its greater nutritional value. "And he could smell that molasses. Two tablespoons of molasses in six loaves of bread, and he could smell that when it came out of the oven. He didn't like to eat the bread. It didn't suit him."

Lois Barton also did Dick's laundry. She remembered signs of masturbation, "because there was always that mess in the shorts to be washed when he brought them to me." When Lois finished the wash, she'd pile Dick's clean clothes by the back door and tell him to take them down to the cabin. "He'd leave them there for a week or ten days and then they'd be dusty from all the traffic, and he wouldn't want to wear them until I washed them again."

Dick often hung out at the Bartons', telling stories and reading his poetry aloud. "I remember him sitting right in the middle of this room while I was working," Lois said, "and reading bits of this and turning the pages in his notebook." Once, Dick read a poem he had written in Eugene High, which Juliette Gibson criticized as "pornographic material and not suitable for a high school kid to be reading in a classroom." Lois Barton recalled "he was so disgusted that she couldn't see the validity of what he had written."

"He told me stories," Lois said. "He told me about his mother. About one of her earlier mates who took him down onto the street in Seattle in his birthday suit and turned him loose down there for people to tease. And he was petrified because he wasn't sure how to get home and pretty uncomfortable about being out there bare naked." Brautigan told Mrs. Barton this story, transporting the actual event, which involved his younger sister Sandi, into the details of his own life story, an early stab at personal mythology.

Dick Brautigan's storytelling revealed how much he disliked his mother. He told the Bartons "she always had a bottle at her elbow and was drunk by 4:00 PM." Lois had a clear impression "that he was aware of her drinking and not very happy about it and that having this succession of male role models had been a rough kind of thing for him." Although by her own admission Mary Lou enjoyed drinking beer, neither Peter Webster nor Gary Stewart remembered ever seeing her drunk. Still, lines from Brautigan's ministory "a glass of beer," (the final entry in "ROCK around the CLOCK") echoed with an enduring sadness: "Mable was sitting in a chair. There was a stagnant dreamy expression on her face. She was holding a glass of beer in her hand."

Toward the end of his stay with the Bartons, Dick began spending more time in Eugene. He wanted to prepare some of his poetry for submission to publishers, and the only available typewriter belonged to Edna Webster. Brautigan timed his visits to coincide with the hours when Linda was away at school. From his many rough-draft notebooks and sheaves of completed work, he compiled four typed manuscripts. The first was "Tiger in a Telephone Booth."

The second manuscript, "Why Unknown Poets Stay Unknown," Brautigan dedicated "For Edna, / and anybody else / who happens / to be around." He included a brief foreword introducing himself and stating his age (twenty-one). After describing his status as an "unknown poet," Brautigan ended with a line so purely in the spirit of his unfettered imagination that he might have penned it at any point in his career: "Let us pretend that my mind is a taxi and suddenly ('What the hell's coming off!') you are riding in it." He mailed the collection to Random House in New York, using 41 Madison Street as his return address.

The manuscript consisted of fifty-three short poems, forty-three of which were published in a 1999 anthology of Brautigan's early work, *The Edna Webster Collection of Undiscovered Writings*. Released by his official publisher, it was nevertheless a crude effort. In the original manuscript, each poem was allotted a single page and given room to breathe (a practice Brautigan scrupulously followed with all his later published books of poetry). To save space, this collection printed them one above the other like literary wallpaper.

Several of the notebooks Dick gave to Edna were also included in this collection and accorded even more savage editorial treatment. Instead of following the author's intentions, where a page often contained only a single word, the little stories were crammed together, a large dot indicating the page breaks. Brautigan, always a stickler for proper layout and design, would have been appalled. His minimalist tales achieved their emotional power by having the reader turn from page to page before finishing a sentence. Printing the individual lines in a single column separated by dots canceled the author's artistic aims as effectively as hanging a painting upside down.

The third fair-copy manuscript Richard Brautigan typed at Edna Webster's house, "The Smallest Book of Poetry in the Whole God-Damn World," contained only thirteen poems and carried a dedication revealing worlds about the author, who also considered himself a genius and expected to die young: "For James Dean. / An American genius. / Dead at twenty-four." These thirteen brief poems displayed a greater degree of sophistication than Brautigan's earlier work. Three of them utilized traditional meter and rhyme, perhaps the only known examples of his poetry to do so. "A Vision of the World" concerned a two-headed sparrow who read *The New York Times* and had his subscription canceled by a little boy "with a / BB gun." In "The Happy Poem," Brautigan wrote of writing a beautiful poem and then burning it. "All things / become nothing, / anyway," he observed. The final poem, "A Western Ballad," sang of Brautigan's desire to find a new life someplace else. "Wander away [. . .]" he wrote. "Never go back."

Richard Brautigan mailed the manuscript of "The Smallest Book of Poetry in the Whole God-Damn World" to the editors of New Directions in New York. He was careful to include a SASE (again, using 41 Madison Street) with his submission. The slender selection had been winnowed from dozens of poems Dick left behind with Edna Webster. One of these, "The Flower Picker," described the agony he still suffered over Linda, whom he called "Libby." She had recently started dating a ninth-grade classmate, a boy she would eventually marry five years later. "JESUS CHRIST! My soul screams when I / think about somebody else making love to her. / Some little boy," Brautigan wrote. "I believe his name is Ed." Other lines lamented, "What I want to know is: why is she 15 and I 21?" and, "I never got to stroke her. / Or kiss her. / Or hold her hand. / Even." And, "I want to walk into a / dark house, her body, and turn on all the lights."

"Little Children Should Not Wear Beards," a forty-seven-page poetry collection, was the final fair copy manuscript that Dick typed at Edna's house, intending it as a submission to Scribner's, the venerable New York publisher on Fifth Avenue. A self-addressed manila envelope survives, with 41 Madison Street as the return destination, but the writing is not in Brautigan's hand. It was written by Edna Webster, who never mailed the poems to Scribner's. The postage stamps on the envelope (twenty-seven cents' worth) were not canceled. The manuscript remained in Edna's possession until she eventually sold it. Along with her other Brautigan papers, it ended up at the Bancroft Library, UC Berkeley, several years after Richard Brautigan died.

Early in May (1956), two disappointing bits of news arrived in the mail. The first came on the eighth to the Bartons' rural route address from Horace W. Robinson of the Speech and Dramatic Arts Departments at the U of O. He enclosed a program of five short plays performed three days earlier in the University Theatre under the billing "Theatre Excitement No. 7." One was a scene from Shakespeare; another, Edna St. Vincent Millay's *Aria da Capo* (not all that exciting in an age of Genet, Ionesco, and Beckett). Professor Robinson thanked Mr. Brautigan "for the opportunity of examining your experimental dramas," saying that he had circulated the three short plays among the other directors on the staff and "they have indicated that they are interesting." The department used "such material" to instruct young actors or for student performances. Having raised Dick's hopes, Professor Robinson concluded: "Your plays are so brief and devoid of character development that they probably would not be useful in either of these categories."

The second letter arrived at 41 Madison Street from The Macmillan Company. It contained Brautigan's manuscript *Linda*. In his brief accompanying letter, Assistant Editor-in-Chief R. L. DeWilton politely rejected the poetry and thanked the author for sending it. Richard took it all in stride. He was already long accustomed to receiving what his idol Ernest Hemingway once called "the sternest of all reprimands."

Around this time, Dick paid his last visit to the Folston home on Hayes Street. Mary Lou was out working in her vegetable garden, wearing her husband's old size 52 mackinaw. "Put the shovel in one hand," she laughed, "and the hoe in the other." Years later, she recalled that her son was furious at what he perceived as a gross indignity. Mary Lou said Brautigan confronted Bill Folston, raging, "You took my mother, a lovely lady, and you made a darn old Indian squaw out of her." Richard detested prejudice in any form, and it's unlikely he ever used these exact words. In any event, Folston, an amiable, good-natured man, never took the bait or replied in kind. Soon after, Dick stormed off, pursued by his angry demons. He had just departed from their lives forever.

It was Hal Barton's understanding when he signed Richard Brautigan out of the mental hospital in Salem that the young man was not to leave the state of Oregon without official permission. Even so, Hal made no effort to block Dick's planned departure. "He just wanted to go," he said. "Be out from under here and get into a new environment where he thought he'd be more accepted." One day in June of 1956, the young poet packed his few belongings in a couple cardboard boxes, each no larger than a case of beer. He didn't have many clothes, although Lois Barton remembered "a half a dozen or more sets of underwear." Much of his writing had been left with Edna Webster, but certain manuscripts and works in progress went along with him. He never returned home to collect any of his things, not even a suitcase. "His nice stuff he left here," Mary Lou said. "He just disappeared, you know."

At dawn, five thirty the next morning, with the sun rising over Three-Fingered Jack Mountain, Lois Barton drove Dick Brautigan and his makeshift luggage downtown. He wore his favorite brown suede jacket. Lois dropped him at the bus station. She didn't buy his ticket or wait to see him off. The Bartons never heard from their resident poet again. He never wrote them a letter or a postcard. "He was just gone and out of the picture," Lois said.

Richard Brautigan did not buy a ticket or board the bus that day. He might have killed time with a couple cups of coffee and a cheap breakfast. When it no longer seemed too early, he picked up his boxes and walked over to the Stewarts' house on Tyler Street. Gary's mom later wrote that Dick "just showed up at the door. He was down and out and wanted to go to San Francisco." Milo Stewart's sister lived in South San Francisco, and he agreed to drive Dick to the city the very next day. Mary Lou later heard a story that her son worked for the Stewarts, helping them paint their house.

Either later that afternoon or sometime the next morning, Barbara was walking north along Willamette in downtown Eugene, when she spotted her brother across the street, heading in the opposite direction. She was taking care of the Guistinas' kids and had seen Dick only once since his release from the hospital. B.J. remembered that he had seemed "just kind of laid-back and sedate and very quiet," in marked contrast to his previous behavior, "always full of energy and things going on in his mind." Brautigan had phoned a few times from up at the Bartons' place to read B.J. his new poetry, but it wasn't the same as before. Dick struck her as "aloof—more wary, standoff-ish." They were no longer close.

On that last day, Dick waved and called out, "Barbara!" to get her attention. He waited for the traffic to clear before crossing over. "Hi. How're you doing?" he said, and they started talk-ing. Barbara remembered that "he had on that brown suede jacket he really liked." After a few moments of casual conversation, Dick said, "Well, I'm leaving." He didn't mention San Francisco or tell her about his long-range plans. "We didn't hug or kiss or anything," Barbara remembered sadly. "He said, 'I just wanted to say goodbye.' And we stood there looking at each other for a couple of seconds, and then he rambled back over to the other side of the street, and that's the last time I ever saw him."

WHEN EDNA WEBSTER expressed a curiosity about Dick Brautigan's family, he brought over a box of old photographs his mother kept hidden in her bedroom. Dick found them one day when his folks were away and took them without asking. They portrayed Kehoes and Dixons. Mary Lou had not saved a single snapshot of Ben Brautigan. After going through the pictures, he gave several of himself as a kid to Mrs. Webster. When Mary Lou discovered the photographs missing, she immediately suspected her son and asked what he had done with them. Dick told her he burned the photos. Unaware of her mother's inquiry, Barbara wanted to look at the pictures on another occasion. She had never seen several and was curious about them. Dick repeated the same story, telling his sister he had burned them all. And that was the last anyone ever said about the matter. This uniquely unsentimental family forgot all about the lost photographs.

Richard had not burned the family pictures. They were packed in one of his cardboard boxes when he left Eugene, among the very few personal possessions he took away with him. Many years later, his daughter grew increasingly curious about her family's history. Every time Ianthe asked Richard to tell her about the relatives she had never seen, he stalled with one excuse or another. She remained insistent, pestering him for information about her unknown uncles and aunts, wanting to know what her grandparents and great-grandparents looked like. Richard promised when she became an adult he would tell her everything she wanted to know.

Richard assumed, given enough time, that his daughter would forget her curiosity. Ianthe never forgot. On her nineteenth Christmas, alone with her father in the huge echoing living room of his Pacific Heights apartment, she finally got her wish. Richard and his second wife, Akiko, had split up earlier in December (1979), and the painful legal thrust-and-parry of divorce had just begun. The near-empty apartment, so recently a proud symbol of Brautigan's enormous literary success, now seemed a sad manifestation of the couple's final unhappiness. Aki had taken the rug and the stereo and much of the furniture. The imitation leather couches and an odd octagonal table were all she had left behind. Even the lamps walked out the door with her. The only light in the room, aside from the flickering fireplace, spilled in from a hallway ceiling fixture.

Richard had just given Ianthe a check for $150. They sat down by the fire for a quiet Christmas evening. Abruptly, Richard set his whiskey glass on the table and jumped to his feet. He left the room, saying he'd be right back. Ianthe fingered the check, contemplating her father's distinctive spidery signature. When Richard returned, he carried a manila file folder. With the deliberate care of someone handling extremely volatile material, he pulled an old Polaroid snapshot from the file and handed it to Ianthe, telling her it was a picture of her grandmother.

Studying the old photo of a sharp-eyed, middle-aged woman smoking a cigarette in the shade of a willow tree, Ianthe puzzled over how her father happened to have such a memento of someone he hadn't seen in almost a quarter century. Richard never corresponded with his mother. It's possible Mary Lou sent him the picture when his sisters attempted to reestablish contact in 1970. More likely he brought it with him when he left home for good. There were several other photographs, all family pictures. Ianthe stared at them, trying to absorb their essence, searching for a connection to link her to an unknown personal history.

After a while, Richard asked his daughter if she was "done looking." She said, "Yes." And he wanted to know if she was sure. Ianthe nodded her head. Without another word, her father, this mysterious man who had so completely turned his back on his own past, took the family pictures from her, stepped over to the fireplace, and scattered the photographs into the flames like a handful of dry dead leaves.

THE LONG JOURNEY taking Richard Brautigan from Eugene to San Francisco began when Milo Stewart set off for the Bay Area to visit his sister. He drove Highway 99 (mainly replaced by Interstate 5), south out of Eugene, all the way to Sacramento, then west on U.S. 40 to Oakland. Richard took this route with Gary's father. He had always wanted to see Reno, so Milo dropped him off in Sacramento. Richard hitchhiked to Reno by way of the Donner Pass.

On a warm summer day in June, he passed under the steel arch spanning Main Street welcoming him to "The Biggest Little City in the World." Richard looked first for a place to bunk for a couple nights. In 1956, Reno had not yet become a sprawling metropolis studded with high-rise casinos. Bisected by U.S. 40, the Truckee River, and its primary dividing line, the Southern Pacific Railroad tracks, Reno back then was just another of the neon-bright honky-tonk oases brightening Nevada's highways at distant intervals in the vast empty desert.

At the time, very few buildings in Reno stood over four stories. Gambling establishments and most of the bars congregated along several blocks of Virginia Street and a rowdy strip on Commercial bordering the tracks from Sierra to Center Streets. The city fathers acted as if no one ever shook a pair of dice or bet on blackjack or cranked a one-armed bandit within the city limits. Reno retained the quiet ambience of its tree-lined neighborhoods. In the words of writer Walter Van Tilburg Clark, it was a "city of trembling leaves."

Brautigan found a cheap room not far from Route 40 in a rundown part of town near the railroad tracks. It was a tiny chamber furnished with a narrow cot in a ramshackle flophouse so depressingly decrepit that he feared leaving his few humble possessions and carried the two cardboard boxes along with him when he set out to explore the sights. The first place on his itinerary was a bookstore. Finding his way proved not too difficult. Reno boasted dozens of casinos but possessed only one bookstore.

Checking the poetry section, Brautigan came across a copy of *Brushfire*, the University of Nevada's literary magazine. Leafing through its pages, he found the work of a young poet named Barney Mergen. The "Notes on the Contributors" mentioned that the author lived in Reno. Surmising he had found a kindred spirit, Richard looked up Mergen's address in the phone book: 112 Ridge Street, way over on the south side, a part of town far removed from the high-toned north-end university neighborhood. Brautigan gathered up his cardboard boxes and started walking.

Barney Mergen lived with his mother and grandmother in what by his own account was "the only honest-to-goodness rickety tenement building between Chicago and Sacramento." Formerly a hospital, the old wooden apartment house stood a few blocks from the Riverside Hotel.

Nineteen-year-old Barney, having completed his freshman year at the university, worked a summer construction job. He had just gotten off and was taking a bath when Richard Brautigan knocked unannounced on the front door. Mergen's grandmother, "scared half to death" by the unexpected appearance of this unorthodox stranger, rushed to tell Barney that he had a visitor.

"There's a strange boy asking for you," she said. He climbed out of the bathtub and toweled off. Dressing quickly, Barney went to investigate. He immediately recognized the accuracy of his grandmother's assessment. Richard towered in the doorway, "thin as a reed," his long wheat-blond hair worn in Dutch-boy bangs cut straight across his forehead just above the eyes. Barney had never seen anyone like him. In those days, men in Reno and everywhere else in America favored crew cuts.

"Hello," the peculiar stranger said, looking straight at Barney. "I'm Richard Brautigan, and I'm a poet." The younger man was very impressed by Brautigan's attitude and the way he had said, in effect, "this is not what I do, but this is what I am."

"He had a sense of destiny about him," Mergen recollected many years later. "That was easy to see."

Brautigan explained he was on his way to San Francisco and needed a safe place to leave his belongings while he looked for work. Glancing about the small cramped apartment, Richard immediately deduced that there was no room here for him. Barney agreed to watch over his two cardboard boxes. "One contained manuscripts, and one held some socks, shirts, and underwear." This composed the sum total of Richard Brautigan's worldly goods.

The two young poets set out together that evening to take in the town. Barney was astonished when Richard told him he had always wanted to see Reno. Mergen was desperate to get out of Nevada and head east, certain all the action was located on some distant shore. Barney couldn't understand why anyone would go even a single inch out of his way just to see Reno.

Nonetheless, he found Brautigan's endless curiosity about everything fascinating. "I loved the way he was sort of opening himself up to the rest of the world," Mergen recalled.

Barney remembered how he and Richard wandered around the main drag together that night, "getting bounced from the gambling clubs because I was underage." In Mergen's recollection "the hostility of the security force was directed more toward him than toward me, because he looked different with those blond bangs and this intense, slightly insane look on his face." They ended up in the coffee shop of the Mapes Hotel, at that time one of the newest and grandest establishments in the city. (Listed on the National Register of Historic Places, the fifty-three-year-old Mapes building was demolished by implosion on January 30, 2000.) When the waitress came to take their order, Brautigan asked for "a watermelon milkshake."

"You some kind of wise guy?" she sneered, sore feet and long shifts not putting her in any mood for whimsy.

Richard smiled up at her "beatifically" and settled for coffee. Barney Mergen felt certain he had just caught a glimpse of the future.

Over the next few days, Richard and Barney spent many hours together, both poor working-class kids setting out on the uncertain path of literature. They bonded further when Brautigan discovered Barney's actual first name was "Bernard," same as the father he had never seen. Quite naturally, they talked about writers, sharing a mutual admiration for the work of Walt Whitman and William Carlos Williams. "Williams for his style. We agreed on the greatness of Whitman."

Barney told his new friend of his chance dinner with Saul Bellow the previous spring while the novelist was at Pyramid Lake waiting for a divorce to become final. For Brautigan, such conversation provided a welcome change from the sort of provincial book talk he had engaged in with friends and family back in Eugene, where Hemingway remained the only author most of them knew anything about. The two young poets discussed F. Scott Fitzgerald. By his midtwenties, Brautigan had read *The Great Gatsby* seven or eight times.

Barney and Richard also talked about Hemingway. "He liked the spareness of the prose," Mergen recalled. "That impressed him. He didn't like anybody who was too ornate or baroque." They discussed Truman Capote, hardly a household name two years before the publication of *Breakfast at Tiffany's*. An autodidact, Brautigan expressed strong opinions about Barney Mergen's scholastic view of literature. "He had a certain amount of scorn for my classroom approach," Mergen said. "That I had done most of my reading of poetry on assignment, rather than because I loved it." Richard mentioned Capote as someone who had eschewed the university, going to work as an office boy at *The New Yorker* straight out of high school. "He idolized Truman Capote for his audacity."

At some point, Brautigan opened his cardboard box and dug out his collected works. "He had these things he would show me that he called novels that were only three or four pages long," Barney Mergen remembered. Richard had packed copies of his recent minimalist notebook experiments. Among them was the manuscript for "i love You." Even after forty years, Barney clearly remembered one of the poems: "for easter / i will give You / a white kitten." In his own work, Mergen was into Richard Eberhart and just discovering Wallace Stevens. "My poetry was totally unlike his. I was trying to write like Dylan Thomas." Brautigan didn't care for Dylan Thomas.

What struck Barney Mergen most forcefully at the time was Brautigan's fully developed "sense of himself." Even in his seminal writing, Richard had articulated a distinctive individual voice. "A lot of his themes were already there. It came out in conversations with me," Mergen said. "When I read those early books, too, *Confederate General* and *Trout Fishing*, it was like hearing him again. They were very evocative. They just sort of picked up where we'd left off in conversation."

Not all of their talk was about books and writing. Richard told Barney enough about his hardscrabble existence to convince the younger man that "his life had been remarkably like mine, only rougher." Brautigan made mention of growing up in "extreme poverty," and living in the "slums," and said that he had been "abandoned by his father." A certain truth informed all his exaggerated claims. The process of personal myth-making had begun.

In an essay written after Brautigan's death, Barney Mergen recalled:

He told me about the time a bunch of men from some service organization had taken him fishing. After an evening of drinking around the campfire, one of the men suggested that they take Richard to a whorehouse, an act of charity common enough in those days, but only if he could prove himself worthy by showing them 10 inches. As Richard told the story, I understand that there were two points to it: one; that he had demonstrated the necessary length; and the other, that the episode proved man's inhumanity to man. Richard's mordant humor was deeply rooted in his past.

Mergen proved to be on the money concerning the sources of Richard's humor, but the story Brautigan told him was mostly fiction. He never drank before leaving Eugene and remained a virgin at age twenty-one. However well-endowed Brautigan might have been, the only brothels he had ever visited were in his imagination. A poem he titled "Love," from the unpublished collection "The Smallest Book of Poetry in the Whole God-Damn World," currently "cooling its alabaster heels" at New Directions even as Richard boasted of fantasy exploits in Reno, ended with the lines "What this / kid needs / is a / meal ticket / at a / whore house."

Richard Brautigan hung around Reno, spending time with Barney Mergen every afternoon and evening for four or five days, until he got word of a construction job in Fallon and hitchhiked sixty miles east into the desert to seek it out. Located on Route 50 in the Carson Sink, Fallon is the county seat of Churchill County and even before Mike Fallon (the town's namesake and first postmaster) built a crossroads store on his ranch in 1896, the place had been a stopover along the emigrant trail to California.

In his memoir, *Downstream from Trout Fishing in America*, Keith Abbott recounted a story Brautigan told him about being so broke one spring in the late fifties that he traveled to Reno for a promised laboring job. Abbott related Brautigan was informed upon arriving that the job wouldn't start for three days. "He had no money for a room and very little for food. On his first night he had a series of comic encounters with a Reno [*sic*] cop who kept finding him curled up on park benches. Threatened with jail, Richard hiked to the outskirts of town and found an old easy chair abandoned in the corner of someone's suburban yard." According to Brautigan, he waited each evening for the lights in the house to go out and then slept in the chair, wearing all the clothes he had brought as protection against the chill nighttime desert air.

This experience stayed with Brautigan for the rest of his life. Two years before his death, he wrote of his "romantic" fondness for neon lights. He liked them because "they remind me of Nevada." Reminiscing about his time there in the middle fifties, he recalled the little towns with their neon lights, "and at night there was the cool crisp smell of sagebrush [. . .] mingling with the neon." In his borrowed backyard easy chair, the flashing casino lights of Fallon glowed like the aurora borealis, a magical Technicolor omen of the future.

After shivering through three cold nights, Brautigan finally started his construction job, and after his first day he received an advance on his pay. With jack in his jeans at last, Richard rented a cheap motel room. In the euphoria of having a warm bed to sleep in, he pulled his pockets inside out, scattering change and crumpled bills all across the floor in ecstatic celebration of his newfound solvency. This began a ritual Richard Brautigan continued for the rest of his life.

The job in Fallon lasted a month or more. Solitary by nature, Brautigan found ample time to write in his off hours. From its earliest days, Fallon boasted two weekly newspapers, the *Eagle* and the *Standard*. One hot summer afternoon, Richard brought his poetry over to a single-story red brick building at 8 Center Street, climbing the pyramidal steps leading to a corner-alcove entrance. The *Fallon Standard* began as a six-column hand-set paper in 1907, the year the town was born. Claude E. Smith had been the editor since 1926, following a four-year stint at the *Eagle*.

A native of Kansas, Smith settled in Fallon with his new bride in 1922. Four decades of Smith's editorials encouraged the area's economic growth. He served two terms in the legislature and was instrumental in getting a naval air station located outside Fallon. Smith published two of Richard Brautigan's poems on Wednesday, July 25, 1956, in a column called "Gab & Gossip." Signing himself C. H. S., the editor wrote: "When it comes to poetry, or any other type of literature, we leave to others the appraisal of what's good. Of poetry we are quite shy. This page, however, carries two short pieces of blank verse by a newcomer to Fallon, Richard Brautigan. They are local. We like them both. Do you?"

"Storm Over Fallon" and "The Breeze" dealt with the weather, a topic always of interest. Even without pay, acceptance provides an author a certain validation, and Richard savored the pleasure of seeing his work in print once again. A little more than a year after publishing the two little poems, Claude Smith and his wife stopped to aid a stranded motorist on Route 50. They were killed together instantly by a speeding car.

Richard Brautigan left Nevada once the job in Fallon ended. He saved enough of a bankroll to make moving to San Francisco even a poor boy's possibility. Less than a year later, he told his new friend, the poet Ron Loewinsohn, a mythic tall tale about being run out of Fallon by the county sheriff because of some unspecified peccadillo with the lawman's daughter. "I found it a little hard to believe," Loewinsohn reflected, years later.

Richard stopped off in Reno only long enough to pick up his possessions at Barney Mergen's place on his way through to San Francisco. "When he came back, it was just one day and he was gone," Mergen remembered. That final night, alone in the casino at Harrah's Club, Richard had a chance encounter with Grace Robinson, the nurse from Eugene High School, down from Oregon for a bit of gambling.

The last person on earth Brautigan wanted to see was someone who knew him from back home. He immediately tried to hide. The nurse caught hold of his arm. "Don't you high-tone me, Richard Brautigan," she scolded. Cornered, Brautigan acted embarrassed. He didn't want to talk and made a quick getaway, heading straight for the westbound side of U.S. 40. Grace Robinson never saw Brautigan again. Nor did Barney Mergen, although he carried a clipping of Richard's poetry from the *Fallon Standard* with him for nearly half a century.

"I N 1955, FRISCO looked like Cow Town, USA," Michael McClure observed in his book *Lighting the Corners*. It was a time when the Hearst Building, a twelve-story terra-cotta-clad tower at Third and Market, reigned as one of the tallest structures in the city. The *Examiner* was published there, competing with two other dailies, the *Chronicle* and the *Call-Bulletin*, all provincial newspapers voicing the Main Street views of small-town rags everywhere across America. The San Francisco Seals ruled the local sports pages. In the midfifties, the Giants had not yet moved west from the Polo Grounds to the frigid windy confines of Candlestick Park.

After the frenzy of the war years, the fifties preferred tranquility. Ike was our president. Everyone loved Lucy. Cars sported tail-fins in an absurdist vision of the future while the urban landscape retained the elegant look of times past. Approaching Frisco on the F-train over the Bay Bridge, the skyline glimpsed through harpstring suspension cables revealed graceful white wooden Victorian buildings clustered on the hills like shoals of distant seabirds. That was the look of the place. Rents were low and red wine cheap. In 1955, it was still possible to leave your heart in San Francisco.

The four-story Montgomery Block was the very essence of that old Frisco, lost now forever. Located on Montgomery Street at the foot of Columbus, the building filled an entire block between Washington and Clay and was the tallest and most expensive structure west of the Mississippi when it went up between 1852 and 1853 at a cost of more than $3 million. The money came from Henry W. "Old Brains" Halleck, one of those larger-than-life characters flocking to Yerba Buena in the ferment of gold fever. Virtually fireproof and constructed on a flexible raft of redwood logs buried beneath the ground, "Halleck's Folly" survived many earthquakes, including the big one of 1906, when the neighboring business district lay in smoldering ruins around it.

Decades before, Sam Clemens and Bret Harte got together for serious libation and literary gossip at the Bank Exchange, the Montgomery Block's corner saloon. Robert Louis Stevenson and Ambrose Bierce came along later. The aforementioned Mark Twain sweated off the booze in the building's basement Turkish steam bath, where he played penny ante with a local fireman named Tom Sawyer, a moniker he never forgot. By the end of the nineteenth century, the Financial District had migrated south, and the neighborhood declined. When rents dropped in the 1880s, writers and artists moved into the skylit studios, making the Montgomery Block the most important literary gathering place in the West.

On one corner stood Coppa's restaurant, beloved by the bohemian crowd for its copious meals and easy credit policy. George Sterling and Mary Austin dined at Coppa's on platters of shrimp and sand dabs in 1906, before heading up Merchant Street to Portsmouth Square to fill the bronze galleon topping the R. L. Stevenson memorial with violets on the eve of the great earthquake and fire. At the opposite end of the block, occupying the southeast corner at Montgomery and Clay, the marble-floored Bank Exchange saloon featured a carved mahogany bar shipped round the Horn by schooner for its 1853 opening. The place was famed for Pisco Punch, invented in the 1870s by its bartender, Duncan Nicol (the secret recipe died with him after the place was closed by Prohibition). Sterling drank here and kept a room upstairs, mainly for love affairs. He lived at the Bohemian Club, which did not admit women.

At one time or another, down through the decades, resident writers included Twain, Joaquin Miller, Ambrose Bierce, Jack London, Gelett Burgess, Charles Warren Stoddard, and Frank Norris (as well as his brother, Charles, and sister-in-law, Kathleen). Later, in the 1930s, poet/ critic Kenneth Rexroth joined the illustrious tenant list, along with Mexican painters Frida Kahlo and Diego Rivera, when the famed muralist stayed here while working on a commission for the California Stock Exchange.

Nearly two thousand long-forgotten literary and artistic residents found refuge over the years in the rabbit warren of studios and converted offices crowding the venerable edifice. The grand old building survived for more than a century, torn down at last in 1959 to make way for a parking lot. Ten years later, the Transamerica Pyramid went up on the site. The tallest structure in town at 853 feet, it has become as potent a symbol of today's San Francisco as the "Monkey" Block was for that fabled city now vanished forever.

When Richard Brautigan arrived in the late summer of 1956, the old bohemia still flourished in North Beach. Three years earlier, a man named Larry Ferling had opened the nation's first paperback bookstore at 261 Columbus Avenue, near the intersection with Broadway, in partnership with Peter Martin, son of the assassinated Italian anarchist Carlo Tresca. The shop took its name, City Lights, from a literary journal (christened in honor of the great Chaplin film), which Martin published out of a cramped office upstairs in the building.

After Martin moved to New York a year later, Lawrence Ferlinghetti (who had started using his true name after sending for his birth certificate to apply for a California driver's license) bought his partner's half of the business. Open from ten until midnight, seven days a week, City Lights Pocket Book Shop quickly became the focal point of the artistic population in North Beach. Newly arrived, Brautigan stopped here to check the notices posted on the community bulletin board and browse through periodicals and poetry magazines.

John Clellon Holmes pinned a new label on older bohemian tendencies in "This Is the Beat Generation," his article for *The New York Times Magazine* (November 16, 1952), but at the time of Brautigan's arrival on the scene the term had yet to gain much currency with the public at large. *On the Road* would not be published until the following year, a month before the Soviet Union launched *Sputnik*. The Russian achievement provided *Chronicle* columnist Herb Caen with the source of his pejorative neologism, "beatnik."

Caen frequently and sanctimoniously objected in print to hearing his favorite city called "Frisco" when this was how anyone even remotely hip had always referred to the place. In *On the Road*, Jack Kerouac wrote of having "eyes bent on Frisco and the Coast" and made energetic prose-poetry out of the evocative name: "That was Frisco; and beautiful women standing in white doorways, waiting for their men; and Coit Tower, and the Embarcadero, and Market Street and the eleven teaming hills." Are Philadelphians offended by "Philly"?

It is impossible to pinpoint the exact beginnings of art movements. Certain events, the 1913 New York Armory show or the first Paris performance of Stravinsky's *Le Sacre du Printemps*, are considered watersheds. What came to be called the "San Francisco Renaissance" had its origins at a poetry reading given on October 7, 1955, at the Six Gallery, a tiny converted auto-repair garage at 3119 Fillmore near Union Street in Cow Hollow at the western edge of the Marina District. Richard Brautigan, often called "the last of the Beats," did not arrive in the city until almost a year later. Prophetically, many of the poets involved in the reading came to play significant roles in his life.

The little garage began its life as a performance and exhibition space in December of 1952, when poet Robert Duncan, his partner, the painter Jess (Burgess Franklin Collins), and fellow artist Harry Jacobus founded the King Ubu Gallery there. They gussied up the old garage with a pair of ten-foot gilt and glass doors salvaged from the Mark Hopkins Hotel and opened with a show of large works on paper by Jess, Jacobus, David Park, Elmer Bischoff, and several other local artists. Rent was $50 a month. Art not often being a profitable enterprise, they had to close their doors after barely a year.

On Halloween 1954 the place opened again, renamed the Six Gallery to celebrate its new proprietors, poet Jack Spicer and five visual artists: Wally Hedrick, Hayward King, Deborah Remington, John Allen Ryan, and David Simpson, all students in Spicer's "unorthodox" English class at the California School of Fine Arts. In January 1955, the Six staged a reading of Duncan's new play, *Faust Foutu* ("Faust Fucked"), starring filmmaker Larry Jordan as Faust; Jess, in drag, as Faust's mother; stern Jack Spicer atypically cast as a gentle Muse; "Mike" McClure as a boy; and the author, who stripped buck naked by the end of his performance, as The Poet.

Spicer, born in Los Angeles in 1925, met both Duncan, seven years his senior, and fellow poet Robin Blaser in Berkeley in the mid-1940s. Drawn together by mutual interests in literature, magic, and homoeroticism, the three formed the nucleus of a group they called the "Berkeley Renaissance." In 1956, Duncan became the assistant director of the San Francisco Poetry Center, founded two years before by fellow S.F. State literature professor Ruth Witt-Diamant, whose flamboyant public gestures often caused the poet to stuff hankies into his mouth to gag back his laughter.

Michael McClure moved to San Francisco in 1954, seeking to study art with Clyfford Still and Mark Rothko. The artist Bruce Conner, McClure's boyhood friend in Wichita, Kansas, introduced to him abstract expressionism, and McClure hoped learning more about such gestural styles would inspire his poetry. He was also interested in following Joanna Kinnison, a young woman he'd met the year before at the University of Arizona. She'd sought greener pastures in San Francisco after a brief first marriage disintegrated. When McClure arrived in the city and found that Rothko and Still no longer taught at the School of Fine Arts, he promptly enrolled in Duncan's poetry workshop at San Francisco State.

Through Duncan, Michael McClure was introduced to Kenneth Rexroth, the grand pooh-bah of the Frisco literary scene. Indiana-born (1905) and an anarchist at heart, Rexroth gravitated to the West Coast in the twenties. He was a generation older than the poets, artists, writers, and filmmakers who flocked to the Friday night soirees in his book-lined second-floor apartment at 250 Scott Street, above Jack's Record Cellar on the outskirts of the black Fillmore District. Rexroth's energy and lively intelligence had nurtured radical thinking in San Francisco for better than two decades. Rexroth wrote a column for the *Examiner* and recorded a weekly radio broadcast for KPFA, tapping into his seemingly encyclopedic font of esoteric knowledge to pontificate on any subject under the sun. A man who cut his own hair and did all the repair work on the beater Willys Knight he drove, Kenneth Rexroth held firm opinions on just about everything.

At one of Rexroth's evenings, McClure encountered the native San Francisco poet Philip Lamantia, proclaimed by surrealist André Breton as "a voice that rises once in a hundred years" upon the young man's precocious first publication at age fifteen. A shared interest in mysticism drew them together, and Lamantia was soon a frequent visitor to the flat Michael shared with his new wife, Joanna. The Frisco art community at that time had a remarkable fluidity. Painters, poets, actors, dancers, all knew one another and supported each other's work in an intellectual, creative, and often matrimonial cross-pollination. The performance of *Faust Fouto* had been a success, and in early September of 1955, Wally Hedrick said to Michael McClure, "That was real nice, that thing we had with Robert Duncan. You wanna have a poetry reading?"

McClure agreed to take charge of the event at the Six Gallery. It was a tall order, as Joanna was pregnant and Michael very busy with a job at the San Francisco Museum of Art. Later in the month, McClure ran into Allen Ginsberg on the street and explained that he was in "a kind of crunch" and didn't have time to organize the reading. "Can I do it?" Ginsberg asked.

"Absolutely," McClure replied, greatly relieved.

In June of 1954, Ginsberg had returned to California from six months of Mexican jungle adventures. He stayed first in San Jose with his sometimes lover Neal Cassady, Kerouac's model for Dean Moriarty in *On the Road*. The sociopathic Denver hipster car-thief and sexual con-man seemed oddly domesticated, living in a nine-room house with a blond wife and three little children. His Mrs., Carolyn, caught him in bed with Ginsberg and kicked the poet out, loaning Allen twenty bucks and driving him up to Berkeley.

In early August, Ginsberg trimmed his hair and shaved off his vagabond's beard. Donning a tweed jacket and preppie tie, he took a square's day job doing market research for Towne-Oller on Montgomery Street. He also fell in love with a woman, an ex-roadhouse singer named Sheila Williams Boucher, and moved into her Nob Hill apartment. Whenever Neal Cassady's job as a brakeman on the Southern Pacific took him to Frisco, he'd get together for wild sex with Allen and, on occasion, a ménage involving Sheila. At the same time, Ginsberg's mentor, William S. Burroughs, had departed his residence in a male brothel in Tangier, sailing for the States from Gibraltar in September, hoping to reunite with his young lover in San Francisco.

A descendant of adding machine money, Burroughs had graduated from Harvard in 1936 and received a small monthly stipend from his parents. Older and better-read than both Kerouac and Ginsberg when they all met for the first time in New York's Greenwich Village around Christmas of 1943, Burroughs engaged in a life of petty crime and drug addiction. One drunken evening in the spring of 1952, a tragic miscalculation in Mexico City jump-started his writing career. Burroughs shot his common-law wife in the forehead while playing William Tell with a six-ounce water glass and a .380 Star automatic. The Mexican authorities charged him with *imprudencia criminal* for the shooting of Joan Vollmer Adams Burroughs, classifying him as a "pernicious foreigner." The shooter soon headed south into the Amazon jungles in search of the elusive hallucinogen *yage*. "I am forced to the appalling conclusion that I would never have become a writer but for Joan's death," Burroughs later observed.

A little drunk after a fight with Sheila one lonely night in December 1954, Ginsberg wandered into Foster's Cafeteria in the Hotel Wentley at the northeast corner of Polk and Sutter. He'd been hanging out here with Michael and Joanna McClure ever since meeting them in October at a crowded inaugural reception for the San Francisco Poetry Center following W. H. Auden's dedicatory lecture. Not finding the McClures, Ginsberg began a lengthy conversation with Robert LaVigne, looking bearded and handsome at a table crowded with "young artist types."

They drifted in the early hours over to the painter's nearby ground-floor Victorian flat on Gough Street. A dumbstruck Allen Ginsberg confronted LaVigne's full-frontal nude portrait of a tousle-haired youth. He found his "pilgrim soul" at last. The subject, twenty-one-year-old Peter Orlovsky, shyly stepped out of his room down the hall. Five days later, Ginsberg took up residence on Gough Street.

Ginsberg's relationship with Orlovsky, which was to span more than four decades, began in its first weeks as a romantic tug-of-war with LaVigne. By February of '55, Peter had moved into an apartment with Allen on the corner of Montgomery and Broadway in North Beach. They pledged eternal marriage vows together one chrome-and-Formica 3:00 AM at Foster's: "a kind of celestial cold fire that crept over us and blazed up and illuminated the entire cafeteria and made it an eternal place." An Oklahoma sunset had illuminated Ginsberg and Neal Cassady seven years earlier when they knelt together in the dust alongside a two-lane crossroad and exchanged similar eternal vows.

In May, Ginsberg was living on unemployment, replaced at the ad agency by a computer, and able to concentrate all his energy on poetry for the first time in months. Heeding some criticism from Rexroth and with Peter off on the East Coast in August, Allen loosened up, not to write a poem, "but just write what I wanted to without fear." He typed out the lines:

"I saw the best minds of my generation
            generation destroyed by madness
                  starving, mystical, naked,
      who dragged themselves thru the angry streets
            at dawn looking for a negro fix [. . .]"

The next day, he shipped a copy of the first six pages of "Howl" to Jack Kerouac in Mexico City. In this draft, Allen titled the poem "Howl (for Carl Solomon)." Seeking to complete an MA in English, Ginsberg had enrolled in the graduate program at the University of California, moving across the Bay at the start of the semester to a one-room "rose-covered cottage" in Berkeley. Peter Orlovsky and his teenage brother, Lafcadio, inherited the apartment at 1010 Montgomery.

A peyote trip celebrating Orlovsky's return to Frisco provided the hallucinatory image of Moloch perched atop the St. Francis Hotel and gave Ginsberg the opening stanzas for "Howl" Part II. By the time he ran into McClure in late September, Ginsberg had already read the poem twice in public. The first time was to a small gathering at The Place, a hip bohemian bar on Grant Avenue, opened two years before by two alumni of Black Mountain College, the legendary avant-garde school in North Carolina.

The second reading (September 16, 1955), part of the Arts Festival held at the Nourse Auditorium on Franklin and Hayes Streets, attracted a much larger audience. The other poets on the bill that night were Jack Nugent, Jack Gilbert, and Guy Wernham, a skinny fifty-year-old Englishman whose mother had once been the mistress of Sir Arthur Sullivan. Jack Goodwin, a San

Francisco composer whose opera *The Pizza Pusher* was to be performed at the festival on the next evening, remembered the event: "The balloon really went up when the 'Howl' thing happened."

Zekial Marko, a flamboyant actor (later, a Hollywood screenwriter) from Salinas, stage-managed Goodwin's opera. According to Goodwin, Marko "horned in and coached the poets while they rehearsed." It was a hot night, and everyone sweated backstage waiting for the curtain to go up. "In Ginsberg we had a genuine Old Testament prophet straight out of DeMille, and Marko made suggestions about tone, volume, tempo, and gesture. The result was electrifying. Ginsberg shouted, wept, chanted, and mopped his brow with a telling little Marko gesture across his forehead on the word 'lobotomy.' The message was drearily familiar, but the presentation was hair-raising." Rumor had it that Marko switched off the microphone when Ginsberg stepped up to read, forcing him to shout out his lines dramatically.

McClure's offer to let him take charge of the Six Gallery reading presented Allen Ginsberg with a perfect showcase for "Howl." He would be the headliner this time and surround himself with poets he admired. Originally guided to Kenneth Rexroth (then a reader for New Directions) through a letter from William Carlos Williams (who had written an introduction to Allen's unpublished poetry collection *Empty Mirror*), Ginsberg sought the older poet's advice in planning the Six Gallery reading. Knowing Ginsberg lived over in Berkeley, Rexroth suggested Gary Snyder, another young poet, a twenty-five-year-old graduate student in Japanese and Chinese, raised among lumberjacks, who had labored on a forest service trail crew and was a regular blue-collar guy, a working-stiff Buddhist, much as Rexroth viewed himself.

Ginsberg found Snyder on Hillegass Avenue, repairing his bicycle in a "Zen garden" backyard. A small, wiry man, browned and hard from the mountains, with slanted cat-green eyes (Robert Creeley called them "wise old-young eyes"), Snyder lived a scholar's life of monastic simplicity in a twelve-by-twelve-foot cottage with straw tatami mats on the floor. Orange crates served as bookcases and writing tables, the only furnishings aside from scattered paisley cushions. Ice axes and coiled climbing ropes hung on the walls; a rucksack neatly packed with nested cookware stood in one corner. Bohemians had flirted with Buddhism since the days of Madame Blavatsky ("In the summer, I'm a nudist, / In the winter, I'm a Buddhist," rhymed Maxwell Bodenheim decades before), but Gary Snyder practiced what he preached, meditating at the Berkeley Young Buddhist Association and publishing his work in their magazine, *Berkeley Bussei*.

The two poets hit it off immediately. William Carlos Williams provided a common meeting ground. Three years before, Ginsberg sent his poetry to the Bard of Paterson, finding at last a sage teacher whose encouragement and advice shaped his voice. In November of 1950, Gary Snyder, then an undergraduate at Reed College in Oregon, had also been profoundly impressed by Dr. Williams during a weeklong campus visit. At the time, Snyder shared a basement flat in a Portland rooming house with two other young poets, Lew Welch and Philip Whalen. They dubbed themselves the Adelaide Crapsey–Oswald Spengler Mutual Admiration Poetasters Society after a reading by Williams rocked them with the power of a hard-blowing jam session.

Snyder agreed to be part of the upcoming "charming event" at the Six Gallery, suggesting that Phil Whalen, due to arrive in Berkeley the next day from a fire-watching job on Sourdough Mountain in the High Cascades of Washington, would happily participate. Ginsberg said Jack Kerouac, his "great poet" friend from Columbia University, was heading into town from south of the border any day now. In fact, Jack had already arrived, jumping freights and hitchhiking, and was high on bennies in Allen's Milvia Street "Shakespearean" cottage, playing Bach's *St. Matthew Passion* full-blast on the Webcore three-speed.

Malcolm Cowley anointed Jack Kerouac "the greatest unpublished writer in America." At thirty-three, Kerouac had just finished *Mexico City Blues*, a long jazz-inspired poem with 242 stanzas, and in the five years since *The Town and the City* (his first novel) failed to earn out its advance, added *On the Road* and ten other books in manuscript to the unfinished epic Wolfeian vision he called *The Duluoz Legend*. He disagreed with Ginsberg on "Howl," urging him not to revise a word, "spontaneity or nothing." He admired the long wailing saxophonelike choruses, so like his own improvisational experiments. Kerouac declined to be part of the proceedings at the Six Gallery, citing shyness, but enthusiastically supported the project.

Michael McClure and Philip Lamantia became the last of the six poets invited to read. Carl Solomon introduced Ginsberg to Lamantia in 1948 at the San Remo bar, a hipster hangout on the northwest corner of McDougal and Bleecker in Manhattan's Greenwich Village. When Gary Snyder suggested they include Rexroth as master of ceremonies, Allen passed the word along, delighting the elder statesman of the Frisco scene, who promptly bought a secondhand pinstripe cutaway for the occasion. Ginsberg mimeographed over a hundred postcard copies of a "goofy" invitation ("6 Poets at the 6 Gallery [. . .] wine, music, dancing girls, serious poetry, free satori"). He mailed out some, posting the others around North Beach in the usual locations: City Lights, Miss Smith's Tea Room, The Place, Vesuvio, the Co-Existence Bagel Shop.

On the afternoon of Friday, October 7, Kerouac and Ginsberg took a bus across the Bay. By coincidence, they bumped into Phil Whalen and Gary Snyder (who also came over from Berkeley together) on the corner of First and Mission outside the Key System Terminal. The group joined Philip Lamantia for dinner at the New Pisa restaurant on Grant Avenue across the Broadway intersection from City Lights. Afterward, they all found separate transportation to the Six.

Ferlinghetti owned a tiny "beat-up" old Austin. He and his wife, Kirby, already had a passenger, and there was only room enough to give Kerouac and Ginsberg a lift. Allen and Jack crammed into the backseat with Gregory Corso ("Wild mad eastside funny Gregory"), their back-alley poet buddy from New York, a gutter sparrow born across the street from the San Remo and drawn to literature at sixteen while serving a three-year bit for armed robbery upstate in Dannemora. At twenty-five, Corso was younger than the other poets packed into the little car.

When they arrived at the Six shortly before eight, the five-hundred-square-foot former garage was already crowded. From varying reports, between a hundred and a hundred and fifty *cognocenti* eventually showed up, a first-time gathering of all the diverse Frisco art and poetry circles. College professors, longshoremen, bohemian poets, journalists, the social set, all crammed together on folding chairs crowding the dirt floor of the two adjoining rooms. Mink coats mingled with blue denim, suits-and-ties rubbed elbows with turtleneck sweaters.

Neal Cassady leaned against the wall in his blue serge brakeman's uniform, bobbing and nodding maniacally to those all around, although most were strangers. Shy Peter Orlovsky stood at his side. Jazz trombonist Charles Richards came in with his wife. Ruth Witt-Diamant, grand doyenne of the Poetry Center, sat primly among the throng. Latecomers lined the back wall or perched on the low platform stage. A festive street fair gaiety prevailed.

Some were present only in spirit. Poet and pianist Weldon Kees was reported to have been in attendance, although he had disappeared on June 20, his empty car discovered on the Golden

Gate Bridge. Most conspicuous in their absence were Jack Spicer (looking for a day job on the East Coast) and Robert Duncan (off in Europe with Jess), the spiritual progenitors of the event.

Jack Kerouac mythologized the proceedings in *The Dharma Bums*, describing the audience as "rather stiff" before he "got things jumping" by taking up a collection of dimes and quarters and rushing out to buy three gallons of cheap California burgundy. The jugs circulated from hand to mouth. Kerouac sprawled on the floor close to the stage. Fred Martin's sculpture (fragments of orange crate draped in plaster-of-paris-soaked muslin) stood behind the podium, "like pieces of surrealistic furniture," according to Michael McClure. Of the six poets gathered on the platform in a semicircle of folding chairs only Lamantia and Ginsberg had read in public before.

Kerouac called Rexroth "Reinhold Cacoethes" ("bow-tied wild-haired old anarchist fud . . .") in *The Dharma Bums*. He dismissed Rexroth's thrift shop tails as his "shabby old coat," yet the emcee's wacky costume perfectly captured the carnival spirit of the evening. In "his snide funny voice," Rexroth introduced Philip Lamantia ("Delicate Francis DaPavia"), the first poet of the night. Lamantia read a group of prose poems by John Hoffman (a friend of his, as well as Ginsberg's and Carl Solomon's), who had died recently of a heroin overdose in Mexico City.

Michael McClure was next in line. (Kerouac called him "Ike O'Shay.") At twenty-three, the youngest of the six, McClure wore a suit for the occasion and read a letter from Jack Spicer, who had departed Frisco in July after being fired from the CSFA. Spicer moved to Boston, where his friend Robin Blaser got him "a low-level job" in the rare book room of the public library. Jack longed to return to the Bay Area. Spicer's letter "got applause from his friends and fans," McClure recalled thirty-seven years later. "It was a practical matter. 'Could anyone help Jack?'"

Michael McClure went on to his own ecologically concerned poetry, reading "Point Lobos: Animism" and "For the Death of 100 Whales." He met both Philip Whalen and Gary Snyder for the first time on the stage at the Six, little realizing how soon they all would be lumped together as reluctant standard-bearers for the "Beat Generation." Spicer and Duncan, founders of the Six (King Ubu) Gallery, would shortly be replaced as the dominant icons in the local cultural pantheon by these unknown young upstarts.

The third reader was Philip Whalen ("booboo big old goodhearted Warren Coughlin a hundred and eighty pounds of poet meat"), whose humorous poem "Plus ca Change" concerned "confronting metamorphic change." Whalen's reading ended around ten thirty, and a short intermission was called. Half an hour later, wearing jeans and a navy sweater, Allen Ginsberg ("hornrimmed intellectual hepcats with wild black hair like Alvah Goldbook") made his way through the crowd to the stage, nodding amiably to his many friends. Fortified by cheap red wine, the poet began reading what would become his best-known work, its title now truncated to "Howl." The burgundy overcame his nervousness, adding timbre to "a small intense voice." Ginsberg spread his arms wide, swaying from side to side at the lectern as he intoned each long line "like a Jewish cantor."

Jack Kerouac beat out time on his wine jug, singing along "(like a jam session)" and cheering his friend with shouts of "Go! Go! Go!" at the end of every line. The novelist was almost completely unknown at the time. Jack Goodwin referred to him as "This Carrowac person" in a letter detailing the event to John Allen Ryan, one of the founders of the Six Gallery, who was away in Mexico. Goodwin described Kerouac "singing snatches of scat in between the lines; he kept a kind of chanted, revival-meeting rhythm going." Soon, most of the audience joined in, enthusiastically shouting, stomping their feet, and snapping their fingers in time with the poem's insistent beat. As

Goodwin reported in his letter, "the people gasped and laughed and swayed, they were psychologically had, it was an orgiastic occasion."

Not everyone was equally enthusiastic. Ruth Witt-Diamant, offended by the wine-drinking and general rowdiness, gestured at Rexroth to tone things down. He ignored her, removing his eyeglasses, wiping away tears of joy. According to other witnesses, he was "visibly annoyed" by the proceedings. Kerouac reported the tears. What has incorrectly come down in literary history as Ginsberg's first public reading of "Howl" lasted twelve minutes. When it ended, the room exploded into a wild roaring ovation. "It was like bringing two ends of an electric wire together," Philip Lamantia remembered. For Michael McClure, "a line had been drawn, and either we had to stand at that line or else we had to step back from it."

Kerouac jumped up to congratulate his friend. "Ginsberg," he shouted, "this poem will make you famous in San Francisco."

Kenneth Rexroth anticipated wider horizons. "This poem will make you famous from bridge to bridge," he said, moist eyes glistening.

Gary Snyder wisely waited for the commotion to die down before approaching the lectern. ("Japhy Ryder [. . .] in rough workingman's clothes he'd bought secondhand in Goodwill stores") The final poet on the evening's program, Snyder read "A Berry Feast" in rich sonorous tones and recaptured the attention of the excited audience. Kerouac found the sound of Snyder's voice "somehow brave, like the voices of oldtime American heros and orators." This last poem, prophetic in its embrace of traditional Native American ways and the natural world, provided a fitting conclusion to the electric evening.

After the reading, the poets, along with their friends and lovers, piled into a rattletrap fleet of secondhand junkers and drove to Sam Wo's on Washington Street, Gary Snyder's favorite restaurant in Chinatown. Ferlinghetti and his wife, not feeling "part of the scene," went home instead. Open until 3:00 AM, the narrow, three-story noodle parlor was better known for the glib rudeness of its impatient waiters than for the quality of the cheap greasy food it served. Snyder taught Kerouac how to eat with chopsticks while the group noisily reviewed the highlights of their triumph at the Six Gallery. No one could quite articulate what it all meant. In retrospect, Gary Snyder judged the evening as "a curious kind of turning point in American poetry." Typically, Jack Kerouac, always the myth-maker, described a more heroic vision. For him, the reading marked "the night of the birth of the San Francisco Poetry Renaissance."

WHEN RICHARD BRAUTIGAN arrived in Frisco in August of 1956, he headed straight for North Beach and made City Lights one of his first stops. The bookstore served as the hub of the bohemian community, with thumbtacked notices on the bulletin board advertising rides, cheap rooms and apartments, lost pets, used vehicles, astrological charts, and sundry other arcane offerings. For a time, Dick Brautigan used "General Delivery" as a mailing address but soon got a room on upper Grant Avenue. His earliest recorded San Francisco domicile was apartment number 38 at 1648 Grant. A letter from D. Vincent Smith written in July arrived about this time from Japan. Smith had decided to use all the Brautigan poems he had on hand for *Tiger in a Telephone Booth* and planned to print copies of the little book soon. Smith promised Dick he'd keep him informed.

On August 27, again through the auspices of D. Vincent Smith, Brautigan mailed a copy of "The God of the Martians," the latest of his minimalist notebook novels, to Harry Hooton in Sydney, Australia. An anarchist poet born in Yorkshire, England, and known as "that flaming archpriest of Neo-Bomboism," Hooton once served eighteen months in Maitland Jail for "unarmed robbery." He had been a fixture in the Sydney bohemian scene since 1942 and published a small literary periodical there called *21st Century, The Magazine of a Creative Civilization*. The first and only issue to date appeared the previous September. Dick used general delivery for his return address but never heard back from Down Under. Hooton died five years later. Brautigan's manuscript did not resurface until after his own death.

By mid-October 1956, when he typed a short postcard note to Edna Webster in Eugene, Brautigan felt sufficiently settled to ask that she send his manuscripts to Grant Ave. "I really need them," he wrote, typing his name ("dick") in lowercase at the bottom. Dick eventually received a return package from Edna. She sent him "The Shortest Book of Poetry in the Whole God-Damn World," recently rejected by New Directions, along with the same brief postcard he had just written to her. Edna did not return the manuscript of "Why Unknown Poets Stay Unknown" (which had come back from Random House early in September with a polite rejection letter signed by editor Albert Erskine) or any of the several notebook "novels." These went into a safe deposit box in Eugene and remained out of sight for the next thirty-five years.

Bill Brown was one of the first Frisco writers Dick Brautigan met, and they remained friends for the rest of his life. Brown, a rugged, powerfully built man with the no-nonsense features of Sergeant Rock, drove a cab in the city at the time and was largely unpublished (*Coyote's Journal* and his novel, *The Way to the Uncle Sam Hotel*, still years in the future). "He'd just blown into town," Bill said, recalling his first meeting with greenhorn Dick. "He heard I knew Bill Williams and selling pot.

"'How's Bill?'

"I said, 'I don't want to talk about Bill.' I was hungover on Lasker's couch. I said, 'I want to talk about Flossie.' So, we went on and on. He was asking questions like 'Where is this?' and 'Where is that, downtown, like on the beach?' He didn't know zip—zip about anything."

Zip came fast in the narrow streets of North Beach. A new world as far removed from Oregon as a rocket ship journey to the moon waited outside the cramped confines of apartment number 38. Within sauntering distance of his rented room, a three-block stretch along Grant Avenue offered almost everything an impoverished young poet might require. The Co-Existence Bagel Shop (1398 Grant), with a cartoonish wall mural by Aaron Miller, served up bargain breakfasts. Cheap dinners and dago red attracted hungry hipsters to the Old Spaghetti Factory (just off Grant at 478 Green Street), where numbers of antique wooden chairs dangled from the rafters high overhead. Miss Smith's Tea Room (1353 Grant) offered booze and poetry readings. For an afternoon java hit, the newly opened Café Trieste (corner of Grant and Vallejo) provided sanctuary and the daily newspapers. Mainly, there was The Place, at 1546 Grant. The public forum this nondescript joint provided prompted Brautigan to send for his manuscripts.

Kerouac called The Place "the favorite bar of the hepcats around the Beach." To Mike McClure it was "the Deux Magots of Frisco." Since opening in 1953, when Leo Krikorian, "a short, husky, ferocious-looking man," bought the bar for $3,000, The Place had attracted a steady clientele of poets, working men, artists, and such local oddballs as Hube the Cube, Red Fred ("a port wine freak" who sat on the counter and played the piano), Boring Boris, Badtalking Charlie (the "crazy black seaman"), and one-armed Paddy O'Sullivan (a faux-cavalier bedecked in Vandyke beard, plumed hat, and a cape).

The Place had a comfortable no-nonsense atmosphere. Fresh sawdust covered the floor every day; a battered upright piano obscured the front window; an antique back bar sported mirrors and columns. Licensed to sell beer and wine, Leo Krikorian stashed Coke bottles full of whiskey out of sight under the sink for the old-time neighborhood Italians who occasionally wandered in looking for a real drink. The bar opened every morning at nine.

In 1954, Knute Stiles, a fellow painter who knew Krikorian from Black Mountain College, became his partner "for about a year," from one April Fool's Day to the next. Leo took the day shift and Knute ran The Place at night. "We were a freak joint," Stiles recollected, "poets of all sizes and ages, some painters, some photographers, some merchant seamen, some radicals, some conservatives."

It didn't take many customers to make a crowd in the bar's four hundred square feet. According to Knute Styles, "We arranged it in such a way that there wouldn't be any single-tabled people, that people would be all kind of together. The smallness of The Place ensured the continuity of the dialogue—it was very hard for anybody to get lost." The barroom had a staircase in the rear leading to a tiny balcony with tables for twelve or fifteen. It overlooked the entire establishment. The first staged event "was Jack Spicer's cacophony band from his class at the Art Institute. They were a very noisy lot—almost drove the customers out really, making noises on the balcony."

Two painters running a bar resulted in a gallery by default. The Place began showing the best contemporary art in Frisco. In 1953, after the close of King Ubu, and prior to its reincarnation as the Six, the city had no galleries adventurous enough to exhibit abstract art. Leo Krikorian's bar on Grant Avenue filled the gap. Among those featured in one-man shows at The Place were Robert LaVigne, Deborah Remington, Joel Barletta, and photographer Bill Eichele.

Jay DeFeo had her first show at The Place after returning from a stay in Paris and Florence with stacks of paintings on paper. DeFeo remembered the barroom walls "sort of plastered with these little drawings," and Knute Stiles recalled that there was so much of her work, "we had to put some of it on the ceiling." The boisterous iconic paintings of DeFeo's husband, Wally Hedrick, hung prominently in the first two annual Dada shows held at The Place. As a couple, DeFeo and Hedrick personified the Frisco art scene, at the time in every way a family affair.

"The bars in the 'Beach' were people's living rooms," said John Allen Ryan, who started tending bar for Leo Krikorian in 1956, shortly before Dick Brautigan arrived on Grant Avenue. Ryan described the establishment's evolution into a hotbed of hipness: "The Place was like a cultural center, poetry in fourteen languages in the toilet, pasted, written, painted on the wall. We had art shows, Blabbermouth Night, poetry readings, jazz. There was always something going on."

Until 1967 there were no true bars in California in the sense of the taverns and saloons elsewhere, two-fisted hard-drinking watering holes where you belly up and toss back your shot. In order to legally pour hard liquor, a California bar in that era had to have a kitchen and also serve food. It had to be a restaurant. All the other joints, places where writers and artists could afford to hang out, served only beer and wine.

Dick Brautigan hadn't started drinking when he first began hanging out at The Place. California law in those days didn't prohibit minors from entering a bar, provided they consumed no alcohol. Tall, awkward, and blond as a newborn child, Brautigan looked younger and far more innocent than most men of twenty-one. He came in shyly and took a table by himself, his perpetual notebook under his arm. Because he didn't ask to be served, Leo Krikorian assumed "he was no more than sixteen."

Wherever Brautigan took his first drink, at 12 Alder Place or Vesuvio or Miss Smith's Tea Room or at Mike's Pool Hall or perhaps slugging it down from a brown-paper-bagged pint on a quiet corner of Telegraph Hill, it wasn't long before the frugal young poet, meticulously noting every minute expense in his notebooks, began devoting ample bookkeeping space to The Place, where a beer or a glass of port cost a dime.

A couple years later, when Brautigan was a drinking man and lived a bus ride away from the Beach up on Potrero Hill, he jotted the following list:

Bus .15
lunch .46
Place .10
Place .10
Place .10
Place .10
Carfare .15
Snack .10
———
1.10

THIS WAS AN exorbitant tally by Richard's pinch-penny standards when his total expenses for all the rest of April came to only $6.55. If Brautigan sipped coffee every day during his first impoverished summer on the Beach in 1956, he drank it at Leo Krikorian's bar. John Allen Ryan remembered the young poet: "He'd sit and write in The Place, in all the bars, he wrote everywhere and carried his notebooks with him."

Richard joined an informal cadre of notebook-toting unknown poets hanging out and gossiping at The Place. There was considerable talk about Gary Snyder, who had left for Kyoto, Japan, in May, his studies funded by a grant from the First Zen Institute of America. Hipsters also chattered about Allen Ginsberg, back in town in September for the City Lights publication of *Howl and Other Poems*. The *New York Times Book Review* had published an article on Ginsberg and the San Francisco scene by poet Richard Eberhart on September 2. Rogue wanderer Robert Creeley with his pirate's eye patch (he lost the use of his left eye before he was five), really set Frisco poet-tongues wagging.

Creeley breezed in from Black Mountain back in March and blazed through the next three months, befriending Ginsberg and Kerouac, typing the stencils for an informal first mimeograph printing of "Howl," brawling and getting arrested, editing the final issue of the *Black Mountain Review*, and running off with Kenneth Rexroth's wife, Marthe Larsen. The affair started with a party bidding Gary Snyder bon voyage on his Japanese freighter.

The next night, Jack Kerouac and Bob Creeley, both drunk, got the bum's rush from The Cellar, a club featuring poetry and jazz. Creeley's lip was bleeding from the bouncer's haymaker. Kerouac invited him to stay at "Marin-an," Snyder's rustic cabin over in Mill Valley. Not much more than a shack, the little place had windows without any glass. Creeley accepted, bringing along Mrs. Rexroth to a eucalyptus-scented Marin County love nest. The cuckolded husband eventually took his revenge in print. A prominent literary critic, Rexroth never missed an opportunity to attack both men with scathing reviews.

Brautigan certainly heard all this dirt and more at The Place. He very quickly fell in with the local scene, roaming North Beach bars and shyly finding his way into boisterous poetry-reading parties. Ron Loewinsohn, another notebook-toting young hopeful, remembered spotting Richard with a group of people he knew outside The Place one evening in the fall of 1956. "A guy you could not miss—very blond—haircut like a pudding bowl." He was with a group of much younger kids, all about sixteen or seventeen years old, wearing a black imitation-leather jacket zipped all the way up. "I don't believe I ever saw him in those days with his jacket unzipped," Loewinsohn recalled. "It was like his protection against the world."

Just back from a hitchhiking trip to the Southwest, Ron wasn't introduced to Richard and didn't know his name or anything about him at the time. Grant Avenue had long been Loewinsohn's "stomping ground." A Frisco kid who grew up in the Mission, he had spent his earliest childhood interned in Manila during the Japanese occupation of the Philippines. Brautigan, long fascinated by World War II, often told Ron that he should write a story beginning with the words "The first time I saw a Japanese soldier." Drawn to North Beach as a young teenager, Loewinsohn had met Kerouac and Ginsberg in The Place. He was also introduced to Robert Duncan but "didn't know him real well," and Philip Whalen, who "became a very good friend." Barely eighteen, Ron had been part of the poetry scene long before Richard made his first reticent appearance.

Soon after this, Loewinsohn saw the tall blond stranger at a party at poet Robert Stock's house way out on Twenty-fourth Street. Stock was also a jazz clarinet player who worked as a bartender at the Co-Existence Bagel Shop. As a poet, he remained a traditional formalist at a time when adherence to the old forms were breaking down. Influenced by the work of the sixteenth-century Portuguese poet Luis de Camões, Robert Stock held workshops that were much in demand and difficult to get into. In order to be accepted, the applicant first had to write a perfect villanelle. ("Do Not Go Gentle into That Good Night" by Dylan Thomas remains the best-known modern version of the form in English.)

Stock's short story "Disappearing Act" chronicled the mysterious disappearance of Weldon Kees. His poetry had been included in the first (and only) issue of *Ark* in the spring of 1947. This local literary magazine, hand-set on a printing press by volunteer labor, took a militantly antiwar posture (what contributor Kenneth Rexroth defined as "philosophical anarchism") in the face of the rampant McCarthyism gripping America. Reborn in March 1956 as *Ark II*–Moby I, when Michael McClure joined James Harmon as coeditor, it again lasted for just a single issue.

Not yet a staple at North Beach bars and coffeehouses, Frisco poetry readings remained informal affairs in 1956. Casual readings often took place at parties like the one at Robert Stock's place where Allen Ginsberg, Peter Orlovsky, and Gregory Corso were all in attendance. At some point during the evening, Brautigan read a few of his poems in the living room. Ginsberg and company were not impressed. "They didn't take him seriously," a partygoer observed. Behind his back, Allen snidely referred to Richard as "Frood." Before realizing he had unwittingly used "their pejorative nickname," Ron Loewinsohn addressed Brautigan as "Frood" that night. Later, he heard Ginsberg call Richard a "neurotic creep."

Brautigan's eccentric behavior doubtless reinforced this disdain. Shy and taciturn, Richard made no effort to hide his bumpkin background, turning his origins into an asset, the cornerstone of his public persona. "I'm just a country boy, come to town on my apple-picking money," he told everyone. It became a favorite recurring joke. "A lot of people ridiculed him," John Allen Ryan recollected, "and that made him even shier. Actually, he had invented a new method of writing. His poetry was unusual; it was mostly prose poetry, which people weren't doing at that time. He invented a new approach that was really his."

One afternoon about three weeks after first encountering Richard Brautigan, Ron Loewinsohn (who knew his real name by now) ran into the blond poet again on Grant Avenue. Dick walked up to Ron without saying a word, his Naugahyde jacket zippered all the way up. Ron said, "Hello." Dick just nodded and handed him an open notebook. On the offered page, he'd written a short poem in his cramped hand:

A Correction

Cats walk on little cat feet
and fogs walk on little fog feet,

Carl.

Loewinsohn laughed. "That's pretty funny," he said, handing back the notebook. Richard folded it up and stuffed it in his pocket, sauntering away down Grant without a word, hip and detached. The moment cemented their friendship, and they started hanging out together. Looking back across the years, Ron Loewinsohn viewed Brautigan from a different perspective, as "a very painfully shy young man who tried everything in the world to cover up his shyness with a veneer of cool reserve."

Another chance meeting occurred late that summer on the streets of North Beach. Philip Whalen and Allen Ginsberg came ambling along, deep in conversation, when they encountered the tall blond stranger headed in the opposite direction. The two older poets stopped, and Ginsberg introduced Whalen to Richard Brautigan without a trace of the condescension displayed at Robert Stock's party. It was a brief encounter. "[Richard] was busy going someplace and went on by," Whalen remembered. He and Ginsberg continued in the opposite direction. Their paths would all cross again in the future.

Having cut his poetry-reading teeth at Stock's party, Dick Brautigan felt ready to climb the stairs to the balcony at The Place. "Blabbermouth Night," an open forum first set in motion by a bartender named Jack Landon, took place every Monday and always drew a raucous crowd. Customers wishing to sound off on any subject striking their fancy used a wooden "soapbox" nailed to the balcony floor as a podium. The barfly audience below roared in either approval or derision.

Poetry readings were more sedate, often scheduled on Sunday afternoons, when the clientele tended to be mostly sober. Before his first appearance on the balcony soapbox at The Place, Brautigan enlisted the talents of Zekial Marko, who coached him on the fine points of presentation, delivery, and the dramatic use of personal mannerisms. Leo Krikorian remembered Richard reading "The Chinese Checker Players," the poem he wrote at the Bartons' after his release from the mental hospital.

Allen Ginsberg left San Francisco for wider horizons in October 1956. Jack Spicer returned to Frisco from Boston a month later, making the same discovery as Robert Duncan and Jess had when they came back to the city from Majorca, by way of Black Mountain, earlier in the year. In their absence, Ginsberg and the Beats had become the hep new cats on the Beach. Duncan took a job at the Poetry Center and moved with Jess to Stinson Beach in Marin County.

Spicer picked up pretty much where he left off, holding court at The Place. Surrounded by devoted acolytes, a coterie he called the "magic circle," Jack pontificated on a wide range of subjects. He regarded the Beats with amused contempt and could not abide either Ginsberg or Kerouac. Dick Brautigan and Ron Loewinsohn were initially put off by Spicer's overt homosexuality. Both outsiders and suspicious of in-groups of any kind, they "affected a kind of contempt" while secretly envying the sense of community shared by Spicer's clique.

Six-foot-tall Jack Spicer appeared much shorter because of his hunched shambling apelike posture, the result of serious calcium deficiency. He had developed a curiously contorted way of sitting to conceal the many cigarette holes burned through the shiny black suit he always wore. Lew Welch described Spicer as "hell-bent on self-destruction." The poet Jack Anderson remembered Spicer as a "hulking bearlike man," with a "beautifully cultivated speaking voice."

Described as "genially ugly," his light brown hair combed straight back above a high forehead, Spicer worked part-time as a private detective during his university years, investigating embezzling bartenders and other petty larceny. Poet Robin Blaser and his lover, James Felts, shared their house with Spicer soon after he arrived in Berkeley in 1945. Spicer's first poetry teacher was wheelchair-bound Josephine Miles, poet-in-residence at the University of California in Berkeley and the lone woman on the English Department faculty. She had a great influence on his early poetry and found him odd jobs to supplement his meager income as a gumshoe.

Robin Blaser remembered "an almost spastic characteristic," a man who "saw himself as un-attractive and dramatized that and played it out. He was an astonishing figure." Jack Spicer was a highly regarded linguist in the academic world. Fluent in German, he had completed all the require-ments for a PhD in Anglo-Saxon and Old Norse except for his dissertation and earned his keep working in universities and libraries, publishing scholarly articles for professional journals under the name "John Lester Spicer." As a poet, Jack Spicer published few works but earned a reputation as a powerful and dramatic reader.

Subsisting on white bread mayonnaise sandwiches, Spicer lived a near-monastic life on Leavenworth, close to Polk Street, in a cramped two-room basement apartment without a telephone, surrounded by stacks of books borrowed from the library at UC Berkeley. A slovenly man, he used his typewriter as an ashtray, the carriage "heaped with butts and ashes." For reasons of thrift, Spicer stuffed his unwashed laundry, stiff from repeated use, into a closet also housing his empty brandy bottles. A visitor described accidentally opening the door. "The stench was incredible, because his closet was totally jam-packed with socks, underwear, and shirts that were beyond the pale."

Jack Spicer's interests, aside from language and literature, were baseball, the tarot, pinball, playing bridge, and movies. He detested popular music. Every evening, until the bar closed at two, he met with his "magic circle" at The Place. At one time or another, the group included George Stanley, Lewis Ellingham, Richard Duerden, Lew Welch, Joanne Kyger, Bob Kaufman, David Meltzer, John Wieners, and Michael McClure. Jack Goodwin recalled Spicer holding court: "A squinting, sneering, adenoidal, hunch-backed Socrates presiding over the nightly poets' table [. . .] the latest tenderfoot on the left, taking notes."

Early on, Ron Loewinsohn and Dick Brautigan overcame their inherent homophobia and sat down at Spicer's table at the Place. The experience provided an education neither had ever received. "Jack was not only a brilliant critic, he was a brilliant teacher," Loewinsohn recalled. "He could give criticism in a way that allowed you to accept it, even when the criticism was painful."

Spicer felt immediately drawn to Brautigan. Both men affected an air of mystery, neither ever revealing intimate secrets. Brautigan, much like Spicer, didn't talk of his past or the family he had left behind for good. Ten years older, Jack Spicer reinvented himself when he first arrived in Berkeley from Los Angeles, a metamorphosis Dick had only just begun. As Ron Loewinsohn observed, "Jack also had a kind of perverse streak in him. He was never predictable. He would make friends with people who the group thought impossible."

Jack Spicer and Richard Brautigan shared the same birthday. Discovering this cosmic connec-tion appealed to the older poet's love of magic and the tarot. Spicer introduced Brautigan to astrol-ogy, initiating a lifelong interest. Jack Spicer believed in a poetry at once communal and imper-sonal, like language itself. Whitman, godfather to the Beats, was not his cup of tea. He wanted poetry to be free of politics and personal voice, liberated from language itself. Dick Brautigan, privately shaping one of the century's most distinctive American literary voices with each rewritten poem, listened hard to Spicer's pronouncements, sifting what he needed, panning gold from the onrushing brilliance.

In November, Brautigan moved away from North Beach to a $6-a-week room in the Hotel Jessie, a flophouse on a little alley south of Market off Third Street behind the Hearst Building and around the corner from Breen's, where William Saroyan used to drink in the late twenties. A parking garage has obliterated the site of the cheap hotel. Jessie is one of a number of tiny streets in the district (Minna, Clara, Annie, Harriet, Mary) named, with a twinkle in the municipal eye, for favorite nineteenth-century prostitutes. The city fathers knew how to celebrate a good time way back when, in marked contrast to the insipid civic spirit now renaming obscure back alleys and dead-end cul-de-sacs for famed local literary gents like Kerouac, London, and Saroyan. Thus far, Frisco lacks a Brautigan Street, although the city recently funded a bronze casting of Richard's poem "30 Cents, Two Transfers, Love," setting it into the pavement at a light rail stop near the corner of Folsom and the Embarcadero.

At the Hotel Jessie, Brautigan wrote continuously, often completing between ten and twenty poems a day. At the end of November 29 seeking a public reading, he sent a batch to Robert Duncan at the Poetry Center, along with a brief cover letter. Spicer encouraged Dick in this endeavor, having credited "three solid years of Duncan" for his ability "to write poetry seriously."

Duncan wrote back early in December 6 fearing his criticism might "seem harsh." He felt Brautigan's poetry "lacks character, signature. They are curiously uninvolved." Although Duncan praised "Titles for Unwritten Poems about America," finding "a certain lively wit at play," he dismissed the others as inadequate. "We must be ignorant of too much in the originals to be amused." Thanks to a private grant, the Poetry Center had scheduled a free workshop in the spring of 1957. Instead of offering a reading, Duncan suggested Brautigan test himself in "the open Forum of your contemporaries." According to Michael McClure, Robert Duncan despised Richard's poetry and even after Brautigan became successful considered him only "a talented stand-up entertainer."

The workshop in question was to be conducted by Jack Spicer. When Spicer returned from Boston "with no job and in a funk," Duncan pulled strings and juggled the bookkeeping at the Poetry Center, coming up with the funds for Jack's "Poetry as Magic" workshop. The prospectus read, "This is not a course in technique or 'how to write.' It will be a group exploration of the practices of the new magical school of poetry which is best represented in the work of Lorca, Artaud, Charles Olson and Robert Duncan." Dick Brautigan did not sign up. He'd had enough of classrooms. In any case, every night at The Place became a Spicer seminar.

Survival remained uppermost on Brautigan's mind. Departing Grant Avenue for 179 Jessie Street was a move motivated by extreme financial necessity. So broke he could barely pay the rent, Brautigan often didn't have enough money to eat. He cadged drinks and looked for money on barroom floors and in the gutters of Frisco. He checked the coin returns of pay telephones in hopes of finding stray nickels. At least an hour every day was spent searching the streets for lost change. More than a quarter century later, Richard wrote of that time while staying in another cheap hotel room in Bozeman, Montana. "I walked a lot," he scrawled in his ever-present notebook. "I walked all over because I didn't have anything else to do and walking around aimlessly is the cheapest thing in the world to do. I applied for jobs, but nobody wanted to hire me."

The squalid room at the Hotel Jessie, where a skinny bar of soap and threadbare sheets and towels were supplied once each week, provided "the entrance to the sleep world" for Richard Brautigan. He washed his shorts and socks in the sink and hung them to dry on a coat hanger suspended in the sliver of sunlight angling in through the dingy window. Richard struggled to come up with the weekly rent. He did not want to lose this last tenuous sanctuary, "a container for my nightmares." Once, utterly without funds, sitting in the bleakness of his room, watching the neon sign flash outside the window, wondering where he might come up with some cash, his eye fell upon an old alarm clock, which he promptly took to a pawn shop, using the pitiful proceeds to buy himself breakfast.

Brautigan's only other liquid asset flowed through his body. He was type A positive, and the Irwin Memorial Blood Bank of the San Francisco Medical Society paid twenty bucks a pint. Richard made his first sale in April when he was issued a Blood Bank Book at the Society's offices at 270 Masonic. Soon after this, he got lucky and found a job as a bicycle messenger delivering telegrams for Western Union in the Financial District. Well-schooled in the art of frugal living, Dick made do on a minimum wage, eating in local cafeterias, writing in his room late at night, enjoying an occasional two-bit triple feature on Market Street. North Beach was a short bus ride away. Liking to walk, Brautigan often saved the fare.

Richard continued mailing out his poetry to little magazines around the country from the Hotel Jessie. The winter issue of *The Caxton Poetry Review* (vol. 1, no. 2) arrived from Ohio, announcing their prizes for the winter quarter. Richard Brautigan had been awarded $1 for "A Correction." Vera Dickerson won $5 for a poem entitled "San Joaquin Spring." All in all, winning a buck felt fine. He could eat for a day on six bits and have change left over for a couple drinks at The Place.

Around this time, Richard paid a visit to the offices of Inferno Press, located in the Hearst Building, just around the corner from his hotel. The editor, Leslie Woolf Hedley, worked for the Hearst Foundation and the Hearst Printing Company. His little San Francisco literary magazine, *Inferno* (declaring itself "the only independent press functioning in California") had published its final issue in 1956 after a six-year run. "In those years we have found ourselves censored, libeled & threatened by mccarthyite fascists," the editor declared as his magazine ceased publication. Hedley thought Brautigan "looked pretty much underfed and lost. He was a very innocent guy. An unhappy kid. We felt sorry for him, of course. And he didn't talk too much about writing. He was going to write poetry, or something of that nature. I asked him if he wanted to show me some."

Richard took to dropping by Leslie Woolf Hedley's office whenever he had a spare moment. The editor was only a few years older but infinitely wiser and more experienced. "After four years in the Army, I can tell you I did not want to see any more tragedies," was how he summed it up. Both men were blond. "You know, you look like me," Richard said to the editor, even though he was seven inches taller than Hedley. He also said he was an orphan, another step in re-creating himself in his new environment. "He kind of thought maybe he was an anarchist," Hedley recalled, "but I think the word was more appealing than the philosophy." Richard also mentioned having a sister, and Hedley guessed that "he must have felt deeply about her because he said he missed her."

When Hedley asked Brautigan how he was getting by, Richard mentioned working as a messenger boy and said he "enjoyed it somewhat." The editor considered being a bicycle messenger "perhaps the second most dangerous job in San Francisco." Leslie Woolf Hedley was sympathetic to young Brautigan. He felt sorry for him "because he seemed pitiful. He seemed very innocent at that time." Richard sat there, talking to the older man, and Hedley listened patiently. "I didn't ask too many questions because I didn't think I wanted to interfere with his life."

When the editor attempted to turn their conversation to the subject of literature, asking Brautigan what he was reading, Richard came back to the Inferno Press office with a bunch of paperbacks. "And it was cowboy stories. Western stuff." Richard, the faux naif, never mentioned Hemingway, Cummings, Saroyan, or any of several other literary writers who were important to him. He did eventually show Leslie Woolf Hedley something he had written. The editor's reply was, "You know, what you're doing, you're writing like a sixteen-year-old."

"Oh, really," Richard smiled. "That's good."

Brautigan also spent a lot of time with Ron Loewinsohn. "They were sparkling friends," Bill Brown remembered. It was, once again, a mismatched Mutt and Jeff pairing, with Ron, like Gary Stewart, standing a head shorter than Dick. Together, they made a curious and distinctive impression on all who met them.

"Two bright young guys," thought Joanne Kyger when she first laid eyes on the pair in the spring of 1957 at an art opening in the East/West Gallery. Twenty-three and brimming with vitality and flair, Kyger had arrived in Frisco the previous February, right around the time *Mademoiselle* ran an article on the San Francisco Renaissance and initiated the uneasy alliance between popular culture and the Beat underground. She came up from UC Santa Barbara, one unit shy of graduation, with her childhood friend the painter Nemi (Emily) Frost, and rented an apartment on Columbus above LaRocca's Bar. She soon found a job at a Brentano's in the City of Paris department store.

The bookstore was something of a crossroads for poets. Joanne had already been introduced to Spicer there. She wanted to join his workshop but was too late. Fifty San Francisco poets had already applied. Spicer winnowed the list to fifteen, through a peculiar "questionnaire" requiring the applicants to answer such odd queries as "What insect do you most resemble?" and "Invent a dream in which you appear as a poet," and "If you had a chance to eliminate three political figures in the world, which would you choose?" The Poetry as Magic Workshop met every Tuesday night that spring from 7:00 to 10:00 PM in a room on the third floor of the San Francisco Public Library. The group sat around a circular wooden table with Jack Spicer always sitting at the eastern compass point, facing toward west.

Spicer assigned a poem topic each week (second assignment: How would you cook a baby?). The anointed fifteen never all showed up together on any given evening. The chosen included John Allen Ryan; Robert Duncan ("sitting in"); George Stanley, who worked as a clerk in the Police Department; Joe Dunn, a member of Duncan's writing class at Black Mountain; Helen Adam; Jack Gilbert; and the "Viking," Ebbe Borregaard, "an imposing and somewhat frightening creature," who had served in Korea after becoming locally famous as a teen runaway when his picture appeared on all the front pages of the San Francisco newspapers.

When Ron and Dick introduced themselves as writers to Joanne Kyger at the East/West Helen Frankenthaler show, she regarded these two younger guys with a jaundiced eye. She had a smile bright as a Pepsodent ad, and her pert good looks deflected attention from her poet's heart and soul. Loewinsohn declared Wordsworth to be his favorite poet. Joanne's knee-jerk reaction ("I had studied with Hugh Kenner and I was from T. S. Eliot") mirrored Ron's when he learned e. e. cummings ("very much passé") had been important to Richard.

Shy Dick Brautigan slyly began a whimsical flirtation with Kyger. "We had this exchange," she remembered. In a bohemian version of boy meets girl, Richard invited Joanne to take him out to dinner. She was the one with a good job. The next night, they went to Chinatown, ending up at "The Hole," Woey Loy Goey Café on Jackson Street, an inexpensive basement restaurant much beloved by the Beats. Kyger, "living on a very tight budget," recalled the place as "the absolute cheapest restaurant you could go to. You could get a bowl of greens and things, with rice, for thirty-five cents. We had this meal together. It was his kind of conversation. I don't know what kind of conversation it was. It certainly wasn't literary."

After dinner, Dick suggested they walk over to the Beach. "And I hadn't really been to North Beach," Joanne Kyger remembered. "I hadn't found North Beach yet, even though I was living close to it." Brautigan showed her around upper Grant Avenue, where he was already known on the street. They quickly ran into Mike Nathan, a young teenage painter. An acquaintance of Richard's, Nathan had a painting displayed in the window of City Lights that portrayed a cop and a priest in the style of Ben Shahn. People thought it a political comment on the March 25 seizure by the Customs Office of the second printing of *Howl*, printed for City Lights in England by Villiers Publications, Ltd. Richard introduced Nathan to Joanne. "Mike Nathan was immediately charming," she recalled. "Totally delightful." Brautigan looked on in dismay while "precocious, lively" Mike commandeered the conversation.

"Richard was so doltish in his behavior." Joanne remembered going off with Nathan soon after when he "offered to take me to the Anxious Asp. Then, for the rest of the evening, I was shown up and down Grant Avenue by Mike Nathan, there was Richard hulking and skulking down the other side of the street, looking balefully across at us. It's not like he was going to come along."

"One thing about him," Bill Brown said of Dick Brautigan upon hearing Joanne Kyger's story, "he never knew how to cope. He didn't have the machinery to handle disappointment."

Loners don't often risk close emotional contact. Too much at stake. Brautigan found safety in solitude, having learned the hard way how much unrequited love really hurts. Reborn in the world of his dreams, Dick Brautigan didn't moon over Joanne Kyger for long. Spinning through downtown Frisco traffic on his messenger's bike, daydreaming of literary fame and fortune, lost in a private paradise only he could enter, he never noticed the zaftig girl with long brown hair who saw him passing on the street from time to time. She'd wave and say hello. Dick didn't even glance at her, pedaling erratically away in complete oblivion. The girl, who wore basic bohemian black, decided the strange boy must be a foreigner unable to speak English, some "misplaced count," possibly Austrian because of his white-blond hair.

fourteen: ginger

HER NAME WAS Virginia Dionne Alder, though everybody called her Ginger or Ginny. Dubbed Ginger as a child, she got her new nickname at seventeen from Lester Rosenthal, her college boyfriend. At UCLA, Les had introduced her to "all the counterculture groups. The anarchists. The Trotskyites. The socialists." A skilled typist, Ginger/Ginny worked for Landelf, Weigel, Ripley and Diamond, a law firm in the Financial District. She shared a cheap apartment on Filbert Street near the top of Telegraph Hill with a roommate, Lenore Yanoff, and with Les Rosenthal, who recently moved back into her life.

Ginny Alder was born in Rexburg, Idaho, in 1934, but her family moved when she was a year old and she grew up in Southern California, in Reseda, in the heart of the San Fernando Valley. She majored in political science at UCLA, also studying journalism and writing for the *Bruin*, the university newspaper. Les Rosenthal brought her to readings in Santa Monica, where she met the poet Stan Persky. It was the first time she had ever heard anyone read poetry aloud. Sue Goya, married at the time to actor/screenwriter Zekial Marko, herself a poet and an habitué of The Place, remembered Ginny as "a great big sexy lady." Donald Allen, coeditor of the *Evergreen Review* and an early champion of Brautigan's work, recalled a "tall, slow-moving, wide-hipped girl." Ron Loewinsohn knew Ginny (as he always called her) through her roommate. Lenore had once been his girlfriend but now was just a pal. He thought Ginny "very articulate and sharp; a delightful person, witty, charming, faithful."

One day, Ron and Dick sat in a North Beach Laundromat watching the dryers spin when Ginny arrived with a load of washing. Ron provided the introduction, but some other magic lit the spark. Ginny invited them both to a party up at her place later that night. In "Gone Since Then," an unpublished short story written in the late 1950s, Richard recalled heading up Telegraph Hill with "R." They climbed the rickety, unpainted wooden Greenwich Street stairway leading steeply up from Sansome Street.

The stairs, landscaped on either side by banks of fuchsia, ivy, lilies, and roses, intersected private paths and country lanes where bohemians once lived among flocks of feral parrots after the '06 quake, building shacks of salvaged lumber in sloping pastures thick with nasturtium, wild mustard, and dog fennel. Dick and Ron soon encountered someone they both knew, a two-hundred-pound brawler called "Big T," coming down the steps with a bunch of his friends. Big T had just backhanded a junkie across the face for "acting like an asshole." The junkie's girlfriend fainted, and it was time to leave the festivities. "Where's the party," Dick wanted to know.

"There." Big T pointed to a house by the stair-turning, every window ablaze with light. "He didn't sound too happy," Brautigan observed.

Dick and Ron "swirled through the party like water through the cooling systems of a car." Tatami mats from Chinatown covered the crooked floors. The place resonated with the discordant vibes of the recent Big T incident. The two young poets were both quickly drunk.

According to Brautigan, Loewinsohn "was on a big Rimbaud kick. He was writing his season in hell and sleeping in the back seats of strange cars." Ginny's apartment had a fabulous view overlooking the Bay. In the nineteenth century, quarries gouged away the eastern side of Telegraph Hill, leaving blasted cliffs in exchange for landfill and ballast. The old wooden building looked down a hundred feet through vines and bushes and treetops to the rusting factories and abandoned brick warehouses clustered among unused train tracks in a "bleak industrial neighborhood" below. Ron climbed out through a window and sat on the roof to enjoy the view, "saying weird things at the stars." The Rimbaud thing shifted into high gear. Dick wandered off looking for a girl to kiss, "and that's how I met my wife, as they say in Rome."

Ginny remembered being struck by Richard's personality. She found him "very naive," an attractive attribute in the world of North Beach cool. She took the tall shy blond boy by the hand, led him to her room, and discovered a total innocent. Ginny had never guessed he was still a virgin. The two became a couple right from the start. Les Rosenthal bowed out gracefully. "They were just absolutely starry-eyed," Ron Loewinsohn recalled. "They were really in love, and it was delightful. They were a delightful couple to be around." Ginny called him Richard, at a time when he was still "Dick" to most of his friends. She had a brother named Richard, so it seemed natural.

Richard had recently vacated the Hotel Jessie and was living in the apartment of a young single mother in exchange for babysitting services. They spoke to each other in a "secret Venusian language" of their own improvised invention. Richard moved in with Ginny after she broke things off with Les. In keeping with the relaxed attitude of the time, all three remained fast friends. Richard quickly became familiar with the wooden steps outside, walking to buy milk and bread at the corner market over on Union and Montgomery. Ginny noticed he could not pass his reflection in a mirror or shop window without looking at himself. She thought Richard wanted reassurance that he was really there.

On his next visit to the apartment after Richard moved in with Ginny, Ron Loewinsohn saw that she had "set up a kind of shrine" to the new poet in her life. Ginny placed a photograph of Richard along with handwritten copies of his poems mounted on cardboard display stands on an orange crate in the company of several "small candles and terra-cotta Buddhas."

During this period, Brautigan continued reading his poetry regularly at The Place. Carol Lind, an artist from Minnesota who lived downstairs from Ginny, painted a large canvas featuring all the regulars that she titled *Which Poet?* Richard was featured prominently in the painting, distinguishable by his long blond bangs. He took a liking to the picture and brought it over to The Place, where he hung it on the back wall directly behind him when he read.

Brautigan was reading a lot of William Saroyan when he first met Virginia Alder. Saroyan's deft early stories spun the straw of life's commonplace moments into magical gold, creating a distinctly personal world in an easy offhand manner. Richard recognized familiar territory. Lean. Minimal. The wise comic voice. Ginny remembered his fondness for Saroyan and others. "He loved Jack London, and he loved Hemingway, and he loved e. e. cummings in the same way. Eudora Welty. But if you asked him if Hemingway was an influence, he would have said no. He said that 'all poetry simply goes into the air and then you breathe.'"

Richard Brautigan felt inclined toward poets who practiced a sinuous stripped-down art. Sappho and Bashō were particular favorites. Robert Briggs, a fellow writer who first met Richard in North Beach in 1957, remembered Brautigan's high regard for the work of Kenneth Patchen and their discussions of Patchen's famous poem "The Lute in the Attic." According to Virginia, Patchen's poetry "was one of the first things we talked about."

Brautigan also admired the Patchen novel *The Journal of Albion Moonlight*, a book whose evanescent charms presaged many of the attributes of his own later work. Briggs recalled Richard's deep concern about Patchen's health. The older poet suffered from a degenerative spinal disease and endured continuous pain. He needed a cane to get around in North Beach and had recently moved to Sierra Court, a dead-end street just off the freeway in Palo Alto, where he was confined to the house under the care of his wife, Miriam.

Always eager for literary conversation, Brautigan never talked about his past. For entertainment, he and Ginny hung out at The Place and other joints along upper Grant. One Sunday afternoon, while visiting Mike Nathan's new storefront studio in North Beach, they encountered a hefty mustachioed painter who took classes with Mike at the Art Institute. Born in Salinas and a veteran of the Korean War, Kenn Davis was the brother of Zekial Marko. Nathan had invited him to have a look at his newfound space, having promised to "break open a bottle of red and celebrate." Davis enjoyed Nathan's company because they both "had the same kind of goofy sense of humor."

Humor later provided a close connection to Richard Brautigan, but when Kenn first encountered "this tall blond guy," Dick "seemed a little off-put by the fact that I was even there."

Mike Nathan quickly made the introductions, calling Brautigan "a wonderful poet." The young painter sounded enthusiastic. "You've got to read his stuff," he insisted. As they shook hands, Davis's name "struck a bell," and Richard turned to Ginny, saying, "Remember that guy? The painting we saw at the Artist's Cooperative last week and I said I really liked it? It had some nice magical provocative kind of qualities." Ginny remembered, and because Mike Nathan had things to do, the three new friends left the gallery together. Kenn Davis, a self-described "sucker for flattery," responded to their enthusiasm for his work. They ended up spending the remainder of the day "just talking—sitting on park benches and stuff."

This first meeting took place a couple months after Kenn's twenty-fifth birthday. "I remember we got into a bit of comic interlude about people who are pushing thirty," Davis said. "Anybody past twenty-five as far as [Brautigan] was concerned was pushing thirty, and that was me." Kenn recollected that not too long after he met Richard, Mike Nathan's "brains got scrambled. The state got their hands on him and sent him off to some sanitarium and gave him shock treatments for about three months. My God, I could barely even talk to him. Mike could have turned out to be one hell of a painter. But after he came out of the hospital, I'd see him on the street and he'd be talking to himself and moving his hands around in the air like he's touching angels." Davis knew nothing at the time about Brautigan's similar ordeal but remembered that "Richard was much more sympathetic with Mike about this."

Dick and Ginny frequently went to the cheap rerun movies at the Times Theater with a group of friends. Along with Ron Loewinsohn and Les Rosenthal, this diverse gang also included Kenn Davis and another artist, Frank Curtin, whose father was an editor at the *Call-Bulletin*. The films they enjoyed were mostly B-movie trash. Frank Curtin and Richard soon became regular drinking buddies, vodka being Curtin's beverage of choice, while Brautigan favored sweet red port at a dime a glass or cheap Cribari jug wine. Ron Loewinsohn remained much impressed with Richard's capacity as a drinker. "He was incredibly able to hold his liquor," he recalled. "He really was astonishing."

A printed form letter, dated April 10, 1957, arrived from Inferno Press soliciting contributions for *Five New Poets*, a softcover collection in preparation and scheduled for release before Christmas. Leslie Woolf Hedley asked for "at least" twelve published or unpublished poems, a brief biography, and a stamped self-addressed envelope. Payment for acceptance would be ten copies of the book. Hedley himself did no editing on this book. Someone else involved with the press suggested the idea, and Hedley said, "Okay. You pick out your own." Dick Brautigan brought a dozen poems to the Inferno Press office.

At the same time, Richard entertained his own publishing notions. One of his poems, "The Return of the Rivers," struck him as worthy of appearing om its own as a broadside. Leslie Woolf Hedley agreed to print a hundred copies at no charge as a favor to the young poet. Inferno Press expected no percentage of any eventual sales. Hedley just wanted to give "orphan" Dick a helping hand.

Sometime in May, Richard picked up the finished sheets of *The Return of the Rivers* and bought a pack of black construction paper. With Ron Loewinsohn joining in, they sat in Ginny's living room folding and gluing the folio pages into improvised black covers. They pasted white two-by-three-inch labels onto the center of the front covers. Richard signed his name in ink above the printed colophon of Inferno Press, a final step in the production of his first "book." Ron thought his new friend "a pretty enterprising young man, always on the lookout to publish, occasions to read, even though he always wanted to make an appearance of being above that."

Many copies of *The Return of the Rivers* were given away to friends. Richard peddled a few in North Beach bars for a buck a copy. The rest went to City Lights and other "obscure" local bookstores. Kenn Davis held a day job at an insurance company and was the only one in the group with a car. He transported copies to Berkeley bookstores in his old Chevy. Ginny remembered "a big argument" over how much to charge. The profits were quickly spent on wine and a couple cheap Chinatown dinners. A surviving copy of *The Return of the Rivers* sold recently on the rare book market for $7,500.

In June, Richard proposed. "Why don't we go to Reno and get married?" he asked in a matter-of-fact way. Ginny agreed. For a wedding present, she gave him a used pink electric Royal typewriter. They rode a bus together to Nevada to tie the knot. Methodist minister Rev. Stephen C. Thomas pronounced them man and wife on Saturday, June 8, with Ace W. Williams (a stranger, who just happened to be in the wedding chapel) and Agnes Thomas, the minister's wife, standing up as witnesses.

After returning from a brief Reno honeymoon, Richard and Ginny moved into a two-room attic apartment with a shared kitchen at 1565 Washington Street, above Chinatown on the slope of Nob Hill right on the corner across from the cable car barn. There was a small struggling theater downstairs, no more than ten or twenty seats. Performances competed with the continuous grinding noise of the cable under the street outside. Late at night, when the Powell–Mason Line shut down for a few hours, Richard and Ginny were startled awake by the sudden silence.

The newlyweds were quite happy in their new apartment, in spite of various inconveniences. The bathroom was off the hall. When it rained, the roof leaked by the door. Love always helps in such circumstances. Ron Loewinsohn remembered how Ginny and Dick "just fell madly in love." He also observed that Ginny was "madly in love with [Brautigan's] work," an asset for an aspiring young writer. Ginny typed his manuscripts, edited his copy, organized his business affairs, encouraged him to keep in touch with editors and publishers. She also paid the rent.

Wanting to do his share, Brautigan came up with an amusing contribution to the family's monthly expense needs. He organized a rent party. Such affairs had been commonplace in New York's Harlem and Greenwich Village during the twenties, when a hot piano player and a bathtub full of rotgut booze provided the come-on. Richard had no live entertainment to offer and invented an ingenious promotional device. He posted handbills all over North Beach advertising the event as a fund-raiser to buy the host a gorilla suit.

Kenn Davis remembered Brautigan's rent party on Washington Street with much amusement. "And we actually had total strangers. Total strangers! Like tourists wandered in and said, 'Where's the guy that wants to buy the gorilla suit?' And here are these guys from like Tuscaloosa or Tampa or San Jose. And Dick was, 'Well, I've always wanted to wear a gorilla suit. Don't you think I'd look great in a gorilla suit?'"

Richard Brautigan wasn't unemployed yet, but his paycheck remained marginal at best. In mid-July he made another trip to the Irwin Memorial Blood Bank. He had quit work as a bike messenger and had a new part-time job "folding pieces of green paper" at an office on Clay Street, down from the Federal Reserve Bank. Brautigan described this experience in Part 3 of "A Couple Novels," an unpublished story from the sixties that survives only in fragments. He had no idea what the green paper was for or why he was folding it. "Nobody ever told me and I never asked."

Part-time employment allowed ample time for writing and provided the luxury of leisure. Richard Brautigan loved to wander the city and people-watch. "He did a lot of hanging out," Ron Loewinsohn said. "He walked a great deal, all around the Financial District, Chinatown, North Beach, that whole area in San Francisco. I don't know that he ever took notes so much, but certainly he was taking mental notes. He would hang out in bookstores, not just City Lights, but any bookstore. He would hang out in parks, sit on a park bench and watch people go along."

Two significant San Francisco literary events occurred during the summer of 1957. Most noteworthy was the *Howl* obscenity trial. On May 29, after federal prosecutors declined to initiate condemnation proceedings, U.S. Customs released 520 copies of the second printing it had been holding since March. Three days later, two plainclothes San Francisco police officers, acting under orders from Captain William Hanrahan of the juvenile division, arrested bookstore manager Shigeyoshi Murao at City Lights on charges of selling obscene literature after purchasing a copy of *Howl* from him. An arrest warrant was also issued for publisher Lawrence Ferlinghetti.

The trial began in mid-August with Judge Clayton Horn, one of four city police magistrates, presiding over a 150-seat courtroom crowded to capacity with reporters and other onlookers. Jack Spicer became a regular spectator. More than legal matters interested him. He was "cruised" at the trial by a young redheaded aspiring painter named Russell FitzGerald, who later became his lover. Counsel for the defense was famed trial lawyer Jake ("Never Plead Guilty") Ehrlich. Nine distinguished expert witnesses (including Mark Schorer, Walter Van Tilburg Clark, Luther Nichols, and Kenneth Rexroth) testified in person supporting Ginsberg's poem.

On the third of October, Judge Horn delivered his decision. Lawrence Ferlinghetti was not guilty of publishing and selling obscene material. (Charges against Shig Murao had been dropped a week after the start of the trial.) The case provided excellent business for Ferlinghetti, ensuring the future success of his City Lights Books publishing venture. "Big Day for Bards at Bay," declared a September *Life* magazine photo essay that made Ginsberg and Ferlinghetti famous almost overnight. By the time the media circus came to an end, more than ten thousand copies of *Howl* were in print.

Richard Brautigan talked about the trial with his friends, Ferlinghetti's legal troubles being a hot topic in North Beach that summer. *Howl* had been prominently displayed in the front window of City Lights all during the legal proceedings. Allen Ginsberg was off in Europe with Peter Orlovsky but remained the man of the moment on the Frisco poetry scene.

When *Evergreen Review*, no. 2, appeared in local bookstores in June, it became the other talked-about event of the summer. Published in New York City, the new periodical devoted its entire second issue to the "San Francisco Scene." Ferlinghetti, Ginsberg, and Kerouac were among the contributors, along with Kenneth Rexroth, Robert Duncan, Josephine Miles, Jack Spicer, Philip Whalen, Gary Snyder, Michael McClure, and Henry Miller. The fledgling *Evergreen Review* was a vibrant publication, focusing national attention on the remarkable literary talent flowering in San Francisco. For a relative newcomer like Brautigan, reading the second issue vindicated his decision to move to the city. Hemingway and Fitzgerald had Paris in the twenties; this time around, Frisco in the fifties was the place to be.

Spicer's contribution to the new quarterly suited Richard's lean aesthetics. Unlike the improvised excesses of Kerouac ("That's not writing; that's typing," waspish Truman Capote hissed on a TV talk show), Spicer's measured, minimal work chose each word with lapidary precision. A remarkable short story, "The Scroll-work on the Casket," presented profound object lessons in his precise (yet curiously oblique) use of language, at once straightforward yet utterly unafraid of the unexpected. To achieve just such a mysterious economy with words became Brautigan's goal.

The freewheeling salon centered on Jack Spicer at The Place found less boisterous surroundings once he began spending every afternoon at Aquatic Park, a convenient cove on San Francisco Bay where the great curving arm of the Municipal Pier embraced the Maritime Museum's collection of nineteenth-century sailing ships. The park fronted the Maritime Museum, a 1939 WPA art deco building, originally a public bathhouse designed to resemble an ocean liner. Rows of concrete bleachers overlooking the tiny strip of beach provided a favorite sunbathing spot. Here, or on the grassy slope above, joined by his friends and disciples, Spicer listened to baseball games on his inexpensive leather-covered portable radio, read books and newspapers, and held forth on the magic nature of poetry, always sitting with his back to the water.

When Spicer's workshop at the public library came to an end that summer, remnants of the group continued to meet informally on Sunday afternoons in the ground-floor Jackson Street apartment of Joe and Carolyn Dunn, where the shades were drawn to ensure privacy and provide the appropriate ambiance. Duncan and Spicer continued as resident sages, with the former enthroned in a plush easy chair, the latter hulking cross-legged on the wine-stained rug. Among the devotees occupying the Salvation Army furniture were George Stanley, Ebbe Borregaard, and James Broughton. Joanne Kyger, having missed out on the Magic Workshop, began attending regularly along with her friend Nemi Frost and another painter, Jerome Mallman.

Later newcomers included two poets barely into their twenties: David Meltzer, up from L.A., where he had befriended Edward Kienholz and Wallace Berman, artists he called the "lumberjacks" because of their beards and rugged shirts, and John Wieners, a former student of Charles Olson's at Black Mountain College, who had moved in October from Boston, where he'd published most of the Black Mountain gang in his magazine, *Measure*. Kyger and Wieners soon became intense friends. He dubbed her "Miss Kids," a nickname springing from her exuberant way of announcing "Kids! I've got a great idea!" in the hey-let's-put-on-a-show manner of the Andy Hardy films. Kyger's late-night cartwheeling in Washington Square was another manifestation of her spontaneous enthusiasms.

Ron Loewinsohn and Dick Brautigan started trooping on Sundays through the Broadway Tunnel under Russian Hill to the Dunns' dimly lit apartment where the ninety-cent jug wine circulated in jelly jars. Ron remembered the positive response to Richard's work right from the first. "I thought it was extremely worthwhile. People got very excited about his stuff. It was unique. None of us had ever seen anything like it before. Part of what made him so bizarre was because he was coming from a direction that really wasn't hip. It was for us totally unexplored."

Spicer soared at a creative peak that summer, writing the poems that formed his book *After Lorca*. Donald Allen, in town for a couple months, remembered Jack showing him a new poem every day at Vesuvio or The Place. Spicer had come to believe "there is no single poem." Poems were serial. They belonged in groups, lived in books. "Poems should echo and re-echo against each other," Spicer wrote to Robin Blaser. "They should create resonances. They cannot live alone any more than we can."

Everyone read to the group, including Duncan and Spicer, with Jack often reading a new poem three times before allowing any comment. When the younger poets presented their work, "Duncan and Spicer were the judges." George Stanley remembered Spicer as the harder of the two. "Duncan was much more willing to allow the possibility of there being something there, and Spicer was much more willing to allow the possibility of there being nothing there, just 'shit!'" Duncan rarely disagreed with Spicer, and the mood stayed genial in spite of the severity of the criticism. "There weren't any grudges," Stanley recalled. "If Spicer thought your poem was shit, that didn't mean he thought you were shit."

David Meltzer called Duncan and Spicer "mentor gurus" and found them an "interesting combination because Robert was this very expansive poet, and Jack was this very reductive poet." Duncan had praised and admired *Howl*, but Spicer had only scorn for the Beats. Ron Loewinsohn said, "Jack would have nothing to do with Ferlinghetti, would not allow his [Spicer's] books to be sold in the store, did not take Kerouac or Ginsberg seriously, dealt with all of the Beat Generation people with a kind of contempt."

Loewinsohn recalled an afternoon when Brautigan read "The Nature Poem" at the Dunns'. Later published in *The Octopus Frontier* and reprinted in *The Pill*, the poem began, "The moon / is Hamlet / on a motorcycle / coming down / a dark road." According to Ron, "Spicer's reaction was to laugh—the deliberate 'ha-ha-ha-ha. That's not funny, that was stupid.' It was pretty intense." Somehow Brautigan, wary and sensitive by nature, took it all in stride. David Meltzer thought this was because Richard "was very much an unacknowledged disciple of Jack." He also remembered how deeply Brautigan craved his mentor's approval. "Richard was very self-conscious, like a lot of writers and artists, even performers, essentially very introverted and shy."

Meltzer recalled the "rigor around the right word" that Richard had reinforced through his contact with Spicer. "I remember we had this long drunken discussion at Vesuvio about James Jones's recent book, *Some Came Running*, his big pulpy thing, which I enjoyed. I was comfortable with both the kind of Whitmanesque expansiveness American style and the reductive." Although he "gruesomely loathed to talk critically," Brautigan thought the Jones book was "terrible. 'Everything is in there,' he just kept on saying. 'Nothing is left out.'"

Early in June of 1957, following a reading by the members of Spicer's Magic Workshop, Jack suggested to Joe Dunn that he was just the man to start a new press and publish the work of his fellow poets. Spicer was certainly aware that his own growing book-length manuscript would soon need to find a publisher. Dunn got a job in the Print Department of the Greyhound Bus Company on Seventh Street. Jack Sutherland, the head of the department, had studied at the Art Institute with Jess and John Allen Ryan. Joe asked if he could come in nights and on Saturdays and use the equipment for his own projects. Sutherland gave his OK, introducing Dunn to the paper salesmen (he had to buy his own stock), and White Rabbit Press was born.

In many ways, the press became a community operation. Robert Duncan drew the original colophon. Jess designed many of the covers. Workshop members sewed the signatures of smaller print runs and assembled the sheaves for *After Lorca* in the Dunns' apartment during their weekly Sunday meetings. Joe Dunn's frenzied methedrine-fueled energy drove the project. He published ten chapbooks under the White Rabbit imprint between November 1957 to September 1958. All were uniform in format, a compact five and a half by eight and a half inches. The first was *Love, the Poem, the Sea and Other Pieces Examined*, by Steve Jonas, a black friend from Boston. The edition of two hundred sold for twenty-five cents a copy.

Richard Brautigan published several new poems in 1957. The "Special San Francisco Issue" (Summer–Autumn, vol. 2, no. 2) of *Mainstream*, out of Palatine, Illinois, featured poetry by Robert Stock, Daniel J. Langton, and other Frisco bards, along with Richard's poem "The Final Ride." The *Berkeley Review* (vol. 1, no. 3) ran two Brautigan poems, "The Return of the Rivers" and "The Horse That Had a Flat Tire." He was also featured in the September–October issue (no. 7) of *Existaria*, "a journal of existant [*sic*] hysteria," published in Hermosa Beach, California. Charles Bukowski, Clarence Major, and Judson Crews were among the other contributors. "The Daring Little Guy on the Burma Shave Sign" and "The World Will Never End" were never collected in Richard's later works.

Jack Kerouac's *On the Road* came out on September 5 and got a rave review in the *New York Times*. It jumped to number 7 on the best seller list. The fall of 1957 also saw Richard Brautigan's work appear in book form, although under more modest circumstances. *Four New Poets*, the little anthology published by Inferno Press, contained four pieces by Brautigan. A slim paperback priced at $1, it featured white wrappers decorated with black handprints.

Along with Brautigan, the other poets were Martin Hoberman, Carl Larsen (editor of *Existaria*), and James M. Singer, all under twenty-five. ("Here are poets representing an articulate segment of a sometime-called 'silent generation.'") Richard's bio identified him as "a young poet born January 30, 1935, in Tacoma, Washington. He now lives in San Francisco, where he is working on a book of poems, The Horse That Had a Flat Tire." Fond of this title, Brautigan used it many times since it first came to him in the mental hospital.

By the fall of 1957, a little over a year after first arriving in the city, Dick Brautigan had become a distinctive member of the Frisco literary scene. In September (his broadside folio "book" for sale in local stores and the Inferno Press anthology about to be published), he was invited to participate in the weeklong 11th Annual Arts Festival in North Beach. As part of the festivities, the

Poetry Center sponsored a number of readings at Fugazi Hall on Green Street. (This theater later became the permanent home of *Beach Blanket Babylon*, a hit of such long-running duration the city renamed the street outside in its honor.) Saturday night was devoted to a "reading from recent works and poems written for the 'Poetry as Magic' Workshop, conducted by Jack Spicer." The daytime hours featured readings by younger poets, most of them Spicer's gang. Richard Brautigan, Ron Loewinsohn, and Ebbe Borregaard all read that same afternoon.

Life looked good for Dick Brautigan. The year after leaving his home base for the uncertainties of life in a distant unfamiliar city found him happily married, published, and an active member of the North Beach community, invited to read his poetry at their annual arts festival. What did it matter if he was mostly unemployed and sold his blood for bar money? His wife had a job, and the rent got paid. Ginny also typed his manuscripts and correspondence. She remembered her new husband pacing in the other room, endlessly muttering, "Oh, the irony. Oh, the pity," dreaming his Hemingway dreams and ironically quoting *The Sun Also Rises* like a stuck record.

One day, Jack Spicer came by Dick and Ginny's place when Virginia was frantic at having misplaced some money she'd set aside for the rent. She'd already looked everywhere without success. Jack said, "Look in all the places you think you've put it."

"I did. I did. I did. I did," Ginny replied.

Spicer's uncanny ability to incorporate elements of magic into the simple details of everyday life fascinated Brautigan. "No. Look in the places where you've already looked," Jack said. He was adamant and kept repeating this instruction. Ginny pulled out her leather wallet. She'd thoroughly searched it before, going through the many compartments and coming up empty-handed. This time, she dug her finger into a "secret" area and there was the folded money. Richard was flabbergasted. He talked about the episode for years. Ginny thought it not so much "magic," but more in keeping with Spicer's views on poetics. Magic for Spicer "was a matter of disturbance, entrance, and passion, rather than abracadabra." Jack once remarked to Robin Blaser "that there was no good source from which to learn magic; it was something we did among ourselves."

Richard Brautigan celebrated his first San Francisco Christmas in a flophouse. The second yule was decidedly more festive. After all his miserable childhood holidays, it was a true joy to have a happy home and a wife he loved. Not even Virginia's illness that season (she had bronchitis) spoiled their happiness. When she felt well enough to go out, Ginny and Dick ran into Ron Loewinsohn on Filbert Street in front of the Saints Peter and Paul Church. He said he had gotten them something for Christmas but had it locked in his car parked nearby. The Brautigans walked back with him, and Ron gave them a parchment leaf from an illuminated medieval manuscript. Dick marveled at the gilded Latin uncials. It was a rare treasure for someone not accustomed to receiving gifts. Richard Brautigan proudly hung it on the wall of his Washington Street apartment.

P RICE DUNN WAS born in Alabama in 1934 and "grew up in the buckle of the Bible Belt." His father worked construction for the Tennessee Valley Authority, a job requiring him to move so often that Price attended forty-two different schools before dropping out of high school at eighteen. A two-year period of drifting followed, during which he hitchhiked up and down the East Coast with a sleeping bag and a duffle. Price found his way to Chicago and out through the Dakotas to Seattle and L.A. It was easy back then for a sober man to find work, "cleaning brick or pearl diving [washing dishes]."

In December 1955, Price Dunn headed north for San Francisco. He got as far as Big Sur. When he became stranded along the highway near Monterey, a long fascination with the writing of Henry Miller compelled Price to backtrack down the coastal route. He soon found the Anderson Creek studio of Emil White and went to work for him, doing odd jobs in return for room and board, not realizing White was a longtime friend of Miller's.

Heavy rains saturated Big Sur that winter. Mud slides after one big storm slammed over the hot springs owned by the Murphy family. Home today of the Esalen Institute, in 1956 the hot springs comprised little more than three rows of motel cabins, open tubs with wooden platforms covered by cedar shake roofs, and a handsome lodge fronted by a broad green lawn running right to the cliff edge. Closed to the public when mud filled most of the tubs, the hot springs looked like it might never open again for another season. The new manager stopped by Emil's one morning soon after the slide and, needing help with the clean-up, hired Price on the spot.

There was more work than a bulldozer could handle and no electricity to boot. The hot springs manager handed Price a shovel. The job paid no wages. Dunn dug out just one of the tubs, discovered the wine cellar, and invaded a pantry rich with fancy hams and smoked oysters. Price had "a wonderful winter," soaking his weary bones while sipping bottle after bottle of excellent cabernet. One fine spring day, a carload of poets drove in for the weekend. When Larry Ferlinghetti, Mike McClure (and his wife, Joanna), Ronnie Bladen, and Jim and Beverly Harmon asked about renting rooms, Price told them the place was closed but they were free to camp. He moved them into an empty cabin. The poets arrived well provisioned with good food and wine. The hot springs remained without electricity, so Price lit some candles and built a fire. He also opened up the main lodge.

Later, down at the baths, Price uncorked the last of the cellar's vintage treasures. When the manager discovered the nonpaying guests, he fired Dunn. "You can't fire me," Price taunted. "I quit last week." The gathered poets were much amused by the heated exchange. "Relax," they told the enraged manager. "Just relax. We'll take him out of here. He can have a ride with us." The poets asked Price if he wanted to head up to San Francisco. "Hell, yeah, sure," he replied. "Why not?"

They bundled into the dilapidated car, keeping the spirit of the weekend joyously alive by driving straight to Berkeley and a scheduled re-creation of the previous fall's Six Gallery reading. Michael McClure was one of the evening's participants. Like most sequels, this repeat performance opted for a grander setting and more-elaborate trappings. Staged in a Berkeley theater where the auditorium was decorated with large Robert LaVigne pen drawings of Allen Ginsberg and Peter Orlovsky making love, the reading featured all six of the original poets. Kenneth Rexroth again served as master of ceremonies.

Price Dunn had the time of his life. He'd never heard of Allen Ginsberg or the others but was immediately swept up into the emotional atmosphere. "It was like a prayer meeting," Price recalled. The stage was set with six wooden throne-sized chairs (one for each poet) left over from a previous theatrical production. Having hitchhiked from North Carolina, Jack Kerouac passed the hat for wine, kept the jug circulating, and led the chanting response when Ginsberg intoned "Howl."

Price went to live in a large house on Scott Street in San Francisco, a block away from Rexroth's place. It was an enclave of poets, shared by Michael and Joanna McClure, Jim and Beverly Harmon, filmmaker Larry Jordan, and Ronald Bladen. Jordan and Bladen had moved a printing press into the basement. "It was a center for things to happen," Joanna McClure recalled. "What you'd call a commune, except they didn't have communes then." Bladen, Harmon, and McClure edited and published *Ark II–Moby I* in the Scott Street house. Price slept in the basement with the press.

Joanna remembered Price as always cheerful and "good-spirited," talking to himself and the cats. She thought of him as the "ultimate primitive." Joanna also recalled the evening Price Dunn headed for the Golden Gate Bridge with suicide on his mind and his weary return the following morning. "Said he spent the whole night sitting out on one of the girders and it was really cold." Less than a month later, after Shig Murao broke his leg in a motorcycle accident, Lawrence Ferlinghetti hired Price to work as a clerk in City Lights.

In August of 1956, when Richard Brautigan first showed up in the bookstore, perusing poetry titles and scanning the bulletin board, Price manned the cash register behind the counter. He thought the taciturn blond stranger "was like a spider man, because he was so tall and stooped." Price never spoke with Richard in the shop but remembered Ferlinghetti "making a remark about that weird poet." On another occasion, after a Brautigan visit to City Lights, Ferlinghetti said, "There's a guy who really hates his mother."

"How in the hell do you know that?" Price demanded. His boss changed the subject without ever answering his question. Before the tall blond poet returned and Price could investigate the matter further, he was astonished to see the hot springs' manager stroll into City Lights. After they exchanged a few good-natured insults, he asked Price if he'd like to return to Big Sur and go back to work for him.

For Price, it was business as usual. One morning a week after returning, he sat in the kitchen of the lodge enjoying a cup of coffee when Dennis Murphy wandered in. He and Price were about the same age and "liked each other immediately." Dennis was writing a novel (*The Sergeant*, published in 1958 and made into a movie starring Rod Steiger, with a screenplay by Murphy), which received the first Joseph Henry Jackson Award while still a work in progress. Price was fascinated by hearing about the process, as he also had literary aspirations. "I need my place over there fixed up," Murphy said. "I need a handyman. Why don't you come to work for me?"

Dennis lived on the other side of Hot Springs Creek on an adjacent plateau along the north rim where his grandfather, Dr. Murphy, had built a huge gabled house back when he bought the springs, hoping to turn the place into a health spa. To Price, it was "like a fantasy movie, a rich guy's castle." Just opposite stood a little six-room cottage. Price moved in and dubbed it "the slave quarters." He went to work for the Murphys, landscaping a new lawn for the big house while Dennis toiled inside on his novel.

The two young men soon became "great friends." Dennis was a "holy terror," a federated boxer who "could fight like bloody hell." Price was also a fighter. He had lost his front teeth long before and now got a new plate (hors de combat) about two or three times a year. Price and Dennis "terrorized the coast," brawling in bars, taking no shit from anyone, eventually getting eighty-sixed from Nepenthy, a restaurant and bar on Highway 1, for being too handy with their dukes. All along, an eventual showdown between them felt inevitable. As Price recalled, "it was going to be who's the fastest gun in the West."

Their OK Corral moment occurred one night in the main lodge. Dennis Murphy came over for dinner, the primary attraction being the bar. At the time, a group of construction workers, hired to rebuild the cabins, had moved in, and Dennis began gambling with them after eating. Price was in the kitchen enjoying a postdinner drink when, *bam*, the door crashed open and Dennis's girlfriend, her face bloody from a solid punch, staggered in. Dennis, drunk and raging, charged after her, sweeping a pile of dishes off a table, intent on mayhem.

Price, the Bible Belt Galahad, stepped up to intercede, and the fight was on. Punching and pummeling, they battled their way out the back door and around the building. Price was not as fast or as skilled but Dennis was drunk, "so that sort of equaled it." The brawl turned into a pure slug-fest lasting nearly an hour. Careening back into the main dining room, Price and Dennis hurtled together through the tall French windows and sprawled on the ground outside, bleeding profusely.

Price was badly cut. Dennis had shards stuck in his back. The manager came around with a hose and washed them down. Afterward, he drove them to Carmel Convalescent Hospital, where Price needed thirteen stitches in his arm. He also needed a new place to stay. He knew a beautiful young woman who had stopped on her way down to meet Pat Boyd, a painter friend who lived south of Gorda. Someone loaned Price a kayak, and he and the girl set off by sea from the hot springs.

It was twenty-five miles down the coast to Willow Creek and Gorda. Pat Boyd and his mother, Madge, lived in a big house surrounded by pine trees on about 225 acres of prime Big Sur real estate. They welcomed the young seafaring couple with open arms. Pat Boyd, "a wiry little guy," had plans to start an artistic community. He and Price went to work together making it real. They dug out an area in the arroyo where a stream flowed, creating a water storage pool. Above this, Price and Pat carved a room-sized space into the sloping hillside. Using telephone poles and ply-wood, they built a small cabin with a deck overhanging the pond.

The dugout building stood high above the ocean, with a northern earth wall. The other three were largely glass, providing incredible views. Sliding shoji screens divided the cabin into a kitchen, a bedroom, and a living room. Price built a huge fireplace into the back wall, carrying sea-rounded rocks up from the beach. The cabin was without electricity and boasted only rudimentary gravity-flow plumbing, but its beautiful setting eclipsed any minor discomforts.

Sometime that spring, Price Dunn found himself at a Telegraph Hill party in hot pursuit of a lovely Jewish girl named Ydra. His long ardent chase lasted until the break of dawn. Everyone else had left the apartment, and the young couple sat together watching the sun come up when they met Ginny Alder, their hostess. She was with the tall blond poet Price had seen the previous summer in City Lights. He introduced himself as Dick. There had been no opportunity to get acquainted during the party, so Price invited everyone to come out for breakfast.

They went to the Star Café on Kearny Street in North Beach, down by the Hall of Justice. Early in the morning, the place was full of cops catching a bite before starting their shifts. Both Price and Richard "collected" great cheap places to eat, and the Star, where a big breakfast cost fifty-five cents, was high on both their lists. The open grill kitchen stood right behind a counter presided over by a Japanese counterman whose adroit movements put Dunn in mind of a ballet.

Price took Ydra back down to Big Sur, a place he had already started calling "Boydland," and they got to know each other a whole lot better for a couple of weeks before she vanished from his life forever. Price returned to the city and "started seeing Richard pretty regularly." They became drinking buddies, hanging out in North Beach, drawn together by a love of tall tales and preposterous wordplay. By then, Richard and Virginia had married and moved to the apartment on Washington Street. Richard and Price often shared a bottle of cheap wine up on Telegraph Hill. When the talk turned to women, Brautigan always said, "The thing to do is find a woman that will support you."

"That's a great dream," Price replied, "if you can do it."

City life had its attractions, but Price was never able to sit still for long and soon headed south again. In due time, he invited his new friends to come down and join him. When Dick and Ginny arrived in August, bringing along six jugs of wine as a house present, Price put them up in his cabin overlooking the pond and moved into a recently built A-frame across the way. The roof beams were so low by the fireplace that it was impossible to move about without cracking your head into the ceiling. The young newlyweds spread their sleeping bags between the dismembered parts of an old Matchless motorcycle Price intended on restoring someday. "It's a $400 bike," he remarked every time Richard complained after tripping over a stray piston. Price made no attempt to reassemble the machine, and it remained a mechanical jigsaw puzzle.

Richard and Virginia stayed in Big Sur with Price for a month on their first visit, gradually adapting to the comparative tranquility of rural bohemia. Brautigan worked on his poetry and engaged in literary conversation with Price Dunn. They disagreed over French poetry. Richard took the odd position that it wasn't of any worth because "you can say anything in French and it sounds good."

Price felt he was "prejudiced" against the musical nature of the language. He insisted that there was some great French poetry and introduced Richard to the work of Robert Desnos and Charles Baudelaire. Brautigan had a nodding acquaintance with their poetry but only read it again in depth at his friend's urging. "He just flipped out," Price said.

In the evenings after supper, they sat talking around the big fireplace. Price was a natural-born storyteller and regaled his friends with tall tales of his wayward youth. In spite of his Southern birth and upbringing, Price did not have a grandfather who fought for the Confederacy. The story existed only as a family fable, starring Great Uncle John as the "Confederate General." Price told the legend to Richard, "laughing about it because I knew it was a total myth."

Meals at Boydland were simple. Fresh vegetables harvested from the garden, abalone gathered at low tide, small rockfish caught when the sea was calm, hard flat bread Price baked with sacks of grain bought in Monterey, rice and potatoes from the same source, and occasionally quail and doves if Dunn got lucky with the .22. There might have been venison, Price being an eager poacher of the neighborhood deer, but he lacked ammunition for his trusty old 30-40 Krag. The only time he used the empty rifle was to terrify a stranded motorist caught siphoning gas out of his truck one night. "I scared the shit out of that son of a bitch!"

Some evenings, conversation became impossible. The moment the sun dipped beyond the western horizon, a mighty chorus of infernal croaking erupted from the perimeter of the pond only a few feet from the cabin. An enormous population of tiny frogs had mysteriously appeared, as if by spontaneous generation, and nothing seemed to quiet them down once they began their amorous *rek-kek-ka-kekking*. Shouting obscenities didn't work. Nor did firecrackers or hurled stones. Price thought perhaps alligators might do the trick, and Pat Boyd bought one at a pet shop. They introduced it into the pond but to no avail. The frogs disregarded the resident reptile and continued their nightly din. If the alligator ate frogs, he didn't eat near enough. He lived on happily in the pond until one night, during the course of a wild drunken party, someone spotted the strange beast and stole it.

A spell of heavy rain greeted the Brautigans' arrival. Ginny remembered that "it rained incessantly for ten days." Housebound, the visitors had no escape from the frogs. The little amphibians became a torture and a torment. Banging a broom handle on the plywood deck shut them up for a few moments, but soon, *peep-peep-peep*, they began again, building to a cacophonous crescendo. For reasons no one could comprehend, the wine Richard and Ginny brought turned out to be sour and remained untouched. Huddled by the fire, with the frogs louder than the rain drumming on the roof, someone suggested maybe wine might shut the frogs up. They rushed outside through the downpour and emptied six gallons of wine into the pond. The frogs croaked on, louder than ever.

Whenever the raucous frog-roar rose to a racket, reading became the only way to pass the time in the evening. Price Dunn remembered one night when he came into his cabin and found Richard reading by lamplight. It wasn't French poetry this time but a Gideon Bible Price kept among his library. A closer look revealed his friend taking notes. "What are you doing?" Price asked.

"I'm checking the punctuation out."

Incredulous, Price laughed. His friend was not joking, and they entered into a serious discussion regarding the importance of punctuation. "A period put in the right place can pierce the heart," Richard said, paraphrasing the Russian author Isaak Babel. An early surviving Brautigan notebook preserved his fascination with counting punctuation. Each page was divided into five wobbly vertical columns labeled commas, semicolons, colons, question marks, periods. Richard dutifully recorded the exact number of punctuation marks, page by page, in each of the columns.

On another evening, sitting at the big fireplace, Price suggested a new way to pass the time in the frog-loud night. "There was always a transient population at Boydland," Dunn recalled. One of those passing through had been a railroad worker from Berkeley named Al, who went "through a lid of grass in a day." Upon his departure, he left two or three ounces of marijuana behind. When Price came across this stash that night, he asked, "You guys want to get loaded?"

Richard didn't smoke and had never tried marijuana, but he made no objection. Ginny also seemed agreeable, so Price "rolled up some joints." When he saw his friend "didn't know how to inhale," Price instructed him in the proper method. "Now, you've got to hold that smoke in," he said. "Suck the air in with it and hold it." Virginia had done this before and didn't need toking lessons from Price. "She got high quicker. Virginia got giggly and laughing." Richard also got stoned, but "he was sort of like puzzled." Soon, the room grew very still, and they sat immobilized, listening to the infernal frogs. "We were just sort of quiet zombies there, not much conversation." That was the only time. Richard and Virginia had no interest in getting high again.

The oddest occurrence during the Brautigans' monthlong stay at Boydland owed nothing to the effects of narcotics. Hitching home from a shopping trip to Monterey one day, Price Dunn got a ride from a heavyset balding businessman driving an Aston Martin. He looked to be about fifty and very athletic. Price also thought that he was crazy. "He was just wacked out. Everybody was after him."

Upon arriving in Gorda, Price brought the paranoid businessman to the cabin and introduced him to Richard and Ginny. The man kept an expensive leather briefcase tightly clutched under his arm as if it might contain atomic secrets. Enlisting his new companions in his conspiracy, the crazy businessman opened the briefcase and passed it around. It was crammed with cash and stock certificates. Price held the briefcase in awe for just a moment and estimated it contained at least $100,000 in tightly bundled hundreds. The stranger snatched it back before he made a more accurate calculation.

The sight of so much loot opened up the possibility of exciting new vistas for Price. "I told Richard, 'I am going to get that money, Goddamnit! If I have to knock that son of a bitch in the head. I never hit anybody, you know, hurt anybody like that. I'm going to be a criminal now. I can see it. My criminal career is starting.'"

Sensing potential foul play, the businessman went into the kitchen and armed himself with a big butcher knife. Richard and Virginia were plainly frightened by all his crazy talk, the cash-crammed briefcase as menacing as a ticking time bomb. "He was talking totally irrationally," Ginny remembered, "and I knew we were going to be up all night." When not waving his knife around, the businessman sat by the fire and held his stock certificates over the flames. Virginia found this gesture "a total yawn." Go ahead and burn it, she thought, it's your money. Price had other ideas and urged him not to do anything stupid.

By morning, the heightened paranoia made the businessman anxious to hide his expensive automobile lest phantom pursuers find it and track him down. Price happily went along with the gag, getting an ax and a machete. The businessman hung on to the knife. They went up to the road and drove the Aston Martin in under the trees. All along, Price schemed how he was going to get his hands on the briefcase. Working together, the two men cut branches and piled them over the car until it was completely concealed. Partway through their camouflaging project, the businessman somehow slipped away unnoticed. "He was real sneaky," Price said. "I looked around and he's gone." As Price had the keys to the Aston Martin in his pocket, he figured all was not lost.

The businessman had answered the call of nature, venturing down to the "beautiful" outhouse with an ocean view that Price had built into the side of the hill. When he returned, the briefcase was gone. The businessman no longer had it with him.

"Where's the briefcase?" Price demanded.

"Don't worry," the stranger said. "I've taken care of it."

Later, Price sneaked back up the hill and searched the Aston Martin without success. He found no sign of the cash-filled briefcase. The businessman seemed in a jolly mood. He had taken to the bohemian life and wanted to join the commune. Back at home in San Jose he had an old truck, a "really good truck," which he offered to give to Price. It would be his initiation offering. Price instantly agreed with this plan. If he could keep the guy around, he stood a much better chance of finding the missing briefcase.

Price and the crazy stranger uncovered the Aston Martin and drove up to San Jose. The Brautigans gratefully stayed behind in Boydland, glad not to be under the same roof with a knife-wielding loony. When the two men arrived at the palatial South Bay home, they found the old truck parked out back. Price helped load it up with "all this shit" his wacky benefactor felt would be useful on a commune. They were just finishing when the businessman's son arrived, accompanied by a lawyer.

After cordial introductions, the businessman's son said, "My father really needs to be under psychiatric care. We appreciate your help. Where do you live? We'll send you back home."

Price agreed. There seemed no other choice. They gave him a lift to the bus station and even bought him a ticket to Monterey. All things considered, it struck him as pretty fair treatment. Price Dunn never saw the wacky businessman again but began searching the hillside around the out-house for the missing briefcase. He probed under the sagebrush and blackberry thickets, rolled over rocks and rotting logs, searched every nook and cranny large enough to conceal a hundred grand. "I went all over that damn hillside down there searching for that briefcase." Price never found it.

Richard and Virginia returned to San Francisco. The journey to Big Sur had been quite a trip. An element of magic adventure imbued the whole experience. It was more than the rustic life. Brautigan had plenty of experience roughing it as a kid. Rural settings also meant little to a country boy who had fled a bucolic environment for the gritty pleasures of the city. Rather, unpredictable Price Dunn provided the magic.

Who else would put an empty rifle to the head of a suspected gasoline thief or bring home a madman with a briefcase full of money or change his teeth three times a year. Price supplied marijuana and introduced alligators into a frog pond ecology. Price and his manic enthusiasms reacquainted Richard with the wonders of French literature. Not long after returning to the city, Brautigan started working on a serial poem featuring Baudelaire as the central recurring character. The Big Sur trip charged Richard Brautigan's creative batteries with the purest high-voltage energy. He had just met his very own Neal Cassady.

sixteen: scorpio rising

J ACK SPICER URGED Richard Brautigan to have his horoscope done, there being no shortage of astrologers in Frisco. The most prominent local stargazer was Gavin Arthur (homosexual grandson of President Chester A. Arthur), who lived in the East-West House, along with his friends Philip Whalen and Gary Snyder. Brautigan could not afford Gavin Arthur's services. Instead, he had an unknown astrologer draw up his chart, an unattributed horoscope probably completed sometime before July 1963, as the blank form on which it was prepared bears a printed address without a zip code.

Richard Gary Brautigan was an Aquarian with his moon in Sagittarius. Spicer queried Brautigan on these and other aspects of his horoscope, offering his own personal take on various sidereal alignments, reinterpreting the importance of having Mercury in the Fourth House (an aspect Richard shared with the mad dancer Vasily Nijinsky), which can indicate a "Utopian fixation."

Peter Miller, who first met Richard in 1969, remembered the writer's ongoing fascination with astrology. "He was very keen on it and very aware that James Joyce was an Aquarius and that he was an Aquarius and that Aquarians are always being characterized as having two sides, the visionary side and then this very strict side, the saturnine side—Ron Loewinsohn was his saturnine friend—and he was very conservative. He had each sign quite declinated [*sic*]. For example, he kept saying, 'All my girlfriends are Aries.' Very fiery. He didn't want it to be an intellectual relationship. That just was not his deal. Maybe it was too intimate."

Because Richard Brautigan had incorrectly given the hour of his birth as one minute past midnight, the half-hour discrepancy caused his astrologer to mistakenly note a rising sign in Libra. Although not much else changed in his chart, the error resulted in a faulty evaluation of Brautigan's personality. Both Spicer and the astrologer likely told him that he was relationship-oriented, friendly and sharing in nature, responsive, gregarious.

In fact, Richard's actual birth at 12:30 AM made him Scorpio rising. His nature was 180 degrees opposite from what his advisers deduced. Having a rising sign in Scorpio indicated a secretive, cautious, reserved, privately creative personality, a much more accurate assessment of Brautigan's nature. To whatever degree Richard believed in astrology, he carried this erroneous sense of self to the grave, preserving the misleading star chart among his papers until the day he died.

seventeen: scaling mount parnassus

1958, YEAR OF the Edsel and the hula hoop, also marked the birth of Barbie and the Xerox copier. America successfully launched *Explorer I*, her first satellite, while, closer to Earth, Charlie Starkweather began his murder-spree love-romp across Nebraska. The enormous success of *Howl* and *On the Road* focused national attention on the tight-knit North Beach bohemian community. America clamored for lurid tales of the bearded, sandal-shod, pad-dwelling, dope-smoking beatniks.

When the poet Lew Welch moved to San Francisco in October of 1957 he still wrote newspaper ad copy for Montgomery Ward. According to local legend, during his brief advertising career Welch penned the immortal line "Raid Kills Bugs Dead." In a letter to Philip Whalen, Lew recorded his immediate reaction to the excesses of the current scene. "Telegraph Hill with its children-type Bohemes was a real shock. Saw one 20 year old in a black greatcoat, pointed patent leather button shoes, black stockings, spiky umbrella, and shaved skull [. . .] it is sad to see that fine section ruined and expensive."

The following summer, a wave of tourists flooded the Beach and roamed upper Grant Avenue in search of bohemian highjinks. In their wake sprang up numerous pottery shops, bead stringers, and sandal makers. The moment Miss Smith's Tea Room closed its doors forever in '58, the Coffee Gallery took its place at the same address, offering poetry, jazz, and the singular talents of Lord Buckley. In May 1958, the *Examiner* began a three-part series on the Beats, which aroused the interest of both curious hangers-on and the local police. Kerouac again unwittingly fueled the frenzy, publishing both *The Subterraneans* and *The Dharma Bums* in 1958, further padding the passenger lists of the North Beach tour buses even as his buddy Neal Cassady was busted for possessing three joints and sentenced to five years to life at San Quentin.

Undercover police nailed Lenny Bruce for obscenity after laughing through his performance at the hungry i. The same bluecoat bluenose attitude compelled Leo Krikorian to take down a Robert LaVigne nude hanging in The Place. "The city fathers decided they didn't want any more lifestyles like those being displayed in the Beach," recalled alto saxophonist Norwood "Pony" Poindexter, who played at both the Jazz Cellar and the Coffee Gallery.

Earlier in the year, Richard Brautigan caught Lenny Bruce's act at Ann's 440 Club during the comedian's first major multiweek performance, when much of the material released on his second album was recorded. Located at 440 Broadway, down the block from the recently opened Enrico's Sidewalk Café, the place was owned by Ann Dee, a cabaret singer whose vocal chords had given out. Formerly Mona's Club 440, Frisco's first lesbian bar, which closed in 1948, Ann's 440 was the spot where a nineteen-year-old singer named Johnny Mathis got his first break.

Robert Briggs described Ann's 440 Club as "a very hard number [. . .] very hard drug scene. Very hard prostitute scene. Very hard criminal scene. Very hard god-knows-what scene." Briggs worked nearby at the Jazz Workshop (474 Broadway) checking IDs. He remembered Brautigan's initial reaction to Lenny Bruce. "Richard was fractured," he said. "Richard was stunned. He was a bit lost for words." Knowing Brautigan to be "very critical with himself and with everything," Briggs recalled that Richard, who might ordinarily have rejected the comedian's act for its raw profanity, "always thought highly of Bruce."

Robert Frank, Alfred Leslie, and Jack Kerouac's classic twenty-six-minute Beat film, *Pull My Daisy*, came out in 1959. That same year, MGM released *The Beat Generation*, a Cinemascope B movie, while a popular television series, *The Many Loves of Dobie Gillis*, introduced a bongo-playing, goatee-wearing character named Maynard G. Krebs to a mainstream audience. Ever-larger hordes of curious beatnik watchers crowded into Greenwich Village and North Beach. By January 1960, The Place closed its doors forever. "I got rid of The Place because the scene had changed," Leo Krikorian remarked. "Everything in the Beach changed, and I didn't dig the scene anymore."

For Richard Brautigan, the decline of North Beach was not a cause for deep mourning. In an unpublished short story ("Going Home to the Locust") he described beatniks as "those grunion of Grant Avenue who throw themselves up onto the cement." Having come to Frisco seeking his future as a writer, Brautigan observed the social intercourse of Hube the Cube, Red Fred, Mad Marie, Badtalking Charlie, and Gene the Scrounge with the dispassionate distance of a lepidopter-ist studying butterfly migrations. Richard was a regular at The Place, yet when the bar went out of business he followed Jack Spicer and his crowd to Gino & Carlo's on Green Street and did his drinking elsewhere.

Gino & Carlo's was an Italian workingman's place, long, narrow, and nondescript, with the old bar to the left of the entrance. Two tables (one called the "poet's table"), stood up front, flanked by the jukebox and a cigarette machine. A couple pool tables occupied the back room. A black metal mailbox hung on the wall up front, waiting to receive contributions for the many mim-eographed publications of the era. Some people called Gino & Carlo's "Jack Spicer's living room," but Don Carpenter remembered it differently. "The bar is a very tough place and it's a very macho place," he said. "When you go into Gino & Carlo's you leave your delicacy behind."

Around this time, Robert Creeley rolled back into Frisco from New Mexico, where he was teaching at a boy's school. One night in a North Beach bar, Ron Loewinsohn introduced him to Brautigan. They hit it off right away. Richard had always been fascinated with World War II, and Bob's wild tales of interrupting his Harvard education to serve in Burma and India in the American Field Service from 1944 to 1945 struck a vivid chord in his imagination. Brautigan and Creeley wandered through the watering holes of North Beach, talking the night away, an echo of the energy Creeley felt on an earlier visit to Frisco in '55, when Ed Dorn, his friend from Black Mountain, met him at the Greyhound bus station (Ed worked at the baggage depot) and they sat up until dawn with Allen Ginsberg, drinking and talking at Dorn's place.

At some point during this later evening, Creeley recalled going up to Richard Brautigan's apartment. Because she had a day job, Ginny was fast asleep. "We sort of drifted in, checked, and then drifted out," Creeley recalled. "And we went classically back to the bar" and "started roam-ing around from there." Just another poets' lost evening on the town. "I can well understand why their marriage didn't work out," Creeley said in retrospect.

His wife, Bobbie, recalled Richard telling her of another episode that indicated his marriage was not made in heaven. The Brautigans were having a dinner party. It was spaghetti as usual. Upset about something, Ginny nagged at Richard as the bowl of pasta made its way around the table from guest to guest. "She won't leave him alone," Bobbie Creeley remembered. At a certain point, Brautigan had enough of his wife's harangue. He reached over, grabbed the bowl of spaghetti, and upended it over his head. Richard put the empty bowl back on the table without saying a word. "He's sitting there quietly continuing to eat with his head covered with spaghetti. It was dripping down his face and onto his shoulders like a wig." Richard laughed out loud when he told this story to Bobbie. "That shut her up!" he howled.

Brautigan continued to see his work appear in print. Early in 1957, the first issue of a quarterly called *Danse Macabre* was published out of a small office in Manhattan Beach, California. Volume 1, number 1, contained poetry by Carl Larsen, Lilith Lorraine, Judson Crews, and on page 18, two poems by Richard Brautigan."

In the fall of 1957, *Hearse: A Vehicle Used to Convey the Dead*, a little fifty-cent magazine, began publication in Eureka, California. E. V. Griffith, the editor, prefaced his hand-sewn quarterly with "carrying poetry, prose, artwork and incidental cadaver [*sic*] to the Great Cemetery of the American Intellect [. . .]" The second issue of *Hearse* came out early in 1958, and "Coroner's Report" on the inside back cover reprinted one of Richard Brautigan's poems from *Danse Macabre*.

Kenn Davis spent a lot of time with Richard and Ginny, sketch pad always close at hand. He drew them together at Mike's Pool Hall and captured Richard eating pork buns (his favorites, bought by the sack at Sam Wo's) in Washington Square. Davis sketched Brautigan reading at The Place on Blabbermouth Night and on the walks they took together through Chinatown, Richard staring in the shop windows, fascinated by the chickens and ducks hanging on display, his poet's eye drawn to the stacked slabs of smoked fish, iridescent gold and silver like some mysterious Asian treasure.

Many of Kenn's sketches were quick thumbnails. He worked them up later into finished drawings. Davis accompanied the Brautigans on several trips to Big Sur, from time to time, he and Richard flew handmade kites down at the Marina Green. Kenn sketched this and the fishing expeditions he and Dick and Ginny took in the spring over to Sausalito, where they dangled their lines off the end of a pier, hoping "for sunfish and such."

Kenn Davis lived in an apartment on Francisco Street. "It had a back porch with marvelous north light." This prompted the artist to ask his friend Dick if he could paint his portrait. Brautigan responded with enthusiasm and sat for Davis "two or three times, an hour or so each," while Kenn painted in oils on stretched linen. Richard posed without his glasses, and his penetrating eyes burned with a mournful gaze. As Davis worked, Brautigan watched over his shoulder from time to time, making encouraging comments. "That's interesting," he said. "That's good."

The painting was shown in the Cellini Gallery as part of the San Francisco Museum of Modern Art's "little extravaganza" called "The Rolling Renaissance." Brautigan hung the portrait in his North Beach apartment, taking it with him from move to move. It eventually went along to the apartment on Geary Street in 1966. When fame followed the publication of *Trout Fishing*, a year or so later, Richard gave the painting back to Kenn, saying "it was not the way he looked anymore." Brautigan had grown his distinctive mustache and had much longer hair. The portrait no longer resembled the public image he had carefully created. There was talk of having Kenn paint a new likeness, but nothing ever came of it.

In February 1958, Richard completed an ambitious nine-part surrealistic poem he called "The Galilee Hitch-Hiker." Always a lapidary writer by inclination, Brautigan skillfully crafted elements of his personal biography with a unique abstract vision. The poem's nine sections were bound together by the recurring character of French poet Charles Baudelaire, whose *Les Fleurs du Mal* explored the discovery of hidden "correspondences" between beauty and vice and was deemed immoral when first published in 1857.

In Part 1, Baudelaire, "driving a Model A," picks up Jesus Christ, hitchhiking in Galilee. The Savior is on his way to Golgotha, where he has a concession "at the carnival." Part 3, entitled "1939," recalled Brautigan's childhood "in the slums / of Tacoma." His mother lets him turn the crank of the coffee grinder, and he makes believe it is a hurdy-gurdy. Baudelaire, the ghostly spectator, pretends to be a monkey, "hopping up and down / and holding out / a tin cup." Part 4, "The Flowerburgers," has Baudelaire running a hamburger stand in San Francisco. Instead of meat, the dead French poet places flowers between the halved buns. When customers demand a burger with onions, "Baudelaire would give them / a flowerburger / instead [. . .]"

Part 8, "Insane Asylum," speaks directly from the heart of Brautigan's painful personal experience and describes Baudelaire going "to the insane asylum / disguised as a / psychiatrist." He stays for two months, the same length of time that Brautigan spent at the Salem Hospital. When Baudelaire leaves the asylum, it "loved him so much" it "followed / him all over / California," rubbing "up against his / leg like a / strange cat." Part 9, "My Insect Funeral," ends the poem on a melancholy note, recalling the tiny cemetery the poet maintained as a child, when he dug little graves under the rosebush with a spoon, burying insects in matchboxes and dead birds wrapped in red cloth.

Later that February, Richard and Ginny returned to Big Sur for another zany visit with their unpredictable friend Price Dunn. Whenever there was a break in the near-continuous Pacific storms, Richard set out to explore the fishing possibilities. After being cabin-bound for five rainy days, he and Price and Ginny wandered far up narrow, rushing Gorda Creek. They scrambled under the manzanita for a mile or so along the mountain side. The deluge had transformed the creek into a rain-swollen torrent. For reasons beyond logic, they elected to cross over.

Sliding down the muddy slope with reckless élan, Price jumped straight into the raging current. Ginny followed, injuring her left knee on an underwater boulder. The water was chest-high and "running really fast." Unable to swim, Richard remained on the bank, clutching his fishing pole, of no help to his wife and best pal. "He was running back and forth on the top of the ridge like a madman." Ginny and Price decided to wade downstream around the tangle of manzanita, where a crossing might be possible. They struggled on, floundering in the rushing torrent. "We just hung on and climbed back out," Virginia recalled. "It was scary."

The winter weather remained wet and cold, rain pelting down against the makeshift dugout. They met Pat Boyd's companion, the granddaughter of Aimee Semple McPherson. Price claimed she had once worked as a part-time prostitute in L.A. Pregnant and recently returned from New Mexico, she called herself Alicia Tree. A couple months later, Price delivered her baby. They all spent a good deal of time gathered by the fireplace, drinking tea. Richard kept busy with his notebook. Among the poems he wrote during the stay was "The Castle of the Cormorants," a mournful, evocative piece in which Hamlet, carrying a cormorant, marries a wet drowned Ophelia.

March 1958 saw the publication of *Hearse* number 3 with two poems by Richard Brautigan, both from the Leslie Woolf Hedley collection *Four New Poets*. The spring issue of *Epos* (vol. 9, no. 3) appeared early in 1958, with Brautigan's poem "Kingdom Come." It was never collected or reprinted elsewhere. The featured poet was Miller Williams, a professor at the University of Arkansas and the father of future singer/songwriter Lucinda Williams.

That same spring, Ron Loewinsohn published his first book of poetry, *Watermelons*. He and Richard Brautigan had fallen out (the first of many schisms between them) and were no longer speaking. When Richard saw a copy of Ron's book he leafed through the pages until he came to a poem once dedicated to him, "beautifully minus a dedication." He smiled and said "Shit," tossing the book aside. Years later, Brautigan eliminated previous dedications whenever former friends offended him.

In May, with Jack Spicer's encouragement, Joe Dunn and the White Rabbit Press published *The Galilee Hitch-Hiker* in an edition of two hundred copies. Richard asked Kenn Davis to design the cover art. "So I showed him some ideas that I had," Kenn recalled, "and he thought this one would work. I did another little rough in pencil and said, let me expand this a little bit." Davis went off for a day or so and came back with a preliminary ink drawing, "kind of semifinished," thinking to do "a more polished version" once he had Brautigan's approval. "But he liked that one just fine. He says, 'Don't touch it. That's great. We'll just go with that.'"

The wispy ink sketch portrays a nearly deserted carnival midway where hot dog vendors and balloon salesmen wander aimlessly beneath a deserted Ferris wheel. Looming ominously in the background, a dark cross towers above Calvary, the ghostly framework of a roller coaster swirling around it in the crosshatched sky. All in all, a handsome little book for a quarter.

Because White Rabbit Press lacked binding equipment, the printed pages and red cover wraps were delivered to Brautigan unbound. Richard, Ginny, and Kenn Davis sat around the Brautigans' kitchen table hand-stitching the little sixteen-page chapbook together with needles and thread, "drinking wine and yakking." When all two hundred were finished, they tackled the problem of distribution. City Lights could be counted on to take a few, but the rest had to be placed in other bookstores through pounding the pavement and knocking on doors. By June, copies of *The Galilee Hitch-Hiker* had been distributed to all the local booksellers.

While making book delivery rounds in North Beach, Richard discovered an intriguing new hangout on the corner of Greenwich and Grant had opened earlier in the month. No sign outside nor any descriptive lettering on the show windows identified the place. Only an oil painting hanging in the window on the Grant Avenue side provided a clue. It portrayed a multiracial group standing around a table, which held a loaf of bread and a bottle of wine. The street people called the place "Bread and Wine."

It appeared to be a coffeehouse. The high-ceilinged thirty-by-forty-foot storefront contained an odd assortment of tables and chairs, crowded bookshelves, and a long counter with a five-gallon coffee urn next to a tall pyramid of inverted mugs. The look was European, clean, functional, entirely secular. Nothing suggested any religious affiliation although the place had been sponsored by the Congregational Church. It wasn't long before poet Bob Kaufman, "the Black American

Rimbaud," dubbed it the "Bread and Wine Mission." His offhand quip stuck. Soon, everyone on the Beach called the corner spot "The Mission."

The pastor of this unorthodox sanctuary was Pierre Delattre, a blond, blue-eyed, twenty-eight-year-old graduate of the University of Chicago Divinity School. Interested in "the history of religion as it applied to literature," Delattre had never intended to become a minister. He wanted to be a writer. Always casually dressed in old tennis shoes, bleached blue jeans, and a hooded white sweatshirt with a large pectoral cross hanging around his neck on a black cord, Pierre Delattre held an undergraduate degree in English from the University of Pennsylvania. He'd also worked construction in Puerto Rico, unloaded a lacquering oven at a tin can factory, and "following in Kerouac's footsteps," toiled as a switchman for the Southern Pacific.

Delattre had come to believe that the true center of spiritual life was not in churches but "out in the streets among musicians and poets." He gave a speech at a large Congregational church in Oakland about how "the institutional church was the greatest impediment to religious life in America." He was approached afterward by Reverend Robert W. Spike, head of the Congregational Board of Home Missions. Spike, murdered a few years later, had been the pastor of Judson Memorial Church in New York's Greenwich Village from 1949 to 1955. He asked Delattre, "What if we found you a place where you could just be present and encourage the spiritual dimension of what's going on in poetry and jazz and the arts in general?" Pierre thought this was a great idea, and the ecumenical coffeehouse was born. The Missions Board rented an empty storefront in North Beach. Delattre was ordained into the Congregational Church. The young minister told his benefactors, "Don't expect me to be trying to convert anybody to Christianity. I want to be equally responsive to Judaism and Buddhism and Hinduism and so forth."

Delattre moved into an apartment above the store with his wife, Lois (an actress and psychologist), and their two children. He commissioned an artist named Del Lederle to paint the picture in the front window. Bread and Wine was open for business. "Almost immediately, we were jammed with people," Delattre recalled. "We had about two poetry readings a week, right from the start, and a lot of stuff going on with drumming and dancing and music. And I had a street theater that was performing inside and outside. It was pretty quickly a center."

Richard Brautigan wandered into Bread and Wine not long after it opened. He was hanging out with George Stanley, a member of the Spicer group known for his garrulous, argumentative nature. Delattre knew Stanley as part of a gang of unruly poets who called themselves "The Disruptionists." Once, they smashed a piano to pieces with sledgehammers, "symbolically destroying bourgeois culture." Another time, a couple of them peed on the floor of the Mission prior to a reading, the ultimate critical put-down.

Richard and Pierre quickly became friends, in part because Brautigan was so clearly his own man and not a part of any group. Delattre also admired Richard's poetry. "He was one of the first of the poets in that area to be really caught up in popular cultural mythology," he recalled. "But rather than using Billy the Kid and other American icons, he was going European, and his big kick at that time was Baudelaire."

A reading at Bread and Wine soon followed. Brautigan was featured on a bill with Ebbe Borregaard, Joanne Kyger, and Gary Snyder. After two years abroad in Kyoto, Snyder had returned to the Bay Area in April and moved back to his simple shack on the slopes of Mount Tamalpais. Joanne and Gary met recently at The Place, and their intricate mating dance began. Pierre Delattre grouped Joanne with the Disruptionists. "I don't know what there was about her," he recalled. "She would walk into a room, and chaos would break out." Kyger confessed to being "totally stoned" with nervous exhilaration on the night of the reading.

Richard Brautigan was also very nervous that night. Delattre remembered how he had to get drunk before he could appear before an audience. "He was very shy, very skittish," downing a bottle of wine prior to his reading. The poets all read by candlelight, sitting on stools beside another stool supporting a big candelabrum. Afterward, Delattre "passed the hat" among the crowd and divvied up the take. Each of the poets received $5. It was the first time any of them had ever been paid for a reading.

Brautigan certainly needed the money. He and Ginny saved every penny for a trip they were planning. For almost a year, ever since a friend loaned them a copy of *Popol Vuh: The Sacred Book of the Ancient Quiche Maya*, they had yearned to travel to Mexico. They had friends living in Oaxaca, and having heard the exchange rate was good, they talked about maybe heading down there. Mexico seemed like an inexpensive and fascinating place to live, plus Ginny spoke some Spanish, so they decided to go south that summer.

The Brautigans gave away most of their few possessions and packed up the rest of their stuff in the Washington Street apartment. Cleaning out a closet, Richard came across Ron Loewinsohn's Christmas gift, the medieval manuscript page. He had tossed it in there after their friendship soured. "The last thing we need around is something that asshole gave us," Brautigan wrote several years later, describing how he in turn gave the manuscript page to a ninety-year-old woman who lived downstairs. Not long after, she moved to the Tenderloin, a single room in the Kit Carson Hotel being all she could afford on her pathetic $70-a-month pension. And that's how Richard imagined the final resting place of the illuminated manuscript, "stuffed under the bed [. . .] surrounded by the smell of boiling celery root."

On June 16, Richard sold another pint of blood, adding twenty bucks to the kitty. They waited for Ginny's federal income tax return, and when the check finally arrived in early summer the Brautigans headed south. They hitchhiked from San Francisco to Nogales, Arizona. It was excruciatingly hot in the desert, never a pleasant prospect when thumbing a ride. While on the road, Richard stopped shaving, deciding to grow a beard.

After crossing the border, the young couple boarded a bargain-basement-priced bus, embarking on an arduous journey along the Gulf Coast past Guaymas to Mazatlán, where they stopped at a cheap hotel. Ginny remembered "a kind of night bus trip to forever." The next leg was much shorter, and they traveled by bus only as far as Tepic, the nondescript capital of the state of Nayarit. They spent the night here. In the morning, another bus took them over the mountains through Guadalajara onto the central plateau toward Mexico City.

Richard and Ginny rolled into the "ass end" of the Federal District, past "a huge ten-mile slum," acres and acres of hardscrabble shacks like a tidewater line of poverty washed up against the gates of the city. They caught a cab at the bus station and asked to be taken to an inexpensive hotel. "I don't know who he thought we were or what he thought we wanted," Ginny recalled. The driver took them to a whorehouse in the Zona Rosa. Their room reeked of cheap perfume. A garish maroon and yellow satin spread covered the bed. Having no place else to go, they stayed for the night.

In the morning, Richard and Ginny found a different hotel, "more like a bed and breakfast," eventually staying in a couple places, wandering around the city, sightseeing for about eight or nine days. One afternoon, Brautigan, sitting by himself in a sidewalk restaurant eating the *comida cor-rida*, observed a couple kids moving from table to table, carrying three or four beige puppies. The kids approached and asked if he wanted to buy one. Richard declined, knowing dogs would not be welcome in his hotel room. He thought the puppies were "cute, but doomed." After the urchins left, Richard reflected on their lives. "The kids had about as much future as the dogs," he scrawled in his notebook twenty-four years later. "In Mexico, I wouldn't bet on the future of anything."

After a week or so, Richard and Ginny took another, more luxurious bus south to Oaxaca, Oaxaca. Here they entered a world far different from the slums and high-rises of the capital. The population of the state and city of Oaxaca consisted largely of indigenous Zapotecs, and the citizens crowding the narrow streets fronted by stately Spanish colonial architecture were all Indian, their faces innocent of any European stain. At the time, there were only nine Americans living in Oaxaca.

Richard and Ginny located their friend John from Marin, who together with his wife and young daughter made up one-third of the Oaxacan gringo population. With John's help, they looked long and hard for a place to live, finally locating a house in the cornfields on the outskirts of town. When it rained, water puddled on the flat roof and the ceiling leaked. For almost all of the three months the Brautigans occupied the little place, several men laid new tile above their heads, a never-ending job. The workmen were always polite, but Ginny thought they were up on the roof "just to observe us."

In the marketplace, observant shawl-wrapped onion vendors were considerably less courteous. These were Tehuanas, women from the Gulf of Tehuantepec on the Pacific Coast, noted for their flashy gold jewelry and rude behavior. Ginny remembered how they loved teasing Richard, calling him *chivo* (goat) because of his new red beard. The Brautigans spent a lot of time sitting in sidewalk cafés fronting the fancy hotels surrounding the Zócalo, Oaxaca's central plaza. One could nurse a drink, watch the evening *pasejar*, and listen to brass band music played in the ornate circular bandstand at the center of the square. The price of a Coke or a brandy entitled a customer to use the hotel lobby's clean tiled bathrooms.

On the plaza, they befriended a ragged twelve-year-old urchin who hung around, selling Chiclets or shining shoes. He approached Richard and Ginny, wanting to give them a shine. They wore sandals, and this became a big joke, laughter cutting through the language barrier. Richard asked the boy if he ever went to school. The kid explained he was a member of the Union of Unsalaried Workers, which ran a night school for boys like him. Richard and Ginny were greatly amused at the notion of unpaid workers joining a union. Perhaps they paid imaginary dues.

The long walk into town often became an ordeal. Rain turned the thick red clay soil of the surrounding cornfields into a nearly impassable gumbo. Staying at home wasn't a whole lot of fun. Frustrated by his inability to learn more than a few words of Spanish, Richard began drinking more and more. Ginny remembered him hurling his brandy glass against the wall, furious at having almost no one to talk with. Brautigan's alcohol problem intensified. For the first time in his nascent drinking life, he was able to afford hard liquor. Brandy was very cheap and the local *mexicalli*, in black ceramic flasks, cheaper still. Distilled from the fermented juice of the agave, rainwater-clear, and potent as liquid fire, mescal was rumored to have hallucinogenic properties.

Fueled by mescal, Richard wanted to get hold of some peyote. Marijuana was readily available, but Brautigan had no interest in *mota*. "We were always looking for peyote," Virginia remembered. "Richard never wanted to smoke marijuana." The search for the elusive mescaline-rich cactus took them as far afield as the little town of Ixtlan, with its fine old colonial church. (A year later, Brautigan wrote a never-published poem titled "Ixtlan," in which he reflected on the cobblestones of Calle de Eternidad, "the Street of Eternity," and drinking mescal "under the century plants.") As far as the peyote hunt, Ixtlan became just another wild-goose chase in a bizarre and futile quest.

Trips up to Monte Alban were more satisfying. An ancient ceremonial center located atop the treeless hills southeast of the city of Oaxaca, thirteen hundred feet above the valley floor, Monte Alban is one of the oldest inhabited sites in Mexico, a sacred mountain top first settled as early as 1000 BC. Constructed around 500 BC, about the time Cyrus the Great roared out of Persia and conquered Babylonia, the fabled temple-city endured through many diverse cultures (Olmec, Maya, Zapotec, Mixtec) until the Aztec conquered all in 1469.

Richard and Ginny explored every inch of the metropolis where ancient architects leveled the mountain top to create a vast central plaza longer than seven football fields. They investigated the restored palaces and frescoed tombs, wandered around the ball court and the observatory, and climbed the looming central temple complex by each of its four monumental stairways. They found numerous obsidian knives. Most of the urban center surrounding the plaza had not been excavated, and quantities of flakes and pottery shards littered the shrub-covered mounds.

The Brautigans ventured south to Mitla, one of the best-preserved sites in Mexico, about forty kilometers from Oaxaca. Aldous Huxley found Mitla "strangely unlike any of the other pre-Columbian ruins." He called the geometric patterns on the low temple facades "petrified weaving," thinking them based on textile designs. Richard and Ginny caught a ride with an amorous dentist who owned a big green Dodge station wagon. The DDS fell in love with Richard's buxom wife after the poet consulted him about a toothache. He chauffeured the young sightseers down to the "Place of the Dead" in a frenzy of unrequited machismo.

After a Oaxacan stay lasting more than two months, it was time to head for home. Ginny thought they remained "a little too long. There was way too much alcohol available." The Brautigans had planned on returning by the same route they had followed down from the border, but when they got to Mexico City they discovered that torrential rains along the Pacific Coast had washed out several bridges and the road was closed in many places. Their only option was to travel up through the interior. Richard and Ginny caught a bus bound for Aguascalientes at midnight.

Two hot and dusty days later they made it to Ciudad Juárez on the banks of the Rio Grande. It was night when Richard and Ginny crossed the border into El Paso and took a room in a cheap hotel smelling of disinfectant. The next morning, they were on the road again, catching a ride to Las Cruces, New Mexico, where a traveling salesman picked them up and drove them as far as Phoenix, Arizona. The Brautigans figured they would spend the night in a hotel there. Richard decided "to try my luck with my thumb for a few minutes before looking for a place to stay." After two vehicles passed them by, a truck stopped and drove the couple straight through, "all the way across the Mojave desert in the cool of the night to be in Los Angeles at dawn."

Back in San Francisco, Richard and Ginny crashed with friends while looking for a new apartment. Although everything seemed much the same, a lot had changed while they were away. Joanne Kyger and Gary Snyder had become an item. At a Sunday afternoon gathering at George Stanley's apartment, Snyder read from his remarkable new work, *Myths and Texts*, sitting underneath a table with Jack Spicer perched cross-legged above. Spicer approved of Snyder's poetry, remarkable considering his scorn for the Beats, an affiliation not entirely of Snyder's choosing.

Literary gossip buzzed about Russell FitzGerald, Jack Spicer's live-in lover, and his blatant seduction of Bob Kaufman ("I took him to the Colombo Hotel and sucked his big cock"). Kaufman, dead drunk at the time, must have had ambivalent feelings about the whole affair, for he married his wife, Eileen, that same year. "Half-Jew and half-black," crowed Robert Duncan, recalling the Kaufman incident years later. He knew Spicer's prejudices and how FitzGerald's betrayal must have stung.

Lew Welch had quit his job in advertising, left his wife, and was driving a cab for a living. He and his college buddies Gary Snyder and Philip Whalen formed a circle, centered on Buddhist-inspired poetry, which included Joanne Kyger, who also lived at the East-West House. Both Welch and Snyder read at Bread and Wine that summer. Kyger noted how Welch said, "That's over," as he hung his wedding ring on a nail sticking from the wall of Marin-An, Snyder's Mill Valley shack. Lew started spending time with Joanne and her pal Nemi Frost. "He's not interested in your poetry," Snyder told his lover. "He just wants to go to bed with you."

Loving Gary Snyder didn't stifle Joanne Kyger's ironic take on just about everything. After Viking published Jack Kerouac's *The Dharma Bums* (in which a fictionalized Gary Snyder is the main character), she and George Stanley formed the Dharma Committee, a mock organization growing out of the weekly Spicer/Duncan poetry meetings devoted to drinking, getting high on Velo inhalers, and having a good deal of hilarious fun. "These are famous times I am sure," Kyger wrote in her journal.

That summer, while the Brautigans were away in Mexico, Price Dunn moved up to Oakland from Big Sur. He arrived with a sculptor named Gene Flores and took up residence in the L-shaped corner storefront building Madge Boyd owned on Fifty-fifth Street. They built a big bedroom/ studio supported on telephone poles. Believing that "a man needs space to breathe," Price always removed all the interior walls with a chainsaw when he rented a new house. In Oakland, Dunn illegally tapped into the PG&E gas line. "I had this big stove with this enormous gas pipe," Price recalled. "This flame would shoot out."

Keith Abbott reported that Dunn held "a firm belief that utility companies had more than enough money and didn't need his cash." He was so frequently delinquent on his phone bills that he listed his new numbers under such pseudonyms as Delmer Dibble, Commander Ralph G. Gore, Jesse James, and Rufus Flywheel. For a time, Price was joined in Oakland by painter Frank Curtin, who was trying to "get straight." They were both broke, taking "slave labor" menial jobs and "playing Captain Garbage, raiding the Safeway garbage Dumpster." Price summed it all up with a shrug. "I mean, it was grim, *grim*." A few months later, he got married.

After a bit of searching, Richard and Ginny found a seven-room apartment with hardwood floors at 461 Mississippi Street on Potrero Hill in San Francisco. The place was much too big, so their artist friend Kenn Davis offered to share it with them. He had no job, and Ginny resented his inability to contribute much to the household. Kenn's saving grace was his car, a two-tone blue and white '55 Chevy, which made the distant Potrero neighborhood seem a lot less isolated from the rest of the city.

The electricity had not yet been turned on when the trio moved in. That first night, the Brautigans stuck a candle on a saucer for light. The dim flickering illumination gentled the chaos of the recent move and suffused the surrounding disorder with a romantic glow. Richard and Ginny made love among the stacks of unpacked carton boxes and rolled carpets. They muted their passion, trying not to make too much noise and wake Kenn, who lay sleeping in the next room.

There was no denying that it was a great pad. The Brautigans filled one room completely with plants. Sliding doors divided the two largest rooms. When these were opened the resulting expansion provided a perfect space for impromptu badminton games. Without a net, the three roommates modified the rules. Getting the birdy caught up in the ceiling light fixture resulted in an immediate out. Ditto if someone opened a door to announce a phone call and the birdy flew into the other room. They played in their stocking feet, sliding over the varnished floor, batting the shuttlecock back and forth, back and forth. "That was a fun time," Ginny recalled.

Kenn Davis recorded this happy domestic activity in his sketchbook. He drew Richard eating watermelon, reading the morning paper, sitting at his typewriter staring out at the rain, and playing indoor badminton. On two occasions, Kenn attempted to teach Dick to drive in the '55 Chevy. Once was in a long graveled area down in the Marina District, a wealthy flatland neighborhood of pastel houses built atop landfill rubble from the 1906 earthquake.

"What I liked about it," Kenn recalled, "was the fact that you could actually drive a car without hitting anybody." He later taught Frank Curtin to drive in the same place. "Frank turned out fine. But Dick, he just never—him and machinery. After about twenty minutes, I realized this is hopeless." The second attempt took place on a camping and fishing trip to Yosemite and ended with similar results. Kenn made better use of his time sketching Richard casting on a trout stream.

One moonlit evening, the three apartment-mates were out having fun near the yacht harbor far from Potrero. Nine years after San Francisco rose anew from the ashes, the Panama–Pacific Exposition of 1915 blazed into life along the waterfront in the Marina. Officially a celebration of the opening of the Panama Canal, the big bash became an enormous party to honor the city's rebirth. The centerpiece of the festivities was the Palace of Fine Arts, Bernard Maybeck's fantasy re-creation of a Roman ruin surrounded by a reflecting pool. Framed in wood and covered with staff (a mixture of plaster and fibrous materials), the romantic structure was intended to last only for the life of the fair. So beloved by San Franciscans, the building was spared while a Turkish mosque, the 435-foot-high "Tower of Jewels," and all the other palaces (education, industry, and horticulture) were demolished.

A half century later, the Palace of Fine Arts itself stood in ruins, lathe work showing through where staff *putti* had crumbled. Kenn Davis found the place "very romantic and secluded." One night, he took Richard and Ginny to this magic spot. Wandering under a full moon, they marveled at the decaying colonnaded dome rising dreamlike above its own wavering reflection. "Entrancing," Ginny recalled.

The trio felt caught up in the zany spirit of romance and scaled the decaying walls of the imaginary moon-pale palace. They climbed upon a shed and from the roof up onto an iron framework supporting the statuary-adorned colonnade. Huge urns perched on large steplike platforms. They climbed these like giant stairs. Iron posts thrust from broken sculpture like time-blackened bones. "The heads were off of a lot of the statues." Ginny remembered fear gripping them when they tried to figure out how to get back down again. "It was scary."

Potrero Hill, a remote neighborhood with fabulous views of downtown San Francisco, provided Brautigan a home, but the focus of his intellectual and social life continued to be in North

Beach. The couple depended on bus transportation to take them everywhere, to work as well as play. Aside from their roommate, Richard and Ginny knew very few other people on Potrero. Their friends Tom and Shirley Lipsett lived at the top of the hill. Ginny and Richard frequently walked up to visit with them. Ginny made friends with a Spanish-speaking sandal maker who lived down the street in a lovely old Arts and Crafts house designed by Bernard Maybeck. Later, the place was torn down to make room for a freeway. She enjoyed conversing in his native tongue as he taught her how to work with leather.

Following the publication of *After Lorca*, Jack Spicer worked on a sequence of cryptic cautionary poems he called *Admonitions*. Not published until 1970, most were written in 1958. Each poem was addressed to a specific friend, but only two (those to Joe Dunn and Robin Blaser) were purely epistolary. Other designated subjects included Nemi Frost, Ebbe Borregaard, Russell FitzGerald, Graham Mackintosh, and Charles Olson. Spicer's poem for Richard Brautigan went straight to the recipient's heart. "For Dick" concluded with the lines, "Look / Innocence is important / It has meaning / Look / It can give us / Hope against the very winds that we batter against it." Having a personalized poem from a man he admired as much as Spicer pleased Richard Brautigan a great deal, but it didn't help buy the groceries, the wolf on the doorstep being more troubling than any poet's wind rumbling like a "sabre-toothed ape."

Ginny continued working for the law firm downtown. Richard wanted to pull his weight, too. After a bit of searching, he found part-time employment with Pacific Chemical Laboratories, Inc., at 350 Clay Street. Richard remained secretive about his peculiar job. He kept it for years, telling few of his friends exactly what it was he did those two or three afternoons a week. Many thought he worked developing photographs. Price Dunn knew it was "some esoteric laboratory where he mixed the brews."

Richard prepared a powdered formula for barium swallows at Pacific Chemical. The mysterious concoction came in two flavors, chocolate and vanilla. (In "The Daily Bread," an unpublished poem written on June 11, 1963, Brautigan described the process: "My job is to weigh / things out, / and so I do it: 400 grams / of cellulose gum, / and four grams of saccharine and / .8 gram of / naconol [. . .]")

Aside from writing, his main efforts went toward trying to get published. Ginny typed up fair copies of his poetry at work, mailing them out in batches to various magazines. Once, with Richard anxious to get poems off to *The Nation* and having no typewriter at home, he and Kenn Davis went downtown with Ginny after business hours to the office where she worked. Ginny can't remember how they got into the building "with a big cardboard box," but they came back down in the elevator carrying an IBM Executive inside it. "Feeling very guilty," Ginny typed all of Richard's poems that night, and they smuggled the electric typewriter back into the offices of Landelf, Weigel, Ripley and Diamond early the next morning, "vowing never to do anything like that again."

Richard Brautigan knew there was no money to be made in poetry. He told Ginny the only book of poetry ever to become a best seller in America was *Spoon River Anthology*. Edgar Lee Masters sold over a hundred thousand copies. Such astronomical sales figures were out of the question for Brautigan, but his experiences with Inferno and White Rabbit Press taught him a valuable lesson: As your own publisher you never got any rejection slips. In early March of 1959, when Gary Snyder returned to Japan and the wrecking crew began dismantling the Montgomery Block (many of the old-time bohemian residents moved to the Hotel Wentley on Polk and Sutter),

Richard and Ginny decided to go for broke and bring out a book of Brautigan's poetry on their own. Long hours were spent around the kitchen table, debating what they should call this new endeavor. They came up with the name Carp Press.

The irony of this off-kilter choice appealed to trout fisherman Richard Brautigan. He also liked the notion of a carp's longevity. "They live forever," Ginny said. "They live on the bottom and are bottom feeders and it had a lot to do with crap. We couldn't really call it Crap Press, so we called it Carp Press. It had to do with the ugliness of the business side of poetry and the longevity of poetry." Kenn Davis recalled that the name also referred to "people who just carp. Richard liked that. To find a simple word that could be a lot of things at once."

Needing a colophon, Richard and Kenn "sat around one evening drawing fishies." As Davis remembered it, "I was showing him some real simple stuff, and he picked up on it very quickly. He did a whole page of them, and we finally picked one that he thought was really great, but the thing was lacking an eye. So, he started drawing eyes in some of the better ones and one in particular had a kind of weird look to it. He says, 'Ooooh! Let's use that.'" The final result looked quite a lot like the primitive piscine symbol used by the early Christian church. So much so that many people asked Kenn Davis if it represented some sort of religious press. "Are you kidding?" he'd tell them. "With a name like Carp?" Brautigan liked the design well enough to utilize it for the rest of his life, sketching it on book inscriptions and posters, making it an integral element of his mock "trout money."

Richard collected two dozen of his best poems to date, including "The Chinese Checker Players" and "The Castle of the Cormorants." He took his title, *Lay the Marble Tea*, from an Emily Dickinson quote, which he used as his epigraph. ("The grave my little cottage is, / Where, keeping house for thee, / I make my parlor orderly, / And lay the marble tea [. . .]") Brautigan arranged the poetry in a cyclical framework; the first ("Portrait of the Id as Billy the Kid") being mentioned in the last ("The Twenty-eight Cents for My Old Age") as a poem he once read in a San Francisco bar. Baudelaire makes an appearance in these poems, as do Hansel and Gretel, Moby Dick, John Donne, Harpo Marx, and Kafka.

Brautigan's long interest in book design, typography, and layout showed its playful side when he arranged seven poems sideways on the page. He and his wife worked together on all aspects of the book's production, paying special attention to the cover. "Richard fussed over every little detail," Ginny recalled. He enlisted Kenn Davis to provide the cover art, an austere ink drawing of a couple seated on tombstones facing one another in a graveyard. A teapot, cup, and saucer rest among the scraggly weeds near the woman, a veiled Emily Dickinson. Davis included a small tombstone with the date of his birth: "RIP 1932."

The man clings to a leafless tree for support. Davis recalled how he and Brautigan had great fun designing the tree as a phallic symbol. "Richard was always looking for something to kind of gently throw in the public's face. Trees are notoriously phallic. And the thing I thought would make it more phallic than anything else was to have the male's arm around it. The fingers kind of coming out from the side."

The Brautigans contracted with Roger Neiss's Litho Art company (his slogan: "When you want another NEISS job—call YUkon 2-6268") to type the copy and print five hundred books. The charge, including sales tax, came to $94.25. "Astronomical," Ginny recalled. The founders of Carp Press made a down payment of $40 to Litho Art in late April 1959 and paid off the balance when they picked up the finished books on the first of May.

Richard and Ginny decided to charge seventy-five cents for *Lay the Marble Tea*. They sent out consignment copies in batches ranging from five to twenty to local bookstores: Discovery, City Lights, Tides, and the UC Corner. Ginny typed formal letters to each. "I think nobody ever expected anything to sell," she recalled. You just do it for the love of doing it."

One early evening in North Beach, Kenn Davis assisted them in delivering copies. "It was getting toward that blue hour," he said. The three friends wanted to see *Room at the Top*, the new English film starring Laurence Harvey and Simone Signoret, but lacked the price of admission. Kenn took fifteen or twenty of the chapbooks "and just hit the bars and started peddling them. Sold one to a traffic cop." Kenn had prior experience in street sales. "Whenever I would get really desperate for money I would do some drawings of the local characters around North Beach and I would try to peddle [them] to tourists." After an hour, Davis collected the admission for all three. Lacking bus fare to Larkin Street, rather than sell more copies, the trio walked through the Broadway Tunnel all the way to the Larkin Theater.

Michael McClure, not yet a friend of Brautigan's, thought *Lay the Marble Tea* "unprepossessing," but found the new little book to be a graceful "katydid hop" forward from *The Galilee Hitch-Hiker*. He felt Richard was "clearly quite literary" and later wrote that "the poems are inexplicable artifacts and penetrating insights into childhood." Philip Whalen, another of the Six Gallery poets, had a different reaction to *Lay the Marble Tea*. "I was very impressed at that time," he recalled. He thought it "really wonderful. The first book from somebody who had his own voice, his own vision, which was quite terrific. It was just totally authentic feeling. It's not like student work or amateur wannabe stuff; it was really there—created material that was on the page."

Like many penniless poets with time on their hands, Richard Brautigan wandered the streets of North Beach, filling his days with chance encounters. One morning in 1959, he ran into Stanley Fullerton, a character as unique and eccentric as himself. Fullerton, a painter living in a $30-a-month room at the Mary's Tower Hotel, had his own survival credo: "rent first, food 2nd, paint & paper, then alcohol." Half coastal Indian on both sides of his family, Fullerton led a hard-scrabble youth and joined the Marines at seventeen, serving in the Korean War as an ordnance disposal man. "There was an extra $75 per month for doing this job plus another seventy-five for doing it under fire." Fullerton left that conflict with a metal plate in his head. After a few months at the Bethesda Naval Hospital and a year at Oak Knoll, in Oakland, California, he was discharged with total disability pay.

Stan Fullerton's wound affected his mind. Once, the metal plate sent him a signal to go out and rob a bank. Fullerton walked into an Oakland savings and loan waving a toy pistol "with a picture of Dick Tracy on the side that made a ferocious *Boing, Boing* when the trigger was pulled." He got away with a sack of money. After running several blocks, Stan wandered around, forgetting what had just occurred. Attracted by a commotion outside the bank building, Fullerton joined the curious crowd, still clutching the toy gun and his loot. He was immediately apprehended. "I was run through the process of California law and put back in the locked ward of Oak Knoll."

The morning Stan Fullerton met Dick Brautigan began when Fullerton bought two gallons of red wine for a buck each at a little store near the Co-Existence Bagel Shop. "I carefully hid one bottle and started for Telegraph Hill with a pocket full of salami and cheese and a sketch book. On the lower part of the hill, I noted that I wasn't alone and that a very tall skinny guy with whitish-blond hair and glasses was taking these great swooping steps to come alongside. He guessed that I needed company to protect the wine from muggers."

Stan remembered seeing Brautigan hawking his poetry chapbook in front of the Coffee Gallery, so they talked and he shared his lunch with the hungry writer. Richard seemed impressed when Fullerton told him several small San Francisco galleries carried his drawings and small wire sculptures of birds. "I found that he had not taken any food for some time and was not in real good shape. Richard needed a certain amount of being looked after, and he very early in his S.F. tenure built a troop of support that involved many folks I never even saw or knew, so our kinship/acquaintance, or whatever it was, was sporadic."

Finances remained tight. Not all the Brautigans' literary endeavors focused on art with a capital "A." Richard, Ginny, and Kenn decided to enter the field of popular fiction. Davis recalled "there were a lot of original paperbacks running around loose and pretty good money made from them for a writer and we thought, why don't we just whip one out and send it off and see if we can sell it." They kicked ideas around the kitchen table at night, eventually coming up with a plot about heroin addicts. The story featured "a lady villain" who died "rather horribly" at the end. Their working title was "Snow White."

Using the pseudonym T. T. Bears (The Three Bears), the team set to work separately. "I typed up a bunch of pages," Kenn said. "Richard typed up a few pages, and of course, we all passed the stuff back and forth correcting our English, correcting our punctuation, correcting the story line and so forth. It was abominable." After about twenty pages, the T. T. Bears team gave up, disgusted with their potboiling efforts. "We never did a thing with it."

During this period, the Brautigans spent many evenings at Bread and Wine in North Beach. There were two poetry readings a week and music every Saturday night. Mimi Fariña and Joan Baez played at the Bread and Wine. Dave Van Ronk dropped in whenever he was in town. Lord Buckley (who influenced Lenny Bruce) performed nearby at the hungry i and the Coffee Gallery, sending an advance delegation of "these gypsylike women" over to the Mission. They stormed through the door shouting, "Lord Buckley—The Nazz!" before the comic monologist, wearing a white dinner jacket and pith helmet, upturned mustache bristling, arrived to perform his bop-talk routine about the life of Christ.

Along with pass-the-hat entertainment, Bread and Wine served free spaghetti dinners to all comers every Sunday night. "We went many times," Ginny remembered. "Free spaghetti nights," Kenn Davis reminisced enthusiastically. "Oh boy, did we go to those." By Pierre Delattre's estimate, the Mission fed about three hundred hungry guests each week. "People would come and volunteer and bring in all sorts of stuff. We had great meals."

Richard Brautigan's reading career in North Beach picked up steam. He and Robert Duncan were among four poets engaged to read weekly at the Coffee Gallery on a rotating basis. The pay was $25 per reading, a princely sum in 1959. Also, the implied prestige of sharing the billing with Duncan must have felt sweet indeed. Less than five years earlier he had curtly dismissed Brautigan's written request for a forum in the claustrophobic world of San Francisco poetry.

During one of Brautigan's turns at the Coffee Gallery, Ron Loewinsohn came up before the reading and said he had something to give him. Richard didn't care very much for Ron at the time and told him to "save it for later." Loewinsohn sat next to Jack Spicer. After Brautigan read his poetry, he handed Richard a poem he had written, saying he always gave a copy to the person to whom he'd dedicated the work. Richard made no reply, remembering the earlier deleted Loewinsohn dedication. "What a chicken shit way to fuck around," Brautigan thought. Was Ron "completely out of his goddamn mind?"

Before the reading, Richard and Frank Curtin had stepped out into the alley for a little taste of "sneaky pete." Afterward, they bought another bottle of "rot gut wine" and headed up the street to the end of Grant Avenue, where they could "crouch under the stairs and drink." Ron Loewinsohn followed them. He wasn't interested in drinking but just wanted to hang out. Richard put him down. Frank had no idea what was going on. He was a friend of Ron's and didn't say anything. Later, Richard read the poem Loewinsohn had given him. It concerned the discarded illuminated medieval manuscript. Richard had similar feelings for Ron's new poem and promptly lost the gift copy.

A new magazine was born in North Beach in the spring of 1959. Three poets, Bob Kaufman, John Kelly, and William J. Margolis, decided to publish a "weekly miscellany of poetry and other jazz designed to extol beauty and promote the beatific life among the various mendicants, neo-existentialists, christs, poets, painters, musicians and other inhabitants and observers of North Beach, San Francisco, California, United States of America." They named their nascent effort *Beatitude*, a term meaning perfect blessedness and one designating Christ's pronouncements in the Sermon on the Mount. It was also the source of Jack Kerouac's seminal remark to fellow writer John Clellon Holmes in 1948: "So I guess you might say we're a *beat* generation."

The founding editors of *Beatitude* comprised an intriguing cross-section of North Beach eccentricity. New Orleans–born Kaufman, one of thirteen children of a German Orthodox Jewish father and a black Catholic mother from Martinique, lived a life that Kerouac described as being "written on mirrors in smoke." He settled in San Francisco after twenty years as a merchant seaman, a career including four shipwrecks, and his life seemed to veer from one disaster to the next.

Pierre Delattre remembered John Kelly as "one of a gang of heroin addicts." Their main man was Hube the Cube, a regular at The Place whose real name was Hubert Leslie and who remained perpetually stoned courtesy of the University of California Medical Center as a $200-a-month drug-testing guinea pig. William J. Margolis was "the epitome of the outsider," according to Delattre. A flamboyant motorcycle-riding anarchist, Margolis had published a magazine called the *Miscellaneous Man* when he lived over in Berkeley, and his spacious old house had been the gathering place of students, poets, leftist longshoremen, Wobblies, and folk musicians.

To keep costs down, these three unorthodox characters planned to print *Beatitude* on a mimeograph machine, a street publication in every way. They placed Allen Ginsberg and Peter Orlovsky on the masthead of the first issue as members of the "bored of directors." This gave rise to the fiction that Ginsberg had been one of the founders of the magazine, when he was not even in San Francisco during the spring of 1959, arriving only later that summer to take part in Gregory Bateson's LSD experiments at the Mental Research Institute in Palo Alto.

Published out of a tiny office at 14 Bannam Alley, *Beatitude* no. 1 hit the streets on May 9, priced at two bits a copy. The first issue contained contributions by Allen Ginsberg, Pierre Delattre, and Bob Kaufman and included "The Whorehouse at the Top of Mount Rainier," a poem by Richard Brautigan. Bob Kaufman lived in the apartment next door to Delattre and spent a lot of time hanging out in his kitchen after the first few issues. He approached the young minister to ask if they might start using the Bread and Wine mimeograph machine to print the magazine. Delattre agreed without a moment's hesitation, and *Beatitude* moved permanently to the Mission. Starting with number 8, until the end of its brief one-year run, the little magazine was published at Bread and Wine with Pierre Delattre serving as its de facto editor. In his memoir, *Episodes*, Delattre recalled the ease of collecting material for the magazine: "I had only to walk down the street and gather poems in my shirt."

Richard Brautigan published four new poems in *Beatitude* no. 4 (May 30, 1959). He also had a poem ("Psalm") printed that same spring in vol. 1, no. 2, of *San Francisco Review*. George Hitchcock (poet, actor, and later the publisher of Kayak Books) worked at the magazine and recalled meeting Richard at the home of a mutual friend who was a *Chronicle* copy editor. The "lean slender long-faced blond young man" introduced himself as being from the Northwest. Hitchcock remembered "a hungry look," and that Brautigan "had a lot of bottled-up hostility."

He also thought that Richard "kept dropping around to peoples' houses around dinnertime because he needed some attention." In George Hitchcock's opinion, "Psalm" was "a slight poem" that "didn't amount to a hell of a lot."

Donald Allen was back in Frisco that spring, gathering material for his upcoming, much-talked-about poetry anthology. Richard Brautigan met him at this time. Allen was a friend of Jack Spicer, whose writing he admired. The word was out, and North Beach poets cornered the editor, touting their work. Lew Welch, then driving a cab and with only one poem published in *Contact 2*, met with Allen and showed him the manuscript of his planned collection, *Wobbly Rock*. Allen marked those poems that interested him and asked Welch to send copies to New York. He made no such request regarding Brautigan's poetry.

Sometime early in June, Ginny Brautigan discovered she was pregnant. It did not come as a complete surprise, as she and Richard had decided some months earlier to have a child. In retrospect, they decided the baby was conceived by candlelight the first night they spent together in the Mississippi Street apartment. At first, nothing much changed in their lives. The impromptu badminton games continued in the big drawing room. Richard fixed breakfast before Ginny walked down the hill to catch a bus to her job in the Financial District. Only now, she would often stop and be sick on the way. Ginny's morning sickness provided a wake-up-and-smell-the-coffee realization. They were going to be a real family in the not-too-distant future and needed to find a place of their own.

After looking around, the Brautigans located a tiny ground floor apartment at 575 Pennsylvania Street on Potrero Hill. The rent was $25 a month. Richard and Ginny had saved a little nest egg and paid for several months in advance, moving in by the end of June. Kenn Davis took a job at the *Chronicle* as a vacation replacement and moved to his own place. Richard and Ginny painted their new apartment: white walls and bright orange floors. Their secondhand furniture received a coat of black as a finishing touch.

The Brautigans added a pair of sleek black cats, Jake and Boaz, to the Halloween color scheme. "Great cats," Ginny remembered. Jake, the favorite, "was really extra smart." In an experimental botanical mood, Richard bought a cobra lily at the local Woolworth's. He replanted the exotic carnivorous plant in an empty Metrecal can and set it on a sunny window ledge, hoping to see it catch and devour houseflies within its hairy honeyed hood. Fate decreed otherwise. It was an election year (1960), and when the cobra lily died, Brautigan stuck a red, white, and blue Nixon button into the dry brown plant as an ironic funeral wreath. He kept this decaying political statement on his desk for many months.

What with marriage, his North Beach poetry life, and the trip to Mexico, it had been a while since Brautigan spent any time on a trout stream. Pierre Delattre owned a station wagon, and his father-in-law had a cabin at Three Rivers in the mountains just below Sequoia National Park. Brautigan and Delattre took four trips together that summer. They stayed at the Three Rivers cabin and fished the water around Kings Canyon National Park next to Sequoia. Delattre remembered Brautigan's conversation as being "tied in with imaginary scenarios built around whatever we happened to be seeing at the time." Once, lost in heavy fog driving through the Tulare Valley, Brautigan fabricated an elaborate fiction "about who we were and what was going on. It was pure invention, not a lot of sentimentality about the past." Richard never talked about his past.

On another trip to the Russian River, Brautigan waded out and caught his limit while Delattre still fumbled with his gear on the tailgate of the station wagon. Richard divided his catch with Pierre so he could continue fishing. Later the same day, they came across a group of picnickers splashing in the river. Brautigan bet he could catch a trout right where the kids were swimming. With a few deft casts, he accomplished this feat. To Delattre's amazement, the swimmers never even noticed. Richard taught Pierre how to fish the riffles. "That was the only place he ever fished. He had all these wonderful mysteries about him. He was very mystical about fishing."

Kenn Davis recalled going fishing with Richard three or four times, mostly up to Yosemite. They camped out, sleeping without tents ("Freezing our butts off!") in surplus bags several degrees beyond inadequate. Once, they set up camp in a snowstorm. "The fishing was terrible," although they saw many trout holding in a clear pool directly below them. When the blue-and-white Chevy languished, inoperable, they hitchhiked up to the North Fork of the Yuba River. Kenn brought along his .38 caliber revolver. Richard objected. "He didn't like handguns at that time," Davis recalled.

A shared rural small-town background meant a mutual familiarity with shotguns and rifles. "I got into one of my modern design modes with Richard." Because he was a Korean War vet, Kenn's affection for firearms carried a certain weight. He was "trying to explain some guns have this wonderful sculptural quality, the precision of the engineering. The balance. And just the look of the thing." Davis's rhapsodic handgun description struck a chord with Brautigan, and years later, Richard echoed his old friend whenever he showed off his sidearms.

By fall, when Ginny's pregnancy began to show, the law firm where she worked dismissed her. It was no big deal. She kept busy with Carp Press correspondence, sending follow-up letters to the many bookstores who had been sent consignment copies of *Lay the Marble Tea*. Terms for sales varied. Most booksellers received a 40 percent discount, while others asked for a one-third markdown. Ginny's diligence in pursuing these matters often paid off. Money kept trickling in, often in very small amounts.

In October, *Lay the Marble Tea* received a favorable review in the little Hollywood magazine *Coastline 13*. Quotes from the poems prompted a reader in San Diego to mail a check for seventy-five cents, requesting a copy the very day his magazine arrived. In the end, the Brautigans actually made some money on the project. "A seedy little profit," Ginny recalled. Their first publishing venture was a success. Carp Press was off and running.

By midsummer, after the first seven issues, *Beatitude* had evolved from an aspiring weekly into a regular monthly publication. *Beatitude* 9, the second issue published at Bread and Wine, came out in September and contained a poem ("Swan Dragons") by Richard Brautigan. A photograph from that time shows William Margolis laboring with a rag on the Mission mimeograph machine while Bob and Eileen Kaufman proofread a newly printed page.

Margolis lived with his girlfriend in a second-floor apartment on Gerke Alley, an obscure cul-de-sac off Grant Avenue. They got into a fight, and she stormed out onto the street. Stoned, Margolis began hurling dishes out the window at his girlfriend, who danced and dodged, screaming abuse, as crockery shattered on the pavement around her. With nothing left to throw, Margolis, higher than a kite and insane with rage, pantomimed dragging himself by the collar and hurtled through the window.

He landed at the feet of his horrified girlfriend, severely injuring his spine. She called an ambulance. His friends were afraid he was going to die. When Bill Margolis was released from the hospital a paraplegic, Pierre Delattre organized a benefit to raise money for Margolis's medical expenses. The event was held at Garibaldi Hall. Richard Brautigan read his poetry, as did Bob Kaufman and Corso and Ferlinghetti, along with participation by numerous other performers and musicians.

In the midst of the festivities, Delattre got word a motorcycle gang was on its way to "beat the shit out of all these beatniks." He ran outside and there they were. Pierre spotted the gang leader and faced off with him. "I'm so glad you came," he improvised. "We're in real trouble. There's this black motorcycle gang from the Fillmore, and they're coming here to bust up this whole scene!" Pierre told them the benefit was for their buddy, who'd been smoking dope when a bunch of guys made fun of his tattoos and someone threw him out the window. Now he had a broken back and would never ride his hog again.

The outlaw bikers were much impressed. "Don't worry, man," their leader told the beatnik priest. "Everything is cool. We'll take care of those bastards!"

Delattre remembered the episode as the "the greatest coup I ever pulled [. . .] They spent the entire time of our production guarding us against themselves."

Richard Brautigan incorporated a fictionalized version of the unhappy Margolis accident into his own personal myth-making during a visit to the office of Inferno Press. Leslie Woolf Hedley had become a de facto "father confessor" for Brautigan, a role the older man "didn't want to play." Hedley found Brautigan "embarrassing," but felt he needed "someone outside of that milieu [North Beach]" to confide in. "I always got the impression that he was an innocent."

Richard told Hedley about drinking cheap port wine and smoking marijuana. "He kind of laughed about it." Brautigan regaled Leslie Woolf Hedley with tales of sex. "I think his love life began at that time," the editor observed. Without mentioning any names, Richard implied that he and "his woman" had been involved in a variety of group sex, "threesomes and foursomes." On one visit to the Inferno office, Brautigan told a story Hedley never forgot. This time, he mentioned someone they both knew. William Margolis was a friend of Leslie Woolf Hedley's. According to Richard, "he was involved in this party with this one girl and Margolis, [who] was insulted by something she said and jumped out of the window."

Richard's part-time work at Pacific Chemical Laboratory left him with ample opportunity for visiting Hedley's office and hanging out with other underemployed poets. He made several new friends in North Beach. Albert Saijo was a nisei, an American born in Los Angeles in 1926 to Japanese immigrant parents. He had been confined in a California internment camp during World War II. His liberation from this unjust indignity came in the form of a draft notice, and Saijo later fought with the Army in Italy. Saijo was "a very swinging but repressed little Jap, really beautiful," according to Lew Welch. Saijo lived at the East-West House at 2273 California Street. Welch and Philip Whalen were his roommates.

Other residents of the "Hyphen House" (as the place was sometimes called) were John Montgomery, Lenore Kandel, and Joanne Kyger. Whenever Richard came over to hang out with Albert, he spent time with the others as well. Saijo, a Buddhist who had often sat zazen at Marin-An with Gary Snyder, was further described by Welch as "a saint," who "builds beautiful things out of old lumber."

In November 1959, Welch and Saijo drove Jack Kerouac back to New York, taking Route 66 to Chicago in "Willy," Welch's battered Jeep. They improvised collaborative haiku about derelict Aermotor windmills and lonely grain elevators all along the way. In *Lighting the Corners*, Michael McClure maintained that, according to Shig Murao, Albert Saijo "got Richard the job testing meat samples that he had in the early sixties." Brautigan remained reticent regarding his job at the chemical laboratory.

Poet Jory Sherman moved to Frisco in 1959, gaining immediate local fame by being arrested for having eight hundred outstanding parking tickets. Sherman's first book of poetry, *So Many Rooms*, was published on the same day he appeared in court, accompanied by his pregnant wife. The presiding judge had little sympathy for Sherman's alibi (the tickets "blew away in the wind") and told him to "Give up being a poet and get a real job digging ditches or something." Sherman was sentenced to spend fourteen weekends in jail.

The local newspapers picked up the story. "Herb Caen went ape shit!" Sherman recalled. Prominent San Francisco attorney Melvin Belli took the case pro bono and got the poet off after only his second weekend in the slammer. Jory Sherman became a local hero in North Beach. "I never had to buy a drink after that." Pierre Delattre "grabbed" him right away, and he gave his very first public reading at Bread and Wine. "Everybody was there," and the event "launched" him.

Jory Sherman no longer remembers when he first met Richard Brautigan. "Richard was so quiet, and I don't think hardly anybody knew him," Sherman recalled. "We were both outsiders." They would meet at Vesuvio on Columbus, always sitting in the back under the balcony. "I liked talking to him. He was different. He was very serious, but he also just had a different path that he was taking." The two poets felt drawn together "because we were just incompatible with everything else." When Richard Brautigan gave Jory Sherman a copy of *Lay the Marble Tea*, he was touched by the gesture.

It was a good time to be a young poet in North Beach. Jory Sherman thought it the most exciting time of his life because of all the "creative ferment." Life was easy. There were readings every night at the Mission, the Fox and Hound, or the Old Spaghetti Factory. Some of these gigs actually paid. Brautigan earned twenty-five bucks each turn from the Coffee Gallery. At the hungry i, Eric "Big Daddy" Nord's bar and nightclub located in the basement of the green-patinated copper-clad 1907 Sentinel Building (now known as Columbus Tower), a poet could always get a free sandwich and a glass of beer. "You didn't have to pay anything in that place." City Lights provided another refuge. Poor poets like Brautigan and Sherman often spent the day there, reading books and magazines without making a purchase. "It was like a library."

Richard made another new friend that summer who seemed to have come from a distant world. In a notebook from the period, Brautigan jotted these words: "Lou Embree: soldier, printer & newspaperman." His spare three-word synopsis only hinted at Embree's exotic history.

Born in British Nigeria, Lou moved with his "Okie parents" to the Pacific Northwest at the age of two. After serving as a machine-gunner in France and Germany during the Second World War and rising to the rank of sergeant, Embree attended college in Idaho, returning to Europe to live the existentialist life in Paris after graduation. Back at home, he worked on tugboats in San Francisco Bay, in a railroad roundhouse in Filer, Idaho, and as a newspaper reporter and editor in Arizona before settling into a career as a linotype operator and printer for a Bay Area avant-garde press.

In the fall, while Ginny kept busy typing follow-up letters tracking consignment copies of the first Carp Press chapbook, Richard's poetry continued to find new publishers. A letter arrived from E. V. Griffith, editor of *Hearse*, saying how much he'd enjoyed *Lay the Marble Tea*. Brautigan struck Griffith as "among the very best and most exciting of the new younger poets." The editor found the poems "sharply beautiful" and "magically alive," inviting Richard to submit new work to his magazine, making no mention of the poetry *Hearse* had reprinted without payment in two earlier issues. Brautigan immediately mailed a batch of poems up to Griffith in Eureka.

September 1959 saw the first appearance of *Foot*, a new magazine edited by San Francisco–born poet Richard Duerden, in his spacious two-story Haight-Ashbury apartment on Rivoli Street. A handsome production, *Foot* boasted clean-set type, sewn signatures, and orange wrappers with a cover design of paired feet by Robert Duncan. The first issue contained five poems by Richard Brautigan, as well as work by Duerden, Philip Whalen, Ebbe Borregaard, and Robert Duncan.

Richard Duerden's artistic philosophy struck a sympathetic chord with Brautigan. "I never look back," Duerden said. "I find it distasteful. The art of my life is like driving on the freeway. I go from place to place, never revise." Duerden was three years older than Brautigan, who wrote "A Poem for Richard Duerden" about the gap in their ages. Still unpublished, the poem imagines "the difference / in years between us, is like a long line of salmon / stacking up in the pools, waiting to / go up the rapids."

Sitting with Brautigan in a North Beach bar, Duerden said, "Richard, I'll tell you what. You write a poem for me, and I'll write a poem for you." Brautigan immediately jotted a few lines down on a slip of paper and passed them over to Duerden.

> *Richard, I'll tell you what:*
> *Richard, I'll tell you what:*
> *You write a poem for me and*
> *I'll write a poem for you.*
> *"Done."*

Duerden read what his friend had written and added a penciled footnote to the right-hand margin: "Well all right." Brautigan told Duerden he was quitting poetry for prose. Duerden asked why. "I don't want to sit at the children's table anymore," Richard Brautigan said.

Jack Spicer's mimeograph publication *J* was another new magazine born that same September. Inspired by the launch of *Beatitude* and "made envious, scornful, and competitive" by Bob Kaufman's editorial participation in a successful venture, he envisioned a deliberately "amateur" magazine at the opposite end of the spectrum from the inbred university journals he detested. Spicer selected all the material for *J* himself, soliciting work from friends and leaving a box for random contributions on the bar at The Place. The first issue, sixteen pages long with a print run of three hundred copies, contained poetry by Robert Duncan, Robin Blaser, Joe Dunn, and Richard Brautigan ("The Fever Monument"), among others. It sold for a quarter.

J made a point to appear homemade. Spicer was influenced by the growing "funk/assemblage" art movement blossoming in San Francisco. Artists such as Bruce Conner (who had moved to Frisco the previous September), George Herms, Jess (pasting up fanciful collages and reimagined comic strips), and Wallace Berman (whose 1957 show at the Ferus Gallery in L.A. was credited with starting the entire trend) were all working with discarded objects (nylon stockings, scraps of fur and feathers, all manner of assorted junk), the throwaway detritus of an overindulgent society.

Wallace Berman's beautiful and singular publication, *Semina*, lasting for only nine "issues" from 1955 to 1964, had a distinctive handmade look, no two numbers being alike either in size or format and each taking up to six months to produce. *Semina* was not for sale. Berman gave the copies away to friends, just as he solicited friends for material and help in the assemblage. It was produced in limited editions, its impact felt throughout the Frisco literary and artistic communities. "*Semina*'s a real outlaw act," Michael McClure observed, "as complex as outlaws in the Old West, as sexy and cool and hip and pop—and at the same time religious." The erudite Jack Spicer was well aware of *Semina*. Richard Brautigan's later seed-packet self-publication, *Please Plant This Book*, paid unspoken tribute to Wallace Berman's visionary creation.

Spicer soon tired of the effort involved in putting out a magazine, even with Fran Herndon assisting with the typing and layout and writing rejection letters. ("'Stick this poetry up your ass!' I had to say. I can't believe I did it. But I did.") *J* quietly folded after five issues. Spicer's attention seemed more focused on his new book of poetry, *Billy the Kid*, which appeared in October with illustrations by Jess. The fifth and final issue (December 1959) ran "1942," Richard's moving elegy on the death of his uncle Edward.

From the start, Brautigan set his sights on broader literary horizons than the small in-group audience delineated by the limited circulation of little poetry magazines. Just as he had submitted short stories to *Playboy* after graduating from high school, Richard mailed many of his new poems to establishment publications back east. His wife handled all the office work, typing the poetry, keeping up with correspondence, making sure the envelopes had enough postage. "I sent dozens of short poems to *The New Yorker*," Ginny remembered, "to *The Nation*, to *The Atlantic*. It was long before he started getting popular."

The fall of 1959 brought Richard Brautigan his first published critical notices. Gene Frumkin, editor of *Coastline 13*, reviewed *Lay the Marble Tea* in vol. 4, no. 1. In "A Step Toward Perception," he praised Brautigan's "crisp, lucid commentary." The autumn issue of *The Galley Sail Review* ran a two-page review by Robert Brotherson, "A Poet and his World." Brotherson praised the opening line of "Sonnet" before proceeding to quote the rest of the poem to demonstrate that "Mr. Brautigan has turned cute on us."

All that fall, Beat-mania turned its mercenary gaze on North Beach. Fueled by intense media attention and the many "beatnik" characters channeled into the American subconscious by the Hollywood dream machine, legions of ordinary Americans descended on bohemia. Daily tour buses cruised by City Lights and Bread and Wine. Pierre Delattre began to feel as if he "was putting on some kind of show." He didn't like the feeling. "When the tour bus passed, the man with the megaphone would point me out in my sweatshirt and cross. I was another monkey in the zoo." In retribution, before quitting Bread and Wine, Delattre and a bunch of North Beach regulars rented their own bus and toured the downtown business district, dressed in outrageous costumes, harassing the "squares" and commenting through loudspeakers on the lifestyles of the men in gray flannel suits.

As the epicenter of hipness moved away from North Beach, the diaspora did not settle in any particular neighborhood. Small bohemian homesteads sprang up in odd corners of the city. Ebbe Borregaard rented two floors of a Victorian house at 1713 Buchanan Street in Japantown and set about converting the space into a gallery. Ginny Brautigan remembered going over during the fall of 1959 to help Ebbe and his wife, Joy, paint the walls white and hang curtains. The place opened as Ebbe Borregaard's Museum. Soon after, in mid-April of 1960, Jack Spicer read the thirty pieces in his new work, "Homage to Creeley," at Borregaard's. The Brautigans were among the enthusiastic gathering of poets (including Philip Whalen, Ron Loewinsohn, George Stanley, and Robin Blaser) crowding into the small rooms to hear him read the poem through three times, with a break for intermission before the last go-round.

Sometime in January (1960), Richard and Ginny traveled down south to Reseda in the San Fernando Valley to visit her folks. Richard's father-in-law, Grover Cleveland Alder, was seventy and about to become a grandfather for the second time. Everyone called the old man "G.C."

Richard liked listening to tales of his youth on a farm in Nebraska and of teaching school and later working as a car salesman in the early adventurous days of the automobile industry, when dozens of different brands competed in the marketplace.

Always a military buff, Richard enjoyed hearing G.C.'s aerial adventures in the First World War. Grover Cleveland Alder flew a de Havilland bomber in the flak-filled skies over France, chasing glory and rainbows in the innocent belief that he would live forever. He joined the Army at twenty-seven and had almost been turned down for pilot training because of his age. He was demobilized in 1919 with the rank of captain. Ginny left Idaho with her parents while she was still an infant and didn't know anything of her history there, so Richard asked G.C. about what he did after the war.

His father-in-law told him about moving up to the area around Rexburg, where he went into banking and ranching, married a pretty schoolteacher almost half his age, and prospered for a time before getting wiped out in the stock market crash of 1929. Four small-town banks and a grocery store gone forever, his ranch mortgaged to the hilt, G.C. began raising sheep, hanging on until 1934, when disease wiped out his flocks. After selling the land to pay off their debts, the family moved to California, where Ginny's father worked parking cars in Hollywood and later as a construction company bookkeeper and real estate salesman. Richard listened to the old man chronicle his rise and fall, observing his not-so-secret drinking. Having a taste for sweet wine himself, Richard shared a glass or two with G.C. He certainly knew where the bottles were hidden in the kitchen. Ginny's father could no longer afford the whiskey he preferred.

After their return to San Francisco, on the evening of Richard's twenty-fifth birthday, Joanne Kyger sailed for Japan aboard the *Nachiharu-maru*, planning to marry Gary Snyder and study Zen. Brautigan had not had much contact with her since their aborted "date" in North Beach three years before and did not attend Kyger's boisterous farewell party at the East-West House. Fed up with other raucous late-night drunken misbehavior, Ginny took off, heading south again to her parents' place. Richard was desperate to get her back. Flat broke as usual, he lacked the funds to go after her and plead his case in person.

Stan Fullerton came to the rescue. At the time he lived on lower Columbus Avenue above a pizza and beer joint, a place Brautigan called "the green shelf." Although Stan was sympathetic to his friend, he believed him to be at fault. "Richard's selfishness always drove people away from him," Fullerton said. The painter understood Virginia's plight. He saw her as "mother earth caring for her dippy genius. Ginny carried the whole ball with dismal office jobs. Richard was her first child. He was not financially responsible, or emotionally able, to handle a whole family." Nevertheless, Stan agreed to help. Always a frugal man (he stored a large canister of Japanese rice along with canned fish and Asian vegetables under his bed), Fullerton saved all his pennies in a large jar. It came to $57 worth of copper. He gave this money to Richard, who used it to travel down to Reseda and bring his wife home.

Sometime early in March ("feeling the spring about me"), Richard Brautigan began a journal. Impending fatherhood enhanced his introspection. Springtime brought him down. Richard called it "the half-assed San Francisco spring" and felt the season went "against the development of myself." It had been over a month since he'd had sex with his wife. This also depressed him. "I felt my body growing away from me like an old man taking out his teeth in the middle of the night."

Try as he might, Richard could not envision the fast-approaching birth of his child. "Skim milk" and a "dirty sock" seemed more real to him.

Ginny went into labor on the morning of March 25, 1960. Richard brought her to the University of California Medical Center at 505 Parnassus Avenue in San Francisco. He stayed by her side until she was taken into the delivery room. Around 7:00 PM, Ginny gave birth to a seven-pound, eleven-ounce baby girl. A photograph of Richard holding his newborn child cradled in his arms with his red beard and bangs cut unevenly across his forehead shows him unsmiling and oddly haunted.

Twenty-five days earlier, Tom and Shirley, their friends at the top of Potrero Hill, also had a daughter. The Lipsetts named their little girl Cadence. Ginny remembered "lots and lots" of discussion on what to call their own new baby. The Brautigans' second choice was Selena, but in the end they settled on Ianthe, the name Percy Bysshe Shelley picked in 1813 for his daughter by his first wife, Harriet. In Greek mythology, Ianthe married Iphis, who lived an intriguing transsexual life. Born a Cretan maiden, Iphis was disguised as a boy by her mother because her father had commanded that all of his daughters be slain. When Iphis fell in love with beautiful Ianthe, the goddess Io (who had herself once been changed into a white heifer by Zeus) transformed her into the man she pretended to be. Taking the edge off the mythological, Richard and Ginny gave their new daughter a middle name: Ianthe Elizabeth Brautigan.

Stanley Fullerton thought Ianthe's nursery room on Mississippi Street "small and ugly," so he bought a few gallons of white acrylic paint and primed the walls, sticking canvas to the still-wet paint. After work the next day, Stan drew life-sized animals on the canvas, colorful long-necked giraffes, droll fat frogs, and various other gaudy amphibians, cavorting about the walls like illustrations from a giant children's book. Fullerton worked "in about four colors." He remembered the paint costing a lot but remained philosophical about the expense. Stan obviously cared for Richard, "who when the mood was upon him could have made the Mona Lisa giggle and beg to be screwed then and there. He had a carnival, perhaps a whole circus, of faces that seemed to turn on and off like the tides controlled by a remote planet none of us had ever heard of."

Richard Brautigan, who had never known his own father, instinctively became a devoted parent. When Ginny returned to work at a new job, Richard stayed home with the baby. Being a modern dad didn't foreclose on Brautigan's freewheeling lifestyle. On the Saturday night before Easter, 1960, ten days after his daughter's birth, Richard decided to take off and see three bad movies on Market Street. "A Western, a film about alligator people, and a crime flick."

Ginny couldn't understand why he wanted "to go downtown and see those shitty films." She wondered why he didn't just stay home and write.

"To hell with it," Richard replied. He was in the mood for B movies. Ginny relented. As long as he was going all the way downtown, why not stop off at a drugstore and buy Ianthe her first Easter bunny?

Richard said he'd "think about it," and caught a bus to Market Street. Once downtown, he made a beeline for Merrill's Drugstore. His destination was not the toy aisle. He headed straight for "the cheap booze section," to pick up a pint of something to take with him into the movies. As he scanned the labels, trying to decide between cheap gin, whiskey, or brandy, his attention was drawn to something odd. Brautigan recorded the moment in a rough-draft typescript he called "Poet's Easter." It was an example of found art, a creative element he came to use with increasing frequency in his writing. "The dishonety [*sic*] of the lables [*sic*] on one of the bottles of brandy catches my eye IDeath supreamd [*sic*] California Brandy."

April 1960 saw the publication of Donald Allen's influential anthology, *The New American Poetry, 1945–1960*, which placed the Beat poets firmly on the critical landscape for the first time. Because of this book, Don Carpenter referred to Allen as "the man who invented the Beat generation." There was much consternation among the Frisco poetry world over who was "in" and who was "out." Among the included were Robert Duncan, Robin Blaser, Robert Creeley, Philip Whalen, Gary Snyder, James Broughton, Philip Lamantia, Edward Dorn, and Jack Spicer (along with the predictable in-crowd: Kerouac, Ferlinghetti, Corso, Ginsberg, and Orlovsky).

The anointed younger poets were Lew Welch, Richard Duerden, Michael McClure, Ebbe Borregaard, John Wieners, Ron Loewinsohn, and David Meltzer. Richard Brautigan was left out in the cold, along with Joanne Kyger, George Stanley, Jory Sherman, and many others. Much jealousy and a sense of betrayal infected several of those omitted. Brautigan displayed no reaction at not being grouped with his contemporaries in this groundbreaking volume.

Life as a new father kept Richard Brautigan "very busy." He mentioned this in a letter to Sam Broder, a new friend from L.A., who he'd met only briefly. Brautigan wrote that he was trying to find the time to write and that some of his poems were being "used by a dance group for a production at UCLA." This also took up a lot of his time. "Telephone rings, a voice says, 'Would you please come to such and such a place and watch us dance to your poems? And let us know what you think of it and we are all dying to meet you.'"

The telephone voice belonged to dancer Ann Halprin, an early Brautigan reader who later resumed her birth name, Anna. Originally from Winnetka, Illinois, and married to noted Bay Area landscape architect Lawrence Halprin, she founded the avant-garde San Francisco Dancers' Workshop in 1955. Anna Halprin always kept on the alert for experimental material that might translate into movement. She had been working with poet/filmmaker James Broughton and came across a copy of Brautigan's *The Galilee Hitch-Hiker* at City Lights several months after its publication. Intrigued by the fanciful imagery, she immediately saw the possibilities of using "The Flowerburgers" as a dance. "In those days, all of us that were working to create new art were very interrelated," Halprin recalled. "We all knew each other. There was a lot of cross-fertilization going on."

Anna Halprin contacted Richard, suggesting her idea for a "Flowerburger" piece. "It never occurred to him that his poetry could be used in performance art." Richard was delighted with the notion and gave immediate approval. John Graham, a member of Dancers' Workshop Company, had been an actor first, and Anna Halprin felt influenced by his "ability to be comfortable with words." No one before had thought to combine voice and movement. "It was the first time dancers had ever used the spoken word," Halprin said. "Now you can't get dancers to shut up."

Watching his own work interpreted in another medium awakened new worlds for Brautigan. Although he never went to any of their rehearsals, Richard was in attendance at the first public performance of *The Flowerburger* by the San Francisco Dancers' Workshop at The Interplayers Theater. This small performance space was founded in 1946 by Kermit Sheets and Adrian Wilson, conscientious objectors who'd met during the war at camp 56 (the "Fine Art Camp") at Waldport on the Oregon coast.

The Flowerburger featured three dancers from the company, Anna Halprin, John Graham, and A. A. Leath. Their costumes came from a thrift shop on McAllister Street. Graham wore tails. Leath had on a black suit. By way of contrast, Anna Halprin was in white, "kind of a funny lacy dress." They worked with three chairs in a line on a bare stage. There was no music. The three dancers took turns reciting *The Galilee Hitch-Hiker*. Instead of doing it straight, they juxtaposed the lines, intermixing words from one poem with those of another, creating an entirely new poem in the process. The dancers declaimed Brautigan's poetry, standing or sitting, sometimes falling to the floor, each performer's movement contrasting with the others. "We were doing a lot of experimenting," Halprin said.

The San Francisco Dancers' Workshop performed *The Flowerburger* many times over the next few years. They took it to the Contemporary Dance Theater on Washington Street and the San Francisco Playhouse on Hyde Street. The performance traveled to UCLA and the International Avant Garde Arts Festival in Vancouver, British Columbia. Closer to home, they danced the piece at San Francisco State University. Ginny Brautigan remembered seeing that performance as well as one by invitation at a private studio seating only fifty at Anna and Lawrence Halprin's Kentfield home in Marin County. The Halprins frequently invited artists for performance evenings in their home. They featured poets Michael McClure and James Broughton in this way, as well as experimental musician Harry Partch. Six years after their first appearance in Los Angeles, Halprin, Leath, and Graham brought *The Flowerburger* back to UCLA. "It was performed on tour all over the country," Halprin recalled.

Having made some money on *Lay the Marble Tea*, Carp Press decided to publish a second volume of Brautigan's work. Richard had written a group of new poems, most appearing in little magazines, and he began to sift through them, thinking about the possibilities of another book. Being at home with a new baby provided the two partners in Carp Press time to plan their next venture. Along with work published in *J* and *Foot*, Richard had written enough new poetry to assemble a fresh collection. He and Ginny discussed the project. Having gone through the process once before made it easier the second time around. One of the new poems, "The Octopus Frontier," gave Brautigan the book's title as well as an idea for its cover.

Gui de Angulo, a noted North Beach musician and photographer, daughter of legendary folk-lorist and anthropologist Jaime de Angulo (who spoke seventeen different Native American languages), was among Richard and Ginny's group of friends. Ezra Pound called her father "the American Ovid." Henry Miller, Angulo's Big Sur Partington Ridge neighbor, wrote that "he had a streak of the devil in him." Gui's pictures of the Frisco poetry scene enjoyed a well-deserved reputation for honesty and skill. Her 1958 group portrait of Michael McClure, Philip Lamantia, John Wieners, and David Meltzer has been frequently reproduced and often incorrectly attributed.

Ginny Brautigan described Gui de Angulo as "very shy [. . .] difficult to talk to," but with "a great sense of humor." Richard had known her since before his first visit to Price Dunn in Big Sur. "She was pretty much closeted down there," Ginny remembered. "Isolated." Life in the city provided a vital contrast. Gui kept busy with her work, interacting with a wide circle of artists and musicians. She visited the Brautigans often on Potrero Hill, taking photographs of Ianthe playing with her mother. When Richard suggested his notion for a book cover, she took to the idea immediately.

Brautigan knew just what he wanted and served as the "art director" on the project. He bought a huge octopus tentacle, nearly six feet long, from a fishmonger in Chinatown. He and Gui de Angulo carried the grotesque appendage up onto the roof of a building in North Beach, and she photographed Richard's bare foot in close-up, standing on the tentacle. "It is striking and just misses being sinister," observed Michael McClure.

Richard gathered twenty-two recent poems for the new collection. Nearly half the poetry included in this latest chapbook had been previously published in Spicer and Duerden's little magazines. Brautigan reprinted the poems without any changes, except for reworking the line structure of "1942," a personal favorite for the rest of his life. By the end of July, finished copies of *The Octopus Frontier* were ready for sale. The Brautigans raised their price to $1 for the twenty-four-page publication.

Earlier in the year, Richard Brautigan bought an inexpensive ring-bound three-hole notebook with brown covers. The first entries were several drafts of a new poem, "The Silver Stairs of Ketchikan," which transformed 2:00 AM baby feeding into a mystical moment. On August 1, Brautigan began another journal in the notebook. After striking out his first two attempts, Richard made a new start: "The idea of this journal is I want to write something other than poems [. . .] I've tried to write short stories but I can't stick with them."

He groped to find a personal definition for his work, stating that he was "deeply involved with the motion of reality in poems," noting his frustration at his "failure to establish adequate movement." He concluded, "I want the reality in my work to move less obviously and it is very difficult for me. Tomorrow my book of poems *The Octopus Frontier* will be ready at the printers and I get the copies [. . .]" Unhappy with what he wrote, Richard crossed out the remainder of the passage.

In the first weeks of August, Ginny set to work writing letters to all booksellers who had received the first Carp Press publishing venture, offering a 33⅓ percent discount on each copy of *The Octopus Frontier* they sold. The return address, 575 Pennsylvania Street, was printed on the chapbook's title page, below Brautigan's crude goggle-eye fish colophon. Richard delivered consignment copies to the local bookshops in North Beach.

In addition to doing all the family bookkeeping and preparing their tax returns, Ginny also diligently wrote everyone who had ordered single copies of *Lay the Marble Tea*, informing them of the new collection. Among the many replies, a crudely printed anonymous card arrived in the mail. ("Dear Sirs: I am very much interested in your carp press. I have a great quantity of surplus carp and am considering sending said surplus to various of our hungry brothers over the water.") Richard recognized Frank Curtin's handwriting.

On August 8, Brautigan read from *The Octopus Frontier* to a full house at the Coffee Gallery on the same bill with Christopher Maclaine, an Oklahoma-born thirty-seven-year-old poet and film-maker. Maclaine's four short movies (*The End*, 1953; *The Man Who Invented Gold*, 1957; *Beat*, 1958; and *Scotch Hop*, 1959) had been well received by the Frisco avant-garde art community.

Addicted to methedrine, Maclaine imbued his work with frantic speed freak energy. Each of his films grew shorter and shorter (the last ran only five minutes). Maclaine made no more movies and died in an asylum fifteen years later. The *Examiner* sent a photographer to cover the "beat-nik" event, but the pictures were never published.

Haunted by the strange brandy label he'd seen in Merrill's Drugstore, Brautigan began enter-taining a peculiar fantasy about a future world where the sun shone a different color every day and the people worshipped in a temple called "Ideath." On a page in his notebook he wrote a possible title over and over: "IN Watermelon SUGAR, IN Watermelon SUGAR, IN Watermelon SUGAR [. . .]" ten times altogether, unable to drive the thought off the page with a new idea.

For the next several pages, Richard jotted notions for a possible work of fiction. He would call Book One "The Fish of the Sky." Proposed chapter headings included "Ideath," "The Priest of Ideath," "The River of Ideath," and "Dialogue with a Priest of Ideath." Among four pages of scattered notes concerning the project, Richard wrote "The setting: torches burning in a circle in the garden with five naked women dancing: their bodies firm enough to be the flesh of trout."

Brautigan roughed out a sample chapter in pencil. He called it "A Brief History of the Trout Fly Named the Beautiful Lady of Death." It began like a fairy tale: "Over a hundred years ago, yes, in the time of tigers, a wise and poetic priest went to the funeral of the most beautiful woman in the land [. . .]" She died at fifteen from a fever that spared her beauty, and she lies in her coffin wearing a dress made from watermelon sugar and holding a statue of Ideath in her cold folded hands. The priest stares at her beautiful corpse "for a long time," entranced because most of the dead have "been torn to pieces by the tigers," their bodies concealed by a covering of flowers. Back in the temple of Ideath, he ties a fly, recording "his impressions of her funeral." The brief chapter ends with a description of the unique fly. "It is the thing we use to catch trout. I fish with the funeral of a beautiful woman. The trout desire it and I take them afterward to the temple of Ideath."

Having set down these notions for his wondrous fantasy, Brautigan went no further with it at the time. Richard knew he would return when he was ready but had other things on his mind. At the top of a fresh notebook page, Brautigan jotted the title for a new story: "*Trout Fishing in America*." He began the opening paragraph several times. First he wrote, "It's come to this [. . .]" A few lines later he started again. "*Trout fishing in America* has come to this [. . .]" On the third try Brautigan found his rhythm: "*Trout fishing in America* has come to mean this. I am watching a shoeshine man walking across the grass in a kind of clocklike arch towards the old Italians sitting under the cypress trees." Richard scrawled in a frenzy, his handwriting often illegible. "I will be old," he wrote further along, "and listen to the same talk and tears will come to my eyes. I'll have to be led naked from the park by troops of Boy Scouts dressed in black. And I will make them feel embarrassed."

What did this mean? He was free-associating, the words tumbling out with zany manic energy. "The park is filled with old people whose sexual organs lie about them like scraps of paper on the ground," he concluded in a wild creative burst, "but the shoeshine man shines the shoes of their penises until they are like new organs. Twenty cents a show or listen to me scream." Reading over what he'd written, Richard didn't know quite what to make of it. Maybe it didn't amount to anything. Just another insane experiment leading nowhere. Perhaps he had a short story after all. Only time would tell.

Not long after *The Octopus Frontier* was published, Richard Brautigan met Don Carpenter, a man destined to become one of his closest friends. Born in Berkeley in 1931, Carpenter moved to Portland, Oregon, when he was seventeen. He hung out in pool halls and joined a tough street gang, the Broadway Gang, which at one time included Gary Gilmore (the subject of Norman Mailer's *The Executioner's Song*) as a member. Carpenter finished high school and started college in Portland in 1949. He soon joined the Air Force and didn't graduate until the fall of 1959.

In 1953, back in town on a thirty-day leave, Don Carpenter met Philip Whalen and Gary Snyder. Later, he visited Snyder in San Francisco, and his introduction to the literary scene eventually lured him back for good. In 1960, married and with two kids to support, Don was studying for his MA at San Francisco State when he first ran into Richard at the home of Bob Miller, a mutual friend. Carpenter knew Brautigan by sight. He had heard him read his short story "Coffee" in North Beach. Don was not impressed. "I hated it. I thought it was horrible writing."

Bob Miller was a rough customer with a high forehead, milky blue eyes, and an "implacable face." He'd also been a member of Portland's Broadway Gang and had done time in San Quentin. A friend of Kerouac's, Miller worked as a housepainter and had a reputation around North Beach as "this extremely tough, funny guy with a good mind." Brautigan knew him from the crowd at Gino & Carlo's.

At Miller's Russian Hill apartment, Don got into a game of three-handed poker with Bob and Richard. "I had never run into anything like this in my life," Carpenter recalled. Brautigan played "surrealist" poker. "His bets and his moves and the cut—the cards he picked and the cards he discarded had no relationship to anything I knew as poker. He plays the way he writes. It never occurred to him that other people had cards, and could defeat his imagination with their cards." It didn't take too much skill for Don to win all of Richard's money that night. He also cleaned out Bob Miller.

Later, they walked down the hill together to Vesuvio and Richard borrowed back enough coin for a couple drinks. Brautigan captured Don Carpenter's fancy right from the start. During the poker game, when Richard excused himself to go to the john, he said, "I have to bleed my lizard," a phrase that stuck with Carpenter for the rest of his life. "I was liking him because he was being charming," Don remembered. "And when Richard is charming, there's no charmer in the world like him." At the bar, all the charm ran out. Brautigan said, "Okay, see you later," and left Don Carpenter to his own devices. "He picked up a girl, and I was left there alone. I never saw him again for the rest of the year. Really pissed me off."

Early one evening in the fall, the Brautigans felt in the mood for ice cream, and Ginny went out to the neighborhood store a few blocks away to pick up a pint of something tasty. While she was away the telephone rang. It was Ginny's brother calling from Los Angeles. Their father, G.C.

Alder, had died that afternoon. His body had been found lying on the floor beside the television in the front room of the rented house in Reseda.

Richard Brautigan hung up and tried to think of the best way to break the news to his wife. He wanted to spare her as much pain as possible, but as he wrote later, "you cannot camouflage death with words. Always at the end of the words somebody is dead." This provided the conclusion for the first paragraph of Brautigan's short story "The World War I Los Angeles Airplane," which went on to chronicle the life of Ginny's father in a partially fictionalized outline list of thirty-three short numbered passages. "33. 'Your father died this afternoon.'"

Ice cream is a poor balm for sorrow. Perhaps the cold confection provided some comfort when Richard broke the news to Ginny after she returned from the store. The next day, she packed and left for Los Angeles with Ianthe. Brautigan was alone and living like a bachelor again for the first time in more than three years. To forestall loneliness, Richard invited his old buddy Ron Loewinsohn over to stay for a spell. He and Ron had patched things up in the late summer of 1960 and were friends once again.

Ron married a young woman named Sue Rosen not long after Richard and Ginny got together, and they also had a new baby. Due to straitened financial circumstances, Ron's wife and boy child, Joe, had gone home to Canton, Ohio, to tide things over. Finding himself another accidental bachelor, Loewinsohn brought his sleeping bag and crashed on the Brautigans' couch. He had the flu. Richard took care of him, cooking the meals (single-guy things like tuna fish salad) and ignoring his friend's complaints. Watching Ron wrapped sniffling in his sleeping bag, Brautigan thought he resembled "a Jew polar bear." (Loewinsohn had been brought up as a Catholic.) Richard jotted down a long poem in his notebook called "We're here," describing their odd-couple living arrangement.

Shortly after Ginny's return from her father's funeral in L.A., the isolation of life out on Potrero Hill began to wear on the Brautigans. Although friends came to visit, occasional parties couldn't dispel the sense of being totally out of the swing of things. "Good god, what do you do out here?" Ginny lamented. "You walk the baby, do the laundry. We got pretty tired of each other's company." Also, there was the uneasy sense that delinquents from the nearby Hunters Point Projects were invading the neighborhood. "It just became crazier and crazier to live there."

From the moment cabin fever set in, a move back to North Beach was inevitable. Their friends Tom and Shirley were also looking to move away from Potrero Hill. After a bit of searching, Richard and Ginny located a ground-floor apartment at 557 A Greenwich Street on the slope of Telegraph Hill. The Lipsetts and their baby, Cadence, moved into unit B at the same address. The entrance led down a long narrow dark passageway to a small central courtyard. Richard set up the pink electric Royal typewriter Ginny had given him as a wedding present on the glass-framed back porch, surrounded by dime store plants. When he looked up from his work, he could see San Francisco Bay and watch the ships departing for faraway ports. Remembering Mexico, he wrote the poem he called "Ixtlan."

Cats always seek distraction when humans are busy doing something else. Jake and Boaz often came to visit while Brautigan tried to work, purring and rubbing against his legs. Quite naturally, he wrote a few, mostly unpublished, poems about his cats. "Spikes" concerned Jake's teeth. "The Eskimo of My Cat" began in mock classical fashion with the line "O Jake." Another poem, "The

Quail," written up on Potrero Hill during the autumn of 1960, told of Jake's abiding interest in three caged quail living next door.

All this time, Richard Brautigan struggled to write prose. "It was a matter of learning how to get people from one room into another, getting them to say some small thing and then back out again through the door." On the sixteenth of September, 1960, Mexican Independence Day, Richard wrote the date on a small piece of paper and tacked it to the wall above his typewriter. It was a date he wanted to remember. "I figured September 16 would mean something other than the date of Mexico's independence. Perhaps some kind of independence for things inside myself." This was the day when Richard Brautigan began to write his first novel. He called it *Trout Fishing in America*.

eighteen: gone fishing

KNOWING THERE WAS no money to be made as a poet, Richard Brautigan determined to break into fiction. His first strenuous efforts began up on Potrero Hill. "He tried to make a transition to prose," Ginny remembered. "He had a desperate time, a desperately difficult time doing that. Most of his short stories kept turning back into poems." Jack Spicer offered to help, although not himself excited by the possibilities of fiction. He had abandoned "The Tower of Babel," an attempt at a mystery novel, after 167 pages. Richard read each new story aloud to Jack and Ginny. Writing in his crabbed hand on lined yellow legal tablets, he struggled to make the brief tales longer than a paragraph or two. After every reading, both his audience members agreed, "For god's sake, take that out. Chop the ending. It's done." Richard sat facing them, looking "rather stricken."

"It wasn't easy for him," Ginny recalled. "Things came to him fully formed." This remained true all of Brautigan's life. He'd scratch down poetry in a single burst on the back of a cocktail napkin or in one of the little notebooks he carried everywhere. When he attempted to rework a poem, the effort usually consisted of writing the same lines over and over again with only the most minor alterations. Richard wrote instinctively, in flashes of magic inspiration, truly evoking the notion of "first word, best word," with none of the accompanying bombast often inflating the work of other Beat poets.

Longer works of fiction are never created in a single moment. They must be labored over, built like a house, brick by brick, board by board, line by line. Richard conceived his work in a photographic manner. Poems arrived as mental Polaroid snapshots, complete and instantly developed. Ginny felt his problem had to do with the difference in form, with having to write "in paragraphs with dialogue." Richard had already written several short stories in Eugene, each with a distinctive voice. He'd disavowed these initial efforts, erasing them from memory, wiping the slate clean, along with his family, his first love, and his hometown boyhood friends.

Brautigan asked Jack Spicer how to go about writing prose. His mentor's advice was oblique. "Throw away the good lines," Spicer said. "Keep the bad lines." He wanted Richard to come up with something new. Ginny remembered the long silent hours of work. "He didn't talk much about it. He and Spicer talked. We talked about it together. He'd say, 'I've got a short story.'"

"We'd say, 'No, you don't. You've got a poem.'"

This is where things stood when Richard pinned the Mexican Independence memorandum to the wall by his desk. Hemingway approved of such tactics "to keep yourself honest." Ginny summed up the breakthrough. "He really created a new form," she said. "Which was a prose poem." Often, the titles of Richard's poems came first, an initial spark igniting the creative detonation. Liking

"*Trout Fishing in America*," his title for the rough, experimental short story scrawled in his note-book, Brautigan decided that's what he'd call the novel he didn't yet know how to write. On the sixteenth, he rolled a sheet of paper into the Royal and wrote straight from the wellsprings of his heart, "As a child when did I first hear about *trout fishing in America*? From whom? I guess it was a stepfather of mine. Summer of 1942." Richard continued typing, the words coming in a poetic flow. He tapped into a lifelong love of fishing, the only part of his childhood he cared to remember.

Silver is not a good adjective to describe what I felt when
he told me about trout fishing.
I'd like to get it right.
Maybe trout steel. Steel made from trout. The clear
snow-filled river acting as foundry and heat.
Imagine Pittsburgh.
A steel that comes from trout, used to make buildings,
trains and tunnels.
The Andrew Carnegie of Trout!

Brautigan ended his initial effort by introducing an interlocutory character named *Trout Fishing in America*, a sort of ghost of trout fishing past, present, and future, who remembered "people with three-cornered hats fishing in the dawn." Reading it over, Richard knew he had a perfect page-long prose poem. Although he had set down a wonderful opening chapter, Richard Brautigan had no idea what he was going to write next. The chapters concerning Brautigan's Oregon upbringing led the charge as the Mexican Army of Independence liberated his mind. He wrote of his Tacoma childhood memories and of hitchhiking to fish the Klamath and of picking cherries "for two-and-a-half cents a pound." Recalling rainy afternoons on the McKenzie and wading the shallow runs of Gate Creek, Brautigan flavored his reminiscences with fern-lined wicker creels and salmon eggs, "using a size 14 single egg hook on a pound and a quarter test tippet," precisely rendered details breathing life into his most abstract fictional notions.

Richard Brautigan continued writing poetry while he wrestled with his novel. In January (1961), Ginny got mad at him for not submitting a chapter from the book for the Joseph Henry Jackson Award and Richard wrote a droll poem about his inactivity. When Ianthe was seven or eight months old, Ginny stopped breast-feeding and went back to work. Richard became the stay-at-home dad, changing diapers and feeding baby food. Fall and winter are often pleasantly mild and sunny in San Francisco. Not wanting to stay cooped up in the apartment, Brautigan carried his daughter over to nearby Washington Square, where she played in the grass while he watched from a nearby bench, notebook in hand.

Sometime early in February (after celebrating his twenty-sixth birthday reading Civil War history, making love with Ginny that night, and writing it all down as a poem the next day), Brautigan sketched out a rough draft in his spiral-bound notebook for a chapter called "The Cover of *Trout Fishing in America*." In what was essentially the same as the version he later published as the novel's opening chapter, Richard described the cover as a photograph of the Benjamin Franklin statue standing in Washington Square "taken in the late afternoon."

The statue was erected at Kearny and Market in 1879 by Henry D. Cogswell, a teetotaling dentist. The marble base supporting the life-sized pot metal statue originally had spigots on all four sides serving mineral water allegedly from as far off as Vichy, France. The earliest existing monument in the city, the statue was moved to Washington Square in 1904. Brautigan's opening chapter described the Ben Franklin monument in detail and told how poor people assembled at five in the afternoon to receive free sandwiches from the Saints Peter and Paul Church bordering on the park. Richard ended the passage by wondering if it was Kafka "who learned about America by reading the autobiography of Benjamin Franklin . . ."

Free sandwiches appealed to Richard Brautigan, as he was always short of cash. To supplement pocket change provided by his part-time job at Pacific Chemical Laboratories, Richard relied upon his old standby, the blood bank. When Brautigan returned the previous October, it had been over two years since he last sold a pint of type A at Irwin Memorial. He paid his final visit to the San Francisco Medical Society in late February 1961. Richard brought his baby daughter along and wrote an unpublished poem, "The Belle of the Blood Bank," about Ianthe watching him with a catheter in his arm.

Work on the novel progressed. Richard Brautigan chronicled his memories of Johnnie Hiebert, the ruptured little brother of the Hiebert twins. He called this early chapter "The Kool-Aid Wino." The original longhand draft differed from the published version only in the ending. In the notebook, Richard wrote that the "Wino" said "To hell with the dishes," and the two kids climbed up onto the roof of the chicken house to drink Kool-Aid from a quart jar "in the shade of a willow tree, its long green branches reaching out over us." The boys held the unsweetened beverage "in our mouths a long time before we swallowed it." Brautigan later cut this final passage.

Three other chapters began as handwritten entries in Brautigan's notebook. The first, originally called "Dostoevsky," became "Sea, Sea Rider." The notebook draft is nearly identical to the published chapter but is half as long, comprising only the final story-within-a-story told to the narrator by the Jewish bookstore owner. The chapter called "The Last Year the Trout Came Up Hayman Creek" went through two rough drafts in Brautigan's notebook with only slight differences between them and the final version in the novel. Of the chapter "Trout Death by Port Wine" (so like a headline in the tabloids Richard adored), only the title remained unaltered when *Trout Fishing in America* finally went to print. In its earlier notebook incarnation, the chapter was completely different, beginning with a memorable line, "Old Roller Skate Wheels was the first dead man I ever saw in my life."

It was Ginny's task to decipher Richard's cramped handwriting and type his notebook entries into legible chapters. There were times when her day job and caring for the baby made this impossible, so Brautigan prepared preliminary typescripts on his own. When he didn't feel like working at home on the big pink Royal standard, he carried a Smith-Corona portable to the cool dim recesses of Gino & Carlo's or some other North Beach hangout. A gift from Price Dunn, who paid $8.60 for the machine after it was impounded in the Monterey Greyhound depot, the Smith-Corona was one of five different typewriters Brautigan used in creating *Trout Fishing in America*.

Anna Halprin's open invitation to Richard Brautigan, asking him to create original works for the San Francisco Dancers' Workshop, found its own oblique way into his novel in progress. He started a chapter he called "The Ballet for *Trout Fishing in America*" on the back porch of 557 A Greenwich Street, inspired by the desiccated, Nixon-campaign-pin-pierced cobra lily plant sitting beside his worktable, he typed, "How the Cobra Lily traps insects is a ballet [. . .] a ballet to be performed at the University of California in Los Angeles."

The previous summer, Jack Spicer and Robin Blaser agreed to start "White Rabbit College," an experimental school modeled on Black Mountain, featuring a curriculum taught only by artists for other writers and painters. The plan involved using Ebbe Borregaard's Museum as the location for their "college." Borregaard insisted on formal contracts, and in the end a seven-week course taught by Robert Duncan on "The History of Poetry" was all that came of it. Duncan's lectures ran on Thursday nights from December 15, 1960, to January 26, 1961.

Duncan also spoke on the next two Thursdays. Borregaard's Museum featured concerts of Baroque music Sunday afternoons at four. Admission was $1.50. Duncan charged a buck. When Richard Brautigan read at the museum at eight thirty on Friday evening, March 17, 1961, a ticket cost seventy-five cents. It was the first public exposure of *Trout Fishing in America*, still a work in progress. During the six months Richard had been writing the book, he showed each new chapter to Jack Spicer, who reacted enthusiastically, offering editorial advice and encouraging the reading at Ebbe Borregaard's place. Brautigan read some of the early chapters set in his boyhood on the creeks around Eugene. He also read a forgotten poem entitled "Alas, In Carrion Umpire."

Richard Brautigan's novel grew by bits and pieces. He had already transformed many childhood fishing memories into poetic fiction, and he included a short story written in the fall of 1959 as a chapter in his expanding manuscript. "A Walden Pond for Winos" is one of the very few chapters in the book not referring to either trout fishing or *Trout Fishing in America*. It is set in Washington Square Park and mentions the Benjamin Franklin statue. A reference to "the cold autumn wind" and the line "At home my wife was pregnant" establish the time frame and indicate the story was written well before Brautigan began work on his novel. In the piece, the narrator and two artist friends share a bottle of cheap port in the park. They talk about committing themselves to an insane asylum for the winter: "Television, clean sheets on soft beds, hamburger gravy over mashed potatoes [. . .] Ah yes, there was a future in the insane asylum. No winter spent there could be a total loss."

Richard Brautigan felt the need for library research. The Mechanics' Institute at 57 Post Street fit the bill. Founded in 1855 in the wake of the gold rush, the Institute had a fine three-story building and a library of over 200,000 books when the 1906 earthquake and fire reduced it all to rubble. The Mechanics' Institute erected a new nine-story building on the site, moving in on July 15, 1910. Two years later, the library collection totaled 40,000 volumes. By 1961, there were close to 160,000 books in the stacks.

Richard Brautigan found his way to the second floor on Post Street to work on *Trout Fishing in America*. As a rule, the Mechanics' Institute Library admitted only subscribers. Richard wasn't a member, not having money to spare for dues, and so couldn't check out any of their books. This presented no problem, as the stacks were open to the patrons. Once Brautigan gained entrance, he wandered along the crowded shelves, conducting his private research without being disturbed.

After finishing work downtown at the chemical laboratory, Brautigan headed to the high-ceilinged main reading room at the Institute. Ginny remembered meeting him there frequently during her lunch hour. Richard also brought Kenn Davis over to the Mechanics' Institute, delighting in showing his friend a place in San Francisco that he "knew nothing about." Kenn sketched Brautigan working in the library, a place looking very much like a private turn-of-the-century club. The flooring of the narrow aisles between the stacks consisted of two-foot-square opaque glass plates. Walking on them made Ginny Brautigan feel "really eerie."

At the Mechanics' Institute library, Richard Brautigan compiled of a list of twenty-two classic books about fishing (with publication dates ranging from 1496 to 1957), which he included in his reworking of the "Trout Death by Port Wine" chapter. Angling writers as diverse as Roderick L. Haig-Brown, Zane Grey, Ray Bergman, and Ernest G. Schwiebert Jr. are mentioned. Another early chapter had its origins in an unlikely source volume, a nineteenth-century cookbook Brautigan came across one day while browsing in the stacks. Intrigued by the antique language, Richard jotted down four odd recipes that struck his fancy. Together they compose almost the entire text of the brief chapter titled "Another Method of Making Walnut Catsup." Incorporating "found art" into his work was a technique Brautigan utilized throughout his career. He first published these accidental discoveries in *Trout Fishing in America*. "We were inveterate billboard readers," Ginny recalled. "We were Dadaist. The best art was chance."

In a chapter called "*Trout Fishing in America* with the FBI," Richard described a wanted poster for Richard Lawrence Marquette he came across in the window of a store on lower Market Street. The suspect was "an avid trout fisherman." Brautigan jotted down the information in his notebook. He described the "dodger" exactly as it appeared, both sides folded under. The arbitrarily truncated description of the fugitive is reminiscent of William Burroughs's "cut-up" experiments, begun in Paris at the same time that Brautigan started on his novel. The facsimile signature of *Trout Fishing in America* ending this chapter is in Richard Brautigan's hand.

"The Mayonnaise Chapter," last in the novel, provides the best-known example of "found art" in *Trout Fishing in America*. Consisting in its entirety of a single letter of condolence that Ron Loewinsohn reported "the author actually found in a secondhand bookstore and reproduced verbatim—including the misspelling in the postscript: 'P.S. Sorry I forgot to give you the mayonaise [*sic*],'" the chapter is essential Richard Brautigan. Although he didn't write a word of it, Mother and Nancy's letter to Florence and Harv reflects Brautigan's easy offhand voice, his concern for average working-class people, his matter-of-fact treatment of death, and his often startling juxtaposition of wildly disparate images. When the nine-year-old letter, intended as a bookmark, fluttered from the pages of a dusty volume, Richard Brautigan made it his own.

Meandering around North Beach and hanging out in Washington Square Park, Brautigan encountered an exotic variety of eccentric individuals. A confirmed "people-watcher," he delighted in these discoveries. Among the more curious neighborhood specimens was a legless tramp who sold pencils on Columbus Avenue near Washington Square. He propelled himself along the city sidewalks on roller-skate wheels mounted beneath a crude handmade board. Everyone on the street called him Shorty. He was a foul-mouthed unpleasant man, frequently drunk and shouting obscenities at passing schoolchildren. This abusive behavior endeared him to the local bohemians.

Ginny Brautigan and Shirley Lipsett often took their new babies to the park, "the only green spot around." They saw Shorty there all the time, waiting for his free sandwich in front of the church. Richard "talked to him a lot," she recalled. Ginny never spoke to Shorty. "Richard almost always found things to say to people." Ron Loewinsohn remembered Shorty. "He was a regular character, and there were a couple of guys from New Orleans, from Pirate's Alley, who were part of that contingent who used to hang around the Benjamin Franklin statue in the afternoon drinking muscatel."

Brautigan made ample use of the offbeat characters he observed in the park. The two "broken-down artists from New Orleans" became part of the chapter "A Walden Pond for Winos." Richard also recognized the comic literary possibilities of connecting Shorty, the unpleasant derelict double-amputee, with a brawling fictional character Nelson Algren named "Railroad Shorty" in "The Face on the Barroom Floor," a short story in his collection *The Neon Wilderness*. Later, Algren recycled the story into a violent episode concluding his novel *A Walk on the Wild Side*, this time calling the truncated strong man "Legless Schmidt." In Brautigan's recollection both characters were named "Railroad Shorty," and he titled a chapter for his own novel in progress "The Shipping of *Trout Fishing in America* Shorty to Nelson Algren." Richard renamed the neighborhood wino and proposed packing him in a crate and sending him to Algren in Chicago, where the old bum might become a museum exhibit.

Something essential was missing from *Trout Fishing in America*. Brautigan had written numerous chapters: nostalgic reminiscences of his boyhood in the Pacific Northwest, oddball recollections of bohemian life in North Beach, offbeat "found art" observations, all possessing an original style and a certain evocative energy, yet taken as a whole, they didn't quite add up to a book. He wasn't writing a conventional novel, but Richard still needed something to tie it all together. He needed to go on a trout fishing trip.

More than a weekend in the Sierras, Brautigan wanted an expedition lasting through most of the summer. Richard and Ginny picked Idaho as their final destination. She'd been born there and had never seen the Snake River, a favorite spot of her father's. Idaho also had the advantage of being closer to San Francisco than either Montana or Wyoming, two other remote Rocky Mountain angling citadels they briefly considered. Ginny had relatives living in Idaho, which provided another advantage. The couple suspected the roads might get worse the further they ventured northeast from California. They could visit her family and take occasional breaks from the rustic joys of camping.

Almost overnight, Richard Brautigan became an amateur cartographer, studying atlases and road maps, following the enticing blue lines flowing between remote mountain ranges with faraway-sounding names: Sawtooth, Lost River, Pioneer, Bitterroot. So many great names. Richard fell in love with the names. He began a list of streams as yet unseen, picking those that sounded the most poetic: Lost Creek, Little Word River, Big Smoky Creek, Silver Creek. Brautigan's projected journey took shape like a poem in his imagination.

A letter arrived from E. V. Griffith, editor of *Hearse*. He apologized for his long delay in responding to the poetry Brautigan submitted. Out of the batch, Griffith was keeping only "The Rain" for the next issue. Under separate cover, he sent a copy of *Promotion*, his new publication, which contained a review of *Lay the Marble Tea* and reprinted two of the editor's "favorites" as a Brautigan sampler. "Hope there is no objection on your part," Griffith concluded.

Richard did object. He learned that E. V. Griffith had already reprinted his poetry in earlier issues without prior permission. "The Rain" was Brautigan's final appearance in *Hearse* (no. 9, 1961). It was also the last time he published his work in "little" magazines for several years. Small presses paid nothing, aside from an implied hipness-by-inclusion. After his success with Carp Press, Brautigan knew he was much better off self-publishing his poetry. Also, he had other things on his mind. He was going fishing.

During the winter and spring of 1961, the Brautigans focused their thoughts on the adventure planned for the coming summer. They "discovered Schedule C," the self-employment form of the federal income tax, and received a $350 refund. With this windfall they bought a rattletrap ten-year-old Plymouth station wagon that embodied the notion of a moving violation. Stan Fullerton came to the rescue. A can-do sort of guy, practical in the many mechanical ways where Richard was all thumbs, Stan took the jalopy over to an automobile graveyard and bought replacement parts from the best of the rusting junkers abandoned there. These included "a new tailgate and lights all around." Fullerton installed the parts "on the spot," trading in what he removed as partial payment on the "new" junk.

Richard required minimal fishing equipment. Preferring to wade wet, he owned neither hip boots nor chest waders. He had no use for a fancy vest to store his flies, leaders, and other tackle. His fly rod was an RA Special #240. Priced at $14.99, the two-piece seven-foot fiberglass rod was a purely utilitarian "smoke pole." With a Japanese Olympus reel and a spool of cheap floating fly line, it was all the gear Brautigan needed for catching trout.

Secondhand camping gear scrounged from friends and scored for discount prices in Army surplus stores transformed the Brautigans' apartment into a makeshift bivouac area. They acquired a tent and sleeping bags, pots, pans, skillets, and a two-burner Coleman white gas camp stove, all previously trail-broke. A Coleman lantern (a necessity for a couple who liked to read late into the night) was the only brand-new piece of equipment that Richard and Ginny purchased, a shopping experience Brautigan transformed into a chapter ("A Note on the Camping Craze That Is Currently Sweeping America") in *Trout Fishing in America*.

The Brautigans gave Jake, their surviving black cat, to their former roommate, Kenn Davis. Boaz met an unfortunate end months earlier. She crawled through an opening in the wooden cover of an unused backyard laundry sink and was unable to climb back out again. No one heard her desperate crying, and she died, like a creature from a Poe story, entombed in the tub.

By June, Richard, Ginny, and Ianthe were ready to hit the road. After storing their few possessions with friends, they vacated the Greenwich Street apartment and loaded the station wagon with all the camping stuff and baby things, along with two orange crates stuffed with books ("Rimbaud, Thoreau, Whitman") and a Royal portable typewriter (the Smith-Corona Price Dunn gave Richard had succumbed to mechanical problems) loaned by Ray Lopez, a barber with a shop in the green-copper-clad Columbus Tower building at Kearny and Columbus where Brautigan got his hair cut. He no longer wore bangs, parting his pale blond hair on the right. Richard also shaved off his beard, but kept the drooping mustache. With high hopes, they headed east across the Bay Bridge in the Plymouth, destined for new possibilities.

Richard and Ginny drove over the Sierras on U.S. 40, passing through Reno, where they tied the knot four years earlier. Somewhere in the Nevada desert, they pulled off the highway and wound down a narrow dirt road into a broad basin fronted by an earthen dam. They made camp on the level surface of a dry lake bed and feasted that night after dinner on a large watermelon bought from a roadside grocery. The watermelon may have provided their salvation. Richard got up to relieve himself in the middle of the night and noticed huge thunderclouds roiling in the dark sky overhead. It was about to rain. A flash flood would inundate their campsite.

Richard woke Ginny, and they set to work striking camp on the double. "We almost killed ourselves," Ginny recalled. "We had all this stuff. We had to cram it in, really fast." If there was no danger of drowning, the possibility of having water up over their hubcaps and getting stuck in the mud in the middle of nowhere seemed very real as the skies opened up above them. The raindrops came down the size of silver dollars. By the time the tent was folded and packed into the Plymouth, along with their books and all the other gear, it was a deluge.

Ginny was terrified. It rained so hard she couldn't see to drive even with the lights on. Richard ran backwards up the road, waving his arms to show her where to turn as the station wagon slid around the slippery curves. Once they gained the paved highway and knew everything would be okay, the whole nasty experience became something they could laugh about, their big trip almost over before it had barely begun.

The Brautigans turned north for Idaho on U.S. 93 at Wells, a tiny truck stop fifty miles east of Elko. Ginny did all the driving. Richard sat, sometimes holding the baby on his lap, staring out at the vast open country. All along the way, he sang a tuneless song of his own invention. "Oh, my Orofino Rose," he crooned, repeating the single line of his simple ditty over and over. (Their trip never took them as far as Orofino.) Pushing on past Twin Falls, they set up camp on Silver Creek, near the tiny town of Picabo, Idaho. Brautigan rigged his rod and set out after trout.

Richard sloshed into the chill mountain water in his blue jeans. During his first week in Idaho, Brautigan fished in Silver and Copper creeks, and on the Little Wood River. He bought a new twenty-five-cent Key brand spiral-bound notebook and began a list that he headed "Names of places where I caught trout, in order of appearance, 1961—Idaho, a travel song, a ghost song." Silver Creek topped the list, followed in short order by the Little Wood River and Copper Creek. Compiling such catalogs became one of Richard's lifelong preoccupations.

The list grew as the summer unfolded. The Brautigans headed next for the Sawtooth National Forest, to a network of narrow valleys between the Smoky Mountains and the Soldier Mountains. They settled in at a campground on Big Smoky Creek, stream number 4 in the notebook. Several other prime fishing sites in the surrounding area were added in quick succession: Paradise, Salt, Little Smoky, and Carrie creeks.

The weather stayed hot and humid, and it frequently rained. During the midday hours when fishing proved unproductive, Richard set up the portable Royal and worked on his novel. The high mountain meadows provided excellent grazing, and many bands of sheep had been herded up to summer pasturage. Brautigan wrote of several woolly ungulate encounters ("Everything smelled of sheep on Paradise Creek [. . .]") and of giving a bottle of beer to a shepherd "who looked like Adolf Hitler."

Large concentrations of lamb on the hoof invariably attracted predators, and Richard listened to the mournful calling of coyotes in the rain. He captured their howls in his singular prose. ("Their voices are a creek, running down the mountain, over the bones of sheep, living and dead.") Salt Creek had been kind to Brautigan. He once caught "seven trout in fifteen minutes," and later eased a beautiful bejeweled Dolly Varden from its swift-moving water.

Richard disliked the printed signs he saw warning of explosive cyanide capsules set out to kill coyotes. He wrote down a mock version of the government warning and had Ginny translate it into Spanish. Both appear in the chapter "The Salt Creek Coyotes," where Brautigan, troubled by what an old-timer in a local bar had told him of the lethal lures, compared the cyanide capsules to the gas chamber at San Quentin.

Richard and Ginny headed west, winding along narrow Big Smoky Road and Shake Creek Road to Featherville, where they turned north through Rocky Bar on James Creek Road to an isolated campground at the edge of the wilderness area beneath East Warrior Peak. Here, Richard fished the Middle Fork of the Boise River and the Queens River, catching trout in both places. Taking a break from camping in the rain, the Brautigans followed the Middle Fork down past Twin Springs and cut through Boise and its expensive motels on their way to McCall, where Ginny had relatives.

The road north through Horseshoe Bend, Banks, and Smiths Ferry followed the North Fork of the Payette River, still muddy from the spring runoff. Route 55 paralleled the west bank of Cascade Reservoir for its entire scenic sixteen-mile length. "The mountains were so beautiful," Ginny remembered. "It was just an untouched place at that time."

The little 1880s town of McCall nestled under the spruce on the southern shore of snow-fed Payette Lake. The area's alpine beauty provided the location for the 1940 Spencer Tracy film *Northwest Passage*. Ginny's cousin and childhood Reseda playmate, Donna, lived in McCall with her husband. She wasn't from Idaho or raised as a Mormon, growing up pagan in Southern California. "She became a Mormon when she was eleven or twelve," Ginny remembered, "but I guess all along her mother and her mother's family were Mormons."

Richard and Ginny drank Mormon-brew decaffeinated coffee and discussed the threat of Communism with Donna and her husband. ("The smell of coffee had been like a spider web in the house.") Brautigan described the visit in a chapter he called "The Teddy Roosevelt Chingader'." He also mentioned buying "tennis shoes and three pair of socks at a store in McCall" and fretted about the lost guarantee. Insignificant banal moments became part of Richard's work from the very start.

Idle conversations with strangers in McCall (store clerks, waitresses, and a ten-year-old girl sweeping a restaurant porch) became another continuing concern in his fiction. The chapter followed the Brautigans back across the high country, where patches of snow still resisted summer. They drove along the South Fork of the Payette River, stopping in Lowman for a strawberry milkshake, and caught their first glimpse of the magnificent Sawtooth Mountains when they looped into Stanley Basin from the north on Highway 21.

The town of Stanley, a random collection of log cabins and double-wides scattered beneath the crenellated cathedral upthrust of the Sawtooth Range boasted "four or five bars." The Ace of Diamonds Club sat derelict with its windows broken out. Richard thought Stanley "a fine town." On Saturday nights, one of the bars hosted a dance called the "Stanley Stomp." Once, hitchhiking through town after fishing, Richard stopped in at a tavern and asked if they had any port wine. The bartender said he didn't think so but took a look anyway and, from behind a bunch of dusty bottles below the bar, pulled out the lone jug of port. He blew the dust off the top and uncorked it. Brautigan "drank the first and last bottle of port wine in Stanley, Idaho."

The Brautigans set up their tent at Unit 4 of the Little Redfish Lake campground, three miles south of Stanley. Right on the lake, the place had a fantastic view of mountains Richard erroneously believed to be in Montana. Best of all, it was free, unlike the Big Redfish Lake campground, charging $3 a week "like a skid row hotel," and crowded with trailers and Winnebagos. Richard and Ginny decided to spend the rest of the summer in Stanley Basin. Their campsite boasted a fine table for eating and work, in addition to a sheet-metal cookstove with "no bullet holes in the pipe."

The Salmon River (the River of No Return) flowed on the other side of the highway. In a letter to a friend, Richard described the fishing as "the best I've ever seen." Ginny had a camera and took pictures of her husband angling, along with potential dust jacket shots of him posed against the gutted hulk of a thirty-year-old derelict automobile. For good times, they gravitated to the Rocky

Bar in Stanley and shook their booties at the "Stomp." Because of the baby, Richard and Ginny crawled into the sack early most nights, too tired to read from their carton-box library.

At first light on July 2, 1961, in Ketchum, forty miles across the mountains as the crow flies, Ernest Hemingway pressed his forehead against the twin upturned barrels of a favorite Boss shotgun, holding the walnut stock firmly against the floor, and tripped both triggers. It was a cloudy day. Richard Brautigan went fishing on Yellow Belly Lake with a forty-year-old Arkansas businessman he met in the campground. All the fellow could talk about was how afraid he was of losing his job. Neither of them heard any news of Hemingway's death that day. Richard didn't learn of his hero's suicide until after returning to San Francisco in the fall, when he happened across the July 14 edition of *Life* with the Yousuf Karsh color portrait of Hemingway on the cover.

Richard didn't include his conversation with the nervous executive in the book. Instead, he recorded a ranting diatribe on the evils of socialized medicine in a chapter called "The Surgeon." The surgeon was a neighbor in the Little Redfish Lake campground. He'd arrived a couple days before in his Rambler, pulling a trailer with his wife and two infant kids aboard. The Brautigans were leaving that afternoon, north to Lake Josephus. All morning, Richard fished alongside the surgeon, listening to him bitch and ramble, holding his own feelings in reserve. Later, camped on the edge of the Idaho wilderness, he shaped his keen observation of the angry doctor into a deft new chapter.

During a near-monthlong stay in Stanley Basin, Richard Brautigan fished the Salmon River, Yellow Belly Lake, Valley Creek, Stanley Lake, Stanley Lake Creek, and Big and Little Redfish Lakes. Even with all the time spent wading streams and lakes, there were many long summer hours for writing. When not working on the novel, Richard maintained a lively correspondence. He wrote letters to Ron Loewinsohn and to Lou Embree, who was forwarding mail from San Francisco.

In a note to Lester Rosenthal in New York City, Brautigan invented a macabre story about Kenn Davis starving Jake to death because he knew Les had never cared for his cat. One afternoon, Richard drew a number of childlike cartoons in a small notebook to amuse Ianthe, adding nonsense captions under the primitive drawings ("Fruit sign after breakfast," "Fish without any bus fare, but he don't care," "Boat that just got over a bad cold," "Watermelon with a sail on its back"). Richard never offered his daughter anything less than the full megawattage of his unique intelligence.

The passages Richard Brautigan wrote looking out across Little Redfish Lake reflected the peaceful happy time he spent in Stanley Basin. Chapters describing sex in a hot spring surrounded by green slime and dead fish and Ianthe playing happily with a pan full of vanilla-pudding-flavored minnows conveyed the primal pleasures of living outdoors and fishing every day. Brautigan was not a purist. He used a fly rod and wrote of fly tying, dry flies drifting like ephemeral angels through his novel, but also mentioned fishing with salmon eggs and something called a "Super-Duper." He used bait and lures without shame. The whole point was catching trout destined for the frying pan. In his notebook, Brautigan jotted down, "Number of times that we ate trout / 9 so far / 6 more." Richard found a writer's paradise in Stanley Basin. "I could not have come to a better place," he wrote to Les Rosenthal.

The Brautigans pulled up stakes toward the end of July, heading north into the mountains to Lake Josephus, situated between the Seafoam Mine (gold) and the Greyhound Mine (lead and silver). The River of No Return Wilderness stretched impenetrably ahead of them. Scattered all along the surrounding plateau, dozens of small isolated lakes beckoned the adventurous hiker. Richard fished Float Creek, Helldiver Lake, and Lake Josephus. Camping in such a remote spot provided ample amounts of solitude. Brautigan crafted two new chapters for his novel: "Lake Josephus Days" and "The Towel," melancholy glimpses into the past and the everyday problems of dealing with a sick baby.

Frost glistened on the morning grass. Chilly nights made campfires a necessity. Their blue smoke drifted down the valley toward the distant clanging of a sheepherder's bell mare. After leaving Lake Josephus, the Brautigans crossed over from Wells Summit and lingered into autumn along Carrie Creek, a spot they'd liked a lot when they fished there earlier. Richard started filling the back of the station wagon with firewood. Although fishing remained excellent, snow might fall any day now. It had been a wonderful trip, but with summer over and cash running low, it was time to head for home.

Back in Frisco, Richard and Ginny found a top-floor North Beach apartment almost right away. Located at 488 Union Street between Montgomery and Kearny ("one unbroken flight of stairs for three stories"), above Yone's Bead Shop, and next door to a Laundromat, the place was a convenient two-block walk from Washington Square. "I can look out the window and see nob hill [*sic*]," Richard wrote in a November letter to Sam Broder. "The lights go on there at night." Brautigan told his friend about the book he'd been working on for over a year and hoped to have finished by spring. "It is called *Trout Fishing in America*. I don't know whether anyone will want it or not, but it will give me a perfect excuse to get drunk and rant and rave about my poor little lost american novel."

Price Dunn showed up to help paint the apartment. The agreement was that he could stay for however long it took to get the job done, one week, two tops, and then he'd be on his way. As Ron Loewinsohn recalled, "The apartment got painted. Price didn't want to move. Richard had to put his foot down. Price moved." In Loewinsohn's opinion their relationship boiled down to: "Price was always wanting a place to crash, and Richard was always putting up with him, putting up with him, and then finding this person in his house that he couldn't deal with."

The Brautigans threw a big housewarming party. Price Dunn got "uproariously drunk." He ended up with some girl he didn't know and couldn't remember the morning after.

Somewhere in the interim they passed out. Richard, Stan Fullerton, and several other cronies carried Price and his "date" naked and comatose from their love nest, depositing them in the bathtub. "A definite giggle session," Fullerton said. Richard's love for bizarre practical jokes came into play, and he poured several packets of green and red food coloring over the unconscious couple. "We woke up in the bath, screaming," Price recalled. "*Aaaaaa . . . !*"

Ginny found new secretarial work. Richard went back to his part-time job at Pacific Chemical, measuring out barium swallows formula two or three afternoons each week. To Richard, everything seemed "all right. Ginny is learning Russian and Ianthe is learning English." The Brautigans returned the borrowed Royal portable to Mr. Lopez and rented an International standard for three months so Richard might continue working on his novel. In the evenings, Ginny neatly typed his notebook entries and rough drafts into legible chapters. When the term on the rental typewriter expired, Richard and Ginny coughed up $65 for a used electric IBM.

After reading the back issue of *Life* magazine with news of Ernest Hemingway's suicide, Brautigan began his first new work since returning from the trip, a chapter he called "The Last

Time I Saw *Trout Fishing in America*." The sudden loss of his artistic "father" triggered memories of itinerant fry cook Tex Porterfield (who first told him about trout fishing) and the winter they spent together in Great Falls, Montana, during World War II. Richard translated these emotions into a fantasy dialogue between the narrator and his eponymous title character. They discussed the narrator's fear that the Missouri River would someday begin to resemble a forgotten Deanna Durbin movie he had seen "seven times" in Great Falls. Popular culture consumes our perceptions of reality, a parasite replicating its host. Fame ate the heart out of Hemingway. Richard Brautigan recognized the symptoms of this insidious social disease yet remained unable to diagnose them when he was himself infected.

Another new chapter ("In the California Bush") grew out of weekend trips Richard and Ginny took that fall across the Golden Gate Bridge to visit Lou Embree and his girlfriend, who lived in the hills above Mill Valley in a rented cabin overlooking San Francisco Bay. Their isolated rural world, eventually erased by four decades of relentless development, was still a tranquil rural place back before the million-dollar homes crowded in under the redwoods. Shielded by eucalyptus trees, Embree's cabin had a cool basement, where Ianthe slept. Richard and Ginny, fresh from a summer-long camping adventure, bunked down outside under an apple tree, rising only when the morning sun rose high enough to bake them in their sleeping bags.

The two couples enjoyed long breakfast conversations, fueled by cup after cup of strong black coffee. Brautigan called Lou "Pard" in his new chapter, recounting Embree's exotic international upbringing and heroic war experience. Richard unleashed his refining eloquence in describing the natural world at Embree's cabin, "the warm sweet smell of blackberry bushes along the path" where he jumped coveys of quail and watched them "set their wings and sail on down the hill." Brautigan conveyed a stronger feeling for nature in a suburban setting than in his observations of the wilderness backcountry along the River of No Return. The "strange cabin above Mill Valley" remained a magical place where running deer startled Richard awake in the dawn.

By Christmas of 1961, Richard Brautigan's first novel was nearly complete, yet he instinctively felt something was still missing. A trip down to Big Sur early in 1962 solved the problem. Price Dunn had returned to the area in the fall of 1961, taking up with a woman with a nine-year-old daughter. He was looking for an affordable home and heard about an abandoned estate high atop a ridge in the Santa Lucia Mountains south of Gorda. The place at Lime Kiln Creek had been built in the 1920s by Victor Girard, an early Los Angeles land developer who Price thought had been a silent movie star. Back before Highway 1 was completed there were no roads along this remote coastline. Girard and his guests came by boat to San Simeon and rode over the same mountain trail used to pack in construction materials for his remote rural retreat.

Forty years later, when Price Dunn wandered up the switchbacks, the land developer was long dead and his palatial "cabin" had burned to the ground, leaving only a fireplace and tall white river-boulder chimney. Brautigan saw it as "a sort of Carthaginian homage to Hollywood." A roofless redwood servants' cottage remained more or less intact along with several convict shacks at the bottom of the hill at Henderson Creek, remnants of the prison labor used to build the highway. It was a beautiful spot. The view from the high promontory was staggering. "You could see all the way to San Simeon—really gorgeous." To Price, the old ruin was a squatter's paradise.

One problem remained. The abandoned homestead had no water. Price Dunn searched around and located a man over in the Livermore Valley who had a donkey for sale. Price bought "Old

George," and the burro packed the water Dunn's makeshift family needed to survive on their ridgetop hideaway. George also carried up a cookstove and other supplies, including a metal roof Dunn purchased in sections at the Cleveland Wrecking Yard in San Francisco. Price nailed the roof on the servant's cottage, snug inside with his woman and her child before the winter rains came.

Richard Brautigan wrote to Dunn asking if he and his friend Ron Loewinsohn might come to Big Sur for a weekend visit. Price agreed and arranged a rendezvous, heading down from his mountaintop to meet them on the highway. "Naturally, we had a jug of wine," Dunn recalled. "I'd been drinking beer, anyway." It was a thirty-minute walk back up the hill along a steep switchback, and suitably fortified, the trio followed the path parallel to Lime Kiln Creek. "We all stopped to take a piss, and we're looking down into the creek, and goddamn, right down there were these two huge steelhead. Big as my leg!"

The trout were holding in a deep pool gouged into the narrow creek. Crazed with excitement, the three young men hurried to dam the lower end with boulders, blocking any possible escape. Leaving Richard and Ron to stand guard, Price rushed home and returned with a garden rake and his machete. Using branches, they drove the fish out of the deep water into the shallow end of the pool. Price waded in, wielding the rake, and somehow managed to stun one of the steelhead. The other got away. Price hacked the huge trout into submission with his machete, and they dragged it onto the shore, carrying their trophy up to the ridgetop cabin. They feasted that night. After a summer in Idaho, where a two-pound cutthroat ranked as a memorable catch, this enormous steelhead struck Richard Brautigan as auspicious.

Price Dunn's colorful cracker patois ("whips and jingles") supplied Brautigan's book with a hangover description. Richard was less impressed with his friend's secondhand metal roof. He thought it "looked like a colander." Not much help with the Pacific rains drumming down outside. Watching leaks drip down around them, Price told Richard he'd bought the roof at the Cleveland Wrecking Yard. Intrigued by a demolition company selling dismantled houses in bits and pieces, Richard peppered Price with questions as they drank their way through the night. A vision of used trout streams sold in sections by the foot sparkled in his imagination.

A few weeks later, back in San Francisco, Brautigan boarded the number 15 bus on Columbus Avenue and rode over to the Cleveland Wrecking Company on Quint Street to check things out. He took careful notes about a thousand different doors and hundreds of toilets stacked on shelves. He observed the discounted laundry marking machine and gallons of "earth-brown enamel paint" selling for $1.10 per can. Richard Brautigan was a stickler for research. He got it all down exactly and described the wrecking yard with minute precision in *Trout Fishing in America*. The place provided a realistic background for his surreal vision of a dismembered trout stream for sale in a junkyard, one of the most striking images in American literature. With this chapter in place, Richard Brautigan knew he'd completed his first novel. It was mid-March 1962.

nineteen: the fastest car on earth

"BRAUTIGAN'S WRITTEN A great poem!" Jack Spicer proclaimed, praising *Trout Fishing in America* in the bars of North Beach. Spicer had supported Richard's book from its very inception, going over the manuscript with him, suggesting revisions and cuts. "Jack was absolutely fascinated with *Trout Fishing*," Ron Loewinsohn recalled, "and spent a lot of time with Richard talking about it." Spicer's advice became subconscious editing. Donald Allen didn't believe any of Brautigan's books was ever edited. "Any time you can get Richard to accept criticism is an unbelievable accomplishment," Loewinsohn observed. "He is so defensive, and so guarded; and Jack was able to get him to make changes."

Jack Spicer also provided introductions to powerful and important literary figures, urging them to read Brautigan's book. Copies of the manuscript went out to local editors Donald Allen and Luther Nichols, and to Malcolm Cowley, far off in Sherman, Connecticut, while Richard Brautigan slaved part-time at Pacific Chemical (which had moved to 41 Drumm Street). Brautigan kept a copy of Hemingway's short stories hidden in the basement of his workplace under an unused pile of old sheets, blankets, and pillows. He'd sneak down and read, sitting on an empty chemical drum, surrounded by "over 100 barrels of barium sulfate."

On his way to work, Richard often stopped off for lunch at one of his favorite cheap cafés, and on March 12, 1962, he began writing what he hoped would be a new novel. He called it"The Island Café." It was a book about lunch. Subtitled "Part of a Short History of Bad Movies in California," the brief unfinished work tapered off into a chronicle of film titles (two weeks of the daily billings at the Times Theater) but remained mostly about eating. Based on the Star on Kearny and the triangular US Café at the intersection of Stockton and Columbus, the Island Café was a place so ordinary it verged on the generic.

Day by day, Brautigan recorded what he had to eat and described the other customers seated at the counter, workingmen, mostly Asians. There was no conversation. From week to week, nothing happened, strangers eating cheap food in silence. The stasis in the entries and a lack of dialogue evoked time's monotonous passage. In this commonplace world, small everyday objects assumed extraordinary beauty: "I also noticed that next to the cash register right up by the flowers in the window there's a toaster and next to the toaster there's a Geritol box. One of those high alcoholic vitamin tonics. The whole arrangement struck my fancy."

Brautigan's observations wove between detailed dietary entries ("March 16 [. . .] boiled beef and noodles, a boiled potato, clam chowder, the same lettuce salad with the French dressing [. . .] and some corn and some crackers and two slices of white bread and two pats of butter and some cream for my coffee and it cost me sixty-five cents"), a poor man's hash house diary reflecting the author's concerns: experimental fiction, the common man, ordinary everyday objects, and the meticulous keeping of lists. Jack Spicer appeared obliquely in the entry for Saturday the twenty-fourth. Saloon-hopping "down on the Embarcadero," the narrator gets drunk and doesn't eat at the Island Café. "For lunch we ended up getting some hamburgers from the bake shop and eating on the grass at Aquatic Park. A quart of beer and somebody with a radio listening to a baseball game."

After fourteen typewritten pages, the difficulties of sustaining this chronological exercise in torpor took its toll. Triple-features from the Times Theater began creeping into the menu entries. Brautigan inserted glimpses of his life among the lists of grade-B movies. One cold day in March, he turned down three films he'd never seen, "the first good bill on at the Times since this work was started," because "a friend is coming over and we're going to talk about a novel he's written. I've had the manuscript for three weeks now." Richard had been working on "The Island Café" about as long. A few entries later, Brautigan slipped his typescript into a manila envelope labeled the Military Industrial Supply Company that he found at work, wrote "Never finished Novel" on the back, and went on with other things.

After leaving Bread and Wine, Pierre Delattre left North Beach and worked for a time as a cabinetmaker. In the fall of 1961, he got a call "from the head of the experimental department of missions of the Presbyterian church," who told Delattre about St. David's, an abandoned church for Welsh immigrants on Fourteenth Street between Guerrero and Valencia in the Mission District. Would Pierre be interested in doing something with the building? Their brief conversation marked the birth of the 14th Street Art Center.

The empty church was huge. Among the dusty pews, Delattre found a number of old hymnals printed in Welsh. "The Welsh always love to sing and perform," Pierre recalled, "and so they actually had two really wonderful stages." The art community got behind Delattre's efforts, helping him brighten the place with a fresh coat of paint. Soon, the center had a sculpture garden and a fledgling film department under the auspices of experimental movie makers Ron Rice and Agnes Varda. Pierre wanted to establish a program of readings like the one he'd had at Bread and Wine. With that in mind, he dropped in on his old pal Richard Brautigan in North Beach.

Richard seemed a bit discouraged about the prospects for *Trout Fishing in America*. He hadn't heard back from Don Allen. "In order to get Donald Allen to publish anything you have to be part of a gang that was really kind of fawning over [him]," Delattre remembered Brautigan saying. "He was joking about what he'd have to do to get Allen's attention." Trying to build up his friend's confidence, Pierre "talked Richard into giving a reading" at the 14th Street Art Center.

Brautigan read through his entire manuscript over two consecutive evenings. Ron Loewinsohn, in attendance both nights, remembered that Richard "did a good job. There was a good deal of reaction to the humor—people did laugh in funny places at the wit. Richard's a good reader. He read clearly. He knew where the punch lines would come in. The pieces are short, so there was a little bit of a break between the pieces. I was absolutely taken with the resonance of the short serious passages, things like 'The Towel,' and the humor, the wit that was there, and was completely taken with the metaphor of *trout fishing in America*."

No record survives of the exact dates of Richard Brautigan's extended reading of *Trout Fishing in America*. Pierre Delattre's best estimate placed it either toward the end of 1962 or early in 1963. The latter date is more likely. "The place was jammed, and they were almost all North Beach poets and aficionados. It was the local artistic community that came," Delattre said.

Ron Loewinsohn recalled things differently. "I would say a sparse crowd, maybe twenty-five, thirty people. And a lot of them were some of Jack's disciples and people who knew Richard and people who were part of this art center." Both Spicer and Robert Duncan were in the audience. Donald Allen did not attend. No admission was charged. Brautigan passed the hat after reading for an hour and fifteen minutes.

Delattre remembered the immediate response as wildly enthusiastic. "They loved it," he said. "I felt that it told Richard that he had a terrific book." Again, Loewinsohn differed in his assessment; Ron found the audience reaction "very mixed, very mixed."

Not long after, the excitement generated by the 14th Street Art Center caught the attention of higher-ups in the Presbyterian Church. "They had a meeting, and these social worker ministers started saying that we were giving all the attention to artists when there are all these people out on the streets who are hungry and drunk and so forth," Delattre said. The authorities demanded half of St. David's be turned back over to them. "In the end, we had to give them the lower floors of the church." Discouraged, Delattre resigned his position and took a job on the waterfront as a longshoreman. He remembered having persuaded Richard Brautigan to read from *Trout Fishing in America* as "one of the things I most congratulate myself on."

The Dancers' Workshop Company of San Francisco continued performing *The Flowerburger* at irregular intervals. After a performance that the Brautigans attended with Tom and Shirley Lipsett, the audience cried out "Author! Author!" Painfully shy, Richard slouched down in his seat, pushing his friend up in his place. Tall, lean, and fair, Lipsett wore similar horn-rimmed glasses and looked a lot like Brautigan. Tom took a bow, a surrogate receiving the accolades meant for someone not yet accustomed to praise.

Inspired by his first accidental collaboration with Anna Halprin's company, Brautigan set to work creating a new dance for them. He called it "a ballet idea" and worked it out first in his notebook, later typing a quick rough draft. Richard described the piece, "Plumbing, Etc.," in a letter to Halprin: "It is about a man who has a great liking for poetry [. . .] he decides to take the plumbing out of his house and replace it with poetry [. . .] I think it's a pretty strange idea." (In a sly dig, Allen Ginsberg replaced the toilet.) "Poetry cannot perform the functions of plumbing, so the man decides to take the poetry out and replace it with plumbing, but he runs into still another trouble, the poetry does not want to go [. . .]"

Brautigan described the stage setting as "a huge pile of plumbing stuff." He envisioned the dance beginning with John Graham sitting in a bathtub center stage, wearing the torn remnants of overalls and hip boots with swim fins attached. "He would then relate the history and events leading up to the present state, one of complete frustration, futility and defeat." At this point, Anna Halprin and A. A. Leath make their entrance, "representing the poetry that doesn't want to leave." The plumbing ballet was never performed. Richard recycled the idea several years later in a short story he called "Homage to the San Francisco YMCA," eventually included in his collection *Revenge of the Lawn.*

In the spring of 1961, Robert Duncan and Jess moved back to the city from their retreat in Stinson Beach, taking an apartment in the Mission District. Duncan began hosting a weekly "salon." Richard Brautigan met fellow poet Jory Sherman in North Beach (usually at Vesuvio) and they walked downtown every week across Market Street to Duncan's apartment. At his salon, Robert Duncan sat in the corner of the main room on a raised platform, reading and talking about literature. "Richard was always quiet at these things," Sherman remembered, "but from our walks together I knew he was brilliant and did not think along ordinary lines."

A more informal poetry group gathered every week at the home of Daniel Langton, "a popular writer" who lived close to Golden Gate Park. Brautigan rode out there with Jory Sherman, who still drove a car in spite of his plethora of unpaid parking tickets. "Danny and his wife were great hosts," Sherman wrote, recalling afternoons of beer and wine and sprightly conversation. Jory Sherman remembered Langton as a "bright, personable type of fellow that you thought was really going to go somewhere. I've never heard from him since."

Brautigan and Sherman spent a lot of time together taking long aimless walks around the city. Fascinated with San Francisco's ornate Victorian architecture, Richard often stopped and studied the fanciful turreted "painted ladies." On one such ramble, they were accompanied by the photographer who took the picture on the cover of Sherman's first book. While he focused his camera on the poets, Richard talked about Victorian houses, expressing a familiarity with them "that went beyond mere architecture."

"I think I am the reincarnation of Mark Twain," Brautigan announced. Jory Sherman believed his friend might have had a point. Richard possessed a "mystic quality." The way he stood with a slight backward slouch, "that brushy mustache, the kind of clothes he wore, the hat. He had a certain otherworldly air about him." Brautigan strongly identified with Twain. Watching him gaze up at the gaudy nineteenth-century buildings with such complete familiarity, Jory Sherman felt Richard Brautigan had stepped out of another time.

In August 1962, Farrar, Straus & Cudahy published Jack Kerouac's new novel, *Big Sur*. Written in ten days at breakneck Benzedrine speed, the book recounted a short period in the summer of 1960 when Kerouac lived in Lawrence Ferlinghetti's rustic Big Sur cabin. The stay was meant to be a solitary writer's retreat, but after three monastic weeks, Kerouac grew restless, returned to Frisco, and launched on an extended binge drunk. Back in Bixby Canyon with a group of friends, including Ferlinghetti, Philip Whalen, Neal and Carolyn Cassady, Michael McClure, his wife, Joanna, and their daughter, Jane, the party continued full blast the following week.

Lew Welch soon arrived with his lover, the poet Lenore Kandel, a Buddhist since the age of twelve, whom he'd recently met at the East-West House. (Kerouac described Kandel in *Big Sur* as "a big Rumanian monster beauty"). All the drinking took its toll on Jack Kerouac. He cracked up, going mad with the DTs. His friends got him sober and shipped the bad boy King of the Beats home to his momma.

By the summer of 1962, Richard Brautigan needed to start a new novel, "The Island Café" having hit a dead end. All around North Beach, the artistic community buzzed with talk of Kerouac's forthcoming book chronicling the recent misadventures at Ferlinghetti's Big Sur cabin. Richard had read Henry Miller's 1957 memoir, *Big Sur*, and saw the literary possibilities of doing his own take on the area. He'd already written a short story about Price Dunn's missing teeth. In July, Brautigan began sketching a sample chapter in the notebook he'd carried in Idaho. He wrote of Lee Mellon, describing his great grandfather, General Augustus Mellon, CSA. "He died in 1906 [*sic*]. The same year Mark Twain died. That was the year of Halley's comet." Richard hoped this odd material would somehow become a novel.

Along with attending poetry salons and Sunday family outings, Richard Brautigan spent more and more time hanging out in bars. David Fechheimer recalled running into him for the first time at the San Gotardo on Columbus. Fechheimer had been living in Europe after hitchhiking penniless across Central Africa "for the better part of a year. I'd picked up a rumor about things going on at San Francisco State, and so I came back." Sick with cholera and bilharzia from his African adventure, Fechheimer thumbed his way to California and enrolled in the English Department out at State.

The San Gotardo (now a Chinese restaurant named Brandy Ho's) was an Italian workingman's bar across the avenue from Tosca. Mixed drinks cost thirty-five cents. "Whiskey and soda, I don't think they had ice," David remembered. "A place where people got seriously drunk, but it was always clean and rather barren." Fresh cut flowers brightened the lackluster interior. Fechheimer had very little money, so he'd buy a glass of soda for twenty cents and go into the bathroom with his own smuggled bottle.

"One night, I threw open the door to a stall and there was this tall, skinny geek, with his half-pint. Sitting on the toilet. Cheapest bar in town. Two guys who were ripping it off." After meeting cute in the San Gotardo men's room, Richard and David became casual acquaintances, although they didn't get to know one another well until the seventies. "We used to see each other and drink a bit," Fechheimer recollected.

Another occasional drinking buddy from this period was a sometime journalist and aspiring writer from the Midwest named Fred Hill. Like Richard, Hill remained perpetually broke, a situation he remedied from time to time by hocking "old trusty," his typewriter. Hill was friendly with Ron Loewinsohn and the Lipsetts, but all Ginny remembered about him was a dramatic propensity for taking drunken bites out of his glass. Hill lived in a succession of low-rent North Beach hotels, notably the New Rex and the Swiss American, where rooms rented for under $10 a week. He and Richard talked about literary matters over cheap drinks, the conversations always returning to Fred's musings about a fantasy woman he called "Miss Delaware."

Price Dunn saw Richard more frequently. "I hitchhiked in and out of town," he said. "There's a wine shop. We'd go over in North Beach and buy a jug and go up on Telegraph Hill and wander around different places drinking." During these rambles, they talked and talked but the conversation tended not to be literary. Richard questioned Price about his sex life. "He always wanted to know about my amorous adventures—the girls!" Brautigan felt the marital bridle chafing. A secret part of him wanted free rein. "I could see their marriage was going down the tubes," Price Dunn observed.

Ron Loewinsohn recalled Richard from that time, "hanging out at bars, not coming home, not paying attention to Ginny, not paying attention to Ianthe, coming home loaded, chasing women." North Beach bar life provided a moveable wino feast. Brautigan sought out thirsty fellow poets at Vesuvio, the Coffee Gallery, 12 Adler Place, Gino & Carlo's, Katie's; any of a dozen different spots. "He wouldn't want the party to break up," Loewinsohn reminisced, "so he would bring everybody home, and then Ginny would be expected to cook and clean up."

One night, he brought home young Tony Aste, a newcomer to town. It turned out Ginny already knew him. Tony had just gotten off a merchant ship a few weeks earlier and had been involved in an automobile accident in North Beach. Bleeding badly from a big gash in his forehead, he needed help in hurry. Ginny and a friend took him to the nearest hospital, "to get his head stitched, and when we got there they wouldn't work on him because he wasn't twenty-one and we weren't his parents—and so, he had a scar."

Tony Aste was an attractive charismatic character. "A charming man," Lew Ellingham recalled. Like Richard Brautigan, he remained a natural loner. Ron Loewinsohn remembered him as "a clever, witty guy—a good-looking guy who had a lot of energy." To David Meltzer, Tony Aste was "a rogue. He could roll a joint in one hand."

Always a wanderer, Aste hailed from Salt Lake City, where he'd spent a troubled youth. He bragged about blowing the doors off the Mormon Temple with a Native American accomplice. While a teenager, he was sentenced to reform school. On his first day of incarceration, he was beaten senseless three times and subjected to eight brutal rapes. "I was so busted up they put me to bed for three weeks," Tony Aste said. "I swore that when I got out I was gonna do the beating and I was gonna do the fucking or they were going to have to kill me."

His toughness offset by an easygoing charm, he quickly make friends. Aste hung out in North Beach with a group of other newly arrived young men who took odd jobs washing dishes, parking cars, bussing tables: the usual minimum-wage, bottom-rung-on-the-ladder employment. Jack Spicer felt an immediate attraction for the lanky picaresque stranger and, according to Lew Ellingham, "treated him like a peer." Spicer nicknamed Tony and his group of friends "the Jets," a sly reference to the rumbling street gang in Leonard Bernstein's Broadway musical *West Side Story*.

Tony Aste, much like Neal Cassady and Price Dunn, was a rugged tale-teller whose stories inspired the poets with whom he associated. Spicer was fascinated by Aste's anecdotes of his rough-and-tumble upbringing. Richard Brautigan first encountered Tony Aste during his nocturnal roaming, most likely at Gino & Carlo's among Jack Spicer's voluble circle. He was drawn to the young maverick and his tall tales, much as he had been attracted earlier to Price Dunn's extravagant misbehavior. For Spicer, the attraction went well beyond adolescent hero-worship. "Jack was chasing Tony Aste's ass all over North Beach," according to Dora Geissler, a close friend of the poet.

Aste shared a Union Street apartment with Lew Ellingham and Stan Persky, a young poet recently returned to San Francisco after a European tour of duty with the U.S. Navy. Right from the start, Persky, engaged in a halfhearted affair with Robin Blaser, fell hard for the inaccessible and impossibly heterosexual Tony. Like the rest of Spicer's circle, he was attracted by the young man's physical beauty and adventuresome charm. "Everybody was in love with Tony Aste," Persky confessed.

Lew Ellingham remembered an afternoon he went over to the Brautigans' to pick up some manuscripts Ginny had typed for him. He thought her smart and literate, impressed that she corrected his spelling without consulting a dictionary. Tony Aste and Richard sat on the couch "playing with this deer rifle." There was no conversation, just the mechanical sound of the two men working the bolt action. Ellingham thought that Richard "seemed to be content to communicate on the level of birdsongs. He understood the role of silence and also the role of atmosphere and interconnections." On another occasion, Lew spent an evening with Richard, and their entire exchange consisted of bouncing a large beach ball back and forth across the room. "An hour may have passed with nothing said—no language."

Late on a fall night, Tony Aste drove Jack Spicer home from the Green Street bars in one of a succession of rattletraps he owned. Jack lived near Polk Gulch on California Street, and they took the Broadway Tunnel shortcut through Russian Hill. Emerging from the tunnel, they were broadsided by a motorist running a red light. Spicer was badly hurt, his ribs crushed. Soon after his release from the emergency room, he moved in with Jim Herndon (later the author of *The Way It*

Spozed to Be and *How to Survive in Your Native Land*) and his wife, Fran, for a period of recovery. Tony Aste walked away from the crash without a scratch.

Luck was also on Richard Brautigan's side. A letter arrived from Malcolm Cowley, and Richard's dreams started coming true. By 1962, Cowley had attained legendary status as a critic. Literary editor of *The New Republic* from 1929 to 1944 (where he published John Cheever for the first time); author of *Exile's Return*, an important history of American "Lost Generation" expatriates in Paris in the 1920s; and editor of *The Portable Faulkner*, the book that rescued William Faulkner from obscurity in 1945. Malcolm Cowley recently ushered *On the Road* from a 120-foot-long scroll manuscript to a best seller at Viking.

Cowley explained it had taken him a long time to read *Trout Fishing in America* because he was engaged with "some writing of my own [a collection of his correspondence with Faulkner] but when I did read it, my, how I did enjoy it." He went on to list what he liked best: "the used trout stream for sale in a junkyard, and the doctor who was giving up his practice in Great Falls, and bathing in Warm Springs, and the general active fancy and good writing. And ending on the word mayonnaise." Cowley feared that the book was "probably too far out for Viking to publish," but promised to bring Brautigan's manuscript to the office for additional readings and editorial comment.

He inquired if Richard had ever considered "trying your hand at a book that was a little more square and salable?" What Cowley had in mind was an inside look at bohemian life in North Beach, Sausalito, and Mill Valley, something along the lines of John Steinbeck's comic take on the denizens of Monterey and Carmel. "More characters, grotesques, coming into the story? And more dialogue? And more humor of situation to relieve the verbal wit? It's something to think about."

Richard sat down that same morning, drafting a reply to Malcolm Cowley for Ginny to type later. Brautigan's letter took a formal, respectful tone. He thanked Cowley twice ("I know how valuable your time is") for reading his novel and called the promised exposure at Viking "welcomed and appreciated." Richard acknowledged Cowley's work. "I read your fine book, Exile's Return when I was in my late teens and it has stayed with me ever since. I have a copy of the November 1926 issue of Poetry that contains 'Blue Juniata.' I like the poems, especially 'Laurel Mountain.'"

Brautigan concluded by mentioning Cowley's suggestions, "interesting, but at present I am writing another novel." He told him he'd been at it for three months and felt the work was "going well," hoping to be done "within a year." Brautigan assured Cowley that the new book had "a more conventional narrative continuity" than his previous effort, but was coy about giving too much away. "It has a Civil War theme with extensive contemporary flashbacks to life in San Francisco and Big Sur." Richard had in fact not yet done very much work on his "Civil War" novel. He had the Price Dunn stories and some lists of Confederate statistics and a few jottings in his notebook. Aside from these sketchy beginnings, his letter to Cowley suggested Brautigan envisioned a different sort of book, one jumping back and forth between past and present.

If Cowley's letter had Richard dancing on air, another from Luther Nichols several days later sent him crashing back to earth. Nichols was the West Coast editor for Doubleday. He wrote informing Brautigan that "after much wrestling and soul-searching back in New York," the publisher had decided to pass on *Trout Fishing in America*. No rejection slip was ever more sugarcoated. "I honestly feel that you're as original and interesting a writer as we have in this area, and humbly suggest that you next try Dial, Grove, New Directions, Angel Island Publications [. . .] houses that are more receptive to unusual works." Nichols offered to write letters of recommendation to "top people" at all the companies he suggested.

Not long after, Brautigan had drinks with Luther Nichols, who suggested sending the manuscript on to his friend James Laughlin, publisher of New Directions. Richard gave his approval. Ten days later, early in October, Malcolm Cowley wrote to say that (as he'd predicted) the Viking editors felt Brautigan's book "was too far out for commercial publication, although they were impressed with your writing." Cowley's second letter possessed the more formal remove of business. He regretted Richard was not interested in "a Vie de Boheme of North Beach," but said "we'd be delighted to see your Civil War novel."

On October 10, Brautigan began keeping a list of his correspondence, starting with a letter to Gui de Angulo. Jack Spicer had initiated the first ripples of interest in Richard's work, and this new compilation provided a measure of the wave's growing swell. On the thirtieth, Brautigan wrote to Thomas Parkinson, a poet and professor of English at Berkeley, whom Spicer urged to read *Trout Fishing in America*. Spicer had worked as Parkinson's teaching assistant while studying for his PhD but had known the professor's aristocratic wife, Ariel, before their marriage. They had been introduced in 1946 on the Berkeley campus by the poet Leonard Wolf, who said simply, "This is Ariel," to which Spicer quipped, "And I'm Caliban."

Tom Parkinson read Brautigan's novel, and he was so "taken up with it and absorbed all the way" that he wrote to Brautigan immediately. He found the book "a continual pleasure and surprise, with nothing false or forced in it." As Parkinson had been Richard Duerden's teacher and had recommended Spicer in 1953 for his job as the head of the newly created Humanities Department at the California School of Fine Arts, Brautigan understood that his opinion carried considerable weight. Richard savored the distinguished professor's final assessment: "It is a work of rare quality, full of radiance and fun and wisdom, and I've never read any other book like it."

By late fall, Donald Allen's voice was the only one not yet heard. Even this omission had an explanation. Allen had embarked on an extended trans-Pacific journey in May and had been living in Japan through the summer. He took an apartment in Kyoto and spent time with Gary Snyder and Joanne Kyger. They discussed Gary's old college roommate Lew Welch, who had been working as a commercial fisherman. After that enterprise failed and his relationship with Lenore Kandel came to an end, Welch moved to a remote spot called Forks of Salmon in Northern California, taking refuge in an abandoned cabin built by an old Wobbly.

When Allen returned from Asia in September of '62, among the pile of unopened correspondence awaiting him was the manuscript for *Trout Fishing in America* and a letter from Lew, who remarked on the rumor of Allen Ginsberg making the cover of *Time* next year, lamenting that somehow the intense media hype had not translated into significant sales. *Howl* had sold sixty thousand copies, not bad for small press poetry but fewer than ten copies per college campus across all of America. Welch speculated on the latent underlying energy of the nation's youth. "We have to hit the young so hard, they will never be the same again." With Lew's letter in mind, Don Allen at last sat down to read *Trout Fishing in America*.

Allen was the coeditor of the *Evergreen Review* and West Coast editor for Grove Press. Don finished *Trout Fishing in America* not knowing when he'd "enjoyed reading a first work so much." He'd been primed by Jack Spicer's passion for Brautigan's book, yet nothing had prepared him for the pleasure and surprise arising from every page. Allen conveyed his excitement to Richard, wanting both Grove and the *Evergreen Review* to have a look.

In mid-December, Allen wrote to Richard Seaver (managing editor of Grove Press) to express his enthusiasm in detail. He praised the novel's "wonderful tone: Western laconic, yet alert both to sound and to play of surrealistic image; when it is really working it's rather like an expert tall tale teller holding you spellbound [. . .] entertained, and yet left with a definite moral point of view." Allen found "many of the sections [. . .] stunningly successful," at the same time emphasizing his belief that the book also worked as a whole.

Following his success with *The New American Poetry, 1945–1960*, Donald Allen, along with Robert Creeley, was coediting a companion anthology of new prose for Black Cat Books. He wanted to use several sections from *Trout Fishing in America* in that volume and suggested to Seaver that "a group of them would be fine for ER." Allen listed thirteen sections from the novel that he "particularly liked." These included "The Kool-Aid Wino," "The Salt Creek Coyotes," and "Lake Josephus Days." He marked two favorites with a triple asterisk (***): "Trout Death by Port Wine" and "The Hunchback Trout," but said it was up to "whoever chooses for ER" to assemble a selection that worked well together.

Donald Allen admitted Brautigan was "far out as they say," but felt "he has much promise [. . .] for one thing he is not satisfied with repeating himself. After this he'll be trying something considerably different." He asked for an "early decision" from Seaver, stressing that "it deserves serious consideration as an Evergreen." Don passed all of this information on to Richard, brightening his holiday prospects. It was indeed the season to be jolly, and Richard Brautigan had every reason to celebrate. Ianthe was two and a half, exactly the right age for Christmas. Her parents gave her a little tree just her size, decorated with plastic toy dinosaurs, and she dragged it around with her from room to room. The future glowed with promise.

The Saturday night before Christmas, Richard and Ginny threw a big party in their Union Street apartment. Their friends considered Yuletide a dreary holiday. The Brautigans "wanted to break the spell of the Christmas gloom." A parade of poets and artists trooped up the long flight of stairs. The crowded rooms rang loud with laughter and an intense rumble of overlapping conversations. All of Brautigan's dreams were coming true.

The nightmare started the following Tuesday, shortly after midnight on Christmas Eve. Richard and Ginny had just had sex. In their ensuing conversation, Ginny revealed she had fallen in love with Tony Aste. Richard asked if they were having an affair. Ginny said yes. Stunned, Brautigan phoned Ron Loewinsohn and told him that he and his wife were separating. "Richard was absolutely devastated," Loewinsohn remembered. He agreed to give Brautigan a place to stay and said he'd be right over to pick him up.

Richard stuffed all his clothes and papers into two suitcases. He gathered his notebooks and manuscripts, stray poems, the beginning chapters of his novel in progress. When Ron arrived, Ginny was in the bedroom trying to sleep. He waited for fifteen minutes while Richard looked high and low for odd bits of his writing. "I spent the time searching for pieces of paper," Brautigan wrote later, "finding pieces of paper, searching and finding, looking among the obvious and the lost for pieces of paper [. . .]" Richard felt "as they must in times of war when an Army Headquarters has to abandon itself before the enemy." At last, they sped off into the night in Ron's car, heading for Loewinsohn's apartment (number 4) at 1056 Fourteenth Street above Market near Castro. It was late, and there seemed no need for further conversation. Richard curled up in a sleeping bag on the couch and fell into a fitful sleep.

He awoke at eight. The small apartment was very quiet. Ron and his second wife, Joan Gatten, slept in the other room. It was a cold clear day, the sun rising over Oakland red as a Japanese battle flag. Richard stared at it, feeling nothing. "The sun is colder than I am" stuck in his head. Not wanting to disturb the Loewinsohns, he went out for a long walk, heading west along Fourteenth Street to Buena Vista Park, a steep wooded hillside rising in an improbable tangle above the urban grid. As the name implies, the park provided splendid views, although Brautigan was in no mood for enjoying the scenery as he wandered among the wild overgrown cypress trees.

Richard stopped off for coffee at the home of friends who lived beside the park. They wanted him to stay for breakfast, but he told them he wasn't hungry and soon left. Instead of eating, Richard Brautigan transformed his feelings into words. On the first page of a spiral-bound notebook, he wrote the title, "The 20th Century Marriage in Flight." Below that, he added a quote from a mournful song originally written in Slovakian in the early 1900s by Andrew Kovaly, a steelworker at a Bessamer mill in Pennsylvania: "Tell Them I Lie Here in the American Land." The song dealt with a tragic accident, a young man killed under an ingot buggy even as his wife and children traveled from Europe to join him for a new life in America. Kovaly had to break the sad news when he met the family at the railroad station. Richard believed he knew just how they felt.

The work took the form of a journal, beginning with the events of the previous night ("A Hell-of-time") In the manner of Kafka, Brautigan referred to those involved only by initial. Ron Loewinsohn became "R," while Richard called his wife "G." Later, Brautigan went back and erased all the "Gs," replacing them with the letter "Y." He had no idea where the manuscript would lead him. Emotional pain made each moment vivid, and it seemed damned important to get it all down on paper.

On Christmas Day, Richard returned to his Union Street apartment. He watched Ianthe unwrap her presents, his daughter's happy laughter a time-warp from another dimension. Afterward, Ginny went for a walk with them. Anyone passing on the sidewalk might have thought they were still a real family. When they got back, Richard busied himself about the place, rearranging furniture. The garbage from their party still stood bagged in the kitchen. Brautigan took it down, cutting his hand on a broken cup when he stuffed it into the can. Richard thought this "strange game" of playing the man of the house seemed "almost like chess." After a while, he ran out of moves. Ianthe cried when he left. "I go get drunk," he wrote in his notebook.

Wednesday dawned cold and clear. After breakfast, Richard and Ron drove Joan to work at the library at San Francisco State and continued for a spin along the ocean before heading home. In the afternoon, Richard walked downtown to his job mixing barium swallows formula. It was several miles from Ron's Upper Market neighborhood to Drumm Street. Along the way, Brautigan passed the Hibernia Bank, where a robber had just been apprehended. Another day in the city.

After work, Richard visited several art galleries. Realizing they were on the same street as Ianthe's nursery school made him sad. He remembered how he used to pick her up at the end of the day. Richard couldn't escape the past. He went to a friend's place for dinner, next to where he lived with Ginny in 1957. After the meal, he fell asleep on the couch, oblivious to his friend's kid loudly playing with his new Christmas toys. The next thing Brautigan knew it was midnight and he was all alone.

Bit by bit, Richard started picking up the pieces of his life, finding solace in his daily routine. Some afternoons, Ron drove him to work, other times he walked. Art galleries provided a constant refuge. Brautigan spent a lot of time looking at paintings. A morning trip to his dentist led to an hour's conversation about hunting and fishing before having a "petite" (the dentist's term) cavity filled. There were dinners with friends, evenings in North Beach bars, conversations with strangers, anything to provide a distraction.

On New Year's Eve, Richard went out with his friends Arthur and Marsha in their new Volkswagen. The young couple, "very much in love," were concerned about him. "After you've been betrayed in the cruelest possible manner, there is little else one can do except to attend a party." Around eleven o' clock, they drove to a large gathering of college students, where Brautigan felt out of place, not knowing anyone. Almost twenty-eight, he was older than the other guests. The apartment's many rooms glowed with colored lightbulbs, yet the lurid ambiance did little to liven things up. It turned out to be a fairly sedate affair.

The host got Brautigan a drink of Canadian Club. ("It's nice to taste whiskey that's got character.") Curiously, he towered over Richard, who stood six foot four. Everyone at the party wore "goofy" comic name tags taped to his or her chest. Names like King Herod, Camus, Sigmund Freud, and Dylan Thomas. Richard Brautigan decided to call himself "Night Flight," although he didn't bother to write it on a name tag. A pretty young blond approached through the noisy gathering. She came on to him with the shopworn line, "Haven't I met you someplace before?" Richard was stunned, not knowing how to reply. His friend Art watched approvingly. He and Marsha both thought it a good idea for Richard to get a girl to take his mind off his problems.

The blond wasn't Brautigan's type. Picking up on his indifference, she drifted back into the crowd. A bit later, he met another woman, tall and slender with straight dark hair. He liked the way she smiled. They started a conversation and sometime after midnight found themselves together on a couch. "She curled up with her head upon my lap." Richard tenderly stroked her hair. It was soft and smelled freshly washed. When she asked questions about his life, he told her he had a wife and a child. He didn't tell her, "I still love my wife though she is an adulteress and has seduced a good friend and they live together now" (he wrote this later in his notebook), "while my daughter, not quite three, plays at their feet like a toy and wakes in the morning to find them in bed together where last week her father slept."

It was suddenly 1963, a new year already ripe with promise and pain. Richard "Night Flight" Brautigan sat stroking a stranger's hair, surrounded by college students. Perhaps not the most auspicious of beginnings, yet one not altogether without hope. He was drinking good whiskey, and women found him attractive. Life remained full of possibilities. Richard devoted eleven pages to the party in his notebook. Together with his earlier entries, they summed up all he had to say about the disintegration of his marriage. He wrote "Finis" midway down the final page. Nine days after his separation from Ginny, the breakup was already ancient history.

The news of Richard and Ginny's split resonated on the bohemian gossip telegraph throughout the bars of North Beach. Jack Spicer saw Ginny and Tony Aste together, a new couple in love, and it struck a powerful chord. The lovers didn't remain under public scrutiny for long. Packing up their few belongings and bundling Ianthe into yet another Aste jalopy (this one without heat), they set off early in the year for Salt Lake City, a trip across a desert so frigid that Tony wrapped his hands in old clothes as protection against the cold. The Rexroth/Creeley/Marthe Larsen triangle, which formed the basis for "Homage to Creeley," had fascinated Spicer when he first heard of the affair in Boston. Now, this new drama already played itself out in his imagination even before the actual events transpired. "Tony" was the first word and the first line in the first poem in the "Book of Gawain," the first of seven "books" in *The Holy Grail*, a poem cycle Spicer had completed four months earlier.

At the end of August 1962, Jack Spicer had been invited to give a preliminary reading of the poem, then still in progress, at Robin Blaser's art-filled apartment during a dinner party attended by Robert Duncan and Jess, among others. The occasion later became something of a scandal. Blaser hoped to reconcile Spicer and Duncan, who'd had a falling-out, but Spicer arrived drunk with his uninvited gang (Stan Persky, George Stanley, and Ron Primack) in tow and attacked Duncan for his poetic affiliations, all the while heaping ridicule on Robin Blaser's luxurious tastes. "Nasty boys," in Duncan's opinion. He remembered the evening as "gruesome" and terminated his long friendship with Jack Spicer that night ("the idea of Spicer is preferable to the actual presence").

"Poetry and magic see the world from opposite ends," Jack Spicer wrote in *The Holy Grail*. His differences with Robert Duncan arose in part from their separate approaches to the occult. Duncan remained "a magician behind the scenes" while Spicer wanted to work his magic in the world at large. For Jack, watching the Lancelot/Arthur/Guinevere drama reenacted before his eyes, months after having written his Grail book, was a reaffirmation of certain deep prophetic magical connections.

For Richard Brautigan there was no magic. Work provided his only distraction. The Loewinsohns set him up with a makeshift office out on the back porch of their apartment, placing a plank over the laundry tubs as a typewriter platform. Brautigan was back in business. "Richard wanted to work on a book because he was so devastated," Ron Loewinsohn surmised. "Writing was one of the ways that he kept himself together." Unhappiness seemed to have concentrated his attention. The pace of his novel in progress picked up considerably. While he wrote, Brautigan played a recording of Shostakovich's *Fifth Symphony* continuously. "Maybe four hundred times," he later claimed.

"He was totally into what he was writing," Loewinsohn recalled. "I would hear, *tappity-tap, tappity-tap, tappity-tap*—peals of laughter—*tappity-tap, tappity-tap, tappity-tap*—another outburst of laughter—*tappity-tap, tappity-tap*." Richard Brautigan clearly enjoyed himself, remembering the wild, wacky times spent down in Big Sur with his unpredictable buddy, Price Dunn. Typing at break-knuckle speed, Richard put everything into the mix: counting biblical punctuation, alligators in the frog pond, a beautiful part-time prostitute, smoking marijuana, the crazed businessman with a suitcase full of money, Price tapping into the PG&E gas line in Oakland, even the "Freezer King of Sepulveda Boulevard."

Brautigan brewed a rich fictional stew, stirring up the adventures of Lee Mellon and Roy Earle, Jesse, Elaine, and Elizabeth, flavoring it with a sprinkling of Civil War anecdotes. Writers often have a difficult time with second novels, trying not to repeat themselves. Richard Brautigan blazed ahead into new territory, never looking back. In *A Confederate General from Big Sur* he accomplished something very special, writing a book rivaling the unique vision of *Trout Fishing in America* while remaining utterly fresh and new.

Listening to all the rapid-fire typing and maniacal laughter, Ron Loewinsohn felt a natural curiosity about what was happening out on his laundry porch. When Richard knocked off for the day, Ron asked, "All right, so I'm going to see some of this stuff? It sounds great, you in there laughing your head off."

"Nope," Brautigan said, smiling slyly and slipping his day's work into a manila envelope. He placed each chapter in a separate envelope, not showing Ron a single word. Loewinsohn had no idea how many drafts Richard went through, nor could he gauge the amount of polishing each page required. "I never got to see it until it was all done."

Ron Loewinsohn's perceptions of his friend's writing methods might have been slightly off the mark. Don Carpenter remembered Brautigan as "an extremely careful writer. He worried a lot about being thought of as a careless writer." Carpenter knew speed was not Richard's main concern. He was interested in the precision of language and worried that his lack of formal education made him vulnerable to misspellings and grammatical errors. "He would conceal the childishness of the way he worked, which was to write each chapter on a piece of paper and then fold it up and put it inside an envelope and write the name of the chapter on the envelope, and then when he had enough envelopes he would stack them in different orders, and when he had the book the way he wanted it he would type it up on his IBM Selectric."

As work on the new novel progressed, the push to get *Trout Fishing in America* into print continued gaining momentum. Donald Allen had shown the manuscript to Lawrence Ferlinghetti, who shared his enthusiasm and agreed to publish several excerpts in *City Lights Journal*, a new editorial project conceived as an annual. For the premier issue, Ferlinghetti hoped to have Allen Ginsberg and Gary Snyder write of their adventurous travels together in India the previous year. Gary and Joanne told Don Allen some of it when he visited them in Kyoto. Ginsberg corresponded often with Ferlinghetti. Richard kept busy running all over town, conferring with Don and Lawrence about the excerpts they wanted to publish. Allen urged Brautigan to send out more copies of his manuscript. "I'm beat," Richard complained in a letter.

At the same time, Brautigan and Loewinsohn began planning a magazine of their own. The past several years had seen a proliferation of small (mostly mimeographed) publications started by poets in San Francisco. Local wits dubbed the era "the magazine wars." After the appearance of *Beatitude* and Jack Spicer's *J*, Richard Duerden started both *Foot* and the *Rivoli Review*. Tony Sherrod put out the one and only issue of *Mythrander*. George Stanley edited the *Capitalist Bloodsucker-N* and Larry Fagin, *Horus* (actually the creation of Stan Persky, who placed Fagin's name on the masthead as a joke). Persky, Lew Ellingham, and Gail Chugg put together the first copy of *M* in the spring of 1962. Most of the same names appeared as contributors in all these ephemeral publications.

Early in 1963, Ron and Richard took a walk in Buena Vista Park, "talking about magazines and how bad they were and how little they did that was worthwhile." Loewinsohn can't remember which of them first said, "Why don't we do one?" Their initial enthusiasm very quickly escalated to "talking seriously about how we were going to do it." Richard had many ideas concerning the form of the project. He suggested they call their new magazine *Change*.

Brautigan also had a vision for the cover. The clean, efficient look of *Life* magazine came to mind. He had seen the tattered remnants of an old billboard transformed into a giant collage by overlapping layers of ancient outdoor advertising. At one time, the three-sheet had heralded a drag strip auto race. All that remained, in foot-high letters, were the words SEE THE FASTEST CAR ON EARTH. Richard enlisted Ron's wife, Joan, as their photographer and posed himself and Loewinsohn in front of the fragmentary poster.

With their cover shot in the can, the editorial team of Brautigan and Loewinsohn settled down to the more mundane details of magazine production: soliciting contributors, planning a budget, establishing a production schedule. While Richard concerned himself with design concepts, Ron took on the more onerous chore of keeping the company books. He did a meticulous job, detailing the cash outlay. Richard shelled out five bucks for stencils and ink while they both shared the $30 cost of a batch of "20 R" paper. They also bought photo paper ($3.07), correcting fluid ($1.25), and a stylus (fifty-four cents).

Like the fastest car on earth, the little magazine zoomed off the starting line. Ron and Richard decided on May Day as their publication date, and deadlines were tight. They paid $6.40 to a lithographer to print up a batch of covers with "Change" boldly above their curious photo like a banner headline. Half of the print run was used for flyers. Ron rented a hand-crank mimeograph machine for $52.50, and the first stencil they cut and ran off was printed on the verso of the covers. Some of these they used for promotion. "CHANGE: THE FASTEST CAR ON EARTH," it read, "For 25¢ these two gentlemen can be brought into the privacy of your living room—Think what can be done for a dollar!"

Soliciting for subscriptions, Brautigan and Loewinsohn met Don Carpenter at a coffee shop on the corner of Columbus and Pacific. "The place was full of poets," Don recalled, "all glowering at each other." Carpenter paid for the coffee. As a part-time teacher, he was the most prosperous of the three. Richard and Ron described their plans for the first issue. Don said it sounded good to him.

"That's just it," Brautigan said. "We would like to offer you the position of first subscriber."

"Thank you," Don said, somewhat flattered. He gave them a buck.

Brautigan and Loewinsohn's ad copy promised *Change* would be a monthly publication out of San Francisco. The first issue offered poetry by Joanne Kyger, Philip Whalen, Richard Duerden, and Ron Loewinsohn; a piece called "Execution Day on the Big Yard," by former San Quentin inmate Bob Miller; and Richard Brautigan's short story "Coffee." Future issues would feature Fielding Dawson, Lew Welch, Jim St. Jim, Edward Dorn, Gilbert Sorrentino, Michael McClure, "& the fastest car on earth." The fledgling promoters concluded, "four months of CHANGE for a dollar, 17 years of CHANGE (204 issues) for $51.00, 85 years of CHANGE (1,020 issues) for $255.00.—What better bargain? Subscribe now! Make cheque or money order payable to the editors."

February and March were busy months for Richard, and there wasn't time for much correspondence. Aside from writing Philip Whalen and Stan Fullerton about *Change*, most of his letters were to Ginny. He still called her Ginny then. By April the salutations had formalized to "Dear Virginia." He told her of the magazine he and Ron were working on and complained about "this income tax business." Ginny had always prepared their returns in the past. "You have done all the other income tax business before and I am quite confident you can handle it this last time." He shipped all his tax records off to Salt Lake City a few days later.

On the twenty-first of March, Richard Seaver wrote to Brautigan at his old Union Street address. He mentioned how much the editors at Grove Press liked *Trout Fishing in America* and selected nine chapters from the novel, suggesting that they publish them in the *Evergreen Review* in "a group of at least three or four at a time." Seaver wanted an option on the book as part of the deal and asked Richard to drop him a note if this sounded agreeable. Grove would then "draw up some fairly simple form of agreement" covering both the book publication and the separate magazine excerpts.

This news greatly improved Brautigan's mood. He wrote a happy letter to Ianthe on her third birthday, sending a little dress he hoped was the right size as a present. No one had ever celebrated his birthday when he was a kid, and the occasion meant a lot to him. Brautigan missed his daughter profoundly. He wrote Ginny, "Perhaps along with the present you might tell her how much I love her and how much her birthday pleases me."

In April, the first issue of Lawrence Ferlinghetti's *City Lights Journal* made its appearance. A photo of a blanket-wrapped Allen Ginsberg graced the cover and an account of his travels in India were featured. In addition to work by Snyder, Kerouac, Burroughs, Ed Dorn, and Harold Norse, the magazine contained three chapters from *Trout Fishing in America* ("Worsewick," "The Salt Creek Coyotes," and "A Half-Sunday Homage to a Whole Leonardo da Vinci") along with a grainy snapshot of Richard Brautigan standing by a wrought-iron gate.

Seeing excerpts from his novel in print helped take Richard's mind off his sorrows, while work remained his main distraction. He was going hell bent for leather on *A Confederate General from Big Sur* and wrote to Thomas Parkinson on the seventeenth to tell him about the new novel in progress and of the *Evergreen Review*'s plans to publish chapters from *Trout Fishing in America*. After this, Brautigan embarked on a flurry of self-promotional correspondence, writing to Malcolm Cowley, L. Rust Hills, and Seymour Krim, among others.

Earlier in the month, a large envelope from the Ford Foundation arrived for Brautigan in care of City Lights Books. Richard had been nominated by Lawrence Ferlinghetti (not mentioned by name) for consideration in a recently announced "one-year program designed to enable a limited number of poets, novelists and short story writers to spend a year with professional resident theater companies." In 1959, the Ford Foundation had sponsored a similar program and twelve fellowships were awarded, with Robert Lowell, Eudora Welty, Richard Wilbur, and Herbert Gold among the recipients. A chronology, a bibliography of published works, and a "general description" of how a residence in a professional theater would relate to "the plans you are currently seeking to fulfill as a writer" were requested. Replies postmarked after May 5, 1963, could not be considered. The final awards would be announced in July.

By the middle of April, *Change* raced toward the finish line. "The magazine was doing extremely well," Ron Loewinsohn recalled. "People were eager to buy, eager to subscribe; people were eager to contribute." To date, they had amassed $152.46 in production costs. On the positive side of the balance sheet, they had twenty-four paid subscribers, including Don Carpenter, Frank Curtin, Diane Wakoski, James Broughton, and a library at Harvard (which bought two) and had arranged with several booksellers, from City Lights on the West Coast to Eighth Street Books on the East, to carry the magazine for a 30 percent discount.

Loewinsohn and Brautigan assembled their mimeographed sheets, stapling the copies together, running the many last-minute errands all such enterprise entails. Pressure took its toll. Richard and Ron had another falling-out. "We had stuff to do on the magazine," Ron remembered, "printers to see, paper to pick up, and Richard had said, 'I'll meet you at nine o'clock,' or whatever. So, he wasn't there, hours later, and we're still trying to catch up, and Richard is complaining that he had gotten all drunked up the night before and was in no shape to do anything. And I just blew up. You know, who the hell told you to get loaded?"

Richard and Ron were no longer talking. This did not bode well for the future of *Change*. Copies had been mailed and subscriptions sold. Freebies had been given to Kenneth Rexroth,

Robert Creeley, Ed Dorn, Charles Olson, LeRoi Jones, and William Hogan, book editor of the *San Francisco Chronicle*. Reality put the brakes on the fastest car on earth. The magazine screeched to a screaming halt. "I did not want to continue by myself," Ron said. "It was a joint project, and we had this blow-up."

Ron did his best to repair the damage. He returned paid subscriptions and collected money from the five bookstores that had placed orders for single copies. In the end, *Change* took in only small change. All told, the magazine earned a total of $8.20. In spite of their differences, the two feuding poets somehow managed to tie up the loose ends left dangling when *Change* crashed and burned. After a final tally on the second of June, Richard paid Ron $45.44, "for expenses incurred in publishing CHANGE, a magazine." Brautigan demanded and received a handwritten receipt from Loewinsohn.

Don Carpenter didn't receive an initial refund and never expected to see his money again. One day, Brautigan approached him on the street. "Ah," said Richard. "I've been looking all over for you. Where have you been keeping yourself?

Somewhat sarcastically, Don explained that he had a wife and family over in Noe Valley, and that "domesticity" kept him "out of the Beach, often for days at a time."

Brautigan pulled an envelope from his pocket and handed it to Carpenter. "This is yours," Richard said. "Your refund from *Change*."

The envelope was stuffed with three-cent stamps. Don didn't mind. "People can always use stamps," he said.

Although he and Ron were no longer speaking, Richard Brautigan stayed on at the Loewinsohns' until he found another place to live. His new quarters, a Spartan room at 1482 Washington Street, on the western slope of Nob Hill, had a tree growing up from the sidewalk outside the window, and leaves drifted in when it was windy. Richard thought this was "nice." In a letter to Virginia shortly after the move, he asked her to write him about Ianthe and hoped his daughter would have "a nice summer."

Brautigan used Washington Street as his return address when he finally got his paperwork off to the Ford Foundation in the nick of time, mailing the required material on Cinco de Mayo, the deadline date. Other mail continued to arrive for Brautigan at the Loewinsohns'. Ron passed along all the letters. Tom Parkinson wrote early in May. He had seen *City Lights Journal* and thought it a shame that no publisher was willing to print all of *Trout Fishing in America*. (Grove Press had turned down the novel, agreeing to publish nine excerpted sections in the *Evergreen Review* and requesting an option on Richard's next work of fiction.) "My own belief is that it would be a smashing commercial success," he wrote. Parkinson asked to see Brautigan's second novel when it was done. He thought it had "an even more engaging title" and invited Richard to read his poetry at the university "in the series of readings that we have each semester." He proposed a payment of $100.

Around this time, Richard met Anna Savoca, a student at San Francisco State, "a very small, intense, highly expressive" young Italian woman from Brooklyn. A mutual friend remembered her as an "anarchic creative kind of person." Fred Hill found her "simian." Brautigan's courtship of Anna began with poetry. Several drafts of eight poems composed during the first two weeks of June, 1963, survive in his notebooks. The earliest, dated June 5, is entitled "Another Poem for Anna," suggesting at least one predecessor ("the impossible / is what we want. / We long for it / like a highway desires an automobile accident / to break the monotony of speed. / Of course nothing is that simple"). Instinctively, Brautigan knew he was in for a wild ride with Anna Savoca.

All along, from the moment she first met Richard, Anna was in love with another guy, named Wally, son of a noted Potrero Hill dowager, whom she eventually married. He was away and unavailable, so she amused herself with the ardent poet. Anna made no secret of her love for the other man. In fact, she mentioned him so often that Brautigan complained to his friends that Anna "Wally-ed him to death." Everything was "Wally this" and "Wally that." Richard had no proper reply, except in his poetry. "Because we leave a lot in names," he wrote for Anna, "more than we intended to. We can't help it, but it's always been this way [. . .]"

These were unsettling times for Richard Brautigan. His novel had been praised by many important literary figures, yet he still couldn't find a publisher. He had become involved with an unpredictable woman who toyed with him like someone teasing an eager puppy. He had almost no money, his only income coming from the part-time job at Pacific Chemical. (Richard wrote a poem for Anna about weighing out the ingredients for barium swallows.) He continued working on his new book even as his writing schedule was interrupted by frequent moves. Starting in mid-July, Brautigan became something of a gypsy, changing his address four more times before the end of the year.

It was frustrating for a control freak like Richard Brautigan to watch his fate being decided by strangers. *Trout Fishing in America* was passed from James Laughlin at New Directions (who thought Brautigan "a writer who shows great promise of becoming a leading literary figure") on to G. P. Putnam's Sons, which forwarded the book to Dell for consideration in the Delta Prize Novel Award. Delta Books decided against Brautigan's novel and sent the manuscript back to G. P. Putnam's Sons, which wrote to Richard, saying "we would be happy to consider it for our list." Brautigan answered on the twelfth, agreeing to their proposal. On the sixteenth, he moved to 1565 Washington Street, where he rented apartment number 3 for $65 a month.

Mail for Richard kept arriving at Ron Loewinsohn's as well at his previous Washington Street address. In time, it all caught up with him. Donald Allen continued acting as his unpaid agent (a service he also provided Lew Welch, squirreled away like a hermit in his remote northern California CCC cabin), so Brautigan didn't have to worry about missed connections in the publishing world.

On July 22 a letter from the Ford Foundation to 1482 Washington Street informed Brautigan that he was not among the applicants recommended for an award by the judging panel. The bad news probably meant less to Richard than a form rejection notice on August 13 from G. P. Putnam's Sons turning down *Trout Fishing in America*. Donald Allen immediately had the manuscript forwarded to Coward-McCann for their consideration. Brautigan happily let Allen lead the charge. Nearing the end of *A Confederate General from Big Sur*, Richard paid more attention to the work at hand than to East Coast editorial politics.

Finances were extremely tight. On the sixteenth, Brautigan paid just half a month's rent, extending his stay in apartment number 3 until the end of August. On the first of September, he moved to much cheaper lodgings at 1327 Leavenworth Street, paying a Mr. Brockson $40 for a month's rent. Here Richard finished writing *A Confederate General from Big Sur*. Alone and missing his little child desperately, he rolled a final sheet of paper into the platen and typed out a dedication: "to my daughter / Ianthe."

Brautigan gave Don Allen a copy of his new manuscript. Allen read it straightaway and was quite impressed. It made him "very optimistic about Brautigan's development as a novelist." Allen wrote that the new book "marks a considerable advance in novel technique" over Richard's initial effort, which he called "in many ways a very original first novel." Although Allen noted that "much of the action is richly comic," he observed that "one soon sees that the author is up to much more than telling funny stories: there is an authentic critical estimate of beatism (for lack of a better word) here."

As Donald Allen had done so much to foster the work of Beat writers, his judgment on the matter carried serious weight. He was not unappreciative of the commercial prospects of *A Confederate General from Big Sur*. "It is very possible that it would get considerable attention from reviewers because of the way it plays off against Kerouac's Big Sur (not closely), for example, as well as other beat books." Allen shipped a copy of the manuscript to Dick Seaver. Grove Press enjoyed a certain cachet as an avant-garde publisher, their backlist including Beckett, Borges, Kerouac, and Charles Olson, as well as most of the European theater-of-the-absurd playwrights. Seaver quickly responded by asking for a two-month option.

Not long after starting what hopefully would become his third novel, a work he called "Contemporary Life in California," Richard went with Anna Sovoca to a birthday party for a friend of hers, a fellow student at San Francisco State. Lois (Loie) Weber was just turning twenty-two on September 28. Anna brought her a wooden bird bowl from Yugoslavia as a gift. Loie's first impression of Brautigan "was of this large hulking strange character with a timid but brooding quality." Anna had told Loie that she was bringing a guy who's "into trout fishing." Loie's husband, Erik, a photographer interested in fishing, struck up a conversation with Richard.

Erik Weber was born in Chicago in 1940 to Communist parents kicked out of Canada by the Mounties. The family moved to Sacramento, California, in 1943 and on to San Francisco a year later. Richard and Erik didn't talk long about personal history or fishing. As soon as Brautigan learned Weber was a photographer, he said, "I need a photographer," believing himself poised on the brink of success, ready for publicity stills and dust jacket pictures. Richard took down Erik's phone number, and they made a tentative agreement to get together for a photo session.

On October 11, Richard Brautigan moved into room number 3 in the Mitchel Art Hotel at 444 Columbus Avenue, paying $9 a week. Quite likely, he was behind on his rent to Mr. Brockton. These were trying times for Richard. He wrote no letters during September and October.

A week later, Brautigan was without a known address until the beginning of December. A year or so later, he told Jack Thibeau that all his books and papers (including the manuscripts for both his novels) were "locked in a cheap hotel room in North Beach. He couldn't pay the rent, and his landlord had put a lock on the door." According to Thibeau, "he had to come up with $27 to get his books out of hock."

Brautigan moved in with his friend Andy Cole, a young Catholic poet from Brooklyn. Jack Spicer referred to Cole, together with Tom Wallace and Larry Kearney, two other Catholic émigrés from Brooklyn, as "the Jesuits." Kearney's first book, *Fifteen Poems*, would soon be published by Graham Mackintosh, who had taken over management of White Rabbit Press after Joe Dunn became addicted to methedrine. Tom Wallace was Nemi Frost's boyfriend. He and Andy Cole had lived for a time at her apartment a couple years earlier.

Around the beginning of October, Ginny returned to San Francisco from Salt Lake City with Tony Aste and Ianthe. Richard had desperately missed his daughter. When he last saw Ianthe at the Union Street apartment she was two and a half years old and cried as he headed down the stairs and out of her life. Nearly a year had passed. The first day he took her to the playground in Portsmouth Square she seemed strange and unfamiliar to him.

"Everything is different about her," Richard wrote in a poignant unpublished short story called "The Deserted Imagination." He sat on a red ceramic dragon in the little park at the edge of Chinatown, watching Ianthe play in the sandbox. Running his hand through her hair, Brautigan watched the sand fall from her tin cup and thought about all the lost time. She used to call him "daddy." He knew "every turn and motion of her body and her mind and took deep pride in that knowing." Now that time was gone forever. Richard felt that he was playing at being Ianthe's father. "We are strangers sitting on a dragon together."

The next night, Brautigan visited Bob Miller and told him his estranged wife was back in town. He mentioned seeing his daughter the day before and that the "vast difference" he noticed in her made him "feel strange."

"Oh, God," Bob Miller said. "Yes, Goddamn it to hell. They change without your being able to do anything about it." Miller had three children of his own. As an example of the enormous transformations that take place during long separations, he told Richard about being incarcerated at San Quentin. Before going into prison "he took a good look around." As the years passed, nothing seemed to change. "Everything remained the same." Bob felt "suspended there." When Miller was finally released he saw the San Rafael–Richmond Bridge standing in front of him for the first time. The bridge hadn't been built when he started doing his time. "Oh, God, Look what they've done!" Bob exclaimed. Vast changes had transpired while everything stood still for him.

Brautigan dealt with his unhappiness by writing about the feelings he experienced. Disguised as fiction, his unpublished handwritten short stories read like journal entries. A piece dealing with his daughter's return he called "To Love a Child in California the Way Love Should Be." The narrator can only spend half an hour with his daughter, "put in an appearance as they say. I had a lot of things to do that day [. . .] She broke into wild joy when she saw me." His daughter is excited by her new sandbox. "Al [Tony Aste] made it for me from bricks and sand." She takes him downstairs to see the sandbox, and they play catch with her ball in the warm California sunshine until it is time for the narrator to leave. "And I told her very carefully and gently and lovely that I had to go out and see some people and that I would see her soon." The little girl starts to cry. "I kissed her goodbye and gave her a big hug and kissed her again and it was not enough, nor would it ever be [. . .]" As he hurries down the stairs, she stands crying on the top landing. "Her voice falling after me saying love over and over again [. . .] It was 12:30 and I had many places to go. I walked down the street to them. They could not come fast enough."

Anna Savoca broke up with Brautigan in early October. Loie and Erik Weber had an older friend, a furniture builder named Clayton Lewis, who lived in Virginia City, Nevada, the old state capital during the heyday years of the Comstock Lode silver boom. Mark Twain began his career in journalism there at the *Territorial Enterprise* during the Civil War, and a hundred years later, the abandoned mines and weathered Victorian buildings became an outpost for what would soon be called the counterculture. Erik introduced Anna to Clayton and they both felt an immediate and powerful attraction.

When Anna told Richard that things were over between them, he grew extremely distraught. In an emotional gesture a few days later, Brautigan cut his wrists at Anna Savoca's apartment, smearing the walls with blood. Anna told Erik Weber about it in vivid detail. "She came home and she saw blood on the walls and all over the place and went into the room and Richard was sitting there with his wrists cut. It was very dramatic." Brautigan's wounds turned out to be superficial, and he did not see a doctor. He had done it to show Anna how much he loved her but she remained unimpressed by histrionics. The gesture made her angry, and she moved up to Virginia City to live with Clayton Lewis. The pair stayed together for about a year before Anna Savoca's ardor cooled. She married her beloved Wally after all. Because the connection to Clayton had come through Erik Weber, Richard became "a little pissed" at him and their planned photo session was postponed.

Evergreen Review number 31 appeared in October. It contained four excerpted chapters from *Trout Fishing in America* ("The Hunchback Trout," "Room 208, Hotel *Trout Fishing in America*," "The Surgeon," and "The Cleveland Wrecking Yard") and attracted more attention among important literary editors in New York. Donald Hutter of Charles Scribner's Sons wrote to Brautigan, "remarkable work—uniquely personal in its voice and astonishingly suggestive—one of the most memorable first exposures to a new writer I can recall." Hutter asked to see the rest of the novel if it wasn't already committed elsewhere.

Donald Barthelme, whose first collection of short stories, *Come Back, Dr. Caligari*, was soon to be published by Little, Brown, worked as an editor of the art-literary review *Location* and wrote to Richard Seaver at Grove Press, saying he and Harold Rosenberg were "very impressed" with the portions of Brautigan's work they had read in *Evergreen*. They were anxious to see more of the book for possible publication in their own magazine and offered a payment "around $150 for an excerpt" of the length that appeared in the Grove periodical.

Richard learned of these recent developments through Donald Allen, to whom the letters had been forwarded. Heady news for a homeless and near-destitute poet. Fame and fortune seemed to glow like a rising moon just beyond the distant horizon. Allen had been working diligently on Brautigan's behalf but suggested to Richard that a New York agent might better serve him at this stage of his career. Don had someone in mind, a man named Ivan von Auw Jr., an associate at the Harold Ober agency, the firm that had once represented F. Scott Fitzgerald.

Richard Brautigan wrote to von Auw immediately. The agent replied to 1482 Washington Street, which Brautigan had given as his return address, saying that he was "interested in principle," but wanted to read Richard's book or at least those parts excerpted in the *Evergreen Review* before giving an answer. "I am very hesitant to take on a new writer unless I have a very strong personal reaction to his work."

Von Auw sent a copy to Donald Allen, who, by coincidence, had already written a letter to him about Brautigan, "a young San Francisco writer with a distinctly original talent." Allen discussed both his novels (the first, "a brilliant Western surrealist [. . .] performance," the second, "closer to conventional story," but "also an elaborate and amusing employment of metaphor"), tracing their wayward course through the treacherous currents of New York's publishing world. Allen said that Brautigan had that day sent off "copies of the two novels for your consideration."

Four days later in Dallas, an assassin's bullets blasted away the dream of Camelot, and the nation's flags hung at half-mast all the way to Christmas. A terrible sadness lingered throughout the land, reinforced by those indelible images (frames from the Zapruder film, Jackie's blood-stained pink Chanel suit, the riderless black gelding with gleaming boots inverted in the stirrups, John-John saluting the caisson, Jack Ruby gunning down Lee Harvey Oswald on TV over and over again) burned into the American psyche like a freeze-frame nightmare.

Richard Brautigan felt part of the collective shock, living like everyone in "a tunnel of mourning," but had problems of his own to worry about: no money, no place to live, no publisher yet for his two unique novels. Although he told Donald Allen that he was "well into his third novel," in truth, he had done almost nothing on "Contemporary Life in California." Brautigan compiled a handwritten list of fifteen possible chapter titles ("April California," "Fame in California," "The Names of the Characters in This Novel," "The F. Scott Fitzgerald AAHHHHHH"), drawing a small box next to each one, planning to check them off in turn as each was written. By the end of November, very few boxes contained check marks.

Things started looking up in December. On the first of the month, Richard moved to apartment C at 483 Francisco Street, not far from Fisherman's Wharf. By some happy coincidence, Ginny and Ianthe lived one block away on Bay Street and he could visit his daughter as often as he wished. Going on four, Ianthe felt happy to be within walking distance of where her father lived. Richard's new place was a sublet, the owners away in Mexico. They were friends of Brautigan's and charged him only $45 a month rent. In return, he had to look after their birds.

The back of the apartment contained a large foliage-filled aviary. Pierre Delattre remembered "twenty or thirty [. . .] little parakeet types." Erik Weber thought they were "huge birds." Price Dunn recalled "a whole bunch of songbirds." Richard's job was to feed them every day and change their water. There was "a little vacuum cleaner to tidy up the aviary when it was needed." One afternoon, Delattre accompanied him to a hardware store in North Beach to buy chicken wire for repairing the cages. Richard Brautigan took the welfare of his feathered charges very seriously.

One Sunday not long after moving in, following a visit with Jack Spicer in Aquatic Park, Richard and Ginny walked with Gui de Angulo along the waterfront toward the Embarcadero, sharing a loaf of French bread they'd bought in North Beach. Like four-year-olds the world over, Ianthe ran on ahead. "There was this vast expanse of cement," Ginny recalled. Not a car or truck in sight. A perfect day for a "recreational" game they played with the seagulls. Richard liked tossing chunks of bread high into the air to watch the eager gulls catch them in midflight.

Ianthe spotted a small animal and ran toward what turned out to be a wharf rat. The rodent bit the child on the hand, and she rushed crying into her mother's arms. "I don't know whether the rat actually bit Ianthe," Ginny said. "I can't remember seeing any puncture marks." Gui sprang into action. She "whipped off her jacket," trapping the rat under the coat. This bold moved spared the little girl a painful series of rabies shots. The Brautigans had the animal tested, and the results came out negative. Ianthe needed only an injection for tetanus in the emergency room. Richard warned his daughter never to pick up strange animals, telling a story of being bitten on the finger in Golden Gate Park while feeding peanuts to a squirrel.

Brautigan got in touch with his old buddy Price Dunn, inviting him to drop by one afternoon. "Richard called me up to come over, and he's got something that he wants me to read." The manuscript for *A Confederate General from Big Sur* rested on a table in the middle room of the apartment. Richard handed Price the stack of pages. "I want you to read this," he said, "and tell me what you think." No mention was made of the subject matter. Price sat down and read the whole thing straight through. When he finished, Richard poured them both some wine. As they drank, he asked, "Well, what did you think about it?" Price knew Richard wanted to see if he was "pissed off or offended in any way."

"It's fantastic," Price told him, knowing his friend had created a wonderful character in Lee Mellon. Price Dunn had enough self-confidence to understand that the Confederate General was fictional, inspired by and at the same time unrelated to him. "It's really a marvelous book," he said. "Congratulations." Brautigan felt satisfied and smiled his sly smile, pure delight dancing in his eyes. Best of all, Price told him "this book will sell because it's closer to the conventional."

Erik Weber captured that same pleased expression when he came over to the apartment later in the month. Richard had called and asked if he wanted to take the photographs they'd discussed earlier. Dust jacket pictures seemed imminent by then. Erik posed Richard in front of the aviary, the birds flitting between perches in the background. It took only eight shots for Weber to know he'd gotten the one he wanted. Brautigan's hair was still cut short on the sides, but his familiar public image began to emerge. The drooping mustache partly hid his smile. He wore a turtleneck under a denim shirt and had discarded his black horn-rims in favor of the round rimless glasses soon to become one of his trademarks. Years later, Keith Abbott described the essence of the photograph: "His open, cheerful, confident expression are [sic] characteristic of his belief in his prospects while his blue work shirt displays the uniform of artistic poverty."

Off in New York, the wheels of commerce continued slowly turning. Coward-McCann turned down *Trout Fishing in America*. Donald Hutter wrote to the old Washington Street address to reaffirm Scribner's interest in the book. Donald Allen discussed Brautigan's work with Arabel Porter of New American Library. She wanted to have a look for their new hardbound series. He also kept in touch with Ivan von Auw, suggesting that the "slicks (Harper's Bazaar, Vogue, Mlle, etc.)" might be interested in publishing excerpts, "before giving Location much of the unpublished balance of Trout Fishing, even though they offer to pay, it might be worth trying a few on the fashion magazines." With this in mind, Allen wrote to Madeline Tracy Brigden, fiction and poetry editor of *Mademoiselle*, urging her to consider using some sections from both Brautigan novels.

All this time, Dick Seaver of Grove Press had been trying to get in touch with Brautigan. He sent a telegram on Friday the thirteenth, and Western Union informed him that they had hung notices on the doors of two different San Francisco apartments. Checking his files, Seaver discovered he had three addresses for Brautigan and realized in all likelihood none of his messages had ever reached Richard. Failing to find him, he phoned Don Allen with news of Grove's decision to become his publisher.

Four days later, having learned of the Francisco Street address, Seaver wrote Richard Brautigan with the good news. Grove Press offered him $1,000 as an advance for *A Confederate General in Big Sur*, at the standard royalty rates. In addition, they wanted an option on *Trout Fishing in America* (with a $1,000 advance payable within three months of the publication of his first novel) as well as an option on his third novel, the terms to be mutually agreed upon after delivery of the manuscript.

Seaver said Don Allen had told him that Ivan von Auw was now acting as Brautigan's agent and would officially transmit the news soon, "if he has not already." Acting in his position of managing editor, Seaver expressed the pleasure of Grove Press to have him as one of their authors. "I think you have done some fine writing, and on the basis of what we have read, am confident you are going to do a great deal more."

Von Auw wrote to Brautigan on the same day, saying Harold Ober Associates wished to represent him. He included the news that Barney Rosset (Grove Press) wanted to become his publisher.

This letter was sent to 1482 Washington Street, and Richard didn't receive it right away. The next day, von Auw wrote again, this time care of Donald Allen, conveying the same information in greater detail. He asked Don to read the letter to Brautigan and then forward it on to him.

After years and years of privation and struggle, Richard Brautigan could not have asked for a better Christmas present. He finally found a New York publisher and had landed a three-book deal in the bargain. By any measure other than his own native Teutonic pessimism, he should have been overjoyed, yet several things about the arrangement troubled him. He spent the holidays brooding over the details and ate his Christmas dinner alone. Hot dogs and beans (beanie-wienie, his old standby) washed down by a bottle of rum mixed with Coca-Cola.

A day or so later, he attempted to delineate his concerns to Ivan von Auw in two letters he never mailed. The first, Brautigan dictated to a friend who took it down in longhand; the second, he typed himself. Grove's recent offer was "disappointing." Richard did not find it "reasonable." Brautigan's unhappiness had nothing to do with money. He was upset by the proposed sequence of his books' publication. I wrote Trout Fishing in America first and A Confederate General from Big Sur second. They were written as the result of an exploratory esthetic. I will not allow the order of this esthetic to be distorted. I believe it should continue to develop in a natural way and be published in the order of its development. I plan on writing a lot of books." For Brautigan, this was a "crucial" issue. He thought of "Contemporary Life in California" as the next in "a whole series of novels based on this conception."

Donald Hutter's continued interest in Trout Fishing in America also gnawed at Richard. If Scribner's published his first novel first, his aesthetic order would remain intact. And what about Donald Barthelme at Location? Shouldn't he get to see some of the requested material? In addition, Brautigan wanted to know what terms or agency agreement Harold Ober Associates proposed. "I hope that we can work out a mutually satisfactory relationship. It is vital to me, particularly at this stage of my writing career, that I have close contact with and careful guidance from a representative in New York."

In spite of his many concerns, Richard remained unable to conceal his glee when he bumped into Don Carpenter in North Beach around this time. "He was really smug and smirking and full of himself," Don recalled, still irritated decades later. "He was on his way, on his way." Brautigan boasted of getting $1,000 apiece for his books from Barney Rosset. Don Carpenter felt sick listening to him. "I never had a more uncomfortable interview with a poet in my life as standing on the corner of Broadway and Columbus hearing him rant about having sold two novels with that incredibly superior bullshit."

On December 28, Richard wrote to Ivan von Auw in New York. He said nothing about his displeasure at having his two novels published out of sequence by Grove. Brautigan also didn't bring up another concern. In the letter he typed but never mailed, he'd been careful to mention he hadn't signed an agency agreement before being informed Grove Press wanted to publish A Confederate General from Big Sur. It bothered him to think of paying a commission to Harold Ober Associates when no work had been done by them on his behalf. Donald Allen, as an editor of the Evergreen Review, deserved all the credit for setting the wheels in motion with Dick Seaver. Richard skirted the issue, playing his cards close to his vest. "If you will tell me something about your agency and something about yourself," he wrote, "I will tell you something about myself, and why I write novels."

Brautigan told von Auw he wrote novels "as a kind of thing to do, never to be of any commercial value, but as a part of learning. I wanted to learn about myself: others: earth and the universe [. . .] I am of course very pleased that the books are of some value, whatever value is, to others. If I am going to have a literary agent, I need someone who will have sympathy with my work. This is an important thing to me at this delicate period in my life." Richard ended by repeating his request that the agent tell him something about himself and his company, "then let's see what we can do."

The last time he saw Richard Brautigan in the sixties, Pierre Delattre paid a visit to the apartment on Francisco Street with the colorful aviary in the kitchen. The front room had been set up like a Buddhist temple with a large statue of the Gautama. "A shrine-thing," according to Erik Weber, who doubted Brautigan ever spent much time there. When Delattre came to visit, the writer guided the priest right on by. Passing the middle room, where Richard had a table with a typewriter and a little lamp set up, Pierre spotted a fresh manuscript copy of *A Confederate General from Big Sur*. "What's in there?" he asked.

"Shhhh! Quiet," Richard whispered, pushing Delattre on ahead toward the bird-chatter filling the kitchen. "My new novel's in there. I kind of stroll in occasionally, write a few quick paragraphs, and get out before the novel knows what I'm doing. If novels ever find out you're writing them, you're done for."

F OR RICHARD BRAUTIGAN, the first week of January 1964 "was a strange time in America." The assassination of President Kennedy cast a dark shadow across the holiday season, seeping sorrow into the hearts of the nation like a poisonous stain. Christmas had never been a jolly time when Richard was a kid. His marriage broke up on Christmas Eve the year before, and he had just spent his most recent Yuletide alone in an apartment full of birds, an occasion he described as "lonesome."

Sometime before Epiphany, walking home to Francisco Street around midnight after a visit drinking coffee with friends up on Nob Hill, Brautigan noticed numbers of newly discarded Christmas trees scattered about everywhere. Stripped of their bright ornaments and twinkling lights, they lay abandoned at the curb and in vacant lots, each one "like a dead soldier after a losing battle." Looking at them made Richard feel sad. "They had provided what they could for that assassinated Christmas, and now they were being tossed out to lie there in the street like bums."

Back at apartment C, Brautigan placed a call to Erik Weber, waking him from a deep sleep. "All he said to me was 'Christmas trees,'" Erik recalled. "Only Richard would call you at two or three in the morning and say something like 'Christmas trees.'" Brautigan remembered phoning around one, but always had a cavalier attitude about late-night conversations. When Erik wanted to know why Richard seemed so interested in Christmas trees, he replied, "Christmas is only skin-deep." Brautigan wanted Erik to take hundreds of pictures of the naked trees discarded everywhere throughout the city. He felt it would "show the despair and abandonment of Christmas."

At the time, Erik Weber had a job at Macy's in the photo-advertising department. He snapped pictures and worked in the darkroom. During his lunch hour the next day, he "just took off and started photographing Christmas trees," wandering up from Union Square, through Chinatown and onto the slope of Nob Hill, aiming his camera at the forlorn trees. Richard had instructed him to shoot them "just like dead soldiers. Don't touch or pose them. Just photograph them the way they fell." Erik did as instructed. Brautigan had no interest in documenting the exact location of each tree. As Weber recalled, "It was just a matter of an accumulation of many, many, many, many discarded Christmas trees."

A sense of secrecy surrounded the entire enterprise. Brautigan often invested his projects with near-paranoid undercover tactics. "We thought we really had something good going," he wrote, "and needed the right amount of discretion before it was completed." Erik spent another lunch hour shooting film and by the weekend had almost 150 pictures of Christmas trees. To speed things up and cover more territory, Richard lined up a friend "who had a truck and used to help him do stuff" to drive them around on Saturday. The friend's only condition was remaining anonymous. He was afraid of losing his job if word got out about his being involved in this weird enterprise.

The three of them drove all over the city, with Erik photographing abandoned Christmas trees in every neighborhood. Up on Potrero Hill after a Chinese lunch, they ran into Lawrence Ferlinghetti, setting out to walk his dog from his small Victorian house at 706 Wisconsin Street. They had just shot a picture of a fallen tree near his place. Erik couldn't remember what Ferlinghetti said to them but thought Richard ad-libbed a reply along the lines of, "Oh, we're just out for a walk." Writing about the incident later, Brautigan reported that he mumbled, "Sort of," as an evasive responsive to Ferlinghetti's query: "Taking pictures of Christmas trees?" According to Erik, Richard said, "We don't want anyone else getting the idea."

The original notion was to produce a small illustrated book. Richard planned a story about a family going to a Christmas tree lot, the poignant moment of choosing the fullest and best-shaped tree to be counterpointed by Erik's photos of all the discards after the holidays were over. Brautigan never wrote that story. Things didn't work out that way. In the end, Brautigan wrote it all down pretty much exactly as it happened. He called the piece "What Are You Going to Do with 390 Photographs of Christmas Trees?"

The story languished unpublished for the next four years, in part because Brautigan made no effort to place it with a magazine. It finally appeared in December of 1968, in *Evergreen Review* no. 61. A full-page collage of Erik Weber's Christmas tree photographs accompanied Richard's text, nine pictures overlapping as if casually dropped on a tabletop, disposable as the discarded trees they captured. Twelve years after its initial appearance, Brautigan included the story as a chapter in *The Tokyo–Montana Express*.

Richard made one small change in the story for book publication. In the original version, every-one was correctly identified by name (with the exception of the anonymous truck driver). Richard appeared as Richard; Lawrence Ferlinghetti as himself; Erik was called Erik. It was Brautigan's ver-sion of photo-realism. By the time *The Tokyo–Montana Express* was published in 1980, Richard and Erik had fallen out of friendship and were no longer speaking. Keith Abbott called the photog-rapher to tell him about the change in the story. Erik went over to Abbott's place to see for himself. Reading the change "kind of pissed" him off, especially after all the work he had done for Richard over the years. In his book, Richard Brautigan changed Erik's name to "Bob."

twenty-one: moosemelon

PHILIP WHALEN LIVED at 123 Beaver Street, a lovely Victorian house built in 1879. Tommy Sales, the landlady, was the ex-wife of critic Grover Sales. She occupied the upstairs and rented out the rooms below. "The rent was very reasonable," Whalen recalled. "The house belonged to a friend of mine, and he very generously gave me this room to live in because I didn't have any money." In an unpublished short story, Richard Brautigan wrote that Philip Whalen "was living his life for poetry and the rest of it could all go to hell."

Set well back off a steep street, number 123 had the look and feel of a country place, fronted by fruit trees and a flower garden. David Kherdian, who wrote *Six Poets of the San Francisco Renaissance*, had a room on the first floor for a while, and Whalen's friend John Armstrong, who became a boatbuilder and moved to Bolinas, was also a resident. "There was a little room off the kitchen where I was," Whalen remembered, "and then there was a larger room past the bathroom and then the big front room." The rooms were arranged in a shotgun row along a long corridor with the kitchen at the rear. Don Carpenter, a frequent visitor, called the place "a poetry household."

At the beginning of 1964, Richard Brautigan lived far from Beaver Street over on the edge of North Beach in his sublet apartment mad with birdsong. After telling Don Allen he was considering Grove's offer for his two novels, Richard wrote to Ivan von Auw on January 6: "You probably have a very good agency, but it does not seem geared to my specific needs as a writer." He asked that Harold Ober Associates return his manuscripts by Railway Express, "collect."

Not having an agent placed Brautigan in a quandary. Donald Allen, his chief adviser, was also the West Coast editor for Grove Press, and a certain conflict of interest remained inherent in their relationship. Richard researched sample publishing contracts, coming to favor one drawn up by the Society of Authors' Representatives, and proposed a single change to Don Allen. Should the author place the book with a movie company, the publisher's 10 percent share of the film rights would instead provide half the advertising budget. The proposal seemed "rather weird" to Allen, but he passed it on to Dick Seaver along with a list of the terms Brautigan expected and conveyed a deal-sweetening tidbit back to Richard. The publishers wanted to submit *A Confederate General from Big Sur* for the Prix Formentor, an international award for unpublished fiction.

The Formentor Novel Prize was established in 1960 in Formentor on the Spanish island of Majorca by publishers (including Grove) from six nations. First awarded in 1961, the prize came with a check for $10,000 (an advance against future royalties) and simultaneous publication in all the participating countries. Jorge Luis Borges and Samuel Beckett shared the honors and the honorarium that first year.

Richard Seaver had no objection to the Society of Authors' Representatives contract. Grove already used it, happy with the boilerplate terms. Seaver offered an advance of $1,000 for each of Brautigan's novels, payable $500 on signing, with the balance coming in quarterly installments. "We would plan to publish A Confederate General in the fall of 1964 and Trout Fishing approximately a year later." Seaver dismissed Brautigan's suggested contractual amendment as "unnecessarily complicated." He stressed the urgency of the matter, putting a subtle squeeze on Richard. Contracts had to be drawn up before Grove could submit the manuscript for Formentor consideration. The prize deadline was at the end of January. Richard Brautigan promptly signed with Grove. He desperately needed the money, and the chance of winning an international literary award proved irresistible.

Richard Brautigan often visited Bill Brown, who had married, had a baby named Maggie, and moved across the Bay to Point Richmond. Brautigan started going over on weekends with Ianthe, renewing what Brown said had become "a kind of aloof, pretty detached relationship." They sat on a pier looking west toward the city, lubricating their literary discourse with quarts of ale. Brown had recently completed a short novel, about his life in a German POW camp, called The Way to the Uncle Sam Hotel. Richard read the manuscript and found the book "a damn good piece of work." He wrote to Leroi Jones in New York, enquiring if Corinth Press might be interested in it.

Bill Brown had a landscape gardening business and occasionally hired Richard on a part-time basis. A woman from Utah owned a place in Belvedere fronting the lagoon. "I'd been going there for years and years," Brown recalled. One time, he brought Richard. "I said, 'Okay, kiddo. You cut the lawn. I've got to go to the nursery. I'll come back with some posies.'" Bill Brown left Brautigan pushing a mower and a little while later "came humming back with some flats of posies in my hands." He rang the bell, and the Utah woman opened the door. "Who's your helper?" she asked. "You better go wake him up. He's asleep on the lawn with one shoe in the lagoon."

Joanne Kyger returned from Japan in February 1964. Her husband, Gary Snyder, followed a month later, his marriage to Joanne more or less at an end. "The move back to the United States kind of precipitated that," Kyger recalled, "there seemed to be all this wonderful freedom." A few days after she got back, Joanne Kyger sent a note to Richard Brautigan through Donald Allen, telling him how much she had enjoyed reading the excerpts from Trout Fishing in America that had appeared in the Evergreen Review. "And I thought, 'Oh, Richard has really jumped a lot from Galilee Hitch-Hiker, and I was delighted by it. And reading it in Japan was fantastic, this incredible, deranged, wonderful little book."

Richard promptly sought her out. Kyger sublet a small apartment in North Beach right behind where her friend Nemi Frost lived. "Richard came by a lot. He was totally hilarious during this period," Joanne Kyger remembered. One evening, loving samurai movies, he acted them all out. "All the way through several of them. Toshiro Mifune. And he was just great. I remember he was lunging around in back of Nemi Frost's storage room. He had a lovely free-floating kind of fantasy that you could get inside of."

Early in February, the Beatles began their first American tour, headlining twice on the Ed Sullivan Show. Neither Richard nor Joanne knew very much about the Fab Four at the time. Beatlemania had yet to penetrate Japan, so Kyger had a valid excuse for being oblivious. "It seemed like at that point the Beatles had just stepped from one place to a whole other theater of the world," she said. Richard and Joanne began collecting Beatles cards in order to learn their names and tell them apart. Which one was John? Who was George? "It was an obsession with us because we'd go back over and over the names."

Sitting at a table at Vesuvio on Columbus with Jack Spicer, the three poets wrote a collaborative letter to Ringo Starr, inviting the Beatles to come to San Francisco. Spicer detested popular music, but somehow Joanne and Richard persuaded him to put aside his hostility and behave like any other adoring fan. (A year later, Spicer began a poem with the line "The Beatles, devoid of form and color, but full of images [. . .]") Kyger doesn't know if they ever mailed the letter, certainly no reply came, but for her the entire event "was part of the fascination of being part of this subculture." She likewise believed Brautigan's interest stemmed from a firm conviction that he was also soon destined for worldwide recognition and fame.

Joanne Kyger remembered 1964 as "a very social occasion" involving Richard and Donald Allen. Don had a beautiful apartment at 1815 Jones Street up on Russian Hill and loved to entertain, serving up "endless martinis." His place was a natural gathering place for visiting artists and writers, while his "old-fashioned manners" made even the surliest rebel feel right at home. Often, after an afternoon cocktail-hour visit, Allen took Brautigan and Kyger out for dinner, an offer the impoverished poets never refused. Joanne sensed at the time that "Richard had already gotten some kind of real confidence in himself. He was playful."

Separated from her husband and not yet involved with anyone new, Joanne Kyger delighted in Brautigan's company. "We used to get into these trips together," she recalled. "It would be some kind of fantasy game where you would actually start acting out. You walk along and your characters would evolve and you'd report back the next day to see how the character was doing." These games involved Richard's lively imagination, yet Kyger intuited an alternative motive. "I remember his spinning out some hypothetical endings to something, one of which seemed kind of like a proposal." She adroitly avoided unwanted complications by "looking at it and taking it on its fictional level," and bypassed uncomfortable difficulties. "I never felt romantically interested in Richard, although he was always a wonderful friend."

In March, sitting in front of his typewriter in the middle room of the apartment on Francisco Street, Brautigan started a brief short story (really more of a prose poem) expressing his disjointed mood. "Drunk laid and drunk unlaid and drunk laid again, it makes no difference," he began, singing aloud with the birds in the kitchen. The brief bit of fiction he composed explored the total lack of attachment in his life without a hint of self-pity. Brautigan called the piece "Banners of My Own Choosing."

Michael McClure can't remember when he first met Richard Brautigan. They knew of one another in the claustrophobic Frisco literary scene but didn't become close friends until late 1963 or early in 1964. Michael's former wife, Joanna, has no memory of Richard when the McClures lived on Scott Street in the late fifties, although she thought he might have come around, as Price Dunn was a resident in their basement. She also doesn't remember knowing Richard during the period when they held court at 2324 Fillmore Street, another art center between 1957 and 1959. "Michael might have seen him," Joanna recollected, "but he was not part of the artists that hung out and showed at the Batman Gallery and did things."

It wasn't until sometime around the end of 1961, when the McClures returned from New York and moved to a house at 264 Downey Street, a two-block-long stretch in the Haight, where they were to stay for the next twenty years, that Joanna began to fit Brautigan into the picture. "I don't think it was right away in 1961 that he was coming to visit." Two years later, Richard became a regular. "He'd come over and sit in front of the fire, and he and Michael would talk books and drink together. I never had feelings of dislike or warmth or liking particularly toward Richard. He was just one of the people that came around, and he was sort of like family."

In *Lighting the Corners*, Michael McClure stated, "For a long period I was probably Richard's closest friend and he was probably mine." Brautigan dropped by Downey Street several nights a week, and they sat on the floor because the McClures were still too poor to buy furniture. They drank Gallo white port, thirty-seven cents a pint at Benedetti's Liquors on Haight Street. "I liked Richard because of his angelic schitzy wit and warmth," McClure wrote in 1985.

Brautigan felt at home with the McClures. "He loved that household," Bobbie Louise Hawkins observed. "Johanna [*sic*] took care of everybody that came in, and Michael was this thoroughly beautiful person with a great sense of style. It always makes you feel good to be around Michael because he has such panache." Brautigan distilled his affection for the McClures' home life into a single poem, "Abalone Curry," where he described their traditional Christmas dinner when Michael prepared his famous abalone curry "in his kitchen that is halfway / between India and Atlantis."

Sherry Vetter remembered going over to the McClures' place with Richard in 1970, the first Christmas they were together as a couple. Brautigan brought a bottle of wine. Since he was flush with his new success, the vintage was a cut above the cheap white port from Benedetti's. Sherry recalled the Spartan apartment: "There was one room like a sunroom where McClure worked, and that was the only place that had any furniture in it." The "funny almost kitchen" had only a sink, a hot plate, and "a little tiny refrigerator."

The big living room contained nothing but colorful pillows on the floor. They sprawled there "Indian style" for the simple repast, which Sherry remembered as "oysters boiled in milk with dollops of butter and salt and pepper and French bread." She considered Michael to be "a prima donna. He thought he was a really handsome knockout dude—lying there with his tight blue jeans on and this little sort of open-collared shirt and this long hair." Sherry thought more highly of Joanna, "a real sweetheart. She was like the sole support."

Bobbie Louise Hawkins agreed that Joanna McClure, who had started her own little kindergarten school, provided the firm foundation for her family by creating "a sense of well-being. Joanna would come back home from the job, come in, be delighted at whoever was there, get her own glass of wine, and be chatty and bright about it. Completely unneurotic. She had a largesse and luxury."

Hawkins believed Brautigan's new fame drove him away from his former friends to his own detriment. "Suddenly Richard made a hit with *Trout Fishing*, and all that was lost for him," she said. "As soon as the fame occurred, all those people sucking up felt real to him. He couldn't distinguish. There would have been some hope for him if he had managed to keep holding on to what had actually given him a home base and anchor. But as soon as that other wash of stuff came in, he went with it. There was nobody there to take care of him."

The artist Bruce Conner had been friends with Michael McClure since their earliest school days together in Wichita and remembered meeting Brautigan for the first time at Downey Street. "Richard arrived looking all thin and pale and gangly and awkward and obviously shy and not very communicative. Words weren't coming out." Conner viewed the new friendship between

Brautigan and McClure with a jaundiced eye. "Michael and I were sitting around talking, and Richard came in, and he said, 'Richard, go in the kitchen and wash the dishes.'"

"Oh, yeah, sure," Brautigan replied, heading dutifully to the kitchen.

Bruce Conner didn't know what to make of this. "Michael, what are you telling him to wash the dishes for?" he asked. "Did he come over here to do the dishes?"

"No. He likes to do things like that," McClure answered. "He likes me to tell him what to do."

Conner remembered Brautigan's "tremulous respect" for Michael McClure. Looking back on those times, he observed, "Michael would push him around, order him around like a little slave. This didn't do much for establishing Richard's value as an independent creature. Maybe Richard did like washing the dishes. I have no idea. Washing the dishes was probably one of the few things he did very well."

Soon after this, Joanna McClure acquired a Russian wolfhound puppy. "Skinny and angular, long-faced and long-nosed," Michael wrote, "and he looked like he had loose threads on his elbows." Bruce Conner remembered the dog as a "tall, gangly, awkward, shy creature." The McClures named him Brautigan. Conner found the situation a bit strange. "Here we were," he recalled. "Richard would come by, and he'd find us over there, and there would be Brautigan the dog. How much more demeaning does Michael want to be?"

Brautigan never mentioned being put out at having a dog for a namesake. He greatly admired Michael McClure, captured in part by his dramatic appearance. "He looks kind of like a dark lion the way he carries himself," Richard wrote in his notebook. "The style of him. But sometimes there is distance in him. A lion floating in space." Wallace Berman took a striking set of four photographs of McClure in 1963, posed frontally nude, his face made up to resemble a lion with a full mane and whiskers. McClure used it on a flyer to advertise a poetry reading, and Brautigan was undoubtedly influenced by it. In *Ghost Tantras*, written in the early sixties, McClure began experimenting with an invented Beast Language, mixing animal sounds ("AHH GRHHROOOR! AHH ROOOOH. GAR.") with his own biospheric metaphysical lexicon. Celebrating this leonine behavior, Richard Brautigan wrote "A CandleLion Poem" and dedicated it to Michael McClure.

Early in 1964, Brautigan still struggled to get his new novel about contemporary life in California off the ground. One evening, eating chicken with the McClures in their kitchen, unable to focus on the dinner table conversation, Richard listened to Jane, the McClures' blond, seven-year-old daughter watching television in the other room, a program about parachuting with the sounds of men bailing out of aircraft, as he pondered the names of the characters in his planned novel. He wanted names with the enduring quality of Echo O'Brien, Flem Snopes, Holden Caulfield, Studs Lonigan, Huckleberry Finn, Dr. Jekyll, Leopold Bloom, Jocko DeParis, Horatio Hornblower, or Hopalong Cassidy. Names with clout. Names a reader would never forget.

Michael and Joanna felt Richard's distance but made no comment. When Joanna smiled at something witty Michael said, Richard mirrored her reaction without hearing a word. Brautigan got up and looked out the kitchen door at the rapt little girl sitting on the couch. He couldn't see the TV screen she stared at, thinking about naming his characters, assailed all the while by the sounds of someone being thrown out of a plane. Returning to the table, Richard requested a favor from the McClures. "Would you please ask your little girl to write a list of words that she can spell and then give the list to me?" he said. "I need it. Would you have her write them in Crayola, please. Somewhere between six and ten words on a sheet of paper. That will be enough."

Michael and Joanna agreed without asking any questions, as Richard knew they would. That was the nature of poets, he reasoned. Brautigan couldn't say why he didn't ask Jane directly. He figured asking her parents "was the best way to do it." The next day, Richard called Michael to remind him. McClure said he'd try to have the list tomorrow. Richard imagined names written in color in "the rough beautiful hand of a child."

The following evening, Brautigan attended a poetry reading in a bar. He drank vodka washed down with a beer chaser and paid particular attention to an attractive young woman in a tight sweater whose response to the work seemed somewhat exaggerated. "She was too excited and laughed too loudly, sometimes even at the wrong places." Michael McClure came in while the featured poet was reading a love poem. He sat down, not seeing Richard, who sat behind him. McClure had a roll of paper and put it up to his eye "like a sea captain," scanning the audience for his friend. Richard attempted a loud whisper. It was no use. He didn't want to disturb the reading. Michael didn't hear him, but the pretty girl turned and stared back at Richard.

During the intermission, McClure found Brautigan and gave him the roll of paper. He said that he and his daughter were very curious about what was going on. Richard assured him they would know all about it soon. Michael wasn't feeling well and had to go. He had only come to deliver his daughter's list. After McClure left, Brautigan began a conversation with the pretty girl in the sweater. She said she was also a poet and had been writing for two years but had never shown her work to anyone. It was a personal thing with her.

When the intermission ended they continued their whispered conversation. People started looking at them, so she said, "Let's go." They left the reading, walking out into the warm sweet rain. The girl wore a raincoat. They ambled along, talking about their lives and about poetry, "her hidden passion." She was twenty-three years old and had a child out of wedlock. She kept her hands in her raincoat pockets. Richard slipped his hand into one of her pockets, and she pulled away. "Oh, now," she said. "I just want to talk about poetry." They continued their conversation about Robert Desnos, the French surrealist Price Dunn had recommended. Brautigan was surprised the girl had heard of him. Neither of them spoke French, and very little of his work had been translated into English.

When Richard tried a second time to put his hand in her pocket, she gently said, "Please."

"I'd like to go to bed with you," Brautigan replied. "Let's talk about poetry while we fuck."

The young woman wasn't interested, and said she'd like to correspond with Brautigan about his poetry. Richard asked her where she lived.

"Here, in San Francisco," she said.

"I live here, too. Why write letters to each other. We live in the same city."

When the girl replied that she'd like writing better, Richard turned and walked away, leaving her standing in the rain. "What about Robert Desnos?" she called after him.

"What about him?" Brautigan answered. "He died in a German concentration camp in 1945."

When Richard got home, he unrolled the papers Michael had given to him. There in brightly colored child printing were the names Jane McClure had chosen for the characters in his novel: "ON CHILDREN . . . LOOG . . . OFF SO . . . HHOG . . . RAN RUN."

Brautigan transformed this episode into a six-page story he called "The Names of the Characters in This Novel." He intended it as a chapter in his new book, but things overall were not going well. Richard wrote only one letter in March, to Ron Loewinsohn, concentrating on his fiction. After several months' work, he had finished just nine short chapters for "Contemporary Life in California." When he finally set the novel aside sometime in April, only twenty-nine pages had been completed.

Other matters remained uppermost in Brautigan's mind. Anxious to place portions of his two completed novels in magazines, a potential source of immediate additional income, he wrote only business-related letters in April. At Donald Allen's suggestion, Richard mailed "Headquarters," a chapter from *Confederate General*, to Madeline Tracy Brigden, fiction editor of *Mademoiselle*, requesting a prompt decision. Brautigan sent another section to the fiction editor of *Esquire*.

In mid-April Richard received a letter from Susan Stanwood, fiction editor of the *Saturday Evening Post*, inquiring about first serial rights for the novel about to be published by Grove Press. Richard mailed her a copy of the manuscript. On the same day, he wrote to Charles Newman, editor of a new literary magazine called *TriQuarterly* published out of Northwestern University. Newman had written to Grove, expressing interest in Brautigan's work for possible inclusion in the first issue. Richard promised to send him something, "within the next few weeks."

Richard Brautigan first encountered Dr. John Doss and his wife at Don Allen's festive 1963 Christmas party. "He seemed like a shy deer," Margot recalled. The Dosses were well-known in San Francisco art and literary circles, both as patrons and participants. Their elegant four-story townhouse at 1331 Greenwich Street on the summit of Russian Hill was long celebrated for the jovial parties they hosted, functioning as what Grover Sales called "the only true salon on the West Coast." A noted local photographer, John was better known as the head of pediatrics at Kaiser Foundation Hospital. Margot started writing a column on walking tours in San Francisco for the *Chronicle* in 1961. William Hogan, literary critic at the newspaper, suggested that she call Donald Allen and show him examples of her work. One thing led to another, and in 1962, Grove Press published *San Francisco at Your Feet*, a collection of her columns, edited by Allen.

Donald Allen's Christmas party guest list also included Robert Duncan, Helen Adam (the Scottish-born balladeer and coauthor of the play *San Francisco's Burning*), Richard Baker (later Baker Roshi of the Zen Center), and Lew Welch, recently returned from his northern hermit's lair to read at David Haselwood and Andrew Hoyem's Auerhahn Press, which had published his first book of poetry, *Wobbly Rock*, in 1960. John Doss also remembered "another guy there who had just written a book on how to fuck."

The Dosses and Richard "hit it off immediately." They invited him to dinner at their place soon after. A cold rain saturated the night, and Richard arrived shivering at Greenwich Street in a torn T-shirt, so chilled and miserable and thin that Margot "immediately went and got a black turtleneck sweater that I had knitted for John when he was in medical school and which he didn't wear much anymore." The cabled sweater became a favorite, and photographs over the years frequently showed Brautigan wearing it.

Margot and John had long been interested in Bolinas (in 1968 they bought a house at 9 Brighton Avenue) in part because it was a magnet for poets and artists. Brautigan had known of the place beforehand, but his new friendship with the Dosses encouraged the notion of relocating to the little coastal town. Early in May, about the same time *Kulchur* (vol. 4, no. 13) published his short story "The Post Offices of Eastern Oregon," Richard quit his job at Pacific Chemical and made the move out to Bolinas. All told, he earned $332 mixing barium swallows formula in 1964.

A letter mailed at the end of April to Francisco Street from Madeline Tracy Brigden at *Mademoiselle* followed Richard out to Bolinas. She said she was sorry to decide against using "Headquarters" in the magazine. Not all his work was being rejected. In May, "September California," a poem, appeared in *Sum* (no. 3), a little magazine in Albuquerque, New Mexico (Ron Loewinsohn was a contributing editor), but small press publication didn't compensate for being turned down in New York.

Richard Brautigan took up residence, rent-free, in an unfinished house located on Dogwood Street up on the Bolinas Mesa. The place was being built by a friend of Bill Brown's, a local contractor named Bob Callagy (later Callagy-Jones, after an affiliation with a Gurdjieff group and the discovery of his true father's name). Eventually, the completed house became the residence of Bay Area TV commentator Mel Wax.

Brautigan worked part-time for Bill Brown during this period. Once, out on a job, Brown gave Richard a shovel and asked him to dig a trench for a septic line. "It's supposed to go between here and here," Bill told him and left. At the end of the day when Brown returned, Richard had dug a trench that was exactly wide enough to fit the pipe but narrower than his shovel. "How in the hell did you do that?" Bill Brown wanted to know.

Joanne Kyger remembered riding the Greyhound out to Bolinas a couple times to visit Richard. They wandered the Mesa and along Agate Beach together, endlessly talking. There was no romance. Joanne spent the night in a separate room and took the bus back to the city in the morning. At the time, the house on Dogwood had no running water and Richard had to use the toilet at a place down the street. "Things are a little crude," he wrote to Don Allen.

Because he didn't drive, transportation into the city was by bus or hitchhiking. Brautigan remained woefully short of funds. While in San Francisco picking up essentials necessary for his rustic life, Richard phoned Michael McClure and found him sick in bed. "My body weighs four hundred pounds," Michael moaned. A month before, they'd had a phone conversation "about the sketch as a literary form and could anything be done with it."

After talking it over, Brautigan suggested they swap sketches. "I'll write one and then you write one in return," Richard said. "How does that sound?" McClure agreed. Isolated in fog-bound Bolinas, Richard struggled for weeks "but there wasn't a sketch in me." Instead, he polished his novels and "wrote a lot of letters to strangers. The letters did not work out the way I wanted them to." After sending a chapter of *Confederate General* to Charles Newman at *TriQuarterly* in May, he wrote the fiction editor of *Playboy*, trying to place sections of his novel. At Don Allen's suggestion, Brautigan contacted Seymour Krim, from 1961 to 1965 the editor of *Nugget*, a girlie rag where he published the work of Gregory Corso, John Rechy, Kenneth Rexroth, John Clellon Holmes, Jack Gelber, and others. Dense fog, heavy as rain, enclosed the unfinished house and limited Brautigan's universe. Sending endless letters to editors made as much sense as staring out the window at the impenetrable gray.

One morning after returning from the city, Richard found a dead rabbit lying outside his bedroom. He didn't like the idea of sleeping so near to death and tossed the corpse into a field about a hundred yards away from his house. Brautigan wrote a couple pages about this nonevent and titled his effort "Railroading: A Sketch for Michael McClure." In a postscript, he stated that "Michael never wrote his sketch, but since then his life has been perfect." When McClure finally got around to responding five years later, he had something much more ambitious than a simple sketch in mind.

Early in May, discouraged by letter-writing and unhappy with the lack of progress on "Contemporary Life in California," Brautigan started work on a new novel. Among his papers, he came across a water-stained three-by-five-inch Velvatone memo book. He had paid nineteen cents for it years before, intending to take it with him when he went on fishing trips up to the Klamath River. "I was going to use it for jotting down little descriptions of nature and my own reactions to those descriptions." Richard noted his original purpose on the front leaf, turned the page, and wrote, "My family was killed by tigers in the act of making love."

Dissatisfied, Brautigan started again: "My family was killed by the tigers before this shack was built. They were killed in the act of making love. When I came home they were lying there. The mark of the tiger was against their (dead) bodies [. . .]" He went on to describe killing the last tigers, "shot full of arrows and then brought to the temple of iDEATH." There they were soaked in "watermelon oil" and set on fire. Writing rapidly, many of his scrawled words all but illegible, Richard sketched out the ideas he'd toyed with in his imagination over the past four years.

He wrote of the "trout chamber" in the "temple of iDEATH" and jotted down the first mention of inBOIL and the atrocities he inspired. ("Cut off their noses with baby knife of iDEATH [. . .] they cut their blood [. . .] fingers, eyes, ears, noses [. . .] But one alone and inBOIL who disemboweled himself.") And at the bottom of the page, Brautigan wrote the name "inBOIL" over again twice, as if to fix it forever in memory.

It wasn't really a beginning, just a few random rough ideas to get the juices flowing. Brautigan made five separate attempts to start his novel, all more or less alike: "I live in an old shack on the top of a small hill, and the walls of the shack are blue wood, and the roof is made from shingles of watermelon sugar." He stored these fragments in a large manila envelope from Flowline Facts—"Chemical Industry Issue," something gleaned from the wastebasket of his former place of employment. On it, Richard wrote "'In Watermelon Sugar'—The Rough."

On May 13, Richard sat down with a sheaf of lined three-hole notebook paper and began in earnest, working with a ballpoint pen. "In watermelon sugar the deeds were done and done again in watermelon sugar," he wrote. "I'll tell you about it." Starting a new paragraph, Brautigan continued,

> *I live in a cabin near the temple of iDEATH. The cabin is small but pleasing and comfortable as my life and made from watermelon sugar as just about every thing here is. We have many fields of watermelon here, carried to the end of the imagination. We use them for our life. It's from them we get everything we need and then take our souls to iDEATH.*

Brautigan reworked this paragraph twice, starting over from the first line, making deft surgical changes. Almost as an afterthought, in the white space above the lined portion of his first page, Richard wrote: "My name is moveable. Just call me whatever is in your mind. What you're thinking that is my name." Brautigan made many revisions as the work progressed but all the magical elements of his new novel were in place right from the start: the narrator without a name (a notion developed into a beautiful poetic third chapter called "My Name"), the talking tigers, iDEATH (which evolved from a temple into a sort of mutable social center), the mutilations of inBOIL "and that gang of his," the Forgotten Works, a sun that changed color every day. Brautigan had worked all of this out in advance in his imagination.

To achieve the innocent voice he wanted for the book, Brautigan reduced his vocabulary to child's primer simplicity. At twenty-nine, Richard was the same age as his nameless narrator. In one of those happy accidents by which art is so often made, he started writing *In Watermelon Sugar* in Bolinas, allowing the casual easygoing bucolic spirit of the place to inform every page. Once again he created something utterly unique. Michael McClure thought it "his most perfect book," one that "might have been written by an American Lorca."

At first, the flow of the work moved slowly, matching the pace of life in Bolinas. Business matters continued to provide a distraction. Susan Stanwood from the *Saturday Evening Post* wrote in mid-May, returning the copy of *A Confederate General from Big Sur*. "I very much enjoyed its wonderful zany humor [. . .] but two things make it pretty impossible for us." She found the comedy "too far-out for the mass magazine readership" and thought the various sections not "sufficiently sustained" for successful excerpting.

A more welcome letter from Charles Newman asked to see three or four chapters of *Confederate General*, "to give a better idea of what you are doing." He offered to pay $75 on acceptance. Richard replied, asking for information about *TriQuarterly*'s first issue. He also wrote back to Susan Stanwood, enclosing two chapters from *Trout Fishing*, along with his story "Two Armored Cars" for her consideration.

Charles Newman answered, saying he looked forward to reading additional chapters from Brautigan's forthcoming novel. Among other contributors, the new magazine would contain essays by Stephen Spender, Arthur Miller, Edward Albee, and Harold Pinter; poetry by William Stafford, W. D. Snodgrass, and Kenneth Patchen (along with his artwork); and fiction by James T. Farrell. Newman estimated the circulation of the first issue to be around three thousand in the Chicago area with another thousand destined for universities. Brautigan sent two more chapters from *Confederate General*, asking to have a look at the galley proofs should his material be accepted.

For $75, Don Carpenter rented Longshoreman's Hall, down near the waterfront on North Point, for a poetry reading billed as "Freeway," held on the night of June 12, 1964, to celebrate Gary Snyder's return from Japan. The three participants were former Reed College roommates Snyder, Philip Whalen, and Lew Welch. The location seemed appropriate, as Welch had worked as a longshoreman and Snyder was a merchant seaman. With the admission set at $1, Carpenter expected to lose his shirt. Lew Welch described the ambience in a letter to Henry Rago, editor of *Poetry Magazine*, "The hall is the funky old place where Harry Bridges won the coast & has a monstrous mural (very well done) showing policemen beating women and children to death—the fuzz mounted on horses with hooves like Percherons, which hooves are crushing the heads of brave men, etc."

An estimated eight hundred people showed up, the largest crowd ever to turn out for a poetry reading in San Francisco. Richard Brautigan hitchhiked in from Bolinas. Jack Spicer maintained "a nonstop, fairly quiet patter poking fun at the readers." Because he forgot to post a ticket taker at the door and hundreds of people squeezed in for free, Don Carpenter nearly did go broke. "I never worked so hard or sweated so much or cursed so hopelessly," he wrote later. In the end, Carpenter made enough to cover expenses, pay the poets a hundred bucks each, and throw a big bash afterward at Tosca, the venerable North Beach café where the jukebox featured opera arias and decades of cigarette smoke mellowed the Tuscan wall murals to an amber hue.

The isolation of country living and preoccupation with his Grove Press publishing deal slowed progress on *In Watermelon Sugar*. By the end of June, Brautigan had completed only seventeen short chapters, several less than a page long. The last chapter he wrote in Bolinas was "Arithmetic," a tale about the talking tigers eating the narrator's parents. A room had opened up at 123 Beaver Street, and Phil Whalen invited Richard to move in, a tempting offer, especially in light of a young woman Brautigan had recently met. Janice Meissner was a pert, petite blond with a devil-may-care attitude. "Glorious-looking woman," Don Carpenter remembered. "Absolutely magnificent. Big tits, nice ass, great legs, great face, lovely hair, good mind. The *works*!"

In addition to being beautiful, Janice had a well-paying job and a nice apartment at 533 Divisadero Street. She was everything Brautigan had ever hoped for in a woman, but being stuck out in Bolinas did not bode well for his romantic ambitions. Early in July, he took up residence with the other poets on Beaver Street. "My room was in the front," Richard wrote about his new home, "with a small marble fireplace and an old rug on the floor that told an ancient story about flowers [. . .] there was a light pouring in like a waterfall through the tall Victorian windows that I never dammed up with any curtains." Plum and avocado trees grew outside the window, and on windy days their branches clawed at the panes. Brautigan thought of it as "having a friendly wildcat hanging on the glass." When Richard wrote Fred Hill of the wonders of his new abode, Hill replied: "Beaver Street? You're loping my mule. Nobody lives on Beaver Street. There isn't any Beaver Street. Come off it, sir."

Early in July, Brautigan started back to work on *In Watermelon Sugar*. He wrote two chapters the first day and three on the following day and three more again on the day after. Richard was on a roll. He began recording the date on each new chapter as he finished it. Don Carpenter remembered that time. He had a family and a day job and owned a car. Don was a close friend of Philip Whalen's, and after he finished his workday, he drove over to Beaver Street to pick up his pal, "and we would go all over rock-hunting or hiking or whatever the hell. I would go past Richard's room and hear him typing. I became attracted to him as a writer hearing him type. It was every day, and it was regular steady typing. Any writer who works every day has got me. 'Cause that's the way it's done. That's the difference between the talkers and the writers. The writers write and the talkers talk."

Shortly after Brautigan's arrival, Lew Welch moved into the middle room on the first floor at Beaver Street. Don Carpenter described him as "tall, thin, handsome, always wearing a crooked smile. Welch liked to think of himself as a hip con-man. He liked to drink and sit in the Jazz Workshop and listen to good music. He loved Sausalito and the No Name Bar, and he loved to play pool and skulk about the Tenderloin." In June, Lew met a new love at the No Name: Maria Magdalena Cregg, a beautiful free-spirited woman born in Warsaw, Poland, in 1924.

Arriving in New York by way of Romania at age sixteen "after being 'squeezed out'" by the invading German and Russian armies, Magda studied art in Boston before relocating to the Bay Area in 1948. She was married to a Marin County radiologist and had two sons at the time she met Welch. Hugh, the older, later appropriated Lew's name in tribute, becoming the rock star Huey Lewis. "She kept him busy guessing," Richard wrote of Lew and Magda's affair, "and going from heaven to hell in the matter of an hour or two."

Phil Whalen remembered that Welch and Brautigan "got along very well, and so it was very nice. No problem. Lewie, of course, was always putting himself down all of the time. He would show you some piece of writing and say, 'Here's that thing that I started.' And you'd say, 'Well, terrific, Lewie.' Mumble, groan, grumble. 'No good, no fucking good.' It's just that he was always very persnickety. He wanted everything to be absolutely perfect. He had this facility for working in his head which was really remarkable. It would take months before he would commit anything to paper, and then he wouldn't like that." Meanwhile, up in the front room at the end of the hall, Richard was "just hammering away at a great rate and having a great time."

When the three poets weren't working they hung out together in the back kitchen. "Gabbled, giggled, and carried on, and eat together sometimes," Whalen said. Don Carpenter remembered, "one day walking into the kitchen, where Phil was sitting and Richard was standing at the stove with a cast-iron frying pan. And he took a can of beans, and he opened them. Van Camp's. And he just put it into the frying pan and was standing there stirring with a fork while Philip and I were talking, I thinking: 'That's the way to eat. There's a direct way.' I was a married man. At dinnertime, I ate a huge meal, all that stuff. But I thought to myself, 'Well, there is how poets eat.'"

The conversation in the kitchen at Beaver Street rivaled that of any North Beach coffeehouse. As Phil Whalen recalled, "Lewie knew wonderful stories and would tell wonderful stories and he had a great fund of anecdotes and tales and whatnot. Very much like Richard." Whalen's memories of Brautigan as a kitchen companion accentuated the positive. "He was always very easy to get along with and very happy and very funny. Whatever he told you, he told you in his own goofy way, and it was always a delight to listen to him."

Price Dunn, who dropped by to see Richard several times when he lived on Beaver Street, remembered the place as "an interesting little commune. There was a poet haven, and they were all living on a pittance, and brilliant, busy working away." Price thought highly of Philip Whalen, considering him "a delightful person," with "a great sense of humor." Dunn recalled the wonderful gab-fests back in the kitchen. "I'd come over there and somebody would be having a pot of soup on, or they'd be making some rice. It was a cheerful, vivacious place. Richard and Philip were just continuous fun; I'm talking about laughing your ass off."

Richard captured the joyful mood in an unfinished piece of fiction he titled "Moose, an American Pastoral." In it, the house on Beaver Street became 321 Moose Street. Philip was called Charles, "a kind and gentle poet in his early forties," and Lew was "a young existentialist named Sam [. . .] prone to excess of joy and depression." He wrote of their poverty and the happy meals back in the kitchen. "Sam did most of the cooking [. . .] but had a liking for fish that could not be satisfied." Richard also mentioned his current project. "I was writing a novel that was very important to me. Occasionally, I drank a little port and I did not have any girlfriends. I met a girl one night and she drove me home on her motorcycle but we didn't do anything more than kiss. We sat on the bed and kissed. She left shortly after that."

Despite his celibate state, Brautigan remained euphoric, his high spirits enhanced by the steady progress of his new novel. Every day, Richard pounded out several more chapters. Some days the tally came to five or six. He steamed along at a great rate, and sixteen days after resuming work on the project, Brautigan finished the first draft of *In Watermelon Sugar*. On July 19, 1964, he typed the dedication on the final page of his manuscript: "This novel is for Don Allen, Joanne Kyger and Michael McClure."

Richard had only written Joanne Kyger one letter from Bolinas, but their friendship picked up without missing a beat after he returned to the city. Being poor together remained a consistent theme. "We would go to the Safeway and fight over who would get the marked-down pork chops," Kyger recalled. During his two-week writing marathon finishing the first draft of the novel he partly dedicated to her, Brautigan called Joanne every day and read her long passages from his work in progress. "He'd always talk about himself and what he was reading," she said. "He was not really very interested in anybody else, particularly. I was there as a listener."

The possibility of winning the Formentor Prize remained uppermost on Brautigan's mind. Ten thousand dollars bought a lot of pork chops. The energy derived from working so well and hard on his new novel bolstered his self-confidence, and he became convinced that the prize would soon be his. In daily phone conversations with Joanne Kyger, he'd say, "Well, I guess I'll hear today, and this might be the last time we'll talk to each other like this anymore because when this thing happens, you're going to be in another world from where I am."

As Kyger recalled, Richard expected to become an overnight sensation, swept up in the whirlwind, much like Jack Kerouac or the Beatles. He talked of going to New York. "He'd just be off the map," she said. "He'd be out there somewhere." Joanne and her new partner, the painter Jack Boyce, "just cracked up" over the whole conceit. "Yeah, Richard, this might be the last day I'll see you," she said to him, tongue in cheek.

In the end, Richard Brautigan did not win the Formentor Prize. The award for 1964 went to Gisela Elsner, a German writer, whose novel, *Die Riesenzwerge*, was published in America by Grove Press as *The Giant Dwarfs*. The news came as a blow for Brautigan. "His whole soufflé deflated," Joanne Kyger remembered, "and Richard went on with his life."

Another disappointment followed soon after. Don Allen sent a manuscript copy of *Trout Fishing in America* to Robert Creeley for his consideration. They were editing a collection of "new American" fiction for Grove together, and Don wanted to include something by Brautigan. For various reasons, Creeley didn't take to the material. "I was in a weirdly funky state of mind," he recalled, "and I decided it was too much a shaggy dog story." At the time, Creeley favored the work of John Hawkes, his friend from Harvard, several of whose nightmarish experimental novels (*The Cannibal, The Goose on the Grave, The Beetle Leg, The Lime Twig*) had already been published by New Directions. "I was trying to get [him] in," Creeley said, "and Don felt, I think reasonably, that for our interests in that book that Jack Hawkes was too European." Maybe it was a trade-off, no Hawkes, no Brautigan. "I just didn't get Richard the first time," Creeley admitted. He stuck to his position and rejected this most American of writers from the *New American Story* anthology. In retrospect, Creeley remembered that essayist and critic Warren Tallman, who wrote the introduction to the story collection, said to him, "It's wonderful stuff, Bob. What's with you?"

Not all news was bad news. Early in July, Brautigan received a handwritten letter from Charles Newman at *TriQuarterly* saying they planned to publish an excerpt from *A Confederate General from Big Sur* in their fall issue. Newman asked for a biographical statement and promised to send a check and the galley proofs "shortly." Richard wrote back the next day with the requested information. *TriQuarterly*'s acceptance offset Susan Stanwood's letter turning down "Two Armored Cars" and the chapters from *Trout Fishing*. "Although they are grand exercises in the ludicrous, they are simply too fragmentary for us. Sorry." She asked to see "more sustained pieces, in which there is some real character or plot development."

A month later, Brautigan wrote again to Charles Newman, wondering "what's happening?" The promised check and proofs had yet to arrive. Grove was releasing his novel in October. Time seemed to be running out. Newman answered that there had been a screwup. *TriQuarterly* had three addresses for Richard in its files and somehow their envelope containing the proofs and a $75 check had gone astray. Nothing could be done about the proofs. They'd run out of time. Newman promised to send another check. He also asked to see more work. The first issue of the magazine was scheduled for September 15.

A check from *TriQuarterly* was mailed to 123 Beaver Street at the beginning of September. On the tenth, Brautigan sent Charles Newman two more chapters from *Trout Fishing in America*, adding, "If you decide to use them, payment on acceptance would be very much appreciated." Always generous with his friends, Richard suggested that Newman contact Philip Whalen and Michael McClure. The editor wrote back immediately, saying he'd get in touch with them both and asking to see "a large hunk" of *Trout Fishing*. "We think very highly of your work here."

Richard took the manuscript of *In Watermelon Sugar* to Jack Spicer, hoping for the sort of dynamic input his mentor had provided for his first novel. Spicer's alcoholism and paranoia had intensified during the three years since the writing of *Trout Fishing*. It was a period in which Spicer produced some of his most powerful work. *The Heads of the Town up to the Aether*, his first copyrighted book (Spicer was opposed to copyright protection on the principle that a writer did not "own" his material) had been published by Dave Haselwood and Andrew Hoyem at Auerhahn Press in 1962. In 1964, Spicer returned to White Rabbit Press, now under the direction of Graham Mackintosh, who designed and printed *The Holy Grail*, the poet's seven-part reworking of Arthurian myth. "In the context of the 'power' that led to such writing," Robin Blaser observed, "I think Richard wanted his place in it, so to speak, beside Spicer—an admirable desire in a young writer."

Jack Spicer turned Brautigan down without a word of explanation. Spicer tended "to let go" of any writer in his circle once he achieved any measure of success. Richard had a book contract with Grove Press, had published in the *Evergreen Review*, *City Lights Journal*, and elsewhere. The new issue of *Evergreen* (no. 33) had just appeared, containing five further chapters from *Trout Fishing in America* ("Witness for *Trout Fishing in America* Peace," "A Note on the Camping Craze That Is Currently Sweeping America," "The Pudding Master of Stanley Basin," "In the California Bush," and "Trout Death by Port Wine"). Brautigan was on his way.

Stung by Spicer's refusal, Brautigan turned to Robin Blaser, who liked him and "cared about his writing." Blaser considered *Trout Fishing* "a masterpiece." Jack Spicer and Blaser had been friends since their time together in Berkeley in the late forties and had exchanged new poems with each other, sometimes weekly, over the years. "Richard would have known that," Robin Blaser observed, many decades later. "There was a kind of magic—North Beach magic—between Jack and Richard. That was not the case between Richard and me." Brautigan had formed "a kind of dependence" on Spicer and "took it hard" when the older poet terminated their working relationship. Needing someone to play the role of mentor, Richard consulted Robin Blaser, a talented poet Jack Spicer treated as an equal.

The resulting connection between Brautigan and Blaser gave rise over the years to the false assertion that Robin Blaser had "edited" *In Watermelon Sugar*. A biography of Jack Spicer recorded this as fact. Not long ago, Robin Blaser set the record straight: "Richard came to me and asked if I would go over his unfinished manuscript. We met, as I remember, two or three times in a bar. Richard read to me, and we talked about the wonderful, strange imagery. If revision resulted, I never knew about it, and I certainly did not assist him in editing *In Watermelon Sugar*, a book I like very much."

Early in September, Richard Brautigan began submitting *In Watermelon Sugar* to magazines. He sent it first to Susan Stanwood at the *Saturday Evening Post* and, on the same day, mailed three more chapters from *Trout Fishing* to *TriQuarterly*. Although the new novel was under contractual option to Grove Press, he held off sending them a copy of the manuscript. They had not yet accepted *Trout Fishing in America* for publication. Richard decided to hedge his bets.

Small irritations kept Brautigan from enjoying the sweet smell of his own success. Topping the grievance list was the dust jacket Grove Press had designed for *A Confederate General from Big Sur*, incorporating a four-color reproduction of a 1959 painting by Larry Rivers entitled *The Next-to-Last Confederate Soldier*. Richard didn't care for it. He also didn't like the dust jacket copy, which stated that one of the "purposes" of the novel was "to give a serious portrait of a 'beat' character and a critique of the beat way of life." Brautigan had no interest in being identified with the Beat Generation and didn't consider himself to be a beatnik. Larry Rivers's painting was tainted by the artist's Beat connections. Rivers was a noted Greenwich Village bohemian and had acted the part of Milo in *Pull My Daisy*. The jacket copy also referred for the first time to Brautigan's "soft and thoughtful whimsy," a description he detested.

Richard Seaver sent Richard Brautigan an advance copy of *A Confederate General from Big Sur* and his accompanying letter informed him of Grove's decision to postpone the book's publication until January of 1965. Seaver feared a first novel published in October or November "might get lost in the shuffle" during the Christmas season. He also took issue with Brautigan's objections to the dust jacket.

Grove had asked Donald Allen to write the copy, but he declined, and the work was done in-house. "I very frankly think it is good jacket copy," Seaver wrote, "and faithfully presents the book. Maybe it does not coincide exactly with your own ideas of presentation, but in my experience authors must at some point let the book go from them and accept others' vision and evaluation of it." In any case, nothing more could be done, as the dust jacket had already been printed. If by chance there should be a second printing, perhaps then the jacket might be modified. Brautigan would never forget this slight. He had very strong ideas about typography, layout, and graphic art. In his future dealings with book publishers, Richard made certain to retain complete design control over his titles.

Luther Nichols wrote to Grove that "Richard is certainly one of the most inventive literary talents we have out here." In November, a letter came from John Ciardi, poetry editor of the *Saturday Review*. "I enjoyed reading Brautigan," he stated. "I don't know what it's about, but one of the nice things about the book is that the reader doesn't need to know. The man's a writer and the writing takes over in its own way, which is what writing should do. Brautigan manages effects the English novel has never produced before." The editors at Grove Press were in blurb heaven, but the book had already been printed, and it was too late to include the quotes on the dust jacket.

By the time Charles Newman wrote again to Brautigan early in October, saying he liked *Trout Fishing* and hoped to see more of it, typographic errors foreclosed on Richard's enjoyment of the moment. A copy of *TriQuarterly* had arrived at Beaver Street. Brautigan thought the first issue "a handsome magazine," but the chapter titled "The Rivets of Ecclesiastes" was printed incorrectly, with several paragraphs out of sequence. Had Richard seen the galleys, he would easily have spotted the error. He remained calm and polite when he contacted Newman about the matter. He requested *TriQuarterly* "print something in your next issue, pointing out that the chapter was not printed correctly." Another disappointment came later in October, when the *Saturday Evening Post* rejected *In Watermelon Sugar*. Susan Stanwood explained, "it was simply too vague and fragmentary for our purposes."

Newman answered Brautigan before the end of October. An editor's "near sightedness" caused the mix-up in Richard's copy. Newman had hoped for "that rarity or rarities, a first issue without typos," but thought that the story "made sense" in its reformatted version. He claimed, "I like it better the way it is printed," while admitting this sounded "ridiculously defensive." *TriQuarterly* offered to print a "rectification" along with the correct version of the final paragraph in their winter issue.

Newman's letter was mailed to 123 Beaver Street. By the time it arrived, Richard Brautigan had moved out. Since returning to the city in July, Richard wrote to Janice Meissner several times. The letters stopped in September, when their romance began to build up steam. Brautigan was primed for a new relationship. In "Beowulf Umbrella," an unfinished short story scrawled in one of his notebooks during the summer, he observed, "My name is Richard Brautigan [. . .] I have not been laid in weeks. I've grown steadily nervous. I've wandered from bar to bar and found nothing, but at the same time I was looking for nothing. I'm 29 years old. I ended up at a place that Philip Whalen says nice people just don't go to. Gino and Carlo's [. . .]" Finding no action there, Richard wrote a poem called "Marriage," reducing wedlock to a simple basic formula: "C sleeps with C. C sleeps with C. C sleeps with C," until enough time passes and "C decides to sleep with D. Then who does C sleep with? Beowulf umbrella."

Janice Meissner had been charmed by Richard Brautigan's wit. She worked for the Schlage Lock Company, an old San Francisco firm founded by Walter Schlage, whose first invention, patented in 1909, was for a door lock that automatically turned the interior lights off and on. To Brautigan, the company name sounded like "Schlock Lock." "Richard thought that was very funny," Joanne Kyger recalled. Janice detested her job. Any man who could make her laugh at her employment woes was worth considering. By the beginning of November, Richard had taken up residence with her in apartment number 4 at 533 Divisadero Street.

From the start, they made a delightful couple. He called her "Candy Pie," and contemporary photographs reveal an affectionate physical chemistry between them. They were pictured holding hands, hugging and kissing, Janice sprawled like a playful kitten across Richard's lap. She stood a head shorter, barely coming up to his shoulder, yet their blond good looks went well together, her happy full-lipped pout the perfect complement to the frowning down-sweep of his Victorian mustache; her dark-lidded sultry eyes exchanging secret glances with his bemused owlish stare.

On November 30, 1964, Brautigan began what he hoped would become a new novel. On a clean page in his notebook, he wrote: "The American Experience by Richard Brautigan." On the next page, headed by the Roman numeral I, he set down a brief opening chapter. "The American experience is an operation illegal in this country: abortion. This is our story. There are thousands like us in America [. . .] in every state, in every city."

Richard began chapter II on a new page. It was also only three sentences long and dealt with his precarious finances. Combining what was left from a publisher's advance, "after paying off certain debts," with the profit from selling thirty-five books of his poetry and sixty borrowed dollars, added to another $120.00 "my woman" had from her job, brought the total to $311. The brief chapter ended here. It was obvious the couple was bankrolling an abortion. Brautigan set his notebook aside at this point, resuming work on his typewriter later.

The second time around, he called the piece "In the Talisman, Looking Out." He typed rapidly, beginning again with the same opening sentence, "The American experience is an operation illeagal [sic] in this country: abortion. This is how we got there, Alvinia and I, how sweet and spinning kisses one night in San Francisco led us step by step, smooth as a highway almost with beginning—I'll kiss you—then to the abortions [sic] table in Tueians [sic]. Mexico." Brautigan then digressed to "invoke a talisman for this book." The narrator felt a story about abortion "must be guided by some kind of gentleness."

The talisman Richard chose was a house. Not just any house, but the old Victorian at 123 Beaver Street. He described it as "a simple two-story white house," with a front yard "divided in half by a stone walk." He left out the fruit trees, but the walk transversed a garden where rhubarb grows "like flowers" and rosemary "pours over the edge of the brinks, in a downward flight of blossoms." Brautigan placed the house "on a hill in San Francisco." He recalled a room with "a table by the window." It was a place where he had been happy. "The room is nice and it makes me feel at home."

Richard described Alvinia (he spelled her name three different ways as if trying to bring the character into focus) in terms he might easily have applied to Janice, "very pretty in a warm black sweater, in her blond body, hair and face." At the end of the second typewritten page (where the narrator imagines himself in the talisman house, watching the girl walk down the hill to meet him through "a high drift of rabipidly [sic] moving fogg" [sic]), Brautigan set the manuscript aside. No documentation survives suggesting Richard Brautigan ever arranged an abortion for any of his partners. Whatever the circumstances, the project stalled, stillborn. Richard had other things on his mind. In early November, he still stewed over the enormous typo in *TriQuarterly* and Charles Newman's presumed failure to respond to his complaint. He dashed off a terse note to the editor: "I would appreciate a reply to my letter of October 6. Thank you."

A few days later, another publishing error provoked Brautigan's ire. That fall, Anna Halprin and the Dancers' Workshop Company revived *The Flowerburger*, performing the piece in November, first at San Francisco State and later as part of the Improvisation Festival at the UCLA Concerts. *Open City Press* printed a review of the first performance ("A Halprin Happening") by John Byrem and published the three poems on which the dance was based ("The Flowerburger," "The Chinese Checker Players," and "In a Café") attributing them to the dancers.

Richard voiced his strong opinions regarding false attribution in a letter. "You did not get my permission to publish these poems and you published these poems without acknowledging my authorship. I do not think this is the way to run a publication and I believe the copyright laws in this country back me up on this point." Richard Brautigan signed his unsent letter, "Yours sincerely, The Flowerburger."

Charles Newman's "nice letter" finally caught up with Brautigan at his new address around the end of the month, and he wrote back immediately, enclosing two more chapters from *Trout*

Fishing in America. TriQuarterly now had seven chapters from the novel. Richard asked for a payment of $100 should they be accepted. The editor replied, doubting the additional chapters would be included in the upcoming winter number, "since we hesitate to publish the same author in successive issues." Newman agreed to the $100 honorarium, asking to "keep the manuscript for a few more months until February," when they would consider it for inclusion in the spring issue.

Richard Brautigan found Newman's request outrageous. He got back in touch with *TriQuarterly* immediately. "I am trying to make some kind of living from writing, and I just cannot afford to have the work I've sent to you tied up any longer without a definite decision." Since sending the first two chapters in September, Brautigan had sent another five. "Unfortunately, the art of living in America depends on a little money to pay the rent and the only money I get is from writing." Richard asked Charles Newman to either accept his work "and pay me for it" or else return the manuscript, "so I can send it some place else."

Not making any headway with his tale about abortion, Brautigan turned his thoughts toward other fiction as Christmas fast approached. The words to an old Appalachian folk song kept echoing around in his brain, and he jotted them down in his notebook: "I'd rather live in some dark holler / where the sun refused to shine [. . .]" Folksingers call such a lyric a "floater verse" because it is easily transposed into any number of songs. "Little Maggie" and "Hard, Ain't It Hard" are among the better-known folk melodies using the verse Richard recalled. Here Brautigan's runaway imagination took over. In the true spirit of folk music, he improvised two off-kilter new lines snatched from out of the blue: "where the wild birds of heaven / can't hear me when I whine." Combining the plaintive traditional lyric with his own inspired invention triggered an idea for a short story.

Richard labored over his opening paragraph, writing two rough versions before starting again on a separate page. He quoted the folk song above his text, appending his final improvised couplet to complete the verse. Folk music continually evolves through the ages, and Brautigan's variant must be seen as a contribution to a long-standing tradition. The last draft in Richard's notebook was almost identical to the first paragraph of the published story.

"The Wild Birds of Heaven," in *Revenge of the Lawn*, is a surreal fantasy about a man named Mr. Henly whose children want a new television set. He buys "a video pacifier that had a 42-inch screen with built-in umbilical ducts," at the "Frederick Crow Department Store." The credit arrangements might have been devised by Franz Kafka. Mr. Henly has his shadow removed by a blacksmith, who nails "the shadow of an immense bird" to his feet in its place. In twenty-four months, when he pays off the TV set, Mr. Henly will get his own shadow back.

The differences between the published version and what Brautigan wrote in his notebook show him wrestling with the imagery of death. The original draft read, "The picture tube was going out and a band of death shadow crept over the edges of what-ever was playing that night and then the static lines that danced like drunken pencils on the picture." In the published version it became, "The picture was going out and that death John Donne spoke so fondly about was advancing rapidly down over the edge of whatever was playing that night, and there were also static lines that danced now and then like drunken cemeteries on that picture."

Another Christmas. Richard was in love and living happily with a new woman. His domestic situation prompted Brautigan to consult Dr. Alex L. Finkle, a San Francisco urologist, in mid-December. He paid four subsequent visits to the doctor, the last in January 1965, paying a total of $55 for his treatment. The nature of his ailment remains unknown, but it was likely a venereal infection. Whether Janice was involved in these medical visits or if she even knew of Richard's problem remains a mystery.

Brautigan's concern for his partner was expressed a year or so later in *Flowers for Those You Love*, a little poem about VD that he gave away for free on the city streets as a printed broadside. "Please see a doctor / if you think you've got it," he wrote. "You'll feel better afterwards / and so will those you love."

Like an ecstatic child waiting for Santa, Richard expressed the joy of his new relationship in a "card" he composed and sent to friends. At the top, he wrote a poem: "All the flowers /that Christmas bring /grow again . . . /grow again . . . /in the houses /where we live." Below the poem, Brautigan drew a childlike schematic of a house with a wavy line of smoke trailing out of the rect-angular chimney. He wrote "Merry Christmas!" inside the house and the date, 1964, riding above the smoke. The little house stood like a blossom atop a tall thin stalk, the way a child might draw a flower with curving leaves pointing like arrows at the two names written across the bottom of the page: Richard and Janice.

twenty-two: aborted dreams

THE NEW YEAR of 1965 blew into San Francisco on a torrent of cold wind and rain. About to turn thirty and with his first novel only weeks away from publication, Richard Brautigan sat down at the typewriter to ponder why he had become a novelist "in a world that I can barely understand." He called his thoughts on the matter "The Why Questions," harkening back to "a creepy childhood in [the] Pacific Northwest." Although Brautigan admitted he'd "never had a very clear picture" of himself, he discussed the origins of his first novel and stated, "all I want to do is to please those I love." Richard was hard on himself when discussing his education. It "was rather slow while being divided into four stages: Timberwolf, [*sic*] loser, hellgramtie [*sic*], kook. Gorky wrote a very beautiful book about his education called My University. . . [*sic*]. If I were to try the same task I would have to call the book my kindergarten. It would be a shameless confession of failure."

Priced at $3.95, *A Confederate General from Big Sur* was published in hardback by Grove Press on Friday, January the twenty-second. Erik Weber's unattributed photograph, taken more than a year before in the aviary on Francisco Street, occupied the entire back cover of the dust jacket. "The novel is changing," Brautigan stated earlier in an interview for "The Book Corner" in the *Examiner*. The jacket flap copy said that he was "now at work on a new novel called "Contemporary Life in California."

In a brief paragraph he wrote for the publisher's press release, Brautigan described himself: "I am twenty-nine years old and was born and raised in the Pacific Northwest. I never cared for school, but lived close to the mountains and listened to people talk. I moved to San Francisco a few years ago, and it's like living on an island. I've left the island a few times to live in Idaho, Mexico and Big Sur [. . .] I just finished a novel, In Watermelon Sugar, and am working on my fourth . . . When I was in my early 20's I wrote poems and published three little books of poetry."

At eight thirty on the evening of the twenty-second, Richard Brautigan read selections from *A Confederate General from Big Sur* at the California Club (1750 Clay Street) a private organization for women that often rented its 1907 auditorium for outside events. An author's reception with an open bar from ten until midnight at the San Francisco Tape Music Center (321 Divisadero Street) followed the reading. Donald Allen mailed out the invitations. Richard and Don each compiled individual lists of the Frisco literary people they wished to come. Brautigan did not include Jack Spicer's name on his list. Allen made sure he got an invitation and wrote personally to William Hogan and Stanleigh Arnold at the *Chronicle*. He mailed Arnold a copy of the *Evergreen Review* containing the *Trout Fishing in America* excerpts. The newspaper published "The Cleveland Wrecking Yard" in their Sunday edition and sent Brautigan a check for $25.

Joanne Kyger and her boyfriend, Jack Boyce; Dr. John and Margot Patterson Doss; Tommy Sales; Gary Snyder and his current girlfriend (who later married Andrew Hoyem); and Ariel Parkinson were among those in attendance at the Tape Music Center. Ariel's husband, Tom, wrote a review of *Confederate General* for the *Chronicle*. Parkinson compared Brautigan's prose to Gertrude Stein and Sherwood Anderson: "fact and fraud and wild whimsey are all reported with an air of detachment [. . .] An absorbing, irritating and terribly amusing book [. . .] An author with the potentiality of Saroyan, its own tone of bewilderment and amusement that brings American humor a new and disturbing voice."

Earlier in January, Richard had called Erik Weber to arrange another photo session. Anticipating that Grove would publish *Trout Fishing* in the fall, Brautigan wanted a dust jacket photo for the book, perhaps one to grace the front cover in accordance with chapter 1. On a fair mild afternoon, they headed over to Washington Square in North Beach. Richard wore pale faded jeans and a plaid wool parka. He was hatless. Erik shot a roll of film, stalking around the Benjamin Franklin monument, taking pictures of Brautigan and the statue from various angles.

By the end of February, Richard and Janice moved to a new apartment just off Divisadero at 2830 California Street, upstairs above Boegershausen Hardware, which owned the building. It was a spacious place with an elegant brick fireplace and a hanging Deco milk-glass ceiling fixture in the main room. The rent was $100 a month, payable to their ironmonger landlords. Such scant furnishings as the couple possessed belonged to Janice. There was a graceful side table and a few wooden chairs, an antique mirror above the mantel, brightly covered futons to sprawl upon, and a long low table they used for entertaining.

Richard's notebook became a tangible repository of their intertwined lives. Along with many magazine addresses, references to "Janice, my blond" appear among the drafts of poems. On another page, Janice wrote out recipes for "honey puffs" and cherry sauce. Still later, she penned notes on silent film stars Theda Bara and Clara Bow. Brautigan later wrote an unpublished poem about Miss Bow. In the same notebook, he also wrote "Seven Poems for Mike Nathan" (four drafts of the same never-published poem, "I changed color into glass, and I drank water from your painting [. . .]"), addressing their shared mental asylum electroshock bond.

Erik Weber came over in March to photograph the young lovers at home. They posed formally, Richard wearing a crew neck sweater and brand-new blue sneakers, Janice looking glamorous in a fur hat and sleeveless dress. Informal shots showed them necking on the futon. Erik thought Janice "seemed to be a real flirt with other people" and later observed that it "drove Richard crazy," but that March they were crazy in love. Brautigan wanted Erik to take pictures of them naked together. "Fucking pictures," Weber recalled, "but it never worked out."

In the last week of March, ten rugrats and assorted parents turned up for Ianthe's fifth birthday party. Soda pop was served in paper cups with a rectangular chocolate cake, five candles burning in a straight line down the middle. The kids were well behaved, almost reticent. Ianthe shyly sucked her thumb and needed some gentle prompting from her dad before blowing out the candles. Both Richard and Janice took a hand in cutting the cake.

Charles Newman returned Richard's manuscripts in mid-February, along with a letter. *TriQuarterly* anticipated a substantial budget increase starting in June, and Newman asked to see more of Brautigan's fiction then ("We are quite interested in your work [. . .]"). Richard replied that he "had written a short novel called In Watermelon Sugar. I would like to find a magazine that would serialize the entire novel or part of it." He said he would send Newman a copy "sometime in June." Three days later, Brautigan mailed the fiction editor of the *Partisan Review* six chapters from *Trout Fishing*. ("A prompt decision would be very much appreciated.") At Donald Allen's suggestion, Richard wrote to Edward Keating at *Ramparts*, sending along a copy of *In Watermelon Sugar*. Again, he asked for a "prompt decision."

Brautigan's most recent publication had been in the April issue of the *San Francisco Keeper's Voice* (vol. 1, no. 4), "an unofficial, informal newsletter that attempts to provide for the animal keepers of the San Francisco Zoo and other interested parties." Richard's poem "October 2, 1960" (about Ianthe, age six months, attempting to eat the phone book) appeared on the "permanent page of particular poetry." Subscribers included such offbeat characters as Anton Szandor LaVey, a consulting hypnotist and "Psychic Investigator" who later founded the Church of Satan.

The reviews for *A Confederate General from Big Sur* began trickling in over the first three months after the novel's publication. Along with Thomas Parkinson's rave in the *Chronicle*, William Hogan praised the novel in the *Saturday Review*, and writing for *Esquire*, Malcolm Muggeridge said that it "provides as good an account as has come my way of Beat life and humor [. . .]" Favorable notices also appeared in *Book Week*, the *Kansas City Star*, the *Los Angeles Herald-Examiner*, the *Toledo Blade*, and *McCall's*, among others.

Unfortunately, the word was not so good in several of the more important critical venues. Two days after the book's publication, Martin Levin panned it in his column, "A Reader's Report" in *The New York Times Book Review*. Philip Rahv was even more unkind in *The New York Review of Books*, dismissing the novel as "pop writing of the worst kind, full of vapid jokes and equally vapid sex-scenes which are also a joke, though scarcely in the sense intended by the author." An anonymous critic in *Playboy* so savaged the book, Brautigan felt the reviewer "recommended that I try finger painting."

Brautigan became the beneficiary of Malcolm Muggeridge's kind words in *Esquire* when Robert Sherrill, one of the magazine's editors, got in touch with him to suggest a writing assignment. Sherrill wanted a story about death row. He contacted Richard in March to propose the idea, planting the seed and saying he'd write soon with more details. When Brautigan didn't hear back from *Esquire* right away, he phoned San Quentin on the first of April, speaking with Associate Warden James Park, in charge of press relations, to ask if he might visit death row. Richard jotted notes as they talked.

James Park had "a friendly, relaxed voice." He explained that the prison discouraged visits due to security and said "it would have to be cleared by Sacramento." He also said that the condemned men had "a closed community. They get upset when strangers come around looking at them like critters in the zoo." Being an official reporter for *Esquire* magazine carried the day. Brautigan made an appointment to visit the prison. Associate Warden Park even offered to show him the gas chamber.

Bob Sherrill wrote at length in early April, suggesting, "the tone of the piece will be the key to it—looking at death's [sic] row as if it were a funny scene, 50 or so inmates revising their appeals, watching TV, working jigsaw puzzles, taking correspondence courses or God know's [sic] what." The editor wanted a story featuring the facts but using "fictional techniques" told from Brautigan's point of view "so as to add up to absurdity rather than the usual horror that grabs by empathy." *Esquire* offered a fee of $600, plus expenses, with a $200 guarantee in case they turned the story down.

Early on a Monday morning, Richard rode the bus from the city over to San Quentin in Marin County. Brautigan was met by Warden Lawrence Wilson, who complained about the over-population problem on California's death row. Forty-eight men were currently awaiting execution. Wilson turned Brautigan over to Associate Warden Park, a clinical psychologist with a degree from UCLA who served the writer tea in his office and provided him with a lengthy information sheet from the California Department of Corrections. The last man executed had been James Abner Bentley (1/23/63 for murder 1 & robbery 1). The total number put to death at San Quentin since 1893 (prior to this date California executions were carried out by the county sheriffs) was 408, of which 214 had been hanged.

Richard Brautigan took copious notes, filling fourteen pages in his notebook with detailed minihistories of various condemned men. ("Raymond Forrest Treloar, 31, a painter, was sentenced to death for the mad dog slaying of a restaurant patron during a hold-up. His partner got life. Treloar said he killed the restaurant patron 'because the guy bumped my elbow.' They also pistol-whipped seven people in the café.") He listed many arcane facts ("Execution usually at 10 in the morning [. . .] 10 to 15 minutes to die [. . .] one ounce pellet of cyanide into solution of dilute sulphuric acid [. . .]") and noted a death row aphorism, "A rich man never goes to the gas chamber," along with the last words of twenty-year-old Alexander Robillard ("I'm not legally a man, but I'm going to die like one. Goodbye and good luck") and of Bernard Gilliam, a Fresno cotton picker, who carried a photograph of President Eisenhower to the entrance of the execution chamber on November 1, 1952, but handed it to a guard at the last minute, saying, "I won't take Ike in there."

Brautigan was curious about what the prisoners ate. "I was not interested in last meals," he wrote, "but in the food they were eating today." Associate Warden Park obliged him by getting a copy of the week's menu from a filing cabinet. It covered every item (breakfast, dinner, supper), from Stewed Prunes to Hungarian Goulash w/ Noodles to Chocolate Cake, that the men in the death house would be served between 4/12/65 and 4/18/65. Brautigan got "a strange feeling" when he saw "Weekly Menu for CONDEMNED ROW" written at the top of the sheet.

There was so much food. Grilled halibut and chicken fried steak featured on the same dinner; "Roast Leg O Pork" and ground round steak were served together on another; short ribs, wieners, and spaghetti constituted a one-meal buffet. The prisoners were to get "Colored Easter Eggs" for breakfast on Easter Sunday. When Richard asked about the caloric content, the associate warden made a phone call and came up with an astonishing figure: "4,500 calories." It seemed odd that caged men should be fed like hogs bound for slaughter. Brautigan asked to keep a copy of the menu, and James Park said OK.

The prison officials wanted to see the article before it was published. Brautigan told them the decision was up to the editors of *Esquire* and headed back to San Francisco on the bus, his precious menu "cradled [. . .] gently" on his lap. That same evening, a friend, "an aspiring Hollywood scriptwriter," stopped by. This was Zekial Marko, whose script, *Once a Thief*, based on his own paperback novel (*Scratch a Thief*), was currently being filmed in San Francisco, starring Alain Delon, Van Heflin, Jack Palance, Ann-Margret, and Marko himself (in the role of Luke, the proprietor of a hip nightspot). They drank bock beer. Brautigan showed Marko the menu. The screenwriter thought it was sick: "Pop Art that hurts. You know the kind that has drawers full of dead babies."

The next day, Brautigan hauled his prison bill of fare over to 123 Beaver Street asking for Phil Whalen's and Lew Welch's opinions. One poet thought the menu "frightening, obscene, and disgusting." The other couldn't believe the vast quantity of food being served. He loved crisp bacon and hadn't had any in a year. Crisp bacon was on the San Quentin menu every day but one during the coming week. "Look at all that food," he marveled. "Why don't they give this food to a poet?" Richard spent the rest of the day showing his curious trophy to various friends, and the reaction was always the same, shock and disgust.

When Brautigan sat down at his typewriter, "The Menu" came quickly, pretty much as it happened, the conversations with his friends and the wardens out at San Quentin. In the middle he placed—as a piece of found art—the original prison-printed menu. Richard mailed the story to Bob Sherrill in New York. In an accompanying letter, Brautigan admitted his story "may be far-out, but that's the way it happened. I had to tiptoe between gallows humor and nausea." He mentioned that the prison officials "seemed pretty nervous" about his article. "They want a gentle anonymous Death Row." Richard asked to be paid soon. "I need the money because it's spring." His expenses for the story totaled $7.59. Sherrill found the piece "fascinating [. . .] everyone on the staff liked it," but warned "it may be a couple of weeks before you will have a decision on whether we'll buy it." Pleased that Richard had worked so quickly, Sherrill hoped "that it will still be spring when you get your money."

Having observed certain malign aspects of the zodiac in May, astrologer Gavin Arthur predicted a huge tidal wave would devastate the coast of Northern California. On the designated weekend, Richard Brautigan recruited Erik and Loie Weber to drive him and Janice south to safety. They left before dawn, arriving quite early in the morning at Price Dunn's current abode along the Carmel River. Erik had no idea who they were visiting. "We'd ask these questions, and Richard wouldn't say anything—noncommittal. We drove in and woke Price up and that huge woman he was with."

The woman's name was Katherine (aka Baby Katherine). "She was quite a character," Loie recalled. She had recently been in a motorcycle accident, and her natural girth was enlarged by the full-body cast she wore under her voluminous housedress. Loie thought Katherine and Price made "such an odd couple." Her left leg also was encased in plaster, causing her to "sort of hobble around. She was crazy about Price, and he used to tease her a lot, and she would act the fool, which she wasn't, she was actually quite intelligent." Only after they all sat down to a big breakfast of fried pork chops did Erik make the connection between Price Dunn and Lee Mellon. Brautigan delighted in keeping everyone in the dark. "Richard never told us, and he never said anything afterwards."

The tidal wave never materialized. They spent the week hanging out and drinking. "I remember Richard a couple of times telling me that Price Dunn was the only person he would trust with his life," Erik recalled. Weber took a couple rolls of film on the trip, mostly posed shots of Richard, Janice, and Loie. The three men went fishing in the Carmel River. The stretch of creek alongside Price's place was "very, very narrow," the banks dense with overgrowth. Richard and Price waded in and managed to catch "a couple of fish." Loie and Erik went down with Richard and Janice to visit in Carmel "a number of times." Loie liked Katherine but thought Janice seemed odd. "I never knew who Janice was," she said. "To me, she was shifting sands."

The first week in June, Form 17 from the IRS arrived at California Street. Brautigan had failed to include a tax payment on his 1964 return and owed the government $261.93. Starting in 1963, before he received even a modest book advance, Richard began itemizing the modest deductions he incurred as a writer. In 1964, these proved insufficient to offset the taxes he owed. On June 28, Brautigan signed an agreement with the Internal Revenue Service, twelve bucks every two weeks until he wiped the red ink off the government books. If Richard earned more than $180 a month, all the surplus income would be applied toward his back taxes.

Brautigan kept his writer's antennae fine-tuned for offbeat article possibilities and learned of a unique burial ground at the Presidio. He gave Erik Weber a call, asking him to participate. Erik had never heard of the military pet cemetery. It sounded interesting, and he agreed to go along. This was not to be a collaboration like their Christmas tree story. "It was Richard being very specific as to what he wanted," Weber recalled. "I'd only been photographing for a year or two, and I wasn't real confident about my own ability, so I followed what he said."

Founded by the Spanish in 1776 to guard the entrance of San Francisco Bay, the 1,480-acre Presidio remained a military reservation for more than two centuries. In 1965, the place was still administered by the U.S. Sixth Army, in charge ever since the United States annexed California from Mexico. In its quaint pet cemetery every sort of household pet from cats and dogs to parakeets, canaries, and goldfish were interred. General "Black Jack" Pershing buried his horse there.

Richard and Erik obtained permission to visit the animal graveyard from the post provost marshal. Brautigan wore his "funny hat," and "his getup was kind of strange." He looked at Erik and asked, "Am I embarrassing you, the way I look and act?" Erik said no, but recalled that "everywhere you went with Richard, people looked, he was so strange-looking." They wandered among the many miniature tombstones commemorating such departed furry friends as Willie (1954–1956), pet hamster of Lt. & Mrs. Davidson, and Old Brown Dog, a "Pal for 19 Years."

With traffic clanging overhead on the freeway overpass leading up to the Golden Gate Bridge, Richard jotted down his first impressions in the same notebook he carried with him to San Quentin. Eric Weber followed along, taking pictures according to the writer's instructions. Brautigan drew little arched childlike tombstone shapes, writing the quaint epitaphs within their boundaries. He listed pet names appealing to his fancy: "Socky, Diehard, Sad Sack, Tiger Sue, Chur, Satan, Caesar, Shorty Johnson, Jet, Duke [. . .]" In all, he took six pages of notes.

When Erik finished photographing he headed back to his car. Richard said he wanted to stick around for a few more minutes. Erik got in the driver's seat and watched his friend staring at the tiny graves as two soldiers came down the hill, rifles slung over their shoulders. The soldiers approached the pet cemetery. One advanced on Richard Brautigan, who paid very little attention until the man jumped forward, his rifle at port arms, shouting, "Halt! Who goes there?" Erik was dumbfounded. "I just sat with my mouth open and watched it rather than photographing it. I thought he was in danger."

Brautigan used the incident with the soldiers to end his story about the pet cemetery. He wrote the piece very quickly over the next week, prefacing it with a quote from fashion designer Rudi Gernreich, the gist of which was "if you're bored, you go for the outrageous gesture." Putting on the "graves and markers and flowers like a Rudi Gernreich coat" became a central metaphor. Richard titled it "Homage to Rudi Gernreich." He mailed the story, along with a selection of photographs by Erik Weber, to Madeline Tracy Brigden at *Mademoiselle*.

A week earlier, Brautigan wrote Bob Sherrill, inquiring about "The Menu" and asking to be repaid for his expenses. Sherrill waited until the end of the month to reply. Everyone at *Esquire* had approved Brautigan's story except for editor-in-chief and publisher Arnold Gingrich, who had the final vote. He voted no. Sherrill said he was "sorry it didn't make it" and returned Richard's manuscript, along with the $200 kill-fee and $7 for expenses, effectively stiffing him out of fifty-nine cents.

Brautigan got his four bits' worth anyway. Sherrill had edited the manuscript, making various cuts (often whole paragraphs) and tightening several other sections. When "The Menu" was eventually published, first in *Evergreen Review* no. 42 (August 1966) and later as a chapter in *The Tokyo–Montana Express* (1980), Richard incorporated Sherrill's changes. The edited version was the one he mailed to Susan Stanwood at the *Saturday Evening Post* and, after she turned it down, to Gerald Rothberg, editor-publisher of a New York–based magazine called *Clyde*.

Gainfully employed, Janice Meissner fit Brautigan's bill regarding a woman who could support him, but she was not the sort to suffer a freeloader hanging around for long. Richard redoubled his efforts to make some money without actually having to go out and get a day job. Pass-the-hat public readings had long been a source of easy coin. Brautigan had already read from *Confederate General* twice and searched for a place to showcase his latest work of fiction.

The Buzz gallery was an artists' commune on Buchanan Street in Japantown. Founded the previous June by painters Paul Alexander (a Black Mountain alumnus), Bill Brodecky, and Larry Fagin, Buzz had been planned to run for only a single year, like King Ubu more than a decade before. George Stanley came up with the name. "We didn't even want to use the word 'gallery,'" Alexander said. "We just called it 'Buzz,' period. Of course, everyone always called it 'Buzz Gallery' anyway whether we did or not."

The gallery provided a residence for the artists as well as a public exhibition space. Nemi Frost, Tom Field, Bill McNeill, Fran Herndon, Jess, Harry Jacobus, and Knute Stiles all exhibited there. Graham Mackintosh printed the announcements and posters. Most of these people were friends and colleagues of Jack Spicer's, yet he was annoyed by the gallery's name, feeling it had been filched from one of his poems. ("I hear a banging on the door of night / Buzz, buzz; buzz, buzz; buzz / If you open the door does it let in light? / Buzz, buzz, buzz, buzz; buzz, buzzz.") Spicer avoided the place like the plague.

Richard Brautigan read all of *In Watermelon Sugar* at Buzz in two parts on two consecutive Saturday nights in July. Don Carpenter was among those attending on both evenings. "Everybody was packed in this little place while Richard read in the most monotonous voice in history." Carpenter remembered seeing Don Allen, Jack Boyce, Joanne Kyger, and Bob Creeley in attendance. Kyger recalled Tom Parkinson laughing "in all the wrong places."

Although he felt "a lot of people were bored by it," Don was "fascinated by what [Brautigan] could do with these few words and ideas." On the way out of the second reading, Carpenter asked Richard how many words he had used in his novel. "You used very few words," Don said. "You only used a couple of hundred words in that whole book."

"His eyes lit up, and he gave me a big hug," Carpenter remembered. "I was the only one that had caught on that he was writing with an extraordinarily limited vocabulary."

Earlier in the spring, Richard had begun work on a novel about his grandmother, "Moonshine Bess." The idea came to him from an unfinished short story he called "Those Great American Dogs." ("I'm thirty years old and live in America and it's too late for me to do anything else now, so American dogs, look at my life. Maybe you can see something I can't see.") In this tale,

Brautigan started to chronicle the lives of various canines he'd had as childhood pets. He ran out of steam after only three pages, concentrating mainly on the escapades of Pluto (left unnamed in the story but described as a "classic american hobo no-good dog"). Brautigan also described four other dogs, including the German shepherd he smeared with fecal matter when he was two years old.

Brautigan started a new story about his grandmother's dog. He first called it "Mark: A 1920s Dog," later amending it to "Mark: A 1930s Dog," and finally just "Mark." Richard began again and again, reworking the first paragraph many times but always using the same opening line, "I guess the only dog I ever loved was Mark, a 1930s American dog." The story described how the big good-hearted police dog died painfully but with great dignity in 1937 when a neighbor lady fed him ground glass. The grandmother responded by pouring kerosene in her neighbor's basement and burning down her house. Arriving at 2:00 AM, when the house was almost gone, the firemen stood around looking sleepy. "'We can't be everywhere at once,' the fire cheir [sic] said." Brautigan pasted a circular photograph of Mark, taken by his grandmother in 1933, at the head of the story.

Richard expanded his dog tale into a novel. Both *Trout Fishing in America* and *A Confederate General from Big Sur* began as sequences of short stories. He quickly came up with a working title, *Revenge of the Lawn*, and drafted an outline of possible chapters. "Mark" was to be chapter one. The second would be called "The Family Tree: the history of the family as related to the pear tree in the front yard. It is a rather strange and weird American family. Perhaps the photograph of a pear tree would be nice."

Brautigan included several other theoretical chapters on his list. "The Neighbor: A very strange man with an unusual dog. The dog drinks trees. The Jewel: A history of the grandmother's breast cancer. The Children: the children of the grandmother. Five girls, two boys. Both the boys die; one at 26, the other 16. The Classic 1930 Appetician [sic] Death: Coyote with comb, mirror and brush. An introduction [illegible] History of each child: this would be a chapter called four American children, and A history of the lawn, the house, the [illegible]."

Following a note, "The Indians that lived where the house was, write a chapter about them," Brautigan listed these titles: "Indian Ghosts, Washington House Ghosts, The Ghosts belonging to my Grandfather and Fueds [sic] and Feats among the Ghosts." The final two entries on his list were "Chocolate Cake: A flashback chapter to the Grandfather watching his mother bake a Chocolate Cake, and The Magic Power of the Lawn."

Richard slipped the nine pages of manuscript and his outline into a manila envelope he marked "New Novel/Notes" and addressed it to Lawrence Ferlinghetti at City Lights Books. He included a short note: "Lawrence, Give me a jingle on the electric telephone when you are through reading this. 567-2293 Richard." Brautigan never mailed this to Ferlinghetti. The envelope remained in his personal archive until his death.

After completing his outline, Richard incorporated several elements from various suggested chapters into a single long short story. He borrowed from his memories of family history: his grandmother Moonshine Bess, her lover Frank Campana and his fear of bees, the pear tree, and the lawn. He started the story with the lines, "My grandmother, in her own way, shines like a beacon down the stormy American past. She was a bootlegger in a little county up in the state of Washington." By Brautigan's standards, it became an expansive work. He called the piece "Revenge of the Lawn," a title originally intended for the novel in which the story was to be a single chapter.

There was a psychic sea change simmering in the American unconscious throughout 1965. The baby boom, a vast population bubble recently come of age, sought enlightenment through mind-altering substances, experimenting with marijuana, mescaline, and LSD. United by rock and roll and postwar prosperity, agitated by the Civil Rights and Free Speech movements, inspired by Beat poets and Eastern mysticism, the Pepsi Generation awakened to a perceived sense of community young people had never known before.

In 1965, lysergic acid diethylamide was still legal and mostly unknown to the public at large in spite of active proselytizing by several charismatic prophets. Timothy Leary, a psychology professor at Harvard, began experimenting with psilocybin and LSD five years earlier, along with his colleague Richard Alpert (later known as Baba Ram Dass). Both were fired by the university in 1963. Leary cofounded a magazine, the *Psychedelic Review*, devoted to experimental drug use and set up shop as the Castalia Foundation in a huge gingerbread mansion on a 2,500 acre Hudson River property at Millbrook, New York, the family estate of a turned-on stockbroker named Billy Hitchcock.

Ken Kesey got his first hit of "acid" (his own terminology) courtesy of the CIA as a paid research subject in one of the Company's clandestine spook projects. "Just say, thank you," Kesey always maintained regarding drugs. These experiments took place in a veteran's hospital, and Kesey used some of his experience working there as the background for his first novel, *One Flew Over the Cuckoo's Nest*. The book was a huge success, and Kesey bought a six-acre retreat in La Honda, in the hills above Palo Alto, California, where the writer and a bunch of friends calling themselves the Merry Pranksters dropped acid, painted their faces with Day-Glo colors, and "freaked freely" in the surrounding woods. Kesey invited the Hells Angels to one of his psychedelic shindigs, turning the wild motorcycle outlaws on to LSD.

Leary and Alpert had recently published *The Psychedelic Experience*, an LSD user manual based on *The Tibetan Book of the Dead*. The Millbrook approach to acid-dropping was Eastern: controlled, meditative, Zen-like. By contrast, the Pranksters were Wild West daredevils with a shoot-from-the-hip, no-holds-barred attitude regarding drug use.

In March 1965, Lyndon Johnson launched Operation Rolling Thunder, the U.S. bombing campaign in North Vietnam and sent the Marines to Danang. In July, LBJ ordered a military buildup that would lead to 185,000 pairs of American boots on the ground in Nam by the end of the year. On October 15, the country's largest antiwar protest took place in Berkeley. Fourteen thousand demonstrators listened to speeches by Allen Ginsberg, Ken Kesey, Kay Boyle, and Lawrence Ferlinghetti, marching to the jug-band beat of "Feel-Like-I'm-Fixin'-to-Die Rag," a tune by Joe McDonald (the demonstration's musical director) and his band, Country Joe and the Fish.

For those on the vagabond fringes of society, 1965 remained a blissful time. The media had to lost interest in "beatniks" and had yet to turn their voracious attention on the new bohemians soon be labeled "hippies." The Beats, who borrowed a good deal of their lingo from the world of black jazz musicians, found it cool to be "hip" or "hep" (as in hep cat) while a "hippy," or "hippy-dippy," was a pretender, some ofay square wannabe without a clue.

Richard Brautigan, who had rejected a beatnik label, would soon find himself in the curious position of being one of the godfathers of the hippie movement. He continued his life as an impoverished artist, his appearance and dress as much a matter of necessity as style. Richard was not immune to the social changes gradually transforming America. Smoking marijuana had emerged from the shadows of seedy basement jazz clubs into a fresh-faced collegiate environment, rivaling beer as the campus intoxicant of choice. Brautigan occasionally shared a joint or two with friends during this period.

Richard and Janice spent frequent evenings over at the Webers' apartment on Geary, getting high and shooting darts. Often, they played all night. "We had a real English dart board," Erik recalled. Brautigan "was really good. I don't think I ever beat him. He was tall and long, and he could kind of reach out and just set the dart in." Pot smoking was a novelty for all of them. One evening, they "got stoned and for something to do we went to Sears, which was across the street."

The happy trio roamed the aisles of the Sears, Roebuck depot on Geary, gawking at the mountainous excess of American consumerism. Attracted by the jewel-like glitter of a button display, Erik and Janice worked their way back to the fabric department, where buttons of all sizes, shapes, and colors were housed in a cabinet crowded with tiny drawers. They began rummaging through them, stoned treasure-hunters marveling over the enchanted baubles. "Janice and I had these buttons all over the place, and Richard's standing up, just frozen and afraid," Erik remembered. "He got very upset that we were acting like this, and he was sure that we were going to get caught, sure that something was going to happen to us." In the end, Brautigan's paranoia got the best of them and they fled the store before being spotted.

Richard's fears were justified. Back in April, armed with a search warrant, eighteen officers from the sheriff's department crossed the narrow footbridge over La Honda creek onto Ken Kesey's property and busted the famous author for possession of marijuana, a felony beef that made all the papers and provided a lively topic of conversation among the literary community. Everyone buzzed about whether Kesey was jailhouse bound.

Financing his bohemian life by writing fiction remained a precarious proposition for Brautigan. Along with the tales of Moonshine Bess he hoped to shape into a new novel, Richard worked on other short stories while still trying to place portions of his first three books with periodicals. On the same day, early in June, he wrote three letters to magazines. He requested that *Ramparts* and the *Partisan Review* return his novels if they didn't plan on publishing selections from them and asked Charles Newman if he would be interested in considering some of his recent work for *TriQuarterly*.

For a loner, Richard maintained a wide circle of friends. After putting in his hours at the typewriter, he embarked on an active social life, always open to the possibility of meeting new and interesting people. A recent friend from this period was actor/poet Jack Thibeau, who had worked as a merchant seaman following a stint in the Marines. Three days after getting off a ship in Frisco, Thibeau walked into a rehearsal for Frank Wedekind's *Pandora's Box* (he knew the woman playing Lulu) and promptly landed the part of Jack the Ripper. At the time, Jack lived in a cheap hotel behind the opera house. With the Civic Center as his backyard, Thibeau began spending time at the main library. One afternoon, he met an attractive librarian named Ann Kincaid. They struck up a conversation, and she invited Jack to lunch. "We started hanging around together, and she took me down to Gino & Carlo's and introduced me to Jack Boyce." It wasn't long before he met Jack Spicer there.

Thibeau remembered Gino & Carlo's as "sort of a salon every Friday night of poets and musicians and painters and longshoremen." Jack Spicer held court over round after round of drinks.

One Friday night, he introduced Thibeau to Richard Brautigan. Around that time, Thibeau needed to find better digs than his $5-a-week hotel, and Jack Boyce brought him back to a big Victorian house on Lyon Street where he lived with Joanne Kyger. The place served as an informal commune and housed a number of transient refugees from Black Mountain. The rent was $125 a month, not a very large sum when shared by all the residents. At one time or another, these included Kyger and Boyce, Lew Welch, Bill McNeill (a Black Mountain painter), and a young artist/filmmaker named Ken Botto, who lived in the garret and used the two front rooms downstairs as his painting studio.

Christopher Maclaine made his last film in 1959, but all over Frisco local artists were shooting in Super 8. The brotherhood of the lens included Larry Jordan, Stan Brakhage, James Broughton, and Bruce Conner. Ken Botto decided to make an autobiographical movie and recruited Jack Thibeau to play the lead. Janice Meissner was cast as his girlfriend. Richard Brautigan had a walk-on as a guy who delivers some fried chicken. Botto shot Thibeau riding a motorcycle borrowed from Gary Snyder. When Jack got into a wreck, Botto kept right on filming in his hospital room. The film (working title, "Rolling Stone") was never finished. A half hour of partly edited footage burned in a fire in 1967, when Botto was off in Europe. Richard Brautigan's film debut went up in smoke.

Brautigan's other near-appearance in a North Beach motion picture came in 1968, when he had a brief part in James Broughton's *The Bed*, an art project much discussed within the bohemian community. Broughton's film showed numbers of (mostly naked) local personalities, one after the other, sitting or lying on the same bed. Brautigan was among those filmed on the bed. "Richard was thrilled about it," Michael McClure wrote. "He was genuinely excited to be recognized as an art-celebrity by a world-known filmmaker like Broughton." Richard Brautigan ended on the cutting room floor, an omission he complained about bitterly to his friends. "For a long time Richard went around with damp eyes, lashing his tail," McClure observed.

Charles Newman finally got back to Brautigan early in July, asking to see his recent work. Richard sent five short stories (including "Revenge of the Lawn") off to *TriQuarterly* four days later. Brautigan's only recent publication had been in the second issue of *Now Now* (a small San Francisco magazine edited by writer Charles Plymell), which ran "Banners of My Own Choosing," a short prose piece written the year before.

Wild Dog 18, a mimeographed magazine published at 39 Downey Street (down the block from Mike McClure's place), appeared for sale in July. Joanne Kyger and Ed Dorn were among the editors. Along with work by Dorn, Kyger, Gilbert Sorrentino, Harold Dull, Lewis Warsh, and Ron Loewinsohn, two new poems (never reprinted) by Richard Brautigan appeared on page 19. "The Busses" and "Period Piece" (a charming bit of magical nostalgia involving an unemployed dragon cutter: "and I remember great green chunks of dragon / sliced and stacked in the ice wagons") accompanied "At Sea," Brautigan's amusing "review" of *Ghost Tantras*, Michael McClure's new book of poetry.

Michael McClure wrote that Brautigan's notice of *Ghost Tantras* in *Wild Dog* "was one of the few reviews that book ever had [. . .] Richard really knocked himself out to please people he liked or loved [. . .] [He] believed in my work the way I believed in his." Always generous with friends and fellow artists, Brautigan had written in April to Donald Hutter, his editorial connection at Scribner's, recommending *The Mad Club*, Michael McClure's newly completed novel.

While Richard Brautigan's star ascended, life became an ever-accelerating downhill slide for Jack Spicer. Recent poems were rejected by *The Nation* and *Poetry*, evoking more amusement than regret from Jack. His drinking increased, and he seemed to subsist on a single peanut butter sandwich (washed down with brandy and milk) each day. Fran Herndon noted the shabbiness of his clothing, observing "a pretty rapid decline [. . .] In the end, in his drunken state [. . .] he was so drunk he could barely lift the bottle [. . .] Jack would just not stop drinking." Lewis Warsh, back for the Berkeley Poetry Conference that summer, recalled seeing Spicer at Aquatic Park one afternoon, "and he couldn't get up. He put his hand on my shoulder and pulled himself up."

The Berkeley Conference was the big poetry game in town all throughout July. Dozens of readings and lectures had been scheduled at the University of California. The list of the invited included Charles Olson, Robert Creeley, Allen Ginsberg, Robert Duncan, Robin Blaser, Gary Snyder, and Jack Spicer. When Leroi Jones had to cancel, Ed Dorn was enlisted as a replacement. Spicer gave a talk called "Poetry and Politics" and later read *The Holy Grail*, his book from the year before.

Aside from these two appearances, Spicer mostly boycotted the conference, hanging out at Gino & Carlo's across the Bay, waiting for his acolytes to bring all the gossip and tales of poetic in-fighting. The notion of fame both intrigued and repulsed Jack Spicer. His final poems dealt with being caught between the siren song of celebrity and the honest dignity of anonymous toil. In one of his lectures, Spicer said, "I don't think that messages are for the poet any more than the radio program is for the radio set. And I think that the radio set doesn't really worry about whether anyone's listening to it or not, and neither does the poet." According to Graham Mackintosh, "Jack was amused by chance."

That summer, Spicer's closest friends all sensed his health was seriously declining. Robin Blaser observed, "It was a very quick downhill path." Jack Thibeau recalled stopping by Aquatic Park around one o'clock on a sunny afternoon in the last week of July and finding that Spicer had not shown up for his regular outdoor salon. Nemi Frost came by with a "bagful of aspirins and all kinds of store-bought painkillers." Nemi tossed the bag down on the grass and said, "If anyone sees Jack, give him this stuff."

Thibeau lived just around the corner from Spicer's one-room apartment on Polk Street and volunteered to deliver the bag. "I went up and banged on his door about five in the afternoon. The room was matted with wet dried newspapers all over the floor. It was like a collage, the entire room. And it was just the bed in there and nothing else. And he was laid out on this bed. I said, 'Nemi asked me to bring this by for you.'

"He says, 'I'm dying.'

"I said, 'Oh, okay.'" Thibeau also brought Spicer a little taste. "A pint of brandy, which was his favorite drink. I left that and the aspirin. He was so ill he couldn't even talk. And so I left and he said, 'I'll see you at the bar tonight.' Which meant Gino's. And I didn't go down to the bar." A couple days later, Jack Thibeau heard the bad news.

Drunk at the end of a long hot afternoon at Aquatic Park (July 31, 1965), Jack Spicer staggered home munching a chicken sandwich dinner. He collapsed in the elevator of his building and lay there for hours, befouled by shit and vomit, his half-eaten sandwich still clutched in his hand. A fellow tenant discovered the sodden body, and the landlady phoned for help. Spicer had no identification in his shabby suit, and the ambulance crew, thinking him just another nameless drunken bum, hauled the poet off to the poverty ward of San Francisco General Hospital in the Mission District.

Spicer lay in a coma for days. When he didn't show up at his usual table at Gino & Carlo's, his friends started wondering, "Where's Jack?" Robin Blaser began searching in earnest and determined that the unknown man lying unconscious over at General was his old friend. The diagnosis was not good. Spicer had pneumonia, jaundice, critical hepatitis, and intestinal bleeding. Blaser hurried across town. After a furious argument with the young doctor in charge, he succeeded in having Spicer moved to a nicer room.

Jack Spicer lingered for three weeks, lapsing in and out of consciousness. During that period numerous friends came to visit. The Gino & Carlo's crowd all stopped by, as did the Herndons and the Tallmans. Robin Blaser was there almost every day. Spicer was often unable to speak. Paul Alexander recalled "he looked radiant—when he would recognize a visitor his smile glowed." Jack Thibeau passed by Spicer's bedside and introduced himself. Spicer's "lips moved, and he was sort of in a coma, and he said, 'Real people . . .'"

Nemi Frost was another he recognized, and he asked her for the all the latest "glossip," struggling to pronounce "gossip." Joanne Kyger remembered Spicer's splinted arm, bristling with tubes, rising up reflexively. She feared he was about to hit her. Get-well cards and flowers crowded the nightstand. The nurses posted Herb Caen's column wishing the stricken poet well up where he might see it had he the strength to look. Everyone understood that Jack was dying.

All through the beginning of August, the waiting room remained crowded with visiting poets and writers. Larry Kearney was there twice a week. Finding it "too painful," Graham Mackintosh showed up only once, as did Robert Duncan. "Duncan came to the door of the hospital common room, but didn't come in," Robin Blaser remembered. "He was not good at handling the illness of others." Stan Persky, Deneen Peckinpah (novelist niece of film director Sam Peckinpah), Bill Brodecky, and Kate Mulholland (Spicer's only serious heterosexual partner) all paid their respects at one time or another.

No one remembered seeing Richard Brautigan at the hospital. He had already said goodbye to Jack Spicer the previous summer. Toward the end, Spicer's attempts at speech grew increasingly garbled. "He was desperately trying to speak what had happened," Robin Blaser recalled. "It was that the extreme of the alcoholic condition separated his mind from his vocal cords." Making an enormous effort, crapping in his hospital diaper from the struggle, Jack Spicer spoke his final discernible words to Blaser. "My vocabulary did this to me," he whispered. "Your love will let you go on."

Spicer died at 3:00 AM on August 17, 1965. He was forty years old. Two days later, the poet and printer Andrew Hoyem dropped by Richard and Janice's apartment on California Street and read Brautigan's short story "Revenge of the Lawn," which Richard still called the first chapter in his "novel about his grandmother." *TriQuarterly* had accepted it for publication, along with a story called "A Short History of Religion in California" (about meeting a group of Christians while on a camping trip with his three-and-a-half-year-old daughter). The two poets talked about the death of Jack Spicer, agreeing that his friends "were quite resigned to his fate."

A day or so later, Robin Blaser hosted a memorial evening for Spicer at his Allen Street apartment. Over two hundred people, including Jack's mother and brother, showed up for this "little wake." Many brought bits of memorabilia, gifts, drawings, and flowers: "Roses just lined the hallway." Larry Kearney remembered the evening as "an extremely drunken event." Robert Duncan came without Jess and proceeded to make out with a stranger in the kitchen. Blaser ignored such excesses, preferring to think of the event as "quite magical."

Richard Brautigan had not been "specifically invited" to Spicer's wake. Don Allen called Joanne Kyger about it, and she in turn phoned Richard. Brautigan told her "he had been thinking about life and death." He had gone down into his backyard and picked "a perfect rose." Richard asked Joanne if she would deliver the flower to Mrs. Spicer if he brought it over in an envelope. Kyger refused. "If you want to do this," she said, "you have to do it yourself." Brautigan never took the rose to Spicer's mother, nor did he put in an appearance at his mentor's memorial.

Brautigan had published a book with a respected New York firm, something Jack Spicer had never attempted and might well have disdained, but it did almost nothing to improve his financial situation. During the five years Richard worked as a part-time laboratory assistant for Pacific Chemical, his income averaged $1,400 per year. Since quitting to devote all his energies to writing, he suffered a pay cut. By the end of August, his income for 1965 totaled only $637.

At the urging of his friends, Richard decided to apply for a Guggenheim Fellowship. In August he wrote to the John Simon Guggenheim Memorial Foundation, requesting application forms. Knowing he would need four references who could offer "expert judgment" about his "abilities," he wrote the next day to novelist William Eastlake and to John Ciardi, asking for their help. The connection to Eastlake, whose singular modern-day "cowboy and Indian" novels set in the desert Southwest (*Go in Beauty*, *The Bronc People*, and *Portrait of an Artist with 26 Horses*) earned him a unique place among contemporary authors, came through Donald Allen. Eastlake had published several pieces of short fiction in *Evergreen Review*.

Shortly after William Eastlake returned from Hollywood, where he'd been working on a screenplay based on his latest novel, *Castle Keep*, Brautigan's letter reached him at his remote New Mexico ranch, near the tiny town of Cuba on the edge of the Jicarilla Apache Reservation. Asking for the older writer's assistance, Richard mentioned a "lack of security" in his life. Agreeing to help with the Guggenheim, Eastlake offered a few words of advice on the subject of security. "Certainly you must realize you are born with all you'll ever get. Money won't help. Success won't help. Red Lewis and Ernie [Sinclair Lewis and Ernest Hemingway] were about the most insecure people who ever lived."

Soon after this, Brautigan got in touch with Michael McClure and wrote to Tom Parkinson (currently living in Paris) to solicit their assistance with his application. McClure was teaching English at the California College of Arts and Crafts. Ironically, this academic position gave his judgment more implied weight with the fellowship committee than his reputation as a poet. Michael immediately agreed to do anything he possibly could to help.

Late in August 26, Richard wrote Bob Sherrill, asking if *Esquire* had come to any decision on his submissions. Four days later, the editor returned "Homage to Rudi Gernreich," with regrets, continuing to dangle the golden carrot. "Close but not quite. Keep trying." About the same time, Tom Parkinson wrote from London (with a Paris return address) saying he'd be happy to write something in support of Richard's Guggenheim application. "I've had some luck in writing for people, but not so much as I'll hope." Both letters arrived at California Street when Richard was down in Monterey staying with Price Dunn. His old buddy operated a hauling business called Blue Whale Movers with his brother Bruce, and Brautigan needed a job. Anything to help pay the bills. As usual, Richard and Price spent their first night together getting drunk.

Brautigan returned to San Francisco in mid-September, having earned a few bucks helping Price with manual labor. He'd managed to get some writing done, continuing to work on the short stories he hoped would develop into a novel. He missed Janice and had written her three letters while he was away, including one just after arriving that he never mailed, perhaps because he'd made a joke out of tying one on with Price. A letter from John Ciardi came during his absence, apologizing for the delay ("I have been off on a 'round-the-world trip'"). He said he'd be happy to provide some words of support on the Guggenheim form.

Richard wasted no time in replying. He wrote three quick letters on the same day. One to Ciardi, thanking him for his offer of help; another went off to Barney Rosset at Grove; and the third, to *Esquire*, nudged Bob Sherrill to make a decision about the Christmas tree story. The next day, he sent several short stories to his old friend Jory Sherman, now an editor at *Broadside*, a men's magazine published out of North Hollywood, California. Sherman read the work immediately and wrote back the next day to say he was sorry he had to turn them down. He enjoyed "The Wild Birds of Heaven," but it and the others weren't right for his publication, "which is pretty much sex-oriented." Sherman asked to see "anything else on hand that might come closer to the mark."

Having received the rejection letter from *Broadside* the day before, Brautigan quickly mailed another new short story to Jory Sherman ("The Rug," based on a Bill Brown anecdote). Brautigan's next order of business was getting his Guggenheim application form in the mail. His responses on the questionnaire were as concise as his poetry. Asked for a statement of his project, Richard replied, "I would like to write a novel dealing with the legend of America and its influence upon myself and these times."

Brautigan's other answers were equally terse. Under marital status, he listed "Divorced" although he and Ginny had not yet filed any paperwork and were not even legally separated. Asked about previous grants and fellowships, Brautigan replied: "I have never received any outside help in my writing." Under educational background, Richard wrote: "I have no education that can be listed here. My 'education' has been obtained by other means." Asked about foreign language proficiency, he replied, "English is the only language I know." His answer to the query "List the learned, scientific or artistic societies of which you are a member" was brief: "I have never been a member of any organization."

Brautigan's paragraph-long project statement concluded: "I would like to write another novel about the fiber and mythology of this country. The locale of the novel would be the Pacific Northwest." Richard's career statement ran somewhat longer, filling an entire page. "I was a little disappointed over a critical reaction that tended to associate [*Confederate General*] with the work of Jack Kerouac, Allen Ginsberg, etc. I did not write my novel in an effort to imitate those writers. Their values and goals are of course valid and have illuminated areas of the Twentieth Century experience, but they are not my values and goals [. . .] As a novelist I am deeply interested in achieving a maximum amount of effect using a minimum of space, and I am also very interested in structure and language." As required, Richard made twelve copies of the three supplementary statements and mailed off his completed application.

Things were not turning out the way Brautigan had hoped when his novel was published at the start of the year. Two months after submitting *In Watermelon Sugar* to Grove, he had not heard back from them. Nor had his publisher come to any decision regarding *Trout Fishing in America*. Adding to his woes, Jory Sherman wrote back from *Broadside* rejecting "The Rug" (later published as "Winter Rug" in *Revenge of the Lawn*). "As it stands, then, there is no way in hell I can buy this," Sherman wrote. "What you have here is more of a slice of life with very little point as it turns out." A letter from Lew Ellingham in New York six days later, soliciting work for a new magazine (eponymously named *Magazine*) didn't do much to help. The little publication was distributed for free ("the two San Francisco outlets are City Lights and Gino & Carlo's."), which meant no payment. Richard sent off a card promising to contribute something.

Seeking serious representation, Brautigan wrote to Elizabeth McKee, a celebrated New York literary agent (her clients included William Styron, John Irving [at the beginning of his career], Charles Webb [McKee had recently sold his first novel, *The Graduate*, to Hollywood], and Flannery O'Connor). Her firm, McIntosh, McKee & Dodds, had been acquired that August by the Harold Matson Company. Richard mentioned his confused relationship with Grove Press, stressing his chief complaint: "Unfortunately, [*Confederate General*] was falsely labeled as a "Beat" novel which is about as good for one as a ten-mile wide hole in the head."

On the day Elizabeth McKee received Brautigan's letter, she wrote him back, expressing interest. McKee requested a copy of *In Watermelon Sugar* with the understanding that Richard wanted her firm to negotiate the contract with Grove. She also asked to see the *Trout Fishing* contract to check the option clause. Brautigan responded immediately. He enclosed copies of his book and contract, saying he had "plus and minus feelings about Grove," again stressing his unhappiness with being classified as a "Beat" writer.

Richard wanted to write another novel "dealing with the legend of America and its influence upon myself and these times [. . .] my trouble so far has not been with writing, but with publishing. That's why I need an agent." Brautigan's outline description of *In Watermelon Sugar* bled away all the magic of his book. Reducing the simple story to its bare bones made it sound banal. ("Previous inhabitants include tigers that can talk, but which have been killed off because the people got tired of being eaten by the tigers.")

1965 became a dress rehearsal for the big Frisco party still to come. Many seminal moments occurred that spring and summer. In April, the first Owsley acid hit the street. This extremely potent LSD was the product of Augustus Owsley Stanley III, a former radar technician and amateur chemist whose ubiquitous aspirin-sized tablets changed colors from batch to batch, keeping one jump ahead of the rip-off artists. High in Comstock Lode country in the Sierras, the Red Dog Saloon opened its swinging doors in Virginia City, Nevada, at the end of July. The house band was an oddball San Francisco outfit called the Charlatans, sporting thrift shop Edwardian clothing and hair so long they made the Beatles look like bankers. The Charlatans became the first psychedelic band, offering a pulsating light show (designed by painter Bill Ham) throbbing across the bar walls in time to the music.

Two other important music venues started up in Frisco soon after. On the Fourth of July, four-hundred-pound Falstaffian local DJ "Big Daddy" Tom Donahue (who ruled the local rock scene) opened a club called Mothers. It took off after he booked a New York band, the Lovin' Spoonful, in August. A little more than a month later, a former pizzeria was transformed by Marty Balin (née Martin Buchwald) into a nightclub he named the Matrix. Balin, an actor/singer living in the Haight, performed with a rock group that became the house band. Their peculiar name, Jefferson Airplane, was an abbreviation of Blind Thomas Jefferson Airplane, a Berkeley gag skewering the pretensions of folk music buffs with mock invented names for "legendary" bluesmen.

Over on 1836 Pine Street, a boardinghouse for wandering musicians managed by Bill Ham, "the light show man," a poet named Chet Helms got involved in a "dope marketing enterprise" called the Family Dog. Helms had talked Janis Joplin into dropping out of summer school at the University of Texas in 1963 and hitchhiking with him to San Francisco. Joplin lasted for a year in the city on her first trip before returning to Austin. Chet's group soon transmuted into a production company. The Family Dog rented Longshoreman's Hall for two weekends in October and put on dances. They called the first one "A Tribute to Dr. Strange," in honor of the Marvel Comics super-hero. The second was dubbed "A Tribute to Sparkle Plenty," after a character from *Dick Tracy*.

Bill Ham set up his light equipment at one end of the cavernous hall. The Dog hired the Charlatans, Jefferson Airplane, and the Great Society to supply the music. Several hundred people showed up on both occasions, clad in all manner of mod finery and thrift shop Edwardian castoffs. They danced under the pulsing amorphous light show to the electric blast of rock and roll, forming impromptu weaving conga lines with happy strangers. Something bold and new had come to town. It was time to party.

By the end of October, Richard Brautigan was in no mood for a party. Bob Sherrill had turned down the Christmas tree story ("Too much, too little, for us. Very funny idea, though. Keep try-ing."), effectively closing the door at *Esquire*. Richard had no other viable notions for magazine articles at the moment. He wrote to Donald Hutter at Scribner's, asking if he'd be interested in reading *Trout Fishing*. Brautigan said he'd been "doing a lot of writing [. . .] I'm trying to give the short story a little workout before I start another novel." Hutter answered a week later, saying he'd be happy to read the book. Richard shipped him a copy the very next day.

That same afternoon brought a curt note from Sallie Ellsworth at the *Partisan Review*. After sitting on the *Trout Fishing* chapters for nearly six months, the magazine informed him that the material had finally been given to Richard Poirier, one of the three editors. "Your story will have to be passed through all three, which will take several months." Ellsworth requested that Richard submit something else should he be rejected. "I found the stories exhilarating," she concluded.

The last week of October, Richard Brautigan went shopping. He bought a used six-string guitar for $16 from the Diamond Loan Company, a hock shop on Third Street. The dawning age of the poet/troubadour saw a new breed of pop star emerge. Donovan and Leonard Cohen received big Bay Area airplay. Bob Dylan, reigning supreme as king of the genre with his AM hit "Like a Rolling Stone," was in town for a series of concerts. Michael McClure experimented with song lyrics. Richard saw an avenue worth pursuing.

Janice and Richard planned a big Halloween party, stocking their place on California Street with wine and beer. Brautigan wrote out the invitations by hand on orange computer cards. Costumes were encouraged. The whole world was invited on Saturday night, October 30. Most of them showed up. Allen Ginsberg came clad in white Indian pajamas. Andrew Hoyem sported a white beret, white tunic with gold buttons, white Australian shorts, and "white shoes and anklets." An unidentified shirtless woman wore a bra with cutouts revealing her nipples. Peter Orlovsky "took the prize" in blue-and-white striped pajamas. Robert Zimmerman came dressed as Bob Dylan.

The place was packed. People crowded in and out all night. Michael and Joanna McClure, Joanne Kyger and Jack Boyce, John and Margot Doss, Erik and Loie Weber along with Erik's sis-ter, Avril, were all in attendance. The noted jazz drummer Elvin Jones, at the time a member of the John Coltrane Quartet, beat on McClure's tambourine so hard that it broke. Nemi Frost lost her purse. Don Allen arrived fresh from a trip to New Mexico, bringing a book from Robert Creeley for Joanne Kyger, who remembered everyone "grumbling about the horrible puke-colored paint Richard had bought [to paint the apartment] because it was so cheap."

Sometime during the raucous evening, a band known as the Fugs made an appearance. The Fugs had come to Frisco to play at Appeal I, a Mime Troupe benefit organized by Bill Graham, who had been the renegade theater group's business manager since 1964. He wanted a grand parting gesture before branching out on his own. Centered on two New York poets, Ed Sanders and Tuli Kupferberg, the Fugs were the prototypical East Village punk band. Kupferberg, an old Beat hero at forty-two, had teamed up the year before with Kansas City–raised Sanders, a young poet who had published with City Lights and edited *Fuck You: A Magazine of the Arts*. About the same time the band got started, Sanders opened a bookstore named Peace Eye. With the addition of two musicians from the Holy Modal Rounders and original songs like "River of Shit," "Kill for Peace," and "I Feel Like Homemade Shit," the Fugs quickly became underground legends.

Their host stood out in the noisy exotic crowd. Richard's high-crowned felt hat added to his towering height. His underpants provided the remainder of his costume. Brautigan's pale pink flesh declared his presence in the dim light like a billboard advertising a nudist camp. The only thing wrong with this description was the expression on Richard Brautigan's face. He was not a happy camper. Reasonable to assume anyone cavorting nearly naked at his own party packed with outrageous counterculture celebrities would be wearing a shit-eating grin, but such was not the case. Erik Weber remembered that Brautigan "had a terrible look on his face. Richard was very unhappy."

Weber felt "uncomfortable" at the party and "probably didn't stay a long time." Looking back, he can't recall seeing Janice that night but knew Richard's misery somehow concerned her. "A big flirt. That's the only thing that seemed to make Richard unhappy, the relationship." Joanne Kyger remembered that Janice went out into the backyard with one of the Fugs "and almost never came back." The gossip making the rounds that night and circulating among the Frisco poetry scene after the party implied that Janice had gone off for a fling with one or more (possibly all) of the Fugs.

Gossip remains painful even if it isn't true. Richard's glum demeanor and hangdog expression indicated he brooded about the Fugs. Brautigan's arcane literary knowledge certainly included the derivation of the group's name: Norman Mailer's bowdlerized euphemism for the English language's most common expletive in *The Naked and the Dead*. (When actress Tallulah Bankhead was introduced to Mailer at the time of his first book's publication, she quipped, "So, you're the young man who doesn't know how to spell *fuck*.") For Richard Brautigan, it was no laughing matter.

Goblins far worse than those troubling the Halloween party haunted Richard in the weeks to come. Elizabeth McKee wrote to say that she and Peter Matson had read *In Watermelon Sugar* and agreed "your writing is very talented and interesting." Even so, they declined to represent him. A couple weeks later, Grove Press rejected the novel as well. Brautigan now needed an agent more than ever. Further complicating the situation, Grove's contract for *Trout Fishing* (McKee doubted she could improve upon the terms) remained in effect even as the publisher expressed no enthusiasm for the book.

Appeal I made history one night early in November. The benefit was held at the Calliope Warehouse (also known as "The Loft"), a former stable and flophouse at 924 Howard Street in the inner Mission south of the *Chronicle* building. The space, once housing a pie factory, was the

Mime Troupe's office and rehearsal area as well as the local headquarters for SDS (Students for a Democratic Society). Bill Graham assembled a splendid array of talent. The Fugs were there, along with banjo player Sandy Bull, poets Allen Ginsberg and Lawrence Ferlinghetti, and Jefferson Airplane, who used the Mime Troupe's loft for their rehearsals.

At midnight, the police tried to break things up, but people kept sneaking back in using the freight elevator, and the dance went on until dawn, when Allen Ginsberg chanted a mantra. The benefit was a huge success. Everyone wanted more events just like it. Ralph Gleason, the *Chronicle*'s jazz critic (who also espoused rock and roll) suggested to Bill Graham that he have a look at the Fillmore Auditorium, an old second-floor ballroom at Fillmore and Geary. Gleason thought it might provide an excellent setting for future ventures of this sort.

A renewed correspondence with Donald Hutter at Scribner's resulted in his reading of *Trout Fishing* (with the understanding that the rights were unavailable). Hutter thought Richard Brautigan "a singular writer, with a strong free talent," and enjoyed the book's "wryness, its sympathy and humaneness, its sense of American place and American foibles" but in the end found it didn't work for him, in spite of "such exploding imagery." Brautigan urged him to read *In Watermelon Sugar*, saying, "I think it is the best thing I have done."

Hutter agreed to have a look right about the time the art gods smiled on Brautigan. The last week in November, Grove Press offered Richard $1,500 as an advance against future work. Payments of $250 a month would start in January 1966, with the option period to last for six months. Any work completed during that time would be submitted to Grove and the payments "considered part of an advance" should they decide to publish.

Richard badly needed the money. His income for the year remained under $1,000. He had an idea for a new novel, and six months bought a lot of writing time. The arrangement with Grove ruled out any possibility of a deal with Scribner's. Unable to consider the novel for publication, Donald Hutter nevertheless enjoyed reading *In Watermelon Sugar* and wrote on the last day of the year to say that he found it "a distinctive work, with some very lovely writing." Hutter considered the book "a more effective novel than TROUT FISHING, a more discreet and consistent fiction." He thought such a "contained, idyllic fantasy" would be difficult to sell but regretted all the same not being able to get involved.

At midnight on December 18, Brautigan attended the premier performance of Michael McClure's play *The Beard* at the Encore Stage of The Actors' Workshop. McClure's two-character one-act, starring Billie Dixon as Jean Harlow and Richard Bright as Billy the Kid, played for only a single performance. The scenery was designed by Robert LaVigne. "A beautiful small set of blue velvet with pinpricks of light." It had originally been scheduled for two performances, but the artistic director of the Workshop got cold feet. It was fund-raising time, and "*The Beard* threatened the acceptable image of The Actors' Workshop."

Loie and Erik Weber went with Brautigan to the opening night of McClure's play. Loie remembered it as "a big event." Looking back over almost three decades, Loie observed Richard's fascination with celebrity. He "was very thrilled at being there and thought it was wonderful and great. I feel like he got really heady around events, important cultural events, because he would talk about it, build it up, talk about it afterwards a lot, and then he would create a story about it. He created stories about the mythological events of his life that he participated in."

Watching the play, Richard took notes for a possible review. He observed that the audience was middle-aged, "average age about forty," and that the actors "both wear clothes from another time. 1890s, 1930s." In the end, Brautigan wrote very briefly about McClure's initial dramatic effort. "A review of *The Beard*. Thursday. I'm sitting here next to a pretty blond girl who has feet so narrow that they could walk around the petals of a flower without disturbing the pollen." That was it. Richard turned his intended criticism into a final backhanded love poem for Janice.

McClure designed his own poster for *The Beard*. He went to a print shop specializing in boxing posters and had 150 printed for the play in the same manner. Bold red and blue block letters bellowing in the beast language: "LOVE LION, LIONESS / GAHR THY ROOH GRAHEER." Photos of William H. Bonney and Jean Harlow stared out on either side like contenders in the main event. McClure made his poster into a poem and papered the town with it. A year or so later, when McClure angled a reading gig for Brautigan at California College of Arts and Crafts, he drew a poster by hand for the event. "It was like a boxing poster of the time [. . .] Richard face forward with his glasses, mustache, and hat. Across from that, I drew his profile, then wrote "DIGGER" under one and "POET" under the other." Brautigan kept this poster in his Geary Street apartment as long as he lived there, along with the original one-sheet for *The Beard*.

On the fifth of December, Richard joined a gathering of published poets, scholars, entertainers, and artists for a group portrait in front of City Lights. Lawrence Ferlinghetti staged the event, inviting all Frisco photographers to "come on down and take pictures of poets." John Doss was among the many shutterbugs snapping away. Larry Keenan, the occasion's official photographer, posed his subjects in rows outside the bookshop's front door. Ferlinghetti, clad in a dark djellaba, towered over the group, opening a striped umbrella above the heads of Allen Ginsberg and Michael McClure. Ranked around them, Lew Welch, Peter Orlovsky, David Meltzer, Stan Persky, Robert LaVigne, Shig Mauro, Andrew Hoyem, Larry Fagin, Daniel Langton, and Committee Theater actor Garry Goodrow, wearing a fez, stood or sat on the sidewalk.

Richard Brautigan, a head taller than most of the others, looked shyly to one side in his trademark high-crowned fawn-colored Stetson. Nemi Frost, a blond ghost in Ray-Bans, appeared and disappeared just over Goodrow's left shoulder in the several exposures Keenan made of the occasion. At one point, the crowd outside City Lights grew so large someone turned on a fire alarm and several engines, sirens blaring, roared up to the store during the photo session.

Variously titled *The Last Gathering* and *Poets at the City Lights Bookstore*, Larry Keenan's photograph quickly became an icon of a fading era. One version graced the cover of *City Lights Journal* (no. 3, 1966). No work by Brautigan appeared in this issue, yet his picture among such a crowd on the front of the magazine ensured that he would forever be associated with the Frisco Beat movement he so vociferously disowned.

Afterward, in the alley between City Lights and Vesuvio, Keenan photographed McClure and Ginsberg chatting with Bob Dylan, who had performed at the Oakland Civic Auditorium the previous evening. Later, they were all ejected from Tosca, across Columbus Avenue from the bookstore, when Lafcadio Orlovsky (Peter's younger brother) accidentally wandered into the ladies' restroom.

December became an intense month. On the fourth, Kesey hosted his second "Acid Test" in a private home down in San Jose ("Can you pass the acid test?") and attracted four hundred participants. The Warlocks, a local blues band, found their groove in the pulsing light show. They had once been known as the Emergency Crew and before that Mother McCree's Uptown Jug Stompers. Soon the group would change its name one last time, to the Grateful Dead.

The evening of December 10, Bill Graham rented the Fillmore Auditorium for Appeal II, hoping to raise more money for the Mime Troupe. He signed some of the area's best bands for the occasion, including Jefferson Airplane, Great Society (featuring a singer named Grace Slick, who would join the Airplane when Great Society disbanded a couple months later), the John Handy Quintet, and Mystery Trend. Graham sold no booze in his upstairs establishment. Admission was $1.50, and the kids lined up two-deep around the block waiting to get in.

The following night, Dylan went onstage at the Masonic Auditorium and, down in Palo Alto, the Pranksters rented a nightclub called the Big Beat for the first Acid Test held in a public space. Jerome Garcia and the Warlocks were once again the featured act. The Pranksters staged two more Acid Tests in December. The last, at a lodge in remote Muir Beach, drew a large confused crowd and resulted in the "classic freak-out" of none other than Augustus Owsley Stanley III, tripping publically off the planet on his own product. Like mating insects, something new trembled in the night air. Until recently an unheard-of rarity, large public "events" featuring rock and roll, lights shows, and LSD became a weekly occurrence.

Chet Helms and the Family Dog hosted more than fifty dances (two bits a head) at 1090 Page Street. The house band called themselves Big Brother and the Holding Company. Their chick singer was Helms's old lady Janis before she split back to Texas. Even as the year ended with a photo-documentation of a fading era, the Age of Aquarius loomed on the horizon, casting a new light on older bohemian trends and energizing the unexpected birth of the San Francisco rock dance culture.

It was definitely party time in Frisco. On New Year's Eve, the Merry Pranksters paraded down Montgomery Street, taking advantage of a traditional end-of-the-year office workers' celebration when shredded out-of-date calendars were thrown from high-rise windows. "Realize that you are in a parade," the Pranksters preached, "and you'll be as beautiful as what you do." Their medicine show came with a pitch for an upcoming mega-event three weeks hence at the Longshoreman's Hall. Bill Graham had signed on to coordinate something truly mind-blowing: the Pranksters' first "Trips Festival." Richard and Janice lived at the center of this festive world. The growing rift between them made participating in the parade impossible.

Alternating with the Family Dog, Bill Graham's Fillmore held weekly concerts where all barriers dissolved, the dancers and the musicians meeting as equals. In mid-April 1966, Chet Helms moved his operation to the Avalon Ballroom on Sutter Street just off Van Ness in Polk Gulch, another upstairs dance hall with a balcony, once a home for swing orchestras. Here the motto was "May the baby Jesus shut your mouth and open your mind." The house band was once again Big Brother and the Holding Company. In June, Helms invited Janis Joplin back up from Texas to return as the group's lead singer. Two psychedelic pleasure temples now beckoned the faithful. In six short months, a wild dervishing frenzy had taken hold of the collective unconscious of Frisco youth.

Buoyed by distant praise and the promise of income, Brautigan made it through the holiday minefield. He worked on a new short story/chapter for the novel about his grandmother while pursuing other literary activities. Like jigsaw puzzles found in summer houses, life's little odd pieces tend to go missing. Just so, the emotional circumstances of Richard and Janice's second Christmas together have been lost to time. One enigmatic clue survived. Brautigan sent Don Allen a greeting card with a photo of a near-naked blond seen from the rear. Her legs were wrapped in a Nazi flag, the swastika prominent below her buttocks. The tattoo on her left cheek read, "Property of Satan's Slaves." Inside, Richard wrote "Merry California Christmas!" and signed both names, "Richard and Janice," in a tiny pinched hand.

Ken Kesey was found guilty of marijuana possession (the La Honda beef) and sentenced to three years deferred with six months' probation. A more prudent man might have considered modifying his lifestyle, but Captain Trips was not one to let the threat of jail stand in his way. Three days later he was busted again for smoking weed with a minor named Mountain Girl on Stewart Brand's North Beach rooftop.

Kesey skipped the February bail hearing for his two drug arrests, and the following Sunday, police investigators found an abandoned bus along the highway near Eureka, California. Painted in gaudy colors, the vehicle carried a sign reading "Intrepid Traveler." A rambling suicide note signed by Kesey lay on the front seat. In part, it read, "Ocean, ocean, ocean, I'll beat you in the end [. . .] I'll go through with my heels your hungry ribs." The note turned out to be a hoax, a fact coming to light soon afterward, when Kesey showed up alive in Puerto Vallarta, Mexico. The novelist was soon joined south of the border by several Pranksters and a large contingent of the Family Dog.

Valentine's Day 1966 provided an ironic backdrop when yet another poisoned barb from Cupid's quiver pierced the troubled heart of Janice and Richard's relationship. The occasion was Joanne Kyger's wedding to Jack Boyce and the festive reception afterward at the Greenwich Street home of John and Margot Patterson Doss. Getting married on a holiday dedicated to love seemed auspicious to a bride walking down the aisle for the second time. James Koller recalled "a party that included champagne without end and dancing—at one point a circle dance ended with all falling to the floor."

Everyone agreed that the trouble between Richard and Janice began with a spilled drink. Janice, looking lovely in "a spangly dress," danced up a storm and in the frenzy collided with a glass of wine. From this point on, conflicting stories veered widely astray. Joanne Kyger remembered going down to the basement with Janice and helping her wash and iron the dress. Margot Doss, who thought Janice "very raunchy," recalled things differently. In her version, it was the Dosses' oldest son, Rick, who volunteered to assist in the dress cleaning. He "took her downstairs, and they wound up screwing in the bathtub." Kyger disputed this. "Margot thinks her sons are the biggest studs in the world," she said. "I was down there with the dress. I thought she was always faithful."

The actual truth turned out to have less import than what Brautigan believed to be true. When Richard asked, "Where's Janice?" he was told she was off getting it on with Rick Doss. Drunk and infuriated, the solid weight of a shot glass clenched in his fist, Richard Brautigan set out to seek retribution just as Dr. John Doss returned home from his shift at the hospital. "He comes tearing down the stairs," Margot recalled, "yelling, 'I'll coldcock that boy!' John came in and grabbed him by the arm and said, 'Richard, you'll have to deal with the old man first.' And so, he calmed Richard down."

Brautigan's method of dealing with emotional adversity always involved immersing himself in work. Although the monthly payments from Grove began in January, Richard did not immediately start writing a new novel. Instead, he continued with the series of stories that had preoccupied him for many months. One was "⅓, ⅓, ⅓," a work of fiction Don Carpenter later called "a two-million-ton short story. It says everything there is to say about writing. In about four pages."

In its own way, Brautigan's association with the distant worlds of publishing remained as curious as the peculiar three-way writing partnership he had described in his new short story. Seymour Krim (now serving as a book scout for Hill & Wang in addition to his work at the *New York Herald Tribune*) offered to show *In Watermelon Sugar* to Arthur Wang, but in the end the publisher rejected it with a cursory note. Over in England, the American writer Stephen Schneck, whose first novel, *The Nightclerk*, had won the fabled Formentor Prize in 1965, told Barley Alison, a director at the publishing firm Weidenfeld & Nicolson, about Richard's new fiction, and she wrote asking to have a look.

The notion of a having a British publisher intrigued Brautigan (*Confederate General* was under contract to Rizzoli in Italy, his first foreign edition, but had not yet found a home in the U.K.) and he sent Ms. Alison the manuscript of *In Watermelon Sugar* after Hill & Wang returned it. In the end, although she enjoyed reading Brautigan's work, Barley Alison also took a pass. "It is just not our kind of book. Fantasy is quite 'difficult' in England any way and we just don't do this kind of book at all."

Brautigan had better luck with little magazines. *TriQuarterly* (no. 5) appeared that winter, featuring two of Richard's stories ("Revenge of the Lawn" and "A Short History of Religion in California"). He liked the issue very much, "especially the poems of Takahashi and the play by Isaac Babel," and showed it to many of his friends in San Francisco.

"A Study in California Flowers," a one-page story, was published early in 1966 in *Coyote's Journal* (no. 5–6), an infrequent magazine founded in Eugene, Oregon, two years earlier when the U of O suspended publication of the *Northwest Review* "because of extreme reaction to an issue which contained work by Whalen, Antonin Artaud, and an interview with Fidel Castro." The editor, Ed Van Aelstyn, along with Will Wroth and James Koller, the poetry editor, took the offending material and started *Coyote's Journal*. They had sufficient submissions for the first four issues and "branched almost immediately into book publication."

Jim Koller had been introduced to Richard Brautigan by Don Allen after a reading in 1960 on his first trip to Frisco from the Midwest. He met Bill Brown around the time Joanne Kyger returned from Japan. By 1966, Brown had signed on as an editor of *Coyote's Journal*. "What we had created then was a super problem for the magazine," Koller recalled, "because no one could agree on anything." Wroth and Van Aelstyn went their separate ways, leaving Brown and Koller at the helm. Many years later, Jim Koller married Bill Brown's daughter, Maggie, who was the same age as her childhood playmate, Ianthe Brautigan.

Around the end of February, Richard received a phone call from Sue Green, who worked for *Art Voices*, a magazine starting up in New York. She had read *The Octopus Frontier* and wondered if Brautigan had any stories he might send her. Two days later, he mailed off a batch of five, including "The Kool-Aid Wino," to the office on East Fifty-seventh Street. Richard had no way of knowing the precarious status of his submissions. The publisher of *Art Voices* was undecided on whether to buy *Art and Literature*, another magazine that had recently folded, or begin his own "from scratch."

Sue Green returned four of Brautigan's stories, keeping only "Kitty Genovese-by-the-Sea," a five-page piece about a pilot named Charles Redgrave marooned on an island with seventeen palm trees eighty miles southwest of Hawaii. Redgrave seals a note in a bottle, setting it adrift on the tide. The bottle is found by a couple walking on a California beach. They think it's a joke and ignore Redgrave's plea for help. Green felt especially fond of this story and wanted to see it in print. Yet, she wrote, "at this point the whole undertaking is out of my control so I cannot promise anyone anything." *Art Voices* went out of business later that summer, and the story was never published, lost like Charles Redgrave's bottled note in a vast ocean of forgotten manuscripts.

Brautigan got the bad news from Sue Green right after his tax returns were due. This time, Richard didn't owe the government any money. His gross income for 1965 (including his *Esquire* kill fee, a $75 reading payment, and twelve bucks from the sale of his poetry chapbooks) came to $940.45. After he carefully itemized his writing business deductions (postage, telephone, and a percentage of his rent and utilities), Brautigan's adjusted income was forty-five cents shy of reaching $400. Facing the financial music of the 1040 form convinced Richard it was time to get to work on his new novel. He had just received his third monthly payment from Grove. His guaranteed income had already reached the halfway mark.

Earlier in March, Richard told Andy Hoyem that he wanted "to go to Vancouver or Pacific Grove" with the money still to come from his publisher. He made no mention of bringing Janice along. In the end, Brautigan stayed put and traveled only into the far distance of his imagination. He had a plan in mind to develop "The American Experience," his unfinished story about an abortion begun eighteen months earlier, into a full-length novel. Reaching back for a painful memory in his youth, he determined to call his heroine "Vida" after the little settlement on the McKenzie River near where Linda Webster once spurned his advances on the covered bridge.

Brautigan actually knew very little about the process of obtaining an abortion. At the time, the operation was illegal in America and many women in California wishing to terminate a pregnancy went across the border to Tijuana for the procedure. Several Mexican clinics competed for their business in a town famous for its bullring and numerous bordellos. As part of his research for the project, Richard embarked on a second trip to Mexico. This time, he did not have to hitchhike. On March 26, 1966, he flew from San Francisco to San Diego on Pacific Southwest Airlines, paying $20.84 apiece for two one-way tickets.

PSA Flight 840 departed at 8:15 AM. Brautigan was up at six in the morning. "Light and gray outside." He brought along his notebook and jotted down everything that he observed on the way to the airport. "I saw a sign with a chicken holding a gigactic [*sic*] egg. Strange." The sign made it into the book, as did Benny Bufano's statue of "Peace" at San Francisco International "towering above us like a giant bullet." Richard even drew a little crude sketch of the gleaming metal artwork.

Scrupulous as a foreign correspondent recording each detail of a battlefield, Brautigan described it all: the terrazzo floors of the terminal, the Formica countertop in the coffee shop, the pattern of familiar California landmarks ("Hollywood, Coit Tower, the Mount Palomar telescope, a California mission, the Golden Gate Bridge [. . .]") on the interior walls of the aircraft, the brief stopover in Burbank, stewardesses in their short-skirted uniforms, a large stain like a coffee ring on the gently trembling riveted wing. It was Richard Brautigan's first flight, and he found the minutiae of the trip fascinating.

Brautigan landed in San Diego at 9:45 AM and took a Yellow Cab into the city. He walked around the downtown, jotting constant notes. A Greyhound bus left every fifteen minutes for Tijuana, and Richard eventually boarded one, paying sixty cents for his fare. Richard's notes during the bus ride made constant reference to "Vida," as if he was really traveling with an imaginary fictional companion. ("I guess he thought that because Vida looked so pure and bautiufl [*sic*] that she must be decanant [*sic*]." Having already seen Nogales and Juarez, Brautigan knew what to expect of border towns. He found them unpleasant. "They bring out the worst in both countries, and everything that is American stands out like a neon sore [. . .]"

Richard wandered the tourist-clogged streets of downtown Tijuana, a new notebook in hand. Having filled the first, Brautigan scribbled notes in a little three-by-five spiral-bound, which fit more easily in his hand while wandering through the crowd. He described the "heroic" welcoming arch, the Government Tourist Building, and a "big modern Woolworth's." The presence of an American five-and-dime in Mexico fascinated Brautigan, and he recorded many impressions of the store.

The one location he didn't describe in his notes was an abortion clinic. Not a single word about what was ostensibly his main objective. Brautigan returned to San Diego that same day, in time to catch PSA Flight 631 home to Frisco at 6:25 PM. Get in, get out, and get the job done with no wasted motion had long been his work motto. The daylong jaunt south of the border had not been intended as a pleasure trip.

Back in the apartment on California Street, Brautigan transcribed his notes into twenty-one detail-packed typewritten pages. He used virtually every observation made on the Tijuana trip in writing his novel. Richard's obsession with accuracy and detail served to counterbalance the extravagant fantasy that he used at the start of the book. The notion of a library housing only unpublished manuscripts stands out as one of Brautigan's most appealing conceits.

At the time, he must have been amused by the notion that only in such an institution would his own rejected work ever find a repository. Richard used the Presidio branch of the San Francisco Public Library as the archetype for this fictional creation, even including the address (3150 Sacramento Street) in his text. For years after *The Abortion* was eventually published, this small neighborhood branch library received numerous letters from true-believing readers who inquired about bringing in their rejected manuscripts. Five and a half years after Richard's death, life imitated art in Burlington, Vermont, when Todd Lockwood founded the Brautigan Library, a repository devoted to archiving unpublished works.

In the novel, the first-person narrator had no name but bore a distinct resemblance to Richard Brautigan. Like the author, he was thirty-one years old and didn't know how to drive. He had worked in "canneries, sawmills, factories" and was "not at home in the world." He had never before been to Tijuana but had visited Guadalajara "five or six years" before. His poverty afforded only instant coffee. In one notable way, Brautigan deliberately distanced himself from his main character. "I felt like having a drink," he wrote, "a very unusual thing for me [. . .]" The narrator lived alone in his strange library for almost three years before Vida Kramar moved in with him.

In many ways, Janice Meissner served as a model for Vida. Richard gave his heroine black hair ("like bat lightning"), but otherwise her physical beauty mirrored Janice's delicately chiseled good looks. Vida and Janice shared a curvaceous figure (37-19-36). "She was almost painful to gaze upon," Brautigan wrote of Vida. "Her beauty, like a creature unto itself, was quite ruthless in its own way." Descriptions of Vida's powerful effect on other men, how they stared at her, awestruck and drooling, and how she brushed off their advances "like flies," had the clarion ring of personal experience. Writing this at a time when things were going so wrong with Janice can't have been easy for Richard. It's hard to lose the most beautiful woman you've ever known. In Brautigan's new novel, the narrator got to keep the girl.

Like Alfred Hitchcock seen in an elevator or buying a newspaper at the start of one of his films, Richard Brautigan had a walk-on part in *The Abortion*. Book 1 ("Buffalo Gals, Won't You Come Out Tonight?") was divided into four sections. The third of these, "The 23," concerned the total number of unpublished books the library had received that day. Always the enumerator and list maker, Brautigan described each in turn, listing every make-believe title and its fictional author.

The ninth of the twenty-three writers to submit manuscripts was Richard Brautigan. Richard described himself this way: "The author was tall and blond and had a long yellow mustache that gave him an anachronistic appearance. He looked as if he'd be more at home in another era." The novel Brautigan brought in was called *MOOSE*. "'Just another book,' he said."

While working on *The Abortion*, Brautigan plugged away at a task he found distasteful, sending out letters of inquiry to editors and agents. "Falling stars," he called these mercenary missives. Don Carpenter, whose first novel, *Hard Rain Falling*, was published by Harcourt, Brace & World in 1966, had recommended Richard to his Hollywood agent, the legendary H. N. Swanson. Known to everyone as "Swanee," the cultured ten-percenter numbered Hemingway, Fitzgerald, John O'Hara, J. R. R. Tolkien, Ross Macdonald, and Agatha Christie among his many illustrious clients. Once, when asked what form of writing was the most profitable, Swanson replied, "Ransom notes."

Don suggested to "Swanee" that *A Confederate General from Big Sur* might make an interesting project for Richard Lester, a director currently red-hot from his recent successes with the two Beatles films, *Help!* and *A Hard Day's Night*. Brautigan immediately sent a copy of his novel to Swanson's Sunset Boulevard office, mentioning conversations with Zekial Marko, who had "a strong interest" in *Confederate General* and "a good idea for a screenplay."

Early in April, Peter Desbarats, editor in chief of *Parallel*, a Canadian magazine published in Montreal, wrote to say that of the three stories Brautigan had submitted, he found "The Wild Birds of Heaven" to be "a blessed if brief deliverance [. . .] from all the muddled words and confused thoughts that silt down on my desk every day." He wanted to use the story in his summer (July/August) issue and offered $125 (U.S.) for the first serial rights. This was welcome news.

As was a letter from H. N. Swanson later in the month. "Swanee" had read *Confederate General* and "found it highly amusing." Although he thought "the market for this type of book [. . .] rather limited," he wanted to try and sell it and asked Brautigan to send him more copies of the Grove edition. He inquired about Richard's other novels, including the work in progress. As Richard had included no return address, Swanson sent his letter in care of Don Carpenter.

Brautigan knew his days on California Street were numbered. In April, he dined twice without Janice at Andrew Hoyem's apartment overlooking Golden Gate Park's Panhandle, a green tree-lined strip eight blocks long and one block wide, running between Baker and Stanyan Streets. One occasion was a formal sit-down affair featuring fricasseed hare. Awaiting the inevitable, Richard plugged away on his novel and tended other unfinished business. He sent H. N. Swanson five copies of *Confederate General*, writing on the same day to Seymour Krim and to Sallie Ellsworth at the *Partisan Review*. The little literary magazine had held chapters from *Trout Fishing* for fourteen months without reaching an editorial consensus. Brautigan begged for an answer. "Please, pretty please with sugar on it, get me a decision on that stuff."

Early in May, Richard Brautigan read from his work at the Rhymers Club in Wheeler Hall on the Berkeley campus, opening the semester's program. The organization, recently founded by Ron Loewinsohn; David Schaff, who once edited the *Yale Literary Magazine*; and graduate student/poet David Bromige (former editor of the *Northwest Review*), had published a single issue of *RC Lion*, their official mimeographed magazine. ("The Pretty Office," a Brautigan short story, appeared in the second issue around the time of his University of California appearance.) Don Carpenter was among the audience for Richard's Rhymers Club reading. Hearing "Revenge of the Lawn" for the first time, he recalled, "I laughed so loud I literally fell off my chair. Right there in public." Andy Hoyem was also present for the occasion. Hoyem made no mention in his daily journal entry of seeing Janice there.

The final breakup came four days later when Richard moved out, taking refuge in Hoyem's second-floor apartment at 1652 Fell Street. For all of the emotional pain involved, the transition occurred without incident. Accustomed to a Spartan life, Brautigan traveled light and made himself at home with a minimum of effort. Space for his typewriter and a place to crash were all he required.

Richard found an ideal roommate in Andy Hoyem, who thought at the time that his friend was only coming to stay for a week or so. A fine poet in his own right, the South Dakota–born Hoyem had graduated from Pomona, served in the U.S. Navy, and worked with Dave Haselwood at the Auerhahn Press, learning the craft of printing using hand-set type. He had recently entered into a partnership with Robert Grabhorn, "the consummate fine press printers in the country at that time," forming the Grabhorn-Hoyem Press. A busy workday schedule kept him at the print shop for long hours, leaving Richard plenty of solitary uninterrupted writing space back at the apartment.

Brautigan made good use of this time. He labored over the growing novel, transforming twenty-one pages of typewritten notes into many short cogent chapters. Everything went in, all the mundane details of the PSA flight, his dislike of San Diego, the old Mexican at the Greyhound station carrying his possessions in a Hunt's tomato sauce box, the Tijuana Woolworth's display window crammed with Easter bunnies and candy eggs, a middle-aged platinum-haired woman wearing a mink coat in the airport café. From these random observed details Richard wove the fabric of his inspired fantasy.

It wasn't all work and no play at the Fell Street digs. Hoyem greatly enjoyed Brautigan's presence and took much pleasure in their witty literary conversations. He thought their time together "was good for both of us." Near the end of May, the two friends hosted a party celebrating the shared birthdays of nineteenth-century French proto-symbolist poet Gérard de Nerval and Robert Grabhorn, who was turning sixty-six. Hoyem had published a translation of de Nerval's *Les Chimères* that year. The two poets mailed out printed letterpress invitations. Jane Rades supplied an elaborately decorated cake, which the guests devoured while sipping punch à l'Aiglon, a Grabhorn recipe featuring Napoleon brandy. The master printer was a connoisseur of obscure beverage concoctions concealing a lethal kick.

Hangovers rarely deterred Richard Brautigan, and no matter how much of Grabhorn's insidious punch he had imbibed the night before, he most certainly was back hard at work on his novel the morning after the party. His steady approach paid off. Four days later, after six weeks at the Fell Street apartment, Richard finished a draft of *The Abortion*. Andrew Hoyem was the first person, other than the author, to read the manuscript. He thought the book "very good, going from allegory to reality, to harsh reality." With the completion of his fourth novel, Brautigan capped one of the most remarkable creative streaks in American literature. Four utterly unique books in five years of work, together with innumerable poems and a distinguished group of short stories, not bad for a country boy come to town with his apple-picking money. Richard Brautigan did not write another novel for eight years.

F ROM 1966 TO 1975, Richard Brautigan occupied a shabby apartment at 2546 Geary Boulevard, near Kaiser Medical Center. No one in Frisco ever referred to it as a boulevard, and Brautigan always wrote Geary Street as his address. The decrepit two-story wooden building stood in the middle of a block across from the Sears depot and just up from the Cable Car Drive-in, a greasy spoon on the corner that reminded Ianthe of a little red caboose. The front windows of the first-floor apartment looked out on the tunnel where Geary cuts through the hill from Presidio to Masonic. When he moved in Richard's rent was $45 a month.

Richard first heard about the place from Erik Weber, who lived in the house next door. In the summer of 1966, the current tenant, a painter named Ori Sherman, planned on leaving for a year and a half to travel around the world. There was no lease, and he wanted someone to "sublet" the apartment, holding it for him until he got back. Erik and Loie Weber suggested Richard. Near the end of June, Brautigan moved out of Andy Hoyem's place on Fell Street and came to stay. When Ori Sherman returned from his *Wanderjahr*, Brautigan refused to leave, citing squatter's rights. "Richard was not giving up that apartment," Loie remembered. "Ori was upset. He was angry, but that was the way it was."

On the afternoon before moving day, Brautigan had lunch with Robert Grabhorn whose press had proofed his manuscript of *The Abortion*. Andrew Hoyem and his wife, Sally, joined them. Afterward they celebrated with Pimm's Cup on the terrace at Enrico's and more drinks in the open arched window at the Condor (home of topless silicone-enhanced Carol Doda), on the corner of Broadway and Columbus. It was warm and clear, perfect for celebrity watching. "Bob Grabhorn panhandled seventy cents out of Allen Ginsberg," Hoyem recalled.

The evening ended in high good spirits at the Fillmore. They were entertained by Frank Zappa and the Mothers of Invention, along with Lenny Bruce, in his final public appearance. Hoyem deemed the comedian's performance "lousy." A month later, Bruce (age forty) died of a morphine overdose in the bathroom of his Hollywood home.

Loie Weber thought of Brautigan as a friend who lived next door. "He was just this oddball character." Nearly ten years younger, Loie found herself drawn to Richard in a maternal way. "I felt his fragility and his vulnerability and how easily hurt he was. How sensitive he was." Right from the start, she did small favors for him. Not long after moving in, Richard, late for an appointment, asked Loie if she would leave a note on his door for his friend Frank Curtin, who had planned to stop by and read his new novel. She quickly jotted down a simple message. "Frank: come on in—read novel—it's on table in front room. I'll be back in about 2 hours. Richard." Loie pinned the scrap of paper to Brautigan's front door and thought nothing more about it. When

Richard returned home the note still hung there, another piece of found art. He took the paper slip into his new writing room, typed up Loie's words verbatim, and made them the dedication to *The Abortion*.

Over the years, Brautigan, never before sentimental about material things, began to fill the cheap apartment with mementos and curious souvenirs. "You know what happens to artists," the photographer Edmund Shea observed, "they become archivists of themselves." Among Brautigan's bizarre trophies were a rusting Nambu light machine gun, a quilted fish, an old-fashioned car horn (with a rubber squeeze bulb) hanging by the unused marble fireplace, a U.S. Army manual on trout fishing, several gold ore rocks from the Great American River on the mantelpiece beside his square inch of Texas and a certificate naming Brautigan an honorary Texas colonel. A laurel leaf crown fashioned by Margot Patterson Doss hung nearby. (Richard came to dinner to celebrate the publication of a new book one day when Margot had been picking bay laurel. She wove the crown for him, and he wore it all evening.)

Loie Weber recognized the mythic importance these objects held for Brautigan. "He assiduously worked at creating his own style, his conscious creation of that apartment as a museum to the current culture then. He would just talk about every artifact. He loved it. The idea of it."

Richard's oddest knickknack was a can of poisoned soup. Kenn Davis remembered a time either in '67 or '68 when botulism turned up in canned soup and San Francisco found itself in the grip of a health scare. Brautigan searched through supermarkets until he "found a can of this stuff with the proper identification numbers on the bottom that said, in effect, if you eat this you will die." He positioned the can in a place of honor on a shelf in his kitchen. Whenever friends came over, he'd point it out and say, "Look, killer soup."

Don Carpenter described Richard Brautigan's dreary apartment as "right out of Charles Addams." The spooky aspects he observed included the ritualistic makeup of his friend's antique brass bed, purchased around 1969, when Richard first began earning serious money. "Had a patchwork quilt on it, and he would lay out this calfskin, rawhide up, orange colored, and on top of that he would place these rocks."

Edmund Shea remembered Richard's "brass bed with this weird arrangement he had on the top of it." The bed was covered by a buffalo hide spread weighted down with totem objects. Ianthe wrote of this as "my father's idea of a Buddhist shrine." Sherry Vetter recalled "that little setup on the bed," quartz rocks rescued from fishing streams, a marble, and "a little metal toy of some kind." She also remembered a daily ritual. "When you got out of bed and you made the bed, you had to put these things back where they were."

From Don Carpenter's perspective, the ritual enlarged to include the entire apartment. Whenever Richard left the place, "I would go outside and stand on the porch and wait, and he would come out and say, 'Wait a second.' He'd go back in the apartment, and I'd follow him back in, and he'd be doing exactly the same routine, checking out every rock in the place, going through the kitchen, making sure the kitchen was okay."

Richard Brautigan's apartment provided sanctuary from the outside world, and his writing room was the Inner Sanctum. He worked in a tiny chamber off the main hallway. To Loie Weber, the room seemed like a cave. "It was so dark and dreary, totally unappealing." The place was a cluttered mess. Keith Abbott referred to it as "that den of debris." A torn blue bedspread screened the nondescript view out the window. Light came from a bare bulb hanging by frayed cord.

A secondhand dining table, surrounded by cardboard cartons stuffed with magazines and miscellaneous papers, served as Brautigan's desk. A squat tan IBM electric typewriter sat square in the middle, all other available space taken up by piles of books and manuscripts. Keith Abbott claimed this "was the one room that few were ever invited in." A notable exception was Richard's daughter, who slept here on "a special little bed" when she stayed overnight. Because she was afraid of the dark, her father always left the hall light on for her.

In the front room/bedroom, the top two shelves of the recessed built-in bookcase, "curiously dust-free" according to his daughter, contained copies of Brautigan's own books as well as the work of various friends. Volumes by Robert Creeley and Roxy Gordon (the authors' photos decorating their front covers) stood facing forward like family portraits. The bottom shelf held a few records, his dial telephone, and a stereo system. On the shelf above, Brautigan displayed rusting keys; an old wire-bound seltzer bottle; many shells, rocks, and feathers; an open dragon-shaped switchblade wrapped in a rosary; a scrap of gold lamé (a gift from Janis Joplin); a card reading "You have been assisted by a member of the Hells Angels"; a strand of barbed wire; and a tooled leather plaque with embossed lettering: "Oh, Flap City. Oh, those leather wings." According to Keith Abbott, this was a spontaneous Brautigan quip often quoted by Lew Welch. The rest of it went, "I didn't get your cherry, and I don't want your prune." Welch later titled his series of absurd plays *Leather Prunes*, delighting Richard.

In the opposite corner, a high-backed Gothic chair occupied a place of honor like a throne. The carved spiraling legs and fading woven upholstery made young Ianthe think of it as "the scary chair," from a haunted house. No one ever sat in this chair. It was reserved for Willard, a three-foot-tall papier-mâché sculpture of an exotic bird. Vividly painted, with absurd round eyes, an enormous beak, long skinny legs, and a belly like a bowling ball, Willard occupied an active place in Richard's fantasy life for years.

The other large art piece in the room was a "collage" by Bruce Conner, who was the first to dub Richard's cluttered apartment The Museum. "When I first walked in there," Conner said, "it was as if I were walking into one of my collages." He later gave Brautigan a wooden stepladder painted black with a hanging row of small red pompons tacked along the front edge of each step. The ladder stood at the foot of the brass bed. In many ways, it remained a work in progress. Richard used the ladder as a showcase for "sacred" objects, notably a copy of William Goldman's shooting script for *Butch Cassidy and the Sundance Kid*, one of his favorite movies.

Bruce Conner recalled another modification. "There was one of those little red pompons with red string that had fallen off, and I noticed that there was an empty glass that the secretary [Loie Weber] had been drinking, a tall sort of cocktail glass type thing that was empty, except there was the red lipstick of the lips on it, and I put it over on the step of the ladder with this little pompon with a string which looked like a maraschino cherry with a stem and put it in there, and I told them, 'Leave this here. This is part of the work.' I felt it was appropriate, a sort of commentary on Richard and his drinking and his girlfriends and his ladder and everything else. But when I was there again, the little pompon was there but the glass was gone."

Conner considered the apartment "a classic cold-water flat," yet told Brautigan that he wanted the place as a painting studio should Richard ever decide to vacate the premises. "It was not one of the greatest places in the world," Bruce recalled. "The bathtub had this sort of brownish-red water. The pipes were so rusted and calcified that it would take about forty-five minutes to fill about six inches of water in the tub, a kind of reddish muddy lump, not very hot at all." This didn't matter as Conner had no plans to bathe in his new studio. Richard told Bruce that when he left "he was going to move out immediately." Conner would have to get hold of the landlord right away. As it happened, Bruce had the flu when he got word that Richard was leaving. He couldn't get out of bed for three or four days and felt this cost him his shot at Geary Street.

Brautigan eventually moved out of the Museum in December of 1974 because the landlord informed him that the building was going to be torn down and all future repairs would now be his responsibility. Richard packed up his eccentric treasures. With the help of Keith Abbott and the trusty old Chevy pickup, everything went out the door, Bruce Conner's stepladder collage included. After Brautigan's death, Ianthe gave the stepladder to Tony Dingman, who later passed it along to actor/photographer Dennis Hopper. Conner remembered seeing the piece at Hopper's place in Los Angeles. "I didn't realize he had it. Dennis was really mystified as to why."

After buying the Bolinas house in 1972, Brautigan commissioned Erik Weber to photograph the Museum. "He said to me, 'Erik, I want you to come and document the apartment. I want you to document everything in it." Weber ended up shooting twelve or thirteen rolls of film. He took pictures from every conceivable angle. Exteriors of the building, front, back, and both sides. Long shots down the narrow hallway. Wide angles of the front room and kitchen. Close-ups of just about everything.

Weber found it a bit peculiar. "He said, 'Erik, I don't want anybody to see these photographs. Nobody to see these while I'm alive.' It is kind of strange to think about. He had me go around and photograph, complete coverage of the place. No one was to see them. And no one did see them. I just left them as contact sheets."

Ianthe Brautigan felt "everything changed" once her father left Geary Street for good. In her memoir, she wrote, "Sometimes I fantasize that if he had never moved, he wouldn't have killed himself. He could have holed up there with his cheap rent and continued his life." Keith Abbott interpreted the move as Richard's need to disengage from his old life once he encountered wealth and fame. Leaving a shabby slum for a newly remodeled apartment at 314 Union Street, on the slope of Telegraph Hill above Washington Square, meant stepping up in the world. Over the years Brautigan lived in the Museum, his rent rose to $75 a month. The new apartment's $365 monthly rate, close to a five-fold increase, represented a dramatic measure of his improving status.

"In his dank apartment the anachronism of Richard's hippie past was all too evident," Abbott wrote. "Young and eager acolytes had passed through, leaving their gifts. A stuffed cloth trout, naive childish calendars, and a handmade quilt for his brass bed were still there, along with mimeo Digger Dollars and 'God's eyes.'" Brautigan never abandoned any of these things. He packed it all in boxes and took it with him after Erik Weber photographed every last detail for some unknown posterity.

Brautigan's departure from the Museum was more gradual than any implied break with the past. Richard had not lived full-time in the Geary Street apartment for years. Toward the end of 1960s, he began keeping company with a number of beautiful, intelligent, self-sufficient women who all had attractive homes of their own. Marcia Pacaud's apartment in Sausalito and Valerie Estes's flat at 1429 Kearny in North Beach were in every way more pleasant places than the Museum. As Keith Abbott recalled about Geary Street, "his dump became a priest hole for him, used only for writing and time away from his social life."

A lingering nostalgia for the Museum haunted Brautigan long after he departed. In March 1979, a little more than a year after his marriage to Akiko Sakagami, Richard moved to a grand Pacific Heights apartment on Green Street. It was a long way from Gino & Carlo's dive on the same thoroughfare in North Beach. Showing Keith Abbott around the huge sunlit place, Brautigan indicated a spacious closet situated at the top of the stairs. "In the old days," he said, "that would have been my writing room. I probably wrote better without a view."

twenty-four: the emperor's new clothes

SAN FRANCISCO HAS always been fond of eccentric behavior. Back in the 1860s, Bummer and Lazarus, a pair of mangy mongrel mutts, had the run of the city, roaming freely through the streets, welcomed in all the eating and drinking establishments along the red-light district known as the Barbary Coast, where the pampered canines received ample handouts from every burly apron-wrapped proprietor. Tough men who'd slip their mothers a Mickey and shanghai their own brothers wept when the dogs died (Lazarus in October 1863; Bummer, two years later, November 1865). Huge crowds followed their funeral processions through the streets of town, and a public monument was eventually raised in their honor.

The most renowned San Francisco eccentric was Joshua A. Norton, a British-born business-man who arrived in the city with the forty-niners, prospered for a time, and suffered a mental breakdown after his financial affairs collapsed. Following a long absence from Frisco, he returned in 1857, convinced he was of royal birth and proclaiming himself Norton I, emperor of the United States and protector of Mexico. The city happily went along with this curious charade, San Franciscans tipping their hats as the Emperor Norton walked the streets in his shabby uniform, plumed top hat, and tarnished epaulettes. In those early days, his majesty was often accompanied on his daily perambulations by Bummer and Lazarus, who became his constant companions.

Norton I issued numerous proclamations over the years, which the local newspapers duly reported with their journalistic tongues firmly in cheek. Two of Norton's decrees were nearly a century ahead of his time. He proposed dumping landfill in the shoals off Yerba Buena Island to create a manmade island there. Another Norton idea called for building a bridge from Oakland to San Francisco by way of Yerba Buena Island. Considered zany at the time, both projects (Treasure Island and the Bay Bridge) have since come to pass. An edict ordering the city to erect a Christmas tree for children in Union Square every holiday season remains in effect today.

A friendly print shop produced the Emperor's spurious currency, which was honored by all the area merchants. Free seats were reserved for him at first-night openings at every legitimate theater, and the audiences rose to their feet in honor when he entered. His imperial majesty was also welcomed in Sacramento, where he would occasionally address the state legislature. The San Francisco Board of Supervisors amended the city charter to grant Norton I a lifetime allowance so that he need not appear in public wearing a tattered uniform. The Emperor ruled magnanimously, handing out free candy to children and worshipping at both Jewish and Christian services to promote religious tolerance. When he died in 1880, after a twenty-one-year reign, ten thousand "loyal subjects" turned out to mourn Norton I, filing past the ornate rosewood casket where his body lay in state. The citizens of Frisco truly loved their mad monarch.

Artists are often eccentrics by nature, and many of San Francisco's more peculiar citizens came from the ranks of the city's literary population. Wild-bearded as an Old Testament prophet, poet Joaquin Miller (born Cincinnatus Hiner Miller in 1837) claimed to be a former Pony Express rider and costumed himself like some outrageous dime-novel hero in jingling spurs, high boots, broad-brimmed sombrero, and a flowing kerchief. Gelett Burgess, in contrast, dressed like an Edwardian dandy, wrote of purple cows, coined the word "blurb," and was fired from his teaching position (topographical drawing) at UC Berkeley for toppling a cast-iron statue of the equally eccentric teetotaling dentist Dr. Henry Cogswell after an all-night revel.

Memorialized by a tiled bench in Ina Coolbrith Park, atop Russian Hill not far from where Burgess lived, George Sterling, "Pagliaccio of the Water Lilies," Greek-profiled protégé of bitter Ambrose Bierce, cut a wide swath through the bohemian exuberance of the early twentieth century. Once, he stripped off his clothing and dove into a moonlit lake in Golden Gate Park to pick a water lily for a female friend. Stirling's boon companion, Jack London, began his career at sixteen as the "Prince of the Oyster Pirates," sailing his sloop *Razzle Dazzle* on late-night raiding voyages into the oyster beds of the Bay. He later worked in a jute mill, shipped on sealing expeditions off Siberia, marched with Coxey's army of the unemployed, served a stretch in the Erie County penitentiary, and joined the Klondike gold rush of 1897. All these adventures transpired before he was twenty-two and started writing in earnest.

Richard Brautigan became a natural heir to Frisco's tradition of artistic eccentricity. In tandem with the sixties penchant for dressing up (Kesey's Merry Pranksters and their outlandish comic book costumes, rainbowed Jimi Hendrix, Sgt. Pepper's Lonely Hearts Club Band, Tiny Tim, and Wavy Gravy), Brautigan evolved his own bizarre sartorial style. "Richard always dressed the same," Michael McClure observed. "It was his style, and he wanted to change it as little as possible." Also involved with his own image-making, McClure considered this an attempt to achieve "the exact style of ourselves."

In Loie Weber's opinion, "Richard was a tragic romantic." From her point of view, his sense of personal style grew out of that disposition. "He had this idealization, admiration for Hemingway," she recalled. "He would periodically just talk about Hemingway. He had a real romantic investment in the lifestyle of Hemingway, the outdoorsman, the seeming he-man. He always talked about his life, image, style, being." Brautigan instinctively understood the futility of imitating Ernest Hemingway's lifestyle. He determined to create a style of his own, one that would indelibly identify him in a reader's mind.

Brautigan's personal image evolved gradually throughout the early 1960s. The duffle coat and flat-brimmed hat he fancied at the start of the decade gave way by 1966 to his trademark apparel, pinstriped suit vest and strands of beads, the high-crowned Western hat and rimless glasses.

Michael McClure described it: "Richard's style was shabby—loose threads at the cuff, black pants faded to gray, an old mismatched vest, a navy pea-jacket, and later something like love beads around the neck." The surplus store navy coat (made famous by Erik Weber's cover photograph for *Trout Fishing in America*) was for cold weather, a not uncommon climatic occurrence in San Francisco. On milder days, Brautigan wore his pinback-studded vest and a turtleneck shirt, sometimes adding a secondhand suit jacket. "Like Baudelaire, Richard is a refined Dandy," wrote McClure. "The impoverished Dandy dresses in the most carefully chosen stylish rags of no-style."

The Mime Troupe ushered in an era of acting out private fantasies in public. The ever-expanding psychedelic-street-people community gathering on Haight Street provided the perfect stage. Along with many of his literary contemporaries, Richard Brautigan gravitated toward the Hashbury. By early 1967, he started showing up in the neighborhood carrying a large shard of mirror. "Have a free look," he told the passing hippies and tourists, holding up the broken mirror so they might study their reflections. "Know thyself!"

Brautigan's mirror came from a trash can full of broken fragments salvaged by the Diggers, who gave pieces to local street kids. "One of the things I liked most about Richard was that he was the real poet of the Diggers," wrote Michael McClure. "He was often on Haight Street passing out papers from the Digger Communications Company [. . .] Richard was doing it because he believed in it."

Richard handed out mimeographed Digger leaflets to runaway flower children showing the location of the nearest VD clinic. He soon started giving away his own broadside poems on the streets of the city. Peter Cohon (who would change his last name to Coyote late in 1967), a Mime Troupe actor who had participated in numbers of free park productions, celebrated this Digger-inspired influence. "One had the sense that you were part of a community of extraordinary people," he said. "And that you were with people that were winners and gifted and gilded and loyal, even though unrecognized. And so the fact that they would give their gifts away for nothing changed the whole perspective on what nothing was worth [. . .] everybody is giving their best for nothing, and it was better than what you could buy."

Brautigan's poetry handouts led to his most fanciful and elegant publishing project, *Please Plant This Book*, a glossy cardboard folder containing eight seed packets, each with a poem printed on one side and planting instructions on the other. Michael McClure thought it "a new image of the book" and "a true poetic act." Brautigan gave them away for free, not just in the Haight but at locations all over Frisco. He stood on crowded downtown street corners in his distinctive hat like some homeless man distributing advertising flyers. "Plant this book," he called to the anonymous passing strangers, holding out a copy as they hurried past. "Please, plant this book." The Emperor Norton would have approved.

twenty-five: **digger daze**

"Y OU NOBLE DIGGERS all, stand up now, stand up now, You noble Diggers all, stand up now." These lines were written around 1650 by Gerrard Winstanley, an agrarian communist who, together with his comrade William Everard, assembled twenty poor spade-carrying farmers on St. George's Hill, Surrey. Winstanley and Everard called their commune the Diggers. They proceeded to work the land, abjuring force, believing in "making the Earth a Common Treasury for All." The Diggers saw no use for money, seeking instead to "neither buy nor sell."

Three hundred and fifteen years later, a group of Mime Troupers rekindled their utopian spirit in San Francisco. In August 1965, the San Francisco police descended on Lafayette Park and stopped the Mime Troupe's public presentation of Giordano Bruno's *Il Candelaio* in midperformance. (The Italian Renaissance philosopher was himself a troublemaker, burned at the stake in 1600 on the orders of the Inquisition.) The play had been adapted from Bruno's writings by former "Quiz Kid" Peter Berg, an intense young writer/director nicknamed "the Hun." Described by a fellow Mime Trouper as "mercurial, charming, coercive, subliminally menacing and intellectually uncompromising," Berg believed in a "guerrilla theater" transforming the audience from spectators into participants to create social change.

The Mime Troupe's director, R. G. (Ronnie) Davis, ignored the orders of the Recreation and Park Commission, which had revoked his group's performance permit on the grounds of obscenity, and staged his show in the park on the scheduled date. Davis was arrested along with two of his actors. On May 2, 1966, the Mime Troupe, led by Davis and "dressed in a variety of costumes from minstrel to commedia," crashed the first luncheon meeting of the newly created Arts Resources Development Committee at the Crown Zellerbach Building.

Composed of "twenty-six prominent business people and civic leaders" and chaired by paper tycoon Harold Zellerbach, president of the Arts Commission, the committee advocated building a huge new cultural center in the center of town. Ronnie Davis read a manifesto to the gathered big shots protesting that no actual artists had been included in their organization. When Davis finished, Zellerbach ordered him and his motley crew to leave his building. Two days later, the annual awards from the Hotel Tax Publicity and Advertising Fund were announced by the city's chief administrative officer. The Mime Troupe, which had received $2,000 over the past two years, was cut off "without a dime."

The following week, over one hundred San Francisco performers, poets, artists, and writers gathered in the Mime Troupe's Howard Street loft to form a "poor man's art commission." The group named itself the Artists Liberation Front, an overtly confrontational political gesture invoking the Communist insurgent National Liberation Front in Vietnam. This boisterous gathering came the day after Richard Brautigan moved into Andrew Hoyem's Fell Street apartment. Richard became an active participant in many ALF functions in the months to come. The meeting was chaired by state assemblyman Willie Brown, who at this stage in his political career sported an Afro and colorful dashikis instead of the $3,000 Brioni suits he later came to favor.

Present among the supportive college professors, architects, doctors, and lawyers were Mime Troupers Davis, Peter Berg, Peter Coyote, and a new recruit named Grogan, recently discharged from the Army, who had simplified his Catholic baptismal moniker from Eugene Leo Michael to Emmett. Lean and angular, his freckled face the map of Ireland, Emmett Grogan moved "through a room with the detached concentration of a shark." In Peter Coyote's excellent memoir of the period, *Sleeping Where I Fall*, Grogan was also described as having "developed a sense of drama in his bearing, his cupped cigarette, his smoky, hooded eyes, which declared him a man on the wrong side of the law, a man with a past, a man who would not be deterred."

Peter Coyote had invited poet Lenore Kandel to the meeting, and she arrived with her lover, William Fritsch (aka Sweet Willie Tumbleweed), "dressed, respectively, in bright red and cobalt blue leather Levi's." Having met at the East-West House, they made a charismatic couple, her long black braid and lustrous glowing skin complimenting his beveled Aztec features and no-nonsense macho presence. A year or so later, "Tumble," a man who clearly expressed his fierce sense of honor in his poetry, became a member of the Hells Angels and roared off into violent karmic alternatives.

Ralph Gleason covered the evening for the *Chronicle*, calling it "one of the most important events in San Francisco's cultural history." Mime Troupe member Barbara Wohl observed, "There were never more anarchists in the same room at the same time." The Artists Liberation Front held its third organizational meeting at the Fillmore on the final day of May. Two weeks later, they met again at the Committee Theater. In mid-July the ALF staged a benefit at the Fillmore with Garry Goodrow of the Committee acting as emcee. Sopwith Camel and Bob Clark's jazz group supplied the music. Allen Ginsberg read "Wichita Vortex Sutra," a new poem. The Committee and the Mime Troupe performed. In his column three days later, Ralph Gleason described the event as "a Mardi Gras, a masked ball, with people in costumes, painted with designs, carrying plasticene banners through the audience while multi-colored liquid light projections played around them."

Freshly funded, the Artists Liberation Front continued meeting throughout the summer. At a press conference held in the band shell in Golden Gate Park in July, plans for a five-day arts festival in September were discussed. In August, Lawrence Ferlinghetti and the ALF denounced Mayor John Shelley and the Arts Resources Development Committee. By September's end, when the Front announced its plans for a series of public fairs in October, word about the happenings on Haight Street had spread through the psychedelic subculture. The Hashbury had become a magnet, attracting fresh arrivals daily. A new community developed overnight like a boomtown.

Richard Brautigan quickly became a nonresident member of that gypsy population. Haight Street pulsed with the immediacy of the new. The Thelin brothers, Jay and Ron, opened the Psychedelic Shop on New Year's Day, and by summer it had become a refuge and a gathering place, providing much the same community bulletin board service as City Lights did in North Beach. At first, Richard went over to the Hashbury to see his friends. Michael McClure had lived in the neighborhood for years. Keith Abbott, a new pal introduced to him by Price Dunn, shared a dingy apartment on Haight Street with his girlfriend, Lani. Although the 38 Geary bus ran every fifteen minutes, Richard almost always walked the twenty blocks from his new place to save the fifteen-cent fare. By the summer of 1966, the feeble trickle of Brautigan's income dried up completely.

Richard's friends looked after him. Loie Weber always made extra when she brewed soup in her big cast-iron pot next door. "Richard at that time was so poor," she remembered. He'd come over often "and just eat soup. He was hungry, and he didn't have much." Erik Weber recalled how "Richard would spend most of his time at our house because he had no phone and no money for food. He'd come down the back stairs, then in the house."

When Brautigan moved into Ori Sherman's apartment there was no refrigerator. Lew Welch and Magda Cregg found a secondhand fridge somewhere in Marin. Lew borrowed a truck, and they drove it over to Geary Street. "That was our gift to Richard," Magda recalled. Other friends made sure the fridge didn't stay empty. John Doss worked as chief of pediatrics at Kaiser across the street, and Margot often left "something in Richard's refrigerator for him—a quart of soup or a pasta with a good sauce."

Something about "the way he said yes and ate it," stuck in Keith Abbott's mind after he offered Brautigan a sandwich one day when the writer dropped by on his way to Golden Gate Park. "We would eat before we went on our rambles," he wrote in his memoir. Keith was another struggling writer from the Pacific Northwest, also an Aquarius born in Tacoma, a connection that struck a chord with Richard Brautigan. Abbott had moved down to Monterey from Seattle the year before, becoming friends with Price Dunn. After Price brought him by Geary Street, Keith saw a lot of Brautigan, who soon included Abbott in his literary world, introducing him to Don Carpenter, Lew Welch, and Mike McClure.

"Richard loved the poems from Spicer's book *Language* [published in 1965]," Keith Abbott wrote later, "and could recite some from memory." Brautigan also introduced Keith to the short stories of Isaak Babel, the great Russian Jewish writer who rode with the red cavalry, and urged him to read Guy de Maupassant. Abbott recalled that his friend "revered" the "simple and clear language" in Sherwood Anderson's story "Death in the Woods." Other favorites in his sparse library ("a writer's library, only literary works, very little criticism") were *By-Line*, a collection of Hemingway's early journalism, and a complete set of *The Greek Anthology*.

Keith and Richard often wandered the city together, trading stories. He recalled this time in *Downstream from Trout Fishing in America*.

> *In those days going around with Brautigan was like traveling inside one of his novels. With friends Richard talked just as he wrote. Outrageous metaphors and looney tune takes were commonplace; one-liners, bizarre fantasies, and lightning asides [. . .] He loved to improvise verbal games [. . .] deadpan, pretending to have no humor at all.*

Often, they spent hours trading tough-guy Bogart movie quips or inventing comic parodies of ancient Chinese poetry. According to Abbott, Brautigan said that these routines "disappeared in their becoming."

Street life provided an ever-passing carnival parade in the Haight, a people watcher's paradise with the park waiting right around the corner. Brautigan described a favorite walk in "The Haight-Ashbury Crawdad," an unpublished short story. "It's beautiful where Haight Street meets Stanyan Street at the Golden Gate Park. I like to walk through the William A. McCavley Memorial Gateway late in the afternoon to sit and enjoy the last hour before sundown." Richard had plenty of time for sitting. His only published novel sold fewer than a thousand copies. Three manuscripts drifted in a Sargasso Sea of rejection letters. Taking a break from long fiction, Brautigan wrote only short stories and poetry that summer.

A decade younger, aspiring writer Keith Abbott regarded Richard Brautigan as an old pro. Richard's very survival, living off his writing, struck Keith as a triumph. Brautigan's life seemed imbued with a "heroic aura." Abbott found optimism to be "the one amazing constant" about his new friend. In spite of poverty and rejection, Brautigan maintained a positive outlook. Richard "clearly regarded his daily life as its own work of art," Keith later observed. It was a simple, uncomplicated life. Morning hours Brautigan reserved for work. After a round of lunchtime phone calls, he spent the rest of the day in pursuit of happiness.

Haight Street had become an exotic bazaar. On any corner, one might observe neo-Edwardian dandies, paleface Indians, blanket-wrapped mock swamis, and a steady procession of guitar-carrying minstrels. At the beginning of the year, twelve empty storefronts haunted the shopping district. By the end of spring, they were filling up fast. In Gear (mod clothing), the Blushing Peony (boutique), Mnasidika (leather apparel), the House of Richard (Mexican ponchos), Far Fetched Foods (aka "Blind Jerry's"), and the I/Thou coffee shop had all opened their doors for business. The old Haight Theater (formerly a neighborhood movie house, a gay porn cinema, and an Assembly of God church) had been leased in May and renamed the Straight Theater. By midsummer, even after large investments from acid king Owsley and the bands Quicksilver Messenger Service and Big Brother and the Holding Company, remodeling was not finished. The partners dreamed large, envisioning a block-sized cultural complex.

While the Straight Theater converted its seating arrangement into a dance floor, ex–Mime Trouper Bill Graham turned the Fillmore Auditorium into a theater, if only for a single evening in July, when he presented the second performance of Michael McClure's *The Beard*. The capacity crowd greeted this amplified original-cast reprisal (backed by "an enormous and beautiful light show with everything from movies of horses running through liquid projections to other projections of movies of little girls skipping rope and clouds passing by") with an enthusiastic ovation.

Graham canceled a second performance after the police informed him that the actors would be arrested and he would lose his license. The next performance of *The Beard*, several weeks later, was at the Committee Theater in North Beach. This time cops were in the audience, filming the cunnilingus scene at the play's climax. When the house lights came up, they busted the two performers for obscenity. An element of the absurd attended the event, considering it was business as usual for the many topless bars in operation that night up and down Broadway.

Early in the year, Bob Dylan gave Michael McClure an autoharp. The poet had been writing songs although he thought himself "totally unmusical." After letting the instrument sit for six weeks on the mantel, McClure started strumming, the first chords in what would be a year and a half spent learning how to play. "I bought an amplifier and stood for hours whanging on the autoharp."

Richard picked up on this and started writing a few songs of his own. He had his pawnshop guitar yet spent very little time whanging on it. Victor Moscoso, the poster artist, who lived at the time with his wife, Gail, on Grant Avenue above the Tivoli Restaurant, remembered Richard dropping by in the evenings. Victor played the guitar, "old-timey Carter Family stuff and moderate bluegrass. Nothing very fancy." Brautigan often fooled around with Moscoso's guitar. "He could strum. He could play a couple of chords. Couldn't sing. He was atonal. Couldn't hold a key." Victor thought Richard sang popular tunes or folk songs. "He didn't sing any of his poems."

Shortly after moving into the Geary Street apartment, Richard sent "Homage to Rudi Gernreich," together with Erik Weber's pet cemetery photographs, to Peter Desbarats at *Parallel*. In July, Desbarats turned the piece down, finding the subject not to his liking. July also brought a rejection letter from Andre Deutsch Ltd. in England. If Brautigan wished to have the typescript of *In Watermelon Sugar* returned, he must include the appropriate postage. Richard's reply snidely requested that the novel be sent "to me in the cheapest way possible and bill me for the postage."

The Grove Press contract for *Trout Fishing in America* expired on July 22. Nine days later, the publishers' option period for *The Abortion* also came to an end. Brautigan had no word from Grove for three long weeks. During this time, he pondered his options, consulting with Don Carpenter and Michael McClure about all the various possibilities. On August 24, Richard wrote to Barney Rosset, terminating any future business relationship. "Grove's lack of interest in honoring the thirty-day decision paragraph in its December 3, 1965 letter to me has forced me to seek another publisher for my work."

The same day, Richard posted a letter to Donald Hutter at Scribner's. Under separate cover, he mailed the editor copies of *In Watermelon Sugar* and *The Abortion*. His letter said the new book "looks good to me. It is a novel utilizing the contemporary energies of California." Richard went on to say that he had always "admired Scribners [*sic*] as a publisher" and had been "encouraged" by Hutter's initial reaction to his writing. Brautigan hoped that "something can come from it."

In the beginning of September, a postcard arrived from France. Tom Clark, a young American poet currently residing in Brightlingsea, Essex, England, had Brautigan's address from Joanne Kyger. He was editing a serial magazine whose title altered slightly with each issue (*Once, Twice, Thrice, Vice, Slice, Ice*). Clark was preparing *Nice*, the latest in the series, for publication, and having read and liked "The Menu" and the chapters from *Trout Fishing* in the *Evergreen Review*, he wondered if Richard might send him something he could use. Brautigan selected "The Armored Car," a surreal tale about his childhood paper route. He had written it during happier times with Janice a year or so before. The story was dedicated to her.

This submission remained a labor of love, as Brautigan knew acceptance brought no actual payment. Richard remained desperately poor that fall. Andrew Hoyem described him as "penniless" in his journal entry for September 10, after they dined together (Hoyem's treat) at Des Alpes, a family-style Basque restaurant on Broadway in North Beach. In return, Brautigan promised to try to get his friend a reading at the Rhymers Club. Two days before, Richard mailed his short story "$\frac{1}{3}$, $\frac{1}{3}$, $\frac{1}{3}$" off to Charles Newman at *TriQuarterly*. He hoped for a quick sale.

The same day, Brautigan sent a copy of *Trout Fishing* to Donald Hutter at Scribner's. Now the editor had all three of the author's unpublished novels in hand. Financial necessity often provides a fertile breeding ground for innovation, and in his cover letter, Richard suggested an idea that demonstrated his uncanny perception regarding the marketing of his material. "What about putting all my novels together as one book?" he wrote. "I think it might be a good way of doing it." Brautigan was years ahead of his time.

By September of 1966, the counterculture community of the Haight-Ashbury had taken on all the aspects, both good and bad, that intense media attention soon would make intimately familiar to the world at large. Hip shops had proliferated throughout the district. Drugs (pot, speed, and acid) were sold openly on the street. The burgeoning population and subsequent housing shortage resulted in overcrowding and ever-escalating rents. Many of the newcomers were destitute and homeless. Panhandling became an everyday problem. In spite of these troubles, a feeling of utopian optimism prevailed. The Age of Aquarius waited just around the corner.

A unique newspaper heralded the arrival of this psychedelic paradise. On Tuesday, September 20, the premier issue of the *City of San Francisco Oracle* appeared in the Haight. Bankrolled by Ron Thelin and edited by a short, bearded poet named Allen Cohen (with the assistance of Michael Bowen, a visionary painter whose studio served as an early office for the paper) the *Oracle*, with its swirling rainbow-hued headlines, looked utterly unlike any other journal on earth.

Volume 1, number 1, contained an article on the Provos, a Dutch anarchist group dedicated to revolutionizing contemporary consciousness. Among their civic activities, the Provos had gathered a number of used bicycles, painted them white, and distributed them across Amsterdam. The bikes were free for anyone to use. You simply pedaled to your destination and left the bicycle on the sidewalk for whoever needed it next.

Emmett Grogan had no love for the *Oracle*, which he felt "catered to the new, hip moneyed class," but found much to admire in the stories concerning "the 'Beatnik-Anarchist Provos' in Holland." Grogan's longtime friend Billy Murcott, "the one he called 'the genius,'" had arrived in Frisco from New York at the beginning of August, and the two often joined in after-hours political bull-sessions around a jug of cheap Cribari wine with Peter Berg, Bill Fritsch, Peter Coyote, Kent Minault, and various other Mime Troupe members. These discussions dealt with the new freedom to which young people aspired. All agreed that "one could only be free by drawing the line and living outside the profit, private property, and power premises of Western culture." Gerrard Winstanley and the Digger rebellion became their model for achieving such lofty goals.

Many in the Haight community espoused universal LSD use as path to utopian ideals. Michael Bowen, busted along with Tim Leary at Millbrook earlier in the year by G. Gordon Liddy (then an assistant DA in Poughkeepsie), had earned the sobriquet "psychedelic ranger-man" for his efforts at turning on the world. Although they both enjoyed getting high, Emmett Grogan and Billy Murcott (Grogan's "almost invisible companion") envisioned a different solution. Toward the end of September, they started sneaking into the SDS office next door to the Mime Troupe loft late at night and appropriating the mimeograph machine to get their message out. The handbills the two ran off surreptitiously were the first of what later came to be known as the "Digger Papers." As Grogan explained in *Ringolevio*, his fictionalized autobiography, "the Papers were an attempt to antagonize the street people into an awareness of the absolute bullshit implicit in the psychedelic transcendentalism promoted by the self-proclaimed, media-fabricated shamans who espoused the tune-in, turn-on, drop-out, jerk-off ideology of Leary and Alpert."

At the end of September, Grogan and Murcott, the anonymous Digger duo, had published at least three of their confrontational Papers. Their ferocious honesty and surrealist verve captured Richard Brautigan's imagination, distracting him from the everyday scramble of trying to earn a living. Tom Clark wrote from England. He liked "The Armored Car" a lot and was including it in *Nice*. The payment was two copies of the magazine. Clark mentioned that he was also "sometimes" poetry editor of the *Paris Review* ("—I mean I suggest poems they sometimes use—"). He asked Richard to send him any "uncommitted" chapters from *Trout Fishing* and said he'd pass them along to "the bigger editors." Clark received no salary, but contributors were paid between $100 and $150. Brautigan mailed him a couple chapters the next day.

When the managing editor of *TriQuarterly* wrote to say that "A Short History of Religion in California" would be reprinted in a magazine called the *Humanist*, Richard answered with a request that he be paid for the second serial rights. When he heard back, it was bad news. Since Brautigan hadn't stipulated any retention of second serial rights, *TriQuarterly* retained stewardship of the copyright. No payment was forthcoming, as the magazine had received none. On the bright side, Brautigan's story picked up ten thousand new readers.

A letter from Donald Hutter dashed all hopes of a sale at Scribner's. Hutter had read *The Abortion*, and although he thought it the best of the three Brautigan manuscripts and admired the "lovely, consistent quality," in the end he felt "a sense of slightness, a feeling of scale too modest and ephemeral for hopes of impressing a general readership." Following this rebuke, Hutter admitted other publishers might not agree with his opinion and offered "to forward the manuscripts to another house." Richard wrote back, asking that the novels be sent over to Charlotte Mayerson at Holt, Rinehart & Winston.

Amid the rioting and curfews following a fatal shooting in Hunters Point, Ken Kesey returned from Mexico, "as salt in J. Edgar Hoover's wounds." He turned up at Stewart Brand's "Awareness Festival" at San Francisco State, flanked by a bodyguard phalanx of Hells Angels. The word was out: "Kesey's back." Five days later, at the time of a full moon, LSD possession became illegal under California law. The date, 10/6/66, caused many in the Haight to think ominous thoughts. The number of the Beast of the Apocalypse in the Book of Revelations was 666.

What a bummer! To exorcize the demons, Michael Bowen and Allen Cohen had planned a big celebration for the sixth that they called the "Love-Pageant Rally." The promotional leaflets the *Oracle* printed contained a "Prophecy of A Declaration of Independence" and urged participants to "Bring the color Gold, bring photos of personal saints and gurus and heros of the underground . . . bring children . . . flowers . . . flutes . . . drums . . . feathers . . . bands . . . beads . . ."

At two in the afternoon, seven or eight hundred new age citizens trooped into the Panhandle waving banners and flags, beating drums and tambourines, joyously blowing trombones, tubas, and conch shells. A flatbed truck, newly painted red, served as a stage for the musicians. Three bands, Wildflower, Big Brother, and the Dead, played that afternoon while the assembly of free spirits danced with frenzied abandon under the eucalyptus trees. As Charles Perry observed in his history of the Haight-Ashbury: "It was one of those ideas people had been waiting for, like the Family Dog dances or the Trips Festival; a gathering to bear witness to the psychedelic life [. . .]"

The multihued Prankster bus stood parked nearby on a street flanking the Panhandle, flying a marijuana leaf flag designed by Mouse (Stanley Miller), the poster artist. Its owner, Ken Kesey, put in a brief appearance but split well before an undercover narc hopped on board asking to see him. The press was everywhere, reporters scribbling notes and five television film crews poking their cameras into the festivities, but the Love Pageant ended up not being the big underground story of the day. After all was said and done, Kesey stole the headlines in the *Chronicle*. In an "exclusive interview" with Donovan Bess, the fugitive talked about life on the lam and revealed his plans for an "LSD Graduation Ceremony" to be held at Winterland on Halloween night. Captain Trips upped the ante once again.

Michael Bowen and Allen Cohen watched the event from a vantage point on Clayton Street. The *Oracle* editors took pride in their achievement. Richard Alpert, Leary's former colleague, came walking by, and Bowen waved him over to ask what he thought of it all. Alpert agreed that the rally was a great success. Allen Cohen suggested staging another similar gathering and wondered what Alpert would call it.

"It's just being," Dick Alpert said. "Humans being. Being together."

"Yeah," said Bowen. "It's a Human Be-In."

Later that night, Bowen and Cohen elaborated on this notion in the "meditation room" at the rear of Bowen's apartment. Plans began to coalesce for a huge public event, something way bigger than the Love-Pageant Rally, a "gathering of the tribes." Over in Berkeley, Emmett Grogan and Billy Murcott appeared in a weeklong Mime Troupe coffeehouse production of *In-Put, Out-Put*, a one-act "comedy-farce" written and directed by Peter Berg. The short run ended about the same time as their unemployment checks. Dead broke, Grogan saw nothing "soulful about panhandling." He resolved to find a way to improve their sorry situation while at the same time benefiting the common good.

Billy Murcott owned a '55 Ford station wagon, and the two men drove to the San Francisco Produce Market on the edge of town. In an hour's time, Emmett's fluent Italian and his experience as a kid in New York City working with an uncle who trucked wholesale produce in Greenwich Village resulted in a jalopy packed with crates of food. Back at Grogan's apartment around eight in the morning, the pair transformed their haul, "tomatoes, turnips, green beans, cauliflower, Brussels sprouts, onions, eggplant, squash, potatoes," and fifty pounds of poultry parts into an enormous stew, using two purloined twenty-gallon milk cans as kettles.

By early afternoon, Billy worked the street, handing out several hundred newly mimeographed leaflets: "FREE FOOD GOOD HOT STEW RIPE TOMATOES FRESH FRUIT BRING A BOWL AND SPOON TO THE PANHANDLE AT ASHBURY STREET 4PM 4PM 4PM 4PM 4PM FREE FOOD EVERYDAY FREE FOOD IT'S FREE BECAUSE IT'S YOURS! the diggers."

Billy and Emmett drove over to the Panhandle and set two steaming milk cans of stew and cartons of ripe tomatoes and fruit on the grass just before four, a block from where the Love Pageant revelers had frolicked. A hungry crowd of fifty stood around waiting, and an equal number soon showed up, tin bowls dangling from their belts. For the next week, Murcott and Grogan hustled wilted produce and day-old bread, boiled forty gallons of stew, and provided free food in the Panhandle every afternoon at four. This turned out to be very hard work as well as a brilliant bit of political street theater. Grogan and Murcott's Mime Troupe compatriots all felt attracted to the project. Peter Berg loved the idea. "Try to keep it going for another week, if you can," he enthused, "and you'll really get your point across."

Volunteer help was soon on the way. A group of young women, some sharing a Clayton Street apartment with a large kitchen, offered to assume the cooking chores. Mime Troupers took over daily delivery of the food to the Panhandle in a yellow VW bus known throughout the neighborhood as the yellow submarine. Blessed with considerable charm and guile, Emmett Grogan continued rounding up the discarded produce every morning.

Two weeks later, Berkeley's left-of-center underground newspaper, the *Barb*, ran "a quasi-journalistic story" on the free Digger Feeds written by none other than Emmett Grogan, who signed himself "George Metevsky," an allusion to George Metesky, the infamous "Mad Bomber" who terrorized New York City a decade earlier. About the same time, Billy Murcott "hustled some dough" and Grogan rented a one-story six-car garage on Page Street. The place was stacked inside with old window frames in various sizes. The Diggers nailed them to the wooden front of the garage and gave the establishment a name: the Free Frame of Reference.

Murcott bolted four two-by-fours together, creating a thirteen-foot-square aperture taller than the former garage it leaned against. Painted a bright golden orange by Emmett Grogan and dubbed the "Frame of Reference," the structure was carried over to the Panhandle every day at four o'clock and propped upright between twin oak trees. When the cans of food arrived, everyone waiting to eat had first to step through the frame before being served, all performers in an elaborate piece of street theater.

Richard Brautigan began hanging out with Emmett Grogan and the Diggers. He took note of Grogan's angry poetic broadsides, the audacious food program, and the opening of the Free Frame of Reference. From its inception, the Diggers' free-for-all emporium became a magnet not just for the needy but also for anyone curious about the mechanics of social change.

Abbie Hoffman visited, taking note of the Diggers' tactics for his own later use in highly publicized political shenanigans. (In August the following year, Hoffman identified himself to the press as "a Digger" after throwing dollar bills onto the floor of the New York Stock Exchange.) Allen Ginsberg showed up a bit later after the Free Frame relocated to Frederick Street, bringing Timothy Leary and Richard Alpert. A group of young runaways chanted "You don't turn us on!" at them.

When Paul Krassner, irreverent editor of the *Realist* (the first true underground publication) came to Frisco, a visit to the Free Frame of Reference stood high on his itinerary. The store, like the food program, was a radical political statement. Everything in it was free. People took whatever they wanted. Whenever anyone asked who was in charge, the answer was always, "You are." Ever the skeptic, Krassner maintained the free store was nothing more than old-fashioned "social work." One of the Diggers told him to give Emmett Grogan ten bucks to see the difference. Nearly always broke himself, Paul offered up a sawbuck, and Grogan immediately set it on fire with his cigarette lighter.

This sort of outrageous gesture tickled Richard Brautigan's fancy. It wasn't long before he established a strong connection with the revolutionary group. Keith Abbott was puzzled by his friend's link to the Diggers. He wrote that their "anarchism attracted him the most, but he admired their public idealism, too." Keith recalled a day when Brautigan asked to borrow both him and his truck to run a Digger errand. Richard regaled him with a story about "a socialite woman" who came by the Free Frame of Reference to make a donation. Brautigan pantomimed all the parts as he told Keith how the wealthy woman wrote a check and handed it to Emmett Grogan, who promptly tore it to pieces. Abbott learned later that Richard had not actually witnessed this event. "Typical of Richard's involvement with the Diggers, which was fueled by equal parts of fantasy, idealism and self-promotion."

Brautigan needed Abbott's truck to pick up a load of pants. When the Diggers wouldn't take her check, the socialite asked what else she might provide. "Clothing," Grogan told her. She arranged for a shipment of factory seconds to be delivered to her address. Richard and Keith drove to her palatial Jackson Street home and picked up the bulky garment cartons, trucking them to the Diggers' free store. The goods didn't last long. Keith Abbott remembered "the word got out on the street, the hustlers descended, and armloads of pants were hauled off, probably for resale in Golden Gate Park."

Jack Thibeau recalled visiting the Free Frame of Reference with Brautigan and Ianthe. They encountered a group of hippies carelessly throwing the free clothing around the store. Offhand remarks revealed the "shoppers" planned on taking the best of the donated goods over to the park and selling them to newly arrived runaways. "You know, Ianthe," Brautigan told his daughter, "I don't like these people because they don't have any manners."

"He had a thing about manners," Jack recalled.

Richard was attracted to the Diggers as much by Emmett Grogan's style and panache as the social causes he espoused. Grogan liked that Brautigan referred to his poems as "tidbits." Their friendship developed at a time when Richard and Erik Weber "were pretty close." Too poor to afford a television, Brautigan brought various members of the Diggers over to Weber's place. Erik's TV provided a big attraction for the Diggers. "They would always come over to watch themselves on the news."

Price Dunn met Emmett Grogan at Richard's Geary Street apartment. "I immediately recognized him for what he was," Dunn recalled. "A real street-smart hustler, a con man—a real opportunist." Price and Emmett were both larger-than-life figures, rival cocks in the barnyard, but the Confederate General "didn't have anything much to say" on the occasion of their initial meeting. Price remained friendly and listened as Grogan outlined his utopian ideals, noting that Richard had fallen "under his spell." Later, talking it over with Brautigan, Dunn maintained that the Digger philosophy was "totally contrary" to their shared values. How was it possible to get something for nothing? "You believe in work," Price said to Richard, "and I do, too."

Early in October, at Don Carpenter's suggestion, Richard Brautigan got in touch with Robert P. Mills, Don's New York literary agent. He sent several reviews of *Confederate General* with a letter providing a career background. "If all three of the novels were published together as a single book it would give a better picture of what I'm trying to do," he wrote. Mills responded immediately, impressed with the reviews. The agent promised a decision once he had read Richard's manuscripts.

Other correspondence involved Tom Clark and writer David Sandberg, who lived under the redwoods in Boulder Creek near Santa Cruz with his girlfriend, Phoebe. Sandberg, thought by some to be "suicidal," owned a reputation as a consummate hustler. Once, he and a friend stripped an abandoned sports car and trucked the parts to San Francisco for resale. Another time, David and Phoebe convinced their parents back east that they planned on getting married in a traditional Jewish ceremony. Checks and gifts flowed in. It was all a ruse. The marriage never transpired.

David Sandberg had edited a single issue of a mimeograph magazine called, variously, *Or*, *O'er*, *Oar*, or *Awwrrrr* and was "looking forward to getting 2 or three poems from [Brautigan] in my morning mail delight" for the forthcoming *OR2*. Richard, chagrined to find himself thirty-one years of age, sent a humorous poem he'd recently written about his nose growing older, along with two others. Sandberg connected with Richard's work. Sometime in the fall he embarked on a project to republish *The Galilee Hitch-Hiker*, out of print for nearly a decade.

Tom Clark wrote to say copies of *Nice* were on their way. Lawrence Bensky, editor of the *Paris Review*, ("he, too, is crazy, unfortunately"), sent back the chapters from *Trout Fishing*, and Clark wanted to print them in *Spice*, which he'd be editing "before long." Richard thanked him and asked for the return of his manuscripts. Tom Clark's magazine arrived the third week of November, and Richard mailed a copy to Janice, his final gift the story in it dedicated to her.

October 20, one half hour after a prerecorded interview was broadcast over a local station, authorities spotted Ken Kesey in a bright red truck, heading south with the afternoon rush hour on the Bayshore Freeway. Apprehended after a chase (including "a brief run on foot"), Kesey soon got out on bail and announced his Halloween Acid Test Graduation would go on as scheduled. At the last minute, Bill Graham changed his mind, denying the Pranksters the use of Winterland for their festivities. Kesey scaled back his plans and held the graduation at the Calliope Warehouse, south of Market on Harriet Street. To Emmett Grogan, "after the hoopla died down" it didn't amount to much more than a "by-invitation-only, private party [. . .] with a lot of booze and plenty of group analysis."

The Diggers threw a Halloween party of their own out on the streets, calling it Full Moon Public Celebration. They passed out fifteen hundred leaflets advertising the event and carried the wooden Frame of Reference over to the corner of Haight and Ashbury, where it leaned against a lamppost. The Digger women, Phyllis, Natural Suzanne, Nina, Sam, Judy, Mona, and Julie, made several dozen yellow three-inch wooden squares, passing them among a gathering crowd soon grown to six hundred. Look through the tiny aperture and change your reference point. Many wore the little frames on cords around their necks like medallions.

The Mime Troupers showed up with two eight-foot puppets made by Roberto La Morticella, the stocky bearded sculptor who called himself La Mortadella. It took two men to manipulate each puppet. Grogan and Peter Berg, Brooks Butcher and Kent Minault worked the controls. Using the Frame of Reference as a makeshift proscenium, they performed a playlet called "Any Fool on the Street." When the police arrived to break up the crowd, a disturbance ensued and five Diggers were arrested.

The quintet (Grogan, Berg, Minault, Butcher, and La Mortadella) appeared before a judge on November 27, and the case was dismissed. On their way out, a newspaper photographer asked to take a picture on the Hall of Justice steps. The Mime Troupers all struck extravagant poses, hamming it up for the press. The next morning, the photo ran on the front page of the *Chronicle*. Emmett Grogan upstaged all the others, sauntering toward the lens, tweed cap at a rakish angle, cigarette dangling from his smirk, forefingers raised in the backward "V," meaning "Up yours!"

Another actor, Ronald Reagan, the former movie star, had been elected governor of California on the eighth of November. A week later, the Psych Shop got busted for pornography (*Oracle* editor Allen Cohen manning the cash register), and copies of Lenore Kandel's book of poetry, *The Love Book*, were seized. While the case against Michael McClure's *The Beard* moved sluggishly through the court system, the poet made music with an outlaw biker. "Freewheelin' Frank" Reynolds, secretary of the Frisco Chapter of the Hells Angels, played harmonica. McClure whanged on his autoharp. He and Frank made the music scene with various groups around the Bay Area, while McClure wrote Reynolds's as-told-to "autobiography."

Richard Brautigan sent a letter to Bob Sherrill at *Esquire*, telling him of McClure's project. "I think the results of this collaboration will be very important [. . .]" Always quick to plug a pal, Richard called his friend "one of the finest poets and playwrights in America." Michael's autoharp playing challenged Brautigan to keep on writing songs of his own.

Late one night early in November, a friend came over to Geary Street with a tape recorder and Richard sat down in front of the mike with his guitar to cut a few tracks for posterity. He wasn't much on technique, tunelessly strumming the same three chords for every song. Brautigan's lyrics possessed a blatant deadpan monotone banality. In a song about riding his horse "to the break in the road," the third verse mournfully begins, "Only got half a horse now." Another song consisted entirely of the word "Hello," sung over and over.

Here are the complete lyrics of two brief Brautigan songs: "Don't touch what you can't see or you might cease to be, / Look around the corner twice; / Turn the light on three times," and "I've been in Idaho. / Drove one afternoon from Rocky Bar to Atlanta, / Had a piece of pie and some coffee / In a café in Atlanta, Idaho."

At times, Richard played for his friends. Joanne Kyger recalled a lengthy party over on Lyon Street at the home of painter Bill McNeill when Brautigan "strummed the guitar and made up very long and winding, aimless songs."

Among the listeners was Helen Adam, the Scottish-born poet whose work in the ballad form impressed Robert Duncan. She had published three books of poetry before moving to the United States in 1939. With her sister, Pat, she wrote *The City Is Burning*, a play adapted into the successful musical *San Francisco's Burning*. "Oh, that one was lovely," Helen Adam said as Richard came to the end of yet another monotone melody. "Can you play that one about grasses on the lawn again?" But the song was lost, an ephemeral bit of improvisation gone in the moment.

Another evening, Keith Abbott remembered Joanne Kyger asking Brautigan, "Richard, whatever happened to your guitar?" Brautigan seemed "extremely embarrassed," Abbott said, "and tried to shut Joanne up," saying he didn't want to talk about that phase of his life. Richard got rid of his guitar not long after the impromptu recording session. Ianthe has no memory of ever seeing the instrument in the apartment once she started spending weekends at Daddy's place.

On the cold November night Brautigan made his tape recording, he had plenty of reasons to sing the blues. Charlotte Mayerson had written asking for more time to reread Brautigan's manuscripts, but in the end Holt, Rinehart and Winston rejected all three novels. Mayerson praised his "writing ability" and "flashes of marvelous humor and style" but called *In Watermelon Sugar* "mannered and 'writy'" and thought *The Abortion* "too derivative of the kind of atmosphere that we've seen so often in Saroyan-like books."

Donald Allen had a friend, a successful attorney, who established the Four Seasons Foundation to publish contemporary writers, particularly the work of San Franciscans. In his new capacity as Four Seasons' editor and publisher, Allen had at last found a vehicle to validate his early enthusiasm for *Trout Fishing in America*. He got in touch with Richard, offering to publish the novel in the coming year.

Soon after that, Richard's friends Bill Brown and Jim Koller got into the act by suggesting they bring out an edition of *In Watermelon Sugar* under their Coyote Books imprint. They had published Philip Whalen, and books by Michael McClure were in the works. At first, Richard resisted the idea. He had a New York agent. Sooner or later, Bob Mills was bound to make a score. Koller and Brown upped the ante, proposing an additional volume of Brautigan's poetry.

Richard, always slow to make decisions, continued dragging his heels. Bill Brown sealed the deal by mailing Brautigan a card quoting a recent Philip Whalen letter: "Coyote would be performing a Great Service Etc. if they would publish THE COLLECTED POEMS OF RICHARD BRAUTIGAN. Dick is a better poet than anyone wants to allow. His books of poetry are all unobtainable—& all of them are very good." Flattery did the trick. Richard agreed to the offer

from Coyote Books. Both publications were to be pilot editions with Brautigan retaining all subsidiary, reprint, and option rights. The arrangement called for the size of the editions to be limited
to a few thousand copies. Richard would receive a straight 10 percent commission on all sales.

At the end of November, Brautigan mailed *The Abortion* to literary agent Robert P. Mills,
saying that he thought it was the only one of his books "that stands a chance right now in New
York." Three days later, Richard heard back from *Esquire*. Bob Sherrill was "fed up with Angels
long ago." Even so, the magazine was running a piece on the motorcycle gang in January. No more
room for Freewheelin' Frank. Sherrill was open to seeing more ideas from Richard and Michael
McClure. Brautigan suggested he and McClure interview Governor-Elect Ronald Reagan. They did
not get the assignment.

For Thanksgiving, the Diggers hustled up twenty donated turkeys (getting them all roasted in
kitchen ovens located across the Haight-Ashbury). They threw a big free feed with all the trimmings
(the "Meatfeast") at the garage on Page Street. The next Monday, Grogan and his pals (identified
neither as Diggers nor Mime Troupers) made the front page of the *Chronicle*.

On the last day of November, Ken Kesey went on trial for his January pot bust and for violat-
ing the terms of his probation. He faced an imposition of his full three-year sentence for the first
charge and an automatic nickel with no parole added on for the second offense. It looked like the
Captain would be spending his next several Thanksgivings in the slammer.

Rain canceled the Diggers' Death of Money and Rebirth of the Haight Parade on December 3
and again when it was rescheduled for a week later. When they finally got their show on the road
the next Friday, it turned out to be a bright, clear day. Around five in the afternoon, the Diggers
started handing out party favors along Haight Street: flowers, candles, penny whistles, two hundred car mirrors liberated from the junkyard, lollipops, incense, and a thousand posters the size of
bumper stickers with the word "NOW!" printed in red letters six inches high.

Young women clad in bedsheet togas gave away hundreds of white lilies. A crowd of about a
thousand gathered for the parade. Richard Brautigan stood tall among them, conspicuous in his
high-crowned felt hat and peacoat. Michael McClure was in the crowd, wearing shades and strumming his autoharp, accompanied by his Hells Angel buddy, Freewheelin' Frank, on tambourine.
The obscenity charges against *The Beard* had been dropped the previous week.

Three hooded figures carrying a silver-painted dollar sign led the unofficial procession, followed by a black-robed surrogate priest waving a glowing Coleman lantern. Behind them marched
four Mime Trouper pallbearers draped in black and wearing huge helmet-like animal head masks
designed by La Mortadella. They bore a coffin covered with black cloth and filled with large
symbolic coins. The crowd, grown to almost four thousand, spilled off the sidewalk and into the
street, blocking traffic. The driver of a stalled Muni bus stepped out and danced with a young girl
to much applause. Avoiding the throng and the traffic jam, the masked coffin-bearers at times were
compelled to parade along the sidewalk.

Emmett Grogan had invited the Frisco Hells Angels, and they rode their choppers down the
white line dividing opposing lanes of gridlocked traffic. At the head of the pack, a "NOW!" plac-
ard attached to the handlebars of his Harley, Angel "Hairy Henry" Kot, recently paroled after a
nine-year bit in San Quentin for armed robbery, grinned beneath his sweeping mustache like a
hirsute kid on Christmas morning. Phyllis Willner, a sixteen-year-old runaway who arrived in the
Haight a few months before with nothing but the clothes on her back, adopting the Diggers as her

new family the same day, stood on Kot's buddy seat wearing a homemade Supergirl costume and holding a "NOW!" sign high above her head. "*Freeeee!*" she wailed.

Right about this time the cops arrived. No permit had been applied for by the Diggers, and their demonstration was technically against the law. Those on the street were in no mood to end the celebration. "We will continue until the Diggers feel it beautiful to stop," one of the manifestos pledged. Six members of the tactical police force arrived in two black-and-whites and a paddy wagon. Two more motorcycle officers cruised down Haight Street on their three-wheelers, admonishing the crowd to break it up and go home. In response, the crowd chanted: "The streets belong to the people! The streets belong to the people!"

The police turned their attentions on Hairy Henry, citing him for a traffic violation for allowing Phyllis to stand on his machine while it was in motion. A routine check of his driver's license revealed Kot's parolee status, and he was immediately arrested. An argument ensued. As the officers attempted to force Kot into their paddy wagon, another gang member, "Chocolate George" Hendricks, came to the assistance of his beleaguered Angel brother. Soon, both men were locked behind the Black Maria's wire-mesh doors, charged with resisting arrest.

Ever since Kesey invited the Angels to his La Honda blast, an unspoken alliance had existed between the acidheads and the outlaw motorcycle riders. George, who gained his nickname from a fondness for chocolate milk, was particularly popular with the local street people. Peter Coyote recalled him as "a big, easygoing guy who liked to hold court in front of Tracy's Donut Shop." When word of Chocolate George's detention spread among the crowd, the Diggers redirected their march toward the Park Station, several blocks away. Chanting, "Free the Angels! We want Hairy Henry! We want Chocolate George!" a thousand people paraded down Stanyan Street and into Golden Gate Park.

Michael McClure marched at the head of the procession, clawing at his autoharp in the company of a young woman blowing a bugle and some guy in a clear plastic raincoat making noise on his harmonica. Richard Brautigan, a head taller than most of the crowd, trooped along with all the rest, several ranks back from his pal McClure. At the police station, the demonstrators encountered "scores of patrolmen" surrounding the building. The crowd lit candles and continued their enthusiastic chanting. Brautigan moved closer, behind Freewheelin' Frank, who sternly confronted a uniformed police officer.

When word came from the station house that bail had been set at $2,500, with 10 percent required to secure the men's release, a new chant went up among the hippie congregation: "Angels in jail, money for bail!" The masked pallbearers passed around the black-draped Death of Money coffin, and everyone gave what he or she could, tossing bills and coins inside. Even the cops chipped in, and bail was quickly raised.

Pete Knell, Frisco chapter president, was pleasantly surprised when the money was handed over. Emmett Grogan observed, "The people had never stood up for the Hells Angels before." Knell shouted his thanks to the crowd and headed downtown to post bond, accompanied by his ragtag brotherhood and many of the marchers. Chocolate George was released that night. Because of his parole status, Hairy Henry was detained in the city prison without bail until his case was heard weeks later.

In the second week of December, Brautigan heard from Bob Mills in New York. The agent had read *The Abortion* and liked it "very much indeed." He agreed to represent the book and proposed sending it on to Dan Wickenden, Don Carpenter's editor at Harcourt, Brace. Richard was very pleased to have this news. Another pleasurable moment in December came with the publication of the second edition of *The Galilee Hitch-hiker*, out of print for eight years. Described as "an or book published by David Sandberg," the slim volume was actually the work of Clifford Burke, called "one of the finest, and arguably the most influential, Bay Area printers of the '60s." Burke ran his Cranium Press out of a garage at 642 Shrader Street in the outer Fillmore. He set Brautigan's nine-part poem in letterpress and printed it as a folio on fine watermarked paper.

The red cover reproduced the Kenn Davis illustration from the first edition. All in all, the book was a simple affair, the signatures stitched together by hand. It sold for seventy-five cents a copy. Sixteen copies were numbered and signed by Brautigan in blue pencil on the verso of the title page, accompanied by his primitive drawing of a fish. A number of unbound sheets were left over after the book's production, and Brautigan gave these away on the streets of San Francisco.

David Sandberg's mimeo-magazine, *O'er #2*, also made its appearance in December of 1966. It was printed on pages of different-colored construction paper and contained three of Richard Brautigan's poems. The one worrying about his nose growing older expressed a genuine concern. When an editor from *TriQuarterly* wrote asking for his help on a projected issue featuring writers and artists under the age of thirty, Richard wistfully replied, "Gee, it's kind of sad to realize that I ain't under 30 any more." He supplied the names of several friends: Ron Loewinsohn (twenty-nine), Erik Weber (twenty-six), Keith Abbott (twenty-two), Steve Carey (twenty-one), and Jeffrey Sheppard, a seventeen-year-old poet to whom Brautigan had recently dedicated "Hey! This Is What It's All About," a bitterly ironic poem about his lack of fame, fortune, and a love life.

Four days before Christmas, Richard Brautigan gave two poetry readings (at 9:00 PM and 11:00 PM) at the Coffee Gallery in North Beach. There was no admission charge. William "Tumbleweed" Fritsch, Allen Dienstag, and Andrew Hoyem also shared the bill. Brautigan and Hoyem had both been invited to be poets-in-residence at the California Institute of Technology in Pasadena for part of the coming month.

The invitation came by way of John F. Crawford, an instructor in the English department, who was collaborating with Hoyem on a new translation of the Middle English poem *Pearl*, which Grabhorn-Hoyem planned to publish as a limited edition in 1967. With this recognition and the planned publication of two novels, the fast-approaching New Year should have shone bright with promise. On Christmas Day, Richard Brautigan wrote, "I am desolate in dimension / circling the sky / like a rainy bird, / wet from toe to crown / wet from bill to wing."

The Diggers supplied enough turkeys to feed five hundred people at the Hamilton Methodist Church on Christmas Eve. This produced the first mention of the Diggers in the establishment press. Ralph Gleason advertised the event ("Christmas Eve for Hippies") in his *Chronicle* column. Perhaps this was unwanted publicity. On December 27, city building inspectors cited the garage on Page Street for two violations of the Health and Safety Code. The Diggers quickly stripped the place, and the next day the officials broke the huge Frame of Reference apart and used the lumber to board up the free store.

twenty-six: rx: dr. leary

"T UNE IN! TURN on! Drop out!" By 1966, Timothy Leary's slacker slogan had resonated out of Harvard Square, sending psychedelic shock waves across American
campuses as it amplified into a national mantra for disenchanted youth. Media hype
elevated the former professor from discredited crackpot to pop guru. In December of 1966, Leary
paid a visit to San Francisco. He was on the road with *Death of the Mind*, his LSD-influenced
stage adaptation of Hermann Hesse's *Steppenwolf*. Around this same time, Dr. Leary encountered
Richard Brautigan at a social gathering in Berkeley.

Brautigan had no interest in LSD and had never dropped acid. "I figure I'm crazy enough,"
he said. "I don't need to test it." His conspicuous involvement with the Diggers made him an
honorary counterculture celebrity and allowed entrée to the inner sanctum of a world where Tim
Leary reigned as one of the principal proselytizing prophets. Always a curious bystander, Richard
possessed a keen interest in observing the charismatic few who marched at the head of the parade.
Drawn into Leary's orbit, Brautigan fell under the spell of the eternal missionary.

One afternoon the following week, Richard and Price Dunn shared a bottle of red wine at the
Geary Street apartment. Slyly and without comment, Brautigan "pulls out this little pouch and
pulls out these papers."

"I'll be Goddamned," Price Dunn said. "What in hell are you doing?" He had not seen Richard
with marijuana since the time he turned him on in Big Sur a decade earlier.

"I met Tim Leary," Brautigan replied, adroitly dramatizing the moment, "and he gave it to me."

Price looked on in amazement. "Richard is rolling a joint," he recalled, "and I couldn't believe
this, and I said, 'God, a disciple of the guru.'"

Richard Brautigan fired up the reefer, doing his best not to cough. He passed the joint to Price,
telling him how he planned to see Timothy Leary again soon. Price roared with laughter. Another
convert. "You son of a bitch," he said. "I can't believe this."

At the same time, word went out on the street that the heat was on. The police were arresting
people for pot possession. Brautigan's paranoia got the best of him. He feared his public involvement with the Haight-Ashbury scene might point a finger his way. He didn't want any dope lying
around his apartment, so he went next door to visit Erik Weber. "He came downstairs with his
stash," Erik recalled, "and told me he wanted me to hide it because he was afraid that the cops
were going to bust him." A few days later, Richard retrieved his celebrity contraband.

Price Dunn recollected his friend's temporary conversion. "We went down on the North Beach
and went to a few places, and Richard had that little pouch, and that lasted about a week, and
then finally one day he walked in and pulled it out, and I started laughing, and he says, 'Oh, shit.'"

Richard joined his friend's laughter, tossing down what was left of Tim Leary's lid onto the kitchen table. "That's more like it," Price shouted. "What are you pretending?"

"You're right," Richard said. "Whiskey is my drink." As a reaffirmation, he poured himself a big glass of Laphroaig, the smoky single malt from the Isle of Skye. The bottle had been a gift from Price. Brautigan savored a potent swallow. It was his farewell to pot. He never smoked the stuff again.

THE NAMBU 6.5 mm light machine gun weighed twenty pounds and in working condition fired 550 rounds per minute. It was Japan's main light weapon for use in jungle warfare and had a distinctive look with a steel bipod supporting the long thin ribbed barrel and a knurled wooden grip (dainty as the handle of a teakettle) mounted in front of the up-curving thirty-round magazine. The grip, curiously old-fashioned in appearance, allowed the Japanese soldier to pick up the Nambu like a suitcase. It was handy under fire when it came time to hustle, and the weapon smoldered in the hell-furnace of combat. A suitcase looks as incongruous on the battlefield as a machine gun does in a living room. Precisely why Richard Brautigan chose the Nambu as his interior decorating centerpiece. It took a visitor by surprise, like one of his metaphors.

This particular piece of war surplus first turned up sometime in 1967 in the basement of an old industrial building south of Market. Kendrick Rand came with his friend Alvin Duskin, who was looking for a space to locate his garment business. The building had been vacant for years. They poked around, checking things out. Duskin had an option to lease the place. Down in the basement, they found the Japanese machine gun just "sitting there" in the middle of "a whole bunch of stuff" like some prehistoric creature crouching alone in the darkness. "So strange," Kendrick Rand remembered.

The antique weapon had languished in the cellar for a long, long time. Rendered inoperable by molten lead poured down the barrel, the valiant old Nambu had become just another bit of abandoned rusting junk. Nobody wanted it. A pacifist at heart, Alvin Duskin expressed little interest in the machine gun but, sensing his friend's excitement, said: "Why don't you take it?" Kendrick picked it up by the curious handle and carried the disabled machine gun away.

What happened to the Nambu next remains uncertain. Kendrick never brought it home. His son, Christopher, was "enamored with such things" but had no memory of ever seeing it back then. Rand probably hauled the gun over to the Minimum Daily Requirement, his place in North Beach. From there, it disappeared into the Frisco poetry scene for a couple of months. Ginsberg was said to have owned the Nambu for a time. Also Lew Welch. Michael McClure denied the rumor that he had once possessed the machine gun. Eventually, it turned up in the hands of Richard Brautigan, who placed it dead center in his front room and painted the outline of a fish on the floor around it.

The Nambu sat there gathering dust and comments for another year or so. It provided ample opportunity for Brautigan to repeat his story of how he learned to read as a small child when he spotted a newspaper headline announcing the bombing of Pearl Harbor. The machine gun also illustrated Richard's theory of why the Japanese lost World War II. Because the Nambu's barrel tended to heat up and warp after a couple thousand rapid rounds had been shot through it, the design allowed for it to be removed and replaced. With the handle welded to the barrel, only six or so fitted into a box one man could carry. The machine guns used by American and Australian troops had removable screw-on handles, allowing twenty barrels to be packed into each wooden crate, giving the Allies a tactical advantage. According to Brautigan, this cost the Japanese the war.

Michael McClure later wrote that the first thing he remembered connecting Richard to guns was "when he was beginning to get goofy with drinking and success and he gave Gary Snyder a broken, vintage Japanese machine gun for his son Kai. 'So he won't lose his Japanese heritage,' said Richard."

Christopher Rand was nine or ten at the time. "Gary was living just outside of Muir Woods," he remembered, "and also was putting together his place up in the Sierras. I was with my mother over visiting him one afternoon and he was just loading up, getting ready to go to the Sierras, loading a bunch of tools into the back of his truck, and lo and behold, he brings out of his shop this machine gun and loads it in."

Not knowing the amazing exotic weapon had ever belonged to his father, Christopher asked Gary Snyder what he planned to do with it. The poet explained he was taking the Nambu up to "Kitkitdizze" in the mountains for a burial ceremony under the pines. The tools of war laid to rest in a Zen peace ritual. Hearing this, Chris grew frantic. He couldn't imagine such a wondrous treasure stuck away forever under the ground. "So, I pestered him and finally he gave it to me."

The Rands had an apartment on Telegraph Hill, and Christopher brought the machine gun back to the city. One day, Richard Brautigan paid a visit and spotted the Nambu. He badly wanted it back. Knowing Christopher was completely into building rockets, "incredible rockets," Richard offered a bribe. Two hundred bucks' worth of rocket gear for the gun. Chris held his ground. Over time it became something of an ongoing gag. Richard forever upping the ante and the stoic little boy refusing temptation. When the Rand family quit the city and moved out to their summer place in Stinson Beach around 1970 or 1971, the Nambu went along with them. "My friends and I would play war games," Christopher recalled, "dig a big foxhole and have the machine gun, and tourists would go by on the beach and see us playing and be kind of . . . dismayed."

The Nambu remained one of Christopher Rand's favorite possessions. He kept it into adulthood, wrapped in plastic and safely stored. In the summer of 1984, he was living in Bolinas and working over at Lucasfilm. One night, he ran into Brautigan at Smiley's. "I tapped him on the shoulder, and he was on his way to being drunk and sort of reeled around and said, 'Don't touch me. I don't know who you are. It's really rude to touch people you don't know.'"

Christopher backed off and hung out with some friends, shooting pool. After last call, Richard started to leave and Christopher followed him outside, introducing himself as Ken Rand's son. It's not surprising that Brautigan hadn't recognized the boy. Chris stood six foot one and weighed over two hundred pounds. After a "cheerful embrace," they bought a six-pack and walked down Wharf Road to the beach "and just rapped for a couple of hours."

"And, of course, the machine gun came up in our conversation, and he goes, 'What do you want *now* for it? I'll still buy you the rockets. What do you want?' It was very funny."

It had been a dozen years since they had last seen each other, and the boy had become a man. They killed the six-pack, trading stories. Richard started tossing the empties out into the ocean. Christopher objected. "I said, 'Hey, that's not cool. What are you doing?' And he said, 'I've picked up so many beer cans I deserve to throw some back if I want.' Strange man."

twenty-eight: bread and circuses

THE HELLS ANGELS threw a big free party in the Panhandle on New Year's Day, 1967, to thank the Haight's doper community for bailing Chocolate George out of jail. Dubbed the "New Year's Wail," and the "New Year's Whale," by the Diggers, who put out a flyer encouraging participants to bring along whale meat, the festivities began at 2:00 PM. Music at the "Wail," performed on an eighteen-foot flatbed truck, featured Janis Joplin and Big Brother, the Grateful Dead, John Handy's jazz ensemble, and the Orkustra, an odd collection of musicians known as the Diggers' house band. (Bobby Beausoleil, the group's top-hatted bouzouki player, later became associated with Charles Manson and was himself jailed for murder.)

Emmett Grogan took credit for planning the whole thing with Pete Knell, but the effort was clearly the work of many Angels and Diggers. The motorcycle club provided a public address system to amplify the rock and roll, along with copious amounts of free beer. "The parks belong to the people!" the crowd chanted when the police cruised by to check things out. Given Richard Brautigan's prominence at the forefront of the march to Park Station, it is impossible to imagine him not grooving among the happy throng at this Digger-publicized event.

The Diggers found a new home for their giveaway emporium at 520 Frederick Street, a storefront with a large basement. They opened for "business" the first week of January, soon after Emmett Grogan stenciled the name, the Free Frame of Reference, above the front window. Among the first visitors were the police, on the lookout for underage runaways and drugs. After being denied entry three times, the cops returned in force around six in the evening with three patrol cars and a Black Maria. Ninety people had gathered within to watch Ben Van Meter's film *Poon Tang Trilogy* on a bedsheet screen. The police ushered them all out, citing fire regulations. Their search trashed the place, causing a disturbance leading to the arrest of four Diggers, including Grogan.

Four days into the New Year, Brautigan took part in a reading at the I/Thou Coffee Shop (1736 Haight Street) along with David Sandberg and young Jeff Sheppard. Another poet, Joe Stroud, had been scratched from the lineup. Sandberg, insecure about his work, referred to his writing simply as "pages." Richard, the featured reader, stepped to the front of the room carrying a large bucket of clams. The minimal advertising for the event, a narrow printed strip of pale green paper, referred to the bivalves as Brautigan's artistic contribution.

About the same time, Richard Brautigan began a brief, intense relationship with a woman whom most of his friends, even those who met her, could not remember years later. Keith Abbott recalled, "She always remained for me just a face. Even after people told me her name, I forgot it just as fast. Her face was an eraser for names." For Loie Weber, "she was like a disappeared person. She was there in image." Her name was Michaela Blake-Grand. She was known as "Mickey."

David Schaff thought her "genuinely crazy." Very soft-spoken with dark red hair, tiny hands, prominent buck teeth, and abundant freckles, Mickey was not a conventionally attractive woman. Creating a distinctive thrift shop style all her own, she wore oval wire-framed granny glasses and dressed in a quaint Victorian manner. Richard called her his muse.

Michaela had been the girlfriend of Andy Cole, Brautigan's old pal and roommate. Richard was fascinated with her in part because Blake-Grand had a degree in textiles and supposedly had submitted a piece of knitting as her thesis. The notion of someone knitting a thesis was a concept right up Brautigan's alley. Contemporary photographs of Michaela show her looking prim and straitlaced like a stern old-fashioned schoolmarm, but in essence she was a deeply passionate woman. Loie Weber remembered Blake-Grand as eccentric and very inverted, possessed with "that kind of quiet, indrawn intensity." Richard's erotic poem "I've Never Had It Done So Gently Before" was dedicated to "M" for Michaela. "The sweet juices of your mouth," he wrote, "are like castles bathed in honey." One evening, she unexpectedly showed up at Jack Thibeau's place and spent the night with him. When Jack awoke the next morning, Michaela was gone, leaving behind a note addressed to "Jick." Thibeau never knew what she meant by that.

Early in January, Brautigan struck up a friendship with Lou Marcelli, a blue-collar guy in North Beach. After working as a letter carrier for the post office and as a fisherman in Alaska, Lou and a bunch of buddies opened a little beer and wine bar called Deno & Carlo at 728 Vallejo Street, next to the police station. "Just five North Beachers," Lou recalled, "didn't know shit about business or how to run a place." At first, the joint didn't do very well. Richard started stopping by when Lou was behind the bar. Most of the time, it was deserted.

Brautigan walked in one mid-January day and asked, "What's going on here?" Marcelli admitted he didn't really know. He said he was just trying to start something up, "with entertainment or whatever." Richard told Lou he'd fill the place for him. "I said, 'Yeah, sure you will,'" Marcelli remembered. "He says, 'You ever hear of Allen Ginsberg?' I don't know Allen Ginsberg from a tub of beans. He says, 'I'm gonna get him here tomorrow night, and there'll be people lined up around the block.'"

This was no idle promise. Ginsberg had flown to Frisco earlier in the month with his longtime boyfriend, Peter Orlovsky, and his sometime girlfriend, Maretta Greer, who'd returned from four years wandering the Himalayas. They came to take part in a Gathering of the Tribes, the great Human Be-In organized by Michael Bowen and Allen Cohen. Allen Ginsberg proved open to Brautigan's solicitations. Richard's friendship with Emmett Grogan helped pull things together. Grogan admitted to being "knocked out" when Richard told him of his idea for the reading.

Brautigan drew a mimeographed poster in the scrawled offhand manner of his recent flier for the reprint of *Galilee Hitch-hiker*. He wrote "San Francisco Poets Benefit for the Diggers" at the top, dotting the page with little cartoon flowers and centering an all-seeing eye in a circle surrounded by the words, "!Free! We love you !Free! We love you." Scattered about this image, along with Brautigan's own moniker, were the names of his friends: Gary Snyder, Lew Welch, Lenore Kandel, William Fritsch, Ron Loewinsohn, David Meltzer, and George Stanley.

Allen Ginsberg's name did not appear on Brautigan's poster, but Richard held true to his word, and the famed beat poet was there at Deno & Carlo on the promised night, January 12, 1967. Aside from the crude flyer, the only publicity for the event were mentions in the *Oracle* and in Ralph Gleason's *Chronicle* column. Even so, more than a hundred people showed up. "The place was mobbed," Lou Marcelli recalled. The occasion launched the North Beach nightspot, which quickly became a popular music venue. Blue Cheer and the Cleveland Wrecking Company played there. Creedence Clearwater Revival got their start at Deno and Carlo.

Because the reading had been called a "benefit," Ginsberg and Gary Snyder dutifully passed the hat for donations. By the time Emmett Grogan and Peter Coyote arrived a considerable sum had been collected. Ginsberg gave Grogan the hat full of money. Emmett announced the only possible Digger benefit was "one where everything was free!" and handed the hat over to the bartender, telling him to count out the bread and buy drinks for the house until it was gone. "That's a Digger benefit," Coyote shouted to much applause. Gary Snyder marveled at the gesture, telling Allen Ginsberg they'd given the money "back to the people!"

The next evening, Andrew Hoyem threw a party he called "Meet My Television Set" at his Fell Street flat. The guest list ranged from fellow poets to Hells Angels and society people. Among the hundred or more who "came and went" were Gary Snyder, Allen Ginsberg, Peter Orlovsky, James Broughton, Thomas Parkinson, and Richard Brautigan, who took off all his clothes "except for bead necklaces and tall hat." Regarding Brautigan's tendency to strip naked at social events, Hoyem observed, "I was always astonished how successful he would be with the girls *after* he'd taken his clothes off."

Antiquarian booksellers David and Dorothy Magee brought the front of a busted TV as a present for Hoyem's machine. Poet/artist Albert Saijo, now working as a Yellow Cab driver, came wearing his cabbie's cap "and obligingly took two guests home." At one point in the evening, Richard Brautigan found himself standing next to Gary Snyder, who sat in an armchair drinking a glass of bourbon on ice. Hoyem recounted the episode: "Richard's dong was in close proximity, so Gary raised his glass and used Richard's dick as a swizzle stick, sending the naked author skyward."

A couple days later, Hoyem received a note from Brautigan: "Thank you for the party. I'm sure I had a wonderful time."

Saturday, January 14, turned out to be a beautiful sunny day, not a cloud in the sky, fulfilling the prophesies of Gavin Arthur, who along with fellow astrologer Ambrose Hollingsworth (once the manager of Quicksilver Messenger Service) had selected the date as auspicious for the big planned Be-In. The Parks Department granted a permit for the use of the Polo Fields in Golden Gate Park, an area large enough to encompass six city blocks, and by midmorning swarms of young people streamed in under the trees, heading for the "powwow." They had been alerted by constant hype on the Bay Area's radio stations, a cover story in the *Oracle*, five eye-catching posters (including work by Michael Bowen, Mouse, and newly arrived cartoonist Rick Griffin), and a press conference two days before at the Print Mint, featuring Gary Snyder and aspiring revolutionary Jerry Rubin.

Twenty thousand people showed up by one o'clock. Gary Snyder officially started things off by blowing a beaded Japanese conch shell, the ceremonial instrument of the Yamabushi Buddhist sect. A group of poets faced the vast crowd, sitting in a lotus-position line along a raised stage covered with Eastern bedspreads. Ginsberg, Snyder, Lenore Kandel, Michael McClure (with autoharp), and Lawrence Ferlinghetti all read their poetry, although at times the public address system failed. They were joined onstage by mantra-chanting Maretta Greer and Freewheelin' Frank, shaking his tambourine. Through it all, Shunryu Suzuki-*roshi*, founder of the San Francisco Soto Zen Center, silently sat zazen behind them.

Richard Brautigan and Andrew Hoyem were not invited to participate with the better-known poets. They wandered among the disinterested crowd, two more foam-flecks amid a sea of faces adrift beneath rippling tie-dye banners and upthrust god's eye totems. The inadequate PA system frequently broke down. The Dead, the Airplane, Big Brother, the Loading Zone, Quicksilver, and Country Joe all played that afternoon, and thousands danced, even if they couldn't hear the music very well. The Diggers gave away a truckload of sandwiches made from several dozen turkeys donated by Owsley Stanley, who also kicked in innumerable hits of White Lightning, the strongest acid he had yet manufactured. At sunset, Gary Snyder produced another blast on his conch shell. Allen Ginsberg chanted "Om Shri Maitreya." As the crowd drifted off, he exhorted them to pick up their trash. The people left the Polo Fields cleaner than they had found it.

Emmett Grogan thought the whole thing a shuck put on by the Thelin brothers' business organization, the Haight Independent Proprietors (HIP), for their own benefit. Not a gathering of the tribes, but "actually more a gathering of the suburbs with only a sprinkling of nonwhites in the crowd [. . .] a showcase for beaded hipsterism [. . .] a single stage with a series of schmucks schlepping all over it, making speeches and reciting poetry nobody could hear [. . .]" They were all just "ham chewers" gathered at "one great big fashion show."

Grogan blamed the HIP merchants for the vast influx of newcomers he anticipated in the near future. In Emmett's opinion, "the truth was that the disastrous arrival of thousands too many only meant more money for the operators of fly-by-night underground-culture outfits, the dope dealers, and the worst of the lot, the shopkeepers who hired desperate runaways to do piecework for them at sweatshop wages. It was a catastrophe [. . .]"

The next day was Sunday, and Richard Brautigan slept in, lingering abed, making love twice with Michaela. By early afternoon, he loaded his travel kit into Andrew Hoyem's car, and the two poets-in-residence set off on the road to L.A. They arrived in Pasadena that night and were accommodated in the guest suite at Ricketts House on the campus of the California Institute of Technology. Impromptu greetings kept them up late. At three in the morning, Richard wrote "The Beautiful Poem" just before going to sleep. Holding his penis while taking a bedtime leak made him think of his passionate morning with Michaela. Richard was so tired, he dated the poem incorrectly, thinking it was still the fifteenth.

Monday afternoon, Richard and Andrew gave a reading at Hoyem's alma mater, Pomona College in Claremont, also the home of Scripps and Pitzer, two other small distinguished schools. Looking more like a sylvan transplant from New England than a Southern California suburb, tree-lined Claremont retained an easy casual charm. Buffered by the three college campuses, fast-food joints and other abominations of the automobile culture had been held to a minimum in Claremont. After the reading (for which Brautigan was paid $50), the faculties of the various colleges hosted a cocktail reception at the home of Irish poet W. R. "Bertie" Rodgers, poet-in-residence at Pitzer. "There was a lot of broken glassware," Andrew Hoyem recalled.

The new ten-day poets-in-residence at Caltech made a contrasting pair. Hoyem appeared "nattily dressed" in a bold-checked sports jackets or a three-piece suit and tie. Brautigan maintained his unique style. John F. Crawford described him as "wearing a floppy Stetson hat, an old vest, adorned from head to toe with two necklaces, a San Francisco dog tag, and Italian studded shoes." He also sported, perhaps only for this SoCal visit, an enormous Mad Hatter bow tie. When a student campus-tour guide spotted Richard walking along the quad, he blurted, "Oh, he can't be a Techer! We're more normal than *that*!"

Brautigan and Hoyem soon established a routine on campus. They dined each evening at a different student residential house, taking their campaign as resident "pied pipers" directly to the undergraduates, a studious scientific lot somewhat shy and suspicious at first. A morning coffee hour with readings and literary discussions provided another way to break the ice. They soon had a small group of fans following their every move. Inspired by steaming mugs of hot black java, Richard and Andrew compiled a list of fifteen amusing coffee quotes, which they called "Student Stimulation Stations." Adding to Dutch and Turkish proverbs and quotes from famous poets (Lord Byron, Alexander Pope, and Wallace Stevens), Hoyem and Brautigan wrote many of the aphorisms themselves. Among others, Richard contributed "The nice thing about coffee is that it's legal" and "It's always midnight on Coffee Standard Time." The poets mimeographed the list of coffee quotations and distributed copies around the campus.

During their free time, Brautigan wrote "Fisherman's Lake," while Hoyem worked on a prose poem he called "Bric-A-Brac." Both poets read before the student assembly. Andrew led off with "The Litter," a long poem his friend John Crawford found "macabre and powerful [. . .] a recounting of his dream visit to the House of Death." Hoyem's gravity captured the attention of the audience. It was a tough act to follow, but Richard worked with a stand-up comic's timing. When he read his lament about his nose growing old and how it might affect his future sex appeal, he won the students over.

Richard wrote to Michaela Blake-Grand three times during his stay at Caltech. He drafted a poem beginning "I feel my blood / joined to the stars [. . .]" and included a copy in his letter to Michaela the next day. "Mammal Fortress" consisted of two short stanzas, the first a plaintive cry, "Where the doe is queen / and the buck is king, / I need you. I love you." Brautigan sent it along with his third letter to Blake-Grand.

The poets-in-residence had a pleasant stay at Caltech. Their 11:00 AM coffee gatherings attracted growing numbers of students. Frequently photographed, Andrew and Richard larked about the campus, paying regular visits to the humanities division to flirt with the secretaries. They sat in on classes, at times "awed and discomfited by teaching, science, and the power of technology." At other times, they simply pursued coeds. Some evenings, they got away from the mysteries of science and drove into Hollywood. Hoyem remembered the sidewalk kids cracking up over Brautigan. "I may not be funny looking," Richard quipped, "but I'll do until something better comes along."

Brautigan found time to speak with his film agent, H. N. Swanson, about *The Abortion*. Swanee liked what he heard and said he'd read the book, "to see if there is a movie in it." It rained all day on Tuesday the twenty-fourth. Richard was bored and wrote a poem about the rain and his ennui, which he called "At the California Institute of Technology." The first lines, "I don't care how God-damn smart / these guys are" got a big laugh when he read them the next morning at the final farewell coffee hour in the lounge at Winnett house.

Brautigan was in fine spirits. Earlier that morning, armed with an introduction from John Crawford, he and Hoyem stopped by the faculty office of world-famous physicist Richard Feynman, who'd won the Nobel Prize two years earlier for his work on quantum electrodynamics. Feynman was a noted prankster, and his varied interests included juggling, Mayan hieroglyphics, lock pick-ing, painting, and playing the bongos. While Andrew and Richard cooled their heels, the secretary discreetly informed her eccentric boss about the visitors. When Feynman heard poets waited, he shouted, "Poets? Poets are always welcome here!" and rushed out to greet them.

The physicist invited them into his office. Richard Brautigan mentioned that there was no rhyme in the English language for the word "orange," suggesting Richard Feynman name some newly discovered atomic particle "torange" to make up for the deficiency. After a discussion of Feynman's "passion for beautiful formulae," the poets hurried off to their reading. Andrew's mood was enhanced by a good-looking blond he met along the way. Brautigan told his friend, "Don't wash that hand, Andrew; it has been shaken by a Nobel Prize winner and a Girl!"

Fifty coffee-sipping students showed up for the poets' final performance. Richard and Andrew read only work they had written while at Caltech. "Le grand farewell appearance" had been adver-tised to be "by popular demand," but things ended on a sour note at Caltech. Brautigan and Hoyem had been promised $300 each. When they went to collect the honoraria, they found $185 apiece deducted from their payrolls for room and board. Richard and Andrew made a final roman-tic poetic gesture, refusing the checks and storming out in high dudgeon.

The poets-out-of-residence had dinner that night at the home of film actor Harry Carey Jr. The next afternoon at a quarter past three, Richard and Andrew sat in a parked car "on a rundown residential / back street," staring up at the Hollywood sign high on the green hillside above the stucco bungalows and flowering jacaranda trees. The Lovin' Spoonful played on the car radio: "Do You Believe in Magic?" Richard pulled his notebook from his shirt pocket and wrote down a poem called "Hollywood." In the fantasy town where celluloid dreams were born, Brautigan, a lifelong movie fan, observed lonely men in shirtsleeves taking out the trash.

Leaving Tinseltown after another day, the two poets drove north to Santa Barbara, a wealthy seaside resort and residential community with uniform Spanish-colonial architecture and a vener-able mission. Hoyem and Brautigan's destination was the home of Jack and Vicki Shoemaker in Isla Vista, ten miles north of Santa Barbara. Shoemaker managed the Unicorn Book Shop (owned by Ken Maytag, whose grandfather made a bundle in washing machines) near the University of California Santa Barbara campus.

Jack went on to a distinguished career in publishing, cofounding North Point Press, Counter-point, and Shoemaker & Hoard. He first got in touch with Brautigan after reading *Confederate General*, writing him a letter saying, "We were going to be putting on a reading series and would pay fifty bucks a reading, plus expenses for travel, would he ever consider coming." Shoemaker soon had a reply from Richard. "I got back a letter from him saying, 'Absolutely. I would love to come. When?'"

Richard and Andrew arrived at Jack and Vicki's place the afternoon of January 27. They enjoyed drinks and conversation before their scheduled reading at the Unicorn, waiting to leave until the Shoemakers' babysitter arrived. Althea Susan Morgan, a tall slender nineteen-year-old redhead who wore her boyish close-cropped hair in a Peter Pan bob, was a sophomore at UCSB. Susan worked for Jack and Vicki four nights a week. Brautigan, always keen for pretty women, was immediately drawn to the vivacious babysitter. At that point, Susan Morgan had never heard of either poet but admitted she and Richard "were instantly attracted to each other."

Brautigan and Hoyem gave a dual reading at the Unicorn, continuing what Jack Shoemaker called "their Mutt and Jeff act—playing off each other. Richard looked quite wild and deranged, and Andrew looked like a librarian." The bookstore, located in the residential neighborhood of UC Santa Barbara, attracted mainly undergraduates to its events, "an audience that was fairly flummoxed and quite familiar with Brautigan and not at all familiar with Hoyem."

The British poet Basil Bunting, a visiting lecturer at UCSB, and his raven-haired daughter, Sima Maria (Persian for "Face of a Virgin," Bunting claimed), were also in attendance. Bunting had worked in Paris in the twenties as a subeditor of Ford Madox Ford's *Transatlantic Review* and had been associated with Pound and Yeats in Italy in the 1930s. At the time, his modernist work was better known in America than in his own country.

After the reading, Richard and the others came back to the Shoemakers' and he invited Susan to join them in the ongoing festivities. She didn't take much persuading and hopped into a VW van with Brautigan, Hoyem, and five or six others. With Jack driving, they headed north about fifteen miles to Gaviota State Park. Along the way, the group smoked "lots of weed," loudly chanting and singing. Richard abstained from the marijuana but accompanied the singers by playing a pair of finger cymbals.

The trail to the Gaviota Hot Springs ascended from the parking area for half a mile through the trees. A waning half-moon made it easy going. The spring was only three or four feet deep and smelled of sulfur, but they had the place to themselves, and everyone quickly disrobed and slipped naked into the steaming water. The rain earlier had stopped, and a phosphorescent ring surrounded the moon. Bats swooped down out of the night, skimming over the tops of the bathers' heads. Mud covered the bottom of the pond, and every movement caused streams of tiny tingling bubbles to rise up between their bare limbs.

They soaked for a couple hours. It was a very romantic evening, so much so that Andrew Hoyem later wrote a prose-poem about the experience for Susan Morgan. He called it "Xenovale." ("In the midst of rising mist a woman's form is discernible. She disrobes and slowly descends to the pool. The outline of her body is blurred, but one may be sure she is statuesque. Her steps are as deliberately delicate as her physique is perfectly proportioned [. . .]" His words made her feel "beautiful," and Susan appreciated Andrew's sensitivity, but it was Richard Brautigan she took home to her Madrid Street apartment that night.

The next day, Richard gave her an inscribed copy of the 1966 Cranium Press reprint of *The Galilee Hitch-hiker*. That evening, the Shoemakers arranged a poets' get-together at their home. Brautigan came with Susan. Bunting brought his daughter. "Both Hoyem and Brautigan noticed her," Jack recalled. "Bunting liked company, and he liked company when he drank. Richard and Andrew both liked to drink." It was the first time Susan saw Brautigan "badly drunk." She remembered Bunting and Brautigan "really hit it off and emptied many bottles." Shoemaker understood their connection. "Bunting liked eccentrics and would have found [Brautigan's] wry, fey self amusing."

Brautigan and Hoyem returned to San Francisco that Sunday. Much had transpired in the hipster community during their fortnight's absence. A dapper dude in a white linen suit had been following Kesey around, hanging out with the Pranksters, and taking notes. Tom Wolfe's series of articles on the Trips Festivals for the *New York Herald Tribune* (combined in 1968 to produce his best-selling book *The Electric Kool-Aid Acid Test*) did more to publicize the hip life than all the combined headlines about the Great Human Be-In.

From Brautigan's perspective, the most interesting media development was a tiny innovative Haight-Ashbury publishing venture launched while he'd been out of town. The Communication Company had its genesis when Chester Anderson, "a fountain of quips and bon mots who liked to play Baroque music on his harpsichord and recorder," came out to Frisco at Christmastime and met Claude Hayward and his pregnant partner, H'lane Resnikoff. Anderson, a thirtysomething bohemian, had published *The Butterfly Kid*, a sci-fi novel set in Greenwich Village, and during a previous stay in North Beach had edited both *Beatitude* and a satirical magazine called *The Underhound*.

Claude and H'lane had only recently moved up to San Francisco from Los Angeles, where Claude wrote for the *L.A. Free Press*. Somehow, he ran into Anderson and they dropped acid together on New Year's Eve. The next day, while coming down, they wandered over to the Wail in the Panhandle. When a burly Hells Angel gave Anderson two beers, one for each hand, Chester knew it was time to move back to San Francisco.

At the end of the first week in 1967, Chester Anderson came to stay at the Haywards' third-floor apartment at 406 Duboce Avenue (corner of Fillmore Street) on the slope of Buena Vista Hill, "a brisk walk" away from the action in the Haight. Hayward worked as the advertising manager for the *Sunday Ramparts*, a weekly newspaper published by *Ramparts* magazine. Peter Coyote described him as "a ferret-faced guy with an easy laugh and furtive manner [. . .] an anarchist by temperament as well as a skilled thief." Emmett Grogan was kinder in his assessment, calling Claude "a Topanga Canyon beat from Los Angeles" with a "graveyard look who though he seldom talked, he made most people laugh just by being around." Grogan also considered him "a slick hustler," a high compliment coming from the consummate con artist of the Haight-Ashbury.

Hayward got Anderson a job as the Marin County ad representative for the *Sunday Ramparts*, a position requiring a minimum of actual work, allowing Chester ample time to explore his new neighborhood. Anderson grew a beard, stopped cutting his hair, and began wearing "beads and things" around his neck. In a letter to a friend, he described himself as looking "quite picturesque, but fairly drab within my environment."

Founded in 1962 as a liberal Catholic news magazine, *Ramparts* metamorphosed into a hip flashy muckraking monthly in 1964, after Warren Hinckle III took over as its editor. Hinckle at that time had failed as a publicist and as a reporter for the *Chronicle*, but in his mudslinging hands the left-wing magazine prospered on the newsstands if not with advertisers. Critic Ralph Gleason served on the editorial board. Jann Wenner, a pudgy rock and roll enthusiast, was the entertainment editor of the Sunday supplement and shared his office with Claude Hayward. The office mascot, a spider monkey named Henry Luce, cavorted between the desks. Claude and Chester fit right in. The unlikely duo talked up the freaks in the acid head community, and Hinckle took an interest in doing a major feature on the hippies. He offered Anderson $2 an hour as a researcher to dig up stories in the Haight.

With his weathered canvas shoulder bag stuffed with composition books, Chester set out on his researching rounds. Among his first interviews, he talked with Emmett Grogan over at poster artist Stanley Mouse's Henry Street studio. Grogan's comment, "Freedom means everything free," got Anderson thinking. Soon he and Claude started rapping late at night and came up with an idea for a news outlet based on the Marshall McLuhan dictum "The medium is message." The *Oracle* wasn't getting the job done. The arty underground newspaper appeared only sporadically and readers had to pay for each copy. Claude and Chester envisioned something more ephemeral and at the same time more immediate, a disposable broadside hitting the streets as often as necessary, many times each day if current events so demanded.

At the Human Be-In, Anderson and Hayward identified themselves as The Communication Company (later commonly abbreviated as com/co) and passed out printed poems and a list of cool places to trip. Three days later, Chester used the second half of his advance for *The Butterfly Kid* to make a $300 down payment to the Gestetner Corporation of California for a brand-new Gestetner 366 silk-screen stencil duplicator and a Gestefax justified electronic stencil cutter. With these amazing machines and an IBM typewriter on loan from *Ramparts*, they set up shop in Hayward's apartment. Able to print up to 10,000 copies "of almost anything we can wrap around our scanning drum," including halftones and art in four colors, The Communication Company was open for business.

Com/co's one-page purpose statement broadside said it all. "OUR POLICY: Love is communication." The list of "PLANS & HOPES" promised

> to provide quick & inexpensive printing service for the hip community . . . to print anything the Diggers want printed . . . to do lots of community service printing . . . to supplement the Oracle with a more or less daily paper whenever Haight news justifies one . . . to be outrageous pamphleteers . . . to revive The Underhound . . . to function as a Haight/Ashbury propaganda ministry, free lance if need be . . . to publish literature originating within this new minority . . . to publish occasional incredibilities out of an unusual fondness for either outrage or profit, as the case may be . . . to do what we damn well please.

The Communication Company lived up to all of these promises. They also pledged "to keep up the payments" on their "MAGNIFICENT" Gestetner machines but, after the initial three hundred bucks, the remaining $672 they owed was never paid. Claude Hayward's mechanical skills (all the more remarkable as he was nearly blind and wore thick corrective black-lens glasses) enabled him to keep the Gestetners running without any technical support from the corporation. Com/co started making some money within a couple months, but the bulk of its support came from Owsley Stanley and various other charitable drug dealers. The Diggers did their part by supplying ream after ream of purloined paper. Com/co held up its end of the deal and printed anything the Diggers wanted. Soon, the neighborhood was flooded with their provocative handbills, a dramatic escalation of Grogan and Murcott's earlier efforts. By the time Richard Brautigan got back to Frisco after his poet-in-residence stint, com/co publications were hitting the streets daily.

On January 20, the Diggers' Free Frame store on Frederick Street (along with Swami Bhaktivedanta's Radha-Krishna Temple, which had set up shop next door in the same building) had a condemned notice posted on the entrance. When Timothy Leary appeared at Winterland a week later, in his one-man Buddha show, he was immediately denounced by a Chester Anderson com/co poem circulated the next day. During a meeting between the HIP merchants and San Francisco police chief Thomas Cahill four days earlier, a new label was pinned on the psychedelic age. Gertrude Stein had famously named the Lost Generation, and Jack Kerouac came up with the term

"Beat Generation." Ironically, it was Frisco's top cop who, in the course of this meeting, said to the gathering of hippie store owners, "You're sort of a Love Generation, aren't you?"

Richard Brautigan looked the part (Claude Hayward remembered him always wearing his trademark navy peacoat and battered Stetson, "usually reeking of patchouli"), as did Chester Anderson, but they were both more than a decade too old to qualify for membership in the Love Generation. The two men shared a greater affinity as fellow writers than mere sartorial similarities. Brautigan felt attracted to com/co because of the Digger connection and their pledge to publish literature originating within the hip community.

Trout Fishing in America proceeded through its various production phases, and Richard expected the book to be out before summer. In addition, with the help of Don Carpenter, who had written a letter to editor A. C. Spectorsky, Brautigan submitted a group of nine stories to *Playboy*, hoping to see them published "together as a group." Although The Viking Press had rejected *The Abortion*, Bob Mills was "convinced the book deserves to be published" and resubmitted it to Arthur Fields at Putnam's. Failing there, he had "a lot of other places in mind."

The planned Coyote Books collection of his poetry prompted Brautigan to work mostly in that medium. Citing a newly written poem, he jotted a possible title in his notebook: "Boo, Forever: Some Poems 1957–1967." He'd also thought a lot about a new novel he planned on writing later that year. What he had in mind was a Western. He'd long loved Western movies, steeping himself in Hollywood quick-draw folklore at countless afternoon triple features and devouring the literature of the West, everything he could get his hands on, from Francis Parkman to Louis L'Amour. Brautigan wrote to Bob Mills about his plan. ("I've always wanted to write a Western and so that's what I'm going to do.")

The landlord padlocked the front entrance of the vacated Free Frame of Reference, officially closed by order of the health and fire departments, and nailed a wire grate over the rear windows. By early February, the Diggers also had to deal with another problem. Their old Ford station wagon had given up the ghost, and it looked like the Yellow Submarine would soon follow it to the automobile graveyard. Without these vehicles, the Diggers had no way to round up the produce they needed for their free food program.

Richard Brautigan came to the rescue. He knew a beautiful young heiress called Flame who wanted to make a donation to the Diggers. Pam Parker, a member of the fountain pen family, had money to burn, Emmett Grogan's favorite pyrotechnic gesture. A "stunning" redhead with pale ivory skin, Flame had much more going for her than mere good looks. Peter Coyote later praised Parker's "fearless humor" and "steel-trap mind." The Diggers asked Brautigan if the mysterious beauty would "go for a pickup truck?"

"Sure," Richard replied without hesitation. Brooks Butcher had been eyeing a '58 Chevy pickup in great condition with brand-new tires. He had Brautigan take him to see Miss Parker and returned that evening driving the coveted truck. The pickup saved the day and became the Diggers' trusty workhorse. Flame in turn became Butcher's "old lady," moving in with him at a Webster Street storefront in the Fillmore District.

The Diggers located a new and much bigger home for their free emporium at 901 Cole, a corner storefront at the intersection of Carl Street. Tall plate glass show windows faced both streets. A surrounding second-floor mezzanine balcony added needed space. The initial rent money came from a wealthy patron, and Peter Coyote, Sweet William, the Hun, and other Diggers cleaned the interior, covering the walls with a coat of donated white paint. Soon, the racks and counters overflowed with discarded clothing, secondhand kitchen appliances, used TVs, and hi-fi sets: a Salvation Army cornucopia of consumer culture throwaways.

Emmett Grogan expressed surprise when Peter Berg signed the lease and began hustling rent money. The Hun had shown only a marginal interest in the two previous free stores, preoccupied with his work for the Mime Troupe. Before long, Berg took over the management of the new establishment, renaming it "The Trip Without a Ticket" and making it the focus for his radical ideas about "guerrilla theater." His wife, Judy Goldhaft, ran a free sewing workshop and taught tie-dye techniques, launching an underground fashion trend that swept the country.

The Hun resigned from the Mime Troupe and devoted all his time to The Trip Without a Ticket, viewing the store as a theater and all of its "customers" as "life actors" in dramas of their own invention. Berg developed his thoughts on the subject into an eight-page manifesto titled "Trip Without a Ticket" ("Guerrilla theater intends to bring audiences to liberated territory to create life actors"), which The Communication Company printed as a pamphlet and distributed for free throughout the city. Another Digger manifesto proclaimed, "the Trip Without a Ticket will be total theater and offer the store as a social art form."

Peter Berg's ideas carried great weight with Richard Brautigan, who spent a good deal of time in his company during this turbulent year. Art Boericke, a professional gardener somewhat older than the other Diggers, remembered seeing Brautigan at Peter and Judy's little cottage in the Inner Mission "three or four times a month," whenever Art came into the city from Marin. "I can hardly remember a single occasion when I was at their home when Richard was not there. I am sure he must have been there a good portion of the week, at least evenings." Brautigan was already a life actor. Over the past decade, he had gradually created the character he inhabited. The Hun's penetrating intellect and radical ideas validated this endeavor.

Peter Berg remembered Brautigan as "very polite and meticulous. He never talked about poverty, the war, racism, or police brutality in his writing. He more or less forfeited political analysis to people like myself." Richard hung out with the Diggers and felt sympathetic with their goals, but his attraction was emotional, not philosophical. As Berg recalled, "If you asked him about the class system he would reply, 'There are no classes in a lake,' his point being that nature is grander than classes."

All this time, the philosophical difference between the Diggers and the HIP merchants had escalated to the point where all sides agreed mediation would be beneficial. Seeking a neutral site for their discussion, they selected Glide Memorial Church, downtown in the Tenderloin at the corner of Taylor and Ellis. Though it had once been a middle-class neighborhood, years of neglect transformed the Tenderloin into a gritty slum where homeless winos huddled in doorways and prostitutes of both sexes plied their trade day and night. These outcasts became Glide's new congregation. Under the dynamic leadership of Reverend Cecil Williams, an exuberant black man who knew in his heart the true meaning of Christian love, the venerable Methodist church opened its doors to the dregs of society. Glide offered a drug rehabilitation program, job placement, daycare, and a free lunch service that fed thousands every week. It was a church close to the Diggers' hearts.

Early in February, both sides gathered in the basement, the conference speakers seated on a circle of chairs surrounded by more than one hundred spectators. The main issue was the projected influx of over fifty thousand young people into the Haight-Ashbury once school let out for the summer. Because of the media attention attracted by the HIP-sponsored Be-In, the Diggers believed the Haight Street merchants had to take responsibility and make contingency plans for the newcomers' welfare. All the store owners had to offer was a rehashed version of the Job Co-op (which hired runaway teenage girls at a buck an hour to sew up embroidered dresses for their hip boutiques) and a proposal by the Thelin brothers to turn the back room at the Psyche Shop into a "calm center" where kids off the street could come down from bad trips.

This enraged Emmett Grogan. He jumped to his feet and launched into a vicious tirade denouncing the HIP merchants as "cloud-dwellers" and "motherfuckers." Strutting like a movie gangster with his IRA cap pulled down over one eye, Grogan berated the long-haired shopkeepers before storming out of the church basement, accompanied by his Digger brothers. Several of the underground weeklies reporting the event ("CLASS WAR IN THE HAIGHT") wrote that he had threatened to bomb any of the stores refusing to donate a percentage of their profits back to the community. The day after the angry meeting, Peter Krug, owner of Wild Colors at 1418 Haight Street, posted a sign in his shop window detailing his business expenses. With a $200 monthly net, the originator of the Job Co-op notion wondered how he might make his business more nonprofit.

Richard Brautigan stayed abreast of the conflicts within the hip community from the safe remove of a perpetual observer. Of far greater interest to him was the February publication in Italy of *Il Generale Immaginario* (*A Confederate General from Big Sur*) by Rizzoli. Grove Press mailed him a copy that he found "very handsome." Grove's edition of the book had sold poorly, but here was another chance, a rebirth. Around the same time, Don Allen discovered a batch of Brautigan's early poems among his papers. His enjoyment rereading them enhanced his enthusiasm for the Four Seasons' planned publication of *Trout Fishing*. Don mailed them to Richard for inclusion in the Coyote Books collection along with a small gift as a "token of [his] admiration." Allen inquired what the poetry books would be called, signing off, "Yours in the faith, Don."

Ramparts magazine came out on Valentine's Day with a lead story on "The Hippies." Stanley Mouse was pictured on the cover, the prototypical acid head. Another poster artist, Wes Wilson, designed a psychedelic title page. Jann Wenner contributed short memos dealing with historical background. The cover story was written by *Ramparts* editor Warren Hinckle III, poison pen in hand. "A Social History of the Hippies" utilized Chester Anderson's thirty hours of interviews for a sneering put-down of the Haight-Ashbury scene. Hinckle called Ken Kesey "a hippie has-been," referred to Emmett Grogan as Frodo Baggins (the questing Hobbit in *The Lord of the Rings*) and compared the counterculture to Fascism and the John Birch Society. Ralph Gleason, who had included a piece on his own observations of the youth movement, quit the magazine's editorial board to protest Hinckle's snide hatchet job.

In spite of the bad press, the Diggers planned an event designed as their response to the Human Be-In. In company with the Artists Liberation Front, who had produced numerous street fairs the previous fall, the Diggers arranged for an organizational meeting at Glide Memorial, site of one of the ALF's public events. Glide by its very nature remained hospitable to the notion of unorthodox community activity, having previously sponsored a liturgical jazz Christmas Happening.

The meeting got underway in the Glide basement. Word went out earlier the same day among the close-knit artistic community. Mime Trouper Peter Coyote, serving as a courier for the event, stopped Richard Brautigan on the southeast corner of Ashbury and Clayton and told him to be there or be square. At the appointed time, Richard stood at the back of the room, taking everything in like an owl "seeking the sources of sound." According to Coyote, the group was "animated by a healthy sense of competition with the Human Be-In, hoping to create an event that would more accurately demonstrate what a free city celebration might be." The basement rang with "whoops of delight" at the outlandish suggestions. It was decided to divide Glide Church into "territories," the various rooms devoted to different happenings, each designed to create, as Grogan put it, "scenes in which they themselves and others would be able to act out their own fantasies."

All present agreed to limit the advertising to word of mouth ("except for a few handbills") and to extend the event for seventy-two hours over a three-day weekend "in order for it to be effective," immersing those attending into "assuming freedom." The officials at Glide were told as little as possible about the actual plans, being assured the Artistic Liberation Front intended to present "a carnival of the performing arts." The free-flowing environmental happening had no rules, except (wink, wink) no drugs would be allowed. Before breaking up for the night, the rowdy group selected a catchy name for their big bash, calling it "The Invisible Circus: The Right of Spring."

Richard Brautigan loved the idea of keeping the location of the Diggers' art carnival a secret until the last possible moment. He made it into a game. When Richard called Keith Abbott down in Monterey the day before the event, requisitioning Keith's van for the Diggers, he revealed nothing about "why or for what. 'Just come,' he ordered. 'You won't want to miss it.'" Brautigan knew the secret was out in the open. Haight Street buzzed with word of The Invisible Circus. The Communication Company printed up a thousand eight-and-a-half-by-eleven red, yellow, and blue handbills featuring a stylized circus wagon to advertise their "72 hr environmental community happening."

Richard phoned Victor Moscoso, asking him to do a poster for the event. Any job for the Diggers was a donation, and Moscoso, currently working in color, scaled back his palette. He selected a black-and-white picture from an art book on surrealism and painted the lettering above it in a single evening. To Charles Perry, the image on Moscoso's small handbill looked like "a human being with a rubber eraser for a face."

Keith Abbott drove up from Monterey on a brisk February morning and hauled the com/co Gestetners, along with stencils and reams of paper, over to Glide from Claude Hayward's apartment. At the church, he humped it all upstairs to the second-floor room Richard Brautigan christened "The John Dillinger Computer Complex." The John Dillinger name, emblazoned on brown butcher paper illustrated with cartoon renditions of a smoking gat and a couple getaway cars, hung on the wall of the Digger newsroom. Claude and Chester got the machines running and a last-minute squiggle-lettered Invisible Circus poster rushed off the press, touting "The John Dillenger Computor [sic]" along with the Lion Priests and the Wind Spinners.

There was even a playroom stocked with toys for kids of all ages. "Paper spaghetti and no rules."

Various factions among the art community claimed fifty rooms in the church and prepared them for happenings. There were rooms designed for confrontation and others reserved for theoretical peace and quiet. Down the hall from the John Dillinger Computer stretched "love alley," a number of separate offices redecorated with mattresses covered by colorful Indian bedspreads and equipped with candles, perfumes, incense, and lubricating oils in preparation as "love-making salons." Elsewhere, a room had been set aside for tie-dying classes, and another was designated as a sewing center. Lenore Kandel staked out her space, and Mouse had a setup for hand-painting T-shirts. Downstairs in the cafeteria dining room, the Diggers prepared to feed the expected masses.

Teams of volunteers, including Keith Abbott, spent the afternoon preparing for the three-day marathon happening. Emmett Grogan trucked over "tons of shredded plastic" he'd scored from a local factory and filled a downstairs corridor waist-deep with the stuff. Rumors spread like mononucleosis. Pig Pen of the Dead was scheduled to play the organ in the chapel, and word went out that Big Brother and the Holding Company would make an appearance. In his Friday "On the Town" column in the *Chronicle*, Ralph Gleason devoted two long paragraphs to The Invisible Circus, stating that Big Brother "will sing and play 'Amazing Grace' at the 11 a.m. regular Sunday services." More talk concerned a "Slo-Mo Destruction Derby" with "junker cars" colliding head-on at low speed in the church parking lot next door. A guy showed up in the afternoon with a bucket full of oysters. Richard Brautigan had sent him out to Point Reyes earlier in the day to buy several dozen from the oyster farms on Tomales Bay. Keith Abbott asked Richard what he intended to do with the mollusks. He received only a sly mysterious smile in reply.

The festivities got under way at 8:00 PM Friday the twenty-fourth, when the Orkustra started jamming in the Fellowship Room. An elevator at the Taylor Street entrance carried visitors up to the Sanctuary and second-floor offices or down to the basement level, where the throb of rock music beckoned. Even as the early arrivals struggled through a hallway filled with clinging plastic shreds, the John Dillinger Computer's first publication rattled off the Gestetners and was distributed to the gathering crowd.

"I Ching Flash One," the first of more than seventy-five broadsides issued that night, reported that the hexagram for the moment from the *I Ching* was "Breakthrough to the Creative." Those who managed to break through the shredded plastic found themselves in a cramped rec room whose low ceiling and close proximity to the boiler made it "sweltering hot." Emmett Grogan described how the Orkustra's amplified music ("blustering with outrageous noise") reached a decibel level so intense that many listeners were brought to tears.

Upstairs, Chester Anderson typed the latest news and rumors onto a stencil. Reporters from the John Dillinger Computer roamed the hallways and brought back stories of what they had seen out among the throng. At 8:27 PM, "Flash Two" was distributed to anyone wanting a copy. In it, Anderson passed along a "usually reliable rumor" that doses of LSD were being given away to "groovy-looking people of all genders" and stated that journalists from the *Chronicle* were on the premises "in a dazed condition. Give them all the help they can use & more."

Anderson mentioned live music "in what I think is the game room," lights and electronic music in the Sanctuary, food in the dining room downstairs, and a UFO "spotted hovering over the bell tower." The Flash declared that "the John Dillinger Computer loves you" and welcomed "all manuscripts, bits of paper, rumors, outrages," promising that readings from the *I Ching* "will be made & distributed as the occasion seemeth to warrant." And on a line all to itself, Anderson wrote: "Emmett Grogan is wandering through the halls. Hail him."

By 9:00 PM, the Orkustra had moved on and Peter Berg presided over a conference "On the meaning of Obscenity" in the Fellowship Room. Sitting with him on the panel at a long table were a minister, a lawyer, and a policeman specializing in community relations. Hundreds of spectators looked on, and a "free pulpit" had been provided for the audience to talk back to the panel. A proclamation from the John Dillinger Computer stated the real obscenity was war and urged the panel to disrobe. After an hour, the conference came to an end when a naked lovemaking couple was carried in on a canopied mattress borne aloft by four sturdy young men as rock music roared and a film of NASA rockets flared onto a paper screen dividing the room. A dozen writhing belly dancers tore through it to the tom-tom beat of drums, a bare-breasted blond in the lead, dancing around the lovemakers.

By 10:00 PM, things started getting out of hand. The crowd in the church had grown so large it was difficult to move from room to room. Keith Abbott described the press in the hallways as "a subway train of human flesh." An effort was made to maintain some semblance of order amid the chaos. Michael McClure and Lenore Kandel read their poetry in the Sanctuary, crowded with stoned participants lighting incense sticks and candles, dripping wax over the rugs and pews. Kandel had taken a break from her room where she deciphered the soles of peoples' feet.

Through it all, the John Dillinger Computer distributed a steady stream of Flash reports: fragments of stoned conversation recorded in the hallways minutes earlier, instant poetry, *I Ching* readings, hallucinatory artwork, and never-ending announcements about everything from a funeral for dead flowers to an argument recorded in a Tenderloin bar across the street. As the Gestetner whirled, Freewheelin' Frank "sat in the corner and painstakingly wrote a poem in the midst of the chaos." One handout declared, "Emmett Grogan has disappeared. So what?"

When the Diggers made an attempt to feed the masses at eleven it proved impossible. A tidal assault of humanity crammed into the dining room. The crowd no longer comprised just the Haight-Ashbury community. By Keith Abbott's account, the swarm included "Tenderloin winos, sailors on leave, escaped mental patients, cruising transvestites, karmic basket cases, tourists and local street trade." Emmett Grogan reported "an old, white-haired, bearded man" in the Sanctuary who "announced he was god and loudly accused the overflow congregation of having taken his name in vain." In Keith Abbott's opinion, "This was not fun."

Around the same time, Richard Brautigan took a break downstairs in a conference room converted into a temporary coffee shop by a group thinking it groovy to run such an establishment. Weary from his efforts with The John Dillinger Computer, Richard shared a cup of joe with an equally exhausted member of the Glide church board. As they sipped their java, a blurred antique pornographic film flickered over and over on a bedsheet hung at one end of the room. The original plan called for each room to change management after an allotted time had passed. The general crush slowed this process, making it difficult to move things around, and the coffee shop had overstayed its assigned tenure.

"The movie was boring," Richard Brautigan recalled, "the people were ugly, and what they were doing was ugly. The two of us drank our coffee and discussed how the craziness was going to end. That was when I noticed that the coffee shop people were packing up their goods and leaving. Just as they left, and the porno movie ended, the sheet split, and out came two strippers with a band blasting bump-and-grind music behind them." The church official told Brautigan he'd had enough. "He was abandoning ship."

Scheduled to read his poetry in the Sanctuary at midnight, Richard determined to go down with the ship. By the time Brautigan arrived, total anarchy had taken hold. To the throb of a dozen conga drums, naked couples copulated on the altar while other nude crazies raced up and down the aisles on bicycles. A statue of Christ was splashed with the blood of an overeager celebrant who "got his head cracked during a scuffle." Thick clouds of incense hung in the high domed ceiling. A pair of frantic doves whirled overhead as dozens of chanting dancers stripped off each other's clothing. Holding candles aloft, they pranced between the rows, dripping hot wax everywhere. A group of Hells Angels got it on in the back pews with a woman wearing a nun's habit who called out, "More! More!" One stoned individual sat cross-legged before the altar, coloring the carved marble tracery with a set of Magic Markers.

Richard Brautigan stepped into this bedlam carrying his bucket of oysters. A moment of unexpected quiet greeted him as he approached the lectern. Setting the pail down, Richard announced he was dedicating his reading to oysters, and all hell broke loose once again. He made a valiant attempt to read a couple poems. Even though he was amplified over a PA system, the mob drowned him out. Bedlam reigned. Brautigan gave up and headed back upstairs to the John Dillinger Computer where he found all the Gestetners broken down from overuse. Only a single mimeo still ran, operated by a speed freak "who was busy cranking out gibberish."

For Keith Abbott, the pandemonium seemed a microcosm of life in the Haight. "What started as an improvised, multi-layered theater experience was soon overrun by a lemming tide of people, most of whom were looney." Emmett Grogan thought the scene "was like the set of an incredible Fellini wet dream." He reveled in the hedonistic carnival, loving the "one big happy prickly pussy crab-lice moment of eternity." Richard Brautigan held himself back from the chaos yet found it amusing nonetheless. More than five thousand pleasure seekers swarmed through Glide Memorial during the first eight hours of The Invisible Circus. Around four in the morning, when the crowd dwindled, church officials pulled the plug. They'd had enough. Around five hundred of those still conscious followed Michael McClure and his autoharp out to Ocean Beach, where they beat on drums and garbage cans until sunup.

As the head of the John Dillinger Computer, Richard Brautigan attended the final meeting when the Lion Priests said enough was enough. Richard told Keith all about it the next day. "Everything had gotten so crazy by that time [. . .] One of the Diggers had selected some speed freak as his representative. Between each speech by the church members, this guy would spew out a rap. It was like counterpoint. Everyone was trying to figure out some way to get the mob out of the church without calling the police and starting a riot." Brautigan recalled a board member who seemed to be in a trance, repeating over and over to himself, "The one thing we agreed upon was no naked bodies on the altar and what did we get? *Naked bodies on the altar.*"

Richard left before dawn. He took the brown paper John Dillinger Computer poster home with him to Geary Street and pinned it in a place of honor on his living room wall. A couple years later, he moved it to the entrance hallway, his poster gallery. Brautigan maintained a close working relationship with The Communication Company after The Invisible Circus. He liked the idea of guerrilla publishing. The Digger practice of giving things away as a form of public theater inspired him to take the stage himself and hand out free poetry on street corners.

Richard began spending time with Claude and H'lane at the Duboce Avenue apartment. H'lane remembered once going to the Fillmore Auditorium with Brautigan. Richard tended to sit it out once the music started, but he actually danced with her that night. The refrigerator in the Hayward kitchen bore a sign reading DIGGERS WELCOME. One evening, Brautigan dropped by when the fridge was empty, and there were six mouths to feed. "No food," H'lane said. Richard had about six bucks in his pocket. He went out, "bought a chicken and some veggies," and returned to cook dinner for everyone.

In mid-March, com/co published "All Watched Over by Machines of Loving Grace," the first of the poems Richard Brautigan brought to them. In a letter to Susan Morgan, Richard claimed the recently written piece was "being made up into a poster." It was issued as a broadside in two different single-sheet formats, ephemeral handouts intended for free distribution. The next com/co flyer featuring Richard Brautigan's work was "The Beautiful Poem," which came off the Gestetners in April. Brautigan wrote "Flowers for Those You Love" on the last day of March. Com/co also published it early in April. The straightforward cautionary poem warned about venereal disease. San Francisco owned the fourth-highest infection rate for syphilis of any city in the nation. By early June, Dr. David Smith opened the Haight-Ashbury Free Medical Clinic at the corner of Clayton and Haight to treat VD and the bad drug trips plaguing the impoverished young runaway street people.

Com/co did not publish everything Brautigan submitted to them. A poem entitled "The Peacock Song" ended up, along with work by Ron Loewinsohn, Keith Abbott, Allen Cohen, and David Bromige, in a manila folder labeled "mss—free poems—unprinted." It remains unpublished to this day. Many of the single-sheet broadsides the Communication Company printed for Richard bore the cryptic initials UPS, standing for the Underground Press Syndicate. Emmett Grogan missed seeing Brautigan's initial com/co publications. Plagued by the bad vibes created by Hinckle's essay in *Ramparts*, Grogan reverted to anonymity.

When reporters showed up at The Trip Without a Ticket, the Diggers told them Emmett Grogan was an invented name. Like George Metevsky, it was a red herring they had cooked up to feed to a voracious press. Emmett Grogan lived only in myth. "Hey, you wanna be Emmett Grogan? Okay, you're Emmett Grogan. Maybe I'm Emmett Grogan, or what about that guy over there in the corner? Or . . ." He was nowhere and everywhere. Stories involving him were nothing but jive, just another shuck. Meanwhile, the real Emmett Grogan borrowed $300 from a black dealer named Super Spade and, a week or so after the Invisible Circus, carrying five hundred tabs of LSD as "emergency funds," hopped a flight to New York using a stranger's student ID.

On Sunday, March 5, the Communication Company staged "Bedrock One," a benefit for itself, at California Hall on Polk Street. Billed as the first in a series of three directed by Chester Anderson and produced by The Experimental Theatre Co-op, LAMF, the event was hosted by Warren Hinckle III, of all people. Perhaps he was thanking Anderson for all the underpaid research. Hinckle got one of his *Ramparts* staff, a young cartoonist named Robert Crumb, to design a poster, one of only two "rock" posters the artist ever drew. It pictured the typical R. Crumb character, a grinning moon-faced idiot with huge feet and a lightbulb screwed into the top of his head.

The lineup for Bedrock One was a grab bag of talent: music by the Steve Miller Blues Band, Dino Valenti, and the Orkustra; light show by the Lysergic Power & Light Company; "happenings" were the purview of the Diggers, the Mime Troupe, Allen Dienstag & the Pack, and the San Francisco Sexual Freedom League. Richard Brautigan & the Caped Crusaders (whoever they might have been) read poetry with a flair inherent in their billing. Admission to the benefit was $2.50. No liquor was served, and minors were welcome (also "CIA agents," according to a com/co flyer, which promised "surprises"). The evening began with a chanting ceremony by devotees from the Radha Krishna Temple, the Diggers' former next-door neighbors with whom they had often quarreled.

Since meeting her in January, Brautigan wrote several letters to Susan Morgan. While still in contact with his muse, Michaela, Richard told Erik Weber that Susan was a "muse from Sacramento." Since the ancient Greeks worshiped nine muses, in an age espousing free love, Brautigan didn't want to get short-changed in the muse department. Susan remembered coming up to visit Richard from Santa Barbara "maybe two or three times. He took me around and introduced me to exciting people." She met Lenore Kandel, Michael McClure, Freewheelin' Frank, and Ferlinghetti. At least once, they went to a concert at the Fillmore. On another occasion, Richard brought her to Lyle Tuttle's tattoo parlor, where Morgan had a small ankh, the ancient Egyptian life sign, inked onto her abdomen.

One afternoon, Susan and Richard found a pile of black folders lying in the gutter. They enclosed pictures of fancy bathroom fixtures. Susan picked one up. "At that time in my life I was not adverse to touching things lying in the gutter," she recalled. On the upper right-hand corner of the cover it said "Albion" in small white printed letters. That night, before having sex, Susan asked Richard to write a poem about Albion. The next morning, while Morgan was out at the store shopping for eggs and bacon, Brautigan wrote "Albion Breakfast" as a surprise. He typed up a copy dedicated "For Susan," signed it, and added the date, March 24, 1967.

"I was never in love with Richard," Morgan wrote Keith Abbott in 1989, "but enjoyed his gawky, sweet ways." It was his acceptance and enjoyment of other people's eccentricities that pleased her most. When Richard told Susan he was looking for a photo to grace the cover of his next book, she happily complied with his request to pose. Brautigan asked Erik Weber to drop by with his camera and took Susan to a thrift shop, where he bought her a lavender satin dressing gown for $1.45. At the time, she thought the garment overpriced, but wore it for years afterward. The night before the shoot, they had dinner over in Berkeley with Ron and Kitty Loewinsohn. A great deal of red wine was consumed. Unaccustomed to drinking, Susan suffered from a slight hangover the next day.

Brautigan stage-managed the event, instructing Susan not to smile. Erik found Morgan a "long pretty" brunette and shot a roll of film, capturing her coy gamine look. Brautigan posed her standing next to the John Dillinger Computer poster and seated in a deep Salvation Army wicker chair. Richard perched in a proprietary manner on the arm. The pictures possessed a studied formality. Susan found them "not very flattering." For Richard, they were strictly business, possible cover shots for one of the planned Coyote Press books.

During this period, Bruce Conner grew much closer to Brautigan. Conner taught at the San Francisco Art Institute, one class of his choice and title each semester. The first course Conner described as "a life drawing class." His caveat was that only women students were allowed to register. "The concept was to see what would happen to an art class that was restricted to one sex," Conner recalled. "And of course, me being a male teaching [it]." Conner had a budget to hire nude models. Once, he hired a good-looking male model and the students were instructed either to draw him or draw *on* him. "That was very popular," the artist observed.

Richard Brautigan modeled for Conner's first or second class. He did not disrobe. Instead, the session became a reading, a Brautigan performance piece. Bruce Conner can't remember any of the students actually drawing. "This was a weird theater they had all come into."

The event had been previously announced, and one young student asked if her mother might attend. "Obviously, she disapproved of Richard," Conner drily observed. "Her daughter was taken out of the class shortly afterwards." The students didn't know what to make of Brautigan. His reading was greeted with "dead silence." Richard commented later to Bruce "that usually when he reads his good poems he gets laughter and stuff." Not this time. "It was a dead response."

Friendship with Conner and Michael McClure brought Richard Brautigan into contact with the Batman Gallery at 2222 Fillmore Street. Founded in 1960 by black-haired Billy Jahrmarkt, a wealthy young man "obsessed with the macabre and gothic," the gallery was named by Michael McClure for the Dark Knight of the funny papers. Jahrmarkt had a taste for black clothing and hard drugs and was so taken with the comic book hero that he started calling himself Billy Batman. The walls of the gallery were painted black, a happy contrast to the sterile hospital white endemic to most art-selling establishments. Batman Gallery's inaugural show featured the sculpture and collages of Bruce Conner. Conner's show was a great success, launching the Batman Gallery "into first place in the avant-garde." Conner observed, "It opened very spectacularly, but then it didn't function very well because Billy was a junkie." Over the first half of the sixties, the gallery showed the work of Jay DeFeo, Wally Hedrick, George Herms, and Joan Brown, all local artists of distinction.

The Beard was published that March by Coyote Books. Shortly afterward, the fledgling publisher ran out of funds and Richard got word that they would not bring out *In Watermelon Sugar* or his book of collected poetry. In spite of this disappointment, Brautigan's primary concern throughout the endless impromptu party of 1967 remained the publication of *Trout Fishing in America*. Robin Blaser contacted him early in the year about submitting a portion of the novel for the first issue of the *Pacific Nation*, a new magazine he was editing. As customary with small literary periodicals, no payment was involved. Richard agreed to let him use the first five chapters from the book.

Having design control meant not informing Donald Allen of every decision. When Brautigan arranged a date with Erik Weber for a cover shoot not long after Susan Morgan's visit, he already knew what he wanted. After auditioning alternative muses, Richard Brautigan chose Michaela to appear with him in the photograph. It was hard to resist a woman who ended her letters with "Cookies" and valued Richard's storytelling prowess above his skills as a lovemaker. They gathered in the Webers' kitchen next door. Erik set up his camera. Richard had a pose in mind with him standing against the refrigerator and Michaela seated to one side on a little wooden stool.

Erik remembered their earlier shoot in Washington Square and suggested packing everything up and moving the whole operation across town. Richard thought this an excellent idea. They all headed over to North Beach. Once again, the statue of Benjamin Franklin became the focal point for the session. Erik Weber arranged his subjects to form a balanced composition. Brautigan stood slightly to the right in his high-crowned hat and navy peacoat. Michaela Blake-Grand, wearing a white skirt, calf-high black boots and a brass-buttoned military-style tunic, a wide lace ribbon tied around her red hair, sat on the low stool to his left. Dr. Cogswell's monument rose impassively between them in the background. Unbeknownst to Richard, the stool upon which his muse perched that day had been built in the furniture workshop of Clayton Lewis, the very man his former lover, Anna Savoca, had run off with to Virginia City five years before. Watching without saying a word, Loie Weber found the business with the stool a "little odd thing."

Erik shot a roll of film. He experimented with different distances, yet the basic pose never changed after the first exposure when Richard stood to the wrong side, tugging on his hat brim with both hands. Once they got started, Michaela reached out to straighten Richard's jacket hem. He and his muse looked very relaxed, engaging in an easy banter. At one point, they cracked each other up. Brautigan endeavored to assume a natural stance, crossing his arms, folding his hands in front of him, placing them on his hips, before finally clasping them behind his back. It wasn't until the twenty-ninth frame that Weber captured the classic image that embodied an era.

When Richard gave Don Allen the photo, he also included prints of the solo portrait Erik took in front of the Benjamin Franklin statue two years before. Allen preferred the earlier picture and wanted to use it on the cover. When Erik heard the news he was adamant with Brautigan. "No, Richard," he protested, "you have to insist that it be this other one. It's much better." Brautigan listened to Erik's advice. Since Richard retained complete control of the cover art, "the rest is history," as Weber later observed.

In mid-March, Richard walked to the Fillmore Auditorium on a Thursday evening in the pouring rain to hear Gary Snyder read from his poetry cycle, *Mountains and Rivers without End*. Snyder sat on the stage floor with a candle burning at his side and read for almost two hours while pictures and colorful light explosions flashed on the wall behind him. Snyder was about to embark on another long trip to Japan, and many of his friends came to wish him bon voyage. Richard listened in the company of Albert Saijo and Lew Welch.

After the reading, a few people hung around, cleaning up the paper cups and candy wrappers littering the auditorium floor. Welch went out and bought a bottle of vodka, smuggling it back into the Fillmore, which did not permit alcohol. Lew and Richard shared a couple of shots, pouring booze into their coffee cups like kids at the prom. Later, Brautigan walked home alone up Geary Street through the rain. He was pleased to see a stream of rainwater pour down from a pedestrian overpass "like a small waterfall." Richard wrote a poem about the evening, lying in bed that night while incense burned on the table beside him.

During the first week of April, the Gray Line bus company began a daily two-hour excursion (Monday through Friday) through the Haight-Ashbury neighborhood. Billed as "the 'Hippie Hop' Tour [. . .] the only foreign tour within the continental limits of the United States," the Gray Line expedition borrowed a page from the past, when tourist busses prowled the streets of North Beach during the beatnik heyday. As then, the interlopers were greeted with a mixture of derision, disbelief, and a certain amount of acid head amiability. Richard Brautigan met the bus with his shard of mirror, reflecting the gawkers' curiosity back into their incredulous faces.

On the same day tour buses started navigating the Haight, an organization calling itself the Council for a Summer of Love held a press conference in a converted firehouse. Composed of representatives from the Diggers, the Family Dog, the *Oracle*, the Straight Theater, and other factions of the hip community, the Council planned to organize art exhibits and "celebratory events" as well as providing "a liaison to the straight world." There was only a halfhearted acknowledgment of the youthful hordes expected to descend on the neighborhood once school let out. In reality, the migration had already begun.

Bolder students heeded Tim Leary's advice and dropped out early. Among them were five young white men from Antioch College in Yellow Springs, Ohio. They had formed a band together the year before, drifting out to Berkeley in the spring of 1967. Antioch required its students to leave the campus every other quarter and work at a real job as part of their education, so the quintet didn't technically "drop out."

David Robinson (lead guitar), Rick Bockner and Thomas Manning (vocals, twelve-string guitars), Lawrence Hammond (lead vocals, bass), and Greg Dewey (drums) all got college credits for being in a rock group called the Mad River Blues Band. Greg Dewey's sister had an apartment in Berkeley on Telegraph across the street from the Caffe Mediterraneum. Her pad served as a convenient rendezvous as the various band members drifted out to the West Coast.

The band abbreviated their name to Mad River and found their own Berkeley crash pad nearby on Blake Street. The group had a good tight sound but like start-up bands the world over had a hard time finding gigs. Not long after they arrived in Berkeley, Richard Brautigan became their benefactor. Each band member tells a different story about how the group first met Richard. Tom Manning and Greg Dewey recalled Brautigan shyly approaching one afternoon after Mad River played at an event in Provo Park, the new hippie designation for Constitution Park. "He wanted to meet us," Dewey said, "pretty bizarre, actually."

Early in April, Glide Memorial Church, having recovered from the aftershock of The Invisible Circus, opened its doors at 8:00 PM for a "Free Digger Poetry Reading." A "Gestetnered" com/co flyer advertised the event as part of the Spring Mobilization against the War. Twelve poets stepped to the podium to read, including Brautigan, Ferlinghetti, Lenore Kandel, Lew Welch, Jim Koller, Ron Loewinsohn, Andy Hoyem, Bill Fritsch, and young Jeff Sheppard. This time, there were no naked bodies on the altar.

Brautigan read at Glide three more times the next year; first, at an event to raise money for the American Federation of Teachers strike fund at the end of February. Richard shared the stage with Muriel Rukeyser, Michael McClure, Kay Boyle, Thom Gunn, Robert Duncan, Denise Levertov, and Lawrence Ferlinghetti, among others. Foremost among the others was Elizabeth Bishop, a Pulitzer Prize winner and former Poet Laureate of the United States, who said she was participating out of curiosity rather than political commitment. She had never seen any of the famous San Francisco poets and "wanted to know what they were like." Bishop smoked pot before the reading and took a liking to Brautigan, who read for about ten minutes. Considering herself "a member of the eastern establishment [. . .] and definitely passé," Bishop thought Thom Gunn's poems and her own "were the best."

The second event, "San Francisco Poetry," came in mid-June, when Brautigan read with McClure, Philip Whalen, David Meltzer, Lenore Kandell, Andrew Hoyem, Joanne Kyger and Bill Fritsch. Keith Abbott was listed on the poster but did not appear, being off in Monterey for the summer. Brautigan's last appearance was as part of a program put on by the Intersection for the Arts, a small coffeehouse ministry (like the Bread and Wine Mission) that had opened its doors three years earlier in a seedy former Tenderloin bar a couple blocks further down Ellis from Glide. Richard shared the bill with Michael McClure. Freewheelin' Frank was in attendance, along with several other Hells Angels. Robert Johnson, Intersection's director, remembered that the occasion coincided with one of Dr. Benjamin Spock's frequent arrests for protesting the Vietnam War.

"[Brautigan] went out and got a newspaper," Johnson recalled. "[He] brought the paper into the church and started shouting and raving. People started throwing things from the balcony, set fire to the drapes." The Hells Angels pitched in to help quiet everybody down. Freewheelin' Frank, who'd had a beef with Johnson earlier on the steps, now helped him get the riot under control. "He got some of his motorcycle guys to take charge."

Angry Arts Week, organized by the Spring Mobe, got off to a jump start with a fund-raiser at Longshoreman's Hall featuring the Dead, Quicksilver, and Country Joe. Plans for a "constructfully disorderful demonstration" at the IRS office downtown to protest the special Vietnam surtax were put on hold. The following Tuesday the Gray Line tour bus was plastered with tomatoes as it cruised through the Haight.

Richard Brautigan did his part for the Spring Mobilization, creating a Friday night event for the Diggers. Peter Berg remembered it as "a memorial to someone who had died." Loving sly wordplay, Richard called his happening "Candle Opera." The com/co broadside, picturing a crude cartoon candlestick, advertised seven bands along with "candles, incense, love, etc." Country Joe and the Fish were the headliners.

Brautigan secured a spot on the lineup for Mad River, telling them about the gig only the day before, when he dropped by their apartment in Berkeley for the first time. (According to music historian John Platt, the first of Mad River's free concerts for the Diggers "was a Be-In held at night in a canyon near San Francisco." Given the timing, the Panhandle event likely preceded it.) The other groups scheduled for "Candle Opera" (New Age, All Night Apothecary, Group Morning Glory, Moebius) were all equally unknown.

The night of April 14 was cold and misty. The crowd gathered in the Panhandle at six, and the Diggers handed out hundreds of free candles. Lawrence Hammond of Mad River recalled Brautigan standing up onstage with the band "and candles all over this flatbed truck." As Peter Berg described it: "Richard had everyone light the candles at the same moment. Women were holding up white sheets; everyone was holding candles; Richard was beaming." Brautigan had achieved his creative vision. Here before his eyes stood a human candelabra, a lyrical take on Digger-style life theater.

Angry Arts Week concluded the next day with a big Spring Mobe peace march beginning downtown on Market Street and proceeding up Fell Street through the Haight, where it doubled in size before overflowing into Kezar Stadium in Golden Gate Park. Richard Brautigan did not participate in the march. He voted for Lyndon Johnson in 1964 because he believed the New Dealing Texan would end the war in Vietnam. When Johnson escalated the conflict, Brautigan felt betrayed and never voted again, maintaining an apolitical stance for the rest of his life.

Com/co published *Karma Repair Kit: Items 1–4*, Richard's numbered four-part poem (the fourth part deliberately left blank) early in April and Brautigan distributed the poem in the streets of the Haight-Ashbury. Kenn Davis, who drove a cab during this period, remembered cruising through the Haight and seeing Richard relaxing on a plastic lawn chair, handing out free poetry to the passing crowd. Brautigan made an effort to ensure special friends saw his newly published work, mailing copies of *Karma Repair Kit* to Michaela Blake-Grand, Susan Morgan, and Wes Wilson, the poster artist whose work advertised the Trips Festival and many of the dances sponsored by Bill Graham and Chet Helms.

Trout Fishing in America had been planned for release early in the summer, but a monkey wrench was thrown into the production schedule when a San Francisco typesetter turned down the job because he objected to a chapter ("Worsewick") that ended with sperm floating on the surface of a hot spring after the narrator and his woman made love in the water. Donald Allen had to rethink his publishing strategy. The Four Seasons Foundation operated on a shoestring, and the loss of the typesetter provided a blessing in disguise. Allen decided to print the book using an offset process and hired Zoe Brown, wife of Brautigan's friend Bill Brown, to type the manuscript and create a photo-ready dummy. The publication date was pushed back until fall.

Brautigan took the news in stride. The Communication Company afforded a more accessible publishing venue, and Richard decided to use the Duboce Avenue facilities for more than simple broadsides. Since his stint at Cal Tech, Brautigan had written a number of new poems, and it made sense to bring out a collection of his latest efforts. As always with his com/co productions (indeed all his earlier self-published chapbooks), Richard acted as his own designer, overseeing every aspect of production.

Erik Weber lived right next door, but Richard wanted a photographer with closer connections to the Haight-Ashbury for his cover shot. At the time, the three best-known camera artists in the Haight were Tom Weir, Bob Greene, and Bill Brach. Both Brach and Greene hung their work in the Psych Shop. Bill Brach owed his singular reputation in part to a number of fine studies made of Janis Joplin. He simply asked prospective subjects if he might take their picture. He did this with Brautigan, and Richard said yes.

Brach didn't find Richard Brautigan especially social. "I used to see him all the time," he remembered, yet they never hung out together. When Bill Brach showed up one afternoon at the apartment on Geary Street, he was visiting the home of a stranger. Brach took a number of photographs of Richard that day. Scouting for an interesting new location, they went down into the basement, where Brach posed Richard in a doorway, sitting in a laundry sink and staring out a small street-level window.

Brautigan favored this last shot and took it with him over to com/co later in April, when it was time to assemble the new book. Hayward had an IBM Selectric in his apartment, and Richard typed up thirty-two of his most recent poems, including all his previous com/co broadsides. Knowing it to be one of his best, he chose "All Watched Over by Machines of Loving Grace" as the book's title poem. Brautigan wrote out the title of each poem by hand and signed his name on the printed title page. Claude can't remember where the paper and ink came from, although he's certain Richard must have supplied it. "There would have had to have been a vehicle involved," he wrote years later, "because 1,500 copies was four cases of paper."

The entire production took only a couple days after Brautigan completed the typescript, which "passed rapidly through the Gestefax." Hayward needed a few hours of "tinkering" to get "the right degree of graininess" for Bill Brach's basement window photo on the yellow cover stock. H'lane helped with the cover layout as Claude manned the Gestetner. Hayward finished the printing "in an overnight burst of energy."

Brautigan assisted in collating the pages, a "tedious" nontechnology of walking round and round the table stacking the sheets. The Communication Company now owned a folder and a stapler and the edition was assembled in a remarkably short time. The haste sometimes showed, as certain copies were bound with pages out of order, others with duplicate pages, pages upside down and missing. Several purpose statements appeared on the reverse title page and front free endpaper. The first of these began, "Permission is granted to reprint any of these poems in magazines, books and newspapers if they are given away free," and the last ended, "None of the copies are for sale. They are all free."

Brautigan misspelled the photographer's name in the second of the statements. "Bill Brock lived with us for a while on Pine Street. He took the photograph in the basement. It was a beautiful day in San Francisco." Brautigan lived alone on Geary Street. Bill Brach shared an apartment on Pine with Mime Troupe actor Peter Coyote and a "crazy artist" named Carl Rosenberg. Brach recalled that a Digger couple lived out on the back porch in a pile of rags, "in squalor like rats." Fifteen hundred copies of *All Watched Over by Machines of Loving Grace* were handed out for free. Richard Brautigan made sure a copy was sent to Malcolm Cowley. Not one was given to the photographer. To this day, Brach has never seen the ephemeral little book.

Andrew Hoyem arranged for Basil Bunting to give a reading in San Francisco at the end of April. Sponsored by the Poetry Center, Bunting read the complete *Briggflatts* (published the previous year) at the San Francisco Museum of Art. Afterward, the Frisco poet community wanted to show him a good time. A small group got together at the home of John and Margot Doss. Lew Welch was there, along with Don Allen. Andrew Hoyem brought his girlfriend (later his wife) Judy Laws. Richard Brautigan came with Lenore Kandel.

They all smoked pot (Richard included) and went out for dinner in Chinatown. Sitting around a big circular table for eight at a Grant Avenue restaurant, waiting in a cannabis afterglow for the food to arrive, the group invented an impromptu game of stud poker, using knives, forks, and spoons in place of cards. "We just made it up as we went along," John Doss recalled. Basil Bunting told a war story about the time his Doberman pinscher ate his commanding officer's toy poodle and got the whole group singing a jingoistic imperial military song. "An old British-army or service-person-overseas kind of song where everybody gets screwed," according to Dr. Doss. The Chinese waiters looked on impassively as the strains of "Troop Ships Are Leaving Bombay" lilted discordantly through their establishment.

After the meal, when the bill was paid, Brautigan and Lenore Kandel "went skipping down Grant Avenue." The Dosses assumed they were headed for a romp in the sack, forgetting that no sane man deliberately cuckolds a member of the Hells Angels. According to Bobbie Louise Hawkins, Brautigan told her that Kandel was one of a quartet of women "he thought of as friends, very distinct from women he thought of as drivers, cooks, lovers." The other three were Joanne Kyger, Joanna McClure, and Hawkins herself.

At the end of April, the Communication Company moved out of the Haight-Ashbury to an office far off in the Richmond District. The new address (742 Arguello Street) was not made available to the public, and community participation dropped off. Chester Anderson had fallen out with com/co over what he felt was a betrayal of the McLuhanite vision he espoused at the start of the enterprise, four months earlier. He and Claude Hayward were no longer speaking.

The hard-core faction in the Diggers demanded that com/co attend mainly to their own political agenda. Digger announcements and flyers occupied an ever-increasing proportion of the available printing time. In addition, the Diggers insisted on donating com/co's services to the newly formed Black Panther Party over in Oakland. The first issue of the party's newspaper was printed on the Gestetner. In May, com/co's output "shrank by more than half."

The huge billboard in front of Brautigan's house on Geary Street advertised Australia that May, with a gigantic picture of a kangaroo. Watching the big marsupial at night made Richard ponder the vitality of the written word versus the raw power of graphic imagery. He noted that the lights on the billboard switched off at midnight and wondered what time it was down under.

After his first two trials ended with hung juries, Ken Kesey pleaded *nolo contendere* on May 2 to "knowingly being in a place where marijuana was kept," a lesser charge carrying a ninety-day penalty. That same afternoon, Brautigan went to see *Billy the Kid versus Dracula*, a horror movie playing in a cheap theater on Market Street. Both men were a long way from the Heilig Theater in Eugene.

At high noon on the fourth of May, the Diggers offered free spaghetti to office workers on the steps of City Hall. When asked what they wanted City Hall to do for them, the Diggers answered, "Eat." Later that month, strange five-foot-high posters appeared all over town, picturing two Chinese tong hit men lounging on a street corner above the slogan 1% FREE. The posters were designed by Peter Berg and stencil artist Mike McKibbon. They borrowed the "1%" from the Hells Angels, who wore the symbol on a patch sewn to their "colors." The motorcycle club referred to themselves as the original "one-percenters." Together with a bunch of other Diggers, the Hun and McKibbon spent the night plastering their work to city walls, fences, and freeway columns. Soon afterward, the tong image appeared as a com/co handbill and in place of George Washington's portrait on a flood of newly minted "Digger Dollars."

Alvin Duskin, the clothing mogul, introduced a plain shirtwaist minidress boldly decorated with large peace symbols in May, creating an instant hit in the local boutiques. On the fifteenth, the Gray Line canceled the Hippie Hop bus tour, even though it had grown so popular there were two trips each day. Traffic congestion on Haight Street was the reason cited. Close to the end of the month, a unanimous jury declared *The Love Book* "obscene and without redeeming social value." Two days later, Lenore Kandel donated 1 percent of the book's profit to the Police Retirement Association. She said this was her way of "thanking the police" for bringing her work out of obscurity. Before the cops raided the Psychedelic Shop, the Thelin brothers had sold perhaps fifty copies of *The Love Book*. After the bust, sales climbed to over twenty thousand. The donation amount was tongue in cheek. Kandel's husband, Bill "Tumbleweed" Fritsch, was a Hells Angel.

At a time when nearly everyone seemed to be living a dream, Brautigan's ascending star in the hip community added further elements of the surreal to his bohemian life. After staying up most of one night writing and drinking red wine, Richard was awakened just before dawn by an insistent pounding on his front door. He lay thinking about it for a while before padding down the long cold parachute-hung hallway in his nightshirt.

A striking statuesque blond named Cassandra Finley stood on his doorstep. She looked like an exotic reincarnation of someone from an earlier earthier time. Her singular dress reinforced this image, ropes of glass beads, black fur-trimmed shoes and gloves, her hood lined with white fleece. She didn't know Brautigan, seeking him out for unknown reasons of her own. Shivering, Richard contemplated her beauty, at a complete loss for words. "I came to be with you," she said.

Brautigan turned without a reply and headed back to bed. The mysterious blond stranger followed him through the chilly apartment. She undressed while he watched, shivering under the covers. Like many gypsy voyagers on the road to Nirvana, Cassandra traveled light, wearing most of her clothes to minimize luggage. She took off several loose cotton blouses and layer after layer of full embroidered skirts. When she was naked (except for her long lapis earrings), she slipped into bed and wrapped a trembling Richard Brautigan in her pliant arms. Cassandra's blond pubic hair excited Richard. He remarked upon it later. In his notebook, Brautigan wrote a prose-poem he called "Magic," saying he had "never laid a blond woman, and being so carefully naive," he wondered if they were "blond all the way down as I am."

Cass Finley didn't stay with Brautigan for long, a few weeks at most. During their brief time together, he took her out to Bolinas one Sunday to visit Bill and Zoe Brown. They liked her, intrigued by her commanding presence. As they returned to the city, their driver worried about finding a parking space. When they neared their destination, Cassandra gave him directions, saying he'd find a spot at the end of the block. Just then, a car pulled away from the curb. Impressed with her powers as a seer, Richard asked Cass to tell him what his own future held in store. She refused. He demanded to know why she kept silent. "Know only I won't be with you," Cassandra Finley replied. She was right on that score.

In mid-May, Brautigan took part in a San Francisco State Writer's Conference, a three-day event at Camp Loma Mar in Pescadero, a small seaside town twenty miles north of Santa Cruz. Over fifty local writers had been invited to participate. Stephen Schneck and Herbert Gold were on the list. So were Don Carpenter, James Broughton, Thomas Sanchez, George Hitchcock, Lester Cole, Lawrence Fixel, Lenore Kandel, Janine Pommy Vega, Bill Fritsch, and Mr. and Mrs. Stan Rice. (In 1967, Anne Rice was an unknown poet while her husband commanded a reputation sufficient to gain him a spot as a workshop leader and featured reader.) "Don't forget your bedrolls," the participants were instructed.

Richard caught a ride south with Andrew Hoyem. He was scheduled to read at eight that night in company with fellow Diggers Lenore Kandel and Bill Fritsch. "Also bring a bathing suit and, of course, some of your work to read," S.F. State advised. Brautigan did not own a bathing suit. His daughter can't recall ever seeing him wear one. What Richard enjoyed was witty conversation and hanging out with writers. The weekend at Camp Loma Mar offered ample amounts of both.

After three days of sunshine, readings, workshops, and literary chit-chat, the conference ended with a "Festival of Feeling" for which the Grateful Dead provided music. Standing among a gathering of talented poets, watching the sun set over the Pacific as Jerry Garcia's blues guitar solos soared into the crisp sea air, Richard Brautigan must have felt like one of the anointed few. His time was surely soon to come.

twenty-nine: willard

RICHARD BRAUTIGAN PROVIDED an accurate description in *Willard and His Bowling Trophies*: "Willard was a papier-mâché bird about three feet tall with long black legs and a partially black body covered with a strange red, white and blue design like nothing you've ever seen before, and Willard had an exotic beak like a stork." He was not making this up. As with all Brautigan's work, flights of imaginative fancy were grounded in the reality of his everyday life. Even the bowling trophies.

Willard was the creation of Stanley Fullerton, one of a flock he made with wire frames stuffed with the Sunday *New York Times*, covered with canvas strips dipped in gesso and painted with whatever was on hand. "I tend to make art objects in great floods or piles," Fullerton later declared, "until I run out of gas or have finished that conversation."

By the middle sixties, the artist lived in Pacific Grove, California, and had acquired a bit of girth. Always a large man, Stan now favored suspenders and a Greek sea captain's cap. This was no mere nautical affectation: Fullerton put out to sea in his gill netter at 3:00 am, "every morning the bar could be crossed," looking for "a fog bank to fish in and hide under." He didn't care much for other people and made no secret of it. "Stan never had a nice word to say about anyone or anything," one old acquaintance recalled. He detested all other artists, with painters topping the list of the despised. That's why he got along with Price Dunn, another irascible iconoclast. Fullerton lived with a large menagerie of cats and exotic birds (mynahs and toucans). "I never met an animal of any sort that I didn't prefer to human kind," he later wrote. "Animals and birds of all sorts come to me. We speak each other's hopes, and we live in harmony till their end comes."

After returning to Pacific Grove from Mexico ("the obligatory hermitage"), Stan got involved "with a sweet young airhead" and planned to leave again soon in a "barely able" pea green 1937 municipal water department tool truck. Price stopped by one day for a visit, hoping to take over Fullerton's Pacific Grove house after the artist moved north to the little town of Marshall on Tomales Bay. About to abandon everything he owned, Stan gave him some of his big colorful cartoonish paintings along with a batch of drawings and etchings. Price spotted the gaudy three-foot papier-mâché bird perched in a corner. "Hey, I like that," he said. "That's nice." Fullerton told him he might as well take the damn thing along with him.

Price Dunn had no idea that Stan made the bird as a "satire" of Richard Brautigan. "A portrait in caricature," was how the artist put it years later, "for in his walk and carriage in early days [Richard] resembled nothing closer than a white stork." Many of these bird portraits had bull's-eye targets painted, in Fullerton's words, "on some portion of their anatomy, something to denote the behavior of the person thus parodied and not dissimilar to the basic behavior of birds." Stan found it "skookum tee hee (a joke of the spirits)" that Brautigan ended up with the bird he had intended as a burlesque on the writer's essential nature.

Price hauled the unlikely looking creature home and parked it on a bookshelf, christening him "Willard," for no particular reason. "I just started a spontaneous fantasy," Dunn remembered. "Poor old Willard, he's an orphan, you know. He's got a speech defect." It began in a bar, Price regaling his drinking companion with tall tales. "I used to have this bird," he told the stranger, "and I loved this bird. So, I made this sculpture of Willard just to remember him by, because I loved him so much." Bit by bit, the fantasy grew, and the legend of Willard was born.

The bowling trophies came soon afterward. Price and his brother, Bruce, had an old truck they used for their moving business, and after a job they found a bunch of discarded bowling trophies left behind by a client. For no obvious reason other than a love for the absurd, Price stacked them around Willard. Bruce Dunn immediately joined in on the joke. "God," he told Price, "I've got some bowling trophies that belong to Willard, too." He brought them over, and soon a shrine was born, the absurd papier-mâché bird surrounded by dozens of gleaming statuettes.

In spite of his strained finances in 1967, when Richard Brautigan came to visit Price in Pacific Grove, they'd go down to Nepenthe, the restaurant located on property once owned by Orson Welles, or up to Monterey and "put on the feed bag. Live high, drink high." One night after dinner at the Sardine Factory, they returned to Price's place and Richard encountered Willard for the first time. "What the hell is this?" he laughed.

"*Shhhh*!" Price fell into his joking mode. "Please don't offend Willard, Richard. You realize this is probably, next to you, my best friend. Willard thinks you're weird." Price went on in this vein, telling Brautigan the history of Willard and making a formal introduction to the artificial bird. "And he says, 'Oh, hi, Willard.' He just buys it hook, line, and sinker. He loves it. It's just the sort of weird fantasy he would like."

The subject of Willard became the theme of the weekend. The painted bird was the only thing Richard could talk about. The next day, he met a girl and went off with her, telling her all about his new friend "Willard," certainly one of the more bizarre pickup lines in the history of romance. When Richard returned and it was time for him to go back to the city he told Price, "I don't know if I can part with Willard."

"You've formed that kind of a bond with Willard," Price replied, enjoying the joke more and more. "Maybe he'll go home with you. Just ask him and see."

Richard went along with the gag, going through the motions of asking Willard to come away with him. "Yeah," he said at last, "he wants to. He wants to go to San Francisco."

"Well, goodbye, Willard," Price replied, a touch of feigned sadness in his voice.

And so the multicolored bird came to live in Richard's Geary Street apartment. On a later trip, Brautigan returned to Pacific Grove and collected all the bowling trophies, bringing them back to re-create the Willard shrine in San Francisco. He treated this sort of nonsense with utmost seriousness. Richard believed Stanley Fullerton had painted Willard's face in such a way that his expression changed from time to time, shifting from serious to apprehensive like "a kind of bird *Mona Lisa*."

Whenever Price came to visit the city, he inquired about Willard, wanting to know all about the bird's recent adventures. When they were drinking, the Willard stories grew ever more convoluted and absurd. "Just a goofy game," to keep the fantasy alive. Over time, the game evolved into an elaborate ritual, the objective being to leave the other guy stuck with Willard. Richard might sneak the peculiar bird under the tarp in the bed of Price Dunn's pickup when he wasn't looking. Price retaliated by smuggling Willard back into town and hiding him in Brautigan's closet. Keith Abbott wrote of Price adopting "his best Southern idiot voice" for the game. "Willard's been getting lonesome for you. It's time for you to take care of Willard again, Richard."

The game went on even after Richard Brautigan was forced by circumstance to move out of the Geary Street apartment. When the rest of his odd collection was "packed up," the painted bird went along with him to live in a two-bedroom apartment on Telegraph Hill opposite Coit Tower. Willard provided a link to the days of impoverished Bohemia. Several years later, Richard started work on a new book. One day, he brought Price Dunn the just-completed manuscript. "I've got something for you to read," Richard said, suppressing a sly smile. Price glanced at the title page: *Willard and His Bowling Trophies.* Now, it was his turn to grin. Once again, his best friend had turned a private fantasy into literature. The book's subtitle, *A Perverse Mystery,* seemed right on the mark.

As Richard saw Price less frequently, he continued the Willard game with other friends. When Brautigan began traveling to Japan in the 1970s, he left the bird with Curt Gentry. "He would say that I would have to soak his beak once a week in bourbon," Curt reported. "And a couple of times he came back and said I hadn't done it, and he would take Willard away." For a while, Gentry kept a framed photograph of Willard on his bureau.

"Even a bird needs to get out once in a while," Richard told Ianthe, explaining why they had to haul the absurd creature along with them on evening excursions. In her memoir, Ianthe Brautigan described a dinner party at Curt Gentry's house when she was seventeen. Richard brought Willard and insisted that he sit at the table with his own place setting and a drink of whiskey. Ianthe didn't mention her father had spent the day drinking with his buddy Tony Dingman, who was leaving the next morning for the Philippines to work as a production assistant on Francis Ford Coppola's *Apocalypse Now.* When Richard called the Gentrys to ask if he might bring Tony along for a final aloha, Gail Stevens (not yet Mrs. Gentry) said no. Her sit-down dinner was planned for twelve, and she didn't want to set a thirteenth place at the table. Brautigan showed up with Willard instead. Gail was not amused. This was the last time Ianthe ever remembered seeing Willard. She thought somehow the painted bird had slipped through her father's fingers, vanishing forever into the vast limbo of detritus littering the soul of our republic.

Willard lives on. One evening in the late seventies, Richard sat at his favorite table in Enrico's enjoying a drink with his actor friend Terry McGovern, who played the part of the high school teacher Mr. Wolfe in *American Graffiti.* Terry lived in Hollywood, but an account for work in commercials kept him commuting back and forth to San Francisco every week. Brautigan had Willard with him, the colorful long-billed bird perched awkwardly on his lap. Every so often when the mood struck him, he dipped Willard's beak into his glass of Calvados. "You have to dip his beak," Richard explained.

"Willard's great," Terry said, just passing the time, and Richard Brautigan handed him the big bird. "No, Richard," the actor protested, "I'm going back to Los Angeles tonight. What the hell am I going to do with this bird?"

Richard smiled. "Just take it," he said. "Make sure to dip his beak."

Later that night, McGovern rode in a cab with Willard down the Bayshore Freeway to the airport. On the flight to Los Angeles, Terry preferred sitting in the rear of the plane, where the seats faced one another and there was more leg room. It was also closer to the drink cart. The stewardesses were entranced with Willard. "They just thought it was the cutest thing in the world, and oh, isn't this adorable and so on and so forth."

After a bit, who should wander back to get his drink refreshed but State Assemblyman Willie Brown. "And he made a big fuss over Willard," McGovern remembered. "And I explained to him that Willard has to dip his beak if you want to be a friend of [his]." The actor dipped the bird's beak into the politician's brandy, and the Willard brotherhood expanded its circle.

Today, Terry McGovern lives with his wife, Molly, in the comfortable Marin County town of San Anselmo, and Willard resides with them. By giving away Stanley Fullerton's curious sculpture (just as the artist had donated the bird to Price Dunn, who passed it on in turn), Richard continued a process of liberation that had become an inherent function of the work itself.

thirty: brief encounter

BY THE SECOND half of the 1960s none of Linda Webster's dreams seemed to be coming true. Her marriage to her boyfriend from high school had not turned out happily. For years, the relationship had been physically abusive. He started beating her when they first began going steady, but she stuck with him. Brutality and fear became the glue binding them together. One savage cut from a can opener left her leg scarred for life. The unseen wounds etched on her heart recorded more permanent damage.

The dysfunctional couple had moved with their daughter to Santa Rosa, California, where Linda, like so many other young women busy with the counterculture cottage-crafts of the era (macramé, decoupage, weaving, throwing pots, winding gaudy woolen god's eyes), took up stringing beads. This eventually led to a successful career as a jewelry importer, but at the time it was simply a distraction from the misery plaguing her life. Over the years, her memories of Dick Brautigan's chaste poetic courtship had evolved into an intense romantic fantasy. "It meant a lot to her to think someone cared that much about her at one time," Linda's sister recalled.

Linda Webster saved all the poetry Richard had written for her but not in its original form, fearing what might occur should her husband happen to discover it. She rewrote each poem in her own hand, substituting her husband's name wherever hers appeared. Should he find and read one, he'd think she had composed it for him. Linda hid the clippings she cut from Herb Caen's column in the *Chronicle* whenever he mentioned Richard Brautigan. She sent these to her sister Lorna, asking her to save them.

Every so often, Linda would sneak down into San Francisco without telling her husband. Her destination always remained the same. Linda headed straight for City Lights Bookstore in North Beach. She knew from the stacks of Richard Brautigan's slim books on sale there that he was bound to show up sooner or later. She spent her time reading the announcements on the bulletin board, hoping to learn of public poetry readings or anything else she might find of interest about him.

One afternoon, hanging out on the Columbus Avenue sidewalk in front of the bookshop, she spotted Richard approaching from across the street. He looked quite different from the callow youth who had courted her a dozen years before, but she recognized the long hair and mustache from the cover photo on *Trout Fishing in America*. The stooped, loping walk remained fixed forever in her memory.

Just before he entered City Lights, she stepped up and asked, "Is your name Richard?"

And in a very quiet voice, he answered, "Yes."

"Richard Brautigan?" Linda inquired.

"Yes."

This was embarrassingly painful. After a pause, Linda got up her nerve to ask, "Do you remember me?"

Brautigan looked at her through his rimless glasses and very quietly said, "No. I'm sorry. I don't."

Linda Webster knew in her heart that there was no way he would recognize her after so many years. She wanted to say, "You used to pick cherries at my grandmother's." But her tongue couldn't find the words. She didn't say a thing.

"I'm sorry," Richard repeated, quiet and polite. He stepped around her and headed for the bookstore entrance.

Linda turned and ran. She ran across Grant Avenue and up through Chinatown, running along the streets onto the steep slope of Nob Hill. She never looked back. She never saw Richard Brautigan again in her life.

thirty-one: summer of love

"IF YOU'RE GOING to San Francisco, be sure to wear some flowers in your hair." So went the Pied Piper lyrics of a tune hitting the charts with a bullet in June of 1967. John Phillips (founder of the Mamas and the Papas) wrote the song for his friend Scott McKenzie. The Diggers responded with a sarcastic broadside lampooning Phillips. Without AM airplay, their message did nothing to stem the rising runaway tide flowing toward Frisco.

Sgt. Pepper's Lonely Hearts Club Band provided a more significant musical event that same month. There had been hints of the drug experience in both *Rubber Soul* and *Revolver*, but now it could no longer be denied: This latest Beatles record was full-on psychedelic. Rich with over-dubbing and orchestration, the new songs spoke straight to the love generation. Everyone hip recognized the LSD in "Lucy in the Sky with Diamonds." Another track dealt with a teenage girl running away from home. The album's message came through loud and clear: "I want to blow your mind . . ."

One look at the cover told the whole story. The Beatles positively glowed, resplendent in Technicolor marching band uniforms, sporting new facial hair and more epaulets and gold braid than a quartet of South American generalissimos. To drive the point further home, arranged behind them stood Madame Tussaud's wax manikins of the Fab Four clad in their dark 1964 mod suits. The times indeed were a-changing.

When Richard Brautigan first heard the Beatles' record, the off-kilter imagery in the lyrics about a woman who "keeps her face in a jar by the door" or a girl "with kaleidoscope eyes" validated his own tangled poetic metaphors. "Being for the Benefit of Mr. Kite," the words taken down almost verbatim from an antique circus poster owned by John Lennon, mirrored Brautigan's fondness for utilizing found art in his work. The Beatles were enormously popular, world famous. An audience receptive to Richard's work was surely out there, ready and waiting.

With summer fast approaching, free rock concerts in the Panhandle became a regular occurrence. Emmett Grogan returned from New York at the end of April and promptly got a permit to stage the "Outlaw Mutation Boogie" after dark with colored lights strung through the trees and two giant kliegs beaming up into the night. He corralled Country Joe, Janis Joplin and Big Brother, and the Grateful Dead into performing. The Dead, beloved within the hip community as the people's band, all lived together in a big Victorian house at 810 Ashbury. They could be called upon to play at free concerts and benefits anytime, night or day. When police arrested members of the band on drug charges early in October, Richard Brautigan commemorated the event with a poem, "The Day They Busted the Grateful Dead." He wrote it was "like hot swampy scissors cutting Justice / into the evil clothes that alligators wear."

Poetry occupied most of Brautigan's creative attention as spring exploded into summer. Knowing a collection was in the works started him sorting through a decade's worth of manuscripts. He had planned to write a piece on the local scene for an issue of *Coyote's Journal* being edited by Bill Brown and Joanne Kyger, but a balancing piece from the East Coast turned out "all wrong" and was rejected, thus letting Richard "off any ambiguous news hook." The assignment, according to Bill Brown, had opened up, giving Brautigan "the freedom to go where you want, if you want, into whatever. OK. There is no hurry."

During that spring, Brautigan made frequent trips to Santa Barbara to visit Jack and Vicki Shoemaker and spend time with Susan Morgan. Once, he took the babysitter up to the Maytags' mountain home, where they ate burnt cheese sandwiches "and made beautiful love." Afterward, while Donovan sang on the radio and Susan slept late, taking up the entire bed, Brautigan wrote "The Sitting Here, Standing Here Poem," which was never published. When Morgan awoke, Richard had gone out. She found the poem sitting on her desk and wrote out a copy. "I felt like I was kind of snooping by looking at what he was working on," she recalled. Brautigan later showed her the poem but never gave her a copy.

On another occasion, a conversation in the Shoemaker living room about the possibility of an "edible book" or a "disposable book" led to the genesis of Richard's notion to print poetry on seed packets. The idea was to have them ready to give away at a "Digger-inspired" summer arts festival called the Santa Barbara "Free-in." Planned as "an all-night affair" on East Beach opposite the Bird Refuge, the event was sponsored by the Unicorn Bookshop and a group known as The New Community. The disposable book project proved too complicated a notion to finish in time. Early in June, when Richard headed south with a "caravan of pickups," accompanied by Lenore Kandel, Bill Fritsch, Jeff Sheppard, and numerous Diggers (who drove the com/co Gestetners down on a flatbed), it had been decided to print and hand out "broadsheets, slogans, and other graphics" in the manner of the John Dillinger Computer.

As the designated spokesman for the Free-in, Richard Brautigan was interviewed by the local newspaper and described the various semiplanned events. In addition to com/co's "on-the-spot" publishing, poetry readings were scheduled, along with light shows by Aurora Glory Alice and Dry Paint and a "happening" directed by an artist known only as Annette. "One novelty will be the serving of food—hot dogs, fruit, soft drinks, etc.—at no charge," the paper reported. Although Brautigan did not predict how many people the Diggers would be able to feed, an estimated crowd of a thousand gathered on the weekend of June 3 for the beach festival.

Susan Morgan, one of the event's organizers, found Richard changed, "so lacking in the sweet quirkiness I had enjoyed." In true Digger fashion, they set off in a VW bus to comb the supermarket Dumpsters for usable fruit and vegetables. Susan felt distanced from Brautigan, who struck her as "full of himself—cresting the wave of new popularity." Her roommate was driving, and to drown Richard out, she and Susan began a loud, rude, speed-fueled conversation "about the price of cantaloupes."

This was the last real contact Morgan ever had with Brautigan. Richard wrote her once or twice over the next couple years, letters lost on the winds of time. Sometime in 1969, when she was living in Bolinas, Susan ran into Richard downtown in the company of a real estate agent. "I greeted him warmly, and he pretended not to recognize me," she recalled more than three decades later. "It was really bizarre and insulting."

The Santa Barbara Free-in featured a huge bonfire. Much of the food prepared for the masses got cooked in giant trash cans. "A variety of local bands played spontaneously," Jack Shoemaker remembered. These included Raw Violet, Underground Railroad, Haley Street Snack Factory, and Alexander's Timeless Blooz Band. Mad River was among the headliners. They traveled down from Frisco with the Diggers, drinking and partying all the way, and played on the beach. Later, they crashed in the sand and slept until dawn.

The crowd had thinned by eight in the morning, but "there were still clusters of 'free-iners' on the beach. As promised by Brautigan, a cleanup committee gathered most of the accumulated trash left behind by the revelers. Even the police deemed the festival a success. Everything was "orderly, relatively quiet." There were no arrests and only fifteen parking tickets handed out. "We hope they're all like this one," the assistant police chief said. The love generation had again staged a huge peaceful outdoor celebration. Here was another manifestation of new age consciousness, this time with Richard Brautigan front and center as the star of the show.

A week or so later, Brautigan escorted Margot Patterson Doss on a walking tour of "Hippie Hill" in Golden Gate Park, a gentle slope of green lawn rising above Kezar Drive and overlooking the Park Police Station. Groves of eucalyptus and oak framed the meadow on either side, providing a quiet retreat where residents of the Haight could sprawl napping in the sun, play their guitars, and pass joints around without any worries of getting busted despite the close proximity of the fuzz. Margot figured Hippie Hill would make good copy for her *Chronicle* column. Ever the attentive guide, Richard asked his friend to make sure she pointed out "the quietness and color of the scene."

Jefferson Airplane's single "Somebody to Love" climbed to number 3 on the national hit parade in June. The *Oracle* published its eighth issue, a hundred thousand multicolored copies sprayed with Jasmine Mist perfume and dedicated to American Indians. On the tenth, a local AM rock station sponsored the Magic Mountain Fantasy Fair on Mount Tamalpais in Marin County. An estimated crowd totaling thirty-six thousand showed up over both days to hear the Airplane, the Doors, the Sons of Champlin, Country Joe, and the Steve Miller Blues Band, but the real action came the following weekend down in Monterey.

Inspired by the Be-In and numerous Digger-hosted musical events, John Phillips and record producer Lou Adler teamed up to present the Monterey International Pop Festival, a three-day extravaganza that the Diggers denounced as "a rich man's festival," the "old star/manager/booking agent syndrome." Nearly 100,000 fans turned out to hear a galaxy of stars ranging from the Who, the Grateful Dead, and the Byrds to Booker T. and the MGs, Laura Nyro, Steve Miller, South African jazz trumpeter Hugh Masekela, and sitar master Ravi Shankar. The festival was filmed by Donn Pennebaker. His footage transformed Janis Joplin, Otis Redding, and Jimi Hendrix from near unknowns to international superstars.

Always a diligent if minimalist correspondent, Richard Brautigan did not write a single letter that June and only one the previous month and in the month following. In all, he wrote just two letters between the first week of April and the second week in August. Something else was on his mind. In mid-June, Richard wrote a poem called "Love Ain't No Tragedy" about the inevitable end of a love affair. With the publication of *Trout Fishing* pushed back until fall, Brautigan distracted himself with romance and poetry.

Unlike the Be-In, the Diggers' planned solstice celebration would be another "Do-In" like the Invisible Circus. An Emmett Grogan manifesto called on the people to "build their courage [. . .]

They will look to their brothers and not men who claim to be their leaders." Around one thousand gathered on Twin Peaks, Frisco's highest point, to greet the dawn on the morning of June 21. Later, they all wandered down to Speedway Meadow, joining the crowd near the Polo Fields in Golden Gate Park, where the Diggers had set up stages and barbecued lamb. Charles Perry reported, "There were archers, magicians, jugglers and many freelancers playing whistles, flutes and guitars, and even a Tibetan liturgical orchestra complete with conch shells, Chinese oboes and six-foot-long trumpets. The Dead, Big Brother, Quicksilver and other bands played, using Fender speakers and amps surreptitiously borrowed by the musicians from Monterey Pop." Richard Brautigan almost certainly joined in. The party marked the official start of the Summer of Love.

Sometime toward the end of June, Richard Brautigan walked into a tiny storefront attorney's office on McAllister Street, not far from the Hastings School of Law. Minimally furnished with an antique rolltop desk and a bright orange rug, the place was homey and inviting and as far removed from mahogany-paneled law office formality as its occupant, Richard Hodge, in his pink corduroy suit, was from the pinstriped mentality of mainstream attorneys. Hodge had gained a local reputation in the Haight for his spirited defense of several Mime Troop members, busted for singing Christmas carols and soliciting alms, and the pro bono work he did at the Free Legal Clinic established by Peter Berg. (Hodge later learned that he had once given free counsel to Charles Manson.)

Dick Hodge had already read *Confederate General*. When Richard walked in unannounced, Hodge immediately knew who he was. "Richard, I'm surprised you didn't come in before now," the lawyer said. Brautigan regarded Hodge "quizzically," a look familiar to the writer's friends. Richard needed legal help to get several Diggers out of jail. Dick Hodge had been recommended by David Simpson, a Digger who met Hodge when they both served in the Coast Guard. "One of my very first clients probably," Dick said, remembering Richard Brautigan's initial visit. "As we talked, he told me he wanted some help in his various publishing affairs." It was a pivotal time for both of them: a young lawyer setting out on his own and a struggling writer on the verge of breaking through to fame and fortune. In time, Hodge came to regard himself as "Richard's conduit to the world of reality."

His connection with the Diggers provided Dick Hodge with a growing and lucrative clientele. Harvey Kornspan, a Digger friend of David Simpsons, had become Steve Miller's manager. The week after the Monterey Pop Festival, the Miller Blues Band backed Chuck Berry at the Fillmore Auditorium, a gig recorded live for an eventual album release. Miller needed some contractual advice, and the Digger axis led him to Richard Hodge. Soon after that, Miller's band signed with Capitol and Hodge negotiated a contract that the pop star's website later described as "one of the most lucrative [. . .] in music history, setting a new standard for future artists." The revolutionary contract gave Miller complete artistic control and secured him a reversionary provision stipulating that after ten years he got back total and complete ownership of his tapes. This one brief clause made Steve Miller a very rich man. Eventually, Richard Hodge represented Kenny Loggins, the Joy of Cooking, Mad River, and Commander Cody and His Lost Planet Airmen, along with a host of other groups.

At the Festival of Growing Things, a rock concert on Mount Tamalpais on July 1, the promoters gave away free flower seed packets to all who attended. If Brautigan wasn't there, he certainly heard about it. Billy "Batman" Jahrmarkt's wife, Joan, went into labor four days later with Richard in attendance. Kirby Doyle, "a mad Irish poet," documented the birth. His novel,

Happiness Bastard, had been published by com/co. Doyle wrote of Richard walking "through the rooms, tall, slightly stooping like a gentle spider standing up."

Claude Hayward drove Dr. John Doss in from Bolinas ("John Doss, way over 6 foot, a tower of a man with those huge gentle hands [. . .]"), and after twenty-four hours of labor, he and H'lane and Doyle witnessed the delivery, along with a crowd of devoted Digger women and the three Bat children, Jade, Hassan, and Caledonia. The baby boy was named Digger by his father. "At the instant Billy Batman called his child by their name the Diggers knew it was given away," Emmett Grogan wrote five years later. "They never used it to refer to themselves again." From that moment on, the Diggers were called the Free City Collective. Kirby Doyle's account of Digger Batman's birth eventually became an anonymous part of *The Digger Papers*.

It is not known when in early July Richard Brautigan first met Marcia Pacaud of Montreal, Canada, but on the twelfth, he wrote a couple of unpublished poems in her sun-bright Sausalito apartment (number 5) at 14 Princess Lane. Both "A Place Where the Wind Doesn't Live" and "The Planted Egg, the Harvested Birds" were dedicated to Marcia, a tall intelligent woman who parted her shoulder-length blond hair straight down the middle. The Pacaud family hailed from Sandstead, Quebec, near the Vermont border, where they lived in a house built in 1867.

Marcia Pacaud had an affinity for poets. She worked at the Tides Bookstore in Sausalito and had been a friend of the Canadian poet and songwriter Leonard Cohen. Richard instinctively understood the path to Marcia's heart was paved with poetry. He told Keith Abbott that she possessed "an inner acceleration." On a single day in mid-July, staying again on Princess Lane in Sausalito, Brautigan wrote five more poems for Pacaud.

These included "Map Shower," a paean to her long blond hair and, finding even her idiosyncrasies adorable, "The Shenevertakesherwatchoff Poem" after noticing that Marcia wore her leather-strapped wristwatch even to bed. Brautigan was enchanted with Pacaud's golden hair, and most of the poems he wrote for or about her made mention of her "long blond beauty." "Richard and his blonds," a friend once commented. Michael McClure observed, "Blond or brunette didn't matter." In McClure's opinion, Brautigan's "sex appeal bloomed with his fame."

Brautigan's shyness had long caused him to be somewhat awkward around women, and when exotic creatures like Cass Finley showed up on his doorstep in the middle of the night it came as a revelation. Magda Cregg told a story illustrative of Richard's ambivalent attitude regarding his sex appeal. One afternoon in the mid- to late sixties, she and Lew Welch and Brautigan were walking down Haight Street, "and Richard tries to pick up a girl, and she refuses him, just in passing, and he goes, 'I wouldn't go to bed with anything I could pick up.'"

The paucity of Brautigan's correspondence during the Summer of Love speaks volumes about the initial intensity of his relationship with Marcia Pacaud. The eloquence of silence, broken only by a mid-August letter to Marcia. One hint of the degree of Richard's passion for his new blond flame came from Don Carpenter, who had met Marcia and found her "a good head, very intelligent woman." Don asked Marcia why, when things had been going so well with Richard, they broke up two weeks after moving in together. She told him "that once Richard knows you love him, he worships you and he drives you absolutely fucking crazy. He gets down on his knees to you."

At age seven, Ianthe had no interest in worshiping Marcia Pacaud. The Canadian woman was always nice to the little girl, but whenever Ianthe came to visit and Richard left her alone with Marcia, she would draw close and whisper, "You're not my mother—go home." This upset Pacaud a great deal, occasionally reducing her to tears. Richard never got angry with his daughter about such behavior. All she had to do was "smile sweetly up at him."

Sometime in July, Richard introduced Marcia to the Webers. Like Americans everywhere, they gathered in the kitchen. Erik got out his camera and started shooting pictures. Richard sat in a wooden chair wearing love beads and his familiar hat and vest, holding his long fingers steepled together. Marcia sprawled at his feet on the geometrically patterned linoleum, a Cheshire cat smile masking her true feelings. She stood up, long and lithe in snug-fitting blue jeans. Erik climbed onto a chair, taking his last shots focusing down into Pacaud's wide-eyed upturned face. Brautigan appeared reduced and diminished, almost lost in the background.

Richard wrote "Horse Child Breakfast" for Marcia Pacaud and her "long blond hair." Michael McClure envisioned the woman in the poem as "a filly [. . .] probably she has a long palomino mane and sleek legs." McClure thought Brautigan's "delicate" poem was "canny and memorable." "It's gorgeous!" he exulted. Richard concluded, "Horse child breakfast / what you're doing to me, / I want done forever."

This was not to be. Brautigan remained incapable of sustaining lasting committed relationships. An unknown girlfriend from this period wrote a curt note breaking things off with him. "The only one of your favorite things I can do with you is fuck, and that isn't enough for me," she declared. "I didn't guess when you said you didn't want a girl as your center just how far away from your center you wanted a girl to be." She ended with a reprimand: "Illusion stomps out reality like an anesthetic stomps out sensation or a boy scout his campfire. and fucking reality will go too. before that does I will altogether. Writing this is unreal." Richard saved her card for the rest of his life.

The single letter Richard Brautigan wrote during the spring and summer of his passion for Marcia Pacaud was to his agent. Bob Mills had written in mid-July to say that *The Abortion* had been read and rejected at Harcourt Brace, Simon & Schuster, Viking, Putnam's, Harper & Row, Random House, and William Morrow. "The consensus seems to be that it's not quite a complete, unified book." Mills didn't send only bad news. Robert Cowley, an editor at *Horizon*, had heard of Brautigan and wanted "an article or two" for the magazine.

Richard responded, saying he'd like to write "about the Diggers in San Francisco." Robert Mills either lost this letter or never received it. When Brautigan wrote again a month later to ask, "What's happening with the Horizon article?" his agent confessed that when the magazine didn't hear back from him in a timely fashion they assigned the piece on the San Francisco scene to someone else. Mills mentioned that the other writer "tried to get in touch with you while he was there, but couldn't find you, they tell me."

A phone call from New York around the end of July provided Brautigan with an opportunity to write about the Diggers after all. William Jersey, president of Quest Productions, a small film company, wanted to do a story about the hippies in San Francisco and called Richard to talk things over. Jersey, a University of Southern California film school graduate who got his start as art director on the Steve McQueen horror flick, *The Blob*, had moved into documentaries. The previous year, he produced *A Time for Burning*, a civil rights film that had been nominated for an Academy Award. In the course of their conversation, they discussed life in the Haight-Ashbury. Richard told Bill Jersey a little of his involvement with the Diggers. They worked up an "idea," and Jersey agreed to pay Brautigan $1,000 for an "expanded treatment."

Quest Productions sent Richard Brautigan a check for $500, the second half payable once a finished treatment was delivered. Should the treatment later be developed into a film script with further work required, Richard would be paid "commensurately." Brautigan signed the enclosed papers, mailed them back to New York, and set to work. He titled his film story "Magicians of Light," a reference to light show artists like Bill Ham and Ben Van Meter.

"Magicians of Light" was to be a movie about making a movie. A New York filmmaker scouts for locations in San Francisco. Many of the scenes take place in familiar Brautigan territory: the Presidio pet cemetery, Foster's cafeteria on Market Street, Golden Gate Park, a "VD Clinic," a light show commune, and "a psychedelic whorehouse" on Telegraph Hill. Richard also suggested additional scenes be shot using actual members of the hip community. "Perhaps people like: Michael McClure/Grateful Dead/Janis Joplin/with/Big Brother & the Holding Company/Bill Graham/Allen Cohen/Red & Jay Thelin/ etc etc etc etc etc."

As an outline for a motion picture, Brautigan's treatment seemed oddly static and lacking dramatic tension. Nothing much happens. The characters wander about almost aimlessly. Scene 18 is typical: "There is another knock at the door. The poet answers the door and it is Willard. He comes in and joins them in the bedroom. Somehow he ends up on the bed, too. They are all sitting there talking. It is kind of nice in a warm magic way. Then they have breakfast."

Richard wrote his fifteen-page screen treatment at great speed in a few days. Impatient, he wrote Bill Jersey: "Hey, I haven't received the second five hundred dollars yet. I'd like to get it soon. I need the money for projects I'm working on here in San Francisco." He received his payment without further delay.

The $1,000 represented the bulk of Brautigan's total income ($1,356.75) for 1967. Richard's gross income for 1965 was only $940.45 and his advance from Grove Press (never earned out) for *Confederate General* came to $1,500. "Magicians of Light" was a slight pedestrian effort with virtually none of Brautigan's unique quirky imagination in evidence. Considering Richard's Digger ethos and the quality of the work he gave away for free, the whole endeavor hints at a rip-off. Quest Productions never made the film.

Brautigan often traveled south to Santa Barbara in August to visit Jack and Vicki Shoemaker. He hung out at the Unicorn and read his work on a weekly two-hour Sunday literary program Jack hosted at a local radio station. Richard sometimes brought Marcia Pacaud along. Jack Shoemaker never really got to know her well. "It was Richard's habit to keep his girlfriends silent and behind him," Shoemaker recalled. "He was an instantaneously jealous man."

Things looked grim in the Haight-Ashbury at the beginning of August. The Summer of Love was turning out to be a bad trip just as the Diggers had predicted. Overcrowded with runaways ripe for the fleecing, Haight Street became a favored hunting ground for social predators and strong-arm artists. Rape was a common, if generally unreported, crime. The waiting room at the Free Clinic remained perpetually crowded with VD sufferers. An epidemic of methedrine hit the street, and speed freaks wandered about like walking wounded, jabbering manically to themselves.

The increased drug trade opened the door to more serious crime. On August 3, a well-known acid dealer named John "Shob" Carter was found stabbed to death in his apartment, his right arm neatly severed at the elbow. The missing limb turned up in the trunk of Shob's car along with his pistol and a large quantity of cash. At the wheel sat celebrated motorcycle racer Eric Frank Dahlstrom, who told the police, "I'm very, very hazy about that arm." Three days later, the body of renowned black dealer Super Spade was found in a sleeping bag snagged on some cliffside rocks near the Point Reyes Lighthouse in Marin County. He had been stabbed in the chest and shot once through the back of his head. Super Spade's corpse had only $15 in a worn wallet, yet friends claimed he had carried nearly fifty grand in cash only the week before.

The bad vibes continued. Chester Anderson feuded with the Diggers and split from com/ co. The Gestetners were moved to the basement of the Trip Without a Ticket. Anderson split for Florida, permanently denied access to the machines. After his return, he moved to the East Bay. Claude Hayward went over to see him, thinking Chester still had the Gestetners. Anderson, crazed on speed, pulled a gun. They never spoke or saw each other again. On August 23, Chocolate George, the affable Hells Angel, was struck by a motorist while driving his chopper on Haight Street. He died of a skull fracture the next day in General Hospital. The whole summer was turning out to be an epic bummer.

A peek into Richard Brautigan's pocket notebook revealed the broad extent of his social contacts in 1967. A page scrawled with telephone numbers compiled a Who's Who of the current scene. Among the names were Lew Welch, Lenore Kandel, The Flying Circus, Marty Balan [sic], Chet Helms, Bill Fritsch, and Sopwith Camel. Another small notebook from 1967 contained addresses and phone numbers for "Emmett," Margot St. James, actor Rip Torn, and Harvey Kornspan (Brautigan misspelled his name with a "C"). The most illustrious contact was John Lennon. Richard had his phone number. Brautigan wrote the address down as "Waybridge [sic], England." Lennon owned Weybridge, an elegant Tudor-style home in Kenwood, a "stockbroker belt" suburb of London.

Rip Torn found his place in Richard's notebook courtesy of Michael McClure, whose play The Beard appeared in Barney Rosset's Evergreen Review. Having published Henry Miller, D. H. Lawrence, and William Burroughs in his long one-man struggle against the U.S. censorship laws, Rosset wanted The Beard (and the controversy attending it) as the first production for his new Evergreen Theater in New York. He suggested Rip Torn as the director for the project (still starring Richard Bright and Billie Dixon), and the actor flew out to Frisco to meet with McClure.

They got together at Enrico's for a lunch of linguini and white clam sauce. Michael brought along Don Carpenter and Emmett Grogan. Both wanted to check the actor out. Also present was Jim Walsh, a New York producer in charge of The Beard, who favored Torn to direct the play. Former child star and current UN ambassador Shirley Temple Black sat at a nearby table. When Rip greeted her with a nod, "she coolly nodded back."

At the end of the meal, Enrico Banducci joined them, treating the table to a round of espresso and Courvoisier. The expensive cognac Brautigan adored but could seldom afford brought Richard into the conversation. At the mention of his friend's name, Michael McClure "started to giggle." Rip Torn would have happily spent the rest of the day at Enrico's, but McClure had made other plans. "We won't wait up for you tonight. You and Richard are going fishing." Shaking his head and laughing, McClure added, "Try to get back before the week ends."

After getting directions, Rip Torn drove his rental car out to Geary Street and parked in the Sears lot across from Brautigan's place. When he rang the bell, the door was opened by "a woman friend," who said, "I'm on my way out. Richard's in the back brewing some tea." Rip found Brautigan presiding over the kettle. He'd met Richard at a sushi bar the previous fall, but Richard had "hidden" from him. This time around, Brautigan was more affable. Over cups of tea their conversation ranged from *The Beard* and the San Francisco poetry scene to *Beowulf* and "fishing for half-pounders in Oregon." Taking note of his "falcon's gaze," Torn thought Brautigan had an anachronistic resemblance to Custer and Mark Twain.

Brautigan organized his fishing tackle, outlining his plans for the day. Numbers of nine-inch fish were "bottled up" in a freshwater pond behind the sandbar at Muir Beach where Muir Creek ran to the sea off Mt. Tamalpais. "Everybody thinks I'm crazy," Richard said as he bent down the barbs on his dry flies with a pair of needle-nose pliers. "That these fish are just rainbows planted by the parks department, but I think they're little steelhead waiting for a rain so the creek will cut the sandbar and they can go to sea." After buying fly dope at Sears, with Rip behind the wheel, they were on their way across the Golden Gate Bridge and up Route 1 to Muir Beach.

Brautigan dismissed Rip Torn's gear. "Bass fisherman," he drily observed, tying up a new nine-foot leader with a 7X tippet for Rip. The actor knew almost nothing about fly-fishing, having previously caught only bluegills on dry flies. Although he didn't cast badly, Torn felt his ability was "nothing compared with Richard's effortless form." Brautigan "caught and released three small fish." Rip caught one.

After that, Richard revealed the ulterior motive for his fishing trip. "We're all friends of McClure's," he said. "We hear you're right to direct his play, but I'm leery of New York and, well, I figured if you checked out as a real fisherman, were telling the truth about that, that you were probably straight in the art department, too." Brautigan suggested they leave the little trout "for the Rain God" and repair for a "sundowner" to the No Name Bar in Sausalito. Here they plotted getting together for "some real trout fishing" at a future date.

Erik and Loie Weber left San Francisco on August 20, planning an extended stay in India.

Two weeks before their departure, Erik took Richard out to the garden behind his Geary Street apartment for a final photo session. It was the only time Weber ever photographed his friend in color. The day was damp and chilly. Richard wore his familiar navy peacoat fully buttoned. ("The coldest winter I ever spent," Mark Twain once quipped, "was summer in San Francisco.") For fun at Brautigan's suggestion, Erik took a picture of him seated in the grass, his right hand cupped around a stray yellow jonquil. This image (used on the cover of *The Edna Webster Collection of Undiscovered Writings*) provides the only example of Brautigan adopting the "flower power" iconography of the 1960s.

The Webers hosted a dinner party for family and friends at their apartment as a way of saying goodbye to Geary Street. Erik's mother was among the guests. Richard brought Marcia Pacaud. They spent the evening making out passionately on the couch, oblivious to the party going on around them. "He was in love with her," Erik remembered. "He seemed like a little kid."

Soon after the Webers left for India, Ernest Lowe, a producer at KQED, the local public access television station, wrote Brautigan, asking if he might be interested in working on a film. No real money was involved. A lifelong love for the movies impelled Richard to say yes. The end result, *Ellen, Age 3, versus American Television*, a six-minute short, starred Ianthe Brautigan's little half sister, Ellen Aste, who now goes by the name Ellen Valentine Spring. Brautigan's shooting script may well be the shortest in film history, consisting of five numbered questions, all variations on the same theme.

The film was made in the kitchen of a Lombard Street apartment belonging to a friend of Brautigan's former wife, Ginny. Ianthe watched the shoot from the sidelines. Richard asked the cameraman, "Are you ready?" and reappeared with three-year-old Ellen. While Ellen ate an orange at the table, Brautigan asked her his questions. "What kind of animal would you like to see on television?"

"Purple," she answered. It was her favorite color.

The other questions remained the same, only the subject changed: "What kind of dinner?" Richard inquired, " toy? . . . bird? . . . person?" Every time, the little girl said, "Purple." At the end, Brautigan asked Ellen if she'd like to see herself on television. When she answered in the affirmative, Richard replied, "Well, I think you will." Cut. The film ended almost as soon as it started. In postproduction, close-ups of the various items were inserted. Because the film was shot in black and white, none of these (ham TV dinner, wind-up pecking bird toy, picture of a Native American, etc.) appeared in purple. There is no record that *Ellen, Age 3, versus American Television* was ever shown on KQED.

Ernest Lowe wasn't ready to give up on the idea of a Brautigan project, and he urged Richard to give it another try. What Brautigan had in mind was an experimental project as vapid as the work of Andy Warhol. Unlike the pop artist's interminably long films, Richard sought the soul of brevity. Not long after, a film team from KQED arrived at Geary Street. Producer Lowe brought cameraman Loren Sears, who worked in sixteen millimeter. Richard had a simple four-page typed script. They filmed in Brautigan's trash-filled backyard, taking numerous close-ups of discarded junk and long tracking shots past broken bottles, headless rubber dolls, and abandoned automobile tires. For the script, Richard compiled a handwritten list of three dozen place names from Yosemite National Park. He called the project *Ghetto Yosemite.*

Most of the work was done in the editing room at the beginning of September. Brautigan wrote Bill Jersey that he was working on his movie, "learning how to edit." He called the process "beautiful magic!" They reduced their footage to a total length of three minutes. Even with this short running time, the film was divided into four "chapters." Each showed the title and credits superimposed over black-and-white photographs of scenic locations in Yosemite. With traffic sounds (sirens and honking horns) in the background, the camera examined various pieces of trash as Richard read a voice-over narration: "This is Ghetto Yosemite located in the Western Addition of San Francisco. A lot of poor people live here. This is their Vernal Fall, their Castle Cliffs, their Inspiration Point [. . .]"

Inspired by the adventure serials he enjoyed as a kid, Brautigan ended each forty-five-second episode with a fey cliff-hanger. The first "chapter" stopped on the word "Half," while the second began with the word "Dome." The second concluded "Merced." The third started "River." Each chapter finished with the phrase "Don't Miss Chapter 2 (3 [. . .] 4) of Ghetto Yosemite" spiraling into focus over a scenic photo of the national park. The next chapter repeated the opening credits. *Ghetto Yosemite* aired on KQED "Channel 9" the next year, and the station sent Brautigan a check for $30.

With Erik Weber off in India, Brautigan looked for another court photographer to take his place. Richard had known Edmund Shea since the days when he worked at the chem lab. They bumped into each other one night at Vesuvio in North Beach and discovered they had friends like Michael McClure and Bruce Conner in common. "We must have talked about art and stuff like that, writing, poetry," Shea speculated. "I drank a lot of wine with Richard over the years." Edmund had produced definitive images of Lenny Bruce, Bill Graham, and various rock-and-roll notables. Brautigan knew he did professional work. It was important to have a photographer he could call at a moment's notice. Richard wanted more pictures of Marcia Pacaud, but she returned for a visit home to Canada in the middle of September. After she left, Brautigan felt at loose ends, making his way down to Big Sur to hang out with Price Dunn.

Partying with the General didn't take his mind off longing for his woman. Richard wrote her a poem ("Marcia in Montreal") and mailed it off in a letter. In all, he wrote her four times between September 17 and October 3, his only correspondence during that period. Perhaps trouble had been brewing before her departure and Richard was trying to smooth things over. A few months after her return they were no longer a couple, although they remained friends and correspondents for years afterward.

Brautigan distracted himself during Marcia's absence with a teenage artist he met in Monterey. Dottie Hochberg was a flower child nearly half his age. She wrote him ornate, elaborately illustrated letters for years following their first meeting, even after she married Gene Godare and had a baby. Richard saved every one.

On Labor Day weekend, Kendrick Rand, whom everyone called "Kend" at that time, opened a coffeehouse called The Minimum Daily Requirement at 348 Columbus Avenue, the triangular corner at the intersection with Grant. The plant-filled MDR provided a cool leafy-green retreat in the heart of North Beach. Rand had been part of the scene in the late fifties but had run a restaurant out on Union Street for the past few years.

At first, business was slow. Richard Brautigan became one of Kendrick's first customers that fall. The Hashbury circus began losing its appeal, and Richard gravitated back toward North Beach. Three years earlier, Rand had seen Brautigan's picture on the back of *Confederate General* and recognized the author as a guy he remembered from Miss Smith's Tea Room or the Bagel Shop a decade before. "Richard came in [to the MDR] a couple of times," Rand recalled. "He would always sit back there all by himself, come in about one o'clock in the afternoon and have his coffee and just take in the scene."

Rand had gotten the notion that Brautigan was "a difficult person." One of the waitresses working at the MDR knew Richard slightly and introduced him to Kendrick. "I used to nod and say 'Hi, Richard,' and 'How are you doing?' and then he started calling me Kendrick, which very few people called me, and I have been Kendrick ever since." The two men started talking more and more on each of Brautigan's subsequent visits. They ended up going out to dinner one night at Woey Loy Goey's, one of Richard's favorite places in Chinatown, where he had dined with Joanne Kyger during his first spring in Frisco. "Sort of like the men's room at Grand Central Station," Kendrick remembered. "All tiled floor, walls, and ceiling and the noise factor is incredible. Very bright lights, mediocre Chinese food, but Richard loved it." Brautigan was intrigued by Rand's patrician East Coast background. "Middle-class suburban yacht club, country club, kind of fascinated him, because [it] was like a foreign world."

Kendrick was separated from his first wife. Richard, between girlfriends after Marcia's departure for Montreal, "started hanging out in my joint." This involved finding inexpensive places to eat. "He knew the cheap restaurants in Chinatown like the back of his hand," Rand recalled. "There was one place he referred to as 'the Pork Chop Palace' where he got three pork chops and a huge mound of either rice or mashed potatoes with pork gravy on it for $1.98. He thought that was fabulous."

Having left his car with his estranged wife, Kendrick was without wheels. His friend Alvin Duskin, the wealthy garment manufacturer and political activist, came to Rand's rescue and gave him a "cherry" black Cadillac Coup de Ville and "a whole new life." Brautigan, antennae finely tuned for anyone who might provide transportation, soon was riding in style with Kendrick. Once, they tooled out to Muir Woods on a fishing foray, winding the big car down through the tight curves on Route 1. They fished Muir Creek where Richard had taken Rip Torn, a ribbon of silver purling between the redwoods toward the beach. Richard spent days planning this trip. "All the preparation that went into this little late afternoon fishing expedition," Rand reminisced. "I mean, many trips to Figoni Hardware to get the right size hooks and some kind of roe. I didn't catch one fish. He caught about half a dozen."

Shortly after its com/co publication, Richard mailed copies of *All Watched Over by Machines of Loving Grace* to a number of important literary editors and critics. Malcolm Cowley wrote a card thanking him for the "*pensees*, like grasshoppers in flight, not my sort of poems, but lively & personal." The title poem was Cowley's favorite. A letter from *TriQuarterly* editor Charles Newman went one better. Newman "particularly" liked the title poem and asked if he could use it in a future issue of the magazine. Brautigan wrote back the next day to give his approval.

When Mad River's six-month lease was up on their Berkeley apartment in September, the band moved across the Bay to a new pad on Oak Street overlooking the Panhandle. "Once we got to the city, Richard became a regular visitor," Greg Dewey recalled, "almost daily." Usually, Brautigan arrived toting a gallon jug of cheap white wine, "Gallo chablis or the like." Richard also brought Emmett Grogan, Bill Fritsch, and Lenore Kandel over to Mad River's flat. Sweet William often came accompanied by outlaw bikers. Lawrence Hammond remembered once "walking into the living room and there were two Hells Angels there. I was kind of intimidated. Richard and Bill were just sitting there grinning. And these Angels were riffing about guns and shooting themselves in the feet. I was watching Richard, and I had the feeling that he was taking it all in and getting ready to write it down. I think he liked to do that, put people together and then sit back and watch."

"Richard was a great guy," Tom Manning said, commenting on the writer's powers of observation. "He was a spacey guy, in the sense that you think he is looking at you and he's seeing you, but he's seeing right through you and behind you and above you at the same time. He was always like that. He was one of the sweetest guys I've ever met in my life." When not sitting back and watching, Brautigan often became quite animated. Hammond recalled how the poet regaled them at times. "When he was really wound up, he would pace back and forth with that funny floppy hat, and his hands behind his back, and just deliver all these lines."

One of the attractions for Brautigan at Mad River's pad was the number of lovely hippie chicks hanging out there. "I always think that he wound up at our place 'cause we generally had these beautiful women around," Dave Robinson recalled. "God bless him, Richard would go after anything that wasn't nailed down. We didn't see much of the women he was with; he was kind of guarded. He was guarding his and eager to meet *ours*!" Tom Manning doesn't remember ever seeing Brautigan with a woman. "I don't know if he kept them away from us on purpose," Rick Bockner said. "I suspect that he wasn't an entirely happy man."

Through Brautigan, the Mad River musicians got to know the Diggers, who took a liking to them. "We were very young, and we didn't know what the hell we were doing," Greg Dewey reflected, "and they were guys who were out there and had been around. They were very kind to us and took care of us. It was a major gift that we had them in our corner. Without a doubt, it was Brautigan who put us in that corner."

In addition to providing gigs where the hat might be passed, the Diggers also supplied free food, and often as not, Richard served as the delivery boy. "When we'd come back and open the refrigerator," Lawrence Hammond remembered, "there'd be all this food in it, and we were *starving*. That was the Digger thing, free food." Knowing firsthand what it was like to go hungry, Richard Brautigan delighted in his Robin Hood role.

Brautigan liked all the guys in Mad River but grew especially fond of Lawrence Hammond, the group's twenty-year-old chief lyricist. For a young man, Hammond "took his craft seriously," which naturally appealed to Richard. Greg Dewey recalled that Brautigan "was fascinated with Lawrence's writing," and they dug rapping with each other. Hammond noted, "We didn't talk about art too much. I don't think he liked to talk about it. If you talked about what you were working on before it was finished, it became very difficult to finish it, for some reason. I seem to remember him commenting on that." Brautigan had a way of talking indirectly about art in his most casual offhand remarks. Greg Dewey remembered one hot summer afternoon in San Francisco when they both felt a moment's relief from a gentle passing wind. "You know that little breeze, Dewey?" Richard said. "That little breeze was just like a poem."

In September 1967, Richard Brautigan focused on the imminent publication of *Trout Fishing in America*. When Don Allen sent the cover material to Zoe Brown early in August, he suggested that the author's name and book title appear "across the top above the photo on the front." Richard quickly squelched that idea. The book's front cover would consist of Erik Weber's photograph and nothing else, no title, no author name, no words of any sort, nothing but this bold iconographic statement. Later, it was rumored that Richard Brautigan first gained a national reputation when all the summer dropouts returned to college with copies of *Trout Fishing* in their knapsacks. A nice story, but the book wasn't published until a month later. The returning wayfarers carried com/co broadsides or *All Watched Over by Machines of Loving Grace*.

Luther Nichols, an early and enthusiastic supporter of Richard's work, maintained a connection throughout the years. When Ishmael Reed, a young African American writer whose first novel, *The Free-Lance Pallbearers*, had just been published by Doubleday, came up from Los Angeles that fall, Nichols asked him if there was anyone in Frisco he'd like to meet. Reed had read Brautigan and said, "This guy's an exciting writer."

Nichols arranged for lunch at Enrico's. Ishmael had been urging Nichols to get Brautigan published by Doubleday, unaware of the editor's initial efforts on behalf of *Trout Fishing* and that his publishing house had recently rejected *The Abortion*. At their luncheon, Reed found Brautigan to be "a private person. He didn't say very much." Ishmael thought Richard looked "very much like the hippie stereotype or the beatnik stereotype," but remembered him saying "he didn't even know those people. He didn't seem to be part of any kind of scene." The lunch at Enrico's launched a friendship lasting through the years until Brautigan's death.

The autumnal solstice marked the temporal end of the Summer of Love. Spiritually, the psychedelic frolic faded out a few weeks earlier when the last of the seasonal runaways packed up their gear and hitched out of town, heading back to school. With the tourists, spare-change artists, and most of the barefoot waifs departed, Haight Street took on a deserted tawdry appearance, like a carnival midway after the bright colored lights switch off and all the rubes have gone home for the night. Unlike the festive zeal greeting the equinox, the fall solstice arrived with little worth celebrating. A planned powwow at Speedway Meadow attracted only about six hundred participants. That night, the Straight Theater hosted an "Invocation of My Demon Brother," a Satanist ritual honoring the birthday of Aleister Crowley. The moon was in the sign of Scorpio. Filmmaker Kenneth Anger and a group calling itself the Brotherhood of Lucifer hosted the event with a Ben Van Meter light show and music by the Orkustra (renamed the Wizard for the occasion). Despite that old black magic, not many people showed. The Hashbury party was over.

In the fall of 1967, Mad River released a three-song EP recording with Wee Records, a local independent label. The record came in a handmade cardboard sleeve the band assembled themselves. Rick Bockner recalled Brautigan joining in on the impromptu assembly line: "That was a fun project. Five guys, a chunk of hash, and some mucilage, gluing the covers together." Wee released a thousand copies. The disc sold well in the Bay Area and got a lot of airplay on KMPX, thanks to "Big Daddy" Tom Donahue, who dug Mad River's sound. This led to the band's signing a contract with Capitol soon after. Because of Richard's prior kindness, Mad River gave him part of their advance and claimed on the liner notes of a 1995 CD compilation that this money "paid for the printing of Brautigan's new novel [sic] *Please Plant This Book*."

Mad River may well have given Richard a sum of money (Rick Bockner thinks it came to around $500), but not all might have gone toward *Please Plant This Book*. Jack Shoemaker stated that he and Vicki provided the funds that paid for the seeds and the seed packets, while Graham Mackintosh donated his time and press to design and print the folded cardboard cover. Brautigan had first approached Claude Hayward at com/co about printing the book. For technical reasons, Claude could not do it for him. "There was a problem with getting the little envelopes through the machine."

"Richard was a great networker, and he played everything very close to the vest," Shoemaker recalled. "It's perfectly conceivable that he would have gotten several hundred dollars from Mad River and several hundred dollars from me and God knows where all. Richard was doing this grand dance, and he would collect from here and give off there. It was the Digger style."

The planning and financing of *Please Plant This Book* became a moveable feast. After its inception at the Shoemakers', the idea got kicked around at several different venues. Brautigan always liked hearing a variety of opinions before drawing his own conclusions. Art Boericke remained certain that the idea for the book "took shape" at Peter Berg's house. Richard appreciated Berg's intelligence and street-theater philosophy and would have sought out his opinion. As a professional gardener, Boericke was able to get the seeds wholesale.

Brautigan made a folded poster paper mock-up of the book he had in mind, drawing the cover in crayon. His childlike sketch showed a black horse surrounded by carrots and flowers, happy bursts of red, yellow, and green. Richard crayoned his name and the title on the cover and typed the eight poems on slips of three-by-five paper. He typed planting instructions on eight similar-sized slips and created dummy seed packets by taping them together. On the back cover, using a thin-tipped Magic Marker, Brautigan wrote, "This Book is FREE."

Richard kept busy raising funds for his giveaway seed-packet poetry project with the actual production still months in the future. Bruce Conner's campaign for San Francisco city supervisor existed in a similar state of flux. While supporting himself as a janitor and a salesman in a knick-knack shop, Conner made time for politics, giving speeches that consisted entirely of long lists of deserts, his run for office partly an art project. A serious side to his electioneering included intense opposition to the war in Vietnam.

Edmund Shea had originally filed for the position but had to drop out of politics after he was busted. Bruce took over in his place. Edmund assisted the campaign by handling the photography for two political posters. One depicted Conner as a baby. The other showed the artist painting an elephant. Bruce Conner also enlisted Richard Brautigan and the Diggers to help. Conner and Peter Berg had been talking about peace and how to achieve that impossible goal. "We were discussing this about the end of the war," Conner recalled, "and the thing to do to end the war was to *end* it and tell everybody it's ended and to celebrate its end and put into people's minds the concept of the war is over."

Peter Berg "and some of the other people who liked to organize such things" focused on "interior theater" and enlisted the Straight Theater for the event. Brautigan wrote a speech for the occasion. The text no longer survives, but Conner remembered it to be, "like many of Richard's things," no more than twenty-five words in length. Brautigan had another publicity idea for Conner's campaign. In 1964, the artist exhibited a group of thirteen canvases, the *Touch/Do Not Touch* series, at the Batman Gallery. Twelve of the uniform black-framed artworks (which Conner was careful never to touch) contained the information do not touch in "museum-sized lettering." On the thirteenth, the same size as the others, Conner applied transfer letters spelling out touch and covered the work with a sheet of glass. Three years later, Richard Brautigan's brainstorm was to photograph the words "Do Not Touch" and reproduce them on sheets of paper.

Bruce Conner took a picture of the center of his work. "We printed them on hundreds of little file cards." At the Straight Theater before Conner spoke, Richard handed out the "Do Not Touch" cards like political flyers. "I'm going up to the balcony," he told the artist, "and after your speech I'm going to disperse them to everyone. It's a grand gesture." True to his word, Brautigan stood at the balcony rail and, when Bruce Conner finished speaking, tossed the remaining cards into the air, and they showered down, fluttering onto the crowd like a pasteboard snowstorm. "They were all over the floor, and virtually nobody picked them up," Conner recalled. "It was sort of a mystery to me why he had chosen to do that." Bruce Conner did not win a seat on the San Francisco Board of Supervisors, but his artist's antiwar campaign possessed a certain oddball appeal, enough to garner him over five thousand votes.

Copies of the first edition of *Trout Fishing in America* (two thousand copies) came back from the printer at the end of September before the official publication date of October 31. Richard inscribed one of the first books out of the box to Don Allen, writing "thank you" and adding two little fish sketches. A week later, Brautigan mailed a copy to Bob Mills, asking his agent to see if "something might be done to interest a New York publisher in the novel." With the book priced at $1.95, at his straight 10 percent royalty, Richard stood to earn under $400 if the first printing sold out, and he was anxious to investigate more-lucrative venues.

Trout Fishing was a slim handsome volume, its dedication ("For Jack Spicer and Ron Loewinsohn") enclosed within one of Brautigan's whimsical grinning fish doodles. The title page, designed by Brautigan, had the words "Trout Fishing in America" arching upward in a tight parabola, "like a bent fishing pole." Erik Weber's photo appeared on the front cover without margins, bled to the edges like the *Life* magazine covers Richard greatly admired. Due to an oversight, Weber's photo credit was omitted.

The back cover contained three "comments" on *Confederate General* from John Ciardi, Thomas Parkinson, and the *Kansas City Star*. A spark of Brautigan's wit glittered below them. Under the heading "Incidental intelligence" he included a quote from an editor at The Viking Press that Bob Mills had forwarded to him after the publishing house rejected *The Abortion*: "Mr. Brautigan submitted a book to us in 1962 called TROUT FISHING IN AMERICA. I gather from the reports that it was not about trout fishing."

A final Haight-Ashbury street ceremony early in October made manifest what had long been evident to anyone not totally stoned out of his mind. Peter Berg, always attuned to effective life theater, organized an event he called the Death of Hippie. A candlelight funeral procession began at sunrise on Buena Vista Hill. "Taps" was played and various hippie insignia tossed onto a fire. The parade, several hundred strong, marched down Haight Street carrying a black cardboard coffin draped in black crepe paper with the words "Hippie, Son of Media" painted on the side. The coffin contained flowers and beads, shorn hanks of long hair, all manner of "hippie paraphernalia." Richard Brautigan brought Joanne Kyger to witness the historic event.

The parade stopped in front of the Psychedelic Shop, where the coffin was placed on a pyre and set ablaze while dozens of veiled mourners knelt in mock prayer. A banner across Haight Street read death of hippie freebie, i.e., birth of the free man. Peter Berg contended that by shedding the outmoded hippie media image everyone would be reborn as a "Freeman." At the end of the ceremony, the Thelin brothers gave away all the merchandise in the Psych Shop. "Everything went," Ron Thelin laughed after it was over. "Even the stuff on consignment." Last to go was the store's sign, carried off and given an anonymous burial. Thelin left a notice in the window of his abandoned store summing it all up: nebraska needs you more.

The funeral was over, but the dirge lingered on. Dramatic obsequies notwithstanding, long-haired hippie drug culture still had a lot of life left in it. Richard Brautigan was among those resurrecting the corpse. In October, he published a final poem with the Communication Company. Although Richard called the first draft of "Boo, Forever," part of "Three Poems to Celebrate the History of Marcia." He initially issued it as a broadside without a title as one of ten different anonymous contributions, all gathered in illustrated wrappers. Brautigan's offering to *Free City News* was typewritten, surrounded by a list of eighty-seven sexual positions and enclosed within the reproduction of an ancient Egyptian drawing. Like all com/co productions, this collection was given away for free.

In the middle of October, a new upstart publication attempted to breathe fresh life into the hippie ethos of sex, drugs, and rock and roll. Bankrolled with $7,500 provided mainly by his family and Ralph J. Gleason, the magazine's consulting editor, Jann Wenner launched *Rolling Stone* as a monthly. It was an inauspicious beginning. Out of forty thousand copies printed of the first issue, thirty-four thousand came back unsold.

The next day after this nonevent (eventually regarded as a publishing landmark), Richard Brautigan appeared at the Unicorn Book Shop in Isla Vista (Santa Barbara) and read the first half of *Trout Fishing in America*. The following evening, he read the second half. The book was nearly two weeks shy of its official publication date. Richard read the whole thing in public, selling quite a few copies while he was at it. A handsome silkscreen poster was produced for the occasion by Chuck Miller, Jack Shoemaker's oldest friend.

By the time of its official Halloween publication date, *Trout Fishing in America* was already off and running. Two favorable reviews of the book had appeared in the *San Francisco Sunday Examiner & Chronicle*, one written by Herb Gold, the other by Don Carpenter, who penned his without reading the book. "He begged me to," Carpenter recalled. "He gave me a copy of the manuscript. I was a smart asshole. If you read [the review] carefully you'll notice that I haven't read the book."

City Lights handled distribution for the Four Seasons Foundation publications, and the slim volume sold well in Ferlinghetti's bookstore. Brautigan wrote an ad, worrying the copy through five drafts in his notebook: "Have you gone Trout Fishing in America yet? Fish strange and beautiful waters with Richard Brautigan as your guide. $1.95 City Lights Books, 1562 Grant Avenue, San Francisco." Don Carpenter claimed the first printing sold out in a week, thanks largely to his rave review.

Brautigan mailed both book reviews to his agent before heading down to his back-to-back readings at the Unicorn in Santa Barbara. Bob Mills promptly sent them on to Rose Marie Grgich, the editor at McGraw-Hill who was considering *The Abortion*. They came in too late. She rejected Richard's novel, saying, "I'm afraid that his book is much too thin and unimportant to be a hard cover book." Her letter marked the twelfth rejection from a major publishing house for *The Abortion*. Mills wasn't quite sure how to proceed. He wrote to Brautigan asking him if he had "any ideas about what might be tried next."

Richard did indeed have a few ideas of his own. While praising Mills for his "zeal," he asked his agent not to submit *The Abortion* anywhere else "for at least a month." Brautigan mentioned "some interesting developments toward my work that might make your job a little easier" and promised to keep Mills informed as they occurred. Through Luther Nichols, Richard had resubmitted *Trout Fishing* (which Nichols called his "magical book") to Doubleday.

It was being offered as a paperback similar to the Four Seasons Foundation edition. Brautigan insisted that the same cover photo be used should the book be accepted. At the same time, Richard sent *In Watermelon Sugar* to Macdonald & Co. in London and to Peter Collier at *Ramparts*. Collier rejected *Watermelon* because he thought it too long and didn't want to cut. He offered instead to "take a look at the short stories you said you were getting together."

The vigorous local sales of *Trout Fishing* greatly increased Richard's visibility on the Frisco literary scene. The December issue of *Ramparts* (vol. 6, no. 5) released in mid-November with a picture of four handheld burning draft cards on the cover, contained Brautigan's wonderful short story "⅓, ⅓, ⅓" (for which he was paid $300) together with Baron Wolman's clever tripartite photo of the author. The same issue contained a "glowing" review of *Trout Fishing in America* by the Formentor Prize–winning novelist Stephen Schneck, who concluded with the observation that something good "was cooking on the American hot plate. Thank you Mr. Brautigan, for a change it isn't naked lunch."

Blair Fuller, a San Francisco–based editor at the *Paris Review*, wrote to Richard in November, saying how much he'd enjoyed *Trout Fishing*. Fuller asked if Brautigan had something to submit to the magazine. This was sweet news indeed, considering the offhand manner in which the magazine had dismissed Richard's work the year before. Another indication of Brautigan's growing local fame appeared in the second issue of *Rolling Stone* (11/23/67). A small ad for the Minimum Daily

Requirement included an endorsement by Richard: "A nice place to eat where it's green and beautiful and open until three in the morning." Kendrick Rand had been out on a date the night after the monthly periodical hit the stands, and when he "swung by" his coffeehouse to take a look in the window he couldn't believe his eyes. "The place was mobbed. I had to excuse myself and go in and work. From that point on, from the [time] before we opened until we closed at night, it was full."

The good news Brautigan hinted at to his agent came to pass early in December. Encouraged by the vigorous sales figures for *Trout Fishing in America*, Donald Allen ordered a second printing of the book. This gave Richard a chance to amend the unintentional omissions of the first edition. Erik Weber got his cover photo credit, and *All Watched Over by Machines of Loving Grace* was added to the list of Richard's books on the catalog page. The best news of all was Allen's decision to have the Four Seasons Foundation publish *In Watermelon Sugar* the following spring, along with a volume of Richard's selected poetry.

The second printing of *Trout Fishing* was scheduled for three thousand copies. Eventually, there would be five printings. The Four Seasons Foundation sold between thirty thousand and thirty-five thousand copies of the book. That was only the beginning. Richard Brautigan stood on the threshold of the enormous fame he had dreamed of since high school. In all its various editions, his first novel, many chapters written in the summer of 1961 along the trout streams of Idaho, sold over two million copies. This was the big one that didn't get away.

The future appeared bright and shining, and all of his ambitions were about to bear golden fruit, yet Brautigan's inbred pessimism continued to hold him in its unhappy grip. Two weeks shy of his thirty-third birthday in January 1968, Richard typed out a poem he called "The Privacy of My Dreams Is Like Death." It began, "I'm so fucking tired of negative / excitement that always leads to boredom / and poor magic." The poet went on to plead for "some nice thing / to happen to my life [. . .]" Commenting on his upcoming birthday, he concluded with "and everything looks like shit / from down here."

It's hard to reconcile these despairing lines with the good fortune smiling on Richard Brautigan when he wrote them. Such behavior might be termed bipolar or manic-depressive. Whatever the label, the inability to forget the bleakness of his early childhood remained a curse from which Richard could never escape. It was a dark shadow shrouding all the rest of his life. Even on the threshold of great success, the seeds of Brautigan's eventual suicide had already been sown. Neither wealth nor fame would ever be enough to prevent the final bloom of that dark poisonous flower already germinating deep within his psyche.

part two:
bushido gunslinger

I N 1967, I was awarded a Wallace Stegner Creative Writing Fellowship at Stanford University and returned to the United States after two years of expatriate life in Europe and the Caribbean. Even in those carefree, long-gone, strong-dollar days, the grant money wasn't sufficient for a family of three to afford Palo Alto rents.

The countercultural revolution was global in aspect: Diggers in San Francisco, Provos in Amsterdam. We were curious to investigate the possibilities of life in the Haight. Living among derelict junkies and spare-change artists was not what we had in mind. Al Young, a fellow writer and former Stegner Fellow, tipped us off to Bolinas. One sunny September afternoon, Tom McGuane and I drove up the coast in his rattletrap Land Rover to investigate. By the end of the day, we'd each rented a place in the little seaside town.

I found a furnished house on Brighton Avenue for $75 a month. It was a long commute out of Marin County, across the Golden Gate, and down the peninsula to Stanford, but the Advanced Fiction Writing class the Stegner Fellows were requested to attend met only each Wednesday evening, so the weekly round-trip wasn't much of an ordeal.

In the spring of 1968, Charlotte Painter, a novelist who taught fiction writing part-time at Stanford, arranged for Richard Brautigan to give a reading at the university. Aqua-colored posters went up around the campus, featuring a caricature of Brautigan ("the greatest American comic novelist in three decades") holding a large grinning fish on his lap. He was scheduled to read to the undergraduates in the afternoon (Thursday, May 9, 1968) and again that same evening at the Advanced Fiction Writing class, which changed the date of its regularly scheduled meeting for the occasion. Having enjoyed *Trout Fishing in America*, I determined to attend both events and set out early from Bolinas in "Bitter Lemon," my battered VW microbus.

I barely made it, arriving at the Tresidder Student Union just as the afternoon reading was about to start. The main lounge was packed. A couple hundred students slouched on couches and armchairs, many crowding cross-legged around the podium at the far end of the room. A number of faculty members, identifiable by neckties and ill-fitting tweed jackets, stood in the back. I edged among them, no other space being available. After an introduction, Brautigan appeared to a smattering of applause. He looked like the photo on the cover of *Trout Fishing*, tall, stooped, wearing jeans, his trademark misshapen felt hat, and wire-rimmed glasses. A shy smile announced he was pleased to be there.

Richard Brautigan told the attentive audience about his recent publishing project, *Please Plant This Book*, the entire edition given away on the streets of San Francisco. One of the anonymous recipients had been a Sausalito grade school teacher who brought the book to class and had her students plant the seeds it contained. When they sprouted, she asked all the kids to write poems about their gardening experience and mailed the results to Brautigan.

With a giggle, gleeful, Richard proceeded to read the work of these fifth graders, one after another. He declaimed their untutored, innocent verse about flowers and springtime and the miracle of growth in mock solemnity. It was an inspired piece of performance art: zany, unexpected, purely in the spirit of the times. The Stanford undergraduates seemed completely into it, laughing and attentive, treated to a welcome bit of guerrilla theater instead of the usual stuffy academic presentation. Back among the restive faculty, I detected angry murmurings and disdainful grumbles. Who did this bozo think he was? Did he really mean to come to venerable Stanford University and read children's poetry?

Indeed he did, and to the apparent delight of the majority of his audience. Several disgusted assistant professors left early. Others stuck around to see if these kiddie poems might just be a warm-up. Perhaps Brautigan would read from his own work soon. Carried away by the students' laughter after each brief fifth-grade poem, Richard howled with mirth, slapping his knee in sheer delight. Altogether, he read perhaps two hundred words. The whole thing, including his introduction and the applause, lasted barely twenty-five minutes.

After the reading, there was a reception and buffet dinner for the visiting poet at the home of Ed McClanahan, then a lecturer in the writing program at Stanford and Wallace Stegner's "aide-de-camp." At the time, McClanahan was by his own description "The Most Famous Unpublished Author in America." This designation came his way courtesy of a 1963 issue of *Esquire* devoted to "The Literary Situation," which featured a centerfold map detailing all the noted writers in the land. On the basis of a handsome advance for an unfinished novel, Ed's name appeared, prominent among the titans, in the bull's-eye of an area called "The Red-Hot Center." His exquisite book, *The Natural Man*, was finally published to much acclaim twenty years later, but in 1968, the literary center had already cooled considerably for McClanahan.

Ed later expressed surprise that I missed his Brautigan fete. Blame it on the isolation of Bolinas. I can't remember how I spent the intervening hours, but at seven thirty that night, I climbed the stairs in the Stanford University Library to the book-lined Jones Room, the inner sanctum of the writing program, on a floor high above the stacks. The five other writing fellows had gathered, along with the graduate students in the advanced fiction class. Wallace Stegner presided over this disparate mélange with gracious forbearance. Gray-haired and handsome as a matinee idol, Stegner possessed an infinite capacity for tolerance, managing to find constructive things to say about work, even such as mine, which he hated.

McLanahan arrived with Brautigan in tow, sober as promised. The party had been timed precisely so Richard would be "in and out quickly," with no time to get drunk. An immediate coolness was detectable from Wallace Stegner. John Daniel, one of the Fellows, remembered "an instant conflict: playful provocation on B's part ('I don't know about you, but I get up, I shit, I write,') met by polite ice on S's ('Well, I suppose you could say that I do all of those things, but . . .')."

Stegner's attitude had absolutely nothing to do with intolerance for alternate lifestyles, as he was a remarkably fair-minded man and amicably shared an office with Ed "Captain Kentucky" McClanahan, whose mode of dress ran to skintight trousers, mod boots, and the occasional red velvet cape. More likely, Stegner had heard of the afternoon's shenanigans and was gravely displeased.

Also, he had little fondness for any writing he perceived as fey. He later described Brautigan's work to the class as being "like the carvings on peach pits."

In studied contrast to his performance in the student union, Richard settled down to give a remarkable reading. Maybe it was the intimate surroundings of the Jones Room, or perhaps he intuited that he was now among peers, serious fellow writers, whereas the business with the children's poems had just been a vaudeville turn. He read a number of short stories he'd been working on over the past decade. They were spare and lyrical, full of surprise and imbued with that quirky melancholy humor that is the hallmark of Brautigan's style. I recall the enormous pleasure I felt on first hearing "Revenge of the Lawn" and "The Ghost Children of Tacoma."

Many of Brautigan's bittersweet stories dealt with episodes from his early childhood during the Great Depression. At one point, Wallace Stegner made a comment that he had come of age in the Depression and had found it an invigorating time, "because when you're down on the bottom, you have no place to look but up."

Richard's smile remained wistful. "I was born in the Depression," he replied, "and all I had to look forward to was World War II."

In retrospect, it seems Brautigan anticipated hostility from Stegner. He came prepared with a short story, unpublished to this day. "Key to the Frogs of South-Western Australia" was less than two pages long and took only a minute or so to read. The title referred to a little twenty-five-cent book the author bought five years earlier because he admired the prose in the opening paragraph. The brief tale ended with the narrator attempting a spontaneous novel, thinking to use "Key to the Frogs of South-Western Australia" as his arbitrary title. Every time he started, he remembered Wallace Stegner's famous short story "Field Guide to the Western Birds" and promptly abandoned his project. The story received only a mild laugh from the listeners, but a subtle point had been made. His simple fiction reminded us we're all writers here, searching for the words to record our secret histories.

I've often wondered if Brautigan wrote the story specially for this particular evening. There's an element of haste in the composition. Not that it really mattered. Reading the story was exactly the sort of wry joke Richard most enjoyed. Afterward, following a brief period of mingling conversation, Brautigan asked if anyone could give him a lift into the city. I quickly volunteered. I was driving back to Bolinas and had to pass through San Francisco on my way. Soon, we were chugging north on 101 in "Bitter Lemon." I felt Brautigan's appraising stare from out of the darkness on the seat beside me. "So," he asked, "how much does this Stegner thing pay you?"

I told him $3,500. Because Stanford gave credits for the advanced fiction writing course, the university required a $300 kickback.

Richard Brautigan drily observed that the modest amount I quoted was more money than he had earned in the past year. After the briefest moment of stunned silence, I laughed and said, "You mean, when I get to be a famous writer like you, I can look forward to a salary cut?" A Wallace Stegner comment from a couple weeks earlier came to mind. He had been asked how many former fellows, after twenty years of the program's history, were now making a living as writers. "Young man," Stegner replied, "you don't understand. You've chosen a profession that doesn't exist." I repeated this to Brautigan, but he didn't laugh. It probably hit too close to home.

When Richard spoke again, his voice assumed a didactic precision I hadn't heard before, a tone that would become very familiar in years to come. His usual gleeful stammer, an eager rush of words on the verge of erupting into bursts of high-pitched laughter, had been replaced by something entirely more formal, each careful phrase intoned like he were reading from a prepared text. He gravely told me of the time, shortly after *Confederate General* had been published four years earlier, when he applied for a Guggenheim Fellowship.

This was a tedious process. Writing samples had to be gathered, forms completed, twelve copies of a "career narrative" submitted, along with letters of recommendation from four distinguished references. Literary heavyweights recommended him. Richard thought he was a shoo-in. Committees work in mysterious ways. In the end, Richard Brautigan's grant application was rejected. "They turned me down with a form letter," Richard said.

I didn't quite know how to reply. It sounded patently unfair, yet an air of slapstick pie-in-the-face absurdity attended the entire episode. Brautigan chortled with wild, unrestrained joy. "Standard rejection slip," he howled.

His infectious laughter had me responding in kind to the cosmic nature of the joke. In telling his story almost as a parable, he forged an undeclared conspiratorial bond. We both shared the sweet taste of freedom, two artists living by our wits. Years later, on a moonlit summer walk, Richard reiterated this heroic belief. "The world is divided into two separate camps," he told me, "sheep and timber wolves. We are the wolves."

Richard delighted in this credo. He knew it was warm and comfortable down in the woolly sheep-fold but preferred the wolf's cool lonely independence, loping unseen at the edges of civilization. It was only natural when we rattled to a stop outside the narrow decrepit wooden building on Geary Boulevard that the old wolf invite his younger lupine comrade in for a "nightcap." Much later, I came to dread all that Richard's late night invitations implied.

A ghostly derelict brooding in lurid mercury-vapor street light, the ancient building was bordered on one side by a debris-strewn lot where twin pylons supporting a vast billboard towered above the squalor. We climbed the stairs under the arched entrance into a dim, damp interior. The glass panes framed in the upper panel of the front door were decorated with Xeroxed Digger Dollars, handwritten poems, peacock feathers, and an El Capitan sardine can label salvaged from an abandoned Cannery Row warehouse, all Scotch-taped in a haphazard collage.

Richard ushered me down a long, narrow hallway. Billowing war-surplus parachutes hung from the ceiling, an interior decorating touch endemic to the period. Richard explained that their purpose was not ornamental but rather to prevent bits of peeling paint and falling plaster from dropping onto the heads of his visitors. I followed his hunched frame past numerous posters (advertising concerts at the Fillmore; coffeehouse poetry readings; Michael McClure's controversial play, *The Beard*; and benefits for the Hells Angels at the Longshoreman's Hall) along a trail of primitively painted red, white, and blue fish outlines (like the early Christian symbol seen mounted on automobiles).

The hall opened into a central room where the dominant decorative feature was a rusted World War II machine gun propped in the middle of the floor, enclosed by a larger version of the happy trout outlines fish-printing the hallway. A small bookcase held a few dozen slender volumes, presumably the work of friends. They were the only books I saw in the apartment. I didn't get a guided tour. Richard led me straight into his surprisingly homey kitchen, very neat and clean with a quaint rocking chair sitting to one side. He sat me down at a round oak table ringed with the ghostly stains of innumerable coffee cups and placed a whiskey bottle between us. Glancing about, I noted an ancient Philco refrigerator dominating the room. On the wall behind it hung a large hand-painted brown butcher paper poster for a reading of *Trout Fishing in America*.

Richard pulled up a chair and filled two large tumblers with bourbon as casually as if pouring tea. There was no ice. Serious talk demanded a serious drink. Our conversation had almost nothing to do with writing or literature. We talked about fishing. When Richard learned I was also a fly fisherman, he beamed with pure undisguised pleasure. We reminisced about the trout streams of our childhoods: his in Oregon's McKenzie River Valley, mine in the Catskills of upstate New York. He told me of secret places in the High Sierra, and we agreed to get together and go fishing. He gave me his telephone number. At the time, I didn't realize Brautigan could not operate an automobile and was simply enlisting a new designated driver. Close to dawn, when the whiskey bottle was a dead soldier, I lurched out into the street and drove cautiously home, thankful for the deserted suburban highways of sleeping Marin County.

I never called Richard's number. Self-conscious about my lowly status as a virtually unpublished writer, I feared being perceived as another hanger-on. My bourbon-drenched night with Richard Brautigan receded into the realm of memory. I had no idea our paths would cross again in four years, in Montana, of all places, at the time a state where I'd never been.

thirty-three: ten-day barons

BY 1968, RICHARD Brautigan's local literary accomplishments and eccentric public art gestures had gained the attention of Herb Caen, Frisco's gossip maven, and he found himself mentioned frequently in Caen's daily *Chronicle* column. Michael McClure had also been in the public eye since the controversy surrounding *The Beard* and was himself often a subject of Herb Caen's three-dot journalism. The two friends turned their newspaper notices into an amiable competition. Whenever either found his name in print he became a self-anointed "Ten Day Baron of Café Society."

"We proclaimed that we were famous for ten days," McClure recalled, "and we rushed off to drink at the sidewalk tables of Enrico's Café, where we could be admired by mortals." Jack Shoemaker recalled that both barons kept scrapbooks of their press clippings and once had "a huge falling-out" over who was more famous, not speaking to each other for a considerable time.

Richard and Michael drank "stemmed glasses of cold white wine" at Enrico's, watching the world pass by on Broadway, fully confident they were being stared at in return. Both Brautigan and McClure possessed a profound vanity and greatly enjoyed showcasing their mutual "baronhoods." Jack Spicer's bitchy behind-his-back nickname for Michael McClure had been "Shameless Hussy." "Michael was a good deal more vain than Richard," Jack Shoemaker said, "but Richard was a great deal more ambitious than Michael."

Brautigan guarded his carefully honed image. He allowed no one but his chosen photographer to take his picture. "Richard only liked to be photographed when he wanted to be," Edmund Shea recalled. Two years later, when Brautigan gained worldwide fame, McClure resented seeing him preening on the terrace at Enrico's. "He seemed to like being there by himself," Michael wrote. "He managed a look that was at once wistful, self-intent, and intriguing." What began as an innocent game of "boyish show-off macho" turned sour once the stakes grew higher than a passing mention in Herb Caen's column.

Brautigan told Robert Mills, his agent in New York, of Doubleday's interest in *Trout Fishing in America*, making no mention of Luther Nichols, their West Coast editor. Doubleday, uninterested in *The Abortion*, offered a two-book contract for *Trout Fishing* and another novel yet to be written. Richard wanted a $5,000 advance. Robert Mills wrote Brautigan in late April, with Doubleday's final proposal, an advance of $2,000 for *Trout Fishing*, payable on signing. They wanted to publish in October, before Four Seasons printed another edition. Mills liked the offer and urged Richard to take it. Brautigan ignored his advice, and the Doubleday deal evaporated.

The appearance of *Please Plant This Book* early in 1968, soon after the publication of *Trout Fishing in America*, gained Richard Brautigan much local attention. Herb Caen remembered first seeing him handing out the seed packet poems on Powell Street. Richard made sure the journalist got a copy in the mail. Brautigan also sent copies to Art Hoppe, John Ciardi, Vice President Hubert H. Humphrey, and Harry S. Truman, among others, using The Glide Foundation (Glide Memorial Church) as his return address. Everyone wrote to say thanks. Humphrey thought it "A most unusual 'book.'" Richard thumbtacked his letter to the wall of his writing room. Truman's secretary thanked Brautigan "for the little booklet of garden seeds."

Brautigan claimed five thousand covers were printed (others think no more than twenty-five hundred), yet it is not known how many copies of *Please Plant This Book* were actually assembled. Some were put together at Jack Shoemaker's place in Santa Barbara, others at Kendrick Rand's apartment in San Francisco, and more done at Graham Mackintosh's printing shop. "When Richard would need some, he'd put together a little crew," Jack said, remembering evenings spent folding cardboard covers.

Dave Robinson of Mad River recalled helping Brautigan glue the folders together in his kitchen as payback for him assisting the band to assemble the sleeves for their first EP recording. "We would sit there and lick these things and the glue tasted *horrible*!" According to Jim Harrison, even Robert Duncan, who professed to despise Brautigan's poetry, lent a hand in the manufacture of the give-away book.

Please Plant This Book's piecemeal production makes the final number open to conjecture. Some estimated fifteen hundred copies. Possibly there were far less. Mad River joined the team of volunteers distributing the free book in public places. Rick Bockner stood on a corner in Sausalito handing out copies. Lawrence Hammond was given several copies, keeping a couple for himself.

The eight colored seed packets in *Please Plant This Book* were carrots, calendula, Shasta daisy, squash, lettuce, parsley, sweet alyssum royal carpet, and a mixture of California native flowers. The prose poems printed upon them constituted an homage to springtime and children. Not one had a direct reference to the seeds inside or the plants they would germinate.

Brautigan made a brief appearance in *Nowsreal*, a Digger film shot between the vernal and autumnal equinoxes of 1968. Spade in hand, he buried a book in a backyard garden. Richard read from "California Native Flowers" in a voice-over, sounding reedy and insistent: "In this spring of 1968 with the last third of the Twentieth Century travelling like a dream toward its end, it is time to plant books and pass them into the ground, so that flowers and vegetables may grow from these pages."

Filmed by Kelly Hart on sixteen-millimeter "roll ends" with Peter Berg in charge of the audio, *Nowsreal* provided an intimate glimpse into daily underground life in the Haight-Ashbury. Beginning with a poetry reading on City Hall steps, the short film featured "Sweet Willie Tumbleweed" Fritsch wearing a red beret, radical young lawyer Terrence "Kayo" Hallinan (years later Frisco's district attorney), and a gay poet named Ama clad in an American flag shirt, a member of the world's most exclusive club, having jumped from the Golden Gate Bridge and survived. Brautigan appeared briefly in one other scene, a tribute to his role as a Digger. Noted Hollywood cinematographer/director Haskell Wexler (*Medium Cool, Bound for Glory, One Flew Over the Cuckoo's Nest*) paid for the final print of *Nowsreal*.

Richard produced one final giveaway broadside along with the *Please Plant This Book* extravaganza. The Communication Company had ceased to function. Brautigan turned again to the skills of Graham Mackintosh, who operated a flatbed printing press. *The San Francisco Weather*

Report possessed far greater production values than any of its Gestetner stenciled predecessors. The broadside showcased "Gee, You're so Beautiful That It's Starting to Rain," a poem about Marcia Pacaud's "long blond beauty." It appeared later in issue no. 45 of the *Paris Review* (Winter 1968). Poetry editor Tom Clark had recently moved from England to Bolinas about the same time that Richard's relationship with his Canadian girlfriend ended in the spring of 1968.

Around the beginning of the year, Brautigan embarked on a project revealing his inherent attitude toward romance. Based on the creation of cartoonist Al Capp, a leap year Sadie Hawkins Day celebration was planned for Golden Gate Park. Richard got together with the Rapid Reproduction Company, a commercial offset lithogapher who'd published several rock concert posters, with an idea for a broadside. *One Day Marriage Certificate* would be available only on February 29, 1968. Richard wrote the text: "This beautiful one day marriage is ours [. . .] because we feel this way toward each other and want forever to be a single day." Blank lines followed for the signatures of the participants. An art collective called The San Andreas Fault supplied an elaborate illustrated border. It's not known how many copies were printed by the Rapid Repro Co. but thus far, only two are know to have survived.

As Richard directed his attentions away from the Haight-Ashbury, he began looking for a North Beach apartment. His search took the form of a prose poem called "The New Apartment Thing." He was looking for a place "that has a sunny window for his plants." Brautigan wished to trade his three-room $65-a-month Geary Street apartment for one in North Beach and was willing to pay "up to $100 a month" and asked that any messages be left at City Lights Bookstore.

Nothing came of it. He kept his place on Geary, yet spent most of his time in North Beach, missing out on the Hashbury street action. One morning, early in 1968, a young artist named Robert Crumb wheeled a secondhand baby carriage down Haight Street, hawking copies of a twenty-five-cent "underground" comic book, *Zap #1*. Crumb had drawn the entire issue himself the previous November. Printed by the beat-affiliated poet/artist Charles Plymell, who kept a small offset press in his apartment, the edition sold out quickly. Like Bruce Conner and Michael McClure, Plymell was a product of the "Wichita Vortex" and had also exhibited his work at the Batman Gallery.

R. Crumb followed quickly with a second printing (raising the price to thirty-five cents). It disappeared even faster. Crumb had a hit on his hands. Other artists admired *Zap* and wanted to participate. S. Clay Wilson, recently arrived from Kansas, teamed up with Crumb, along with poster artists Rick Griffin and Victor Moscoso, to produce *Zap #2* a couple months later. Each artist worked in his own distinctive style. The end result was mind-boggling. Not since Depression-era eight-page Tijuana bibles had pornography and the funny papers so happily united. Janis Joplin became a big fan. The *Zap* audience also bought *Trout Fishing in America*.

Mad River cut their first album for Capitol sometime in the late spring or early summer, at the recording studio of Golden State Recorders on 665 Harrison Street. The band had grown disenchanted with the degenerate post–Summer of Love scene in the Haight and had relocated back across the Bay to Berkeley. They were assigned a veteran L.A. producer, Nik Venet, who had worked with the Beach Boys and Bobby Darin. He'd recently had a top-twenty hit with "Different Drum" by the Stone Poneys (featuring a very young Linda Ronstadt).

The band invited Richard Brautigan to take part in the session. They wanted to acknowledge Richard's generosity when they first arrived in the Bay Area broke and hungry. Greg Dewey recalled the invitation "was one of those drunk night ideas." There were no rehearsals. Brautigan got together with the guys at the studio and read his poem "Love's Not the Way to Treat a Friend," accompanied by David Robinson and Lawrence Hammond, playing a tune written by Robinson.

It was not an easy session. The band members had to direct Brautigan how to read his poem in sync with the music. "Richard had absolutely no concept of how to read it," Greg Dewey remembered. On the first try, Brautigan read the entire poem before Hammond and Robinson finished the music for the first verse. "It was harder than he thought," Dewey said. "I think he had considered that songs are a lot like poems, but he had never considered how you have to perform the poem within a song."

In the end, everybody was happy with the results. Lawrence Hammond wrote to Brautigan a couple weeks later, saying "he was pleased," in spite of a hang-up involved firing producer Venet. "Working with him is like having Otto Preminger make a movie of Woody Guthrie's memoirs," Hammond reported when Capitol Records finally released the album, *Mad River*. The cut featuring Brautigan's poem was not included on the LP.

For the first time, Richard hired an accountant to prepare his tax returns. His gross income for 1967 totaled $3,081. Esmond H. Coleman, CPA, an English major during the Depression before switching to science, became Don Carpenter's friend when they both taught part-time at the University of California. Through Carpenter, Coleman got to know Gary Snyder, Phil Whalen, and Brautigan. Over time, he worked for all of them, handling their accounts. "I was sort of simpatico," Coleman said. "We talked the same language. In between debits and credits, we would talk about literature."

Coleman met Richard in 1964 when Don took him to an early reading of *Confederate General*. From time to time after that, he ran across Brautigan at Vesuvio and because the poet never had any money would occasionally buy him a drink. Once, when Coleman was at the North Beach bar with his wife, Richard approached him and said, "One of these days, I'm going to need you. I'll have a lot of money and I'll need an accountant."

"I never thought he was a great novelist," Coleman admitted, but he found Brautigan very thorough in his record keeping. "Meticulous in a kind of disorganized way," he said. "He'd come in with a bag of stuff, every little tiny fucking receipt. Everything! If he bought biscuits at the store he would have a receipt for it. Shopping bags full of receipts."

Coleman considered Brautigan's life as "something out of Dickens. He was a very lonely boy, and he learned to be a loner, and he was basically a loner. His relationships were not really deep. I don't think he was able to give much or accept much. He was sufficient unto himself, or at least he liked to think so."

Throughout the month of June, at twenty-three separate venues throughout San Francisco, an "Underground Art Celebration: 1945–1968," featured painting, music, films, dance, sculpture, drama, photography, memorabilia, environments, lectures, and poetry. Ken Maytag and his brother, Fritz, who owned Anchor Steam beer, put up some of the money to fund the various events, which were collectively designated the "Rolling Renaissance." David Meltzer had a hand in organizing the poetry end of the festival. Meltzer invited Brautigan to participate along with more than two dozen readers, including Allen Ginsberg, Michael McClure, Lew Welch, Lawrence Ferlinghetti, Kenneth Patchen, Robert Duncan, Philip Whalen, and John Wieners.

Fritz Maytag threw a huge party at his brewery. Things soon started getting out of hand. Maytag didn't have a liquor license and worried that the commotion might attract the attention of the police. "It's my beautiful bubble you're bursting," he shouted down from his office at the cavorting crowd. Allen Ginsberg reacted by taking off all his clothes. Irving Rosenthal (former editor of the *Chicago Review* and *Big Table*, who had recently moved to Frisco to edit *Kaliflower*, a free weekly newsletter published by the Digger-inspired Sutter Street Commune) also stripped naked, except for his fingerless gloves.

David Meltzer can't remember Richard Brautigan actually reading at the "Rolling Renaissance." He recalled him stealing food and wine at Maytag's party "to bring back to his tribe." Richard remained a Digger at heart. "What struck me is we were giving it away, and he was stealing from us and then giving it away," Meltzer said. "That was a strange cognitive."

At the end of June, a letter arrived from William P. Wreden, a San Francisco dealer in rare books and manuscripts. He enclosed a copy of "The Story of Joseph Francl," which he planned to publish in a fine press limited edition of five hundred copies. Originally written in German, Francl's journal was a transcript of a mid-nineteenth-century diary kept by an emigrant from Bohemia who trekked west to the California goldfields, leaving a young wife back home in Wisconsin. Wreden wanted Brautigan to write a ten-page introduction for the book. He was interested in having "a contemporary literary interpretation of the phenomena of pioneer overland travel."

Richard accepted the assignment and wrote an off-kilter, oddly moving introduction, bringing his own peculiar sensibilities to the 114-year-old manuscript. The book was published at the end of the year as *The Overland Journey of Joseph Francl* in an edition of 540 copies. Wreden hosted a reception early in 1969, celebrating the book's launch at his Post Street showroom. His invitation quoted a line from Richard's introduction, describing Francl as a man "who cared for his beer and other liquors, too."

Trout Fishing in America's San Francisco success did not go unnoticed in the New York offices of Grove Press, and they decided to bring out a trade paperback edition of *Confederate General*. The avant-garde poet/novelist Gilbert Sorrentino, working as an editor at Grove, thought it might be a good idea to reissue the book with cover art in the manner of the Four Seasons' singular *Trout Fishing* photo. He wrote Don Allen, setting the wheels in motion. Allen got in touch with Brautigan. Edmund Shea being unavailable, he contacted Bill Brach, asking him to handle the photography.

Richard showed up in Golden Gate Park with a baby alligator and a hippie girl wearing a full-length belted smock. Years later, Brach couldn't remember the young woman's name. She had straight dark hair hanging well past her shoulders, parted in the middle. With a broad nose, thick eyebrows, and full lips, she possessed an exotic ethnic appearance. Brautigan posed her between two columns holding the eighteen-inch-long reptile, her long dress dragging on the ground, looking a bit like a gypsy. Bill Brach took several shots.

Richard brought his favorite prints over to Don Allen. He wanted the title printed in red across the top of the photo and "Turn to page 100 for an interesting story about alligators . . ." at the bottom of the cover. Allen didn't think the alligator had sufficient light but sent the picture off to Grove.

Gilbert Sorrentino spent the next two weeks working with Grove's production team on the cover design. He respected Brautigan's work and had recently written a favorable review of *Trout Fishing in America* for *Poetry* magazine. Sorrentino wanted to satisfy the author's wishes. It was not to be. Grove decided to keep the same Larry Rivers cover art they had used on the hardcover edition.

The gypsy girl was perhaps only a brief fling after Marcia Pacaud's departure. Richard soon met Valerie Estes, who had majored in home economics in college and went on to earn a PhD in anthropology. Brautigan was attracted by her quick, lively mind. He liked to say that "there was no more powerful aphrodisiac than intelligence in a woman." Valerie later worked as an assistant to Donald Allen. He expressed surprise at what she "saw in this guy who was sort of unattractive." Estes thought Brautigan "physically not very attractive," but felt "his presence was much more than the sum of his parts." Brautigan "was truly charismatic, and you don't say that about too many people."

"Richard was always on the make, you know," Valerie Estes said. In the era of free love, Estes carved a few notches herself, but Brautigan "had more notches on his gun than almost anyone." Tall, attractive, and dark-haired, an Aries with large intelligent eyes and the brains to back them up, Valerie Estes grew up in Berkeley and Reno, Nevada. She moved to San Francisco in February of 1967 after almost four years of wandering in Eastern and Western Europe, West Africa, and the Middle East with her husband, Bob Morrill. (In an odd coincidence, Bob's best buddy in Catholic school, from first grade all the way through graduation, had been Barney Mergen, who befriended Richard when he passed through Reno in 1956.)

Morrill got a job as a corporate attorney, and the marriage lost most of its luster. Valerie split in September '67, leaving their place on Russian Hill for a tidy three-room Kearny Street apartment on the slope of Telegraph Hill. That fall, Valerie volunteered to register people for the Peace and Freedom Party, a radical new political organization. Eldridge Cleaver was their candidate for president. She set up a card table in front of City Lights and handed out leaflets. One day, pamphlet in hand, she approached a bearded man with "great blue eyes," asking "if he might be interested in signing up for Peace and Freedom."

"Sure," came the laconic reply, "but I think my name is on that pamphlet." The man turned out to be Lawrence Ferlinghetti. They began "some sort of friendship," which led to a brief affair and a general introduction "to the City Lights crowd, although not to Richard."

KQED recruited Estes to help out with an arts festival planned in Washington Square Park in May 1968. She was given the task of finding poets willing to read at the festival. While living in Greece, she had met a poet named Robert Dawson. Having seen Dawson's name on a poster advertising a reading in the Haight, Valerie wondered if it was the same man. She went to hear him read, and they renewed their friendship. Dawson gave her Richard Brautigan's name and phone number.

When she called Richard about the arts festival, he said he'd like to talk to her in person about the matter. "What I now realize was he probably liked my voice on the phone," Valerie recalled, "you know, the potential, and he had no intention of reading."

"Why don't I come by tonight?" Brautigan asked in his most winning manner.

"I'm having dinner with some friends," Valerie replied. "I can't do it tonight."

Richard thought this over. "Well, I'll come by and pick you up after dinner."

Valerie's friend Betty Kirkendall, a reporter at the *Chronicle,* lived in the neighborhood. After their meal, Richard arrived right on time. "I think we probably went back to my house, and I really don't remember clearly," Valerie said. "I'm willing to put money on it that we drank a lot of wine and ended up in bed."

Brautigan did not read at the art festival in Washington Square Park. He accompanied Valerie to the event, which was a great success. Bob Dawson read, along with several others lost to time. "Richard and I rather quickly became some kind of an item," Valerie recalled, "enough so that I didn't see Lawrence any longer. In fact, I didn't see anybody else. All right, that wasn't true, but all things considered my percentage of time with him was fairly high."

For Richard, being with Valerie became a self-fulfilling prophesy. Around this time, he wrote an (unpublished) short story in his notebook he called "An Apartment on Telegraph Hill." Largely autobiographical, the story contained several revealing personal revelations. The narrator was a sculptor, whose work "had long ceased to yield any satisfaction." He "had no interest in women except to get occasionally laid when I got bored with getting drunk and it took a really good woman to get me away from the bottle," and dreamed of having "a girlfriend on Telegraph Hill." He fantasized about her apartment full of "lots of fine stuff." Brautigan wrote, "Coming from a poor family, I've always been attracted to women above my station."

Richard soon took up residence in Valerie's North Beach apartment at 1429 Kearny Street (the address was changed to 1427 when the building was remodeled), while maintaining his squalid museum out on Geary Boulevard. Richard had always been self-sufficient and preached a form of sexual equality, but Valerie remembered that she "always did the cooking, except when Richard made his spaghetti sauce. Breast of lamb was another thing." When Brautigan bought a cheap cut of meat, what he called "a protein wallop," at their local North Beach market, he'd bring it home and roast it. Valerie recalled him "throwing this hunk" in the oven. "I don't know what else we ate with it. Red wine, probably."

The three-room Kearny Street flat was reconfigured to suit Brautigan's work needs. The middle room, which had been Valerie's bedroom, was converted into an office for Richard. They moved the bed into the front room, and Brautigan brought over his electric typewriter, setting it on a table painted purple. In October, he wrote a poem he called "The First Lady of Purple," which he dedicated to Valerie. Richard worked "from mid- to late morning, and then he would wander the rest of the day," she recalled. He composed directly on the typewriter and "was pretty disciplined about it. When he was writing he drank almost nothing." His work "was something that was very private," Valerie said. "He didn't share this with anybody, including me."

"Alcohol was always the escape." Valerie Estes knew the part booze played in Brautigan's work habits. Whenever Richard "finished whatever that piece of work was then the constraints were removed and he drank again." In the downtime, he wrote poems. Poetry never had the constraints of discipline that prose did. "He didn't work on the poems. He didn't set aside time to work on the poetry," Valerie said. "The poems were on napkins. So, he drank during that time. Poetry came during the interims of the prose work."

Several of these poems were written for Valerie. "As the Bruises Fade, the Lightning Aches" celebrated their robust sex life. Brautigan was proud of his ability to withhold his climax for an extended period of time. Valerie felt he was mainly concerned with his own pleasure, never asking what she might enjoy. They were noisy lovemakers. Their neighbors in the building on Kearny Street complained often. Of the pair, Richard shouted the loudest.

Valerie first met Don Allen through Brautigan. He took her to a cocktail party at Allen's apartment in honor of the expatriate writer Kay Boyle, recently returned to the Bay Area. There were eight or ten people present, and Estes remembered drinking "a lot of wine." Lawrence Ferlinghetti was among the guests. They all piled into the back of his little pickup and drove to a restaurant. Allen was taken with Estes and asked her to be his assistant. In need of a part-time job, she said yes.

Once, after Donald Allen fired her, Valerie and Richard went on a trip to Kirkwood Meadows, an isolated spot in the Sierras near Carson Pass, where Barden ("Bart") Stevenot, her new boss, owned a mountain retreat he planned to turn into a ski area. Crews of loggers and dozer operators were already at work in a high valley with the greatest variety of wildflowers in all California. At the time, the only structure on the place was the Kirkwood Inn, a venerable log building along what once was the Kit Carson Emigrant Trail. Built in 1864, the old inn had seen some wild times. The saloon and a kitchen were downstairs, with places to bunk above. Stevenot asked Valerie and Richard to move to another bed at the far end of the building because their raucous sex kept him awake at night.

One evening following an afternoon's fly-fishing on Caples Creek, Stevenot took Valerie and Richard to dinner at the J&T, a Basque family-style restaurant in nearby Gardnerville, south of Carson City across the Nevada state line. After their meal, they walked up to the Overland Hotel for a drink. An old woman saw them passing and, fearing a hippie invasion, phoned the sheriff's office. When the deputies arrived at the Overland bar, they spotted Richard playing the slots, the only longhair in the place. A tough local lawman looked hard at Brautigan and asked, "How long ya been here? How long ya stayin'?" He made his meaning clear. Hippies weren't welcome. Bart Stevenot was furious, threatening to call his lawyer. "They gave that the consideration of asking us to leave town at our earliest convenience. They had never run into the likes of Richard yet, with the granny glasses and Buffalo Bill hair."

Back on Kirkland Meadow, the Outcasts of Gardnerville went over to June Roof's bar, a two-hundred-square-foot establishment where Stevenot's construction crew did their drinking. At first, "the guys had regarded Richard with suspicion," Bart recalled, "but after several nights hoisting drinks with him they had bonded to the extent that no one was going to throw their new best friend out of some Nevada lowlife town, and they volunteered in their somewhat impaired state to go down and clean up the deputies." While appreciating their motives, Stevenot and Brautigan politely declined the offer.

A letter came near the end of July from Roger L. Stevens, chairman of the National Endowment for the Arts. Brautigan had been selected to receive an award of $500 under the Literary Anthology Program, established in 1966 "to give greater circulation to work that originally appeared in magazines with limited circulation." Robert Duncan, Anne Sexton, and Louis Simpson were the final poetry judges this year, and Richard's poem "It's Raining in Love," published originally by *Hollow Orange*, was one of twenty-nine they selected to receive the award. The $500 came in the form of an unsolicited grant and did not have to be declared as income to the IRS. The poem would be published the following year by Random House in an anthology edited by George Plimpton and Peter Ardery. Two weeks later, Phillip Burton, the congressman from the Fifth District of California, wrote Brautigan to offer his "personal congratulations."

Back in June, a memorandum had arrived from Gordon Ray, president of the John Simon Guggenheim Memorial Foundation. Ray had written to inform Brautigan that Josephine Miles, poet and professor of English at UC Berkeley, had suggested Richard might be interested in applying for a fellowship. Accordingly, he enclosed an official statement and a set of application forms. There was no great rush in submitting the paperwork, which wasn't due until autumn. Anticipating a fall publication date for *Watermelon* and *The Pill*, Donald Allen, West Coast editor for the *Evergreen Review*, arranged for Richard's five-year-old piece about abandoned Christmas trees to appear in the December issue. Brautigan received $100 from the magazine. Around this time, Richard asked Dick Hodge to draw up the papers to dissolve his marriage to Ginny.

That spring Brautigan wrote a series of radio ads for KSAN to help out his pal Lou Marcelli. Richard and Lou often started their days together with coffee at the Minimum Daily Requirement. Kendrick Rand remembered them as being "great buddies." Three or four days a week they'd leave his place and head for the "double bill for a dollar movie theater on Stockton in North Beach." He recalled that "they had their special seats."

Marcelli recently expanded the musical offerings at his North Beach bar to include a weekly dance program out at Muir Beach. Lou hosted bands such as Time and the Cleveland Wrecking Company at the community lodge (now the popular Pelican Inn) for a $1 admission charge. These Muir Beach dances proved so successful that he soon also offered programs on Friday and Saturday nights at 8:00 pm.

Brautigan's radio spots took the form of military recruitment ads for the "DenoCarlo Naval Base." The featured band was announced as providing "drill instruction [. . .] It's a chance to serve your country, by dancing and playing in the sand." Another advertisement featured an "interview" with Chairman Mao of the Chinese People's Republic. The lodge at Muir Beach saw plenty of good times during this period. Lew Welch wrote his much admired poem "Wobbly Rock" while seated on a stone nearby. Magda Cregg hosted a big party at the inn to celebrate her lover's achievement. "Everything had gone off perfectly," she remembered. "There was enough food. The music was great. Everyone was dancing. Everyone was high. Everyone was having a wonderful time." At that point, Brautigan picked up a brick and threw it through a window."

"Richard! Why did you do that?" Magda scolded. "You sonofabitch! You ruined my party!" Brautigan turned to her and said, "I don't want things to be predictable."

For some time now, Michael McClure had been playing autoharp and making music with Hells Angel Freewheelin' Frank. McClure wrote "Oh Lord, Won't You Buy Me a Mercedes Benz," an offbeat little song that Janis Joplin liked to sing. It became the final track she ever recorded. In August of 1968, Joplin released *Cheap Thrills*, her last album with Big Brother and the Holding Company. The cover art was by R. Crumb, who "took speed and did an all-nighter." Crumb "wasn't crazy about the music" but "liked Joplin OK" and did the work for $600. "My comics appealed to the hard-drinking, hard-fucking end of the hippie spectrum," the cartoonist later wrote, "as opposed to the spiritual, eastern-religious, lighter-than-air type of hippie." Joplin and Brautigan lodged firmly in the former camp.

Richard had been familiar with R. Crumb since the artist did the poster for Bedrock One the year before. Victor Moscoso, who worked on *Zap #2*, provided a stronger connection. Valerie Estes remembered going with Richard to visit the artist and his buxom first wife, Dana. Their apartment struck her as one of the dirtiest places she'd ever seen, quite an achievement in those funky crash pad days. Brautigan took note of the Crumb/Joplin/McClure axis. Richard liked the idea of transforming his poetry into song lyrics. When Janis suggested she might try a couple on her next album, Brautigan immediately began gleaning his work for suitable selections.

Keith Abbott, recently moved back to the city to attend San Francisco State, remembered stopping by Richard Brautigan's Geary Street apartment around this time. Richard enlisted him and his 1951 Chevy pickup to drive over to Janis Joplin's place in the Haight. Brautigan told Keith about his plan to deliver two poems to Janis for her to sing. Abbott didn't say anything, remaining skeptical. Sensing his friend's enthusiasm, he kept his mouth shut on the subject. "He was quite high about this chance," Abbott recalled in his memoir.

The two poems Brautigan had chosen were "The Horse That Had a Flat Tire" and "She Sleeps This Very Evening in Greenbrook Castle," both surrealist fairy tales. When they arrived at Joplin's Victorian house, the singer wasn't at home. Richard and Keith were greeted by two of Pearl's "tough, leather-clad girlfriends" who took Brautigan's poems "with thinly veiled contempt" and showed them to the door. Janis never used either.

The month of August also saw the publication of *The Digger Papers*, a compilation of many of the handout broadsides the Diggers had distributed through the Haight over the past year and a half. The twenty-four-page pamphlet appeared in two different versions. Paul Krassner distributed it as issue no. 81 of his magazine the *Realist*, which sold for thirty-five cents. In return for this, Krassner printed an extra forty thousand copies, all given away without charge by The Free City Collective, the Diggers' new name for themselves. None of the contents was copyrighted, and all contributors were anonymous. Those in the know recognized who was who.

The stellar lineup included Allen Ginsberg, Gary Snyder ("A Curse on the Men in Washington, Pentagon"), Lew Welch ("Final City, Tap City: Crack at the Bottom of It"), and Richard Brautigan ("All Watched Over by Machines of Loving Grace"). Peter Berg contributed his revolutionary diatribe "Trip Without a Ticket." His "1% Free" Tong hit men poster graced the back page. Kirby Doyle's account of the birth of Digger Batman was included, along with a "Free Huey" collage/advertisement by Natural Suzanne. Taken together, the *Papers* provided an accurate compendium of the Digger ethos.

Richard Brautigan saved copies of *The Digger Papers* for the rest of his life. The ephemera from this fleeting period remained potent in his memory long after the utopian dreams they chronicled faded like rainbows in the mist. For Emmett Grogan, whose seminal handouts jump-started the whole thing, the dream died every time he stuck a needle in his arm. By his own confession, he was his own worst enemy, no longer any good at finding and distributing free food, no use to his long-suffering woman.

Scag has a way of sneaking up and taking over when you're too stoned to pay attention. To kick his forty-pound habit, Grogan took refuge out in Marin County at a hideout commune Peter Coyote and a friend named Bob Slade had established on a three-hundred-acre ranch near the tiny crossroads town of Olema. Brautigan wrote a poem, dedicated "For Emmett," called "Death Is a Beautiful Car Parked Only" about his friend's cold-turkey agonies. ("You hotwire death [. . .]")

The Democratic convention in Chicago that August took street theater to a bizarre new level. Several underground characters performed upon the world media stage provided by the riots. Abbie Hoffman took a star turn in a Digger-inspired role. The Diggers held Hoffman in low esteem. Emmett Grogan called him "Abbott." One morning, Abbie woke Peter Berg by pounding on his door and shouting, "I bet you think I stole everything from ya, dontcha?"

"No, Abbie," Berg replied, rubbing sleep from his eyes. "I feel like I gave a good tool to an idiot." He closed the door and never spoke to Hoffman again.

Sometime that summer, Leonard Cohen showed up in North Beach. The Canadian poet/song-writer/singer had recently enjoyed considerable success from his recordings of "Suzanne" and "Bird on a Wire," hit singles providing a much larger audience than counterculture poets usually enjoy. Cohen happened into the Minimum Daily Requirement and took a liking to Kendrick Rand. He began bussing tables as a lark. The place was packed. "You need help," the poet said, "You're too busy here."

"Well, good help is hard to find," Rand replied.

"I know how to work." Leonard Cohen put on an apron.

"I didn't pay him a penny," Kendrick recalled. "He just loved it. And he worked his ass off."

Leonard Cohen worked for free at the MDR for a week or two. This was great for business. Word quickly spread, and the usual crowd grew to unusual proportions. According to Kendrick Rand, Leonard "was stalking Richard." Brautigan didn't come by the coffeehouse for the entire time the Canadian poet worked there. Rand regarded Leonard Cohen as "handsome, very person-able," and thought "Richard was a little jealous of that." Richard probably avoided the Minimum Daily Requirement because of Cohen's close friendship with Marcia Pacaud.

Earlier in the spring, Kendrick Rand rented an apartment on Vallejo, half a block up from Grant Avenue. He wanted it so he could have a place where his two young kids could come and stay. Kendrick gave Richard a key to the long narrow railroad flat. "He used to hang out there a lot during the afternoon." It gave him a retreat in North Beach to escape to and write "or whatever he did." Rand made sure there was always "a jug of burgundy" on hand.

Kendrick had a friend named Paul Lee, who taught at UC Santa Cruz and was involved with Tim Leary's *Psychedelic Review*. Through Lee, Rand arranged for Brautigan to give a reading in Santa Cruz, and they drove down together in the big Coupe de Ville, taking Kendrick's kids along for the ride. This trip involved a lot of preparation, "checking the best way, when should we leave, what should we wear. That was how Richard operated back then."

As fog-bound San Francisco summer moved into the warmth of fall, Brautigan busied himself with his Guggenheim application. For his references, he lined up Josephine Miles (who had initi-ated the process) and novelists Kay Boyle (introduced to Richard by Don Allen), Herb Gold, and Stephen Schneck. His statement of project was particularly concise: "I would like to finish a book of short stories." Brautigan listed his marital status as "divorced," although legally this was not yet so, and when asked to give a summary of his education, he once again stated, "I have no education that can be listed here."

Asked to supply a brief account of his career, Brautigan began, "It's hard for me to write about my 'career' because it doesn't seem like a career to me at all. It's just what I do with my life and what I choose to write about and what happens then." After summarizing his publications, readings, and awards, Richard concluded, "the thing that I have enjoyed the most was writing and putting together 5,000 copies of a book of poems printed on seed packets. The book is called Please Plant This Book, and it was given away free. There are now thousands of gardens growing from this book, and that pleases me."

Early in October, a letter arrived from Luther Nichols, who wrote that "there are two exceptional younger writers on the West Coast—you and Tom Robbins." Nichols described Robbins as a former art and music editor, a columnist, "and a beginning novelist" who had avoided reading Brautigan at first, afraid of being influenced by writing he'd heard might have an affinity to his own. Finally, he succumbed and read a copy of *Trout Fishing*.

"Read it?" Tom Robbins wrote to Luther Nichols,

No, I didn't read it. I inhaled it as if it were Acapulco gold, I sucked it as if I were an infant prince and it were the royal wet nurse, I licked it as if it were the frosting left on the spoon that iced the Cake of the World. Now I carry it with me everywhere I go; close to my heart as if it were a love letter from the Only One. Any publisher who would refuse to print TROUT FISHING IN AMERICA is a candyass cretin, a study in imbecility. For Richard Brautigan is, to use the vernacular, where the new literature is at! He is the writer of the future.

It pained Nichols to know his own publishing house was among the dozen or so to have rejected *Trout Fishing*. The imbecile cretins continued rejecting Brautigan's work. Two days later, a distressed Blair Fuller of the *Paris Review* returned Richard's short stories, saying "George Plimpton did not take to them." Fuller sent his sincere regrets, adding that he had just seen Irwin Shaw, who was "very enthusiastic" about *Trout Fishing*, and that Kay Boyle mentioned Brautigan "with enthusiasm" in an interview Fuller had done with her for the *Paris Review* series.

Boyle's published enthusiasms greatly enhanced Brautigan's prospects for winning a Guggenheim. Also in early October, Apple Records contacted Richard via Barry Miles, asking if he'd be interested in working on a spoken word album. Brautigan wrote back, suggesting his idea for the record and offering to send Miles a tape of himself reading "The Pill versus the Springhill Mine Disaster." Miles was off in Italy, but Apple responded that Richard's idea was "exactly the type of thing he wants to do."

One October evening, Richard and Valerie took a cab to the airport ("a big splurge") to pick up her friend Bunny Conlon, who flew in from Las Vegas the day after the funeral of her husband, Jack. Valerie had worked for John Francis ("Jack") Conlon in Washington, D.C. back in 1962, when he was chief of staff for Nevada Senator Howard Cannon. Richard and Valerie brought the new widow to her suite at the Mark Hopkins and joined Bunny for dinner. Instead of going to the Top of the Mark, they ordered room service and ate in Bunny's suite. Brautigan sat on the floor, pulling a book of verse from his pocket. "Richard read poetry to me," Bunny recalled, thinking it was something Persian, Rumi perhaps. She found it very sweet and comforting. "All evening he read this beautiful poetry to me. And I didn't know who Richard was. But, I thought he was a lovely person."

The next day, Richard and Valerie invited Bunny over to the apartment on Kearny Street for brunch. Bunny took a cab down from Nob Hill to North Beach. When she gave the driver the address, he said, "Oh, that's where Richard Brautigan lives."

"You know Richard?" Bunny asked, somewhat perplexed.

"Everybody knows Richard," the cabbie replied. "He's had his picture on the cover of *Time* magazine."

Bunny was shocked. Who was this famous guy her friend had hooked up with? Although Brautigan's picture never graced the cover of *Time*, the cab driver's wisecrack had the eerie ring of prophesy. Richard and Valerie "got a big laugh out of it" when Bunny told them what the cabbie said. Such praise didn't qualify for a baronhood, but it provided a giddy glimpse of what the future might hold.

When Halloween rolled around, Valerie didn't buy any candy because she was certain no trick-or-treaters would ever come. Richard felt differently. Her apartment was on Telegraph Hill, an Italian neighborhood populated by families with a lot of kids. He became so adamant that Valerie ran down to the store, returning with a carton full of little boxes of Chiclets. To celebrate the occasion, they bought two pumpkins. While Valerie prepared dinner, Richard carved his into a jack-o'-lantern with "one round eye and one triangular eye and a not-very-bright witchy smile." Valerie carved her pumpkin while the food cooked. She took a "modernistic" approach. Richard thought the end result looked "like an appliance."

No trick-or-treaters rang their doorbell. At seven thirty they sat down to a meal of red cabbage and sausages with baked apples for dessert. They expected their meal to be interrupted, but not a single goblin, werewolf, or warlock came while they ate. Around nine, they went into the bedroom. Richard brought the bowl full of Chiclets along in case someone came to the door. Nothing. Not a sound. Half an hour later, they started making love. Less than a minute later, they heard "a cyclone of Halloween shrieking" outside their front door. They looked at each other in silent laughter but made no move to answer the doorbell's insistent ring. The Chiclets sat untouched all night. Richard and Valerie were no longer at home. Brautigan wrote the episode up as a short story he called "Halloween in Denver."

The Four Seasons Foundation simultaneously published *In Watermelon Sugar* and *The Pill versus the Springhill Mine Disaster* on November 19, 1968. According to his wishes, Richard Brautigan's name did not appear on the front cover of either book, only along the spine. Uniform in size with *Trout Fishing*, the two were better designed, both volumes produced by Edwards Brothers of Ann Arbor. Lovely young women graced the photographic covers. Over the next four months, both titles sold a combined fifty thousand copies. In 1969, Richard earned over $7,500 in royalties from the Four Seasons Foundation.

Donald Allen submitted several poems not included in *The Pill* to the editors of *Poetry*, the venerable Chicago magazine that earlier in the century had championed the work of Ezra Pound, T. S. Eliot, and Robert Frost. Visiting editor Daryl Hine wrote Allen to say he was keeping both "Love's Not the Way to Treat a Friend" and "Wood" for future publication, asking for Brautigan's address. He needed to send a payment and the proofs directly to the author.

Evergreen Review no. 61 published "What Are You Going to Do with 390 Photographs of Christmas Trees" in December. A full-page photo collage of Erik Weber's shots of discarded Christmas trees accompanied the piece. *Evergreen* paid Weber an additional $100. They mailed the check to Richard. He wrote to Erik in India, asking if he should take it over to Erik's mother. "So much for Christmas trees," Richard wrote. "I finish one thing and then something new comes along. It gives life an interesting pace."

Richard brought Erik's check to his mother's house at his request. Brautigan spoke with her and Weber's sister, Avril. They all felt it was a shame that Erik and Lois had broken up so far away in India. Brautigan had "faith" that Erik was "doing what is right." A couple days later, Richard airmailed copies of *In Watermelon Sugar* and the *Evergreen Review* to India with "very much love from America."

Erik and Loie soon got back together. Weber wrote to Brautigan, asking him to send some LSD. Richard declined, writing back, "I'm very sorry but I can't help you out with your request." Reading the letter on a hot tropical night in India pissed Erik off so much he smashed a swollen mosquito with it and mailed the bloodstained page back to Brautigan.

By any reasonable standard, 1968 had turned out to be a bummer year. In February, Neal Cassady died from exposure and drug overdose beside the railroad tracks outside of San Miguel de Allende, Mexico. The old hipster was not the only casualty. Day by day, week after week, month by bloody month, the Vietnam War escalated further into inevitable catastrophe. Over thirty thousand young Americans had already been killed in Southeast Asia. H. Rap Brown proclaimed violence "as American as cherry pie," heralding the assassinations of Martin Luther King, Jr. and Robert Kennedy, both cut down by an increasingly familiar media figure, the lone psychotic gunman. "Burn, baby, burn!" became a new urban battle cry. Every evening, cities across riot-torn America burst into flame on the nightly newscast. The Yippies went to the Chicago Democratic National Convention, making their usual Dada-anarchist political statement with a porcine candidate named Pigasus, and found themselves swept up in a police riot they had helped to instigate. To cap things off, Richard Milhous Nixon got elected the thirty-seventh president of the United States.

Even so, 1968 had been a very fine year for both Jann Wenner and Richard Brautigan. *Rolling Stone*'s first anniversary issue ("Forty Pages Full of Dope, Sex & Cheap Thrills") featured an interview with John Lennon and pictured on the cover John and Yoko nude from the rear. It sold like mad and generated a ton of publicity. After twelve uncertain months, the little music magazine was here to stay. A celebrity-hound forever on the scent of copy, Wenner got in touch with Brautigan in early December, asking if he wanted to write for *Rolling Stone*. Richard, a keen observer of his own career path, intuited that the magazine's youthful rock-and-roll readership was his audience as well. It made sense to appear in a publication celebrating Janis Joplin and the Beatles. Also, Jann offered to pay.

Brautigan told Wenner he had lots of short stories. At a time when *Rolling Stone* advertised for reviewers and writers to submit their work for free, Jann appreciated the worth of featuring a celebrated author in the magazine. At $35 per story, he also knew a bargain when he saw it. Wenner paid Richard $100 for the first three, "Crazy Old Women Are Riding the Buses of America Today," "Fame in California," and "A Need for Gardens," all published in December, in issue number 24.

The next ten issues all contained stories by Richard Brautigan. At one point, Wenner increased the payment to $50 for each piece and invited Richard to "come in some time and yak about it with me." Brautigan published a total of nineteen short stories in *Rolling Stone* during the coming year. At times, when the supply ran short, Jann Wenner dashed off a quick note: "Richard: We've run out of your stories; we need a new bunch [. . .]" Once, the editor scrawled his plea on the payment check stub: "We need more stories NOW! To the rescue please!"

The publication of *Trout Fishing in America* sent ever-widening ripples through the sluggish East Coast literary establishment. Stephen Schneck told his New York agent, an aggressive and intelligent young woman named Helen Brann at the Sterling Lord agency (which also represented the work of Jack Kerouac), about the novel. Schneck mailed her copies of Richard's books, and she read them straightaway. Immediately catching the vibe, she contacted Brautigan, offering to act as his agent. Helen Brann was hooked. Her every instinct insisted she'd just found a winner.

The new year of 1969 began bright with promise for Richard Brautigan. His three books published by the Four Seasons Foundation were selling briskly, Apple was about to produce a recording of his work, and a powerful New York literary agency wanted to represent him. In January he wrote to Daryl Hine at *Poetry* magazine asking him to withdraw "Love's Not the Way to Treat a Friend" from pending publication. Brautigan had other plans for his poem.

Early in January, Ralph Gleason urged Janis Joplin to ditch Big Brother and the Holding Company. He said the band was unworthy of her talents. A few days later, the blues singer followed his advice. Janis began putting together another group, and word went out among the hip community that she was looking for a great new name for the ensemble. During this period, Richard Brautigan ran into Janis from time to time. Valerie Estes recalled meeting her at Enrico's one afternoon. For some impromptu reason, Joplin gave Estes one of her earrings.

On another January afternoon, Richard and Price Dunn sat people watching on the terrace at Enrico's when Janis Joplin came by and joined them. With the income from the *Cheap Thrills* album, Janis treated herself to a Porsche and had it repainted in swirling psychedelic images by Dave Richards, one of the roadies for Big Brother. "How do you like my car?" the singer grinned.

After a few drinks, Janis drove up a few blocks to Gino and Carlo's. They had been drinking wine but switched to hard stuff at the literary workingman's bar. "Richard was really getting off being with Janis Joplin," Price recalled, "because everybody recognized [her]."

Richard and Janis played pool. Price observed them from the bar. "They were just wild and crazy," he recalled. Eventually, the trio set out in search of dinner. After a hard day of physical work, Price "wanted a substantial meal, but no, they didn't want to eat roast beef." They ended up at the Old Spaghetti Factory on Grant Avenue and continued drinking. "Come on, have another one," the rowdy crowd demanded. When one round was finished, the next stood waiting. Price Dunn had a low opinion of Spaghetti Factory fare: "god-awful. This appalling shit, sauce like colored food dye." An abundance of booze lubricates the most discriminating palate, and they wolfed down their abysmal pasta with the gusto of the gloriously drunk.

Their inebriated conversation centered on Joplin's quest for the perfect name for her new band. "She wanted Richard to come up with a name," Price recalled. "Oh god, how drunk we all were." Price staggered out into the night, wisely leaving his car in a garage, and took a cab home. Brautigan had no answers for Janis Joplin at the Spaghetti Factory. Finding an appropriate band name haunted his imagination for days. Janis listened politely when Richard finally told her his perfect choice, "Out of the Cradle Endlessly Rocking." His inspiration came from the first line of a Walt Whitman poem originally published in 1859. Unimpressed, Joplin called her last two groups the Kozmic Blues Band and Full Tilt Boogie.

Valerie Estes lived in an apartment in the same building as V. "Valhalla" Vale, the keyboard player (as Vale Harnaka) in the six-man blues/rock band Blue Cheer. He shared his birthday with Richard Brautigan, and they decided to hold a joint party on January 30. It was an open house. A large boisterous crowd wandered between Vale's place and Estes's apartment.

Janis Joplin was among the many revelers celebrating Richard's thirty-fourth birthday, along with Bill Brown, Lew Welch and Magda Cregg, Emmett Grogan (who brought a horde of Diggers), and Chinese American novelist/playwright Frank Chin, "the first Chinaman to ride the rails," he claimed, referring to his job as a brakeman on the Southern Pacific Railroad. Dr. John Doss remembered Joplin wandering through the crowded party demanding, "Where's the dope?"

Valerie Estes said, "Janis was drunk and looking for more Southern Comfort." It was Grogan who "was trying to score heavy-duty dope." Margot Patterson Doss was introduced three separate times to Emmett Grogan, whom she already knew. "Why do people keep introducing me to Grogan?" she asked Bill Brown.

"Margot," Bill replied, "don't you realize that there is a valley between the ying and the yang that neither you nor Grogan could ever cross?"

A couple weeks later, Barry Miles arrived in Frisco from L.A. Having no place to stay, he headed straight over to Richard Brautigan's Geary Street apartment. A supremely self-confident fellow, Miles had some apprehension about his first meeting with Richard. Allen Ginsberg, a mutual acquaintance, put down Brautigan's work to Miles, calling it "shallow and contrived." In an elaboration of the pejorative nickname, "Frood," that Ginsberg hung on Richard back in 1956, the Beat poet started calling him "Bunthorne" behind his back. (Reginald Bunthorne was the lily-carrying aesthete in Gilbert and Sullivan's 1881 operetta *Patience*, a character meant as a parody of Oscar Wilde.)

When Miles arrived at the Museum, which he found "an obvious bachelor pad, scruffy but pleasant," Brautigan led him straight to the kitchen, the apartment's social hub. Miles later described Brautigan as "tall and gangling," saying that he "affected the image of an old prospector or western pioneer." Keith Abbott and Valerie sat waiting at the big round kitchen table. Richard presented Keith as his "best buddy," and Miles came to regard him as Brautigan's "constant companion."

On that first afternoon, the pair had a little fun at the Englishman's expense. Miles informed them that he was called only by his last name. Taking this as his cue, Richard began addressing Keith as "Abbott," telling Miles that his buddy also went by a single name. Their tongue-in-cheek gag had a lasting effect. Thirty-four years later, Miles published his memoir of the sixties, and the old hoax found its way into print. "Abbott, as he was known, made continual runs to the fridge for beer," Miles reported, none the wiser after all that time.

The telephone became a central image in Richard's concept for his spoken word album. On the first track, Brautigan spoke to an unknown caller about the chaos the sound engineers left behind in his Geary Street apartment. Richard said it looked like something dropped from outer space. "The place is just surrounded with electronic equipment. We have four microphones, stands, amplifiers, speakers, wires all over [. . .] all we need is a body to cut up and bring back to life . . ."

The gear was there to record segments of what Richard called "the sounds of my life in San Francisco." These included the rustle of taking off his clothes, splashing in his bath, the scrape of a razor along his whiskered cheek, and, *click*, a light switching off when he went to bed at night. He also included a long rambling conversation with Price Dunn about what to have for dinner. In Miles's 1997 biography of Paul McCartney, he mentioned recording "hours of tape of Richard [. . .] sitting around the kitchen table drinking beer with his buddy Price."

The studio sessions took place south of Market at the Golden State Recorders, where Brautigan had previously worked with Mad River. Brautigan read the "Hunchback Trout" chapter from *Trout Fishing* as well as chapters from *Confederate General* and *In Watermelon Sugar*, and a representative selection of his poems from *The Pill*, four of which, he declared on tape (a deliberate dig at Valerie) were dedicated to Marcia Pacaud. He also included a selection of four short stories from his planned collection. Miles, unduly influenced by Ginsberg, missed the point completely, claiming he "wanted to capture the whimsical, almost precious, innocence of Richard's work." In order to "create an accessible public surface," Miles overdubbed Brautigan's *Trout Fishing* reading with the purling sounds of a mountain stream, adding a ringing telephone and the wail of an ambulance siren.

Rounding up eighteen of his friends to all read the same poem resulted in Brautigan's most inspired contribution to the record album. Originally written in April 1966, and later published during the Summer of Love as a com/co broadside, "Love Poem" was only twenty-seven words long but provided an impressive amount of what Tom McGuane once called "perfect power-to-weight ratio." Richard used this poem because Ianthe had memorized it when she was about eight years old. He paid his daughter $11 for reading "Love Poem" on his recording. She spent it all on Cracker Jack and Archie comics.

Richard's diverse reading group included Valerie Estes, Michaela Blake-Grand, Margot Patterson Doss, Betty Kirkendall, Michael McClure, Price Dunn, Donald Allen, Peter Berg, Bruce Conner, KSAN DJ Alan Stone, *Chronicle* columnist Herb Caen, and David Schaff, whose book of poetry, *The Moon by Day*, had been published by Donald Allen's Four Seasons Foundation. They all assembled in the recording studio at the designated hour without any notion of what Brautigan expected them to read.

Celebrated photographer Imogen Cunningham, then eighty-five years old, was a surprise guest reader. The connection to Cunningham came through Margot Doss, her neighbor on the western slope of Russian Hill. Valerie picked the elderly photographer up in a rented Mustang with Miles and Richard, chauffeuring them all over to Golden State Recorders. David Schaff recalled that Cunningham "wasn't particularly socially adept," but "Richard had an interesting quality in his affection for people who were strange, who were nonthreatening strange."

"Each one of us had to figure out a different way to read the poem," Margot Doss recounted. Michael McClure read with a calculated poet's intonation. Bruce Conner put on a performance, yawning his lines like a dreamer emerging from sleep. Anthony Storrs, a Hispanic/black man who called himself "Antonio," read the poem in Spanish. David Schaff remembered him in retrospect as "a Six Degrees of Separation type of character, except with more edge." Don Allen read twice, once alone, and again at Brautigan's suggestion, in tandem with Schaff. Alan Stone used his sonorous DJ's intonation, while Peter Berg, always the contrarian, turned a simple declarative statement into a query. Only the women put on no act, reading honestly and without affectation. Brautigan's straightforward language struck a resonant chord within them all. Richard did not read his own version of "Love Poem." He concluded by reading "Boo, Forever," a different sort of poem about the loss of love, set to the whirling mechanical sound of a metal top slowly losing its centrifugal energy as it spins to a stop.

Throughout the month of February Brautigan's mail brought a constant stream of good news. Missy Maytag wrote inviting Richard to read again at the Unicorn ("Come to Santa Barbara and cheer us up"). A week later, he traveled down and earned $150 at the bookshop. Jack Shoemaker mentioned the UC Santa Barbara Renaissance Fair coming up in April, and Richard agreed to participate. When Kendrick Rand heard about the university's offer, he told Brautigan, "You're worth more than that. This is ridiculous. You are selling yourself really too cheaply." Richard thought it over and said that if he got more money, he'd pay for an airline ticket for Kendrick to come down with him.

A more lucrative invitation arrived from the United States International University (California Western) in San Diego, a private liberal arts college with an enrollment of around sixteen hundred students. The school was organizing a Creative Arts Conference in August and wanted Brautigan to conduct a two-week prose workshop and give "one evening's reading or presentation for the general Conference." The university offered a contract for $1,200, plus the use of a suite without cooking facilities on campus. Meals at the commons were available at a 20 percent discount.

A discordant note came in a letter from the Guggenheim Foundation, informing Brautigan that he had once again not been nominated for a fellowship. Having been invited to reapply made this second rejection specially galling. News from Helen Brann in New York turned the Guggenheim business into an ironic joke. Sterling Lord submitted his three-book proposal to a number of publishing houses. The agency was running an auction. E. P. Dutton bid $7,500, Random House upped that to $12,500, and Doubleday, which had earlier rejected *Trout Fishing*, eventually offered $17,500.

An interlocutory judgment of dissolution of his marriage to Virginia Alder arrived at Richard Hodge's Kearny Street office during the first week in March, and Richard breathed a little easier. Single again, he was off the financial hook. Brautigan no longer had to fear losing a big chunk of the good fortune coming his way in a divorce settlement. Wanting to meet Helen Brann and have a look at the famous Sterling Lord agency, Richard planned his first trip back east.

An upcoming visit to New Mexico was on Brautigan's mind when he ran into Gary Snyder at a party after a reading at California State College. Feeling expansive with a $125 paycheck in his pocket, Richard picked up the tab and got drunk with Snyder. Recalling Gary's studies in Japanese Buddhism, Brautigan improvised a brief "Zen" poem for his inebriated fellow poet: "There is a motorcycle / in New Mexico." Richard called it "Third Eye."

Six days later, he and Valerie embarked on an eccentric cross-country sojourn. They flew first to Albuquerque and journeyed up into the mountains to Santa Fe, where they stayed in a house and studio on Canyon Road rented by Bunny Conlon and her artist brother, Al Eylar. Bunny had been born in New Mexico and, after her husband's death, came home to live with her young son, John.

The next day, Richard and Valerie visited Professor Charles G. Bell, a Southerner and close friend of the novelist Walker Percy. Bell ran the poetry reading program at the Santa Fe campus of St. John's College. Trained in physics, Bell, himself a poet and novelist, studied English literature as a Rhodes Scholar at Oxford. He spent a summer at Black Mountain, meeting Charles Olson and Robert Creeley, who first suggested meeting Brautigan. Bell found Brautigan "a boisterous sort of man," but arranged for him to give a reading at St. John's the following Monday.

Richard and Valerie borrowed Al Eylar's car, setting off on what she described as "the Brautigan Hegira." They traveled west, first to Los Alamos, not knowing their plates had long expired. For years, Eyler painted over the date sticker with the appropriate color to avoid paying the registration fee. It was snowing when Richard and Valerie rattled into the birthplace of the atomic bomb. Stopping at the local Safeway for a sack of groceries, Richard felt "there was a clinical feeling to the town" and wrote a poem about the experience, "The Sister Cities of Los Alamos, New Mexico and Hiroshima, Japan."

Outside Los Alamos, Richard and Valerie visited Bandelier National Monument, wandering around in a world of flat-topped mesas and sheer-walled canyons, investigating ancient Pueblo dwelling places nestled among the junipers and piñon pines. Next, it was west to Grants, where Richard wanted to see the huge radiation lab. The following morning, they backtracked east and south to the Acoma Pueblo, the oldest continuously inhabited city in North America. Coronado's army arrived in 1540. The Spaniards were the first white men to see the pueblo. Until 1929, when a Hollywood film company built a dirt road along the side of the 367-foot sandstone mesa to shoot *Redskin*, the only way up was a precarious series of ancient footholds carved into the living rock. The road was still unpaved when Richard and Valerie visited forty years later.

Saturday afternoon, they drove north, heading to the Chaco Canyon in the San Juan Basin, for a thousand years the center of the Anasazi culture. In 1969, the place remained remote. Brautigan and his lady explored the area without the supervision of uniformed park rangers. At Pueblo Bonito, built against the cliff face of the canyon wall, they climbed rickety wooden ladders into the archaeological ruins of what had once been the largest apartment building in North America.

While Richard stared at the ruins of an ancient civilization, Helen Brann sat in her East Side apartment at 14 Sutton Place South, surrounded by the glittering towers of Midtown Manhattan, worrying about how to welcome her eccentric new client when he arrived the following week. Helen had overnight guests that weekend. Seymour Lawrence and his wife, Merloyd, were in town from Boston, his home since college days. Lawrence attended Harvard and had been friends there with Robert Creeley when both were undergraduates. Together, they had started a small magazine called *Wake*, serving as its coeditors.

Sam Lawrence had long known Helen Brann, having used her as a reader when he was at the Atlantic Monthly Press. He had started there in his midtwenties as special assistant to the editor. Within three years he was the director and editor in chief. He was afflicted with lifelong stuttering, but his impediment did little to slow him down. At twenty-eight, Lawrence was the youngest publisher at the firm. During his twelve-year tenure, he brought in Richard Yates, Sean O'Faolain, Kenneth Muir, and Katherine Anne Porter. Lawrence missed a couple, having rejected both *On the Road* and *The Subterraneans*. Kerouac derided Sam as "that little queen," dubbing him "Little shit S."

After the Atlantic Monthly Press, and a stint as vice president of Alfred A. Knopf, Sam discovered he didn't care for corporate life and walked out, starting Seymour Lawrence, Inc., in Boston. He made an arrangement with Dell to copublish his books as the Delacorte Press. The first novel Lawrence published under his own imprint in 1965 was a reissue, the first "completely unexpurgated" edition of *The Ginger Man*, by J. P. Donleavy. Four years later, Lawrence brought out *Slaughterhouse Five*, elevating Kurt Vonnegut Jr. from an obscure "science fiction" writer into a best-selling author and firmly establishing himself as a literary publishing powerhouse.

"Do you know a restaurant where I can take a very tall hippie writer to lunch?" Helen asked Sam, while getting him coffee and orange juice in the morning.

"Who's the author?" Sam said.

"You've never heard of him; his name is Richard Brautigan."

In fact, Sam Lawrence had heard of him, earlier in the month, from Kurt Vonnegut, who "mentioned that he had heard of a hippie writer on the West Coast that he had never met, who is creating a cult of his own." His name was Brautigan.

Sam could barely control his excitement. "My god, Vonnegut was just talking to me about this guy," he blurted.

Helen told him she was running an auction on the three Brautigan books. "I should have him," Sam said. "How much have you got?"

"I've got fifteen thousand so far."

"You've got twenty," Sam replied, making an offer that soon became the deal. Lawrence also recommended Pete's Tavern down by Gramercy Park for Helen's lunch with Richard. (O. Henry had been a steady customer fifty years earlier.) From that point on, Lawrence became a great champion of Brautigan's work. Where Don Allen considered Jack Kerouac to be "a greater writer" than Richard, Sam thought that Brautigan was "a much better poet and writer than all the beats together, including prose writers like Kerouac."

Saturday night, while Helen Brann entertained the Lawrences, Richard and Valerie pushed on to the tiny town of Cuba at the edge of the Jicarilla Apache Reservation, where William Eastlake owned a ranch. Most of the roads along this leg of the trip were gravel, and somewhere en route they lost the muffler on Al's car. "Don't know if we paid for it or not," Valerie reminisced. "Probably not. Many of us were less reliable then."

After a breakfast of ham and eggs in Cuba, Richard and Valerie drove to William Eastlake's ranch for lunch. The noted author had also invited Lucia Berlin, a young short story writer. Born in Juneau, Alaska, in 1936, Berlin spent most of her youth living in mining camps across Montana, Idaho, Arizona, and Chile, wherever her itinerant mining engineer father found work. A dark-haired beauty, she had modeled for Sears in the 1950s. Berlin suffered from scoliosis, a form of spinal curvature Brautigan also endured. She had published her early stories in the *Atlantic* and the *Noble Savage*. Eastlake told Lucia he wanted her to meet "this brilliant new writer." When she read *Trout Fishing*, Berlin remembered "being dazzled by that book."

Later in the day, Brautigan and Estes headed on to Taos, where the spirit of D. H. Lawrence haunted the quiet adobe streets. Richard wrote a poem here that he dedicated to Valerie. "All Girls Should Have a Poem" is a single sentence broken into four lines expressing the poet's desire "to turn this God-damn world upside down" to please the woman he loved.

After returning to Santa Fe, Richard gave a reading on the evening of the seventeenth at St. John's College. Charles Bell remembered the poet as "a showman, a spectacular character and quite a reader. He paced around the room, and then he jumped up on the table." Afterward, a collection was taken among the student audience, netting Brautigan $25. The money covered gas expenses for the past few days. Charles Bell promised he would endeavor to have the college pay the poet an additional fee.

Early the next morning, Richard and Valerie left with Bunny on a trip up to the tiny village of Abiquiú. The noted eighty-one-year-old painter Georgia O'Keeffe had made her home there ever since buying and restoring an abandoned hacienda in 1945. A noted recluse, O'Keeffe first visited New Mexico on a trip to Taos in 1929. In spite of her reputation as a hermit, Brautigan kept saying he "wanted to meet Georgia."

"Well, nobody meets Georgia," Bunny told him. "People that live in her village don't even know she's famous, and she doesn't want anybody to know she is." Richard was persistent. He wanted to give O'Keeffe a copy of *Please Plant This Book* and kept saying, "Tell me where she lives. Take me there and let me try to get her to talk to me." Valerie remembered Richard giving away copies of this rare publication "very selectively to people." She considered him "the world's greatest PR man."

Bunny directed them to O'Keeffe's house in Abiquiú. Richard got out of the car, holding a copy of his seed-package book, and approached a large front gate. He rang the big bell hanging there. Nothing happened. He rang again. Still no reply. An elderly Spanish-looking woman dressed in black hobbled out the hacienda door. She limped to the gate and asked, "*Que quieres?*"

"I'm Richard Brautigan," the poet replied, "and I'd like to give my book to Georgia O'Keeffe."

"*Dame,*" the tiny old woman said. She put her arm up and Richard handed her the book. "*Gracias,*" she said, turning without another word. Richard watched, speechless, as the taciturn crone walked back to the house and closed the door.

Frustrated and upset, Richard returned to the car. Bunny and Valerie sat silently watching him. "I don't know why she couldn't have let me see Georgia," he complained.

"You just did," Bunny told him.

The following day, Richard and Valerie said goodbye to Bunny Conlon, who was returning home to Washington, D.C. shortly. They agreed to visit her there when then they got to the East Coast in three days' time. The couple traveled next to Placitas, a small settlement north of Albuquerque, where they stayed with Robert Creeley and his second wife, Bobbie Louise Hawkins. Creeley had settled in the area in 1956, after a four-year stay in Europe, followed by another two years teaching at Black Mountain College. Creeley had received an MA from the University of New Mexico in 1960, capping an academic career interrupted when he dropped out of Harvard in 1946. Publishing five books of poetry between 1952 and 1956 was an accomplishment far more distinguished than any mere college degree.

The Creeleys lived in a beautiful century-old adobe house with earthen floors soaked in the blood of slaughtered oxen and buffed for a hundred years or more to a polished cordovan sheen. "A wonderfully romantic touch," Creeley observed. Renewing his acquaintance with Bob Creeley meant a lot to Brautigan, who considered himself "a minor poet." Not only was Creeley a major poet, at this time almost unheralded, enhancing his appeal to Richard, but the older man had lived a life of far-flung adventuring that made Brautigan's own provincial high jinks pale by comparison.

All the next day the wine and conversation flowed. At one point, Brautigan told the Creeleys that when he and Valerie first "were thinking about trying to live together," he took some of her furnishings and moved them over to his apartment "to see how the furniture would get along." Richard had always invested mystic importance in inanimate objects. "That was an incredible business," Creeley recollected with a laugh.

The next morning, Richard and Valerie flew from Albuquerque to Los Angeles. While Valerie visited with friends, Richard headed over to the Apple office in the Capitol Records Building on Vine Street just north of Hollywood Boulevard. The thirteen-story circular tower, designed to resemble vinyl forty-fives stacked on a turntable, was built in 1956 and housed the recording company founded by songwriter Johnny Mercer. A red light on a rooftop spire blinked out the word "Hollywood" in Morse code at night.

After a hamburger lunch in the cafeteria, Brautigan met with George Osaki in Apple's art department to discuss the layout for his record album sleeve. They hit it off. Richard felt Osaki understood what he had in mind. Brautigan asked if the prints Edmund Shea had supplied would suffice for mass reproduction. Osaki said they'd work just fine. Apple held an additional five pictures of Brautigan in their files, but Richard preferred the cover photographs be used for all publicity, "as it will establish a visual image of the record." He also agreed to write a publicity release and send it from New York the following week. Brautigan insisted on being informed of all changes and demanded "final approval on any publicity, advertising, artwork, and on the master." Richard Hodge put the finishing touches on the contract, stipulating these points.

The following morning, Richard and Valerie flew to New York. They stayed in a room at the Chelsea Hotel on West Twenty-third Street, a red brick Victorian with ornate wrought-iron balconies. Built originally as the city's first cooperative apartment house in 1884, it was the tallest structure in New York at the time. Since converting to a hotel in 1905, the Chelsea provided sanctuary to writers, artists, and musicians, including Mark Twain, Sarah Bernhardt, O. Henry, Edgar Lee Masters, Virgil Thomson, Tennessee Williams, Brendan Behan, Arthur C. Clarke, Christo, Arthur Miller, and George Kleinsinger, composer of *Shinbone Alley* and *Tubby the Tuba*. Thomas Wolfe wrote *Look Homeward, Angel* in a room at the Chelsea. Dylan Thomas died while a resident. His namesake, Bob Dylan, composed the song "Sad-Eyed Lady of the Lowlands" there. William Burroughs once had a room, as did pop artists Larry Rivers, Claes Oldenberg, and Jim Dine. Andy Warhol celebrated the hotel in his film *Chelsea Girls*. Richard Brautigan was happy to add his name to the illustrious guest register.

That evening, Valerie and Richard had dinner with poets Anne Waldman and Lewis Warsh at Max's Kansas City, a restaurant on Park Avenue South made trendy by the patronage of the Warhol circle. Waldman and Warsh, both twenty-four, had been a couple ever since they met in San Francisco the summer of 1965, when Anne came out to the Bay Area to attend the Berkeley Poetry Festival and Lewis lived in a spare sublet apartment on Nob Hill. The next year, they founded and edited *Angel Hair*, a literary magazine lasting (for six issues) until 1969.

A native New Yorker, raised in Greenwich Village and educated at Bennington College, Waldman went to work for The Poetry Project at St. Mark's Church in-the-Bowery after she and Warsh returned to the city. In 1968, Anne became the program's director, and over dinner with Brautigan (Richard feasted on steak and lobster tail) she asked him if he would like to read there the following week while he was in town. The honorarium would be $50. Richard agreed on the spot.

The next morning, Richard and Valerie took a train from Pennsylvania Station to Washington, D.C. They stayed with Bunny Conlon in her house close to Capitol Hill. Bunny remembered Brautigan's kindness to her four-year-old son, John, who was sick and wouldn't take his medicine. "Richard said, 'Go outside and don't come back for half an hour and he will have taken his medicine.'" She obeyed his instructions. Brautigan worked the special magic he had always had with children. The medicine went down without further complaint. John "was really happy and I was just amazed that [Richard] could get him to do it. He was wonderful with kids."

On a morning in the last week of March, Bunny drove Richard and Valerie on a tour of nearby Civil War battlefields. Richard wanted to see Manassas, now a suburb of the greater District of Columbia metropolitan area. A century before it had been the site of the two battles of Bull Run, military engagements so close to the capital that curious civilians rode out in their carriages with picnic baskets "to see the Rebels run." Instead, they witnessed a complete rout of the Union forces.

From Manassas, the trio drove on to the Wilderness, a wooded area in northern Virginia ten miles west of Fredericksburg, where the forces of the North and South engaged in two bloody battles nearly a year apart, in 1863 and 1864. In the first, now known as the Battle of Chancellorsville,

General "Stonewall" Jackson was mortally wounded by his own troops after the Confederates had flanked and nearly annihilated the Union army under the command of General "Fighting Joe" Hooker. The second Wilderness campaign comprised a number of engagements in May and June, with Lee and his army facing off against the Federals, now commanded by Ulysses S. Grant. After a horrible slaughter at Cold Springs, Grant withdrew, having lost sixty thousand men.

At one of these historic places, Richard got out of the car "and started running around and marking, taking big steps, measuring the battlefield." Bunny and Valerie remained in the car, watching him with amusement. Valerie commented that Richard ran "like a wounded antelope," because "he had one leg shorter than the other." When Brautigan rejoined them he said, "I wish I had come here before I wrote *The Confederate General*. I would have written it completely different." According to Bunny, she and Valerie "just about died laughing. But he was serious. He was very serious."

That night, Richard and Valerie had dinner with Conlon in Old Town Alexandria, where Brautigan ate cherrystone clams for the first time in his life. The next day, they were back on the train, heading north to Boston. They stayed in Cambridge with Ron Loewinsohn and his future wife, Kitty. Loewinsohn was attending Harvard, working toward a PhD in English literature, and had arranged for his old North Beach pal to give a reading the following evening at Quincy House.

For a reunion feast, they all went to Durgin-Park, a Boston landmark since 1827, still doing business in a decaying and disreputable part of town. A noisy place with famously rude waitresses, tin ceilings, bare lightbulbs, and long wooden communal tables, the restaurant had been a favorite of Valerie's ever since she traveled up from DC on weekends seven years earlier to visit her fiancé, a student at Harvard Law.

The morning of March 25, Richard and Valerie took another historic tour, driving up to Lexington and Concord (Valerie remembered visiting these revolutionary battlegrounds had "probably" been her choice). They drove on to Walden Pond, where Henry David Thoreau built a rude hut on his friend Emerson's land and lived for two years and two months without gainful employment. When Brautigan surveyed the scene, he described an empty paper box in the snow in his notebook.

That same night, presented by the Quincy Poetry Forum, Brautigan read his work in the dining hall at Quincy House, a venerable Harvard undergraduate residence on the banks of the Charles River. A modern architectural "behemoth" had been added on in the sixties, and the influx of new inhabitants gave the place a reputation for rowdy exuberance. Admission was $1, and Richard received $270 for his performance. Valerie stole the show at Quincy House with her homemade outfit, a fur miniskirt and vest constructed from a thrift shop mink coat. It was one of her "favorite hippie outfits."

In the morning, they traveled back to New York by train and again checked in to the Chelsea. Although their room had no view to speak of, it came with a kitchen, and Richard and Valerie cooked their own breakfasts. The current residents of the old hotel included Gerome Ragne of *Hair*, artists Claude Pelieu and Mary Beach, filmmaker Sandy Daley, pornography writer Florence Turner, as well as Patti Smith and Robert Mapplethorpe, both young and unknown, and Leonard Cohen, who was keeping company with Marcia Pacaud.

In one of life's awkward coincidences, Marcia occupied a room upstairs from Richard and Valerie. She was in town "on a long-term basis" for EST training. "I was always incredibly jealous of her," Valerie said, "because she was blond and she was beautiful and she was all these things that I wasn't and Richard, it may have been unconscious, but Richard didn't hesitate to talk about Marcia and how blond and beautiful she was."

It was Brautigan's practice to introduce each new girlfriend to her successor. ("My lovers become my friends.") Valerie remembered they "ended up being a threesome in some of our roamings." At some point during their stay, Marcia even fitted Richard for a new pair of Levi's. Valerie managed to anesthetize her feelings ("we were drunk so much of the time"), but after a week of uncomfortable togetherness, she exacted a small measure of revenge when they all went out to eat at Max's Kansas City. At this point in time, Richard's favored libation was the Brandy Alexander, a cocktail composed of cognac, crème de cacao, and heavy cream. Valerie recalled that they drank "lots and lots. I was stupid enough to drink along with him." After dinner, awash on an ocean of brandy, they drifted out of the restaurant and hailed a taxi. "Richard got in on one side of the cab and I got in on the other," Valerie said, "and I shut the door and left Marcia outside." They roared off with Miss Marcia Pacaud of Montreal, Canada, standing alone and inebriated on the curb.

On the evening Richard and Valerie returned to Manhattan from Cambridge, Brautigan read his poetry at St. Mark's Church in-the-Bowery, his second reading in two days. The cornerstone of St. Mark's was laid in 1795. Located on Second Avenue between East Tenth and East Eleventh Streets and enclosed by an iron fence, the old churchyard, with its trees, grass, and weathered eighteenth-century tombstones, remained a rare pastoral oasis amid a concrete urban wasteland. Richard read on the altar of the barrel-vaulted sanctuary on the same program with Aram Saroyan, son of William Saroyan, one of Brautigan's favorite writers.

In the eight days remaining on their trip, Richard and Valerie took in the town. They went to see *Dracula*, checked out the Old Masters at the Metropolitan Museum, and spent time with J. D. Reed, a twenty-eight-year-old poet whose first book, *Expressways*, had just been published in hardback by Simon & Schuster. Something of a wild man, J. D. Reed distinguished himself from the herd mentality through bizarre fits of unpredictable public behavior.

On Lawrence Ferlinghetti's introduction, Richard linked up with Claude Pelieu and Mary Beach, an art-scene couple in residence at the Chelsea. Mary, an American heiress raised in France, began painting at an early age and had been interned for a time by the Nazis during World War II. She was a relative of Sylvia Beach, proprietor of Shakespeare & Co. and the first publisher of James Joyce. Claude, fifteen years younger, was born in France and had his premier show in Paris at the Galerie du Haut Pave, under the purview of Henri Matisse and Raoul Dufy. He met Mary Beach in 1962 and they traveled together to San Francisco, where they formed creative liaisons with Ferlinghetti, Allen Ginsberg, and Charles Plymell. Claude worked in collage, wrote poetry, and translated the Beat writers into French. He gained a measure of notoriety in New York after he pissed in Norman Mailer's pocket at a party in the Dakota.

Pelieu and Beach accompanied Richard and Valerie on a visit to Ed Sanders's avant-garde Peace Eye Bookstore, housed in a former meat market on East Tenth Street. Sanders had preserved the original Hebrew lettering painted on his show window: strictly kosher. Brautigan harbored no ill feelings from his Halloween party four years earlier when the Fugs took a shine to Janice.

Richard and Valerie went to the Met during the afternoon. They had dinner at Levine's, a few blocks uptown on Park Avenue South from Max's. Billed as a "Jewish/Canadian" restaurant,

Levine's featured closed-circuit TV cameras focused in all directions. Every booth had its own small-screen set so the customers could all watch one another watching wach other.

On March 29, Bunny Conlon traveled up from DC and took a room at the Chelsea. She had lunch with Valerie. By nightfall Estes felt sick. Bunny and Richard went out to eat, leaving Val with the color TV, promising to bring back deli food. They went to a restaurant near the hotel. Brautigan drank "a lot of beer." After they ate, the waiter brought the bill. Richard said, "Okay, let's go."

"What about the ticket?" Bunny asked.

"No. It's taken care of," Brautigan said. They walked out the door and down the street.

Somebody yelled at them. Bunny turned and saw the waiter running in their direction. "You forgot to pay for this check," he shouted.

Richard looked at the man "like there was something wrong with him," and said, "Well, I don't have any money." The waiter didn't find this a plausible explanation. "Don't you know who I am?" Brautigan demanded.

"I don't give a damn who you are," the waiter snarled, "this is what you owe me." Bunny paid for their meal on the street, and settled the matter.

The day after Richard's reading at St. Mark's Church, he met with Helen Brann. He told Valerie the purpose of their trip was for him to sign a contract with the Sterling Lord agency, but Richard had no formal arrangement with Helen until December of 1973, when she started the Helen Brann Agency. On the day Richard was scheduled to fly back to San Francisco, Helen was on the phone with Seymour Lawrence, hammering out the a deal.

Sam wanted to publish a hardback edition with all three books in a single volume. This had been Brautigan's vision for some time. Helen Brann asked for $20,000 in advance for the hardback omnibus edition of *Trout Fishing*, *The Pill*, and *Watermelon Sugar*, agreeing that Dell could simultaneously publish the three titles separately as trade paperbacks with a 14 percent royalty going to the author. (Don Allen would get 1 percent until a hundred thousand copies of each had been sold, after which Brautigan was to receive 15 percent.) The other terms were also advantageous to Richard. He kept 60 percent of any paperback or book club sale, instead of the usual 50 percent, and retained the right of approval of book jacket design and typography. It was an incredible deal for an author with absolutely no national track record.

Instead of Pete's Tavern, Helen Brann took Richard and Valerie to lunch at Maxwell's Plum, a trendy expensive East Side restaurant. (Valerie considered it "an in-crowd place.") Helen told her new client of the progress she had made in her negotiations with Sam Lawrence. The posh surroundings, fine food, and expensive wine provided Brautigan a preview of the literary fame he'd spent so many years pursuing. Later in the afternoon, Richard and Valerie boarded a plane and flew back to San Francisco.

Life took a different turn for Richard and Valerie after their return. She started graduate school over at Berkeley the very next day, enrolling in three classes. Brautigan went to a party. The weekend before the assassination of Martin Luther King, Bill Brown hosted a big bash at his house up on the Bolinas Mesa. Coincidentally, J. D. Reed had come out to visit Tom McGuane, a classmate from Michigan State, who moved to Bolinas in the fall of 1967 after completing a Wallace Stegner Fellowship at Stanford. Aspiring young writers, McGuane and Reed were drawn to the gathering at Brown's place to mingle with what Tom described as "the then very vivid San Francisco literary scene." Charles Olson and Allen Ginsberg were among the guests. Freshly harvested mussels in seaweed provided the main fare. The party lasted though the afternoon and late into the night with everyone getting enormously drunk. McGuane remembered running amok and nearly driving his Land Rover off a cliff when a Zen Buddhist asked him to help return a live crab, discovered among the mussels, to the sea. A fan of *Trout Fishing*, McGuane encountered Brautigan for the first time at Bill Brown's party. "I remember specifically telling [Richard] the moment I met him how much I admired the book and him for writing it," Tom recalled. "Above all his graciousness and his pleasure in being admired and his good manners."

Brautigan had been disappointed five years before when Grove Press published *Confederate General* and his dreams of a New York success were rudely shattered. His advance had been small and the book poorly promoted. Once Helen Brann called to say that Seymour Lawrence had accepted their terms, he knew things would never be the same again. The advance against royalties was $20,000.

Brautigan's total income between 1965 and 1968 came to less than $7,000. Richard didn't want the Internal Revenue Service to gobble up his good luck and asked that the money be paid out in four annual payments: $5,000 each January 1, beginning in 1970. Knowing he had almost four years of financial security ahead provided a nearly incomprehensible life change. For Valerie's twenty-eighth birthday (April 9), Richard took her for drinks at Enrico's and then on to dinner at the Mandarin, an expensive restaurant in Ghirardelli Square. He gave her a poem ("Valerie's Birthday Poem") written that afternoon.

The next day, Brautigan embarked on a blitzkrieg mini reading tour. First stop, Cañada College, a two-year school in the hills near Woodside above Redwood City, thirty miles south of San Francisco. Richard spent the morning in Palo Alto, hanging out at the Free You with Ed McClanahan and Gurney Norman, another young writer from Kentucky. The You was a Digger-inspired free institution of higher learning operating within a stone's throw of Stanford. Richard gave the Free You "All Girls Should Have a Poem" to print in their giveaway magazine.

Kent Crockett, an English professor at Cañada College and a friend of McClanahan's, had invited Brautigan to kick off the "Holy Moly Reading Series." He arrived in Palo Alto to drive Richard and Ed up to the new college auditorium, still in the final stages of construction. The college was not yet a year old. Brautigan was the first to perform there. Worried that noise from the construction backstage might disrupt the reading, Crockett got permission from the college president to tell the workers to take off for an hour and a half. Kent Crockett introduced Richard, and the poet looked out at the audience of colorfully dressed young people, smiled, and said, "Ohhh . . . you're all so beautiful."

Five minutes into Brautigan's reading, in absolute silence, a large wooden frame slid down behind him from the set storage loft overhead. This provoked slight tittering from the audience. Looking "a little perturbed," Richard continued with his reading. After another five minutes, the wooden rectangle rose silently back up into the flies. The audience laughed louder this time. Angered, Richard carried on his reading. For a third time in fifteen minutes—the workmen were testing the stage equipment—the big frame made another silent appearance. When the renewed laughter subsided, Brautigan was clearly annoyed. "Well, I think this reading is over," he said. Seated in the audience, Ed McClanahan thought Richard "behaved in a sort of ugly fashion."

"It was high tension at that point," Kent Crockett recalled. "This audience had come in just expecting the most easygoing guy in the world, and by this time there was a tension through the entire [crowd]." Crockett went backstage and had a word with the workmen, who apologized and agreed to knock it off. Crockett assured Brautigan everything was going to be fine, and he resumed his reading. A malevolent fate continued to plague him. Five minutes later a stray dog wandered down the main aisle, metal tags jingling, all the way to the stage. "The dog scratched and made a lot of noise," Kent said, "and walked out, which caused another titter of laughter."

Once decorum had been restored, a second dog repeated the previous canine's performance. At this point, Richard declared a recess, and everybody took a break for a few minutes. When the audience returned, Brautigan resumed reading as if nothing had gone wrong, "and as it continued," Kent Crockett remembered, "the tension that had been in the air, the sort of palpable tension, diminished and diminished and disappeared, and by the end of the reading everybody in the audience was much in love with Richard. And he with them." The students talked about the experience for months afterward.

Later in the afternoon, Brautigan went with Crockett, McClanahan, and a number of students for a picnic lunch at the Pulgas Water Temple, a circular neoclassical structure built in 1938, a few miles north on Cañada Road. The temple marked the spot where water from the Hetch Hetchy in the High Sierras spilled out of the aqueduct into Crystal Springs Reservoir. Richard relaxed beside a tranquil reflecting pool while the students "smoked dope and played Frisbee." Ed McClanahan found Brautigan at the picnic to be "just in the best form. In a weird way, he made up for his misbehavior." Ed had always considered Richard to be "volatile, he was a Jekyll and Hyde kind of thing."

The poet had a 6:30 pm plane to catch. Kent Crockett raced him down the Bayshore Freeway to the airport in his '57 Chevy. Brautigan was scheduled to read in Isla Vista at 8:00 pm. The First Annual Spring Renaissance Faire at the University of California, Santa Barbara had started off with a parade four days earlier. Intended to be "experience-oriented," the faire provided pottery wheels, clay, and rolls of butcher paper for finger-painting. Participants were encouraged to come in costume. After musicians and folk dancing, poetry readings rounded out each evening's entertainment. Lew Welch and David Meltzer read Monday night, Gary Snyder on Tuesday, Brother Antoninus on Wednesday, and Richard Brautigan brought the festivities to a conclusion Thursday at eight.

Richard was met at the airport and whisked straight to the University Methodist Church in Isla Vista. After remarking he'd been back east for about three weeks, Brautigan said, "It's so great to be back in California" and began with recent poems. He read "April 7, 1969" and the one he wrote for Valerie's birthday the day before, and "Third Eye" (for Gary Snyder), along with other work composed during his recent trip. Richard had serious competition for the UC student audience. Canned Heat, fresh from their hit rock single, "On the Road Again," performed in Robertson gym at the exact same hour, sharing the bill with Poco as well as the Ace of Cups, an all-girl band. There was one thing in Brautigan's favor: Admission to the concert was $2.50, while the poetry came for free.

The next day, while Valerie had lunch in San Francisco with Lawrence Ferlinghetti, Richard read again at Santa Barbara City College. The school's Forum Committee had been "enthusiastic" when they first approached him before his trip east, but as a junior college that had "lost its last three bond elections," they had no funds left in their 1968–1969 budget, according to Lorraine Hatch, on behalf of the college. The Associated Students, who did not sponsor forums or readings, "agreed to siphon $100 out of some unidentified fund" and hoped Richard might do "a short program" for that amount. "He showed up on time and read like an angel," Hatch enthused afterward.

Back in Frisco, Brautigan's professional life shifted into higher gear. To counterpoint all the high stakes business correspondence from New York, a short letter from Charles Bell in New Mexico awaited his arrival. It contained a check for $30, official payment for his reading at St. John's College, along with Bell's apology for the paltry size of the fee and his assessment of Valerie as "the tenth Muse lately sprung up in America."

Richard earned another small sum in April, when he sold "Not the Way," the poem he had withdrawn from *Poetry*, to the *Rolling Stone* for $10, a 25 percent paycheck improvement over the other periodical, which paid only fifty cents per line. Around the same time, annoying news arrived from Christopher Cerf at Random House, who wrote to apologize for "the very regrettable error" in *The American Literary Anthology, Number 2*, which had just been published. The editors were "all dreadfully embarrassed" to have omitted the last thirteen lines of Brautigan's poem "It's Raining in Love." Cerf promised to correct the mistake in the second edition if the first sold out (it didn't) and to print the entire poem again in full in volume 3 of the *Anthology* (which never appeared).

The contracts from Dell were ready by the middle of the month when Helen Brann sent them to Richard for signing. Sam Lawrence wrote Brautigan saying they planned to release the one-volume hardback edition in "late-September–early October," requesting a biographical note. Richard phoned the requested catalog material in to Helen Brann. Sam and Helen had discussed a possible new title for the hardbound edition "at some length." Brautigan was adamant on the phone "that there not be a title." What Richard wanted was the front dust jacket to simply list the titles of his three books, prefaced by "Richard Brautigan's."

After some discussion, Helen and Sam decided Brautigan was right. Before departing for Europe, Sam put Richard in touch with Rosalie Barrow, Dell's director of production, who would coordinate and oversee all details involved in the book's design. Richard's idea was to use the cover art from the current Four Seasons editions to precede each section in the hardback omnibus and incorporate the original typography. Brautigan told Helen he planned to gather all three women from the previous covers together for a dust jacket photo shoot. She thought this was an excellent suggestion.

While Richard concerned himself with the details of book publication, his relationship with Valerie rapidly unraveled. Busy with school, she spent long days in Berkeley, often not returning to the city until late in the evening. Once Valerie stayed over with a friend to finish an assignment. Richard sounded disappointed when she phoned to tell him. Valerie gave him her friend's number and said to call if he got bored. Around ten thirty, he called, drunk, and rambled on and on, insisting, "I love you more than you love me." (Valerie believed this to be "true." In her journal, she tried modifying her judgment with "perhaps," and then "probably," crossing out both words.) Brautigan also ranted about the Apple record, a veiled reference to Miles, with whom Valerie had a brief affair. When she argued, Richard hung up. Later, he called back suggesting they not see each other anymore.

Valerie felt she loved Richard in her way but couldn't live with him and was unable to commit. She'd criticized him to such an extent that she wondered if it might be "ballcutting." The next night, when she returned home to Kearny Street, Richard called in a good mood and came over soon after. They made love, preparing and eating dinner while still naked. Valerie experienced no awkwardness during their nude meal, her first, wondering only if she should place her napkin in her lap.

One night in late April, Richard arrived for dinner at Valerie's apartment and announced, "I've been making love to another woman." Valerie kept right on cooking, her chest pounding, thinking of her own recent transgressions. Their meal went half-eaten. A long painful evening followed. Valerie wandered around with her wineglass trying "not to lash out with criticism." Brautigan claimed his "unhappiness" as the reason for "noticing" a nineteen-year-old "chick" at Enrico's who kissed him twice and slipped away into the crowd. Although at one point she suggested they "end it all," Richard spent an uncomfortable nightmare-filled night with her, feral cats howling outside on the street while Valerie's cat Zenobia and her kittens scrambled for safety under the bed. The next morning, they parted at seven at the bus stop when Valerie left for school. They agreed she'd call if she wanted to see him. On the ride over to Berkeley, "despondent at the loneliness" she knew would come, Valerie thought about how she really did love Richard but wanted some time apart, "to test our feelings."

Brautigan's difficulties with Miles had a lot to do with jealousy. He resented the record producer's relationship with Valerie and her continuing ambivalent feelings. When Miles wrote her about Brautigan's record, confessing that "Apple is in the process of being destroyed" and that he was "trying to sneak in as many spoken word albums as possible," he mentioned he'd be back in California in May or June and wished to see her.

Miles received the record sleeve artwork and layout Brautigan had designed with the help of George Osaki. He was upset because Richard wanted a production credit and wrote back to remind him that the "contract is held by Miles Associates." Not even the Beatles demanded such an accommodation. To mollify the situation, Miles offered a 5 percent royalty instead of the original 3 percent. He casually mentioned finding three breaks in the tapes when they arrived in London—he reedited, resulting in a loss of an inch of tape (one-fifteenth of a second). This infuriated Richard, who demanded that Apple use a copy of the "Sounds of My Life" track held by Golden State Recorders for their master. "I am very interested in the timing of that track and want it just like the way we recorded it in San Francisco." The loss of one-fifteenth of a second was inaudible to the human ear, but Apple went along with Brautigan's wishes.

Between classes at the end of April, Valerie phoned Richard and said, "Why don't you move to Kearny?" They hadn't made a permanent split the previous week. Without knowing quite why, she felt better about them as a couple. Estes hinted they set a time limit, suggesting the first of June. They were still friends. Valerie wanted to make the best of it even though she continued to think of Miles. "What I don't need is another married man affair on my list," she wrote in her journal, but the Englishman provided a convenient "crutch." She did not intend to sleep with him again, yet she enjoyed his company, and it was comforting to know, "Well, there's always Miles."

By the time Brautigan moved back in with Valerie, he had sent all of the design material for his book, including the front cover photograph, off to Helen Brann. He was very specific about what he wanted. This included printing the back cover in blue with the word "mayonaise [sic] in white an inch above the center of the cover." He asked to see color samples "so that I may choose the blue."

Brautigan also spelled out his minimalist notion for the front flap copy and specified the two quotes that were all he wanted to appear on the back flap. He instructed that the three titles of his books run in blue across the dresses of the women on the cover, but allowed Roz Barrow to "work out the best design and balance." Richard insisted "the three books should be reprinted exactly the same as the original editions with all the Four Seasons Foundation imprints on them and everything, back covers, etc." By exercising his contractual design approval, Brautigan imposed a found-art aesthetic on the uncomprehending world of commercial publishing.

Another domestic crisis flared up early in May. Richard had promised to "be home at six" and cook dinner. At seven, he phoned Valerie to say that "the college artist chick" he had planned to meet at Enrico's was late, so he would be delayed. When Richard arrived at eight, smiling, drunk, and sheepish, Valerie was stone-cold sober. "Why are you late?" she demanded. He'd never change, she gibed, muttering he was a "pushover" around "chicks." Furious, Valerie rushed about the apartment, shoving Brautigan's belongings into a Safeway double bag.

Richard made for the door. "U.S. mail," he shouted. When Valerie said she wouldn't mail his things, Richard told her to throw them away and was gone, leaving her "alone and shaking."

The situation over in Berkeley only added to Valerie's emotional difficulties. The University of California owned a vacant lot one half block east of Telegraph Avenue between Haste Street and Dwight Way that volunteer students and local street people had landscaped, converting the abandoned urban space into People's Park. When the University attempted to resume control, claiming they wanted to build a soccer field, and surrounded the lot with a chain-link fence, the students protested. After being initially dispersed by law enforcement, over two thousand demonstrators marched "to take back the park." Police and sheriff's department deputies responded with tear gas and shotguns. More than one hundred were injured and an uninvolved onlooker accidentally killed.

Within a week of Brautigan's walkout, he was once again ensconced in Valerie's apartment. Soon after, Richard instructed his agent and publisher to use Kearny Street as his new address. At 5:17 am on the morning of May 13, he woke up at Valerie's side and felt her breasts, but he had a plane to catch and had to forgo any further pleasure. "Alas, I must fly away [. . .] And there is no time to enjoy the weather of her breasts [. . .]" Richard jotted in his notebook as he cruised east on TWA flight 703, eating breakfast at "500 miles an hour."

Brautigan changed planes in Chicago, heading for Durham, North Carolina, and a reading at Duke University. Along the way during the long trip, he composed several poems in his notebook: "Donner Party," "Flight Handbook," "Fake Protien [*sic*]," "Late Starting Dawn," and "Tongue Cemetary [*sic*]."

Brautigan was paid a total of $454.50 at Duke including expenses. After the reading, he got together with a bunch of students and aspiring writers in an off-campus apartment, drinking homemade beer until he passed out on the couch. Three days later, Richard flew back to Chicago. He dined on Chinese food that night, and the next afternoon at three, presented a poetry and fiction reading in the Quantrell Auditorium at the University of Chicago. Brautigan was billed as an "Experimental Prose Writer and Poet," and received $425 for his efforts, with an extra $175 thrown in for expenses. After less than a week on the road, he returned home to San Francisco with more than a thousand bucks in his pocket.

In addition to his big reading score, Richard continued to earn other small sums throughout May and June. He sold four more stories to *Rolling Stone* for $30 apiece. Jann Wenner published something by Brautigan in almost every issue that spring and summer. Knox College in

Galesburg, Illinois, gave Richard $15 for a one-time "amateur performance" of *Trout Fishing in America*. (The Sterling Lord agency received a $3 commission.) Strangest of all, a graphic designer named Audrey Sabol paid $300 for "non-exclusive rights" to make a wall hanging incorporating Brautigan's poem "Xerox Candy Bar."

Richard understood the critical importance of his new book's presentation. Brautigan determined not even the tiniest detail would escape his exacting attention. At the end of May, a memo about these special provisions circulated among the upper echelon of the publishing firm, reminding those in power of this extraordinary concession and ensuring that Richard's ideas would be taken seriously. "You're the boss," designer Roz Barrow wrote when she sent him three blue color samples as possibilities for the book's cover.

One of Brautigan's many concerns was the correct spelling of "mayonnaise." In the last line of the concluding chapter of *Trout Fishing*—a found-art letter—Richard ends his book with the word misspelled as "mayonaise." The question arose, which spelling to use on the back of the dust jacket, one "n" or two? At first, for his own "specific reason," Brautigan favored just one but in the end changed his mind and decided to spell it in lowercase with two "n's." He also insisted on keeping the "i" in *Trout Fishing in America* lowercase.

There were also photographic problems. A proof of the cover art arrived with the top of Brautigan's head cropped off. "I think the photograph would be a little more effective if we had all of my head in it," Richard wrote back. Brautigan had long insisted he wanted the covers on the Delta editions to look "exactly like" those used by the Four Seasons Foundation, but noticed Roz Barrow was using the fourth printing. That cover was slightly different from the others. The fourth printing had "the top of Benjamin Franklin's head missing. This is not very good." Richard wanted the cover to be identical to the one used on the Four Seasons Foundation's third printing.

Small annoyances arrived from time to time to distract Brautigan from his intense concentration on every tiny detail of his book's production. A form letter from Apple Records announced that their L.A. office was closing, a death knell for Richard's album. All correspondence should be forwarded to Joel Silver (the future action film producer) at Abkco Industries, Inc., in New York. In July, Alix Nelson, an editor at Simon & Schuster, wrote "enclosing a set of uncorrected galleys for William Hjortzberg's [*sic*] first novel, ALP [. . .]" She thought it "an important literary debut" and "a hilarious one as well." She hoped that Brautigan might enjoy the book and offer some comment. Richard made no reply of any kind.

Valerie continued her precarious relationship with Richard through the month of July. Some weekends, they rented a car and drove up to Sonoma to visit Ianthe, who lived there with her mother. On other occasions, they rode the bus out to Bolinas, getting together with friends such as the Browns, Joanne Kyger, and Jack Boyce, or to Marin City to visit Lew Welch and Magda Cregg. Richard called Pat Slattery, who handled Apple's business in Hollywood, around the middle of the month, thanking her for the work she'd done on his behalf. She was bowled over. In her five-and-a-half-month "employment nightmare," she had not received a single call or letter of thanks until Brautigan picked up the phone.

Richard and Valerie planned to watch the *Apollo 11* moon landing at the apartment of their friends Fritzi and Michael Dorroh. They came over for a homemade chicken enchilada dinner. Richard had recently cooked his spaghetti and meatballs for Mike and Fritzi at Valerie's place. After eating, they sat on the couch staring silently at the television screen, "listening to everything Walter

Cronkite told us." Fritzi remembered how they "were all amazed at this historic event." When Neil Armstrong took his giant leap for mankind, Brautigan reached for his notebook. Inspired by the TV image of the astronaut's fat squash-shaped footprint in the moon dust, he jotted down a draft of his poem "Jules Verne Zucchini." He contrasted the cost of the moon mission with the number of people dying of starvation back at home. Richard added the single word "Earth" above the date at the bottom of the poem.

By late July, Brautigan felt the ever-increasing acceleration of his own liftoff toward stardom. Helen Brann sold two of his short stories ("The Weather in San Francisco," which Richard had written when he lived with Janice Meissner on California Street, and "The Auction," a tale of his impoverished boyhood in the Pacific Northwest) to *Vogue* for a total of $500. These were the first pieces of Brautigan fiction to appear in a national mainstream magazine.

Sam Lawrence contacted Brann, expressing interest in Brautigan's new volume of poetry, which Donald Allen planned to publish in December. (The rights were to revert to the author after a total printing of twenty-five thousand copies.) Jonathan Cape Ltd. bought the British rights to Brautigan's three books. Ed Victor, an American who worked for Tom Maschler at Cape, loved Richard's work and got approval to make an offer. Victor's sarcastic intelligence and superior attitude made him a natural fit among the Brits. "I don't think we paid very much money," he recalled.

Early in August, following another disagreement with Valerie, Brautigan moved back to Geary Street. Aside from having brought his typewriter and a few changes of clothing, he had never actually moved in, so this didn't involve more than filling a couple shopping bags with his stuff. A week later, Richard and Valerie had dinner at Enrico's. The next week they went to see the film *Midnight Cowboy*, so the split was not yet a complete separation.

Mad River's eponymous first album had not been a hit. The band members' names mismatched with their pictures on the sleeve, and Capitol had sped up the tracks in postproduction. This made Mad River's music "sound like the Chipmunks." *Rolling Stone* panned the release, which didn't sell. Greg Dewey called it "one of the biggest heartbreaks of my life."

When Capitol failed to renew their contract, the band got another chance and recorded a second album in Berkeley with their old pal Jerry Corbitt of the Youngbloods as their producer. *Paradise Bar and Grill* turned out better and was released at the end of July. The record included Richard Brautigan's musically accompanied reading of "Love's Not a Way to Treat a Friend" (recorded the previous year) as its third track on side A. Richard received a check for $136 for his performance.

In August, Brautigan was invited by his friend Lew Welch to join in a reading for a group of prisoners at San Quentin. Welch had been having a hard time that summer, suffering from depression and "big changes [he didn't] seem able to handle very well." These included the approach of his forty-third birthday, making him "feel old and feeble," and his fifth attempt at going dry and "stopping the booze absolutely." The event marked Richard's first return to the big house since he researched "The Menu" in 1965. He and Welch agreed the prisoners were among their "warmest and [most] appreciative audiences." The convicts' favorable reaction was the only recompense the poets received that afternoon. They donated their time.

Preparing for his trip to San Diego to direct the prose workshop at California Western's Summer Conference, Richard asked Edmund Shea to make him a series of black-and-white slides of punctuation marks to be projected onto a screen. Long accustomed to working with artists, Shea never questioned Brautigan's odd request and had the slides ready before he left. Two days prior to his departure, Richard sent a letter to Sam Lawrence listing the writers he wanted to receive complimentary copies of Delacorte's hardcover three-in-one edition of his books. Along with friends like Don Carpenter, Lew Welch, Ron Loewinsohn, and Michael McClure, and long-standing supporters such as John Ciardi, Tom Parkinson, Josephine Miles, and Kay Boyle, Brautigan added Herbert Gold, Anne Waldman, and Ishmael Reed to his list.

Don Carpenter described the San Diego beach campus of United States International University as being "on the sandspit." He said the suites the school provided for the participants were "little barracks, it was horrifying." Robert Creeley described them as having a "plastic cement block design." Richard called the place "Stalag 19." The poster advertising the event featured an Edmund Shea photograph of Brautigan, clearly the "star" of the weeklong celebration. Along with Brautigan, the literary gathering included Carpenter, Creeley, Edward Dorn, Stephen Schneck, Michael McClure, and Jim Morrison, lead singer of the Doors, who was there to present his sixteen-millimeter documentary film, *Feast of Friends*.

After the screening, Morrison sat out on the lawn "in a circle of poets and writers with a few of the students," passing around a bottle of whiskey. Don Carpenter remembered the rocker "making an ass of himself." Creeley recalled "this awful sad evening" and Morrison as "extraordinarily drunk."

Creeley quoted T. S. Eliot, and Jim Morrison began teasing him, "the vulnerable square, the poet." Morrison grabbed the whiskey bottle (and here the memories of eyewitnesses vary). Don Carpenter thought the rock star broke it over his own head, while Creeley remembered "and he just goes *whop* on the head of his friend Babe, and the bottle breaks. Wow!" In his book *Lighting the Corners* Michael McClure recalled the Jim Morrison incident, remembering it both ways.

> It was the middle of the night. Everybody was extremely intoxicated. We were sitting out on the greensward. Creeley had his clothes off and was rolling down the hill, drunkenly yelling that he was his body. It was wonderful. Richard Brautigan was sitting under a tree brooding about noble Brautigan thoughts. Jim, Babe, and I were there sort of cross-legged under another tree. I don't remember what anybody was saying, but Jim reached over with a bottle and broke it over Babe's head. I said, "Jim, that was a rotten thing to do," and he said "Oh yeah?" and he picked up another bottle and broke it over his own head.

Bob Creeley had a notion about the nature of Brautigan's "noble" thoughts. "Richard, he's not at all pleased by this," Creeley said. In fact, Brautigan "was very turned off by Jim Morrison." According to Creeley, "he loathed that sense of public disorder or public indifference." Richard hated having broken glass lying about and borrowed a flashlight to look for pieces of the whiskey bottle. Bob Creeley recalled him earlier "on the beach picking up plastic." For his part, Jim Morrison jumped to his feet and sauntered off. Two "sad groupies" passing by asked, "Where do you think they're going?"

"Nowhere you'd like to go," Creeley muttered.

Three days later, at a party following Carpenter's reading at the Solomon Little Theatre, Creeley and Don sat and talked with a student when Richard approached and said, "We have to leave now."

"Why . . . ?" the student protested. "Hey, the party's just getting started. What do you have to leave for?"

"You'll never know," Creeley told him. "We have to leave 'cause Richard said so." Soon after, they were all barreling down the San Diego Freeway in a Volkswagen with the Creeleys up front and Brautigan and Carpenter seated in the rear. Bob and Bobbie were "arguing like murder," Don recalled. Suddenly, Creeley hit the brakes and stopped the little car beneath an underpass on the freeway. Richard and Don sat terrified in the backseat, "waiting for the semi to hit us, you know, from Mexico, highballing it north with all the toilet seats." An accident was avoided after Bob got out, walked around, and opened the door for Bobbie. She took his place in the driver's seat, and they sped off into the night.

On another occasion, Bobbie Creeley remembered going to "this funny bunkhouse" where they all were staying, to pick up Richard. "We were going to go up the coast to this woman's house to have something to eat and sit on the beach and then come back." Brautigan was sleeping in his room, naked, covered only with a blanket. When they woke him, Richard sat up, the blanket across his lap. Bobbie noticed his body was covered with bruises, "the kind of bruise that looks terrible when it starts to get yellow." Don Carpenter stuck his head into the room, took one look, and said, "God, that woman should go to prison."

Brautigan gave his presentation on August 23 in the Little Theatre auditorium. Creeley had read his exquisitely honed poetry the evening before, and the students doubtless expected a similar performance from the author of *Trout Fishing in America*. Richard neither read nor gave a talk. Instead, he stood at the back of the hall with a projector, showing Edmund Shea's slides of punctuation marks. Don Carpenter sat in the audience. "It was terrifying at the beginning," he remembered, "because they didn't know what to do. This went on for forty-five minutes of punctuation marks. There aren't that many punctuation marks. There were repeats!" Brautigan remained silent, not saying a word as he changed slide after slide.

"The students just sat there in that auditorium frozen with wondering how they were supposed to react to this. And he would hit one, like the semicolon and then the comma. And the comma would be up there five minutes and then the colon. And after a while you can hear first this one and then that one and then this one start to get it. And you hear the laughing. And it's like when Mark Twain got up and told the same story six times in a row until they started to laugh. He was going to tell it as many times as it took for them to get the idea that that's what was going on. And that's what Richard was doing. Pay attention to these punctuation marks, and as soon as we got that, it was like you were real stupid if you weren't laughing."

Don Carpenter also recalled one afternoon sitting outside under a tree surrounded by a circle of students. "I've never had this experience at another writers' conference," he said. "I was explaining to them how I felt about certain literary matters. There was Richard sitting there listening to me. Not adding anything, not trying to be another teacher or anything like that. Just one of the students. It was really flattering, an enormously charming thing to do." Carpenter chuckled at the memory. "The fact that there were a number of pretty girls sitting there wasn't at issue, although it certainly became an issue later in the evening. I think I'm the only poet there that didn't get laid."

Don Carpenter should have brought his wife along. Most of the other poets did. Bobbie Creeley came with Bob. Michael McClure had Joanna by his side. Ed and Jenny Dorn were there with their baby son, Kidd, their first child, born two weeks before on the D. H. Lawrence Ranch near Taos. Most of the social activity was purely domestic. Bobbie Creeley remembered sitting on the grass with Richard, talking about their childhoods. Brautigan told her he'd stay in a place for three months and then move on.

"Why did you move so much?" she asked.

"One of my stepfathers had been a fry cook," Richard replied.

Bobbie understood completely. Her own father had been a fry cook, and she moved around a lot as a child. "Fry cooks," Bobbie said, "rank below itinerant evangelists and used car salesmen as a bad credit risk."

Brautigan told her the story of the time his mother abandoned him in Great Falls with Tex Porterfield. Bobbie Creeley recalled that Richard felt this was "the crowning blow."

"We didn't even like each other that much," he said.

"How did he treat you?" she asked.

"Well, he treated me well enough. I'd come to where he was working after school, and he'd give me $5, and I'd go out and eat dinner."

Brautigan formed a lasting new friendship at California Western's Summer Conference with Roxy and Judy Gordon, a young Texas couple who had come down to San Diego from the Fort Belknap Reservation in northern Montana. Half-Choctaw, half-Scottish, Roxy Lee Gordon had been adopted as "First Coyote Boy" by the Assiniboine (Nakota), who shared the reservation with the Gros Ventres (A'aninin). At twenty-four, already an accomplished storyteller and songwriter, Gordon had his own distinctive look, lean and lanky, wearing cowboy garb and mirrored aviator sunglasses. He wrote about his friends up on the rez and of some time he and Judy had spent in Colorado working for VISTA (Volunteers in Service to America). Roxy recalled how "Richard liked a short story I wrote. He hooked on to me. I think also he liked I had a car." Newly pregnant, Judy was thinking about where she would have her baby. Brautigan suggested the Gordons come up to San Francisco. "I had to find San Francisco on the map," Roxy Gordon remembered.

Richard's teaching engagement at U.S. International lasted another week, until the following Friday. Most of the other writers cleared out once their presentations were over, but Schneck and Dorn stayed to read during the second week of the conference. The day after Brautigan's reading, Don Allen hosted a big literary gathering at his place in Frisco. Bob and Bobbie Creeley were there, along with Michael and Joanna McClure, both poets having already departed San Diego. The guest list also included Lew Welch and Magda Cregg, Joanne Kyger and Jack Boyce, David Schaff, and Warren and Ellen Tallman. Valerie Estes came wearing a flowered black silk chiffon dress.

Along with gossip about Brother Antoninus and Joanne's tales of the La Mama theater troupe coming to Bolinas and ripping everybody off "without giving a single performance," Bob Creeley and Valerie talked about Charles Olson's letters. Creeley didn't understand them either. Bob insisted how fond he was of Richard. "It was the first and last thing he told me," she wrote to Brautigan the next day. Allen's party was just the sort of fashionable bohemian social event that so frequently found a mention in Herb Caen's column. Maybe this one resulted in an additional bar-onhood for Michael McClure. Richard Brautigan had no regrets far off in San Diego. His days as a baron had come to an end. A coronation into the hierarchy of true literary royalty lay just ahead.

thirty-four: the great public library publishing caper

I T ALL STARTED with an obituary. Richard Brautigan tore the column from the back pages of the *San Francisco Examiner* in September of 1968, another piece of found art. He kept it among his personal papers for the remaining sixteen years of his life. The headline read, "Mrs. Myrtle Tate, Movie Projectionist." The widow of Yancey S. Tate died at Kaiser Foundation Hospital at the age of sixty-six and had been a "longtime member" of the International Alliance of Theatrical Stage Employees and Motion Picture Machine Operators of San Francisco Union, Local 317. Richard wrote "Mrs. Myrtle Tate, Movie Projectionist," a poem about "one of the few women who worked as a movie projectionist."

Richard's friend actor/poet/screenwriter Jack Thibeau had experimented with a series of Xerox poems later published in New York by Roger Kennedy and transformed by Mabou Mines, the experimental theater group, into *The Saint and the Football Player*, "a massive performance piece," with music by minimalist composer Philip Glass. Thibeau showed this work to Brautigan. "He didn't know what they were," Jack recalled, "but he liked the concept that you can put the dimes in, Xerox it, and you're published."

Richard Brautigan was not looking for a cheap form of alternative printing. For the past couple years, his close affiliation with the Mime Troupe, the Diggers, and the Artists Liberation Front had directed his creative energy toward happenings and street theater. *Please Plant This Book* was one result of this collective thinking. Richard's participation in Candle Opera and The Invisible Circus were others. When Jack Thibeau told him about Xerox publishing, new possibilities for public performance blossomed in his imagination.

Richard made all the arrangements. Poster artist Victor Moscoso remembered getting a phone call from Brautigan. "He said he had a friend, Jack Thibeau, I may have known Jack. And it was Richard's idea to go down to the Public Library and produce a little book." He had a simple plan. Each of the artists would have his own page to design in any way he pleased. Creative improvisation was encouraged. Richard Brautigan told them to bring their library cards.

Important cultural events needed recording for posterity, so Richard called his photographer friend Edmund Shea, asking him to come along with his camera. More to the point, Edmund owned a car. Not just any old jalopy, but a beautiful classic 1939 flathead straight-eight Packard. They would ride in style. Early in December, the foursome was ready to roll. Richard phoned ahead to the Main Library down at Civic Center to make all the arrangements. He wore a turtleneck sweater, a filigreed medallion (the number "13" enclosed within a circle) on a chain around his neck, the standard navy peacoat, and a new wide-brimmed, high-crowned hat with a leather band. Valerie Estes came with him. At Richard's suggestion, she brought along Zenobia, her purebred

Siamese cat. Jack Thibeau recalled the drive downtown in the big gangstermobile. "Edmund picked us up one at a time like we were going to rob a bank."

Thibeau remembered "the PR department waiting for us at the door" when they arrived at the neoclassical beaux arts building on the corner of Larkin and McAllister. He was surprised to see Ann Kincaid, the librarian who had befriended him when he first arrived in the city four years before, among the greeting committee. The quartet was graciously escorted inside and led up the broad marble steps to the high-ceilinged, book-lined Reference Room housing the coin-operated Vico-Matic copy machine. A sign mounted on the device boasted: vico-matic copies anything in seconds for 10c bound books, checks, letters, resumes, contracts, legal briefs, etc. (It was a dry copier, actually a Thermofax, not a Xerox, thus explaining the severe age darkening that later obscured the photo-sensitive paper.)

Brautigan had come prepared with rolls of dimes, and he fed a coin into the copier. Turning to Jack Thibeau, he suggested, "Why don't you go first?" Although up until that moment, Thibeau had no idea what he was going to do, he immediately said, "Okay." For no particular reason, Thibeau had brought along a package of little stickum gold stars, the kind fifth-grade teachers affix to prize essays. He sprinkled these over the glass plate on the machine. Unzipping his black jacket and pulling up his shirt, Thibeau laid his bare chest down on top of them. With the coat collar pulled up over his head, Jack used his jacket as a hood to block the outside light. One dime followed another and photos of Jack Thibeau's hirsute pectorals adrift among the stars, page after page, rolled out of the Vico-Matic. Seven years later, Jack landed a job in the Philippines as Martin Sheen's body double on *Apocalypse Now* because his chest hair matched that of the star.

Next came Victor Moscoso's turn. He, too, had bought a number of stars of different sizes at a stationery store. As Edmund Shea circled around them taking pictures, Victor laid the stars out on the copy machine and provided Zenobia's brief moment of fame. With Valerie assisting, Victor placed the cat on the glass plate and dropped dimes into the machine. Another original art page was born.

Richard Brautigan produced his page by centering a copy of his poem about Mrs. Myrtle Tate on a background of newspaper movie ads, including *The Graduate*, *The Shoes of the Fisherman*, and a revival of *Gone with the Wind*. As a final touch, Richard placed his library card at the bottom of the page. He had also prepared a title page, *The San Francisco Public Library: A Publishing House*, which contained the following information, "This magazine was created and Xeroxed at the Main Library in the Civic Center using their ten cent Xerox machine on December 5, 1968 by: Victor Moscoso, Jack Thibeau, Richard Brautigan."

Richard had prepared small slips of paper with a typed statement: "This is one of seven numbered and signed copies." The line below contained a typed number. These were printed on seven of Brautigan's pages, and he signed them all. In addition, Thibeau and Moscoso each signed an undisclosed number of their own pages. According to librarian David Belch, no more than twenty copies were printed. Richard bound each one together with three staples and placed all the copies, together with all the stars and other original material, in a large yellow photography paper box.

Jack Thibeau recalled the moment: "He sealed it with some stuff and said, 'Well, that's that.'" Eventually, each of the participants received a signed copy. "They shriveled up and died within a year," Jack said. Moscoso was disappointed that they got so dark. Today, the few surviving copies have turned almost entirely black. Even so, a collector wishing to purchase one from a rare book dealer should be prepared to fork over at least $2,000 for the ephemeral item.

A LONG-STANDING URBAN MYTH holds that the sequence of small stars on the covers of *Playboy* magazine (actually a code indicating various regional editions) stands for the number of times head honcho Hugh Hefner slept with the Playmate of the Month. Likewise, it has also long been rumored that the women on the covers of Richard Brautigan's books were all at one time his lovers. As Don Carpenter said, "Richard's sexual archive is reflected on his book covers."

Michael McClure summed it up when he wrote, "Richard was crazy about beautiful women, smoothly glabrous ones with long hair and big eyes." Don Carpenter remembered "lots of women," getting straight to the point. "Richard did a lot of fucking. A lot of fucking! *A lot!*" Brautigan worshipped the women he loved, elevating a select few to the lofty status of "muse." Some of these he sought to immortalize by placing their pictures on the front covers of his books.

The first muse thus anointed was Michaela Blake-Grand, pictured on *Trout Fishing in America*. By the time Don Allen published the novel, Mickey had slipped from muse status to the less exalted position of old friend and pen pal. The current muse was Marcia Pacaud, although even that relationship was on the wane when she set out one morning early in 1968, wearing a sleeveless cotton frock, to take some pictures with Brautigan and Edmund Shea. This was the first photo shoot Richard and Edmund worked on together.

The trio was heading for a railroad tower south of Market that Brautigan thought would make a good backdrop when they happened across a large hole in the ground at the corner of New Montgomery and Market Streets. It was an excavation site for the Bay Area Rapid Transit (BART), then under construction beneath the surface of Market Street. Edmund had read Richard's poem "The Pill versus the Springhill Mine Disaster," although he was not familiar with most of the other poetry in the planned collection. There had been some discussion about the book's title, and when Edmund peered down into the hole he said, "Well, gee, here's our mine."

With no cops in sight, the threesome sneaked down into the gaping excavation. Large steel girders reached up like piers to support the sidewalk above. Marcia slipped off her shoes (but kept her watch on) and perched winsomely on a pile of rubble, bare arms crossed over her knees. Edmund snapped several pictures of Marcia alone and then a bunch more with Brautigan posed with her. In some he sat at her side. One shot seemed utterly characteristic of Richard. He stood behind Marcia, his arms over her shoulders, clasping his hands together as if in prayer while she gripped his elbows.

Later, when Brautigan went over the contact sheet with Shea, he selected a photograph of Marcia Pacaud sitting alone for the cover of the poetry book he would dedicate to her. Shea thought Brautigan included women in these pictures "because he liked girls. All of his writing is kind of romantic in a way. Loving, feelings and things like that. I think our only thing was to do good pictures."

Their second effort at making a good picture came soon after, when Edmund arrived at Brautigan's Geary Street apartment to shoot the cover for *In Watermelon Sugar*. This time, the muse of the moment was but a passing fancy, a woman no one, not even Edmund Shea, seemed to remember. Richard never wrote her any letters, although he corresponded frequently with his other lovers. Her name was Hilda Hoffman. A graceful Virgo, she had only recently moved to San Francisco from New York, where she had been a member of a singing and dancing troupe. For a brief period, she had been Paul Krassner's girlfriend, although he recalled only her hippie sobriquet and even that recollection remained vague, "Morning Dove . . . Morning Glory . . . Morning Star, something like that." Brautigan wrote a poem for Hilda that later appeared in *Rommel Drives on Deep into Egypt*.

As always, Richard took charge, directing the whole operation. They went to work on the rickety stairs leading down from Brautigan's kitchen to the trash-filled backyard. Stacks of old newspapers stood in sodden piles on the landing. Hilda parted her long fine blond hair straight down the middle and wore a cute little summer minidress ending just above the knees. Richard posed her standing alone on the stairs holding a mop, evoking the domestic qualities of Pauline, one of the characters in his novel.

Richard got in on the act himself, sitting on the stairs a step or two behind Hilda, peering owlishly over her right shoulder. Edmund took a couple double-exposure shots as an experiment, showing Hoffman's face framed in the doorway while her full figure hovered ghostlike in front. "I always liked that," Shea remembered. Richard felt otherwise. After looking over the contacts, he chose a medium-close two-shot, which appeared on the front of the book.

The next cover girl was indeed just that, a two-year-old child. She was obviously the only early model with whom Brautigan was not intimately involved. Caledonia (Jahrmarkt) Batman was the daughter of art gallery owner Billy Batman. For someone whose father was a junkie, she appeared remarkably well-adjusted. Bill Brach, who to this day has never read any of Richard Brautigan's books, encountered Caledonia playing at a cookout in the backyard of a Digger house in the Haight-Ashbury. Many Diggers were in attendance, including Billy and Joanie Batman, Peter Berg, and Peter Coyote.

Bill Brach aimed his camera at Caledonia and took several pictures as she wandered barefoot through the grass. Brach can't remember if Brautigan asked him to take the photos or saw them at a later date. In any event, Bill was never paid for his work. This was appropriate under the circumstances, as the photographs appeared on the cover of *Please Plant This Book*, which was given away for free. Brach printed the pictures in an old-fashioned oval format suggesting nineteenth-century daguerreotypes. Brautigan used three on the folded cardboard covers of his book. Two were close-ups, and the other showed Caledonia from behind, walking away from the camera. Ianthe Brautigan felt jealous when she saw another little girl pictured on one of her father's books. Over the years, Ianthe has often been incorrectly identified in rare book catalogs as the child pictured on Brautigan's singular publication.

The notion of a record album featuring the work of Richard Brautigan first sparked into life in London in October of 1968, when Barry Miles brought a list of poets and writers over to Paul McCartney's three-story Regency house in St. John's Wood. The Beatles started Apple Corps in

April 1967 as a holding company to avoid paying millions of pounds in taxes. The logo came from a René Magritte painting of a big green apple (*Le Jue de Mourre*) owned by McCartney. A year and a half after the start of the Apple record label, the Beatles formed a division devoted to inexpensive spoken word and experimental releases. John Lennon christened it Zapple. ("A is for Apple. Z is for Zapple.")

In the midst of these trendy times, the only thing London lacked was a hip bookstore on the order of City Lights. Peter Asher (half of the pop group "Peter and Gordon" and married to Marianne Faithfull), John Dunbar (brother of Jennifer Dunbar, who would later marry Ed Dorn), and Miles decided to open Indica, a gallery/bookshop at number 6 Mason's Yard. Paul McCartney helped paint the walls and put up shelving. John Lennon met Yoko Ono at an Indica art opening.

John published quirky poetry and gained a reputation as the "avant-garde" Beatle, but it was Paul who first explored experimental ideas. McCartney wrote, "When [John] was living out in suburbs by the golf club with Cynthia and hanging out there, I was getting in with a guy called Miles and the people at Indica." Paul regarded Zapple as "the point of connection between Apple and Indica Bookshop." He and Lennon chose Miles "as the *de facto* label manager."

When Miles brought his literary checklist over to McCartney's Cavandish Avenue pad, Richard Brautigan was known in England only through *Trout Fishing* and *Confederate General*, but had gained a reputation sufficient to be ranked alongside Allen Ginsberg, Henry Miller, William Burroughs, Kenneth Patchen, Charles Olson, and Lawrence Ferlinghetti on the list of luminaries. Zapple's plans included not just poetry, but electronic music, lectures, avant-garde theatrical productions, "anything off-beat."

Miles first contacted Brautigan early the previous October, before the Zapple name had been coined and the division was known as "Words from Apple." Richard wrote back, saying he was interested and proposing a notion to record his vision of America.

In January 1969, Miles flew to America to begin recording the initial projects in the low-budget series. Miles traveled first for five days to Gloucester, Massachusetts, to record Charles Olson reading his poetry. He stopped next in New York for a session with Ken Weaver, the drummer with the Fugs. Weaver hailed from Texas and hoped to have an album of "Texspeak," a folksy ramble showcasing his gifts as a good-old-boy redneck raconteur. Miles recorded hours of tape, but no album was ever released.

After two hectic weeks on the East Coast, it was on to California with a detour to Los Angeles, where Miles met Charles Bukowski, who at that point still worked for the post office and was almost totally unknown. Having never read in public, Bukowski felt nervous about reading with anyone listening, so Miles "wired up an Ampex 3000" along with a microphone and stand in the living room of the poet's "run-down" East Hollywood house and left the equipment and a dozen reels of blank tape. This field session became Bukowski's first professional recording. Miles told Buk he'd collect the finished tapes in a week or so and headed north to Frisco.

Miles arrived "a bit exhausted from traveling and constant work." Richard was ensconced at Valerie's place on Telegraph Hill. "He moved in to Kearny Street and more than once," she said, "because, of course, we fought a lot." The low-budget nature of the Zapple project prompted Miles to inquire about cheap lodging. Valerie "volunteered" that he could sleep on her couch. "Miles in turn hired me as a gofer, for want of a better word," she said. Miles remembered it was Richard who suggested Valerie for the job as his "assistant."

Like Brautigan, Miles didn't drive a car, so he rented "a shiny green" Ford Mustang. Part of Valerie's job involved serving as his chauffeur. Miles also recorded the work of Michael McClure and Lawrence Ferlinghetti while in San Francisco. Golden State Recorders on Harrison Street had several other acts booked in February, so juggling his schedule between the three poets left Miles with a bunch of free time. He and Valerie took to cruising about the Bay Area together in the Mustang. They explored Mount Tamalpais and Muir Woods. Valerie introduced her boss to the No Name Bar in Sausalito. Inevitably, they drifted into a brief love affair. Valerie found skinny Miles to be a fantastic lover, the best she had been with up to that point in her life. (She ranked both Brautigan and Ferlinghetti "lousy" in bed.)

Wanting to keep their fling a secret (Miles had a wife back in London), the couple spent many nights in L.A. While commuting from San Francisco to Los Angeles, Valerie and Miles crashed at Frank Zappa's spacious mock-Tudor house high in the Santa Monica Hills. From there, they drove together over to De Longpre Avenue to collect the Charles Bukowski tapes.

Buk had a hangover. A middle-aged woman in a black slip and fishnet stockings skulked about. Valerie retained distinct memories of the "bad boy" poet's place. "I can still see the beer cans." Never mind the pile of car tires stacked in the corner of the living room. During their time in L.A., they visited folk singer Phil Ochs and the novelist Stephen Schneck (who was a friend of Valerie's) and attended a performance by the as-yet-unrecorded Alice Cooper at the Whiskey A G-Go.

From the start, Brautigan's relationship with Miles was strained. "Miles and Richard were not each other's greatest fans," Valerie observed. Class differences played a part. Miles, a proper English chap, was "somewhat uppity," in Valerie's candid assessment. Creative disagreements during the recording sessions were rubbed raw by jealousy. Miles hoped to finish the project in two weeks (his instructions had been to "get as much recorded as possible" and edit in London).

When Miles flew home, he left six hours of completed tape with the engineers in San Francisco. He thought the album was "by far the best" of everything he had recorded while in the States and was sure the Beatles would "dig it." Miles felt the record was a "true expression" of Richard's work. A "followup album might be a good idea." He wrote to Brautigan from London, saying he hoped "none of the things that happened caused you any pain as none was intended."

Richard Brautigan insisted on complete design control over the record album, as he had with all his books. He brought up the matter during a phone conversation with Miles in London early in March. Miles replied in a letter: "The series is designed for people to 'do their thing,' so this is wanted. I will make sure that the contract gives you design control over the cover etc. etc." Richard wanted an album with no writing on the front, much like the cover for *Trout Fishing*. Miles insisted that "the title must go on the front. "We have issued records with no writing on the front but it cuts sales drastically because no-one knows what the album is. It's different with books because they are displayed spine-out so people can read the title that way." Miles thought "a black and white photograph with simple lettering would do it." Apple authorized him to pay for a photographer.

Brautigan pressed ahead with the album cover project and brought in Edmund Shea to handle the photography. The photo session took place in Valerie Estes's apartment. Edmund framed most of his pictures in the front room. He had not heard the tapes. Richard told him telephone calls played a part, and they used Valerie's phone as a prop. Richard posed Valerie before a pair of closed double doors holding her black rotary-dial telephone. At one point, Shea took a few shots of Valerie talking on the phone. Not wanting to fake a conversation, she dialed a friend. Valerie thought of Edmund as "a round elf" and observed that he worked well with Richard because "he didn't bicker with Richard over what Richard wanted."

Brautigan chose Valerie's outfit, a paisley tunic she disliked with three-quarter-length sleeves and matching trousers that looked as if they had been made from an imported Indian tablecloth. He had her braid her long dark hair into two thick strands, something else she didn't like. The picture Richard eventually selected showed his girlfriend smiling and holding her phone with the receiver firmly nested in the cradle. "He had some image that he wanted," Valerie commented. "I have very negative feelings about that photograph."

Edmund Shea spent five hours taking pictures. Part of the time he shot from the street outside the building. Valerie leaned out one window, singing. Richard listened intently from another window. Looking at the contact sheets gave Brautigan a new idea. He liked the pictures of Valerie holding the phone and asked Edmund to take some of him in a similar pose, to suggest they might be calling each other. Shea did this work over at Brautigan's apartment on Geary Street. Richard posed holding out the phone's receiver, extending it at arm's length toward the viewer.

Brautigan's telephone had a toggle switch installed on the side, enabling him to turn the machine off when he wished. "It's really an incredible thing," Richard said. "It gives you control over the telephone. I'm not a victim of it." With the switch off the phone would ring but Brautigan couldn't hear it. It was Richard's habit never to answer the phone after eleven o'clock at night. "Whenever the telephone rings after eleven o'clock, I just automatically assume that it's not going to be good news," he said. "Years and years of practice of answering the telephone at that time of night, bum trip after bum trip. Now, I just don't answer the telephone anymore."

Forsaking the scruffy pea jacket and pinback button-studded vest that had defined his image, Richard Brautigan attempted a sartorial makeover for the record album cover shoot. He wore a new turtleneck sweater (a gift from Valerie), a dignified thrift shop broad pin-striped jacket, and his number 13 medallion. He looked prosperous and well fed, as befitted a man whose income for the first two months of 1969 surpassed his total earnings the year before.

The day before leaving on his trip to New Mexico and New York in March, Brautigan wrote to Miles, telling him that the title of the album was to be *Listening to Richard Brautigan*. "It is direct and to the point." He agreed with the notion of black-and-white photographs. "I may use two or three photographs on the record, but I am not going to send negatives. I am going to send prints because the developing is very important and I always like to have it done in a way that pleases me." He decided finally to use two photos, one of himself and the other of Valerie, a big smile wreathing her face, both holding telephones. Brautigan asked that Shea be paid a $300 photographer's fee and that Valerie receive $50 for modeling.

Brautigan traveled east in part because Seymour Lawrence bought the rights to his three Four Seasons Foundation books for a single omnibus reprint edition. A couple months earlier, Richard proposed the same arrangement to his former agent, Robert Mills, also representing Don Carpenter. Don happened to be sitting in the agent's New York office at the time Richard made his call, "collect, of course." As Don recalled, years later, Richard "yammered at the agent that he wanted *Trout Fishing*, *Springhill Mine Disaster*, and one other book brought out as a trilogy, in one volume. And Bob Mills was saying, 'This is utterly impossible. I can't have you as a client. You know, Don is here right now. I'm sorry, etc.' and hung up." Somewhat chagrined, Carpenter confessed at the time he agreed with Mills. "It was utterly hopeless," he said, laughing at his own folly in the same breath. "Sold like fucking hotcakes!"

Richard Brautigan set to work organizing a cover shoot for the forthcoming omnibus edition of his books. Toward the end of April or early in May, with Erik Weber still wandering in India, Brautigan again recruited Edmund Shea for the job. Richard's first notion involved getting all three former cover muses together for a photo shoot reunion. When that proved impractical, he had a new idea. Brautigan persuaded his daughter to be part of the project, assuaging her hurt feelings over *Please Plant This Book*. Seeking some sense of continuity with his best-known work, Richard got in touch with his original muse, Michaela Blake-Grand. She agreed to pose with him once again.

Edmund arranged to take the photographs in the kitchen of a friend's apartment half a block down Sacramento Street from his place. "Richard had been in the kitchen and stuff, so he liked the idea of shooting it there." At the photo session, Brautigan orchestrated everything as if directing a movie. He made sure the frying pan Edmund once used to cook him an omelet hung prominently on the white pegboard wall in the background. It added to the homey feel, with the white-enamel stove, coffee can potted plants, and hanging herbs. The tableau Richard Brautigan posed before his found-art stage set deliberately evoked formal family portraits of the nineteenth century.

In a way, it was family. Ianthe sat at the center, wearing a dress with a big bow. Skilled with a needle, Valerie Estes designed and sewed it for her. Ianthe's right arm pointed straight out from the shoulder. Her father stood behind her, hands on his knees, hunched slightly forward. Michaela sat to her left, hands hidden behind the folds of her gown. Mickey played the part of the mother in this family portrait, and for many years afterward, people assumed it to be a photo of Ginny.

Richard's hair hung to his shoulders, longer than on the *Trout Fishing* cover. He wore a loose-fitting black T-shirt with the number 13 medallion dangling around his neck. Brautigan thought Mickey and Ianthe's floor-length costumes should evoke a connection between current hippie styles and the sentimental appearance of a bygone era. He carefully instructed Valerie on how he wanted his daughter's dress to look. All three participants bore deadpan expressions of Gothic solemnity.

The photo session lasted for hours. Ianthe remembered the pain of holding her arm out, take after take. Her father explained his idea for the cover to her. How she was pointing at the front dust jacket flap, which would have no text other than a simple greeting: "Welcome, you are just a few pages away from *Trout Fishing in America*." She remembered it as "a very low-key day," but nine-year-old Ianthe's fantasy of a career in modeling was forever shattered by the experience.

Richard wanted to print the dust jacket photo on the front cover as well, so the book looked the same, with or without a jacket. Children's books often had covers identical to the dust wrapper art, as did the hard back publications of such gifted graphic artists as William Steig and Robert Osborn. Brautigan insisted that Shea be paid a decent fee. "Book publishers hate to pay real money for covers," Edmund observed. He spoke from experience. Sam Lawrence offered $25 each for the use of the Four Seasons cover photographs in the Delta editions. Edmund Shea was to receive a total of $175, including his new photo for the cover of the Delacorte hardback. Edmund submitted a bill for $1,500 for his services. Sam Lawrence hit the ceiling, fuming that "we usually pay $50–$100 for all rights—jackets, promotion, etc." After much prodding from Richard, Sam upped his offer to $450.

One Sunday evening before Christmas in 1969, a beautiful twenty-four-year-old woman named Beverly Allen, a self-described "blithe spirit" who worked as a house model at Saks Fifth Avenue, walked into the Caffe Trieste with her "jittery" friend Patricia MacDermott, an aspiring actress. Allen had recently returned from music studies in Rome, after a brief failed marriage to a Berkeley professor who served on the Greek Atomic Energy Commission. Brautigan stood just ahead of them in line for the espresso machine. Beverly recognized the writer at first glance.

The two young women struck up a conversation with Richard, and they sat down together with their coffee at a small table. "He clearly had his eye on Patricia," Beverly Allen wrote in a twenty-eight-page memoir. "This bothered me." To get the poet's attention, Beverly began inserting lines from his poetry, so fresh in her mind, into the conversation. The first one took Richard by surprise, "an amusing coincidence," but by the third or fourth his light blue eyes clouded with suspicion. "Do you know who I am?" he inquired.

Beverly replied, "Do you know who *I* am?" When Brautigan learned she was a professional model, he immediately offered her a job posing for the cover of his forthcoming book of poetry, *Rommel Drives on Deep into Egypt*.

Beverly thought the title "singularly unattractive," but agreed to participate. Brautigan explained to her that all the covers of his books featured photographs of women, "his wife, or later, his girlfriends, who were significant in his life at the time." With a new book of poetry due out soon, "he had no wife or girlfriend whose photo he could use." Neither of Richard's wives ever appeared on his book covers, but it was widely assumed that Mickey Blake-Grand was whom Brautigan referred to as "my woman" and "the woman who travels with me" in *Trout Fishing in America*.

Richard and Beverly set a date for the cover shoot in mid-January 1970, the day before she was scheduled to fly back to Italy. The week of New Year's Eve, Brautigan phoned her with an invitation to dinner at his place on Geary Street. He would show her some of the poems from the book. Feeling like a "glamorous model by day and lonely little furball by night," Beverly didn't hesitate. Richard cooked his famous spaghetti. Only one burner on his ancient stove actually worked.

Once, when Brautigan scrambled some eggs for Lawrence Hammond, the musician asked, "Richard, how long has it been like that?"

"Ever since I've been here," Brautigan replied. "I've become good at one-burner cooking."

It was a cold night. Richard's kitchen window fogged with steam from the boiling water when Beverly arrived bearing "a bottle of wine and a painted papier-mâché Mexican doll." Brautigan gave her a tour of the museum. "At first glance, the apartment seemed cluttered because there was so much stuff," she later wrote, "but then I noticed how incredibly orderly it all was. We sat in the kitchen and ate spaghetti and drank wine and told each other about our lives."

Once they started talking, any thought of the *Rommel* poems fell by the wayside. Beverly told Richard about her childhood in Oakland, where she was born to Swedish immigrant parents and attended public schools. She graduated from UC Berkeley with a degree in music, married an older professor, and moved to Greece. Richard in turn wove a tale of his impoverished youth in the Northwest.

"He could spin a yarn," she recalled.

Beverly enjoyed Richard's stories, but what really impressed her was how intently he listened to what she had to say. Years later, she wrote, "I can still feel how it felt to have Richard listen to me." Cheered by the wine, they laughed and played records. Brautigan stacked sides on the changer, "and every now and then said listen to this about a song that came on." One of his LPs was Bob Dylan's recent *Nashville Skyline* album. Her brief memoir provided a tantalizing hint about what might have happened next. "It never occurred to me to bother how many women Richard might have played that for, or how many times a young woman warm with wine and his radiant attention, having noted the big brass bed in his bedroom, would have simply followed the song's instructions."

When Beverly Allen left the Geary Street apartment for her family home in Oakland later that night, she gave Brautigan the painted Mexican doll (her "taliswoman") as a keepsake. A few days later, she dashed off a semipoetic handwritten note on Saks Fifth Avenue stationery, wishing Richard a happy new year. "If I could write poems I would write about a man I met the other night [. . .] And we, like the birds, can embrace the illusion of dream, the illusion of reality, the illusion of illusion." When asked what she remembered of meeting Richard, Beverly always replied, "His gentleness."

Two weeks later, on a grim cold wet day, after staying up late the night before packing for Italy, Beverly drove her mother's De Soto across the Bay Bridge and over to Geary Street. Richard and Edmund Shea waited for her at the Museum. Richard had asked Beverly to wear something that evoked "some kind of Nazi stereotype." She was dressed in tall black boots, a yellow miniskirt she'd picked up in Berkeley, a T-shirt, and a long black vinyl raincoat from Saks. The original plan had been to go out to the beach, but rain and mist foreclosed on that notion. They headed instead to the children's playground in the Panhandle of Golden Gate Park, "where Richard knew there was a sandbox."

Brautigan had discussed the imagery he wanted with Shea beforehand, and they brought along a five-and-ten-cent store kid's tin pail and shovel. With these props and Beverly decked out in her shiny black raincoat, they set to work. A sense of silliness and fun informed the entire shoot. Richard was the director, instructing Beverly to play the part of a "spy-woman." She obliged by acting "at being some kind of Veruschka," her hair loosely pulled back into a single braid. "It was fun. It was a tremendous amount of fun. It was absolutely playful." As the day progressed, it grew colder and colder. Years later, Beverly wrote, "I remember sitting on the damp sand in that sandbox, feeling cold, growing weary of being there."

Toward the end, it started raining in earnest, and they broke out a big umbrella. Edmund took his final shots of Beverly crouching beneath it, her damp hair unbound and flowing, and of Richard on the slide and holding the umbrella protectively above her. (Later that year, when *Confederate General* was published in England, Jonathan Cape Ltd. used the picture of the two of them under the umbrella on the front cover of the book.) They were all "freezing cold" at this point. Edmund snapped one last picture of the lithographed tin pail and a crumbling cone of molded sand, and they hurried out of the rain.

After a "giddy" stop at a donut shop for hot chocolate, they returned to Geary Street, where the general mood of hilarity and jovial bonhomie continued. At some point in their animated conversation, they ended up lying on the kitchen floor with their heads resting on each other's bellies. Their combined laughter reverberated through their bodies with manic circularity. At that moment, Edmund Shea fell in love with Beverly Allen.

Edmund left shortly after cupid's arrow pierced his heart. He kept his unrequited secret passion locked away in a private mental drawer for the next twenty years, while she went on to become a tenured full professor of Italian, French, and comparative literature at Syracuse University. After Edmund's departure, it was time for Beverly to leave. Her mother was preparing a farewell dinner, and she had to get back to Oakland. Richard walked her through the rain to where she had parked on Geary, but she'd left the headlights on and the battery was dead. A call to AAA delivered a jump start, and Beverly took off into the rush hour traffic. Her last glimpse of Richard was in the rearview as he stood on the sidewalk in the steady drizzle, waving goodbye. They never saw each other again.

Dell had enjoyed a tremendous success with four of Richard Brautigan's books, but a contractual dispute resulted in a change of publishers. In August 1970, *The Abortion* and *Revenge of the Lawn* moved to Simon & Schuster. As before, Brautigan retained the right of approval over book design, advertising copy, typography, layout, and dust jacket art. He began discussions with Edmund Shea about his plans for the cover of *The Abortion* before the switch to S&S. Erik and Loie Weber returned from India that April. Richard saw them in New York City in May, where Erik photographed him visiting his new agent's office. Richard said nothing about Erik doing the covers for the forthcoming books. Erik's *Trout Fishing* photo was becoming world famous, yet Richard decided to stick with Edmund Shea's work. Richard later told Edmund he was the best photographer of women.

Richard knew exactly what he wanted for the cover of *The Abortion*. He talked everything over with Edmund. "He'd tell me what he had in mind generally," Shea said. "I never read any of the books before I did the pictures." A good part of the novel was set in a library, so Richard decided to make the Presidio Branch of the San Francisco Public Library the background for his photo shoot. Brautigan used the real address, 3150 Sacramento Street, for his fictional library in the book. "The library was between his house and my house," Shea observed, "so we obviously walked by there on occasion."

With the location selected, Richard found the perfect woman. Victoria, a local folk/pop singer, used only her first name professionally, not altogether unwise as her last name was Domagalski. Petite, with high cheekbones and straight black hair hanging to the middle of her back, Victoria was a lovely woman who closely resembled Richard's description of Vida, the heroine of *The Abortion*. She lived with her manager in a huge Victorian apartment. In Brautigan's estimation she was "a fantastic cook." He'd had dinner at her place "three or four times." Once, Victoria served him lamb; another time it was paella; later she made "something Italian."

On the night of the "incredible Italian meal," Richard brought Sherry Vetter, a twenty-one-year-old Catholic girls' school teacher he had recently started dating. Sherry remembered Victoria as "a beautiful girl, beautiful body, beautiful face, long shiny hair, meticulous housekeeper." Victoria served "ravioli and all this stuff" that Richard loved. Throughout the meal, he kept praising her cooking. Finally, Victoria had enough. She smashed her plate down on the table. "Richard, I can't take these compliments," she said. "All I did was stop at the Italian deli on the way home."

After dinner, they repaired to the living room, which was furnished with nothing but cushions on the floor and a grand piano. Victoria had set Richard's poem "1942," about the death of his uncle Edward, to music, and she sang it like a song that night while her guests lounged around the piano on cushions. Sherry thought Victoria's "voice was as beautiful as Joan Baez, Joni Mitchell, Judy Collins." She believed Victoria could have been a big star, but her manager "really screwed her totally." Richard politely complimented the song, but Sherry could tell he didn't like it. Victoria wanted to publish the music "and make it something, but he was against that."

Whether Richard and Victoria were ever lovers remains open to conjecture. Sherry Vetter believed that "she was never a girlfriend." Victoria had an album (the eponymous *Victoria*) about to be released, with distribution by Atlantic, at the same time as the publication date for *The Abortion*. She agreed to appear on Brautigan's book cover if he wrote the liner notes for her stereo LP. On the fold-out record jacket, Victoria posed as an odalisque, sprawled across piles of oriental cushions in flowing harem pajamas like a concubine in a sultan's seraglio. She composed all of the songs on her album and recruited Herbie Hancock to handle the keyboard chores in the backup trio. In his brief essay, Richard discussed Victoria's evident skills in the kitchen and, after listening to the album tapes, concluded: "I think Victoria sings as well as she cooks."

For *The Abortion* cover shoot, Victoria wore high snug black boots and a minilength trench coat. She had the exotic look of a mod foreign agent. "He thought she was beautiful," Edmund Shea recalled. Victoria posed on the library's portico, perched on the iron railing, staring up at Brautigan with large skeptical eyes, her full lips set in the beginnings of a frown. Wearing jeans, a plaid shirt, and a thrift shop suit jacket, Richard leaned against a smooth stone column on her right, staring straight into the lens without his glasses, his gaze as penetrating as a raptor's. Edmund took several pictures of Brautigan inside the library next to a bookshelf. In these shots, Richard wore his wire-rimmed spectacles and exchanged the single-breasted jacket for a castoff pin-striped vest.

Michael McClure expressed disdain for the cover photograph on *The Abortion*. Edmund Shea remembered he made "some comment about Richard standing consciously very sexy in this picture." McClure thought Brautigan deliberately posed with the cockiness of a rock star. In truth, Richard didn't choose the picture that became the book's cover. Edmund described the selection process. "We would take a lot of pictures and then Richard would pick the ones he wanted [from a contact sheet] to have them blown up in print and then winnow it down."

Brautigan respected Shea's judgment and usually went along with his final selection. For *The Abortion*, Richard preferred another photograph to Edmund's pick. "The way I got him to pick the one I wanted was to put them both up on the wall, side by side, and I made him stand on the other side of the room and asked him which one he saw." The obvious choice became the cover of *The Abortion*. The sexual vanity McClure ascribed to Brautigan was, in fact, Edmund Shea's astute editorial decision. Richard rewarded Edmund, using his sales clout with Simon & Schuster to dramatically increase the photographer's fee. Edmund had trouble collecting, but in the end S&S paid Shea "real money." He received $1,500 for his work on *The Abortion*, "which I don't think they would pay me today."

Simon & Schuster picked up the deal Dell refused. It was a two-book package, the second to be a collection of Brautigan's short stories. By the time the contracts were signed, Richard had already decided that Sherry Vetter's picture would grace the cover of *Revenge of the Lawn*. Sherry, whose actual first name was Elizabeth, hailed from Louisville, Kentucky. Following her graduation from the University of Dayton in Ohio, she spent eight months in the Peace Corps in Ivory Coast. After getting sick and returning to the States in 1970, she got a job teaching fifth grade at Notre Dame, a private Dominican girls' school in San Francisco. "I was just a straight girl," Sherry said. "That's what drew [Richard] to me. I was probably his first straight girlfriend."

Sherry remembered a dinner party at the home of Richard and Nancy Hodge not long after Richard asked her to pose for the cover. The conversation centered on *The Abortion*, recently published, "and someone was bugging Richard about Victoria's beauty, and said to him, 'You know that people are going to buy this book because there's a pretty girl on the cover and not for what's in it.'"

Brautigan disagreed with this point of view. He was "pretty much pissed off" and thought it was a stupid idea. "I'm not worried about putting pretty girls on the covers of my books," Brautigan said, nodding toward Sherry. "In fact, this pretty girl sitting right here is going to be on the cover of my next book."

Feeling ornery, Sherry quipped, "No. I've changed my mind. I don't want to be *on* the book, I want to be *in* the book."

Richard smiled at her. "I could never write about you," he said. "You are real life."

Sherry Vetter met Richard Brautigan for the first time early in 1970 at an Irish pub in North Beach. She was there with her friend and roommate, the artist Yuri Nishiyama, and a fellow named Don, who acted as their escort. It was a cold January Frisco night, and Sherry wore a baggy sweater, jeans, and tennis shoes. She had on no makeup, and her auburn hair hung loose about her shoulders. Richard got into a conversation with Yuri, who was familiar with his work. Sherry kept thinking, "I know I've seen this guy's face before." In fact, she'd gone to a poetry reading a few months earlier, but came in late while Brautigan was at the podium and didn't catch his name.

Richard was attracted by Sherry's face. There was a "wholesomeness" about her. Brautigan thought she looked like an "American teenage girl next door kid sister." When he asked Sherry for her phone number, she wrote it down on a piece of paper, which she folded into an airplane and sailed out into the middle of the dance floor. Richard later recalled, "It landed at the feet of some people who were dancing to a drummer so different that he could have been pounding away in another galaxy."

"See you later," Sherry said, taking off with Yuri, "her smile breaking into a sixteen year old giggle." Brautigan hurried out onto the dance floor to retrieve the paper airplane from under the feet of the stoned dancing couple. The gyrating space travelers regarded him curiously. "But what the fuck difference did it make," Richard thought, once he had his treasure in hand. "You make a cute couple," he told the pair and walked away, clutching the airmail phone number.

A two-week courtship by phone began. The first time Richard called, he got Sherry's roommate. He didn't leave a message and tried again two days later. This time, Vetter was on the line. "I guess you took some flying lessons in the last couple of days," she said.

"I've had a lot of them," Richard replied. Sherry "wasn't into hippie guys," and kept some distance between them. Brautigan called night after night. He read his poems over the phone to her. This produced the desired result. She accepted Richard's invitation to dinner.

Sherry arrived at his place right on time, seven o'clock sharp. Brautigan regarded her with amazement. She no longer looked like the kid sister girl next door. She wore lipstick and enough mascara to emphasize her large green eyes. Her auburn hair was bound up on top of her head. In her ankle-length black velvet skirt and matching high-collared velvet jacket over a white lace blouse, she looked elegant and modishly old-fashioned. "I don't remember you being so short," Richard said, trying for nonchalance.

"Bastard," she said with mock seriousness, pushing past him and heading down the long hallway leading into the hundred-year-old Victorian apartment. After glancing at the front room, Sherry stepped into the kitchen. "I thought you were rich and famous. Why do you live in a dump like this?"

"My money is currently tied up in wheat futures," Richard said, matching her mocking tone. "While we're currently on the subject of grains, would you like a drink?"

"A glass of white wine. We'll toast your wheat futures, so you can get out of this goddamn rat hole." She sat down in a green wicker rocking chair. "Really, you should think about better ways of investing your money. I have a feeling that your wheat futures aren't that promising."

When Richard gave Sherry a glass of white wine he wondered why she didn't take off her jacket. He wanted to know what her body looked like. Fifteen minutes later, after another glass of wine, Sherry still had not unbuttoned her coat. "Aren't you warm with your jacket on?" Richard asked. "The dinner reservations I made aren't until an hour, and it only takes a few minutes to get there. Why don't you make yourself comfortable? Don't worry, I'm not going to get you drunk and try to seduce you."

"I don't trust you," Sherry said with a smile. "Are you sure you made reservations for dinner? I think you're trying to use the wine to take advantage of a little person's limited alcohol capacity."

"You found me out," Brautigan confessed.

"It wasn't hard to do. You may write books but you can be read like one, too."

"The lady's too smart for burning."

Sherry smiled and started unbuttoning her velvet jacket. "The wine does make me hot," she said. "Maybe your plan is working. A man who has all his money in wheat futures has to get lucky sometime." She finished unbuttoning her coat but didn't open it.

This drove Richard crazy with anticipation. "What in hell did her body look like!" he thought.

"I'm certainly hot," Sherry continued, holding out her empty glass. "Can I have a little more wine? Maybe it will cool me off."

Richard filled her glass from the jug in the fridge, facing away from Sherry.

When he turned back toward her, wineglass in hand, she had removed her black velvet jacket and sat with her arms resting on the arms of the rocker, grinning like Sylvester after swallowing Tweety Bird.

Richard stopped dead in his tracks. Sherry wore a sheer antique lace blouse. She wore no bra beneath it. "I saw her sitting there with her breasts totally exposed under the delicate transparent blouse from another century," Brautigan wrote many years later. Vetter had the face of a teenage girl, and "an incredibly erotic body with very large breasts." Richard felt momentarily at a loss for words.

"The wine, please," she said, still smiling.

Richard thought it looked like the smile of someone having a great deal of fun and trying hard to conceal it. "If I can still move, I'll try to bring you the wine," he said at last.

"I certainly hope that you can move," Sherry replied, her mischievous smile a promise of further surprises still to come. This began a relationship that was to last, on and off, for almost a decade.

"I was supposed to do the photograph for [*Revenge of the Lawn*]," Erik Weber said, "but Richard was pissed at me." He and Brautigan got together in New York that May and Weber took a number of pictures. Richard was mad about a photograph taken of him leaning against a wall in Helen Brann's office. The picture ran in *Mademoiselle* when the magazine published three of Brautigan's short stories in July. "Richard thought it was the worst photograph ever taken of him," Weber said, "so he decided to use Edmund Shea, rather than me."

The photo session for *Revenge of the Lawn* took place in the kitchen of Sherry Vetter's Noe Valley apartment. She lived in a big Victorian building "with Yuri and several others—one girl from Sweden—it was great. We had fun." Brautigan had the idea to include a chocolate cake in the picture, a visual reference to a line in the title story. "He believed that he was six years old and it was a cloudy day about to rain and his mother was baking a chocolate cake."

Two cakes were used for the cover shoot. Sherry baked the first herself at Richard's request. She remembered Edmund Shea took pictures for about two hours. "Periodically Richard would say, 'Okay, now change clothes.'" Sherry went through six outfits, searching for just the right look. One choice, "a white nylon thing that was like a halter top," was particularly revealing. Edmund suggested she lean over and gouge big pieces out of the cake. She tore into it, eating chunks by the handful, at once innocent and carnal, "a sexual thing," Sherry said. "And Richard thought that was great."

Sherry's cake was totally destroyed. Richard went out and bought another from a local bakery. Sherry changed her outfit a final time, choosing her Swiss grandmother's handmade lace blouse she wore on her first date with Brautigan. Grinning broadly, Sherry perched on the seat edge of her press-back oak rocking chair with the store-bought chocolate cake on the white linen-covered table in front of her, and Edmund Shea took the cover photograph for *Revenge of the Lawn*. After the story collection was published, the Noe Valley pastry chef baked "a facsimile cake" and placed it in the professional shop's front bay window surrounded by a half dozen copies of Brautigan's book.

The baker's modest window display provided a memorial to Richard Brautigan's singular vision of book design. *Revenge of the Lawn* was the last of his works to feature photographic covers with attractive young women. Three years later, Simon & Schuster published his new novel, *The Hawkline Monster*, and a decision was made to distance the book from Richard's earlier "hippie" publications. *Hawkline* had a traditional mainstream look with commercial dust jacket art.

In 1976, *Sombrero Fallout* followed with an elegant dust jacket painting by John Ansado of a lovely Asian woman holding a black cat. A simultaneous publication in Japan by Shobun-sha featured a color photograph of Japanese American actress Mie Hunt, who had appeared in the raunchy 1971 British film *Sex Clinic*. The photo created an entirely different mood from the American dust jacket painting. Hunt, hair bobbed and coiffed like silent movie star Louise Brooks, sat on a stool, one hand between her legs, lips painted Chinese-lacquer red, black dress slit to reveal her naked inner thigh. A wanton, depraved look glazed her heavily mascara-rimmed eyes. It could well be a poster for one of the soft-core porn movies Brautigan came to love in Japan.

When Jonathan Cape brought out the English edition the following year, Richard had a final chance to dabble in art direction. He didn't ask his girlfriend to pose for him, hiring a professional model instead. The Brebner Agency charged him $225 for the services of Mia Hara, a charming Japanese model. Erik Weber took the photographs in Richard's Union Street apartment. It was all strictly business. Brautigan maintained final approval, but left the designing to the professionals.

In 1980, when *The Tokyo–Montana Express* was published, a photograph of Richard and his friend Takako Shiina floating in a small green boat off the coast of Japan near the town of Ajiro appeared on the back of the dust jacket. Ten years earlier it would have graced the front cover of the book. Instead, the dust jacket featured only the title in large slanted red letters above a photograph of a medallion depicting Japan's last coal-burning steam engine. Richard had seen the bronze disc in the transportation museum in Tokyo. The same train image was used in the book to divide the chapters.

Brautigan promoted the photo to the front wrapper of the Delta trade paperback edition. "Cover concept" was credited to the author. Shiina, Richard's soul-sister, owned The Cradle bar, his favorite hangout in Tokyo. She sits apart from him, leaning against the gunwale, resting her head on her shoulder. A feeling of utter resignation pervades the image. Wearing a black cowboy hat and shirt, Richard slouches in the bow, his hands forming an inverted steeple between his knees. He stares wistfully off into the distance as if searching for something precious he's lost forever.

thirty-six: satori

RICHARD BRAUTIGAN TOLD his friend Jack Thibeau this story. It began one night in North Beach around 1970, when fame first exposed Brautigan to the blinding limelight of national attention. Richard picked up not only the tab, but a comely young admirer as well. She was just his type: willowy, blond, a hippie chick with few acknowledged inhibitions. Richard brought her back to his apartment on Geary, where the contrast between the low-rent surroundings and his newfound celebrity only intensified her ardor. Within the confines of his recently purchased brass bed, she gave him the sort of blow job he had once described in a poem as "a circle of castles" around his penis.

When he climaxed, the young blond spat his ejaculate into the palm of her hand, prodding the viscid substance gently with a fingertip as if examining some precious treasure, bright pearls from the crown jewels of an emperor. Looking up with stars dancing in her eyes, she murmured in wonder: "Richard Brautigan's sperm . . ."

thirty-seven: fame's feathery crowbar

"**R**ICHARD'S GETTING LAID by a bevy of 18-year olds," Keith Abbott wrote to a friend after a visit to San Francisco. Abbott regarded this as "only a convenient shorthand symbol" for Brautigan's newfound fame. He was equally impressed by expensive dinner tabs, endless cab rides, and complimentary tickets waiting at the Fillmore. Like a rock star, Richard "strolled around and collected accolades from the kids. Brautigan hitchhiked until the end of his life whenever necessity dictated but rarely rode a bus again once the money started rolling in. Richard's itemized expenses for 1969 were more than double his total income for the previous year. By 1971, the cab receipts in his income tax folder were bundled together with rubber bands in wads thicker than packs of playing cards.

Among the few luxuries Brautigan bought were a television set and the antique brass whorehouse bed he had long coveted, most useful for a man beset by groupies. Not all were one-night stands. Doralyn Foodym, a fellow Aquarian and student of anthropology at Berkeley, recalled "a time when we were very fond of each other." Once, in an "absurd" moment, her Mustang was towed away after Brautigan "moved it," one of several hints that he really knew how to drive when he wanted to. Doralyn remembered sitting on the brass bed at Geary Street with Richard, talking about Edmund Shea, when he told her that there were lots of things she'd be better able to understand as she grew older. At the time, she "resented the comment like hell," but five or six years later, she wrote to Brautigan from Copenhagen, where she was about to receive a PhD from the Institute of Social Medicine, to say he had been right. Now she knew how odd it felt "to be with those who are naive but don't know it yet."

As the summer of 1969 wound to a close, the book design for the Delacorte omnibus edition was completed to Brautigan's satisfaction. Sam Lawrence wrote, calling it "beautiful [. . .] I'm grateful to you and Roz Barrow for making it possible." An ad was prepared for the *New York Times Book Review*, the *Village Voice*, and the *Sunday Examiner & Chronicle* in San Francisco. It featured a triple photo of Richard's face above the heading, "The great three-headed Brautigan is now at your bookstore." Franklin Spier, Inc., the advertising agency responsible, thought it "wacky, to be sure," but a "stopper visually," something with appeal for the Brautigan audience. The opening line of their copy read, "From out of the West comes the thundering typewriter of the great Richard Brautigan just in time to save avant-garde writing from the bad guys." The text went on to quote the well-worn John Ciardi quote from the back cover of *Trout Fishing*, adding "Mmmm, that right, Kimo Ciardi."

Brautigan hated this ad, and it did not run. Instead, Delacorte followed his detailed instructions to the letter. Richard's own design for a new advertisement had no cute Lone Ranger references, only a photograph of the book's cover. He simplified the text and included quotes from *Time* and the *Examiner & Chronicle*, eliminating the Ciardi blurb entirely.

Again, Richard's instincts were more on the money than the crass selling notions of the Big Apple publishing wizards. Sam Lawrence recognized a winner and wrote Brautigan, "I like the way you've changed the ads." Orders began "literally pouring in" at the beginning of September. The "extraordinary" demand for the three Delta paperbacks (scheduled for publication in November) was so great a planned first printing of twenty thousand copies for each title had to be increased to fifty thousand each before the end of September. The Delacorte hardback had its publication date moved ahead to October 31, but the first edition still bore the date September 1969. A second printing had to be ordered by November 5.

One afternoon during the third week in September, Richard and Valerie showed up at the Minimum Daily Requirement with Abbie and Anita Hoffman, who were in town trying to raise money for Abbie's fast-approaching conspiracy trial in Chicago. Paul Krassner was on his way up from Los Angeles with some film they had made of the riots during the Democratic National Convention the previous summer. Brautigan had an idea that the MDR might be a good place to show it and dispatched an employee over to Kendrick Rand's Vallejo Street apartment to say Hoffman wanted a word with him. By the time Kendrick arrived at his restaurant, "Richard had a fair amount to drink." He and Valerie got into a fight, ending when she poured a pitcher of beer over his head. "They soon left in a huff," Rand remembered. "I stayed up until about three in the morning with Abbie." Kendrick agreed to let Hoffman show his film at the MDR the following Sunday.

Rand had some trouble rounding up a projector but "finally got one from someone who was connected with the Committee [Theater]." With only word of mouth for advertising, "the place was mobbed." They showed the film against the back wall and people who couldn't get in stood out on the sidewalk staring through the big picture window. Richard and Valerie, at peace once again, sat with Kendrick and his wife, Annie. "It was a wonderful night," Rand remembered.

By early October, Brautigan had received invitations to read at more than ten colleges. John Barth wrote asking him to come to the State University of New York at Buffalo. Richard had been suggested to Barth, who managed the reading program, by Robert Creeley, recently arrived in Buffalo as part of the English faculty.

The second week of October, Brautigan participated in a writers' conference at the College of Marin in Kentfield, California. Among the other authors were Kay Boyle (who gave the keynote address), Jessamyn West, William Stafford, Caroline Kizer, and Josephine Miles. After conducting a morning seminar, "On Writing," Richard read his work at eight o'clock Saturday evening on a program with Stafford and Miles. For three days, he was paid $180, plus $10 for expenses.

Two welcome royalty checks arrived early in October. (The first, from the Four Seasons Foundation, totaled $3,000; a second, for $695.53, came from Grove Press. After *Rolling Stone* bought two more short stories for $30 each, Helen Brann wrote Jann Wenner demanding a "new payment schedule." Wenner balked, writing Brann he "would be sorry to discontinue this feature, but we cannot afford to pay the kind of money you are demanding." He offered "$50 per short story, irrespective of length." Richard accepted. The publicity value of appearing in *Rolling Stone* was worth it.

Before the end of the year, Brautigan sold the periodical two more stories at their new rate. The smallest amount Richard earned in 1969 came from *Poetry* magazine, which sent him a check for

$3 when his poem "Wood" appeared in the October issue. Somewhat belatedly, Heliotrope (a San Francisco outfit self-described as "a learning environment open to anyone," with courses including Swedish massage and a celebration of dusk), mailed an honorarium of $20 in October for printing Brautigan's poem "Critical Can Opener" in their summer catalog.

Jack Kerouac died in St. Petersburg, Florida, on October 21, 1969, of massive gastrointestinal hemorrhage brought on by cirrhosis of the liver. A lifetime of heavy drinking caught up with him at last. The King of the Beats was dead. Around the same time, Brautigan, the heir apparent, called Rip Torn in New York. Brautigan had cooked up a fishing trip to Deer Creek in Big Sur with Price Dunn, and they wanted Torn to join them. Rip remembered his words "tumbling over each other and the funny chortling noises he made."

The actor left the matter up in the air. "If I can get a real cheap flight," he said. Torn's wife, the actress Geraldine Page, was heading for Hollywood soon to star opposite Clint Eastwood in Don Siegel's psychosexual Civil War drama, *The Beguiled*. She decided to fly out early with Rip and the kids and be part of the adventure. Rip brought along a two-person kayak. The Torns landed at SFO and rented a station wagon, loading the luggage and strapping the kayak to the roof before driving into San Francisco to pick up Brautigan. Richard stashed Willard, his papier-mâché bird, in back along with his gear. After stocking up on road refreshments, they headed south to Monterey.

The Torns and their two-year-old daughter and twin diapered sons stayed with Price's brother, Bruce, and his wife. The Dunns seated them on cushions at a round table, serving linguini with pesto. Keith and Lani Abbott joined the party. Keith found Rip Torn "high strung and nervous," a chain-smoker of hand-rolled cigarettes. Richard told Rip that Price "knew every inch of Big Sur." Abbott declined to join their fishing adventure. "Price hadn't been in the Santa Lucia Mountains for years," he observed.

Gerry put off the trip to L.A., staying at the Dunns with her sons and young daughter. Rip roared down the Pacific Coast Highway with the wild boys in search of the mythic Deer Creek. Richard claimed the stream had "a lot of trout, maybe some steelhead." Around noon, they turned off onto a narrow dirt road. The ride in was rough. They reached an abandoned farm on a turn overlooking what Torn described as "a deep gorge carved by the tiny glint of water far below." The fishermen had found Deer Creek.

Armed with beer and fishing rods, they scrambled down past abandoned farm machinery into a canyon choked with poison oak. Forty minutes later, the quartet reached bottom and discovered "the creek was nearly dry." Sinkers and rusting hooks decorated the surrounding bushes; trees were draped in tangled monofilament. "Looks like an army of hippies has bivouacked here," Brautigan quipped. After a halfhearted attempt at fishing—Richard caught a water snake—they decided to head for home. It took three hours to struggle out of the gorge.

Along the way, "Richard started to chortle," improvising a humorous riff on their predicament. "Rip, do you think Hollywood would be interested in a series called 'The Blunder Brothers'? We've got a fine cast here. We could profit from our blunders, and looking at this crew, I doubt we'd run out of script [. . .] What do you think? Hell, this bunch could never run out of blunders." Laughing harder, Brautigan announced two cold beers waited in the truck. "First up on top gets 'em." Price and Richard "poured on the coal," leaving Rip and Bruce far behind.

When the stragglers finally made it out of the canyon, Brautigan tapped his pocket watch. "We've been here [. . .] thirty-five minutes," he said. "Time to have a game of cribbage." He tossed

Rip a can of beer. "Here—we saved you laggards a brew to share." Back at the Dunn's place in Monterey, Richard related his adventures with the Blunder Brothers. Weaving Willard into the fantasy, he concocted a fable about "capturing the dreaded water snakes of Big Sur." It was all in fun, but Keith Abbott felt "under the fantasy was a sour feeling, as if Price and Bruce hadn't come up to the mark."

Richard Brautigan arrived in Boston just before Halloween, when Delacorte published his big three-in-one book. Sam Lawrence owned a fashionable brownstone townhouse on Beacon Hill, "very unlike the hippie atmosphere," and when Brautigan came to visit, Lawrence remembered him dropping to his knees and staring at the floor.

"What are you doing down there?" Sam demanded.

"This is real pine," Richard muttered in awe. "Real pine."

To Sam Lawrence such domestic refinements were no big deal. His house had the original pine floors with "an orangy, lemon patina." Richard reminded Sam that neither Edmund Shea nor Erik Weber had been paid for their photographs on the Delacorte and Delta editions of his books. Lawrence promised to take care of the matter. Weber was still in India, so Sam would have Roz Barrow send the check to the Chelsea Hotel in New York, where Richard was headed in the morning.

When Richard returned to visit Ron Loewinsohn in Cambridge, he came across a green and white pinback button advertising an alternative educational institution at the Grolier Book Shop, the oldest and best-known literary bookstore at Harvard. Sam Lawrence introduced Brautigan to the owner, Gordon Cairnie, an early supporter of his work. "He always had Richard's books," Lawrence said. "Even the early ones." The pins were on sale to benefit eight little storefront establishments located all around the Cambridge area, collectively called the Trout Fishing in America School. Founded by Peter Miller, a Williams College graduate (a second-year student at the Harvard Graduate School of Education), with five other like-minded academics, the experimental school provided a learning environment where kids who didn't particularly like formal academics could earn a high school diploma. The curriculum ran from English, math, and science to criminology, theories of revolution, and motorcycle repair. Tuition was $10 a month.

Brautigan got hold of Miller's phone number and called him up. "I heard you named a school after my book," he said. Peter Miller "was shocked to hear from the guy."

"I want some pins," Richard told him. "Saw some pins." Miller said the school sold the pins to earn extra money. Brautigan asked to come over and buy a few, and soon after, he showed up with Ron Loewinsohn. Richard told Peter about his upcoming reading at Harvard. Brautigan became a benefactor of the school named for his novel. "He was great," Miller recalled. "When his book came out, he would send us a box of books, which we would sell. We didn't have any money." From time to time, Richard visited one of the eight Trout Fishing schools. "He would come," Peter Miller said, "he'd sit there all afternoon. He could find somebody who was real shy who he'd end up talking to. It was very sweet."

In and out of Cambridge for book signings and other business prior to his reading, Brautigan stayed with Peter Miller and his girlfriend, Kat, in their apartment on Broadway near Harvard Yard. Richard's presence caused immediate tension on the domestic front. "He was murder on anyone's girlfriend," Peter remembered. "It only took him a moment to get jealous. He wanted real attention."

A big parade for Trout Fishing in America, Inc., on the first day of November provided a happy moment. Around fifty students, teachers, and parents marched along Massachusetts Avenue through Central and Harvard Squares to Cambridge Common, where they gathered for a rock concert by three local groups: Peace, Catfish Black, and Cloud. They carried signs; banners; red, yellow, and blue balloons; and large staff-mounted papier-mâché fish. The parade included a pair of balloon-decorated motorcyclists, two guys running for the city council, and a cheetah named Natasha riding in the backseat of a battered station wagon. Recalling Brautigan's happy participation, Peter Miller said, "He got in it, walking down the street. It was great. It was the sweetest side of the sixties."

Richard went with Peter Miller on a return trip to Walden Pond, along with John Stickney, a visiting *Life* magazine reporter, who had volunteered to teach a journalism course at Trout Fishing in America. Brautigan knew what to expect from his previous sojourn with Valerie and expressed dismay at all the litter strewn around. "Where the hell are all the trash bins?" he fumed. "What would Henry David Thoreau think if he could see this place now?" Pointing at a discarded beer bottle lying submerged on the bottom, Richard calmed his indignation with wit. "Look there! Right below the surface. A glass-backed trout is sleeping."

By the time of Richard's reading at Harvard, he "almost had a room" in Peter Miller's apartment, having stayed there "four or five times." Brautigan told Miller of his plans to write a history of the Confederate side in the Civil War. "We didn't have a dime," Peter said. "So he would say, 'Come on, let's spend this money,' and we go to the public market and buy five bags of groceries and fill up all the cupboards."

Richard Brautigan was "honored" to be reading at Harvard, as Peter Miller recalled. "I'm going to read at Harvard," Richard announced to the students at the Trout Fishing in America School, "but I want you all to come. The whole school." When Brautigan mounted the podium in the "neoclassical lecture hall," they were all there. "Twenty-five or thirty of 'em," Peter Miller said. "Little ones, short ones, tall ones, fat ones, all went and got onstage. Very ragtag."

The Harvard students in the audience looked equally ragtag. John Stickney described them as "the hirsute, sueded, fadded, and fringed crowd of neo-surrealistic young people." At one point during the reading, a cat wandered onto the stage, stared curiously at the poet, and sat at his feet. Richard swigged chablis from a gallon jug and read his poetry for about half an hour before jumping down, amid shouts for more, inviting the crowd to take his place onstage.

Brautigan urged his fans to come up and read their favorite work, either his poetry or anyone else's. Numbers of students took up the challenge, reading all manner of poems and even a political manifesto. Upon hearing an absurd newspaper article, Richard clapped his hands in delight. Someone began playing a blues harmonica into the microphone, and couples started dancing in the aisles. "I love chaos," Brautigan declared.

At one point, Richard suggested to the students that they read "Love Poem" over and over as it was done on his recording. Several of them accepted his invitation, experimenting with different voices and inflections. Sarah Ulerick, a Radcliffe freshman, read the poem with a Southern drawl. She charmed Richard, and later they walked together across Harvard Yard toward the reception, talking in fake German accents. Brautigan knew he'd score tonight. "I'd like to get to know you better," he said.

"What would you like to know?"

"Do you use contraceptives?"

When she said "No," he lost interest and drifted on to other possibilities. His paycheck for the evening came to $400.

Another attempted pickup during his time in Cambridge didn't end quite so politely. Brautigan was drunk, out on the town with Peter Miller, and asked a young woman to come home with him. When she refused, Richard "got real pissed" and kicked a dent in the front door of her car. According to Miller, Brautigan "threw some money on the ground and walked away from it. It was not his greatest moment."

Richard took great pleasure in being hailed as a poetry hero on the Harvard campus. His happy mood dampened when friends in the know pointed out a discrepancy between the just-published Delta edition of *Trout Fishing in America* and the original Four Seasons Foundation printing. Brautigan had decreed that both editions be identical. The Four Seasons' press plates had been purchased to facilitate this plan, but the new edition was ever-so-slightly different. Pages 42 and 77 of the original edition had included the facsimile signature of Trout Fishing in America, written in Richard's distinctive crabbed hand. On the same pages of the new Delta printing, the two signatures were conspicuously absent. The book had already gone into a second printing, and fifty thousand copies had been shipped to bookstores across the country.

An "extremely unhappy" Brautigan telephoned Helen Brann to complain about the situation. She wasted no time expressing her displeasure to Sam Lawrence. Richard insisted that "the dropping of this signature changes the entire meaning of both these chapters, not only in structure, but continuity of feeling." He considered it a breach of his contract.

Two days later, Richard contacted Helen with a suggestion for how Delta might rectify their error. He wanted the publisher to run ads "as simple as possible, pointing out the omission" and instructing readers to go to a bookstore and get stickers bearing Brautigan's "Trout Fishing in America" signature, which could then be pasted into the appropriate spots in the novel. Richard knew this would be expensive. As it was the printers' fault, they should bear all the costs of such an enterprise.

Soon after, Peter Miller, his girlfriend, Kat, and John Stickney saw Brautigan off to Buffalo. Stickney talked about writing an article on Brautigan for *Life,* and Richard instructed him to give Helen Brann a call. Peter and the Trout Fishing school gang headed up to Vermont for Thanksgiving. Richard spent the holiday at the home of Bob and Bobbie Creeley in Eden, New York, a small town about fifteen miles south of Buffalo. He discussed the problem of the missing Trout Fishing signatures with the Creeleys, who convinced him the bookstore sticker notion would never fly due to the prohibitive costs involved. Bobbie came up with a simpler solution.

She proposed a long thin newspaper ad running the full length of the page, a column of Richard's repeated Trout Fishing in America signatures. The short text, written by Bobbie, warned those who bought the novel of the defect on pages 42 and 77. "Please cut out and paste where necessary. The extras are for your friends. P.S. Congratulations! You have one of 50,000 collector's items." Brautigan suggested Bobbie Creeley be sent "a size 12 navy blue maxi coat" as payment for her freelance copy writing,

Bobbie never got her coat. In the end, the problem was solved by Dell designer Rosalie Barrow. The resourceful Roz came up with a number of rubber stamps reproducing Richard's Trout Fishing in America signature. She mailed these to all Dell warehouses across the country, instructing the recipients to stamp the missing signatures on the appropriate pages. "The line should be stamped in black ink and kept clean." This fix involved only Delta copies not yet shipped, creating two future categories of collectible books, those with the stamped signature and copies that had none.

"Warmly received," Brautigan appeared before a "packed hall" at SUNY Buffalo. John Barth wrote, "The campus prided itself, in those years of antiwar sit-ins and teargassing riot police, on being 'the Berkeley of the East.'" Richard brought along Edmund Shea's punctuation slides and had a reel-to-reel tape recorder set up beside the lectern. After being introduced by Barth, Brautigan greeted his audience, "pushed the Play button [. . .] and disappeared into the auditorium's projection booth." While everyone listened to the tapes recorded for Richard's Zapple album, "the invisible author projected slides of giant punctuation marks: five or ten minutes each of a comma, a semicolon, a period," which John Barth thought were "entirely without bearing on the taped recitation." This went on "for a very long three-quarters of an hour."

Robert Creeley, also in the auditorium, felt it "was very charming." Barth held the opinion that "had it been anybody but Brautigan, that audience would never have sat still for it." Even Creeley believed the students really "wanted him to read." Barth found the whole affair "eye-glazing." When the tape came to an end, a "beaming" Brautigan reappeared and "gestured grandly toward the tape machine."

"There you have it, folks," Richard announced, "the twentieth century."

Hearing this, one of John Barth's "seriously avant-garde graduate students" leaned toward him and quipped, "Yup, about 1913." For this performance, Brautigan was again paid $400.

In San Francisco, Richard got back together again with Valerie on the first of December. September had been a rough time for both of them. They had been mostly apart for the past couple months. He told Valerie he'd cried himself to sleep every night in September, dreaming of her continuously, kissing and loving her in his troubled slumber. Hoping to resume their relationship, Brautigan took her shopping at I. Magnin's, an upscale department store, and bought her "a wonderful [Burberry-style] full-length tan overcoat."

They went to see *Butch Cassidy and the Sundance Kid*, which immediately became Brautigan's favorite film. Flattered by all this attention, Valerie "responded totally." She had been feeling "so horny, hurt, alone," and after a "long drunken evening at Enrico's" they staggered up the hill to her apartment for passionate lovemaking. The next day, one of her neighbors asked Valerie if she'd heard someone "freaking out" in the middle of the night. Estes didn't know how to reply.

Early December brought an announcement from New York of a "free" Bay Area concert by the Rolling Stones, at the conclusion of their eighteen-venue *Let It Bleed* U.S.A. tour, a "thank-you gift" for their American fans. The Stones began touring two months after Woodstock. They played twin evening shows in Oakland in November, charging ticket prices double those of other leading bands, such as the Doors. Acting through the Grateful Dead, the Stones management contacted the Diggers. The Peters, Berg and Coyote, suggested a multiple-stage event in Golden Gate Park, to "ensure a collaborative frame of reference and minimize divisions between the community and its entertainers." This collective approach didn't sit well with the Stones. Their manager, using Emmett Grogan as a go-between, got in touch with the Hells Angels, saying the Rolling Stones "wanted to do something for the people." In exchange for a hundred cases of beer, the Angels agreed to act as "security" at the proposed concert.

After the city denied the band use of Golden Gate Park, the location for the event, scheduled for Saturday, December 6, changed twice more in a three-day period. Finally, on Friday, twenty-four hours before the start of the concert, the Stones announced the event would take place at the Altamont Speedway, in the bare rolling hills near Livermore in Alameda County on the east side of the Bay. Hells Angel Bill Fritsch called the place "a goddamn, fucking, bereft pasture. In the middle of nothin'." Numbers of wrecked stock cars lay scattered around the old track. Sweet Willie Tumbleweed described the barren location: "Couple barbed wire fences. Cow shit. Not even a barn." Thousands of eager fans waited through the night for the gates to open at seven on Saturday morning.

Thousands more joined them as the day progressed. By the time the music started, over four hundred thousand people were in attendance. Richard and Valerie joined the vast crowd. They needed a ride and inveigled Lew Welch and Magda Cregg to take the long way round and swing through Frisco to pick them up on their way from Marin City. "We had to park miles away," Magda recalled. As they walked along over the empty golden hills, joining the approaching throng, people began recognizing Brautigan and called out, "Hey, Richard! Richard! Richard!"

"He was feted everywhere," Cregg said, "and this made him feel very good."

"What a sweet California morning," Richard Brautigan remarked amid the adulation.

Once they arrived at the performance area—where hot air balloons soared overhead, tie-dyed banners waved in the wind, and a four-foot stage (built for an earlier location and transported here the night before) stood surrounded by three-story-high scaffolding hung with huge speakers and dozens of lights—the two couples separated. Lew and Magda didn't see Richard and Valerie again for months. Brautigan, cashing in on his celebrity status and friendship with the Hells Angels (particularly Bill Fritsch), went backstage, where the other illustrious gathered.

Owsley Stanley, the acid mogul, chatted with the organizers of the Woodstock Festival. Survivors of the Berkeley Free Speech Movement mingled with the rock aristocracy of San Francisco. Timothy Leary, between court dates, was there with his wife, Rosemary. Emmett Grogan roared in on his "chopped red Harley fandango '74." No love lost between Grogan and Leary, the psyche-delic guru considered the founder of the Diggers "a junkie street-warrior, darling of the chic leftists [. . .] a notorious *agent provocateur* and seeder of dissension."

Rolling Stone had dispatched writers John Burks and Greil Marcus along with photographer Baron Wolman to cover the event. They arrived the night before and soon saw this outlaw impromptu happening was not going to be Woodstock West. Santana started playing at 10:00 am. As the group broke into their second song, an enormously fat man stripped off his clothing and began gyrating wildly amid the mass of people crushing in close to the stage. All at once, several Angels leaped forth, sawed-off pool cues in hand, and beat the naked kid into a bloody pulp. Jefferson Airplane were up next. When singer Marty Balin pleaded for sanity, he was coldcocked by an Angel and lay comatose on the stage as his band played "Somebody to Love." Things were getting out of hand.

The Grateful Dead had been scheduled to follow the Airplane but canceled at the last minute after the attack on Balin. The Flying Burrito Brothers took their place and played beautifully. Their set was interrupted by the roar of choppers when the Oakland Angels arrived and drove their bikes down through a crowd pressed as close together as rush hour commuters. Up next came Crosby, Stills and Nash, their delicate harmonies upset by the violence erupting around them. The Angels swilled beer and bashed at an overenthusiastic crowd attempting to clamber up onto a stage built too low for safety.

Gatz Hjortsberg was at Altamont, along with his wife and young daughter and several friends from Bolinas, who had given them a ride. Just back from his first stay in Montana, he marveled at the size of the crowd, equal to half the Treasure State's population. The Bolinas contingent had set up with blankets and picnic baskets high on the hill above the stage. Here the mood remained happy and calm. The music sounded far away, like the approach of a distant parade. Children played; food and joints circulated freely; the only violence to be seen was through a pair of binoculars. The little Bolinas group headed home at sunset, before the real trouble began.

As it grew dark and cold, bonfires built of creosote-treated fence posts were lit. The fiery scene reeked of damnation. More than an hour passed, and still the Rolling Stones had not appeared. The impatient crowd grew increasingly restive. Backstage, the band chatted and tuned their instruments. Furious, Bill Fritsch told Mick Jagger, "You better get the fuck out there before the place blows beyond sanity." When Jagger replied they were "preparing" and would go "when good and ready," Sweet William got really pissed. "I want to slap his face," he said. "I told him, 'People are gonna *die* out there. Get out there! You been told.'"

At last, the Rolling Stones came onstage, surrounded by a cordon of Hells Angels. Mick, whiskey bottle in hand, broke into "Sympathy for the Devil." Camera crews recorded the event. The Maysle brothers filmed it all for their documentary, *Gimme Shelter*. The anarchy reached its apex during the opening verses of "Under My Thumb." Meredith Hunter, an eighteen-year-old black man wearing a lime green suit, leaped toward the stage, stoned out of his mind on meth and brandishing a pistol. In an instant, Alan Passaro, a former Gypsy Joker who had prospected the Frisco Chapter of the Angels for eight months prior to gaining membership, rushed toward Hunter.

One shot was fired before Passaro, in what Bill Fritsch described as "a classic street move," twisted Hunter's arm away, reached behind with his free hand, drew his sheath knife, and stabbed the black man to death. That single wild round saved Passaro from a death sentence. The Maysles captured it all on film. "We didn't know that we'd get lucky," one of the brothers later remarked. A slowed-down snippet from their movie was introduced as evidence at Passaro's trial, leading to his acquittal on the grounds of self-defense.

A few months later, after Erik Weber returned from India, he and Richard got into a conversation about the Altamont incident. "Jesus! What a bunch of assholes these Hells Angels are," Erik remarked.

"Oh, no," Brautigan replied, siding with the Angels. "Mick Jagger's life was in danger. They were protecting his life and had every right to kill the guy."

Richard's fellow Digger Emmett Grogan adopted a similar position, saying in an interview, "And Meredith Hunter dying like a sniveling maniac instead of like a determined man—that was his fault." Any way you sliced it, Hunter's savage killing provided an unforgettable demonic moment and perpetuated Altamont as the symbolic end of the flower-power sixties, a dark and bitter Götterdämmerung for the Love Generation.

Just as the shining promise of the sixties gave way to the cynicism of the Nixon years, Richard Brautigan's own star ascended. Work done in obscure poverty during the hippie decade now cast its golden light upon him. Money, previously in short supply, came in abundance. Helen Brann asked Delacorte for an advance of $50,000 for *Rommel Drives on Deep into Egypt*, once again to be paid in annual $5,000 installments. Sam Lawrence counteroffered $35,000 (still an enormous sum for a book of poetry), which was accepted, the entire amount to be paid in full 120 days after publication.

Delacorte wanted to publish the books as quickly as possible to capitalize on their success with the other three Brautigan titles. Richard exercised his creative control, suggesting that *Rommel* be designed by his friend Andrew Hoyem and the type set at Grabhorn-Hoyem, Andrew's San Francisco press. Sam agreed. For the first time, on the page listing his prior publications, Brautigan marked his earlier poetry chapbooks with a footnote, declaring them "Out of Print." He also included *The Abortion* on his list, with an asterisk proclaiming the book was "Not Published."

Soon after, Brautigan had his serendipitous meeting with Beverly Allen and arranged for the rainy-day sandbox photo shoot. By mid-January, the cover photograph arrived in Sam Lawrence's Boston office. Edmund Shea had not yet been paid for his previous work for Dell and inscribed the accompanying card "Peace, love." Richard decreed the title be printed on the dust jacket in all capital letters, like "a headline." An instant dispute arose when Brautigan insisted that his name not appear on the front cover. Seymour Lawrence hated the idea, feeling "very, very strongly" that it would considerably "damage sales potential."

Helen Brann sided with Sam on this one, advising her client that "from a practical standpoint and a professional standpoint," his name should be on the cover of *Rommel*. Richard won her over on the phone the next day, explaining his design concept in great detail and pointing out that neither his name nor his image appeared on the cover of *The Pill*, which continued to sell extremely well.

Brautigan had it all his way, right down to the blurbless flap copy. Each contained only a single poem: "Jules Verne Zucchini" on the front flap, "Critical Can Opener" gracing the rear. On the back cover, traditional home of the author's photo, Richard placed Edmund's picture of a tin toy pail and a crumbling sand cone.

Things were not well for Timothy Leary as the sixties came to an end. In January 1970, a jury in Orange County, California, found him guilty of marijuana possession charges, the result of a Laguna Beach bust a couple years before, when two roaches were found in the ashtray of his car. Already appealing a twenty-year federal sentence for a previous pot bust at the Mexican border in Laredo, Texas, in 1965, Leary got ten years maximum. He was sent first to Chino State Prison for psychological testing (ironically, tests Leary had developed himself) and later on to the California Men's Colony–West at San Luis Obispo to begin serving his term.

To celebrate Richard Brautigan's thirty-fifth birthday, John and Margot Patterson Doss hosted a huge party at their town house on Russian Hill. Lew Welch wrote a poem to celebrate the occasion:

JANUARY 30, 1970
Dear Richard,
On this very day, in 1889, Franklin
Delano Roosevelt was born. Had he lived,
He would now be 81 years old.
Would he have liked your books?
What present would he give you on

this mutual birthday?
A chest of California grapes?
Lew

About 250 guests joined the festivities. "I think the whole literary scene in San Francisco was in our living room," John Doss recalled. "People were packed like sardines," Margot added. Herb Caen, one of the throng, wrote in his column the next day that if a bomb had fallen on the Doss home it would have wiped out the West Coast literary establishment. Richard came early and placed little trout pictures he had drawn all over the house. "In every room," Margot said. "In every bathroom."

At Brautigan's request, the party was catered by Kentucky Fried Chicken. "Buckets and buckets, because that's what Richard wanted to eat that time." A life-sized plastic statue of Colonel Sanders greeted arriving guests in the front foyer. At some point, a wandering wit placed a fat joint in the Colonel's hand, setting the tone for the ensuing hilarity. The Dosses had the foresight to remove their carpets, sparing them from trodden bits of greasy spilled chicken. John took the car out of the garage. They used the space for dancing. He decorated the place with paper kites and played colored lights over them. "Like disco, before disco was disco," Magda Cregg recollected.

Things got out of hand when Joanne Kyger and young Billy Burroughs, son of beat patriarch William Burroughs, had a disagreement that Margot Doss described as "this awful set-to." Both were quite drunk, Burroughs perhaps more so. Magda Cregg remembered that Joanne liked to fight. Another time, "she threw a jug of red wine at LeRoi Jones." The dispute came to an end when somebody escorted young Burroughs out the door.

Margot carried the birthday cake, aglow with three dozen candles, into the dining room, and everybody congregated around the big table. "Richard, you have to blow out the candles," Margot said.

"This is the Age of Aquarius," Brautigan replied. "The candles will go out by themselves."

Gary Snyder started chanting "Om." Others joined in. "He got the whole room just vibrating," John Doss recalled. And, as if by some miracle, the candles began dimming.

"They came up again as soon as the chanting stopped," Margot said.

"It was a very magical moment," added Dr. Doss.

Valerie doesn't remember going to Richard's birthday party at the Dosses', but they were still seeing each other at least twice a week during February and March. Brautigan had already begun his courtship of Sherry Vetter. Valerie was happier with him than at any other recent time, feeling "an openness like we've never had before." She worried that perhaps she was just using him "for service." At times, Valerie felt "ugly, selfish, lonely" and didn't want Richard to kiss her, yet she took the time to measure and hand-sew a tailor-made Confederate-style military coat for him.

Roxy and Judy Gordon followed Richard's advice and traveled up to San Francisco. They found a place to live in Oakland and set about looking for Brautigan. Roxy knew the hip spots to go but thought getting there was some kind of miracle. "I don't know how in the hell I even found North Beach," he reminisced. Roxy hadn't called Richard, and he was nowhere to be found at Enrico's. The Gordons "stumbled upon a little Italian restaurant" across the street. This was the celebrated Vanessi's. By coincidence, Brautigan walked in while they were eating their spaghetti.

Spotting an obviously pregnant Judy, Richard borrowed a military expression. "You're on point," he said.

Flush with Delacorte money, Brautigan took the young couple to "many, many parties" and treated them to long afternoons at Enrico's, buying lots of what Roxy considered "expensive wine." Lew Welch and Gary Snyder joined them for a libation from time to time. Welch told Roxy and Judy that Richard was "a baby beatnik and the father of the hippies."

Brautigan and the Gordons hung out a lot together. "He was always coming over to our house in Oakland," Judy said, "and we were always going over to his place on Geary Street. We went up and down the coast. The three of us would go to these different bars and restaurants, famous places that he wanted to expose us to." The Gordons went to several of Richard's enthusiastically attended readings and witnessed firsthand the rush of fame sweeping like a tidal wave over their new friend.

Aside from her husband, Richard was Judy's only visitor at the University of California hospital while she nursed newborn J. C. (John Calvin) Gordon. She remembered the perfect fit of Richard's gray Confederate coat and how proud he was of the "striking" outfit. Brautigan wore it for the first time when he came to see her. "He looked so, so fine," Judy said. Roxy and Richard walked along the hospital corridor together and looked down at the Haight through the big plate-glass window. By that summer, "things went weird again" for the Gordons and they headed back to Texas. Richard dedicated *Rommel Drives on Deep into Egypt* to Roxy and Judy.

One day, Richard dropped by Greg Dewey's place in Berkeley. Dewey had left Mad River, on the verge of breaking up around the time their second album was released, and played drums now with Country Joe and the Fish, one of the most popular bands in the world. He had performed at Woodstock with them and was riding almost as high as Brautigan. "He was getting famous, so was I," Dewey recalled. The two old friends spent the day catching up and sharing a bottle. "Busily drinking me under the table, as usual," Greg said. At one point, Richard asked, "So, what are you planning on doing? Are you going to get rich, or famous, or both?"

Greg Dewey hadn't given the matter much thought. He figured if you got famous both things happened at once. "Well, you know, famous," he replied.

Richard regarded the younger man with unexpected gravity. "You better plan on getting *rich*," he said.

Good news kept coming Richard's way. By the end of February, Delacorte ordered a third printing of twenty-five hundred copies for the clothbound edition of the *Trout Fishing* omnibus. Thus far, Dell had sold over six thousand copies. A week later, the Literary Guild ordered five thousand copies as an alternative selection during the months of July, August, and September.

Brautigan did his part to help sell copies. Enrico Banducci agreed to let Richard have a book-signing party at his sidewalk café on Broadway. Brautigan started selling and signing books at Enrico's at eleven in the morning. Banducci went home soon after that. When he returned around nine thirty that night, as was his practice, Richard still sat beside a stack of books, signing, signing, signing. City Lights brought them over by the case, all air expressed from the East Coast by the publisher. "Richard, why don't you get a stamp," Enrico said, "and stamp those books. Stamp in your signature. What's the difference?"

The line outside stretched far down the block. Banducci remembered "it was really chaotic." Toward the end of the evening, Brautigan was getting drunk and his ordinarily minuscule signature grew larger and larger until it was about two inches high and took up most of the page. There wasn't enough room to contain his gigantic scrawl. "I won't be able to write a fucking word for days," Richard told Enrico. All told, Brautigan sold and signed over a thousand copies of the omnibus edition that night.

Originally scheduled for early in April, *Rommel*'s publication date was delayed by a strike. Orders for hardbound copies were finally shipped on the last day of the month. The Delta paperback edition was released at the same time. Richard's contract with Dell obligated his publisher to run a full-page advertisement in the *New York Times Book Review* within four weeks of publication, as well as smaller ads in six other notable periodicals and in every college newspaper where *Trout Fishing* had been advertised. The page in the *Times* cost $3,210. The total expenditure for all ads ran to $9,007. It paid off. Within five months, *Rommel Drives on Deep into Egypt* was in its fifth printing with over 120,000 copies in print.

For Richard Brautigan, 1970 became a year of travel. In February, Helen Brann requested a $500 expense check for Richard from Dell. Mid-March, Brautigan returned to Boston, staying again with Peter Miller and visiting the Trout Fishing in America School. After a couple of days, Miller's girlfriend, Kat, presented him with an ultimatum: "Him or me!" Helen Brann traveled up from New York with Roz Barrow, joining Brautigan and Sam Lawrence on a trip to the printer, double-checking to make sure everything was in accordance with the work sent to them by Grabhorn-Hoyem.

Back in New York in early April, Richard stayed at One Fifth Avenue, a twenty-seven-story art deco hotel built between 1927 and 1929 at the intersection of Eight Street and Fifth just above Washington Square Park. The room rate was $25 a day. On the ground floor, the hotel housed a restaurant and bar decorated all in white with salvaged remnants of the luxury Cunard liner *SS Caronia*, launched in 1905 and scrapped in 1933.

By chance, Erik and Loie Weber were in New York at the same time, having come over from England on their return from India. They were visiting Loie's parents. Erik was surprised to get a call from Richard. "I don't know how he found out where we were or the number, but he did." Having been in the Far East for three years, the Webers suffered from culture shock. Seeing an old friend in such a new light only added to their confusion. "It was hard for me to grasp," Loie recalled. "The Sterling Lord agency, Richard's books, the money. He was really getting known, so Richard the personage was emerging, and that wasn't the Richard I knew for ten years before."

Erik and Loie hung out with Brautigan for a week or more. They went with him to a celebrity party. Rip Torn and Andy Warhol were among the other guests. "I remember Richard was very impressed that Andy Warhol was there," Loie said. Warhol was with one of his Factory leading ladies, Ultra Violet or Viva Superstar. "A not-real female," recalled Loie, who "had just come back from a totally other culture" and felt the alienation of sudden reentry. "This is too weird," she thought. It got weirder. Warhol pulled down the top of his companion's gown, exposing her superbreasts for a barrage of snapshots.

When Erik Weber, who had very little money after three years in Asia, saw that his *Trout Fishing* cover photo had been used on the Delta edition, he wrote to Sam Lawrence asking for a payment of $200, "as soon as possible, so we can go back to the West Coast." Erik also resumed his role as Richard's court photographer, expressing astonishment at his friend's newfound afflu-ence. "When I left him [to go to India], he was still in rags," Erik said.

Weber went with Richard to the Getty Building on Madison Avenue, where the offices of the Sterling Lord agency were located, and took pictures of him in the lobby and standing in the elevator, holding the doors open. This upset the doorman, who came over and said, "No more photographs," trying to kick them out. They had to call upstairs and have Helen Brann explain it was OK.

Erik took several more shots in Helen's office. Richard looked prosperous in his new herring-bone tweed jacket and long woolen scarf, his hair coiffed in a modified pageboy cut. The haircut was Loie's work. "That's what he wanted," she said, "and I helped him to do that. Crafting his image, his style. Because he had that look [long hair] for so long, and then he debated and debated, and looked, and talked." Richard described the hairstyle he had in mind to Loie. "I don't think he hardly did anything impromptu," she said. "He was one of the most measured, the most cal-culating people, terrified of being caught." Loie also thought Richard now "seemed a little more lighthearted."

When Keith Abbott saw Weber's New York pictures for the first time, he found Brautigan's poses "studied. He knows what he wants to look like." Keith thought Erik captured "Richard shin-ing in his newly minted fame." They showed his "clearest attempt to break free of his social class." Carefully posed in his agent's office, "he is in on a joke. His fingers are on his temple, mimicking the standard thoughtful back cover author poses. He smiles at his unbelievable good luck."

Brautigan's lingering smile might have resulted from a chance encounter with Carol Brissie, an attractive young woman who worked at the Sterling Lord agency. She spent time with him and the Webers during his brief stay in New York. Wanting to see more of Richard, she tried to reach him the night before he left for Cambridge but called too late. Richard flew with Erik and Loie to Boston. "It was the beginning of Richard's largesse," Loie recalled, "of having money, having his friends be with him."

In Cambridge, Brautigan introduced the Webers to Ron Loewinsohn and the Trout Fishing in America School people. *Life* sent photographer Steve Hansen to take Brautigan's picture seated on the sidewalk in front of one of the storefront schools with the students and faculty assembled behind him. Erik Weber captured the event with a photograph showing Hansen crouched over his tripod-mounted camera and Richard posing in the background. Erik and Loie returned to San Francisco about the same time Brautigan came back from Boston. Flat broke, the Webers moved in to a little house on Rhode Island Street on Potrero Hill.

Newly pregnant, Loie started working for Richard as his secretary/girl Friday. She remem-bered the apartment on Geary Street looked much the same as it had before she left for Asia. Her first job was organizing Brautigan's chaotic files. Richard bought a new filing cabinet. "We spent a week, two weeks, billions of little pieces of paper and making piles. Because he had things in paper bags, things in envelopes. Brautigan had one file for correspondence with fans. Another, where Richard disposed of requests from assorted crackpots and pushy wannabe interviewers, was marked "Pests.".

Loie also took dictation, typing business letters. Richard carried the typewriter out of his sacred writing room ("this dank little cavey place that was totally unappealing") into the kitchen, and she worked at the round oak table. At times, they collaborated, writing letters together. "We had quite a lot of laughter over the writing of some of those letters," Loie recalled. She felt Richard tried to cope with his new fame "with a certain grace and integrity." He seemed more relaxed and had even stopped biting his nails. "He was a worrier, a fretter, a nail-biter," she remembered. "The same attention to detail, that same gnawing mentality that went into crafting his style and his work, a lot of that was also internally applied to himself."

All during the first year of Richard Brautigan's enormous success, his life seemed touched by magic. Later, Richard frequently complained of the ill treatment he received at the hands of critics and book reviewers. This time around, in the bright spring of his fame, praise came his way in rushing laudatory torrents. Even a mass-market magazine like *Newsweek* proclaimed, "Brautigan makes all the senses breathe [. . .] He combines the surface finality of Hemingway, the straightforwardness of Sherwood Anderson and the guile of Baudelaire."

J. D. O'Hara, writing in *Book World*, observed, "Brautigan at secondhand is all too likely to sound merely whimsical and cute. He is not; what underlies these games is a modern fatalism, not maudlin fatheadedness." Dan Wakefield called Brautigan "a real writer," on the front page of the *Los Angeles Times* Books section. In the *New York Times Book Review*, Thomas McGuane wrote "These books are fun to read," comparing Brautigan's style to Kenneth Patchen, Thoreau, W. C. Williams, and "the infrequently cited Zane Grey."

Across the pond in London, Tony Tanner in the *Times* described *Trout Fishing in America* as "a minor classic" and "one of the most original and attractive novels to have come out of America during the last decade," while John Coleman in the *Observer* found the novel "a pleasant surprise [. . .] an excellent and pretty original compilation [. . .] streets ahead of Burroughs or Kerouac [. . .]" The esteemed Guy Davenport declared in the *Hudson Review*, "Both these works show Mr. Brautigan to be one of the most gifted innovators in our literature."

On the other hand, Jean Stafford lamented in *Vogue* that she did "not understand [. . .] Richard Brautigan's what-you-may-call-its." Stafford had been puzzled by Richard's work, and before writing her review, she called Sam Lawrence at home one night at 10:00 pm, "in her cups and rambled on about Brautigan." She wanted the "lowdown" on the author "and why the book looked the way it did." Sam assured her "there was no 'lowdown,' just what was in the book." She still didn't get it.

After receiving his graduate degree from Harvard early in April, Peter Miller found himself wondering what to do next. The Trout Fishing in America School ran along on its own energy, and Miller felt at loose ends. Peter mentioned this when Richard phoned to ask how things were going. "Why don't you come out to California?" Brautigan said.

Miller had never been to the West Coast. Richard sent him an airline ticket, and he flew out for the first time. Brautigan's hospitality included providing a place to stay in San Francisco. Richard invited Peter to crash for a while at the Geary Street apartment. Miller remembered the Museum as "the weird one with all the stuff on the floors."

During Peter's visit, Richard received a call from Michael McClure, who needed to dig up a pipeline in his backyard. "We'll go help him," Brautigan said. He and Miller headed over to McClure's place. They put on work gloves, but the poets appeared unfit for manual labor. Richard and Michael stood around talking while Peter got to work with the shovel. "I dug this fucking hole," he recalled, "because that's just not what they did."

Brautigan's audience consisted mainly of college students who did not concern themselves with book reviews. Richard gave twenty campus readings in 1970. All but one were in California. Fifteen had been arranged by the California Poetry Reading Circuit, a division of the Writing Center of the English Department at the University of California. They planned a spring tour, beginning the last week of April and running until the end of May. Richard traveled to Stanford, Pomona, Cal Tech, USC, many branches of the University of California (Berkeley, Irvine, Santa Cruz, Davis, and Santa Barbara) and state colleges in Sacramento, Chico, Sonoma, and Humboldt County. Brautigan always drew a large crowd. "Wherever he reads his audience runs into thousands," Sam Lawrence wrote in a letter to the Dell hierarchy.

Brautigan began his California tour at Berkeley. Wearing his tweed sports jacket, he read to a packed house at the Wheeler Auditorium. After dinner and many rounds of drinks, Ron Loewinsohn brought him to a "depressing graduate student party" at a house close by the campus. The moment Richard and his companions "burst into the room," the atmosphere at the effete academic gathering noticeably altered. "That's Richard Brautigan . . . That's Richard Brautigan . . ." everyone began whispering. Richard was in a surly mood. When asked "Are you really Richard Brautigan?" he replied with a curt "No!"

Jayne Palladino, a twenty-six-year-old PhD candidate in comparative literature, was among the partygoers that night. Married at eighteen and only recently divorced, Palladino had not been having a good time. She'd been looking for a polite means of escape when Brautigan barged in, hostile and obnoxious. She thought he seemed "much too big" for this company, which felt "oppressively small" to her, and she took an immediate liking to him for being different. Feeling emotionally vulnerable at the time, Jayne expected Richard to treat her badly when he struck up a conversation. At first, he was "perfectly awful," a bragging boastful drunk laying his "famous author trip" on her. Soon, Brautigan made her laugh and listened to her ideas about poetry, becoming increasingly gentle and entertaining. Amazed that he seemed to actually like her, Jayne Palladino was further astonished when Richard invited her to dinner at his place. Although "terrified," she agreed to the future date.

Ed McClanahan introduced Brautigan the next afternoon at Stanford, the second reading on the tour. Richard asked those standing in the back to come down and take the empty seats up front. He told the students about the cat sitting on the stage during his Harvard reading the previous fall. "At Stanford, it's a dog," he said. "At the University of California, it's probably a frog." After reading from *The Pill*, Brautigan launched into more-recent work. After "Jules Verne Zucchini," he said, "I was not overjoyed with this *Apollo 13* shot. I thought it was a tremendous extravagance and waste of human energy and time and material. I didn't feel very good about the first one either. The poem's about that. I think we should wheel and deal down here." His remarks were greeted by a slight smattering of applause. "Two people who want to live on Earth," he quipped.

Earlier in April, Richard called Rip Torn in New York. "I'm getting another Blunder Brothers act together. Interested in a Feather River adventure?"

"Damn right!" Rip yelled.

The day after Brautigan's Stanford reading, Torn rendezvoused in Frisco with Brautigan, Price and Bruce Dunn, Peter Miller, and Paul Kantner, the lead guitar player for Jefferson Airplane. The sextet set off for Sacramento in "another old car." Sacramento State was a scheduled stop on

Brautigan's California reading tour. They had to be there before one in the afternoon. Torn considered Richard Brautigan "a splendid reader." This was a true compliment as it came from one of the finest performers of the time. The audience at State was energized by excitement. Richard focused on a pretty redheaded nurse who stared up at him, "enraptured."

The party food provided after the reading proved inadequate. The participating poet had been promised a meal, but "all they had were dips and cheese balls and cheap wine." Richard concentrated on the redhead. Leaving the party without her, he said to Rip, "I talked too damn much and ruined it. I scared her off. Dammit!" They crashed not far from the campus at "an upstairs back-of-the-house apartment with a screened-in porch." Along with a half bottle of Jim Beam and "a few beers," the boys augmented the party's meager fare with a vegetable stew enhanced by liberal doses of bonita flakes, lemon, and Tabasco.

Rip Torn described the scene in "Blunder Brothers: A Memoir." "Down to his skivvies, Richard headed for the mattress on the porch. He poked his head in the door. 'Ah, dammit! No blanket. I hate to ask you, but I'd hate worse to have to get dressed again.' I was going to sleep in the car, where the bedding was. 'Sure, Richard, I'll get you one.' He sighed and scratched. 'You see, I talked too much.' But as he lamented, there came a shy knock at the door, and in walked the redheaded nurse. By the time I got back up, they were out on the porch and on the mattress."

Rip brought the blanket and a snort of Jim Beam, invited onto the porch by Richard, who said they didn't care if he looked. "She's beautiful. Give old Rip a look. It'll keep him warm." Torn left the bourbon behind. The nurse worked an early shift and was gone before anyone else awoke. She forgot to cover "the bare-assed poet," and Richard caught cold in the chill dawn.

He had another reading that afternoon at UC Davis, ten miles from Sacramento. The Blunder Brothers provided the ride. After Davis, Richard had four days off from his tour. Or so he thought. A change of scheduling made him pencil in Sonoma State for the morning of May 4. With only three days left for fishing, they drove straight from Davis to Sierra City, in the Tahoe National Forest. By the time they made camp, it was dark.

Richard camped much the same as he had as a boy, sleeping on the ground wrapped in a blanket. They bivouacked right off the road in a clearing gnarly with exposed roots and rocks. Rip wrote of motorcycles roaring by at five in the morning. Fishing the North Fork of the Feather proved slow the next day. "Nobody got any fish," Miller said. Richard called it "fishing over mausoleums." They decided to head to Oroville for chicken fried steaks. At a grocery/tackle shop, stocking up on hooks and jars of salmon eggs, they learned from the proprietor that the Feather had been rendered sterile through the misguided efforts the Fish and Game Department. He told them to give the Yuba River a try.

The gang fished the rushing snowmelt of the Yuba that afternoon. Miller admitted to not being much of a fisherman. "I didn't know how to fish," he said. "I just went up with these guys. And Bruce didn't know how to fish." Even so, they all had a great time. Rip, a passionate fisherman, marveled "at how a trout could come rocketing up to snatch a bit of bait in the tumbling white water." He admired the "effortless grace" of Richard's casting. The poet was poetry in motion."

They fished with spinners and eggs, catching trout in water tumbling past rusted mining machinery. Tired of bait-fishing, Brautigan rigged Torn's line with a light tippet and a Royal Coachman. "See right there?" Richard pointed. "That big boulder in the cascade? There's fish behind that boulder. You can't see them because of the bubbles, but they can't see you either. Cast right where that rill comes over that crack in the stone."

Rip did as instructed and hooked into a two-pound rainbow he had to chase down the river, the fish cartwheeling in a quicksilver dazzle above the current. Examining the big rainbow's stomach contents, mainly "sticks and gravel," Brautigan shared more of his Trout Fisherman in America expertise. "These are caddis houses or casements," he said, pulling a tiny cream-colored larva from its shell. "And this little fellow is the caddis worm. I've caught a lot of fish using these on a fine hook."

Having landed enough trout for dinner, the gang gathered at "a ghostly old gold camp [. . .] on the river, across the road from a high butte." Richard got out his cast-iron skillet and displayed a streamside cooking technique he'd perfected during boyhood excursions on the McKenzie. He fried the fish with bacon and onions. In another pan, they cooked up spuds and parsley, a great feast, augmented by lemons and ketchup. "Nothing compares with fish that are taken right from the water to the flame," Rip Torn reminisced.

By nightfall, Richard wasn't doing so well. Once the sun went down, it turned very cold. Rip felt "it was like opening the door on a freezer." Brautigan shivered and shook, the phlegm rattling deep in his chest at every breath. He'd speared himself with the barbecue fork while cooking, and his hand was red and swollen. Rip thought it resembled a "lobster claw." Bundled in his blanket and wedged between two boulders, Richard trembled in his sleep. Bruce Dunn wondered, half-seriously, whether he'd make it through the night.

Rip suggested strong medicine, proposing a run to the nearest bar. After covering Brautigan with an extra blanket, Rip and Bruce set off in search of hooch. The best they could come up with was some cheap California rotgut brandy scored at a local roadhouse. It must have done the trick. Brautigan, much the worse for wear, made it to Sonoma State in time for his reading the next morning.

At the end of the first week of May, Brautigan read to an audience of about seven hundred at the First Unitarian Universalist Church in San Francisco, sponsored by the San Francisco State College Poetry Center. There was a $2 admission. Helen Brann flew out for the occasion, pleased to see copies of Rommel in bookstores all over town. It was the first time Helen heard Richard read from his work. Kendrick Rand sat in the pew behind her. He brought a half-gallon of white wine "to share with him in anticipation of sitting around afterwards." Richard grabbed the jug in its concealing paper bag, carrying it up with him onto the simple Unitarian-style sanctuary, a raised oval stage covered with Oriental carpets. Brautigan poured a glass of wine, setting it on the pulpit to his left, and placed the jug at his feet within easy reach. Richard wore jeans, a blue vest, and a long blue woolen scarf. Terry Link, a reporter for Rolling Stone, thought it looked "almost like a priest's stole."

As the church filled with people, Brautigan swigged wine and paced the platform, nervously swinging his arms. Every so often, he'd "do a few knee squats, like an athlete warming up," Link observed. Richard began the reading with recent poems. "Voluntary Quicksand," a reaction to the shootings at Kent State, was written that very morning. Other poetry written during the past few weeks he referred to as "short, flat, funky poems," saying they "lie like mush on a page." The audience reaction was muted. Perhaps the sepulchral atmosphere in the church had something to do with it. "I have a feeling this whole audience is prose writers," Brautigan quipped. "For a while I thought I was reading in a mortuary. I guess a church is the same thing."

Changing the pace, Richard switched to more familiar material from *The Pill*. "Surefire things," Kendrick Rand said, "that always sort of got the audience going." This time, "they bombed." Brautigan tried to talk his way out of a tight spot. Between sips of wine, Richard said the purpose of the poet was not to write good poems, but instead "to work out the possibilities of language and the human condition." The biggest round of applause came when he announced his upcoming book of short stories would contain two "lost" chapters left out of *Trout Fishing in America*.

Afterward, Brautigan asked Kendrick Rand, "Well, what did you think?" His friend told him that the reading "went over like a lead balloon."

"I guess," Richard replied.

"I mean, everyone's sitting in pews and there's the Bible and the hymnal in front of you and you're up there reading your poetry about your dick and screwing," Rand said. "I think everybody was aware that they were in a church and they really felt uncomfortable with the subject matter."

Helen Brann hung out with Richard for the next couple days. "It was like walking around with a movie star," she recalled. He took her to his favorite restaurants and bars. When they walked along the street together, strangers approached to ask for his autograph. Richard always took the time to stop and talk politely with his fans. "He was marvelous with them," Helen said. "He was very more composed and more charming than a lot of movie stars that I've been with."

Not everyone was an autograph-seeker. Many who passed them on the street simply said, "Hi, Richard," and Brautigan would return the greeting.

"Do you know that person?" Helen asked.

"No," Brautigan replied. "I've never seen him before in my life."

At Enrico's or Vanessi's, "quiet places" where they went to eat, pretty young girls would come over to him, which absolutely delighted him. "When he came east it didn't happen at all," Helen Brann observed. "Nobody knew him really. He was never happy in New York at all. It was an alien place."

Brautigan was scheduled to read at UC Santa Barbara in the middle of May. His $200 Reading Circuit Tour standard fee was double what he'd last received there. Richard honored his year-old pledge about demanding more money, buying Kendrick Rand a ticket to fly down and attend the event. Valerie Estes, Kendrick, and his girlfriend, Annie, waited for Richard at the terminal. Carlos Santana and his band were on the same flight, also heading for a gig in Santa Barbara. Kendrick and Richard knew most of the musicians, and they partied together on the short trip down the coast.

The church where Brautigan read this time was not "a big stone edifice" but a more modern structure with folding chairs. Kendrick observed Richard off the top of his form that night after three events in three days. "It wasn't his greatest poetry reading." Valerie had looked forward to a fun weekend in Santa Barbara with the Rands, but Richard heard from Gary Snyder about a ceremonial walk around Mount Tamalpais he promised to attend. He decided, to her "dismay," to return immediately to San Francisco. This meant sitting up all night on a Greyhound bus. Kendrick Rand observed "he had a commitment and that was one of the wonderful things about Richard."

Jack Shoemaker traveled down to a reading in Claremont with Richard during this period, when he telescoped his appearance to what he called a "quick trick," extremely short readings, "to leave them wanting more." Shoemaker thought Brautigan's abbreviated turn "annoyed lots of folks who felt ripped-off by Richard accepting a decent fee and then reading two dozen short poems." At Claremont, it was all over in under fifteen minutes. Brautigan "cackled" and walked off the stage.

The California Poetry Reading Tour ended at 8:00 pm, on May 27, at UC Santa Cruz. Posters around the campus advertised the event as a "poetry diddey-wah." Lew Welch shared the stage. Brautigan began by begging for something to drink: "Water, water. Can anyone get us a pitcher of water?"

"They promised us water," Welch complained. "We came here for free, man." Not exactly the truth. Richard received $200 for his appearance.

Waiting for water to arrive, Brautigan and Welch discussed the reading order. Richard listed a number of new poems, and Lew asked, "What are you rejecting?"

"Lighthouse," Brautigan replied.

"All right. Enough! Enough!" the audience cried.

After more easy bantering, Richard read a few of his most recent poems. "It's very hard to follow Richard," Lew said, when he took over the podium. "Oh, he's bringing out his new book, folks. He has a new book every two weeks. They call it prolific. You know what we say about girls when they do that?"

"The muse has made me an easy lay," Richard replied.

"Right on!" Lew Welch shouted.

Rommel's sales remained brisk, propelled by the energy of Brautigan's meteoric success, but this time around the reviews were somewhat less than scintillating. Many of the poems were slight, even by Richard's minimalist standards, and four were merely blank pages with titles attached. "A cloying, cute, half-assed collection of rather uninteresting tripe," sniffed the *Los Angeles Free Press*, suggesting Brautigan "may yet turn into the Rod McKuen of the hip set." Jonathan Williams, poet and publisher of the Jargon Press, wrote in *Parnassus 1* that "there is less here than meets the eye [. . .]" saying Brautigan "writes for kids who eat macrobiotic food [. . .] You'd starve to death on these no-cal poems."

In early spring, two East Coast journalists showed up in Frisco wanting to talk with Brautigan. Richard had met John Stickney in Boston. The proposed *Life* magazine article had been approved, and he was in town on assignment. Stickney spent some time at "the Museum" and traveled with Richard and Valerie up into the mountains outside the city, where photographer Vernon Merritt posed Brautigan crouching on a rock beside a stream turbulent from recent rains. They spotted a celery stalk sweeping along on the runoff, and Richard launched in on an improvised verbal riff, his voice rising in high-pitched excitement: "That could be the first hors d'oeuvre! Suppose there were more, an entire table full of them, canapés and all? Then a bar, with drinks and setups for everybody! And finally an entire cocktail party, man, floating down this crazy stream!"

Brautigan was more reserved when he met Bruce Cook in a North Beach coffee shop. Cook, the book review editor of the *National Observer*, was writing about the Beat Generation. Richard sat at the top of his list of younger authors "who had come to be known as writers of the 1960s." Richard brought Valerie to the interview but didn't have much to say. He had known most of the principal actors in the beat drama and had shared an apartment with Welch and Whalen, but

Brautigan remained reticent about the whole affair. "My involvement with that was only on the very edge," he told Cook, "and only after the Beat thing had died down."

Brautigan described his work methods, typing away at a hundred words per minute, which reminded Cook of Kerouac's "old Spontaneous Prose technique." "I get it down as fast as possible," Brautigan acknowledged. "I can't spend time on character delineation and situation. I just let it come out." Whenever he got stuck, Richard went out and saw two or three movies, "the worse they are the better," and that got his juices flowing again. Cook thought Brautigan appeared "spooked" and "uneasy," uncomfortable that he had said too much. Before rushing off in such a great hurry he almost left Valerie behind, Richard mentioned Michael McClure. "McClure's a good friend," he said. "You ought to talk to him about this stuff. Not me."

As Brautigan came to the end of his California Reading Circuit tour in the third week of May, Helen Brann was wheeling and dealing with Sam Lawrence on the terms for a new two-book contract. She reached for the sky, demanding an advance of $200,000 for *The Abortion*, with an additional $100,000 for a collection of short stories.

"Shocked," Sam made a counteroffer of $150,000 for both titles combined. In a private memorandum to the upper echelon of his publishing house dated May 25, Lawrence wrote he had read Brautigan's new books with much enjoyment.

> No question about his being a writer of the 1970s. His style is as controlled and as pure as Hemingway's. He looks at the world with the eye of a wise humorist and at the same time, with a child-like lyric innocence. I can readily see why the thousands of kids who make up Woodstock Nation read him so voraciously. He cuts through the sham and hypocrisy of American life. He writes with true sentiment, a deep feeling for nature and the beautiful qualities in people—with a marvelous sense of comedy. He's the genuine article, an "original." We should make every effort to keep him as an author.

Helen Brann came down $100,000, but her asking price still remained too steep for Dell. By early June, they struck a deal. The advance for the two books would be $175,000. Sam had been willing to offer another fifteen thousand but played his cards close to his vest and happily accepted Helen's lower bid. Brautigan retained all the same rights of author's design approval held in his previous contracts.

Flush with newfound success, Richard went shopping for real estate. The first week of July, he wrote a personal check for $500 as earnest money on a building at 418–420 Union Street on Telegraph Hill in North Beach and signed a buy/sell agreement with Nob Hill Realty. The sale price was $60,150, with a down payment set at $13,500. Two days later, the seller approved the agreement but upped the purchase price to $65,000, with the down payment raised to $28,000 in cash. Brautigan resented this and canceled the deal.

Sam wrote to say he was "delighted to be publishing Richard's two new books. Our hopes are high." Brautigan contacted Roz Barrow to confirm Grabhorn-Hoyem's role in designing and supervising the typography. He wanted no repeats of the corporate meddling that had botched the first Delta printing of *Trout Fishing*. Soon the Dell deal began unraveling. Helen Brann found a discrepancy in the Richard Brautigan contract she had just received. On page 1, clause 4 specified that the two new books would be jointly accounted with Brautigan's four previously published titles. This meant after one year, any unearned advance for the new books could be recouped from the earnings of the earlier publications. At no point in the negotiations had Helen ever agreed to such a proposal. Sam Lawrence was out of the country in Oslo, Norway. Outraged, Brann got in touch with Dell, holding up the deal until the matter was resolved.

Around the same time, a letter arrived for Brautigan from Spring Lake, North Carolina. It came from someone named Sandra J. Stair, who turned out to be Richard's youngest sister. She had been married for the past three years to a soldier away in Vietnam, leaving her to care for his young daughter from a previous marriage. "How many nights have I layed [sic] awake praying that I would see you again," Sandra wrote. "How many times had [sic] I had a problem wanting to talk with you and wanting you to understand. *Please!*"

When Richard didn't reply, Sandra wrote back. She complained about the oppressive summer heat in North Carolina and of the frightening thunderstorms. "When I'm all alone like tonight the fears that I've kept out of sight and out of mind during the day seem to apear [sic] before me like a ghost . . . I hate this place . . . I'm just about to go out of my mind waiting to hear from you [. . .] So please, Dick. Write or call me please." She signed herself "Your Devoted Sister, Sandi."

Sandra had been eleven years old when Richard had last seen her. He didn't know how to relate to this strange grown-up woman writing from North Carolina and had nothing to say to her. Coping with the demands of fame caused Brautigan to occasionally cluster an entire month's correspondence into a single intense letter-writing day. When Loie Weber began working for him, she took over the chore of recording the daily tally of his correspondence in the two-bit stenographic notebook.

On July 18, the last of eleven letters Brautigan dictated to Loie was a brief note addressed to his sister. "Dear Sandra, I appreciate your feelings towards me but many years have passed and all I can do is wish you a happy and rewarding life. I am sorry if this seems blunt and I am sorry if it causes you any pain. Again: thank you for your interest in me and I wish you good luck." He signed off with "Best wishes." Richard saved a carbon copy of this letter.

Jayne Palladino almost canceled her dinner plans with Richard Brautigan at the last minute. She knew he was smart. For unknown reasons, she feared he had a "subtle master plan" to hurt her in some way. She suspected his invitation was just a ruse but got a grip and journeyed over to Geary Street at the appointed time. Jayne was not reassured by the look of the neighborhood and rang Brautigan's doorbell with trepidation.

Much to her surprise, Richard behaved in an utterly charming manner. He greeted her with a kiss and a glass of champagne. In the kitchen, Jayne found that he had carefully prepared a large platter of appetizers, little hors d'oeuvres, crackers spread with salmon and caviar. No man had ever gone to the trouble of doing something like that for her before. Even more amazing, Brautigan appeared as obviously nervous as she was, "maybe even a little more so."

They settled into an engrossing conversation about literature, and Jayne felt a bit foolish about her earlier paranoia. She loved the excitement in Richard's voice when they talked about poetry and found it "really infectious." As a graduate student in literature, Palladino was thoroughly versed in the canon and found Brautigan "immensely well read," often in areas she knew almost nothing about. And as they laughed and talked, sipping champagne and polishing off the canapés, Jayne noticed "this huge army of ants marching up and down" in a line across the kitchen floor.

Her first instinct was to grab the Raid. Richard refused to kill the insects. "He insisted that the ants had as much right as anybody else to be in his kitchen." Jayne stayed for the night. They didn't see each other again for more than a year.

When Sam Lawrence returned from Europe, he tried to hammer out a solution to the contract problem with Helen. Three of Richard's short stories (part of *Revenge of the Lawn*) had appeared in the July issue of *Mademoiselle* and piqued his interest. Sam worked at the last minute on a proposed payment schedule for Brautigan's advance, spreading the $175,000 over a three-year period.

Richard expressed his concerns to Robert Briggs in San Francisco, who wrote a memo to Lawrence, stating, "he already has more money than he wants." Briggs felt Brautigan was "very sharp about not changing his life styles [*sic*], only eating and drinking better, traveling more comfortably and having the obvious privacy 'fifteen, twenty thousand per yr can bring.'" He noted Richard was "very concerned with how he is being published." Briggs spoke with him "about being published by heavy front money and leaving himself open to the definite and inevitable exploitation necessary to retrieve such sums [. . .] slick paper, smashing advts. etc.," writing Lawrence that "Richard is/ was horrified by this and is most pleased about the weight of the Delta line and the manner we have handled his cloth sales, as limited as they have been." Sam Lawrence took encouragement from his West Coast representative's assessment of the situation.

Richard Brautigan left San Francisco on a journey to London in mid-July, his first trip abroad. Roxy and Judy Gordon had breakfast with Richard before driving him to the airport. "He gave our waitress this huge tip and it just blew [her] mind," Judy remembered. "He just kind of grinned about it. He really liked waitresses to have big tips." Helen Brann met Brautigan's plane in New York between flights and convinced him of the disadvantages of joint accounting. She sold Richard on the wisdom of seeking another publisher in case things didn't work out with Dell.

It turned out to be a timely meeting. Brann stuck to her guns in the contract dispute, and the publishing firm wrote to her "just for the record" that Dell no longer wished to negotiate further and was "withdrawing all offers on the Richard Brautigan books."

The attitude of the Dell hierarchy (excluding Sam Lawrence) can be summed up by a Robert Briggs aside in his memo: "It might be of relief to us to let someone else paddle the Brautigan ship while we float behind, smiling, with our four Brautigan titles."

Richard traveled alone. He had wanted Valerie to accompany him, but when he asked her, she refused. Even telling her that his English publisher was covering all expenses didn't make her change her mind. Knowing the Creeleys planned to be in London around the same time prompted Richard to call Bobbie. She was part of the extended support group he turned to for advice. "Valerie won't let me just take her to Europe and pay for everything," he whined on the phone.

"Would she go if you loaned her the money?" Bobbie inquired.

"I've asked her that. I told her I'd give her the money. I've told her I'd loan her the money." Richard sounded desperate. "I've told her, and she just won't go. She just won't go."

"Well, Richard," Bobbie Creeley said, "I think maybe she doesn't want to go to Europe with you because you're famous."

Brautigan didn't get it. What difference should that make? Bobbie explained to him the weird thing that happens with fame. How "if you're next to a person who's famous, you're made completely unreal because people who adore that person treat you better than they would think you deserved if you weren't affiliated with [the famous] person. They treat you like you're special, but actually you're kind of an annex."

Brautigan arrived in London jet-lagged on the morning of July 21. His two-week foray deliberately coincided with the publication of the English editions of his books. Ed Victor at Jonathan Cape arranged for Richard to stay at the Ritz Hotel at 150 Piccadilly in St. James's. "I put him up at the Ritz because I thought it was a great joke," Victor recalled with his mocking patrician smile. A five-star hotel built in 1906, the Ritz overlooks Green Park toward Buckingham Palace, another elegant London residence.

When the bellman escorted Richard into his sumptuously furnished bed chamber, one of 133 Louis XVI–style rooms and suites each individually decorated in the hotel's signature colors, blue, peach, pink, and yellow, he had no way of knowing about the fourteen-year hardscrabble journey it had been for the hotel's new guest, all the way from a $6-a-week flophouse on Jessie Street to damask-covered antiques and twenty-four-karat gold leaf detailing, with gift baskets of flowers and bottles of expensive wine waiting from his publisher.

A letter from Tom Maschler, Richard's editor at Cape, awaited at the Ritz, inviting him to lunch that day if he wasn't too exhausted. Maschler wanted to greet his new author and discuss "one or two tentative arrangements" the firm's publicity director had made for "a television appearance and a broadcast and so-on." Brautigan chose not to do any interviews. Walking to the Jonathan Cape offices later in the day, Richard grew confused and stopped to call for further instruction, stepping into one of those red public telephone booths bearing the royal crest once so common in London. Brautigan picked up the receiver. Before he could put in his coins—crossed lines were quite common then—he heard a very proper, cultivated, upper-class English voice say, "Whatever happens, my name must be kept out of this." Richard hung up the phone. "It was a total Brautigan moment," Ed Victor observed after hearing the story.

Richard and Ed went for dinner on his first night in town and later meandered through a sequence of clubs and pubs. They returned to the Ritz quite late and extremely drunk. Richard had dressed up in Valerie's "Confederate" coat for the occasion. Victor thought he looked "very strange. He had a hat, the hat had a big feather. He had a real kind of hippie outfit, like some old army uniform or something." When they reached the hotel, the front entrance was locked. Richard knocked on the glass. The night porter came over, took one look at Brautigan, and turned away.

"I live here," Richard pleaded again and again, pressing his face to the glass and knocking. "I live here . . . I live here . . ." The porter sternly shook his head. Only when Ed Victor, impeccably dressed in his tailored suit, stepped forward to explain things did the porter relent and open the door. The following week, Victor hosted a party for Richard Brautigan at his home. Richard returned to the Ritz by himself this time. He was learning his way around.

Brautigan's friend from San Francisco, the private detective David Fechheimer, was also staying at the Ritz during this period, engaged in another of his mysterious capers. He and Richard went carousing together one evening and got rip-roaring drunk. Recalling his previous difficulties gaining entry, Richard approached the hotel from Green Park, where the Ritz had a private terrace and Italian garden surrounded by a colonnaded brick wall. Brautigan observed that if he climbed up on a park fence, he'd be able to access the colonnade. Soon, he and Fechheimer were clambering aloft. "Doing sort of a Harold Lloyd," the detective remembered.

Richard walked drunkenly atop the colonnade. The wall ascended a slight hill in graduated steps so that their wobbling progress took Brautigan and Fechheimer higher and higher. A hotel doorman, formal as a Balkan general in his uniform, appeared in the garden beneath them. "I say, sir," he said. "Can I get you a ladder, sir?" One was produced, and the two inebriants descended, making the most novel entrance in the sixty-four-year history of the Ritz.

Fechheimer recalled one evening when there was "a whole bunch" of London's illustrious gathered in Richard's hotel room. "It's hard to remember what a celebrity he was for a while." Among the group was the supermodel Jean Shrimpton ("just gorgeous"), who stretched out on Brautigan's bed, which "had a step up to it and spills of white bedspread and piled pillows." It didn't take Richard long to head over and lie down beside her. He stared silently at the twenty-eight-year-old beauty for a long time before saying, "I think I'm in love with you."

"Don't worry," the Shrimp replied, "you'll get over it."

In truth, Brautigan didn't feel comfortable at the Ritz. "Richard hated hotels," Bobbie Creeley said. "He hated the Ritz." Back in San Diego he had told her, "I can't stay in a hotel." The Creeleys were in London for a couple of months. They had been loaned a huge, art-filled flat in Chelsea by their friend Allen Powers, an heir to the Philips Electronics fortune. "About five blocks to Kensington Gardens," Bobbie recalled, "King's Road, Brompton Road. Rolls Royces stacked." Brautigan spent a lot of time in the Powers flat with the Creeleys.

"Richard would come for dinner and then simply stay and stay and then go to sleep on the couch because he couldn't stand going back to the Ritz." When they all went out to a restaurant, Brautigan always returned home with them, ending up on the couch for the night.

Allen Powers's flat was every bit as imposing as the Ritz. Robert Creeley remembered the "incredible" art collection. Powers's father had collected the abstract impressionists, while Allen concentrated on more-recent American pop artists, of whom he was the second largest collector in England. "Every wall had at least three paintings on it," Bobbie recalled. Even the bedroom where the Creeleys' daughters slept had "huge uprights" to store "these gigantic paintings." It was like living in a museum.

One night, Richard came by after a trying day spent with lawyers. "He's already looped," Bobbie remembered, "and in this mournful voice he says, 'I know what they carry in those briefcases now, Bob.'" They sat drinking vodka around a metal enameled table stamped with "This Is Not a Work of Art," which of course was a very valuable art object. Andy Warhol's silkscreen portrait of Elizabeth Taylor stared down at them from the wall above. At some point, Bobbie began to register that she was "on the cusp of one of those drunken evenings with everyone talking [at once]."

According to Bob Creeley, "Richard was getting more and more depressed and more and more teary about the amount of money [he was suddenly earning]."

Bobbie couldn't stand it. "Give it to me, Richard," she said. "I know what to do with it." Unable to bear any more aimless conversation, she told them, "I'm going to bed," leaving the two poets wrangling around the art table.

In the privacy of her room, Bobbie engaged in "this wifely thing of lying in bed listening to the conversation." The meandering drunken discourse continued until she heard her husband exclaim in alarm, "Oh, god, look! Did I do that with my chair?" Robert Creeley had just discovered a "ping pong ball–like depression" on the surface of a huge Barnett Newman painting. Newman died the next day, and the damaged piece quadrupled in value overnight. "I felt like I killed him when I heard the news," Creeley said.

"Should we try and fix it?" Bobbie heard her husband say through the wall. "Maybe we shouldn't touch it." She resisted an impulse to get up and help. "Fuck it," she thought, pulling the covers up over head. After a while, Bob Creeley came to bed, carrying a reservoir of rage and ready to start an argument. It was 3:00 am. Bobbie wanted none of it. "To hell with it." She got up and put on a wrapper. Slamming the door behind her, she headed back through the apartment with Bob in hot pursuit.

"Okay, Richard," she said, "You and Bob can take this up because this is yours. I'm going back to bed."

"For Christ's sake, Bobbie," Richard complained, sitting up on the couch. "It's three in the morning." He lifted his sheet demurely.

This cracked Bobbie Creeley up. The gesture with the sheet reminded her of the coy young maiden in "September Morn." They soon got into "this incredible argument" over who would be the first to phone for a taxi. Richard got a cab and went back to the Ritz. Bobbie took another cab and checked into a different hotel. Bob was left in the apartment with his sleeping children to dolefully survey the big dent in the Barnett Newman painting.

They all met "sheepishly" the next afternoon and went off together to the Tate Gallery to look at the Whistlers and Turners and Blakes. Brautigan particularly liked the "later atmospheric abstracts" of J. M. W. Turner, having been "profoundly impressed" by a traveling show of the early nineteenth-century landscape painter's work in San Francisco.

When Allen Powers called and heard about the damaged Barnett Newman painting, he told Creeley not to worry, there was an art restorer who lived downstairs in the building. He said, "You just put some moisture on the back and it will straighten itself out." Powers also told Creeley the American sculptor John Chamberlain, famous for his crumpled automobiles, "was throwing chairs around up there," and had injured the Newman painting while staying as a previous guest.

To repay the Creeleys' generosity, Richard Brautigan took them all to dinner at the Ritz, which boasted "one of the most beautiful dining rooms in the world." First, he showed them his own room upstairs, a bedchamber Bobbie described as an "incredible iced cake." Their most pressing problem involved the dress code, jackets and neckties being required for gentlemen. The cravat was not an item of apparel favored by Richard. He didn't know how to tie a Windsor knot or even a simple four-in-hand. Bob Creeley did it for him, knotting the borrowed tie first around his own neck before slipping it off and snugging it up under Brautigan's collar. "Don't take it all the way off," he told him, "so you can save it for future use."

In the Ritz dining room, things went from bad to worse. Bobbie remembered the whole "nightmarish" experience as "ghastly." None of them understood the menu, much of which was written in French. The haughty, disdainful waiter provided no help, maintaining an attitude of supercilious superiority as his guests squirmed in discomfort. Their ineptitude much amused a couple seated at the next table, "obviously having the time of their lives listening to these Americans be completely stupid and out of it." They settled for the simplest possible fare. The Creeleys' daughter Kate wanted "spaghetti and an artichoke." The waiter dutifully wrote it down. Their other daughter, Sarah, ordered a hamburger, "with great aplomb," Bob Creeley thought. Bobbie said they all eventually "came up with something," but couldn't remember what. "We were suddenly so provincial and so stupid," she recalled. "Here we all were in London, and this should be wonderful and interesting, like artists abroad, and we just had no style for it."

They still managed to have fun together. One day, Richard joined the Creeleys and their daughters on an hour-long train trip to Brighton, a seedy and disreputable seaside resort. Londoners came down for a weekend "on the razzle," wandering from pub to pub in search of something wicked. As with her more glamorous American cousins, Vegas and Atlantic City, there is a lingering air of the underworld to Brighton, the pervading atmosphere of criminality Graham Greene captured in his novel *Brighton Rock*. Brautigan and the Creeleys met up with thirty-one-year-old Surrey-born poet Lee Harwood, whose first book, *title illegible*, was published in 1965.

Harwood had lived in Brighton for the past three years. "It's always good to be by the sea," he explained. Together, they explored the Lanes and Marine Parade with Bobbie recording their adventures on her eight-millimeter movie camera. They dutifully trooped through the Chinese-style interiors of the Royal Pavillion (completed in 1823), the ornate onion-domed pleasure palace designed by John Nash for the prince regent (later George IV) for his saturnalian escapades. Unlike the British and French thrill seekers who came in search of sin, Richard and the Creeleys took an evening train back to King's Cross Station.

On another afternoon, Bobbie Creeley prepared a big picnic lunch and organized a fete on Hampstead Heath, a favorite spot since she was nineteen and studied painting in London. Situated between the hilltop villages of Hampstead and Highgate, four miles from the sprawling city, the Heath provided an open, rolling greensward very popular with Londoners. In the summertime, magicians, clowns, and Punch-and-Judy shows entertained the children and band concerts calmed their parents. On windy days, kite fliers gathered on Parliament Hill to launch their fanciful creations skyward. Bobbie invited Stuart Montgomery, Lee Harwood, and a couple others, along with Richard and her husband and kids, filming it all with her home movie camera.

Back in New York, Helen Brann phoned Jonathan Dolger, an editor she knew at Simon & Schuster. Dolger, a native New Yorker from a literary family, had worked in publishing since 1962, starting out in the S&S publicity department. Helen explained her recent difficulties at Delacorte, the whole joint accounting mess, and asked if Dolger would be interested in acquiring Richard Brautigan for the identical terms. Brann's timing was calculated and precise. A year or so before, Robert Gottlieb, Simon & Schuster's editor in chief, had decamped for a similar position at Alfred Knopf, taking with him twenty-one of the firm's top literary authors, including Joseph Heller and Bruce Jay Friedman.

It proved an ideal situation for the agent. Simon & Schuster was actively searching for new writers to fill the vacuum left by Gottlieb's departure and additionally was developing two new trade paperback lines, Fireside Books and Touchstone Books, perfectly suited to showcase Brautigan's work. They were Jonathan Dolger's project. A fan of Brautigan's, Dolger pounced at the opportunity, immediately phoning Richard Snyder, president of S&S, who was vacationing on Fire Island. Within three or four hours, they hammered out an acceptable deal. Helen Brann sent over the proposed Delacorte contract, which S&S adopted with all of Brautigan's stipulations, omitting only the language regarding the joint accounting.

When Richard returned from England at the end of the first week in August, the new contracts were ready for his signature. He stayed over in New York for another week, and Simon &

Schuster gave a party for him. "A lot of the younger kids in the office were very excited about this," Jonathan Dolger recalled, "and wanted to meet him." Helen Brann came to the party. So did Carol Brissie, who no longer worked at Sterling Lord. Richard spent the entire afternoon talking only with her. Carol had left in January to take a job at Dancer Fitzgerald Sample, the Madison Avenue advertising agency. Dolger surmised it was a case of "Richard essentially being Richard and being shy didn't talk to anybody. Except one particular girl, naturally. I remember people were upset about it, not annoyed, just disappointed."

Carol Brissie was not in the least disappointed. She called Richard her "blond bear" and spent "a very happy week" with him in New York. She had been "near despair." It was "a pretty black time," and the week with Richard provided a bright spot. When Brautigan asked about her astrological sign, she didn't have a clue. Richard made a calculated guess that she was either Aquarius or Libra rising. Carol promised to have her horoscope charted and let him know if he was on the money. The *Life* article came out on August 14, just as Brautigan prepared to depart. Carol enjoyed reading it, finding it "very real." Right after Richard left town, she came down with trichomonas and went on medication for a week. She waited until Brautigan returned to Frisco before writing to delicately suggest he "might want to have a checkup."

On a plane bound for North Carolina, Mary Lou Folston found a copy of *Life* in the seat pocket in front of her. Leafing through it, she came across the article about her son. A photograph filling the bottom half of the piece's last page showed Richard and Ianthe walking across a street on Telegraph Hill. This was the first time Mary Lou had ever seen a picture of her ten-year-old granddaughter.

Brautigan detoured down to Texas on his way home from New York, stopping off in Austin for a visit with Roxy and Judy Gordon. They were living near Bee Cave, a little town on the outskirts west of the city. Their friend Bill Wittliff, a publisher, photographer, and eventually screenwriter (*Black Stallion*, *Barbarosa*, *Legends of the Fall*, *A Perfect Storm*, and *Lonesome Dove*) had arranged for them to look after A. C. Greene's ranch, San Cristobal. Abilene-born, Alvin Carl Greene, "the dean of Texas letters," was a journalist, historian, author, and Dallas television news commentator. At the height of his success, Greene had published the critically acclaimed *A Personal Country* the year before. Roxy and Judy occupied a smaller place close by Greene's sprawling rock-and-adobe-walled main residence. They had the use of the big house for parties when friends came out from Austin.

With Brautigan as a houseguest, fishing topped the agenda. "Richard always wanted to fish," Judy said. The Gordons took him further west out to Hog Creek, a tributary of Pecan Bayou that connected Lake Brownwood with the Colorado River. Roxy's parents had a log cabin there. Brautigan got a Texas license, and they fished, not for trout, but warm-water species: perch, bass, and catfish. "I discovered Richard was not the famous fisherman," Roxy, a lifelong angler who knew something about technique, recalled. "Couldn't fish and didn't know what to do when he caught one." Judy was more specific. "He would bop them on the walkway."

Visiting graveyards was another favorite Brautigan pastime. One sweltering afternoon when the temperature soared to 105 degrees, Roxy and Judy drove Richard to the cemetery at Byrd's Store, a tiny settlement close by the Hog Creek cabin, where he took notes and watched an old man with skin cancer raking the graves. Looking at the dry landscape surrounding him, Brautigan judged the view to be "godforsaken."

"Godforsaken is beautiful, too," Judy Gordon replied.

Another time, Bill Wittliff took Richard and Roxy to the old Rosario Cemetery, outside Austin. Brautigan scribbled twenty-six pages of notes in his fifteen-cent Velvatone memo book. Of particular interest was the Manderfield Tomb, a crumbling ruin distinguished for its decay even in this decrepit necropolis. Richard made crude sketches of the dilapidated mausoleum. "The Manderfield Tomb is the eyesore of the cemetary [*sic*]," he wrote. "The death slum . . ." Brautigan was fascinated as always with the overt symbols of mortality, and his copious note-taking was intended as research for a projected poem or short story that he never wrote.

Back home in Frisco, after his Texas sojourn, Richard bragged to Joanne Kyger about his time in London. "I got to run with the Creeleys," he boasted. He began spending more time with Sherry Vetter. At first, she met him for lunch from time to time when Ianthe was visiting. "He got to me because here was this little girl who couldn't handwrite," Sherry recalled. "She didn't know math. She could barely read, and I started out tutoring her."

At the time, Ianthe lived up in Sonoma with her mother and attended a "free school," which Brautigan thought, not without justification, wasn't providing a proper education. He wanted her to go to a "regular school." Ianthe told her father she hoped to be a veterinarian. "She was really interested in animals and stuff," Sherry said, "and he knew she could never be that unless she had some math and some science."

Richard, for his part, tutored Sherry in his literary preferences, trying to influence her reading tastes. He introduced her to the work of McClure, Snyder, and Creeley and to classic writers "he thought were really great, like Baudelaire and Sappho." He recited poetry to her. Vetter recalled Phil Whalen's poem "Three Variations All About Love," a personal favorite, misquoting it slightly: "Behind my eyes at Benares, Over my shoulder at Port au Prince." They took long walks together, studying the turn-of-the-century San Francisco architecture. "He loved Bernard Maybeck," Sherry recalled, "especially the copper gutters."

Brautigan often recited favorite poetry from memory to Sherry Vetter during the course of their ten-year relationship. Richard would say, "Let's recite the Robert Creeley poem." He referred to Creeley's "Just Friends," from the 1962 collection *For Love*, the first line, "Out of the table endlessly rocking," a variation on Walt Whitman's famous opening. Sherry remembered wandering hand in hand through Golden Gate Park with Richard, singing old Gershwin tunes. One time in Bolinas, Brautigan, Whalen, and Vetter walked down the street crooning the old George and Ira Gershwin song "Our Love Is Here to Stay" at the tops of their lungs. Philip and Sherry improvised little dance steps. *"In time the Rockies may crumble, Gibraltar may tumble, They're only made of clay . . ."*

Richard introduced Sherry to Lew Welch at the No Name Bar in Sausalito. He gave her a copy of *Courses*, a chapbook published by Dave Haselwood in 1968. "Sign it, Lew," Richard said. On the back cover, Welch wrote out a poem from the book:

Comportment
Think Jew
Dance nigger
Dress and drive Oakie.

Earlier in the summer, when Brautigan was still in New York, Welch sent Richard a sequence of seven postcards on his journey north and west from Colorado. Lew had spent five weeks as

⌃ Richard Brautigan fishing a riffle on the Yellowstone River, Paradise Valley, Montana, ca. 1980. Acrylic painting by Greg Keeler.

⌄ Lincoln Elementary School, Eugene, Oregon. Sixth grade class photo, 1947. Richard Brautigan is seated behind a desk at the far right. Always marching to a different drummer, Richard is one of only two students not wearing a Native American headband.

›› Senior class photo, *The Eugenean*, Eugene High School Yearbook, 1953. Perhaps the only photo ever taken of Richard Brautigan wearing a necktie.

˅ Shack built by Harry Taylor, ca. 1930. Richard Brautigan lived here for five months in 1956 in the care of the Barton family after his release from the mental ward of the Oregon State Hospital. It was his last residence in Eugene. Photo by Quintin Barton.

⌃ Richard Brautigan reading from *The Octopus Frontier* at the Coffee Gallery in North Beach (San Francisco), August 8, 1960. Photo by "Edgren." Courtesy: Greg Miller.

⌃ January, 1965: Richard Brautigan and Janice Meissner in their apartment above Boegerhausen Hardware at 2830 California Street, San Francisco. Photograph © Erik Weber.

⟫ January, 1965: Richard Brautigan posing by the Benjamin Franklin statue in Washington Square Park, San Francisco. First cover shoot for *Trout Fishing in America*. Photograph © Erik Weber.

≪ Richard Brautigan reading Michael McClure's play, *The Beard*, aloud after dinner at Erik and Loie Weber's Geary Boulevard apartment, March, 1965.

≫ Richard Brautigan taking notes in the military pet cemetery at the Presidio, San Francisco, for his short story, "Homage to Rudi Gernreich / 1965." May 23, 1965. Photograph © Erik Weber.

>> Price Dunn, "the confederate general from Big Sur" (bottom) and Richard Brautigan (top of ladder), on a trip Richard made with Janice and the Webers to escape a tidal wave which never materialized. Mouth of the Carmel River, Carmel, California. May, 1965. Photograph © Erik Weber.

⌄ San Francisco, March 24, 1967. Out-take from the cover shoot for *Trout Fishing in America*. Richard Brautigan and Michaela Blake-Grand cracking up while posing in front of the Benjamin Franklin statue in Washington Square Park.

⌃ Making music in the McGuanes' kitchen, Deep Creek, Montana, August, 1972. Clockwise from Lower Left: Jimmy Buffett (with guitar), Bob Junsch, Marian Hjortsberg, unknown woman in doorway, Mary Chatham, Richard Brautigan, Gatz Hjortsberg (partly concealed by wall) and Tom McGuane (on mandolin). Photograph © Erik Weber.

⟨⟨ Photo shoot for *Willard and his Bowling Trophies* at Brautigan's apartment on Geary in San Francisco, September, 1975. Richard has his hands folded into a finger steeple familiar to all his friends. Unhappy with how he looked in these pictures, Brautigan used an earlier portrait by Jill Krementz on the back of the *Willard* dust jacket. Photograph © Erik Weber.

⌃ Michael McClure (seated on chopper) and Richard Brautigan, standing on Haight Street across from Benedetti's Liquors, 1968. Photograph © Rhyder McClure.

⌃ Richard Brautigan at Muir Beach, Marin County, California, February, 1969. Photograph
© Dr. John Doss.

>> Richard Brautigan seated on the rim of his bathtub at The Museum in 1969 wearing the "number 13" medallion he favored at the time. Photograph courtesy Michael Ochs Archives.

⌄ Helen Brann's office at the Sterling Lord Agency, 660 Madison Avenue, New York City, April, 1970. Seated in the foreground, flush with his new success, Richard Brautigan looks like the proverbial cat that swallowed the golden canary. In the background, Brann wheels and deals on the phone. Photograph © Erik Weber.

⌃ The Museum. Richard Brautigan's funky apartment at 2546 Geary Boulevard, San Francisco,occupied the entire first floor of this decrepit building. Richard lived here for nearly a decade, from 1966 to 1975. Photograph © Erik Weber.

» Marcia Clay, age 17, (1970). Marcia and Richard used this photograph on an invitation to their mutual January 31, 1980 party at Brautigan's 2110 Green Street apartment. Photographer unknown.

» Snack time at McGuanes' kitchen, Deep Creek, Montana, August, 1972. L to R: Jim Harrison, Becky McGuane and Richard Brautigan. Photo © Erik Weber.

☆ On the terrace at Enrico's Sidewalk Café, March, 1981. L. To R.: Curt Gentry, Don Carpenter, Richard Brautigan and Enrico Banducci. When word went out that *People* magazine was organizing a party at Enrico's to celebrate Brautigan, only Don and Curt showed up. Photograph © Roger Ressmeyer.

« Richard Brautigan at "The Great Buddha of Kamakura," a 45-foot-high bronze sculpture dating from 1252 AD. Kôtoku-in Temple, Kamakura, Japan, Spring, 1977. Photographer unknown.

➤➤ Richard in love, Pine Creek, Montana. Summer. 1980. Photograph © Masako Kano.

⌄⌄ The Montana Gang (plus some folks from the bars in Livingston), upper Deep Creek, October, 1980. L. To R. (top row): Dr. Dennis Noteboom, Terry McDonell, Rosalyn "Roz" Mina, unknown, Thomas McGuane IV, Max Hjortsberg, Terry de la Valdène, Becky Fonda, Peter Fonda, Justin Fonda, Pete Stein, Ursula "Ushi" Butler, Guy de la Valdène and Michael Butler. (Middle row): Marian Hjortsberg, "Willie Boy" Walker, Benjamin "Dink" Bruce, Russell Chatham, Sandi Lee, Heather Hume, Jeff Bridges, Lorca Hjortsberg, Susan Cahill, unknown woman, lawyer from Hawaii and Dana Atchley. (Bottom row, seated): John Fryer. Laurie McGuane (baby Maggie on lap), Tom McGuane, Richard Brautigan (Teddy Head on lap), Phil Caputo and Tim Cahill. Photograph © Michael Abramson.

≪ Richard Brautigan in Oahu, Hawaii (December, 1981) holding a puzzled barnyard rooster while wearing his new "Fighting Chickens" tee-shirt. Photograph © George Bennett.

≫ Greg Keeler and Richard Brautigan, Bozeman, Montana, Spring, 1982. Greg helped Richard secure a part-time appointment as a visiting writer at Montana State University. Having recently broken his leg, Brautigan is still using a cane. Photograph © Linda Best.

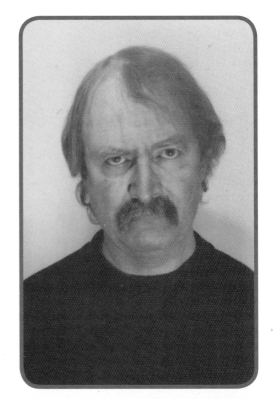

>> Amsterdam, January, 1984. Brautigan's Japanese visa application photo. "Yes, Europe has been good to me."

⌄ Richard Brautigan's mailbox, Pine Creek, Montana, November, 1984. An anonymous admirer left a bunch of flowers shortly after news of Brautigan's suicide was released by the press. Photographer unknown.

poet-in-residence at the University of Northern Colorado in Greeley. Magda and her son Jeff were along on this trip.

Coincidentally, Welch mailed one of his cards from Livingston, Montana. Another one, post-marked the previous day in Rock Springs, Wyoming, read in part, "The talk is about a hippy who ate the heart of a man he killed." This referred to the cannibal murder of a social worker by two itinerant hitchhikers earlier in the year at La Duke Springs, along the Yellowstone River, about forty miles south of Livingston. Brautigan promised Lew Welch to try and get Helen Brann to represent his new poetry collection, *Ring of Bone*.

In mid-September, Tim Leary escaped from the minimum security prison in San Luis Obispo. Helped by the Weather Underground and disguised as a bespectacled, bald businessman with a fake passport identifying him as Mr. William McNellis, Leary, along with his wife, Rosemary, flew first to Paris and then on to Algeria, taking refuge with the exiled Black Panther Party. In an ironic reversal of fortune, they became the virtual prisoners of Eldridge Cleaver, ex-con, informa-tion minister of the Black Panthers' American Government in Exile, and author of the best seller *Soul on Ice*.

As Richard's affair with Sherry Vetter moved forward, he felt the need to check her out astro-logically. One afternoon, sitting around with friends who were amateur astrologers, Richard offered Sherry's birth statistics and they drew up her chart. Later that day, he knocked on her apartment door in Noe Valley. Sherry found Richard standing outside with a little packet of hand-written papers in his hand. "I've had your horoscope done. You've got every house on fire," he said, with deadpan solemnity. "We can't see each other again. This is the end."

Sherry cracked up. "I thought that was the funniest thing I had ever heard," she said, "because I didn't even know what sign I was." Sherry also found it amusing that Richard had used the expres-sion "on fire" to describe the aspect of her various houses, instead of "in fire." Brautigan wasn't jok-ing. He treated the entire matter with utter seriousness, but the young woman's laughter got through to him and he relented, handing over his handwritten notes, which she discarded.

In spite of astrological misgivings, Richard Brautigan knew deep down that Sherry Vetter was a keeper. She was good for him. "You are my map to this other world," Richard told her not long after they started going out together. "For twenty years, I've eaten spaghetti with no sauce and no meatballs. But now, I want to get into this other world." Acting as his guide, Sherry took Richard to a party at her brother's house across the Bay. Blaine Vetter worked as a headhunter in the com-puter industry and lived in a fine house on top of the Berkeley Hills. Later, Richard often played basketball with Blaine on the little court he had at his place, but on that first night, Sherry recalled, "everybody was all dressed up in suits and Richard had his regular outfit," consisting of blue jeans, a white T-shirt, and his black high-top kangaroo-hide shoes.

Feeling angry "because everybody was sort of looking down their noses at him," Brautigan stormed out of the party. Sherry ran down the driveway after him. She knew he couldn't go any-where because she was the one with the car. "Those people," Richard fumed. "Those people are all dying of terminal ordinary. I make more money in a month than they do in a year." It was the first time that Vetter realized Brautigan was rich. All the money in the world would never be enough for Richard to escape his impoverished past.

The following summer, on a fishing trip with Vetter to the Upper Sacramento River, Brautigan once again felt completely out of place in the off-season Mount Shasta ski resort where they spent a couple nights. "Voice of the snow dead," Richard wrote in his notebook. "And I am always on the outside looking in. The air is blue. Alone, blue and dead. I feel like Gatsby. I've never been skiing. I've never been in a place like this before. I am humbled [. . .] It's my childhood again. And always outside looking in."

If Sherry Vetter served as Brautigan's road map into the brave new world of prosperity, Loie Weber provided him with a compass. Not that she told him which way to go; instead, Loie validated Richard's choice of direction. "He liked to control everything," she recalled. "I think he was one of the most measured, the most calculating people. He was terrified of exposure, and he chose his friends carefully. One of the reasons he asked me to work for him was that he already knew me. I was safe."

Able at last to afford a color television, Richard watched all the talk shows and studied the self-promotional efforts of other well-known authors. "He talked with me a lot about his strategizing in terms of interviews and noninterviews," Loie said. "Richard was very aware of how available Kurt Vonnegut was in every way to the media, and he didn't want to do that. [Brautigan] was very much sought after by a lot of the media, TV and magazines and newspapers and all kinds of others, the amount of letters that would come in, and he took a very hard-core stance. He was giving nothing to nobody. He was going to be sort of a mystery, unavailable."

Erik Weber's take on the situation differed. Richard "wouldn't go on talk shows," he said. "I can understand why. He's not spontaneous. To be sitting there and have somebody ask him a question or make a joke. He'd sit there with a stupid grin on his face and not say anything." Weber believed Brautigan feared a vast talk show audience far removed from the undergraduate hippies buying his books. "It would have taken him into different places. I think Richard was afraid of all those places."

Brautigan's mysterious inaccessibility not only kept the outside world at arm's length, it served occasionally to give a cold shoulder to old friends closer to home. When Robert Briggs, who represented Ballantine Books on the West Coast, got David Meltzer a contract to do an interview/anthology with ten Bay Area poets, Meltzer wanted to include Brautigan. By the time *The San Francisco Poets* appeared early in 1971, the cast had dwindled to five: Rexroth, Ferlinghetti, William (Brother Antoninus) Everson, and Lew Welch, along with Richard, who offered six poems he'd published in *Rommel*. Jack Shoemaker signed on to the project to assist Meltzer with the interviewing. Because David "didn't get along with Richard very well," Richard became Jack's assignment. "It was my job to convince Richard to participate," Shoemaker recalled, "and to smooth the way for there to be an interview, which Richard didn't like and would never grant."

This presented a considerable problem. The lengthy interviews constituted the main body of the book. The other four poets talked honestly and often in great depth with Meltzer and Shoemaker. Brautigan balked, refusing the Q&A. Instead, Richard gave them a charming inconsequential essay four paragraphs long, which he called "Old Lady." Much annoyed, Meltzer refused to include it, insisting on a proper interview. His position was "Richard won't be in this book on those terms." Brautigan withdrew from the project.

"When Ballantine found out that Richard had pulled up stakes, they put a tremendous amount of pressure on David and on Briggs," Shoemaker recalled. "They said, 'You can't lose Brautigan. He's one of the most famous people in the book.' So we had to agree that we would print this little self-interview Richard produced." David Meltzer "hated it" but did as instructed in order to save his book. Five years later, when the Wingbow Press reprinted it as *Golden Gate, Interviews with 5 San Francisco Poets*, Meltzer dropped Brautigan and all his poetry.

Busy dealing with the many demands of fame, Richard Brautigan produced little new work during 1970 and 1971. Every mail delivery brought fan letters, requests from editors, and assorted odd inquiries. Richard never answered any of these letters. They all went into files labeled "Unrequited Publishers" and "Pests."

Brautigan's work continued to appear in major and minor publications throughout 1970. The demand for his material remained high. Helen Brann sold "Homage to the San Francisco YMCA" to *Vogue* for $350. Along with the three pieces in *Mademoiselle*, other work was published in the *Evergreen Review* (nos. 76 and 84), the *Dutton Review* (no. 1), *Rolling Stone* (no. 63)—"Greyhound Tragedy" became the last of Brautigan's stories published by Jann Wenner, who could no longer afford him—and *Playboy*, who called Richard a "*hip huck finn*," paying $2,000 for three short tales they collectively dubbed "Little Memoirs."

Brautigan asked Erik Weber to take his photograph for *Playboy*'s "On the Scene" section. In one shot, Richard reclined fully clothed on his new brass bed, legs provocatively spread in a parody of a Playmate's centerfold pose. "The absurd humor of the situation shines from his face," Keith Abbott wrote. The *Playboy* editors didn't appreciate the joke. They printed another of Erik's pictures in the magazine.

Brautigan was especially pleased when fiction editor Gordon Lish bought "The Lost Chapters of Trout Fishing in America" for the October issue of *Esquire*. In addition to a $1,000 paycheck, the acceptance washed away the residual bad feelings left over from failing to get "The Menu" published in *Esquire* six years earlier. *Esquire* no longer played around with Richard Brautigan. They wanted more of his stuff and said so. After two Standard Oil Company tankers collided in San Francisco Bay off Fort Point late in January 1971, and the resulting oil spill provided a hint of future ecological disaster ("Quite likely every lagoon and marsh in the Bay Area will be sterile forever," an alarmed Lew Welch wrote Jim Koller about the event), the magazine called and offered Brautigan an assignment. "*Esquire* is interested in us doing a story on the spill," Richard told Erik Weber on the phone. "Me doing a story and you photographing it."

Brautigan went over to the famed surfing area under the Golden Gate Bridge to observe the cleanup, watching volunteers with pitchforks toss what he took to be hay onto the water to soak up the petroleum tide. He scribbled notes, filling all fifty-five pages with rapidly scrawled random observations ("black, gooy [*sic*] [. . .] the smell of the fucking oil [. . .] oil on the bow of the ferry going to S.F."). Composing the story, Richard made almost no use of his notes, relying instead on memory and metaphor. "The air is overwhelmed with the stench of oil like rotting dinosaurs covered with chocolate syrup." He wrote many drafts of a piece he eventually called "Hay on the Water."

Esquire wanted a full-page photographic illustration. After Erik Weber spent all day taking pictures on different beaches, Richard sent him out into the countryside to photograph fields of grass ripening into hay, farmers cutting hay, cows eating hay, chickens laying eggs in nests of hay, an ironic contrast to the oil-sodden bales floating in the Bay. When someone pointed out to Brautigan that it was not hay but straw, he attempted to rescue his efforts, retitling one of the later drafts "Straw." It was no use. None of Erik Weber's photos fit the bill. Richard abandoned the project. "Forget it. It's over," Brautigan told Weber when he called. "Hay and straw are different things, so that ruins the story."

Brautigan collaborated with the Webers on another project based on Loie's pregnancy. Erik took a series of photographs showing her belly growing ever larger "like the waxing moon." He shot pictures until the birth of their daughter, Selina. Richard wrote a brief page-long text to go with the photos. The Webers called it "The Coming of Moonrose." Richard had Andrew Hoyem design the layout and sent it off to Helen Brann. She received the proposed little book without enthusiasm. Nothing ever came of it. "It wasn't her cup of tea," Loie said. "It wasn't enough Richard. It was a little too esoteric."

In the last week in August, six months after publication, Brautigan received his advance for *Rommel Drives on Deep into Egypt*. Minus a 10 percent commission for the Sterling Lord agency, it totaled $31,500, a considerable sum for a slim book of poetry, more than most poets earn over an entire career. In November, Harvest Records (a division of Capitol) released *Listening to Richard Brautigan*. Mad River's recording *Paradise Bar and Grill*, also on Capitol, came out about the same time. Richard received $5,000 for his spoken word album, considerably more than Apple's initial offer. Brautigan printed his telephone number on the record's front cover, and his fans barraged him with calls. He wasted no time changing the number.

One old friend never heard Richard on vinyl. Janis Joplin died of a heroin overdose in L.A. on October 4, 1970, at the Tropicana Motel on Santa Monica Boulevard. Pearl was only twenty-seven years old. As Joplin's meteoric career faded to black, Richard Brautigan's rising star blazed ever more brightly. Four months after Dell published its first three Brautigan books, 100,000 copies of each title were in print. By the end of 1970, they sold between 7,000 to 10,000 copies per month. Six months later, the sales figures for *Trout Fishing in America* had grown to 265,000 copies.

As part of the festivities celebrating the opening of the new University Art Museum at Berkeley, Richard was invited to share the bill with Gary Snyder and Robert Duncan at a poetry reading on an afternoon early in November. Snyder, Duncan, and Brautigan read outside in the sculpture garden. The minimalist composer Steve Reich performed indoors in the galleries later that evening. A surviving photograph from the event showed Brautigan keeping alive the old bohemian esprit. Seated beside the two older poets, Richard swilled whiskey from a bottle concealed in a brown paper bag.

All through the fall of 1970, Brautigan kept on top of the design process for the two books about to be published by Simon & Schuster. He arranged with Edmund Shea to take the cover photograph and consulted with Andrew Hoyem about the book's layout and typography. By coincidence, the designer in charge of production at S&S was Helen Barrow, sister of Roz Barrow, who held the same position at Dell. At the end of December, Brautigan received $25,000, his first advance payment from Simon & Schuster. A second installment of $75,000 followed in January. The same day, he received an additional $5,000 from Delacorte, the annual contracted amount for his three-book omnibus edition deal. As icing on the cake, a production company paid Brautigan $1,500 to use his poem "Horse Child Breakfast" in a film.

In early February 1971, Richard traveled to the Universities of Texas and Colorado, flying first to Austin and then on to Boulder on the same trip. He received $750 (plus expenses) for each one-day stint. Roxy and Judy Gordon arranged for Brautigan's gig at UTA. Judy recalled, "That was the largest, biggest reading ever, up until that point." After the reading, Bill and Sally Wittliff hosted a big party for Richard at their home in Austin.

The four-day literary festival at the University of Colorado proved a more sedate affair. The event also featured Ishmael Reed, Charles Wright, Peter Beagle, and Joanna Featherstone. Richard had never been to Colorado before and stayed only for a single day, even though he'd been told it was "beautiful in winter." These were his only college readings in 1971.

The Abortion was published by Simon & Schuster in March 1971, released simultaneously in a cloth edition and as a Touchstone Paperback. The beauty of Richard's photographic covers was that they became ads unto themselves and instantly translated into various other forms of print promotion. Edmund Shea had been paid handsomely by S&S, yet had not received anything from Dell after all this time. Shea found it "incomprehensible," sending a third bill to Rosalie Barrow. Altogether, the tab for all his photographic services totaled $1,500.

Dell offered Shea $750, "in full settlement of all his claims." Edmund rejected this. He moved to England for a year, using his *Abortion* S&S cover proceeds to bankroll his travels. On December 14, Dell increased their offer to $1,000, "the best that we can do." Edmund Shea stuck to his guns, holding out for the full amount. In the end, he received his $1,500, which paid his way back home to the States from Kano, Nigeria.

Richard Brautigan thought of his manuscripts and papers as treasures worth preserving. The sudden onslaught of fame increased his appraisal of the small personal archive stored in cardboard boxes at Geary Street. A casual conversation with Robert Duncan suggested the Bancroft Library at UC Berkeley might be willing to store his papers for him. In February, Brautigan sent a carton of typed manuscripts, galleys, page proofs, and early first editions over to Berkeley. The small collection included rare treasures: a copy of *The Return of the Rivers*; manuscripts of *Trout Fishing, All Watched Over by Machines of Loving Grace*, and *Rommel*; the original production material for *Lay the Marble Tea*; and the galleys, page proofs, and production notes for *Please Plant This Book*.

Richard wrote to Robert Duncan in March, outlining his conditions concerning access to the material he was storing at the library. He stipulated none of the items were to be made available to members of the public without first obtaining his written permission. Thus began a seven-year pas de deux between Brautigan and the Bancroft. James D. Hart, director of the rare book library, wrote to Richard in June, saying how happy he was to have Brautigan's work "on deposit," assuming "that someday students of your writing will be able to make use of the materials."

At the beginning of December, Hart spoke on the phone with Brautigan, suggesting that an "informal agreement" be drawn up regarding the placement of his papers. Later that month, Jack Shoemaker deposited more archival material (*Revenge of the Lawn* and *The Abortion*) at the library in Berkeley. Hart followed up with another letter to Richard. He said the Bancroft "would like to think of owning a fine Richard Brautigan collection but we are somewhat uneasy about serving merely as a place of storage without any likelihood of becoming the place of ownership."

Hart included, in duplicate, the agreement mentioned earlier. He asked Brautigan to sign and return one copy to the library. Richard didn't write back and never signed the agreement. For the next half-dozen years, the Bancroft Library served as the somewhat unwilling curators of a Richard Brautigan collection they did not own.

Around the middle of March, a six-page letter arrived for Richard from "the fat little fingers of the sister of yours whom [*sic*] once upon a time was like a second shadow [. . .]" B.J. was now Barbara Fitzhugh, married and living in Portland, Oregon. After all these years, Barbara still didn't get along very well with her mother and limited her trips back to Eugene to "about twice a year whether I need to or not [. . .] I'm the outsider in the family." Barbara enclosed snapshots Rex Sorenson had taken of her and the kids on his recent visit to Oregon. She said she'd thought of her big brother often over the years. "If you'd like to write, I wish you would," she concluded, "and if you don't, I can understand that also." She signed, "As Always, Love, Barbara Jo." Richard never wrote back, but he saved her letter and the snapshots until the end of his life.

On the weekend Barbara's letter arrived, Richard was away in Monterey with Sherry Vetter. They made several trips there that year and the next, flying down (airfare was $10.80 one-way) to spend time with Keith and Lani Abbott or with Price Dunn, always staying at Borg's Motel in Pacific Grove. Brautigan had been scheduled to give a reading at the Ninety-second Street Y in New York on March 30, but for unexplained reasons, the event was canceled.

In April, when Sherry's car was in the shop for repairs, she rented a Chevy Malibu and drove Richard up to Mendocino for a long weekend, his first vacation in two years. A friend had loaned her a cabin on the edge of the picturesque coastal town. Brautigan promptly came down with the flu and spent three days in bed "staring out at the trees."

Richard ran a high fever and sweated through the nights. On the third morning, he wanted to have sex ("perhaps to break the monotony") but couldn't get an erection. His sickness had taken its toll. Brautigan sat staring forlornly at Sherry's diaphragm lying on its plastic case as she playfully lifted his bathrobe and prodded Richard's wilted penis with her big toe. She went into town around noon to have coffee with a friend.

Brautigan tossed in bed, burning with fever and staring through the windows at the drizzle-shrouded trees. Unable to take it anymore, he struggled out of bed and into his clothes. He found an old girl's bicycle leaning against the outside of the house and pedaled slowly for half a mile to a graveyard close by Mendocino. Always fascinated by cemeteries, Richard wandered feverishly among the tombstones under an overcast sky, reading the epitaphs of long-dead Californians. Brautigan was back in bed, snug under the covers, staring at the gloomy trees, when Sherry returned from her coffee date, bringing him a glass of orange juice.

At the end of April, Brautigan sent a check for $50 to the Sonoma State College English Department, along with a short letter explaining that he had been overpaid by that amount for the reading he gave there the previous year. Around that same time, Kendrick Rand was shutting down the Minimum Daily Requirement for the very last time one cold windy evening when Richard and Sherry stopped by on their way to La Bodega for dinner. Rand planned a permanent move to his place in Stinson Beach and was closing the coffeehouse forever. Richard suggested a drink in celebration, and, after their meal, he and Sherry rejoined Kendrick on the terrace of Enrico's, where they polished off "a bottle or so of wine." Richard's newfound affluence bankrolled a recent passion for expensive French white wine. Aside from that, Kendrick saw little difference in Brautigan. "He didn't really change that much."

After their first bottle, Richard pulled a letter from *Playboy* out of his peacoat pocket. "I gotta show you some of this," he said, handing it to Kendrick. The message expressed a warm appreciation for Richard's work. "Since you are part of the family now," the letter concluded, "please feel free to avail yourself of the services of the Playboy Club." It was signed by Hugh Hefner. From where Rand sat, he looked straight down Kearny Street at the lighted facade of the Playboy Club several blocks away. "Hey, Richard," Kendrick pointed at the distant nightclub. "You ever been in there?"

"No," Brautigan replied.

"Well, by god, let's go down there!"

They hailed a cab. A woman dressed in the club's signature abbreviated bunny costume greeted them at the door and asked if they were members. When they said no, she told them only club members were admitted. Richard produced his letter. "I've been invited here by Hugh Hefner," he said.

They were allowed in out of the cold to wait in a foyer while word of the letter worked its way up through the chain of command. The intrepid trio made their way to the lobby. There, a nest of scantily clad bunnies parted at the approach of "the madam." She looked them over. "Everyone else is in three-piece suits," Kendrick recalled. "Real Montgomery Street." Thinking to call their bluff, the madam said, "Well, I understand that you are the guests of Mr. Hefner?"

"Yes." Richard handed her the letter. "He's invited me to come to the Playboy Club and avail myself of the services."

The madam managed to say, "Just wait a moment. We'll accommodate you." After a while, they were escorted up the stairs from the lobby into a large gaming room where numerous bunnies attended the businessmen shooting pool. More stairs in the multilevel club led to a dining area, while another set descended to the toilets. "They had taken a table and placed it there with three chairs and sat us in this little foyer off the men's and ladies' room," Kendrick related. "I'm sure we were the first and last people ever to sit there." Richard, Sherry, and Kendrick ordered double Jack Daniel's and "proceeded to get very drunk." When members came down from the game room to use the facilities, the raucous trio pretended to be bathroom attendants and greeted them with rude insults. "It was quite an evening."

After leaving the Playboy Club, Kendrick said to Richard, "This is my last night in North Beach, and somehow, in all the years of North Beach, I have never been into a topless place." Richard admitted he hadn't either, and they decided to correct this unfortunate oversight, weaving their way into the Garden of Eden. "Pretty drunk," they stuck around long enough to watch "the male-female act of love" before departing.

The Simon & Schuster editions of *The Abortion* sold well, but not as well as the Brautigan books published by Dell/Delacorte. Jonathan Dolger attributed this to the S&S sales force being unfamiliar with Brautigan. The tepid reviews the novel received didn't help. Clarence Peterson, writing in the *Chicago Tribune Book World*, called *The Abortion* "a whimsical delight," but he went on to say it "appears to have been written in no more time than it takes to read it." Steven Kroll (*Washington Post Book World*) also enjoyed the novel, yet said "it seems of little consequence." Robert Adams bluntly stated in the *New York Review of Books*, "It isn't a bad book. It just isn't much of a book." Harshest of all, in the *New Republic*, Jonathan Yardley referred to Brautigan as "the Love Generation's answer to Charlie Schultz. Happiness is a warm hippie."

The same spring *The Abortion* appeared, Brautigan produced the last of his Digger-inspired giveaways. Jack Shoemaker had planned to move to Oregon in 1968, but stopped off in Berkeley for a few months to work at Serendipity Books, Peter Howard's newly established first-edition emporium on University Avenue. Three years later, he was still there.

Shoemaker never did make it to Oregon, staying on at Serendipity for six years. While there, he launched the Sand Dollar Press, the first in a series of distinguished publishing ventures. Because Serendipity planned to have a booth at the New York Antiquarian Book Fair in the spring of 1971, the notion of printing something by Richard Brautigan to hand out to the fair-goers made perfect sense. The end result, *Five Poems*, a seventeen-by-eleven broadside (Serendipity labeled it a "wideside") became the most attractive of all Brautigan's "free" publications. Printed with red titles and black text on heavy cream-colored paper by Clifford Burke's Cranium Press, the broadsides owned a finished professional look lacking in the earlier com/co handouts.

A long letter arrived from Jayne Palladino. She'd run into Richard for a few minutes at Ron Loewinsohn's poetry reading in Berkeley a couple months earlier. Thinking about the positive effect he had on her life made her want to see him again. Attempts at phoning him failed because he changed his unlisted number so often and kept his phone unplugged for most of every day. In her letter, Jayne suggested a walk into the Berkeley Hills. Brautigan waited months before calling her. By then she was in love with someone else, so they didn't get together.

California Living, the magazine section of the *San Francisco Sunday Examiner & Chronicle*, published "A Taste of the Taste of Brautigan" in mid-May. There were seven short enigmatic poems, accompanied by photographs, "conceived and executed by Richard with his good friend, photographer Edmund Shea." Edmund took the pictures before departing for England. In his introduction, the editor confessed "while the temptation is great for this magazine to do a definitive personal profile of Richard, he prefers to let his writing speak for him . . . for now."

While everything continued to get better for Richard Brautigan, old friend Lew Welch fell on hard times. Depression and booze took their toll. Like Jack Kerouac, his drinking had reached pathological levels. "Stark raving mad," Welch described himself as "such a bad alcoholic I can barely function." He and Magda parted company.

Cregg left the country to travel in Colombia, South America. "I was so much worse than I knew," Lew wrote to her. "It must have been awful for you to watch [. . .] I really know now where Kerouac was—how the spirit dies so there isn't even fear anymore & the body dies so there isn't any love or courage possible." Jack Shoemaker's Sand Dollar Press had recently published a second edition of *The Song Mt. Tamalpais Sings*. At the time, *Courses* was the only other Welch title still in print.

Lew had a plan. Allen Ginsberg gave Welch his share of the hundred-acre communal property up by Nevada City where, on his portion, Gary Snyder built the log home he called "Kitkitdizze." Welch planned to dry out at a friend's Washington farm during the spring and build a cabin in the Sierra that summer. Letters from Gary instructed Lew on the protocol and criteria for selecting a cabin site, defined the "general code" comembers had agreed upon for land use, warned of fire danger, and offered useful tips on well drilling. Work on the eight-by-twenty log structure was set to start late in June.

Welch arrived in the mountains by mid-May, living in his van while he set up camp. He needed a crew of five, including two carpenters, and had to supply all their food during construction as well as buying lumber. Lew had $3,000 set aside, but it wasn't enough. He wrote Magda, pleading for a loan of $1,000. He planned on asking Richard and Don Carpenter for money. Isolation gripped him. "It's funny," he wrote, "but everybody seems somehow a stranger."

Lew Welch had long been struck by the large number of suicides among poets. Ten years earlier, in an unfinished letter to Robert Duncan from Ferlinghetti's Bixby Canyon cabin, where he binged with Jack Kerouac, he stated, "The other possibility, *the only other possibility*, is suicide." On May 22, Welch named Don Allen as his literary executor in his journal. In his agitated state, he misdated the entry as "March 22." "I never could make anything work out right and now I'm betraying my friends," he wrote. "I can't make anything out of it—never could. I had great visions but never could bring them together with reality. I used it all up. It's gone [. . .] I went Southwest. Goodbye." Lew took his pistol and walked away from camp, disappearing into the mountains. He was never seen again.

Early in June, the Sunday *New York Times Book Review* published "The Mercy Killing," a parody of Richard Brautigan by the respected novelist Walker Percy (*The Moviegoer*). Sharply barbed on the surface, a literary parody is at heart a sincere compliment. In order for a reader to get the joke, the subject of a parody must be famous enough to be recognizable, possessing a distinctive individual style. Hemingway and Faulkner had unique voices and were readily parodied. Brautigan, too, had his own literary voice. Percy's mocking send-up acknowledged Brautigan's widespread fame.

The Brautigan burlesque was sandwiched between parodies of James Baldwin and Donald Barthelme, distinguished company for a young writer recently arrived on the national scene. "The Mercy Killing: A Love Story, by Richard Brautigan" poked fun at *The Abortion* while misinterpreting the actual work. Walker Percy had the misguided notion that Brautigan celebrated illegal abortions. Even a cursory reading of the novel reveals otherwise.

Richard and Sherry Vetter traveled often to the mountains on fishing trips. Sherry owned a baby blue Volkswagen "bug" and did all the driving. "We would load up the car with my fishing gear, ample extra clothes and a box full of cooking utensils and food," Brautigan wrote ten years later. "The important thing that we did not take with us was sleeping bags because we always stayed in motels or cabins, most often with kitchens so we could cook, which included lots of trout that I caught."

Their longest trip to the upper Sacramento River lasted three weeks. Richard and Sherry took Ianthe, on her summer vacation, along with them, the day after Brautigan attended the Whole Earth Demise Party at the Exploratorium in San Francisco. To celebrate the final issue of the *Whole Earth Catalog*, editor Stewart Brand swirled through the crowd robed in black like a monk and gave away $20,000 in cash. Copies of a Lew Welch poem were also handed out. Most partygoers had no idea he'd gone missing and was very possibly dead.

Shortly before they left, Richard called Sherry and told her that his daughter didn't have any clothes. Would she please help her buy what she required? "She particularly needed a swimming suit, and she was *so* skinny," Sherry recalled. "I did buy her this real cute dress, but none of the bathing suits would fit her." Sherry sewed a little two-piece reversible suit for Ianthe. "She wore that thing over clothes and under her clothes every day for the three weeks."

Swimming suits were essential. Sherry loved to swim, and Richard described her bathing costume as "a very daring and delicious bikini." Richard made sure the motels where they stayed always came with swimming pools. Richard and Sherry drove north across the Golden Gate Bridge, stopping at Ginny's place in Sonoma to pick up Ianthe, and then straight on up to Redding, a distance of 239 miles, with Sherry behind the wheel for the entire trip. They stayed at the Hyatt Lodge, which had a pool and cost only $15 a night.

During the day, Sherry and Ianthe spent much of their time swimming. Brautigan liked to sit poolside and watch them. "Richard was always watching," Sherry recalled. "Watching for little things, like the way you moved and the way you walked and the way you swam." Brautigan had his own take on this. In his unpublished memoir "American Hotels," he observed, "Sherry was so graceful in the water that I liked to watch her swim, other than for obvious reasons, so often that I would eat by the pool and watch her splash around."

What gave Richard the most pleasure was when Sherry jumped out of the pool and squirmed into his lap, dripping and giggling. "Even though she was in her early 20s," he wrote, "because she was so short, and innocent of face, she looked 15 or 16. I was in my middle 30s and looked a little old for my age, so it created some consternation with the people that we encountered [. . .] because we were obviously lovers." Richard and Sherry "often adjourned to our room and made love like healthy fire." After a nap, they went fishing in the afternoon. Sherry didn't fish but brought along a book and sat on the bank reading under a tree. "I would just sit and watch," she reminisced. "It was so incredible to watch him fish."

Sherry remembered the folks they scandalized around motel swimming pools. "All these men were sort of dressed down in these L. L. Bean fishing gear outfits, and their wives—they were rich guys!" On this trip, the trio ventured up to the little town of Dunsmuir and stayed at the Venice Motel on the edge of the Shasta-Trinity National Forest. "This one particular guy followed Richard around for a couple of days to learn how to fish." He was fascinated with Brautigan because Richard used so little gear. Brautigan waded wet in high-top tennis shoes. Aside from his fiberglass pole and a fern-stuffed wicker creel Sherry liked to sit on, he had none of the highly priced equipment favored by the Abercrombie & Fitch crowd.

Richard, Sherry, and Ianthe had dinner one night with this man and his wife and two kids. Sherry remembered the evening as "kind of fun." Richard and Sherry went into town that day and bought a couple bottles of wine, "and the guy was flabbergasted that this old, weird hippie knew anything about wine." Brautigan also knew how to charm. "Richard had a way, wherever we went, of meeting and talking to and becoming friends with the oddest assortment of people," Sherry recalled. "Many, many different kinds of people from all different social categories, from the poorest to the richest."

Years later, after their fishing trips faded to distant memories, Sherry told Richard that she had never enjoyed driving across endless miles of California backcountry. Worse, she actually hated the fishing, all the hours she spent watching Brautigan wading in trout streams. Only the books she brought along to read on the bank kept her "from going stark raving mad."

Two weeks after returning to San Francisco from their trip to the upper Sacramento, Richard Brautigan flew to New York. Again, he stayed in $25-a-night rooms at One Fifth Avenue. Brautigan was in town to meet his new editor at S&S and get to know some of the production people at the publishing house.

After a small welcoming party at the S&S offices, Richard Snyder (later CEO and chairman of the company) suggested they all go up to Elaine's Restaurant. Long a bastion of literary and showbiz celebrity, Elaine's, on Second Avenue between Eighty-eighth and Eighty-ninth streets, like Toots Shor's famous gin mill long before, gained a reputation for exclusivity based on brash rudeness and the arrogance implied by serving mediocre food for inflated prices.

Brautigan wanted to go there, Jonathan Dolger observed, because he felt "it was some sort of acceptance." Widely regarded as the "in" literary hangout, Elaine's was, according to Dolger, "under the best of circumstances a terrible place. It's noisy and the food isn't any good." Even so, Snyder, Dolger, Brautigan, Helen Brann, Christopher Cerf, and "two or three girls" got into cars and headed uptown. According to Helen Brann, "Elaine treated us like shit, and we got a horrible table, and the food was not to be believed, it was so terrible, and the service was lousy, and everybody got drunk, and nobody had a good time."

After every drink, Dick Snyder grew louder and louder, while Brautigan, inherently shy, became ever more quiet. At one point, Jonathan got up to visit the men's room and Richard followed him in. "Can we get the fuck out of here," he pleaded. Helen, Jonathan, and Richard made their escape like "liberated slaves, away from all these people." Dolger recalled heading downtown on First Avenue like Dorothy, the Tin Man, and the Scarecrow skipping along "the Yellow Brick Road" to Brann's Sutton Place apartment and a final tranquil nightcap.

Helen's apartment often served as a place of refuge for Brautigan when he was in New York. She claimed she never cooked ("I try not to cook dinner for clients or anybody else"), but Brann realized how much Brautigan enjoyed the sanctuary her apartment provided, "so maybe I would have a couple people over. I would give parties for him. Very small. Just people he knew and liked." Helen felt flattered that Richard ate everything she cooked. At the time, she owned two small dachshunds, Denver and George, who loved Richard. Brautigan didn't care for the dogs, yet they seemed especially fond of his blue jeans, and when he sat in Helen's big chair in the living room, they would bite at his cuffs.

For "serious business conversation over breakfast," Brann and Brautigan went to the Edwardian Room at the Plaza Hotel, an elegant corner restaurant with views of both the park and Pulitzer fountain. For dinners they favored The Palm, a high-end steak joint with bold celebrity caricatures painted on its tobacco-colored walls. Jonathan Dolger remembered how Richard always ordered a "cull," a lobster with a very large claw, a specialty at The Palm. "A genetic aberration. Huge thing." It was a big step-up from beanie-wienies.

Richard left New York before the end of July, taking a TWA flight to Albuquerque. Roxy and Judy Gordon had moved to Moriarty, a small town east of the Manzano Range, forty miles from Albuquerque. Roxy had recently published his first book, *Some Things I Did*, with Bill Wittliff's Encino Press in Austin (which had also issued *In a Narrow Grave* by Larry McMurtry). Roxy's book, an account of his VISTA training and other adventures, was dedicated to Brautigan ("whose favorite gun is the Colt Navy .36") and to his wife.

Roxy and Judy had started a country music magazine, *Picking Up the Tempo*. The Gordons tried to interest Richard in outlaw country music, teaching him the names of various singers and urging him to listen to Waylon Jennings. Ianthe later encouraged her father to do the same. Eventually, Brautigan used an imaginary Waylon singing a make-believe C and W song at the Grand Ole Opry to conclude his novel *Sombrero Fallout*.

Richard brought Roxy a present, "a wrecked old straw cowboy hat" that had once belonged to the experimental novelist Rudolph Wurlitzer (*Nog*, *Flats*), who had achieved some measure of pop culture fame by cowriting the screenplay for *Two-Lane Blacktop*. Roxy and Judy gave Richard a lift up to Santa Fe, getting a flat along the way. Brautigan took a $9 room at the De Vargas Hotel. While there, he got together with several Santa Fe friends. Richard phoned Jorge Fick to say he was in town. Brautigan first met Fick, a local painter who'd known Bob Creeley at Black Mountain, during his trip to Santa Fe with Valerie Estes in 1969. Jorge thought he was calling from the bus station. "He was living his own story," Fick recalled. "He was the pearl in the oyster."

Brautigan returned to San Francisco and resumed his life where he'd left off, dictating his correspondence to Loie Weber, hanging out with friends, picking up again with Sherry Vetter. In mid-August, they went on a five-day fishing trip to the North Fork of the Yuba River in Nevada, returning to the general area of his previous Blunder Brothers misadventure. Sherry was attempting to write at this time. On these long drives she often discussed technique with Richard. He criticized her poetry, telling her what was good and what was not and why.

Brautigan was fond of Gustave Flaubert, who spoke of "the moral imagination of the reader." Richard explained to Sherry that what he meant was "that you can't tell the reader everything, you have to leave room for the reader to make [his] own moral choices about things that are happening."

Working on a poem, Brautigan utilized an instinctive anti-intellectual method he called "floating." He instructed Sherry in this technique, saying, "Let your mind float through it first and then, floating through it, you'll find it. You'll find the way that the words have to line up." She'd been working on a poem she called "Father's Day Out," about a phone conversation between a woman and a man who had not spoken for a long time. Sherry felt "the first couple of sentences were not good." Richard offered to help. Sherry loved the opening line he came up with, amazed at how it floated off the top of his head: "After years of restraint he returned to me his mind unaltered in the use of clever cutting innuendo."

Vetter observed that at the literary dinner parties they attended, when Richard told a story about people everybody present knew, he never used any actual names. "He would change little things to hide who it was." After one party, Sherry asked Richard, "Why didn't you tell them who that was? It would have made it more interesting."

"If you use the name it's gossip," Brautigan said. "If you don't use the name, it's fiction."

Earlier that year, Brautigan's lawyer Richard Hodge and his law partners bought 273 Page Street, an elegant two-story Victorian mansion built in 1877 with two original fireplaces gracing the eighty-foot living room. Located near Hayes Valley, an area where the outer edges of the Tenderloin, the Mission, the Haight, and the Fillmore converged, the ornate old silver-gray house became the legal hub for Hodge, Green & Zweig. During the seventies, the place acquired local fame as a salon and party palace.

Nancy Hodge, a slim, attractive brunette who had once been the bareback riding champion of California, possessed impeccable taste and decorated the venerable mansion with gleaming antique furniture, a grand piano, Persian carpets, and crystal and brass fixtures. Thursday nights developed into a regular open house at Page Street. Musicians, poets, journalists, artists, lawyers, and ex-cons gathered together amid the candlelight and floral arrangements, sipping drinks before twin blazing fires, helping themselves to fine food arranged on silver platters beneath a cut-glass chandelier. Being a close friend and esteemed client, Richard Brautigan was a frequent guest, mingling with local notables Commander Cody, Jessica Mitford, Congressman Pete Stark, Boz Scaggs, and Toad the Mime. "A house can be like the map of a mirror / reflecting a decade and the people / who come and go in it," Brautigan wrote, celebrating 273 Page Street in his 1978 poem "San Francisco House."

Tom McGuane was among those who came and went. A couple years after buying the mansion, the Hodges hosted a party for McGuane on the occasion of the 1973 publication of his third novel, *Ninety-two in the Shade*. Tom brought Robert and Katherine Altman. The film director was interested in acquiring the movie rights to McGuane's book. In Altman's honor, pornographic movies played in the basement law library.

James D. Houston was at the party, talking with Altman for "only three or four minutes." Even in such a short time, he was impressed with the director's amazing powers of observation. "You recently had a mustache," Altman said.

"That's right," Jim replied. "I shaved it off last week."

At one point in the evening, Brautigan and Don Carpenter cornered Altman and began lecturing him. "You've got to learn something, mister," Tom McGuane remembered them saying. "You're not in L.A. anymore; you're in San Francisco." The verbal assault lasted for more than half an hour. "Their whole pitch was San Francisco is the center of the civilized world. Self-righteousness with a little Orientalism laid in."

Don Carpenter recalled the evening with chagrin. "Altman sat there, and we passed a bottle of wine around among us while I excoriated the man for his career. For his destruction to *The Long Goodbye*. Just a complete drunken asshole, no worse behavior on earth."

At last, Altman had enough. "Listen, boys," he said, "I've heard as much of your shit as I'm going to listen to." With that, "he read them the riot act." All the while, Richard Hodge sat on a couch chatting amicably with Altman's wife, who assured him of the great career awaiting him in Hollywood. Hodge had hoped the party would help broker the arrangement between Altman and McGuane. In the end, things didn't pan out.

Revenge of the Lawn was published in the fall of 1971 by Simon & Schuster simultaneously in hardback and as a Touchstone trade paperback edition. Richard traveled to New York for a publication party. While in town, he got together with Sam Lawrence, down from Boston on business. Brautigan also went out to Connecticut to spend a weekend with Rip Torn and Geraldine Page, who were starring in *Marriage and Money* at The Westport County Playhouse.

Torn was at a point in his career when he "had been eighty-sixed from films, television, and Broadway." Summer stock was his last resort. Richard called him before he opened in Connecticut, wanting to come fish in the Catskills. Rip told him he "barely had time to piss, much less fish." He'd probably be able to see him only at night after performances. Once Torn found some time, he called Brautigan in the City with an invitation to spend a couple days talking and fishing. Richard caught the New Haven train at Grand Central, alighting in Westport where Rip, Gerry, and the kids were staying at a farmhouse by the salt pond.

Brautigan seemed "itchy and perturbed," the moment he set foot in the home where the Torns were guests. He didn't care for their hosts. After dinner, the head of the household told stories about the old days in Connecticut. Rip enjoyed the tales and, staying up late with Richard afterward, asked if he enjoyed them, too. "Hell, no!" Brautigan retorted. "They're so goddamned middle-class. I come across a continent to talk with you and what do you do? You sit around bullshitting with those damn people. I'm going to see your plays, we're going to fish, and I'll ride back to the city with you and your family because I want you to go to my publishing party."

"Okay, General," Torn said.

Rip and Richard did fish the Saugatuck River, which flowed into Long Island Sound at Westport. They hoped to catch some sea-run browns but only landed "five small bluegills and one stunted bass." The Torns did not attend Simon & Schuster's party for Brautigan, and he traveled back to Manhattan by himself. Richard was standoffish and didn't talk to anyone at the party "except one particular girl" he had his eye on. Jonathan Dolger and Helen Brann felt upset and disappointed. They had hoped to take their star author out to dinner with some people they knew, but Richard made other plans.

While sales of *Revenge* remained brisk, cresting on the wave of Brautigan's enormous initial success, the numbers fell short of the totals racked up by the three Delacorte titles. The reviews were something of a mixed bag as well. "Brautigan at his most puppy-mannered and inconsequential," sniffed *Kirkus Reviews*. "At its worst, [it] sounds simultaneously like a clumsily written children's book and a pretentious piece of avant-garde impressionism," carped Anatole Broyard in the *New York Times*.

On the plus side, Sara Blackburn called Brautigan an "American folk hero" in the *Washington Post Book World*, and Larry Duberstein, writing in the *Saturday Review*, proclaimed *Revenge* to be "one of Brautigan's best books, and at his best he is a writer of surprising talent and vision."

Collaborating in the December 9 issue of *Rolling Stone*, Gurney Norman and Ed McClanahan turned their review into a lively discussion on the art of the short story, detailing the many ways Richard expanded the boundaries of the form. Norman, contrasting Brautigan's humor with his perception of Ernest Hemingway's lack of same, observed, "Suicide may have been inevitable for Hemingway, but you'd never think such a thing about Faulkner, Flannery O'Connor or Brautigan."

Richard was so pleased with their review he invited Gurney and Ed out to lunch in San Francisco. They were scheduled to pick Ken Kesey up at the airport at 4:30 pm and figured a free meal courtesy of Brautigan would be a fine way to start the afternoon. When they arrived at Geary Street around noon, Richard greeted them with a fifth of Maker's Mark bourbon, an improvement on Ed and Gurney's jug wine tastes.

After laying the dead soldier to rest (Gurney was the designated driver, so Ed and Richard did most of the drinking), they headed out to a posh Japanese restaurant, where Ed recalled they feasted on "inscrutable Oriental comestibles" washed down by quantities of Pouilly-Fuissé (a pricy French white Brautigan favored) and numerous snifters of Courvoisier. McClanahan dimly remembered them all having "a raraparooza of a fine old time."

When the hour arrived to head down to the airport and collect Kesey, Brautigan elected to go along for the ride, suggesting they all come back to the City and go out to dinner. Kesey, in town for a two-day residency at Stanford, immediately fired up a doobie in Norman's VW bus. Richard insisted they stop at a liquor store for another fifth of Maker's Mark. By the time they made it back to Geary Street, nobody was feeling any pain.

Brautigan called Sherry Vetter, inviting her over, and the discovery that the winsome schoolteacher hailed from Louisville (Norman and McClanahan were fellow Kentuckians) occasioned round after round of toasts "to Southern womanhood." Before long, the second bottle of Maker's Mark joined the empties.

Richard called ahead to a fancy Chinese restaurant, reserving a booth and ordering up a banquet known as "The Feast." This was composed in part of several whole fishes, which were consumed along with a fresh deluge of Pouilly-Fuissé. Around this time, things got a little strange. McClanahan later claimed the fellow didn't exist, but Sherry remembered a fifth man with red hair she thought was Ken Kesey's "valet."

She had a conversation with him in the restaurant hallway, and he referred to the gathering of writers as "the knights of the boothtable," telling her that they all already hated one another or would shortly, "a bunch of guys who were praising each other face-to-face, and also putting down each other's foes, and what would they do behind each other's backs?" The redheaded stranger was hardest on Kesey. "Can you imagine," he said to Sherry, "writing three hundred pages and expecting the world to support you for the rest of your life?"

After dinner, the rowdy sextet repaired to Enrico's for round after round of Irish coffee. Seated at the sidewalk café on Broadway, they loudly engaged in the popular local diversion of "spotting cheesy local celebrities" among the passing crowd. Amid shouts of "There goes Herb Caen!" and "There goes Mel Belli!" Brautigan grew sulky over the misguided notion that Kesey had been making a pass at Vetter. His unpleasant mood came to an abrupt end when Gurney, who had not been drinking and had wandered off on "a meditative stroll" through the side streets of North Beach, reappeared suddenly in front of Enrico's. In a single motion, Ken and Richard jumped up, shouting in enthusiastic unison: "There goes Gurney Norman!"

It had been a wild and woolly night. A relatively sober Gurney ferried Ken and Ed safely home to Palo Alto. The next morning, looking back from deep in the black hole of his hangover, McClanahan couldn't remember very much of the festivities, but "one thing remained luminously clear: From the Oriental inscrutables to the Irish coffee, from the first drop of Maker's Mark to the last drop of Poozley-Foozley, Richard had paid for *everything*."

James D. Houston recalled a similar evening two years later in 1973, not long before the party at the Hodge law office. He and his wife, Jeanne, had a book signing at Minerva's Owl on Union Street for *Farewell to Manzanar*, their memoir about the Japanese internment camps. Brautigan, always interested in Japanese culture and history, made an appearance and met the Houstons for the first time, inviting them to join him for dinner after the event.

"He really had a festive spirit about him," Jim Houston recalled. When the book signing ended, they all repaired to Vanessi's. By this time, the guest list had expanded to include Leonard Gardner, author of *Fat City*, and his companion, writer Gina Berriault, as well as a couple of other writers. The headwaiter knew Richard as a regular customer, greeting him with formal effusiveness: "Right this way, Mr. Brautigan."

Once they were all seated, without a word from Brautigan, several dozen blue point oysters appeared on the table. "He had a great generosity that way," Jim said.

"He loved doing it," Jeanne added. "I thought he was a very nice man. I didn't think it was ostentatious or anything like that. I felt like he just wanted to share his success."

Jeanne Wakatsuki Houston recalled a conversation she had with Richard about a letter she wrote to him in 1971 when Jim's book *A Native Son of the Golden West* was first published. She had asked in all innocence for any help Brautigan might offer to support her husband. Although Richard didn't reply at the time, he remembered Jeanne's letter and was touched by it. "I was very moved by your loyalty," he told her that night at dinner.

In his memoir, Keith Abbott documents another instance of Brautigan's spontaneous generosity. One evening, when Richard was running errands with Keith, they encountered a large group of artist amigos, Joanne Kyger, Robert Creeley, and his wife, Bobbie Louise, among them, on their way from a gallery opening in search of new adventure. Richard invited the whole crowd to dinner, saying he wanted to start repaying the many favors they had all done for him over the years.

Abbott doesn't mention the name of the restaurant. Vanessi's for classic Italian fare and the Great Eastern with its live tanks for Chinese seafood remained longtime Brautigan favorites. Richard proved a "genial host, directing the conversation from one writer to another." He graciously picked up the tab for the entire party and invited everybody back to Geary Street for a nightcap.

In 1970, Richard and Don Carpenter were among the first customers to belt one down at Perry's, on Union Street in Cow Hollow, another upmarket joint with the look of an Upper East Side New York City saloon, an imitation "right down to the ceiling tiles." Notorious as a singles bar pickup palace, Perry's also owned a reputation as a writer's hangout, frequented by newspapermen like Charles McCabe, a close drinking buddy of Richard's going back to the Jack Spicer days at Gino & Carlo's.

McCabe, "a literary Falstaff" whose prose style had been compared to Samuel Johnson and Montaigne, often composed his *Chronicle* column, "The Fearless Spectator," at the Green Street watering hole, drinking Rainier ale in his favored spot at the end of the bar by the window. "McCabe was a falling-down drunk," Price Dunn recalled, observing that his friendship with Brautigan eventually "soured." Don Carpenter remembered that Brautigan and McCabe used to meet for lunch once every week.

One day, someone told Brautigan that McCabe was laughing at him, making fun of him behind his back. "And Richard never saw McCabe again," Carpenter said. "Just on the basis of what that guy said, never went to lunch, never talked to him. If he saw him he turned the other way. He would have nothing to do with him. McCabe had no idea why and then just became virulently hateful about Richard. And printed terrible items about him in his column. But it was all Richard's fault for believing some fucking gossip."

Curt Gentry, another Brautigan crony who got his start in journalism, began palling around with Richard in the early seventies. The first time Gentry remembered going out to the Geary Street apartment was the first occasion he recalled spending any "real time" with Brautigan, "right after he had discovered Bob Dylan." Richard played the same record over and over about a dozen times "until everybody left." This was probably around 1970. Beverly Allen noted Brautigan's fondness for Dylan when she met him.

Curt and Richard hung out a lot together at Perry's, "picking up girls, getting drunk." Gentry spent four years in the Air Force during the Korean War (mainly editing a military newspaper in Japan) and had worked at the *Denver Post* and the *Chronicle*. The noted book critic Joseph Henry Jackson talked him out of a career in journalism: "If you write second things all day you're not going to write stuff at night." By the time Gentry became friends with Brautigan, he had several published books to his credit, covering prostitution (*The Madams of San Francisco*, 1964), the Tom Mooney case (*Frame Up*, 1967), the search for the Lost Dutchman Mine (*The Killer Mountains*, 1968), and the Gary Francis Powers U-2 misadventure (*Operation Overflight*, 1970).

"Richard had this terrible habit," Curt Gentry recalled. "He'd invite a couple of girls over to the table at Perry's. We'd sit down, and one of them said something that would offend him, or didn't come on to him the right way, or didn't seem to know who he was, then Richard would just go off and leave us after we'd ordered the food and I'd be stuck with the bill and the two ladies." Curt cured his friend of his bad behavior one night when two women who were roommates joined them at their table at Perry's "and Richard stomped out." Gentry took both the girls home with him that night. "When I told Richard about that the next day, he never did that again."

Most Frisco establishments tended in those days to be either bars where you went to drink or restaurants where you went to eat. What distinguished the Washington Square Bar and Grill and

Perry's and Enrico's was that all three provided both amenities. They were places where you could linger through the afternoon drinking and then stay on for dinner in the evening. Gentry enjoyed Enrico's, which had "a real street sense to it." Women working in the neighborhood strip clubs came in for something to eat "when they got off their shift at two o'clock. They served food from two till four after the bar had closed, so you got to know the hustlers, got to know the hookers, the musicians that worked around." Curt remembered one time when he and Richard "decided to see how long we could last at Enrico's. Started at eleven o'clock in the morning when they opened, and we left at four o'clock the next morning."

Enrico Banducci had ample occasion to observe Brautigan. The bluntness of Richard's approach astonished him. "There was a Tahitian girl," Enrico remembered, "and he would just fall over himself."

"I've got to fuck her," Richard told Enrico.

"You just met her," came Banducci's incredulous reply.

"Enrico, there is a feeling you don't understand," Brautigan said.

"Well, no . . ."

"There's a feeling that comes over me, and I know it's in her, too. I know she wants to fuck me. And I've got to fuck her. I'm going to ask her."

"Well, let me get out of here." Enrico anticipated an embarrassing disaster. "I don't want to see."

From a safe vantage point at the bar, Banducci watched Richard make his approach. "He walked like his feet never touched the ground," Enrico observed, describing Brautigan's prancing footwork. "And you know what? They got up and left together! I said, 'Holy Christ! Is that what you have to do to make a sale? Just say, 'I want to fuck you.'" And that's all he said to her, and she just said, 'Okay. Let's go.' He looked at me and out he went."

Not every assignation produced such a satisfactory outcome. Don Carpenter recalled the many lunches he had with Richard at Enrico's during "the golden period when he was rich." They sat outside as various onlookers were drawn to their table. "There are people in North Beach who flat fucking loved Richard because he's the most famous person they knew and he likes them and treats them well." Brautigan used all this attention to hunt for women. He'd go over to a pretty girl's table and say "I'd like to buy you lunch. Could you join us at our table? We'd like it very much if you could."

Carpenter noted this practice often led to disaster. "He's been burned a number of times. The girl is sitting with him and he's buying her drinks and it's all worship. 'I love your work.' And then the girl's husband would show up. She called her husband: 'I'm with Richard Brautigan. Come.' And he'd get burned."

The worst burning had a promising start. One rainy evening Richard picked up a woman at Enrico's. He paid for her drinks, looking over his shoulder all the while for a husband who magically didn't show up. The love god smiled, and the woman offered to take him home with her. She lived far off in South San Francisco. Brautigan hailed a cab on Broadway, and they drove through the pouring rain to the far outer reaches of the city. When they pulled up in front of her building, Richard played it smart. "Where do you live?" he asked the woman.

"I live there on the fourth floor," she replied.

"Which apartment?"

The woman pointed it out. "That's the apartment. Right there."

Brautigan told the cab driver, "You wait here, and if everything's okay, I'll wave to you from the window. Otherwise, you wait for me, okay?"

The driver agreed, and Richard went inside with the woman. He checked out her apartment, and everything seemed fine, so he went to the window and waved down at the cab, which promptly drove off into the night. At that moment, awakened from his sleep, the woman's husband strolled into the room. Brautigan walked back through the downpour, reaching his place soaked around six in the morning.

Later, relating the unfortunate episode to Don Carpenter, Richard said, "All the way home, walking through the rain in South San Francisco, I kept saying to myself, 'You've earned this, Richard. Enjoy yourself. You've earned this. You've worked for it.'"

On other occasions, Brautigan's appetite for casual sex got trumped by an overabundance of enthusiasm. Don Carpenter told of a couple different barroom pickups. "Two times, not once, but two times we picked up girls," Don recalled. "Once we went up into the hills of Sausalito with the girls, and once we went over to my house. But what happened then was exactly the same, both times.

"At one party, I was in a room with one girl, and she was on the phone, lying on top of me, and we were sharing a joint. Much younger than us. We shouldn't have been with them in the first place, but they hustled us out of a ride home from the Trident. The next thing I know, I look up and Richard is standing naked in the doorway saying, 'Let's go. Come on, let's go,' and the [other] girl comes in and says, 'What's the fucking matter with this guy?'"

The other time Don remembered: "We were over at my house. My living room was very small, and I was kneeling at the television set attempting to tune in Johnny Carson. I heard a girl behind me say, 'Umm, I think it's time to go.' I turned around and Richard was stretched out full length on the couch, naked. And the girls were sort of standing there looking a little tense. So I had to drive them back to Sausalito to the No Name Bar."

Don Carpenter also attested to Richard's kindness and generosity with his old friends. "There was no change in personality," Carpenter stated, addressing a charge that Brautigan became crazed by fame. "There was no change in character. The important things to a guy like Brautigan were loyalty and respect and honor, and those things never altered with him. He was an absolutely loyal man."

Several times, Don and Richard planned to dine together at the Washington Square Bar and Grill, the upscale watering hole that first opened its doors in 1973. It was known familiarly as "The Square" to its habitués until Herb Caen started calling it the "Washbag" and the new nickname stuck. On their way into the restaurant, they would be accosted by Jack Micheline, "this drunk old poet."

Micheline, author of *North of Manhattan* and *River of Red Wine*, had been affiliated with the San Francisco Renaissance. He was part of the local literary scene since the heyday of the Beats, and his wild unpredictable misbehavior earned Micheline a reputation as "a precursor of Charles Bukowski." Don Carpenter got "pissed off" because when he wanted to have dinner with Brautigan, Micheline "would start monopolizing Richard's time drunkenly."

"Instead of getting rid of Micheline," Don said, "Richard would have him to dinner and feed him and just be the sweetest guy in the world. Pay for it, be kind to him. Richard was recognizing something that I wasn't. Jack Micheline needed him. Needed to be seen with him, sit with him, have dinner with him. Didn't have any money for dinner. You don't ask poets to order their priorities."

Curt Gentry recalled Brautigan's kindness and generosity to Bob Kaufman. Drink and drugs had taken a toll on the black bard of North Beach. It was difficult to ascertain if Kaufman's ten-year vow of silence, embarked upon after John F. Kennedy's assassination, was the result of moral indignation or psychosis from years of substance abuse. Rumored to have first used the term "beat-nik" before Herb Caen popularized it in his newspaper column, Kaufman had fallen on hard times since his glory days as one of the founders of *Beatitude*.

Gentry remembered how Kaufman "was always hitting on [Richard] for money, you know, a dollar here and a dollar there," at a time when the culture-shocked poet had been eighty-sixed from every bar on the Beach. Brautigan never turned him down. Even if Kaufman had already put the bite on him earlier in the evening, "Richard would give him a dollar."

Cow Hollow remained far from Bob Kaufman's regular haunts, and the old beatnik poet never put the bite on Brautigan outside Perry's. Michael McClure occasionally accompanied Richard on his forays to the pickup palace after he introduced Michael's work to Helen Brann. She agreed to represent him and placed McClure's first novel, *The Adept*, a phantasmagorical murder mystery involving a hippie coke dealer, with Sam Lawrence at Delacorte. Brautigan joined Allen Ginsberg and Robert Creeley in providing enthusiastic blurbs for the book, calling it "a beautifully written psychological thriller." Michael repaid these small favors by finally completing the "sketch" he had agreed to exchange with Richard five years earlier.

"The Richard Brautigan Story" by "Miking Malecho" was a bizarre sixty-one-page quasi–science fiction fable, divided into two sections. McClure wrote the first part in the late sixties, mentioning Richard's "new blond girlfriend." The fictional narrator is "Captain Paranoia," a Halvmart, half-Martian, half-human, whose "face is a mask of rage!" He and his androids engage in relentless struggle against the Martians who have taken over the world and "secretly kidnapped" Richard Brautigan, replacing him with an android replicant. The meandering eighteen-page narrative is accompanied by thirteen cartoonish portraits of Brautigan. McClure deftly captured his friend's ironic bemusement.

The second part, called "The Brautigan Mystery: Volume Two," runs for forty-three typewritten pages, a series of "Letters to a Young Poet, by Guru Maximus (Compiled by the Editors of the College of Philandery)" purportedly published by the "Institute of Erethric Priapism, second edition, 153rd printing." The letters were "addressed to Mr. Richard Brautigan who is still struggling in the Philandery Program," trying "to achieve the degree of Doctor of Philandery." No illustrations this time. The allusions to Perry's date the manuscript to sometime after 1970.

McClure wrote of

THE THREE Ps
1. Pussy.
2. Perry's.
3. Peach brandy.

Guru Maximus instructed Brautigan in the subtle arts of Philandery, urging him to use "The Pocket Watch Technique." Set a large pocket watch in front of the twenty-three-year-old secretary he is attempting to seduce and say, "You've got nineteen minutes until screwing time, Toots."

Richard saved the manuscript until his death. Michael McClure didn't keep a copy and thought the piece had vanished.

Most of Richard's encounters at Perry's were one-night stands, while Sherry Vetter remained his "main old lady." A lone wolf like Brautigan spent much time by himself or in the company of male friends. In late September, when Richard was sitting on the terrace of Enrico's drinking wine with Erik Weber, a waiter told him he was wanted on the phone. A minute or so later, Richard informed Erik the call was for him. It was bad news. Weber's sister, Avril, had committed suicide, hanging herself from a tree behind Margot Patterson Doss's house in Bolinas. She was three months shy of her thirtieth birthday.

Stunned, Erik wandered out of the restaurant onto Broadway. Richard followed. He knew Avril and was familiar with her mental problems but still disapproved of her final decision. They walked together up a side street to Weber's truck, and Brautigan told him that suicide "was a chickenshit thing to do." Taking your own life was cowardly. Loie Weber had a different view of the situation. She regarded her sister-in-law's death as an example of Brautigan's gift for "foreknowledge."

Richard began writing *In Watermelon Sugar* in Bolinas in 1964. The novel in part was an allegory of the Bolinas lifestyle. Margaret, one of the main characters, commits suicide by hanging herself with her scarf from an apple tree. The narrator sees this tragic event reflected in the Statue of Mirrors. "Everything is reflected in the Statue of Mirrors, if you stand there long enough and empty your mind of everything but the mirrors, and you must be careful not to want anything from the mirrors. They just have to happen."

For Loie, the mirrors and their prophetic reflections were a symbol of foreknowledge. "Richard was a very intentional person," she said, "So, Margaret hangs herself, and the narrator is with Margaret's brother at the time, and Richard was with Erik at the time when Erik's sister killed herself."

By the fall of 1971, Brautigan had $105,835.57 deposited in his Wells Fargo savings account. He needed to invest some of this money but was instinctively suspicious of large financial institutions. "He didn't like banks," his accountant, Esmond Coleman, observed. "He didn't like the stock market. He didn't trust that. He was a sort of Henry George sort of tax man. He thought the only thing worthwhile was real estate. That's all he felt was of lasting value."

Richard and Sherry spent frequent weekends in Bolinas, staying at the Dosses' house downtown on Brighton Avenue or at the home the Creeleys bought halfway up Terrace Avenue. "Oh, a normal one!" Margot Doss said when she met Sherry for the first time. "One who talks. A normal one who dresses normal." The Creeleys moved to Bolinas with their family, and Bob commuted to the City to teach at San Francisco State. Crouching under stands of dripping eucalyptus, the Creeleys' place stood on an acre of land granted as payment to the town's original surveyor. Bob thought it "looked like an old New England farmhouse."

Richard loved staying with Bob and Bobbie, where he was apt to encounter lively conversation and interesting strangers. This was the time Bob came to know Richard best. "For me [he] was an excellent friend," Creeley said. Sherry remembered many evenings when the poets gathered. She thought the writers' talk was "not dialogue, all monologue."

Richard and Sherry started driving around with a Bolinas real estate salesman from the Sharon Agency downtown. "Looking at all these fancy houses," Sherry said, "the straight people houses." When the Realtor showed Richard number 6 Terrace Avenue and told him the story of the Chinese girl's ghost, Sherry tried talking him out of buying the place. "He wanted to get it because it was relatively cheap compared to the other places and it was huge."

When Richard and Sherry first visited the house she found it eerie and dark, but she thought all the old furnishings original to the place were "cool." Sherry noted many bouquets of ancient dried flowers displayed everywhere. "Hibiscus, old and fragile like pale crinkled crepe paper in white jugs," she wrote in her journal, "hydrangea, flower heads, perfectly preserved like mummy flowers in blue Ball jars." They evoked the spirit of Mary Elizabeth Parsons, who lived there at the turn of the century. Alfred B. Parsons, current owner of the house, was her direct descendant. Parsons, a hay merchant, lived south of Sacramento, in the tiny town of Clarksburg. Earlier that July, he leased his "summer bungalow" out for a year. Another improbable six-degrees-of-separation coincidence: David and Tina Meltzer became his tenants.

Richard began seriously considering purchasing 6 Terrace Avenue in late October of 1971. The sale of the house included furnishings, and Mr. Parsons had the Sharon Agency prepare a partial inventory in November, listing kitchen appliances, numerous beds, dressers, tables, lamps, and several antiques: a piano, a pair of rocking chairs, two marble-top dressers. The Meltzers, who had been in the house for only three months, hadn't expected to have their home sold out from under them quite so soon. When the actual sale appeared imminent, David and Tina made an effort to convince Richard to let them continue living in the house.

They invited Richard and Sherry over for a dinner party. Brautigan and his girlfriend drove out from the City and took a room in Tarantino's tiny motel, tucked behind Smiley's. The Meltzers were vegetarians. Tina slaved all afternoon to make a tomato and tofu quiche, the sort of meal they considered a feast. Everybody sat around a big round table in the main room, the two couples and the Meltzers' two children. "Cute little leany-beany scrawny kids," Sherry recalled.

Once the food had been served and Richard well plied with wine, David broached his plan, how they might stay on as caretakers, making sure the pipes didn't freeze, keeping the house aired out and stocked with provisions. If Brautigan wanted to come for the weekend, all he had to do was call ahead, and "they would just split and stay somewhere else."

Richard paid close attention to David's proposal. The food wasn't to his liking, and he wasn't preoccupied with eating. Sherry found the vegetarian tomato-tofu quiche almost inedible. "I ate my piece, but Richard didn't touch his. I mean, he touched it, but like one bite." Later, when they were lying in bed in the little motel room with the kitchenette, Sherry asked him, "Well, are you gonna do it? You know, let them stay?"

"No," Richard replied. "I'm not going to let them stay. That food was horrible."

"It was the food that killed her," Sherry later observed. Tina Meltzer's culinary efforts spoiled any chance of remaining in the house on Terrace Avenue. The Meltzers quickly modified their plans, deciding to leave the country once their lease was up. "We were going to emigrate to Europe," David Meltzer said. "We were exiling ourselves."

Early in December, Alfred Parsons came by the Sharon Building in Bolinas and modified the inventory before signing it. He had decided to keep the studio couch, the two rocking chairs, an oval mirror, one of the marble-top dressers, and the andirons in the fireplace. The Realtor wrote to Brautigan about these changes, suggesting the items were "easily replaceable" and "not worth ruffling [Parsons's] feathers over." He sent along the inventory, together with a copy of the original 1890 deed.

In mid-December, Richard put down $1,000 in earnest money, and Parsons and his wife signed a Bill of Sale, a Grant Deed, and an Assignment of Lease transferring the remaining portion of the Meltzers' lease over to Brautigan. Richard deposited the money he'd need to close into his checking account and flew down alone to Monterey for New Year's Eve with Price, staying at Borg's Motel in Pacific Grove. He returned to Frisco on the second, writing a personal check for $31,799.55 to the Western Title Guaranty Company two days later. Payment in full.

When Bruce Conner heard Richard bought a house in Bolinas, he was "dismayed." Conner thought Brautigan's motivation grew out of his "competitive tendency with other writers, you know, drinking at bars and hanging out at bars where writers hung out." Bruce considered Bolinas a literary hotbed crammed with "poets and writers and editors." It seemed Richard "was going to one-up them and have a bigger house than anybody." Knowing Brautigan couldn't drive and didn't own a car, Conner asked his friend why he planned on living "way out there in Bolinas."

"I bought it. I'm gonna go there when I retire."

Conner felt even more dismayed. "Richard, writers don't retire," he said. "There's no way you are going to retire."

"Yeah. I'm going to retire there in my old age."

Bruce Conner saw this in a different light. Artists don't retire. Conner thought Brautigan picked this remote house as somewhere to go when it was time to die.

Home ownership did not mean immediate occupancy. The Meltzers' lease still had six months to run. David made sure his $150 rent check arrived on time each month. Richard recorded the sums in his income notebook, adding them to a running tally of royalty payments and foreign rights advances. He took out a $50,000 insurance policy on the Bolinas house in January.

Jayne Palladino wrote to Brautigan in early February. She went by the name of Walker now. Her last love affair had ended painfully. She had passed her PhD exams. Freed from academic pressure, she felt life to be good once again. Jayne hoped to get together with Richard sometime soon.

Sherry often came by Geary Street in the afternoons after school with stacks of fifth-grade papers to correct. Richard assisted with the homework, marking errors in the young girls' writing assignments. Once the phone rang and Brautigan wandered from the room, dragging the long cord behind, engaged in an intimate conversation. A few minutes later, "a really pretty woman" arrived. She was beautifully dressed and sat on the bed opposite Sherry, who was correcting papers. The woman took off her boots and slipped off a pair of "silky knee-high stockings," cuddling back onto the bed. "What is going on?" Sherry thought. She was twenty-one and considered herself a straight girl. "The idea of ménage à trois was something I had seen in the movies," she said. Sherry started "getting a little picture here of something." She excused herself, grabbed up her coat, papers, and car keys, and bolted out the door.

Brautigan called her the next day. He was furious. "Why did you do that?" he demanded. "That was so rude! What did you think was going on?"

Sherry shouted, "I never want to see you again," and slammed down the phone. A couple hours later, Richard arrived at her apartment door, carrying a frozen duck under one arm and a shopping bag containing cans of escargot and a hardback copy of the *Larousse Gastronomique*. "This was his apology," Sherry recollected. "Will you please cook this duck? And here's the cookbook, and here's the escargot. I remember saying to him, like, never do that to me again. Never try that again. And that was all that was ever said about it. I cooked *canard à l'orange* and the escargot and everything was happy again."

Whenever Sherry spied a hard brick-shaped inedible loaf of what Richard called "hippie bread" lying on his kitchen table, she knew it came from a rival. Brautigan would say to her, "I met this girl on the bus, and then she took me to her house, and we made love, and then she gave me this bread."

Outraged, Sherry responded, "God, you probably got a disease from her, and now you'll give it to me!" Although he called her "his main old lady," Sherry knew "there would be all these other ones." She remembered Richard's attitude when he told her Bob Creeley was "dumping Bobbie" and running off to Majorca with a young blond. He boasted to her of the times he and Edmund Shea boarded a city bus and bet each other a dollar who could pick up a girl first. "Get into her pants first," Sherry elaborated. "I mean, that was exactly the way they phrased it. Whoever got laid first."

Bad boy grab-ass philandering didn't always bring Brautigan much joy. Ron Turner, founder of Last Gasp Comics, recalled an evening in March of 1972 when things weren't going so well for Richard. Ron, an ex–Peace Corps volunteer, had met Brautigan at The Pub, a bar at Masonic and Geary, a gathering place for artists where Richard often hung out. Allen Ginsberg was in town, on his way to Australia for a monthlong trip with Lawrence Ferlinghetti.

That night, Allen was visiting with Richard at the Museum, while Ron hosted a huge Last Gasp party at The House of Good, an old deconsecrated synagogue. This beautiful building, located a few blocks further downtown on Geary, had been converted into a dance hall by Jonas Kovach (aka John Kovacs), an Auschwitz survivor and former Haight Street gay bar owner hoping to compete with Bill Graham's Winterland. Turner hired several bands for the Last Gasp event and had all his comic publications displayed for sale.

Shig Murao, manager and co-owner of City Lights, came with his girlfriend, among fifteen hundred partygoers at The House of Good. As the evening settled into its groove, Murao's girlfriend, tripping on acid, returned after leaving and confronted Turner near the front entrance. "Shig's had an accident! Shig's had an accident!" she blurted. Ron asked what he might do to help and soon found himself on a street corner a block away from his big party. "The car was a mess, and [Shig] was a mess, and they took him into jail," Turner recalled. "And so, I've inherited his girlfriend who is stoned out of her mind." Trying to help, he asked where she and Shig had been going.

"To see Allen over at Richard's house," the girlfriend replied.

He was shorthanded that night and didn't want to leave the Last Gasp shindig, but Ron did the right thing and loaded Shig's girlfriend into his van, driving her over to Brautigan's place. Richard met them at the door, beverage in hand. He looked depressed, mumbling, "So, you want something to drink?" shambling into the kitchen to pour them both whiskey. Ensconced in the front room, Allen Ginsberg sat "all dressed in robes and white," reading his poetry to a group of about fifteen devoted young men, who were "just hanging on every word."

Brautigan seemed dressed in a peculiar fashion, uncharacteristically wearing a necktie. While Ron attempted to describe the predicament: Shig's accident, his own giant Last Gasp function, how Allen seemed obviously engaged—"I don't know what to do here"—the girlfriend noticed Richard's necktie for the first time. Entranced by the vibrating colors, she exclaimed, "That's the most beautiful tie I've ever seen in my life!"

Brautigan burst into tears. "That's the nicest thing anybody has said to me in days," he sobbed. Shig's girlfriend embraced Richard. "He's bubbling away," Ron said. Turner finally caught Ginsberg's attention. "Allen," he said, "We've got a problem. Shig—"

"I'm staying with Shig," Ginsberg interjected.

"Not unless he gave you a key!" Ron told him about Shig's accident, told him Shig was in jail. Ginsberg went into immediate action, manning the phone, calling various police stations, "bing, bing, bing," until he located Shig. "He's thinking really fast," Ron recalled. "The bail was something like $500 to $800, and I said, 'I don't think I've got that kind of money on me.'"

"No problem," Ginsberg said, pulling up his white gown to reveal a bulging money belt containing his Australian travel stash. "He must have two grand in there," Ron thought, watching Allen count out the bail money. They bundled into Ron's Ford van, gloomy Richard, Shig's tripping girlfriend, all fifteen Ginsberg fans, and Allen "sitting on the engine mount." After dropping the fan club off on Polk Street, they proceeded to the cop shop on Ellis. Always the loner, Richard went off on his own then, vanishing into the night while Allen Ginsberg found himself surrounded by a crowd of autograph-seeking policemen. "Only in San Francisco," Ron Turner said.

Robert Creeley used to stop by the Geary Street apartment to visit Brautigan and hang out at the Museum either before or after teaching his class at San Francisco State. "Those were really terrific times," he recalled. Creeley remembered one occasion when he and Brautigan were "together in some classic gathering in drunken company." They started sneaking out of the room. Brautigan "looks back at all these people variously plopped about and says, 'Let's leave them with a "Gentle on the Mind" number.' Most happy times."

Brautigan started seeing Jayne Walker again from time to time, cooking her occasional meals at Geary Street or going out for late-night ribs at soul food joints in the Fillmore. Other times, he took her to restaurants in Japantown, a dozen or so blocks down Geary from his apartment and to his favorite sushi bar in the Japan Center. Brautigan made it "perfectly clear" that he had been previously married and felt "that sort of exclusivity was a terrible mistake." He told Jayne he would always have many partners, and at the time, she thought, "Maybe that's a good idea." True to his word, Richard maintained his relationship with Sherry Vetter and continued prowling Bay Area bars in search of a random piece of strange.

One afternoon, Brautigan wandered into the Trident in Sausalito. Located at the end of a pier out in the Bay, the Trident was an upscale restaurant by day and a classy jazz club at night. Richard spotted some friends having a late lunch and joined them at their table. The journalist Mark Dowie (later an editor at *Mother Jones* who wrote the award-winning exposé of the Ford Pinto) sat with his fiancée, his sister, Ann, and her boyfriend, a married artist named Dugald Stermer. Brautigan knew the Dowies and Stermer. He pulled up a chair, sitting between Dugald and Mark's girlfriend, Mary Ann Gilderbloom, a tall, willowy young woman who, at five eight, weighed only 103 pounds.

Mary Ann, a fan of Richard's work, was fascinated by the way the staff ("beautiful women in diaphanous blouses") fawned over him as he entered. Brautigan ordered a drink, and she noticed he was staring at her. "He has this way of looking at women when he's in his cups," she recalled. "And he was looking at me." Mary Ann was "kind of like oblivious" during this period of her life, a naive trait she felt was part of her charm. Richard was certainly charmed. He leaned in closer and asked, "Can I ask you out on a date?"

"Thank you very much," Mary Ann replied, "but I am engaged."

"Well, should you break up with the gentleman, then can I date you?"

"That's lovely," she said. "Certainly. You'll be the first to hear." Nothing more was said of it.

Early in April, feeling a need to get out of town for a while, Brautigan caught a Continental flight to New Mexico and traveled up to Santa Fe for two weeks. This time around, Richard stayed at La Fonda, at $21 per night a much classier establishment than his previous lodging in that city. As always, he got together with the Gordons, Jorge Fick, and other friends in the area. Partied out after a week, ensconced in room 422, Richard began his first work in months, writing a sequence of eight poems.

Throughout the spring, as the term on their lease for the house in Bolinas was about to expire, the Meltzers maintained an amiable correspondence with Richard. David wrote regarding the regular bills, garbage pickup, propane, etc. Brautigan stayed away but arranged to have the roof mended. David, Tina, and the kids left at the end of June, and Brautigan drove out to Bolinas with Sherry Vetter in her little blue VW bug to take possession of 6 Terrace Avenue. On the way, they stopped at a hardware store, stocking up on brooms, mops, and about a dozen kerosene lamps, shoving them into a little car already stuffed with sheets, towels, and pillows. As Sherry busied herself cleaning the house, sweeping away cobwebs and removing squirrel nests from the outdoor cooler in the kitchen, she heard Alfred Parsons drive up in his white Mercedes.

Richard went out to greet him. Sherry watched from the deck balcony as Richard counted out money from his pocket into the old white-haired man's hand. Brautigan later told her that he was paying for the house in cash, $30,000 in hundred-dollar bills. As the purchase had been made by check back in January, this clearly wasn't true. What Richard actually paid for and just how much money he really gave to Mr. Parsons remains a mystery, his illusionary transaction another curious practical joke.

Richard and Nancy Hodge were among Richard's first Bolinas visitors, spending a weekend there shortly after he took possession of the place. Brautigan had a strange woman with him on that occasion. She wasn't familiar to Brautigan's attorney and his wife, who both knew Sherry Vetter. Richard had gone out to the house with Sherry a few days before, cleaning, moving furniture, and preparing a guest bedroom for the Hodges "with fresh flowers and fresh sheets on the bed."

At a Page Street dinner, Brautigan had asked Nancy Hodge to make curtains for the Bolinas house. Prior to their visit, Nancy bought the material ("he told me what he wanted") at a fabric store on Geary Street. Nancy brought her little portable sewing machine and spent "about ten hours" stitching up the curtains.

Tina Meltzer had gotten in touch with Richard before the end of May, sending news of their upcoming June rummage sale. At Brautigan's request, she sent him a list of the larger household items (braided rugs, bookcases, and antique dressers) they had for sale. Among the offerings was an "autoharp with case $20." Richard wasn't interested. Having gone through an unsuccessful guitar phase, he had no further aspirations for an alternate career singing folk songs in coffeehouses. He left the autoharp strumming to his buddy Michael McClure.

Richard and Michael were not friends much longer. "It was Richard buying the house that David and Tina lived in right out from under them and their two children that was the straw that broke my camel's back," McClure wrote in 1985 about why he quit speaking to Brautigan. David

Meltzer emphatically denied any such assertion. "There are all kinds of stories that like Richard threw us out and all that," he said, "That's absolutely not so. These stories I think were generated by friends in Bolinas."

Erik Weber had a different take on why Richard and Michael's friendship ended. From his perspective, it was all about money. "That's what Richard told me," Erik recounted. "He said, 'Michael asked me for a lot of money, and I turned him down.'" An earlier loan to McClure had gone unpaid. When Erik Weber's truck needed major repairs, he borrowed $2,000 from Brautigan to get the job done. Erik promised to repay the amount in monthly installments, and after he did just that, Richard told him on the phone, "You're the only person who has ever paid me back. Unlike Michael."

Siew-Hwa Beh, Richard's girlfriend in the mid-1970s, heard much the same story years later. "When Brautigan made money, McClure wanted to borrow money from Richard for a down payment on a house," she said. "Richard refused to loan the money because he felt that if he did that it might break up their friendship. He felt that once he loaned friends money things become different. But their friendship ended anyway because he wouldn't give him the money."

Brautigan had strong feelings about such transactions. In a fatherly way, he once gave his daughter some advice. "Never loan your friends any money," he told Ianthe, "or you will always be disappointed." It was best, he counseled, always to consider any "loan" to be a "gift." That way, when there were no expectations, there could be no regrets. In 1978, Ron and Kitty Loewinsohn needed to come up with a large sum for the down payment on a house they wanted to buy in Berkeley. Richard gave them the money, but the Loewinsohns considered it a loan. Influenced by Brautigan's own plaque-making proclivities, which Ron observed on a trip to Montana in the summer of 1974, he nailed an engraved bronze plaque to a post in the basement of his new house. It read: the richard brautigan memorial house.

"Ron paid him back every cent," Kitty said. Loewinsohn earned the money teaching summer school. Kitty thought "this was one reason why Richard really trusted Ron, although it was in the context of a whole life they had shared. He just felt that this was a man who kept his word, and if he said he was going to pay him back, he would do it." She sensed that Brautigan "had had unfortunate experiences with other people."

Don Carpenter recalled a time when his debt to Brautigan totaled $4,000. After Simon & Schuster paid Carpenter $25,000 for *Turnaround* in 1980, he started paying Richard back. Every time the publisher sent him an installment, he'd "slip a grand off each payment and send it to Richard," along with a formal letter saying he hadn't forgotten about the debt. "I never got $4,000 of pleasure more anywhere in my life than paying that off," Don said, "because it made him so fucking happy. He never expected to see that money again."

Around the same time, Sherry Vetter became a benefactress of Richard's philosophy when he gave her $500 to help finish building a house. "About a year after he gave it to me, I said to him that I was gonna pay him back when I sold the house," Sherry recalled, "and he said, 'Nah, forget it. Do you know how many thousands of dollars my friends owe me? Five hundred bucks is nothing.'"

Money matters aside, another possible cause for the schism between McClure and Brautigan might have been envy. Sam Lawrence once told Gatz Hjortsberg that the entire Frisco crowd was jealous of Richard's sudden and unexpected success. Richard had taken Sam out to a Marin

County picnic in Mill Valley, where Sam sensed Michael's envy during a conversation with the poet. Keith Abbott wrote in his memoir about hearing "rumblings of displeasure. The remarkable sales of Brautigan's Delacorte Press books had created a backwash of envy and jealousy among the writers" in San Francisco.

Abbott also quoted Peter Berg regarding his final break with Brautigan. The former Digger felt disgust, rather than jealousy, when considering his old friend's preoccupation with an ever-growing fame. "Richard would talk about how many books he sold last week," Berg told Abbott. "It was constant, to the point where that was his only conversation, and I started calling him Richard Career. That was the end of our relationship."

Perhaps the final words on the matter belong to McClure, who wrote "an angry poem" about Richard in the year of their breakup. He called it "Nineteen Seventy-two," and the opening lines sound harsh and accusatory:

SO, AT LAST YOUR PERSONALITY
HAS BECOME A COPROLITE!
((Fossilized shit!))

A few lines further along, Michael got to the heart of the matter:

BUT STILL I CAN HARDLY BELIEVE
that you sit there telling me:
about the women you fuck,
how much money you make,
and of your fame.
As if
the last twenty years
never happened.

It is impossible not to detect an undertone of deep resentment beneath the surface outrage of McClure's words. It comes as no surprise that he "hoped [Brautigan] would never see the poem" when it was published two years later in the collection *September Blackberries*. An important era in Richard Brautigan's life had clearly ended. Michael McClure's poem provided a bitter epitaph, not only for a lost friendship, but also for those heady bohemian years when poverty, obscurity, and art provided the matrix for a profound outpouring of literary creativity.

I N THE SUMMER of 1972, Richard Brautigan, Jimmy Buffett, photographer Erik Weber, and I set off for Sixteenmile Creek, a legendary Montana fishing spot. Our directions veered some-what askew. Finding Sixteenmile on a map, flowing out of the Shields Valley (named for Sgt. Shields, who passed through with Lewis and Clark), we assumed driving north on U.S. 89 was the best way to go, unaware the fishery was located mainly on the huge CA Ranch across the Meagher County line eighteen miles southwest. The correct approach was from the Gallatin Valley, via Maudlow.

Instead, we found ourselves in Ringling, a ghost town named for the circus family whose huge surrounding ranches once grew hay to feed their traveling menageries and the draft horse brigade hauling gilded show wagons down Main Street America. We were an odd quartet, a literary lumi-nary accompanied by three unknown artists. At this point, Buffett's career appeared to be faltering. He'd struck out in Nashville, bailed from a failed marriage, released an unsuccessful first album in 1970 (*Down to Earth* sold a total of 324 copies), and recently started working day jobs while sing-ing in Key West bars at night. The songs he wrote over the summer were soon to make him famous. This trip resulted in "Ringling, Ringling," a melancholy ditty that later graced Buffett's *Living and Dying in 3/4 Time* album (1974).

Ringling was indeed "a dying little town." All that remained of the bank was the fireproof vault, standing stark and alone amid the surrounding debris. Only the bar survived, a squat log building crouching beneath a towering aluminum Matterhorn of discarded beer cans glittering in the late morning sun. We stopped to ask about access to fish Sixteenmile and got the bad news, staying on for most of the afternoon, doing our part to enlarge the alpine empties pile.

Erik Weber remembered an aloof Brautigan sitting at the end of the bar, while the rest of us horsed around playing pinball. "He was talking to the person running the place, this older woman. But he wouldn't relax. He wouldn't have any fun."

Hoping to rescue what was left of the day, we headed later up through White Sulphur Springs to the Musselshell, a slow-moving river the color of coffee and about as fishable as an irrigation ditch. Before we encountered the final sad truth of a fruitless fishing trip, conversation in the car volleyed amiably from front seat to back. Richard grouched about bad reviews from the East Coast literary establishment. I replied that the harshest criticism I ever received came from Ben Stein, a former state senator who had edited the remarkable journals of Montana pioneer Andrew Garcia. *A Tough Trip through Paradise* was a book I much admired. When I bumped into Stein and his wife outside Sax & Fryer in Livingston the previous winter, I told him so.

Stein said he'd recently read my first novel, *Alp*. The senator further observed that it was the most depraved and disgusting book he'd ever encountered, so foul he felt compelled to carry it out back behind the barn and bury it in a manure pile.

"I said, I hoped a beautiful rose grew in that spot," I told Richard, who grinned behind a lattice-mask of steepled fingers. "Stein said the only other books that ever caused such a violent reaction were 'that *Trout Fishing* abomination! and Tom McGuane's *The Sporting Club*.'" The senator claimed to have hurled both volumes into his fireplace, burning them.

"Hmmmm," Richard pondered, covering his sly grin. "I wonder if he ever thought of drawing and quartering a book."

thirty-nine: my home's in montana

I N THE SPRING of 1968, having sold *The Sporting Club* to Simon & Schuster and ready for a new adventure, Tom McGuane picked the town of Livingston off a map of Montana. It was no random choice. Fly-fishing dictated his selection. The Yellowstone River flowed through Livingston. The Madison and the Gallatin lay within an hour's drive. All were blue-ribbon trout streams, and Yellowstone National Park, fifty-seven miles to the south, held the promise of back-country wilderness angling.

That summer, Tom and his wife, Becky, rented a nine-room, two-story brick house on H Street. The rent was $28 a month for the ground floor only. They were soon joined by Jim Harrison, J. D. Reed, Dan Gerber, and Bob Dattila, all fellow alumni of Michigan State.

Harrison, whose first book of poetry, *Plain Song*, had been widely praised, published a second, *Locations*, during his stay in Livingston. Gerber's brief but spectacular career as a Trans Am driver ended with a near-fatal crash when he ran his Ford Cobra into a concrete wall at 110 miles per hour and "ricocheted into other possibilities." Among these was *Sumac*, a literary journal Gerber founded and was coediting with Harrison. The first issue was due out in the fall. Dattila, not yet the aggressive literary agent known within the publishing world as "the Hun," worked in the rights department at McGraw-Hill. The unfurnished H Street house had wall-to-wall carpeting. Everyone unrolled his sleeping bag and crashed.

McGuane returned to Montana the following summer. Duane Neal, a professional outfitter, loaned him a small ranch in Paradise Valley, where the Yellowstone flowed north out of the park toward Livingston. Harrison, at work on a sequence of ghazals, joined the McGuanes again, funded by a Guggenheim Fellowship. By the end of August, Gatz Hjortsberg and his family rattled up the gravel road past the Pray post office in a VW microbus. *Alp*, his first novel, was scheduled for publication in the fall. Between fishing trips, the three young writers worked at separate rustic workbenches in Duane Neal's barn, portable typewriters clattering, surrounded by curling uncured deer hides and dismantled farm machinery.

By September, armed with movie-money from *The Sporting Club*, McGuane bought fourteen acres on Deep Creek, about twelve miles south of Livingston. The land surrounded an old ranch center, complete with corrals, a log barn, several venerable outbuildings, and an ancient root cellar carved into a nearby hillside. After hanging drywall to conceal the knotty-pine paneling in the farmhouse living room, Tom and Becky departed for Key West, where they maintained a winter residence, a modest one-story conch bungalow enclosed within a minijungle of tropical foliage.

McGuane's enthusiastic review of *Trout Fishing in America* appeared in the *New York Times Book Review* in mid-February 1970. More than a year went by before Brautigan exchanged letters with McGuane. Having just read and admired *The Abortion*, Tom wrote Richard in March of 1971, inviting him to come and visit either in Key West or Montana. Brautigan replied in April. McGuane wrote back in May, saying he would be out on the coast in the summer to do a magazine piece on Point Reyes, and would call when he arrived, adding, "I would love to see you."

Tom wrote again in September. He was "just sitting down, with glee," to read *Revenge of the Lawn*. McGuane thanked Brautigan for sending him a copy and wished Richard had come out to Montana that summer. Another year went by before Brautigan took McGuane up on his offer. By the summer of 1972, the ranks of the expatriate population in Paradise Valley had grown. The Hjortsbergs returned the previous fall, after sojourns in Mexico and Costa Rica, buying a three-story nineteenth-century farmhouse across the road from the Pine Creek Methodist Church.

Landscape painter Russell Chatham, his wife, Mary, and their baby daughter arrived in the spring, leaving a rented apartment upstairs at the Druid's Hall in Nicasio, California, for a stucco-covered former schoolhouse with a wood-burning basement furnace, high at the upper end of Deep Creek above the McGuanes' place. A superb fisherman, Chatham had for a period of years held the world's record for a striped bass taken on a fly.

In Key West the previous winter, McGuane made a number of intriguing new friends. Jimmy Buffett, a twenty-five-year-old country singer from Mobile, Alabama, earned a marginal living as a Key West bar singer and perfected the beachcomber lifestyle he later celebrated with great commercial success in "Margaritaville," his 1977 hit. He and Tom ran amok together, brother berserkers howling at the moon and crawling at dawn down the yellow line dividing Duval Street.

Harrison and Chatham came south that winter for the tarpon season, as they had the year before. Jim Harrison had made his first trip in the winter of 1969, before the McGuanes bought their Ann Street house and were living in a rented place on Summerland Key. The two men fished together on Tom's secondhand Roberts skiff. While hanging out at the marina one day, they encountered a tall aristocratic fellow with an unflappable demeanor. Woody Sexton, a famed salt-water fishing guide and mutual friend, introduced them to Guy de la Valdène.

An American-born French count on his father's side and a member of the socially prominent Guest family on his mother's, Guy lived a life devoted to sport, dividing his time between fly-fishing and bird hunting. Harrison later wrote, "Valdène is the best shot, and also the best saltwater flycaster I know, but I should add that this apparently isn't very important to him." The three became fast friends. When Chatham joined them in the Keys the following year, he rounded out a Rabelaisian quartet devoted to the robust pleasures provided by the pursuit of fish, game, mind-altering substances, and attractive young women.

One evening that summer, Brautigan sat at a table in Enrico's with Erik Weber and Bob Junsch. He'd known Brooklyn-born Junsch for about four years, since back when Bob tended bar at Mooney's Irish Pub on Grant Avenue. Junsch shipped out frequently as a merchant seaman, but was currently "looking for a ship," and when Brautigan mentioned driving to Montana, he was along for the ride. "Richard mentioned this trip very much like it was a business venture," Junsch said, "and he offered it to me more or less like a job, you know, as his driver."

Brautigan wanted to rent a car, a really large car. Bob rented a "big comfortable station wagon" from Hertz, putting down $650 of Richard's money as a deposit. In the second week in August, the expedition headed east over the Sierras and across Nevada, bound for Montana. Erik Weber had previously discussed going on a fishing trip with Richard and went along as the designated photographer. Bob Junsch had never seen that part of the country before and greatly enjoyed himself. Richard "was a great passenger," he said. "Terrific passenger for the long drive."

The trio planned to make it straight through in a single twenty-four-hour driving marathon but ran into car trouble in Idaho. The rental started "limping along" outside of Twin Falls. Junsch recalled that the "rear end went out." Weber remembered a bald tire. They pulled into Twin Falls for the night and negotiated for a new car the next morning at the local Hertz office. Brautigan remained aloof while Weber handled the bargaining. "Richard would have nothing to do with this. He had a hard time in pulling things like that," Weber said. "He just stood in the background while I conducted the business and got us a new car and a few days off the rental price."

When Brautigan and his pals arrived at the McGuanes' place on Deep Creek they found a full crowd already in attendance. "It was a wonderful summer," Tom's wife, Becky, said, "because everybody was at the house, which was about twenty-seven people. The main thrust was what were we going to have for dinner." Among those lining up for chow were Jimmy Buffett; his girlfriend, Jane; their chum Roxie Rogers; Guy Valdène and his gorgeous blond wife, Terry; Bob Dattila (who had operated his one-man Phoenix Literary Agency out of a studio apartment on New York's East Side for the past couple years); Jim Harrison; Scott Palmer (a young man who worked for the McGuanes); and Benjamin "Dink" Bruce, another friend from Key West, whose father hung around with Hemingway in the thirties, all drawn to Montana by what Don Carpenter called Tom McGuane's "magnetic Irish warlock personality."

Everyone, men and women alike, was attracted to McGuane. Six foot four with hair hanging down past his shoulders, shooting from the lip, punning one-liners faster than the speed of delight, Tom reached new manic heights during the summer of 1972. He had taken up the mandolin and riffed duets with guitar-playing buddy Buffett. Hard at work on a new novel set in Key West, McGuane unwound at night presiding over roundtable literary discussions in his kitchen, half-gallon jugs of bourbon and vodka fueling the energetic conversation. Becky, a petite honey blond barely five feet tall, provided the domestic glue binding this disparate social mix with her cheerful disposition and hearty crowd-pleasing meals.

Brautigan was impressed with Becky's pint-sized beauty. When he phoned Sherry after arriving, he said, "I want you to lose weight. I want you to become devastatingly thin." According to Sherry, "devastating" was a favorite word of Richard's at the time. Five feet tall and 108 pounds, Sherry reacted to her lover's request to lose weight with dismay. "God," she thought, "I only wear a size 2. *Where* can I get any thinner?"

Becky made the new visitors feel right at home. She set Richard up in the guest house, a converted one-room log chicken coop a stone's throw from the main building. Weber and Junsch bunked down in the back end of a long living room, divided in half by a Sheetrock wall. The first night, everyone gathered as usual around the round oak table in the kitchen. Tom McGuane's initial impression of Brautigan was of someone "helplessly odd under all circumstances, pauses in conversation, some of the places you weren't used to. He started stories late in the story. He had a penchant for honing in on crazy seemingly inappropriate details."

Erik remembered he and Bob "felt very comfortable, having a good time," but Brautigan proceeded to get quite drunk. "He was really loaded," Weber recalled, "annoying the hell out of everybody. The only way Richard could really talk to people that he didn't know too well was just to get totally smashed."

Late that night when everyone else was asleep, Brautigan, an insomniac, wandered into the mud room/pantry to get some ice for his drink from an old Norge refrigerator where cases of beer and soda were stored. The machine was not a defrost model, and the ice trays had frozen fast in the freezer compartment. Tugging at them, Richard pulled the whole outfit over on top of him, breaking the door off the freezer. "I heard this terrible crash," Becky recalled. Brautigan moaned, "Oh, no . . . Oh, no . . . What am I going to do?"

What Richard did do was wake up Erik and tell him to "get going and fix the freezer door." This was the sort of chore Weber normally handled for Brautigan, but he was too tired and told his friend to "fuck off." After Erik rolled over and went back to sleep, Richard started creeping up the stairs, whispering, "Becky . . . ? Becky . . . ?" in a plaintive tone.

"What is it, Richard?" she answered, thinking his voice seemed so soft he really didn't want to wake her, yet "the whole house sounded like it was coming in."

"I have a present for you," he answered.

"You do?"

"Trout money," Brautigan said. "I have tons of trout money for you." He tiptoed into the McGuanes' bedroom with about forty sheets of typing paper, each hand signed and featuring a stylized drawing of a fish, his Carp Press logo. Becky thought they looked like something her son Thomas might have drawn when he was four or five.

Tom found Richard's behavior that night completely "inappropriate, crawling up and down the stairway dead drunk writing trout money on pieces of paper, pushing it into your room, saying you're going to be richer and richer."

"These are worth a fortune," Richard said.

"What am I supposed to buy with it, Richard?" Becky asked.

"I would suggest you buy a new refrigerator."

"Well, I was going to get one tomorrow, anyway."

"You were . . . ?" Brautigan sounded extremely pleased. "That is just marvelous, because you could put these in your safe deposit box and someday they will be worth a lot of money."

"Richard thought that everything he touched was worth something," Erik Weber observed. "Anything that had his name on it was going to be worth a lot of money." Twenty years before, Brautigan had given Edna Webster his early writing saying it would be her "social security."

After handing the McGuanes a fortune in trout money, Richard crept back downstairs and exacted his revenge on Erik for refusing to help with the broken freezer door. One by one, he collected every chair in the house. As silently as possible for a staggering drunk, he assembled them over Weber's sleeping form, stacking a makeshift cage above him. Alerted by a strange noise, Erik awoke to find himself imprisoned within Richard's peculiar creation. "I couldn't get out of the goddamn bed," he said, "without knocking down all of these chairs."

After that, things settled into the usual summertime routine, badminton games out on the small patch of lawn in front of the McGuane farmhouse ("Badminton was the game of the year that year," Dink Bruce recalled), a road trip up north to Ringling, fishing on the Yellowstone or over at Armstrong's Spring Creek on the west side of Paradise Valley, and long literary conversations around the kitchen table at night. After the initial trout money fiasco, McGuane found Brautigan to be "pleasant and very nice to have around." Tom was surprised to discover that "he was a product of a very normal evolution in literary history. He liked the mainline, liked to talk about Mark Twain, William Faulkner, Ernest Hemingway, Sherwood Anderson."

Dink Bruce found Brautigan to be "standoffish." He observed that "Richard was basically quiet and sort of subdued about meeting everybody. He and McGuane got into arguments about things." Bruce eventually warmed toward Brautigan when he offered to assist in repairing a used Saks Fifth Avenue panel delivery truck Bruce had converted into a camper. Dink was installing a vent in the roof, and Richard wandered over to watch. "Can I help you?" he volunteered. Dink told him to get into the truck and hold things steady while he stood on the roof and put the screws in. "I thought that was pretty nice of him," Bruce said. "I didn't know him from Adam's apple."

At this point, Brautigan still fished as he had as a boy, without waders, no vest or net, only a minimal amount of gear besides his rod and reel and a simple canvas creel. For the first time in his life, Richard found himself in the company of world-class anglers. "He was not a very good fisherman," Guy Valdène observed. Jim Harrison had his own opinion about Brautigan's technical skills, noting, "He had awful line control as they call it, just awful. But he kept at it." Erik Weber, who knew nothing of fly-fishing at the time, accompanied the boys to Armstrong's Spring Creek, where he photographed Richard casting from the shore. He said that after observing the difference in everyone's technique, "once I saw Jim Harrison out there, I couldn't believe it. It was like two totally different ways of fishing."

Every year on the third weekend in August, the Crow Nation hosted a large powwow and Indian rodeo on their reservation on the Little Big Horn River south of Billings. It was just the sort of festive hoolihan the gang at McGuane's place couldn't resist. Well-supplied with whiskey and accompanied by John Fryer, a self-taught expert on Montana history, they all set off for Crow Agency in high spirits. Everyone except for Richard, awaiting Sherry's arrival, and Becky, who remained at home because she knew the trip was really a guy thing. The boys were gone for two days and found Brautigan in a snit when they returned. Erik said his friend seemed "very angry, upset, and not saying anything, not talking."

Richard's bad mood lifted once Sherry flew up from San Francisco for his final week in Montana. She remembered, on her first night at Deep Creek, sitting around the kitchen table eating Becky's freshly baked apple pie, along with Tom, Guy and Terry, Jim Harrison, Jimmy Buffett strumming his guitar, Erik and Bob, and a young journalist, "sort of a nerdy guy, short with glasses, dark hair," who had a tape recorder. Richard was furious at the thought of having his words recorded. "He practically broke the thing," Sherry said. "He was really angry."

Sherry stayed with Richard out in the remodeled chicken coop. She hated the place and thought "it was full of fleas." No fleas live in Montana, but there are plenty of other small biting insects. Sherry was also bothered by Brautigan's inability to see beneath the surface of the domestic situation surrounding him. Richard had been completely dazzled by the McGuanes, "hung the moon on them," in Sherry's country idiom. He adored Becky and was "smitten with Tom. Thought Tom was so great."

One night, when he and Sherry were having "a little argument" in bed, Richard held up the McGuanes as paragons of marital bliss. Sherry couldn't believe what she was hearing. How could her lover be so oblivious to what was going on right under his nose? She patiently explained what she had observed in her first few days, detailing the rift in Tom and Becky's marriage. "Richard was flabbergasted," Sherry said.

Several times, to repay the McGuanes' generous hospitality, Erik Weber cooked large Indian meals in a wok over a charcoal fire out in the yard. He acquired these exotic culinary skills during his travels on the Asian subcontinent. Tom remembered Erik cooking for as many as fifteen people at a time and regarded this as Richard's attempt at reciprocation. "He'd impose on you to the point he'd recognize his imposition," McGuane said, "and then do some tremendous thing to pay you back. He'd see that his people cooked for a few nights."

On their last weekend, Richard and Sherry went to the Jaycee Centennial Rodeo in Livingston with a bunch of McGuane's other houseguests. Before the bull rides, they watched skydivers drift down from the clouds into the arena at the Park County Fairgrounds. On a Monday morning near the end of August, Brautigan, Vetter, Bob Junsch, and Erik Weber bundled into the rental car and made "a beeline back to the city," driving straight through to San Francisco.

Two days later, Richard wrote a letter of thanks to Tom and Becky. He knew an era of his life was drawing to a close. Up in Montana, Brautigan encountered an unexpected literary scene. Something different. At Tom McGuane's place on Deep Creek, he met a group of writers who enjoyed trout fishing, drinking whiskey, and shootings guns as much as he did—writers who rejected trendy urban coteries, yet remained passionate about art and literature. And in Tom McGuane, Richard found another attractive charismatic madcap whose free-spirited energy invested the rowdy misbehavior of the group surrounding him with near-mythic import.

Brautigan hired Erik Weber to photographically document his Geary Street apartment shortly after they returned from Montana. Shooting pictures, Weber noticed numbers of cardboard boxes filled with packing material, and he had the feeling Richard was preparing to move out. Brautigan kept the Museum for almost three more years, until the building was condemned, but psychologically he had already departed. Weber's photos provided an elaborate time capsule of Brautigan's former life.

Brautigan began spending more time in Bolinas. The fogbound town made a fireplace welcome even in August, but when Richard tried to light a fire he discovered a hive of bees blocking the chimney. They swarmed into the room in a raging cloud. Brautigan hired a couple guys to tackle the problem. The bees proved a greater menace than ghosts. Joanne Kyger believed Richard invented the story of the female Asian spirit because he wanted to live in a haunted house, but she joined in the "fantasy" with the same playful spirit as when they watched *Batman* on TV together in 1965.

"He had a quirky sense of humor," Kyger said. Joanne's contribution to the haunted mansion make-believe involved helping Brautigan build a nest in his house on Terrace Avenue. "It was in an upper back room," she said. "We built this kind of thing for the ghost child to stay in. We had some twigs, and we had some feathers. It was just an elaborate fantasy sort of nest. You could get into those things with Richard."

The house in Bolinas provided Brautigan a place to entertain friends and a home for Ianthe when she came to visit. These were the first extended periods she'd ever spent with her father. She picked out her own bedroom up on the third floor, but nighttime presented a problem. Whenever the old house creaked in the wind, Ianthe thought "the ghost was going to come and visit me." The nest in the room next door was not a fantasy for a girl of twelve. The Mickey Mouse sheets and a happy face nightlight provided no consolation. Ianthe moved downstairs to a little second-floor bedroom closer to where her father slept.

In the daytime, the house transformed into a magical place. The deck was "wonderful," and a secret passage connected two of the third-floor bedrooms through a closet. Ianthe found cupboards stuffed with mysterious musty magazines from the thirties and forties. She read a batch of letters written during World War II to a girl named Polly. She played an off-key piano downstairs. Sherry taught Ianthe how to bake chocolate cakes in the spacious kitchen.

Over Easter vacation, when she spent a week in Bolinas, Ianthe and her father had a debate about the TV. Richard wanted to watch the Lakers game, Ianthe preferred *The Brady Bunch*. A bet was proposed. "We did a lot of wagering together," Ianthe wrote in her memoir. "I got most of my allowance raises from winning bets."

Betting with Brautigan "often involved elaborate preparations." Father and daughter searched the backyard for perfect-sized pinecones. Teasing was part of the process, and Richard firmly insisting he was going to win. The bet involved tossing the pinecones at a wastepaper basket from a measured distance. Whoever made three baskets in a row was the winner and got control of the television. "He let me win," Ianthe wrote, "and I was allowed to watch my program, only cutting to the game during commercials."

"He was so good to her," Sherry recalled. "And she loved him so much."

Ianthe hung out on the beach near the Jefferson Airplane house, hoping "that this time the band would be home and someone famous would come to that gate and use the speaker phone." No one ever did.

The Bolinas house provided ample space for dinner parties, and the second floor filled often with hard-drinking writers and poets. When the Creeleys came, the drink and talk went on until dawn. Sherry cooked elaborate meals, assisted by Nancy Hodge whenever she and Dick were on the guest list. Brautigan prepared his signature spaghetti dinner for Joanne Kyger, Bobby Louise Creeley, and Ron Loewinsohn, who brought his new girlfriend, Kitty Hughes, a graduate student at Berkeley, where he was teaching.

Kitty's parents hailed from Nebraska. She was a second cousin to Bruce Conner. Kitty studied at Bryn Mawr and the University of Pennsylvania and taught at Norfolk State, a black college in Virginia. Two of her colleagues there had known Loewinsohn at Harvard. Later, when she encountered them again at Berkeley, they introduced her to Ron. Tom and Becky McGuane also arrived for the spaghetti feast. Kitty Hughes thought they "looked sort of yuppie." Becky struck her as "a suburbanite." Kitty wondered what she was doing in this crowd. "She was perfect in some way," Hughes recalled, "but she was also the domesticated kind of trophy of this guy."

The first time Tom McGuane was introduced to Dick and Nancy Hodge, he showed up in Bolinas with a woman no one knew. Ianthe enjoyed all the wild evenings, "marathons [. . .] filled with a kind of foot-stomping, boisterous noise that chased all my kid fears away." After a harrowing few days when Ianthe had been sick and throwing up, Brautigan phoned Sherry Vetter. "You've got to come up and get her," he pleaded. "She's driving me crazy. I can't get any work done." Inspired by his Montana trip, Richard had started the Western novel he had dreamed of for so long. He had not written a novel in six years and was desperate to avoid any distraction.

Vetter taught a fifth-grade class in the City. She regarded his request as "way beyond what a regular friend would ask." Sherry called him on it. "This is what you do," she told Richard, "you never say please and you never say thank you. The request is always really beyond friendship. You're trying to get people to prove over and over that they love you and you want them to fail. Because then it would prove that they really don't love you like your mother didn't."

Sherry still found the time to drive out to Bolinas. She sat in the little blue bug, with Ianthe beside her and the motor idling, preparing to depart, when Richard appeared at the open driver's side window. "He did a deep plié, his hands on the car door." After repeated entreaties of "Daddy, Daddy, will you miss me?" answered by multiple pledges of devotion and an urge that they "get out of here," Ianthe reached over to Richard and said, "Think of me."

Brautigan stared past Vetter at his daughter. "I think only of you," he said. The "beautiful sweet" moment hung in the air.

Sherry took Ianthe shopping and then drove her up to her mother's place in Sonoma ("the flies on the ceiling of the hippie house kitchen, the women forlorn, overwhelmed"). She hesitated on her return at the fork in the road. Either back to the City or over the hill to Richard. He'd begged her to come back, but his recent heavy drinking argued against it. Sherry turned right toward Bolinas, a place she always thought of as "spooky. God, did the sun ever shine over Bolinas?"

She arrived back at Brautigan's house in the late afternoon. He had already gone to Smiley's. Richard left her a note: "I am at the bar." Sherry felt happy being alone. She sat in the growing dark, "listening to the ocean, distant, murmuring." Later, she read and prepared an omelet, glad "not to have to smile and listen to philosophical gibberish: writers' conversations." After eating, Sherry picked up Ianthe's scattered play clothes and got ready for bed, putting on a pair of pajamas but not unpacking her canvas bag. Snug in the big brass bed on the second floor, she phoned Ianthe, who asked for her dad. "He's in the bathtub," Sherry lied.

"Go holler at him and get him. Make him talk to me!"

"He'll call later, but don't wait up in case he forgets."

Sherry prowled the house, examining the bouquets of dried flowers gracing every corner, ghostly decorations from the past she believed had been placed there by Mary Elizabeth Parsons seventy years earlier. She followed her own advice and didn't wait up for Richard. After she fell asleep, nothing disturbed her until she heard an approaching car around three in the morning. Sherry awoke as someone delivered Richard from the bar. She felt vulnerable in bed. Not knowing Brautigan's "state of inebriation" made her jump from under the covers and run into the kitchen.

The door to a screened-in outdoor cooler stood in the far wall. Sherry and Richard had long used this secret vantage point to observe who was coming to visit before deciding whether to lie low. She opened the cooler door and looked down through the bottom slats at the back stairs leading up to the second-floor redwood deck, "like a child in a hide-and-seek game." Richard stood at the foot of the stairs, clutching both railings, "leaning forward, waiting for his head to clear."

Brautigan threw back his head and called, "Sherry . . ." Getting no answer, he started laboriously up.

Sherry watched from above, frozen, unseen, and "by the weaving of his body, the looseness of his limbs, the shadow of his long torso cast across the hillside below him from the floodlights affixed to the house," she saw he was quite drunk. Four steps up, Brautigan's right foot broke through a rotten tread, catching his leg, fracturing the femur when he tried to jerk it free.

Richard wailed in pain. He lurched forward, disappearing from view.

Sherry left the kitchen and walked to the French doors opening out onto the deck at the other side of the house. As she fiddled with the lock, she heard him coming and "a great overwhelming anger" rose within her. It squeezed the breath inside her chest. Sherry saw Richard's "white face leering through the glass" at the door. She pushed the door open and sent Brautigan "reeling across the deck in a crazy dance. Winding down like a top off its spin."

Richard spun out of control, screeching, arms flailing. He collided off-balance with the railing and seemed in danger of toppling over. Sherry rushed out into the heavy ocean fog, tripping on a deck chair, grabbing the back of Brautigan's broad leather belt before he lost complete control. "Die now!" she thought, her inner rage ablaze, knowing a simple push would send him to his doom. Instead, Sherry pulled Richard toward her, and he collapsed in her arms.

"My leg," he cried. "I broke my leg!"

"Come inside." Sherry helped Richard to the bed and calmed him with coffee. Pulling jeans and a windbreaker over her pajamas, she set off through the night to the home of Dr. John Doss, who had given up his lucrative city practice to become "a hippie doctor" in Bolinas. The Dosses were not at home, but their three sons slept with their girlfriends in a converted garage behind the big Victorian summer house. Sherry woke them, pleading, "Please. I can't get him down the steps by myself."

Jock Doss returned with her and helped Brautigan into Sherry's VW. The long day of driving had come full circle. "For the fourth time in one day," Vetter recalled later, "over the hill and back into the city with the man she says she loves folded up like an accordion in the front seat of the bug, moaning out at every sharp curve."

Sherry drove Richard to Kaiser Permanante near his apartment on Geary and waited while Dr. Daniel Boone from Kentucky set his leg. Something had changed in the past few hours. Sherry felt "the first break" in their friendship. She took Richard the final few blocks home, and had her last sight of him, leg encased in a fresh white cast, pulling himself backward up the front steps of his dilapidated building.

Over the next few days, Richard phoned, pleading, "What am I gonna do?"

"You'll have to get somebody else to take care of you because I'm not going to do it," Sherry said. She didn't see Brautigan again for four months.

Richard told his daughter he broke his leg in broad daylight, tripping over an exposed root while walking on his property. No mention was made of Smiley's. Ianthe remembered the difficult time her father had getting about on his crutches, hating every invalid moment. "He did a lot of hopping around the Geary apartment, the sight of which made me giggle." Brautigan felt imprisoned by his immobility. "Hopping got old very fast," he told Ianthe.

A copy of the first book-length critical study of his work arrived in the mail. *Richard Brautigan*, a slim 206-page paperback original by Terence Malley, a young professor at Long Island University, was the second volume in a series of "critical appreciations" called "Writers for the Seventies." Richard didn't particularly care for Malley's interpretations of his writing but wrote a short letter thanking the author for sending the book. Around the same time, Houghton Mifflin published *The Best American Short Stories—1972*, edited by Martha Foley. Along with work by Robert Penn Warren, Ward Just, and Cynthia Ozick, the book included Brautigan's story "The World War I Los Angeles Airplane." The "East Coast literary establishment" Richard griped about had recognized his work along with the cream of contemporary American literature.

When Sam Lawrence came "out to frolic" for five days in San Francisco at the end of October, Richard, feeling miserable and incapacitated, spent only a brief amount of time with him. Sam thought of Richard as "the prodigal son" and longed to have him back under his imprint. Brautigan liked and admired the publisher but had been very unhappy with Dell's poorly designed first paperback edition of *Trout Fishing*. He resented the extra work imposed on him when the production department ignored his design specifications.

Housebound with a broken leg, having Loie Weber handle all the correspondence from her home on Potrero Hill, Brautigan worked on his novel. Richard had wanted to do a Western for years. His recent trips to Texas, New Mexico, and Montana charged his imagination. Standing out in the desolate Rosario cemetery taking notes on the crumbling Maderfield tomb suggested the notion of a cowboy gothic. After traveling to Texas, Richard jotted down a possible title for just such a book: "Which then from Death Will Come, A Gothic Western." In his next four-by-six notebook, Brautigan listed fifty-seven possible titles, ranging from the prosaic ("Nurse on Nightmare Island, "The Witch of Blackbird Pond," "Mansion of Evil") to the poetic ("Winterwood," "Echo in a Dark Wind," "Nor Spell, Nor Charm"). "House at Hawk's End" hinted at his eventual choice. Random notes followed: "Possibility of combining gothic novel with western ending," he wrote. "A large gothic house in eastern Oregon." The ideas took shape. "Have the plot that you've already written arrive the house and the book ends with them walking into the house and the door closing after them [. . .] Chapter with Mary Shelly [*sic*] as she is making love and all she wants to do is write [. . .] There are always beautiful young women on the covers of gothic novels. The dark mysterious power of gothic novels."

On another notebook page, Richard sketched an enigmatic outline:

Structure of novel.

Part I: Gothic Covers

Part II: Tuna and Saddle

Part III: Thanatopsis

Ending: They are changed into a gothic cover. Or, they go into the house, the door closes, then the girl runs out. She looks behind her. She looks terrified but really she is smiling.

Again, as had been his practice ever since starting on *Trout Fishing*, Richard Brautigan began working on a new novel by setting down random notes. When the time felt right he knew the work would come in a rush of energy. The only new work since returning from Montana was either poetry or short pieces like "The Last of My Armstrong Spring Creek Mosquito Bites," an off-kilter fishing reminiscence Brautigan wrote in Bolinas several days after his visit with the McGuanes.

In November, Mary Ann Gilderbloom returned to San Francisco after "four or five" months in Europe. She had left abruptly after Mark Dowie broke off their engagement with an unexpected "Dear Jane" letter. Back in the city, Mary Ann found a place to live on Ninth Avenue, a "hippie enclave" in the Sunset District, and got a part-time job as a bookkeeper at Philobiblon, a bookstore at 50 Maiden Lane, just off Union Square. Before long Gilderbloom was one of three comanagers.

Richard Brautigan was the first person to call Mary Ann upon her return from Europe. "I hear you're free," he said and asked her out. They soon started dating regularly.

Richard's courtship proved both courtly and romantic, with many "long talky dinners." Lots of time was spent in the Geary Street kitchen, where he would read poetry while they drank "copious amounts of Courvoisier with a Cointreau top." Brautigan brought Mary Ann out to Bolinas, telling her he had recently purchased his house and adroitly avoiding any mention of Sherry Vetter. "The place in Bolinas actually kind of freaked me out," Mary Ann recalled. "It was kind of creepy. I wouldn't have spent a weekend alone in that house."

Gilderbloom made herself useful at the Bolinas house. Skilled with a needle, she sewed all the cushions for Richard's dining room. She prepared pancakes from scratch for breakfast while Ianthe squeezed fresh orange juice. One day, randomly browsing through an old wooden chest, Mary Ann came across a 1901 edition of *Wedded and Parted*, a novel by Charlotte Braeme, originally published in 1883. The heroine was named Lady Ianthe. "Look at this," Mary Ann said, showing the book to Richard, who passed it along to his daughter. Ianthe, long convinced her name was unique, found this literary coincidence "a bit startling."

Bolinas provided Brautigan and Gilderbloom a vibrant social life. There were lively parties at the Creeleys'. "He was such a decent man," Mary Ann said. "More drydock than Richard." She recalled their heavy drinking. "I remember going to the Creeleys' one night, and there were a whole bunch of people, and the house was just warm and ripe. Bobby Louise was such a woman. She had this voice and this sexiness about her."

Gilderbloom recalled spending time at Don Allen's house in Bolinas. "Really incredible evenings at the Allen household, which was nice and small and totally intimate and wonderful warm and filled with a soft yellow light." Don also entertained in the daytime. "We'd all be at his house on a Sunday afternoon," Mary Ann remembered. "A whole bunch of us were sitting on the front porch and somebody pulled out a joint. They were passing it around, and it came to me, and [Richard] came and he put both hands on my shoulders, and I passed it right by. He didn't expect it of me." Once, in a glow of good spirits after an agreeable bohemian soiree, Brautigan told Gilderbloom that "when he died he wanted to be burned in a big fire-pyre on the Bolinas beach. Then you can just ship me out on a big wooden raft."

When his walking cast came off for good in November, Richard flew down to Monterey for a long weekend of frolicking with Price Dunn. As always, he stayed at Borg's Motel. Brautigan returned to San Francisco just before the end of the month and departed the next day for New York, flying on American with his daughter, Ianthe's first trip to the East Coast. They checked in to a suite at One Fifth Avenue for a two-week stay, and Richard stocked the place with an ample supply of Courvoisier.

Ianthe had a fine time in New York. Her father gave her cab fare and expense money. She went ice skating at the sunken Lower Plaza in the heart of Rockefeller Center and attended the ballet at Lincoln Center on her own. Treating her like a grown-up, Brautigan brought Ianthe to dinner at Helen Brann's Sutton Place apartment. Bored with the literary shoptalk, she spent the evening playing with Denver and George.

When Ianthe wanted to see more of the city, Richard asked Gatz Hjortsberg, a native New Yorker, to guide them on an improvised tour. In town to attend a *Playboy* awards banquet at the Four Seasons (an abbreviated version of his novel *Gray Matters* garnered Best First Contributor), Gatz had been trampled by a rodeo bull the month before on assignment for *Sports Illustrated*. "All covered in hoof-prints," Tom McGuane observed.

Late in the morning of the day the *Apollo 17* lunar module set down on the surface of the moon, Richard and Gatz, both limping, explored Manhattan, an adventure planned for their daughters. Ianthe enjoyed looking after six-year-old Lorca, holding her hand as they hurried across crowded streets and down into numerous subway stations. Their first stop took them far uptown, to Fort Tryon Park.

They came to see The Cloisters, a branch of the Metropolitan Museum of Art located on a four-acre hill at the upper end of the park. Built around enclosed quadrangles with architectural elements salvaged from several abandoned French Romanesque and Gothic monasteries, The Cloisters housed a portion of the Met's astonishing collection of medieval art. Unfortunately, the place was closed on Mondays, a fact lost on Brautigan's native-born guide. It was a clear windy morning, and the intrepid quartet wandered around the exterior terraces and sere winter gardens.

By lunchtime they were famished. Gatz led his charges from the very top of Manhattan to the Fulton Fish Market on the East River just below the Brooklyn Bridge. In the midnineteenth century, the area bustled with activity, alive with ship chandlers' shops, sailmakers' lofts, counting-houses, and warehouses, the very heart of the port of New York. China clippers moored in every slip, upthrust bowsprits angling out over South Street. This was the city familiar to Herman Melville. By 1972, the place teetered on the precipice of oblivion. All Melville would recognize from the great age of sail were old Federal-style red brick buildings, constructed between 1811 and 1813, now mostly boarded up, slate tiles slipping off their mansard roofs. The Fulton Fish Market, built in 1822, was one such survivor.

Richard found the old neighborhood fascinating. Gatz brought them to Sloppy Louie's, a venerable seafood restaurant across South Street from the Fish Market. The place remained at heart a workingman's joint, with sawdust-covered floors, mirrored walls, a pressed-tin ceiling, and twelve bare wooden tables scarred from decades of use. Sloppy Louie's served an extensive variety of fresh seafood at reasonable prices. Richard, Gatz, and their daughters ordered from the daily menu hand-lettered with wet chalk onto a large mirror at the back of the room.

After lunch, they walked for a couple blocks along South Street, turning west on Maiden Lane and continuing south to Wall Street through the coffee-roasting district. Gatz directed his party into the heart of the Financial District. Much to Richard's delight, he pointed out the large bomb scars pockmarking the marble facade of J. P. Morgan & Company, remnants of an anarchist attack in 1920 that killed thirty-eight innocent pedestrians.

Continuing westward on Wall to Broadway, they spent a short time exploring the Trinity Church cemetery, where Richard lingered for several intense minutes staring silently at Alexander Hamilton's tomb. Soon, they all headed south down Broadway, urged along by the daughters, who anxiously anticipated their final adventure of the day, a trip to the Statue of Liberty.

The ferry trip across the upper bay over to Liberty Island took fifteen minutes. After disembarking, the four gawking tourists traversed the back end of the small island, sharing an unspoken excitement. Even Gatz felt an unfamiliar thrill. Like his companions, he had not been here before. Native-born New Yorkers never do anything so corny as visiting the Statue of Liberty.

The interior of the giant statue was even more amazing than its dramatic exterior. An elevator carried them up through the ten floors of the pedestal, after which they climbed a circular iron staircase for the next twelve stories. They ascended slowly. Richard's recently mended broken leg caused him considerable discomfort. Up in the crown, the incredible gull's-eye view of the harbor and the Verrazano Bridge provided an ample reward for the rigors of the climb. A pale winter sun hung low over New Jersey. The day was ending.

It was cocktail hour back in Brautigan's suite at One Fifth Avenue. Richard got two water tumblers from the bathroom, filling them both to the brim with Courvoisier: his idea of a proper drink. Brautigan downed the first as if it were tap water and poured himself another. Gatz had a harder time, taking small cautious sips. He'd hardly drunk a finger or two before it was time to leave for dinner. Richard gave his twelve-year-old daughter some money to take Lorca to a Greenwich Village restaurant before heading out into the night.

Brautigan reserved a large table at Max's Kansas City. When he and Gatz arrived, most of his guests were already there. Bob Dattila, Marian Hjortsberg, and the actress Jada Rowland were among the group. Marian and Gatz had been having marital problems. She and Lorca came earlier to the city without him, staying in Jada's Midtown apartment. Jada and Gatz had been friends since high school. She debuted on Broadway at age four with Katharine Cornell and created the part of Amy Ames on the soap opera *The Secret Storm* when she was eleven, staying with the show for its entire twenty-year run. Jada came with another actress friend. Penelope Milford had appeared recently on Broadway in *Lenny*, a play about the late comedian Lenny Bruce.

Richard called for bottle after bottle of Pouilly-Fuissé. When the raucous conversation turned literary, Penny Milford said that her favorite writer was Richard Brautigan. The long table fell silent as she went on, enthusiastically describing her great affection for his work. By degrees, it became apparent that Penny was unaware the man with the long blond hair and drooping mustache seated at the head of the table was Richard Brautigan. Someone finally nudged Penny and told her the truth. "No, it can't be," she insisted. Everyone chimed in, insisting the tall stranger was Brautigan. Penny took a longer look, overcome by acute embarrassment. Richard beamed with undisguised pleasure.

For the rest of the meal, Brautigan focused his attentions and charms on Penny. When the party drew to a close, Richard picked up the $93.60 wine tab. Penny invited everyone to her loft downtown for a nightcap. Jada, Marian, and Gatz piled into the cab along with Penny and Richard, not ready to call it a night.

Penny Milford's loft occupied an entire floor of an old industrial building, one vast room providing most of the living space. Against a bare brick wall at the far end, brass cymbals gleaming in the dim light, a drum kit seemed somehow out of place. Penny fixed everyone drinks. The conversation subsided into a gentle murmur. It was well past midnight. Like a deflating balloon, essential energy transpired from the occasion. Penny's boyfriend burst into the room. He was Richard Gere, an unemployed and as-yet-unknown actor. Richard Brautigan leaned toward Gatz. "We better go," he whispered. "No percentage in sticking around."

Jada dropped them off at Richard's hotel suite. Ianthe and Lorca were fast asleep. Brautigan offered more Courvoisier, but Gatz felt too queasy for another drink. He burned with fever. Marian also felt sick, so Richard kindly gave them his bed for the night, sleeping on the couch in front of the television. Gatz and Marian had the flu. In the morning, the fruity smell of spilled cognac nauseated them and they retreated to Marian's aunt's place in Connecticut to recuperate. Two days later, Richard and Ianthe returned to San Francisco.

Back on Geary Street, Brautigan got word of an unexpected surprise. The same day Richard flew back from New York, *Apollo 17* astronauts Harrison Schmitt and Eugene Cernan had lifted off from the moon. They had discovered a small crater about the size of a football field and less than thirty yards deep that they named "Shorty," in honor of Trout Fishing in America Shorty. On the rim of this crater, the astronauts had made an even more important discovery, a yard-wide patch of bright orange dirt vented up as a fumarole from deep beneath the moon's surface, "the greatest single find made during America's six explorations of the moon."

Back on earth, the new year of 1973 began badly for Timothy Leary, who had slipped away from the Black Panthers in Algeria, taking refuge in Switzerland. His wife, Rosemary, left him, and the acid guru took up with Joanna Harcourt-Smith, a jet-setting playgirl. The pair traveled on to Afghanistan, where they were immediately busted in Kabul, set up by Leary's son-in-law. In January, accompanied by Federal Narcotics Bureau agents, Leary was flown to Los Angeles. He wound up at Folsom Prison facing twenty-five years of hard time, by ironic coincidence in a cell across the corridor from Charlie Manson.

Preoccupied with typographical nit-picking involving the forthcoming Dell editions of his first three books, Richard Brautigan did little new writing. He continued taking notes for his projected Western novel but had not yet started on the book. He fussed with Loie Weber over the correct spelling of "harpsichord," the accidental addition of an "a" by a typesetter, and changing the word "while" to "a while" on the page proofs. Brautigan had Helen Brann insist that Dell pay Loie $4.50 an hour to "go over" the page proofs, comparing them to the corrected galleys. Dell refused to pay the $90 billed by Brautigan for Loie Weber's editorial services. In the end, Sam Lawrence wrote Richard a personal check, insisting that if he wished to check the galleys again "it will have to be at his own expense."

Ken Kesey wrote Brautigan in February, telling him about *Spit in the Ocean*, his new alternative magazine, and asking if he might be interested in becoming an editor. The theme of the first issue was to be "Old in the Streets." Richard said he was not an editor. He offered a poem instead. "The only literary activity I am interested in is writing," he wrote to Kesey, "and as you know, at best, that is like having a bull by the balls at midnight in a bubble gum factory." He wished Ken good luck with his new project.

Jayne Walker (formerly Palladino) wrote to Richard in mid-February, saying she'd like to see him, having recently had an "absolutely outrageous" dream about him. She included her phone number. She would have called but Brautigan had changed his number so often. Richard got in touch with her. They soon started keeping company again.

Brautigan took Walker out to Bolinas for the weekend. Jayne found the place "ultragloomy, the creepiest house, a horrible house," and couldn't figure out why he'd ever bought it. "Incredible cobwebs" hung down from the "cathedral ceiling." She thought he'd just moved in. Jayne couldn't stand it. When Richard left the room, she got a broom from the kitchen and started "swatting at the cobwebs." Brautigan raced back into the room, greatly disturbed.

"Don't touch those cobwebs," he shouted. "I love those cobwebs. I want them to stay exactly the way they were." Jayne knew nothing about the resident Chinese ghost but thought Richard wanted his own haunted house, an Addams Family mansion.

The next morning, Robert Creeley, a poet Jayne greatly admired, came over for breakfast. Richard had turned her on to modern writers, and she took a graduate seminar in contemporary poetry with Tom Parkinson at Berkeley in the summer of 1971, writing a long paper on Creeley, Robert Duncan, and Charles Olson. Jayne had the feeling Brautigan invited Creeley over as a special treat for her. She sensed that Richard and Bob "were very uncomfortable with each other, and they talked with difficulty." Jayne detected a certain shyness in their relationship. She was also struck with the way Creeley talked "in really short bursts, only two or three words at a time. Just like his poems." This was the only time Jayne Walker visited Richard in Bolinas. She never saw Robert Creeley again.

Whenever Walker went to see Brautigan on Geary Street they launched into lengthy and detailed conversations covering everything from literature to politics. "He was really fascinated by San Francisco city politics," she said. Richard cooked for her once or twice, but most often they got so caught up in their heated talks that it would suddenly be ten thirty or eleven at night and they would head over to some late-hour soul food place on Fillmore Street for a couple orders of ribs.

Brautigan repeatedly returned to certain conversational topics. His literary reputation provided a favorite theme. He expressed frustration at begin typecast as the hippie writer. "Not that he didn't do everything in the world to encourage this identification," Jayne recalled with amusement. Once Richard "talked on and on about all of the ways in which he wasn't a hippie. He just spoke with such horror and contempt of the drug culture. He really didn't believe at all in the hippie rejection of the work ethic." Jayne was convinced by Brautigan's reasoning. "He obviously does come from a different generation," she said.

Brautigan kept in touch with Gatz Hjortsberg, who patched things up with Marian. Gatz suggested that on his next Montana trip Richard might stay at the Pine Creek Lodge & Store, less than a quarter mile up the old East River Road from his place. The establishment's name was misleading. There was no lodge. The Pine Creek Store, a simple one-story log building with a front entrance of river rock, was built in 1946. A number of simple cabins were added later on the other side of an irrigation ditch flowing beside the store. Most resident tourists incorrectly assumed it to be Pine Creek. Only the first two cabins, built of logs and closest to the road, had any substance; the others were little more than plywood shacks. They could be rented daily, weekly, or monthly.

Dave and Sue Dill, a young couple from Long Beach, California, had recently purchased the Pine Creek Lodge. They redecorated the store, putting in a lunch counter where Mrs. Dill served sandwiches and home-cooked meals. Dave was a fly-fisherman, hoping to guide and sell his own hand-tied flies. In March, Gatz gave Richard's name and address to Sue Dill. She mailed Brautigan a copy of their recently printed brochure. Richard got back in touch, reserving the Dill's best cabin for the coming summer.

In April, Richard filed his tax return right on time. Brautigan's gross earnings for 1972 came to $101,826. Esmond H. Coleman, CPA, reduced this to an adjusted gross income of $95,001. Brautigan's tax bill came to $36,458. He had already prepaid $24,990 and sent the IRS a check for $11,633 including a $165 penalty for underestimating his tax payments. Mr. Coleman received $300 for his services, double Brautigan's charitable contributions for the year. Not that Richard wasn't generous. Keith Abbott never saw him refuse a panhandler.

Richard Brautigan first met his Japanese translator around this same time. Kazuko Fujimoto moved to California from Tokyo when her husband, David Goodman, resumed his graduate studies at Stanford. Unhappy with Palo Alto, they relocated to San Francisco. One afternoon, the Goodmans went to lunch at the Suehiro restaurant in Japantown and Fujimoto spotted a man with long blond hair seated with a friend at a nearby table. Kazuko decided it must be Brautigan. Gathering her nerve, she approached his table and said politely, "Not to disturb your lunch but

I would like to introduce myself. I am the Japanese translator for your *Trout Fishing*." Brautigan seemed very pleased to meet her. Fujimoto told him she had some questions about the book but knew this was not the proper occasion. Richard gave her his address, and they agreed to get together sometime soon.

A week or so later, Kazuko phoned and said, "I'm coming, and I'll bring some lunch. Am I right to assume that you don't eat sandwiches?" A few days later Fujimoto drove over to Geary Street with a freshly baked salmon soufflé. Kazuko was "very touched and impressed" that Richard had prepared steamed asparagus. Knowing the importance of the visual in Japanese cuisine, he had lined up the stalks in a "very nice way." She thought, "This is a sensitive thing to do."

After their lunch, Richard and Kazuko had "a nice conversation" lasting several hours. She recalled, "He was very generous in answering my questions." Aside from the Rizzoli edition of *Confederate General*, foreign editions of Brautigan's work were a recent manifestation of his growing popularity. He told her that usually he had no interest in knowing what went into the translations of his work because, through friends, he had discovered many errors had occurred over which he had no control. Brautigan wanted to make sure the Japanese version was "right." Richard told Kazuko that in the 1972 Dutch translation of *Trout Fishing*, his reference to a "tropical flower" had mysteriously transmogrified into a "gay man." Fujimoto recalled Brautigan was "horrified" by this error. She resolved not to make the same mistakes.

One thing Kazuko observed in the Museum, along with the line of crude fish outlines painted on the hallway floor, was Richard's inflatable trout. Fujimoto thought it funny. Brautigan told her he took it with him when he traveled, keeping it in his shirt pocket. "And when the attendants come around and ask what I want to drink," he said, "I tell them maybe a martini or something like that and I take [the balloon fish] out and say, 'One more for this guy.'"

Fujimoto and Brautigan met several times afterward in coffee shops and restaurants to discuss the progress of her translation. She asked many questions. Richard was always thoughtful and concise in his answers. Impressed with her thoroughness and professionalism, Brautigan instructed Helen Brann to include a clause in all his Japanese foreign rights contracts stipulating that Kazuko Fujimoto was to be his designated translator.

Richard continued seeing Jayne Walker from time to time throughout the spring of 1973. That summer Walker left on a trip to Europe and Brautigan started dating a young Japanese American nurse named Anne Kuniyuki. Don Carpenter recalled that no one ever saw her. Richard "would call her up and she would come over at eleven or twelve at night when she got off her nursing shift." Anne Kuniyuki hailed from Honolulu, Hawaii, and aspired to be a potter. Along with a full-time job, Anne studied ceramics at the San Francisco extension of the University of California. When she first met Richard, she needed to find a new apartment. Her busy life demanded juggling her job with school and the drudgery of house-hunting. Richard Brautigan brought Anne Kuniyuki to dinner often at Page Street and to Richard and Nancy Hodge's home in Berkeley. Nancy remembered that Brautigan seemed "quite fond" of Kuniyuki.

Around this time, Richard started writing the Western he had toyed with in his imagination for so long. He followed the scheme he worked out in his notebooks: combining two different genres, a cowboy story and the gothic novel. As always, he incorporated many elements from his actual life.

Set in 1902, Brautigan's story opened in a pineapple field in Hawaii, both a sly joke (the islands are the westernmost point in the United States) and a nod to Richard's recent friendship with Anne

Kuniyuki. Like his gunslinger, Cameron, Richard Brautigan was a counter. This habit formed in Brautigan's youth and stayed with him throughout his life. Staring out a car window, Richard silently counted the telephone poles flicking past or the number of cows in a distant field. Brautigan compiled a five-page chart in an early notebook, counting the punctuation marks in an unnamed text. Many writers make lists of possible titles for their books. Brautigan's list for *The Hawkline Monster* ran for pages. For more than a decade (late 1962 to September 1973), Richard compiled a dated list of every letter he wrote. In a brief poem written on the first of September, Brautigan wryly commented on his counting proclivities. The complete text of "Nine Crows: Two Out of Sequence" reads: "1, 2, 3, 4, 5, 7, 6, 8, 9."

Brautigan set *Hawkline* in eastern Oregon, where he'd hunted deer as a teenager. Richard described hills "that looked as if an undertaker had designed them from leftover funeral scraps." The twenty-one-room Hawkline Manor stood alone amid this desolate landscape. Brautigan's imagination recaptured Mrs. Manerude's four-story, thirty-room mansion in Eugene, where he'd worked odd jobs after school as a teenager. Another autobiographical touch found in *The Hawkline Monster* involved Professor Hawkline, who conducted strange experiments in the basement of his mansion, combining various ingredients into a toxic stew called The Chemicals. What random thoughts of Dr. Frankenstein and other B-movie mad scientists flashed through Brautigan's mind when he mixed barium swallows formula down in the basement of Pacific Chemical?

In the third week of August, Richard packed his fishing gear, some clothes, books, and his unfinished manuscript and flew to Montana. He took a cab over the Bozeman Pass to the Pine Creek Lodge in Paradise Valley and settled into one of their rustic cabins. A couple days later, Roxy and Judy Gordon drove in to join him, accompanied by their four-year-old son, J.C. (John Calvin), and a German shepherd named Mike. The same day, Art and Suzy Coelho showed up to join the party with their son, Eli, and a dog called Milo.

Art Coelho (Brautigan spelled it "Quehlo" in his notebook) was raised on family farms in California's central San Joaquin Valley. A writer and painter, the grandson of Portuguese immigrants from the Azores, Art first met Roxy and Judy back in 1969 when they were heading down to San Diego after their VISTA service. Art had been in Austin two years earlier and attended Brautigan's reading at the university.

Peter Miller, now settled in Seattle, remodeling houses and working with a contractor on Pioneer Square, had plans to start up a bookstore in the market area with the writer Raymond Mungo (author of *Famous Long Ago*, a memoir about cofounding the radical Liberation News Service in the sixties, and *Total Loss Farm*, a comic chronicle of life on a rural commune). They hoped to find an old building and restore it. Almost on a whim, Peter drove out to Montana, blasting straight through "like an auto assassin," to keep his buddy Richard company.

The plan was for all of them to head down to Crow Fair together. Brautigan didn't want to miss the powwow for a second time. Richard arranged for the Gordons to meet Thomas McGuane, and over drinks in Tom's kitchen, Judy found it "so funny" how these two "giants danced around, trying to outdo each other." Jimmy Buffett had returned for another summer visit. Much impromptu music resonated on the premises. Buffett's first major-label album, *A White Sport Coat and a Pink Crustacean*, had just been released. McGuane wrote the liner notes, commenting that Buffett's music lay "at the curious hinterland where Hank Williams and Xavier Cugat meet."

While Brautigan, Buffett, and McGuane retreated into the farmhouse for booze and literary gossip, Peter Miller, the Coelhos, and the Gordons played mixed-doubles badminton on the patch of reconstituted prairie passing for a lawn. Later that evening, fueled by the afternoon's libations, Richard read his poetry aloud after supper to a captive audience back at the Pine Creek Lodge. Eventually, both couples left Brautigan to his insomnia, escaping to their own separate cabins for the night.

The next day, they got a late start. After a leisurely breakfast, the couples set off in two cars for Billings, where they dropped Milo off at Art's rented pink house on Burnstead Street. By the time they departed for the powwow, driving south toward Hardin, it was late afternoon. They didn't arrive in Crow Agency until twilight.

Brautigan wrote in his notebook: "There were thousands of Indians from all over America and hundreds of tepees and pickups and campers and tents [. . .]" Art Coelho had been adopted into the Yellowtail clan of the Crow Nation and had participated in their grueling Sun Dance ritual two years earlier. The group found their way to the camp of Pie Glenn, a Yellowtail on his mother's side, where they were invited guests. After gifts of food and tobacco were exchanged, the visitors were made welcome as if they were blood kin. Sleeping places were prepared for them in the lodges, and everyone shared in the communal evening meal.

Saturday night was the main event at Crow Fair, featuring family giveaways and a fancy dance competition. Dancers in their feathered finery had come from all over Indian country to participate. A steady drumming throb accompanied the wailing chants. Rising dust clouds drifted like fog in the floodlights' glare. Food stalls encircled the dancing ground. The smell of fry bread and corn dogs sizzling in boiling fat scented the nighttime summer breeze.

Richard Brautigan, tall and blond, cut a distinctive figure in the crowd the next morning with his shoulder-length blond hair, drooping mustache, and high-crowned hat. Numbers of young laughing Native American children followed him around, calling him "General Custer" in a good-natured teasing way. Richard had long been interested in Custer and went with the Gordons to explore the Little Bighorn battlefield. Later, exhausted by sightseeing, Brautigan took a nap in the Custer National Cemetery on Last Stand Hill. A group of Livingston people (John Fryer, Joe and Carolyn Swindlehurst, the Hjortsbergs, and Dr. Dennis Noteboom, newly arrived with his beautiful young wife, Patricia, after two years of medical service on the Pine Ridge Reservation in South Dakota) were among those watching the dance competition.

Gatz accidentally encountered Richard among an ocean of unfamiliar faces. He could tell at a glance his friend had had a snootful although the reservation was legally dry. Brautigan, ever sly and evasive when it came to personal details, told him he had been invited to sleep in a tepee that night, implying a mysterious affinity for Native Americana and never letting on his connection to Art Coelho and the Yellowtails. Gatz, who planned to sleep with his wife and friends on a tarp spread on the nearby hillside, took this as a measure of Brautigan's fame and was duly impressed.

Richard, Peter, the Coelhos, and the Gordons left Crow Agency early on Sunday morning, not waiting for the horseback parade in the afternoon, the official end of the powwow. Roxy and Judy drove Richard and Peter back to the Pine Creek Lodge and soon were on their way home. Although they stayed in contact over the years via phone calls and letters, they never saw Richard in person again.

Sue Dill got Brautigan settled in for a long stay in cabin number 2, the most desirable residence as it was farther from the road. Richard always had trouble sleeping. He discovered the first night that his bed wobbled, so he jammed a paperback copy of *War and Peace* under one of the legs to level it.

Peter and Richard fished together after returning from Crow Fair. They talked about basketball and Brautigan's plan to buy property in Paradise Valley. Richard asked Peter if he might be interested in a house-building project. Brautigan also wanted to take in a number of consecutive professional basketball games in Seattle. Miller promised to look into both requests, and almost as quickly as he had come, he was off again, back to the Pacific Northwest.

Five days later, Anne Kuniyuki wrote Richard a brief note asking, "Would you dig my coming to visit you." Because of appointments, the approaching start of the school year, moving out of her apartment, and the demands of her job, it had to be the first two weeks of September. Brautigan never felt entirely comfortable without a woman. When her letter arrived, Richard hurried to the glass public telephone booth by the highway and called Anne to invite her up to Montana. They made plans for her to come and spend a week.

Anne Kuniyuki flew into Bozeman early in September. Richard paid for her airline ticket and arranged for a rental car. The day Anne traveled up from San Francisco, he wrote two new poems. Armed with a set of dictated directions, she found her way over the hill to the Pine Creek Lodge and cabin number 2. Anne stayed with Richard for nine days before returning to San Francisco. She was much impressed with the area's scenic splendors and "had an incredible super beautiful time."

With Anne at the wheel, they toured the surrounding countryside. She sat on the banks of the Yellowstone and watched Richard fish. They drove into Livingston and Brautigan rented an Olivetti typewriter at Gateway Echo office supply. Back in a "very foggy" San Francisco, Anne found it hard to come down from the "high" of being with Richard in beautiful sunny Montana. She kept flashing back on the experience and mailed Brautigan "a package of goodies" as a thank-you.

Brautigan conducted many of his business affairs in the outdoor telephone booth. Most of his calls were to Helen Brann and to his secretary, Loie Weber. He needed to dictate letters. On September 6, Loie initialed seven letters on the long-running correspondence list. These were the last recorded in the compilation Brautigan began in a stenographer's notebook eleven years earlier.

Richard made several calls to Valerie Estes. Early in October, Brautigan phoned her four times in two weeks. She speculated about their former relationship: "He's a good person and sometimes I think he was right—in a weird theoretical—or distanced—way, the best person for me." Richard first called Valerie earlier in September to offer a research job. He needed work done for *Hawkline*. The pay was $5 an hour.

Helen Brann stopped off in Montana for a single night on her way out to San Francisco. Helen had recently parted company with Sterling Lord and was starting a new literary agency under her own name. Brautigan arranged with the Dills to have one of the Pine Creek cabins ready for her arrival. Originally from Colorado, Brann felt an immediate rapport with Montana. When Richard came by her cabin, Helen admired the prized new dark blue cowboy hat he wore. Without a moment's hesitation, Brautigan took it off and "popped" it on her head. "It's yours," he said. The hat became a treasured possession.

The McGuanes hosted a dinner party that same night, and Richard brought Helen along to join in the fun. Buffett had left, but Charles Gaines (*Stay Hungry*, *Pumping Iron*), had arrived.

A Virginia country gentleman, Gaines's impeccable manners and courtly, easygoing demeanor nicely complemented his buffed bodybuilder's physique. Dan Gerber was another visitor. Everyone assumed he and Richard had previously met, but somehow they had missed connecting the past. At one point during the evening, Brautigan approached Gerber, and they shook hands. "Why, I know who you are," Richard said, "and I know you know who I am, you know, but we've never met."

The raucous crowd around the table in the McGuanes' kitchen included Gaines's wife, Virginia, Gatz and Marian Hjortsberg, and several attractive young women. This was the first time Helen Brann had ever observed Richard among his peers. She'd spent time with him in New York, in the company of editors and publishers, but it was not the same. "I'd never seen him with his pals. I was really struck by the difference between Richard and the other men there," she said. "Richard was being as funny as he could be, excruciatingly funny, and the fellows loved him for his humor." Brann found her impressions difficult to describe. "I have the feeling that he was completely out of his water," she said. "Not his depth. These men were so alien to him he was like another being. He was not effete exactly, but if you sat there as a woman, and all these guys were sitting there, and Richard, his hands and his voice and his being, he was in fact like a poet out of some other century, with these great big he-men!"

Much alcohol was consumed. Brann observed that Richard "got absolutely soused, and he found some broad that he really liked and decided to go off with her." Helen was furious. She didn't know the way back to Pine Creek, and Richard seemed ready to abandon her. "I bawled him out," she recalled. "Get me back," Helen insisted. "You have to get into this truck with me." The other guests were "just thrilled" by her outburst. Brautigan behaved in a "very gallant" manner and climbed into the pickup beside her, riding shotgun and providing directions as they "rattled back" to the lodge. Once there, Richard went straight to bed.

Helen Brann had to catch an early flight the next morning. Brautigan, always the good sport in such moments, was up at five, knocking on her cabin door. Brann stumbled out of bed, hungover, finding Richard smiling on her doorstep, a cup of hot coffee in one hand and a jigger of brandy in the other. He poured the brandy into the coffee and handed her the cup. "He was incredibly kind and dear to me," Brann recalled.

During her brief visit to Montana, Helen Brann was pleased to learn of Brautigan's progress on his new novel. Richard resumed a steady writing schedule on the rented Olivetti, and *Hawkline* grew throughout September. He wrote no poetry in the month following Anne Kuniyuki's departure. Two lines of the novel might have been lifted from a Brautigan poem: "Finally they came across something human. It was a grave."

By mid-September a number of Richard's friends arrived in Pine Creek for a monthlong stay. Jim Harrison, Guy de la Valdène, and Bob Dattila all took up residence in adjoining cabins at the Dills' lodge. The boys were out for a good time, which meant a lot of eating, fishing, drinking, and recreational drugs. Harrison left his wife, Linda, at home in Michigan. Guy did the same, but brought along a new girlfriend, putting some distance between himself and a complicated family situation back in Florida. Dattila, who was divorced, came with his seven-year-old son, Andrew. "It was a really mellow time somehow," Bob recalled. He had a Polaroid camera and recorded the activities around Pine Creek, snapping instant photos of the fellows lounging on the front steps of their cabins, drinks and cigarettes in hand.

Bob Dattila and his son had returned to New York by the time Dick and Nancy Hodge came to Montana in the final week of September. Richard arranged for a rental car to be available, but the Hodges arrived two days later. No one came to greet them in Belgrade. Brautigan sent instructions to drive to a motel in Livingston. He had rented a room to watch a football game with his friends as the Pine Creek cabins had no television. The Hodges walked into the room and encountered McGuane, Harrison, Valdène, and Russell Chatham for the first time, all laughing, drinking, and shouting. A self-described "naive little girl," Nancy thought, "Oh, good grief! What am I in for?" She soon discovered these big loud rough-looking men were "immeasurably polite, sweet, considerate, sensitive, darling guys that completely belied the way they appeared."

After the game, Brautigan took the Hodges to the Sport on Main Street and then on to another bar. Dick and Nancy were not big drinkers, so they mainly soaked up the Western atmosphere. Next morning at the Pine Creek Lodge, Nancy was up at first light. "It was just so gorgeous there." She encountered Richard stepping out of cabin number 2, coffeepot in hand. He walked her to the irrigation ditch running through the property (like all newcomers, she thought this was Pine Creek). They knelt in the dew-damp grass and filled the pot with cold running water. Nancy asked if it might be polluted from cattle grazing further upstream. Brautigan pointed out it was clear and fast-moving, a bit of romanticism on his part. The well water in Richard's cabin was far less likely to contain giardia.

Dick and Nancy sported brand-new, skintight black North Beach Leather pants, party clothes bought for a Montana party season. On one occasion up at the McGuanes', Guy Valdène had coolers packed with seafood flown in fresh from Key West. Shrimp, stone crab, plump glistening oysters. Richard provided bottles of Calvados and cases of Pouilly-Fuissé. "Nothing is too disgusting!" became the party cry of the summer.

Quieter moments included fishing trips to Yellowstone Park and tranquil soaks at Chico Hot Springs. Richard and Dick spent much time together. Brautigan had been looking at real estate and wanted his lawyer's advice before the Hodges left Montana on the last day of September.

The property that most interested Richard stood on the opposing bank of Pine Creek from the Hjortsbergs' place. It had been a several-hundred-acre sheep ranch recently subdivided into ten-acre parcels, one of the first such projects in Paradise Valley. A crude new gravel road cut across the pasture. Otherwise, the landscape bore no visible changes. The lot Brautigan was eyeing contained the original ranch house, crouching squat and stuccoed under the cottonwoods along East River Road. A magnificent hundred-year-old redwood cow barn towered on the hill behind the house. Numerous dilapidated outbuildings completed the picture.

"I think I've got the place next door nailed down," Richard told Gatz over coffee one morning in the Hjortsberg living room. Knowing others had been looking at the property (including young Dr. Noteboom and his wife), Gatz asked, "How do you know that?"

"I offered a thousand more than the asking price."

"It's yours!" Gatz agreed.

Jayne Walker returned to Berkeley from Europe in mid-September and tried getting in touch with Brautigan. Surprised to find him still "up in the wilderness," she wrote several postcards saying she hoped to see him soon. Richard made a beeline to the phone booth, begging her to take a quick trip to Montana. He was excited for her to see the "ranch" and meet his new friends. The problem was Jayne's standard poodle. Richard swore he wouldn't be able to sleep with a dog padding around in his tiny cabin. Jayne found a place to board her dog and flew up early in October. A rental car awaited her at the Bozeman airport in Belgrade. The first night in cabin number 2, Jayne learned more about Brautigan's insomnia. He couldn't sleep with an electric blanket, claiming it made a "terrible noise" that kept him awake.

Jayne had a "splendid" four-day weekend in Pine Creek. There were dinners with Tom and Becky and Gatz and Marian. Marian owned a gentle Tennessee walker named Sundance, and Jayne took him for a leisurely ride down to the Yellowstone. Richard set the whole thing up. "He was just like a kid. So excited," Jayne said, "that I got to do this."

In the same little-kid spirit, Richard walked her over to the place he was in the process of buying and showed her the most precious kid-treasure of all, the manuscript of his just-completed novel (but did not let her read a single word).

Richard told Jayne of his admiration for Gatz, who, unlike the other writers, actually lived year-round in Montana and had a working spread, raising pigs, chickens, and rabbits and tending a large organic garden that produced what McGuane called "mutant plants." Richard dubbed his new neighbor-to-be "Farmer Gatz" and "raved" to her about the Hjortbergs' fantasy farm with its saddle horses, restored root cellar, orderly flower beds, and well-tended lawn. She felt Richard held up his friend's life "almost as a kind of model." Walker believed Brautigan dreamed of creating just such a place for himself, "if he were strong enough, pure enough." She knew such dreams floated on clouds of alcohol. "It was scary how much he drank," Jayne said. "I wouldn't have thought that anybody could drink that much and live. Much less function."

Jayne Walker flew back to San Francisco. Richard bought the Olivetti he'd been using to finish his novel for $212, minus the first month's rent. He also paid Guy Valdène $175 for a .20-gauge Ithaca/SKB shotgun. Guy got the .20-gauge in a trade from Harmon Henkin, a burly bearded Maoist writer from Missoula who liked to hunt and fish and frequently drove over to the Livingston area with a carload of sporting goods to barter. Swapping vintage fly rods, shotguns, pistols, cameras, and hunting rifles had become a current passion in Tom McGuane's circle. Valdène got swept up in the swapping energy, becoming the new owner of Henkin's scattergun. Once he realized he would never use it, already possessing a considerable arsenal of his own, Valdène sold the shotgun to Brautigan.

Brautigan "went racing all around town and found somebody to put a plaque on the stock of the gun," Valdène recalled. The little brass oval was engraved with the words "Big Fish." Richard gave the shotgun to Jim Harrison in celebration of a recently caught trophy brown trout. Before the catch-and-release ethos became universal, Dan Bailey's Fly Shop in Livingston hung signboards on the walls, bearing the silhouettes of their customers' fly-caught trout weighing over four pounds. These were known as "wall fish." When Harrison earned his own spot on the wall, Richard started calling him "Big Fish." Soon after, Brautigan wrote a story he titled "A Gun for Big Fish."

Jim was a frequent recipient of Richard's spontaneous generosity. When Harrison published a new book of poetry, *Letters to Yesenin*, with Dan Gerber's Sumac Press, Richard sent him *The Collected Poems of Yesenin in the Russian Language*, the joke being that Jim didn't read Russian. Enclosed with the book was a big picture of a wrecked freighter christened the *Yesenin* in the poet's honor, suggesting if Harrison kept at it, someday he too might have a tramp steamer named after him. Jim acknowledged Richard's deep love of literature. "I mean," Harrison observed, "this is a guy that spent a lot of time in the library."

The Indian summer days remained warm and crystal clear. It cooled off quickly once the sun went down. The nights grew chill, perfect for long conversations around a wood fire under the pines, whiskey glasses in hand. Harrison and Brautigan talked about collaborating on a Jack Spicer project. Richard urged Jim to read Ishmael Reed, especially his poetry collection, *Chattanooga*. The second week of October, Richard took his 228-page typescript of *The Hawkline Monster* into Livingston to be photocopied. He ordered four complete copies, three wrapped for postal shipment. His last task on the book was typing the dedication: "This novel is for the Montana Gang."

On October 17, Brautigan signed a "contract for deed" for the Pine Creek property. At first, Richard bought only the house, the barn, and ten acres, but as time went by, to protect his privacy, he acquired the surrounding lots, two south along the road up to the tree line bordering an irrigation ditch at the top of the hill, another back behind the barn. Eventually, Brautigan owned a total of forty acres, which he insisted on calling his "ranch," although a working spread in Montana, one large enough to earn a meager living, would run several hundred acres at the very minimum.

Ianthe arrived toward the end of October on her first trip to Montana. Unlike his absentee practice with guests and visiting girlfriends, Richard actually went to the airport to greet his daughter. In 1973, the main terminal at Gallatin Field was a small cinder-block building. There were no Jetways, and portable stairs were wheeled out for arriving and departing flights. Ianthe remembered glimpsing her father from the plane window, seeing him waiting on the tarmac, his fine blond hair blowing in the afternoon wind. From the start, Ianthe was "enchanted" by Montana, impressed by "its sheer magnificence and the size of the mountains." The shy, skinny thirteen-year-old felt equally drawn to the rambunctious Montana lifestyle her father and his rowdy friends enjoyed at Pine Creek.

Ianthe liked the storytelling best of all. For as long as she could remember, her father and his friends "got together primarily to tell each other stories." As a child, she spent many long hours listening to the fanciful tales of poets and artists. In Montana, she found herself in the company of wondrous word magicians. "Jim Harrison told his tales in a very laid-back style that I loved," she wrote, years later, in her memoir. "Tom McGuane used his deep dramatic voice to hold everyone [. . .] When my father told a story, he would usually get excited and his voice would rise in the air, leaving the last word to collapse into laughter." At night, after a delicious trout dinner prepared by Jim and Guy, snug in her cabin bed, she was "lulled to sleep by the fluid sounds of their voices drifting in through the open window from where they sat nearby on old battered picnic tables."

Each day became a new adventure for Ianthe. Jim Harrison gave her fly-casting lessons on the lawn beside the cabins. Richard worried that she might hook herself in the eye. After a couple long afternoons of instruction, Ianthe admitted that she wasn't cracked up to be "a fisher person." Even so, she accompanied her father and his angling buddies on outings to the Firehole River in Yellowstone Park, and to a series of beaver ponds on upper Mill Creek where Richard like to fish for pan-sized brookies. The highlights of her Montana trip, aside from time spent at Chico Hot Springs, all revolved around social events. Particularly memorable were a big cookout for many guests under the pines at the lodge and a party at Tom and Becky's where, when no one was paying attention, she got drunk for the first time on the Calvados left over from the Key West seafood pigfest. She had never before noticed that her father "drank a lot. Everyone drank, but he seemed to go one step farther." Ianthe slugged down her first surreptitious sip "in an attempt to understand him."

Harrison and Valdène departed before the end of October, heading for Jim's place in Lake Leelanau, Michigan, for the start of grouse season. Harrison immediately dashed off a couple typed letters to Brautigan. Already missing the convivial Pine Creek fraternity, he lamented, "So I suspect I shouldn't have left Montana when we were having so much fun. Fun must dispel all residual calvinism and be sought damning the cost. Laughter. Booze. Fishing. Sweet oysters [. . .]"

The Michigan bird hunting had been fine until the rains started, and they shot seven one afternoon. This prompted praise for the gift Ithaca .20-gauge. "I will always treasure the shotgun. It's neat. In the pantheon of gifts it's up there with a flyrod and three hymens." Guy left Lake Leelanau for Philadelphia once the shooting got rained out. The bad weather compelled Jim upstairs to his writing studio to resume work on a projected screenplay. He agreed with Brautigan's assessment: "You were right. We must carry our griefs alone like a hair ball or blood clot. In the dark night of the soul it's always Peoria."

Ianthe left for California around the same time the boys departed. On his own again, his novel off in the mail, Richard looked for possible venues for shorter pieces. Throughout October, he stayed in mail and phone contact with Helen Brann, hoping to facilitate just such an assignment. McGuane, Harrison, Hjortsberg, and J. D. Reed all supplemented their literary incomes by freelancing for *Sports Illustrated*. This struck Brautigan as an enticing proposition. Through his agent, he proposed articles on hunting and basketball to Patricia Ryan, the text editor at the Luce publication. Although Pat found "the notion of Brautigan on basketball intriguing," the magazine already had a staffer working on a piece about the SuperSonics, and she regretfully declined. Ryan did offer Richard a *Sports Illustrated* assignment, which included a guarantee, and he promptly had Helen Brann submit "A Gun for Big Fish" to her.

Richard had lots of time to think about the house he bought. Every time he walked through the empty rooms, he considered the renovations he wanted before he moved in. Brautigan gave Peter Miller a call and asked him to come to Montana and have a look at his new place. Richard made arrangements for Miller to fly to Bozeman on the first weekend in November.

It was snowing when Peter arrived. "God, this is cold," he thought. Brautigan showed him around the Pine Creek property, and Miller agreed it had tremendous potential. It was the wrong season to begin a big construction project. Richard and Peter agreed to meet again in the early spring and finalize their plans.

Richard Brautigan left Pine Creek at the end of the first week in November, flying out of Bozeman on a $139 Frontier flight that routed him through Salt Lake City to New York. This time he stayed for two weeks in room 1207 at the Fifth Avenue Hotel, 24 Fifth Avenue. The rate was $23 a night. A lot of Richard's time in the city was spent hanging out with Bob Dattila and eating expensive meals at The Palm. Harrison wrote, after his return to Frisco, hoping he "had a Gotham gala, replete with girlbum stew." Brautigan likely got together with Carol Brissie, who had been out in San Francisco during July, when Brautigan treated her to a memorable scampi dinner at Vanessi's.

Brautigan discussed market strategy for *The Hawkline Monster* with Helen Brann. She wanted a $75,000 advance for the hardcover and quality paperback rights, with a guaranteed first printing order of twenty-five thousand copies. Richard would retain the approval of dust jacket design and ad copy accorded him in his previous S&S contract. All this sounded fine to Brautigan, who asked his agent about having Simon & Schuster bring out a new collection of his poetry. Helen thought this was an excellent idea. She advised waiting until after they made the *Hawkline* deal before proposing it.

Brautigan left New York on November 21, taking an American Airlines flight to San Francisco. Ensconced again on Geary Street, he got back in touch with Jayne Walker, and they resumed an on-again, off-again relationship. She often met him at Enrico's, where he spent almost every late afternoon drinking with his buddies before heading next door to Vanessi's for dinner. Walking down Broadway alone always seemed "quite a trial" for Jayne. It was a neighborhood of strip clubs and topless bars, and she feared people would assume she was a hooker.

Walker had brought back "a fair amount" of saffron from Spain. "Richard was immediately struck by the brilliance of my move," she said. He knew saffron was worth its weight in Kryptonite in the States and yet relatively inexpensive in Spain. Brautigan became obsessed with acquiring some of the uncommon spice. To that end, he proposed a trade to Walker. He would give her a signed copy of *The Octopus Frontier*, already a rare and desirable early Brautigan title, in exchange for some of her saffron.

"Richard would never have signed a book for me because he was so completely paranoid about letting anybody sell his signature," Walker recalled. Brautigan had been "horrified" to learn that some of his old friends were selling his letters now that he had become famous. A bargain was struck. Richard had "a very clear idea in his mind of what the book was worth on the market because he always kept track of stuff like that." They measured out a quantity of saffron in his kitchen, "not that much really," and Brautigan signed a copy of his book for Jayne. A couple days later, he phoned her in Berkeley, furious because he had just learned the true value of his saffron and discovered it wasn't worth as much as a signed copy of *The Octopus Frontier*. Walker refused to renegotiate the trade. "A deal is a deal," she told him.

At the end of November, Helen Brann mailed Brautigan a $500 kill-fee check from *Sports Illustrated*, which had rejected "A Gun for Big Fish." She was trying the story next with *Esquire*. A week later, Brann sent Richard his new Simon & Schuster contract for *The Hawkline Monster*. They settled upon a $50,000 advance for hardcover and quality paperback rights, with a straight 15 percent royalty on the hardcover edition. Helen added a clause stipulating a full-page ad in the *New York Times* within one month of publication. Along with the book contract, Brann enclosed copies of an exclusive agreement with her new agency for Brautigan to amend as he wished. Richard made a few changes, eliminating the agency's control over "ideas" and "recordings" and striking out all language entitling Brann to deduct expenses such as postage and telephone calls from his account. In his own hand he added, "You will handle the magazine sale of my poetry only at my discretion." After a week of scrutiny, Richard signed both documents and mailed them back to Helen in New York.

Helen Brann wanted to move forward with plans to market the motion picture rights for *Hawkline*. She had entered into an arrangement with theatrical agent Flora Roberts to represent that side of her business. Roberts, a Bronx-born New Yorker, had worked as an assistant to legendary Broadway producer Kermit Bloomgarden before becoming an independent agent in the early 1950s. Among her long-term clients were Ira Levin and Stephen Sondheim. Roberts sent a manuscript copy of *Hawkline* to film director Peter Bogdanovich for his consideration.

All in all, 1973 had been a very good year for Richard Brautigan, ending on a fiscal high note when Helen Brann sent him a check for $45,000 in December, his advance from Simon & Schuster for *The Hawkline Monster*. In a mood to celebrate, Richard took his daughter and Anne Kuniyuki on a trip up to Mendocino over Christmas. They stayed at the Sea Gull Inn, which provided a pleasant refuge from the cold, foggy weather. Ianthe was sick the whole time, coughing continuously on the drive north. She believed because Anne worked as a professional nurse, she would take care of her. Things didn't work out that way. Ianthe thought Anne was very nice, "but she was no healer."

1974 began on a prosperous note. In January, Brautigan received $15,000 from Dell, the third of his contracted annual advance payments for his three-book deal. Helen Brann wrote that *Esquire* was taking "A Gun for Big Fish," enclosing a check for $900. Another January letter came with $250 from *Mademoiselle* for Brautigan's recent seven-part poem, "Good Luck, Captain Martin." Simon & Schuster offered a $20,000 advance for Richard's new poetry collection. They did not want to publish the book until September of 1975 to avoid any sales conflict with *Hawkline*. Jayne Walker sent him a telegram at the end of January offering to cook "a fine dinner" for his birthday. Brautigan quickly accepted.

A letter from Jim Harrison came that same month. Jim had "had a wonderful time with [*Hawkline*] last night between midnight and three, the best hours of any day, the first untainted hours. Boy did I ever want to fuck those Hawkline sisters." Harrison thought it his favorite of all Brautigan's books, and ventured that Richard might have a hit on his hands. "It is metaphysical fiction and then some [. . .] It is so opposite, and vitally, any naturalistic ideas of fiction while copping their best techniques."

During the next six weeks, Brautigan spent time with both Anne Kuniyuki and Jayne Walker. The contracts for the poetry collection arrived at Geary Street the third week in February and were immediately signed. During this period, Brautigan helped Kazuko Fujimoto with her Japanese translation of *Trout Fishing in America*. He was impressed with her "knowledge and perception" of his book. When Helen Brann sent the contracts for the Japanese edition of *The Abortion* on March 12, he urged his agent to get Fujimoto (just finished with her work on *Trout Fishing*) the job of translating that book, too. An advance of $20,000 for the new poetry book was mailed two days later.

Brautigan flew down to Florida at the end of March. He stayed in an upstairs bedroom at the large airy home of Guy and Terry de la Valdène on White Street in old town Key West. Richard wrote poetry, swinging in the hammock on the Valdènes' screened-in porch. Guy kept busy working on a film about his passion, fly-fishing for tarpon, which he and his brother-in-law, Christian Odasso, who spoke only French, were codirecting. Financing came from the Valdènes' family. "We blew more budget money on food and wine," Guy confessed. "I mean we ate like pigs."

They had a French crew and a tight five-week shooting schedule, up every morning at six, except on days when they were weathered in. Christian was a professional filmmaker with some experience. Guy knew where to find the fish. He had been a still photographer for *Sports Illustrated* and *Field & Stream*. "The thing didn't quite work," Valdène later admitted. "We wanted to bring a bunch of writers and sportsmen together and really try to capture the fishing and also get a lot of new views and check out the Key West scene."

To this end, Guy Valdène recruited Jim Harrison, who flew in from Michigan with Dan Gerber, and Tom McGuane, who wintered in Key West. For about a week, Brautigan wanted no part in the film. Guy attributed it to Richard's "standoffish" disposition, calling him a "tall ostrich in the corner." Brautigan followed his own agenda. He bought a "goofy" secondhand bicycle with high handlebars. Valdène recalled that "he'd just cruise the streets of Key West, back and forth, all day long."

Richard's schedule also included working on a regular basis. He rented an Underwood electric typewriter ($15.60 a month) to type final drafts of the poetry he wrote longhand on sheets of unlined paper. Dink Bruce observed that Brautigan seemed a bit uncomfortable in the tropics. "He didn't like the heat."

On his first day in town, Richard picked up a beautiful nineteen-year-old girl with "childlike eyes and a fragile mouth." Knowing he was old enough to be her father added "a certain delicious something" to their lovemaking. Brautigan joined his fishing pals and the film crew for nightly feasts and drinking bouts. At the time, the Pier House was downtown Key West's most luxurious hotel. Its bar, the Chart Room, provided the locals their main hangout.

Tourists frequented Sloppy Joe's, a converted icehouse on Duval Street that had misappropriated the name of Hemingway's old 1920s drinking hole. The original Sloppy Joe's, now renamed Captain Tony's, was tucked away around the corner on Green Street. The Chart Room was a small intimate bar with sliding glass doors opening out onto the patio. Conchs (natives of Key West) gathered here to pick up the local gossip and play liar's poker, a game using bank notes instead of cards with the serial numbers providing the hands.

One night at about nine or ten o'clock after a long day's filming, the gang was kicking back in the Chart Room. Numbers of people wandered back and forth between the bar and the pool. Without a word, Guy stripped off all his clothes and jumped naked into the water. Soon, one after another, everybody took off his or her clothing and jumped in. Dan Gerber remembered "there must have been twenty or thirty men and women" paddling around together.

Foster, the Chart House security guard, didn't know what to make of the situation. In the end, he peeled off his makeshift uniform and plunged in to join the fun. Almost the only one not to go skinny dipping was Brautigan, never reticent in the past about appearing nude in public. Richard didn't swim. He stayed fully dressed in his jeans and tall black cowboy hat, running gleefully back and forth into the bar to buy bottles of Dom Pérignon and pass them out to the hedonistic bathers.

About a week after his arrival, Brautigan traveled up to Miami to meet his daughter, who was flying in alone from California. As always, Richard allowed Ianthe plenty of freedom. They took many long walks through the old town together, especially at day's end, when they'd head down to the waterfront and watch the incredible Technicolor sunsets. Because there was no more guest space available at the Valdène's home, Ianthe stayed with Tom and Becky McGuane, who turned their son's room over to her. Every morning she awoke to the sight of Thomas, an angry displaced seven-year-old, glaring at her from the foot of the bed. Otherwise, she felt very comfortable at the McGuane's and had no trouble sleeping, unlike her father, who took Valium to combat his chronic insomnia. The drug did the trick, but Richard found it prevented him from dreaming, so he gave it up. "I don't dream," he said, "and I have to be able to dream."

A permissive father, Brautigan still remained very protective of his daughter. One night everyone went out to a traveling carnival that had set up in town (going full-blast through Lent in true Key West pirate tradition). Richard took Ianthe along, and the gang stood in line for the whirling rides and lost their pocket money on dubious ball-tossing games. Brautigan allowed himself to be filmed anonymously among the merrymakers but would not permit the French crew to focus their cameras on his daughter.

A devoted swimmer, Ianthe spent much of her time in the water. She was disappointed to discover there was no surf in the Keys. Becky McGuane gave her a cute little bikini to wear at the beach. Terrified by dangers of the deep, Richard warned his daughter to beware of being eaten by barracuda. "Don't wear any flashy rings when you go swimming," he told her. "Not if you want to keep all your fingers." To ensure her safety, Brautigan arranged for Ianthe to swim at the Pier House pool. When she asked if he'd like to join her, Richard replied, "I just swim at night."

After a spell of heavy weather things broke clear just when Guy happened to have some unexpected free time on his hands. "You wanna go fishing?" he asked Brautigan. Ianthe romped about in the tropical sunshine wearing shorts and a halter top, but remembered how her father's fair skin, so prone to burning, required him to cover up completely in trousers and long-sleeved shirts. Richard agreed to go out onto the flats and sat incongruously fully clothed in the fishing skiff, wearing a high-crowned black cowboy hat (Valdène remembered it as being "about two feet taller than his head"), while the rest of the gang stood around bare-chested in shorts, the wind whipping their salt-bleached hair. The camera crew came along in Dink Bruce's boat. McGuane, Harrison, and Scott Palmer joined them in Tom's skiff. Guy promised Richard that he wouldn't be filmed. Guy needed shots of jumping tarpon, and the three boats set off toward the Pearl Basin in search of fish.

Far out on the vast pellucid ocean wilderness surrounding the tiny island of Key West, where stillness and the endless open sky provided a welcome contrast to the frantic party frenzy of the tourist-crowded town, they came across a large school of tarpon. Outboard engines were switched off and tilted up out of the water to avoid spooking the fish. The camera boat and McGuane's skiff waited behind as Valdène, a bandanna wrapped around his forehead, pirate-fashion, silently poled upwind toward the feeding fish, elusive silver shadows in the sea grass. "I literally poled for forty minutes after this school of fish. I could see them rolling just out of range."

Knowing Richard desperately wanted to hook and play one of the huge tarpon but wasn't skilled enough to make the cast, Guy did it for him, double-hauling the weight-forward line, expertly shooting the fly out toward his quarry. After many attempts, casting again and again, he finally had a take and set the hook. "I want you to feel the power of this thing," Valdène said, handing the rod to Brautigan. For a few ecstatic electric moments, Brautigan played the big fish until it broke off. "He was so happy he was howling at the top of his lungs," Guy observed. "So excited he literally couldn't talk for fifteen minutes." Dink's boat was too far out of camera range for Christian to get a shot.

That night at dinner, still high from his tarpon experience, Richard asked Guy, "You want to film?"

High himself, having recently smoked a joint, Guy replied, "Why not?"

They shot the interview out on the porch. Richard swung in the hammock. Guy sat beside him in a wooden chair. "Tell me about the fish," he asked, camera rolling.

"Massive," Richard replied enthusiastically. "Very powerful. Extraordinary! So extraordinary as to create immediate unreality upon contact with the fish [. . .] Everything went into slow motion. My mind couldn't deal with it anymore." Brautigan's poetic imagination provided the appropriate metaphor. "The water is almost like marble breaking—liquid marble coming up—silver Atlantis coming out of the water."

What particularly impressed Richard was that all the fly-rod-caught tarpon were unhooked and released unharmed once they were brought to the boat. "Hemingway said a thing about material possessions that I think is a beautiful thing," he mused, swaying in the hammock, his expressive hands forming shapes in the air before him. "He said you can never own anything until you can give it away. And the ultimate keeping of the tarpon would be the releasing of it, and the killing of him then just becomes something that people block out on the walls, whereas if you release him, you have him in your mind forever alive."

Watching from behind the camera, Dink Bruce almost couldn't believe what he saw. "Because here [Richard had] been sedentary this whole time, but he knew that Guy was up against the wall and he knew he needed a piece of Richard on this film because he's selling it, it's French TV, right? And they really liked Richard. And he put out this ten-minute special effort for Guy."

Valdène shouldered the blame for the main fault of the final cut. He felt they had "fabulous footage" of wild fish and the Key West scene, but thought he didn't include enough coverage of his writer pals because he didn't want to be "a pain in the ass." Instead of bugging Tom, Jim, and Richard for repeated filmed interviews, Guy more or less let them off the hook. "When we got to the editing, we had hundreds of thousands of feet that were not specific enough," he said. "So, in the movie it was like what are these guys doing?"

Tarpon, the finished film, with a musical score by Jimmy Buffett, was eventually presented on French television, but the first showing was at Richard Hodge's Page Street law offices later that year. Richard and Nancy hosted the celebratory event as one of their regular Thursday night soirees in the posh Victorian mansion. Guy Valdène was the guest of honor.

Others in the invited audience included Richard Brautigan, Curt Gentry, and Don Carpenter. Richard's cinematic concerns at the time were more involved with *Hawkline*'s chances in Hollywood than his friend's fishing movie.

Back in March, Flora Roberts had forwarded a copy of a letter from Peter Bogdanovich to Brautigan in Key West. The filmmaker found *Hawkline* to be "a very intriguing and beautiful story," but it was not something he was interested in directing himself. Roberts next planned to submit the book to Arthur Penn (her "very good friend") and, if that didn't pan out, to Sam Peckinpah. Tom McGuane's first original screenplay was soon to begin filming in Montana, and the notion of scoring copious quantities of Tinseltown coin seemed a distinct possibility to all of his ink-slinging amigos.

After a visit lasting "two or three weeks" in Key West, Brautigan flew back to San Francisco with Ianthe. Richard returned his daughter to Ginny's care and resumed a busy romantic life, keeping simultaneous company with Jayne Walker, Anne Kuniyuki, and Mary Ann Gilderbloom, none of whom knew the others existed. Mary Ann remained his current main squeeze, dining with Richard at Vanessi's as often as three times a week. "There was copious amounts of drinking," she recalled. "It's amazing that I staggered through it."

Olav Angell, Brautigan's Norwegian translator, had recently arrived in town to consult with Richard about the upcoming edition of *Trout Fishing* to be published by Gyldendal in Oslo later that year. This necessitated much heavy drinking. One subject they discussed over multiple shots of aquavit concerned the handwritten signature of Trout Fishing in America. In the original Four

Seasons edition, this had appeared as a printed facsimile of Brautigan's own cramped penmanship. The production department at Gyldendal had struggled to render Richard's peculiar signature in Norwegian without success. The aquavit did the trick. Under Olav's tutelage, Richard carefully wrote the words "Orretfiske i Amerika" on a sheet of paper for Olav to bring back to his publisher in Norway.

It was time to collect Mary Ann after work for the evening's frivolities. Brautigan and Angell, in the company of another Norwegian writer, arrived at Philobiblon dead drunk. "Richard was only halfway there," Gilderbloom recalled. They all bundled into a cab and headed to Enrico's for further drinking. "We sat there and drank and drank and drank," she said. "Then we went into Vanessi's and sat in a booth in the back and continued to drink." Mary Ann realized she had crossed the line of her capabilities. She was far drunker than she had ever been before. Fearing she might get sick, Gilderbloom staggered to the bathroom and decided it was time to go home. There were people she knew from the book industry having dinner in the restaurant, and she had no intention of embarrassing herself in front of them.

When she returned to the booth, Brautigan ordered her another drink. Mary Ann declined, saying she had to leave. "It was the one and only time I ever saw him get really pissed at me," she said. Richard didn't want "his lady to be drunk and out of line and then drop out of the party," but he walked her outside to Broadway and hailed a cab, giving her $20 for the fare. Brautigan concluded his Norwegian translator's last night in Frisco with a wildly inebriated cable car ride. The next afternoon, Richard called Mary Ann to apologize for how he had treated her the previous evening. "Oh man, I feel really bad," he said.

Brautigan flew up to Seattle at the end of the third week in April to confer with Peter Miller about the remodeling project on his new Montana home. Peter introduced him to John Marshall, the contractor he was working with, "a wild man who drank forty cups of coffee a day." Marshall was from New Orleans. "Richard liked him, although he was sort of wary of him." Brautigan described the project he had in mind and asked, "Why don't you come?"

Miller and Marshall thought it sounded great, agreeing to get a crew together and be out in Montana in a matter of weeks. While in Seattle, Richard noticed all the houses for sale. "How much for this house?" he asked Peter, pointing one out.

"Twenty-five thousand dollars," Miller said.

"Buy me five," Brautigan replied. "I want to buy five houses up here."

Nothing came of it, Peter recalled. "I don't know that I even took him seriously."

Preparing for a return to Montana, Richard decided it was time to upgrade his fishing gear. While he had been content since childhood with bargain basement equipment, Brautigan's new fishing companions, McGuane, Harrison, and Valdène, favored the finest tackle as a matter of aesthetics and dependability. McGuane suggested the R. L. Winston Company in San Francisco. One afternoon Richard set off with Keith Abbott and his shopping list to investigate. Keith related how Brautigan "often enlisted my aid before trips, especially for any equipment purchases, not only because I owned a truck, but also because he relied on second opinions to counter his sometimes screwy, overamped takes on reality."

The R. L. Winston Company, a venerable Frisco fly-rod-building firm established in 1929, was located in a nondescript cement block building on Third Street, south of Market, an area better known for winos and panhandlers than fly fishermen. In this environment, Winston maintained a profile so low as to be almost invisible. Brautigan had come prepared with a wallet stuffed full of hundred-dollar bills.

Doug Merrick, present owner of the company and a master rod-builder, barely raised his head in his backroom workshop when he buzzed them in. He wasn't impressed when Brautigan dropped McGuane's name. Richard was in a mood to splurge, but steered clear of the pricey custom-made split bamboos that were Winston's specialty. Merrick also sold excellent fiberglass rods. Brautigan bought a couple in differing lengths, along with the appropriate reels and properly weighted fly lines. Abbott felt he was "validating his new savvy friends and, by extension, his new fascinating life as a celebrity."

Richard's final purchase was a pair of chest waders. "I never owned or needed them before," he told Merrick. "When I was a kid, my waders were tennis shoes." Comparing various brands, Brautigan decided he wanted them extra-long, sufficient for the Yellowstone's deep, swift-moving water. As he contemplated the baggy, clownlike waders, Richard's inherent paranoia brought various scenarios for disaster to mind. "What happens if these fill with water?" he asked. "I could drown."

"Son," Doug Merrick drawled in his confident Western manner, "to fill those waders with water you'd have to climb up on a rock and dive headfirst into a stream."

Brautigan returned to Pine Creek in late April with all his new fishing gear, anxious to keep a close eye on the ongoing construction project. The Dills welcomed him back to their lodge, but Richard was unable to take up residence in cabin number 2, his favorite. He had to settle for number 1, the noisier cabin close by the narrow highway.

A young couple from Los Angeles had rented cabin number 2. Michael Haller was an art director and production designer who had come out after Easter with his wife, G., and their two sons, Eric and Bret, scouting locations for *Rancho Deluxe*, the movie Tom McGuane had written. They chose to live in the valley, rather than in town with the rest of the cast and crew, so the boys could attend the Pine Creek School, a traditional two-room country elementary school about a half mile down the road.

By the beginning of May, *Rancho Deluxe* was shooting all over Livingston and Park County. The film was directed by Frank Perry (*David and Lisa*, *Diary of a Mad Housewife*, *Play It as It Lays*), and McGuane's offbeat script had attracted a diverse and talented cast, including Jeff Bridges, Sam Waterston, Elizabeth Ashley, Slim Pickins, Clifton James, Harry Dean Stanton, and Richard Bright (who had starred as Billy the Kid in Michael McClure's *The Beard*).

Jimmy Buffett signed on to write the musical score. He also contributed an original song, "Livingston Saturday Night," which he performed with a local band in a scene filmed in the Wrangler Bar. In an uncredited appearance, actor Warren Oates played harmonica with Buffett's group in this scene. Oates had wandered up to Montana to hang out with his actor pals. He lived in a large motor home dubbed the "Roach Coach." Bob Watkins, an old sidekick from Kentucky who had once done time for bank robbery, served as the designated driver and all-around majordomo.

Because Michael Haller had to be on the set almost every day, G. became a stay-at-home mom. Always a good neighbor, each morning after he finished writing, Brautigan tapped on the door of cabin number 2 and visited for a while. Usually it was to quote a line or two of poetry, often his own. "Sometimes he would ask my opinion," G. recalled. "'What do you think?' And it really didn't seem to matter what I thought, but it was just throwing something out. And one morning, when he came over with his little recitation for the day and he said, 'What do you think?' And I said, 'It sounds like William Carlos Williams.' And he was flabbergasted because it was William Carlos Williams. 'Today is William Carlos Williams's birthday.' And we celebrated William Carlos Williams's birthday."

They read Dr. Williams's poetry aloud. Brautigan told G. how much he admired him. "This man who could have a full-time medical practice and be delivering babies and bandaging wounds and doing all this and be a family man, because he was successfully married and had children, and that he could also write poetry and be a champion for all these writers."

Richard's admiration sprang from self-awareness. He possessed virtually no skills other than his ability to write. What was curious about the day's celebration was that Williams had not been born in May, a fact well-known to Brautigan. Just the previous fall, he wrote "September 3, The Dr. William Carlos Williams Mistake," a poem stating that Williams had been born on September 17, 1883, not on September 3.

Throughout the late spring, Richard lived alone in cabin number 1. As much as he might have wished for female companionship, recent events prevented that happy possibility. Anne Kuniyuki's mother died one morning early in May, and she flew back to Hawaii the next day, having just gone home to Honolulu a couple weeks before. (She sent Brautigan a coconut on that previous visit.) Kuniyuki returned to San Francisco before the end of May. It had been a hard time for her, and Richard flew down for a few days to keep her company.

Much as she wanted to come out to Montana, it was not to be. Anne stayed in the city, checking Brautigan's mail and forwarding anything he deemed essential. She also kept an eye on the Bolinas house from time to time. In June, to stimulate his imagination, she mailed him a photo of her wearing "an honest-to-god real live muu-muu" taken at her mother's Honolulu yard the previous month.

Kuniyuki might not have made the effort had she known about Jayne Walker, whom Richard was also trying to entice out for a visit to Montana. Walker felt nervous and frustrated by the demands of writing her dissertation and the anxiety arising out of her impending move to Ithaca, New York, where she planned to teach at Cornell in the fall. For a while that June, she toyed with the notion of taking "a working vacation," but found herself stuck in the middle of a chapter and felt she had to finish it before allowing herself any time off. Feeling too broke to phone, she wrote Brautigan a somewhat hurried letter hoping she might make the trip to Montana early in August.

Living at the Pine Creek Lodge meant Brautigan could check in regularly on the progress of his remodeling project just down the road. At the last minute, John Marshall had backed out, deciding not to come to Montana. Peter Miller was left in the role of sole contractor. "Which I was probably only half-fit to be, but Richard said, 'Let's do it. It will be fine.'" So, Miller set about putting together a makeshift crew. Eventually, he signed up fifteen.

Peter came out to Pine Creek with his girlfriend, Cathy Rogers, and stayed in one of the Pine Creek cabins while waiting for the crew to assemble. A trained naturopath, Cathy hung cheesecloth sacks full of tansy on their screened windows to ward off the bothersome nighttime mosquitoes. When Brautigan spotted these sachets the next morning, he had a fit and ripped them all down. Furious at this violation of her privacy, Rogers got into a "big fight" with him. "I'm paying for it," Brautigan shouted, stalking off in a frenzy.

"Too spooky." Peter Miller felt shocked by the incident, having always regarded Brautigan as a paragon of the New Age Male. "He hates women," Rogers said. Miller failed to recognize that Brautigan's outburst was not occasioned by any deep-seated anger toward women. It erupted out of his general displeasure with manifestations of the "hippie subculture." This did not bode well for the immediate future. The ragtag crew Peter Miller assembled was a caricature crosssection of the dropout counterculture.

"It was just like the sixties revisited," one of the crew members recalled. "All kinds of women with long dresses, families and dogs and children." Several of the recruits were veterans of the Liberation News Service Commune in Vermont. A woman named Emily had been hired just to cook. There was John Fenu, a former big-time acid dealer everyone called Spaceman, who arrived with his wife, Justine, and their baby. One young guy showed up with a custom wooden box housing twenty-three handmade English chisels of all different sizes. It was his contention these elegant tools were all a fine craftsman needed to complete any job.

Peter Miller found himself with a dilemma on his hands. Without the talents of John Marshall to motivate his unskilled crew, very little real work was getting done. Straw boss Miller didn't feel up to acting as the official foreman, so he contacted Ron Little, a former ski racer turned carpenter, whom he'd known back in Cambridge. Little lived now in Aspen, Colorado, where he and a friend named Tom Kyle were partners in a construction business. They had just lost a bid and decided "what the hell," a job camping out in Montana sounded like a good deal. They packed up their table saws and radial arm saws and "big game boxboard tools" and drove north.

Ron Little had known Richard Brautigan since Peter Miller introduced them six years earlier, when the writer came east to give his Harvard reading. Ron didn't do drugs but "knew the difference between bourbon and scotch," so he and Richard starting hanging out together. Little took Brautigan to a Boston Irish workingman's bar "called the Plow and Shield or something like that."

Over drinks, Brautigan told Little about his surefire method for attracting unattached women. "Richard gave me a nudge and reached down and unzipped his fly and said, 'This always works, this never fails. There will always be girls.'" The technique seemed not to go over so well at the Plow and Shield. When nobody paid any attention, Brautigan pulled his underwear out a bit for more emphasis. Soon, "a couple guys in the barroom started to get fidgety" and came over to tell Richard to button up. "They didn't put up with that kind of shit."

When Little and Kyle arrived in Pine Creek, the long-haired vegetarian crew offered a cold reception. The first order of business was a dispute over whether to allow the power tools into their project. Ron and Tom felt a touch of wry annoyed bemusement when the communal work crew voted on permitting them to use their professional equipment at the work site. The irony underlying this new age egalitarianism was that only Little and Kyle, out of all the gathered company, knew anything about building houses.

At first, Kyle and Little shared Richard's discomfort. The crew all camped out in the main house. On their first night, when everyone was trying to get some sleep, the Fenus' three-year-old toddler kept "walking around, waking people up, screaming and crying." Ron reflected on what he termed "hippie equality." No one spoke to the child or complained about his bad behavior. When Ron's suggestion that the kid be put down at a normal hour was ignored, he set up a tent out back. He and Tom slept there. Three days later, Tom started keeping company with Emily, one of the two camp cooks, and moved back into the house to sleep with her. For the remainder of the job, Ron had the tent to himself.

To facilitate keeping an eye on things, Brautigan borrowed a bicycle from Gatz Hjortsberg and pedaled back and forth between the Pine Creek Lodge and his new house a half mile away. Richard told G. Haller how honored he was that his friend, whom he knew to be of modest means, had trusted him with so valuable a possession. G. remembered watching Brautigan pedal off every morning after he finished writing, wobbling down two-lane East River Road. "He looked like the witch from *The Wizard of Oz*," she said, "with his big black hat and black boots and his Levi's. A great big grasshopper."

Brautigan's first order of business at the construction site involved lengthy discussions with Miller and Little regarding what he had in mind. Peter recalled that Richard "loved" the Hjortsbergs' gracious turn-of-the-century home across the creek and hoped to re-create some of the amiable ambiance of their place. Both the kitchen and the only bathroom in Brautigan's house were tiny. Brautigan wanted them enlarged. The front of the house by the main entrance had been divided into two smaller rooms. It was quickly decided to take out the wall between them.

All the work scheduled for the main house involved the downstairs. The bedroom above required no modification. This was to be a guest bedroom. Richard, long plagued by insomnia, didn't care to sleep upstairs when parties might be raging below. An old unused coal shed stood not far from the back kitchen door. Brautigan asked to have it made over into his personal bedroom. Then, he could sneak off from any festivities and be assured of privacy.

The construction of his writing studio was a primary concern for Brautigan. As the huge old barn stood empty and unused, "there was an intuition" to locate the studio somewhere within the building's spacious interior. Ron Little came up with the notion of constructing it like a tree house sitting high up in the rafters under the barn roof. Richard liked this idea, "sort of isolated," and Ron sketched it out for him in the dirt on the barn floor.

After these preliminary discussions, work began in earnest with Ron Little acting as the de facto foreman. The A. W. Miles Lumber Company in Livingston (a venerable institution founded by the nephew of famed Indian fighter General Nelson Miles) had a quantity of fine redwood on hand, so the crew bought a large amount for their project. "All they had was redwood," Peter Lewis recalled, "the most beautiful redwood."

"Nobody was working off plans," Little recollected. "It was making it up as you go along." Ron did the basic stuff, "roughing, working on supports, foundations, checking to make sure what we built would stay up." Tom Kyle handled the finishing work, "building cabinets and drawers and covers." All along, they tried to keep the rest of the crew occupied, assigning tasks equal to their abilities.

When the wall dividing the two rooms at the front of the house was demolished, a surprising discovery was made. Beneath the stucco, laths, and plaster, the house had originally been built of logs. Brautigan was delighted by the unexpected revelation. It thrilled him to know that his house had a secret history.

Another chance discovery greatly pleased Richard. When the bathroom wall was knocked down to enlarge the space, a hospital baby identification bracelet was found behind the toilet tank. Made from plastic beads back in the forties, it had been fastened around a newborn's wrist or ankle. Round blue beads signified the baby was a boy. White square beads spelled out the child's last name: Shorthill. Brautigan's place had originally been part of a larger ranch belonging to David Shorthill, a Union officer who came to the Paradise Valley in the 1860s. Richard felt this connection to a veteran of the Civil War, however far removed, was a rare treasure. He saved the baby bracelet for years.

Aside from these two discoveries almost nothing about the remodeling project pleased Brautigan. "He hated the crew," Peter Miller said. "Mostly because they were different than he was. They didn't drink. They had their girlfriends and kids." Gatz Hjortsberg remembered Richard grumbling about the crew. "Those bean sprout eaters," he fumed, "those fucking granola heads!" Even though he griped about their eating habits, Brautigan brought Jimmy Buffett over to the construction site for a vegetarian dinner prepared by the cooks on the crew. No matter how much work they accomplished in a very short time, Brautigan always found something to complain about. "We were working under a deadline," Ron Little recalled. "We had like four weeks."

Attempting to defuse the tense situation, Peter Miller created a task for Brautigan. "We gave him the job of straightening nails," he said. "Pulling and straightening nails." Quantities of scrap lumber had been torn out of the house and coal shed. Richard "would sit there all afternoon, pulling nails from boards and straightening them, putting them in the right baskets." The crew had no plans to recycle either the wood or the nails. "We didn't give a shit whether the nails ever showed up again or not," Miller said. "He just needed a job. It was a perfect job for him. And he liked it because he didn't have to bother with anybody. He was not handy and didn't pretend to be handy."

"Kurt Vonnegut doesn't do this," Richard quipped, extracting yet another nail from a broken board.

Ron Little, Brautigan's drinking buddy from Cambridge, was the only member of the crew Richard actually seemed to like. Peter Miller thought it was because Ron was also alone. "I kind of hung out with Richard," Little recalled. "I drank whiskey, and he'd get a bowl, fill it with ice, and get a bottle and drive around in a pickup and talk." Brautigan appreciated Little's skilled craftsmanship and liked the way his future studio was progressing. Whenever he saw Ron he'd say, "You are the one guy there. You and Tom knew what you were doing but those other sons of bitches, they even screwed up my bathroom wall." Ron remembered Richard really hated the rough textured surface of the bathroom walls.

Ron Little brought a .44 Magnum revolver with him from Colorado, bought originally to scare away the bears on a fishing trip to Alaska. Brautigan was impressed by the powerful handgun. Little was a take-charge sort of guy. Once, when a crew member's mangy little dog bit one of the children, Ron ran over and petted the animal to calm it down. Without asking anyone, he took the dog toward the Yellowstone and shot him. Ron "liked that kind of keeping control of shit," Peter Miller said.

Little stayed in touch with Brautigan for a couple of years after the remodeling project was finished. "Rich and I liked each other," he said. Ron stopped to visit whenever he passed through Montana. The last time they were together was a summer when Ianthe was staying with her father. Little arrived one evening, and he and Brautigan sat up late drinking whiskey. "And he talked to me about Hemingway," Ron said. They had been discussing what it felt like for Little when he quit the international ski racing circuit. Richard mentioned "about how Hemingway had shot himself with a shotgun." This conversation stayed in Ron's mind for years because suicide had not been on his mind. "[Brautigan] brought it up," he said.

Living just across the creek, the Hjortsbergs frequently wandered over to Brautigan's construction site to admire the work in progress. They thought more highly of the craftsmanship than Richard did. "He didn't like it," Peter Miller once told Gatz. "You liked it. We were always pleased that you liked it." There weren't many other onlookers. Jeff Bridges stopped by one day when he wasn't working on McGuane's film and praised the laminated redwood countertops Tom Kyle had put together in the kitchen. "See, they've beveled the corners," Bridges said. Brautigan wasn't paying attention.

The filming of *Rancho Deluxe* remained the big news. It was hard to get away from the production. Many local residents were cast in small speaking roles. Scott Palmer and Gatz Hjortsberg, both short of coin, worked as understudies for Jeff Bridges and Sam Waterston, the most menial jobs on the production. In spite of a lifelong interest in the movies, Richard Brautigan visited the location only once. Later, he told G. Haller he thought there were a lot of people sitting around doing nothing. "He didn't quite understand the down time," she said.

Brautigan proved more capable when G.'s son Eric had a bicycle accident on Deep Creek Road near the McGuane place. Richard and Jimmy Buffett had been visiting with Tom and brought the unconscious boy back to the Pine Creek Lodge. Eric had a broken nose. After he regained consciousness, it was feared he might have a concussion. Brautigan called Dr. Dennis Noteboom in town and described the boy's symptoms. Eric wasn't vomiting or showing other overt signs of concussion. Dennis said to keep him in bed for a day or so.

Richard and Jimmy hung around swapping stories for the amusement of the temporary invalid. They talked about how they disciplined themselves to get their work done, perhaps providing backhand moral guidance for the boy. It wasn't all talk of noses to the grindstone. Buffett told a wild story about a dispute he once had with a business associate. It ended when Jimmy performed a wild tap-dance on the roof of the fellow's car in his golfing shoes.

Harry Dean Stanton became Richard Brautigan's closest friend among the *Rancho Deluxe* cast. Born in Kentucky in 1926, the character actor with the weathered basset hound face had appeared in thirty-two films prior to his role as ranch hand Curt in McGuane's opus. *Cool Hand Luke*, *Two-Lane Blacktop*, *Pat Garrett and Billy the Kid*, and *Cisco Pike* were among the best known, and Stanton went on to notable parts in *Alien*, *Wild at Heart*, *Pretty in Pink*, and *Paris, Texas*. Harry Dean had served in World War II, an experience that intrigued Richard, whose longstanding love of military history attracted him to anyone with firsthand knowledge.

One afternoon, Brautigan and Stanton drove back from a binge in Bozeman along Trail Creek Road, an old gravel byway connecting Paradise Valley with Chestnut, a former coal mining town now reduced to a meager handful of ramshackle buildings alongside I-90. Harry Dean abruptly put on the brakes and jumped from the car. He climbed through a barbed wire fence and ran out into the pasture, dragging back a weathered section of wood about four feet long with rusting iron attachments on either end. It was the tailgate to an ancient and long disintegrated wagon. "What do you want with that old piece of junk?" Richard asked.

"Oh, man." Stanton enthused, "won't this make the most beautiful coffee table?"

The drinking bout continued at Brautigan's place. When Harry Dean headed back to his motel room in town he left the old tailgate behind. Stanton never returned for it, and Brautigan eventually propped the relic up against the trunk of a cottonwood tree in his front yard, affixing a long narrow copper strip on which he had engraved: the harry dean stanton coffee table. The tailgate leaned against the tree trunk for almost a decade, until Richard's death.

Mary Ann Gilderbloom arrived late in May for a short stay at the Pine Creek Lodge with Brautigan. Richard borrowed Tom McGuane's truck and had Scott Palmer drive over to the Bozeman airport to pick her up. After that, Mary Ann became the designated driver. At the time, the Livingston social scene revolved almost entirely around the cast and crew of *Rancho Deluxe*. Gilderbloom recalled an evening in town at the Wrangler Bar. Richard and Mary Ann were just leaving after much heavy drinking when they spotted a guy veering down the street with a guitar slung over his back. "That's Jimmy," Brautigan said. "Let's give him a ride home."

"Let's go and have another drink," Jimmy Buffett replied.

This seemed a fine idea, and they all went back into the bar. "We commenced to drink some more," Mary Ann remembered.

At one point, Buffett and Stanton sat down in front of the Pong machine for a drunken mano a mano. Pong had become the bar game of choice for the *Rancho* crew. McGuane even wrote it into a scene in the film. The pair sat before the glowing video screen, so drunk their heads were nearly touching. Observing from behind, Mary Ann said to Richard, "That would be a fabulous album cover."

Later that night, Gilderbloom drove Buffett home to McGuane's house in Tom's truck. "I drove really slow because he sang to me the entire way," Mary Ann recalled. "Drunk as a skunk. It was hilarious. It was one of the funniest nights in my life."

The remodeling project was nearly done. A tremendous amount had been accomplished for $15,000, a relatively modest sum. Only a few finishing touches remained before the ragtag crew would disperse into the rest of their lives. They were all sleeping one night when Stanton and Brautigan showed up in the dark house, skunked to the eyeballs. How it started was anybody's guess. Richard's critical appraisal of their craftsmanship took a violent turn. Ron Little was awakened in his tent by the sudden commotion, dogs barking, babies crying, women screaming. Little shoved his .44 Magnum into the waistband of his jeans and hurried to investigate.

He found Brautigan raging in the kitchen, armed with "a great big thirty-two-ounce framing hammer." With Harry Dean urging him on, Richard smashed at the newly completed ceiling. "This is the way I wanted the ceiling, goddammit!" he shouted. The wall was next. "This wasn't the wall I was after," Richard hollered, hitting it with the framing hammer, a heavy dangerous tool with a hatchet blade on one end. Everyone stood around terrified, the children wide-eyed, unable to deal with his insane behavior.

Ron Little was pissed. "The job was almost over, and I was ready to go home, and he was wrecking things." As Brautigan prepared to swing the hammer again, Little stepped up and grabbed it out of his hand. Taken off balance, Richard fell to the floor. When Harry Dean started to say something, Ron told him, "You get the fuck out of here, man."

Turning to assist Brautigan, Little said, "Richard, you're going to bed. That's enough. You've banged this place up plenty. You've scared the kids. You've scared the dogs. You can call it a night now."

Stanton moved slowly toward the door, continuing to mutter encouragement to the recumbent Brautigan. Ron tried to get Richard to his feet, telling him it was over for the night. If he had any problems they would talk about it in the morning. Harry Dean had gotten into his rental car and started the engine, still yelling at Richard, trying to egg him on. This really pissed Little off. He stepped outside, raised his .44 Magnum, and fired at the car, knocking out a headlight. In the darkness, a two-foot flame erupted from the muzzle of the revolver.

"Made a hell of a racket," Ron said. "A gun that big and that loud has a tendency to get everybody's attention." It sobered Stanton up in a hurry. "Scared the shit out of him," Little recalled. Harry Dean floored it. His car spun around a couple times in the driveway, a maneuver known among hot-rodders as a doughnut. Mad as he was, Ron Little began to find the whole thing amusing. "I thought about killing the fucking car and make him walk back into town," he said. Instead, Ron fired a second shot into the ground beside the driver's side door, causing Harry Dean to concentrate wonderfully on his driving. The actor got control of the car and sped off into the night.

The construction project, including patching up the kitchen, came to an end a couple days later, about the same time *Rancho Deluxe* wrapped. To celebrate both events, Richard Brautigan threw a big housewarming party at his new home on the first Saturday in June. Most of the cast and movie crew were invited, along with the much-despised hippie carpenters. Harry Dean was there. Ditto Jeff Bridges and Sam Waterston. Tom and Becky McGuane mingled in the crowd. Marian Hjortsberg brought over a roast suckling pig to the feast. After a long, cold, wet spring, the bright sunny afternoon came as a welcome treat.

G. Haller thought the party "was to honor the crew and Peter for the wonderful work that they had done." She remembered Richard as being "very proud" of the redwood craftsmanship. At one point in the festivities, Brautigan took her over to a large cottonwood in the backyard, pointing out where he planned to plant his garden. G. felt concerned about the lack of sunlight. "Oh no," Richard assured her, "this is the place to put the garden because the tree had been used as the slaughtering tree for all the animals on the farm." He assumed the spilled blood enriched the ground beneath the cottonwood.

Ron Little sat off by himself, observing the proceedings, when a very pretty young blond woman approached, carrying two beers. She gave one to Ron and sat down next to him. After she asked his name, they chatted for a minute before she wondered what he did. "I'm just a carpenter," Ron said, "a simple carpenter." Without another word, the blond got up and walked away.

In a curious twist, a young couple who worked as the rural route mail carriers crashed Brautigan's party. They brought a preacher along with them and proceeded to get married among the merrymakers while various children pelted them with tossed grass. Taken off guard, Gatz Hjortsberg was drafted as their reluctant witness. After the ceremony, they used the potluck as their reception dinner. G. Haller recalled that Brautigan at first seemed very upset by the unexpected nuptials, but quickly adopted a philosophical attitude. "You don't want to ruin the party," he told her, "so you just kind of let them do what they are going to do."

By the next afternoon, almost all of the remodeling crew was gone. Peter Miller never had another conversation with Richard in his life. One day, several years later, he bumped into Brautigan on a San Francisco street. "Hello," Peter said.

"Nice to see you," Richard replied, walking on his way without another word. They never saw each other again.

The last of the crew to leave was John "Spaceman" Fenu and his family. Their truck had broken down, and Spaceman was working on his transmission beside the barn when Brautigan came striding up the hill from his newly completed house. "You have to get off my property," he said. Spaceman, basically a quiet guy, just stared at him, uncomprehending. "You have all the rest of great big Montana in which to repair your truck," Richard told him. Fenu got the message. He somehow managed to start his outfit and drive away, leaving Brautigan all alone in his new home in the mountains.

forty: **over easy**

N THE FALL of 1973, Richard Brautigan came into Livingston one evening for some serious drinking. He headed straight for the Wrangler, the bar of choice among the Montana Gang. The much-beloved watering hole has been replaced by a succession of restaurants in the on-going yuppification of the West. Back then, Livingston was still a railroad town, boasting twenty-four bars and an equal number of churches. A fellow could tie one on every Saturday night and pray off his hangover on Sunday without ever hitting the same joint twice for six straight months.

Two rival drinking establishments stood on Park Street, across from the Northern Pacific depot. The Wrangler featured rock-and-roll bands and catered to a scruffier long-haired crowd, in those days most likely blue-collar guys, carpenters, and auto mechanics, not hippie weirdos. Next door was the Longbranch (now sadly transformed into a Chinese restaurant), a shit-kicker cowboy bar with country music and a frieze of the local ranch brands running around the walls. Most nights, customers wandered back and forth between the two long narrow rooms. Eventually, an interior door was cut through the dividing wall. Music came mainly on the weekends. The rest of the time, folks shot pool, played the Pong machine, and got slowly and religiously drunk.

Richard spent a lot of time at the Wrangler. Cindy Murphy, a local gal who tended bar for proprietor Bob Burns, remembered him often arriving alone. Brautigan sat by himself drinking all night without saying a word to anyone. Cindy recalled that Richard always tipped well. Mary Burns, the owner's daughter, was about nineteen when Brautigan started coming into her father's place. He told her he was planning to raise ducks. "I ordered a bunch of baby ducklings," he said. "They're coming in soon on the train." After that, whenever Mary saw him in the bar, she'd ask about the ducks. Had they arrived yet? "Nope. Not yet, any day now." This went on for a couple of years until it dawned on her that he was pulling her leg.

One time, standing at the Wrangler Bar, Brautigan was accosted by a weary salesman in a rumpled plaid polyester suit, wide necktie undone. After a difficult and frustrating day, the fellow radiated truculence and glared red-faced up at Richard. "You hippies certainly have it made," he said, his voice acid with disapproval.

Whiskey glass in hand, Richard peered down imperiously through his bifocals at the angry little man. "I am not a hippie, sir," he declared, enunciating each word precisely. "I work for my living."

On another occasion, Richard came into the Wrangler with Tom McGuane and Jim Harrison after a day of bird hunting. Dick Murphy, Cindy's brother, remembered it was "a pretty crazy night in there." McGuane and Harrison elbowed to the bar, shouting out drink orders. Richard had something else on his mind. "Brautigan's got this paper sack," Dick recalled, "like a big grocery bag, and he's got it kind of necked down, funneled down from the top, and I'm watching him, and he's got people sticking their hands in there, and people would scream. 'Stick your hand in there,' he'd say, 'so you can tell what it is.' The girls especially would all come out screaming."

Murphy himself gave it a try. The bag contained seven or eight dead grouse. "There were so many in there that they were all still warm, of course, and so all you felt was this kind of plump feathered bodies. It was pretty funny. He was getting a big kick out of it."

One night, after knocking back round after round of Black Jack and water, no ice, a drink known locally as a "ditch," Richard and a group of fellow patrons straggled across the street to Martin's when the Wrangler closed at 2:00 am. An all-night café slinging hash seven days a week in an Italianate brick building that once served as a dining room for the Northern Pacific passenger depot, Martin's had a Renaissance villa exterior that matched the baggage room, one of three imposing structures built between 1901 and 1902. Inside, the place was pure 1950s moderne, Formica-topped tables and a color scheme running to pumpkin and aqua. Dedicated Livingston barflies all headed to Martin's for a greasy breakfast after last call.

The crowd from the Wrangler numbered about ten, including Cindy and Richard, an artist named Donna Bone, and a couple guys who recently moved to Montana from New Jersey. They sat at a long table in the middle of the large, high-ceilinged room. Orders were taken: eggs prepared various ways, hash browns, omelets, short stacks, biscuits and gravy. At some point, Brautigan, who hadn't been saying much, got up and walked silently away from the table. No one really paid attention. Richard was quite drunk, yet moved with a certain lurching dignity. Cindy Murphy remembered a gradual awareness of the displeasure building behind her, a barely perceptible murmuring, an uncomfortable mirthless laughter: the uneasy sound of people wondering if the joke was on them.

The folks at the long central table spun around to see what was going on. They beheld Richard, passing from group to group, deliberately sticking his finger in everyone's food, one plate at a time. He did so with casual indifference, like a royal taster working the house at the king's request. The stunned reaction behind him wasn't exactly that of a lynch mob, but people were plainly puzzled and patently pissed. The bunch from the Wrangler looked on in helpless bewilderment, having no ready explanation for their companion's peculiar behavior and expecting a massacre at any moment.

Brautigan wove between the tables, serene as a drunken angel, dipping his finger dispassionately into the cheese omelets and sunny-side-ups on his way to oblivion. There were perhaps thirty other customers, railroad workers and ranch hands, the usual late-night crowd, and nothing like this had ever happened to any of them before. Not looking back, Richard made his way to the cash register by the door. He picked up the tab for everyone in the place. Three dozen free breakfasts anointed by the touch of the poet.

RICHARD BRAUTIGAN'S NEW Montana home and the Hjortsbergs' place to the north across Pine Creek shared a common underground gravity-feed water line. It was an ancient affair, the iron-bound wooden conduit laid sometime before the end of the nineteenth century. The line fed off two source boxes, the lower one, for use in winter, was located directly in the creek; the uppermost placed in an irrigation ditch running only in summer. A control valve regulated the flow down the branch line to Brautigan's house.

In the spring of 1974, while Richard's house was being remodeled, Gatz walked him up through the woods, attempting to explain the intricacies of their antique waterworks. The valve control was of special interest as Brautigan planned to shut off his supply in winter. Richard, unmechanical as always, proved a disinterested student. He preferred discussing books, his own work in particular. Brautigan told Hjortsberg about his "five-year plan." Richard explained he would write a new book in a different genre every year for the next five years.

The first of these genre novels, *The Hawkline Monster: A Gothic Western*, had already been written. By the time Brautigan moved in to his remodeled house, the book was three months away from publication. There were no interviews or plans for a book tour. Once again, the designer in charge of Simon & Schuster's book production was Helen Barrow. Richard Snyder, president of the company, had some new ideas about how to publish Brautigan. Instead of releasing *Hawkline* simultaneously both in cloth and as a trade paperback, Snyder decided to bring it out first as a hardcover.

The new marketing approach called for a corresponding shift in the overall book design. Instead of placing Brautigan's photograph on the front cover, Simon & Schuster hired noted dust jacket illustrator Wendell Minor, who produced an evocative sepia-toned painting of the turreted Hawkline Manor. Brautigan approved Wendell Minor's cover. Jonathan Dolger recalled that Brautigan loved Minor's work. Richard asked his friend John Fryer to take his dust jacket photo. Fryer, a talented amateur photographer, maintained a professional darkroom in the basement of his store in Livingston. Early in June, shortly after his housewarming party, Fryer took a photo at Pine Creek. Richard wore jeans, a dark untucked Western shirt, and the high-crowned black hat he had favored in Key West, his long blond hair hanging free past his shoulders. John Fryer was paid $125 for his work.

The Hawkline Monster: A Gothic Western was published in August of 1974 with an initial printing of forty thousand copies. No text accompanied the author photo, nor was there any biographical information about Brautigan printed inside on the flaps. Helen Brann agreed with Dick Snyder. Publishing Brautigan's new novel in a more traditional format would lead to increased hardback sales. By the beginning of October, Simon & Schuster had sold enough books for Jonathan Dolger to order an additional printing of ten thousand copies. The usual array of naysayers lined up to lambaste Richard for "triteness and banality," "self-indulgent whimsy,"and "irreverence and obscenity." In the *New Statesman*, Julian Barnes regretted the novel's "watered style and paper-thin narrative." Roger Sale (*Hudson Review*) said, "It is a terrible book, deeply unfunny, in no need of having been written." There were a few exceptions. *Playboy* called *Hawkline* "certainly Brautigan's most simultaneously unified and eclectic work," while *Booklist* raved, "With just the right blend of cowpoke humor and touches of the macabre, Brautigan hilariously spoofs the traditional western as well as the classic horror tale."

Even as the bad notices started rolling in, there was much to celebrate. *Hawkline* was selling well, and Hollywood came calling, checkbook in hand. After *Rancho Deluxe* wrapped, Michael Haller returned home to Los Angeles and talked enthusiastically about *The Hawkline Monster* with his friend, director Hal Ashby. Haller first worked with Ashby in 1971, as the production designer of *Harold and Maude*, and again on *The Last Detail*, Ashby's third film as a director, finished the year before and featuring rising star Jack Nicholson. Michael thought that *Hawkline* was a perfect lead role for Nicholson. Harry Dean Stanton was eager to play the other hired assassin cowpoke in the story.

Taking a giant step into the deal-making process, Brautigan traveled down to Los Angeles to meet with Ashby. Richard had never been fond of L.A., which he called "this strange sprawling city of gothic vegetation and casual clothing where I am changed instantly into a child thinking that all eight million people here somehow work in the movies." Hal Ashby brought Brautigan to a lunchtime meeting with Jack Nicholson at the actor's home high up on Mulholland Drive. Brautigan, understandably apprehensive at having to sell himself and his work to Nicholson, fortified himself with ample doses of bourbon whiskey.

More cocktails followed chez Jack. By midafternoon, Brautigan, far from being nervous, felt no pain at all. Richard played an afternoon game of "horse," one-on-one basketball, with Jack Nicholson at a hoop the actor had set up in front of his garage. They bet $50 on the outcome. Brautigan, six inches taller than Nicholson, won the game and the wager. As they sat around the living room later that afternoon, the conversation touched on financing. Richard launched into a lengthy discourse detailing his disdain for money. To demonstrate this scorn, Brautigan resorted to an old Digger tactic. He took out his wallet and removed all the bills, including his basketball winnings, slowly tearing them into tiny pieces. Ashby and Nicholson looked on in astonishment as Brautigan scattered the bank note confetti into an elongated crystal bowl on the coffee table. Jack had another business meeting scheduled at that hour, so Hal and Richard politely took their leave.

The moguls arrived as Ashby's car pulled out of Nicholson's driveway. Jack had no time to tidy up, and the bowl of shredded money sat on prominent display as the small talk started. It was hard to ignore. One of the big shots, knowing Nicholson was a collector, asked, "What is this? Some kind of art piece?"

Jack flashed his famous grin and strung the guy along, telling him it was a conceptual work designed to express the artist's contempt for commerce. "You know," he said, improvising the gag as he went, "people just like make contributions."

Quick as a high-roller tossing down a bet, the mogul whipped out his wallet and tore up a wad of hundreds, dropping the pieces into the crystal bowl. It was the start of a long-running comic tradition. For years afterward, the bowl full of torn money sat on Jack Nicholson's coffee table, a memorial to Richard Brautigan, as sucker after sucker ripped up his bankroll in the name of art.

Nicholson would not commit to the *Hawkline* project until he read a script. Hal Ashby negotiated a deal with Helen Brann and Flora Roberts early in June 1975. Dick Hodge worked for seven and a half hours, helping to facilitate the deal. Ashby obtained the underlying film rights to *The Hawkline Monster* and contracted Brautigan to write the screenplay. The amount agreed upon for both came to $125,000, although, separate from his screenwriting fee, Brautigan received only a $10,000 option against an eventual sale price.

Ashby hoped to make *Hawkline* his next picture, planning to start shooting in Montana in the summer of 1976. Richard hired a private secretary, Glenise Butcher, to assist him in typing the many preliminary drafts of his screenplay. Glenise, a beautiful young Englishwoman, proved extremely useful to Richard. Not only was she a swift typist, she could take dictation in shorthand.

Don Carpenter served as Brautigan's "in-house critic" on the *Hawkline* project. In 1972, Don wrote and coproduced the film *Payday*, starring Rip Torn as a self-destructive country-and-western singer modeled on Hank Williams. The film featured original songs by *Playboy* cartoonist and children's book author Shel Silverstein, who had worked with Don on *Stars and Stripes* in Japan during the Korean War. *Payday* received a standing ovation at the Cannes Film Festival and impressed Richard Brautigan, who regarded his friend Carpenter as his unofficial ambassador to Hollywood.

Brautigan brought Glenise Butcher over to Carpenter's place and had him explain the format and structure of a screenplay. She took it all down in shorthand. After learning the structure, Brautigan began writing the script. The previous year, when Gatz Hjortsberg had scored his first Hollywood assignment, Richard offered some advice. "You know the secret to writing screenplays, don't you?" he quipped. "You have to leave all the writing out."

Brautigan's *Hawkline* screenplay ran very long. Industry standards dictate anything over 120 pages to be an unwieldy epic. His script was peppered with wry Brautiganesque touches, like adding a line of dialogue after a description of an owl sitting in the rafters of a barn:

> OWL
>
> *Hoot!*

"He called me up maybe, what, six thousand, seven thousand times, with little line changes and things like that," Don Carpenter recalled. "And then he brought over his first draft with Glenise to take notes. He would read the scene to me, and I would tell him what I thought about how the scene would play and what I thought should go into it, what should come out. What he was interested in getting from me was how to make a drama, how to make a dramatic scene. I've never done a better tightrope job in my life. I didn't touch content or style or approach."

After reading the final draft of *Hawkline*, Carpenter told Brautigan "it was one of the best screenplays I'd ever read, and there was no chance it would ever be made into a movie, because it's schizophrenic." Don considered the script "beautifully written, beautifully, beautifully written." He thought the only way a Brautigan movie could ever get made was "to not try to make it like every other movie, not try to make it conform to any kind of movie, but to make it a Brautigan movie, so that it's totally weird from beginning to end."

Richard refused to believe Don's dire predictions. He wrote down his friend's words, "This screenplay of *Hawkline Monster* will never be made into a film," and passed the paper across to

Carpenter. "You sign this," he said. Don signed. "I'm going to make you eat that in public," Brautigan said.

"I will eat that at the Beverly Hills Hotel," Don replied, "at the Polo Lounge at the Beverly Hills Hotel. I will pay for lunch on the day this film is completed."

By midsummer, Brautigan finished his 145-page first draft of the screenplay. Ashby and Haller enthusiastically awaited its arrival in L.A., but Richard refused to mail it. G. Haller speculated that it had to do with a previous trip made to Hollywood during his first *Trout Fishing* fame. A big-shot producer courted Richard with a dinner invitation to his Beverly Hills home. Brautigan was "limoed" up to the mogul's mansion and served an "obscenely long three-foot [baked] trout." The sight of it made Richard feel like he was some rube from the hills who only ate trout. All through the meal, the talk focused on the genius of *Trout Fishing*. After dinner, the producer offered Richard $250 for an option on the book. The experience made Brautigan leery of movie executives. G. was dispatched to Montana "to find and deliver the script."

G. brought along her two boys, and they stayed once again in a cabin at the Pine Creek Lodge. As soon as they settled in, she walked over with Eric and Bret to pay a call on Richard. Brautigan announced that he was going to take the kids fishing. G. felt disappointed when their destination turned out to look like a trout farm. It was Armstrong's Spring Creek, which also supported a fish hatchery. Richard took pains to set the boys up and show them what to do. "He was very, very emphatic about the kids catching fish," G. recalled.

All of them caught fish. Richard invited the Hallers back to his place that evening for a trout dinner. Ianthe was spending the summer with her father and helped him prepare the meal, assisted by Tony Dingman, who had come to help with the chores and drive Brautigan around. Siew-Hwa Beh, Brautigan's new girlfriend, rounded out the party.

Born in Penang, Malaysia, of Chinese ancestry, Siew-Hwa first came to the United States in 1963 at age eighteen on an American Field Service scholarship. She returned to the States two years later with $100 in her pocket, two suitcases, and another grant. She was one of the first women to attend the UCLA film school. The writer-director Paul Schrader was among her classmates. Frustrated by the subordinate position of female students expected to make coffee instead of movies, Siew-Hwa scraped together $600 in 1969 with her roommate and created *Women & Film*, the world's first feminist film magazine.

In the late fall of '74, Siew-Hwa dated a Chinese journalist named Min who wrote for several local papers and was a friend of Brautigan's. Min brought her to a bar in North Beach, where Richard spotted Siew-Hwa through the boisterous crowd. "There was a lot of dancing," she said, "and I had no idea that he was so smitten."

Five feet, one inch tall and extremely thin, Beh wore tight pants and no bra under a sleeveless, collarless bib. Brautigan described her a few years later in a short story ("A San Francisco Snake Story"): "She was very intelligent and also had an excellent figure whose primary focus was her breasts. They were large and well shaped. They gardened and harvested much attention wherever she went."

When Richard approached Siew-Hwa to make his introductions, she asked him what he did for a living.

"I write," Brautigan said. "I wrote *Trout Fishing in America*."

"Well," Siew-Hwa replied, "I really am not into fishing."

That she didn't know Richard was a writer "turned him on," Siew-Hwa later recalled, "because he had never met anybody who was educated who'd never heard of him. He was thrilled that I didn't know him."

Brautigan wheedled Beh's phone number from Min and called her a couple days later. "He called me only when he was drunk," she said. "I guess he was too nervous." Their first conversation was a lengthy recounting of an argument he'd recently had with his ex-wife, Ginny, about Ianthe's dental problems. Virginia wanted to have the bad teeth removed and Richard thought she should save them. "You've got to have your own teeth to chew your own food," he told Siew-Hwa.

"What is this guy, nuts?" she thought, making a rude reply and hanging up. Brautigan never got discouraged, and he tried again. "His strength is that he was persistent," Siew-Hwa related, and she agreed to go on a date with Richard. He invited her to his new North Beach apartment on Union Street. "He cooked for me," Siew-Hwa said. "As the evening wore on he paid me a lot of attention. He read to me, and I've never had anybody spend time reading to me. And I was so charmed." After the first couple dates, their passion grew "so intense" that they couldn't bear to stay apart and Beh moved in with Brautigan. Ginny told Siew-Hwa, "You are the woman Richard has been waiting for. You are the one."

Fueled by their mutual passion and a shared love for the movies, Siew-Hwa adopted a partner's proprietary interest in Richard's film script. This came to the fore at the Pine Creek fish dinner with G. Haller and her kids. "Siew-Hwa was very challenging at the end of this visit," G. recalled. "Kind of challenging my credentials. It's like 'Who are you?' and 'What are you doing here?' Like maybe she could make a better deal."

They all watched television after dinner. Eric and Bret fell asleep on the couch, and Ianthe covered them with a blanket. The grownups "sat and talked and talked" until it was time for G. to wake her kids and walk them back down the center of the road to their cabin at the Pine Creek Lodge. The Hallers returned to L.A. the next day without the *Hawkline* screenplay. Eventually, Brautigan mailed his script in, addressing it to "The Beautiful Hal Ashby."

Richard waited a bit too long. By the time his script arrived, Ashby was preoccupied with the production details of *Bound for Glory*, his Woody Guthrie biopic starring David Carradine. Mike Haller assured Flora Roberts in August that the project was still "in the works." By early October, more than six weeks had gone by with no word from Hal Ashby. Richard Hodge wrote Flora Roberts to say Brautigan had expressed "a great disinterest in working further on the screenplay, given the problems of communication to date."

All was silent on the Hollywood front until the middle of March 1976, when Helen Brann wrote to Richard: "I understand that Hal Ashby is stirring the pot again and that maybe a movie will be made of THE HAWKLINE MONSTER." Ashby had other pots to stir. He was busy with another project, *Coming Home*, a tale of injured Vietnam vets featuring Jane Fonda and Jon Voigt. Penny Milford received a Best Supporting Actress Oscar nomination for the role of Vi.

Ashby continued to express interest in *Hawkline*, paying $10,000 in June to renew his option for another six months. He renewed again in December, adding an additional $10,000 to Brautigan's bank account. False promises and outright lies prevail in the film industry, but this kind of capital investment signified a genuine desire to make the picture. Richard told Keith Abbott, visiting Pine Creek in the summer of 1976, that his goal now was to earn $1 million in Hollywood. "'One million dollars a year,' he kept repeating, almost as if hypnotizing himself," Abbott wrote in his memoir. "'I'm going to make one million dollars in one year.'"

The road leading Brautigan toward the $1 million mirage proved both long and winding, as such routes tend to be in Tinseltown. Hal Ashby trudged the same path. While looking for his leads in *Hawkline*, he set his sights on *Being There* (1979), starring Peter Sellers and arguably his finest film. Along the way, Richard's "Gothic Western" grew in popularity, appearing in England as well as in translations in Japan, Italy, France, Spain, Holland, Germany, Denmark, Norway, Sweden, and Finland.

By November 1976, *Hawkline* had sold 49,211 hardbound copies in America and an additional 73,750 in quality paperback. The mass-market paperback, released in September, had already reached 160,985 copies in sales. These figures were not lost on Hal Ashby, who planned to move ahead with Jack Nicholson. Harry Dean Stanton had been dropped in favor of Dustin Hoffman.

In June of 1977, Hal Ashby again renewed his *Hawkline* option. He hoped to begin shooting in Montana that fall. Dustin Hoffman, yet to sign on the dotted line, stood in the way of starting principal photography. Hoffman never signed. Ashby and Nicholson moved ahead to other projects. Ashby had already spent what Helen Brann described as "a small fortune" on option payments, and did the sensible thing, buying the film rights to Brautigan's novel outright.

By 1982, Ashby, slowed by health problems, turned the director's chair over to Mike Haller, assigning himself the role of producer. A deal was made with Universal Studio, and Gatz Hjortsberg signed on for a couple drafts of a new *Hawkline* script. Completed, bound copies were delivered to the executive offices high atop the tall glass executive building known as the Black Tower. Thom Mount, head of motion picture production at Universal, was fired that same weekend. On Monday morning, his successor, Frank Price, swept the desk clean of all Mount's projects.

The Hawkline Monster languished in development hell once again. New drafts were written. Mike Haller tried one himself. Nothing came of them. Hal Ashby died in 1988. Haller ten years later. It seemed for a time as if their dream of a *Hawkline* movie might follow them into the grave. Ianthe Brautigan later regained the North American rights to her father's book, and another deal percolated in the promised land.

Richard Brautigan began work on the second book of his five-year plan early in 1974. This time, there was no need for a long list of potential titles. He knew what he wanted right from the start: *Willard and His Bowling Trophies*. Brautigan appended a subtitle, *A Perverse Mystery*. This had been his practice since writing *The Abortion: An Historical Romance 1966*.

Willard became Richard's first project in his new writing studio high in the rafters of the barn at Pine Creek. On the first day of summer in 1974, seated at his desk in front of the big picture window facing the Absaroka Mountains, he wrote "46 pages, behind 2" in the date square of a spiral-bound 1973/1974 reminder calendar. He had completed nearly fifty pages of his new novel, but Brautigan felt he was two pages behind schedule. He recorded his daily page tally in his calendar, a process Hemingway called "keeping yourself honest." The totals varied. Some days Richard wrote eight pages; often it was only two or three. At the end of the first week of July, he exclaimed: "hot dog! 14 pages 38 pages ahead."

July was a productive month, many eight- or nine-page days. On the seventeenth, a thirteen-page day, he jotted "finished" in the date square. After a three-week break, the daily tally began again on August 11, continuing, with another three-week hiatus at the end of the month, until September 26, when Richard wrote "finished" following an eight-page day.

Willard takes place over the course of several hours in a single evening, ending tragically "a few moments past one in the morning." The backstory of the Logan brothers' three-year criminal hegira in search of their stolen bowling trophies wanders haphazardly across the roadmap of America, but is almost an adornment embroidered onto the texture of the novel. The events emotionally involving the reader all take place in Bob and Constance's apartment in a three-story building on Chestnut Street in San Francisco, where the author lays bare secret desires and embarks upon an investigation of his private sexual nature.

Unlike Bob, his fictional hero, Richard's predilictions for S&M were not occasioned by sexually transmitted diseases. A taste for bondage predated Brautigan's herpes infection by many years. Richard told his lovers a story about when he was young and newly arrived in San Francisco. He claimed his first love affair was with an older woman who enjoyed being tied up. She instructed Brautigan in the practice. Because sex was a new experience, he learned to associate bondage with intercourse. Richard claimed it had "ruined him" for traditional sexual activity. There's no way of knowing the truth. Richard's first sexual partner was his wife, Ginny. She was born a year earlier than Richard, hardly "an older woman."

Sherry Vetter recalled one evening in her early twenties when she had recently started dating Richard. She wandered down the long front hallway at his Geary Street apartment, "and I'm discovering the doors leading to different places." Sherry opened one and stared into a narrow closet. A row of wire coat hooks screwed into the wall held five or six silk neckties. Brautigan came up the hall from the kitchen. "I didn't know you wore ties," Sherry said. He slammed the closet door. "Richard, you're always telling me we can't go to certain restaurants because you refuse to wear a tie," she protested, following him down the hall. "You've got perfectly nice ties in there!"

Not too long after that evening, Sherry Vetter found out why Brautigan collected neckties. "I used to say to him, 'Richard, it's so amateur. It's so silly. Why are we doing this? I mean, for one thing, it's silk ties. Do you think I could not untie this? I mean, nothing here is real. It's so silly.' And he'd stand up and stamp his feet up and down, and he'd say, 'Just do it! Just do it! I don't care how silly this is!'"

In 1982, more than ten years after Sherry met Richard, when they'd both married and divorced others, she saw him for the last time. They "holed up" in the Kyoto Inn, a high-rise Best Western hotel in San Francisco's Japantown. Sherry awoke to find Richard standing beside her "ripping up these white sheets.' This struck her as so funny she couldn't stop laughing. Richard sat down on the other bed and laughed along with her, taking off his glasses, laughing until tears formed in his eyes. He gave up the sheet-tearing and looked over at her nude figure. "I like the way your body matured," Richard said sweetly, and they dressed and went out for a late night dinner.

Another of Brautigan's lovers close to the end of his life echoed Vetter. "It was nothing serious, and it was a game," she observed. "And I knew it was a game. It was kind of silly. Sometimes I would say, 'Richard, do we have to go through that tonight?'

"And he'd say, 'Well, maybe just a little one. Maybe just the wrists and nothing else.' It was like we'd bargain. 'Just the wrists and nothing else. Not the feet and the gag and the . . .' He would say that. He was so funny. He'd say, 'I'm just going to tie you up. It's okay. It's not going to hurt.'

And do it. 'There. That's nice.' You know, talked like he was talking to a kitten he was petting. Very bizarre."

Sherry Vetter later insisted, "Every girl you'll talk to will tell you it was totally so amateur, such a joke." One time when her brother called the apartment, "Richard and I were fooling around, the tying-and-gagging stuff." Richard jumped out of bed and answered the phone. When Sherry's brother asked for her, Brautigan said she couldn't come to the phone, adding by way of explanation, "She's all tied up." Vetter also remembered how, after a bondage session, Brautigan begged her never to mention what they did in the privacy of their bedroom. "Don't ever tell anybody about this," he said. "I'll never write about this."

"And then he did," Sherry reflected almost wistfully. "And remember who the girl was who got tied? It was me. The big green eyes, remember that?"

Another of his former girlfriends said, "The fact is it's only when he was really drunk that he would have the slightest inclination to tie people up." Brautigan never willfully caused his partners any physical pain. Although Richard practiced what many consider deviant sexual behavior, he wasn't a sadist. He regarded bondage as something playful and no more wicked than wearing sexy lingerie.

Lawrence Wright reported in *Rolling Stone* that girls would warn each other about Richard's "penchant for bondage" in the restrooms of North Beach bars. There was a young woman, a one-night stand Brautigan picked up at a midseventies Russell Chatham art opening in Livingston, who appeared the next morning, ashen and shaking, in the Hjortsbergs' kitchen pleading for coffee and a ride to the Greyhound station. No mention was made of gags or silk neckties. She'd obviously just had an unpleasant and totally unexpected experience. Three of Richard's girlfriends complained to Margot Patterson Doss about what they felt was weird sexual behavior. She got on his case about it. "But, Margot," Richard replied, "I always tie them up loosely, and I never hurt them."

Don Carpenter had lived in Japan in the fifties and felt that *Willard and His Bowling Trophies* was "a Japanese sadist novel." Richard's game plan was to write books "each in its own way a surrealistic version of a popular genre." Elaborating further, Carpenter observed, "Sadomasochism is the national sport of Japan." Brautigan was well versed in contemporary Japanese literature, having read and admired the novels of Yukio Mishima, Kōbō Abe, Yasunari Kawabata, and Junichiro Tanizaki. He had long appreciated classic Japanese poetry, especially the work of Bashō and Issa.

It wasn't just Brautigan's sexual habits and his pet papier-mâché bird that made it into *Willard*. He added a three-volume set of *The Greek Anthology*, one of his favorite literary works, to the narrative mix. Richard owned these books. His description was specific: "a 1928 Putnam edition, a part of The Loeb Classical Library, with gold lettering on a dark cover." The anthology, a collection of mostly anonymous ancient Greek poetry, songs, epigrams, and fragments, first compiled by Meleager in the first-century BC, held great appeal for Richard.

It's easy to see the influence of *The Greek Anthology* on Richard's work. Much of his poetry depended on fragmentation for its effect. What was left out, the empty spaces, give many of his poems their power. Four *Anthology* selections (all used in *Willard*) sound almost like Richard's poetry. ("Deeply do I mourn, for my friends are nothing worth." "I know the tunes of all the birds." "And nothing will come of anything." "The dice of Love are madnesses and melees.") The author of the last is known. His name was Anacreon. Brautigan used this quote as an epigraph for the novel.

A second epigraph for *Willard* came from a quote attributed to Senator Frank Church of Idaho: "This land is cursed with violence." When Helen Brann wrote the senator to verify the quote, Church replied that he remembered making the observation to a reporter when word arrived of Robert Kennedy's death in June 1968.

Willard and His Bowling Trophies was the only one of Brautigan's books that bore no dedication. Many years later, Siew-Hwa Beh claimed Richard intended to dedicate the novel to her. Brautigan asked to use her photo on the dust jacket. She refused, saying, "You are not going to collect me the way you collect other women." Siew-Hwa had not met Richard when he completed *Willard*. The book was published in the late summer of 1975, and they were living together by then. The day after publication, Don Carpenter phoned Siew-Hwa. "Well, he paid you the highest compliment," Don said. "He never put a name there because the book was supposed to be for you."

Toward the end of summer, Dell asked Brautigan if he'd be interested in writing an introduction for a planned American edition of *The Beatles Illustrated Lyrics*. Having enjoyed his own tenuous personal connection to John Lennon, the Beatles, and Apple Records, Brautigan agreed. In October, Richard wrote a brief essay at the Pine Creek house. "The Silence of Flooded Houses." He quoted a couple lines from "Eleanor Rigby" for poetic emphasis and mailed the piece off to Helen Brann, never anticipating the tempest in the corporate teapot engendered by his simple reference.

In September, Brautigan called Erik Weber, saying, "I want a photograph for *Willard*." He also hired Loie to proofread the *Willard* manuscript. Erik journeyed over to Geary Street from Potrero Hill. Richard was not in the best of shape. He was full-bearded and overweight, his shoulder-length hair thinning on top, and his image no longer reflected the ethos of a generation. Erik took ten shots in the apartment, the last film he ever exposed in the Museum, all grim frowning portraits of Brautigan. At the All American Bowling Trophy Supply, a simple storefront selling bowling balls and other nine-pin paraphernalia, Erik photographed him frowning in front of the entrance.

The next stop was a bowling alley on Chestnut Street. Weber fired off eighteen frames (Brautigan grouped with golden trophies, peering over a gleaming rack of balls, kneeling before an altarlike wall, balls shelved like polished skulls behind him). One of these became the cover of the British edition. Another graced *Loading Mercury with a Pitchfork*, Richard's first collection of poetry in six years.

Weber remembered Brautigan wanted to "cover his belly. He didn't want people to see it. Felt embarrassed by it, a very vain person." Around this time, Richard suggested Erik take photographs of him naked in the bathtub with his feet sticking out. "We couldn't do it," Erik recalled. "He said no. I don't want to do it now because my stomach's too big."

Brautigan received a $50,000 advance for hardcover and quality paperback rights for *Willard and His Bowling Trophies*, identical to what he got for *The Hawkline Monster*. Helen Brann also secured a straight 15 percent hardback royalty. Again, the dust jacket art featured a striking painting by Wendell Minor, a stylized portrait of Willard surrounded by gleaming golden bowling trophies. Early in 1975, unhappy with Erik Weber's pictures, Richard contacted Jill Krementz, noted photographer and wife of Kurt Vonnegut Jr. Five years earlier in New York, Krementz took pictures of Brautigan in his new-look pageboy haircut.

She sent proofs for Richard to consider. He selected a pensive head shot for his *Willard* author's photo, uncharacteristically not wearing his glasses. Jill Krementz wrote Brautigan in May asking which of the other photographs he liked. She wanted permission to use them. "Your book will be coming out in no time at all and I'm sure I'll be getting requests."

When *Willard* appeared, it was not a critical success. The reviewers stood in line to slam it. Cole William, writing in the *Saturday Review*, called it the worst novel of 1975. "Up to the author's usual standards: fey and wispy." In the *New York Times Book Review*, Michael Rogers suggested, "Perhaps Brautigan should make a retreat from the novel form." When the novel came out in England the following year, Julian Barnes sneered in the *New Statesman*: "It's like following a cartoon strip [. . .] one step back for every two forward, terrific of course, for those with spaced-out memories." *Willard* had fewer foreign sales than Brautigan's previous books. It appeared in translation only in Japan, France, Spain, and Germany. Even Don Carpenter was no fan of the novel. "I hate that book so much I may not even have [a copy]," he stated. No matter. *Willard* sold thirty-five thousand copies by October 10.

By the time the bad reviews came out, Richard was hard at work on his next novel. Brautigan planned to write his own take on the contemporary Japanese novel, compressing the story's time-span into a single hour. The emotional compression used by Japanese writers also attracted Richard. A deliberate shattering of an antique teacup provided the dramatic high point in Kawabata's novel *Thousand Cranes*.

The "I-novel," a particularly elusive form of twentieth-century Japanese literature, possessed great appeal for Brautigan. The term first came into use in the 1920s, when critics used it to describe the intensely personal autobiographical sketches written "for a closed circle of fellow writers" in the early years of the new century. Toward the end of the Meiji period, works such as Tayama Katai's "The Quilt," published in 1907, and the comic satire "I Am a Cat" (1905), with its supercilious feline narrator, the first fiction by Sōseki Natsume, "the Charles Dickens of Japan," came to define this "new" form.

In the 1950s, following Japan's traumatic World War II defeat, a revival of the I-novel saw a restructuring of the form. This reflected an introspective examination of the old historical ideologies and the inevitable downfall of the quest for Empire.

Brautigan's first four works of fiction might be regarded as American I-novels. The anonymous first-person narrators in *Trout Fishing* and *In Watermelon Sugar*, assumed by the readers to be Brautigan himself, fit the parameters set down by Tomi Suzuki in *Narrating the Self: Fictions of Japanese Modernity*: "a mode of reading that assumes that the I-novel is a single-voiced, direct expression of the author's self, and its written language is transparent." Suzuki further explains, "the reader's belief in a single identity of the protagonist, the narrator, and the author of a text makes a text an I-novel."

Brautigan had been familiar with Japanese poetry since high school. It is not known when he first encountered the I-novel. *Sombrero Fallout* lacks a first-person narrator and cannot be considered an Americanization of the I-novel, yet one of the "characters" in the book is a black cat, Richard's sly homage to Natsume's fictional feline. Along with its compressed single-hour span, the book's curious structure sets it apart from Richard Brautigan's other long fiction. There are only two characters in *Sombrero Fallout* (three, including the cat). The two are an unnamed "very well-known American humorist" (coincidentally born one year before Richard), a man "so complicated that he could make a labyrinth seem like a straight line," and Yukiko, his beautiful

Japanese ex-girlfriend, who owns the cat, black as "a suburb of her hair." The novel deals with the aftermath of their two-year affair and the writer's torment over the breakup.

The book's main action is purely imaginary and takes place in a wastebasket, where one of the American humorist's failures, a torn-up first draft about a frozen sombrero fallen from the sky, reassembles itself and continues on its own. The blackly comic political satire evolving within the wastebasket provides the book's title, but the manic slapstick violence is a diversion from the emotional heart of the novel. Nothing truly dramatic occurs during that hour ("slightly after ten" until eleven fifteen) on a rainy night in San Francisco, but Brautigan's evocative rendering of the American humorist's anguish carries the reader deep into the lonely catacombs of heartbreak.

In describing the humorist ("It was difficult to find a bookstore that did not carry at least one of his titles"), Richard reached deep inside for details almost autobiographical in their intimacy: "He was often very bored and he did not think twice about telling other people about his boredom." "He was a very shy person when he was sober. He had to be drunk before he could make a pass at a woman." "He had an attractive but very erratic personality. He allowed his moods to dominate him and they were very changeable. Sometimes he would talk too much and at other times he wouldn't talk at all. He always talked too much when he drank [. . .] Some people thought that he was very charming and others thought that he was a total asshole." "He never lacked things to worry about." "He had been suffering from insomnia [. . .]" "There was only one person in the world who would call her that late at night." "His basic approach to life [. . .] was to have it as confusing, labyrinth-laden and fucked up as possible."

Taken together, these small telling touches form an accurate psychological profile of the author. Michael McClure noted the resemblance between Richard and his nameless character. In an essay on Brautigan, McClure found this interesting "because Richard is presenting a highly and carefully doctored self-portrait. I wonder when he is presenting himself and when he is deliberately not doing so. I wonder when he is presenting himself and thinks he is not—and vice versa." When Gatz Hjortsberg read *Sombrero Fallout*, he told Brautigan he thought it was very courageous for him to write so honestly about himself.

"That wasn't me!" Richard snapped without a moment's hesitation.

Internal evidence indicates the character of Yukiko was based on Anne Kuniyuki. Aside from the obvious connection that both are Japanese, there is the musical near-anagram-like similarity of their names. More telling, Brautigan's description of the first meeting of Yukiko and the American humorist mirrors his own initial encounter with Kuniyuki. "When he turned around on his bar stool, very drunk, which was a condition not unknown to him, he saw her sitting at a table with two other women. They were all wearing white uniforms. They looked as if they had just gotten off work." The fictional Yukiko had a job as a psychiatrist in the emergency room of a San Francisco hospital. Anne was a nurse. They both wore white uniforms and worked the night shift.

The city of Seattle provides another connection. Anne Kuniyuki moved from San Francisco to Seattle not long after her mother's death. She kept in touch with Brautigan, writing him tales of her night-shift nursing adventures. Three pieces of her pottery had been accepted for exhibition at the San Francisco Art Festival in the first week of August 1974. Kuniyuki planned to fly down for the event. She and Richard broke up soon afterward. By that fall Brautigan was keeping company with Siew-Hwa Beh.

Toward the end of *Sombrero Fallout*, Richard introduced Norman Mailer as a character in the wastebasket insurrection plot. The famed American novelist arrives by airplane as a war correspondent and is annoyed to discover the other reporters are more interested in interviewing him than covering the actual story. Brautigan portrayed Mailer in the novel as heroic. "The soldiers were amazed by Norman Mailer's courage [. . .] Again and again he exposed himself to tremendous concentrations of townspeople firepower."

Sombrero Fallout was nearly done by summer's end, and Brautigan worked only sporadically on the novel. The journal he kept between August 30 and November 3, 1975, maintained an accurate tally of his writing life. On the first of September (Labor Day), Richard wrote eight pages in the morning and fished on Mission Creek and the Yellowstone all afternoon. In the evening, he read the galleys of Ed Dorn's *Gunslinger* and wrote a blurb for his friend's book-length poem. Brautigan did not work on *Sombrero* again until September 22. His journal records only four writing days during the month and lists an equal number of hangovers, including a "hideous" one (Thursday, September 25), which "ruined the whole goddamned day. I didn't get any work done. Bad Richard!"

At the beginning of October, John Hartnett, Helen Brann's assistant, mailed Brautigan five copies of his long-awaited Dell contract for *The Beatle Lyrics Illustrated*. Payment had been held up for a year due to a permissions disagreement straight out of Kafka. The book's British publishers objected to a quote from "Eleanor Rigby" Richard had used in his short essay. They felt he should pay for the privilege of including this copyrighted material. After much legal wrangling, the bizarre situation got straightened out. The Brits agreed that "since they have sold all book rights in the lyrics to Seymour Lawrence/Dell," Brautigan's publisher had the right to give him permission to include the excerpt from "Eleanor Rigby" in his introduction. Once signed copies of the contract were received, Richard could at last be paid $750 for the introduction.

Brautigan worked hard on the final stretch of his novel in October, taking time out to copyedit the manuscript for the book of poetry Simon & Schuster agreed to publish two years earlier, now titled *Loading Mercury with a Pitchfork*. Richard finished the edit on October 10 and mailed it to his publisher, working on his novel in the afternoon. That evening, he and Tony Dingman picked up Siew-Hwa, Curt Gentry, and his girlfriend/research assistant, Gail Stevens, at the Bozeman airport. They stayed up late, drinking and talking. Brautigan got very drunk, ending up in a bitter fight with Siew-Hwa. He didn't work on his novel again for another eight days.

In the home stretch at last, Richard started back on his book in earnest and worked hard for the next four days, finishing the draft in the last week of October. Brautigan spent the next day proofreading the manuscript. He felt the novel was "in beautiful shape," but planned to make "minor corrections" before mailing it to his agent the following Monday.

Again, episodes of heavy drinking and hangovers intervened. Brautigan "basically just suffered [. . .] There are so many things to do and I went to bed with a feeling of not having done anything." Richard pulled it together the next day and finished his corrections for *Sombrero Fallout*. Tony Dingman drove him into Livingston. He Xeroxed the manuscript, mailing a copy to Helen Brann. Two days later, he closed up his "ranch" for the winter and flew to San Francisco. Negotiations with Simon & Schuster began as soon as Brann delivered the novel to the publisher. Contracts were drawn up by mid-December. S&S once again paid Brautigan a $50,000 advance, guaranteeing a straight 15 percent hardback royalty. Richard wanted the money before the end of the year. Helen made it just under the wire, mailing him a check on the thirty-first.

Simon & Schuster delayed publication of Brautigan's new book of poetry in 1974 because they feared conflicting with the sales of *Hawkline*. They took another pass the following year, exercising the same caution regarding *Willard*. In 1976, they abandoned this strategy, releasing both *Loading Mercury with a Pitchfork* and *Sombrero Fallout* within six months of each other. The hardback edition of *Loading Mercury* came out first, early in the spring, followed by a trade paperback released in June.

Richard wrote his own one-paragraph dust jacket flap copy for *Loading Mercury*: "written in the inimitable Brautigan style: delicate, full of insight and the ability to see and describe the possibilities and complications of the world in a lucid and totally original way." Such self-promotion might seem underhanded but was a common practice in the publishing industry. Sam Lawrence later asked Richard to perform the same service, writing: "This is a trade secret but our best catalogue and jacket copy are written by the authors (Donleavy, Vonnegut, Wakefield, Berger)."

For *Mercury*'s dust jacket photo, Brautigan chose one of Erik Weber's pictures from the batch he had previously rejected for the cover of *Willard*. Superimposed over a silver background, the two-year-old photograph showed a bearded Richard kneeling, gazing straight into the camera, his denim shirt untucked. It was printed on both the front and back covers of the dust jacket, die-cut out of the previous background of bowling balls. *Mercury* was dedicated to Jim Harrison and Guy de la Valdène.

Robert Creeley supplied an enthusiastic blurb ("Weirdly delicious bullets of ineffable wisdom. Pop a few."), but these were almost the only words of praise the book received. Michael McClure considered it "dry and trashy." *Kirkus Reviews* called *Mercury* "a fey little volume" and wondered if Brautigan might be "a surrealist Rod McKuen." Joseph McLellan, writing in the *Washington Post Book World*, said that the collection "shows no growth, a lot of cuteness and just enough substance to keep you reading." Jonathan Cape declined to reissue the book in the United Kingdom. Even the devoted Japanese failed to bring out a translation. The only foreign edition was a Danish translation (not published until 1978).

The galleys for *Sombrero Fallout* arrived in Pine Creek around the Fourth of July, shortly after Brautigan returned from Japan. A day or so later, Richard was working hard on the final revisions in spite of recurring insomnia aggravated by jet lag. Keith Abbott came out to Montana for a month or so to help Brautigan with much-needed ranch work. He observed, "being such a perfectionist, [Richard] was usually a basket case after reading proofs."

When the bound page proofs for *Sombrero Fallout* arrived near the end of July, along with the dust jacket copy, Richard enlisted Keith's help in rewriting his publisher's clumsy work. Abbott remembered Brautigan as being "scornful" of what Simon & Schuster sent to him. According to Keith, Richard tried to find "a way of talking about his work that avoided the 1960 hippie buzz words." Brautigan called this "the dewhimsicalizing of his literary reputation." He was not altogether successful. The flap copy he rewrote contained such observations as: "The lover dreams cat purr dreams of her dead father while the hero agonizes over tuna fish sandwiches and the possibilities of a simple seven-digit phone call."

Simon & Schuster published *Sombrero Fallout* in September 1976, releasing a first printing of thirty-five thousand copies. The dust jacket featured a striking painting by John Ansado of a beautiful reclining Japanese woman staring with candor at the reader. A photograph of Brautigan seated outdoors on a boulder in his high-crowned black hat (one of a batch John Fryer took for *Hawkline* two years earlier) filled the back cover.

Away in Japan all spring, Richard hadn't had time before his deadline to arrange for new photographs to be taken. John Fryer dreamed Brautigan's novel was titled "That Bat You Took." Richard was greatly amused and convinced Fryer his dream title remained a serious contender. John wrote Jonathan Dolger at S&S in July requesting a $175 photo payment. He got his money, but the publisher printed his name incorrectly as "John Freyer" on the copyright byline.

A Japanese edition, translated by Kazuko Fujimoto, was published simultaneously by Shobun-sha in Tokyo. Richard felt proud of the international popularity this mutual venture celebrated, although the reviews for *Sombrero Fallout* were mixed. Barbara A. Bannon in *Publishers Weekly* called the book "an amusing trifle for Brautigan fans," while a writer in the *Bookletter* said, "*Sombrero Fallout* may be the best novel Richard Brautigan has written [. . .]" Robert Christgau, writing in the *New York Times Book Review*, claimed, "One senses yet another artist who feels defeated by his audience and longs for simpler times," but Charles Casey, in the *St. Louis Post-Dispatch*, stated, "it's [sic] touchingly funny moments and it's [sic] interesting experimentation make it one of Brautigan's best."

A letter from Philip Whalen, sent from the Zen Mountain Center in the Carmel Valley and dated "7:IX:76," offset any residual bad feeling occasioned by the negative reviews. Whalen "enjoyed SOMBRERO FALLOUT. The tone & colors are exactly Japanese [. . .] the mixture of hysteria, violence, sentimental feeling and hair get it down exactly." Phil had also read *Loading Mercury with a Pitchfork* and said the poems "maintain your unique sound. I can think of only two other poets whose work is inimitable—Gregory Corso and Robert Creeley—I am swamped with jealousy and shame."

By the time the first reviews of *Sombrero Fallout* appeared, Brautigan was close to putting the finishing touches on the fourth of his five-year-plan genre novels. Early in 1976, Richard began jotting ideas on a series of four-by-six note cards. "Dreaming of Babylon," he wrote on one, along with "A Private eye novel 1942–1976." Below that, enclosed in a penciled circle, he added, "1924–1946–1951–1967–1976." Whatever the other dates meant at the time, Brautigan decided to set his new book in 1942. He planned to write a detective story. Along with his title, he had already worked most of it out in his imagination.

Richard hired Loie Weber to research the project. He had been paying her $5 per hour to work for him, but agreed to raise her salary "retroactively." Having narrowed the time period to "a couple weeks in 1942," Brautigan needed a day-by-day compilation of long-gone San Francisco events and weather. Knowing his subplot involved the Babylonian daydreams of his dim-witted gumshoe hero, he also asked Loie to research ancient Babylon. For planned scenes in the morgue, Richard demanded what he called "specific information." Loie Weber spent a couple weeks at the Civic Center library looking "at all the newspapers during that particular time period." She took careful notes in a Velvatone notebook.

Loie spent forty-two hours on research, not including a quick "follow-up" to the California Historical Society for copies of period restaurant menus. She spent $45 on supplies, saving all the receipts, as Brautigan was a stickler for such details. Loie also took a trip to the San Francisco morgue, where she interviewed the coroner, who showed her around the autopsy room and gave her an odd souvenir, a coroner's office toe tag used to ID the corpses. She passed it on to Richard. Loie recorded her observations in clinical detail.

Brautigan "didn't use this information at all," Loie recalled. She never typed up her notes, giving Richard her legible and meticulously rewritten notebook. He selected the items of interest to him and ignored the rest. Brautigan wanted to know everything in advance, all the details in place, so there would be no surprises. Asked why Richard avoided taking literary risks, Loie replied, "That's not the way his mind worked."

A curious coincidence occurred while Loie Weber worked on *Dreaming of Babylon*. She was an avid gardener and did some indoor cultivation for a woman whose live-in lover happened to be a private detective. Loie found this interesting. They started chatting. Loie told him she was researching a detective novel for Richard Brautigan. The detective was David Fechheimer. He pretended he didn't know Brautigan but said he really admired his writing.

"So, he's sort of picking my brains," Weber recalled. The canny Fechheimer played his part to perfection, feigning ignorance and eliciting tidbits of information about his pal Richard. The hapless C. Card, Brautigan's fictional shamus, lacked the savvy intelligence to pull off such a stunt. If Richard had wanted to create a clever detective, he would have interviewed David about trade secrets. Instead, he never said a word to Fechheimer about his book until it was done.

In spite of consistently strong sales figures for the four Brautigan titles they had published, Simon & Schuster treated their contractual obligations to the author with cavalier indifference. In April, S&S failed to run a full-page ad in the book/movie section of the *New York Times* upon the publication of *Loading Mercury with a Pitchfork* as stipulated in clause 27 of Brautigan's contract. A half-page ad advertising *Sombrero Fallout* appeared in the June 28 issue of *Publishers Weekly*, sandwiched between full-page ads for new novels by Rona Jaffe and Lois Gould and sharing its space with a book called *The International Book of Wood*. Simon & Schuster had always announced Brautigan novels with full-page ads in *PW*. This time, the publisher failed to show Richard the ad copy first, another contractual breach.

Helen Brann knew Richard, away in Japan, would react with "complete dismay" upon seeing the ad. She wrote Jonathan Dolger to complain, "If someone at Simon & Schuster had intentionally set out to wound and upset a major American author, he or she could not have done a better job." On the phone with Brann that same morning, Dolger (whom Brann believed had "done a thoughtful and excellent job for Richard over the past few years") told her, "we feel Brautigan is so well-known that he doesn't need a full-page ad." This attitude elicited a "wave of shock" in Richard's agent.

The shockwave's reverberations resonated deep within Helen Brann's negotiating strategy for *Dreaming of Babylon*. In November, she flew out to San Francisco to meet with Brautigan and several other clients who lived in the Bay Area. Helen found Richard in an "up" mood but thought "he was drinking too much." Brann "had this gang of writers sitting around" in her suite at the Stanford Court Hotel, among them Keith Abbott, whom she signed up a month earlier on Brautigan's recommendation. Keith thought Richard seemed much the same as he had in Montana in the summer, "drunk, morose and harried [. . .] that night he looked like a corpse." Helen and a friend "had to sort of bundle [Richard] up and get him home somehow. Get him into a cab." Richard managed to give his agent a manuscript copy of *Dreaming of Babylon*, which Brann promptly read. She "loved" the novel and brought it back with her to New York.

Knowing Seymour Lawrence had been patiently waiting in the wings for the return of an author he referred to as "the prodigal son" in Dell Publishing internal memos, Helen Brann submitted a bid to Simon & Schuster more than doubling Brautigan's previous advances. S&S countered with an offer of $100,000, twice what they'd paid before. Helen immediately rejected it. When Simon & Schuster held firm, she wasted no time getting back in touch with Sam Lawrence.

Brann sent Lawrence manuscript copies of Brautigan's new novel along with *June 30th, June 30th*, a book of poems written in Japan earlier that year. She offered Sam the hardcover, quality paperback, and mass-market paperback rights for the United States and Canada, asking for an advance of $200,000 for *Babylon* and an additional $50,000 for the poetry. She wanted a straight 15 percent royalty on both trade editions with an increase to 17 percent after twenty-five thousand copies were sold.

This generated a flurry of interoffice memoranda at Dell, examining Richard's prior sales figures and the details of the S&S offer. Lawrence expressed his enthusiasm without any equivocation. "This is an opportunity to restore a genuine and original talent to our list," he wrote to the top Dell executives on New Year's Day 1977. "It's a moment I've been waiting for."

Two weeks later, Helen and Sam hammered out a deal. Lawrence would pay Brautigan an advance of $125,000 for *Dreaming of Babylon* and an additional $25,000 in advance for *June 30th, June 30th*. These amounts were for the hardback and quality paperback editions only. The mass-market paperback rights were reserved for the author, along with "all the usual subsidiary rights," dramatic, first serial, subsidiary, and translation. Unlike Brautigan's previous Simon & Schuster deals, the royalty for the trade edition started at 12 percent, rising to 15 percent only after sales totaled fifteen thousand copies. Helen gave Sam an option on "Richard's next full-length work," insisting on Brautigan's right to final design approval of all dust jacket and advertising art and copy.

Simon & Schuster had a contractual right to top any offer from another publishing house by 10 percent. If they exercised this clause, Brautigan would remain an S&S author. They had previously offered an advance of a hundred grand, but Simon & Schuster bean counters refused to cough up an additional thirty-seven-five, and the deal with Dell went through. In mid-February 1977, Helen Brann delivered signed contracts for *Dreaming of Babylon* and *June 30th, June 30th* to Sam Lawrence. After an absence of seven years, the prodigal had returned.

Richard contacted Erik Weber and arranged for a dust jacket photographic session at his Bolinas house. Brautigan bought a new hat for the occasion, a wide-brimmed tan fedora with a two-inch silk band to evoke the sort of headgear a hard-boiled shamus might wear. Weber shot three rolls of film, mostly of Richard wearing the hat, either talking on the phone or staring sternly at the camera. There were shots of Brautigan writing in his notebook and the fedora alone, perched on a chair and sitting on a dresser. Another dozen showed the hat sitting on Richard's bed in obvious defiance of the old superstition.

Much later, a friend looked at Erik Weber's contact sheets and said, "Do you know it's bad luck to have your hat on the bed?" Erik immediately thought, "Richard must have known that. He knew stuff like that." Eight years later, Brautigan died standing in front of this same bed in Bolinas. He never wore the fedora again after the afternoon photo session with Weber.

In the end, Richard decided to have no photograph on the *Babylon* dust jacket. He approved one of Erik's pictures (a straightforward portrait of Brautigan wearing the unfortunate hat) for use in the advertising campaign. Richard felt one of the reasons the eastern critics had been so unkind to him had a lot to do with the "overuse" of his image on earlier book covers. Sam Lawrence objected to not having an author photo on the novel ("I for one am always curious to see what an author looks like") but relented in the end. "If Richard is adamant and wants no photograph at all, so be it."

Brautigan wrote his own flap copy in the past, but this time around he enlisted the help of Don Carpenter in early February 1977, asking him to take on the task. Don agreed and composed every word of the wry dust jacket notes. Sam Lawrence, thinking they were by Richard, pronounced them "beautiful."

It was Carpenter's contention that Brautigan wrote all of his "genre" novels as "attempts at movies. Richard, without ever admitting it to anybody, wanted very badly to make movies, very, very badly. He was extremely interested in the movie business, and he was all over me about movies and about getting movies made." Carpenter was Brautigan's conduit to the film industry, a friend who had actually written and produced a movie. "He loved, and I loved, to talk movie lingo," Don said, "because as a linguistic phenomena I love it, and he loves linguistic phenomena, and so we would talk movie language."

Back in late January, before enlisting Carpenter's copy writing assistance, even as the final details of the Dell contract were still being negotiated, Richard and Helen Brann had a long phone conversation about the *Babylon* dust jacket art. They decided Wendell Minor, who had designed the covers for both *Hawkline* and *Willard*, was the perfect man for the job. In talking it over, they also agreed they preferred the *Hawkline* art. Brann wrote to Sam Lawrence, who passed on their suggestion to the art director at Delacorte Press.

Soon after, Brautigan left on another trip to Japan. By mid-February, Wendell Minor finished a preliminary pencil sketch for the front cover of *Babylon*. Because Richard had been hard to locate in Tokyo, Sam Lawrence sent a copy of the drawing to Helen Brann to forward to him. Brautigan never saw a copy of Minor's work.

Early in March, Richard phoned Helen Brann from Tokyo with his own brainstorm for the *Babylon* cover art. Brautigan proposed either a drawing or a photograph in the style of Diane Arbus, showing an old-fashioned refrigerator, the kind with a drum-shaped cooling fan perched on top, situated against a seedy, murky background. The fridge door hung partway open with a woman's naked foot dangling out from inside. Helen liked the idea and passed it along to Sam Lawrence.

Brautigan's suggestion was not used. An artist named Craig Nelson provided a circular painting portraying a disheveled private eye with a pencil-thin mustache, staring down at the sheet-covered corpse of a lovely blond, like an illustration from a pulp crime magazine. Richard formally approved the design and dedicated *Babylon* to his agent: "This one is for Helen Brann with love from Richard."

Dreaming of Babylon: A Private Eye Novel 1942 was published on September 27, 1977, in a first hardcover edition of thirty thousand copies. Seymour Lawrence had suggested a first printing of twenty-five thousand, but Helen Brann strenuously objected, pointing out that Simon & Schuster had never printed fewer than forty thousand copies of any of their hardcover Brautigan editions and had gone back for second printings every time. According to Richard's wishes, no photograph appeared on the dust jacket.

The back cover featured five quotes from magazine articles praising Brautigan (none dealt specifically with *Babylon*). It was an odd mix, from *Newsweek* and the *National Geographic* to the London *Times Literary Supplement* and a translation from *Le Monde* in Paris. The final quote, from the *National Observer*, had to be cut down to only two brief lines because Richard objected to being called "a kind of cracker barrel surrealist" and actively hated having his work referred to as "the kind of thing Mark Twain might have written had he wandered into a field of ripe cannabis with a pack of Zig-Zag papers in his pocket."

Delacorte Press launched *Babylon* in the beginning of October, with a full-page ad in the *New York Times Book Review*, as stipulated in Brautigan's contract. Richard wrote the copy and provided a wry heading: "America's favorite avant-garde novelist is now 35 years behind the times." He sent Seymour Lawrence a gift-wrapped bottle of the publisher's "favorite drinking material," Black Label Jack Daniel's, to celebrate the book's publication. "Big Jack," Sam called it, quoting Frank Sinatra, "to distinguish it from Little Jack, the Green label." At Brautigan's urging, Lawrence sent a copy of the novel to Norman Mailer.

Dreaming of Babylon was not a critical success. Joe Flaherty, writing in the *New York Times Book Review*, said "Brautigan delivers a litany of screwups and lame jokes. It's the ice age seen through Fred Flintstone." Rob Swigart, in the *San Francisco Bay Guardian*, called the novel "a cotton candy souffle, pretty to look at but not very wholesome." The Chicago *Sun-Times* panned the book as "a sleek but sophomoric parody." Even Brautigan's hometown paper, the *San Francisco Examiner*, sneered that his genre writing "is like doing the crossword: it might be kind of fun, but it isn't writing."

Worse was yet to come. The *New Yorker* in its "Briefly Noted" section went for the jugular: "Richard Brautigan has mastered all the forms of children's fiction [. . .] and children's fiction for adults is what this pretty skimpy book is all about." When the novel appeared in England the reviewers were even more unkind. Thomas M. Disch howled at the head of the pack, in the *Times Literary Supplement*, "Mini-chapter by mini-chapter the mindless tale advances with resolute pointlessness and a total mastery of anticlimax [. . .] The book is a vacuous daydream." In the *Spectator*, Mary Hope joined in, "There is not much point in parodying a style unless there is a valid alternative statement to be made; this is just a thin idea, made thinner by the disparity between the master's theme and the pupil's variations."

Michael McClure found *Dreaming of Babylon* to be "awful, pathetic." After reading a third of the book, he felt "stuck [. . .] there's barely any coherence of a story." McClure found it hard to concentrate on the novel. "This little universe was hardly worth creating," he wrote, "and barely has enough energy in it to sustain the fact of the ink on the page."

Seymour Krim, an early supporter of Brautigan's work, felt just the opposite. "Reading him is effortless," he wrote. "His books seem to write themselves without the usual sweat and pain we associate with serious writing [. . .] it is brother writers who are always taught a lesson when they pick up the latest Brautigan." Krim gave *Babylon* a favorable review, perhaps the only serious writer and critic to do so. Writing in the *Chicago Tribune Book World*, Krim stated that Richard "sees things for what they are with a cool but merciful eye [. . .] People who have regarded Brautigan as a novelty who would sooner or later deflate never reckoned with the iron in his

charm. A successful vision is not manufactured overnight. Years of an earlier alienation [. . .] produce muscle in the imagination even when it is most lightly handled without an ounce of literary
self-consciousness."

Sales figures were disappointing. *Dreaming of Babylon* sold only eighteen thousand copies,
hardbound, leaving twelve thousand of the first edition to languish on remainder tables. (In contrast,
Hawkline eventually totaled forty-nine thousand hardcover sales and even the perverse *Willard*
reached thirty-nine thousand.) *Babylon* was reissued as a Delta trade paperback in September 1978
and was published in the United Kingdom the same year by Jonathan Cape Ltd., with translations
in Japan, Germany, France, and Spain.

Dreaming of Babylon became the last of Richard Brautigan's "genre" novels. Although he fell
short of his five-year-plan goal, writing a book in a different style for each of four straight years
was a proud achievement. Brautigan never mentioned why he decided not to go for book number 5.
Spending more time in Japan became a priority. Richard had found an intriguing new world to
engage his imagination.

forty-two: stockholm

ONE BRIGHT SUMMER morning in the early seventies, the sort of cloudless azure day that gave A. B. Guthrie the title for his best-known novel and Montana a catchy logo for her license plates, Richard and I bounced along graveled Pine Creek Road, heading for town in my green 1949 three-quarter-ton Chevrolet pickup. As we rattled over the thick wooden planks of the old iron bridge spanning the Yellowstone, Richard appraised me with his penetrating owlish stare. "You know, Gatz," he said, his voice assuming a solemn tone. "I've been thinking recently that I've got a good shot at the Nobel Prize."

I didn't know quite how to react. Was he kidding me? Richard was a wry practical joker, and I instinctively sensed him luring me into some elaborate comic hoax.

"How do you figure that?" I replied. Not wanting to play the dupe, I endeavored to keep my voice neutral.

Richard spoke slowly, his manner at once scholarly and judicious. He explained that his work was the bane of the "eastern critical mafia," his commercial popularity ensuring perpetual bad reviews from the literary establishment. In Europe, the opposite was true. There, he was taken seriously as an artist, especially so in the Scandinavian nations.

As Richard continued his deadpan brief, point by pedantic point, a slow numbing realization crept over me. The man was serious. I wondered how to react to something that on face value struck me as utterly preposterous. By disposition, I fell naturally into a subordinate role. Being six years older and having the distinction of fame and financial success gave Richard a dialectic advantage. Although there existed between us the unspoken notion of all artists equal together in the crucible of creation, he nevertheless assumed the position of elder statesman, emphasizing the predilection of the Nobel judges to choose work disdained in its home country, yet acclaimed and much appreciated by a superior European culture. "I fit the bill perfectly," he smirked.

"Don't you think you're a little young for the Nobel Prize?" I observed. Convinced my thrust had skewered the inflated balloon of his ego, I experimented with a superior grin. Richard never missed a stroke. "Kipling had it at forty-one," he parried. *Touché!* I said nothing more on the subject, steering the conversation toward fishing as we drove the rest of the way into Livingston.

forty-three: throwing a hoolihan

I N THE EARLY 1970s, when Richard Brautigan moved to Montana, it was still possible to regard the state as the Last Best Place. Wide-scale subdivision had yet to drive property values into the stratosphere, and there was nary a sign of the dot-com billionaires whose extravagant hilltop McMansions and designer-fringe Rodeo Drive faux-Western fashions forever altered the hometown character of the area. Even after the cataclysmic social changes rending the fabric of American life in the sixties, Livingston retained the innocence of an earlier time. It was still *Leave It to Beaver* and John Wayne in Big Sky Country.

One freedom enjoyed in Montana was the right to bear arms. A resident can buy a handgun without any waiting period, just lay his money down on the counter and walk out of the shop with a brand-new six-shooter. Unconcealed weapons may be carried or worn openly in public places, as evidenced by the ubiquitous gun racks visible through pickup truck rear windows in every town in the state. Having grown up hunting and owning firearms, Brautigan understood the gun culture of Montana and soon acquired a small arsenal of his own.

When Richard flew back to Montana in June of 1974, he brought his old pal Price Dunn along with him. They took a cab over the hill from the Bozeman airport. Brautigan gave the Confederate General an immediate tour of his newly renovated ranchette. Richard brought Price out to the barn for a tour of his rafter-high tree house studio painted a vivid robin's egg blue on the inside.

Back at the house, Richard wasted no time before showing off his Winchester gallery gun, recently acquired from Harmon Henkin. "He asked me if I wanted to do some plinking with the .22," Price said. Dunn took the antique pump-action and a box of shorts, heading off alone through the cottonwoods behind the house. Hundreds of years before, this had been the Pine Creek streambed, and the flow of water carved a steep embankment along the northern edge of what was now subdivided hayfields.

Below Brautigan's towering barn, the old ranch dump sprawled down a cut bank hillside, with decrepit washing machines and kerosene stoves, coils of baling wire, fifty-gallon drums, and archaic farm implements, all swept up in an avalanche of broken bottles and rusted tin cans. It provided an excellent site for shooting as the steep slope afforded a safe backstop. It grew dark by the time Price fired the last of his shells and headed back to the house. He had found the shooting "boring." A far more interesting exercise in marksmanship awaited him.

Richard had started drinking early. "He was soused," Price recalled, "and I just joined him." They had a few together. Around midnight, Richard suggested it might be fun to go out on the back porch and blast a cap or two.

Price attempted dissuasion, knowing the danger of shooting in the dark. He turned the conversation toward other topics. Richard mentioned "maybe" learning to drive. He proposed a Model A Ford as his training vehicle. Price thought this absurd. "Time must have a stop," he quipped.

Brautigan agreed. To emphasize the point, he picked up his Winchester rifle and took a shot at the electric clock hanging above the refrigerator. Richard's aim was off by about three inches. "You missed it," Dunn observed.

"No. No," Richard insisted. "The point is you aim as close to the edge as possible without hitting the clock."

And so began a bizarre night of drinking and indoor marksmanship. After a number of near misses, Brautigan attempted a long shot from the adjoining bathroom and hit the clock dead center. The rules of the game immediately reversed. "We sat there and drank the rest of that bottle of whiskey," Dunn recalled, "and shot the shit out of that clock. Richard was really far more juiced than I." By the time they called it a night, the two sharpshooters had blasted at least fifty rounds through the kitchen wall, blowing the unfortunate clock asunder.

The next morning, surveying the results of their nocturnal shenanigans, Richard and Price made a disturbing discovery. While the bullets they'd fired penetrated the Sheetrock kitchen wall with small neat holes clustered close together like a shotgun's pattern, the mushrooming slugs splintered through Brautigan's brand-new redwood siding when they emerged out the other side on the back porch. Much expensive craftsmanship had been utterly destroyed, a problem that required a swift application of the checkbook. Richard immediately phoned for help. When the carpenter surveyed the bullet holes in the kitchen, Brautigan shrugged and said, "I had some friends over last night, and they got a little frisky." In Montana, this passed for a reasonable explanation. A couple days later, the exterior of Richard's house looked as good as new.

Brautigan left the bullet holes in the wall above the fridge undisturbed. He found a plain wooden picture frame at a secondhand store in Livingston, just the right size, and hung it around the damage. Only the bullet-punctured dial remained from the clock. Richard replaced it in its original position, hanging the dial within the frame from a protruding nail. Later, Brautigan attached a small brass plaque to the bottom of the frame. On it he'd had engraved: shootout at ok kitchen. r.b. and p.d.

This framed memorial to a drunken boisterous night remained in Richard's kitchen for as long as he lived at Pine Creek. After his death, his daughter sold the place to a speculator, who resubdivided the forty acres into smaller lots and took the frame and riddled dial away with him as a trophy, leaving the bullet holes intact. After a resale, the new owners, out of respect for an author they never knew, preserved the cluster of gunshots as if it were a work of art.

Brautigan enjoyed shooting (and having his guests shoot) at a variety of objects (TV sets, pachinko machines, various books, an old bathtub) from off his back porch. Richard's gonzo target practice became so frequent Tom McGuane dubbed his friend's back porch "the lead Disneyland." Once, when the nocturnal gunplay grew especially loud and annoying, Brautigan's neighbor John Dermer, a refrigeration mechanic who lived diagonally across the road in the parsonage of the Pine Creek Methodist Church, shut off the gravity-feed water line and refused to restore the flow until Richard called a truce on his late-night fusillades. Without water, Brautigan had his Livingstone lawyer, Joe Swindlehurst, propose a deal. Richard and his friends would shoot off the back porch only between the hours of 5:00 and 7:00 pm. Dermer agreed and turned the appropriate valve.

Toward the end of June, Ianthe Brautigan flew out from California to spend the summer with her father, her first opportunity since infancy to have that much time with him. The moment she glimpsed him from the plane window, Ianthe felt "an overwhelming sense of joy." A friend drove them over to Livingston. After a quick tour of town and a stop at the local IGA for groceries, they pulled into the state liquor store, where Brautigan bought gallons of wine and a case of bourbon. They stopped on their way home at the Tastee-Freez, Richard's favorite spot for burgers and fries. For the rest of the drive, Ianthe listened to "the bottles clinking together in the trunk."

The year before, on her initial visit to Montana, Ianthe noticed for the first time that among a crowd of heavy drinkers, her father drank the most. Richard Brautigan "drank a lot." On her second summer in Big Sky Country, she observed he was drinking even more. It scared her. Her father was having blackouts and acted suicidal. He came into her bedroom drunk at three in the morning to read newly written short stories. Once, Richard appeared in Ianthe's doorway early in the day with a bar of soap in his hand. "This is my last will and testament," he said. Another "bright and sunny morning," Richard told his daughter, "If you weren't here, I would have killed myself last night, but I didn't want you to find the body."

Summoning a courage she still finds amazing, Ianthe attempted to talk with her father about his drinking. Brautigan had raised her to believe that she could discuss anything with him, but when she said he was drinking too much, Richard flew into a rage. "After spending several nights listening to him in a drunken rampage, saying every hurtful thing he could think of, I realized I had made a mistake," Ianthe wrote in her memoir. One night, he cornered her in the bathroom, a drink in hand. "Just what do you think you're doing?" he raged. "When you are eighteen, you're on your own. Don't expect anything from me then."

Reasoning with her father failed. Ianthe took a more drastic course of action. Once, when Brautigan was out on the town, she searched through the cupboards for all the bottles of George Dickel she could find. Richard favored this brand of expensive bourbon and bought it in quarts by the caseload. Ianthe gathered them up, uncorking each bottle one by one and pouring the contents down the sink drain. She worked quickly, hoping not to get caught in the act. When Ianthe was done, the kitchen reeked of whiskey and all the booze was gone.

Brautigan never noticed. Staggering in drunk later that night, he simply assumed he'd drunk it all himself and headed for town to buy another case in the morning. As the alcohol consumption increased, things went from bad to worse. Most of Richard's friends remained unaware of any serious domestic problem, but Ron Loewinsohn, who came out for a four-day visit during the second week of July, left Montana wondering how fourteen-year-old Ianthe was possibly going to survive.

In his deepest imagination, Richard Brautigan envisioned his Pine Creek place not as some backwater bastion of boozy bacchanalia but rather a bucolic utopia where he might fulfill his childhood fantasies, no longer a dirt-poor ragamuffin berry-and-bean picker but the lord of the manor raising crops of his own. He promised his daughter as much, telling her Montana would be their new home. She could choose her own bedroom in a house untroubled by ghosts. He would buy her a horse. Richard made good on his pledge. Ianthe picked out a front room with several east-facing windows. She also got the promised horse, a part-thoroughbred bay mare named Jackie.

For the house, Brautigan bought a gas stove, matching washer and dryer, and a two-door refrigerator, all brand-new, "seventies yellow," the first such appliances he had ever purchased in his life. The big new hospital-white chest freezer embodied all of his agrarian dreams. As Ianthe noted in her memoir, "He bought this freezer with intentions that never came to fruition, secret dreams about the ranch and the life he meant to live there."

Inspired by the "back to the land" lifestyle of his next-door neighbors, Brautigan envisioned his own self-sufficient farming operation. The year before, Gatz bought two wiener pigs at $45 each. By the end of the season, one went into his freezer, conveniently wrapped and labeled in paper packages. The other Hjorstberg kept over the winter and bred in the spring, hoping to establish his own wiener pig business. Nine piglets resulted. Unfortunately, the market price dropped to $15 per wiener. Brautigan bought four pigs at this bargain price, thinking to get a special tax deduction for raising livestock on his forty-acre spread. Richard referred to his tiny swine herd as "the porkers." They provided much amusement throughout the summer, continually escaping from their pen and rampaging through the surrounding countryside.

In June, Brautigan bought fifty baby chicks for $14 at Agrineeds in Livingston. The price included postage. The little yellow birds were mailed from a hatchery in Great Falls. Richard's old farmstead (complete with tumbled-down corrals, decaying brooder coops, abandoned sheds, and the monumental barn where the lower-level dairy cow stalls were packed three feet deep with densely compressed manure) retained a ghostly reminder of a prosperous agrarian life a half-century before. Vat-loads of elbow grease might see the place functioning again. Shoveling out the barn would require a Herculean effort equal to the Augean stables, but the chicken coop presented a simpler task. Gatz Hjortsberg got things in order for Brautigan, rebuilding the roost and cleaning the old nesting boxes. By the time the chicks arrived, a crude wire-mesh fence enclosed their little yard under the cottonwoods.

Chickens are funny creatures. Richard, like everyone who has ever watched their mindless clucking antics, was amused. He eventually wrote three short stories about chickens that appeared in *The Tokyo–Montana Express*. One of his flock had a club foot and walked with a distinctive wobbling limp. Brautigan named her Gimpy. She became his personal favorite. By fall, after Ianthe returned to California, the birds were full-grown and ready for slaughter. Richard had no intention of wielding the ax himself and enlisted Marian Hjortsberg to organize the task. Her husband bowed out. Over the course of the summer, Gatz had already killed his share of rabbits and chickens.

Marian recruited Russell Chatham's wife, Mary, and a newly married young lawyer and schoolteacher, Kent and Becky Douglass, to assist her. Kent and Becky had arrived the year before from Colorado and quickly became part of a small community of local professional people, artists, and writers. Marian organized the event. She set three large kettles boiling over separate fires. Mary got the job of gathering up the chickens. Kent was assigned as the hatchet man. Marian and Becky scalded and plucked the beheaded birds. Richard gave specific instructions. His pet, Gimpy, was not to be killed. In the frenzy of slaughter, one bird out of fifty looks very much like another, and Gimpy went to the block with all the rest.

"It was a horrible scene," Becky Douglass recalled. When it was over they were all splattered with blood. The crew received half the poultry in recompense for doing the deed. The other twenty-five went on the grill for a potluck Brautigan hosted that same evening. Marian told him that Gimpy, terrified by the carnage, had run off into the woods and they had been unable to find her. When the thirty-five other guests arrived, bearing casseroles, salads, and pies, the four butchers were still drenched in blood. After several stiff drinks and a couple helpings of freshly grilled chicken, none of it mattered anymore.

Later on, things started to get rowdy. Richard brought out some of his arsenal and urged those who felt like it to blast away at the flies on the kitchen wall. Most of the guests took off in a hurry. The next morning, head throbbing with a hangover and disgusted with his newly shot-up kitchen, Brautigan wandered down into the woods behind his house looking for Gimpy. The little crippled chicken was nowhere to be found.

Richard had recently acquired a number of cooking utensils, including a giant skillet the size of a manhole cover. Showing off his new pots and pans to Gatz earlier in the summer, Richard lamented, "You know how when you break up with a woman she always runs off with the cooking stuff?" His neighbor, married to the same woman for twelve years, didn't have a clue. Assuming his most authoritarian didactic voice, Richard endeavored to further his friend's domestic education. "I'm thinking of having a plaque made," he said, pointing to the three-foot handle of the Paul Bunyan–sized skillet hanging on the wall. "I'll attach it right there."

"What will it say?" Gatz asked.

Richard smiled. "When you go, this stays."

Jack Thibeau remembered an earlier time when Richard wanted to go shopping and they took the California Street bus downtown. On the way, Brautigan told a story about a girl he'd been living with. When she moved out, she took all the kitchenware. A week later, she called and said, "Richard, I still love you. Come over. I want to cook you a nice dinner. And please bring that Dutch oven."

"Well, he went over, and she cooked the meal in the Dutch oven," Jack said, "and, of course, kept the Dutch oven." Thibeau and Brautigan got off the bus on Powell Street and walked down the hill to Macy's on Union Square, where Richard bought a new set of pots and pans.

Brautigan had no live-in girlfriend during the summer of 1974. Off and on, he'd been seeing both Jayne Walker and Mary Ann Gilderbloom. Mary Ann came out in May for a brief visit, and Richard invited Jayne in June, but she didn't make it. She thought she might come in August. Close to the end of the month, Jayne wrote from Ithaca, New York, where she had a teaching appointment at Cornell. "I'm so sorry that I couldn't come to see you this summer," she apologized. Walker really cared for Brautigan and hoped they might find time to get together if he traveled east in the fall.

Mary Ann became a frequent visitor to Pine Creek that summer, making two trips in July, one lasting five days, the other just a long weekend. Much private time was spent secluded with Brautigan in his exterior bedroom, the remodeled coal shed standing several yards away from the kitchen door behind the house. Inside this separate structure, a south-facing window had been covered over to reduce the sun's direct glare. In its place, Richard had Russell Chatham paint a window-sized landscape providing an artistic interpretation of the former view. The room's other window faced north. It was covered by a translucent blue drape, making the interior glow like a grotto with aqueous light. One afternoon after napping, Brautigan read aloud to Mary Ann from the manuscript of *Willard*, his work in progress. He planned on reading her the entire book.

"I fell asleep," Gilderbloom recalled.

Richard woke her and started laughing. "Okay, this is the way I'm going to treat it." He threw his manuscript across the room. As the pages wafted to the floor, Brautigan looked down at his supine companion. "You didn't like it," he said.

"You know," Mary Ann replied, "it's just a little bit too weird for me."

Prior to her first July trip to Montana, Richard phoned Mary Ann with a special request. He had developed a taste for Jurgensen's, a high-end, limited-bottling, sixteen-year-old bourbon that was the house brand of an expensive specialty food shop of the same name on Union Street in Cow Hollow. He wanted Mary Ann to stop by the store and pick up a case for him. At Jurgensen's, Gilderbloom discovered the staff knew Brautigan quite well and their exclusive bourbon was on sale. When she got home, Mary Ann phoned Richard with the good news, asking if he wanted to buy "a little extra."

For Brautigan, this was like winning the Irish Sweepstakes. "He had me buy like tons of it," Gilderbloom remembered. She bought eleven cases, total cost of $1,069.46, tax included. "It was delivered to my house, and it sat in my closet for a long time." Mary Ann brought two cases of Jurgensen's to Pine Creek when she flew up for the Fourth of July. The remaining nine remained in Gilderbloom's closet like hidden treasure. "And so, when [Brautigan] was down from Montana, he would usually come over in some kind of stupor and say, 'Can I have some bottles?'"

Richard called Mary Ann in San Francisco with another request before a trip to Montana in September. He'd grown tired of trout and "really good red meat." Brautigan asked her to go to Swann's Oyster Depot on Polk Street and order a quantity of seafood and shellfish. The day before she left for Montana, in mid-September, Swann's delivered $59.50 worth of seafood to Philobiblon on Maiden Lane (two pounds of shrimp, two live lobsters, forty-eight small oysters in the shell, and six skin-on salmon filets), packed in ice for travel.

Mary Ann brought the ice-cold package with her on the flight to Bozeman. Richard hosted a party, a big seafood feast. Dessert was chilled watermelon. Everyone sat out on the back porch, spitting seeds over the rail. Black thunderclouds massed to the west. A powerful electrical storm blew across the valley, jagged lightning streaking down, heading straight over the Yellowstone toward Brautigan's place. "It kind of went right behind the porch but never touched the house," Gilderbloom recalled. "It was so bizarre."

Dick and Nancy Hodge came out for a visit in the summer of '74 and found things relatively tranquil. Richard's attorney "always brought out the best in my father," Ianthe observed years later. Brautigan loved a cheesecake Mary Ann Gilderbloom baked. To preserve the recipe, Brautigan asked Gilderbloom to write it out and give a copy to Nancy Hodge. "Long after he had stopped seeing Mary Ann," Nancy recalled, "when Richard would come to dinner, he had me make her cheesecake."

Brautigan bought his daughter's horse from Lexi Cowan, a twenty-year-old rancher's daughter. Tall and lean, with bright blue eyes and short blond hair, Lexi drove a '66 Mustang and impressed Ianthe with her patient intelligence and wide-ranging competence. An accomplished horsewoman, she worked for a Livingston veterinarian and carried in her purse an eclectic selection of personal effects: "pliers and horse-worming medicine as well as exotic colors of lipstick." Lexi warned Richard about discarded barbed wire, so common on old ranches, and potentially lethal for a horse. They all spent hours searching out strands of ancient rusted wire coiled like serpents in the underbrush. Although he "knew absolutely nothing about horses," Ianthe wrote, "my father was good at that sort of thing. He found lots of wire."

Throughout the chaotic summer, Lexi became a fairy godmother to Ianthe. In Montana, vets pay house calls, and she started stopping to check on Jackie on her way home from work. Her visits coincided with the start of Brautigan's cocktail hour. If things looked bad, Lexi found some excuse to take his daughter away for a drive down the valley. "She had an uncanny sense for when my dad was about to go on a binge," Ianthe recalled.

Price Dunn came back to Pine Creek in September, after Ianthe returned to California to begin her freshman year in high school. He kept Brautigan company and served as his hired driver. Price left a month later, receiving $700 for chauffeuring services. Three days later, Richard flew on Northwest to Traverse City, Michigan, traveling north to Jim Harrison's place in Lake Leelanau. It was bird hunting season. Dan Gerber and Guy de la Valdène were there for the start of the hunt. Woodcock and grouse provided the quarry. Another hunter, Geoffrey Norman, a former Green Beret and currently a senior editor at *Esquire*, also joined their party.

Snow covered the ground, unusual for Michigan at that time of year. Brautigan went with the others into the woods, his first day of hunting in more than twenty years, following an eager dog coursing the frozen ground searching for scent. Harrison's other dog was down, and they had taken Linda's favorite, a "semi–gun shy" Airedale bitch. Gerber remembered Brautigan "huffing and puffing and just sort of exhausted."

Richard found himself alone and heard "something move" behind him, spinning around to see "a beautiful cottontail rabbit." Brautigan looked over the beaded sight of his .20-gauge shotgun. "He's dead on arrival," he thought. The bunny started hopping away. "And I just stand there with the gun," Richard recounted, years later. "It was in range for maybe five seconds. And I just let it hop away. And I thought, 'The rabbit doesn't need me to pull the trigger. When I pull the trigger the rabbit's going to be dead.'" Brautigan knew at that moment he "had lost forever the whole thing of hunting." He just stood there with the gun and felt good, thinking if he'd lost something, perhaps he'd gained something, too.

Guy Valdène recalled that Richard "had absolutely no interest at all in shooting. He just liked to wander around in the woods. He'd be trailing a hundred yards behind. You'd turn around and he'd be sitting under a tree looking at the trees or plants but always content." By the end of the afternoon, the Airedale disappeared. They called the dog, waiting and searching for an hour and a half. Cold and tired, everyone wanted to go to the bar. "Let's tell Linda that we didn't take the dog," Brautigan suggested.

After his first, and last, outing, Richard didn't join the other hunters again. He stayed behind in Harrison's orchard to write poetry. One night, Brautigan got into a big wrangle with Geoff Norman about his experiences in Vietnam, demanding to know how Norman could justify having "actually killed people." In recompense, the next day Richard took a Polaroid picture through the big plastic-covered kitchen window of a horse standing in Jim Harrison's field. Dan Gerber thought it looked "like an impressionist painting, quite pretty actually." Brautigan signed and dated the photo, giving it the title "Horse Number 8."

At the time, Jim Harrison was having a hard time financially. Writing *Sports Illustrated* pieces provided an unsteady source of income. After three highly-acclaimed books of poetry in the sixties, Harrison branched into fiction, a preferable alternative to teaching college lit courses. He had published two novels, *Wolf* (1971) and *A Good Day to Die* (1973), but found it hard to set aside enough free time to start on a third. Brautigan noted the situation, saying nothing at the time.

Richard took off for New York on the first of November and checked into the Sherry Netherland Hotel at Fifth Avenue and Fifty-ninth Street, the most luxurious Manhattan hotel where he had lodged thus far. Brautigan paid $55 a night for his room, more than double the rate of One Fifth

Avenue, three miles to the south. Richard had breakfast with Helen Brann across the avenue at the Plaza. Mostly, he hung out with friends. Harrison and Valdène had also come to New York about the same time. They ate together almost every night at The Palm, where Richard favored the cull lobsters at thirty bucks each. Bob Dattila's office/studio apartment on Forty-ninth off Lexington was just down the block from the restaurant, and he joined the boys in their nightly feasting.

One evening, after polishing off a gigantic expensive lobster, Brautigan blurted, "Listen. I've got to find a girl. I've got to get laid." Dattila didn't recall Brautigan usually speaking this way. Having more than his share of street smarts, Bob told Richard about a lovely young Puerto Rican prostitute he'd picked up three months earlier.

"She's not like the normal hooker," Dattila explained. "She's like cheery and it's fun. It's not like some sort of tawdry thing. So, if you want to get laid and you want to spend like a hundred bucks to do it, I can arrange that." Richard thought this an excellent suggestion. Bob said she was always at the same spot every night. They all piled into his car and drove uptown to find the girl. After the arrangements had been made, Dattila took them back to his apartment and said he and Jim and Guy would return to The Palm. When Brautigan and the prostitute concluded their business, they could join them for drinks. They'd buy the Puerto Rican girl dinner if she was hungry.

Dattila, Harrison, and Valdène sat waiting at The Palm, having round after round. A half hour went by, then an hour. After an hour and a half, they got worried and walked back to Bob's apartment. Nobody was there. "What the fuck?" They phoned One Fifth Avenue, incorrectly assuming Brautigan had a room there. The desk clerk, checking old records, told Dattila that Richard had checked out.

A couple weeks later, Bob Dattila spotted the Puerto Rican girl. Thinking he might bring her back to his place, he cheerfully approached. "Hey, how you doing?"

"You son of a bitch!" she retorted. "Your friend tried to kill me! He threatened to kill me." Dattila didn't know what she was talking about. "He said he wouldn't take off his boots and he said he had a gun in his boot and if things didn't go right he said he was going to shoot me."

"He was kidding," Bob said.

"No, he wasn't kidding!"

At this point, the girl's pimp came across the street. "That guy mistreats my woman and I'm going to kill you," he threatened.

In Bob's expert opinion, "Richard ruined a perfectly good whore."

Brautigan lay low. He avoided Harrison, Valdène, and Dattila. Curt Gentry and his wife were also in town. Richard made much of The Palm, telling the Gentrys of the splendid huge lobsters and monstrous steaks. "He'd build up and build up," Curt recalled. "No, we won't go tonight. No, we won't go tomorrow night." He put them off, carousing with his wild-man buddies. Close to the end of Brautigan's stay, a more sedate family dinner seemed in order.

On the way to the restaurant, Richard worried that perhaps "they wouldn't serve him." He told the Gentrys the management had changed. "We got there," Curt said. "They rolled out the red carpet the second he came in. Turned out he'd been going there for a month [sic] and almost every night and dropping $100 and everything."

Richard took an American Airlines flight back to San Francisco in November. Soon thereafter, he met Siew-Hwa Beh for the first time in a North Beach bar and began disengaging from his relationship with Mary Ann Gilderbloom. Remembering Jim Harrison's monetary plight, he called him in Michigan. "I sense that you are trying to write your novel and don't have any money," Brautigan said. "Is this true?"

"Yeah," Harrison replied without much enthusiasm.

"I thought so!" Richard said, changing the subject. Three days later, a check for $5,000 from Brautigan arrived in Lake Leelanau. "An enormous amount of money at that time for me," Harrison recalled. It enabled Jim to write his third novel. In 1979, when Harrison had a great financial success with *Legends of the Fall*, he paid Richard back.

By the end of December, Brautigan had to vacate his old apartment on Geary Street. He dismantled the Museum and packed a decade's worth of memorabilia away in cardboard boxes. At the end of January, Keith Abbott came over with his pickup truck to help Richard move his stuff over Telegraph Hill. He rented a dolly and furniture pads. The job took thirty-two hours, spread out over five days, coming to an end in early February, when Keith drove a load of trash to the dump in Marin County. He charged eight bucks an hour for his labor and sent Brautigan a bill for $234.61, including expenses.

Leaving the Museum forever represented another break with Brautigan's impoverished bohemian past, one every bit as dramatic as his move to Montana the previous year. Richard's new apartment at 314 Union Street seemed a galaxy away from the ramshackle slum out on Geary. Near the top of Telegraph, just a block from Pioneer Park, Union Street angled so steeply the facades of the trim wooden houses took on a near-trapezoidal shape.

A couple flights up in a recently remodeled building, Brautigan's flat consisted of a long hallway, a front bedroom, bathroom, and kitchen with a sunny back room that Richard used as a writing studio. Coit Tower provided a dramatic view out the rear windows. Of all the Museum's yard sale treasures, only Willard gained entrance on Union Street. The rest remained sealed in the moving boxes. "Packed up," Brautigan told his daughter. Ianthe liked the new place with its clean efficient kitchen, shiny linoleum, and the recently purchased matching furniture. "I loved the fact that he now owned something as ordinary as a couch," she wrote in her memoir.

Another important milestone, Richard's fortieth birthday, came on January 30. Clocking forty represents a turning point. Kazuko Fujimoto's translation of *Trout Fishing in America* had just been published in Japan in an edition of twenty-five hundred copies, which sold out almost immediately. Another edition was promptly printed and another after that, the novel staying continuously in print. It was time to celebrate. Richard wanted to mark the occasion with a memorable party. The Hodges offered to host one in their elegant Victorian law office.

"Richard loved Nancy because she was the most competent hostess in the world," Dick Hodge said. "He was in awe of her."

Nancy Hodge planned a sit-down dinner for twenty-four. The law library in the Page Street basement held a custom redwood slab table accommodating that number. They had beef Wellington for the main course. Brautigan picked up the tab, buying twelve bottles of Côte de Beaune, twelve bottles of Korbel brut, six bottles LPx D champagne, and six bottles of Châteauneuf-du-Pape. The wine bill came to $273.51. Food costs were $356.73. Nancy spent a week making preparations, cooking the whole dinner herself with the help of two assistants. No detail escaped her attention. She got things right.

Richard compiled the guest list, including many of his old friends. Price Dunn, Joanne Kyger, Ron Loewensohn and Kitty Hughes, Don Carpenter, Tony Dingman, Curt Gentry, and Margot

Patterson Doss (Dr. John Doss being "away in India or something") all received invitations. Jim Harrison, Harry Dean Stanton, Gatz Hjortsberg, and Bob Dattila flew up to Frisco together from Los Angeles. Poet Don Marsh and his wife, Joan, "friends of Carpenter's actually more than Richard's," but great admirers of Brautigan and his work, came into town from Carmel Valley. "Everything was absolutely magical from the time someone walked in the door," Nancy recalled.

There were elaborate bouquets of hothouse flowers, hundreds of candles glittering like captive fireflies throughout the ninety-eight-year-old mansion. Nancy placed mirrors on each step of the stairs leading down to the law library. Every room scintillated with witty conversation and the sparkling play of candlelight on cut crystal and polished mahogany.

Full-scale high jinks began in earnest at the dinner table, the preceding cocktail hour having been relatively sedate. The low-ceilinged law library, long and narrow, echoed and amplified the shouted jokes and raucous laughter. Nancy "spent the whole night running back and forth" between the kitchen and the improvised dining room.

Jim Harrison called for everyone's attention, saying he "wanted to share a letter that he had received." Harrison stood, unfolded the letter, and started to read "this dry-eyed, flowery tribute" to Brautigan. After a few minutes, he paused, saying "there's some other stuff in there you have to read because, you know, I can't read it out loud." At this point, Jim passed the letter around. It went from hand to hand, and everyone who looked burst into spontaneous laughter. The "letter" was a blank sheet of paper.

During the feast, Bob Dattila dropped beneath the long redwood table, crawling along between the seated diners. Seizing a beautiful young blond by the legs, Bob hauled her off her chair, pulling her down into his private netherworld. Gatz Hjortsberg sat across from the woman. He thought it looked like a subterranean gopher feeding on a dandelion. The golden flower held her head up high, and suddenly she was gone, disappearing into darkness, fast in the rodent's grip.

After dinner, before the ceremonial cutting of the birthday cake and coffee service upstairs, Nancy Hodge organized a tour of the venerable house. About a dozen guests followed her up the wide carpeted steps, past a towering mahogany newel post crowning the bottom of the banister where Price Dunn's previous rowdiness sent an antique crystal globe perched on top tumbling to a shattering conclusion. Entrance to the parlor on the second floor was gained through a pair of pocket sliding doors, a theatrical Victorian decorative touch designed to make a dramatic impression. When Nancy slid open the doors, the tableau revealed within was not what anybody had in mind.

Displayed on the couch before the gathered party guests, Margot Patterson Doss had her dress up over her waist, with bad boy Price Dunn kneeling on the carpet, his head buried between her outspread legs. Hearing the commotion behind him, "Price turned around with this big goofy smile on his face."

"Hi, everybody," he grinned.

"Oh . . . ! Uh . . . ! We'll see you later." Nancy discreetly pulled the twin doors closed.

Back downstairs, the assignation above dominated the conversation. Dattila, one of the wide-eyed onlookers, "thought it was incredibly charming," and remembered the guys commenting on Price's "heroic bravery." Harry Dean Stanton, "the consummate Hollywood insider," seemed "shocked" by what he saw, Dattila recalled. "She's kind of old for that," the actor observed.

Joanne Kyger, another eyewitness, found this misbehavior on the part of a woman she regarded as "our sturdy Scots walker" a bit hard to fathom.

Richard seemed quite pleased by it all. "That's my pal," he said of Price. "What a service! What a humanitarian guy!"

Nancy, the consummate hostess, took it all in stride. "It was absolutely a hilarious night," she recalled. "I think Brautigan was very joyful and was having the time of his life." He had every reason to be happy. The next day Sam Lawrence wrote to Helen Brann reporting the approximate sales figure for the four Brautigan titles under the Delta and Dell/Laurel imprint was one and a half million copies.

Three days following Richard's birthday bash, Keith Abbott transported the last of Brautigan's possessions from Geary Street over to the new Telegraph Hill apartment. Not long after moving in, Richard met Nikki Arai, a Japanese American photographer and art dealer, a neighbor who lived on Windsor Place, a residential alley off Green Street only a block or so away from Brautigan's residence. Arai had recently broken up with her boyfriend, Simon Lowinsky, who had also been her business partner, and was feeling "very down on men."

Lowinsky and Arai had operated the Phoenix Gallery in Berkeley. A photo exhibit there on People's Park in September and October of 1969 showed her work along with that of Alan Copeland. This led to the publication of *People's Park*, a collection of their photographs she edited together with Copeland. Arai and Lowinsky moved to San Francisco in the early seventies and opened the Simon Lowinsky Gallery. They traveled often to Holland to buy the work of printmaker M. C. Escher, which they resold in Frisco for inflated prices. Copeland considered this "a Ponzi scheme."

It was nevertheless a lucrative endeavor. Nikki Arai drove a Mercedes Benz SL convertible and lived in a luxury apartment. She had flair. Brautigan was immediately attracted. When Nikki brought Richard to her boudoir the first time, he discovered she kept a pair of shackles attached to the headboard of her bed. She once told Alan Copeland, "I just love running a razor blade over warm flesh." This was a bit more bondage and S&M than Brautigan had bargained for, and their affair was short-lived. But a link had been forged. They remained friends for the rest of her life.

Very soon thereafter, Siew-Hwa Beh moved in with Brautigan at 314 Union Street. Living with this intelligent, outspoken, liberated Malaysian woman whom, from the very start of their relationship, he called "an avenging angel" charged his life with high-voltage emotional intensity. At first, he felt delirious with happiness. Don Carpenter remembered when Richard met Siew-Hwa, "he just couldn't stop talking about it. He was so happy, he literally walked into lampposts."

For Beh, the two years she spent with Brautigan felt like ten. "You know how you can spend a whole lifetime with someone and never have that intensity of intimacy?" she said. "The first seven, eight months were so ideal it was like I felt in my soul and in every way that I had come home. All my life I had looked for a playmate, another person to play with me. I never had a boyfriend or even a girlfriend who was such an ideal playmate. Our life was so unreal. He never had to go to an office. We read poetry. We talked a lot. We loved to eat. We had great sex."

There had been previous lovers, and Beh had been married for four years while in college, but still she admitted, "I was so new to a whole sexual life because I came from a place where you're not allowed to be sexually that free." Part of the new freedom included bondage. The ever-independent Siew-Hwa set her own rules in that department as well. "I was into freedom and being able to express myself," she recalled, "and I said, 'Only if you allow me to tie you, too.' I think no woman had ever told him that and I think that thrilled him."

The open give-and-take early in their relationship extended beyond the bedroom into even more sacred territory, Brautigan's work. Unlike any previous muse, when something Siew-Hwa said in conversation inspired the writing of a poem, she teased him, saying, "What part of the commission do I get from this?"

Intrigued, Richard told her, "They're paying me $200 for this poem; I'll give you sixty bucks for it."

"That's good," Siew-Hwa said. "Next poem. Muses have to eat, too."

Beh believed Brautigan paid her so much attention that he spoiled her "in a sense." He enjoyed drawing baths for her. While the tub filled, Richard lit numbers of candles on the window ledge and the vanity top and along the edge of the sink. After Siew-Hwa immersed herself in the steaming water, he brought in a "cold, cold bottle of white wine," usually Pouilly-Fuissé, and sat on the toilet seat and just stared at her. "It's like he noticed everything about it," Beh recalled. "He would look at me in silence like he was trying to hold on to every moment."

Richard liked taking a book into the bathroom and reading to Siew-Hwa as she washed her hair. Often, they cracked jokes during these intimate bathing moments. "He looked so angelic," Beh said, "but other times he would look melancholy, like he couldn't believe this would ever last. He would be so simple and yet so complex at the same time. We were both very conscious about class. We both felt we were outsiders. We understood each other because in many ways I was just as primitive as he was. As kids, we would just run around the streets wild. And I enjoyed being a loner with him. Two outsiders found each other."

Together night and day during those first months, Richard and Siew-Hwa forged a unique bond. "It was a wonderful gift," she said. "I couldn't have dreamt of a better dream." Beh described Brautigan as "the perfect house-husband. He cooked every day. I would just love it," she said. A perfectionist in the kitchen as well as in his writing studio, Richard took care to get things right.

"He was a gourmet," Beh recalled. "He knew his wine and his food, and he knew every corner of every street, so he would go to different delis. He was playful. He was like this eternal child who would keep discovering and rediscovering and having the joy to discover again." At home, Richard and Siew-Hwa didn't watch much television, but their nighttime ritual before sleep involved watching *The Tonight Show* with Johnny Carson. Beh noted that Brautigan was not "placid" in his television watching. "He had a unique way of seeing things," she said. "He could turn anything that's mundane into something funny or witty. And that was such a joy because that was a real gift."

Richard shared his love of basketball with Siew-Hwa. Professional and college games provided more opportunities to nest in front of the television set. Another aspect of popular culture Brautigan greatly enjoyed was country music. He introduced Siew-Hwa to Dolly Parton by playing her the song "Coat of Many Colors." "You're a feminist," he told his Malaysian girlfriend, "you must listen to Dolly Parton, who was really quite a feminist before her time." (Ianthe remembered her father playing Parton's "Jolene" over and over again during the summer of 1976.)

The second week in April, Jim Harrison and Guy de la Valdène arrived in San Francisco for a short visit. They stayed with Brautigan at his new sun-filled apartment. Russ Chatham came over from Marin to join the fun, later described as a "riotous couple of days." The boys were in a mood to party, wanting to visit the Golden Gate Foundation, an upscale fifteen-room Pacific Heights brothel at 2018 Bush Street. The place had opened several months earlier, quickly gaining a sub-rosa reputation by discreet word of mouth. They also gave out gold calling cards, "a member organization" advertising the "preservation of fine traditions."

The problem for the gang was a shortage of funds. This was no two-bit whorehouse. Prices ranged from around fifty bucks a pop to $300, depending on the customer's sexual preferences. Sitting at the bar at Vesuvio on Columbus Avenue, the boys discussed their dire financial straits. Richard came to the rescue. He dug through the pockets of his old army jacket and started "pulling out bills." Brautigan found between $1,100 and $1,300 in the faded fatigue coat and turned it all over to his buddies. Curt Gentry joined their party. He had published a book called *The Great Madams of San Francisco* a decade earlier and had a long-standing scholar's interest in brothels.

Richard accompanied the gang to the cathouse on Bush Street but didn't partake of its main attraction. They trooped under an ornate iron gate and up twenty steps beneath a drooping oleander tree to the canary yellow doorway of the Victorian mansion housing the Golden Gate Foundation. After being treated to "free" drinks (champagne), the boys took bubble baths upstairs with the girls of their choice, before retiring to the six tangerine-lit, sumptuously furnished bedrooms.

While his friends caroused, Richard had drinks in the bar, where he encountered Joseph Alioto, mayor of San Francisco. "What are you doing?" Brautigan inquired.

"I'm sort of running the town," His Honor replied.

Kitty Desmond, the madam, billed as the "executive planning director," listed her occupation as "researcher." She had been granted a business license by the city to operate an "emotional therapy research foundation." Her place was raided by the police a month later and shut down for good. Russell Chatham found himself unable to collect on an arrangement to trade a large nude painting for "a dozen glorious pieces of [Kitty's] matchless ass [. . .]"

After returning from Montana in the fall of 1974, Brautigan's monthly tab at Enrico's and Vanessi's provided an accurate yardstick of time spent at his favorite North Beach establishments. In December of '74, Richard charged $556.04 at Vanessi's and another $238.51 (mostly drinks) at Enrico's. More than a convenient watering hole, Enrico's served as a quasi-private club for its regular customers.

In his newspaper column, Herb Caen described "an ordinary day" at Enrico's. Caen stood inside at the bar with Charles McCabe, taking it all in. Over "at the family table," Scott Beach played his handmade psaltery for editor Blair Fuller. "Nearby, Barnaby Conrad was arguing movies with Mel Torme. A newly bearded Herb Gold, just back from Haiti, toyed with his eggs-in-hell while listening to Enrico practice his violin." Out on the sidewalk terrace, Richard Brautigan sat "scribbling poetry on an old envelope." A couple tables away, Evan Connell occupied his time "staring into space." Dressed to the nines "except for an incongruous white tennis hat," J. P. Donleavy paused for a drink on his way to visit John Huston in Mexico. Caen felt the scene rivaled the fabled Algonquin Round Table from the 1920s.

Herb Caen neglected to mention Ward Dunham, Enrico's affable, bearded Herculean bartender (and occasional bouncer), who gave the place much of its character. Born in Denver, Dunham came to San Francisco in 1965 after getting back from Vietnam. Before signing on at Enrico's, Ward worked as the night manager at a club called the Roaring Twenties while studying history and journalism at San Francisco State during the day.

Belying his formidable appearance, Dunham was a skilled calligrapher, whose incisive Gothic lettering was much prized by collectors. Broadway riffraff commingling with high society, "low-lifes coming into contact with the social elite of the city" at Enrico's, provided Ward with a front-row seat for the world's most fascinating street theater.

Enrico's seemed designed for the inside crowd. "All the good stuff to eat was never on the menu," an old regular recalled. "You had to know what to ask for. "Dirty hamburgers were Enrico's evocation of the hamburgers you ate as a child at the drugstore, with a little thin slice of pickle and a little thin slice of onion, perfectly done for a dollar and a quarter. If you wanted the Enrico hamburger it was big and thick and on French bread and inedible."

Sometime in the fall of 1974, Brautigan reconnected with private detective David Fechheimer at a party at Men Yee's lavish Pacific Heights apartment. At the time, Yee and a friend named Pat Bell planned to go into the publishing business together. "They were going to do a Book of the Month or something like that," Fechheimer recalled. "Some crazy scheme." Richard and David started a conversation at the party and ended up spending the next couple days together, "drinking and talking and screwing around."

After that, they met regularly through the winter and spring of 1975 at Enrico's. Once, sitting together drinking at Brautigan's favorite table, they were approached by a young man. "Obviously a star-struck graduate student wanting to be a writer," Fechheimer said. The aspiring author asked Richard's advice regarding his potential literary career.

"I think I can help you," Brautigan replied. "I'll be willing to sell you some verbs. You're going to be a writer, you're going to need a lot of verbs."

Not knowing quite what to make of it all, the young man asked, "How much do verbs cost?"

"Well," Richard said, "they start at a dollar."

Still unsure where this was leading, the young man handed Brautigan a dollar bill.

Richard took the money, folded it, and put it in his pocket. "Go," he said, without cracking the hint of a smile.

Along with good food and energetic sex, a passion for the movies provided another enthusiasm Brautigan shared with Siew-Hwa Beh. He and his new love often saw several films on a single day. They watched Lina Wertmüller's *Swept Away* one morning (they liked it) and, after a lunch of creamed herring on Union Street, went to *Three Days of the Condor* (which they hated) at the Northpoint Theatre. Following a quick pizza dinner, they dropped over the hill into Polk Gulch and saw *The Harder They Come* ("a sweet movie") at the Lumiere, the venerable art film cinema on California Street.

At the time, Brautigan was writing his *Hawkline Monster* screenplay while Beh continued to work on her magazine dealing with women in film. Richard was "very pleased" by this tangency, Siew-Hwa noted, "because he thought it would really strengthen our relationship." She told Brautigan that Hal Ashby was the perfect director for the *Hawkline* project and was entirely supportive. "He was very puritanic," she said. "He never drank anytime he worked."

By the first week of May, the work had been going really well and Richard's script was nearly done. He decided to celebrate, advertise, and mock his good fortune all in a single gesture. At San Francisco Posters in North Beach, he ordered 250 custom one-and-a-quarter-inch white pinback buttons printed with sold out. why didn't i think of it sooner? in blue letters. At a tourist novelty shop near Fisherman's Wharf, Brautigan bought a couple dozen white cotton T-shirts and had the same slogan stenciled on the front in blue. Throughout the summer, he gave these souvenirs away to his friends and acquaintances. The inner circle received the shirts.

As the *Hawkline* screenplay wound to a conclusion, Richard made plans to return to Montana for an indefinite stay. Siew-Hwa would spend a lot of time with him at Pine Creek but needed to pursue her own career in San Francisco and planned to travel back and forth as her schedule demanded. Unable to drive, and knowing he'd be living alone twelve miles from town with a teenage daughter who had only a learner's permit, Brautigan cast about for a companion to serve as a chauffeur, provide entertaining company, and help with the cooking. He found the perfect candidate in Tony Dingman.

Richard Brautigan had been introduced to Dingman by Lew Welch in the fall of 1969 at the San Francisco opening of American Zoetrope, Francis Ford Coppola's and George Lucas's new production company. Tony had been studying poetry with Lew for about a year as part of a UC Extension course. Dingman's sister, who introduced the film director to his future wife, Eleanor, provided the connection to Coppola.

Born in Los Angeles, Tony graduated from Stanford University in 1960, then worked for a year as a social worker in L.A. before moving to San Francisco. Dingman spent the next three years at UC Hastings College of the Law. After failing to pass the bar exam three times in a row, he hit the road in the summer of '66, living for fourteen months in Brazil teaching English as a foreign language.

When he returned from Rio in February of '68, Tony found work on Coppola's production of *The Rain People*. "They needed to give a poor fuck-up a job," he said. Having been a Bekins moving man the summer before he left for South America, Dingman had a Teamsters card and became the transportation captain on the shoot. After spending the summer shooting in a dozen eastern states, Coppola and Lucas (associate producer on *Rain People*) returned to Frisco and found a first home for the fledgling Zoetrope in an unused warehouse.

Richard and Tony hit it off immediately at the launch party and quickly became fast friends and drinking buddies. "Things were good for a long time," Dingman recalled. "He never pissed me off. I never pissed him off." Both men shared the virtue of punctuality. Ianthe remembered Tony as "one of the few people who could get along with my father for long periods of time."

By the summer of 1975, the ranks of the Montana gang had realigned. Tom and Becky McGuane split up. Tom sold his original screenplay, *The Missouri Breaks*, to producer Elliott Kastner, at the same time finessing a side deal to direct the film version of his novel *Ninety-two in the Shade* himself. While shooting in Key West that winter, McGuane fell in love with Margot Kidder, the picture's female lead. By the time the movie wrapped, Margot was pregnant. Becky moved out, divorcing him in March.

Beautiful, bright, and big-hearted, Becky didn't remain a grass widow for very long. A handsome movie star waited in the wings. Peter Fonda, one of the leads in *Ninety-two in the Shade*, had his eye on the petite blond throughout the shoot in Key West. "I couldn't help but notice that Tom wasn't paying close attention to his promise or duty," Fonda wrote in his memoir, *Don't Tell Dad*. "He was after every skirt in town."

Regarding his own feelings for Becky, Peter stated, "From the get-go, I had thought she was a gold mine." To celebrate their love, Dink Bruce carved rings for them from a sabadilla tree growing in Becky's backyard. When Ianthe attempted to get some answers from her father regarding "all the couple shuffling," Richard declined to satisfy her curiosity. "If I tried to keep track of the substance of my friends' love lives, that's all I would have time to do."

When school got out early in June, Ianthe flew to Montana with her father. Tony Dingman followed a week later, flying Western to Bozeman. Ianthe later wrote she "always felt very safe when Tony came to stay with us." Owning an automobile was essential. Richard and Tony soon went used car shopping. They settled on a big white ten-year-old Plymouth Fury. Brautigan dubbed his new set of wheels the "White Acre."

Richard remained in a good mood through the start of the summer. Work on his novel was going well, and in the middle of June, Helen Brann sent him a huge batch of foreign contracts, twenty-one altogether, for five different books from countries as varied as Finland, Japan, Holland, Sweden, Norway, and Mexico.

With Tony Dingman ensconced at Pine Creek, life ran a bit smoother. He helped manage the house, did the shopping and pitched in with the cooking. Tony also nursed Richard through the worst of his drunken nights and never objected when Ianthe played her favorite Bob Marley records over and over and over. Both being poets, Brautigan and Dingman respected each other's work time. Tony recalled that Richard had only one hard-and-fast rule: "No yogurt in the refrigerator."

Summer in Montana was houseguest season, and a steady flow of visitors began appearing at Brautigan's Pine Creek home. Curt Gentry and his girlfriend, Gail Stevens, were among the first to arrive, showing up in time for the Fourth of July, always a rambunctious holiday in cowboy country. Gentry had enjoyed an enormous success in 1974 with *Helter Skelter*, his hardcover bestselling account of the Manson killing spree, coauthored with prosecutor Vincent Bugliosi. The book received an Edgar Award for best true crime book of the year from the Mystery Writers of America.

Flush with best seller earnings and a new woman on his arm, Curt Gentry felt in a mood to party in Montana. July had been unseasonably cool and wet with sky-blackening thunderstorms and hailstones bigger than cherry bombs. Cowboys never complain about rain, and the Independence Day festivities went on without interruption. After the town's annual parade, the main event was the Livingston Roundup, a three-day rodeo spanning the second, third, and fourth of July. Held in conjunction with other three-day rodeos in the nearby cities of Red Lodge, Montana, and Cody, Wyoming, the Roundup attracted talent at a national level. The hands competed in all three towns over the long weekend, potentially tripling their winnings if Lady Luck rode with them all the way to the whistle.

Most of the Montana gang was in attendance at the fairgrounds arena the night Curt, Gail, and Tony Dingman came with Richard and Siew-Hwa to the rodeo. The Hjortsbergs were there, as were Tom McGuane and Margot Kidder. Gentry recalled that when the announcer asked all the native Montanans to stand, "Richard was up before anybody else." The rodeo was a long affair, with two rounds of every event and a halftime show featuring trick riders, trained bison, and a clown whose chaps-wearing monkey rode a bucking border collie.

The Missouri Breaks, directed by Arthur Penn, was in production at locations in Nevada City and the vicinity around Billings. Starring Marlon Brando and Jack Nicholson, the cast included several familiar faces. Harry Dean Stanton was back, as a member of a horse-thieving gang, along with Randy Quaid and Frederic Forrest. Stanton and Forrest became very close and hung together throughout the shoot. Siew-Hwa Beh idolized Brando, and Harry Dean told her he would introduce them. Richard, knowing of Marlon's fondness for Asian women, fell into a jealous snit, afraid his girlfriend might run off with the movie star, and the proposed meeting never took place.

McGuane's coterie made regular excursions to Billings to visit the set. One afternoon, Tom McGuane, along with Forrest, Stanton, and a group of other movie people, rode up to Brautigan's house on horseback. Richard had prepared for this unexpected visit. He bragged of a new possession. The best thing he ever had, Brautigan claimed. Anticipating hot summer weather, he purchased an electric fan. Richard brought the machine into the room, turned it on, and focused the air flow on Harry Dean, who was "stoned out of his mind." At the same moment, Siew-Hwa switched on a portable tape recorder. "Harry Dean, I'm your biggest fan," the recorded voice chimed. "Harry Dean, I'm your biggest fan." Everyone laughed. Curt Gentry got the impression that Stanton didn't have a clue what was going on.

During his stay, Curt also observed that Richard and Siew-Hwa "were fighting just constantly." In spite of the bickering, Gentry thought Brautigan's girlfriend "had a pretty good sense of humor." He noted that she was able to put up with his friend's numerous idiosyncrasies "but wouldn't do any work for him, cooking or anything."

Richard did the cooking, aided by Tony and Ianthe. At times, the wives of his guests pitched in. Gail did her part during Curt's short stay. Terry de la Valdène, Guy's lovely blond wife, took "over the organization of the kitchen" during their several visits that summer. "Terry and I would wash the endless dishes together while she told me funny stories about growing up," Ianthe recalled. The two of them grew very close. Guy observed Ianthe "sort of used Terry as a mother figure."

The Valdènes always arrived bearing boxes of shellfish and oysters packed in ice, along with cases of top-shelf booze. They stayed in the bedroom on the second floor of Brautigan's house. Jim Harrison usually came at the same time without his wife, Linda. Being a solo guy, Jim was relegated to a smaller room at the bottom of the stairs on the left, a grade above Tony Dingman's quarters, which Guy described as "a miserable little room."

Brautigan arose early, even if drinking heavily the night before, and went to work on *Sombrero Fallout* in his writing studio high in the big red barn. Later came a substantial breakfast, frequently prepared by Richard, who favored hearty fare, biscuits and gravy or Hangtown fry or eggs with sausage and bacon. On occasion, he served his friends fried rice or turkey dressing in the morning. Afternoons, the boys went fishing. "We were great pals," Guy observed.

Harrison had finished a first draft of the novel Brautigan's loan set in motion, but he was stuck for a title. Jim based the main character on his mother's only brother, who died in the 1919 flu pandemic, imaging his life story had he lived. At one point, Jim told Richard, "I'm having trouble with a title."

"I charge a quarter for titles," Brautigan replied.

"I'll take three," Harrison said, giving him six bits.

"It's about a farmer, right?"

"Yeah."

"How about calling it *Farmer*?"

"Okay."

In the evenings, numerous dinner parties provided the agenda, Paradise Valley being a moveable feast in the summer of '75. Tom McGuane became a frequent host on Deep Creek. Margot Kidder was pregnant but didn't let it slow her down. She kept busy filming a behind-the-scenes, making-of documentary on *The Missouri Breaks*, transforming the converted chicken coop/guest cottage into her office.

Becky had divorced Tom and bought Wilbur and Doretha Lambert's place adjacent to McGuane's spread, The Raw Deal Ranch. She wanted their son, Thomas, to have only to walk across a hayfield when he wanted to see both parents in a single day. Peter Fonda flew Becky down to San Antonio, where he was shooting *Race with the Devil* with Warren Oates. He rented the best room in the city's finest hotel and filled her suite with hundreds of yellow roses (a symbol of loyalty), an extravagant floral welcome marking the beginning of their life together. They got married on Armistice Day in Sonora, Arkansas, where Peter was working on another film, Jonathan Demme's *Fighting Mad*.

Back at home, high jinks and misrule remained the order of the day. Practical jokes abounded. One night, Jim Harrison, exhausted from the day's frolicking, left early from a party at the Hjortsbergs', hoping to get some much-needed shut-eye, and found a stranger bunked down in his guest room bed at Richard's. Returning to the party and too polite to ask about his replacement, Jim failed to notice Richard's sly unconcealed grin. Knowing his friend planned an early departure, Richard slipped out ahead and placed a dummy made of pillows in Harrison's bed. A coconut served for a head.

Harrison exacted his revenge a few nights later, when, after a late evening of drinking, he smeared butter all over the doorknob to Richard's exterior sleeping cabin. Guy de la Valdène remembered Brautigan's schedule seemed to be one "bad" drunken day followed by two "good" sober ones. "He said he couldn't write otherwise." Guy, being a good listener, was often on the receiving end of Brautigan's late night bull sessions. "At three in the morning the guy can barely get the words out of his mouth," he recalled.

The manic hilarity seemed to reach its zenith with a mammoth food fight at Tom McGuane's place. The season's war cry, "Nothing is too disgusting," rang in the air as the dinner guests ran from room to room, pelting each other with leftovers. Their clothing befouled, the women stripped down to bras and panties, transforming into fierce mashed-potato-hurling amazons. The entire downstairs was trashed. This sophomoric bacchanal might reasonably have provided the conclusion to the summer's mischief, but reason seldom plays a part when anarchy rules the roost.

"We knew it was going to happen," Guy de la Valdène said in retrospect. A couple weeks later, Brautigan hosted his own big dinner party. In preparation, Richard removed his favorite possessions from the walls of his combination living room–dining room, taking down a Japanese flag and a treasured Russell Chatham painting completed earlier that year. The canvas had "1942," Brautigan's poem about the death of his uncle Edward, penciled on the surface over the gaunt image of a tree. Richard's guest list included Siew-Hwa, Tony Dingman, Guy and Terry, Gatz and Marian Hjortsberg, and Bob Dattila, out for his annual rural frolic but lodging elsewhere.

Tom McGuane and his large household of visitors were also invited. These included Moira Hodgson, petite blond Irish food critic and author of several cookbooks, and Margot Kidder's longtime friend from Canada, writer Rosie Shuster, a gorgeous brunette with a killer wit. Rosie's father had been half of the Canadian comedy team Wayne and Shuster, and her artist uncle, Joe, had created the comic strip *Superman* (with high school buddy Jerry Siegel) as a teenager in Cleveland.

Rosie married her junior high sweetheart, Lorne Michaels, in 1972 and was on her way to New York to work on the writing staff of *Saturday Night Live*, a show he was producing for NBC. Their marriage wasn't working out. She had a traveling companion, Stuart Birnbaum, also a comedy writer, in tow. Once, heading through the swinging doors into the Longbranch for a night of two-stepping, Shuster quipped to her friend Kidder, "You know how to tell the cowboys, don't you, Margie? They're the premature ejaculators in the big hats."

The dinner table conversation at Brautigan's place was raucous and entertaining, everyone shouting amid the laughter. Richard had prepared vast quantities of his signature spaghetti sauce, and the Hjortsbergs brought fresh vegetables and a large green salad from their garden. At the end of the meal, Dattila made his apologies and ducked out. Moments later, Brautigan said, "Terry, you're one of my favorite friends in the world, and this is why I'm gonna do this." He picked up a pitcher full of red wine, reached across the table, and poured it over the top of Terry de la Valdène's head.

"What the fuck!" she exploded. Guy was equally shocked. Richard had always placed Terry (and Becky McGuane) "right up on a pedestal—always the perfect gentleman."

Brautigan went on to calmly explain his motives to Terry. "The reason I'm doing this," he said, "is had I started this food fight and not gotten you involved, you would have gone upstairs and missed all the fun."

After that, all hell broke loose. Terry reached into the pot of spaghetti sauce and hurled a handful at Richard's face. In seconds, the entire party grabbed leftovers and flung them at the first available target—everyone except Margot and Siew-Hwa, who ducked into the safety of the bathroom and locked the door. Moira Hodgson, wearing a white antique crocheted Irish lace blouse, her coppery hair arranged in an elegant coiffure, ran upstairs for the safety of a guest bedroom.

The battle raged on for fifteen or twenty chaotic minutes. Marian Hjortsberg poured a bottle of sweet sticky liqueur all over her husband. The others ran back and forth between the kitchen and the dining room, flinging cold spaghetti, booze, and wilted salad. When all the leftovers were gone, they raided the garbage pail, hurling coffee grounds and orange peels, whatever came to hand, pelting each other with filth.

After the trash was exhausted, Guy filled the garbage can with water and doused it over the survivors' heads. Brautigan's downstairs had been reduced to shambles, walls an abstract spaghetti sauce action painting, floors slick with water and trampled leftovers. Somewhat chagrined, the befouled and bedraggled gang took their leave. McGuane blew his Land Rover's horn for stragglers. Marian ran to rescue Moira Hodgson from her hiding place. "It's all right now," she said. "It's over. You can come down now."

Moira tiptoed like an immaculate princess through the wreckage. Brautigan made a little formal Japanese bow, holding out his hand to escort her through the doorway. In on the plot, Richard laughed his excited high-pitched laugh. Jim Harrison waited in hiding on the front porch, pressed against the wall with a half-gallon of mountain red. When Moira stepped out, he upended the bottle over her head. The cheap burgundy poured through her perfect hairdo, streamed across her face, and stained her antique blouse a deep purple.

Moira stood stock-still in disbelief, and her Celtic temper built. Her features darkened. "Bitch!" she exploded, thinking Marian Hjortsberg had set her up. Moira whirled around and slugged Marian so hard she "went flying to the other side of the room." Everyone was laughing "just like satyrs."

The next day, Ianthe awoke to the *swish* of a lawn sprinkler. She looked out her bedroom window at the front lawn and saw the dazzle of the oscillating spray in the morning sunlight. The sprinkler sat dead center on the stained living room rug, "going slowly back and forth [. . .]" After it dried out, the rug showed few battle scars. The interior of the house was another story. Guy went into Livingston and bought several gallons of latex paint. Tony Dingman repainted the kitchen and the living room ceiling. He left a small patch of the original yellow in the kitchen where Brautigan had calibrated his daughter's growth with pencil marks.

At fifteen, about to start her sophomore year in high school, Ianthe no longer stood against the kitchen wall to be measured. Her mother planned a move from Sonoma Valley to Hawaii. Ginny and Richard talked things over, deciding it would be best for Ianthe to spend the winter with him and attend school in Montana. Before Labor Day, Terry de la Valdène took Ianthe into Livingston and registered her at Park High. They shopped in town for new school clothes. Brautigan took an interest in his daughter's education, asking about her reading assignments. Her English teacher had assigned Faulkner's "The Bear," and Ianthe found it boring. Brautigan loved Faulkner. He wanted Ianthe to be properly introduced to his work, having her read *As I Lay Dying* instead.

In the last week of August, John Fryer gave Richard a small notebook. Brautigan said he wanted to keep track of how he spent his time every day. "This book is a record of my reality," he noted on the first page. "It is not a diary. I am writing it because I am curious about what I do with my life." Between the end of August and the first Monday in November 1975, Richard maintained an accurate day-by-day autobiographical compendium. He recorded daily events, the trivial and the important.

Brautigan noted everything he had for breakfast ("a hamburger with some grapefruit juice," "country sausage and eggs [. . .] at a truck stop café," "fried rice," and "fried potatoes and deer steak [. . .] I made a really good gravy and poured gravy over the potatoes. It was a fine breakfast.") He detailed the number of hangovers he suffered (fourteen over the two-month time span). Most remarkable were his omissions. Richard made no mention of fifty-one days when he had almost nothing to drink. When he drank, Brautigan really tied one on, but there were periods (some lasting almost three weeks) when he imbibed nothing stronger than wine with dinner.

Richard's nondiary detailed his writing life during the completion of *Sombrero Fallout*, including descriptions of several short jaunts to San Francisco, when he left Ianthe in Tony Dingman's care. A four-day fishing trip to Vancouver Island, British Columbia, in September was also recorded. Brautigan flew from Bozeman to Seattle (with stops in Great Falls and Spokane, "a long and boring flight"), where he spent the night in a TraveLodge. The next morning he met Russ Chatham and two other fishing companions. They took the car ferry to Victoria and drove nine hours north to Port McNeill, the final fifty miles on a dirt road.

Along the way, they stopped at the harbor city of Nanaimo and bought nonresident angling licenses for $15 at Murphy's Sporting Goods. Brautigan listed his address as 314 Union St., San Francisco, although he always claimed Montana as his primary residence when buying his annual local permit. The fishing in B.C. proved terrible. Richard caught the only salmon. Eating wild blueberries in the woods provided a more interesting activity.

Brautigan left his friends, flying on Pacific Western to Vancouver and on to San Francisco, where Siew-Hwa picked him up at the airport. Richard was gone from Montana for ten days before returning to his daughter. He resumed his urban life in Frisco, breakfasting with Don Carpenter at Mama's Café on Stockton Street, lunching with Ron Loewinsohn in Japantown, going to the movies, hanging out at Enrico's, making love and fighting with Siew-Hwa.

The mercurial seesaw nature of Richard's relationship with Siew-Hwa was duly recorded in his journal. A sampling of the early entries spelled out their domestic tribulations. "Siew-Hwa and I got into a big argument [. . .] I slept in a separate bed again." "I had a good day with Siew-Hwa. Didn't argue and made love." "We almost had an argument but fell asleep before it could get off the ground." "Siew-Hwa and I continued arguing until I left to go to the airport." "I talked to Siew-Hwa on the telephone. It went alright. We didn't argue." "Siew-Hwa and I started off the day with a terrible argument. It lasted until 3:00 pm when we found something better to do that pleased us a great deal."

Siew-Hwa's volatile behavior stemmed from a fierce independent spirit. On her many trips back and forth from San Francisco, Beh always paid her own way, unlike most of Brautigan's former female companions. Arguments with Richard frequently grew out of heated conversations, intellectual disputes escalating to a shouting match. Between outbursts they enjoyed a special harmony, loving and nourishing. The day before Siew-Hwa arrived for a visit early in September, Richard went fishing on Mill Creek and caught two brook trout for her breakfast. Later, they drove to Yellowstone Park. Brautigan fished the Gibbon River until twilight. They spent the night at the Old Faithful Inn, dining very late on "mediocre" Rock Cornish game hens.

After "a horrible lunch" the next day, Richard vowed to bring his own food the next time he visited the Park. "It is a mistake to eat any food that is cooked for you at Yellowstone." He and Siew-Hwa toured Geyser Basin, viewing the steaming pools and geysers. Brautigan found the colorful algae "beautiful, like other worlds." After leaving by way of West Yellowstone, Brautigan fished the Gallatin River in the afternoon. They drove down Gallatin Canyon to Bozeman, checking into the Holiday Inn, where they marveled as "lightning mixed itself in the sunset." After dark, they watched the Miss U.S.A. pageant on TV. The next morning, Richard saw Siew-Hwa off at the airport. They'd enjoyed four harmonious days without even the hint of an argument.

On the first of October, Brautigan had breakfast in the morning with Don Carpenter, returning to Montana from San Francisco later in the day. Back in Pine Creek, he paid Tony Dingman $2,000 "for services rendered: specifically as chauffeur-painter, for the months of June, July, August, September, 1975." That night, Richard went to a party at Tom McGuane's. He got "very drunk," staying up until 5:30 am. The next day was lost in a hangover fog.

On the second Friday in October, after Richard worked on his novel and watched the last few moments of a high school football game in Livingston, he and Tony met an incoming flight bringing Siew-Hwa, Curt Gentry, and Gail Stevens. Back at Pine Creek, Brautigan "drank a lot, got maudlin and fought with Siew-Hwa." The next morning he woke up with a "horrible hangover." Brautigan spent the day in bed, out in his little sleeping cabin. "It seemed to be the best place for me," he reflected. Richard got up as it grew dark and joined his friends and family in the main house, joking "about being a vampire cowboy." Curt cooked a massive steak Brautigan thought was delicious. Later, Harmon Henkin dropped by and stayed up with Richard until one in the morning, discussing future trades.

On Sunday, Richard prepared a spaghetti dinner for fifteen, while he and Curt "talked about fame." Brautigan went to bed very late. Once again, he drank too much "and disappointed myself by doing so." It snowed that night, the first serious storm after a languid Indian summer. The surprise splendor of more than a foot of new snow on the ground brightened Richard's morning hangover.

Everyone reveled in the early winter. Ianthe built a snowman. Wild snowball fights spontane-ously erupted. "We were like children," Brautigan wrote in his journal. After the morning's frolic, when Richard took what Curt Gentry called "his weekly bath," Curt, Siew-Hwa, Ianthe, and Gail filled a washtub with snow, carrying it to the bathroom window. They raised the window in whispered silence and dumped the whole freezing load in on top of the placid bather. Whooping, Richard ran from the bathroom "stark naked out into the blizzard," grabbed a shovel, and decapi-tated Ianthe's snowman.

According to the improvised kitchen schedule, it wasn't Brautigan's night to cook. He was pissed when he had to do it anyway. Harmon Henkin and a girlfriend had been invited to dinner. Siew-Hwa didn't like Harmon and refused to cook for him. After a big fight, Beh locked herself in a spare bedroom. Brautigan "wouldn't speak to her." He prepared rabbit he'd bought from Gatz. After dinner, Richard and Harmon "got into some trading." Brautigan traded Henkin "a .22 cali-ber Ithaca carbine for a very good fly reel, a winter vest, a waterproof jacket and a dozen muddler minnow flies."

A late night of drinking and trading followed by a bout of insomnia left Richard feeling "like shit" the next day. He and Siew-Hwa were barely speaking in the morning. Richard used his exhaustion as an excuse to stay home and not go with Curt, Gail, and Siew-Hwa when Tony drove them all to the airport. A nap didn't help. Neither did lunch at Martin's Café, where the food was "terrible." Another nap in the afternoon "didn't help either." Brautigan solved the problem by getting very drunk during and after dinner "with a bunch of people" at Becky Fonda's place. They got into a snowball fight out front, and Richard lost his eyeglasses.

Waking up the next morning with another hangover, Brautigan wrote "What's new?" in his makeshift journal. Tony drove him up to Becky's, and they found his glasses in the snow. Hangover therapy included a long afternoon nap, watching "very bad television," soaking in a hot tub, and reading *Helter Skelter*. Richard wrote "What a horrible story" about Curt's book, intending it as praise. His day ended with a long nonargumentative telephone call to Siew-Hwa lasting until 3:00 am.

The morning's hangover marked the beginning of a ten-day stretch of relative sobriety and consistent hard work. Brautigan received word from Helen Brann on October 16 that *Willard* had sold 35,500 copies as of the tenth. "I was immensely happy," he wrote in his daybook. Richard allowed only three hangovers to disrupt his industrious progress toward the conclusion of *Sombrero Fallout*. He finished on the twenty-second. "Hooray!"

The next day remained very cold. Richard spent most of the morning and afternoon proof-reading his manuscript. A letter from Siew-Hwa arrived with the day's mail. Beh bared her heart in two handwritten pages. "I feel unconsolable, spiraling in unspeakable grief," she wrote. "I can no longer feel your care only your violence, aggression, denials, and self centeredness." They had lived together for just eight months, yet Siew-Hwa observed, "I wake up every morning house sit-ting with a ghost lover [. . .] I am lost to the world and can speak only to/from my loneliness. I'm waning fast becoming an apparition. Our love was too young and fragile to weather the constant premature pummelling of your many years of historical grievances."

Richard brooded on the contents of Beh's letter for the rest of the day. He cooked dinner for David Dill and Judy and Stuart Bergsma, who lived nearby on the Deep Creek bench, getting very drunk as the evening wore on. Once the Bergsmas departed, Brautigan and Dill, whose wife had recently left him, sat up drinking and talking about love until 2:00 am. After Dave went home,

Richard called Siew-Hwa in San Francisco. Discussing the contents of her letter precipitated a big fight. "I got mad at her and hung up," Brautigan wrote later. After slamming down the receiver in a fury, Richard gathered all the telephones in his house and burned them in his cast-iron Franklin stove. "They burn with a strange blue flame," he observed.

Ianthe slept through the whole thing. When she awoke the next morning, she smelled gas. "I could tell by a peculiar silence in the house that people had been drinking all night," she wrote in her memoir. Ianthe found "a nest of odd wires" coiled among the ashes in the fireplace, all that remained of the phones. Gatz Hjortsberg remembered seeing a two-inch piece of coiled blue wire lying like a cartoon pig's tail on the fender. A hangover didn't help Richard deal with the problem when he finally woke up. He was at a loss on how to handle the telephone company. "They want to know what happened with my phones. I can't tell them I burned them, can I?" Brautigan asked his daughter.

Richard wanted Tony Dingman to take care of the problem. Tony just laughed at him, so he walked next door to Gatz's place and called Mountain Bell himself. "They sort of disappeared," he stammered, answering the dread question. Dingman drove Brautigan into town, where Richard personally collected his replacement phones from the front office. Brautigan made no mention of any of this in his daily compendium. The fifth and last entry for the day had him using his new instruments: "A total, total stranger called me up on the telephone. They told me that they heard I was dead. I told them I wasn't and that made them happy."

The cold weather held through the next day, a Saturday, and not much got accomplished. Richard took Ianthe into town to shop for daffodil bulbs. He wanted to see flowers in the spring-time, he said. Deep inside, Brautigan wasn't really sure about what to do next. With his novel finished, he had no current work on hand. Tony would be leaving soon. A chinook blew up in the evening, and the temperature rose, but Richard felt winter creep inexorably closer. The prospect of spending several frozen months housebound with his daughter seemed less and less like something he wanted in his immediate future.

Brautigan had dinner that night at the Hjortsbergs' and drank only three glasses of red wine. "I was a good boy." Back at home, he puttered about in his sleeping cabin for a while before going to bed. Vanessi's and Enrico's seemed a million miles away. Tossing and turning, struggling with his persistent insomnia through the night, Richard restlessly decided to close his Montana place for the winter and return to San Francisco.

Ianthe got the news on Sunday without "any advance warning" after she'd planted the daf-fodils. She was devastated. "Another part of my world collapsed," she wrote in her memoir. "I knew the truth: [My father] couldn't take care of me. The ranch was an illusion. My bedroom was false. Anything he gave me would be taken away [. . .]He just couldn't manage it." Ianthe found herself in a quandary. Her mother had just moved to Hawaii and she didn't want to uproot and move halfway around the world. She felt exhausted and "couldn't imagine" having to start again at yet another new school (the eleventh she had thus far attended). Lexi Cowan and her older married sister, Deane, came to Ianthe's rescue, offering to take her in and look after her for the rest of the school year.

Both Cowan sisters lived on Mill Creek, where their parents had ranched, about ten miles south of Brautigan's place. Deane shared a double-wide with her husband, Ralph Bischer, a Vietnam vet, and her son by her first husband who had died in the war. Lexi had a house across the creek. Ianthe left with only a suitcase and her little cat, Mittens, originally smuggled into the household over her father's objections. Richard opened a bank account for his daughter, promising to send money every month. He also established charge accounts at several clothing stores and at Sax & Fryer's. A week or so later, Ianthe returned with Lexi and rode her horse through the snow to Deane's Mill Creek pasture. She had no memory of saying goodbye to her father. For his part, Richard made no mention of his daughter's departure in his daily record.

Brautigan's little "journal" avoided emotional issues but detailed the trivial issues that preoccupied him. An entry three days before taking off from Pine Creek was typical:

Sunday, October 26, 1975, Pine Creek.

1. I did a lot of things today getting ready to leave Montana on Thursday.

2. Lou Erickson, the fencer, came over and we spent a couple hours talking about things that I wanted done concerning fencing and cleaning up the place.

3. I felt bad all day because Siew-Hwa and I had a huge argument over the telephone again and I also had trouble sleeping last night.

4. I went over to Gatz's and got very drunk. I was melancholy and talked about my writing. I probably sounded like an asshole.

Hjorstberg remembered this evening vividly. It became one of those nights, causing Marian to remark, "For once, I was glad I was the wife, so I could go upstairs to bed, while you had to stay down in the kitchen and be the host." After Richard drank all the whiskey, he went to work on the vodka and the gin. Once the hard stuff was gone, he demolished the liqueurs, polishing off remnant bottles of crème de menthe and Kahlua. All the while, Brautigan remained relatively coherent, but his stutter grew more pronounced. He focused on a single thought, repeating it over and over and over like some insane mantra. Gatz listened to Richard's rambling rant, a smile frozen on his face, mentally repeating a silent prayer, "Please, God, make him go home. Please, make him go home." It was past four when Richard finally departed.

A hangover wasted the next day, and Brautigan went to bed "with a feeling of not having done anything." On Tuesday, Richard finished correcting *Sombrero Fallout*, took the manuscript into town to make Xerox copies, and mailed one off to Helen Brann in New York. During the afternoon, he and Tony washed White Acre, keeping the promise they'd made to the car at the start of summer. The rest of the day was devoted to packing, after which Brautigan and Dingman went up to the Bergsmas' for a fine roast lamb dinner.

Wednesday, October 29, was Richard's last day at Pine Creek for 1975. He and Tony stayed busy preparing the house for the winter. They drained the pipes, unloaded the fridge, and shut off the gas to the stove. Brautigan organized all of his business papers up in his tree house office in the barn. That afternoon, he brought his chainsaw, his television set, his fishing rods and tackle, along with an arsenal of assorted firearms, over to Gatz and Marian's for safekeeping. On learning Margot Kidder had given birth to a baby girl earlier in the day, Richard wrote a short poem to celebrate the occasion. Because the child had not yet been named, he left a blank space in the title when he typed the poem. Later, although she was called Maggie from the start, he wrote the baby's given name by hand: "Margeret [*sic*] in October."

Richard and Tony spent the night at the Holiday Inn in Bozeman, flying out to San Francisco the next morning. Siew-Hwa failed to meet them at the airport, which precipitated "a horrible argument later on." Brautigan started drinking and "didn't stop," heading out in the evening for a drinking tour covering half a dozen bars. "No good came of it," he observed later. Brautigan had nothing to eat until one in the morning, when he wolfed down a hot dog. "Some dinner." A "hideous hangover" followed the next morning, accompanied by fighting with Siew-Hwa.

Over the next couple days, their ongoing argument continued, interrupted only by eating out in restaurants and going to the movies. Brautigan ended his daily record-keeping experiment on November 3. He breakfasted with Don Carpenter and had lunch with Curt Gentry. The day was warm and pleasant. Richard's penultimate entry read, "I'm trying to get my shit together here in San Francisco, i.e. the rest of my life." Much of the "shit" Brautigan needed to deal with stemmed from his turbulent relationship with Siew-Hwa. He took the path of least resistance by getting out of town six days later.

Richard flew to New York on American Airlines. He spent a lot of time with Helen Brann, dropping by her apartment so often that she felt compelled to write him after he left town, explaining that because her office was located in her apartment building, she could not "see clients except by appointment [. . .] If you have manuscripts to leave off or pick up they must be left with the doorman. We are always happy to see clients, but you must call us and make an appointment first."

Helen Brann was a tough cookie, hard to get along with and often disagreeable, but she and Brautigan enjoyed a special relationship that went beyond the usual agent/client arrangement, verging into an improbable friendship. Richard had recently brought her two new clients. One was Don Carpenter. Brautigan thought Brann might find a new home for his out-of-print books. The other was Peter Najarian, a young writer who had been a Stegner Fellow at the time Richard read at Stanford in 1968. Gatz Hjortsberg reintroduced them when Peter came out to visit that fall. Peter had published *Voyages*, a well-received but poorly selling novel, with Pantheon in 1971. Helen called Richard "a great scout!" Brautigan contemplated spending the winter in Key West and invited Brann to come down and enjoy some time in the sun.

Richard changed his mind and his plans once he got back to San Francisco. He would travel to Tokyo instead. Brautigan had several reasons for wanting to visit Japan. Four of his books had been published there that year. Kazuko returned to America that summer for a vacation. She was working on the translation of *Confederate General*. Earlier in August, still in Tokyo, she received a disturbing phone call from the firm planning to publish *The Pill versus the Springhill Disaster* in Japanese. Brautigan's contracts all stipulated Fujimoto was to be his official translator, but this outfit had another idea. They asked her not to do the translation.

Natsuki Ikezawa, a thirty-year-old poet, novelist, and essayist, had requested the assignment, and the publishers wanted Kazuko to step aside. She found this "quite odd," replying she "was not in a position to alter the terms of a contract between them and [Brautigan]." Early in September, Fujimoto wrote Brautigan from Racine, Wisconsin, reminding him that item 17 in his publishing contract stipulated that she was the designated translator. By coincidence, Helen Brann also wrote to Richard on the same day addressing this very problem. Brann speculated if they "stuck to our guns," they could force the Japanese publishing firm to drop the Ikezawa translation, but said she "didn't see that we can do too much about this at this point."

Richard and Siew-Hwa had dinner at the Washbag with Kazuko and her husband, David, in mid-September. Fujimoto planned on taking a short trip down to Big Sur to ensure the "accuracy" of her *Confederate General* translation before returning to Tokyo. Kazuko told Richard that she wanted to work next on either *Revenge of the Lawn* or *Willard and His Bowling Trophies*. Brautigan's journal entry for the day included this observation: "I was pleased to know my work is popular in Japan."

Ianthe flew to Hawaii from Montana over Christmas break to spend time with her mother and half siblings. She had not seen her father since just before Halloween. On her return, she stopped off in San Francisco for a brief visit. Ianthe stayed a week longer than she expected, coming down with a bad case of bronchitis. She ran a fever of 102. Brautigan walked his daughter down Telegraph Hill and across Columbus Avenue to see a doctor but was too preoccupied with other concerns to stay and learn what was wrong with her. He didn't leave Ianthe enough money to both buy antibiotics and take a cab home. After she filled her prescription she walked back to Union Street, "too tired and sick to cry." She was only fifteen but "felt like an old, old woman whose life was coming to an end."

Preoccupied with applying for a Japanese visa, breaking up with Siew-Hwa, planning his trip, and "drinking nonstop," Brautigan paid scant attention to his daughter's illness, although he handed her money "by the fistful." Ianthe ordered takeout food and somehow "managed to keep things together," with the help of Siew-Hwa's nursing. After Richard also came down sick, Siew-Hwa took over all the cooking chores despite being "mad as hell" at him. When Ianthe asked what was going to become of her, Richard said she could either accompany him to Japan and attend a boarding school there, or go back to Hawaii and live with her mother. Neither option sounded very attractive. Ianthe planned on returning to the loving circle formed by Deane and Lexi Cowan in Montana, and as soon as she was well enough to travel, she did.

In an interview years later, Siew-Hwa Beh declared, "Richard destroyed the relationship. He started initiating a lot of destructive things that would cause rifts, like staying away until all hours of the night." Brautigan never brought anyone home to the apartment but started seeing a "Latino [sic] woman who he had no feelings for." Siew-Hwa didn't understand why he started cheating. "Now there are three of us," Richard told her after he returned from one of his assignations. When the Latina woman called the apartment and Siew-Hwa answered the phone, she wasn't jealous. "I felt so much compassion for the situation," she said. "He was troubled, and the darkness started to descend, and I didn't know what to do."

Brautigan never brought other women home while Beh was in residence, but when they were apart it was another story. Sherry Vetter remembered spending time with him in North Beach during this period. She recalled the Union Street apartment in detail. The back room Richard used as a writing studio was bright with sunlight, something Brautigan, with his pale sensitive skin, couldn't tolerate. Richard seemed unable to make up his mind whether to have curtains installed or get wooden blinds instead. "It was the problem of making the decisions of what to buy and what was right or what was stupid," Sherry said. "So he did nothing." Brautigan left in place the cheap pull-down roller shades that came with the apartment for the duration of his tenancy.

One afternoon, Richard sadly told Sherry about Siew-Hwa Beh, "his Chinese girlfriend," and how she had called him a male chauvinist pig and told him he would have to reform. At this point in their relationship, Brautigan and Vetter had become close friends and were quite comfortable discussing other partners. Sherry found this particular moment "so poignant and so sad." Richard looked over at her and asked, "Do you think I'm a male chauvinist pig?"

"Oh, no, Richard," she replied, "you're not a male chauvinist pig," adding in the same breath, "Can you loan me $500?"

"Certainly," he said and wrote her a check.

Throughout all of this, Beh remained faithful to Brautigan. "I trusted myself never to sleep with anybody," she said, "and also I knew Richard couldn't handle it." There was someone interested in her at the time, but Siew-Hwa never mentioned it because she knew it would make Brautigan jealous. "I had no idea how deeply jealous he could be. Because he told me how so many times he would come home to the apartment and his girlfriend or whoever was in his life at that time was fucking someone else in bed. And I said, 'What did you do, Richard?'

"He said, 'Sometimes I just sat there and watched them.'"

Beh, priding herself on her monogamy, felt deep sympathy as Brautigan related one bygone betrayal after another. She stayed loyal to Richard in spite of the tensions wracking their relationship. "I have to be loved not hated," she told him, "accepted not suspected." Throughout all their differences, the couple continued to live the celebrity life of successful artists in San Francisco, dining frequently at Vanessi's and the Washington Square Bar and Grill.

One evening at the Washbag with Tony Dingman, Tony suggested Francis Ford Coppola might like to join them. Richard was ecstatic. Tony made the call and said Francis would soon be on his way. And the long wait began. They waited and waited. A couple hours went by. Coppola stood them up. Brautigan glowered in petulant fury, unaccustomed to such rude behavior from fellow celestials. On another occasion, things went better. Harry Dean Stanton brought Al Pacino over to the Union Street apartment. After a bit, they all went out to join Jack Nicholson and Angelica Huston for the evening. Siew-Hwa, a student of cinema, was away and missed the party, to her lasting regret.

Brautigan had every reason to be annoyed when Coppola snubbed him at the Washbag. Sherry Vetter recalled their "crazy little relationship." She remembered one evening in North Beach when Richard and Francis competed in a mano a mano marinara sauce cook-off at Tommaso's, an Italian restaurant that opened in 1935 on Kearny, just across Broadway from Sentinel Tower, the venerable pre-earthquake building owned by Coppola and the headquarters of Zoetrope Productions.

Brautigan continued to have breakfast and lunch regularly with Dingman, Don Carpenter, and Curt Gentry. Carpenter had mixed feelings about these meals. "Richard very much liked to call me during working hours," Don remembered. "If he knew I was working on a novel, he might call me every day for a month to go to breakfast. He'd call between six and seven, when I was just getting started. 'Come on over.' And I was so deeply in his debt, financially, as well as a number of other ways, I had to do it. So, I'd drive over to the city. There he would be with a big bag of laundry or something, and we'd go by the laundry and then we'd go by the various breakfast places. He would make the decision as to where would meet, what we would do, where we would go, who would pay—he would always pay—that is how he controlled."

On his way to visit Richard one afternoon, Keith Abbott spotted Bob Kaufman, the Beat poet, on the corner where Stockton crosses both Columbus Avenue and Green Street. Kaufman waited for the light to turn red and started to cross the busy intersection, "exactly the opposite of what you're supposed to do." The city traffic screeched to a halt as Kaufman, hands trembling, "wired on whatever," shambled erratically from corner to corner. Abbott considered this a "disgraceful performance."

When Abbott got to Brautigan's Union Street apartment, he was harshly critical of Kaufman's behavior. Richard sat his friend down at the kitchen table, pouring them both a glass of whiskey. He explained how he first met Bob Kaufman back in the early days of the North Beach poetry renaissance, relating "little anecdotes about Bob's sense of humor, how he defused things, how he was hounded by this one cop [. . .] Sort of gave me Bob Kaufman's history." Brautigan launched into another story about Kaufman, a sweet man and a pacifist at heart.

One night on the Beach in some forgotten gin joint catering to interracial couples, an enraged bigot approached Kaufman and his date and started harassing him. "This guy just pushed Bob to the breaking point." To make his point, Brautigan mimed the action in slow motion. How Kaufman picked a wine bottle off his table (Brautigan's hand moved slowly through the air a couple of inches) and cracked it over the loudmouth's head. Richard's tone grew more serious. He told Keith that he'd only seen something like that once before in his life. "It came out of left field," Abbott recalled. Brautigan told his friend about the time one of his stepfathers (most likely Tex Porterfield) hit his mother on the head with a cast-iron frying pan and knocked her out cold.

Earlier in the year, Richard met Klyde Young, an old friend of Bob Junsch. Young, a house-painter who lived in Mill Valley had been to Japan when serving in the Merchant Marine. Conversations about his upcoming trip to Tokyo led Brautigan to ask Young if he'd paint the Bolinas house. Klyde thought the place "was in pretty bad shape. Sometimes you couldn't get the front door to lock because it was warped." Noticing how badly the house was overgrown with trees and shrubs, Young suggested he cut some of them down. "Who wouldn't want to see the ocean if you've got an ocean view house?"

Richard wouldn't hear of it. He liked the seclusion. Brautigan also wouldn't move a number of old pine-needle-covered stoves and refrigerators in his backyard. Richard told Klyde he liked to go out and look at them because they reminded him of dinosaurs. The house painting job also proceeded in an eccentric manner. Young ended up staying a long time and living in the place. "He wouldn't say, 'Paint the house.' He'd say, 'Paint this room,' and then he'd disappear for weeks and the next time I'd hear from him, he'd say, 'Okay, paint this room. Okay, start painting the windows. Okay, now paint the eaves.'"

This went on and on, the work proceeding in reverse order. During the wet winter months, Brautigan had Young work on the outside of the house. "So there were days when I couldn't do anything outside," Klyde recalled. During the warm months, Richard had him working inside, "because he did it backwards." Over the long haul, they got to be friends.

Brautigan's passport was issued on April 4, 1976, with a photo showing him long-haired, smiling smugly, very pleased with himself. He received a Japanese visa for a stay of two months early in May and left immediately for Tokyo. Siew-Hwa stayed at Union Street for another day before moving to temporary quarters in Berkeley. She returned to Richard's apartment several times to clean and do the laundry.

At Brautigan's request, Beh installed a timer for the lights in the living room, setting it to go on at 8:30 pm and switch off at 2:30 am. Richard wrote her a "long" letter, and she replied, telling him of everything she had done. Siew-Hwa made occasional trips to Bolinas, checking that "everything was okay" at Richard's house. She cleaned the place and installed another light-timer, set to switch off at 2:00 am.

Beh's memory of her first visit to the Bolinas house remained vivid. Brautigan told her the story of the ghost dwelling upstairs, convinced the spirit was trapped in the building. Siew-Hwa proposed he install a mirror above the stairs to free the ghost. She recalled a Chinese folktale relating how ghosts didn't know they were dead until they chanced to look in a mirror and saw no reflection. Once a deceased spirit recognized it had passed away, it could move on into an afterlife.

Around the first of June, Siew-Hwa traveled to Kingston in Ontario, Canada, where her exhusband had a teaching position in the Department of Film Studies at Queen's University. Richard wrote a long and "formal" letter. She wished it had been more personal and intimate. After Beh arrived in Canada, Brautigan phoned her from Tokyo. Japan was "a tremendous experience," but he felt exhausted, having stayed up all night writing. Their conversation went badly. When Siew-Hwa told him she was thinking of going to Malaysia, he replied, "That's fine, certainly. You should do what makes you happy."

Brautigan flew back to San Francisco from Japan on June 30. Tony Dingman planned to return to the Philippines and continue working on Francis Ford Coppola's *Apocalypse Now* once the sets destroyed by Typhoon Olga were rebuilt, so Richard found himself without a drinking companion/ designated driver for the summer in Montana. He also needed some work done at his place and figured it was too late in the season to hire anyone locally. Keith Abbott recalled Brautigan literally calling him "in a panic," begging him to come up to Pine Creek. At first, Abbott declined. "Richard, it's summertime," he said. "It's my big season. It's when I make money here in Berkeley and I just can't do it."

Richard told Keith, "I'll pay you whatever you make in a day."

Abbott said he liked to "write in the morning and then go out and work." Brautigan said fine. "He just sort of badgered me into coming up," Keith related. Richard agreed on a daily wage and gave Keith a plane ticket to Montana. Considering it a "paid vacation" and planning on staying a month at most, Abbott arrived on the Fourth of July. A Dodge rental car awaited him at the airport, paid for with Peter Fonda's credit card. Brautigan claimed he had no plastic because writers were anathema to banks. Keith didn't buy it, considering Richard wealthy and successful, the owner of two homes. He thought Brautigan's unspoken pride on being denied a credit card was "one of his grandiose romantic fantasies" tinged by a "whiff of megalomania."

Keith arrived on the night of the nation's bicentennial and went to the rodeo at the Livingston fairgrounds with Peter and Becky Fonda. Richard had something else to do. He was not with his friends in the bleachers. Ianthe had been competing in the Rodeo Queen Contest. His daughter's horse, Jackie, had broken her leg and had to be put down. Distraught, she tried riding Deane Cowan Bischer's troublesome palomino but couldn't adequately control the mount and only appeared in the arena processional on the first day of the three-day rodeo. Perhaps Richard knew of Ianthe's disappointment and chose not to attend. Thirty years later, Ianthe still wondered why her father didn't come to see her if he was actually in Montana.

After the rodeo, Brautigan connected with Keith Abbott for a tour of Livingston's bars. At the 2:00 am closing time, they repaired to a wild outdoor Montana party gathered around a telephone pole bonfire. Driving home in the rental car, Richard told Keith, "Put it up to a hundred." Alarmed, Abbott accelerated to seventy. Brautigan demanded he go faster. Keith eased the sedan over the century mark. Abbott was puzzled by his friend's request because he knew Richard's sense of caution. In California, Brautigan never wanted speed and always made Keith drive on the inside lane of the Golden Gate Bridge, fearing a head-on collision. That night, Richard bragged how Montana was a renegade state, extolling the virtues of "Cowboy Freedom." Abbott felt Montana provided Brautigan "license to override some of his strongest taboos."

The Fourth of July proved a true Independence Day for Timothy Leary, many miles to the south in Santa Fe, New Mexico. He was finally released from federal protective custody. Leary's initial freedom from prison in 1974 came the old-fashioned way. He ratted out all his old friends. The ex-professor cooperated fully with authorities. Among the names he named were those of his former attorneys and his ex-wife Rosemary, currently hiding underground.

Leary later moved to L.A., hanging out with the Hollywood B-list. While a steady contributor to Larry Flynt's low-brow skin magazine, *Hustler*, he went on tour "debating" his old nemesis, fellow ex-con G. Gordon Liddy. The psychedelic guru and self-proclaimed "neuronaut" promoted the wonders of the Internet, extolling space travel to colonize other planets.

A couple days after the bicentennial, Richard Brautigan came over to the Hjorstbergs' for a late breakfast. He arranged the gathering himself, sly and mysterious when pressed for details. Marian baked a coffee cake and got out the homemade jam. Richard approached formally along East River Road. He wore an obi-belted, block-printed white cotton *yukata*, the summer kimono used by both men and women, his long hair flowing around his shoulders. He carried a colorful stack of exquisitely wrapped packages. Ianthe followed many yards behind, a distance suggesting that she had no connection to the strange-looking man farther up the road.

Following coffee, toast, cake, and genial conversation, Richard, with elaborate formality, gave a gift to each member of the Hjorstberg family, complete with head bows above his prayer-folded hands. The presents were not elaborate (a scarf, a mechanical tin toy, some stationery), but the gift wrapping was extraordinary, each box an extravagant example of *tsutsumi*, the Japanese art of wrapping. It was Brautigan at his finest, thoughtful, generous, a connoisseur of the perfect moment.

Across the creek, Keith Abbott observed the other side of Richard's personality, finding his old friend "harried, manic and humorless." Brautigan had several projects requiring Abbott's immediate attention. Having bought thirty acres to the south (three adjoining subdivision lots) to protect his privacy, Richard wanted the irrigation ditch at the upper end of the property cleared out so he could get some water on his new pasture, maintaining his deeded water rights, liable to forfeiture if not used. He also needed the fences repaired and the tall grass around the house cut down before it became a fire hazard. Raised on "a stump ranch" in Washington, Keith was familiar with the tools of the trade. Up at the crack of dawn, Abbott "really wanted to get out of the house," and away from Brautigan. His old friend seemed "in an extremely volatile state."

Keith borrowed Tom McGuane's old Dodge Power Wagon, rented a field mower in Bozeman, and cut down the tall dry grass around the house, revealing a large swampy area in the front yard under the cottonwoods. Water seemed to percolate up from beneath the surface, puddling a short distance from the house. When Abbott told him, Brautigan erupted in a furious tirade, damning the phone company for the problem. Earlier in the year, Mountain Bell laid a new cable through the valley, cutting a trench along the length of the borrow pit along the road on the other side of Richard's house. Brautigan felt sure this had caused his water problem.

In what Keith Abbott described as a "vendetta" against the phone company, Richard spent the next several days haranguing various Mountain Bell executives and supervisors. A telephone crew was dispatched to line the ditch across from Brautigan's place with bentonite, a clay formed from the decomposition of volcanic ash capable of absorbing considerable volumes of water. When this didn't solve the problem, Richard resumed his tirade in between calls to Richard Hodge, who advised him to contact local lawyer Joseph Swindlehurst. Joe told Richard he had a legal right to protect his property.

Richard hired a backhoe to dig out the borrow pit. Keith Abbott tried to talk sense, taking his friend for a walk to the top of the neighbor's sloping pasture across the road. An irrigation ditch ran along the side of the hill. Abbott explained gravity caused the water to flow down the slope toward Brautigan's house. "You got it wrong, pal," Richard replied, insisting he was within his rights to dig out the ditch. "My lawyer will handle this," Brautigan said.

The backhoe arrived the next morning to dig up the ditch. Before long, the operator severed Mountain Bell's cable, knocking out telephone service to every home in the valley on the east side of the river south of Brautigan's place. The phone company dispatched a repairman to deal with the problem, and Richard's paranoia kicked into high gear. Fearing confrontation, he sent Keith out to talk with the man, who said it was no big deal, backhoes often accidentally cut phone cables in rural areas. Brautigan didn't buy this, convinced he would be hit with a massive lawsuit. He stewed over this until four in the morning, when he called Richard Hodge in San Francisco.

Earlier in the year, Richard had phoned his lawyer in the middle of the night from Japan. Dick Hodge had not been amused. He was trying significant murder cases and had to get up early in the morning. "Richard," he sternly told his client, "the next time you call me after midnight, there better be a body on the floor and a smoking gun in your hand." Mindful of Hodge's prior admonition, Brautigan said, "I remember what you told me. I want to know if you think this qualifies? I just caused the power to go out in three states."

Richard settled down after the hysteria of the Mountain Bell fiasco subsided. Taking a break one afternoon, Keith offered to sight-in Richard's pride and joy, and old .22-caliber gallery gun from the twenties. Brautigan okayed the project but declined to accompany Abbott to the dump behind his house, where piles of rusted junk provided convenient targets. "No, I don't like to go shooting with anyone else," he said cryptically. "I had an accident when I was young." He remembered Donald Husband's death when he was fourteen, weaving the accidental shooting of a classmate by someone else into the fabric of his personal mythology.

Keith tried hard to be sympathetic to his old friend's eccentric behavior. Brautigan had just broken up with Siew-Hwa Beh but continued to have angry long-distance "shouting matches" over the phone. Lingering jet lag exacerbated his insomnia and increased his alcohol consumption. Knowing Richard eschewed all drugs but booze, Keith was "shook" to discover his buddy had a prescription for Stelazine, "which knocked him out for two or three dreamless hours." Brautigan drank between one and three liters of wine with dinner, finishing every evening with copious quantities of whiskey. Abbott warned mixing alcohol with drugs might prove to be a lethal combination.

Richard ignored this advice, and Keith took matters into his own hands. Knowing Brautigan didn't enjoy drinking alone, Abbott started making long afternoon explorations into the surrounding canyons, delaying the start of the cocktail hour. On his shopping trips to town, he would "forget" to buy any brandy or whiskey. Instead of the 1.5-liter wine jugs Richard favored, Keith brought home the smaller 750-milliliter bottles. This undisclosed intervention, along with a pleasant fly-fishing trip, cooled Brautigan down for a time.

Despite peaceful interludes, life remained chaotic at Richard's place. Keith began looking for a way out. Watching Brautigan set fire to a signed copy of a book by Raymond Mungo (Mungo had made a mildly disparaging remark about one of Brautigan's books) and having a paranoid Richard tear up a page of his calligraphy practice (Keith chanced to use a few lines from a recent conversation as his text) made him determined to leave. The unexpected arrival of Bud Swearingen and his two teenage sons delayed Abbott's departure.

An affable Texan, Bud spent considerable time in Montana. Swearingen was an accomplished fly fisherman and showed the boys his favorite spots. Keith Abbott reported Brautigan's "black moods vanished" during the Texan's visit. The trio provided "distractions and companionship." Keith recalled, "Life became a real pleasure, almost like the old days. When [Richard] got untracked from his problems, his humor was infectious."

Once the Swearingens departed, Brautigan slipped back into neurosis. His depression alleviated only when the bound page proofs for *Sombrero Fallout* arrived in the mail. Keith helped Richard work on the dust jacket copy, "as he obsessively wrote and rewrote the description of the novel." Making up for his seven-month absence from his daughter's life, Brautigan flew in her longtime childhood friend, Cadence Lipsett, to keep Ianthe company. They picked her up at the Belgrade airport, Keith Abbott driving. Richard sat in the backseat being "incredibly funny and charming." He called Cadence by her mother's name, "Shirley," comically correcting himself. Not long after, Abbott made Brautigan's "preoccupation with his book" an excuse to leave early. Before booking his flight to California, Keith arranged for a local company to continue the irrigation-ditch-clearing project.

Around this time, Brautigan invited Ed and Jennifer Dorn to come up to Montana for a visit. "He was a generous host and an enthusiastic cook," Jenny wrote nine years later in an article for the *Denver Post's Empire Magazine*. Richard took them trout fishing and down to soak in the "scruffy, but marvelous" outdoor Chico Hot Springs pool. Jenny observed Richard "was such a keen student of life that he even turned the pathetic, worn-out cowboy nightlife of Livingston into a tour de force."

Their last night at Pine Creek, the Dorns sat up late with Richard, arguing about the Symbionese Liberation Army, a radical outlaw organization that had committed a string of bank robberies and murders two years earlier. They received nationwide press coverage when they kidnapped the heiress Patty Hearst. After being "brainwashed," she joined the gang as "Tania," her new revolutionary nom de guerre. Brautigan said he "did not like the idea of revolutionaries running around killing people." Jenny considered Richard "a reasonably well-off landowner" unable to support any kind of revolution.

Needing a driver after Ed Dorn's departure, Richard called Don Carpenter, asking him up to Montana for a couple weeks to a month. Carpenter declined the invitation. "I told him that I refused to be at his beck and call," Don said. He never visited Richard's place in Montana. Next, Brautigan phoned Loie Weber, who had split up with Erik and just might be free.

"He wanted me to come out for a month and drive him and sort of hang out with Ianthe," Loie said. She looked at it as a job, not just helping out an old friend, so she "wanted benefits beyond just a certain amount of money." She felt her specific needs should be met because she was giving up all her other work. Brautigan said he'd think it over.

A couple days later, Richard called Loie back. "I've thought about it and I'm going to make other arrangements," he said. A subtle dynamic shift had occurred in their long relationship. "He just went ice cold," Loie recalled. "I had crossed the line, and I was 'dead meat' from then on. He used that phrase." She never worked for him again. Once, at a later date, Loie went to lunch with Richard in San Francisco. She told him what she was working on and asked for advice. "He was very sweet, very attentive, very generous, very distant, very formal," she said. "I don't know if we ever talked again after that. I had no desire to talk to him. I felt we weren't really friends anymore."

Brautigan finally got hold of his old pal Price Dunn, living on Hawthorne Street in San Francisco. He asked Price if he'd like to come to Pine Creek, adding that he really needed somebody to help him out. "Well," Price replied, "I can come up and stay awhile."

Price arrived not long afterward, flying into Bozeman. Richard met him at the airport with Maria, his current petite Philippine girlfriend from Marin County, at the wheel of an Avis car rented once again with Peter Fonda's plastic. "Richard always made a big production about my eating," Price related, so they headed straight to a local steak joint before driving over the hill to Pine Creek.

In the morning, Brautigan prepared a big ham-and-eggs breakfast. After eating, Brautigan took Price out to the barn to show him his studio. For several days, Brautigan entertained Confederate General Dunn with fishing trips to Armstrong's Spring Creek and the nearby Yellowstone River. They caught a mess of little pan-sized trout, bringing them home for supper. The only problem between the two old friends involved Price's snoring. "I snored like a grizzly bear," Dunn admitted. Plagued by insomnia, Richard moved his pal down from the upstairs bedroom, switching places with him in an effort to get some sleep. When this didn't work, Brautigan abandoned the main house, taking his girlfriend and retreating to his outside sleeping chamber in the reconstructed coal shed.

Richard needed all the sleep he could get, worrying over the dust jacket copy for *Sombrero Fallout* while at the same time working on his book of Japanese poems. A ghost from his past had also returned to haunt him. Back in May, Edna Webster, now calling herself Edna Webster Jensen, mailed a batch of Brautigan's early unpublished adolescent work to Durrett Wagner at Swallow Press in Chicago, asking him to publish them. She claimed the copyright belonged to her.

Wagner wrote to Dell, Brautigan's former publisher, for further clarification. Dell forwarded his letter to Helen Brann, who contacted Brautigan. Richard had no wish to see his early poems published, calling them "juvenilia, and highly imitative." When Brann wrote back to Wagner, she stressed the work in question legally belonged to Brautigan and they could not grant him publishing rights. Richard insisted "the matter be handled with as much tact as possible." He had not been in touch with Edna Webster in over twenty years. Having her haunt him with memories of his anguished youth troubled his intermittent sleep.

Brautigan was additionally plagued by a severe outbreak of herpes. Not surprisingly, his girlfriend, Maria, was bored. No sex and Richard's preoccupation with his work was not her idea of a good time. "He wasn't giving her as much attention as she wanted around the house," Price observed. "She was probably sexually frustrated."

Hoping to lift Maria's spirits, Richard enlisted Price to drive her into town for the afternoon while he prepared dinner. They went to the Wrangler Bar. "She spent the whole damned afternoon drinking and hanging out," Dunn recalled. Not wanting to get drunk himself, Price left the bar and drove across town to visit Sandi Lee, Russell Chatham's girlfriend. She worked for the phone company as a long-distance operator and knew the inside dope on just about everyone. Unable to remember the exact address and not recognizing Lee's house, Dunn returned to the Wrangler and nursed a beer, watching Maria "out there dancing around with the cowboys like she was ready to get jumped." As it grew later and later, Price lost track of the time. Maria was in no mood to leave. "I just wanted to get out of the fucking bar," Price said.

When they hadn't returned by dark, Brautigan walked next door to the Hjortsbergs', seeking company. Gatz and Marian had taken the kids on a three-day camping trip to an old prospector's cabin on Gold Prize Creek, midway between Warren Oates's place and Sam Peckinpah's wilderness hideout. A slender attractive young woman named Terry Cousins, who worked as a housekeeper for the Fondas, the McGuanes, and for Brautigan, was house-sitting. Richard liked her, and Terry poured him a drink, sitting down at the kitchen table to talk. Around nine o'clock, Terry's date arrived.

Thirty-one-year-old writer Toby Thompson came to Paradise Valley that summer to interview Tom McGuane for a planned book on the sixties. He'd published *Positively Main Street, An Unorthodox View of Bob Dylan* in 1971, and *Saloon*, his cross-country travelogue about old-time barrooms, was due out in the fall. Thompson met McGuane in Key West in 1974 while researching *Saloon*. He found much had changed during the intervening couple years. Tom's ponytail had given way to a haircut "redneck short," none of his films had been a hit, and ex-wife Becky had married Peter Fonda. Toby rented a $4-a-night room at the Murray Hotel in Livingston. While waiting for his interview, he bumped into Terry Cousins one night out honky-tonking.

This was their second or third date. Toby, "trying to get [his] head back together" on the ragged side of a recent divorce, thought he just might get lucky. Suddenly, there sat Richard Brautigan, "looking his most imperious self," having a drink with Terry. "I know you're up here writing a book about McGuane," Richard said. "I want you to know that anything I say or do tonight is totally off the record, and if you write anything about me, I can assure you that you're going to hear from my lawyers."

In spite of this, Brautigan and Thompson "hit it off." Richard "sort of invited himself along" on Toby's date with Terry. They headed first to the Old Saloon in Emigrant, fifteen miles to the south in Paradise Valley. The Discords, a local cowpoke band, played that Saturday night. "Three guys standing there with guitars," Thompson recalled. "All of them playing chords—nobody even playing a lead line—and singing these old cowboy tunes." Toby, Terry, and Richard stayed on until about one in the morning, dancing and drinking Jack Daniel's.

Thompson found Brautigan to be "a great raconteur and loveable in his own way." Several of the cowboys in the bar knew Richard and came over to engage him in conversation. Toby was impressed by his "easygoing eccentricity." Brautigan interrupted the conversation to make several phone calls, hoping to reach Price and Maria at home.

Thompson talked about the pain he felt over the breakup with his wife and how he was trying to understand what it was about writers that made it so difficult for other people to live with them. "This business of being a writer just cost me a marriage," Toby said above the high lonesome music.

"Only one?" Richard queried with a sly grin.

The trio ended the night at the Chico bar. At the 2:00 am closing hour, Toby ordered three double Jack Daniel's in plastic go-cups for the drive back to Pine Creek. They all piled into the front seat of Thompson's Jeep Wagoneer and set off along the East River Road. Not realizing Richard didn't drive and knew nothing about automobiles, Toby believed Richard when he said, "The thing about this road is you can drive absolutely as fast as you want."

"I took off. About seventy-five miles per hour," Thompson related. Within a mile, the Jeep's front wheels dropped into a bathtub-sized pothole a foot deep. "Every emergency light in the vehicle went on," Toby recalled. "All three glasses of Jack Daniel's coated the inside of the windshield. The wipers are going—the flashers are going—we were airborne, going to the fucking sky."

Thompson regarded Brautigan in a new light. "What the fuck is this guy telling me?" he thought, knowing he could no longer trust Richard. They managed to get the car started and limped back to Pine Creek, greeted by an empty driveway. Price and Maria had not returned from town. Toby switched off his ignition. He sensed beneath Brautigan's drunken surface he "had become more and more furious." When Richard got out, Toby couldn't start his car. He and Terry set off on foot for the Hjortsbergs' place.

Inside his house, Brautigan vented his rage, smashing furniture, hurling chairs against the wall. The noise woke Ianthe in her small bedroom just off the main living/dining area. It sounded like her "father was breaking everything he could in the living room." She whispered, "Cadence." Her friend's eyes widened in the dark. For the first time, Ianthe felt "truly scared."

"Let's get out of here," Cadence said. The two teenagers tiptoed in their nighties to the bathroom and climbed out the window, fleeing barefoot through the night to the Hjortsbergs' house. They found Terry and Toby still up in the kitchen and used the phone to call the Cowans. Deane drove down from Mill Creek and took Ianthe and Cadence home with her for the night.

Price and Maria got back to Richard's place around three. Years later, Dunn remembered it as "eight or nine o'clock." The first thing Price saw as he pulled into the driveway was his empty suitcase. All his clothing had been thrown out onto the lawn "like garbage." Richard stood glaring on the porch, "drunk as a lord." Dunn scrambled about, stuffing his things back into his bag. Brautigan advanced on him. "Get the fuck out of here," Richard demanded. "I'm going to kill you, beat the shit out of you!" Brautigan pulled off his glasses and took a swing at Price, so inebriated he nearly fell from the effort.

"Richard, will you stop this?" Dunn said. "I am not going to fight you. There's no way in hell I'm going to have a fight with you."

"You don't want to stand up and fight like a man?"

"You know," Price said, "I'll talk to you in the morning." Knowing his friend "was just crazy drunk," and thinking it was all "bullshit," Dunn felt sure the whole unpleasant incident would blow over by the next day, when Brautigan was sober.

Price gathered up his bulging suitcase, and he and Maria headed down the road to the Hjortsbergs' place next door, seeking refuge. Toby and Terry were about to go to bed when they barged in. Almost immediately, Richard called, demanding Terry come over to keep him company.

Pissed off at her compliance, Toby went to bed, alone. Inheriting this big slice of Richard's troubled life had not been part of his plans. He regretted letting "a lot of crazy drunks" into the Hjortbergs' "obviously meticulous" home. Price Dunn did not remember Toby Thompson. Dunn's version of the story had Gatz and Marian finishing dinner in their kitchen when he showed up with Maria. Price claimed Maria didn't stay long, but headed back to make up with Brautigan. He remembered spending the night in the guest room downstairs.

When Dunn returned the next day, Brautigan was in his kitchen fixing breakfast. "Good morning, Richard," Price said good-naturedly. Richard, his face gone hard as stone, ignored his oldest friend, refusing to speak. Dunn got some ham out of the fridge and started making his own meal. "Are you still of the same mind?" he asked. "You're sober now, right? You're hungover, but you're coherent."

"Yep," Brautigan replied, cold as the inside of his refrigerator, "I've made up my mind."

"Well, fine," Price said, "if that's the way you feel about it. I can't believe this, but that's the way it goes. All that bullshit you were talking about last night." Richard left the kitchen without another word. Price ate his breakfast alone, in shock that an eighteen-year friendship, the longest of his life, had ended so abruptly. "How could he imagine I'm going to be trying to fuck his girl-friend?" he pondered. "For one thing, I wasn't even attracted to her. She wasn't my type. Didn't make my music fly."

Not believing what was happening, Dunn got his gear together. He put his bags in the trunk of the rental car, accidentally dropping the keys beside them. "Everybody was in a hurry," Price remembered. Someone slammed the trunk lid shut, locking the keys inside. The tension notched up several degrees. Dunn found a hammer and a screwdriver in the tool chest. "I didn't give a rat's ass, you know," he said. Without another word, he chopped a hole in the trunk lid and pried it open. The end result looked like a bomb had gone off inside. After retrieving the keys, Price took off with Maria.

His first stop was at the Cowans' place on Mill Creek to tell Ianthe he was leaving. She had known Price all her life and thought him "the funniest storyteller" of them all. "I just wanted you to know that we are splitting," Dunn told her. "Things are just too crazy here."

When Toby Thompson wandered back over to Brautigan's place around ten or eleven, all was quiet on the emotional front. He ran into Price and Maria on their way down the road. Richard "had truly shown them the door," Toby observed. "The outrage and surprise on everybody's face was so intense. They didn't look guilty. They just looked like they'd confronted a crazy man." Not wanting to disturb Brautigan, Thompson didn't go inside the house. "He was clearly nursing a bad hangover and was asleep." When Toby tried to start his Jeep, the engine still wouldn't turn over. He called AAA for assistance.

Price Dunn left the damaged rental at the airport. When Peter Fonda got the bill from Avis, with additional damage charges, he couldn't comprehend the jagged hole ripped through the trunk lid. Brautigan and Dunn never spoke again. Once, later in the summer, they ran into each other at Enrico's. Price had finished a glass of wine and started for the john just as Richard came out of the men's room. "He looked right through me," Dunn recalled. Brautigan walked past without a word, straight back to his table.

Maria wrote Richard a polite and friendly thank-you card once she returned to San Francisco. Scant mention was made of the recent discord. Maria said she was thinking of Richard and Ianthe, who "were so kind during my visit." She missed Montana and "all the lovely people you introduced me to," but cautioned, "try not to break any more fireplaces and chairs, really! just stick to writing and fishing." Maria signed off with love and the hope that she might see Brautigan again soon. "Onward thru the fog."

Summer rolled along. The disastrous severed friendships became just another blip on the community radar. Tom McGuane married Margie Kidder not long afterward in a tiny private ceremony with only the witnesses, Wilbur and Doretha Lambert, and Marian Hjortsberg, as offi-cial photographer, in attendance. Parties continued full tilt. Houseguests arrived in droves. Richard made sporadic trips to San Francisco between visits. Prior to one such journey, Siew-Hwa came out to travel back with him. As the fabric of their relationship unraveled, Brautigan and Beh's intimacy intensified. Even after leaving for Malaysia in November, she wrote Richard asking him to describe the smell of her body.

Around this time, Russ Chatham brought Dan and Ginny Gerber by for a drink. The Gerbers had been staying with their three young children at Chico Hot Springs. "It was a disaster," Dan recalled. Richard insisted all five Gerbers move in to his place. Polite refusals were resolutely swept aside. Gerber remembered Brautigan as an "extremely gracious host." The first night, Dan and Richard sat up late drinking. Gerber felt uncomfortable when Richard talked of his recently com-pleted book of poems. "I'd never really cared much for Richard's poetry," Dan confessed.

Later, up in the barn in Richard's studio, Richard handed Dan the poems from Japan one by one. "It was an evening filled with dread," Gerber confessed, but he responded to the work, and things "turned out happily." Richard fibbed to Dan, saying he was the first person to whom he'd shown the poetry. Gerber said "good things," and Brautigan was "delighted. He was just so happy."

Richard and Siew-Hwa left for Frisco soon after, insisting Dan, Ginny, and the kids use the house for as long as they wished. Finding a new designated driver to replace Price Dunn topped Brautigan's priorities. The list of friends available for the job had dwindled to zero. Richard thought some anonymous admiring student of English literature might better fit the bill. He phoned his old amigo Ron Loewinsohn, currently teaching at UC Berkeley. Ron told him he'd do what he could.

Peter Lewis, one of Loewinsohn's undergraduate students, studied at Reed College in Oregon for a year before dropping out to travel in West Africa, eventually enrolling in Berkeley in 1973. Lewis designed his own course of study to satisfy the degree requirements and worked closely with Loewinsohn. One afternoon during the summer of 1976, Ron asked Peter if he knew anyone who might want to go out to Montana for a period of time. Loewinsohn said a friend of his needed someone to take care of his property "and essentially to take care of him."

"What about me?" Peter Lewis asked.

"Well, that's fine," Professor Loewinsohn replied. "If you want to do it, that would be fine." At this point, Ron revealed his friend in Montana was the famous author Richard Brautigan. This was "neither here nor there" to Peter, whose own "literary affections went in a somewhat different direction." Brautigan at the time was "a cult figure in Berkeley," but Lewis regarded working for him mainly as "an opportunity to get out to the country and have some time to read and write and do something that seemed in and of itself pretty novel."

Loewinsohn provided "an introduction" to Brautigan. Peter Lewis drove over to North Beach from Berkeley, parking near Richard's building on Union Street. Peter never forgot that afternoon. After climbing a couple flights, he found the apartment door ajar. Stepping inside, Lewis saw Brautigan for the first time, a towering six-foot, four-inch "albino in his jockey shorts in agony."

Richard suffered from severe back pain. He immediately loped down the hall to his bedroom and collapsed on the mattress. "Just in miserable shape, moaning," Peter recalled. Siew-Hwa Beh hovered in the background, unable to provide any help. She left soon after Lewis arrived. From his brief glimpse of the couple's dynamics, Peter observed they shared "a very tempestuous relationship." Lewis himself suffered from a chronic back problem and knew what to do, taking charge of the situation.

Brautigan lay in "a terrible position." Lewis rearranged his bed, placing pillows under his knees and supporting his lower back. After getting Richard "all squared away" with hot compresses on the pain points, Peter finally enquired, "Is there anything you'd like to ask me?"

"No," Richard replied, his pained grimace easing into a smile, "you've got the job." He never mentioned the curious coincidence of having another Peter Lewis in his life, erasing the founder of the Trout Fishing in America School forever from his memory.

The appropriate arrangements were promptly made, with a modest stipend for Lewis, basically just beer money, in addition to room and board. Brautigan bought Lewis a plane ticket to Montana and gave him a small amount of cash to get from the Bozeman airport to Pine Creek. At first, before things grew "uncomfortable," Lewis had a delightful time, enjoying late August in Montana, hot cloudless afternoons easing into long balmy evenings and clear star-spangled nights. Peter's duties seemed modest. He drove Brautigan around, did the cooking and laundry, and occasionally mowed the lawn. Only later in September, when hunting season opened and guests began arriving, did things start to change.

Not long after Peter Lewis arrived, Ianthe left to live with her mother and begin her junior year of high school on the Big Island of Hawaii. Lewis noted that Brautigan spent very little time with her. "Even when she was there," he said, "He would sort of attend to his own regimen of writing or drinking or whatever else he needed to do." Ianthe struck Peter as mature beyond her years. She seemed very solicitous around her father, manifesting "an almost maternal demeanor toward him."

By the start of bird season, Ianthe had departed and things became more hectic around the Brautigan household. Streams of visitors arrived almost daily. Harry Dean Stanton, "a phenomenally gentle and lovely individual," came for a short stay "but he wasn't very comfortable" and soon left to find other accommodations. Bob Dattila showed up with his new girlfriend, a young magazine writer from Texas. They also remained only briefly. Every new set of guests demanded a corresponding celebration, and Peter found himself cooking for groups of eight to ten people almost every other night.

When Guy and Terry de la Valdène arrived for a two-week visit, they brought along four cases of liquor (Jack Daniel's, Calvados, Stolichnaya, and Chivas Regal). By the time they left, only a couple bottles of scotch remained. The night before the Valdènes' unscheduled departure, much of their booze was consumed at a boisterous dinner party for sixteen for which Peter Lewis did all the cooking. By the end of the evening, the place was a shambles, the dinner table littered with "glassware and china and half-empty platters." They all felt too drunk and tired for any cleanup. Everyone except Brautigan staggered off to bed, leaving the mess for morning.

Alone in the early hours, Richard drunkenly calculated the time difference between Montana and Japan and phoned his friend Takako Shiina in Tokyo. Not yet asleep in his small corner of the house just off the laundry room, Peter heard Brautigan make the call.

Through the thin wall, Lewis listened to the muffled conversation. Richard went to the bottom of the stairs and called up to the guest bedroom "in this nasal, whining drawl."

"Guyyyy . . . ? Guyyyy . . . ?" Brautigan crooned. "Come down and speak to my friend in Tokyo."

Peter heard Guy tossing upstairs, cursing into his pillow. "Shit! I can't believe this," Guy muttered, figuring if he just stayed under the covers, refusing to budge, Richard would eventually give up and leave him alone. Brautigan continued his whining and pleading. It was four in the morning, and Valdène had no intention of getting out of bed. In complete frustration, Richard hung up the phone and ran amok in his dining room, smashing plates and throwing glasses everywhere. His berserk rage escalated. He upended the table, sending all the china crashing to the floor. In a final frenzy, Brautigan hurled two of his heavy chairs at the wall, punching holes in the Sheetrock.

Terrified, Peter Lewis cowered on the other side. "It was the most extreme outburst of physical anger and pain that I think I'd ever witnessed close at hand," he said. "I felt like Chicken Little with the sky coming down on my head."

With nothing left to smash, Richard's anger subsided. An "eerie calm settled upon the house." He picked the telephone out of the wreckage and "very pointedly, very systematically" proceeded to dial Takako's number in Tokyo once again. With the connection made, Brautigan returned to the foot of the stairs. No longer whining, he called out in a completely matter-of-fact tone: "Guy [. . .] I'd like you to come down and speak to my friend."

Utterly resigned, Guy descended the stairs with dignity. He took the receiver from Richard and, "in his most gracious county manner," conducted an extremely polite conversation with Takako Shiina. Guy asked about the weather in Tokyo and how business was going in her bar. He said "he was in Montana with his friend Richard and they were having a lovely time." After perhaps forty-five seconds, Valdène handed the phone back to Brautigan and returned upstairs to bed.

The next morning, Guy and Terry cut their visit short and moved on to Tom McGuane's place for the remainder of their vacation. The phone rang while they were sitting in the kitchen making their plans and having coffee. Richard was still in bed, so Peter Lewis answered the call. It was the telephone company demanding to speak with Mr. Brautigan. Not knowing what else to do, Peter handed the phone to Guy. It turned out the calls to Japan had gone on for so long the charges totaled hundreds of dollars. Mountain Bell demanded an immediate payment. As a curious denouement to the previous night's antics, Valdène assured them in his dignified way that they would have their money in short order.

Peter Lewis knew he would be the one responsible for cleaning up the mess in the dining room, but the sight of it pissed him off, and he did nothing for most of the day. He typed a small card, making it look like an art label: trashed dining room, 1976, r. brautigan, and tacked it to a column where Richard would be sure to see it. Peter wanted to present the scene to his employer as a perverse performance piece. Brautigan usually was up at eight in the morning to go to work. This time around, "he finally stumbled from his bunkhouse at two or three the next afternoon."

Another night around one, a "crazy, weird sound" was heard in the woods out back of the house. Coyotes often came through the property, knocking over the trash cans, but this new noise sounded strange. Richard, "as usual, shitfaced by this hour," stumbled into the laundry area next to Lewis's room. Peter opened his door and found Brautigan rummaging around in the cupboards above the washing machine, a shotgun gripped in one hand. He was looking for shells.

Earlier that summer, reports of mutilated livestock had appeared in local newspapers. Horses and cattle had been found with their genitals and udders surgically removed. Several of these animals turned up in Paradise Valley. There were wild rumors of bloodthirsty interstellar alien invaders. Brautigan waving a shotgun made Peter Lewis nervous. "Anything could have happened," Lewis said. "He was that drunk."

Richard told Peter about the cattle mutilations. "He made cryptic weird references to some sort of satanic rock-and-roll plot to destroy the purity of Big Sky country." Brautigan wanted Lewis to learn how to use the shotgun in case he heard someone disturbing the horses. "He encouraged me to simply go out and shoot to kill anybody that I might see in the pasture and reassured me that I'd receive the applause of all the ranchers in the valley." Providing firsthand instruction, Richard grabbed a box of shells and stumbled out onto the back porch, where he proceeded to fire "twenty rounds or so" up into the trees, "branches coming down all over the property."

John Dermer complained to the police. Half an hour later, the front doorbell rang. Two stern-faced state troopers confronted Brautigan. They told him his neighbors were upset and that he ought not to be shooting in the middle of the night. In a "slurred and halting" manner, Richard launched into a wild explanation about a feral cat constantly harassing him. The policemen asked him to put his gun away and "not to engage in these bouts of midnight sharpshooting." After they left, Brautigan congratulated himself on talking his way out of an uncomfortable situation.

Beyond all the houseguests, Lewis observed, "It was a particularly social stretch. It was really a party frenzy. There were endless parties." Richard did considerable entertaining that season. There were frequent dinner gatherings and potlucks at the homes of all the Montana Gang. Russell Chatham had a three-day exhibition of his new paintings at the Danforth Gallery in Livingston during the second week in September, with an artist's reception on the last day. These events attracted unattached young women curious to meet an eccentric collection of the locally famous. Brautigan frequently picked up eager celebrity hunters and brought them home to Pine Creek.

Peter Lewis recalled young female groupies appearing sheepishly in the kitchen the morning after on at least a half-dozen occasions. Brautigan would roll over and "pretend not to know her or recognize her." The "totally embarrassed" girl wandered over to the main house "not knowing what to do or say or how to get home." Peter always made her coffee and said, "Hop in the car. I'll drive you." He had not anticipated this task when he accepted the job.

Peter Lewis could not remember a time during his stay when Richard was alone. "I certainly never really saw him by himself," Lewis said. "There were a few evenings when just the two of us were at the house." When Toby Thompson dropped by, he and Brautigan sat out on the back porch, "talking, drinking, and staring at the stars." Thompson thought "it was clear that [Brautigan] wanted somebody to be a kind of protégé," finding that Brautigan's knowledge of early twentieth-century literature was "really quite impressive."

Thompson asked Brautigan about his influences. Richard mentioned André Gide and Knut Hamsun. Brautigan also discussed the influence of Japanese writers, "particularly the genre of the Japanese I-novel." He told Toby that "he primarily considered himself a poet" and laughed about how he had kidded Tom McGuane about it. "Hey," Brautigan had said, "Look. I'm a poet, and I've already published eight novels, and you guys are struggling with your third or fourth."

Thompson extended his Montana visit and stayed on in his cheap room at the Murray. He asked Brautigan for a blurb for *Saloon*. Richard came through with "This book is a good place to get a drink." Toby "was hoping for something a bit more expansive," but thought it "classic Richard Brautigan." Thompson hoped to interview Brautigan for his sixties book. Richard remained elusive, telling Toby he didn't want him to write anything about what was happening in Montana. At the same time, Thompson felt that Brautigan really wanted to be included.

When Brautigan came into town, he often wandered into the lobby of the Murray. If he encountered Thompson, the pair embarked on bizarre shopping expeditions. Toby remembered poking around in Anthony's when Richard spied a collection of miniature felt doll hats, all in different colors, little fedoras and derbies and tiny Stetsons. "These are going to Rancho Brautigan," he said, buying the whole lot. Brautigan took them back to Pine Creek and hung them on a row of nails driven into his dining room wall.

Another time, Richard and Toby went to dinner at a steak joint in the ghost town community of Cokedale, named for the ruined stone coke ovens lining the gravel road, remnants of the turn-of-the-century Montana coal industry. Brautigan liked this restaurant for its excellent meat and because the owners had decorated the place with a collection of tiny shoes. "They were all over the walls and the ceiling," Thompson recalled, "weird little tiny sneakers. Richard loved that."

Peter Lewis was an aspiring writer. Unlike Toby, he had yet to publish anything, and Richard rarely talked with him about literary matters. Once, Brautigan burst into Lewis's room while he was writing and told him to grab the vacuum cleaner and follow him to the barn. Richard led the way up the multilevel stairs into his writing room. Peter was shocked by the enormous number of flies ("hundreds of flies, thousands of flies") inhabiting Brautigan's studio. "I know that had I tried to do anything there I'd have gone nuts," he said.

Brautigan attempted to defend his private space against the invading insects by Scotch-taping the seams around the edges of the big picture window. Scotch tape had also been plastered in "odd patterns along the door jambs." Richard asked Peter to vacuum up the dead flies littering nearly every surface of the office. Lewis went to work: floors, windowsill, Brautigan's desk. Richard yanked the vacuum nozzle out of Peter's hands and started using it like a hunting rifle to suck the buzzing flies out of the air. "He just went nuts."

On a couple occasions, Brautigan shared literary thoughts with Lewis. Richard once observed that there was "only room for one general in Livingston." Peter felt Richard was "upset that McGuane seemed to be leading the charge at that particular moment in literary history." Lewis intuited "he clearly felt he was working in the shadow of McGuane's burgeoning reputation."

Another time, when they sat together out on the back porch, Brautigan spoke of the ways in which great American novelists had achieved significant fame after their first publications only to be panned in midcareer. Brautigan mentioned Hemingway and Faulkner. Lewis understood he clearly meant to be included in the same league. "He felt he was writing in the tradition of the great American novel," Lewis recalled, "and would assume his rightful place in the pantheon."

When poet Ken McCullough and Brautigan returned to Pine Creek from a workshop in Missoula, they engaged in a long literary conversation that struck Peter Lewis as "as close to a statement of his credo as I ever heard him deliver." They discussed the metaphysical poets. Peter remembered Richard maintaining "that there were two things that he most fervently believed." One was, "Somehow in the act of making love one died. That you achieved death in lovemaking." The other was "specific information," a point Brautigan stressed often in literary discussions. "He kept repeating this phrase over and over again," Peter recalled. "Specific information."

Brautigan's disenchantment with Tom McGuane's growing success came to a head one afternoon at a party given by Russell Chatham's girlfriend, Sandi Lee, at her small Livingston home on

D Street. Richard had recently begun telling his younger writing colleagues that they hadn't "paid their dues." Over barbecue at Sandi Lee's, Brautigan said this to McGuane and touched a nerve. Tom's volatile Celtic blood rose darkly to his face. Brautigan ignored this warning sign and pressed on with his non-dues-paying admonition. McGuane, his face the color of an eggplant, exploded. "You," he bellowed at Richard, "you're nothing but a pet rock! A fucking hula hoop! You should get down on your knees every day and thank God for creating hippies!"

The pair suddenly grappled in front of the astonished partygoers, lurching into Lee's tiny bathroom, slamming the door behind them. The argument continued, muffled and indistinct, the angry words punctuated by the sound of blows. When the door burst open, Brautigan, pink and flushed, stormed off. McGuane had nothing more to say on the subject of dues payment.

Peter Lewis recalled another incident revealing Richard's preoccupation with his rightful place in the literary pantheon. A postcard arrived from Donald Allen congratulating Brautigan on the recent publication of *Sombrero Fallout*. Don wrote that he considered him "one of the great American writers working in the humorous vein of Mark Twain." Allen's praise was not received well. "Richard was furious," Peter remembered, "just beside himself." Years before, Brautigan had claimed to be Twain's reincarnation and deliberately cultivated a Twain-like nineteenth-century appearance. Now, he resented the comparison, especially the designation of humorist. Lewis regarded the outburst as "an absolute misgauge of his own importance as a literary figure."

Compared to the manic emotional turmoil engulfing Brautigan's place, the Hjortsberg household next door struck Peter Lewis as a "bastion of conjugal and literary sanity." He often walked over to buy eggs from Gatz and Marian and felt their home "projected a calm that was the complete opposite of Rancho Brautigan. It seemed to represent all that was sane and good about the literary enterprise."

Peter also became aware that "Richard was very paranoid." Whenever Lewis went into Livingston to run errands and shop for groceries, Brautigan rummaged through his personal papers. "I was writing a lot of poetry at the time," Peter recalled, "and he seemed to feel somewhat challenged by my daring to undertake my own literary life under his roof. I was a threat to him." Lewis complained about this to Toby Thompson. "God, he's driving me crazy," Peter said. "He comes into my room, and he goes through my stuff, and he pulls the pages out of the typewriter and reads them. Things that I'm writing."

Thompson thought Peter Lewis "was freaked out about it." Peter told him Richard had said, "Everything you have is mine!" In addition to suspecting Brautigan of snooping through his work, Lewis was convinced Brautigan listened in on his telephone conversations with his family and his girlfriend from an extension in another room. "That upset me tremendously," he said.

Peter had taken the semester off from Berkeley and hoped to stay in Montana through the fall. He found Paradise Valley "beautiful and compelling." He also enjoyed meeting "a bunch of very interesting people." Now, Lewis toyed with the idea of leaving. "It became clear that my position there was really untenable. [Brautigan] was becoming increasingly violent." The final straw came at a small dinner party at which Harry Dean Stanton was the guest of honor. "Richard started to lace into me about my poems and who I chose to read and the composition of my library," Peter recalled. He also said Brautigan "made reference to some of those phone conversations. That's when I really put the whole thing together."

Lewis blew up, lambasting Brautigan about his "Hooveresque" behavior. Harry Dean, "who saw himself as a peacemaker," came to Peter's defense, attempting to defuse the tension and calm Richard down. Lewis realized at that moment it was time to leave. A couple days later, while driving Brautigan to the Bozeman airport for a flight to San Francisco and his "fix of Chinese food and movies," Lewis told him he wouldn't be there when he got back. Lewis remembered saying he "was very, very sorry," maintaining he "simply couldn't continue to work for him given the situation." Richard expressed disappointment, apologizing for his behavior. He respected Peter's decision and made no attempt to cajole him into staying. "That was that," Lewis said.

Before he left late in September, Toby Thompson came for dinner at Brautigan's place. Guy Valdène prepared an elaborate meal. He and Jim Harrison had spent the day bird shooting, and a brace of rough grouse hung from the rafters of the porch ceiling. Halfway through dinner, Richard noticed one of the Hjortsbergs' cats prowling around. "Watch this," he whispered to Toby. "Watch this."

Brautigan snuck out onto the porch and cut down the grouse, stuffing them into his coat pockets. Back in the dining room, Richard feigned great concern. "Geez," he said, "those grouse aren't there. The cat got your grouse."

Harrison and Valdène ran out onto the back porch. "They were furious," Toby Thompson recalled. "Just really furious."

After dinner, the boys all headed into town for a nightcap (or two, or three) at the Wrangler Bar. A couple hours later, drinking with Guy and Jim, Richard reached into his pockets and pulled out the grouse. "I'll be darned," he said, setting the dead birds down on the bar in front of his friends. Valdène and Harrison were pissed. "They knew they'd been had," Thompson observed.

After Toby Thompson returned home to Cabin John, Maryland, Richard lacked a regular drinking buddy. With no designated driver and the weather growing ever colder, Brautigan arranged for the usual end-of-season shutdown, emptying his refrigerator, hiring someone to drain his water pipes, and bringing his television set, fishing rods, and gun collection over to the Hjortsbergs' for safekeeping. Back in Frisco, it was business as usual for Richard: watching double features, breakfast at Mama's with Don Carpenter, hanging out at Enrico's.

Early in November, Helen Brann traveled to San Francisco to meet with her new clients, some (Don Carpenter and Keith Abbott) recommended by Richard Brautigan. Brann hosted a cocktail party at her suite in the Stanford Court Hotel, Richard and Keith among her many guests. Brautigan brought along a manuscript copy of his latest novel, *Dreaming of Babylon*, to give to his agent.

Journalist John Grissam was also at the party. In collaboration with Dr. Eugene Schoenfeld, who had long written a medical advice column for the underground press under the pseudonym "Dr. Hip," Grissam was at work on a book of interviews on the subject of jealousy and asked everyone in the room about experiences with the green-eyed monster. Swilling bourbon, Brautigan did not participate in these discussions. Richard ignored Grissam, making phone calls in the other room. As time went on, it became clear the journalist was one of his fans. Grissam told Brautigan of his perceptions about the freedom enjoyed by rich and famous writers. Richard deflected these comments. As the whiskey took hold, he sat down on the rug beside the journalist, insisting fame meant nothing, only the work counted. Grissam remained adamant. Surely the money provided by fame provided a boon to a writer.

Brautigan exploded. Reverting to one of his favorite Digger gestures, he tore up a $20 bill and scattered the shreds over Grissam. "This isn't real." he shouted. "You think this is real? This is nothing." As Grissam gathered up the torn banknote bits and stuffed the pieces into his vest pocket, Richard dropped to his knees beside him, grabbing one of the journalist's legs, banging his foot against the floor. "This leg is more real than any of that," Brautigan insisted.

Grissam explained his leg had "mysteriously atrophied" at the disastrous end to an unhappy love affair. Brautigan became suddenly solicitous of Grissam and apologized to him, leaving the hotel suite shortly afterward. To Keith Abbott, it seemed as if Brautigan "had gone instinctively to the source of another person's pain [. . .] doomed to return constantly to his own pain." Whatever Grissam may have felt about Richard's finding the source of his inner agony, he was grateful for the gift of the torn-up double sawbuck. "The next day, I Scotch-taped the pieces together," he said, "exchanged the twenty at a bank, and paid my phone bill."

Not long after this, Brautigan encountered filmmaker Nicholas Roeg. Their evening concluded over a bottle of Jurgensen's at Richard's Union Street apartment. By 1976, with the release of *The Man Who Fell to Earth*, forty-eight-year-old Roeg's reputation as a cinematographer had been eclipsed by growing recognition of his skills as a director. His first three motion pictures in the director's chair, *Performance*, *Walkabout*, and *Don't Look Now*, were all praised for technical innovation and offbeat insights into human relationships.

Late into the evening, a dispute arose between Brautigan and Roeg over the age of the whiskey they were drinking. Richard owned the bottle and maintained that it was eighteen years old. Nicolas insisted it was much younger. A check of the label revealed the bourbon to be sweet sixteen. Brautigan immediately claimed victory, claiming he'd owned the bottle for two years. Roeg refused to accept this false logic. A struggle ensued. Richard pushed Nic down a long flight of stairs in his apartment building, landing the Brit in the emergency room with a broken foot.

Years later after Brautigan's death, Jack Thibeau attended a New Year's Eve party at Helena's, a private celebrity supper club obscurely located in an industrial section of Silver Lake, a Los Angeles district east of Hollywood. No sign marked the large gray stucco building housing the exclusive hideaway, formerly the dance studio of proprietress Helena Kallianiotes, whose gold-spangled belly-dancing costume hung framed under glass against a far wall. A close friend of Jack Nicholson, Kallianiotes enjoyed a sporadic film acting career, most notably as the tough lesbian hitchhiker in *Five Easy Pieces*.

The glittering party swirled on toward the new year, when Thibeau spotted Nicolas Roeg seated at a candlelit table with his actress wife, Theresa Russell. When the moment seemed right, Jack approached them. "Mr. Roeg," he said, "I am a friend of Richard Brautigan's."

Roeg immediately pushed a chair aside for Thibeau. "I just wanted you to know that Richard's favorite story when he got drunk was about how he broke your leg," Jack told the director.

"Richard broke my leg?" Roeg replied, looking totally nonplussed. "Do you know that for three days I stayed in my hotel room in San Francisco waiting for the police to come and get me because I thought I had killed him?"

As she listened to the conversation, Theresa Russell's "jaw dropped." She asked Jack how he knew Richard. The other guests at the Roeg's table were also curious, chiming in: "How did you know Richard? How did you meet Richard?"

"Well, I met him in North Beach," Thibeau explained. "We used to drink wine in alleys together."

Nicolas Roeg rose to his feet, holding his drink aloft in a toast. "Here . . . Here . . ." he exclaimed.

Roeg and Brautigan never spoke again after the whiskey dispute at Richard's apartment. "So neither one knew what happened," Thibeau said years later, "and it sort of drifted off into a memoir for both of them."

Shortly after pushing Roeg down the stairs, Brautigan gave up his Union Street apartment. He planned on returning to Japan for an extended stay and didn't want to pay rent for an unoccupied place. Siew-Hwa Beh had left for Malaysia in November, so Richard arranged with Keith Abbott to truck her belongings over to Berkeley. His own larger possessions went into storage. The smaller stuff, books and manuscripts, his clothing and personal mementos, Richard packed in several large "beautiful trunks."

Curt Gentry had purchased a modern house on Russian Hill with money earned from *Helter Skelter*. "It was an incredible house," he recalled. Curt lived there with his second wife, Gail, his former girlfriend, whom he had married six months earlier. Brautigan called him and asked if he could come and spend the weekend, saying he was going back to Japan soon. Curt agreed, and Richard arrived with his new trunks in tow. "Well, the weekend passed," Curt said, "then a month passed. Almost three months later, Richard was still there. I gave him his own keys, and he'd come and go, but he was wearing awfully thin."

One annoyance involved taking all of Richard's telephone messages. The Gentrys got Brautigan his own phone for his bedroom. Curt and Gail quarreled frequently, but Richard didn't hear their arguments ("He was the only one in the neighborhood that didn't") and decided during his extended stay that marriage could be a wonderful and happy thing. Richard immediately adopted the role of pampered husband, asking Gail when she planned to change his sheets, even though she had just changed them the day before.

All along, Richard kept telling the Gentrys that he planned on leaving "in a couple days." Things came to a head when Gail received a telephone call from Japan Airlines confirming Brautigan's reservation two months ahead. "That was it," Curt said. "I had to tell Richard to leave." Brautigan was furious. "He got very, very mad," Gentry recalled, "and he got very drunk, and so he didn't come home that night." Actually, Richard did return to the Gentrys' house with Tony Dingman in the middle of the night to collect his trunks. Brautigan told Dingman he was "never going to speak to [Curt] again."

Richard and Tony hailed a cab at one o'clock in the morning and hauled Brautigan's trunks to the Fairmont Hotel at the top of Nob Hill. When they attempted to check in, the desk clerks at first were hesitant to admit a staggering drunk with shoulder-length hair dressed like a refugee from the Summer of Love. Richard grew indignant and started throwing down $100 bills, shouting, "I can buy this place." Dingman persuaded the management Brautigan was a world-famous author, and his friend was given a room.

The next morning, the Gentrys arose at their usual hour, walking around quietly not to disturb Richard, whom they assumed was still sleeping upstairs. When Curt went up at last to wake him, the phone rang. It was Brautigan, calling to say he needed to come and get something. Gentry didn't understand. He thought Richard was calling from the guest bedroom on the other line. Things got straightened out, and Brautigan collected his stuff, leaving only Willard, his papier-mâché bird, behind at the Gentrys'. Not long afterward, on February 19, 1977, Richard flew to Tokyo, his second visit to the Land of the Rising Sun in less than a year.

forty-four: kids

ALTHOUGH HE OFTEN said he didn't like children, Richard Brautigan possessed a natural rapport with kids. As Keith Abbott observed, "Children generally liked Richard, recognizing an ally in anarchy." Brautigan's daughter, Ianthe, became the main beneficiary of his talent for thinking like a child. She felt young peoples' affinity for her father stemmed from his recognizing and sharing their latent fears. Richard was terrified lightbulbs might explode at any moment. This made perfect sense to a kid. As a child, Brautigan felt afraid of statues. He thought they were actual people covered alive with molten metal. He often walked blocks out of his way to avoid passing a statue. Hearing of this irrational fear struck a familiar chord in the haunted imaginations of children.

Richard and Ianthe often played games together. Waiting for elevators, they made bets on which car would arrive first. When she was around ten, Brautigan took his daughter to lunch with Bruce Conner. Richard and Bruce played a private game similar to the dirty dozens. The object was to ridicule and insult the other guy as comically and outrageously as possible without ever laughing or even cracking a smile. This went on until the bill arrived. After sitting straight-faced through the meal, Ianthe suddenly burst into gales of hysterical laughter while walking away from the restaurant. "Hey!" Brautigan said to Conner, "she understood the point of our game and was playing along with us."

Richard never missed a chance to instruct Ianthe on his own peculiar view of life. He once told her that people were crazy when they were alone. The protective wall of solitude allowed an individual's innate insanity to emerge. People talked to themselves and did various other strange things when they thought no one was looking. Then, Brautigan explained, the phone rings or the doorbell chimes unexpectedly and they are suddenly sane once again.

From her earliest childhood, Richard shared his love of the movies with Ianthe. A weekend dad, Brautigan didn't simply regard moviegoing as an easy way to spend time with his kid. Richard's genuine passion for film stretched far back into his own boyhood. He didn't take his daughter to family movies suitable for children, light fare like Disney. They went to pictures that he was interested in seeing. Ianthe was treated to films like *Slaughterhouse-Five*, *Chinatown*, *Amarcord*, *Sleeper*, and *The Rocky Horror Picture Show* at a relatively tender age. During one "brief horrifying period," they attended nothing but Japanese samurai films. Ianthe developed a liking for the Blind Swordsman series.

Although he never wore a watch, Brautigan had "a thing about time" and liked to arrive at appointments ahead of schedule. He always got to the movies early. He and his daughter often spent a quarter of an hour sitting together in an empty theater, eating popcorn and staring at a dark screen. They both enjoyed comedies, becoming "hysterical with laughter." In her memoir, Ianthe recalled her father's "wild, whooping laughter" filling the auditorium. Watching *Young Frankenstein*, Brautigan laughed so hard that he stuck his hand into his supersized soda instead of his popcorn.

Richard walked out of the theater when he didn't like a movie. Ianthe remembered him leaving with her during Woody Allen's *Manhattan*. Brautigan disliked *Black Moon Rising* so intensely he headed for the exit shortly after it started, this time in the company of Siew-Hwa Beh. Exiting a movie he didn't enjoy was Richard's way of saying that just because you get served crap, you don't have to eat it.

At fifteen, Ianthe needed eyeglasses, and her father brought her to an optometrist. A developing interest in boys caused her to worry about her appearance. Ianthe shared her fears with Brautigan. "Remember that Dorothy Parker poem?" she asked her father. "'Men seldom make passes at girls who wear glasses.'"

"Wrong!" Richard immediately replied. "Boys don't make passes at girls without asses!"

Brautigan took pains to treat Ianthe's burgeoning sexuality with dignity and offer serious advice. "Don't ever get involved with someone who has more broken wings than you do," he told his daughter. He also warned her of the dangers of VD. Acutely aware of his own herpes problem, Richard advised Ianthe to always take a close look at a man's penis before having sex. Not one to avoid frank talk with his daughter, Brautigan cautioned her to "never do speed. You can come back from anything else. You can come back from heroin. But not speed." He also instructed Ianthe to "always take care of your body [. . .] Keep your body safe."

On a lighter note, Richard taught his daughter to love practical joking. In her memoir, she mentioned a time when she came home from school and was "considerably put out" because her father had eaten all the chocolate chip cookies she had baked. A couple days later, she found chocolate chip cookies hidden all over her room, in her shoes, in the desk drawers, under her pillow. Chocolate chip cookies turned up in odd places for weeks.

On another occasion, Richard appeared one morning in Montana wearing a Japanese kimono and cowboy boots and launched into an impromptu dance routine, reducing Ianthe and her friend Cadence to fits of uncontrolled laughter by "singing off-key, pretending to tap-dance [and] flapping around the kitchen [. . .]"

Siew-Hwa Beh recalled an evening on Union Street in 1975 when Brautigan was fixing diner. "I pulled this joke on Ianthe," he told her, "and I knew it was the last time I could pull this joke on her." His daughter was fifteen and growing wise to Richard's tricks. "I was with Ianthe, and we went into a shop with all these clocks," Brautigan continued. "I said to Ianthe, 'Ianthe, what time is it?' And she ran around trying to look for a watch so she could see the time. She kept asking the people around whether they had a watch so she could tell the time, but the whole shop was filled with clocks." Richard laughed at the memory of his joke as he stirred the spaghetti sauce. "I just had to pull it on her," he said, "because it would be the last time I could get away with it."

In retaliation, the next year, Ianthe and Cadence Lipsett turned all the clocks in the Montana house back an hour while Brautigan worked in his studio out in the barn. With his concern for time and punctuality, Richard was furious with them when he found out the joke was on him. Resetting the clocks had thrown off his schedule. Cadence remained unrepentant. "He's blowing this way out of proportion," she told Ianthe. At the same time, Cadence held Richard in high regard. "He was so articulate and precise in the way he explained things," she said. "One of the great things about your dad was that he was never condescending when he talked to us."

In his memoir, *Downstream from Trout Fishing in America*, Keith Abbott wrote about helping Richard move his possessions out of the Geary Street apartment. On the final day of the project, he brought his seven-year-old daughter, Persephone, along with him. The little girl was sullen and bored. Brautigan suggested she sweep his bedroom floor, where he still emptied the coins out of his pockets every night. Persephone dragged the broom into the empty room. The little girl's mood changed the moment she saw what littered the floor. Brautigan "could barely contain himself" and hurried onto the back porch to fetch an empty mayonnaise jar for Persephone to collect the pennies, dimes, nickels, and quarters she had swept up. Keith Abbott remembered "the look on Richard's face as he stood in the doorway, his hangover banished, watching delightedly [. . .]"

Not all parents appreciated Brautigan's subversive connection with their children. Dan Gerber's wife, Virginia, was "sort of horrified" when they stayed with Richard at Pine Creek and he regaled their kids, especially ten-year-old Frank, with wild tales from his youth. "You know," Dan recalled, "it would be things like stealing stop signs away from the streets and causing accidents." Brautigan related other pranks, included the episode of hiding rotten chickens in the freezer of the local market and his trick of sticking a garden hose through the open window of a neighborhood house when the residents were away and turning on the water. The Gerbers were appalled, but their children sat enthralled by Brautigan's juvenile delinquent memories.

Fascinated by Richard's towering redwood barn, Lorca Hjortsberg had frequently journeyed across the creek to play in its spooky deserted cow stalls. Her family's own leaning red barn, populated with chicken coops and workshops and a functional hayloft, lacked the labyrinthian mysteries of Brautigan's cobweb-draped basement-level byre, the floor caked three feet thick with ancient dried manure.

Two summers later, shortly after school got out in June, Lorca complained to her father about all the trash littering Pine Creek Road between the Yellowstone River and old Highway 89. Gatz organized an impromptu cleanup, enlisting his daughter, her best friend, Polly Story, and her three-year-old brother, Max. They worked all morning and into the afternoon, picking up discarded bottles, cans, and Styrofoam takeout boxes. When they finished, the gravel road was clean and the back of the Hjortsbergs' '49 Chevy pickup piled high with stuffed black plastic trash bags. Gatz posed the kids leaning nonchalantly against the heaped garbage sacks and took a quick snapshot.

When Richard Brautigan returned from his second trip to Japan at the end of June, he was fascinated by this photograph. Like discarded Christmas trees, rubber bands scattered across a city sidewalk, or a decrepit West Texas graveyard, there was something about the image that caught his fancy. He began talking with Lorca about the great trash pickup, trying to get to the heart of a story. Their conversations led to a curious and unexpected conclusion. Richard suggested he and Lorca collaborate on a screenplay.

The entire project may have been nothing more than a fancy to capture the imagination of a ten-year-old girl, nevertheless Brautigan, professional to the core, insisted Lorca agree to follow a rigid writing schedule. He asked her to come over to his house every afternoon to work for at least an hour. Being taken seriously by an adult has great appeal for a child, and she immediately agreed. To seal the bargain, Richard proposed they both sign a formal agreement. He found a paper napkin from the Tastee-Freez, his favorite fast food restaurant, and drew up a contract with his ballpoint pen.

The fragile document became its own work of art. At the top, Brautigan printed "The Contract" beside one of his iconic fish drawings. In block capitals below that, he wrote the name of their project, "GARBAGE TRIUMPHS OR 'JUST GARBAGE.'" Inside a much larger smiling fish sketch at the center of the napkin, the words "For a movie" were superimposed above "Share and Share a like [sic]." The signatures of Richard and Lorca appear beside the place of signing, "Pine Creek, Montana." Richard added the date and the deal was done. Brautigan carefully folded the contract, preserving it in an empty plastic Dan Bailey's Fly Shop box.

An element of make-believe crossed over into the realm of reality, so often the case in the movie business. It seemed very real to a girl of ten. Thirty years later, Lorca still treasured her paper napkin contract with Richard Brautigan. She recalled going next door to Richard's house every day around noon, knocking on the door of his sleeping quarters, and working with him in his kitchen while he drank a cup of coffee. Brautigan employed a Socratic method. After instructing her in screenplay format, he asked Lorca questions about the story, and she wrote down the ensuing action in a school notebook.

The plot involved a conflict between the "good Indians" and the "garbage Indians." The project lasted for week or so, until Richard took off on one of his periodic trips to San Francisco. Lorca can't remember what became of the "screenplay," or even how much of their project was actually completed. Her memories of the script's contents remain equally vague. What she never forgot was the magic of "collaborating" with a famous writer who took her ideas seriously and stimulated her imagination with his own.

Bret Haller, Mike and G.'s youngest son, remembered a different sort of collaboration with Richard Brautigan. Bret, who later followed his father's film career footsteps and became a movie producer, recalled Brautigan as "definitely one of those guys that if you were gonna get on your bicycle and go riding around in Pine Creek, he was one of those guys you'd want to go visit. He would have an open-door policy, and you could go bug him if you wanted to. 'Let's go hang out with our pal Richard.'"

One time, Bret took sick and couldn't go to school, staying home in bed. Richard came over to visit, as he had when Eric Haller broke his nose earlier in a bicycle accident. Brautigan brought along a model airplane kit, some jars of paint, and a tube of glue. He had owned the kit for some time, and the boys admired the Stuka JU 87 dive bomber, depicted on a colorful box-lid illustration. The Stuka was a formidable aircraft used by the Germans to great effect as an antitank weapon on the Russian front during World War II (Stuka is an abbreviation of *sturzkampfflugzzeug*, German for dive bomber), and the model airplane kit piqued Richard's abiding interest in WWII.

It took several days to assemble the airplane. Brautigan came over every morning to sit with the sick boy and work on their project. The Stuka had upswept gull wings and a fixed undercarriage and landing wheels, an ugly and instantly recognizable aircraft. Richard told Bret of the Stuka's fearsome capabilities as they pieced and glued the model's parts together. A rear gunner sat behind the pilot. The two-man Stuka dove at close to eighty degrees. It carried either one five-hundred-kilogram bomb or four fifty-kilogram bombs under the fuselage, and the wheel covers contained the "Trumpets of Jericho," sirens screaming during the dive "to shatter the morale of enemy troops and civilians." Richard and Bret painted the plane a camouflage pattern and mistakenly applied the swastika decals backward on the wings.

Bret Haller still owns the model Stuka dive bomber he built with Richard Brautigan. More than just a youthful memento, it's a reminder of a very special friendship. Bret remembered Richard "certainly wasn't one of those stern adults. He was a kid."

Brautigan concurred with everyone's assessment of the eternal kid dwelling within him. In a poem, written in Japan in June of 1976, he had this to say:

Age: 41

Playing games
playing games, I
guess I never
really stopped
being a child
playing games
playing games

forty-five: tokyo throes

PLANNING FOR HIS first trip to Japan preoccupied Richard Brautigan through the early months of 1976. He had Helen Brann decline an invitation from the State Arts Commission of Washington set early in May because he would be out of the country. In mid-April, Gary Snyder answered a letter Brautigan had written asking for insights into Japan. Snyder's travel advice reflected his own unique interests. "Tokyo will absolutely take you over," Gary wrote. He urged Richard to visit the National Museum and have a look at the rooms full of "naked medieval sword blades." Snyder knew Brautigan would appreciate how they all seemed alike and yet each was subtly different. "Purity," Gary called it. Along the same lines, Snyder included a list of temples in Kyoto "worth doing" (Ryoan-ji, Toji, Todai-ji, Horyu-ji), balancing this aesthetic tour by recommending Cid Corman's Kyoto ice cream parlor and Horagai ("conch shell"), a coffee shop run by an old friend in the remote Tokyo district of Kokubun-ji.

For a couple months before he left for the Philippines to work on *Apocalypse Now*, early in '76, Tony Dingman lived in Richard Brautigan's Bolinas house. Richard sometimes came out on the weekend, but mostly Tony was alone, "waiting to leave," and working with Klyde Young, painting and fixing up the bathroom. "I met him like late compared to a lot of the guys," Tony said, "but once we got to be drinking partners things were good for a long time."

Brautigan wrote to his Japanese translator seeking information. "I'm so glad we have cleared up the business about The Pill versus the Springhill Mine Disaster," he told her. He planned to arrive around the end of April and remain until early June. He had heard the Imperial Hotel was "a good place to stay in Tokyo, centrally located, etc.," and wanted to know what she thought about the idea. Kazuko reassured him that the Imperial was a five-star world-class hotel. Richard promptly booked a reservation.

Brautigan arrived at Haneda (Tokyo International Airport) on May 13, 1976. Having already obtained a valid travel visa from the Japanese Consul-General in San Francisco, he was unexpectedly detained by emigration officials. He had listed "writer" as his occupation on the entry form. Taking a hard look at his scruffy appearance, the officials decided Richard must be a "technical writer." Seeking such employment in Japan might deprive a legitimate citizen of a job. Brautigan was not allowed to enter the country.

Desperate, Richard phoned Curt Gentry, who was staying at the Hotel New Otani with his fiancée, Gail Stevens. A couple days earlier, Curt and Gail had overheard an American speaking perfect Japanese in a bar. Piqued by his own dwindling knowledge of the language, Gentry approached the stranger and introduced himself. "I had read *Helter Skelter*," Len Grzanka remembered, "and was really impressed." Grzanka lived in Tokyo, working on a Harvard PhD and teaching English part-time at Tsuda women's college. Len took Gentry and Stevens to a number of art galleries the next day ("Gail had a black belt in shopping") and went out on the town at night with Curt.

Gentry phoned Grzanka to inform him of Brautigan's plight. "My sponsor in Japan was the Minister of Justice," Len said, "so I had a little bit of clout." Grzanka found his way to where Immigration authorities held Richard. He explained Brautigan was not a *teknakada* (technical writer) but a *shosetska*, "an author. And when I said *yimina shosetska*, a famous novelist, they backed off and let him in."

Brautigan took a cab to the Imperial Hotel, the oldest and most prestigious in Tokyo. Located across from the forty-acre Hibiya Park, adjacent to the emperor's palace grounds, the hotel had a long and distinguished history. The first Imperial was built in 1890. Frank Lloyd Wright was commissioned in 1916 to design a replacement. His "Maya-revival-style" structure opened in June 1923, and survived the 7.9-magnitude Great Kantō earthquake, which leveled most of Tokyo months later. Wright's Imperial also made it through the Allied bombing of World War II, only to fall to the wrecking ball in 1968. (The Japanese saved the facade, entrance lobby, and interior reflecting pool, reconstructing them in 1976 at the Museum Meiji-Mura, a collection of historic buildings in Nagoya, outside of Tokyo.) By the time Brautigan arrived that same year, two new European-style high-rise buildings had been constructed to form the resurrected Imperial Hotel.

At the front desk, oppressed by the opulent formality, Richard also felt the haughty scrutiny of the hotel staff. He had no credit cards and was asked to pay cash, up front, for his room. Being mistaken for a hippie drug dealer, the second indignity suffered since arriving in Japan, drove Brautigan to the sanctity of his posh quarters, where he spent the evening drinking and watching television. He wrote "Kitty Hawk Kimonos," his first Tokyo poem, about the two young women in kimonos "standing beside a biplane" that he saw on his TV screen that night. Richard didn't understand a word of Japanese but felt an affinity for the "old timey airplane" and the women's "very animated / and happy conversation."

The next morning, Brautigan went for a walk, beginning his habit of exploring the remote neighborhoods of Tokyo on foot. He wandered through the back streets of the Shibuya District wanting to see his first Japanese bird. Richard was surprised to hear the sound of a rooster crowing. He jotted down a poem ("Crow") in his notebook.

The management of the Imperial remained adamant about payment up front from Brautigan, every single day. When it seemed things couldn't get any worse, the hotel asked him to leave. Richard appealed to Len Grzanka for help. He called the Imperial "and tried to straighten things out with them." "They just said no," Len recalled with a chuckle. "*Yanayatsu* . . . He's disgusting." Richard complained about the situation to all who would listen. The next afternoon around three, he traveled to Kazuko Fujimoto's Tokyo apartment in the Harajuku/Aoyama District, with the hotel problem uppermost on his mind. Brautigan brought a bottle of Hennessy cognac, most of which he drank himself. Kazuko's other guests were Katsuya Nakamura, publisher of Shobun-sha (Brautigan's Japanese publishing house) and Kaitaro Tsuno, Shobun-sha's editor in chief.

Later, they all went to dinner at Szechwan, a fine Chinese restaurant in the Roppongi District, the most international area of the city. After their meal, Kazuko and her husband, David Goodman, brought Richard and the men from Shobun-sha to The Cradle Bar, also located in Roppongi. Both Shinjuku and Ginza boasted a greater number of restaurants and nightspots, but the high density of discos and bars in a much smaller district intensified Roppongi's pleasure-seeking atmosphere. The

Cradle opened in 1971 on Stars and Stripes Avenue (Seijoki Dori), a thoroughfare named for the nearby offices of the U.S. Army newspaper. The basement bar had become a favorite Tokyo hangout for writers, artists, and filmmakers by the time Richard Brautigan first walked down the stairs five years later. Known to its devoted habitués simply as Cradle, the place owed its congenial ambiance to the warmth and curiosity of the proprietress, forty-two-year-old Takako Shiina, whose father had translated *Alice in Wonderland* into Japanese in 1927. He later became a screenwriter and, between 1931 to 1941, directed fifty films under the name Saburou Aoyama.

In 1968, Takako met English playwright Arnold Wesker (*Chicken Soup with Barley, The Kitchen, Chips with Everything*). She was recovering from the tragic and unexpected loss of a child and had embarked on a pilgrimage, walking from temple to temple. Wesker had been invited to Tokyo as part of "Wesker 68," a festival celebrating his work. Takako Shiina was one of three translators hired to serve in shifts during the official program. "I came to her at a vulnerable time," Wesker recalled. "There was something about the way we hit it off, and she took courage."

Takako decided to open a nightspot congenial to artists. Initial funding came from a wealthy American she met during a trip to the States. Shiina built the bar and block of flats. She lived upstairs with her actor husband. Takako asked Arnold Wesker to name the bar. "Well, you're creating a place that's going to be sort of a comfort for artists," he mused. "Call it The Cradle."

Wesker described the look of the subterranean boîte: "You went down a flight of stairs into the basement, and you turned right into The Cradle. Turn right again and you're looking down the length of The Cradle. On the left is a bar, and on the right there might have been bar stools or there might have been sofas. And further along, you stepped down into a well, and there was a table with lots of armchairs around it. That's really all it was."

Brautigan wrote, "There is a sunken living room with a fireplace and comfortable couches to encourage pleasant conversation while eating and drinking good things." The walls of the bar were covered from floor to ceiling with theatrical posters, the majority advertising plays by Wesker, along with framed photos of Shiina's father directing his films. A piano and a guitar stood available for anyone who wanted to make music. Recordings of every sort provided good listening, everything "from jazz to classical to country and western." When no music played, "there is much sound of laughter, but sometimes there is just the silence of people thinking."

Much later, Richard observed, "The Cradle cannot be described in common terms. It is not a restaurant. It is not a living room. It is not a bar. It is not a home. But it is all of these things created by one woman . . . Shiina Takako. The Cradle is her vision of how life should be as a gathering place for people. It is designed totally for pleasure and creative exchange. We need all of that we can get in the world." The Japanese always placed the family name first. Although he spoke virtually no Japanese, Brautigan adopted this tradition right from the start, a pretention he clung to while never making any effort to learn the language.

Kazuko Fujimoto introduced Richard Brautigan to Takako Shiina, and they became friends immediately. The editor Kaitaro Tsuno was an old friend of Takako's. She had met the Goodmans through him. This was the first time either Brautigan or the publisher of Shobun-sha, had ever come into her bar. Richard launched into a tale of woe about his shabby treatment at the Imperial. Takako suggested a solution. One of her regular customers managed the first-class Keio Plaza Hotel in the Shinjuku District. She called, and he agreed to give Brautigan a 50 percent discount, "the best discount rate they ever gave." After that, Richard "was at The Cradle every night," Shiina recalled.

Forty-seven stories high, the Keio Plaza (built in 1971) was the world's tallest hotel. A short walk from the Shinjuku Station among a cluster of other towering buildings, it was described by the *Tokyo City Guide* as a "concrete and glass skyscraper of the most undistinguished kind. Interiors are more of the same." The hotel made up for a lack of charm with impeccable service and a very convenient location. Brautigan wrote a postcard picturing his slablike hotel to Gatz Hjortsberg shortly after arriving, describing Keio Plaza as "a typical Japanese inn" with "an excellent view of Los Angeles."

Richard Brautigan checked into room 3003 on the thirtieth floor of the Keio Plaza. It was "a very long room, cheery and bright." On a clear day, the view from his huge window took in Mount Fuji, the sacred Fuji-san, forty miles distant. It was the rainy season, and the iconic volcano was often obscured by clouds. One morning, after spending the night drinking, Richard returned to his room at sunrise. Very drunk, he took off his shoes at the door, a Japanese practice he thought was "cute," and walked to the window. There stood Fuji in all its snow-capped glory, "absolutely clear like a crystal vision of itself." Brautigan felt he could have touched the mountain had been able to open the window. He lay down on his bed and fell asleep. When he awoke in the early afternoon, the clouds had rolled back in and Mount Fuji was gone. Richard wondered if he would ever see it again.

Brautigan resumed his ambulatory explorations in his new neighborhood. He made sure to take along his passport, his small leather-bound notebook, a ballpoint pen, an English-Japanese dictionary, and a little card with the name and address of his hotel printed in both languages, available at the front desk and very useful late at night when dealing with cab drivers. Bit by bit, Richard filled his room at the Keio Plaza with "plants and wall hangings, all objects that I would find in the course of a day's wandering."

Curt Gentry occasionally accompanied Brautigan on his urban adventures, observing later that "Richard made no effort to get to know the Japanese or to visit the country. I tried and tried to get Richard to come out, to go with us down to Kyoto. To go somewhere. Richard just would not leave Tokyo." Gentry observed that Brautigan "had some overinflated ideas of his own importance. We'd be walking down the street in Tokyo. Richard looked particularly strange—out of place—tall, blond, with that mustache, a Levi jacket. The Japanese would turn and stare at him and kind of laugh as he went by."

Brautigan's ego went into overdrive. "You know," he told Gentry, "everybody in Japan recognizes me from my book jackets."

Richard and Curt's adventures together in Tokyo were mainly nocturnal. "[We] did quite a bit of drinking and playing around," Gentry recalled. Brautigan's preferred nighttime playground was the Roppongi District, and the Café Cardinale became another of his favorite hangouts. It was the sort of place where all the male customers were foreigners while the women were all Japanese. Gentry recalled Richard talking "about the ugly Americans and such," at the same time he eagerly joined in the gaijin barroom mating dance at the Café Cardinale. "American Bar in Tokyo," a poem Richard wrote early in June, summed the place up in ten deft lines: "young conservative snobbish / American men, / drinking and trying to pick up / Japanese women [. . .] It is very hard to find any poetry / here."

The funniest moment Curt Gentry recalled occurred around four in the morning after a night on the town. Richard insisted on walking his friend back to the New Otani, the largest hotel in Asia, sprawling across a ten-acre traditional Japanese garden. Both men were quite drunk. They staggered into the entrance area, where an escalator carried guests up to a more formal lobby. At the bottom of the escalator, Richard and Curt discovered two well-dressed hotel employees staring down from above.

"Assistant manager and bus boy," Gentry remembered, "and they are bowing, and we're down at the bottom of the escalator, and we're bowing, and they're bowing, and we're bowing, and this kept going on." Brautigan whispered to Gentry that Japanese culture dictated whoever bowed last lost face. "So we had to bow last. We're standing at the bottom wondering why it's taking so long to get to the top," Gentry said. They failed to notice that the escalator had closed down hours before. "The Japanese are too polite to tell these two drunks that we have to walk up."

Curt Gentry believed Richard "didn't explore Tokyo that much," but Brautigan's poetry notebook told another story. The poems Richard jotted down during his first couple weeks in Japan ranged over a diverse swath of Tokyo real estate. He wrote of winning a can of crabmeat and a toy locomotive in a pachinko parlor and the triumph of ordering his first meal, "curry and rice," in a Japanese restaurant. He described watching a fly on a red brick in Mitsui Plaza in Nihonbashi in the Chūō District close to the waterfront. Other poems described an "Egyptianesque" Japanese model ("Her lips are so red / they make blood / seem dull, a / useless pastime") and the signs on shuttered bars in the Ginza on a rainy afternoon ("brightly-colored / kites").

Brautigan's poetry notebook became an emotional diary of his first exposure to Japan. He wrote of small details, off-kilter and obliquely observed, recording drunken observations of the nightlife and his difficulties with the language. His more bizarre misadventures often went unobserved in his poems. One such incident involved an excursion Richard took with a couple friends to the nearby port city of Yokohama, a half-hour's train ride from central Tokyo.

Brautigan traveled to Yokohama to visit the "floating world," where he sought out The Nunnery, a notorious whorehouse he'd heard about in Tokyo. All the prostitutes here dressed as nuns, adding an element of mysterious blasphemy. When the girls came downstairs, charms hidden beneath chaste black habits, the "nuns" guided their clients first to a steaming bath, next to a massage table; serene sisters of pleasure ushering the devoted supplicants on to private cells in the cloister.

Along with discovering exotic brothels, "Richard had this thing about finding out that the liquor was cheaper if you bought a bottle," Curt Gentry recalled. The customer purchased a full bottle, and the bartender wrote his name on the label, pouring him drinks until the booze was gone. If not, he was free to come back another time and claim what remained. One night, Gentry and Brautigan bought four bottles, each in a different bar. The bartenders wrote their names on the labels in flowing Japanese ideographs, which neither Richard nor Curt could read. All of their booze went unfinished, and neither could remember the locations of any of the bars.

The poetry Brautigan wrote during this period described aching loneliness. His poem "The 12,000,000" started with the lines, "I'm depressed, / haunted by melancholy" and concluding "I know I'm not alone. / Others must feel the way / I do." Two days later, a new poem, "A Study in Roads," began, "All the possibilities of life, / all roads led here." Richard listed all places he had lived or visited in his life and concluded: "Having a drink by myself / in a bar in Tokyo before /

lunch, / wishing there was someone to talk / to." Brautigan often spent the night alone in his hotel room listening to the whisper of rain against his thirtieth-floor window. "I love the rain [. . .] / I'm slightly drunk: / people walking by in the street, / a bicycle."

A tropical depression spawned ten days earlier in the Pacific east of the Philippines grew to typhoon strength and hit Luzon with winds exceeding 115 miles per hour. For the next week, Typhoon Olga drifted across the island like a psychopath on a rampage, leaving two hundred people dead, thousands homeless, and most of the sets for *Apocalypse Now* destroyed. Jack Thibeau had already shot his brief scene ("soldier in trench") before the typhoon shut the production down at the end of May. When Tony Dingman told Jack that Richard Brautigan might be in Tokyo, Thibeau got a three-day government pass allowing him to travel to Japan without a visa and caught a flight from Manila as soon as the airlines resumed operation.

Thibeau had been drinking hard for days and continued on the plane. Drunk when he arrived in Tokyo early in the morning, Jack knew only that Richard might be staying at the Keio Plaza. Thibeau caught a cab around four AM. The ride from Haneda to Shinjuku took a long time, and Jack didn't reach the hotel until nearly six. He wandered into the restaurant, where numbers of Japanese businessmen were having breakfast. They looked on in disbelief as Thibeau knocked back bottle after huge bottle of Asahi beer. "Just to build up the courage to find out if in fact Richard was in the hotel."

Fortified with Asahi, Thibeau collected his bags and made his way into the lobby. Picking up one of the house phones, he asked to be connected with Richard Brautigan's room. After several rings, Brautigan answered.

"Richard, this is Jack Thibeau."

"Where are you?"

"I'm in the lobby."

"Come right up!" Brautigan roared.

Thibeau arrived at room 3003, and the two old friends stared in disbelief. "We were both two hallucinations looking at each other," Jack said. Richard had been up all night, drinking, his table littered with bottles. They drank and talked for another couple hours before Brautigan phoned the hotel manager and got Thibeau a room right down the hall. "We both felt that we saved each other's lives at that time," Jack recalled.

The next three days were a perpetual party for Brautigan and Thibeau. Richard "was very free in Tokyo," Jack recalled. "He was like a child bounding around in some marvelous newly designed playground. He loved it there. He just thought that Tokyo was the erotic capital of the planet Earth." Thibeau felt his old friend "was in some kind of medieval frame of mind." Richard delighted to know Shinjuku, the area where he lived, was a red-light district, "the floating world." He told Jack there were illicit love affairs going on in every room in every hotel in the city. "I'm staying in the foremost love hotel in Tokyo," he boasted.

Brautigan and Thibeau partied nightly in the bars of Shinjuku and Roppongi. Jack noticed Richard was having difficulties with the language. "He had about two phrases in Japanese that he knew," Thibeau said. One was "*dozo*," which meant "please." The other, "*sumimasen*," meaning "I'm sorry" or "excuse me." These had to work for all forms of communication with non-English speakers. "And the more he got drunk, the more they got blurred together," Jack remembered. "It was just a series of "*sumimasen . . . dozo . . . sumimasen . . . dozo*. He had no ability whatsoever in the language." From Thibeau's point of view, Brautigan "just walked around like some kind of orphan. 'Can I have a beer and that girl over there?' *Sumimasen*."

Observing this behavior, Jack asked Richard what he planned to do about it.

"I'm thinking of writing a book," Brautigan replied. "I'm going to call it, 'How to Learn Japanese . . . In One Million Years.'"

Richard brought Jack to The Cradle and introduced him to his friend Takako. One "crazy" night, Brautigan invited Thibeau out to dinner. The plan was for Jack to meet him at The Cradle, where Takako would join them for the evening. Somehow, they all got their wires crossed, and Takako had gone on to the restaurant ahead of them. After several confused telephone calls, a beautiful "young" woman sitting at the bar took charge of the situation. Thibeau remembered that she wore what he called a sloped English hat. The woman phoned Takako at the restaurant, telling her she would bring the lost boys safely to their dinner date.

They all hopped in a cab. It was an extremely foggy night in Tokyo, and the driver got lost. Frustrated, the trio left the taxi and found a public phone. Their benefactress called the restaurant once again. The proprietor said he would send some of his waitresses out to find them. By this time, Brautigan had "taken a fascination" with the mysterious woman in the sloping hat. As the three walked along, the waitresses came running through the swirling fog.

The stranger in the English hat, so helpful and friendly, suddenly ran off in the opposite direction. Richard chased after her, but she disappeared into the fog. Brautigan and Thibeau continued to the restaurant and dined with Takako Shiina. Later, all three returned to The Cradle for a nightcap. About four in the morning, when Jack was fast asleep in his hotel room, the phone rang. It was Richard. "That woman we were with tonight is sixty-five years old," he said. "Good night, Jack."

One afternoon during his brief stay, Jack went with Richard to a pornographic movie theater, "this boring soft-core porno" Brautigan enjoyed. Richard bought the tickets and kept the stubs, mentioning they were "for the IRS." Once inside, Brautigan sat Thibeau down. "I'll be back to get you in an hour," he said, returning as promised. "I knew better than to ask Richard where he had been," Jack said, "because that would have ruined it. You never ask questions like that."

Another drizzling afternoon, when Richard and Jack stepped from the Keio Plaza to catch a cab, Brautigan took hold of Thibeau's arm and hauled him out beyond the protective entrance canopy into the falling rain. "You know," Richard told his friend, "you think you know everything." He pointed up into the storm-tossed sky. "Those hawks know everything." Riding a thermal, spiraling through the dark clouds, the twin silhouettes of gliding raptors turned above them.

After Thibeau departed, Brautigan again recruited Curt Gentry for his nighttime barroom forays. Literary conversation occupied a good deal of the time that the two writers spent together. Curt Gentry had been friends with Yukio Mishima, the esteemed Japanese author, who had on three occasions been a candidate for the Nobel Prize and whose spectacular ritual death by seppuku six years earlier made headlines around the world. "Richard was fascinated with him," Gentry recalled, "fascinated by his suicide."

Celebrated as a novelist, playwright, poet, short story writer, and essayist, Mishima created his own private right-wing army, the Tatenokai (Shield Society), and dedicated it to renewed nationalism and veneration of the emperor. On November 25, 1970, armed only with swords and daggers in the samurai tradition and dressed in uniforms Mishima designed himself, the famous author and four members of the Shield Society gained entrance to the office of the commandant at the Ichigaya Military Base, the Tokyo headquarters of the Eastern Command of the Jietai (Japan's Self-Defense Forces), barricading the door and tying General Mashita to his chair. Mishima went out onto the balcony and harangued the one thousand soldiers ranked below to rise up and overthrow the existing government. The troops drowned out his speech with jeering mockery. Mishima returned to the commandant's office and committed ritual hara-kiri. After the author sliced open his abdomen with a dagger, his second decapitated him with a sword. A startling photograph of Mishima's severed head on the commandant's Persian carpet appeared in *Life* magazine, fascinating Richard Brautigan.

Brautigan "really pushed" Gentry to use his influence to arrange an introduction to Yoko Sugiyama, Mishima's widow, who lived under the protection of the Shield Society. "I went to some trouble to try to set up a meeting," Curt recalled, "and I got her to agree to see him. Richard never followed up. And I'd keep reminding him of it, and he said he was too busy or he would always make excuses." Gentry thought Brautigan was unwilling to "go out of his way to get to know the Japanese." To Curt, Richard remained the eternal observer. "He wanted to know Mishima from a distance and not try and get closer to him."

Richard did meet a number of distinguished living Japanese writers during his first stay in Tokyo, mainly through his nightly visits to The Cradle. Shiro Hasegawa (described by Kazuko Fujimoto Goodman as "a writer of great integrity"), best known for his collection of short stories, *Tales of Siberia*, ran into Brautigan at Takako's basement bar, "slumped against the wall" after a hard night's drinking. Hasegawa wrote a poem for him, "Dickinson's Russian," a comic riff on Richard's short story "Homage to the San Francisco YMCA," about a man who replaced his plumbing with poetry. Brautigan used this poem, in its original form and in a translation by Fujimoto, at the beginning of his poetry collection *June 30th, June 30th*.

The music critic and writer Tadasu Tagawa also met Richard at The Cradle. At the end of the first week in June, they traveled by car to Osaka, in the Kansai region at the mouth of the Yodo River on Osaka Bay. Created by the warlord Hideyoshi Toyotomi in the sixteenth century as a commercial center separate from the imperial powers of Kyoto, Osaka gave rise to a merchant class at first despised by the nobility. The Toyotomi clan built the great Osaka Castle between 1583 and 1586.

That evening, Richard and Tadusu attended a performance of the Black Tent Theater Group in Gifu, a suburb of Osaka, on the bank of the Nagara River, where *ukai* (cormorant fishing) had enjoyed an unbroken thirteen-hundred-year history. The birds are controlled, several at a time, by handlers manipulating long leashes that prevent them from swallowing the salmonid *aju* they caught. Brautigan watched the fishermen on their boats in the river, blazing fire-baskets dangling over the bows. He saw fish rising and thought of the Yellowstone and the trout awaiting him when he returned to Montana in the summer.

Later that night, something grotesque and unpleasant occurred between Richard and Tadusu. The next day, they returned to Tokyo together on the bullet train from Nagoya, Japan's fourth-largest city. Speeding through the Japanese landscape at 120 miles per hour, Brautigan, still drunk from the night before, ranted and raved about the events of the previous evening. He blamed all the ills in the world on his new friend, telling Tadusu to consider him dead. Richard took Tadusu's hand, saying, "My flesh is cold to you. Dead."

Tagawa's eyes filled with sadness. Brautigan forbade him to read one of his books again, knowing how much he loved them. By the time the train reached Tokyo Station, Richard's unwarranted anger had subsided. He took Tadusu's hand again, saying, "I'm alive for you. The warmth has returned to my flesh." Back in his room at the Keio Plaza that night, Brautigan phoned Tagawa. "Are you fine?" Tadusu said.

"Yes, I am fine," Richard replied.

The next day, Brautigan awoke at 4:45 am, ate an early breakfast, and recorded the entire episode in a long poem, "Lazarus on the Bullet Train." First light revealed another cloudy morning in Tokyo. A little before eight, he wrote a brief letter to Don Carpenter, addressing the envelope first, one of his old habits. Richard predicted he would have a long day and stay up all night. "I love Tokyo at night."

Kazuko Fujimoto had had a serious abdominal operation six days before. On the evening of the ninth, Brautigan went to the Toho School of Medicine Hospital to see his recuperating translator. David Goodman accompanied him. "I don't think he would have been able to get to the hospital on his own," Fujimoto speculated. Richard watched Kazuko eat her dinner. This made him feel sad. She seemed so tired. Fujimoto remembered Brautigan as being very quiet and sweet. "I don't think he said any jokes," she recalled. "Usually he said some jokes and he is the one who is the most amused." Richard's discomfort inspired his poem "Visiting a Friend at the Hospital."

Curt Gentry had been wrong about Brautigan's willingness to engage with prominent Japanese intellectuals and misjudged his friend's interest in traveling beyond the municipal boundaries of Tokyo. Richard, for his part, never brought Curt to The Cradle, his newfound hangout where he met local poets and writers. Brautigan fell back on his long-standing habit of compartmentalizing his friends. The Cradle was private territory he would not share with Gentry. Let his old friend think the Café Cardinale remained his favored Tokyo stomping ground. Curt and Gail left Japan in late May. Early in June, they traveled to Hawaii. On the thirteenth, Gentry celebrated his forty-fifth birthday by marrying his research assistant at the top of Mount Tantalus, overlooking the Punchbowl Crater, Diamond Head, and downtown Honolulu.

Brautigan spent more and more time downstairs in The Cradle. His friendship deepened with the proprietress, Takako Shiina. One night after hearing her sing, Brautigan wrote a poem for Takako. They drank through the night together, sharing conversation and intimate secrets, fellow travelers on what they called the "Calle de Eternidad," an echo of Brautigan's visit to Ixtlan, Mexico, sixteen years before. In the wee hours, Richard and Takako decided that they were brother and sister on a spiritual plane. Brautigan didn't leave The Cradle until just before sunrise. In a cab on his way home to the Keio Plaza, he jotted down "Day for Night," his final poem of the day: "the streets are blankets, / the dawn is my bed. / The cab rests my head. / I'm on my way to dreams."

For two days in the second week of June, Richard wandered about Tokyo with a broken clock belonging to Takako Shiina, trying to find its exact replacement. Brautigan had destroyed the clock during a moment of drunken excess. The Cradle was decorated with many beautiful antiques, and the clock had been part of Takako's collection. "He had to go all over to find one just exactly like it," Don Carpenter said, remembering the story Richard told him, "and bring it to Shiina." Two poems resulted from his quixotic clock quest, both dedicated to Takako. By mid-June, Brautigan had completed nearly forty poems.

One drunken incident at The Cradle never became a poem. On this night, a young Japanese musician played the guitar Takako provided for her musically inclined customers. Richard stood at the bar, getting "drunker and drunker." Reaching over, he took the guitar. Strumming in his plink/plunk fashion, Brautigan sang an off-key version of "Oh, Shenandoah" over and over. Takako thought it was the only song he knew. When the Japanese musician tried to take back the guitar, Richard flushed with drunken anger and hurled the instrument into the fireplace, reducing it to kindling. Takako was furious. She told Brautigan he could never come back into The Cradle until he bought her a new guitar, "exactly like the old one."

Richard pulled out his wallet and asked, "How much do you want?"

Brautigan told a friend he broke the guitar because the unnamed Japanese troubadour played songs with "anti-American sentiments." He had to hunt all over the city to find a replacement guitar that matched the one he destroyed, a repetition of his previous clock search. His nightly forays to The Cradle became an integral part of his life in Tokyo. No poem recorded the moment, but Richard found the exact instrument and was soon back at his favorite spot at the bar.

During the early morning hours of June 12, Brautigan stayed at The Cradle well past closing time. The day before, he wrote six poems. He felt so proud of this accomplishment that the sixth was a commemoration of the previous five. It was a night to celebrate. Richard drank and talked, hanging out with Takako as the hours slipped away. Their conversation touched on Japanese history. The emperor Meiji began his rule in 1867 at the age of fifteen and brought Japan into the modern world, taking it from a medieval nation where samurai fought with swords to a world power that, by the time of Meiji's death in 1912, had defeated both China and Russia in major wars. Japan went from feudal armored knights to battleships and locomotives in a single generation.

The talk got around to the Meiji Jingu, the shrine devoted to the deified souls of the emperor and his consort, Empress Shoken. Built in 1920, and situated in a 178-acre park in Shibuya-ku in central Tokyo, the Meiji Jingu served as both a Shinto spiritual center and a recreation and sports area. When she learned that Richard had never been to the shrine, Takako proposed a late night reconnaissance. Fueled by drink, Brautigan agreed.

An hour before dawn, Richard and Takako climbed over a stone wall, sneaking into the gardens of the Meiji shrine. They were both drunk, falling down "like comedians" as they staggered through the cultivated forest. They wandered under a forty-foot wooden main gate (*torii*), the tallest in Japan, built from ancient *hinoki* tree trunks in the shape of a rooster's perch. Legend said a rooster's crow woke the sun goddess and first brought light to the world.

At dawn, Richard and Takako came to a small meadow, grateful they had not been spotted by the police. They lay down together fully clothed on a bed of sweet green grass. Brautigan cupped his hand over Shiina's breast and kissed her. She kissed him back. "That's all the love we made," he wrote in a poem ("Meiji Comedians"). As day broke, fearful of getting caught, they left the shrine garden and went their separate ways.

When Richard woke up alone that afternoon in the Keio Plaza, the first thing he saw were his mud-covered shoes. This last trace of his amorous exploration of the Meiji Jingu made him feel "very good." He did not sleep with Takako, but felt OK about it. Seeing his shoes pleased him so much he wrote another poem, "Meiji Shoes Size 12." Brautigan wrote two more poems that day, both tinged with doubt and sadness. The next day, Richard Brautigan wrote another poem in his notebook. "Tokyo / June 13, 1976," mourned his departure from Japan in sixteen days. No mention of Curt Gentry and Gail Stevens's marriage on the same day, Curt's birthday, on Oahu. Curt had written Brautigan about his Hawaiian trip and impending nuptials, but Richard had other things on his mind.

One morning, Brautigan sat in the cafeteria at the Keio Plaza having his breakfast when he saw the world heavyweight boxing champion, Muhammad Ali, stride like a god into the room. Less than a year after the "Thrilla in Manila," Ali came to Tokyo for an exhibition match with Antonio Inoki, the top wrestling star in Japan. The champ was also staying at the Keio Plaza. For the next week, Richard saw him every day, "walking quietly around the hotel in the company of various people."

Whenever Brautigan switched on the television in his room, he'd see Ali, hyping the upcoming bout "on just about every program." Always an astute observer of popular culture, Richard paid special attention to the champ's appearances. "The most interesting thing about the whole affair was that there were two Mohamid [*sic*] Alis," he wrote later in a notebook. "There was an extravagant one who was clowning and jumping around on television and there was a quiet sincere almost shy one that I saw every day in the hotel."

During his remaining two weeks in Japan, Brautigan's poetry, written daily in his notebook, recorded his life like a diary. "The Red Chair" reported an erotic film Richard went to see one evening. In the poem, Brautigan used the noun "voyeur" as a verb, ("feeling, voyeuring every detail of their passion"). This species of neologism has become commonplace. The newspeak of television, politics, and the military altered our language, transforming *transition, scope, parent, text,* and *leverage* into verbs. Back in the 1970s, it was an almost unknown practice. Brautigan, always a stickler in his careful use of language, deliberately chose "voyeuring," knowing the word would make his reader feel uncomfortable, wanting just that reaction to the perverse decadence of the soft-core porn he had seen.

During Brautigan's last week in Japan, Tony Dingman traveled up from the Philippines and hung out with his old pal in Tokyo. Typhoon Olga halted the production of *Apocalypse Now* for four weeks. During the hiatus, Dingman was out of a job. Detouring to Japan on his way back to the States seemed like fun. Richard brought Tony to The Cradle twice, the second time on Dingman's last night in the city. They had a wild time together. Brautigan wrote almost no poetry during his friend's visit.

Awake at five on the morning of June 25, unable to go back to sleep, Brautigan went downstairs to the Keio Plaza cafeteria for an early breakfast. As he sipped his first cup of coffee, Richard was surprised to see Muhammad Ali come into the room. "There were very few people in the cafeteria at that hour," he observed, "but they were also startled to see Mohamid [*sic*] Ali there because everybody in Japan knew he was going to fight that morning. Mohamed [*sic*] Ali acted as if it were any other morning, anywhere at any time."

An attractive young Japanese woman sat at the counter. Without saying a word, Ali approached her and began massaging her neck. Taken by surprise, she turned and stared at him. The champ smiled down at her, his big powerful hands kneading her shoulders and neck. No words were exchanged. Ali massaged her neck for another ten seconds or so and a smile spread across her pretty face. "Then, he stopped and continued to his table. The Japanese girl did not turn and watch him."

The big fight was broadcast on national TV and shown on 150 closed-circuit locations in the United States. Ali, described as out of shape for his victorious match in April with a "tough young brawler" named Jimmy Young, threw fewer than a dozen punches in his fifteen-round bout with Inoki, who had recently defeated Olympic Judo Gold Medalist Willem Ruska. The rules for their fight had been radically changed two days before the match. Inoki could kick at Ali only if one of his knees remained on the ground. Still, the Japanese wrestler and martial artist hammered away at Ali's legs with his feet, lying on his back for almost the entire fight, which ended in a draw. Muhammad Ali left the ring with damaged, bleeding legs (he later suffered blood clots), pocketing more than $6 million for his pains.

As Brautigan's time in Tokyo drew to a close, he reacted emotionally with a final burst of new poetry. He wrote four poems on June 28, three of them about different aspects of love. Richard spent his last full night in Tokyo at The Cradle. He got "very drunk" and wrote an odd poem, "Stone (real." It compared his inebriated condition to Bee Cave, Texas. All the while, Takako Shiina sat silently watching him. Richard left Japan on June 30, flying out of Haneda at nine thirty at night. Traveling east into the sunrise, he jotted a final poem in his notebook. "Land of the Rising Sun" noted that as he crossed the international date line high above the Pacific it became the thirtieth of June all over again.

Tony Dingman left Tokyo two days earlier. He met Brautigan at the airport and drove him into San Francisco to Curt Gentry's house. Richard stayed with Curt and Gail for a couple days before heading up to Montana for the summer. During his visit, Brautigan read the Gentrys the entire manuscript of the poetry he'd written in Japan. He did so without a stop. Once finished, he confessed he had no title for the book. With the final poem fresh in her mind, Gail Gentry suggested he call it "June 30th, June 30th." "There's no other title that fits," she said.

Back in Montana, Brautigan focused on revising his poetry manuscript. He made almost no changes, adding only a few words to a couple poems near the end of the sequence while also working on the galleys for *Sombrero Fallout*. Writing an introduction for *June 30th, June 30th* occupied most of Richard's time in July. The subject was his uncle Edward, killed during WWII in Sitka, Alaska. Brautigan wrote how this caused him to hate the Japanese people when he was a child during the war.

The introduction chronicled Richard's reading Bashō and Issa. After moving to San Francisco, Brautigan learned to love Japanese food and saw hundreds of Japanese movies. He "slowly picked up Buddhism through osmosis" by hanging out with poet friends like Gary Snyder and Philip Whalen. Richard admitted the poetry in his book was "different from other poems that I have written." Each bore a date. He acknowledged the quality of the work to be uneven but "printed them all anyway because they are a diary expressing my feelings and emotions in Japan and the quality of life is often uneven." Brautigan's stay in Tokyo brought the Second World War to an emotional conclusion. He finished his introduction in his Pine Creek studio in early August. His last sentence came straight from his heart: "May the dead rest eternally in peace, waiting for our arrival."

Brautigan returned to San Francisco in mid-August, wanting some urban pleasure after mailing the completed manuscript of *June 30th, June 30th* off to his agent. John Hartnett, who took dictation and typed Helen Brann's letters, wrote a personal note, saying he had never "read a more moving or evocative group of poems." The poetry reinforced itself, and by the end of the book,

Hartnett felt that "it was all—from the introduction to the last poem—one poem." Hartnett concluded: "It's an impressive, powerful, lovely work."

Richard sent a copy of the manuscript to Jim Harrison, who shared John Hartnett's enthusiasm. "What can I say?" Harrison wrote Brautigan. "It is your work that has touched me the most deeply. [. . .] It is not a succession of lyrics but finally ONE BOOK." Jim concluded his letter with the highest praise. "I love the book because it is a true song, owning no auspices other than its own; owning the purity we think we aim at on this bloody journey."

During the second half of August, Richard received a wedding invitation from Ron Loewinsohn and Kitty Hughes. They were getting married on the first of September at the Sebastopol home of London-born Canadian poet David Bromige and his companion, writer Sherril Jaffe. Brautigan declined, saying he had to fly back to Montana the day before the ceremony. Loewinsohn wrote Brautigan a sarcastic note, mentioning how many people at the reception had asked about him, wondering if he was "going to show up." Ron said he thought they all believed him when he explained his old friend's need to return immediately to Pine Creek. Loewinsohn ended by saying "how touched & pleased Kitty & I were with the telegram of congratulations that your driver sent us on our wedding day."

Brautigan's stay in Montana was brief. With no driver in residence, life at Pine Creek felt fairly constrained, and it wasn't long before he packed the place up for winter and returned to San Francisco. By the start of October, Richard was living again on Telegraph Hill. Anxious to be off to Japan, Brautigan lingered in the city, waiting for word from his agent regarding the ongoing contract negotiations for *Dreaming of Babylon* and *June 30th, June 30th*. His various behavioral excesses during this period (pushing Nic Roeg down the stairs, tearing up $20 bills in Helen Brann's Stanford Court suite, moving in with Curt Gentry and his new wife under false pretenses) did not prevent Richard from keeping his nose to the grindstone. He stayed in constant contact with his agent, offering his input on every aspect of her deal-making.

Late in October, Takako Shiina flew to America. She was on her way to visit her young lover, Ryu Murakami, a twenty-four-year-old Japanese writer who published his first short novel, *Almost Transparent Blue*, earlier that year. *Blue*, written while Murakami was still a student, dealt with youthful promiscuity and drug use, and although some critics denounced the book as "decadent," it went on to sell over a million copies and win both the newcomer's prize for literature and the Akutagawa Prize (a pocket watch and 1 million yen) in 1976. Murakami was staying in Manhattan at the Waldorf-Astoria, covering the New York City Marathon, then in its sixth year, for a leading Japanese periodical.

Takako stopped off in Los Angeles, en route to New York. Brautigan was there at the airport to meet her plane, accompanied by Don Carpenter and Melissa Mathison. (Mathison had worked as an assistant on both *Apocalypse Now* and *The Godfather II*, as well as serving as Francis and Eleanor Coppola's babysitter. She later wrote the screenplays for *The Black Stallion* and *E.T.: The Extra-Terrestrial*.) They all went to dinner at Lucy's El Adobe Café, a small, dark Mexican restaurant located on Melrose Avenue directly across the street from Paramount Studios. Much beloved by actors and musicians, Lucy's was the place where Linda Ronstadt was introduced to California governor Jerry Brown, launching their much-publicized romance. Richard ordered "a big pitcher of Margaritas" to wash down the typical campesino fare.

Afterward, Brautigan escorted Takako to their separate rooms at the secluded Sunset Marquis Hotel in West Hollywood. Situated on a tree-lined cul-de-sac a half block south of Sunset Boulevard, the Marquis was another trendy celebrity hangout, redolent of privilege, the low buildings clustered around a central pool. The next day, after sleeping off her jet lag, Takako felt ready for a more vibrant night on the town. She and Richard joined Harry Dean Stanton for dinner at The Palm on Santa Monica Boulevard. The pricy steakhouse was the West Hollywood branch of the New York restaurant much beloved by Brautigan.

After eating, the trio ventured further west along Santa Monica to the Troubadour, where Waylon Jennings performed that night. Founded in 1957 by Doug Weston (whose proprietary credit was emblazoned on the sign above the entrance), the Troub became a hotbed of emerging talent from its very start. Lenny Bruce was busted there for obscenity the year the club opened. The Byrds, Buffalo Springfield, Joni Mitchell, the Pointer Sisters, Neil Young, and Elton John (in the United States) all had their debuts at the Troubadour. Cheech & Chong and Tom Waits were discovered during the Troub's famed Monday night open mic amateur "hootenannies." Waylon Jennings had played at the Troubadour several times previously, and the large crowd milling on the sidewalk outside the box office testified to his recent full-blown stardom as an "outlaw" country singer. The place was sold out, but Harry Dean knew the management and snuck his friends around to the back door. They went in through the office and quickly found good seats out front for the show.

When the music ended, Richard, Takako, and Harry Dean walked two doors down the block to Dan Tana's, an unpretentious Italian restaurant that, in the twelve years since its opening, had become a popular hangout for actors, studio execs, professional athletes, and mob wise guys. With red-checkered tablecloths, roomy booths, and chianti bottles hanging from the ceiling beams where strands of Christmas lights glowed year-round, Tana's looked more like a New York or Chicago joint than a Hollywood in-spot. Not having room for another big steak, Brautigan and his pals enjoyed a couple of copious cocktails before heading back to the Sunset Marquis, where they sat drinking around the pool until dawn. Takako stayed in L.A. for only two days before flying on to New York. Richard had arranged for a room at the Gotham Hotel and bought theater tickets for her and Ryu Murakami to see *A Chorus Line* and *Equus*.

Takako Shiina stopped off in San Francisco on her way back to Japan. Brautigan met her at the airport, and they traveled by taxi to his apartment on Union Street, where he made her comfortable in his office, converted into a guest room for the occasion. During her short stay, Richard brought Takako over to Bruce Conner's house. The artist presented her with signed copies of his books. Brautigan also arranged for a party in Shiina's honor at the Page Street law offices of Richard Hodge. She knew almost no one among the ten or so guests, but Don Carpenter provided a familiar face.

Before Takako left for Tokyo, Richard took her to Bolinas. Margot and John Doss were heading to their house downtown and provided a convenient ride. Brautigan's place had the cold look of unoccupied emptiness. Richard wasted no time before escorting Takako up the road to Bob and Bobbie Creeley's old farmhouse. The Creeleys were congenial and articulate hosts. Takako recalled great bunches of drying marijuana hanging from the rafters. When the first joints were rolled, Richard declined, but insisted that his friend from Japan, who didn't smoke, should give it a try. Takako took the first hit of pot in her life that night. It made her sleepy. When they all drove downtown to eat at a local restaurant, she dozed off in the car and missed out on dinner.

A discotheque called Dance Your Ass Off became one of Richard's favorite playgrounds in San Francisco. Located near the intersection of Taylor and Columbus, the place started up in the midseventies, featuring a logo of a girl dancing, a surprised expression on her face as she looked down to see her butt splitting off from her body. Don Carpenter described it as "a pickup joint. You'd go there to dance and meet chicks." He, Brautigan, and Curt Gentry started showing up at Dance Your Ass Off not long after the disco opened for business.

Richard Brautigan was not a dancer. His fame trumped fancy footwork when it came to picking up chicks. Carpenter recalled that Richard liked Dance Your Ass Off because "the guy who ran the place gave [him] a lot of special privileges." Every time he came in, the manager called Herb Caen. Brautigan got his own designated table with drinks, "many of them free," doubles coming on the double. Around this time, Don remembered, Richard first mentioned his attraction to "Oriental women."

Drunk on a Wednesday night, Richard sat at the Dance Your Ass Off bar, "humped over" his glass of bourbon when Jude Acers, the disco's resident chess player, whose name was inscribed on the club wall, approached, escorting a beautiful young woman wearing a clinging low-cut black dress. Acers, small, pale, brilliant, pockmarked, introduced Richard to Marcia Clay, a twenty-three-year-old painter, who had recently moved back to San Francisco after a peripatetic life in France and Japan. For about six months, Clay lived in an apartment right behind Dance Your Ass Off. The loud soul music kept her awake every night until three. Fed up one evening, she went to the club, cut to the head of the line, and complained to the bouncer.

"Come on in, lady," the big guy said, and Marcia Clay found herself a regular customer. The club was the hangout of writers and hip blacks. Clay showed up often and danced all night long. "It was very sexy," she recalled. Dr. Che, the friendly two-hundred-pound black bouncer, who looked like a classic genie out of a bottle, all solid muscle with a shaved head and gold earring ("a very sweet guy actually"), made sure she got safely home every night. During the summertime, Dr. Che worked as a rattlesnake killer on Mount St. Helena in Robert Louis Stevenson State Park. He and Jude Acers were among the "funny entourage" Marcia got to know at Dance Your Ass Off. The "crazy," celebrity-fancying "chess genius" liked bringing her glasses of 7UP.

This Wednesday night, Acers didn't offer Clay a soft drink. "I want to do you the biggest favor that anybody has ever done for you," he said.

"What's that, Jude?" Marcia asked.

"I'm going to introduce you to Richard Brautigan."

"Oh yeah, okay, sure, fine," she said. Secretly, the proposition excited her. She'd never been much of a reader as a kid but Brautigan was the first writer, other than J. D. Salinger, whose books Clay actually picked up and read in high school. At fourteen, a flower child who didn't do drugs, she had been very impressed with Brautigan's book *The Pill versus the Springhill Mine Disaster*. Along with several of the poems it contained, it had been dedicated to a woman also named Marcia. "That struck me as being significant," she recalled.

"Is that Richard Brautigan?" Marcia Clay thought nine years later, staring at the tall drunken man slumped over his whiskey. Marcia didn't drink. She liked to dance. "Well, what are you sitting there for?" she said, her inner flower child challenging the famous writer. "Why don't you come dance with me?"

Richard hated to dance. Marcia lured him off his stool and dragged him out onto the disco floor. "What is this?" he mumbled, never at his best in situations over which he had no control. In spite of his awkward, embarrassed movements, she danced with him under the strobe lights, talking all the while, saying "whatever came to mind," to keep his self-consciousness from getting the upper hand. Richard looked at his vivacious young partner "with this already obsessive stare." Clay was fascinated with Brautigan.

Marcia kept throwing questions at Richard as they danced. Brautigan had a puzzled look on his face. "You're very intelligent," he said at last.

"Yeah, well what else is new?" Clay thought.

Between dances, their heated conversation continued almost without a stop. Once again, intelligence in a woman provided a powerful aphrodisiac. Encountering someone as gorgeous and smart as Marcia Clay hit Richard like a double whammy. Whiskey consumption caused him to grow repetitive. On three separate occasions during the evening he told Clay, "What concerns me the most is that we live and die here."

They became friends. Clay went to visit Brautigan at his Union Street apartment the very next conversation. Soon, she started seeing him every night. They were never physically lovers. She slept with him "many, many nights, but we never had sex." Clay meant she'd never had intercourse with Brautigan, although they made out like bandits. One time it got so close, they had an absurd argument at three in the morning over whether it had actually happened. "We had a curious relationship," Clay recalled. "I was never attracted to him to be his girlfriend, but he was really infatuated with me. I was a female counterpart that was not a lover but was a lover."

The real glue holding their semiplatonic relationship together was always enlightened, lively talk. From the start, Brautigan remained as fascinated with Marcia Clay's mind as with her obvious physical attributes. The first night she visited his apartment, Marcia regaled Richard with tales of her exotic life. It sounded even more interesting because of its brevity. Clay was born in Kansas City, Missouri. Her mother, Anita Clay Kornfeld, was a Southern writer who published an autobiographical novel, *In a Bluebird's Eye*. Their big house in K.C. hosted frequent parties packed with writers, artists, and jazz musicians. Miles Davis and J. J. Johnson "and all kinds of wonderful black musicians used to come and perform at the house." Miles was the first man ten-year-old Marcia ever saw naked. He'd spent the night and wandered out into the hall past the room where Clay and her sister played an early Saturday morning game of Monopoly. "Just this shadow of a man," she recalled.

Marcia began painting at thirteen, first exhibiting in major galleries four years later. She dropped out of high school and moved to Paris. For a time, Clay "hopscotched" between France and the United States. Fluent in French, Marcia became involved with a Frenchman, "off and on," for three years. To maintain her independence, she'd head for Japan. Clay would sell a painting to buy a ticket to Tokyo, where she lived "much like a sponge" off the good graces of her affluent friends. "I was not an ordinary person," she said, "I was just odd."

Brautigan spent time with Marcia Clay almost every day before he left for Japan. They lived only a few blocks apart in North Beach. "We just started having a wonderful time," Clay remembered. Marcia had never been a drinker. After she started keeping company with Richard, she was drunk every night. One evening, Marcia became so inebriated she had difficulty navigating the steep hillside streets down to Enrico's from Brautigan's place at the intersection of Union and Montgomery. Richard hauled her up onto his shoulders and carried her piggyback, "*clump, clump, clump*" down the precipitous Kearny Street stairs. "I mean, I could have been dead," Marcia recalled. "It was crazy, and I loved that kind of craziness."

Clay also loved Brautigan's extravagance, recalling how they often took a cab from North Beach "all the way over" to Japantown to eat dinner in a restaurant he liked. He always took her into a Japanese bookstore and bought "five or six books at a time."

"I need somebody to talk about Japanese literature with," Brautigan told her, "and so you have to read this so I can talk to you about it."

"I saw him like some kind of father figure," Marcia said years later, "because he was older and he loved me, protected me. He was also kind of strict. I just sort of felt like a little girl." Richard treated Marcia like she was special. He bought her presents and planned special things for them to do. For some reason, she didn't see herself yet as a grown woman. "I was very comfortable feeling like somebody's little girl," Clay said. "And he liked me being a little girl."

Marcia Clay especially appreciated Brautigan's acute sensitivity. In spite of her extraordinary beauty, Clay possessed an underlying shyness, the result of having been born with cerebral palsy. Her left arm remained a little shorter than her right. "It changed my psychology somehow," Marcia admitted. Her slight handicap made her "an overachiever." Richard recognized "that fighting position of wanting to strive to get something."

Brautigan noticed how Clay attempted to deflect attention from her cramped left hand by wearing her watch and all her rings on her right hand. One day, with the formal ceremony Richard so often adopted, he took both of Marcia's hands in his and said very sincerely, "This right hand is very beautiful; it doesn't need any jewelry. Put your jewelry on your other hand; it needs all the help it can get."

Most of Clay's women friends couldn't put up with Brautigan. "Why do you want to waste your time with a guy like that who is always drunk?" they told her. Marcia felt otherwise. "For me, it fit," she said. "It fit. Some kind of intellectual, personal thing." She didn't view Richard as just a drunk. Clay saw him as "so alive, so intense, so strange, so bright, and such a deviant."

All these attributes came into play one night while having dinner at Vanessi's. Marcia got an obstinate bit of food stuck in her teeth. She complained about it, and Brautigan jumped to his feet, rushing out of the restaurant. When he returned, he handed her a brand-new toothbrush. It felt like magic, being caught up in his imagination. "If I went somewhere with Richard," Clay said, "I was with Richard Brautigan. It didn't matter about the rest of the world because I was with somebody who was fantastic and the world knew it."

Around this same time, Ron Loewinsohn and Kitty Hughes invited Richard over to dinner at their rented house in the upscale Rockridge District of Oakland. Earlier that day, a friend of theirs, a PhD professor in the Berkeley English Department who had just broken up with her academic boyfriend, called Kitty and said she was feeling lonely. Could they fix her up with someone? As Brautigan was already coming over, Kitty invited her friend. The lady professor had a flamboyant manner and "came on pretty strong." She said she was "feeling cuddly" and began "making rather overt gestures" directed at Richard, who was "turned off by her" and immediately backed away.

Kitty Hughes felt that Brautigan was "looking for a vulnerable spot." When the professor mentioned that she had done her PhD thesis on Samuel Beckett, Richard went on the attack. He insisted Beckett's characters were like "comic book figures," mere caricatures. "He really started letting her have it," Hughes recalled. Brautigan bore down on the startled professor. "How can Beckett be taken seriously as an author?" he demanded, reducing her to tears as he repeated his "caricature" insult over and over.

Kitty thought Richard "totally undermined this enterprise" her friend had worked on for a good part of her life. The professor was crying, "quite upset by this treatment." Brautigan showed no remorse, Hughes observed. "In fact, I think he felt almost good about it. I think he felt he'd fended her off, too." It was the only time Kitty ever remembered seeing Richard, who was "usually good humored about his goading of people," attack someone quite so viciously.

Before leaving the country, Brautigan wanted to complete the preparation of his will. Richard's main concern was that his daughter not dispose of his literary works in the case of his death. Richard Hodge engaged the San Francisco firm of Ferguson, Hoffman, Henn & Mandel to prepare the document. William Mandel sent Hodge two copies of a preliminary draft for his review. Previously, Mandel's firm had advised Brautigan that his estate as "presently constituted" did not have sufficient liquidity to cover any attendant inheritance and estate taxes. Brautigan's taxable estate, including literary rights, cash, and realty holdings, was conservatively estimated to value between $500,000 and $750,000. The combined projected taxes on this amount were calculated at $100,000 to $200,000. Mandel advised Brautigan to buy term life insurance to provide the needed liquidity and suggested putting Brautigan's literary works into a trust. To satisfy Richard's desire not to have them sold piecemeal, he included this idea in the preliminary draft of the will.

Brautigan took off for Japan on February 18, arriving at Haneda on February 20, again losing a day in travel due to the international date line. It was cold and snowing in Tokyo. Richard checked into the Keio Plaza Hotel, taking a suite on the thirty-fifth floor. Late at night, he made a beeline for The Cradle, his friendship with Takako Shiina undiminished after an eight-month hiatus. During the day, he wandered the city with his notebook, often spending the afternoons at a café in Mitsui Plaza he had visited often the previous year.

Brautigan liked it among the skyscrapers, surrounded by "concrete, steel, and glass." An artificial waterfall in the plaza pleased him. A modernistic civic fountain, the waterfall flowed over a tall flight of brick steps. With his eyes closed, the waterfall sounded "just like any waterfall anywhere in the world." Richard went into the café only if there was a table by the window where he could see the waterfall. "If a window seat was not available, I would not go inside."

Not long after arriving in Japan, Brautigan made plans for his daughter to visit over her upcoming spring break, timing the trip to take place during the annual cherry blossom festival. Following the celebration of her seventeenth birthday on March 25, when her mother baked a cake with "Sayonara, Ianthe" written in icing on the frosted top, she took off for Tokyo. Richard got her a room on the twenty-sixth floor of the Keio Plaza. Years later, Ianthe wrote that the nine-story distance separating their quarters "reflected the reality of the relationship."

Knowing his daughter loved to swim and the hotel had no pool, Richard arranged a pass for Ianthe at a neighborhood health spa. The seventeen-year-old found Tokyo empty and dreary in the daytime. With a confirmed night owl father, Ianthe was often alone early in the morning and spent her time either swimming in the health club pool or exploring the enormous Keio Plaza, riding up and down in one of the twenty-five elevators, wandering among its twenty restaurants and nine bars and lounges, peeking into the two wedding halls, hanging out in the bustling lobby.

Ianthe discovered her father was on a "drinking jag." Even so, he gave his daughter the "Brautigan tour" of Tokyo. This included playing pachinko (Richard teased her on their second night together when she won a pair of socks playing pachinko and had to carry them around for the rest of the evening), admiring the realistic plastic food displays in restaurant windows, watching karaoke singers at midnight under a pink canopy of cherry blossoms, touring an area Ianthe thought of as "the Tokyo equivalent of Times Square," where every movie marquee under the neon aurora seemed to advertise Barbra Streisand's film *A Star Is Born*, and dining on never-ending portions of sushi, "pretty much all we ate."

During the "tour," they ate at a restaurant with low tables and little benches. Brautigan instructed his daughter in chopstick etiquette, how to place them properly on her bowl. "Never put them this way," he said. "It means death." That night, they were served a whole grouper "lined with sushi." Another evening, Richard brought Ianthe out to the Tokyo suburb where Len Grzanka lived. On Brautigan's previous trip to Japan, Len took him to his favorite neighborhood sushi restaurant. Grzanka told the proprietor, Kiamatsu Soji, a third-generation sushi chef who lived upstairs in the building with his family, that Richard was "a famous American novelist."

Soji immediately hung a closed sign the door, brought his wife and daughter downstairs to meet Brautigan, and proceeded to serve his honored guests a fantastic array of piscatorial delights, all without charge. So much sake was consumed that Richard couldn't make it home and had to crash at Len's apartment. Memories of that evening prompted a return visit with his daughter. Once again, Soji closed his place down for a private party, slicing up sushi of the highest order while Grzanka served as translator. As before, the entire feast was on the house.

Len Grzanka was writing a (never-published) novel at the time. He asked Richard to take a look at the manuscript, and he "gave it a cursory glance." Brautigan also gave his friend some advice. "Len," he said, "you've got to write what you know about. If you don't have fun writing it, nobody's going to have fun reading it." Richard elaborated on his point, trying to explain how personal experience might be shaped to serve one's fiction. "I'd like to write something about putting on a Donald Duck suit and robbing the Bank of America at high noon," he said, "but, I could never put on a Donald Duck suit."

Most of Brautigan's activities were nocturnal. Occasional daytime excursions broke the pattern. Once, Richard and Ianthe took the bullet train down to Kyoto, where they "spent a long quiet afternoon at the Moss Temple," a place of incredible beauty, the eighth-century temple sitting within a lush fourteenth-century garden where forty varieties of moss had been carefully cultivated to create an idealization of the natural world. Ianthe so enjoyed crouching beside her father, watching the splash of a waterfall over moss-covered stones, that she bought a poster at the temple's gift shop. She kept it for years until it was torn and tattered.

They picnicked at another park. Richard tried to convince his daughter that one of the warning signs actually said watch out for monkeys. She "had a hard time believing that there were wild monkeys on the loose." Ianthe made a wish at every temple they passed that day. Kyoto, Japan's former capital, a beautiful city of many ancient temples, repositories of untold forgotten hopes and dreams, had long inspired the wishes of those in need. Back in Tokyo, when her father bragged to his friends about her wish-making, Ianthe was surprised to discover he had noticed the secret supplications.

While she was away in Japan, half of Ianthe's Hawaiian high school burned to the ground. The ensuing crisis extended her vacation by another week, unexpectedly giving her extra time with a father she seldom saw. Many of the hours spent together ticked away in bars. Brautigan "liked sitting around drinking until two or three in the morning." Although Ianthe was underage, it didn't seem to matter in Tokyo. Ianthe ordered screwdrivers, the only drink she knew by name. "I had learned firsthand that alcohol could cut my pain," she wrote years later in her memoir. On the plus side, during her stay in Japan, Ianthe kicked a brief but short-lived "attraction" to Valium.

The company they kept in these various drinking establishments consisted mainly of artists and writers. Ianthe paid scant attention to the frenzied conversations lurching forward in fits and starts as those capable of translating attempted to clarify obscure points in Japanese or English. The early hours of the new day nearly always found them at The Cradle. Richard was still going strong, but Ianthe "could hardly keep [her] eyes open." Takako Shiina's maternal instincts kicked in, and she found a comfortable couch where the teenager could lie down and get some much-needed rest.

Brautigan surprised his daughter with the spontaneous gift of "a beautiful watch on a gold chain." Probably intended as a belated birthday present, it was not offered to her as such. "This watch meant a lot to me because he thought up the idea himself," Ianthe later wrote. "Most gifts he gave me were things he knew I wanted." A promised trip to Fuji never took place because Richard was too hungover on the scheduled date, but he made things up with his daughter the next day with an unexpected trip on the bullet train to watch the filming of a TV series on location. Another evening, they traveled by cab all over Tokyo, one more example of paternal spontaneity. That night, Richard took Ianthe to an experimental theater performance, her first ever. "I remember they were eating a lot of cabbage onstage."

The most significant moment during Ianthe's trip to Japan involved a meeting that may not have seemed all that important at the time. One night, Richard introduced her to "a spectacularly beautiful woman" who, as is customary in Japan, gave her a simple gift, "little paper birds." Her father had been emphatic "that the relationship was important." Ianthe had met many other girlfriends before and remembered the woman's "small white car" best of all. The woman's name was Akiko Yoshimura. Her relationship with Brautigan would change his life forever.

forty-six: the paradise valley ladies' book club luncheon

WHEN BECKY DOUGLASS first encountered Richard Brautigan in the summer of 1973, she was twenty-three years old and still wore her hair in pigtails. Stuart and Judy Bergsma, a recently arrived young couple, were having a potluck at their Deep Creek ranch (later the home of Peter and Becky Fonda). Richard sat on the log cabin's porch steps, head cupped in his hands, too drunk to enjoy the spectacular view of the Yellowstone Valley and the Absaroka Mountains spread in a VistaVision panorama before him. Becky Douglass smiled as she carried her casserole up to the house. Richard tugged at her skirt in passing. "You want to fuck?" he inquired, matter-of-factly: the very first words she ever heard him utter.

Over the next four years, Becky Douglass had ample occasion to observe Richard's often eccentric behavior on display in many different party settings. She'd been introduced to several of his girlfriends, but most often he came by himself, catching a ride with the neighbors when there was no resident driver. Richard was always an enigma. His wry charm provided an easy draw-bridge to casual conversation, spanning the deep moat of reserve enclosing his intensely private nature. He had a way of eliciting one's darkest secrets without ever revealing anything intimate about himself. Quite naturally, the whole gang was curious when Richard showed up in Paradise Valley with a brand-new Japanese bride in the fall of 1977.

The women in the community had started an informal book discussion club that met on a rotating basis for lunch once each month at the homes of the various members. It was a diverse group, numbering between twenty and thirty, ranch wives and their daughters, ranging in age from Madge Walker, who was in her seventies, to young Becky Douglass. Marian Hjortsberg was part of the group, as was Eileen Story, wife of a state senator whose grandfather trailed the first herd of Texas longhorns into the territory just after the Civil War.

What more appropriate gathering than a ladies' book club for a writer's wife to get acquainted with her neighbors? On the afternoon in question, the luncheon was being hosted by Deane Cowan Bischer, in her double-wide under the cottonwoods at the lower end of her parents' place on Mill Creek. The title of the book under discussion has been long forgotten, but what happened that afternoon burned indelibly into the memories of everyone present. Akiko Brautigan certainly had not read the designated book. Her knowledge of English was still limited. She was not going to the Bischers' place to talk about books.

Aki wanted to make a good first impression and chose her outfit with great care. Elegantly stylish, she wore a trim gray suit with a straight skirt, high heels and hose, matching hat, white gloves. The effect was sleek and sophisticated; above all, Western not Asian. At the Bischers', she couldn't have looked more out of place had she arrived naked. All the other women were casually dressed in jeans, denim skirts, whatever felt comfortable. Mrs. Brautigan's formal attire looked distinctly urban, with nary a nod toward cowboy chic, making her appear all the more alien. When a local gal wanted to put on the dog, she came dolled up like a rodeo queen in a purple pantsuit and matching high-crowned Stetson.

All the women welcomed her, trying to make this frightened beautiful stranger feel comfortable. They assumed everybody dressed this way in Japan. Deane introduced Akiko to the book club as a "guest," and she stepped up to meet them all in turn with a sweet polite smile highlighting her delicate face. As she took each woman's hand, looking straight into her eyes with the utmost sincerity, Aki repeated the same greeting, every word clear and precise, the polished result of much careful practice. "How the fuck are you?" Akiko Brautigan said sweetly to the book club members, one after the other, holding their hands, meeting their gaze with forthright candor. "How the fuck are you . . . ? How the fuck are you . . . ?"

It was obvious that she didn't understand what she was saying. Aki's kind and gentle manner belied any profane intentions. Becky Douglass took her aside and did her best to explain the mistake. Akiko's face hardened into fury as she understood. How carefully Richard had coached her on exactly what to say. What an apt pupil she had been. Her anger burned within, fueled by the thought of the sly smile on her husband's face as he enjoyed his little joke back at home. The buzz of conversation resumed, ending the embarrassed silence. Everyone did her best to pretend that nothing out of the ordinary had happened. Literary chitchat would never seem quite the same again.

AKIKO NISHIZAWA WAS born in 1944 in a Sapporo military dormitory on Hokkaido, the northernmost of the Japanese islands. An American invasion of the homeland seemed inevitable. Okinawa had not yet fallen, and its amber grain fields seemed a world away from the sparsely populated, forested wilderness of Hokkaido, home of indigenous salmon, bear, and the "hairy" Ainu, Japan's unique white-skinned aborigines. Two years later, when Aki left Hokkaido, the war was over, the atomic age had begun, and the American army occupied her country.

The Nishizawa family moved to the small fishing town of Ishinomaki in the northern Tōhoku region, about a two-hour train ride from Tokyo. Her father worked as an engineer at a pulp factory splintered off from a large conglomerate that had been broken up by antitrust action. The company opened a new plant in the Inland Sea area to the south. Like gypsies, the Nishizawas made another move.

Both Akiko's parents were very traditional. The factory where her father worked was called "a society factory." Every family employed there became part of a rigid class structure, common laborers at the bottom of the ladder, each successive corporate position ascending from rung to rung into the stratospheric realm where the president of the company presided like a minor god. As Akiko's father worked his way up to president, her family's social status rose along with him. "Living in that sort of society," she recalled, "everybody treated me as a special kid."

On the surface, Akiko behaved like a typical "daughter in a box," the Japanese term for a young woman from a good family who remained modest, chaste, and above all, obedient. Beneath her demure surface, Aki was a rebel, the "black sheep in the family." While her sister agreed to an arranged marriage, a "photo marriage," and she considered her brother to be a "very square guy," Akiko became argumentative and affected an interest in Communism.

After graduating from high school (a three-year course in Japan), Aki attended a university in Tokyo. Her parents considered her a traditional girl and made sure she roomed in a private all-female dormitory. She studied English literature, but her grasp of the language remained poor. "I never study anything in the university," she said. What interested her was personal freedom, "real life and with boyfriend." Dropping out before graduation, Akiko went to work for "some cultural organization" involved in music and the lecture circuit.

One day, Akiko saw a big want ad in the Japanese national newspaper. Sony was preparing to buy Columbia Records and in the process of forming a new company. There were no age, sex, or education limitations for those seeking employment. At the time, this was rare. Until the passage of an Equal Opportunity Law in 1986, only a third of all Japanese corporations would accept job applications from women who had graduated from four-year colleges.

Employment possibilities were even more limited for those without degrees. Sony required only that the applicants submit essays describing why they wanted to work in the new corporation. Figuring millions of people read the national newspaper and Sony would be deluged with applications, Aki sent in a radically brief essay simply stating her qualifications and declaring, "Why don't you ask me to meet with you?" Sony liked this approach and invited Akiko for an interview with their top executives. They wanted to test her English language skills because the job involved working closely with their American joint venture companies.

"But my English was so bad because I hate it," Aki later confessed.

Akiko got the job in spite of her obvious shortcomings as a linguist. She became part of the company's international division, later known as CBS/Sony, working in what the industry called A&R (artistry and recording). Aki married an advertising man named Yoshimura. Female employment was uncommon at the time, and it was even more rare for a married woman to work outside the home. Aki's English had improved, and one of her responsibilities involved showing visiting American artists, such as Pierre Boulez, Leonard Bernstein, and Isaac Stern, around Tokyo.

Akiko worked mostly with foreign talent, but she sometimes produced the work of contemporary Japanese artists. This included public relations, and she had many contacts in the publishing industry. Promoting a record she was about to release, Aki met with an editor who frequently exchanged inside dope on what was new, hot, and hip with her. Aki saw a copy of a Richard Brautigan book in the man's office. She had read Japanese translations of Brautigan's work in university, first *In Watermelon Sugar*, later *Trout Fishing* and *The Abortion*. Akiko was excited. "Oh, did you read that?" she asked.

"Yes. Very unique book," the editor replied.

Several months later, early in 1977, the editor came to see Aki. He spoke to her about Brautigan. "Do you know that author is in Japan right now," he said "and is staying in Keio Plaza Hotel."

"Shall we call him?" she asked.

The editor gave her the number. Akiko phoned the Keio Plaza only to be told that Richard had checked out. When the desk clerk heard the disappointment in her voice, he said, "No, no, he is supposed to be back again." A week later, Aki called the hotel a second time. Again, she was told Richard had left. "Mr. Brautigan is in the Gifu area to watch the *ukai* [cormorant fishing]. He's supposed to come back by now."

Soon after, Aki tried the number again. This time he was there. The front desk connected her with Richard Brautigan's room on the thirty-fifth floor. "And my heart started beating like some small girl talking with some superstar or something." Brautigan spoke rapidly, excitedly, as if he'd tuned in to her own exhilaration. "I just talked with the telephone operator in Montana," he said, "and asked what the weather looked like." Akiko didn't quite know what to make of it all. She felt perplexed. "That kind of conversation," she remembered. "And blah, blah, blah . . ."

Ice broken, Richard asked the stranger on the other end of the line three quick questions. First: "How did you get this phone number?"

"Oh, by a certain way," Aki answered coyly.

Brautigan sounded pleased with her reply. "Are you a journalist?" was his second question.

"No."

"Who are you then?"

"I am working in the music industry," Akiko said.

"Oh, that's okay." The melodic voice was not a threat to his privacy. Richard immediately asked Aki for her phone number. And she gave it to him.

Small talk can be difficult with someone you've never met. Brautigan launched back into his rapid-fire free association, talking about the Japanese television program he was watching, a detective cartoon.

Akiko forgot about their odd conversation. She thought, "The famous author is never going to call me." He did call and asked her out for dinner. "My god!" she remembered with a certain wonder. Although still married, Aki accepted Richard's invitation.

On the appointed evening, Akiko drove to the Keio Plaza Hotel. She brought a stack of Brautigan's books in Japanese translation with her, hoping he might sign them, but took only *Trout Fishing* when she rode the elevator to the thirty-fifth floor, leaving the others in the car. When Richard opened the door to his suite, the famous author greeted her wearing the summer kimono called a *yukata*. "Kind of bizarre," Aki remembered. "Unusual. So, I thought, hmm, strange." In spite of his unorthodox dress, Brautigan was gracious and polite. He immediately offered Akiko a drink and some appetizers. She recalled smoked salmon on plates decorated with a trout pattern.

Aki noticed something else. In one corner of the room, Richard had assembled a makeshift altar to himself, arranging several of the Japanese translations of his books into a personal display. "Like a little shrine to worship his own book," Akiko thought.

Later, Brautigan removed the *yukata*. Clad in his typical blue jeans, he took Akiko out to dinner at Szechwan, the Roppongi District Chinese restaurant Kazuko Fujimoto brought him to the previous year. Afterward, he brought her to The Cradle and introduced her to Takako Shiina. By this time, Richard was very drunk, having alternated between whiskey and sake all evening long. Aki had never known an alcoholic. "That's the tragedy, I think," she said in retrospect.

They quickly became lovers. Richard's courtship ritual had long included preparing an intimate spaghetti dinner complete with his famous sauce. He soon stirred up something al dente for Aki. Tracking down Italian ingredients was no problem in cosmopolitan Tokyo. The logistics of finding a place to prepare the feast presented a far greater obstacle. A two-burner hot plate in his suite at the Keio Plaza was out of the question. Asking Kazuko or Takako to use either of their apartments eliminated any possibility of romance. Brautigan played his ace in the hole and called Len Grzanka, a bachelor who lived alone.

Grzanka agreed to let Brautigan use his suburban apartment for the planned pasta tryst. Richard wanted privacy, so Len generously vacated for the night. When Grzanka returned the next morning, "the place was a disaster." Not only did he find the unmade bed a tangled testimonial to a night of passion, but Len also observed that Richard "didn't wash a single plate. He burned sauce in a bunch of pots. There was sauce all over the place."

Around this time, Delacorte sent the uncorrected galley proofs for *Dreaming of Babylon* to Tokyo. Brautigan went to work on them with his usual obsessive concern for detail. Daytime hangovers and night owl habits dictated an eccentric schedule. Richard's most productive time came in those predawn hours after he returned to his hotel suite from The Cradle. As always, he depended on his friends to supply advice on the fine points of grammar and vocabulary. Len Grzanka's position as an English professor elevated him to the top of Brautigan's local list of potential advisers.

"He had a habit of calling me up at about 2:00 or 3:00 am to look up words in the dictionary for him," Grzanka said. "He'd keep me up for hours."

This didn't sit well with Len, who had to rise at six and take a long train commute to get to work at Tsuda College by eight. He repeatedly explained his situation to Brautigan, pleading with him to call during the day. It didn't seem to make any difference, and the late night phone calls continued. "Richard basically had no consideration for anyone else," Grzanka observed.

As Richard's relationship with Akiko intensified, he became increasingly emotionally dependent on her. "We thought we could stimulate artistic creativity together," Aki recalled. While she regarded herself as basically a positive and optimistic person, she recognized Brautigan's inherent negativity. "Every minute he always had some kind of negative energy kept within him," she said. Because she was interested in his mind and loved his work, she wanted to give him all she had, both mentally and from her heart. "I was small, but I was open," Akiko observed. "And he was touched by my openness and my small things."

One night, Richard cried bitter tears. "I never thought I was loveable," he told her. "I was abandoned by my mother. I was abandoned by my first wife. And so, I thought I [would never be] loved by any women anymore." Aki realized "he had some big complex about women." She knew Brautigan believed she was the one who could give him everything. For a time, she believed it, too. In spite of her imagined role as a liberated woman, Akiko understood how much she relied upon her husband. "So, I was not independent at all," she said. "I was dependent." In Richard, Aki saw a way out of her predicament. Richard represented freedom from all the traditional restrictions of Japanese culture, from being the daughter in the box. She didn't understand how completely he wanted to possess her.

Even as their affair grew in intensity, Richard and Akiko spent more time apart than together. She still had her day job and a husband at home. He retained a loner's instinct for solitary nocturnal wandering. These aimless evenings often ended at The Cradle. One night at the bar, Brautigan encountered Ryu Murakami, who had just finished his second manuscript (*War Begins Beyond the Sea*) and was in "a dreamy mood," almost as if intoxicated. Meeting Brautigan, Murakami told him, "I've just done my writing that'll be published soon as my second novel."

"Hmm," Richard mused, turning his head away.

"What a fellow!" Ryu thought. "He didn't even congratulate me." Brautigan struck him as being in a bad temper.

Suddenly, Brautigan turned back to face Murakami. "The important one should be the third," Richard told him. "You can write your first novel based on your experiences. And the second should be done using the technique and imagination which you've learned from the first novel. The battle for the writer, just to begin after using up his experience and imagination." Richard's words shook Ryu out of his happy, dreamy state.

Junnosuke Yoshiyuki, an older and more respected Japanese novelist, also became acquainted with Richard Brautigan around this time. Born in 1923, Yoshiyuki was the oldest child of author Eisuki Yoshiyuki, who died in 1940. After dropping out of the University of Tokyo without a degree, Junnosuke began working as a magazine editor but devoted his leisure hours to drinking, gambling, and consorting with prostitutes. His novels included the *City of Primary Colors* (1951), *Sudden Shower*, (1954, winner of the Akutagawa Prize), *Room of a Whore* (1958), and *The Dark*

Room (1969, winner of the Tanizaki Prize). Prostitution and sex provided a constant theme in Yoshiyuki's work.

Akiko recalled that Richard "had a very good relationship" with Junnosuke Yoshiyuki. Richard's interests in soft-core pornography and his great affection for the writing of Junichiro Tanizaki certainly helped form a bond between the two men. According to Aki, they saw each other several times while Brautigan was in Tokyo.

One nameless night, back at the Keio Plaza, inebriated on love and booze, Brautigan placed an early am phone call to Don Carpenter in Hollywood. "Four o'clock in the morning," Carpenter remembered. "Drunk as a fucking goat." Richard wanted to tell Don about his newfound love. "I've met the most beautiful woman," Brautigan stammered. "We're going to get married as soon as she divorces her husband."

"Oh, god," thought Don Carpenter, struggling to clear his sleep-clouded brain. For the first and only time, he told his old friend an unpleasant truth he knew Richard did not want to hear. "If she'll leave him," Don said, "she'll leave you."

Akiko's husband suggested she marry her lover. When she told Yoshimura about her involvement with Brautigan, he took the news with equanimity. "Well, you better ask him to marry," Yoshimura remarked to his wife.

"Why?" Akiko was amazed.

"Because marriage is to protect the woman," he said. "And without having that I won't divorce you."

Caught up in the stress of the situation, Brautigan suffered a severe attack of herpes. A sexually transmitted disease never enhanced a new love affair. Condoms offered no protection from embarrassment. Desperate, Richard called Helen Brann for help. Brautigan had only recently received an extension permit for an additional sixty-day stay in Japan, and he had no intention of returning to America for treatment. His agent consulted with her own physician, who suggested a doctor in Tokyo. Richard sought an immediate appointment.

Brautigan got a call from Dan Gerber, in Tokyo with his Zen master, Kobun Chino Otogawa Roshi, and Bob Watkins, a friend from Montana. They planned on spending a few days in town before heading on for a longer stay in Kyoto. Dan had been studying Buddhism and sitting zazen for about four years, since the depression he felt following the death of his father in 1973. Kobun, Dan's teacher, was born in 1938 and raised in Jokoji, the Soto Zen temple in Kamo, Japan, where his father had been chief priest. He came to America in 1967, invited by Suzuki Roshi to help establish the Tassajara monastery in Carmel Valley.

Kobun read *Trout Fishing in America* not long after its initial publication by the Four Seasons Foundation. Much later, Gerber gave him a copy of Kazuko Fujimoto's translation, and he "was amazed how different it seemed to him in Japanese than it did in English." Dan remembered his master "sort of laughing" at "what a different book it was in Japanese."

Brautigan met them for lunch at their hotel. Afterward they walked about the city. Richard told Dan "how fascinated he was by the design of everything in Japan." Gerber thought this was because Brautigan couldn't read Japanese. "Everything was pure design." Dan admired Richard's quality, "ideal for any artist," of being "a stranger in the place that you live. Richard had a wonderful ability to look at things like a child."

As Brautigan and Gerber walked the streets of Tokyo in the company of a robed Japanese Zen priest, they attracted considerable attention from the passing pedestrian swarm. Both tall, blond, and undeniably Western, they stood out, head and shoulders, above the crowd. "I was quite a sight in Japan," Dan remembered. "Everybody always asked if I was John Denver." Gerber recognized this simple cultural misunderstanding. Brautigan attributed the crowd's fascination with a pair of tall white strangers as a direct consequence of his own celebrity. "I'm very well known in Japan," Richard commented smugly to Dan.

Another day, an angry Brautigan arrived at Gerber's hotel by taxi, outraged because the cab driver had just pulled an "Amerigoo," on him. "Amerigoo" was Richard's term for the way Japanese took advantage of foreigners, thinking them dumb Americans. On this occasion, Brautigan's cabbie took him the long way around to Gerber's place. "He would be alternately delighted and then infuriated by what he called Amerigoo," Dan remembered.

Brautigan complained of his recent herpes attack. He said it happened whenever he got upset. Richard wasn't sure "whether the herpes had erupted because he had gotten upset" or if it was the other way around. "The two things coincided," Gerber observed. Richard made no mention of Akiko by name. He told Dan about a "mysterious" relationship with a married Japanese woman. "She would appear on her terms," Gerber said, recalling the story, "and make love to Richard and then disappear." Brautigan's emotions swung, week after week, from exhilaration and delight in everything Japanese to deep depression and disgust at the never-ending Amerigoo. Richard told Dan that "he was on an emotional roller-coaster within a roller-coaster. Lying in bed in his hotel listening to people fucking through the wall next door." Hearing his friend's story, Gerber thought, "Anybody would be unhappy living in a luxury hotel as a hotel guest month by month."

Brautigan wanted to show his friends something special. After lunch, he guided them to a little plaza at the north exit of Shibuya Station, pointing out a life-sized bronze statue of a dog. In the early 1920s, Hachi ("Hachikō"), a white male Akita, accompanied his master, Hidesaburō Ueno, a professor at the Imperial University, to Shibuya Station every morning on his way to work. Each afternoon, the dog went back to the station to meet the professor when he got off the 3:00 pm train. On May 21, 1925, Ueno suffered a stroke and never came home again.

For almost a decade, Hachikō waited at Shibuya Station, rain or shine, day in and day out, for a best friend who didn't return. The faithful dog touched the heart of Tokyo. His death on March 8, 1935, waiting in the exact spot where he'd spent so many devoted hours, made the front pages of every newspaper in the city. Funds for the *chuken* monument were raised by public subscription. Over time, the statue became the most popular meeting place in Tokyo.

Takako Shiina told Brautigan the legend of Hachikō and took him to the Shibuya Station exit plaza. Richard loved the story. They often visited the site together. Richard knew Hachi's story would touch Dan's heart and deliberately staged this poetic street theater to please his old pal. Curiously, Brautigan never wrote a single word about the faithful dog.

Gerber, Kobun Chino Otogawa Roshi, and Bob Watkins left Tokyo the following day. Richard came to their hotel to see them off. With all the luggage, they decided to take two cabs to the station. Richard and Dan traveled in one; Kobun and Bob in the other. The two parties separated on the way to catch the Kyoto train. "One problem being in the Tokyo station is that everything is in Japanese," Gerber recalled.

Lost, unable to either speak or read the language, Dan recalled running up a long flight of stairs, Richard huffing and puffing alongside him, both hauling heavy bags, only to find themselves on the wrong platform. "Richard took it upon himself," Gerber said. "It was very important to him that I make my train." They ran back down the stairs and raced to another platform, reaching the departing train with just moments to spare. Brautigan handed the last bag aboard as the doors closed on his red exhausted face. Gerber later joked that he expected to read a Kyoto headline the next day: american author dies on railroad platform. "This was the gracious host part of Richard," Dan said. "I also think he was very happy to see somebody from home."

On the train, Kobun reflected on meeting Richard Brautigan. "He's incredible," the Zen master said, laughing softly to himself. "What is he doing living here? Why does he stay in Japan? He is miserable here."

Not long after his friends departed, Richard went to see the physician recommended by Helen Brann's doctor. Things did not go well during the consultation. Brautigan suffered further "pain and mental anguish" after applying the prescribed medication to his afflicted member. Richard complained to Helen, who responded with an apologetic handwritten letter. "I feel that you are desperately unhappy," she wrote, "and I'd give anything within my limited power to help." Brann felt Brautigan should return to San Francisco, "where you are so loved and missed." She wanted him to come back for the ABA (American Booksellers Association) convention being held in Frisco in May. Sam Lawrence thought Richard should be there to promote *Dreaming of Babylon*. Helen felt sure Dell would pay Brautigan's travel expenses.

Richard did not return for the ABA convention. He remained in Tokyo, where the weather turned hot and humid. Knowing he would not be back in Montana for some time, he wrote to Gatz Hjortsberg, asking that he check on the placement of a new cattle guard on the road near his home and deal with any potential fencing problems arising from tearing down a nearby shed. About this same time, he shipped his corrected *Babylon* galley proofs off to Helen Brann in New York.

After three weeks, Dan Gerber returned to Tokyo and gave Brautigan a call. Richard said he'd take Dan out and show him the city's vibrant nightlife. Brautigan picked Gerber up at his hotel in the early evening, a time the Japanese call "the hour of the pearl," and walked him to a nearby park. It was one of the very few parks in Tokyo that did not close before five o'clock and had become a popular trysting place for young couples. Richard mentioned this to Dan, indicating all the paired-up men and women sitting primly on the benches. They waited for darkness, when they could make out in relative privacy. This discreet mating ritual charmed Brautigan. "These people would go to the park and sit there very dignified until it got dark." What tickled him most were all the public signs depicting what Gerber described as "a bear in black, sort of like a ghost, lurking up out of bushes over benches." The signs meant "Beware of Peeping Toms."

Brautigan wanted to show Gerber the mysteries of Tokyo at night. He took Dan to the Roppongi District. Gerber considered it "the Via Veneto of Tokyo." They went to a number of "very brassy bars." Dan felt, "the Japanese had seen a lot of American movies of the forties and fifties of what American nightclubs were supposed to be like." Gerber remembered Brautigan being amused by the sight of "these absolutely glorious, gorgeous Japanese women" fawning over groups of American and European businessmen. "Geeks and nerds who in a bar in the States would be lucky to find any woman who would give them the time of day."

Brautigan insisted "there were two kinds of Japanese women in Roppongi." Those interested in European and American men who wore their hair long and straight. The others, interested in Japanese men, had permed hair cut short. Gerber thought it was a "very innocent evening," walking around, taking in the passing crowd and the bright flashing neon. In their ongoing conversation, Richard told Dan about the whorehouse in Yokohama where prostitutes dressed like nuns.

Asked if he'd been a customer there, Brautigan insisted he had never paid for sex in his life. Emphasizing his denial, Richard gestured in the air with his right hand, writing an invisible script. "Ink for the pen," he said.

Brautigan told Gerber a story about traveling to Seoul, Korea, "with this mysterious woman that he was seeing." Richard said he had to leave the country every sixty days to renew his Japanese visa, necessitating a "miserable" overnight trip to Seoul. None of this was true. Brautigan never journeyed to Korea. Not with Akiko, the mystery woman, nor anyone else. When he needed to extend his visa, Richard went to the Immigration Department and had a sixty-day extension permit stamped into his passport.

As Brautigan's departure date approached, he tried planning for Akiko to come to America with him. Richard had given up his San Francisco apartment before leaving for Japan. Not having a permanent place to live provided additional complications. An incident late one night in Takako Shiina's basement bar brought matters to a head. Inebriated when he wandered into The Cradle, Brautigan got increasingly more drunk. The American screenwriter Leonard Schrader sat at the bar talking in Japanese with Ryu Murakami and Kazuhiko Hasegawa, a film director.

Between 1969 and 1973, Leonard Schrader lived a double life in Japan, teaching American literature at Doshisha and Kyoto Universities during the day and hanging out with the Yamaguchigumi family, the preeminent Yakuza gangster clan in Kyoto, at night. Leonard used this experience to cowrite his first screenplay, *The Yakuza* (1975), with his younger brother, Paul, who gained international fame the next year with a script for Martin Scorsese's film *Taxi Driver*.

That night at The Cradle, Brautigan made several drunken attempts to insinuate himself into their conversation. They had no interest in talking with a boozy American who spoke no Japanese. Richard grew more insulting. He probably mixed up the two Schraders, confusing Leonard with Paul, who had treated Siew-Hwa Beh unkindly when they were film students at UCLA. Brautigan decided such behavior deserved retribution.

Stammering and repetitive, Richard grew increasingly nasty, drunkenly deriding Schrader. Kazuhiko Hasegawa had enough of hearing his friend abused by a loutish stranger. Rising suddenly, the film director flattened Brautigan's nose with a sudden karate chop. Richard stood dumbfounded, his bleeding, broken nose mashed like roadkill. Without a word, the director then reached out and took hold of the damaged proboscis, tugging it straight with a deft twist.

Speechless, bloodied, and humiliated, anesthetized by oceans of booze, Brautigan watched in a fog of disbelief as Takako Shiina asked her bartender to fill a bucket with water. Kazuhiko Hasegawa sat on a couch, savoring his triumph. Takako poured the water over his head. It was a July night, but the director fretted he might freeze to death on his way home from The Cradle. Takako promptly brought Richard to a hospital. A sodden memorial to the event, the couch at The Cradle took a long time to dry.

Observing Richard's broken nose a day or so later, Akiko said, "Why don't you go back right now. That would be better and I'll come to follow you."

Brautigan asked if she wanted his old nose the way it was before.

"Yes," she said. "I like your nose very much. So, please fix it."

Knowing he needed nose reconstruction, Richard phoned Erik Weber in San Francisco before his departure. He asked if Weber had the latest pictures taken of him. Erik said yes. Richard wanted copies. "I just stopped what I was doing and ran in the darkroom," Weber remembered. He made several prints. They got to Brautigan on time, and Erik charged him a "very minimal" fee of $3 or $4 per print.

"He was pissed off at me," Weber said. "He thought I should have given him those prints without charging him. It was real petty. His idea of paying me back would be to take me to a $20 or $30 lunch." After fourteen years, Weber and Brautigan's long friendship started to unravel.

Richard Brautigan flew home to San Francisco from Tokyo on June 19. He stretched his stay to the limit, departing a day before his extension permit was due to expire. Richard called ahead, alerting Tony Dingman of his arrival time. At 9:00 am Tony and Jack Thibeau waited at SFO when Brautigan's jet touched down. Richard traveled light, making room for two bottles of duty-free cognac in his carry-on bag.

Dingman and Thibeau drove Brautigan to the Russian Hill home of Dr. John Doss. Jack no longer remembers what was said about the broken nose. Dr. John had a look at Brautigan's damaged snout. Margot and John believed Richard "got in a wrangle in the airport with someone about his nose and this guy evidently was a karate expert and popped him on the nose and broke it."

"It's OK until tomorrow," Dr. Doss said after a quick examination. "I'm going to get you to see a specialist, and he'll set your nose, and everything will be fine." Tony and Jack drove Richard over to Nob Hill, where he took a room at the Fairmont Hotel. In the morning, he went to see an ear, nose, and throat guy recommended by John Doss, and everything turned out just as predicted.

Staying at the Fairmont did not turn out so happily. One morning around two, suffering from insomnia, a day or so after checking in, Brautigan phoned the Dosses. "Margot," he pleaded, "can I come and stay in your house awhile. All I can hear are toilets flushing and people fucking."

"I felt very sorry for him and said all right," Margot Doss recalled.

Brautigan checked out of the Fairmont and caught a cab over to 1331 Greenwich Street. The Dosses put him up in their unfurnished guest room. John inflated a new nine-by-twelve air mattress to serve as a bed. "He was with us for a month," Margot remembered.

"I think it was only about a week," her husband corrected. "It just seemed like a month."

Brautigan wasted no time before calling his old girlfriend Sherry Vetter and inviting her over. Sherry had known John and Margot Doss "from a long time back." She had no reservations about visiting Richard in their home. They soon got it on upstairs in the guest room. Their energetic lovemaking was no secret to the Doss household. The air mattress "made all this incredible noise."

Sherry remembers Richard lying on the bed in the Doss guest room "with his nose bandaged up." She sat in a chair facing Brautigan while he read her the stories recently written in Japan in a funny nasal voice. Sherry's friend Yuri Nishiyama had told her that Richard's nose was broken at The Cradle in Tokyo when he asked a young musician, "a really lousy singer," to knock it off and the Japanese troubadour smashed his guitar into Brautigan's face.

Richard received the page proofs for *Dreaming of Babylon* at the Doss household. Sam Lawrence asked Brautigan to also send him the descriptive copy for *Babylon*'s inside dust jacket flaps. Richard called Don Carpenter, one of several trusted "ghost editors," for help. "You have to write the praise about yourself," Carpenter said. "The trick is to get a friend to do it. Then you edit it as best you can." Don proofread every book after *In Watermelon Sugar*. "Which should it be, one word or two? Is it hyphenated? Is this a colon or a semicolon? He went over everything, time and time again." Carpenter came to Brautigan's aid again on *Babylon*. "The wild praise in the back of the book was written by me," he said. "I could say all those things because I believed them."

During his brief stay with the Dosses, Brautigan continued heading out nightly to favorite haunts in North Beach: Enrico's, Specs', and Vanessi's. Specs' (which opened in 1968) had a long, storied history. Until 1949, when the previous owner, Henri Lenoir, moved across Columbus to start Vesuvio Café, Specs' was called 12 Adler Place. Herb Caen, Barnaby Conrad, and Kenneth Patchen all hung out there in the years after WWII. Alcohol provided Richard an introduction to total barroom strangers. One evening, after a chance meeting at Specs', Brautigan brought his momentary new best friend back with him to 1331 Greenwich Street.

The next morning, Dr. John Doss, always the first in the family to rise, came downstairs to the kitchen to make breakfast. He was astonished on discovering Brautigan "with some Swedish poet sitting at the kitchen table with two or three bottles of whiskey out there and tumblers." The pair were still drinking and yammering at each other "in this incomprehensible language" of their own invention. To Dr. Doss, it seemed like a "mythic, shamanistic confrontation." He had no idea "what the hell was going on."

Deep in his heart, Richard knew such louche behavior was not conducive to lasting friendships and set about looking for a place to live. While Brautigan wandered about North Beach looking at real estate listings with Jack Thibeau and Tony Dingman, they strolled down Grant Avenue in search of refreshment. Tony "jumped out in front of Richard" without a word, and "started ripping matches one at a time out of a matchbook." Dingman lit them and tossed each burning match into the air. "Just this little fireworks of matches," Thibeau recalled.

"Pyrotonia," quipped Richard.

Brautigan's good humor stemmed from Akiko's impending arrival. He happily told all his friends about her, describing her grace and classic beauty. "The only time I ever saw him really happy, like a kid would be happy, I mean really excited and delirious," said Ward Dunham, the bartender at Enrico's, "was when Aki was going to come here from Japan. That was the happiest I ever saw him."

Effusive with joy, Richard paid a call on Marcia Clay in her spacious new apartment/studio on Stockton Street. He wasted no time before telling her about meeting Akiko. Marcia thought his first descriptions of Aki "already mythological." Brautigan's fiancée was not only "incredibly beautiful" but very intelligent and best of all familiar with his work. Richard told Marcia about the evening Aki first visited him at the Keio Plaza. "And, of course, I fell in love with her," he said.

It didn't take long for Brautigan to find a new apartment with "a sweeping view" on Telegraph Hill at 1349 Kearny, between Union and Green Streets, just a block away from where he'd lived with Valerie Estes in the late sixties and not far from his previous digs on Union. With a large overhanging bay window, Richard's new sun-filled apartment stood on the second floor of a small two-story duplex. Brautigan's rent was $525 a month. The convenient location provided another easy stroll down to Enrico's, Vanessi's and Chinatown. As soon as he was comfortably settled in, Richard sent for Akiko, who had quit her job at Sony. She arrived around the end of July and stayed a little more than three weeks. "And, he said, 'I'll introduce you to all my friends which is much better than me,'" Aki recalled. "And this was true."

Among the first to visit were Ed and Jennifer Dorn, who by chance lived in an apartment directly across Kearny Street from Brautigan. Richard invited them over. Jenny observed that the couple "appeared to be very happy, and Richard was more than ever tiptoeing around and using quaint Japanese mannerisms." Akiko struck her as "quite beautiful." Brautigan had his new love serve tea and read them poetry in her native tongue.

Shortly after her arrival, Richard brought Aki over to 1851 Stockton Street to meet Marcia Clay. Brautigan prepared Clay for the meeting with an "avuncular" phone call. Concerned that Akiko knew no one in America, Richard asked Marcia to become her companion. She considered it "an appointed friendship: YOU WILL BE MY WIFE'S BEST FRIEND, an edict à la Richard." Brautigan described Aki's "friendless plight" with a touching concern bordering on pity. With this in mind, Clay "was surprised to see a buoyant, bright-eyed, sure-footed young beauty enter my place that day." Akiko wore a pleated, patterned skirt, patent leather shoes, and white knee socks. She carried a tiny lettered Japanese handbag. "A living doll," Marcia thought.

"Smug and smiling," Richard sat back watching them interact, very pleased with himself. Marcia and Aki hit it off immediately, and their friendship, still strong today, lasted decades longer than Brautigan's brief relationship with his Japanese fantasy.

Richard proudly escorted Akiko to all his favorite places, Enrico's and Vanessi's and "the little Japanese breakfast place on Columbus," where friends gathered to eat and drink. Brautigan's bride-to-be met them all. The couple enjoyed strolling through the Chinese markets on Stockton Street. "Chinatown is his favorite place to walk in the morning," Aki said. Richard favored a small place selling barbecued pork. He'd buy a half pound or so and get them to chop it into small pieces to go, so he and Aki might enjoy an ambulatory breakfast, nibbling on bits of pork from a paper sack as they took in the sights.

While the happy pair embarked on various moveable San Francisco feasts, an unseen clock kept ticking. Before Richard and Aki could tie the knot in America, she first needed to get a divorce back in Japan. Her husband wanted assurance that Brautigan planned to marry her. To set the wheels in motion, Richard Hodge sent a telegram to Japan, a legal declaration that matrimony was indeed Brautigan's avowed intention. Soon afterward, Akiko returned to Tokyo to fulfill the final legal residency requirements for the dissolution of her marriage.

She checked into room S-805 at the Hotel Okura in the Minato-ku. One of the finest hotels in Japan, the Okura was built on the grounds of the Okura Art Museum. The hotel boasted a traditional Japanese garden and two swimming pools, one for summertime use only. Free to take a dip in either one at her leisure, Aki truly swam laps of luxury. "I'm marrying with someone who has everything," she said. Richard Brautigan picked up the tab. It came to almost $7,000.

Divorce remained uncommon in Japan. With their strict code of conduct, most Japanese regarded divorce as bringing shame on the family. None of this mattered very much to Akiko, who had defied convention for most of her life. Nor did it matter that in Japan, after almost every marital split-up, no alimony was ever awarded to the departing wife. "So, I give everything to my ex-husband," Aki said, "because I was working together with him. We bought the house, apartment house. And I left my car to him."

Akiko believed that she and Richard, with his poet's soul, understood each other completely, united by a great shared passion. The sexy, charming, poetic letters she wrote him almost daily from the Hotel Okura reflected this belief. The very first was in itself a poem, where "one pure white ship / a grand white ship" sailed "slowly—slowly—slowly" toward her new love, her new life.

At the end of August, Aki replied to what she called "the most beautiful letter I ever had in my life!" Her brief note to Richard consisted of only three lines ("I touched you!" she enthused at the start). Her conclusion made it magic, a graphic design taking up half the page. Akiko transformed her final word, "Love," into an undulating calligraphic wave. Numbers of iconic fish poked their startled heads from the swells, while one beautifully rendered specimen leaped high into the air, twisting with a deft sureness of line suggesting ancient Japanese shodō. Brautigan had for decades rendered crudely drawn fish as a personal hieroglyph. This graceful interpretation of his most potent symbol must surely have moved him.

With Akiko stoking the fires of his imagination, Brautigan began working on a series of short stories about his experiences during his first two trips to Japan. His workday also focused on the design and production of his two forthcoming books. Early in July, he told Helen Brann he wanted an illustration on the front dust jacket's cover of *June 30th*. Richard rejected a purely typographical cover and declined using any quotations on the front of the book.

Brautigan needed immediate help with the cover for *June 30th* and gave Erik Weber a call. Taking the book's title as his cue, Erik suggested using a picture of the departure stamp in Richard's passport, a bold circle with its titular date at the exact center of page, colored red and looking like an ancient Japanese seal. Richard loved the concept. Erik took photos of the page in Richard's passport. They worked up a dummy layout and sent it off to Sam Lawrence.

Akiko's impending arrival gave Brautigan pause for thought. Commitment had never been his strong point, and now he awaited a new bride. "This better work," his daughter told him sternly. "You better not screw this one up." Prior to Aki's arrival, Richard went for a long walk with Kitty Hughes along the bluffs above Agate Beach in Bolinas. He was "determined that he was going to make this one work." At the same time, Brautigan was "really afraid that the marriage would fail." Kitty felt that he was "girding himself up." She also thought Richard had a fantasy image of the ideal Japanese woman.

"Wait till you see her," he exulted. "She has classic Japanese features, like out of an old painting."

The magic letters from Aki arrived almost daily. The last day of August, she wrote with news of Sadaharu Oh's 755th career home run. ("BANZAI!!!") The next day, her letter radiated pure happiness. "It's September! It will be the most exciting month for ever." Akiko said she'd put a handmade calendar up on the wall of her hotel room so she could check off the dates one at a time ("the days are disappearing day by day") until the hour arrived for her to fly to America. To get things ready for his fiancée, Richard traveled up to Montana. While a hired cleaning crew freshened the Pine Creek house, Brautigan visited friends, giving away inscribed copies of his new novel.

All along, Helen Brann had been after Brautigan to get the descriptive copy for *June 30th* to Seymour Lawrence. Helen mailed Sam the catalog copy after Richard read it to her by phone. He called it his "most intimate book" and identified himself as "one of America's most popular poets."

Brautigan had Helen fill in the blank when he dictated, "There are _____ copies in print of Richard Brautigan's three previous books of poetry." His agent did the math: 600,022.

Brautigan received finished hardcover copies of *Babylon* early in September. He inscribed one ("This copy is for Ron and Kitty Loewinsohn") while having dinner with his friends at their place in Rockridge. After their marriage, Kitty kept her own name, Hughes, but Richard always referred to her as Kitty Loewinsohn.

Akiko left for San Francisco in the last week of September. Her mother, Fusako Nishizawa, dictated a typewritten letter to Richard on the same day, having unsuccessfully attempted to phone him from the Hotel Okura that morning. "I am feeling such a sadness to lose my precious treasure," she told her future son-in-law. She asked Richard "to be nice with my daughter" and wished them both "to be very happy together." It was September 20 all over again for Aki when, far across the international date line, she reunited with Brautigan. The lovers were again in each other's arms.

Richard and Aki began their lives together in the apartment on Kearny Street. Fond of the view, Akiko loved living there. Whenever Brautigan went out, he brought back some small gift for his bride-to-be. Once, he gave her a stuffed cloth turtle. Aki called it "Tootsie," Richard's private nickname for her. "He called me Tootsie," she said, "and I thought this is a tootsie." Each little offering had its own delicate ceremony, "spiritual or sacred." When Brautigan bought a bouquet of white daisies, he made sure to place a vivid blue iris at the center. "He was enchanted," Akiko recalled.

Kitty Hughes met Aki for the first time a couple days after her arrival. "She seemed very shy and retreating," Kitty recalled. "This sort of submissive Japanese female." Hughes thought she was a fantasy for Richard, an "image" he had created in his mind. "It became quickly apparent that Aki was in fact quite a strong woman," Kitty said. "She was very aware of American culture and wanted to come here. She was more complicated than Richard thought."

Early in September, Brautigan asked Erik Weber to come over to Kearny Street and take some photographs for *June 30th, June 30th*. Akiko had gone out for the afternoon. Erik shot more than a dozen pictures of Richard wearing jeans and a rumpled denim work shirt, some in the apartment, others up on the roof of the building. Combed back off his forehead, Brautigan's shoulder-length hair was obviously receding. In almost every frame, he appeared in tremendous pain, a puzzled, stricken look on his face. Richard grew angry when he looked at the pictures for the first time. "These are terrible," he said. "I don't want anyone to see these." Brautigan used no photograph on the cover of *June 30th*. These pictures were the last Erik Weber ever took of Richard Brautigan. Weber mailed Sam Lawrence an invoice for his work on the front cover design for *June 30th*. Before receiving it, Lawrence wrote to Brautigan, "The design for JUNE 30th, JUNE 30th is fabulous. My gratitude to you and to Erik Weber."

In the weeks before Aki's arrival, Brautigan discussed revisions to his will with attorney Bill Mandel. A revised copy from the law firm was ready to be mailed. Mandel called Richard, and he went to his office on Columbus Avenue to read the new draft firsthand. The changes added Akiko Yoshimura as a beneficiary. In the updated document, Brautigan's personal effects went first to Aki, next to Ianthe, should the recently divorced Mrs. Yoshimura not survive him. His real estate holdings (Bolinas and Montana), were to be divided "by agreement," between his daughter and Akiko. If they could not agree, the property was to be sold with the proceeds divided between them.

The will's provisions for a trust remained as originally written. Lifetime income from Brautigan's literary estate was to be split equally, one half going to Ianthe, the other to Aki. Richard Hodge, Ron Loewinsohn, and Helen Brann were named as trustees, his agent appointed as a de facto literary executor. The will specified Brautigan's remains be cremated without any funeral or memorial services. Richard signed the document in the presence of Mandel and another member of the firm, who acted as witnesses. When Brautigan returned to the Kearny Street apartment later in the day, he "very seriously" told Akiko, "I just changed my will."

This announcement had a special resonance for his future wife. Richard often told her he would end his life before he turned fifty. Brautigan never specifically used the word "suicide," but Aki knew what he meant. "I didn't take it that serious," she said, "but always he was like a play. He was saying, 'My life has to be [over] before fifty. He worshipped the way that Hemingway died." Richard also told Akiko what he wanted done with his body after death. "Please cremate me," he said, "and flush the ashes in the toilet bowl."

"Wow!" Aki replied, not knowing if he was kidding. "Your body is so big I'm afraid that flush going to be stuck."

Richard "wanted to marry right away," but didn't want the ceremony to take place in San Francisco, fearing his local celebrity might transform the occasion into media-mania. Around the end of September, Brautigan called Tony Dingman, asking him to come to Montana when he left with Aki. The idea was to get married in some quiet courthouse in the middle of nowhere. "He wanted to marry somewhere in Montana," Akiko recalled. "It's such a beautiful place." With Tony at the wheel of the Plymouth Fury, they drove across the wide reaches of Montana. "Richard wanted to show me how grand the state was," Aki said. Whenever they crossed the Missouri River in "White Acre," Brautigan started singing "Oh, Shenandoah," at the top of his lungs. "One of the happiest time for us."

While making plans for their wedding, Richard went fishing. This involved a trip to Dan Bailey's Fly Shop to buy a license and a new supply of flies and leaders. Brautigan loved poking around in fishing tackle stores. He thought of them as "cathedrals of childhood romance." As a poor kid in Oregon he could only afford the most minimal fishing gear and spent "thousands of hours worshipping the possibilities of rods and reels." Now he could buy anything his heart desired.

At the same time, Richard resumed his writing life, working on short stories, this time about his life in Montana, all possessing his signature oblique poetic point of view. One concerned spiders seeking shelter in his house from the cold. Another, "Autumn Trout Gathering," was about Richard's preparations for his first day of fall fishing, and Aki reminding him to bring some Kleenex along on his trip to the spring creek. "Cat Cantaloupe" told of luring the Hjortsbergs' cats over "with extravagant promises of cat delicacies."

Not being year-round residents, Richard and Akiko had no cats of their own. They did have plenty of mice and welcomed regular visits from Pandora or Queever. One night, the couple ate not-quite-ripe cantaloupe with their dinner. Dissatisfied, they set their plates on the floor and were astonished to see the visiting cat make a meal of their leftover melon. This formed the basis of his story, Brautigan again coaxing something amusing from the mundane.

Back before meeting Aki, when Richard lived alone at Pine Creek, he had a way of cadging special treats from the Hjortsbergs, often showing up in his neighbors' kitchen at breakfast time, coffee cup in hand, looking for "a hot cup of joe." Gatz and Marian raised their own pigs, and Brautigan developed a special fondness for the bacon they produced. "He was always trying to weasel a rasher of bacon," Marian remembered. "He'd come over weaseling and wheedling."

"Hmmm. Do I smell bacon?" Richard would say. "Have you been cooking bacon recently? I'll bring you quart of real maple syrup if you cook me breakfast with your real bacon."

One day Richard got wind that Gatz was going grouse hunting. "And he shuffled over with those long, black, funny boot shoes he used to wear," Marian recalled, "and he started rubbing his hands together like Uriah Heep."

"If you get enough grouse," Brautigan said, "I have a nice bottle of Pouilly-Fuissé. If you were to invite me over."

In those days, the Hjortsbergs made their own wine and could never afford anything as extravagant as imported Pouilly-Fuissé. This was a tempting offer. But Gatz bagged only a brace of grouse that afternoon, just enough for two. The next morning, the birds plucked and cool in the fridge, Marian stood washing the breakfast dishes, looking out the long kitchen window, when she spotted Queever dragging a freshly killed grouse across the front lawn. "I ran out in my bathrobe and grabbed the grouse," she said. "The extra grouse for Richard." Marian roasted the game birds. Brautigan came over for dinner, bringing along two bottles of Pouilly-Fuissé. "We had a very fine dinner," she remembered, "and I don't think we ever told him it was caught by the cat."

Problems started for Richard and Aki when they applied for a marriage license. A blood test was required, and the application asked for information regarding race and religion. This greatly angered Richard. Things went from bad to worse. At a subsequent interview, Brautigan was asked to produce his birth certificate. "He was upset because they asked about his father," Akiko said. "All of a sudden his face changed." Richard flushed with rage, "and he turned around and was gone."

"I don't want to marry here," he told Aki. She knew it was because he did not want to discuss his family roots with anyone. "For some people it's not that big matter," she said, "but for him I think it was."

Brautigan and his bride-to-be returned to San Francisco. Tony Dingman stayed on alone at Pine Creek. Richard said he'd be back in a week or so. "And then it became October and then November and then it became December," Dingman recalled. "And they kept saying 'We'll come, we'll come.'" Each week, Brautigan phoned Dingman to say, "I'll be up. We'll be up." Tony remembered spending most of the winter alone in Richard's Montana place. "It was kind of neat," he said. "I wrote a whole bunch of stuff."

That fall, Margot Patterson Doss was introduced to Akiko Yoshimura at a party hosted by Don Allen. "I thought: Here's this poor young woman from Japan who has no friends here." Margot wasted little time remedying the situation. A Japanese couple, Fumio and Mieko Wada, lived immediately across Greenwich Street from the Dosses' house on Russian Hill. Margot brought Akiko over to meet them. "They entertained Richard and Aki many times," Doss recalled. "We spent a number of wonderful evenings at Mieko's and Fumio's."

By the end of September, negative reaction to *Dreaming of Babylon* began its ugly critical yawp, newspaper reviewers across the country rushing in for the kill. The bad reviews depressed Brautigan. Casting about for a lifeline, he began asking friends what they thought of the book. Bruce Conner was among those cornered. "It was the first time he had asked me anything like that," Conner said, "and I don't talk about other people's work. I just don't do it. I think it's inappropriate."

Bruce didn't like Richard's novel. "I didn't want to tell him that I didn't like the book." The only thing Conner could think to say concerned a reference to a seventy-five-watt lightbulb in the first chapter. It felt wrong to him. "The book was supposed to be a period piece, which I think was in the 1940s. People didn't have a lot of bright lights in their homes." Conner had worked in a grocery store as a kid in Wichita, Kansas, and remembered all the bulbs there being forty-watters.

"I don't think seventy-five-watt bulbs were popular," Bruce told Richard. "This upset him a great deal because the only thing I could talk to him about was a seventy-five-watt bulb, about his whole novel, and 'Yes,' he'd researched it, and 'yes,' there were seventy-five-watt bulbs in the 1940s." This composed the "sum total" of Bruce Conner's criticism of Richard Brautigan's work.

In November, Brautigan phoned his lawyer, Richard Hodge, and asked for his help. He and Aki yearned to get married, but Richard didn't want the ceremony to take place in San Francisco because he feared his fame would be a "big story" and he and Akiko would be hounded by the press. Hodge came to the rescue. He had a friend, Contra Costa Superior Court Judge Patricia Herron, whom he had known since his two-year stint as a deputy district attorney in Richmond when he first arrived in the Bay Area.

Pat Herron agreed to marry the eager couple, in "complete anonymity," in her home on Point Richmond. The wedding day, December 1, 1977, was warm and clear. Judge Herron lived in a spacious New England–style home overlooking San Francisco Bay. Other than the bride and groom, only the witnesses, Richard and Nancy Hodge, and the presiding judge were in attendance. It was the first time the Hodges ever met Akiko. They thought she was "charming." Aki wore a soft blue-green dress she had brought from Tokyo. Richard dressed in jeans as usual, adding a jacket for the occasion, along with a dressy pair of cream and gray two-tone lizard cowboy boots for a touch of class.

The ceremony took place out on the deck. A bright sun glinted off the wave-tossed bay. Brautigan hated convention and asked Judge Herron to keep the official proceedings as brief and simple as possible. Richard Hodge served as best man. Aki brought Tootsie, her stuffed toy turtle. In Japanese and Chinese legend, turtles symbolize long life. She didn't carry a bridal bouquet or flowers of any kind, thinking this "quite nice" because it was "not ordinary." It was all over in a matter of moments. As Judge Herron pronounced them man and wife, Richard picked a strand of parsley and wound it around her ring finger. "This is your wedding band, dear," he said, laughing with loud satisfaction.

A champagne toast followed the no-frills ceremony. Akiko remembered the "beautiful curved crystal, special wine goblets." Afterward, the wedding party went out for a late afternoon lunch at a fine local neighborhood restaurant. An aura of happiness surrounded the occasion. For the moment, it seemed the good times might last forever.

forty-eight: rattrap roulette

O THER THAN HIS two-month daybook experiment in 1975, Richard Brautigan did not keep a journal. There have been times when I've regretted that I didn't either. Had I even guessed (way back when Richard was my pal and next-door neighbor) that someday I'd be his biographer, I'd have been a proper little Boswell, jotting down every overheard witticism, scribbling away after each shared adventure, keeping the record straight. Without a written chronicle of times gone by, I have to rely on memory, so often an unreliable instrument.

Perhaps my most serious blackout occurred in the fall of 1977. Gary Snyder had a weeklong residency at Montana State University and came over one afternoon to visit Richard. Not that I've forgotten Gary Snyder. I'd admired his writing since college and was thrilled when Richard and Aki invited me and Marian to dinner so we could meet him. I remember that evening very well, not so much the food, but the conversation.

Snyder seemed laid-back and affable, although every word revealed an accumulated wisdom underlying his regular-guy persona. Aki told me that he spoke the best Japanese of any gaijin she'd ever met. She had not yet perfected her own English, but her eyes sparkled with a keen intelligence as she went on in her sing-song accent. "Funny thing about Gary," she said, merriment dancing in her topaz gaze, "in America he all time wear his Buddha robes, but in Tokyo, he only wear cowboy hat." I said I knew just what she meant.

Later that same week, Marian and I reciprocated by hosting a dinner of our own. This is the evening I don't remember, an omission that seems all the more incredible as the following events all transpired under my own roof. My mind remains a blank slate, but fortunately I have the detailed testimony of one of our invited friends supplementing what I have inexplicably forgotten. The guest list included Richard and Akiko; Gary Snyder; Peter and Becky Fonda; poet/novelist Dan Gerber; his wife, Ginny; and Bob Watkins (who later ran a trading post near Taos) and his girlfriend, Sandy.

Having eleven seated at dinner meant breaking out the monogrammed silver and cut-crystal wineglasses, our finest embroidered Irish linen tablecloth spread across the dining room table. There would have been candlelight and a centerpiece of autumn leaves and flowers (aster, phlox, orange Japanese lanterns). Marian was a superb cook. The multicourse meal would have been exquisite, climaxing in coffee, brandy, and a pie made with apples picked from the hundred-year-old tree growing in our front yard. (The secret to the flakiest crust anyone had ever tasted was lard, rendered from the pigs we sent to slaughter every fall.) After dinner, everyone repaired to a spacious living room, heated against the chill night by a barrel-shaped antique wood stove. I remember none of this, evidence of the quantity of red wine I had consumed with dinner.

With elaborate tact and courtesy, like a trained diplomat, Richard had arranged for Gary Snyder to read his poetry that evening. Everyone gathered around as Snyder thumbed through paperback editions of his work, giving voice to lines hewed with a woodsman's skill and shaped by the wisdom of a true sage. "Gary read this lovely poem," Dan Gerber recalled. (The lament of the brain-dead: Japhy Ryder reading in my living room and I can't remember a damn thing.)

Afterward, there was "a lot of heavy drinking going on." The party mingled in shifting conversational groups of twos and threes. At one point, Richard wandered off, perhaps to the kitchen to refresh his whiskey glass. At that time, Marian and I had a rodent problem. I'd set a rattrap in the pantry, where we kept the bags of dog food the big ones favored. These gadgets looked like an ordinary wooden mousetrap only much larger, a comic book exaggeration of the commonplace. When Richard returned to the living room, he carried the cocked rattrap in his hands.

He proposed a bizarre entertainment. The idea was to toss the trap around the room from person to person. The object: not to have the infernal thing go off and get your fingers snapped. "Well, Snyder was, I mean, he was just kind of like, *shhh*, these people are crazy," Dan Gerber told me, describing the mock horror on the face of the guest of honor. But Gary played the game with backwoods gusto, catching the rattrap as if he'd done it all his life, flipping the thing across the room to another potential victim. It was thrown from hand to hand three or four times and never went off.

Disappointed by the lack of action, Richard balanced the rattrap, still cocked, on top of a door frame. He jumped up, banging the trap with his head to spring the mechanism. The rectangular metal bow snapped shut, cutting a large gash in his forehead. Richard's delighted laughter broke the stunned silence. He refused all offers to tend the wound and went around "very proudly" for the remainder of the evening with blood dripping from his brow. I don't remember any of this.

forty-nine: banned in the boondocks

FTER THEIR WEDDING, Richard and Akiko planned to travel to the East Coast. Helen
Brann's office made hotel reservations for them in New York. Brautigan hadn't had much
contact from his agent for several weeks, and the lack of attention troubled him. Richard
depended upon Helen for much more than deal-making. He considered her a friend and expected
undivided loyalty from his friends. Brautigan brooded on the matter until he could no longer stand
it. After a long night of drinking, he phoned Helen Brann at 1:30 am. It was past four in the morning in Manhattan.

Helen had often spoken with her needy client at odd hours, but she was in no mood to deal
with Richard on this particular night. Her "dear, dear friend" Pat Hemingway, someone Brautigan
had met and liked, had been diagnosed with cancer two and a half months earlier. The day before
Thanksgiving, Pat had been released from the hospital and came to stay with Helen Brann, who
was nursing her when Richard called. She was in no mood to set aside her friend's medication
to deal with Brautigan at this late hour. Their curt conversation ended abruptly. Richard said he
would not speak with her again until after the new year and hung up.

Deeply insulted by his agent's continuing "lack of communication," Brautigan sank deeper
and deeper into a melancholy funk. Three days later, he sent a telegram to John Hartnett, who had
joined Helen Brann as a coagent: "Cancel hotel reservations. Not coming east." Richard had told
Helen he would call "next week concerning business," but made no mention of his recent marriage
to Aki. Helen knew "something [had] gone terribly wrong" and "searched for a clue to what [she]
might have done to offend him."

Brann wrote Brautigan a heartfelt handwritten letter, apologizing for her lack of communication and explaining her current painful situation with Pat Hemingway. Helen asked Richard
to call her. "I am worried and anxious to hear from you." Richard did not call. Neither did he
write back to Brann. Instead, he sent a comforting letter to her friend Pat, perceptively describing
Hemingway's "special qualities." Subsequently, Brann placed several phone calls to Brautigan, all
answered by his wife. Her partner, John Hartnett, also failed in several attempts to reach Richard
directly. Akiko was running interference.

Soon afterward, the newlyweds returned to Montana and resumed their low-key life at Pine
Creek with Tony Dingman as their unofficial resident jack-of-all-trades. December days were
short and often gloomy in the Northwest. Freezing weather canceled the fishing possibilities,
although the Yellowstone River remained legally open to anglers year-round. Housebound, surrounded by acres of frozen snow, Richard, Aki, and Tony all looked for amusing ways to pass the
time. Brautigan had his morning writing schedule. Dingman wrote poetry, but had no long-range

projects under way and mostly worked in short bursts. Tony turned his attention to a thousand-piece jigsaw puzzle.

The picture on the box cover showed a harbor scene, boats bobbing at anchor beneath a cloudless blue sky. Dingman set to work on the dining room table. After three days of solitary concentration, the puzzle remained 80 percent complete, everything done except the sky. Dingman avoided the puzzle. He sat in a rocking chair in the front room, staring in mournfully at the dining table. "I can't finish it," he said. "The blue sky is hopeless." Brautigan got the vacuum cleaner, plugged it in, and vacuumed the puzzle, piece by piece, off the table. Tony had never seen his friend look happier. "He loved it," Dingman recalled. Richard returned the vacuum cleaner to storage. "There was just too much blue," Tony said. Soon after, Brautigan wrote a short story he called "Blue Sky."

Richard and Aki went back down to San Francisco for the Christmas holidays. After a spell of rural solitude, Brautigan welcomed the energetic bustle of city life. The Hjortsbergs had left to spend the winter in Haiti; Tom McGuane and his new wife, Laurie, were off in Key West; Russell Chatham had departed for parts unknown. None of the Montana Gang was around, and the weather had turned bitterly cold.

Brautigan's San Francisco friends all greeted Akiko warmly. John and Margot Doss thought the world of her. Don Carpenter sounded enthusiastic albeit sexist. "A very beautiful, very accomplished, very intelligent woman," he said. "The best pair of tits in Japan, bar none." Jack Thibeau remembered Aki as "very pleasant." Although Ron Loewinsohn liked Akiko, he adopted a more pragmatic view. Richard "thought he had gotten the archetypical geisha, who would walk three feet behind him," Ron said. "But Aki was really very modern and very tough."

The Brautigan's new friends, Fumio and Mieko Wada, hosted a grand New Year's Eve party in their honor a month after the wedding. They had entertained Richard and Aki several times previously, "a number of wonderful evenings," parties including Japanese film stars, models, and Nō theater actors. The Dosses, who lived across the street, were among the New Year's guests and remembered a ceremonial dinner "on a tremendous big tray, a big fish in the center surrounded by smaller fishes surrounded by even smaller fishes." All the specialty seafood had been hand-carried to San Francisco from Japan by friends of the Wadas. "Richard loved this," Margot Doss recalled. "It had been done especially for his benefit. That was an enchanted night. We all had such a good time."

Don Carpenter recalled a drunken evening spent at the Wadas' place with Richard and Aki. Fumio's job involved working with a computer in a closet. Don thought he might be a Japanese spy. When he mentioned this to Brautigan, "he sort of didn't deny it." As the evening progressed, Carpenter got very drunk and blacked out. "As I did when I was a drinking person," he confessed years later.

Don woke up about four in the morning in the spare bedroom of the Brautigans' apartment. After an hour of lying in the dark, "eaten by guilt," he got up and left the building. Outside on the street, not seeing his car anywhere, Carpenter reached into his pocket, coming up with "a huge bunch of keys that did not belong to me." Don left them under the doormat and went home.

Later in the morning, after coffee and reading the *Chronicle*, Carpenter called the Brautigans' number. When Richard heard Don's voice on the line, he hung up. Don called back, "wondering what dreadful shit" he had caused. This time, Akiko picked up the phone. "I wanted to tell you about the keys under the door," Carpenter said.

"You broke Richard's glasses and you bit me," Aki shrieked.

"What! I did what?"

Brautigan grabbed the phone from his wife as Carpenter stammered in "this guilt paroxysm." Before he could utter a word of apology, Richard said, "I don't want to talk to you, goddamn you, asshole!" and slammed down the receiver.

Don immediately wrote Richard a letter "of abject apology with no literary attempt to palliate my evil." He literally begged for forgiveness. During his "guilty hangover," another friend, Bill Hamilton, the cartoonist, phoned him. Carpenter told the story, and the artist laughed. Hamilton made a drawing of the episode showing an obviously hungover man on the telephone. The caption read: "I did not break your glasses. I did not bite your wife." It ran in the *Chronicle* and a number of other newspapers in Hamilton's feature, "The Now Society."

Brautigan got a big kick out of the cartoon. He had long since forgiven Carpenter for his louche behavior. "I think Richard thought that Hamilton had class," Don observed, "because Hamilton is always telling people or hinting that he is related to Alexander Hamilton."

In January, J. D. Leitaker, principal of the Anderson Union High School in Shasta County, California, removed five of Richard Brautigan's books (*A Confederate General from Big Sur, Trout Fishing in America, The Pill versus the Springhill Mine Disaster, The Abortion: An Historical Romance,* and *Rommel Drives on Deep into Egypt*) from the shelves of the school library and from the classroom of V. I. Wexner, who, for the past eight years, had taught Developmental Reading in Anderson, a small lumber mill community twelve miles southeast of Redding in the Siskiyou foothills. Wexner, a 1963 Princeton graduate, had been having great success encouraging his students to read by offering complete freedom of choice and providing a wide and varied cross-section of literature from which to choose. A native New Yorker who had attended an experimental high school, V. I. must have seemed an unconventional teacher in conservative Shasta County. For his part, Wexner considered Principal Leitaker to be a "bully."

Leitaker's "suspicion" arose the previous month when Wexner ordered new books for his class and a discrepancy appeared between the titles as written on the purchase order and the full titles printed on the receipts received by the head of the school's reading program. Wexner had shortened two of the titles to *The Springhill Mine Disaster* and *An Historical Romance.* "I think the instructor could find works of a similar nature without the sexual references and the profanity that is in these books," Leitaker said.

This wasn't Brautigan's first brush with censorship. Two years earlier, in April of 1976, Stefanie Rose, a Long Island high school teacher (Carmel, New York), wrote to Richard asking for his help. She had been teaching *In Watermelon Sugar* as part of her literature of fantasy course for three years. A month earlier, "a rather outspoken member" of the community had pulled his children out of the Carmel School, citing Brautigan's book as the reason. In an official complaint, this parent claimed "the explicit sexual passages" and "the completely aberrational behavior depicted" led to "the criminal corruption of my son's morals." Although a teacher's committee, formed in response to this complaint, found nothing "wrong" with *In Watermelon Sugar*, Rose thought the "fireworks are still flying." In the end, the Carmel School District took no action against Richard's novel, but clearly trouble was brewing from coast to coast.

Unaware of the controversy swirling about his author's work in Shasta County, Seymour Lawrence made a business trip to San Francisco. Among his many appointments, an invitation to

1349 Kearny Street came as a pleasant diversion. Richard Brautigan greeted Sam with a bottle of top-shelf bourbon. The other guests were Richard and Nancy Hodge. Lawrence and Hodge met for the first time, qualifying the occasion as a business deduction. Akiko prepared a "fine dinner" and charmed everyone with her considerable talents as a hostess. The recent marriage seemed destined for success.

When Richard and Aki returned to Montana at the end of January, their pleasant insular life with Tony Dingman picked up again without missing a beat. "Some very, very good times," Tony recalled. "Lots of cooking, lots of drinking, lots of laughs."

Occasionally, their isolation was interrupted by the arrival of a guest. One frozen day with the snow very deep and the temperature locked at thirteen below zero, Tony drove Richard over the hill to the Bozeman airport to pick up Harry Dean Stanton, who was flying in from Los Angeles for a short visit. Brautigan imagined the look of shock on Harry Dean's face when he first saw the frozen landscape after having left the palm trees of L.A. only hours before. They drove the stunned actor back to Pine Creek along a road Brautigan described as "an icy sword cutting starkly through country that wore winter like a suit of albino armor."

On the way, they encountered six huge crows eating an abandoned truck tire in the middle of the road. Black and insolent, they made no move to fly as the car approached. Tony swerved around them, their double-ply dinner uninterrupted. "You've got some winter here," Harry Dean said. "Those crows are hungry." Brautigan later recorded the incident as a short story in *The Tokyo–Montana Express*.

Early in February, Tony got the impression that Richard and Akiko "wanted to be together on a honeymoon or something," so he boarded the Northern Pacific at the Livingston depot and took the train back east to visit his sister in Boston. His timing left something to be desired, his arrival coinciding with one of the worst New England blizzards of the century. He got stuck in New York and, with much effort, finally made it to Boston. Montana now seemed a balmy paradise to Dingman.

Brautigan spoke on the phone with his agent early in February. He told Helen Brann he had decided it would be better to publish *June 30th, June 30th* in mid-October, rather than in March, as previously scheduled. If the book was published in March it would have only a couple months to catch on with college and university students, Richard's strongest audience, before the summer break. A mid-October pub date provided almost the entire school year for Brautigan's market. Richard wanted all of Jim Harrison's letter used as the jacket copy instead of cutting it down to a blurb. Brann conveyed Brautigan's wishes in a letter to Sam Lawrence in Boston.

Helen planned to leave for a vacation in the Virgin Islands. On the eve of her departure for St. Thomas, she spoke by phone with Richard. Her client had changed his mind once again about the dust jacket copy for *June 30th, June 30th*. Brautigan still wanted to use the Harrison letter in its entirety but asked that the publisher cut a long praise-filled paragraph ("the most intimate book Richard Brautigan has ever written [. . .] a unique look at Japan as seen through the eyes of one of America's most popular poets") he had composed himself, substituting a simple biographical statement.

The same day, V. I. Wexner sent an open letter to members of the Anderson High school board. He asked to appear before the board when they met to discuss the banning of the Brautigan books. Wexner told the board members, "Richard Brautigan is a serious writer" and that his books were "no more bawdy than Shakespeare or Chaucer." Intuiting most of the board might be unfamiliar with Brautigan's work, he urged them to read *In Watermelon Sugar*, the title he "would recommend first, if a student wanted an unusual book."

The Anderson Union High School District Board of Trustees, which eight years earlier had banned J. D. Salinger's *A Catcher in the Rye*, held a public meeting on Wednesday, February 22, to deal with the issue of the Brautigan books. Forty-four people, mostly parents, teachers, and former students, were in attendance for the ninety-minute discussion. The faculty Professional Relations Committee and the school administration's Administrative Council, acting under a district policy on resolving disputes over instructional material, both recommended that three of the books, *Trout Fishing*, *The Pill*, and *The Abortion*, be removed from the high school shelves. The committees differed on the acceptability of *In Watermelon Sugar* and *Revenge of the Lawn* and left the final decision on these books to the board of trustees.

After a comment period where one parent said, "We are sick of people teaching our children barnyard morals," and an impassioned plea for academic freedom by V. I. Wexner, Trustee Frank Yanger made a motion to prohibit the three books, stating, "I read one of them and, frankly, thought it was garbage." The board agreed with his assessment and voted to ban the three, citing Brautigan's work as "unfit" for Anderson High School. The next day the news broke in the *San Francisco Chronicle*. He didn't know it yet, but Richard Brautigan had just joined an exclusive and distinguished club. At one time or another, *1984*, *The Grapes of Wrath*, *To Kill a Mockingbird*, *Huckleberry Finn*, and *The Diary of Anne Frank* had all been banned in America.

At the time, Brautigan was more concerned with the status of his foreign editions. How many were still in print? Had any of the rights reverted back to him? Spurred on by Akiko, he wrote Tom Mori of the Tuttle-Mori Agency in Tokyo, his Japanese representative, asking these questions. Receiving no reply after two months, Richard had Dick Hodge handle the matter for him.

Brautigan continued working on his Montana stories during this period. Richard's short fiction often explored the poetic possibilities of the mundane. He wrote about buying lightbulbs and the much-anticipated spring opening of the Tastee-Freez, whose fast food he loved (the Big Tee burger, crispy onion rings, milk shakes in fifty flavors). Brautigan read each new short story aloud to Akiko, always first to hear them. "At that time, I have to be like a kind of a secretary," she said.

Margot Patterson Doss wrote a weekly Sunday column, "San Francisco at Your Feet," for the *Chronicle*, and on March 5, it took the form of a letter to Richard. She began with a quote from *Trout Fishing* and thanked Brautigan for his $39.97 check covering the last phone call he made to Aki in Tokyo while her houseguest the previous year. Margot used the money to buy a new umbrella. The column described the Fish Roundabout at the Academy of Sciences (Steinhart Aquarium division) in Golden Gate Park. The Roundabout, "a surreal indoor ocean surrounded by wall-to-wall carpeting," swirled upward like an aquatic Guggenheim Museum. The display struck Doss as an ideal Brautigan environment. "If you get any inspirations on how to fish this place, please let me know," she wrote.

The morning the column appeared, someone read it to Richard over the phone. Brautigan so enjoyed the piece, he called the Dosses and said, "Margot, I'm going to go out and catch you a trout, and I will bring it to you on ice." Richard proved true to his word. He caught the fish, flew the next day with it in a hand-carried cooler down to San Francisco, "put it on this beautiful tray of ice," and proudly delivered it to 1331 Greenwich Street, a grand, extravagant Brautigan gesture.

Richard spent most of March and April in San Francisco. The art department at Dell didn't like the *June 30th* cover design based on Erik Weber's passport stamp photograph. They planned on not using it and refused to pay Erik for his work. Richard still had complete design control, and his friend appealed to him for help. Brautigan intervened, insisting the publishing house follow his original instructions.

Dell went through the motions. They paid Weber for his pictures, but graphic designer Walter Harper modified Erik's original concept of a centered passport stamp resembling an ancient Japanese seal. Harper used a more realistic image of the stamp, setting it off-center and turned at a slight angle. Weber hated this but demanded a design credit on the dust jacket. The Dell art department had the last laugh. Weber's credit read: "Jacket illustration adapted from photograph," misspelling his name "Eric."

On April 6, Emmett Grogan's body was found on a New York City subway car at the Coney Island–Stillwell Avenue station, the last stop on the Brighton Beach Line of the old BMT. He had died from a heroin overdose. The fast-living Digger outlaw had come to the end of the road. Brautigan had lost track of Grogan over the years since they hung out together in the Haight but retained an interest in his old friend. A copy of Emmett's crime novel, *Final Score*, published two years before his death, was one of the few books Richard kept in the small built-in bookshelf at Pine Creek.

Richard and Aki returned to Montana at the end of April. The lengthening days grew warmer. Pleasant sunny fishing weather blossomed between the snow flurries. Tony Dingman "rode the dog" from Boston to San Francisco. Two days after Dingman got off the Greyhound bus, Brautigan phoned him from Pine Creek, saying, "Come on back." Tony flew up to Montana, and life with Richard and Aki picked up as if he'd never left.

Weather permitting, Brautigan and Dingman played "horse" under the basketball hoop at the Pine Creek School after the kids went home in the afternoon. "Richard was a very, very competitive guy," Tony said. "He would get crazy if he would lose." Both men wrote every day. "We kind of encouraged each other because it was fun," Dingman remembered. A bit shy, Dingman almost never showed his poetry to Brautigan, although he remembered "one time Richard read some stuff I'd been doing up there."

Brautigan worked on his short story sequence. Reading his work aloud to his wife started Richard thinking about a framework for his new fiction. He determined some of the stories should have a Japanese focus, deciding to return soon to Tokyo and write about life observed there. "There should be a book of short stories about life in Montana and Tokyo. I thought the contrast would be interesting and dramatic." Brautigan planned on traveling alone to Japan. He explained this to Akiko, telling her she couldn't go with him for "residency requirements."

Many evenings were spent drinking and carousing. "We had some good times," Dingman said. Warren Oates stopped by to join in the fun whenever he was up from L.A. at his place on Six Mile. One time, a San Francisco friend of Tony's sent a lid of grass in the mail. Dingman smoked the weed, and his whiskey consumption tapered. His friend said it was Mexican weed. Brautigan read a magazine article about the U.S. government's drug policy of aerial spraying marijuana fields in Mexico with a dangerous chemical herbicide called Parquat. Richard pointed this out to Tony, who started coughing. Soon, he coughed more and more.

"It's the Parquat," Brautigan insisted. "It's the Parquat!"

Dingman's cough worsened. Finally, he flushed his stash down the toilet. "Richard loved it," Tony remembered, "he thought that was the greatest." The cough went away. Tony learned later that the marijuana had been grown in Sacramento. "It was psychosomatic, man," Dingman said. "There was no Parquat."

Bourbon-infused evening conversations ranged freely from country music to politics to litera-ture to girls and back again, but one topic generally remained off-limits. Brautigan never talked about his childhood. "I never asked, and he never volunteered," Tony recalled. "We had a truce at that level." Richard did briefly mention he had lived in Great Falls for a time as a child. Akiko was curious, wanting to know more about her husband's early life.

To please his wife, Brautigan planned a return trip to Great Falls, the only time he ever delib-erately revisited a scene from his childhood. They picked a bright sunny day for the six-hour round-trip drive, setting out in "White Acre" with Tony at the wheel and Aki entranced by the sprawling enormity of the Montana landscape. Reaching the little city on the Missouri River, their first destination was the Great Falls grade school Richard attended for a few months when he was nine. After a bit of driving around, they found the old brick building. Brautigan got out and walked to the entrance, taking hold of the doorknob. "He remembered sticking his tongue on this doorknob," Dingman said. "It froze, and they had to come out and pour warm water to get his tongue off."

Akiko told the same story six years later to journalist Lawrence Wright, only from a different perspective. "It was so cold," she said. Richard "put very great stress on the coldness of the door-knob. He was scared of it. He would touch the doorknob and go home again."

After finding his old grade school, they searched out the establishment where Tex Porterfield had labored as a fry cook. Tony recalled it as being "a kind of a *hofbrau*." Brautigan stared at the building where he had once lived, a place he hadn't seen in thirty-four years. "One of my step-fathers used to work here," he said. "After he got off work, he used to come upstairs and beat me." Richard's stories of his hardscrabble youth varied, depending on his audience. He once told Rip Torn he was only four when the fry cook tied him to the bedpost while away at work, saying, "He gave me enough slack so I could get to the can and, more important, so I could get to the corner and look out the window."

His long-distance trip down memory lane finished, Richard said, "Let's go," and Tony Ding-man drove them back to Pine Creek.

April drew to a close. Brautigan made plans for his trip to Japan. He wanted to leave at the beginning of June. Aki mentioned that her mother was celebrating her sixtieth birthday right around that time. Richard wrote to Fusako Nishizawa, telling her of his intended itinerary, saying he hoped to see her on her birthday. Brautigan and his wife headed back to San Francisco at the end of the month. They discussed traveling on to New York for a week in the middle of May. Richard reasoned such an excursion might take the onus off his upcoming solo jaunt to Japan.

A peevish five-page letter from Helen Brann, written on her new stationery with the letter-head "THE BRANN-HARTNETT AGENCY, INC.," reached Brautigan soon after he returned to San Francisco. (John and Helen established a partnership at the beginning of 1978.) "I have tried to reach you several times in the last couple of weeks leaving messages on your answering machine or with Aki, and you have not returned my calls." Brann got to the point by page 3: "On a larger issue, Richard, I am very distressed that the spirit of cooperation seems to have gone out of our relationship; I cannot work with a writer who avoids talking with me, who communicates with me through a lawyer, or who seems to take offense when I cannot take a non-emergency call long after my office has closed." Helen clearly felt her professional and personal relationship with Richard was coming apart at the seams. She ended, "I only know I will not continue as things are now."

Richard read Helen's letter several times. He underlined key passages with a pencil. On the first of May, Brautigan wrote Brann a formal typed reply. Half as long as Brann's, his letter was a lengthy message for a terse correspondent. Richard addressed the matter with cold logic. He agreed their ten-year relationship was too important to throw away "because of a misunderstanding," and that unless they reestablish that relationship "on a professional footing," it would be best to "each go our separate way."

Brautigan wrote a note to Seymour Lawrence a week later. There was "a good possibility" that he and Aki would be in New York the following week. Richard promised Sam to "bring the seagull," continuing a shared private joke. The next day, Brautigan visited Marcia Clay. She'd moved to a new and larger apartment on Stockton Street. Richard "snailed his way back into my secluded circles," she wrote in her diary. Clay felt "inspired" after Brautigan's visits but did not "particularly appreciate his sexual advances," calling his tongue probing between her lips "a lugubrious eel."

Richard brought books of poetry along when he visited Marcia. "Elizabethan poetry," she said. "Japanese poetry. We would read poetry together." Brautigan read Clay's writing and offered suggestions, helping her edit. When he didn't come around, she wished to "spend more moments of complicity" with him. Marcia felt Richard one of the "rare men" who loved and understood her. "I don't particularly mind his drunkeness [sic]," she confided in her diary, "but do find it distasteful to consume his kisses."

Another evening early in May, Richard sat down at the end of the bar in Enrico's. The conversation touched on messages sent in bottles across oceans. Brautigan was leaving for Japan in a few weeks. The crowd decided to experiment. Ward Dunham produced an empty Drambuie bottle and soaked off the labels. The regulars were invited to write private messages on little slivers of paper and slip them inside.

A couple hours later there were almost forty messages in the bottle. Along with Brautigan and Dunham, other secret-message writers were Dwain Cox, Tony Dingman, Donna Galloway, David Fechheimer, and Ward's wife, Marian. After all the messages had been inserted, Calligrapher Dunham sealed the cork with red sealing wax, adding a wax seal on the side of the bottle. "It resembled the cross-section of an evening in an American bar," Brautigan wrote, describing the bottle's contents.

Mrs. Nishizawa, Akiko's mother, responded to Richard, her "barbarian son," on May 12, saying she was "deeply touched" by his letter and was "happy to be with you on my Kanreki day," when all the members of her family planned to gather together to celebrate her sixtieth birthday. She had picked two days after Brautigan's planned arrival in Japan as the date for the celebration. No mention was made of her daughter's absence. The Nishizawa family accepted Richard's explanation that immigration regulations prohibited Aki from leaving the United States.

Richard and Akiko did not travel to New York in May. Before leaving for Tokyo, Brautigan spoke with Helen Brann about using a new photograph of himself with the *June 30th, June 30th* ads. He told Helen about the Tokyo monument to the faithful dog. Richard wanted his picture taken there by a top Japanese photographer within a week of his arrival, stipulating Delacorte provide a fee of $500 for the project. Sam Lawrence received Brann's letter, circling the amount, writing $300 in the margin. Richard had design approval, but Sam controlled the purse strings.

Brautigan arrived back in Japan on the first of June. He always traveled light, with minimal luggage. He made sure to pack the sealed Drambuie bottle full of messages from Enrico's, and *Hello, I Must Be Going*, a 586-page book about Groucho Marx by Charlotte Chandler. Akiko sent him off with a small gift for her old friend Yoko, married to Hiroshi Yoshimura, a music scholar and composer known for his "sound chaos" theory. She hoped Richard would get together with them during his stay.

Brautigan checked into the Keio Plaza Hotel (room 3324), bringing a bottle of imported cognac from the duty-free shop as a gift for the manager, ensuring a continuation of his discount. On Saturday, Richard attended his mother-in-law's *kanreki* celebration. In accordance with tradition, Mrs. Nishizawa wore the symbolic color red to mark the occasion. The Japanese word for baby means "red one." At sixty a person is reborn, completing the twelve-year Chinese zodiac five times, once for each of the five elements. Richard greatly enjoyed the party but never wrote a word about the event.

Brautigan resumed his familiar routine in Tokyo. He woke up late in his hotel room, ate some breakfast, wandered about the city, pausing to write a story or two in various cafés. After dinner with friends or a double feature at a soft-porn movie, Brautigan ended the night at The Cradle, returning very drunk to the Keio Plaza, where he fell asleep with the television set on and the sound turned down low so the musical Japanese voices murmured "like the sea at descending tide."

Richard had met the photographer Shimpei Asai when he took some pictures for the Japanese edition of *Sombrero Fallout*, published the previous year. Two years younger than Brautigan, Asai had received a prize from the Japan Advertising Photographers' Association in 1965 and had photographed the Beatles during their 1966 visit to Tokyo. The second week in June, Brautigan and Shimpei traveled to the Shibuya Station. Brautigan wore jeans, a denim shirt, and a cowboy hat. Asai posed the author by the bronze statue of Hachikō, holding on to the pedestal, the faithful dog standing a foot taller than Richard's ten-gallon headgear. Shimpei took his pictures from an angle. It made for an interesting composition, yet Richard seemed diminished. After making a final selection, Brautigan asked Asai to send copies directly to Sam Lawrence and Helen Brann.

On June 12, the 7.4-magnitude Miyagi-ken Oki earthquake trembled through Tokyo for thirty terrifying seconds. The capital suffered slight damage, but the city of Sendai, 180 miles to the north, took the brunt of the quake. Twenty-eight people died, 1,325 were injured, and 1,183 houses collapsed. The night before the temblor, Richard got very drunk. Akiko teased she'd heard a rumor that he was "swinging" with an 8.5-magnitude hangover.

Several days later, Richard had dinner with Japanese novelist Kenzaburō Ōe (*Nip the Buds, Shoot the Kids*; *A Personal Matter*; *The Silent Cry*), who won the Nobel Prize ten years after Brautigan's suicide. Oe and Brautigan had much in common, both being born in 1935, both growing up poor in rural forested communities, both experiencing World War II from the wide-eyed perspective of small children. Richard had long admired Oe's writing. On this occasion, Richard's new friend Kenzaburō pulled a pair of goggles from the bag he carried and put them on.

The other customers in the restaurant stared at them. Brautigan acted as if this were perfectly sane and rational: lots of well-dressed Japanese men wear goggles in fashionable restaurants. The latest fad. All the while, he kept thinking, *"Please take the fucking goggles off."* Perhaps Oe was a mind reader. After a couple minutes, he removed his goggles and replaced them in the bag.

Brautigan felt a surge of relief. The night returned to a semblance of normality. The two writers talked about the earthquake. Oe's firstborn son, Hikari, had been born with a cranial deformity and suffered from a mental disability. (Oe's 1964 book, *A Personal Matter*, dealt with this family tragedy.) Oe told Brautigan he was trying to explain to his son about earthquakes in a way that Hikari could understand so he would not be afraid. Kenzaburō told Richard he'd been unable to find the right words.

"Does he understand what the wind is?" Brautigan asked.

"Yes," Oe said.

"Tell him that an earthquake is a wind that blows through the ground."

Kenzaburō Ōe liked this suggestion. Richard Brautigan was pleased that his companion didn't put his goggles back on.

Akiko had gone to visit friends in Seattle, which she found "too quiet," missing "something crazy, or energy." "I miss you crazy man," she wrote her husband. "Living away from you, I realized how special person you are." Aki used her time in Seattle fabric shopping for the house in Montana, a place in dire need of a woman's touch. Northwest Airlines was on strike, and Akiko took Amtrak back to Montana at the end of June. Waking up in roomette 5 at 8:00 am, she saw the wide Missouri outside her window surrounded by "amazing green" bright with yellow wildflowers. Throughout the day, the Missouri seemed to appear at least a hundred times. "I sang a song 'Oh Shenandoah, I long to see you . . .' in my heart."

Toward the end of June, Takako Shiina's younger brother, the stage actor Keisuke Nakai, drove Brautigan a hundred kilometers southwest of Tokyo down to Ajiro, a small fishing village on the Izu peninsula. Takako owned a condominium in Ajiro, a place renowned as a hot springs resort and fishing spot. Nine months pregnant, Takako came along on the trip with her brother's wife. Richard brought the sealed Drambuie bottle.

Takako's condo faced west, overlooking the Sagami Gulf. Unable to sleep the first night of his visit, Brautigan stood at a window around one in the morning, looking down at the lights on four squid-fishing boats anchored below on the dark surface of the sea. The fishermen used their lights to attract squid. Richard thought they looked like a constellation of stars in the night sky.

The next morning, Takako rented a boat to take everyone fishing. Richard had planned to bring the message-filled bottle and launch it into the unknown, but he accidentally left it behind because he couldn't stop thinking about the squid fishermen "fishing until dawn and maybe having a drink or two before going to sleep." When Brautigan realized his mistake, they returned to shore, setting back out to sea not long afterward with the bottle in hand. After setting it adrift, they spent the rest of the hot afternoon fishing. Takako caught a large octopus, which she cooked for dinner along with the rest of their catch. Exhausted from the struggle of hauling the big mollusk up from the depths, Takako rested her head against the gunnel, shaded by her broad-brimmed straw hat. Richard, who hadn't been fishing, sat in the bow, staring back at the shore when Keisuke shot the picture of them that later graced the back cover of *The Tokyo–Montana Express*.

The episode of the squid fishermen and the forgotten Drambuie bottle became short stories that Brautigan wrote in his notebooks during two months in Japan. Richard also transformed an evening he cooked spaghetti for Takako into fiction. They dined with her husband and another

Japanese stage actor in the kitchen of the Shiina apartment upstairs above The Cradle. Richard discovered a bucketful of *dojyo*, tiny live eels, a couple feet away from the stove, swimming "in circles like science-fiction children of spaghetti." Takako had bought them fresh to make a special soup.

Another night out became "The Eyes of Japan." This hot, humid June evening began when Richard and Takako had drinks at her father's house with director Kirio Urayama and Choichiro Kawarazaki, a famous Japanese actor. After leaving her parents' place, they all went to dinner at Kawarazaki's "Western-style" home. Here they drank sake on the rocks. Choichiro's wife, Eiko Ito, a retired television star, prepared snacks. The actor exclaimed, "I am the lion of my own house." Later, he helped his wife prepare dinner. Brautigan thought they made "a very efficient kitchen team."

Brautigan wrote notebook stories about a wide variety of everyday subjects. One told of a tall young woman, "wearing a simple white dress [. . .] faded pink socks [. . .] very cheap white, plastic shoes," who thanked Richard in English for offering a seat on the Yamanote Line train. Another was about a "beautiful and very sad poem" concerning unfaithful women by Shuntarō Tanikawa. Others described his dinner with Kenzaburō Ōe and watching a Japanese stage production of My Fair Lady in Tokyo with Takako. There was even a story about a story Takako told him of why the bartender at The Cradle didn't come to work one day (he was at the funeral of a young friend who committed suicide by jumping from a hospital window after his arm was amputated).

Shuntarō Tanikawa's work eschewed haiku in favor of the sonnet form. He'd translated Mother Goose and Charles Schultz's *Peanuts*, and was a poet Richard Brautigan much admired. He liked the man's "quick and honest" intelligence. Almost the same age (Tanikawa was three years older), they were introduced at The Cradle. One evening, Shuntarō took Richard and Takako to the home of Thomas Fitzsimmons, an American poet visiting Japan with his wife. Born in Lowell, Massachusetts, in 1926, Fitzsimmons had gone into World War II as an underage merchant seaman shortly after Pearl Harbor. By the war's end, after Hiroshima, he demobilized. In the years following, he worked as a writer/editor at the *New Republic* and the *Asahi Daily News* in Tokyo.

Tanikawa joined Brautigan for lunch at the Keio Plaza on another occasion. Their conversation ranged over "Western movies, poetry, the difference between Japan and America, literature, Montana weather, writers [they both] liked." At one point, Tanikawa paused, searching his mind for something he wished to say. When at last he spoke, his tone was flat and confessional. "I live with three people over eighty years old," Shuntarō said. He didn't explain himself. Tanikawa shared an apartment with his elderly parents and an old aunt. Taken by surprise, Richard didn't know how to reply. He felt unable to come up with an answer. "It was one of the most extraordinary things a person has ever said to me," he observed. The two men sat silently staring at each other and "The time seemed endless like growing old." Brautigan wrote down the episode later, calling it "Four People in Their Eighties."

One of Brautigan's strangest notebook tales grew out of his persistent insomnia. Early on a mid-July morning, Richard wandered about the lobby of the Keio Plaza, observing the hotel's Teletype as it came alive for the day. Brautigan carefully recorded the wire service machine's preliminary clattering keystrokes, noting all the many repeated apostrophes ("''''"), recurrent letter "M"s and the common typist's warm-up phrase, "THE QUICK BROWN FOX JUMPS OVER THE LAZY DOG," in an "almost religious chant." Richard wrote it all down. He called the story "Subscribers to the Sun."

Back in Pine Creek, Akiko fell ill, running a fever. An "awful" conversation with her drunken husband depressed her all the more. She walked down the road to ask for help at the Pine Creek Lodge and found everyone desperately hungover. Aki thought summer must make everybody crazy in Montana. "No one is normal except Gatts [sic] and Marian's family," she wrote to Richard, inspired by Marian Hjortsberg's recent visit to her sickbed. The two women talked through the afternoon as woolly fluff drifted down like snow from the cottonwood trees.

Akiko's illness, combined with the isolation of Montana life, intensified her loneliness. In desperation, she called Don Carpenter. "I can't understand," she pleaded. "Why did he do this? He married me. He brought me over here. We had a good time for a while, and we came to Montana, and then he went back to Japan. He's left me. It's been a month. Why did he do that?"

Don couldn't think of what he might say to calm Aki down. He knew he couldn't tell the truth. There was no way Carpenter could say what he was thinking: "You've married a man that you've never met. You don't know this guy, and he doesn't know you. And he's had an obsession with Oriental women for ten years and you're just one of them."

Don said none of this. He did the best he could in the moment. "Akiko," he said, "don't you realize that you've married a crazy man?"

Aki's fever broke, and she felt better. She worked on fixing up the house and started a garden in the weed-choked plot out back. Akiko tilled the earth and pulled weeds, planting various Japanese vegetable seeds. This made her happy, working up a healthy sweat. When she was done, she tapped herself on her back in the traditional manner of Japanese farmers, "*ton, ton, ton.*" Realizing she would see her husband again in less than a month filled her with joy and helped conquer her loneliness. She wished she'd been able to control her feelings and wanted him to know this was the first time in her life she'd ever lived alone. "I love you so much," she wrote in a letter to Richard.

Far off in Japan, Richard had returned to Tokyo from his trip to the Inland Sea. He enjoyed seeing other parts of the country, but as his wife observed, in his heart he was "the Tokyo-boy!" Akiko's friend Yoko Yoshimura had seen Brautigan's name in *Asahi Shimbun*, one of Japan's oldest and largest national daily newspapers. She had not yet contacted him, apprehensive that her limited understanding of English would make communication difficult. Yoko had approached an interpreter, but he mistakenly thought Hiroshi Yoshimura, away on a concert tour, had been Akiko's first husband and, wanting to avoid any possible conflict, declined to help. Because of this misunderstanding, Richard and Yoko never got together during his long stay in Japan and Akiko's gift went astray.

Northwest Airlines remained on strike. Aki called the carrier "North-worst." She planned a trip to the East Coast. The only available ticket involved traveling by a circuitous late-night route on Delta. Before departing, she wrote a letter to her aunt in Japan, describing her loneliness and a fear that Richard might not come back. Akiko also described the bondage her husband had introduced into their sex life. Was this normal? On a lighter note, she worried the cabbages she'd planted might not survive during her absence.

After a couple days in New York with a visit to the Museum of Modern Art, Akiko traveled upstate to Bard College in Annondale-on-Hudson to join Ron Loewinsohn and Kitty Hughes, who were spending the summer there. Ron's friend Leon Botstein, the president of Bard, arranged for them to live in a "wonderful" house on the campus at the end of a green field stretching down to the Hudson River. Kitty remembered Aki as "kind of unhappy" that summer. She took long walks with Akiko while her friend looked for wild greens. "These are like we have in Japan," Aki said, picking plants she took home and cooked for Ron and Kitty.

By the end of July, Brautigan had written fifty-two new short stories. Back in San Francisco, after a three-week stay with the Loewinsohns, Akiko bragged of her husband's achievement to Marcia Clay when they spent an evening together. On the first of August, Aki waited at the airport as Richard's plane touched down, ending his two-month visit to Japan. The newlyweds resumed their life together on Kearny Street. Brautigan made his mind up to move out, wanting a new place to live. Akiko "really loved" their little home on Kearny and didn't understand why Richard "was unhappy about it."

The task of searching for a new apartment fell to Aki while Richard took care of business. He got together with his secretary and read aloud the stories he'd written in his notebooks in Japan. His often illegible handwriting required this procedure. Glenise Butcher had recently gotten married and now used her new husband's last name, Sibbern. She took everything down in her steno pad in shorthand, typing up clean copies later. Among the stories Brautigan dictated were "A Different or the Same Drummer," "Fantasy Ownership," and "Harem."

The second week in August, Akiko brought Francis Ford Coppola to lunch at Marcia Clay's apartment. Clay met Coppola the previous year in the Napa Valley town of Yountville, at a show of her artwork in the local theater. Afterward, Marcia sat with Francis and his wife, Eleanor, at a table for four at "a very private dinner" at the French Laundry, a Yountville restaurant occupying a stone building built in the 1880s. The restaurant gained its curious name because the place housed a French steam laundry in the 1920s.

"A friend of mine is well acquainted with you," Marcia said to break the ice. "Richard Brautigan."

"Does he tie up your feet and hands?" Coppola inquired, taking Clay completely off guard. The film director explained he'd heard of these things from his girlfriend, Melissa Mathison, who had once enjoyed a brief fling with Brautigan. Marcia found it "really strange" for Francis to talk so openly in front of his wife, while at the same time feeling "very defensive" of Richard.

"Richard Brautigan has some faults," she said, "but he is my friend." Clay explained she had never been Brautigan's lover. She "wasn't attracted to him that way" and therefore had no comment regarding bondage. Coppola couldn't resist a final jab at Richard. "He makes terrible spaghetti," Francis said.

Marcia Clay believed Francis Ford Coppola had "an enormous crush" on Akiko Brautigan. On the day they came for lunch, Marcia thought Aki was "leading [Francis] around by the neck on a leash because she was the first Asian woman that he'd become smitten with. He was just staring at her with great big, round, absorbent eyes." Brautigan's close friends, Curt Gentry and Don Carpenter, gossiped that his wife was having an affair with Coppola. Clay regarded their relationship a harmless flirtation. Aki "was very aware that she had a mystique and effect over a lot of Richard's friends," Marcia observed. She also noted that Francis "was willing to have some kind of a fling with a married friend of a friend while he was married."

Lunch at Clay's apartment stretched out to "three or four hours [. . .] it was a kind of marvelous exchange." At one point, Coppola said, "This would be wonderful just to have women looking after me all day." Marcia considered him to be "very old-fashioned Italian." Confirming this,

Francis accusingly asked, "Why aren't you married?" Clay, only twenty-four, found his question "sort of strange." Coppola was always friendly to her after that afternoon, greeting her warmly whenever their paths crossed on the streets of North Beach.

June 30th, June 30th was published simultaneously in hardcover and paperback on August 11. Three thousand hardcover copies were printed. Sam Lawrence sent Brautigan a congratulatory telegram, mailing a copy of the book on the same day, asking Richard "to write something nice and return to your erstwhile publisher." A box of complimentary copies followed. Richard began inscribing and signing, giving them away to friends.

At the same time, Akiko searched for a new apartment. She found one to her liking up between Polk and Larkin on Russian Hill, the second floor of a three-story building at 1264 Lombard Street. It was an attractive Spanish-style building with twin sets of double bay windows perched over one of the steepest streets in the city. The floor-through flat pleased Richard. "Why didn't I buy a place earlier?" Brautigan complained. "It's ridiculous to buy now. Everything's so high."

After she found their new digs, it became Aki's job to pack them up and move them there. While she worked, Richard was nowhere to be found. "On the moving days he would disappear," she said. Akiko called Bekins. The moving van arrived at Kearny Street on the last day of August and trucked all their stuff across to Russian Hill.

Brautigan devoted most of August to business, reconnecting with his agent as if nothing had happened between them. Early in the month, Helen Brann informed him about everything that happened while he was away in Japan. The advertising schedule for *June 30th* was of primary concern. Helen told Richard a planned ad in the Sunday *New York Times* would consume most of Dell's $6,000 advertising budget. Knowing his books never sold as well on the East Coast, Brautigan suggested it might be better to spend the money at the *Los Angeles Times* and *Rolling Stone*. Sam Lawrence called Brautigan. After a lengthy conversation, the publisher agreed to run a four-fifths-of-a-page ad for *June 30th* in the Sunday *New York Times Book Review* with a panel across the bottom announcing the publication of the Delta edition of *Dreaming of Babylon*. The money saved would allow for additional advertisements in Chicago, L.A., and San Francisco newspapers.

Brautigan took his mind off work at night, sitting at a bar, most often Enrico's, drink in hand. These nocturnal excursions remained strictly stag. Japanese husbands traditionally behaved in this manner, so Akiko perceived nothing unusual. After the bars closed, dead drunk, Richard rang Marcia Clay's doorbell. She often painted until dawn. Visitors at three in the morning were not unusual. Clay enjoyed Brautigan's conversation even when he was inebriated. He described "the forms of the thought process and reasoning." Richard imagined "horizontal thought" (instinct), opposed to "vertical thinking" (reason). Often, Brautigan passed out on Marcia's bed. In the morning, he phoned Aki, inviting her for breakfast.

One late September evening at Specs', Richard ran into journalist Ken Kelley, a hard-drinking thirty-year-old Irishman who possessed an aura of one doomed to an extravagant destiny. For a period in the late sixties, Kelley worked as the personal secretary for Huey P. Newton, information minister for the Black Panther Party. Funded by John Lennon and Yoko Ono, Ken cofounded *Sundance*, which lasted for only three issues in 1972. The magazine provided Kelley a springboard into his long career. Kelley became an interviewer for *Playboy*, *Penthouse*, *People*, *Mother Jones*, and other national publications.

In her autobiographical novel, *Lovers and Tyrants*, Francine du Plessix Gray based her character Elijah Stewart on Ken Kelley, age twenty-two, "very tall and very lean, with long curling light-brown hair, a light growth of beard, deep-blue eyes with very long dark lashes. His features have a classic beauty, the nose is aquiline, there is a certain hardness to his thin, crisply chiseled mouth [. . .] There is a violence about his beauty which has to do with the fact that one cannot possibly conceive of him as ever getting older."

At thirty, after a decade of drink and drugs, Kelley still possessed remarkable good looks, offset by immeasurable amounts of charm. Armed with an expense account from the *Examiner*, Kelley started buying Brautigan drinks at Specs', wanting an interview. Ken told Richard how they met in 1974, at a spaghetti dinner party in his apartment at 1722 Larkin Street. Other guests included photographer Annie Leibovitz, Jann Wenner, George Butler, and Charles Gaines, whom Kelley had met in Birmingham, Alabama, earlier in the year, during the filming of Gaines's novel, *Stay Hungry*. Ken had been the house sitter/babysitter for director Bob Rafelson. *Stay Hungry* featured Mr. Universe, Arnold Schwarzenegger. This led to Gaines's book *Pumping Iron*, with photographs by George Butler, who directed the 1977 documentary film of the same title.

Back in 1974, Brautigan arrived late at Kelley's place, bearing a bottle of Dickel and a Japanese print. Ken served spaghetti, poured a glass of 101-proof Wild Turkey, and put a Hank Williams side on the turntable. Richard came to see Charlie Gaines, whom he'd met in Montana. They all piled into Annie Leibovitz's sports car and headed over to some "strange bar" George Butler wanted to see. "Of course, Richard stood out like a sore thumb in those situations," Ken recalled. "You could see him physically get nervous."

When they parted, Ken asked, "Where do you hang out?"

"Specs'," Brautigan replied, keeping his favorite place, Enrico's, to himself.

Ken Kelley tracked Richard Brautigan down at Specs' four years later. Over their next few evenings together, at Vanessi's, for dinner, to Perry's to watch the stockbrokers and lawyers picking up women, Kelley followed Brautigan armed with a ballpoint pen and a ruled legal pad. Their Q&A never saw print, but Richard used the time to observe Ken's investigative technique. In a drunken way, it was an audition.

Kelley's hasty notes revealed the inner workings of Brautigan's mind. "To me, words are just shadow and wind," Brautigan told him. "Life is too short for one-liners." After eighteen books, Richard confessed he was "just barely getting to know what's going on," saying twenty years of thinking produced a half hour of work.

"Living and dying is the only thing to write about," Brautigan said. During their peripatetic nights together, the drinks kept coming and coming. Kelley's scrawl grew indecipherable. "Don't think in terms of public recognition," Brautigan lapsed into his repetitive stutter. "I'm really interested in people living and dying here. The books I write describe living and dying here." Reflecting on his insomnia, Richard said, "Life keeps me awake."

Brautigan dubbed Truman Capote "one of the best writers in America," praising *The Grass Harp* and *A Tree of Night*. Brautigan picked Capote's stories "Miriam" and "Jug of Silver" for special commendation. "Can't write anything better. Best American short story writer." Brautigan thought Tennessee Williams the "best American playwright ever produced," calling *The Glass Menagerie* and *A Streetcar Named Desire* the "best American plays."

Richard told Ken he started writing at seventeen. He wanted to write novels, but he said he used poetry to understand crafting sentences. Poetry was "telegraphic." It took Brautigan eight years, "learning how to write sentences," before he attempted *Trout Fishing. Confederate General* required eight drafts; *In Watermelon Sugar* three drafts. Richard called *The Hawkline Monster* his "only narrative novel, A to Z." He told Ken his next work would combine Tokyo, Montana, and San Francisco.

Kelley asked Brautigan about his musical preferences. Richard's favorite song was "May the Circle Be Unbroken" (performed by Mama Maybelle Carter). The soundtrack from *Chinatown* stood high on Brautigan's top ten. Richard told Ken about his introduction for the Dell edition of *The Beatles Illustrated Lyrics.* Proud of this association, Brautigan considered Lennon and McCartney's songs "some of the best writing ever done."

After several boozy nights of genial schmoozing, Kelley asked Brautigan if he was ever called anything but Richard. "When anyone calls me Dick, I know they want something from me," Richard said. "A nickname is unnatural familiarity. You should know people before you use nicknames."

On October 3, the ACLU filed suit against the Anderson Union High School District in Shasta County. V. I. Wexner, along with William Woods, a fellow teacher, and three students (Donna Cartwright, Mary Osterday, and Brenda Galey) from Anderson High School, had filed a complaint with the ACLU, asking for legal help. Brautigan's publisher, Seymour Lawrence, joined the lawsuit. Sam flew out to San Francisco the previous week to consult on the matter. He had breakfast with Richard. A "splendid afternoon tea and Jack Daniel's" at Brautigan's apartment before flying to Mendocino to buy "a redwood house perched on a cliff over the Pacific."

Margaret Crosby, the ACLU attorney representing Wexner and Woods, declared the case was "without precedent regarding publishers' rights to disseminate information free from government censorship." The ACLU suit demanded the five banned Brautigan books be returned to the classrooms under a court order. Private practice lawyer Ann Brick volunteered for the ACLU. She stated, "By no stretch of the imagination could any of the Brautigan works be considered obscene. The school officials are trying to pick and choose so that students see only the social and cultural views of the administration."

Not wanting to have the matter "clouded by his presence," Richard Brautigan left town for Montana with his wife after a $94.74 farewell binge at Vanessi's. Before departing, Brautigan released a press statement (September 24, 1978):

On our Apollo 17 mission to the moon in December, 1972, the astronauts named a crater after a character from one of the books that is forbidden to be taught at Anderson High School. I do not think it is the policy of the United States Government to name the geography of the moon after a character from a dirty book.

The crater is called Shorty.

The book is Trout Fishing in America.

If Trout Fishing in America can get to the moon, I think it should be able to get to Anderson High School.

Tony Dingman met Richard and Akiko at the Bozeman airport, driving them home to Pine Creek. Dingman stayed on in Montana over the summer, looking after Brautigan's place. Their congenial country life resumed as if uninterrupted. Aki showed Richard a letter from her aunt in Japan, written in Japanese. Akiko translated for her husband. Her aunt told her not to worry about the cabbages. They would grow and do well. The aunt treated Aki's bondage concerns in the same matter-of-fact manner. Some men have certain tastes, she wrote to her niece, it's nothing to worry about.

Brautigan did almost no writing in Montana that fall, although a few stories grew out of Tony Dingman's comic automotive misadventures and other ordinary events. A $400 offer in the local paper for a cherry 1953 Oldsmobile that turned out to be only an engine block became fiction, along with a tale about buying a $30 cake at a church bake sale and another concerning the time Tony failed to drive forward from an intersection in a small Montana town with no stop signs.

In early October, Brautigan plunked down $16,500 in cash to Maverick Realty as a down payment for two little houses on South Third Street in Livingston. Richard worried what to do with his money. Brautigan told Dick Hodge, "he didn't want to invest it in stocks, bonds, [or] anything to do with capitalist America. He had no interest in a tax shelter or any other sort of passive investment. He thought that was kind of dishonest." Richard went through a long list of investment possibilities. "Basically when he was done there was nothing left but real estate."

Brautigan told Hodge that he didn't want to become a landlord. Tony Dingman remembered, "His legacy from his mother was 'The rich steal from the poor.' Period." The two houses Richard bought, a little compound clustered on the same side of South Third, were rental properties. Numbers 107 and 107½ were housed in a single structure. Number 109, set back off the sidewalk, was an older sandstone building used early in the twentieth century as a photographer's studio. The total purchase price for all three units came to $57,500. Their combined monthly rental income totaled $507.50.

On October 27, Richard signed a deal at Maverick Realty to buy another property in Livingston, a $52,000 purchase of a two-story brick building built in the 1890s at 311½ West Callender Street. Once the residence of a local tailor, and commercially zoned, it currently housed the Carden Big Sky School (a day care preschool). The down payment was $26,970. Brautigan paid off the balance at the closing on November 9, before he returned to San Francisco.

When Gary Snyder held a weeklong residency at Montana State University the previous fall, Richard phoned the MSU English Department, leaving a message inviting Snyder over to Paradise Valley. Previously, Greg Keeler, the thirty-two-year-old poet and literature professor who'd arranged for a National Endowment matching-fund grant to bring Snyder to the university, stuck a note on Brautigan's mailbox, "asking if you ever might want to come and read in Bozeman." Keeler never heard back. Returning from visiting Richard and Aki, Gary told Greg he had urged Brautigan "to get more involved with the Montana community."

A year went by. Brautigan made a second call to the secretary of the MSU English Department. Richard wanted a residency of his own at Montana State. He invited Greg Keeler and two undergraduates from the Associated Students of Montana State University (ASMSU) programs board over to his house in Pine Creek for dinner. At the bottom of the note to Greg, it said "bring wine." When the three showed up at Brautigan's place on a snow-covered November afternoon, Keeler clutched a half-gallon of Almaden chablis.

Born and raised in Oklahoma, Keeler came from an academic family. His parents both taught at Oklahoma State University. Greg received his MA there and a PhD from Idaho State but was by no stretch of anybody's imagination a stereotypical academician. When Brautigan opened the front door, Keeler observed that he and Richard both looked ("tall, blond, and pink") and dressed ("torn work shirt, blue jeans, and cowboy boots") very much alike.

To distance himself from Keeler, Brautigan took issue with all his literary opinions. He called Flaubert a "sack of shit," and referred to William Stafford (one of Greg's favorite poets) as a "cunt" because Stafford had once told Brautigan that his children enjoyed reading his books. Later, Brautigan picked up Queever, the Hjortsbergs' long-haired cat visiting from across the creek, and tossed him into Keeler's face.

After a bit, Richard settled down, recognizing Greg more a kindred spirit than a stuffy academic. "You're just a sprout," Brautigan said upon learning Keeler's age. He was very gracious to the students and deftly blunted their initial awkward attempts to talk business. "Let's not worry about that stuff yet," Richard said, "you're in the country now. Relax." They all sat down to a "very good" spaghetti dinner. Aki, who Greg thought looked "beautiful and appropriately inscrutable," mentioned that she was interested in finding some local Japanese friends and perhaps continuing her education in Bozeman.

Late that night, having stuffed his guests with pasta and plied them with copious amounts of booze, Richard abruptly turned the conversation toward negotiation. "Welp, let's have a ballpark figure," he said.

The two students, drowsy with drink and teetering on the edge of sleep, looked at one another in confusion. They weren't quite prepared for this. Restricted by the limitations of their ASMSU budget, which had to cover a variety of events over the school year, they fumbled for an appropriate amount, something affordable yet not insulting. Thinking of the $100 fees offered to other speakers, one of them groggily offered "Four . . ."

"Four thousand it is," Brautigan shot back. To the astonishment of the bewildered students, the deal was done.

A week later, Greg Keeler and his wife, Judy, who also taught at MSU, invited Richard and Aki to their home in Bozeman for a reciprocal dinner. Akiko, the designated driver, took them over by way of Trail Creek Road, Brautigan's favorite graveled back route, traversing the Gallatin range from Paradise Valley and connecting with I-90 at the old coal mining town of Chestnut. Richard had insisted that Greg return home this way the previous week. He and Aki had escorted Keeler and the two sleeping students as far as the junction with Highway 89 on the east side of the Yellowstone.

The two students were once again in attendance at the Keeler's, watching in amazement as their $4,000 visiting author leaned so far back in his host's "cheap wicker Kmart love seat" that he toppled over backward. They also watched Brautigan work his way through Greg and Judy's liquor cabinet, swilling down Canadian whiskey, gin, vodka, and rum after polishing off the wine and bourbon. Richard became drunk and drunker, lapsing into "a small Oriental voice and getting very serious." Keeler, who dubbed Brautigan "The Captain," called "this late night voice the Imperial Mode."

Around midnight, the students were almost asleep on the couch. "Any more liquor?" Richard demanded. Greg rustled among the empties, finding only dead soldiers. Every drop had been consumed. "Time to go," Brautigan said. Keeler remembered neither wife being much amused by the abrupt departure. Judy took an instant dislike to Richard that evening. Aki also "didn't seem too thrilled about the exit." She had to drive her inebriated husband home over the Bozeman Pass. For Greg Keeler, the evening began an improbable and enduring friendship.

The Brautigans returned to San Francisco in the middle of November. On the sixteenth, an anonymous group called "Concerned Citizens" published an eight-page newspaper under the headline "Does ACLU Push Smut?" The paper contained excerpts from *The Pill*, *Rommel*, *Confederate General*, *The Abortion*, and *Trout Fishing*, along with the disclaimer "We regret the necessity to print and review this material, but we feel there is no better way to inform you of this but to let you see for your self." The excerpts were all deliberately selected to emphasize sexual content.

The front page printed a quotation from *Biographical Dictionary of the Left*, by Francis X. Gannon, referring to "the Communist Character of the American Civil Liberties Union," along with a statement directed to the "Dear moral and Christian people of Shasta County." The piece was signed "Morton" (Morton Giesecke), and read, in part, "I have looked over these books in question, and I judge them to be vile and foul to my tastes, they are contemptible by the light of God's Scriptures. I feel that material of this sort will lead to further moral decay and perversion of all that is good and decent in our American Society."

The distant buzz of Birchite gadflies greatly annoyed Brautigan. Keith Abbott recalled him spending an entire evening talking about "his current censorship problems." Richard knew every detail of the case. He repeated them over and over, quoting the public statements of the principal and the school board. "The next step to look for is book burning," Brautigan solemnly warned Abbott, "just like the Nazis."

Other literary matters distracted him. Richard had long resented how Grove Press handled *A Confederate General from Big Sur*. Barney Rosset continually reissued the novel in small printings while Brautigan's other titles were selling tens of thousands of copies. Sam Lawrence dreamed of acquiring the one that got away. After protracted negotiations and with the considerable help of Helen Meyer, chair of the board of the Dell Publishing Company, Sam's dream came true in mid-November when Dell bought the rights to *Confederate General* for a single payment of $15,000.

Lawrence planned to reissue the book in September 1979, simultaneously as a hardcover edition and a Delta trade paperback. To get the ball rolling, Sam asked Richard for his new jacket art suggestions. Lawrence also needed fresh front and back flap copy from Brautigan before the end of the month. Richard mailed new dust jacket copy for *Confederate General* to Helen Brann, which reflected long-standing resentments. Written in 1962–1963 when he was twenty-eight years old, the novel was about the year 1957, "a preview of things to come in America." The book "sold less than a thousand copies and was immediately forgotten," Brautigan wrote. "It was reprinted in 1968 and identified with the hippie movement and thought to be a description of the way they lived, though the book took place eleven years before when the hippies were still in grade school."

"This is a new edition," Richard concluded. When John Hartnett mailed Brautigan's flap copy to Sam Lawrence (Helen Brann was in the hospital, recovering from an operation), he included the author's thoughts on the jacket design. Richard wanted "a silver/gray background (not foil) with the title and his name in scarlet (not red)." On the back, Brautigan asked for "just a small confederate flag, centered."

Don Carpenter remembered having lunch with Richard and Aki at Vanessi's around this time. A friend of Aki's was visiting from Japan, and they were showing her the town. "Right in the middle of lunch, somebody said the word 'banzai' in some context or another," Don recalled, "and Richard went into a furious tirade and stamped out of the restaurant and we all had to run after him."

Brautigan's angry outburst came because he believed "'banzai' meant emperor worship and he had lost friends in World War II and didn't want that word used in his presence." In fact, 'banzai' was a victory cry meaning "a life of ten thousand years," used as often in sporting events as on the battlefield. Carpenter and the two women spoke Japanese. To placate Brautigan, they all pretended his version was correct. "I mean, the guy had surrealism for breakfast," Don observed.

Richard discovered a new watering hole, the Albatross Saloon on Columbus at the intersection of Kearny and Pacific. Once the hub of the Barbary Coast, the corner joint was first called the Billy Goat Saloon and reopened a year after the 1906 fire as the Andromeda Saloon. Jack Dempsey, future heavyweight champ, worked as a bouncer there in 1913 and 1914. New owners rescued the venerable dive from oblivion in 1977, stripping layers of paint from the ancient bar, removing a false ceiling to reveal the original pressed tin, and installing a 1916 Pukka Walla vertically rotating ceiling fan. The drinks were generous and the food all priced at $2.50. The Albatross became a hip hangout. Francis Ford Coppola entertained visiting French filmmakers there.

Richard Brautigan celebrated his forty-fourth birthday at the Albatross Saloon. He had such a good time the management asked him to write a few words celebrating their establishment for future advertising. Richard obliged them, just as he had Kendrick Rand a decade earlier. "The Albatross Saloon provides a beautiful remembrance of days long since gone in San Francisco, never to return," he wrote. "The Albatross is like eating and drinking in the past."

Brautigan also spent time with Marcia Clay, savoring her beauty and keen intelligence. Once, after Richard complained about the fragile state of his marriage, the subject of obsession arose. "He was a very obsessive person," Clay observed. Brautigan didn't want to hear about it. What Marcia had in mind was bondage. "How can you expect her to stay interested in you when you tie her up?" Clay demanded.

Brautigan reacted furiously, breaking off their friendship. "I'm not going to talk to you for six years," he proclaimed and stalked out. Marcia felt devastated. "The loss of Richard in my life is one experience that has had a real effect on me," she wrote in her diary. "The romance of his friendship was suddenly put into value [. . .] My regret with Richard was to have created a split when, deep down inside I longed for the unity. There's the immaturity. What is gone is gone—for now at least. I continue to hope that we will again be close."

Another old friendship ended at Richard and Nancy Hodge's Page Street Christmas party. Erik Weber was among the many guests. Brautigan arrived later, already drunk, in the company of people Erik didn't know. They hadn't spoken in a month or two. Richard walked right by without acknowledging him. Later, leaning against the office wall, Weber found himself close to Brautigan. "Richard was pissed at me," Erik remembered. Brautigan launched into his list of complaints, and Akiko walked into the room. Weber had never met his wife before. Richard made no introductions. He looked at Aki "with this drunken sheepish grin."

"When men are having a discussion," Brautigan said, "the women . . ." With a dismissive wave of his hand, he signaled for Akiko to leave. Erik found the gesture "really rude," as if the wife was expected to always walk behind her husband. Richard went on to castigate Erik about the cover for *June 30th*. The hardcover edition had not sold very well, and Brautigan blamed Weber. He had insisted Delacorte go with Erik's design. "That was it. He owed me no more," Weber recalled. "That was it, the end."

As the new year of 1979 got under way, evidence began to surface that members of the John Birch Society were behind the banning of Brautigan's books up in Shasta County. Faced with such intolerant right-wing enemies, Richard decided to help the ACLU dig up information for their case. He got back in touch with Ken Kelley, who had passed some sort of unspoken test with his initial interview. While they were sitting around Brautigan's office discussing the project, Richard tossed a manila file folder onto Kelley's lap. An identification label read "First Amendment."

The folder contained news clippings and documents on the removal of Richard's books from the library of the Anderson High School library in Shasta County. Brautigan had an undercover assignment for Kelley. He wanted him to go up north to Anderson and poke around, dig into the background of the individuals who opposed his books. "I want you to call Maggie Crosby first," Richard said.

Ken didn't recognize the name. "Who's Maggie Crosby?" he asked. Brautigan explained that she was an attorney with the ACLU of Northern California. This was Kelley's final test. If he pulled it off, Richard promised an invitation out to Montana the next summer. "You'll meet people you've never met before in your life," he enthused. "You'll see mountain ranges climbing up under the sky." Brautigan told Ken he'd take him trout fishing and promised to sit for a formal taped interview.

"You can be the cosmic Sherlock Holmes," Richard said.

Kelley contacted Maggie Crosby, and she filled him in on the details of the case. Not long after that, Richard invited them both over to his place on Lombard Street for dinner. Ken knew "conceptually" that Richard had a wife, but "it never came up in casual conversation at all," and he was taken slightly off guard on meeting "some Japanese person wearing Japanese clothes." Akiko prepared an Italian/Japanese dinner: teriyaki steak and pasta con pesto, in accord with Brautigan's wishes. When they discussed the censorship case, Maggie Crosby said she had "pretty solid evidence" that several of the parties involved were members of the John Birch Society. Ken Kelley's job was to substantiate her case. Ken recalled this in great detail. Maggie Crosby cannot remember ever meeting Kelley.

In mid-January, Ken bought a $47 round-trip ticket on AirWest and traveled to Redding, a forty-minute flight from the Bay Area. He rented a Budget car, driving twenty-five miles east to Shingletown, where he located the rural home of V. I. Wexner, who put him up during his two-week stay. Ken talked with V. I. (Ken's host went only by his first initials) about his teaching techniques in the developmental class, focusing on how the censorship of Brautigan's work deprived some of his students of the only books they'd ever shown any interest in reading. "I think," Wexner told him, "the library has room for six books by Richard Brautigan."

Identifying himself as a reporter, Kelley roamed across the school district, interviewing a wide range of participants in the case, including superintendent Frank Robertson; Albert Davis, president of the school board; various students; Leonard Neutze, operator of Anderson Glass Company; and boat mechanic Morton Giesecke (the latter two Christian fundamentalists who supported the book ban and gave John Birch Society publications to Ken). "It's poison," Giesecke said of Brautigan's writing. "It will destroy the minds of the kids." After admitting all he had read of Brautigan were the excerpts published the previous November in the one-shot eight-page "Concerned Citizens" newspaper, Giesecke remarked, "You don't have to explore every corner of a septic tank to know what's in it."

Ken Kelley had his own secret undercover methods when it came to investigative journalism. If the subject of an interview objected to being taped, Ken made a point of turning off his machine and scribbling away in a reporter's notepad, with another active recorder hidden under his clothing. Kelley always got every word on tape. When Albert Davis left the quiet of his trustee's office, Ken followed him into a noisy basketball game in the high school gym and everything Davis said came through loud and clear above the clamor. Back in San Francisco, Kelley turned his research findings over to Richard Brautigan, who was so pleased he promptly extended Ken the promised invitation to Montana.

On February 15, Judge William H. Phelps of the Superior Court for Shasta County overruled the defendants' demurrer to the ACLU complaint, ordering that Brautigan's books be returned to the Anderson High School library. He appended an opinion that the books "could be placed in a restricted area, inaccessible to minor students unless they provided evidence of parental consent." Both the plaintiffs and the defendants immediately appealed Judge Phelps's decision.

It took ten years, long after Richard Brautigan's suicide, for the book-banning case to be finally decided. On April 25, 1989, the California Court of Appeals for the Third District, in a two-to-one decision, ruled in favor of the plaintiffs and the ACLU. The prior judgment restoring the banned books to the school library was affirmed while the provisions "addressing restrictions on the classroom use of the Brautigan books and a system of prior parental consent for access to them" were struck from the ruling.

The court's opinion strongly rebuked the school district for claiming their authority to remove books from the high school library, even those not deemed obscene, on the grounds that their contents were not "socially acceptable to the people of the district." The concurring judges ruled, "The problem is all the more serious because the type of action, book-banning, is the archetypical symbol of repression of free speech and because it occurs, in a manner of speaking, 'in front of the children.'"

The Court of Appeals noted that allowing the school board to remove nonobscene books based on "the nebulous terminology 'pervasive vulgarity' and 'educational unsuitability'" would upset the "complex and closely balanced questions of state and federal constitutional law." Such action "would afford a disruptive and divisive focal point for pressure groups to politicize the public educational system. Every book in the library would be a litmus test of the Board's adherence to conventional views" and "the narrowing of the breadth of school library collections to the blandest common denominator." Poetic justice enhanced the court's opinion with a footnote quoting, in its entirety, Richard Brautigan's poem "Education" (from *The Pill versus the Springhill Mine Disaster*, one of his banned books), saying that it "foreshadowed [. . .] this state of affairs." This would have delighted Richard had he been alive to read the final decision.

fifty: rashomon

EARLY ONE JULY morning when dew glistened on the ripening grass and the mountain air retained a chill memory of the previous night, I wandered over to visit my neighbor Richard. In an hour or two, the relentless summer sun would burn the deceptive freshness out of the day and send all creatures in search of shade, but for the moment, the crisp, crystalline clarity seemed like a sneak preview of paradise. Usually it was Brautigan who came calling at breakfast time, coffee mug in hand, looking for a hot "cup of joe" and the latest gossip. Since his recent marriage, he'd grown more domestic, preferring to stay home with his delicate Japanese bride.

I recalled a moment on Richard's back porch a week or so earlier. My friend sat on the rail, leaning against a support post as he watched Akiko picking wildflowers under the cottonwoods. She wore a flowing, patterned kimono, her dark hair immaculately coiffed, and moved with such grace that every delicate step seemed choreographed. Brautigan's mooncalf grin revealed his unrestrained joy. "Isn't she beautiful?" he whispered, a teenager in love.

The front door stood open when I stepped up under the archway onto the recessed alcovelike porch. A screen door obscured the interior of the house. Hearing voices, I called out a greeting and let myself in. This was standard procedure in Montana at the time. No one ever locked his door, and a certain casual informality prevailed. Before I got halfway across the narrow combination living/dining room in front, a bizarre tableau framed by the kitchen doorway stopped me dead in my tracks.

Just beyond the unintended proscenium, Richard Brautigan knelt on the linoleum floor. He was shirtless and barefoot, wearing only a faded pair of blue jeans. Shockingly pink and bristling with curling blond hairs, he appeared almost larval, an enormous golden caterpillar. His potbelly pillowed over the waistband of his jeans. He clutched a serrated bread knife in both hands, pressing the tip against his navel, staring pleadingly up at Akiko. His wife seemed to tower above him in spite of her slight stature. She wore the same kimono, the obi belted tightly about a narrow waist. Her hair sprang in a wild Medusa-like disarray around a pale oval face contorted with rage. "You no commit seppuku," she shrieked. "You got no guts!"

I stood transfixed by embarrassment, not quite comprehending what was going on in the kitchen, and found myself eye to eye with Aki, her beautiful face transformed into an inchoate demonic mask. Backing silently to the door, I felt certain Richard had not noticed my intrusion in the intensity of the moment. The air of unreality seemed so tangible as I walked home it felt like I was floating above the ground. I wondered what exactly I had seen. A melodramatic domestic dispute? Inexplicably intense sexual game-playing? The rehearsal of an amateur Nō play? None of it made sense. No matter what the truth, I knew for certain I would always remember the unexpected moment as something abstract: a dream fragment, an image projected on smoke, a terrifying glimpse into the unknown.

fifty-one: trouble and strife

I N MID-FEBRUARY OF 1979, the Brautigans started looking for another new apartment. Things hadn't worked out at the place on Lombard Street. A quiet single lady rented the flat below them, and Richard's constant pacing in his heavy cowboy boots disturbed her tranquility. Complicating matters, the landlord's daughter lived right upstairs, always available to receive the frequent complaints. The night Ron Kovic came to visit provided a final lease-breaking fiasco.

Kovic, a decorated (Purple Heart, Bronze Star with a "V" for valor) Vietnam vet, had become one of the leading opponents to the war after he was paralyzed from the chest down during his second voluntary tour of duty with the Marines in Indochina early in 1968. His powerful memoir, *Born on the Fourth of July*, was published in 1976, the same year Kovic addressed the Democratic National Convention. Ron and a lady friend arrived at 1264 Lombard by taxi. Brautigan and the cab driver carried him up to the second-floor apartment in his wheelchair. Kovic was also a heavy drinker. Richard wasted no time in uncorking a bottle of whiskey.

Loud music and laughter-punctuated conversation reverberated through the Brautigans' apartment. "Heavy discussion," Akiko recalled. Increased whiskey consumption took the hilarity up a notch. Richard and Ron started throwing eggs at the wall. Aki decided it was bedtime and dimmed the lights, "a hint that they should be a little bit quiet." The hint went unnoticed. Akiko headed for bed with "big music still going on." When she awoke a couple hours later, the racket in the other room had not diminished. "It's time for sleep, babies!" Aki shouted. This did the trick. The carousing ended. Ron Kovic and his companion spent the night. In the morning, everyone nursed hangovers when the phone rang. The landlord's daughter was calling. There had been one too many raucous nights.

Ianthe remembered "a hysterical evening" at the Lombard Street apartment when her father brought Dennis Hopper home with him from North Beach. At nineteen and hoping to study acting, she was intrigued by Richard's Hollywood connections. Ianthe had gone with Richard to a screening of *Apocalypse Now* at Francis Ford Coppola's house and met the actor portraying a drug-addled photojournalist in the film. Hopper's character was partly based on legendary British war photographer Tim Page, celebrated for his reckless courage in Vietnam. After a traumatic head wound, Page became a caregiver for amputees and other gravely injured veterans during his year-long recovery in the United States. One of those wounded soldiers was Ron Kovic.

Akiko went to bed early the first time she met Dennis Hopper. Brautigan headed out alone to a party. "I'm going to kidnap Dennis Hopper," Richard told his wife when he phoned later, interrupting her sleep. Aki awoke to find her husband and the actor standing beside her bed. "Here's Dennis," Richard said. "I kidnapped him."

"He knew I admired [Hopper] so much because of *Easy Rider*," Akiko remembered. Richard "always asked me to cook some noodle, the ramen. Hot noodle. Chinese type of a noodle to the guest. Middle of the night. Very late."

Richard Brautigan loved hearing Dennis Hopper quote from Shakespeare, especially the *Hamlet* soliloquies. Drunken snatches from the Bard resonated through the apartment when Ianthe went off to bed. In the morning, she found her father asleep and Hopper raging about the kitchen, hunting for something to drink. Dennis recruited Ianthe in his search. He and Richard had consumed nearly all the booze in the house. Ianthe uncovered a bottle of a peculiar Chinese liqueur "with a small pickled lizard lying in the bottom."

Furious at her husband and his friend for staying up all night, Akiko had left much earlier. She grew more angry when she returned and discovered Hopper still in the apartment swilling down lizard juice. "Shit, shit, shit!" Aki shouted. Ianthe had never heard her "classy stepmother" swear before. Another morning, Akiko sat her stepdaughter down at the kitchen table to discuss Richard's alcohol problem. Ianthe was unable to provide any help. The child of an alcoholic, she had become a classic codependent. She thought things had gotten "much better" since her father married Aki.

Rude, drunken behavior inevitably takes a toll on love. One night during this period, Robert Briggs witnessed the Brautigans' marital discord firsthand. Briggs had gotten married a year or so before and his wife, Diana Saltoon, was "rather a Zen zealot." Richard invited them over for dinner to meet Akiko. From the moment they entered the apartment, they knew the Brautigans "weren't getting along." Aki, "a wonderful cook," had prepared a gourmet French meal. Richard worked his way through a bottle and a half of George Dickel, growing increasingly abusive with every swallow. "Diana did not like the way he treated Akiko," Briggs observed.

"They might have had a lovers' quarrel or something," Diana Saltoon recalled. "She was a little bit sensitive and a little bit uptight. She was obviously younger, much younger than he."

"He didn't know what to make of her," Briggs said. "She was far too sophisticated for him and yet he was very much in awe of her." This was the last time Robert and Diana ever visited with Richard and Akiko.

Aki soon discovered the new apartment of her dreams on the second floor of 2170 Green Street. Situated between Webster and Fillmore on the lower slope of Pacific Heights, a district known as Cow Hollow, it had once been the home of Lotta Crabtree, who began as a pint-sized red-haired child entertainer dancing in mining camps and went on to a notable career in the American theater. Crabtree commissioned the famous "Lotta's Fountain" at Kearny and Market in 1875. Her fountain once kept company at this intersection with the statue of Benjamin Franklin, which was moved to Washington Square, where it became part of Richard Brautigan's personal mythology.

Brautigan had never lived in such a classy neighborhood. The grand sunny apartment had sweeping views of the Bay and the Golden Gate Bridge from the rear windows. Ianthe described the living room as "cavernous." Their building stood next to the Leander Sherman mansion, built in 1876 with a three-story ballroom where Paderewski and Lotta Crabtree both performed.

The Brautigans moved in to the palatial Green Street apartment by the first of March. The place was much more spacious than any previous residence, and their possessions weren't sufficient. Akiko had the perfect solution: time to go shopping. She bought rugs and lamps and big black imitation leather couches. Richard left all the interior decorating decisions to her.

Brautigan got a phone call from James D. Houston, hired by Bantam Books to edit an anthology, part of a paperback series on American literary regions. Jim signed on to oversee the volume covering West Coast fiction. He wanted to include excerpts from *Trout Fishing in America*. The other authors accepted $300 or $400 for reprint permission. Brautigan's publisher "wanted something like $1,800."

Jim told Richard this was "going to be a one-of-a-kind collection, and it's going to define West Coast literature, and I want you to be in it."

"How much can you pay?" Richard asked.

"Well, they wanted $1,800. We're looking at three or four hundred."

"You call them back and tell my agent that we'll take whatever you can pay," Brautigan said, "because I want to be in that collection."

"He greased the wheels," Houston recalled, "and we settled on, I think it was $350. The money wasn't as important to him as being in that [book]. He knew that this was going to put his work in the context that was important to him."

"It was something he did as a favor," observed Jeanne Wakatsuki Houston, Jim's wife. The book was published later in the year. Richard's work was included alongside selections by John Steinbeck, Raymond Chandler, Tillie Olsen, Jack Kerouac, Ken Kesey, Tom Robbins, Ishmael Reed, Thomas Sanchez, and Wallace Stegner.

Brautigan's residency at Montana State University began the second week in April, his first public appearance since 1971. Richard, always a scrupulous guardian of his image, gave careful thought to what he would do and say before the gathered students. Greg Keeler recalled that week (April 9–13) as "all sort of a blur." The faculty found Brautigan a place to stay in Bozeman so he wouldn't have to commute over the pass from Paradise Valley. Aki had remained behind, decorating their new San Francisco apartment.

The Keelers hosted a party for Brautigan. Other nights, Greg and Richard hit the local bars, evenings lost in a fog of booze. One afternoon, Brautigan phoned Marcia Clay in Frisco. She was startled to hear his voice. She recognized it instantly, although he didn't announce himself by name. Richard sounded "cloudy" on the long-distance line, but Marcia thought "his voice was so real, just the same as ever." Brautigan wanted to know if Clay had "gone to bed with such and such." Angry, Clay said no. Even if she had, it was her own business. "Right," Richard said.

She was happy to hear from Richard. A month earlier, Marcia wrote in her diary, "I miss him. I want his company late at night when there is only solitude and I know there is no one, before or since, but Richard that I can talk to." Anxious to go out for a swim, Clay knew Brautigan was capable of talking for hours, so she said goodbye and headed for the pool.

Brautigan's duties as poet-in-residence included giving a formal poetry reading in the Student Union. He donned a sport jacket for the occasion and attracted "a small audience." A larger crowd turned out for his performance at Cheever Hall, where he interspersed his readings and anecdotes with recordings by Pink Lady, an all-female Japanese pop group. Richard went fishing on his last day in Montana. Greg Keeler drove him to an irrigation dam on the West Gallatin River north of Four Corners. David Schrieber, an MSU senior writing a novel as an independent studies project, came along. Keeler described it as "an impromptu trip." They had no waders and brought only a couple fly rods and several Woolly Worms flies.

Deep windblown snow banks piled against the edge of the irrigation ditch. Greg led them toward his favorite spot. Another fisherman saw them and started running to get there first. "Look at his little feeties go," Keeler said. Richard loved this, repeating "little feeties" with great pleasure. They beat the interloping angler to the chosen hole, and the stranger sulked off with what Brautigan called "a crumpled Charlie Brown mouth."

The three anglers were after mountain whitefish, a species native to Montana but not favored by fly fisherman because of their sluggish fight and small suckerlike mouths. Richard wanted three big whitefish for a special dish Akiko prepared. By day's end, Brautigan's departure time fast approached and they had only landed two. Keeler rose to the occasion, "walloped" his Woolly Worm on the surface, "and caught a large stupid whitefish." Quota in hand, the fishing trio hurried back to town. Greg filleted the whitefish and packed them in rock salt (a requirement for Aki's recipe) before driving Richard to the airport just in time to make his plane.

The day after Brautigan's return to San Francisco, he and Akiko brought her salted whitefish dish over to a party at Francis Ford Coppola's. Richard reported to Greg Keeler that his catch had been a "hit." On the last day of April, Marcia Clay reported in her diary that Francis planned to take Aki to Washington, D.C. to dine with President Carter and the Japanese prime minister. She heard this from Richard, who referred to the president as "that peanut farmer." Brautigan had "reappeared" on Clay's threshold early in the morning ten days before, "persistently ringing the doorbell." She was delighted to see him. "I've been in Dante's waiting room for so long," she wrote. "A thousand flowers are opening for this new spring. Metaphors won't do."

Aki did not travel east with Francis Coppola. She journeyed west instead, flying home to Japan during the second week in May. Her first few days were spent recovering from jet lag at her parents' home in Yokohama. Brautigan sent a number of small gifts for the family with her. Fusako Nishizawa, Akiko's mother, wrote him a thank-you note, her first handwritten letter in English, reworked six times, addressing Richard as "Dear my third son." Shocked by the exorbitant price of fish in Japan ("my appetite immediately going away"), Aki enjoyed vegetables from her mother's garden, homemade sushi, and fresh bamboo shoots, a delicacy unknown in America.

Akiko traveled up to Tokyo in mid-May, staying at the home of her friends Yoko and Hiroshi Yoshimura. On her first night in the city, Aki stopped by a bookstore in Roppongi, pleased to find they stocked her husband's books. *Trout Fishing* was in its eleventh Japanese edition. The next day, she had lunch with Tom Mori, Brautigan's agent in Japan. Akiko also met with an editor at Japanese *Playboy* to discuss publishing Brautigan's short stories. They were sent to the magazine by the Tuttle-Mori agency.

On the twenty-first, Akiko got together with poet Shuntarō Tanikawa in Shibuya. He brought along the second volume of his complete poems and gave it to Aki. Walking through "the endless stream" of the crowded district, they both confessed to feeling "almost dizzy" from the swarm of people. Aki found Shuntarō a "really beautiful man." They met to discuss Richard's wish to write an article on Shuntarō. Brautigan also hoped someday they might give a lecture together. Akiko asked about Shuntarō's planned contributions to the *CoEvolution Quarterly*, an offshoot of the hugely successful *Whole Earth Catalog*. Former "Merry Prankster" Stewart Brand, the creator and editor of both the *Quarterly* and the *Catalog*, had contacted Brautigan four years earlier, asking him to contribute commentary on a recent article the magazine had published about the feasibility of space colonies. Richard declined the first offer, but agreed to help this time around.

Akiko explained to Shuntarō everything her husband told her on the phone, and he seemed pleased, saying he would gather selections of his collages for "the visual message" *CoEvolution* had requested. For safety's sake, Shuntarō asked Aki to hand carry the material back to the United States with her rather than send them by mail.

The next evening, Akiko dined at an excellent sushi restaurant with Akira Yasuhara, an editor at the literary magazine *Umi*. During Richard's last trip to Tokyo he had spent an evening drinking with Yasuhara's boss at The Cradle. Akira offered Aki a business proposal. *Umi* wanted to publish a long work of fiction by Brautigan. Yasuhara suggested *In Watermelon Sugar* as an example of the length he wanted.

The editor also offered to arrange a meeting with Mieko Kanai, a thirty-two-year-old poet and short story writer Richard admired. Kanai published her first story ("Love Life") at age nineteen. *Rabbits*, her collection of fantastic tales, came out in 1976. Brautigan was intrigued by Kanai's habit of always wearing large dark sunglasses whenever she was seen in public. Richard told his wife he wanted to have a conversation with the young writer.

Brautigan planned on going to Key West, but in mid-May, Helen Brann phoned with news that Targ Editions, a letterpress publisher of fine hand-bound signed limited editions, wanted to bring out a collection of Brautigan's recent short stories. The offer was $1,000 total payment for a single edition of 350 copies. The money would be paid upon delivery of the complete manuscript. The stories were already written. Richard had only to pick and choose the ones he wanted.

Targ Editions had been founded the previous year by William Targ, upon his retirement as editor in chief of G. P. Putnam's Sons. Targ's illustrious career in publishing spanned more than three and a half decades, highlighted by his purchase of *The Godfather* for a $5,000 advance after two other publishers turned the book down. Mario Puzo's novel became the most profitable work of fiction ever published by Putnam's. Targ was first drawn to Brautigan's work as a book collector, not as a publisher. He wrote Sam Lawrence early in 1970, asking for a copy of the new Delacorte edition of *Trout Fishing*. Targ started reading Brautigan and found his writing "pretty hypnotic [. . .] He is an original and the stuff reaches out to you. A touch of Whitman is there, too [. . .] A most happy encounter."

William Targ collected the early first editions of a writer he called "the sanest of all living authors." In a short time, he had amassed almost ten little books, along with Brautigan's phonograph record, "a delight." When Richard moved from Delacorte to Simon & Schuster in 1971, Targ wrote Michael Korda, one editor in chief to another, requesting a signed first edition of *The Abortion*. Eight years later, Helen Brann mailed a one-page Targ Editions contract to Richard Brautigan after appending a single added clause stipulating the author retained "final approval of the galleys of the work" and that Targ's published book would "agree in every aspect with the text as supplied by the author."

Richard selected twenty stories written in 1977 and 1978. He took his time. A month went by before he mailed them to his agent for submission to William Targ. Brautigan then returned to work in earnest, writing new short stories based on his notebook observations. "I didn't do much writing on the book," Richard later observed, "until the spring of 1979."

When Akiko returned to San Francisco from Japan early in June, Richard read her the beginning of a new novel based on his childhood in the Pacific Northwest. This was a project he'd attempted years before but "got nowhere with it." While selecting the stories for William Targ, Brautigan made a fresh start. Thus far, he had written fewer than two thousand words. "I was influenced by the introspective style of the Japanese 'I' novel," Brautigan later observed, "and started writing [. . .] in that style." The working title was "The Pond People of America."

Aki listened closely as her husband read his new manuscript. Chapter 4 began, "In April it was spring and I began my discovery of the ponds, which led me step by step down the road to the pond people and into their camp and into their pond houses and into their pond furniture and everything pond." Akiko gave careful consideration to what she heard and "suggested that the material should not be written in the form of an 'I' novel, but as an American novel, that the material demanded an American approach." Brautigan later stated, "I thought her suggestion a good one, so I converted the beginning of the novel to an American novel, which took changing only the first few pages of the beginning." Richard never showed his work in progress to Aki again.

Brautigan came up with another title. Early in June 1979, he started writing the first draft of "So the Wind Won't Blow It Away," incorporating much of the work already done on "The Pond People." He based his new title on a song he'd heard over and over the previous summer. "Dust in the Wind," by the soft rock group Kansas, had peaked at number 6 on the charts. The song's chorus was about everybody being only dust in the wind. The intimation of mortality struck a sympathetic chord within Richard. He heard it echo in his imagination when he wrote an epigraph for the new novel: "These events are only being recalled to preserve a little more of our original American dust."

Brautigan set the draft aside to concentrate on his final story selections for William Targ. Seymour Lawrence came to San Francisco on business around the middle of the month. The Brautigans took him out for drinks and dinner on his last night in town. Aki gave Sam a number of beautiful Japanese postage stamps, not realizing that he was a serious collector, making her spontaneous gift all the more delightful to the publisher. Not long after, Richard assembled twenty stories, dividing them equally between Japan and Montana. Most were less than a page in length. He called the little collection *The Tokyo–Montana Express* and dedicated it to Richard and Nancy Hodge. Less than a year later, Brautigan could not remember when he first came up with the title. Did he think of it at the time of the Targ submission, or was it earlier? "It is difficult to judge the precise time of creative inspiration," he observed, "because so many years of thought go into writing and nobody knows how the human imagination works anyway." Richard had Akiko sign the Targ Editions agreement as a witness and mailed it off to Helen Brann along with the selected stories.

Brautigan's agent sent the whole package on to Targ by the end of June. He read the stories immediately. They exceeded his "highest expectations." Targ felt it was "a delightful book" and thought the title "an inspired one." Four days later, the little volume was in production. Targ assigned Leonard Seastone of Tideline Press to handle the typographical design and letterpress printing. He hoped to have finished books ready for mailing by the first of December.

David Fechheimer was getting a divorce and had moved out of North Beach. A friend, Swiss filmmaker Barbet Schroeder (*Barfly*, *Single White Female*), introduced him to German director

Wim Wenders (*The American Friend*; *Paris, Texas*; and *Wings of Desire*), who had come to San Francisco to develop Joe Gores's novel *Hammett*, into a film with producer Francis Ford Coppola. Fechheimer and Wenders shared an apartment on Lyon Street. The detective had been contracted to write a biography of Dashiell Hammett, but Lillian Hellman refused to talk with him and the project remained in limbo. Fechheimer had already researched the first thirty years of Hammett's life (pre-Hellman) and had been hired as a consultant on the Wenders-Coppola film.

Fechheimer did not introduce Wim Wenders to Richard Brautigan. They probably met at Enrico's, where Wenders frequently hung out. Tony Dingman was at the bar every night and likely provided the connection. One evening, Brautigan invited Wenders home for dinner. They took a cab to Green Street where Aki ("Akiko-san") prepared an excellent meal. There was a lot of drinking. Richard got "especially" drunk, according to Wim.

At one point, Brautigan brought out a copy of the German translation of *Trout Fishing*, asking Wenders to tell him if it was any good. Wim looked at the opening pages and let Richard know what he really thought. Wenders "found the translation a bit clumsy, or formal." His opinion angered Brautigan. From Wenders's point of view, "it all became a big blur in his mind." Richard started insulting his guest as if he'd been the translator. "Soon I was the ugly German in general," Wenders recalled, "responsible for the war and the Holocaust."

Before Wenders comprehended what was happening, Brautigan stood in front of him, aiming a rifle. Very frightened, Aki negotiated an opening so Wim could make it to the stairs. "I remember a pretty steep staircase," he said. As Wenders made his way to the front door, Brautigan stood above, aiming at him, drunk and confused. Wim thought that Richard "in some other operatic way" was in total control "holding the gun steady." Aki stepped in front of Wim, and Richard lowered his weapon. Wenders "literally escaped" out the front door. "I was scared shitless!" he remembered.

The Brautigans returned to Montana in time for the Livingston Roundup, the town's three-day Fourth of July rodeo. Tom and Cindy Olson, a young couple who built a log home overlooking the Yellowstone at the far back end of the subdivision behind Richard's place, had been house-sitting for the writer and his wife. They met Brautigan a couple years earlier when they rented the parsonage of the Pine Creek Methodist Church across the road from the Hjortsberg's house.

Cindy's younger brother, Sean Gerrity, also camped out at Brautigan's, bunking in a VW microbus. He had done odd jobs for Richard the previous summer. Brautigan asked the Olsons to stay in his house before he came back, sweep up the mouse droppings and cobwebs, maintain a lived-in feel. They moved out before Richard and Akiko arrived. Aki was distraught. She had looked forward to having some company.

Brautigan's protective jealousy around his wife had grown into paranoid fantasy. One day, he accused Sean of wanting to screw Akiko. Gerrity came close "to decking him." On another occasion, Richard made the same accusation to Greg Keeler. "You want to fuck her," Brautigan raged, "and I'll tell you why you want to fuck her. Because you want to fuck me. I am a famous writer, and you want to fuck me, but you are afraid of such things, so you want to fuck my wife instead."

By the middle of July, houseguests started showing up. Tony Dingman was the first to arrive. Not exactly a guest, Tony helped with the shopping, cooking, and driving and served as Richard's in-house drinking buddy and literary sounding board. A week or so after Dingman's arrival, Ken Kelley made his first trip to Montana, rewarded for his diligent undercover work in Shasta County. Richard and Tony picked him up in the afternoon at the airport in Belgrade. On Brautigan's instructions, Kelley brought along two expensive bottles of Calvados. They drove back to Pine Creek just before sunset. Dingman took off soon afterward. He was having a fling with a local girl who lived across the road and no longer spent his nights at Richard's place.

Brautigan poured himself and Kelley a large glass of Calvados (Ken thought it tasted like "turbo-charged ambrosia") leading his guest on a walk through the woods behind his house. Richard wanted to show Ken something he called "really sacred." They followed game trails meandering between the cottonwoods toward the setting sun, a golden nimbus of newly hatched gnats whirling above their heads. Knowing Kelley hailed from Custer's hometown in Michigan, Brautigan spun tales of the Indian Wars as he led Ken onto a narrow bench overlooking a number of ancient teepee rings on the Hjortsbergs' property.

"Richard is turning himself into an Indian," Kelley recalled, "dancing on the warpath." Brautigan launched into an impassioned diatribe about freedom and gun rights and the Constitution, wanting Kelley to understand he was now in God's Country and had left effeminate, liberal San Francisco far behind.

Back at the house, Akiko performed her own war dance. She and Kelley did not get along. Ken thought of her as "Witch Woman." The problems started when Kelley was shown to the upstairs bedroom. He suffered from a bad back and found that the bed "sagged terribly." When Ken placed the mattress on the floor for support, Aki objected. "This isn't the hotel, you know," she said. Kelley slept instead in a hammock on the back porch. "I wanted to wake up under the Montana sky," Ken said. "I didn't want to be confined."

Kelley awoke the next morning, and the first thing he saw was the Hjortsbergs riding their horses down the gravel road past Brautigan's big red barn. He didn't know who they were at the time. Later, Richard told him about how Gatz had called to let him know the house next door was for sale. "If it hadn't been for Gatz I wouldn't be here," Brautigan said. He also praised Hjortsberg's writing, loaning Ken a copy of *Toro! Toro! Toro!* "almost like handing me the Gideon Bible. Here's this little gem."

Akiko showed Ken her garden. "I had to earn my keep," Ken recalled. "I had to weed her garden." He looked her straight in the eye and said, "I certainly don't want to trample on your turf here. I'll stay out of your way, and you don't have to feel threatened by me. We can just pretend to be friends." He thought they'd made a deal.

Later, Brautigan escorted Kelley into his separate sleeping quarters, where he housed his fire-arms. To Ken, it looked like "a dungeon in the woods. There was something military about it. There were a lot of guns on the walls, sort of an armory." Richard wanted to expound further upon the previous evening's Code of the West. He handed Kelley a gun, "a pistol. A big one. A long old-fashioned Wyatt Earp kind."

Lesson number 1: "Never touch a gun unless you know or determine that it is loaded." Ken checked the cylinder, and sure enough, the piece was armed and ready. He felt that this was "the introduction to the sacredness of Montana. Where guns meant something. Because this was how battles were fought, heroic battles. This is the West." What Brautigan had in mind was something more than a simple history lesson. He envisioned literary ritual sacrifice.

That evening, Brautigan brought a bootleg Hungarian edition of *In Watermelon Sugar* out from the main house, along with a can of Campbell's tomato soup. "Look what they've done to the back cover," Richard demanded. "They made me look like a hippie Joe Stalin." Brautigan set the paperback book on a cottonwood stump, propping it up with a fork from the kitchen. He placed the soup can in front of it. Brautigan took the first shot from the back porch. The tree stump stood thirty or forty feet away at the far reach of the light. The weapon of choice was a .45 automatic. Richard squeezed one off with a loud roar that made Kelley jump.

Brautigan missed the stump. Next, it was Ken's turn. Kelley didn't like guns. Richard told him not to shoot "from the safety of the porch."

Brautigan led Ken into the darkness. "He decides this is where the Indians would do it," Kelley recalled, "and he said, now, just aim and fire." Ken didn't know what to expect. He raised the pistol, snapped off the safety, sort of aimed, and pulled the trigger. KA-BOOM! The weapon's report and recoil stunned him. He "felt something weird." He was covered with a wet red fluid running down his face and dripping off his nose.

Shocked, Kelley looked at Brautigan. "He was bleeding with a smile on his face." Ken had hit the target, and he thought the bullet ricocheted and struck Richard. He felt an instant flash of horror, "truly gargoylian," before realizing the Campbell's can had exploded on impact and sprayed tomato soup all over him and Brautigan. The next morning, Kelley collected the shattered can and bullet-punctured paperback, putting them in a plastic bag he kept for the rest of his life. "I was enough of a cultural historian," he said, "to know I should have that."

Kelley had passed some unwritten test, and Brautigan agreed to a formal interview.

On the first of August, the two men sat down with a tape recorder running and drinks in hand. They began by talking about poetry.

"I love John Donne," Richard said, his voice unnaturally precise.

"Byron?"

"Too fucking romantic," Brautigan shot back. "Blake I love," adding emphatically after a pause, "I love Milton." Lapsing into "Imperial Mode," Richard made a solemn pronouncement. "I have tremendous problems with Byron, Keats, and Shelley."

Ken Kelley changed the subject, posing a typical journalistic query: "Who's your favorite writer of the twentieth century?"

"I'm too old for that question," Brautigan demurred.

"Favorite Shakespearean play?"

"*Hamlet.*"

As the conversation continued, Richard loosened up, further expounding his personal opinions about modern literature. "Hemingway is the best short story writer in America," he declared. Asked about books he liked, Brautigan listed *On the Road*; *They Shoot Horses, Don't They?*; *As I Lay Dying*; Fitzgerald's Pat Hobby stories; and *The Sea Wolf*. Richard called Jack London "an extraordinary writer," immediately pronouncing *Martin Eden* to be even better than *The Sea Wolf*. Flannery O'Connor and Henry James were two writers Brautigan didn't care for.

The discussion turned to Richard's recent teaching stint at Montana State, an experience he hoped to repeat, only next time he wanted to work with grade school through high school students. "One week," he said, "get in and get out. I'm going to teach William Carlos Williams, the early Eliot. I'm going to teach Stevens." Kelley ended by asking Brautigan what he thought of certain popular modern writers. Richard said he hated Carlos Castaneda and didn't like Gabriel García Márquez. "I'm not interested in neurosis," he said. "I'm not interested in dramatic epics. I'm interested in specific information."

Within days of Ken Kelley's interview, Richard and Nancy Hodge, along with their three-and-a-half-year-old son, Aaron, arrived in Montana for a short stay with the Brautigans. Around this same time, Fumio and Mieko Wada, Richard and Aki's friends from San Francisco, also came to visit. An immediate party celebrated the arrival of the guests. Jim Harrison, staying at the Pine Creek Lodge, and Becky Fonda joined in the fun. The festivities began at Chico Hot Springs. Nancy Hodge remembered that "they played pinball and drank at the bar, and we swam."

"It was a two-tiered thing," according to Ken Kelley. "There was the official party and the unofficial party. The official party was to welcome the Hodges. That was held in Chico." Richard and Nancy left the hot springs early with Aki because they had to get their son to bed. Things got rolling when the others returned to Brautigans' house. Tony Dingman warned Kelley that "word is spreading there's a Richard Brautigan party, and anything could happen because he doesn't do this very often." Before long, a variety of scruffy locals arrived, looking for a good time.

Ken's "unofficial" party included playing a game of Go with Akiko and a one-legged Vietnam vet acid dealer on crutches. Kelley swallowed a tab, assuming Brautigan had done the same. Before his memories of the event grew "more and more psychedelic," Kelley clearly recalled being humiliated by Aki at the Go table. "She was, 'I beat you again, ah hah hah hah!'"

"Great," Ken said. "I was hoping all of us could play an American game like Ping-Pong." Pent-up emotions boiled over. Ken resented Akiko for demanding he work in her garden. His ensuing diatribe included repeated use of the word "Jap." Aki fled in tears into the kitchen. Brautigan watched the entire episode, saying nothing to Kelley in the moment.

Ken staggered outside, tripping under the stars, while the Hodges' "official" party continued on another wavelength in the kitchen. Unlike the journalist, Dick and Nancy did not drop acid. Neither did their host, in spite of what Kelley believed. Brautigan preferred his enlightenment straight from the bottle. By midnight, booze had taken him to a new level of satori. Richard had a thing about perfection, whether crafting a line of prose, reviewing a contract, or concocting his spaghetti sauce. Earlier in the evening he'd regaled his attorney about the craftsmanship and harmonious beauty of a pistol owned by a friend. A phone call had been made, and the loyal pal drove the acclaimed gun over to Brautigan's place for everyone to examine and admire.

Around midnight, while the group in the kitchen debated the merits of heading into town before the bars closed versus calling it a night and simply going to bed, Richard declared Dick Hodge had to cement their friendship by shooting into the ceiling with the perfectly crafted pistol. Hodge declined. He didn't like guns and wanted no part of drunken six-gun shenanigans. Brautigan insisted. If Dick wouldn't fire the revolver, he'd do it himself.

Hodge grew politely aggressive with Brautigan. Dick never drank much and was the most sober person in the house. Little Aaron lay fast asleep in the room directly above their heads. "I love you, you know," he told Brautigan, "but I really don't want to shoot this gun. I don't want to wake my son." Richard still didn't get it. Tony Dingman and the pistol's owner had to wrestle the weapon away from him, removing the bullets.

"The next morning, Richard Brautigan was all apologies," Nancy recalled. "He was all over me for an hour the next morning about how sorry he was." Ken Kelley beat a strategic retreat earlier, heading across the creek to the Hjortsbergs'. He introduced himself with effusive Irish charm. Soon, he was begging for asylum. "Look guys," he said, "give me a break. Please help me. You won't even notice I'm here. I'll sleep outside."

Aki came over a bit later, seeking sympathy from Marian. "Oh, that monster Richard," she wailed. "That monster, Richard." Akiko had already confided in Nancy Hodge, who arrived soon after to go riding with Marian. Afraid of horses, Ken Kelley hung around the barn overhearing mutterings about bondage while the women saddled up. That evening, Dick and Nancy discussed moving in to the Hjortsbergs', but there was no more room at the inn. Kelley was already ensconced on the couch in the library alcove next to the spare bedroom where Gatz's mother stayed.

Brautigan "comes over, very grandly" Kelley remembered, "to show this is just a big cosmic joke." Richard proposed "a joust," a Ping-Pong tournament to be held in his barn. He stewed over Ken's racist comments to Aki: an insult demanding revenge. Brautigan's wife had been a junior high school Ping-Pong champion. Kelley challenged everyone to play the game. A public humiliation seemed in order. Richard asked Ken to oversee the construction of a regulation-sized Ping-Pong table and provide a spaghetti dinner for the spectators and participants. Kelley pleaded poverty.

"So," Brautigan asked, "how much money have you got in the bank?"

"Quite a curious question," Kelley replied, "but I'll answer it: $12,000."

"All right, then," Richard said. "You can afford it."

Brautigan wanted a spaghetti feast like the one Kelley hosted for fifty people at his Larkin Street flat the night they met five years before. Ken said he'd make enough to feed everybody.

The next morning, Kelley enlisted Sean Gerrity to take charge of the Ping-Pong table project. They went to the hardware store in town and bought a sheet of three-quarter-inch plywood, several two-by-fours, brushes, cans of green and white paint, everything they needed, before setting to work in the barn. Knowing Brautigan's perfectionism, they double-checked the accuracy of their measurements, making sure their plans conformed to rule book specifications. Sean and Ken finished the table in a day. "It was perfect," Kelley recalled.

Avoiding the construction project, Richard Brautigan took Aaron Hodge fishing at Armstrong's Spring Creek. His parents, Aki, and the Wadas all went along, "a whole entourage," turning the event into a picnic. "It was just wonderful," Nancy Hodge recalled. "That was something Brautigan did spontaneously. He was the one that suggested taking Aaron."

Akiko spent the afternoon shooting photographs. Richard wanted to teach his wife to fish and had bought her a seven-and-a-half-foot Scott fly rod, a Hardy Lightweight reel with a five-weight double-tapered line, and a pair of chest waders. Aki thought the baggy waterproof boots were very funny, like something a clown would wear, and she did not bring them to the spring creek. Aaron was having a wonderful time in Montana, excited about his first fishing trip. Neither Dick nor Nancy knew or cared anything about trout fishing. Richard knelt beside Aaron, carefully explaining the knots and which fly was the best. "He did everything for Aaron, step-by-step," Nancy said. "He was just a sweetheart."

Aki recorded it all with her single-lens reflex Nikon. Richard made the cast for the little boy and set the hook on the strike, handing Aaron the rod. The kid thrilled to the electric action of the fight. Brautigan helped him play, land, and release the trout. Richard Hodge thought of it as his friend's "idea of perfection. Richard wanted to catch the perfect fish and take it through like a little set piece."

The next afternoon's Ping-Pong tournament provided drama performed on a bigger stage. Everyone gathered in the cavernous redwood barn, and the teams were selected. Aki, Sean Gerrity, Ken Kelley, the Wadas, Marian Hjortsberg, and the Hodges all signed up for a round-robin elimination contest with quarter- and semifinal rounds. Richard Brautigan did not play. He appointed himself the judge of the event. One round of the semifinals pitted Ken against Aki, a true grudge match. "It was vicious playing," Kelley recalled. In the end, Mrs. Brautigan prevailed.

The final game for the championship matched Richard Hodge against Akiko. Brautigan wanted his wife to win. "He didn't like a loser at all," Aki recalled. "So, I have to be his hero all the time. As a wife, as a secretary, or the friend. I have to be perfect for him." It was not to be. Akiko lost to Dick. Richard, acting as an impartial judge, called the final point against her. Aki's loss put a damper on the spaghetti party.

Greg and Judy Keeler came over from Bozeman with Dave Schrieber. They brought along a bright, attractive MSU student as a date for Tony Dingman. When Greg first arrived, he spotted Ken Kelley in the living room and thought him "a loud smart-ass." Keeler, "still fascinated with the newness of knowing Richard," didn't notice his host's sour mood. Richard seemed playful, bouncing two-hundred-pound Greg on his lap "like a baby." A little later, Brautigan took Keeler and the MSU coed up to his barn-loft office and gave them "a wonderful but sad reading" of "Shrine of Carp," one of his recent Japanese stories.

The trouble started after serious drinking got under way. Brautigan, insulated by the private sanctuary of booze, refused to talk about his wife's defeat in the recent round-robin tournament. Late in the night, when the Wadas and the Hodges had gone off to bed, Richard staggered out to the barn with an ax. Accompanied by Dave Schrieber, he laid waste to the offending Ping-Pong table, smashing it into splinters.

After revenging himself on an inanimate object, Brautigan returned to his house. He found his .45 and threatened to shoot a hole in the floor. "Richard, there are children sleeping upstairs," Aki protested, trying to stop him.

"It's my floor, and I'll shoot it if I want to," Brautigan raged. In the end, he was talked out of indoor gunplay, "so the kids could sleep in peace." Schrieber gathered up all the ammunition he could find and snuck it out of the house, and all the survivors (not including Richard) went over to the Hjortsbergs' for a hot comforting sauna.

In the morning, the wrecked Ping-Pong table provided novel breakfast conversation. "It didn't look like anything you'd ever seen before," Ken Kelley recalled. "It was a giant rubble." When Aki observed the destruction, she took a piece of white chalk and drew a circle around the wreckage, like a cop outlining a homicide victim. Greg Keeler came over later, and Richard said, "Pardon the mess. We had to deal with a rude houseguest this morning." Brautigan told Keeler he'd thrown Kelley out because he'd broken Akiko's favorite lamp.

Ken related a different story, claiming he wasn't sleeping in the room when "the little Japanese toy lamp" was broken. "It got knocked over by somebody I'd never met," he whined, "so because I wasn't sleeping there to protect it, and should have been, that was my fault."

Richard and Nancy Hodge left early that day, driving off to the Bozeman airport with their son. Later in the afternoon, Ida Hjortsberg, Gatz's mother, came to the back door, with a large shard of shattered Ping-Pong table she'd found in the woods while hunting mushrooms with her five-year-old grandson, Max. "Does this belong to you?" she asked. Akiko accepted the fragment, knowing her husband had hurled it out into the cottonwoods, possessed by his incomprehensible demons.

Soon after the Hodges' departure, Jimmy Buffett showed up in Montana. The Brautigans were recovering from houseguest overload, so he stayed at the Pine Creek Lodge with Jim Harrison.

Richard and Akiko planned a dinner party to welcome their friends. Aki prepared a huge pot of borscht, one of her specialties, slaving in the kitchen for most of the day. Harrison, Buffett, and their group arrived very late, long after most of the other guests had already eaten. They'd spent the day floating the Yellowstone with a fishing guide and lost track of time, often the case when the trout are rising.

Brautigan was not pleased. He watched the late arrivals, silently furious, as Buffett wandered about his kitchen, drawling, "Hi, I'm Jimmy," to everyone he encountered. After wolfing down a couple bowls of borscht, Harrison, Buffett, and their entourage abruptly departed for Chico Hot Springs. Richard and Aki "felt snubbed." Cleaning up after the last guest departed, the Brautigans decided it might be a good time "for a sort of second honeymoon."

The next morning they booked a room at the Bozeman Holiday Inn, heading over the hill in the evening for dinner with Greg and Judy Keeler. The Brautigans arrived at the Keelers' with Richard "sullen" and in full "Imperial Mode." The previous evening's perceived insult remained foremost on his mind. It was all Brautigan could talk about, "before, during, and after" the dinner. Richard repeatedly whispered, "Hi, I'm Jimmy," muttering "popular culture" as a disgusted assessment.

Later in the evening, Brautigan instructed his wife to go on ahead to the motel room "and prepare your body for me." Aki complied, but not without a sardonic dismissive rolling of her eyes. The night wore on. Richard, unable to let go of the perceived Buffett/Harrison snub, kept returning to the topic, over and over again. He called this "tracking." Keeler wondered if his friend believed the process of repetition might somehow "exorcize" his demons.

Close to midnight, after hours of "tracking," Brautigan announced it was time to drive over to Pine Creek and "settle some business." Greg Keeler had grave misgivings about this endeavor but fell dutifully into line, chauffeuring Richard over Trail Creek Road in his Mazda station wagon. Outside cabin number 2 at the Pine Creek Lodge, Brautigan instructed Keeler to "push this cabin with your car. I want it moved." Although he was a Buffett fan and hoped someday to meet Harrison, Keeler complied, easing his car up against the log structure and giving it a little bump. "Now flash your lights and honk your horn," Richard instructed. When Keeler hesitated, Brautigan did it for him, having immediate second thoughts about his act of retribution. "These guys are big and can be pretty mean," he said. "They could sue me for all I'm worth. Quick, let's go to my house and hide on the floor."

Back at Rancho Brautigan, supine in the dark kitchen, they lay staring at the ceiling while discussing the impact of Japanese films on Richard's work. Around two in the morning, Brautigan remembered his wife waiting in a room at the Holiday Inn and suggested a return to Bozeman. As a conciliatory gesture, the delinquent husband had Greg stop at Denny's and ordered fried shrimp to go. "She loves them, and they should be a perfect peace offering." The order took so long, they both had a burger and fries while waiting. Keeler dropped Brautigan off at the motel at some ungodly hour, wishing him good night and speeding off toward home.

The next day, Richard and Aki pulled up in front of the Keelers' home on Linley Place. Greg watched as she slammed the brakes, sending Richard's head thudding into the dashboard. Greg had a vision of Akiko bouncing the "measly shrimp [. . .] off his face and chest, one by one" as he begged for forgiveness. Richard stopped by the Keeler's place just long enough to tell Greg his wife had been pulling the dashboard stunt all morning.

With the house quiet after all the guests had gone, Brautigan returned to the novel still called "So the Wind Won't Blow It Away." Richard planned a mid-September trip to Japan to continue working on his sequence of short stories. When the Tokyo office of the International Communication Agency (or ICA, later renamed the United States Information Agency), learned of Brautigan's travel plans, they invited him to participate in a program conducted under the auspices of the American Embassy.

Anxious for work in hand before his author left the country, William Targ wrote Brautigan in August, asking where to send the limited edition's colophon page for signing. Targ finally spoke on the telephone with Akiko near the end of the month. The next day, he mailed 350-plus colophon pages to Montana in a beat-up tan attaché case. Richard and Aki took it with them when they left for San Francisco before the end of the month.

Brautigan worked steadily on his novel, finishing a first version at the end of August. On the title page he typed, "This is a very rough draft and will be rewritten extensively. It is not publishable in this form." On September 5, Brautigan received a special visa from the Japanese Consulate-General permitting him a 120-day stay in Japan "for cultural activities." Akiko assisted him in getting this and wanted to accompany her husband on his trip to her homeland. Richard convinced her she wasn't allowed to leave the country because she'd applied for American citizenship. Aki didn't know if this was true. An obedient wife, she swallowed her hurt and anger, staying home on Green Street. Always a professional regarding work, Brautigan sent the signed colophon pages back to William Targ before taking off for Japan.

The day of his departure in mid-September, Richard phoned Helen Brann, telling her he planned to be out of the country for three months. Brautigan did not share this information with his wife. Akiko found out about his plans weeks later from her family in Japan. She wrote to Richard the first week in October: "Is it true that you gonna stay in there until the end of the year??? Zeeeeeee!! This means (Oh NO!) Not with joy," hardly the words of a contented spouse. A mutual friend observed Brautigan "was so naive" and "didn't feel it was necessary to change his way of living around women."

This was Richard Brautigan's fourth trip to Tokyo. He had been there every season but fall and was looking forward to experiencing a Japanese autumn for the first time. He would have to wait. Mid-September remained hot and sultry. Richard resumed his old habits in Tokyo, moving in to a room on the thirty-fifth floor of Keio Plaza and heading out to The Cradle every night.

During his first couple days in the city, Brautigan visited his in-laws, promptly writing Aki that everyone was taking good care of him. He asked his wife if she missed him. Not that Richard lacked for company. Bruce Conner had been invited to Japan by the ICA to host a presentation of his short experimental films. He arrived for a month's stay. Brautigan got him a room on the same floor of his hotel. "They gave him a good price," Conner recalled, "and I got the same kind of price."

Richard offered a bit of advice about what to expect as a first-time foreigner in Tokyo. "When you go to Japan, Bruce," he said, "just imagine how people would relate to you if you were a giant cactus on roller skates rolling down the sidewalk."

Conner felt this attitude provided "an excuse for Richard to be a little obnoxious." Brautigan brought his friend to The Cradle "many times," reintroducing him to Takako. Bruce observed that the bar "was like in a way a second home for [Richard]. He expected everybody to speak English. He didn't make any effort to speak Japanese other than, at most, two dozen tourist phrases, and he pronounced them just horribly."

Brautigan claimed "it didn't make any difference," confiding to Conner that "the proper behavior in Japan is that it doesn't make any difference what you do in Japan. You are a barbarian in their eyes."

Spending time in a bar with Brautigan provided Conner with another insight into Japanese customs. "They have a different attitude toward drunks," he recalled. Drunks were taken care of kindly. No one roughed them up or tried to steal their money. "So, this is heaven for Richard." One evening, his role as Brautigan's drinking buddy backfired on Conner. Richard had a fearsome capacity for holding his liquor. Trying to keep up with him was an exercise in futility. Out for a sushi dinner with Brautigan and some of his Japanese friends, Conner made the mistake of attempting to match him drink for drink.

By the end of the meal, Bruce was sloshed. When the bill arrived, Richard asked Bruce if he'd like to help pay for the dinner. Deep in his cups, Bruce offered some pocket change. Richard felt this to be an insult to his friends but bottled up his indignation until later that night when they were back at the Keio Plaza. He phoned Conner's room in a fit of fuming anger, threatening to come and beat him up. Drunk enough to take Richard at his word, Bruce slid his security lock into place just as Brautigan came lurching in a fury down the hallway. Unable to gain entrance, Richard hurled himself at Bruce's door, cursing and screaming. He kicked and pounded with his fists, creating an enormous disturbance.

Bruce Conner thought being in Japan with Brautigan "would be a splendid opportunity. I could make contact with people through Richard and [he] could show me things about Japan." Conner and Brautigan had planned back in San Francisco to work on a screenplay together. After making a number of short experimental movies, Bruce wanted to direct a feature before he turned fifty and "felt that because of Richard's involvement it would be easier for me to see about getting funding for the film." Living on Brautigan's floor in the hotel seemed ideal to Conner. "This is great," he thought. "We'll have breakfast together."

Things didn't work out that way. "I didn't see [Richard] for days at a time," Bruce remembered. "He'd lock himself into his room, saying he was busy writing. Or he had an appointment, or he was doing an interview, or I couldn't get him at all." Conner kept busy. Brautigan had introduced him to people he knew, and Bruce worked with a film crew he'd organized before his arrival. Every time Bruce mentioned the screenplay project, Richard said, "Oh, I don't want to talk about that now. I've got other projects."

Brautigan finally found time to talk with Conner about their proposed script. Bruce recalled "his premise and concepts of the film were so completely the opposite of any ones I had because what Richard came up with was a bunch of guys planning a bank robbery and virtually everything was taking place in one room. There were seven or eight people, and all they did was sit and talk and play cards and drink. All of the humor was verbal. All of the action was verbal."

After several meetings that went nowhere, Conner said, "Look, Richard, there's nothing really here to do a movie about." Bruce had a concept he thought might save the day. The idea was to focus on the artificiality of filmmaking. A boom mike would hang down in the middle of a scene.

Actors might talk directly back to the director. The clapboard marking each shot would not be edited out of the final cut. Both men wanted Robert Mitchum to star. Conner proposed having the bank robbers plan to meet at a movie theater. The final scene would show Mitchum standing in a queue outside under a marquee bearing the picture's actual title. The lead actor turns to the camera and delivers a final line: "This better be a good movie."

Bruce championed this concept. They had a beginning. They had a punch line. Richard couldn't grasp a visual approach, remaining locked into his dialogue-heavy structure. Bruce gave up. "I think you ought to write it as a book," he said.

On a warm Monday evening, the first of October, Brautigan presented a program he called "My Life, My Book," at the Tokyo American Center under the auspices of the recently reorganized United States International Communication Agency (USICA), a branch of the State Department established to promote educational and cultural exchanges between the United States and foreign nations. A week or so earlier in September, he gave a similar presentation at the American Center in Sapporo, his wife's birthplace, on the northernmost island of Hokkaido.

Takako Shiina was in the audience along with several members of Aki's family. Richard brought Akiko's mother a special present from Hokkaido. After the American Center reading, Mrs. Nishizawa wrote her daughter a four-page letter describing Richard's "lecture" as "unique, humorous and delightful, with dignity." She enclosed a clipping from the *Weekly Asahi Magazine* about the event.

The next night became Bruce Conner's turn to take the stage at the American Center. Both Richard Brautigan and Takako were in attendance. The films screened included *Cosmic Ray* (1961), *Take the 5:10 to Dreamland* (1977), *Mongoloid* (1978), and Conner's most recent production, *Valse Triste* (1979). After the screening, Takako took Richard and Bruce to an old traditional Tokyo sukiyaki restaurant. Bruce Conner assumed that Takako Shiina was Richard's girlfriend.

During their meal, Brautigan remarked to Conner, "Whenever I think my mind's going, I'm going to get rid of myself. I could blow my brains out." Richard made a gesture with his forefinger, miming a pistol barrel inserted into his mouth. "He also said he'd never told anybody that before," Conner recalled.

"Why would you want to do it that way?" Bruce asked. "Can you imagine what a terrible mess this is for somebody to clean up? How disgusting it's going to be?"

"Well, I won't be there to do anything about it," Brautigan replied. "Why should I care?"

"Hey, man," Conner said, "your mind is going already. What's the big event?"

After their planned film collaboration crashed and burned, Richard and Bruce continued to lunch together nearly every day. "He would talk about how he couldn't find a sock in the morning," Conner recollected. "How he looked all over the place for it. He talked about his tax problems or any number of mundane and stupid things." These trivial subjects were the basis for much of Brautigan's short fiction and had a creative importance for him that was lost on his listeners.

Bruce Conner had long been interested in the country music from the thirties, forties, and fifties that he'd listened to as a kid in Kansas. He liked all the old-time stuff, hillbilly music, Western swing, rockabilly, and had collected "dozens of records." He made tapes of some of these and brought the cassettes along with him to Japan and played them for Brautigan, a big fan of Dolly Parton's more commercial country music. Richard didn't care for Conner's tapes. "He said that it reminded him of when he was a boy," Bruce reflected, remembering their conversation. "He didn't want to hear those songs because he was living with his mother and there would be these men that would just sort of come in and carry her away. He'd be abandoned."

What "impressed [Brautigan] was the interviews, the publicity, the publication," Conner observed. Richard enjoyed being perceived as "an important artist" in Japan "because an artist who is recognized is respected much more in their gestures than many other people. The social relationship is quite different." One night at The Cradle, Brautigan used his cachet to benefit his friend. Richard and Bruce were drinking and schmoozing with several corporate executives from NHK-TV and Brautigan was "badgering them into giving Bruce Conner an exclusive tour of their most recent Samurai production."

Early in October, Bruce went to dinner with Richard and Akiko's sister. Richard told Bruce about visiting his wife's family "a few times" and that "things were a little bit awkward." Even so, he felt "everything was going along fine." This evening proved otherwise. Bruce remembered "the sister was as combative and irritating and insulting as you could be." She spoke English well, making it impossible to miss the point. Conner felt familiar with the refinements of Japanese etiquette and understood "that she was obviously not being very nice." A few nights later, she had an opportunity to up the ante.

On the night of October 10, Richard Brautigan was scheduled to give a reading at Jean Jean, a performance space housed in the Yamate Church in Shibuya-ku. Bruce Conner took the subway with Richard from their hotel. When they emerged from the station, passing the bronze statue of Hachikō, it started to rain, a gentle autumn sprinkle. Brautigan told Conner, "I'm gonna go across the street and pick up something at the drugstore."

"Take my umbrella," Bruce said. He had one of those compact folding spring-loaded bumbershoots. "Here. I'll open it for you." Conner pushed the button, and his umbrella expanded with a *snap*, splattering water all over Brautigan.

Delighted, Richard exclaimed, "This is marvelous! I like the rain."

Bruce loved his friend's reaction, "like he had received a wonderful gift. It was a jewel-like event."

Takako Shiina and a large contingent of the Nishizawa family were also in the Jean Jean audience with Bruce Conner that night. Richard shared the stage with his friend, Japanese poet Shuntarō Tanikawa, a collaboration set in motion during Akiko's visit to Tokyo the previous May. Tanikawa went on first. During a ten-minute break between readings, Aki's sister inconspicuously slipped out of the theater.

When the audience returned to their seats, Bruce Conner observed an empty chair standing alone, a deserted island in a sea of spectators. A dozen minutes or so into Brautigan's presentation, after he read a new poem titled "The Link," a member of Jean Jean's staff came onto the stage, interrupting the proceedings with an important message. Word had just arrived of a medical emergency. Akiko's sister had collapsed in a nearby department store.

The entire Nishizawa clan, "all of Akiko's family, mother, father, brothers, cousins, got up en masse" and walked out of the hall together without a word. Richard stood on the stage, watching in stunned silence. Bruce Conner felt it was all a stunt, "obviously a bad, naughty trick which [Aki's sister] had planned ahead of time." In his opinion, there was "nothing wrong with this woman. She hated Richard."

Afterward, Bruce Conner conversed with Shuntarō Tanikawa about Richard. Conner felt Tanikawa admired and liked Brautigan but was critical of him "in very small ways." Takako told a story about a time when she and Richard and Shuntarō went out to dinner together and the Japanese poet said, "Richard, your problem is you don't understand women." Brautigan's response was a nervous, high-pitched laugh, "Hahahahaha!" He dealt with Tanikawa's remark by treating it as a joke.

Takako Shiina took note of the Jean Jean program in her journal. She had no recollection of the Nishizawa family's mass walkout. Shiina recalled Brautigan was "always complaining about Aki and didn't get along with her family." Bruce Conner later admitted that some of Akiko's relatives "probably didn't know what was going on" when they were informed of the department store emergency. Richard told Bruce that Aki's mother and other family members came to his door at the Keio Plaza about four days afterward "with gifts, apologizing and tearful."

In mid-October, Aki left San Francisco on a trip to the East Coast with Marcia Clay, who was having an exhibition of her paintings at the Zenith Gallery in Washington, D.C. They stayed at a friend's apartment in a building full of artists next door to the gallery. The trees had just begun turning color. Akiko was charmed by the capital city. "Lots of old buildings are made by brick like in Europe," she wrote her husband.

In Tokyo, "summer seemed to be going on forever." In the middle of October, Richard Brautigan sat in a little student café and wrote "Tokyo Stories, Brautigan" on the cover of a pocket-sized notebook. He began jotting down short pieces inside, completing six that first day. He thought they might be an addition to the work he'd already done for *The Tokyo–Montana Express*. The subjects were mostly everyday and commonplace (crickets, leaves, a man measuring the Shinjuku Station platform), just what Bruce Conner complained about as topics of Richard's conversation.

Typhoon Tip, the largest and most severe tropical cyclone on record, half the size of the United States (1,380 miles) in diameter, roared into Tokyo on October 19, 1979. With winds in excess of 80 miles per hour, the storm had diminished from its peak force of 190 miles per hour but still packed considerable punch, killing forty-four people as it careened across Japan. The nineteenth started out warm, clear, and sunny. In the late afternoon, Richard Brautigan went for a walk in the beautiful park surrounding the Meiji Shrine.

Suddenly, the sky darkened and wind whirled into chaos. Rain sheeted down, debris went flying. Hit by the force of the typhoon, Brautigan braced himself between a tree and a park bench, hanging on with all his strength. The storm lasted about twenty-five minutes, passing away to the north around sunset. The air cleared. The evening light shone with an unearthly glow as Richard emerged, soaking wet and smiling, through the Main Torii, Japan's tallest wooden Shinto gate, at the entrance to the shrine.

Anita LoCoco, a young American woman who lived nearby in the Harajuku District, had been on her way to an acupuncture appointment, cutting through the park, when the storm overwhelmed her. Once the typhoon passed, she staggered on her way, a bit traumatized. She recognized Brautigan from his book covers, his face "kind of glowing." They were both drenched, with the bewildered look of survivors after a catastrophe. LoCoco introduced herself and struck up a conversation.

Brautigan and LoCoco walked around the park together, dripping wet. She told him how she'd grabbed onto a tree when the wind came up and had been lifted parallel to the ground, "like in a cartoon." Laughing, feeling "exhilarated" from it all, Richard commented that the typhoon "was like a life/death experience." Anita told him about coming out of a reading he'd given at Lone Mountain College, eleven years before, tripping on acid and seeing "the crescent moon with Venus in the middle." Brautigan remained pleasant, though a bit formal, chatting amicably while keeping his distance. After ten minutes or so, they parted company and walked away into separate lives, never to meet again, a chance encounter after a storm.

All along, Richard wrote new short stories in his little notebooks, working at sidewalk cafés and supermarket cafeterias. He finished four the day after the typhoon, another four on October 22, and an additional six the following day, when cold autumn weather finally arrived in Tokyo. Many of these brief tales involved going to soft-core porn movies. By his own admission, Brautigan watched "between eight or nine porno movies every week" while in Japan. "Richard had this absurd obsession with pornography and sex which did not involve very strong interpersonal relationships with women," Bruce Conner observed.

One evening, Brautigan took Conner along with him to the movies. The artist/filmmaker thought in Japan he'd see "worthwhile" work by great Japanese directors (Kurosawa, Inagaki, and Shindo), but "99 percent of the theaters seemed to be these porno movies." The pornography presented was not the XXX features shown in adult theaters in the States. Certain cultural taboos prevented "kissing on the screen." All the sex was simulated, "never too closely depicted," Bruce recalled. Bondage and rape were popular themes in Japanese soft-core porn.

Brautigan told Conner he was studying Japanese porn films because he planned to write a book about them. "Instead of sightseeing or going on the town to traditional sights like temples and parks, museums and nightlife," Richard scrawled in his notebook, "I watch television and attend porno movies to find my Japan. This is the Japan of fantasy and imagination [. . .] I think that to come to some understanding of a country you must first try to understand its fantasies." At porn theaters, he observed "the basic dream life of Japanese men at its lowest possible denominator." Out of his seventy-six stories written in Japan, only ten were directly about pornographic movies. Others involved actors, models, and television commercials, all satellites orbiting his central theme, part of the book he planned in his mind.

Sometime in mid-October, Brautigan met writer/singer/actor Akiyuki Nosaka at The Cradle. A hard-drinking brawler, Nosaka was a rebel hipster masked by dark glasses. He burst onto the scene in the 1960s with a series of poignant stories about adolescent youth adrift in the chaos of war. He was best known for his novels *The Pornographers* (1963) and *Grave of the Fireflies* (1967), a powerful autobiographical story about struggling to survive starvation with his little sister in the ruins of Kobe after the 1945 American firebombing raids. As a *chanteur*, he used the stage name Claude Nosaka. The two literary outsiders formed a drunken bond. Richard had a presentation scheduled in the American Center in Tokyo. Akiyuki was set to give a lecture at the Yonago hospital at the same time. They agreed it would be a fine idea to travel together and share the experience.

The two writers planned a three-day trip. Nosaka suggested to Mr. Isohachi, his friend at the Tokyo American Center, that he and Brautigan make the trip without a translator. Near the end of the month, they set off on the bullet train. Along the way, both got totally drunk. Through his shades, Nosaka observed Brautigan with a hipster's acid dispassionate reserve. He considered him an American Davy Crockett clone, overweight, pale skin splotched by red patches.

Akiyuki had a secret agenda. He planned on writing about the episode and asked Richard numerous questions. Nosaka's published account of his trip with Brautigan appeared as a short I-novel, *Nichibeisakegassen* (Japan–USA Drinking Battle), in December 1979. Japanese I-novels (*shishosetu*) often distort the truth for artistic reasons. In his novel, Nosaka claimed the first Japanese translations of Brautigan's books stated that Richard had been born in Minnesota in 1930, and he assumed they were both the same age.

When the fictional Nosaka inquired about these biographical details, the make-believe Brautigan insisted they were true and said he worked as a journalist in Europe during the Korean War. The fictional Richard told Akiyuko that he'd gone dancing at a fireman's hall in Minnesota to celebrate America's victory after VJ Day. In his book, Nosaka mentioned how this greatly upset him. The real Akiyuko had been a starving orphan in a burnt-out city at the time.

In spite of the fabrications, many of the I-novel's details reverberated with the clarion clarity of truth. Nosaka described his visit with Brautigan to Yonago, where instead of giving a lecture, Akiyuki reverted to his Claude persona and started singing. This soon became a karaoke session. Richard got into the act, belting out "Buttons and Bows" and "Rock Around the Clock."

Afterward, Brautigan, Nosaka, and a number of doctors and nurses waited for a taxi outside the hospital, on their way to a *ryoutei* (a restaurant serving traditional old-fashioned Japanese food). They were startled by the heavy sound of a falling body hitting the ground. Brautigan walked back along a path through the shrubbery and encountered the corpse of a fifty-year-old cancer patient who had committed suicide by leaping from a fourth-floor window. He returned ashen faced as white-clad hospital personnel hurried to the scene. "Dead," Brautigan said.

At the restaurant, Richard seemed in deep thought, drinking heavily. Every time the waitress poured his sake cup full, he said, "*Arigatogozaimasu*," but when one of the doctors asked his opinions on euthanasia, Brautigan made a reply that Nosaka was incapable of translating. Later, at their hotel, Akiyuki invited Richard to his room, where they continued drinking beer. Nosaka wanted to talk about death, but Brautigan, pale with fatigue, expressed no interest in the topic. "Life is life," he said. "Death, I do not understand. I saw the face of the dead for the first time." Akiyuki likely made this up, as Richard had seen his uncle Edward in his coffin. Brautigan wrote of his uncle's death several times but never mentioned a suicide in Yonago.

"I saw a lot of death," Nosaka replied in his I-novel.

Brautigan fell asleep on the sofa beside Nosaka's bed. The fictional Akiyuki stared at him, bewildered that his companion had witnessed death up close only so late in life. He had read five of Brautigan's books in translation before embarking on this trip and was surprised to find no mention of the deaths of friends or family members in them.

The next morning, the two writers parted company in Mineyama, on the platform of the bullet train exchange station connecting Tokyo and Kyoto. A discussion between them had been scheduled to take place in Osaka after Brautigan's Kyoto reading, but Nosaka called it off. He thought Brautigan behaved like a "sissy" at the Yonago hospital. In his I-novel, Nosaka described Richard reacting in a similar fashion when he witnessed another suicide after someone walked in front of his train. This was pure fiction.

Brautigan's own version of this event mentioned traveling on the Tango 8 bullet train to Kyoto for his October 31 USICA presentation at the American Center. Brautigan was working on "The Empty Nest," a short story about a Tokyo porn theater and had just written "[. . .] wants to see these girls in action acting erotic fantasies with interruption" when something dramatic occurred. One of his party, sitting at the front of the car, got to her feet and started toward him, "a look of total horror on her face." Eyes filled with tears, her cheeks flushed and red, she looked to Richard "as if she was going to throw up."

"What's wrong?" he asked. "What's going on?"

"A child was just hit by the train." As she spoke, the Tango 8 express came to a stop. Everyone in the car hurried to get a look at the accident. The child had been struck at a crossing. A crowd gathered outside, making it difficult to see because the body lay so close to the train. The child was struck only a glancing blow to the top of his head. On his way back to Tokyo later that night aboard the Hikari 6 bullet train, Brautigan learned that there had been no concussion and the kid required only several stitches.

Having fulfilled his commitment to the International Communication Agency, Richard was free to leave Japan anytime. He still had seventy-three days left on his cultural visa, taking him through the holidays into the new year. Brautigan had an hourlong book signing scheduled at a "famous" Tokyo bookstore on Sunday, November 4, and wanted additional time to write more Japanese stories. Richard penned a letter to Aki, saying he planned to extend his stay.

On her return from the East Coast, Akiko began working for $3.50 an hour at a Victoria's Secret shop. She was getting used to life without Richard, making her own way in the world again. Aki had also been hired as an interpreter and driver for a Japanese film crew sponsored by Suntory whiskey. Their schedule included travel to Chicago, Albuquerque, and Sacramento to interview the reggae star Bob Marley, scientists at the Solar Energy Lab, and the mayor of California's capital city. Akiko would be on the road between November 12 and 17. She wrote to her husband agreeing with his decision to stay on in Tokyo to complete his writing project, but the tone of her letters had grown matter-of-fact and much less affectionate.

Caught up in his work, Richard remained oblivious to Aki's feelings. The day of his return from Kyoto found him scribbling away furiously at a sidewalk café table in Tokyo. By late in the afternoon, Richard had written eight new short stories in his spiral-bound notebook. He thought this was one of the best writing days he'd ever had in his life. The stories were about piano movers, looking for fish under the surface of a pond where actors simulated sex in a porno film, an alcoholic dreaming of all the bottles he'd emptied in his lifetime, and a little French girl eating an ice cream cone. They had little to do with Japan. He might have written them anywhere.

During the coming week, Richard wrote another twelve stories, dining alone every night for nine days. Brautigan always found company over drinks at The Cradle later on, but drunken conversation with strangers in a bar wasn't quite the same. On the second Friday in November, Richard wrote "Japanese UFO," the title story for his planned book on Japanese pornographic movies. It began, "This is a fantasy, a science fiction book about Japan. It even has UFOs in it." The story is a rumination on drive-in movies. Brautigan had been thinking about them "off and on for five years." He'd also been thinking about God, perhaps "3,972,411,000 times." Richard connected his religious speculations with drive-ins. "The screen god just starts them movie-less every night." He compared drive-in theaters to the Roman Coliseum and "the great ancient structures of Mexican civilization," and concluded, "it's Friday night in Tokyo. Once it was Friday night in Montana and people went to the drive-in movie show. Then they stopped."

Thinking of his projected book-length "Japanese UFO," Brautigan wrote another tale about porno movies that night. His subject was the instrumental music played in the intermissions between films. While the Japanese men in the audience took naps, read newspapers, or ate ice cream purchased "from an old woman who walks up and down the aisle," Richard listened to the banal music. Little by little, Brautigan heard something familiar, an instrumental version of "Dust in the Wind," the top-twenty hit from the summer of 1978 that had influenced the new title for his novel about his childhood in the Pacific Northwest.

Three days later, after eating his dinner alone in a supermarket cafeteria, watching the shoppers go up and down on an escalator, Richard wrote, "I'm beginning to imagine that I will spend Thanksgiving by myself in Tokyo." He had just received enough money to stay another month. He ended a third story with, "Home is a sweet sound [. . .] Tomorrow I'll make my reservations. I want a rest waiting for me just to be on the safe side."

Brautigan finally made his plane reservations in another couple days. He also wrote the final three stories composed during his sixty-six-day stay in Japan. The last was "Woman in a Snake Skin Coat," an image he'd carried around in his head for over a month. It was late in the evening, and alcohol consumption made his writing clumsy. The story concerned his uncomfortable feelings of "nervous repulsion" while waiting for the down elevator on his floor at the Keio Plaza, standing next to a middle-aged woman in a full-length snakeskin coat. Once he finished, Richard wrote "The end," added the place and date, and scrawled beneath the story:

Happy Birthday
Merry Christmas
Fuck 'm
Fuckm

Brautigan departed Tokyo Sunday the eighteenth of November at 4:40 pm, flying eastward on Japan Airlines flight 004. Thanks to the international date line, he arrived in San Francisco at eight thirty in the morning of the same day. Richard returned to a deeply troubled marriage. Altogether, he wrote seventy-nine new stories while in Japan. Brautigan would pay a heavy emotional price for this never-published work.

Jimmy Sakata opened Cho-Cho, his Japanese restaurant in North Beach, in 1960, when he was thirty-six years old. It's impossible to say when Brautigan first started coming into the place. Sakata recalled that he'd been a customer for some time. "I never paid attention to him," he said, "I didn't know who he was." Jim first took notice of Richard "when he started to come with his Japanese wife." He remembered how they'd sit in the back "and have powwows." They still remained strangers to him. "She'd be crying or something." Tears were again on the menu when they stopped by after Brautigan's return from Tokyo.

By that time, Richard had introduced himself and Aki to Jimmy. "He said he was a writer, showed me a book." Sakata couldn't understand why they were together, "except for some sexual attraction." Jimmy didn't think Akiko could speak English very well and saw this as detrimental to a relationship. The way Sakata saw it, Aki "came over here, followed him here, came after him." He didn't know it at the time, but Akiko's tears in the back shadows of Cho-Cho that night were washing away any hope of reconciliation.

Nancy Hodge planned an elegant Thanksgiving dinner to welcome Brautigan home. The Hjortsbergs had also been invited. Gatz set off on Tuesday with his two young children, driving down from Montana, "My Sharona" blasting out of the car radio. He'd become involved in an extramarital affair over the summer. To even the score, Marian flung herself into a fling with Ken Kelley. She'd flown on ahead to San Francisco to spend time with her new lover.

Gatz arrived at the Hodges' home in Berkeley late Wednesday afternoon, bringing along a fruitcake his wife had baked as a house present. On Thanksgiving Day, Hjortsberg drove into San Francisco with the kids to pick up his wife at Kelley's place on Larkin Street. Designated the Brautigans' driver, Ken took his car over to Green Street to collect Richard and Aki. With his long legs, Brautigan occupied the entire backseat of the little automobile. Kelley was forced to make amiable chitchat with Akiko, whom he detested. "I felt insulted that she was riding even in the same car as me," Kelley recalled.

Nancy Hodge remembered Thanksgiving dinner as "one of these long, laborious meals. We ate all this wonderful stuff. Everyone seemed to be in a pretty good mood." After dessert and the last of the red wine, Richard suggested they all go into the living room and dance. It was about five in the afternoon. Nancy brought in champagne, frigid in an ice bucket, setting it on a glass table with a number of crystal flutes. The three couples danced on the rug in front of the fireplace. "Brautigan wanted everybody to be very happy that day," Nancy said.

Ken Kelley remembered things differently. "It was like the Last Supper," he said. "Richard was being rude to everybody. He was very drunk." According to Kelley, Brautigan was "pinning insults" on Hjortsberg, who "was going out of [his] way to be a gentleman, trying to presume some dignity in the situation." Perhaps his perspective as Marian's lover put things into different focus. In spite of laughter and dancing and champagne, all three couples at the party were headed for divorce.

The Brautigans were the first to split. Akiko blamed it on Richard's alcoholism. "He tried to quit," she said. "So many times. When he was sober he was so sober. He was so sincere and so sweet and tried to make up [for] the previous day. And he tried to quit so many days. And it didn't work. We loved each other [but] can't live together because of alcoholic things."

Margot Patterson Doss told a different story. She claimed that Akiko, hurt and angry over being left behind when Richard took off for Japan without her in September, jumped into an affair with Fumio Wada. Fumio's wife, Mieko, had gone on a trip to visit her sister in Germany and didn't return to San Francisco until early October. "For three weeks it was a hot little affair," Margot remembered. If her story was true, the relationship must have started not long after Brautigan departed for Tokyo.

Truth almost always gets lost in the poisonous fog of gossip. Whatever the real story, Aki and Fumio teamed up to host a "bachelor party" at Sunday noon, the last day of September, on the deck of the Wadas' Russian Hill house. They served pot stickers. The guest list included curious neighbor Margot, along with Tony Dingman, Shig Murao, and others. "When Richard came back she told him about [the affair]," Patterson Doss claimed, "and that's why they got divorced."

For whatever reason, shortly after the Hodges' Thanksgiving dinner, Richard and Akiko decided to separate. One weekend afternoon, they took Ianthe to the neutral setting of Enrico's to break the bad news. "She was kind of crying," Aki recalled. Ianthe couldn't understand why people who loved each other would want to do such a thing.

All at once, Ron Kovic rolled up to their table in his wheelchair. Ron never mentioned it, but Akiko thought he must already have heard rumors of their impending breakup. Kovic carried a knapsack with him. He asked Brautigan to close his eyes and slid a blue telephone out onto the tabletop. Ron took it with him so he could plug in anyplace his travels landed him.

Kovic asked Richard to guess what it was. Brautigan touched the phone and said something Aki thought "very beautiful," his words lost in the emotional moment. "Obviously, Ron tried to make him laugh," she said, wishing she could have been just such a friend. "Because he knew he's down and he's sad."

Akiko moved out of the Green Street apartment the first week of December, relocating to Los Angeles. Brautigan drank his troubles away at Enrico's. "There was a lot of bitterness," Ward Dunham recalled. "He would sit at the bar every night and was not happy about how it was going." One day, Aki sent word that she wanted to come over to the apartment "and take a bunch of stuff out that she wanted." Richard had no desire to stay home and see her but wanted someone there to keep an eye on things. Brautigan asked Dunham to help, and he got his wife, Marian, to go over to Green Street while Richard sat at the bar in Enrico's. "God, he was in the blues," Ward said.

Brautigan busied himself with work. He read many of his recent Japanese notebook stories aloud to his secretary, Glenise Sibbern, who took them down in shorthand, typing fair copies later. A good deal of time was spent on the phone with Helen Brann. As soon as Richard arrived back from Tokyo, his agent sent him the Targ Edition galleys for *The Tokyo–Montana Express* by express mail. Brautigan went right to work, correcting them by hand. He express-mailed them back to Brann's office, and she sent them by messenger over to Targ on the last day of November, six days after the author received them in San Francisco. When his wife walked out, Richard received more bad news. Helen Brann phoned the same day to say that Targ, in a last-dash effort to get the book out in time for the Christmas market, planned to publish it without his corrections, inserting an errata slip instead.

Brautigan, a stickler for typographical accuracy, was very upset. Brann reminded William Targ of their May 23 agreement granting Richard "final approval." The published text must agree "in every aspect with the text as supplied by the Author." Targ was not happy. Neither was his printer, Leonard Seastone, of Tideline Press, who phoned Brautigan, pleading with him to change his mind about the inclusion of an errata slip as "a personal favor." Furious, Richard phoned Helen, complaining about these backdoor tactics.

Brann and Targ hashed out their differences on the phone. The publisher agreed to postpone the book and insert all Brautigan's corrections. He had no other choice. This upset William Targ so much he wrote a peevish note to Helen Brann, claiming the "errors" Brautigan discovered were "of the most trivial sort." He griped about having to buy more paper, reset pages, disrupt the binder's schedule, and postpone publication until spring. "A modest errata slip would have prevented a delay."

Soon it was Christmas. Richard wandered alone through the huge apartment, so empty now since Aki left, taking most of their possessions along with her. There was no tree or any holiday decorations. The place felt abandoned. All along, Akiko kept calling him, "wanting more and more stuff." She refused to talk about anything else, except one time when she phoned and wished Brautigan a merry Christmas.

When Ianthe came over on Christmas Eve, after her father gave her a gift check and burned the family photos in the fireplace, he started talking about his past, something he'd never done before. Brautigan told his daughter the story of throwing a rock through the Eugene police station window and being committed to the state mental hospital. He talked about electroshock treatments and seeing his mother for the last time shortly after his release. In retrospect, Ianthe came to believe her father contemplated suicide even then. Years later, she wrote that she thought he "wanted to make sure that I knew everything there was to know about his past before he died. He didn't want me to find out from a newspaper or magazine."

When something troubled his mind, it was Brautigan's habit to spend a lot of time on the phone late at night, calling friends for advice. Hearing the despair in Richard's voice, Jack Thibeau, always a dependable nocturnal consultant, offered to come up from Los Angeles and spend the weekend with his old pal. Seymour Lawrence got to Frisco before Jack arrived, hosting a gala event in the Pavilion Room of the Fairmont Hotel on Nob Hill. Between 6:00 and 8:00 pm on Friday, December 28, Sam sponsored an invitation-only champagne reception to honor Tillie Olsen and Richard Brautigan, two of the San Francisco authors he published under his own imprint at Delacorte Press.

Tillie Olsen was forty-nine years old before her first book, *Tell Me a Riddle*, a quartet of short stories, came out in 1961. It was an immediate success. The title story in the collection won the O. Henry Prize for best American short story. A high school dropout, Olsen had been a labor organizer and a member of the Communist Party in the 1930s. Sam Lawrence had published both *Yonnondio: From the Thirties* (1974) and *Silences* (1978) at Delacorte. This independent, crusading woman was the same age as Brautigan's mother.

Jack Thibeau traveled up from L.A. the next day. He enjoyed getting together with Richard as something unusual often occurred. On a recent trip, sitting at a sidewalk table at Enrico's with Brautigan, Thibeau was amused when Richard bought a couple roses from Millie, an old woman who sold flowers on the Beach. "She was sort of a dwarf," Jack recalled. "On the scene every night at every bar. Come in and have a couple drinks and sell flowers. Everybody knew her." After buying the roses, Brautigan "disappeared down the street," returning with an envelope and some stationery.

Richard wrote a quick note and put it in the envelope with the flowers. Out on the sidewalk, he flagged down a passing taxi. "I'll give you $5 to drive over this envelope and then pull back over it," Brautigan told the confused cabbie. "The cab driver couldn't believe it," Jack observed. He drove back and forth over the envelope, pressing the roses flat. Richard paid him five bucks and the bewildered driver took off in search of other customers. Satisfied with the results, Richard Brautigan wrote Takako Shiina's name and address on the front and mailed the tread-mark-decorated package off to Tokyo.

This time around, Thibeau met Brautigan at the Hyatt Regency Hotel, which opened six years earlier in the Embarcadero Center across from the Ferry Building. The luxury hotel had featured prominently in several Hollywood films, notably *The Towering Inferno*, *High Anxiety*, and *Time After Time*. Richard and Jack went immediately into the bar. The first thing Richard asked was, "Do you have any money?"

"Yeah," Jack replied. "I have a couple hundred bucks."

"Well, give it to me," Brautigan demanded. "I'll give you a check."

Thibeau handed over all his cash. He wasn't worried as he had several credit cards, financial instruments utterly unknown to Brautigan. Jack didn't ask Richard the reason for his request because he knew "it was part of a ritual." The Hyatt was the site of the ninety-fourth annual Modern Language Association Convention. Ten thousand college teachers came to town to present papers and attend seminars on language and literature. Richard Brautigan had been invited to appear on a panel chaired by Dennis Lynch, a graduate student at Northern Illinois University. The subject was "Zen and Contemporary American Poetry." Lynch called it "a focal point of the convention."

The other panelists were poets Robert Bly, Gary Snyder, and Philip Whalen, along with translator Lucien Stryk. Whalen and Snyder had both known Brautigan for more than twenty years. Each man talked about how Japanese culture influenced his work and then read poems illustrating that effect. Richard mentioned his forthcoming book of short stories, *The Tokyo–Montana Express* as well as "Japanese UFO," a novel in progress. Governor Jerry Brown and his girlfriend, singer Linda Ronstadt, sat among a crowded audience that numbered almost one thousand.

After the panel discussion, Brautigan picked up another audience member, an attractive young assistant professor from the State University of New York Binghamton. She was working on a book about Sylvia Plath. Intent upon seduction, Brautigan didn't mention he detested Plath because she stuck her head in the oven and killed herself while her little kids were in the house. Afterward, the prof went out to dinner with Richard and Jack and they all headed back to Brautigan's place on Green Street for a nightcap. The comely academic ended up spending the night with Richard in his grand master bedroom.

The next morning, Thibeau was up early making coffee in the kitchen when the young lit professor wandered in, looking somewhat disheveled. "I'm so embarrassed," she said.

"Why?" Jack asked.

"I mean, I just met this man, and I come home and spend the night with him. It's embarrassing."

"You've got it all wrong," Thibeau told her. "That's not the way things work in your academic world, but this is show business."

"Oh, really?" The professor smiled. "Am I in show business?"

"Yes. It's all all right."

"Oh, that's wonderful," she said.

Later, when Thibeau told Brautigan the show biz story, he cracked up. "Richard always was in show business," Jack reminisced. "Richard was like a rock star."

Before Thibeau left for Los Angeles, Brautigan gave him a check for $200. It was the last time Jack ever hung out with Richard.

THE OLD SALOON in Emigrant, Montana, hadn't changed much since it opened in 1902. A narrow single-story brick shoe box of a building, it stood close by the railroad depot on the Park Branch of the Northern Pacific back when a train ran down from Livingston to the north entrance of Yellowstone Park at Gardiner. The depot was long gone, and so were the tracks, torn up when the line was abandoned in 1972. After Prohibition, the Old Saloon survived for a time as a soda parlor. The management finally threw in the towel and locked the doors in the early 1920s. Forty years later, in 1962, when the new Highway 89 opened to traffic, the owners swept the board floors clean and started pouring whiskey once again.

Aside from replacing the carbide lights with electricity and the ice chests with refrigeration, there were few concessions to modern times. Gold pans from the miners in Emigrant Gulch still hung on the walls. A big cast-iron wood stove offered heat, with indoor sport provided by a pool table in the rear. An ancient, goose-necked electric cigar lighter adorned one end of the bar next to the old Superior Quality cigar cutter. The brass cash register dated to 1904. A color television set hanging above the entrance to the tiny grill kitchen provided an anachronistic connection to the present.

The poet and songwriter Greg Keeler remembered an afternoon in the early eighties, when he, Marian Hjortsberg, and Richard Brautigan paid a visit to the Old Saloon after attending a barbecue party at the Paradise Valley home of former Montana governor Tom Judge. Richard's sour mood on this occasion stemmed from his dislike of "yuppies," many of whom had been in attendance at the governor's place. As Greg recalled in his exquisite memoir, *Waltzing with the Captain: Remembering Richard Brautigan,*

> *The three of us went in, and there was one of the wealthiest, most egotistical people we had seen at the party. He sat at our table, pretty obviously flaunting his acquaintance with Richard. Several cosmic cowboys were at the bar behind us when Richard decided to change the tone of things, took out his Buck pocket knife, opened it, and started stabbing away at our table. He then dropped the knife in Mr. Upwardly Mobile's whisky. The whole bar took a deep breath, and I wished I was back in Richard's kitchen eating beany weenies. But Marian saved the day. She daintily plucked the knife from the whisky glass, licked the blade, folded it up and put the knife down. The general breath was exhaled, unheard applause went around the bar, and things calmed down.*

ON ANOTHER AFTERNOON not long afterward, Brautigan came into the Old Saloon with Marian and Becky Fonda. They were all three sheets to the wind and navigated erratically to a small table in the rear. Lynne Huffman, an aspiring writer whose career as a railroad brakeman had been cut short after being dragged sixty yards by a slow-moving train, sat at the bar with a couple cowboy pals. They sipped drinks while watching a noisy football game on the TV. Richard scowled with displeasure. Marian did nothing to stop Brautigan this time when he got up and approached the bar, disgusted with the raucous boob tube. "Would you mind turning it down?" Richard mumbled. "We'd like to play the jukebox." It was difficult understanding him, and Lynne Huffman had to translate for the cowboys.

All eyes remained fixed on the screen. A wind-weathered wrangler said, "We're watching the game." Richard returned to his table. Several moments later, he was back. This time, he proposed to buy everyone a round if they would lower the volume. Again, nobody bothered to turn his way. "We've already got drinks," another cowpoke observed laconically.

Richard slumped away without a word. Loud cheering continued with every televised play. Dropping quarters in the jukebox would have been a waste of money. Brautigan's agitation grew. He walked up to the bar once again. Always penny-wise and pound-foolish, he said, "I'll pay you $100 if you'll just turn it down a bit."

The cowboys swiveled on their bar stools, regarding Brautigan through narrowed eyelids. He towered storklike above them with his drooping General Custer mustache, long blond hair straggling out from under an absurd Elmer Fudd cap topped by a little woolen fluff-ball. "We're not interested in your damn money." The monotone reply sounded final. Richard nodded, getting the message at last, rejoining Marian and Becky at their table.

"Who is that guy?" one of the cowpokes asked Lynne Huffman. Lynne explained that he was Richard Brautigan, a writer and a poet who lived nearby.

"Well," the ranch hand drawled, his words coming smooth and easy as a knife blade drawn across an oiled whetstone, "you better tell your friend not to come back to the bar or he'll be Richard 'Rest-In-Peace' Brautigan."

fifty-three: midnight express

A S THE FIRST year of a new decade began, Richard Brautigan sat alone, brooding in his cavernous empty apartment. His mind was troubled by the supposed betrayals of his wife, a woman he referred to hereafter as "that cunt" in conversations with friends, love and hate always the unpredictable heads and tails in the coin toss of love. Richard often fell asleep on the couch at night while watching TV. Early one morning about three, he awoke to the flickering of an old black-and-white Western, just in time to hear Gabby Hayes yell, "Why she's got Californy fever!" Brautigan picked up the phone and called Greg Keeler in Montana to tell him about the singular moment. "To Richard," Keeler wrote later, "this seemed like the ultimate existential commentary on what had happened with Aki."

Not wanting to give Akiko any advantage, Richard hired an attorney. Sandra G. Musser was a partner in the San Francisco firm Musser & Schuler. She had represented Curt Gentry in his divorce. Brautigan signed a petition for the dissolution of marriage on January 9, 1980. In it, a man known to worry over every comma in a contract requested that all his copyrights, various real estate holdings, contracts, and royalties, as well as "a portion of the household furniture and furnishings," be confirmed as his separate property. Musser submitted the document to the California Superior Court in the San Francisco City Hall the next day.

Work provided Brautigan a distraction from emotional pain. He plunged straight into completing a longer version of *The Tokyo–Montana Express*. He had started back on the project in December. Sometime during the interval, Richard recalled, "a friend suggested that the narrative voice behind the stories was perhaps more interesting than the stories themselves." Thinking about this advice and wanting to create something that "was not simply a book of random stories," Brautigan decided to incorporate previously published material into his new book.

Richard was also influenced by his longstanding admiration for William Faulkner, who considered *Go Down, Moses* to be a novel and was shocked when Random House first released it in 1942 as *Go Down, Moses and Other Stories*. When the book was reissued in 1949, Faulkner insisted his original title, *Go Down, Moses*, be restored. He wrote to his editor, Saxe Commins, "*Moses* is indeed a novel," chiding that only a publisher would ever see it otherwise. Brautigan had read and enjoyed Joseph Blotner's 1974 two-volume biography of Faulkner.

Richard added his preface to the limited 1968 edition Joseph Francl book to the mix, along with "The Menu" and "Homage to Rudi Gernreich," as well as "An Eye for Good Produce," "The Last of My Armstrong Creek Mosquito Bites," and the story about discarded Christmas trees he did in 1964 with Erik Weber. Stories published in *Outside*, *TriQuarterly*, the *CoEvolution Quarterly*, *Evergreen*, *California Living*, and other publications were also included.

By adding copyrighted work from an earlier period to his book of short stories, Brautigan thought he "converted it into a novel." Not everyone agreed with his assessment.

Robert Briggs told him flat out not to call the book a novel.

"What do you mean?" Richard replied.

"Just what the fuck I said," Briggs shot back. "Call it a book by Richard Brautigan."

More practical reasons demanded Brautigan designate his new book a novel. Twenty of the stories were in the forthcoming Targ edition bearing the same title. In a prefatory paragraph written for William Targ, Richard referred to the slim volume as "this small collection of short stories." He was married to Akiko at the time and worried about the possible division of community property. Brautigan wanted to put as much distance as he could between the limited Targ printing and the big book he hoped to sell to Seymour Lawrence.

Richard assembled all the various "stations" on *The Tokyo–Montana Express* toward the end of January and shipped the whole package off to his agent in New York. She sent it to Dell as part of a previous option agreement. Helen Brann made an immediate deal with Sam Lawrence, confirming their verbal agreement on a $35,000 advance, payable on signing. The other terms remained identical to the *Dreaming of Babylon* contract, including a first refusal option on Brautigan's next book.

Near the end of January, Sandra Musser received a letter from Verna A. Adams of the San Francisco law firm Savitt & Adams. She had been retained by Akiko to represent her in the divorce proceedings. Adams requested Brautigan's financial records and other documents pertaining to his writing career. On the twenty-eighth, Akiko signed a partial financial declaration asking for spousal support to enable her to maintain her accustomed lifestyle. "My husband and I enjoyed a luxurious standard of living prior to our separation," Aki stated. She alleged that Brautigan's income was "substantial," asking that he "be restrained from molesting or disturbing the respondent" and "from selling any property except in the normal course of business."

Earlier in January, Richard got together again with his old friend Marcia Clay. They decided to cohost a huge party as a diversion from his marital troubles. "We hatched it up together," she recalled. The apartment was empty, most of the furniture gone. It seemed the perfect opportunity for one last big blowout. They scheduled the event for January 31, the day after Brautigan's forty-fifth birthday, to celebrate the start of a new decade. "We'll have ten years of your paintings," Richard said, "and I'll do a poetry reading from the past ten years of my writing."

Marcia designed a small printed invitation card, "most elegant," with a "really gorgeous" photograph of her at seventeen on the cover. It read: "One evening of ten years 'Art by Marcia Clay' at the home of Richard Brautigan who will read (don't worry, briefly) six or seven poems of his last ten years." Clay used her parents' connections and contacted Pat Steger at the *Chronicle*, informing her of the planned party. Steger made mention of the coming affair in her social column. "Richard was like a kid when he saw that," Marcia remembered.

Clay chose sixty of her paintings for exhibition, hammering nails into the bare walls of Brautigan's apartment to hang them. On the day before the party, Richard received a surprise birthday present. A telegram arrived at 2110 Green Street from Seymour Lawrence. "The Tokyo–Montana Express is a wonderful experience," Sam wired. "I am filled with admiration for this wise and wonderful book. I had the same sense of discovery and astonishment as with Trout Fishing."

At seven in the evening of the thirty-first, hordes of invited guests and assorted gate-crashers began arriving at Brautigan's second-floor flat. By the time the party reached its peak, three hundred people packed into the place. Among the milling throng, one man caught Marcia Clay's eye. Born in China to Russian parents and raised in Japan, Alexander Besher wrote a weekly business column for the *Chronicle*. His friends all called him "Sasha." Before the party was over, Marcia started calling him Sasha, too. They soon began spending a lot of time together. By the end of the year, they were married.

Nothing was said at the time, but the big decade-launching party marked the end of Marcia and Richard's friendship. When Clay removed her paintings from Brautigan's apartment, she left nail damage behind in the walls. "The landlords got pissed about all the holes," she recalled, "and they made him pay for them." It cost Brautigan about $400 to patch up the damage. He never mentioned this to Marcia, bottling up his resentment. The schism widened once he met Clay's new husband. "This man I'm not interested in," he told Marcia. For his part, Sasha "couldn't stand Richard," she said. "He called Richard a wimp. He called him a fink." Clay had become a wife. Brautigan was never much interested in other people's wives.

Sometime in February, fed up with his marital woes and clomping about in his lonely, empty apartment, Brautigan flew to Vancouver in British Columbia. Not much is known about this trip. Richard went to the anthropology museum at the University of British Columbia to look at Pacific Northwest totem poles. He also took in some Chinese movies at a theater in Chinatown. It was a time of solitude, a familiar condition for Richard.

Back in Frisco, alone and depressed, Richard phoned his former lover, Siew-Hwa Beh, who was living in Berkeley. He told her he'd broken up with Akiko because she'd been unfaithful. "Aki slept with someone," Brautigan said in despair. "I couldn't believe that this friend slept with my wife." Richard never mentioned any name, saying only, "This friend is a close friend. I didn't know I would be so betrayed by a friend." Siew-Hwa knew in her heart how much this hurt him, "because he was too fragile." Beh had always been monogamous in her relationships and understood how much an outside affair would hurt Brautigan. "Once you are with Richard, you are with Richard," she observed.

Beh headed straight to Green Street and consoled Brautigan. He said he wanted them to get back together again. "Why did you marry her?" she asked.

"I never wanted to marry her," Richard replied. "I never wanted to marry her! You left me, so I wrote to her and she wanted to come and see me. When she got here, she said she couldn't stay unless I married her to get her a green card. I never wanted to marry her! I never wanted to marry her!"

Brautigan's desperate insistence unnerved Beh. She started to cry. "Crying and crying and crying," she recalled. The winter afternoon darkened into night. They had no dinner. Richard's blood sugar plummeted. "Richard had a sugar thing," Beh recalled.

"I've got to get out of here," Brautigan shouted. "I can't deal with this. I'm hungry. I've got to get out of here!" Richard stormed out, leaving Siew-Hwa alone, crying in the empty apartment. This was the last time she ever saw him.

A little later, Siew-Hwa ran into Kitty Loewinsohn in Berkeley. They started discussing the Brautigans' split. Kitty told her "about how much she and Ron helped Aki about this and that." Siew-Hwa thought Kitty forced herself "to be naive and blind." Something her friend said struck a chord. At that moment, she "knew it was Ron Loewinsohn who slept with Aki."

Beh called Brautigan soon after this conversation. "Richard, is it Ron?" she asked. Brautigan made no reply. "He kept quiet," Siew-Hwa said. "He didn't say a word. He would not say a word. That was the way Richard [was] faithful to people."

Brautigan's long-standing habit of pestering his friends late at night for advice on everything from punctuation to contractual nuance went into overdrive in March. Keith Abbott found these drunken monologues "unbearable." Richard recounted the tiniest legal detail of his impending divorce "over and over, as if his memory were gone." At one point, he told Keith, "I guess the only thing I can do is write. If that's so, then that's all I'll do."

Brautigan phoned Sandra Musser often. Richard said Akiko was "trying to destroy me." He described his wife as "a pathological and very clever liar," claiming to have heard she'd told someone she only married him to get a green card. Brautigan's fury boiled over. He accused Aki of having had another lover, far back when "she was cheating on her husband with me." He raged about overheard gossip. "She fucked an American pop star trying to get to the United States."

After repeated phone calls from Akiko, Richard hung up and called Sandra Musser. He wanted his attorney to inform Verna Adams that they "would take serious action if Aki ever tried to get in touch with me again."

While protecting his privacy, Brautigan took steps to pry into his wife's personal affairs. Richard asked a friend, a "very perceptive person" who didn't want his identity revealed, to investigate Akiko's feelings. Under the guise of lending a sympathetic ear, the friend encouraged Aki to divulge a number of confidences. He reported everything back to Brautigan. Akiko said she still loved Richard and felt "very bitter" about the failure of their marriage. She didn't want to go to court, proclaiming her fondness for Ianthe. The undercover friend thought they "could definitely get together and work things out."

Helen Brann and Seymour Lawrence "consummated" their deal for Richard Brautigan's new "novel" early in February. The advance remained unaltered, and another $25,000 was added if either Dell or Laurel published a paperback edition. The author was also to receive a straight 15 percent royalty on all hardback sales and retain 100 percent of the subsidiary rights (British, translations, serial, dramatic, radio, film, and TV). Sam planned to publish in October. Helen got her dates confused and assumed the book was coming out in September.

Helen called Richard with the good news. Having final design approval, Brautigan wanted to avoid the production problems he'd encountered on *June 30th, June 30th*. Kathy Simmons would now oversee all the details involved in coordinating catalog copy, advertising, flap copy, and jacket design. Brann put Brautigan in direct touch with Simmons. The Delacorte contract was finalized on February 12.

A finished copy of Targ's edition of *The Tokyo–Montana Express* arrived at Helen Brann's office a week later. It was a beautiful book hand-set in Garamond on laid Guttenberg paper, with a title page printed in three colors. Limited to 350 copies, the slim hardbound volume was priced at $50. Helen instructed William Targ to ship the author's copies to Brautigan's address in San Francisco.

At the end of February, a check for $1,000 went out to Akiko from Sandra Musser's office for "spousal support," in accordance with an agreement with Verna Adams. Richard signed his Delacorte contracts a week later. Richard's ten complimentary author's copies of the Targ edition never arrived. He called Helen Brann and complained, leaving the matter in her hands. With

Brautigan's court date two days off, he told Sandra Musser he "thought they were running pretty close." Richard heard Aki wanted $1,600 a month in support. He thought this was "ridiculous." With time running so short, he asked his attorney to get a postponement. Sandra told him she was ready to go to court the next day.

On March 11, Sandra Musser filed an Income and Expense Declaration signed by Richard Brautigan. It spoke volumes about the author's declining popularity. In 1977, Brautigan's net income was $94,799 ($77,813 was a release of royalties earned between 1966 and 1977 but held back by Dell Publishing). His 1978 net income fell to $16,464. By 1979, it was only $15,620. In addition, the declaration stated "that because *Dreaming of Babylon* failed to realize the projected sales, Dell Publishing has reduced Petitioner's advance against book publications from $125,000 per book to $35,000 per book." As a result, Richard anticipated his net income for 1980 to be between $15,000 and $16,000.

Musser and Brautigan walked into the courtroom on Thursday, March 13. Sandra instructed him not to wear a denim jacket and jeans. "Richard couldn't understand why not," she reflected years later. They had not been told Beverly Savitt, Verna Adams's partner, would be waiting for them. Savitt went on the attack. Their entire strategy up to this point had been based on mutual cooperation. Brautigan expected to make an offer between $750 and $1,000, based on his net income. The court awarded Akiko $1,900 a month in support, a judgment using gross income as its basis. "Bam!" Richard wrote, describing the episode a couple months later.

Most evenings, Brautigan went looking for action at Enrico's. Failing to find old friends or attractive women, he'd sit at the bar and tell his troubles to Ward Dunham over several snifters of Calvados. "After Aki left," Dunham said, "he was never happy after that." One evening, Richard mentioned to Ward that he felt haunted. "You deserve to be haunted," Dunham replied.

Other nights, Brautigan would amble down to Cho-Cho on Kearny Street and spin a tale of woe for Jimmy Sakata. "Fuck it!" Jim told Richard. "You worry too much. Just say fuck it. Nobody can take everything from you. You have your life, your freedom."

Brautigan brooded over the March 13 court order. He felt he had "received short shrift in the hearing," and instructed his attorney to request a transcript. Richard was upset that he had not been allowed to provide oral testimony to rebut what he felt were the "exaggerated claims" of Akiko's counsel regarding his income and standard of living. At his urging, Sandra Musser filed a petition for a modification of the court order. Musser concluded the petition stating Brautigan's testimony "may not change the court's ruling but it will result in petitioner feeling as though he had his day in court and the matter will be equitably resolved."

On April Fools' Day, having decided to give up the expensive Green Street apartment, Richard rented a narrow studio upstairs above the entrance to Vesuvio Café (255 Columbus), across the alley from City Lights. Known as the Cavelli Building since a bookstore by that name opened there in 1913, it sported an Italian Renaissance Revival second story added five years later. The move represented a return to Brautigan's earliest days on the Beach. Beret-wearing Henri Lenoir, proprietor of Vesuvio and a fixture on the bohemian side of Frisco since the early 1930s, had known Brautigan for twenty-five years. Richard was exactly the sort of tenant Lenoir enjoyed having. The rent was $125 a month.

Richard placed his desk (a hollow-core door resting across twin filing cabinets) directly in front of the lone window looking toward City Lights and installed shelves along the side walls.

Brautigan's big office electric typewriter sat dead center. Most of his papers remained stored in stacked cardboard boxes. Instead of thumbtacking artwork to the walls, he had everything properly framed. A large poster advertising *Rommel Drives on Deep into Egypt* dominated one side of the office. Brautigan also displayed original Bruce Conner art, a drawing and a collage, from the early sixties. It was a much more upscale office than his previous workplaces.

A week later, Sandra Musser filed a Request for Admission of Facts and Genuineness of Documents with the court. Outraged by his wife's claims on his literary and real properties, Brautigan prepared the list of eighty-four numbered items requesting "separate and truthful responses" from Akiko. Brautigan endeavored to establish a "sole claim" to the Bolinas property and all his books written and copyrighted before the 1977 marriage. He specified that he did not "edit, amend or update" any of these works between December 1, 1977, and December 31, 1979, and that the $20,000 received in 1978 came from Hal Ashby productions for the film rights to *The Hawkline Monster*.

Two telling domestic details enlivened this legalistic compendium of bank accounts, bookkeeping, and book titles. Number 6 stated: "That Mrs. Brautigan spent only two days at the Bolinas property, including one overnight, while married to Mr. Brautigan." Item 7 provided fine-tuning: "That Mrs. Brautigan's sole contribution to the Bolinas property was to assist in cleaning the premises to ready it for rental." To obtain precise information regarding Richard's various bank accounts and tax returns for the Request for Facts, Akiko met once with Esmond Coleman, Brautigan's accountant.

Around this time, producer Francis Ford Coppola pulled the plug on his production of *Hammett* in Los Angeles. The director, Wim Wenders, stopped filming. With his film job on hiatus, Tony Dingman came up to San Francisco and moved in with Richard on Green Street. Dingman was always good company for Brautigan, knowing how to make him laugh. Tony also provided a willing butt for Richard's teasing and practical jokes, accompanying him on his daily rounds to Cho-Cho and Enrico's.

Brautigan, Dingman, Ward Dunham, and Curt Gentry developed a shorthand alphabetic code to describe the slutty aspects they most admired in the passing parade of women. "VPL" stood for "visible panty line," a fashion statement they believed indicated easy virtue. "VPL at two o'clock," someone would call. All heads at the bar pivoted to watch the designated ass bobble past. "WS, WS," meant "will suck, won't swallow" and was used to share secret information about those who'd gone out with one of the group. "The great thing about it," Gentry recalled, "you could do it in front of people and they didn't know what you were talking about."

From time to time, Tony Dingman arranged impromptu gatherings at Brautigan's apartment, seeking diversions to take his friend's mind off his troubles. Far across town, Bruce Conner had the same idea. He invited Richard over to dinner in spite of his wife's objections. Jean Conner had been offended by Brautigan's habit of accepting an invitation and then canceling at the last minute if something better, often a date with a young woman, came along. Jean relented, and Bruce tendered an invitation to Richard.

Even as dinner simmered on the stove, Brautigan phoned the Conners to say he couldn't make it. Bruce heard the sound of loud voices in the background. A party was under way at Richard's place. Absolutely furious, Conner jumped into his car and drove all the way from Glen Park over to Pacific Heights. He stormed up the stairs and pounded on Brautigan's apartment door.

"Where's your address book?" Bruce demanded when Richard opened up. "Where's your address book?"

Confused, Brautigan said it was on his desk, back in the office. Conner pushed past him. As soon as he found the address book, Bruce turned to the "C" section and erased his name, address, and phone number from the page. Conner left without saying another word.

Richard kept busy all through April, working on the dust jacket and ad copy for *The Tokyo–Montana Express*. The minimal inside front flap material would be the final sentence from Brautigan's introduction to *The Overland Journey of Joseph Francl*, followed by "one stop on the route of the Tokyo–Montana Express." Richard concocted a brief statement of self-praise, referring to his "daring imagination, humor and haunting compassion." The inside back flap copy consisted of "Umbrellas," one of the shortest stories in Brautigan's collection: "Another stop on the Tokyo–Montana Express." Richard instructed his publisher not to use the words "a novel" to describe his forthcoming book in any of the ads.

A court order filed on April 18 directed Richard Brautigan to pay for his wife's attorney's fees and costs. By the twenty-seventh, these totaled $2,700. Discouraged by what he perceived as the failures of his legal counsel, Richard fired Sandra Musser, replacing her with Joel A. Shawn, a lawyer in the San Francisco firm Friedman, Shawn, Kipperman & Sloan. This led to additional expense. Brautigan had to pay a $3,000 retainer and sign a three-page agreement promising to keep the trust replenished to the tune of $2,500. Sandra Musser believed all of Richard's problems were caused by ego.

Sam Lawrence came out to San Francisco toward the end of the month. Brautigan always had fun with his publisher. Lawrence brought good news. Richard had been invited to read at the Poetry Center at the Ninety-third Street YM-YWHA in New York on November 24, during a three-month reading and book-signing tour for *The Tokyo–Montana Express* Delacorte had in the works. There were plans for paid college lectures to coincide with Richard's promotional appearances. The Boston booking agency Lordly & Dame, Inc., had been contracted to make the arrangements.

Sam met Enrico Banducci for the first time over the course of several jet-fueled conversations. The restaurateur offered to host an autographing party for Richard's new book at Enrico's. They agreed the launch party would take place on the publication date, Wednesday, October 26, between 2:30 and 6:00 pm.

The *Chronicle*'s Sunday magazine, *California Living*, informed Sam they would feature an interview with Brautigan, together with a selection from *The Tokyo–Montana Express*, in their October 26 edition. More good news arrived. Richard's friend, poet Ed Dorn, currently teaching at the University of Colorado, had arranged for Brautigan to be writer-in-residence in Boulder from mid-July to the first of August. A speaking engagement at the Chautauqua Auditorium in Chautauqua Park had been scheduled for July 19. Lawrence anticipated the audience to number around two thousand.

Tony Dingman's company didn't dispel Brautigan's gloom. Aki's ghost still haunted the spacious Pacific Heights apartment. The place had been her choice. Faced with Akiko's financial demands, Brautigan was eager to escape the burden of the high Green Street rent. Tony helped Richard haul his typewriter and filing cabinets, boxes of papers, books, and the various drafts of current literary projects over to his new office above Vesuvio. The black Naugahyde sofa went out to the Bolinas house. So much miscellaneous junk remained, Brautigan rented space number A-32 ($90 a month) at the Army Street Mini-Storage under the Southern Embarcadero Freeway. Richard trucked numbers of carton boxes over there before departing Green Street forever.

After leaving palatial Pacific Heights, Brautigan checked in to a cheap SRO residential hotel in North Beach. The tiny room brought back painful memories of Richard's penniless days in the fall of 1963 when he couldn't afford the rent on a similar shabby crib and the landlord had locked him out, holding his manuscripts for ransom until he paid up. This time, Brautigan felt his wife had hijacked his life.

Akiko called Don Carpenter often, "to try to get me to take her side in this fucking thing." Don said Richard's notion of loyalty was that he shouldn't even talk to her. Carpenter thought the Brautigans' breakup was "the most horrifying divorce I've ever heard of in my life." Richard "was really savaged by it. He was unable to deal with the concept of the way women and lawyers come after you in a divorce situation." To illustrate his point, Carpenter recounted an episode when "the lawyer reopened the divorce case over a pair of Czechoslovakian duck decoys that someone had given Richard. He's sitting in a restaurant waiting to meet the lawyer to sign the papers. The lawyer doesn't show up. Hours go by." When Brautigan asked his attorney what went wrong, he was told Aki wanted the decoys. "The whole fucking thing collapses over two duck decoys!"

Petty legal infighting took its toll on Brautigan. Tony Dingman understood Richard's deep depression. Alone in his cheap hotel room, working his way through a bottle of Jack Daniel's, Brautigan swilled down a handful of pills and lay back on his narrow bed for the final glide into eternity. In the morning, he woke up as usual, an all-too-familiar hangover made even more bitter by failure. "He knew that he could not dose himself with pills," Dingman said. "He was just that strong, a horse, a bear, and he knew he was just going to have to blast himself. It was inevitable."

Richard always told Tony, "We never get out alive." In retrospect, Dingman felt Japanese culture and poetry, which elevated suicide to a status at once honorable and romantic, had an undeniable appeal for Brautigan. "He was pulled to it," Tony observed. "It was irresistible."

Richard started walking to Enrico's early, right after it opened, now that he lived in the neighborhood. He made a new friend, Richard Breen, a decade younger, often the only other person at the bar in the mornings. They found themselves eyeing each other from opposite ends. "A conversation was pretty inevitable," Breen observed.

Richard Breen was the son and namesake of an Academy Award–nominated Hollywood screenwriter. Raised in the San Fernando Valley, he became fond of Frisco during his college years at the Jesuit-run University of San Francisco. Breen never graduated but acquired a taste for scotch, "pretty much my college experience." For most of the seventies, he worked in L.A., writing scripts for television private eye series: *Mannix*, *Shaft*, *Ironside*, and *Columbo*, "dozens of different shows."

Breen used his residual checks to buy drugs and "had a hell of a time." He was young "and got bored real quickly," so he gave up Tinseltown for Fog City and took a job parking cars at the Flying Dutchman lot next door to Enrico's. He called it "the most significant car lot in the Western hemisphere." It was a good job for a writer. "It made for great copy," Breen said, "because all the weirdos were coming to me instead of me going to the weirdos." Breen's tales of "catering to the insane" attracted Brautigan. Richard soon found his way to the valet shack, clutching a bottle, to observe the weirdness first hand.

They made a strange pair: Breen in his long white valet's coat, Brautigan wearing a denim jacket and a cowboy hat. "I'd have my bottle of Beefeaters," Breen recalled, "and he had his bottle of Calvados." Sometimes, Brautigan stayed there all by himself. "Richard used to hang out in a shack on the parking lot whether I was there or not," Breen said. "Just sit there and watch the movie go by."

A parking lot at night can be a dangerous place. Breen remembered customers pulling knives on him and having to talk his way out of bad situations. "Richard would never do anything to help out. He'd just take two drinks instead of one from his bottle, figuring if things were getting hairy it's your fault for putting on a white coat." Street people and petty criminals gravitated toward a parking lot, according to Richard Breen. "They don't have a car, but they come up and ask for directions and ask for money, offer to sell drugs."

The passing riffraff also sold stolen merchandise, stuff fallen off a truck. Breen claimed Brautigan bought "three hot television sets that I know of. It was irresistible to Richard. He had to buy something hot. Thought he was getting a deal." There was no electrical outlet in the valet shack, no place to plug in appliances. It was never certain if the hot TVs even worked. Brautigan just left them there and forgot about it. Breen sold them back to the thieves at a lower price. "I made a killing," he said.

A further excursion into crime cost Richard Breen his job at the Flying Dutchman lot. Sometime at a later date, Brautigan needed to "extract some stuff" from his unit at Army Street Mini-Storage. Breen "snatched a car from a monthly-parker" at the lot and with Tony Dingman for company, they set off for the storage unit. At a stop sign along the way, a Toyota pulled up alongside with a beautiful Chinese woman at the wheel. They all sared at her. "She was gorgeous," Breen recalled, "a fox."

Brautigan was mesmerized. After a moment, she drove off into traffic while they headed on toward Army Street. Richard had misplaced his key and had to hire a locksmith to get into the storage unit. After Brautigan retrieved what he needed, they dropped Tony off "someplace in the area."

Richard looked hard at Breen. "We have to find that chick," he said.

"OK. How are we going to do that?"

"Drive around."

For the next seventy-two hours they did exactly that, roaming the Bay Area in search of the mysterious Chinese woman, fueled by liquor store stops (whiskey for Brautigan, gin for Breen) and frequent cocaine scores to keep the driver alert. It was like a gonzo version of *American Graffiti*. Once, they spotted an Asian woman and followed her across the Bay Bridge to Oakland. "Just bizarre shit." At some point, Breen got worried and swapped licence plates on the stolen car. After three crazed days, they were cruising through Daly City when the Toyota driven by the Chinese woman pulled up alongside them.

"It's the same chick." She'd been following them. Her window was open. Brautigan rolled his window down.

"It's about time," she said. Breen thought this was "really freaky."

"Too late," Brautigan said, rolling his window back uup. "We better get this car back," he said to Breen. "It's over."

"What do you mean it's over?"

By the time they returned to the lot on Broadway, it was all over for Breen. He'd been fired from Flying Dutchman. "Golly," he told Brautigan, "I stole somebody's car just so you could go down and see dust on furniture."

The first week in June, an inter-office memo at Delacorte Press warned about production delays for *The Tokyo–Montana Express*. Sam Lawrence moved the party at Enrico's to November 6, with the *California Living* article reset four days earlier. The next evening (June 6) at 8:00 pm, Richard Brautigan appeared at the Fourth Annual San Francisco International Poetry Festival at the Palace of Fine Arts in the Marina. Fourteen months of planning had gone into the event. Seymour Lawrence boasted a month earlier to colleagues that the entire day would be devoted to Brautigan. Richard, in fact, shared the stage with six other poets, including John Thomas, Michael Ondaatje from Canada, and his old friend Amiri Baraka (LeRoi Jones).

Throughout May and June, Richard discussed divorce strategy with Joel Shawn, his new attorney. Richard jotted random thoughts on a legal pad. He questioned Shawn on the skills of the opposition: "Savett [*sic*], can you handle her? She ate Sandra like candy [. . .] Savett [*sic*] is tough. How can we settle this thing without going to trial?" In his jumbled lists of possible settlement amounts, Richard noted Akiko's $7,000 Japanese hotel bill and estimates of her legal fees. He mentioned her possessions in Montana (sewing machine, skis) and household items in Bolinas, including an oak bed, an oak dresser with a marble top, and a dulcimer.

Richard made a point of wanting to keep the 1969 Plymouth Fury bought before their marriage and all the fishing equipment he'd given Aki. Brautigan's biggest fear was that she might "destroy" him. "I'm at the best part of writing in my life," he wrote, "and I don't want to lose it to her [. . .] she fights for the written book. Make it a national case. If we [illegible] for the Tokyo–Montana Express make it a national case. ACLU."

The galleys for *Tokyo–Montana* were ready early in June and sent to Brautigan for his corrections. Delacorte began mailing bound promotional uncorrected proof copies before the end of the month, a publicity quest embracing most of the usual literary suspects (Barthelme, Malamud, Updike, Barth, Matthiessen, Capote, Algren, Saroyan, etc.) as well as Brautigan's longtime writer pals. A number of curious selections (Willie Nelson, Loretta Lynn, Senator Mo Udall, Robert Mitchum, Marisol, Walter Cronkite, Joan Mondale, and Bob Dylan) were added to the list.

On July 1, 1980, Richard Brautigan was deposed under oath by the opposing counsel in their San Francisco office. As soon after that as possible, he took off for Montana. The Hjortsbergs' marriage was also disintegrating. Gatz had moved to a rented furnished apartment in Livingston. Richard continued his habit of wandering over for coffee in the morning. Much to his surprise, he found himself becoming friends with Marian. He told her that he never related to the "wives."

Sitting on the porch one morning, Brautigan said, "You were always up to your elbows in brine or in the midst of changing a diaper, so to me you were a nonhuman. I mean, you didn't interest me at all. I'm just overwhelmed and delighted that you actually have a sense of humor."

"Thanks, Richard," Marian replied, not without irony.

She never cared much for Brautigan before that summer. "I wasn't overly fond of him," she said. "He wasn't very open or friendly. He just cultivated the friendship of the more macho element. If Richard didn't show you his charming side, he was not at all charming. He never showed me his charming side, and I obviously didn't show him mine."

That July, Brautigan turned on the charm. It wasn't long before he and Marian became lovers. One day, he took her hand and said, "I think we should go to bed now."

At first, she resisted his advances. "I really cared for Richard," Marian recalled. "I had no desire to be with him because of who he was. I also wasn't wildly attracted to him." Their mutual affection grew so strong "that it was fine when we did do it." Marian was careful not to take things too seriously and fall in love. "I'd seen his patterns," she said. "It would have been a disaster. I would have been devastated. He was capable of being a loyal friend. He was incapable of being a faithful lover."

One afternoon in the second week of July, Greg Keeler was hanging out at Pine Creek when four Japanese journalists drove up to interview Brautigan. They did a double take when they saw the two friends standing together in the front yard, "tall, blond, and pink" like enormous twins. The quartet, who all seemed to be named Ken, represented FM Tokyo and Pioneer stereo. They had come to record a program for their Welcome to Hard Times series. Pioneer manufactured a car stereo called "Lonesome Carboy." They had already used Warren Oates in their Lonesome Carboy commercials and wanted to add Richard to the list.

The Japanese audio technicians recorded sounds of gunshots and the whistling Montana wind. Keeler remembered them wandering around the place, following Brautigan with a microphone and tiny "miraculous" recording devices "while he struck noble poses and made majestic sweeping statements about the West." Richard went into full Imperial Mode in front of the mike. "To me, a good sentence, an accurate clear sentence, in writing," he declaimed, "is the same as a bullet, moving and hitting its target."

Later, Brautigan took his antique .22 caliber Winchester pump-action rifle down behind the barn to the dump for tin can plinking. "This gun sounds like the past," he said, "it is a repeating rifle. The action is like poetry." Richard was eager to publicize his forthcoming novel. Pioneer wanted to sell car stereos. The finished radio piece incorporated sounds of chugging steam engines and wailing train whistles, while the author intoned, "My name is Richard Brautigan. We are now on the Tokyo–Montana Express . . . going here and there, everywhere and nowhere at the same time."

Not long after this, Seymour Lawrence traveled out to Montana to spend time with Richard. They had much to talk about. Lordly & Dame had already booked seven engagements for Brautigan, at $1,500 per appearance. These were at small, little-known colleges. Sam planned to make the most of it, scheduling tandem book signings at prominent local bookstores. Lawrence had arranged for copies of Brautigan's titles (hardcover Dell and Laurel editions) to be stocked in Aspen, Boulder, and Denver in time for his university residency. He also had posters with the author's photo advertising *The Tokyo–Montana Express* shipped to all the bookstores and the Colorado Chautauqua Association.

During Sam's brief visit, he and Richard went for dinner at the home of Brautigan's neighbor Bob Gorsuch, a handyman and jack-of-all-trades who did odd plumbing and electrical jobs for the writer. Bob not only looked after the Pine Creek house, he took care of all the repair and maintenance for Brautigan's three rental properties in Livingston. Lawrence enjoyed "a real sense of Montana hospitality" and one of the best steaks he'd had in a long time. A large rattlesnake Gorsuch kept preserved in his deep freeze also impressed the publisher.

On a Sunday afternoon in mid-July, Gatz Hjortsberg drove out to Pine Creek from Livingston for drinks with Richard and Sam. The three men sat in the sunshine on Brautigan's back porch, talking shop and sipping bourbon. At one point, Richard advised the younger writer to patch up his strained marriage. Speaking from firsthand experience, he cautioned Hjortsberg about the rocky pitfalls of divorce. Gatz collected antique tin windup toys. The colorful novelties stood ranked on shelves in his third-floor office in the house across the creek. "If you don't put things back together," Richard said, "you can kiss your little playthings goodbye."

The next day, Brautigan left for Boulder, Colorado. He checked into a white, high-ceilinged corner room at the historic Hotel Boulderado at Thirteenth and Spruce Street. Since it first opened its doors in 1909, the block-long red-brick Edwardian building had housed presidents and statesmen as well as Ethel Barrymore (1915), poet Robert Frost (throughout the 1920s), and both Louis Armstrong and Duke Ellington in the 1960s, a time when most other neighboring hotels would not open their doors to black guests. Unlike the sleek, modern Keio Plaza, the hotel had real charm and an understated elegance with a curved stained glass ceiling arching two stories above the tile-floored lobby.

Poet Edward Dorn moved to Boulder in the fall of 1977 on a one-year contract as "visiting poet." He was invited back the next year, and the year after that, for what the Dorns believed was temporary employment, just another episode in a nomadic academic life stretching over two decades across six different campuses. They were happily surprised when Ed was offered "a tenure-track position" at the start of the eighties.

The Dorns' half of a "duplex one-floor" on 1035 Mapleton was "the only rental on a street full of mansions." Their friend, writer Ron Sukenick, called it "the worst house on the best street in Boulder." For the next thirteen years, the place that "seemed to hang in the boughs of the trees outside" hosted what Jenny Dorn designated "a continual party": visiting writers passing through, college students hanging out at all hours, school friends playing with the Dorns' children, Maya and Kidd, all made the one-story home on the steep hillside echo with laughter and lively conversation. The Dorns' kitchen became Boulder's only true salon. Brautigan joined the crowd immediately upon his arrival.

Richard came to the Dorns' kitchen every day and met Simone Ellis there. Simone dropped out of prelaw in 1974 to attend the Naropa Institute, a school founded the same year by Chögyam Trungpa Rinpoche (named for an eleventh-century Indian sage), Tibetan Buddhist and Oxford University scholar. Ellis worked as Allen Ginsberg's personal assistant while helping promote the new unaccredited Buddhist institution. The Beat Generation founding fathers swarmed to Naropa like moths drawn to a bright new flame. Simone moved to San Francisco in 1979 to study film at the Art Institute. Gregory Corso's wife, Lisa, invited Ellis to rent an extra bedroom in their apartment on the edge of Chinatown. Lisa Corso moved out, and Simone and Gregory soon became lovers.

She returned to Boulder in the summer of 1980, to visit the Dorns and show her short films in their living room. Simone's mentor, Stan Brakhage, one of America's most influential twentieth-century experimental filmmakers (*Dog Star Man* and *Window Water Baby Moving*), and poet Anne Waldman were among the impromptu audience at the Dorns'. Ellis had enjoyed Brautigan's writing since her student days. They hit it off from the start. Simone was surprised by Richard's "chivalrous" nature, finding his behavior "very Japanese."

The next Saturday night, July 19, Richard Brautigan gave "a little talk and read from his work" at Boulder's historic Chautauqua Auditorium. Wendy Serkin made the arrangements. Ginger Perry, a friend of the Dorns' and a member of the CU Creative Writing Program, put up $300 to fund the publicity. Built of wood in 1898 and surrounded by forty acres of public park under the rugged ramparts of the Flatirons, the huge deteriorating auditorium had been recently restored. Portions of the original dirt and sawdust floor remained. It was still possible to see daylight through cracks in the walls. Chautauqua, born in 1874 on the shores of Lake Chautauqua in upstate New York, provided adult education in a summer camp setting, a rural platform for dramatic readings, lectures, sermons, live musical performances, and orchestral productions. By the height of the Chautauqua movement in the 1920s, several hundred permanent facilities, like the one in Boulder, prospered around the country.

Ed and Jenny Dorn sat among the "old-timey" audience of a thousand "freckled, ginghamed women and their freckled, ginghamed children and their homespun fathers." Simone Ellis went with them. Dorn recalled Richard had been "very impressed" to learn Billy Sunday and William Jennings Bryan both spoke from the same stage. "He liked those old echoes." Brautigan was in top form and was rewarded by "gentle reflective laughter. " Ed felt the audience of hill people "obviously loved him." Jenny filmed the entire event with her eight-millimeter movie camera.

The next afternoon, Richard went with Simone and the Dorns to a faculty/student garden party at Ginger Perry's home at 744 University. Brautigan's Chautauqua reading had been a success. Wendy Serkin paid Ginger back and offered to supply all the food and booze if she would host a party for the visiting author. Drink in hand, bored with the academic professorial chitchat, Brautigan scanned the large gathering until his eye alighted upon Masako Kano, an attractive young Japanese graduate student invited by Perry, a fellow classmate in Professor James Kincaid's comparative literature summer course.

Still a virgin at twenty-three, Masako was the perfect "daughter in a box." Born in Tokyo into a strict, conservative family, she finished college at twenty and won a scholarship to the master's program at Hofstra University. This pleased her father, Masamichi Kano, a linguist, translator, and critic. Versed in twelve languages (including Latin and Greek) Kano spoke English with a British accent although he had never been to the United Kingdom.

Masako entered Hofstra in the fall of 1979, studying English and American literature under the direction of Dr. William D. Hull II, a distinguished poet and scholar. Her father allowed her to take a summer course at CU only after arranging for her to live in the Boulder home of a friend, Dr. Joyce Lebra, professor of Japanese history at the university. Dr. Lebra treated Masako like a daughter, giving her a large teddy bear. Masako named it Winifred Whimsy Bear.

Masako means "feminine elegance" in Japanese. She immediately caught Richard Brautigan's attention. "I noticed a very peculiar-looking guy was watching us," Masako said. Kano had not gone to Brautigan's Chautauqua reading. She attended a university performance of *Hamlet*, a Freudian interpretation where the prince of Denmark wore pajamas and got cozy with his mom. Richard approached the group of students and asked Masako where she was from. "Japan," she told him. Thinking Richard was an English professor, Kano launched into a discourse on literary theory. Brautigan stopped her.

"Are you hungry?" he asked.

Masako had just eaten an appetizer. "Well," she said, "I'm going to move on to the main course."

"Why don't you sit underneath that nice tree, and I will bring you food," Richard replied. While she waited, someone told her Brautigan said he wanted to see how she ate.

As a "very modest Japanese girl," Masako did as instructed even though she found his reported remark quite unpleasant. In Japan, it was considered very rude to watch someone eat. Brautigan brought her a full plate and a plastic fork. Because of the difference in their heights, Richard fetched a small chair for Masako. He sat on the ground beside her. After some time passed and Kano had not taken a single bite, Brautigan said, "I'm waiting for you to eat." Masako explained that etiquette in her homeland dictated against watching other people eating. "I know that," Richard replied. "I know that."

Brautigan told her about his four trips to Tokyo, describing in detail events that had happened to him in Japan and the people he'd met there. Masako felt Richard's storytelling transported him back to Japan. She was fascinated. Before she knew quite what was happening, Brautigan started feeding her, picking the food off her plate with his fingers and slipping it delicately between her lips. "I ended up eating it," Masako recalled in amazement.

Before long, consumed by a mutual attraction, they were kissing passionately beneath the big tree. The dutiful daughter broke out of the box. "What a woman," Ed Dorn said, watching the amorous pair from a short distance. "What a woman."

"Is he talking about me?" Masako demurely asked Richard.

"Yes. Of course."

Masako said it was the first time anyone had referred to her as a woman. "I was always called a girl in New York."

"It's a very good start then," Richard told her.

A fine gentle rain began misting around them. Most of the guests headed indoors. Brautigan wanted to remain outside, sheltered under the big tree. When the rain let up, he suggested they escape from the party. Masako said she probably should go back to Professor Lebra's house. Her father's friend was nice but very strict. She needed to feed the professor's Burmese cats. Brautigan said he'd walk her home, and they strolled off together. Masako didn't know Richard had come to the party with another woman. They left the gathering without saying a word to Simone.

Brautigan and Kano wandered down a gradual slope to the Farmer's Ditch, a narrow creek spanned by a sturdy little bridge. Richard asked Masako to sit on the rail. She confessed that she'd watched a performance of *Hamlet* instead of going to his reading. Masako had never read any of Brautigan's books. Richard suggested they each try to describe the other as Shakespearean characters. Masako couldn't think of any of the Bard's creations who reminded her of Brautigan. "You're more like, not a character," she told him. "You're like a mountain cat."

This greatly pleased Richard. He explained that this animal was called a puma. Thinking about Masako's "character," Brautigan decided she was like Puck from *A Midsummer Night's Dream*. From that moment, these became their pet names. In private, she called him Puma and Richard always affectionately referred to Masako as Puck. When Brautigan asked how old she was, Kano lied, embarrassed at being a twenty-three-year-old virgin. Masako told him she was twenty-one. "Oh," Richard replied. "You're the same age as my daughter."

Brautigan visited the Dorns nearly every day during his stay in Boulder. The next afternoon, he sat in their kitchen, drinking beer with Ed. "However obnoxious his behavior might have been the previous evening, it was easy to forgive him," Jenny observed. "His mischievous or drunken behavior was more like that of a naughty boy than a disturbed adult." On this day, forsaking an oft-repeated lament about his "complicated and painful divorce proceedings," Richard was regaling his friends with tales of budding romance, when one of Ed Dorn's former students stopped by.

Brad Donovan, whose master's thesis at CU had been a book of poems ("sort of mainline stuff"), had started collecting a year's worth of unemployment and was looking for a place to live with a ski area nearby. Over "a few beers" with Ed, Richard told Brad about Bozeman, Montana, "saying how much fun [it] was." Brautigan told Donovan the Bridger Bowl ski hill was a fifteen-minute drive from town. He should check the place out. They talked for a while about fishing. Brautigan invited Donovan to come up and fish with him on the Yellowstone. Brad reciprocated, asking Richard to a barbecue the next afternoon at a friend's house in the country "four or five miles north of Lyons," where he was staying with his wife, Georgia. There would probably be some handgun shooting.

In their conversation at the Dorns', Brad noticed "Richard was not quite into the Boulder scene because it was so centered on Naropa." Brautigan's issues with the tiny Buddhist institute reflected his independent spirit. He'd certainly heard of an incident at a Halloween party in 1975 when visiting poet W. S. Merwin and his girlfriend had been forced to strip naked by the "Vajra Guard," Trungpa Rinpoche's personal goon squad. Ed Dorn had secretly distributed mimeographed copies of *The Party*, a compilation of eyewitness accounts by former Fug Ed Sanders. Dorn's good friend, poet Tom Clark, wrote "When the Party's Over" for the *Boulder Monthly*, an article expanded in 1979 into *The Great Naropa Poetry Wars*, an eighty-seven-page book designed and printed by Graham Mackintosh, who had published *Please Plant This Book*.

Richard always found such strong-arm tactics offensive. His low tolerance for fatuous pretension kicked into high gear when he learned that Allen Ginsberg and Anne Waldman had named Naropa's literature program the "Jack Kerouac School of Disembodied Poetics." Donovan had no connections to Naropa, and Brautigan seemed "very relaxed" talking with him.

The next day, Richard and Masako went to the cookout at Joe Wilson's place on the road to Estes Park. Among the half-dozen guests were writers Wayne Moore and Roger Echo-Hawk, a Pawnee tribal historian. Wilson had a long-barreled .38 Colt, and everyone, including Masako, took turns shooting it. She had never fired a gun before. Empty beer cans provided the targets. Brautigan badly wanted to show the young Japanese woman that he was a good shot, but the others "were much better than he," Masako observed. "Made him a bad mood after that," she said.

Brad Donovan noted that Masako "was kind of standoffish. She pretended she didn't understand English." He was later surprised to learn Kano was writing her master's thesis on William Butler Yeats's connections to Japanese Nō drama. In truth, Masako was self-conscious about her command of the language despite being a graduate student in the history of American and British literature. "My English was not perfect," she confessed. The third time Masako saw Richard, he put her language skills to the test.

Brautigan took the young woman to his corner room at the Boulderado. She went with him naively enough, thinking she was much too young for him to be interested in her. Masako sat on his "very big bed" watching Brautigan standing by the window. "Well, you said you would read some of your poems for me," she said. "Now it's time. Why don't you read for me?"

Richard picked a small volume off the dresser top. "Here is a book," he told her. "I actually want you to read aloud for me." Brautigan handed Masako a copy of *June 30th, June 30th*, asking her to read the preface. She read very slowly because he "wanted to hear every word" as she pronounced it. At first she thought Richard was judging her and strove to perform well for him, but as she got into the content, reading about his uncle Edward's experiences in the aftermath of the attack on Pearl Harbor, she reflected on how the details of the Pacific War had been overlooked during her primary education.

When she finished, after a long silence, Brautigan asked her to read it again and she did. "How did you know?" he asked at the end of the second reading.

"What?"

"How could you understand?"

After that afternoon, Richard and Masako endeavored to spend as much time together as possible. She found him "always very gentle, kind of fatherlike," and felt completely natural around him. With Richard, Masako no longer had any need of pretending to be an adult. He made her relax. Richard held back his sexual desire, giving Masako the impression that he simply enjoyed going out with her and wanted to show her the natural and cultural sides of Colorado.

At the end of July, Sam Lawrence wrote Brautigan in Montana, thinking he had returned from Colorado. He hoped Richard hadn't run into any rattlesnakes. "Only adoring fans. Screaming for your books and your body." Lawrence didn't know how on the money he was. Sam had good news. The number of bookstores requesting autograph parties on Brautigan's reading tour was "building beautifully." Best of all, the Quality Paperback Book Club picked *Tokyo–Montana* as its featured alternate selection for January 1981.

Richard continued his daily sojourns to Ed and Jenny Dorn's kitchen. Simone Ellis also remained a regular visitor. One afternoon, she showed up with the stuffed head of a small female grizzly bear her father shot in 1955. It was among Simone's most treasured possessions, a connection to her dad's Native American heritage. She had taken it with her when she went off to college. One of the reasons Ellis came back to Boulder that summer was to retrieve her totem animal from a former roommate who held it for ransom until a number of "borrowed" books were returned. Brautigan took one look at the taxidermy bear head and fell in love. Many toasts were lifted to the ursine trophy. Richard had to have it. Simone explained the powerful family connection, how the head attained totem status. Ellis agreed to only loan it occasionally to Brautigan after calling her father for permission.

In order to spend time with Richard, Masako found ways to sneak out of Professor Lebra's elegant condominium with its swimming pool and beautiful gardens. "I was little bit in prison, I think," she recalled. It was easy in the daytime when Kano had a class schedule. After dark, she pretended to go to the library or came up with other excuses. When Brautigan met her in the evenings, they'd stroll down Pearl Street, a pedestrian-friendly thoroughfare closed to automobile traffic, for dinner at a favorite Italian restaurant. Pearl attracted numerous musicians, buskers, mimes, and clowns. Masako remembered Richard, "when he was in a good mood, just dancing around me" in time to the ambient street music.

Their pas de deux continued as July slipped away into August. One afternoon, she waited for him outside a restaurant. Brautigan snuck up from behind and covered her eyes with his hand. "I have something special for you," he said, "so please close your eyes."

She did as he instructed. "He was kind of humming and dancing in front of me," Masako remembered. "Can I open my eyes?" she asked.

"Yes."

Brautigan handed her Simone's stuffed grizzly bear head. Masako remembered the trophy as "kind of a family cult thing," a "spiritual thing." She hated it on first sight. The mounted head was not meant as a present. It didn't belong to Richard, but from that day on the bear played a continuing role in their lives. Brautigan named it "Teddy Head." He borrowed it often, carrying it to parties, making a joke of the doleful decapitated bruin.

Summertime in Boulder was "a carnival thing," Masako recalled. Pearl Street throbbed with musicians and itinerant performers. Wherever Brautigan went with his lovely Japanese companion "he was always surrounded by people." Richard asked Masako to dress in a colorful Indian sari and carry Teddy Head on many of these excursions. "So I looked quite noticeable."

On other occasions, Brautigan carried the stuffed bear head himself. Then, he wanted Masako to hold her teddy bear, Whimsy. Kano understood the symbolism of the image, knowing their delicate dance could lead in only one direction. When Richard asked Masako if she used birth control, she told him she didn't need to worry about "those things" because she was a virgin. "I was kind of pretending I knew everything," she confessed. "I was desperate to get rid of my virginity."

Thinking Kano was only twenty-one, "Richard was a little bit hesitant." Masako felt she had "missed something very important," but "was waiting for the moment to come." All along, as her relationship with Brautigan developed, she thought "it's a chance for me to become a woman. So, I didn't want to let him go." Masako had never had a serious boyfriend. In Tokyo, if a young man ever called, her father answered the phone speaking Chinese or Russian and scared him off.

The gateway to womanhood swung open for Masako Kano one hot August afternoon in Richard Brautigan's room at the Boulderado. "I wanted to become a woman," she said. In "waiting for the moment to come," Kano allowed her imagination to invest the act with romantic elaboration. "Maybe too much imagination," she recalled. Teddy Head, perched above them on the bureau, grounded their lovemaking in reality. The stuffed bear stared down with blind glass eyes.

"Always watching us," Masako said.

Brautigan was gentle, approaching the anticipated union as a serene ritual. Once it happened, Masako asked, "Was it really? Did I become a woman? Is that it?"

She noticed Richard was crying. "I don't want to lose you," he said. "You have to come with me." Brautigan insisted she travel to Montana. He told her how beautiful and peaceful it was there. Masako could work on her Yeats thesis in tranquility. He had academic friends at MSU, Greg Keeler and others, who could help her. Masako had to finish her summer course at the University of Colorado first, but promised to come once it was over.

Brautigan had never discussed his divorce proceedings with Kano. A "Marital Settlement Agreement" had been successfully concluded. By the first of August, both Richard and Akiko had signed the document. Aki was awarded $15,000 in cash, plus $1,400-a-month spousal support, beginning on the signing date and running through the end of December 1981. For his part, Brautigan retained all his earnings since the separation, his real property in Montana and Bolinas, as well as the rights to all of his literary works, including the as-yet-unpublished *Tokyo–Montana Express*. All things considered, it wasn't such a bad deal for Richard. He even got to keep the Plymouth Fury and all the fishing gear he'd bought for his wife.

As Brautigan's time in Boulder drew to a close, Masako continued sneaking out to spend afternoons with him in his hotel room. Richard wanted more. He dreamed of holding her in his arms through the night and couldn't wait until she came to Montana. Brautigan planned a weekend getaway in Estes Park. First he had to get permission from her protector. Dr. Joyce Lebra was a formidable individual. Born in 1925, she was the first woman to earn a PhD in Japanese history in the United States and the last person to interview Yukio Mishima in 1970 before his suicide. She had lived in Japan for ten years. Lebra knew far more about Asian culture than Richard Brautigan could begin to imagine.

Richard called Dr. Lebra "the witch professor." He arranged for a private meeting. "A kind of session," according to Masako. "Joyce wanted to make sure Richard would protect me." Kano told her chaperone she was taking a course taught by Brautigan. This was a fabrication. As a writer-in-residence, Brautigan did not conduct classes at CU. He presented himself in a professorial manner during his interview with Dr. Lebra and persuaded the stern scholar to give him permission to whisk her old friend's daughter off on a weekend rendezvous. The decision caused Lebra some concern. Many of her Japanese friends were horrified. She immediately phoned Masamichi Kano in Tokyo. Kano, "an iconoclast in a society that doesn't foster such," responded calmly, saying "something like, 'she will use her own judgment.'"

Masako's heart, not her head, made the call. She went up to the beautiful home of a gun collector in Estes Park at the eastern entrance to Rocky Mountain National Park. After shooting more guns, the couple went for long walks. Masako felt "so simpatico" with the older man, remembering Richard stopping to make a comment about falling leaves that resonated within her. Brautigan introduced Kano to a creature she called a honeybird. A feeder filled with colored sugar water hung from the eaves of the house, and a jewellike miracle darted out of the trees to hover and sip. It was the first time Masako had ever seen a hummingbird.

At four the next morning, Richard staggered into the Dorns' kitchen, encountering Ed and Simone Ellis having a late-night conversation. Teddy Head sat on top of the refrigerator. Brautigan had to have it. He started weeping. "Let me take it back to the hotel just for the night," he pleaded. Pissed at Brautigan's foolish behavior, Ed told Richard to take the damn thing home for the night and go. Brautigan swooped it up and headed out into the early dawn, catching a cab straight to the airport. He kidnaped Teddy Head. When Dorn phoned the Boulderado the next morning, he was astonished to learn Brautigan had trashed his room and departed without taking his manuscripts, his clothing, or a crumpled pile of cash.

Back in Montana, Richard resumed long-standing habits, heading across Pine Creek in the mornings for coffee with Marian Hjortsberg and more frequently for glasses of white wine on her porch in the evening. Marian's younger sister, Rosalyn, who lived nearby, often joined them for a chablis nightcap. Embittered by his bruising divorce, Brautigan enumerated his grievances against Akiko. Marian, equally angry at her two-timing husband, eagerly joined in the litany of complaint. They compiled long lists, itemizing every bit of perceived abuse.

Vampires provided an appropriate metaphor for such perfidious spousal misbehavior. Fueled by cheap Almaden, they groped for the right name. "Vorpal is coming!" they cried, evoking Lewis Carroll's vorpal blade. The name that eluded them was Vlad the Impaler. They settled on Vopol. Doubled up with laugher, Brautigan cried, "Vopol is coming and the list grows" after each bitter expletive. Rosalyn went to Bozeman the next day and had T-shirts made for Richard and Marian with vopol is coming and the list grows printed across the front.

Toby Thompson had not been to Montana in four years. At the beginning of August, he checked into the Murray Hotel in Livingston with his new girlfriend, poet Deirdre Baldwin. It was a "crazy" relationship and Toby was "under a lot of pressure." Thompson called his old bachelor pal Brautigan, who invited them out to dinner. Masako was still in Boulder and Richard was alone. He asked Toby to pick up a fifth of George Dickel on his way out of town. Said he'd pay him back but never did.

Brautigan was drunk when Thompson and Baldwin arrived at Pine Creek. Richard greeted them at the door, giving Toby a big kiss on the lips, his newest affectation. Thompson was disgusted. Brautigan "really took umbrage" and expressed his displeasure by "making snotty comments" about Deirdre upon learning she was a poet "with her own small press."

"His nose in the air," Richard played the part of a perfect host, preparing "this really marvelous dinner." Brautigan served spareribs, fresh corn, and salad, preparing it all himself. "He was a very good cook," Toby recalled. Thompson thought Richard's manner seemed different. "He was self-possessed in a way that made him standoffish." When Brautigan offered Toby a vacant rental apartment he had in town, rent free, Toby declined. He knew conditions would be attached.

One Sunday in mid-August, Lynne Huffman strolled around Gardiner, the little Montana town at the north entrance to Yellowstone Park. He was dating a "savage," a summer park employee up in Mammoth. They found their way into the Blue Goose Saloon on West Park Street and ran into Jeff Bridges playing the upright piano in the cool recesses of the nearly empty bar. This chance encounter set a pub crawl in motion. The group enlarged as it wandered northward down the valley. By the time they got to Chico Hot Springs, Toby Thompson, Deirdre Baldwin, and Dink Bruce had joined the crowd.

The celebrants found Gatz Hjortsberg and his girlfriend, Sharon Leroy, having cocktails in the tiny Chico bar. When Richard Brautigan arrived, the whole thing turned into an enormous dinner party. Later, Brautigan got up and left. After he didn't come back, Lynne asked his date where Richard had gone. "I think he's going to Japan," she said, not knowing that Japan would soon come to him.

Another August evening, just before Masako flew up from Boulder, Toby and Deirdre were in the Wrangler Bar, waiting for Brautigan with Gatz and Sharon. When Richard came in with Marian's sister, Roz Mina, Thompson thought they looked a little surprised to see Gatz, who was "sort of out of favor" for his marital misdeeds. They had just come from the Empire Theater, having watched *The Empire Strikes Back*, the second installment of the *Star Wars* trilogy. "How did you like the movie?" Toby asked Brautigan.

"I feel like I just spent three hours in a pinball machine," he said.

Brautigan mailed Masako Kano an airline ticket to Montana. In his meeting with Dr. Lebra, Richard had mentioned the possibility of just such a trip, suggesting the classmate who brought

Masako to Ginger Perry's party might come along as a chaperone. In the end, Kano just ran away and escaped. She arranged to sleep at her classmate's place. Instead of taking only enough for an overnight, she packed everything, including Whimsy, her teddy bear.

Brautigan sent a young cowboy who worked occasionally for him to pick Masako up at the Bozeman airport. He was Ianthe's boyfriend from Park High in Livingston, back when she had hoped to become a vet. Masako remembered the drive, "the beautiful panorama to Livingston." When the pickup pulled onto the short curved driveway, Richard sat waiting on the fence. They'd not seen each other for two weeks. "Good afternoon, Mr. Brautigan," she said.

Brautigan soon introduced Masako to Marian Hjortsberg and Roz, along with other friends in the Pine Creek area. Marian had an antique upright piano in her living room, and Masako, musically inclined, came over in the afternoons to play. Greg Keeler made the trip from Bozeman to meet the comely graduate student. His first impression was one of impending doom. "He was so big and old and American," he wrote later, "and she was so tiny and young and Japanese." Keeler also saw how well they got along and how happy she made Richard in spite of his divorce woes. Late one night, Brautigan read "The Love Song of J. Alfred Prufrock" aloud to Greg and Masako, turning his kitchen into "an odd little classroom." Keeler was surprised to learn Richard liked T. S. Eliot. As a rule, he avoided academic poetry.

"Dobro Dick" Dillof owned a local reputation as a lady's man. It had a lot to do with his dark good looks. At certain angles he resembled John Garfield, although none of the women who fancied him had ever seen those old black-and-white movies. He almost never took off his battered cowboy hat, preserving a mysterious allure until his Stetson hung above them on the bedpost. His wondrous skills as a musician also proved powerfully attractive, as did his vagabond troubadour persona. He lived in a sheepherder's wagon parked behind the Pine Creek Lodge, and a steady procession of dewy-eyed farm girls paraded through for a serenade.

Dillof was a good friend of Ed Dorn, whom he first met a year or so before while playing a concert with Fiddling Red at the Hummingbird Café in Indianapolis, Indiana. "Thought he was brilliant," Dick said of Dorn. "Hit it off right away." As a wandering minstrel, Dillof had crisscrossed America for years, hitchhiking and hopping freight trains. Dick and Red's Midwest tour ended around Thanksgiving, and they stopped in Boulder to visit the Dorns on their way back to Montana. When Ed heard their destination, he casually mentioned that he knew Richard Brautigan, who had a place near Livingston.

Back in his sheepherder's wagon under the fir trees behind the Pine Creek store, Dillof had no idea that Brautigan lived just down the road until Marian Hjortsberg introduced them one August afternoon. As they talked, Richard was delighted to learn Dobro knew Ed Dorn, "who he considered a big brother." Brautigan invited Dillof over, and the musician walked in on a phone conversation with Aki. Richard sat on the couch, speaking loudly, "in a big round voice" so Dick could hear. "Let me get this straight," Brautigan intoned, "you took half of the money I make writing my books, sweating my blood. Half of my money you took in the divorce and you want to be my friend? That's very interesting. Could you tell that to a friend of mine here." Richard handed Dillof the phone. Dick didn't want any part of it.

Having gotten off to an amicable start, Brautigan introduced Dillof to Masako. Later, at a picnic, she expressed an interest in seeing his "cart." Dick saw nothing wrong with inviting her over for a peek at the sheepherder's wagon. Masako felt no impropriety about making such a visit. Dillof and Roz Mina were obviously lovers. Kano observed them at the picnic "very nice and very close and being in love."

Brautigan was often busy in the mornings, rewriting the "hamburger" passage from *So the Wind* over and over "because he wanted to get it exactly right." Masako didn't mind the separation. She "loved being alone and just strolling around." Richard told her to do whatever she wanted. One morning Masako walked up the road for a look at Dobro's horse-powered mobile home.

The sheepherder's wagon was as compact as the interior of a sailing ship. At the far end, above an ingenious Chinese-puzzle arrangement of cabinets and drawers, a built-in bed occupied almost a third of the living space. Arching translucent canvas roofed the tiny tidy compartment. Other amenities included a twin-lid wood-burning cookstove and a table that folded down from the wall. Dick added a windup portable Victrola to play his collection of old-time 78s and decorated the interior with nineteenth-century advertising flyers. The wagon also housed his exotic collection of antique musical instruments: guitars, Dobros, fiddles, concertinas, prairie zithers, and autoharps.

Masako's was the briefest of visits, only a few minutes at most. She found Dillof taking a nap. He groggily offered to show her around. When Brautigan heard about it, he hit the ceiling, furious as a suspicious old rake upon learning his latest conquest had been to the boudoir of a younger rival. "He's very jealous," Kano recalled. Masako told Richard not to worry. Dick was in love with Rosalyn. Nothing had happened, so the event blew over without incident.

Later Masako met Roz's husband, Mina E. Mina, a Coptic Egyptian whose family had fled to Canada during the Nasser revolution. She asked Richard what would become of such a complex triangle. Mina was an actor frequently away for long periods, looking for Hollywood work or touring in his one-man show based on the writings of Charles Bukowski. Richard laughed. "She loves her husband but she is in love with Dobro Dick too," he explained. "You have to learn about this."

To make amends for even the presumption of betrayal, Dillof offered a demonstration of his antique instrument collection at Brautigan's place, along with lessons for Masako. Marian and Rosalyn got wind of this. In retribution for a recent Richard prank, they planned to retaliate with a stunt of their own. The afternoon that Dobro Dick brought the autoharps, banjos, and National steel guitars over to Richard's place, the two sisters headed for town. At the hardware store, inspired by the paintings of Hieronymus Bosch, they bought a number of large metal funnels, fitting them on their heads like hats.

It grew dark in Pine Creek. All remained serene at the Brautigan household. Richard had gone fishing earlier. Masako filleted his catch and made trout sushi. According to his wishes, she dressed in her special cotton kimono, the obi belted tight. Brautigan had planned a tranquil evening "of Zen-like perfection" and had arranged Dick's exotic instruments around his long dining table, placing cut daisies and dried flowers into the sound holes. "To make me surprised," Masako recalled.

Dillof stopped by Marian's house on his way over to Brautigan's and encountered the sisters preparing their costumes: black capes, Donald Duck and Arabian masks, topped off by funnels tied to their heads. "I don't know if we should do this," Dick protested.

"Dobro, you're the biggest prankster of them all," Marian remonstrated. "We *have* to do it."

Decked out in outlandish getups, the trio snuck down East River Road to Richard's house. Inside, tranquility prevailed. Green tea and trout sushi had been prepared. "We are kind of celebrating," Masako recalled, "kissing each other as usual, and suddenly there is noise." They looked out the windows and saw three masked Boschian zanies cavorting on their porch.

Brautigan struggled to maintain an inscrutable composure. "He wanted to laugh, but he was going to one-up us," Marian remembered. "He wasn't going to fall for it."

Richard came to the front door. "Is there something I can do for you?" he solemnly asked the masqueraders, taking the wind out of their sails.

"He turned the whole situation around so that we ended up feeling like complete assholes," Marian Hjortsberg said.

Brautigan and Kano's new life together soon found a harmonious groove. Richard wanted Masako to see Yellowstone Park because "it's really wild." On an overcast, rainy day, inauspicious for sightseeing, Brautigan remained determined to go. Brad Donovan joined the party as the designated driver. They wound up past Mammoth Hot Springs, climbing high onto the Yellowstone Plateau toward the Upper Geyser Basin, where Masako got to see Old Faithful.

After observing fumaroles and mud volcanos, they strolled along the banks of the Firehole River. When Kano commented on the numerous bleached bones and animal droppings, Richard produced a small volume from his satchel on a shoulder strap. It was a scatological encyclopedia. Like an amateur coprologist, Brautigan proceeded to identify the various types of excrement they encountered.

Greg Keeler remembered watching Richard teach Kano to fish, "like his little girl, and she loved every minute of it." Kano called Brautigan "my old Puma" and "Papa" and "Big Fuzzy Bear." Richard was delighted. "Isn't she cute as a bug's ear," he whispered to Keeler as they watched her practice fly-casting. "I can't believe she's real." Greg fished with them on Little Mission Creek, where John Fryer lived during the summers, and up Mill Creek to Brautigan's favorite beaver ponds.

Richard had a morning ritual. He got up first and always put George Benson's record *Breezin'* on the phonograph, saying it got him going. Next Brautigan started a pot of coffee percolating and made fresh-squeezed orange juice while "lots and lots of bacon" fried crisply on the griddle. Masako found Richard "quite domesticated in that sense." To commemorate their union, they took photographs of Whimsy Bear and Teddy Head posed together in an open field behind Brautigan's house.

After breakfast, Richard usually went to his barn-loft studio to work for a couple hours. They spent the afternoons together, fishing with Greg Keeler, going to picnics (one at the Fondas' spread involved flying kites with Jeff Bridges), playing one-on-one basketball at Pine Creek School (Masako had shot hoops in high school), and making love outdoors. "To be honest," she confessed, "we made a lot of love."

The lovers had a special secret place down in the woods near a number of old tepee rings on the Hjortsbergs' property. Richard told Masako, "there's no wind there." They'd bring a blanket and perhaps a pot of coffee to the spot, just across the creek from a mysterious oblong stone formation that long ago supported the frame of a large Salish bark lodge. It was rumored

Daniel Boone spent the winter here on a trip up the Missouri to the Yellowstone River sometime around 1810, when the old trailblazer was in his seventies. It was a magic place, imbued with a timeless aura.

At day's end, Richard and Masako watched the sunset blazing over the Gallatin Mountains, sitting on the hood of one of Brautigan's junker cars parked in front of his barn, the windshield providing a convenient backrest. The "pink clouds running all over the sky" amazed Masako. When electrical storms rumbled into the valley, they took refuge in the house, watching the thunder and lightning from the upstairs bedroom window. At every fiery strike, Brautigan made a sound like "Oooh . . . Oooh!" Storms like this never happened in Tokyo.

Late summer provided her introduction to bondage. Richard was very coy about broaching the subject. Brautigan had prepared a separate bedroom downstairs for Masako. Sometimes he wanted to sleep alone in his little house outside, he explained, and she needed a private space of her own. Their lovemaking was a moveable feast, often in this room, other times upstairs or outdoors or in Brautigan's tiny private sleeping building. After sweeping it clean, Richard decorated Kano's little chamber with a "very nice Indian couch" and a basin of flowers.

One morning Masako found a letter in Japanese strategically placed on the table ("a funny thing"). It was the note Akiko's aunt had written two years before, offering reassurance about her husband's sexual proclivities. Kano remembered reading about "tying up things. Some men have some tastes, so don't worry about so much." She thought "the physical condition of the letter seemed to suggest it had been read many times," and she was certain Brautigan placed it deliberately in her room.

This was Masako's first love. She trusted Richard. She thought, "That's the way. This is just how things are done in the West." Brautigan had already taught her that you could be married and still have "a summertime love with anybody." In "observing everything," Kano made the connection with "the young geisha girl, tying only the hands." Richard explained that by binding her, making her wait without any touching, her "body would be more open and expecting."

One rainy day, Richard had just tied Masako in the upstairs bedroom when the telephone rang. He excused himself and went down to answer the call. Brautigan became totally involved in the conversation. After a while, Masako fell asleep. When she awoke, she was still bound and Richard wasn't there. "I was so afraid," she remembered. "He just forgot me." Masako started shouting, "Richard, please come back!" This became a funny story, Kano admitted, after Brautigan returned to untie her before his game playing turned into a nightmare.

Toby Thompson and Deirdre stopped by Pine Creek one afternoon to visit Brautigan and encountered Brad and Georgia Donovan just up from Colorado. Toby assumed they were Bozeman people. Thompson thought Richard was moving away from the Livingston gang and spending more time with Bozeman friends. Greg Keeler planned a party later in the evening to welcome the Donovans to Montana. First Brautigan wanted to go fishing.

Richard invited Toby to join them, both on the stream and over at Keeler's. Georgia and Deirdre said they'd take Masako into Livingston and teach her to shoot pool. Thompson "could tell [Brautigan] was a little queasy about this." The boys headed to Mill Creek to fish Richard's favorite water, the beaver ponds at the lower end of Arch and Peg Allen's ranch.

Brautigan positioned Brad and Toby on a pair of promising riffles and headed through the willows to his secret spot. Richard loved fishing these beaver dams, their shallow pools filled with eager little brookies. "I remember him trotting back with this huge plastic bag full of fish," Thompson recalled. Brautigan kept more than twenty small brook trout for a fish fry scheduled on the next day.

It was late when they got back to Pine Creek. The women hadn't returned from town. Brautigan grew agitated. The big sky darkened. They would be late for Keeler's party. Masako remembered, "Richard got very upset" when she came back from town with Georgia and Deirdre. Brautigan knew Deirdre least well, so he blamed it all on her, determining never to see her again. "He just shut the door," Masako observed.

Brad Donovan recalled "a real fast ride" over Trail Creek Road with Toby, trying to get to the Keelers' and finding Thompson "a little bit standoffish." At the party, Masako observed a lot of MSU faculty members among the gathering. Richard got very drunk. He took Toby aside and told him, "I believe a man should be able to control his woman." Later, Thompson's profession came up in conversation with Donovan. Brautigan warned, "Whatever you do, don't call yourself a journalist. Journalists piss in the water we have to drink."

Toby and Deirdre went to Richard's fish fry the next night, and he treated them cordially. They were around the area for another couple weeks. Brautigan "refused to get together at all," Thompson complained. "He practically would not take my phone calls." Richard and Masako had a big Labor Day party at Pine Creek, for which he cooked Swedish meatballs. Greg Keeler brought a bunch of smoked whitefish. Marian Hjortsberg tossed a large green salad from her garden. Jeff and Sue Bridges came. Cindy Olson was among those shooting guns off the back porch. Toby and Deirdre were not invited.

At summer's end, Ianthe came out to Montana from San Francisco where she'd been part of the ACT therafter program. Three years younger than Masako, Ianthe believed they were both the same age. To Greg Keeler they looked like "international sisters." They liked each other right from the start, although Ianthe kept her distance at first. When Masako noticed her holding back, she "asked her directly what is wrong." Ianthe spoke honestly, telling Masako she'd had a "traumatic relationship," giving her love to another Japanese woman. When her father married Akiko, she became Ianthe's de facto mother. When they split, she felt "really hurt." Along the way, "she suffered from Aki and Richard's fighting." Once it was all out in the open, Ianthe and Masako became good friends.

Masako was particularly impressed by the easy rapport between Ianthe and Richard. She recalled sitting on the couch one afternoon after they'd all been drinking, listening to a conversation she couldn't completely follow. Brautigan and his daughter talked about Montana summers gone by, laughing together as they remembered one time in 1978 when they were "crawling under the table." Kano found their close connection "a wonderful thing," a father and daughter relating as friends.

When one of Masako's wisdom teeth became impacted, Richard took her to see Dr. Jim Smith, his dentist in Livingston. She needed to have it extracted. Brautigan was writing on the day Masako's surgery had been scheduled, so Ianthe drove her into town. When she first arrived in Montana, Richard told his girlfriend she must learn to drive, but that was as far as it went. After the operation, Dr. Smith wrote out a prescription and instructed Masako to "tell your father . . ." Having known Akiko, Smith assumed Kano was her child. Brautigan found it very funny when he heard the story. Afterward, from time to time Richard teased Masako, calling her "my daughter."

Masako spent a couple days recovering, mostly napping in bed. While asleep, she bled from her mouth and the blood stained the pillowcases. A year later, when Kano was back in Japan and Brautigan believed their romance had ended forever, he slept on the blood-stained pillows, "possessed by the artifacts of our affair."

As if to turn her from him, Brautigan told Masako, "I'm not beautiful." At first she found it funny. "You need a young beautiful boy," he went on. "Maybe you should make love with a young beautiful boy." This hurt her feelings. At times, being so much younger she "felt more like Richard's exotic pet than a real girlfriend."

"I was so much in love," Masako confessed, not understanding why Brautigan would say such a thing to her. Deeply troubled, she talked it over with Ianthe. The real daughter reassured her honorary sibling, "He didn't mean that."

Another emotional moment came when Masako found Richard weeping on the couch after a phone conversation with Akiko. She didn't know what to do. "It's really disgraceful," Richard said. Masako felt he suffered from "losing of face." She was very worried. Not knowing what to say to her lover, she called Don Carpenter in California. Masako had spoken with Don before when he phoned from Mill Valley and Richard put her on the line with him. Carpenter had been drinking then. He told her about serving with the U.S. Air Force in Japan and a beautiful girl he'd met there. Masako felt a connection. This time she asked him what to do about Richard. "Maybe you can talk to him?" Don had again been drinking. He instructed Masako not to tell Brautigan she'd phoned him but to say he just happened to call before she handed the phone to Richard.

Before long the days grew shorter. As summer drew to an end and the time for Masako to return to Hofstra approached, Richard began maneuvering to keep her in Montana. Greg Keeler gave Kano a copy of *The Autobiography of William Butler Yeats* to help with her thesis. Brautigan concocted a plan for her to transfer to MSU and complete her graduate work there under Keeler's direction. Masako explained all her work thus far had been with William Hull. Richard told her to phone her professor or write a letter. "So you don't need to go back."

Working for the other side, Joyce Lebra called Masamichi Kano in Tokyo to apprise him of the situation. Masako's parents became "quite worried." Her father asked about Richard Brautigan among his intellectual circle and was told he was "not the type of man" for his daughter to be involved with, "too old and too bohemian." Not a serious marriage prospect. Masako knew her parents "were very confused. They didn't want this kind of thing happening to their daughter."

Masako regarded Professor Hull as "a fatherly figure." When she phoned him to say she didn't plan on returning to Hofstra, Hull informed Kano that her actual father had been in contact. "You should call him," her professor advised. Masako phoned home. Mr. Kano didn't want to speak with Brautigan. His daughter put Richard on the line anyway. They talked for a while. Masako thought it sounded "quite friendly." Brautigan told Masamichi Kano that he had a daughter Masako's age and understood how he felt. The conversation made her father more concerned. Knowing Richard was planning a nationwide reading tour, Kano made him promise not to reveal his daughter's identity.

Masamichi Kano left Tokyo for New York at the end of the third week of September, scheduled to return on October 6. He sent word to his daughter that he expected her to see him while he was in the United States. Brautigan didn't want Masako to go, but she was "still under the protection of [her] parents" and felt compelled to obey their wishes. Richard believed her father was taking her away from him. Masako promised she'd come back soon. At the Bozeman airport, she studied the reflection of her crying eyes in Brautigan's sad blue gaze.

When Masako flew off to New York, she left most of her belongings behind in Pine Creek. A couple days after Kano's departure, a letter arrived from Nikki Arai in San Francisco. She'd had new stationery printed and wanted to know how Brautigan liked the letterhead. A trifling thing, but hearing unexpectedly from an old friend provided a bit of welcome distraction. Back under her father's influence, Masako knew she would break her promise to Richard and never return to Montana.

Masako stayed at the home of Edgar Lynn Turgeon, a professor of economics at Hofstra. "Richard got very upset," she recalled. Once he learned Turgeon and Professor Hull were both gay, he "was really at ease about me staying there." When she told him she had decided to complete her thesis with Professor Hull, Brautigan said she was too serious and analytical. "You can be relaxed," he said, suggesting Greg Keeler's "literary assistance" would offer a different, more creative approach toward her work. Masako knew he proposed an "artist's attitude," not the scholarly discipline the Yeats thesis demanded.

Brautigan called Kano repeatedly at Professor Turgeon's Long Island home in the middle of the night, which she found annoying. Richard vented his frustrations to his daughter so often that Ianthe finally phoned Masako herself, begging her to come back. As a final gambit to force her return, Brautigan held onto Kano's belongings. She repeatedly asked him to ship her things, "including my teddy bear," to the East Coast. Richard resisted. As long as he kept her stuff, he clung to the impossible belief that she might come back.

Around this time, a Montana writer named Steve Chapple (whose book *Don't Mind Dying: A Novel of Country Lust and Urban Decay* had just been published by Doubleday) arrived at Brautigan's place in Pine Creek with his girlfriend, Kathy. He'd come to interview Richard for the *San Francisco Chronicle*. They talked in the kitchen, where Teddy Head guarded the door, working their way through two fifths of George Dickel between the late afternoon and 3:00 am.

Brautigan told Chapple he planned to move to Japan for a year. "*Trout Fishing in America* is not taken as a rolling picaresque hippie novel in Japan," he said, "but rather as a questioning of man's relation to the environment." When Steve asked about the influence of Montana on his writing, Richard replied, "Montana has reestablished my proximity to heroic nature."

It grew dark. Their conversation continued as the first dead soldier was laid to rest.

Having put potatoes in the oven earlier, desperate for food, Kathy tossed a salad and slid steaks into the broiler around midnight before collapsing on the couch beside Whimsy Bear. Richard compared *Trout Fishing* and *Tokyo–Montana*. The first, he said, "was a book written by a boy. This book is written by a man. I'm no longer a boy. That's the difference."

As they wolfed baked potatoes and rare meat, Brautigan spoke about mortality. "I don't give a shit about death, man," he proclaimed. "I have no fear of it at all. I'm interested in the role it plays in others. It defines our lives. I use death to emphasize life. Death is the electricity of life. People wouldn't take life seriously if they didn't know it would turn dark on them."

Speaking with his mouth full, Chapple asked how he could be so unconcerned about death. "I almost died once," Richard told him, completely lucid in spite of downing an ocean of whiskey. "I was eight. Appendicitis. I got peritonitis and filled up. At the hospital they talked of my autopsy. I went to a place. It was dark without being scary. It was dark without dimensions. There were no memories there. It was so spectacular, Steve, dark without being warm. The reason I'm not afraid of death is that it would have been okay."

The interview ended three hours before dawn. Brautigan informed Chapple, "Now I'm following the future."

Part of that future meant accepting Masako would not return to Montana. Conceding all was lost, Richard packed up her stuff a few days later and sent it east to Professor Hull's house. Putting Whimsy into a cardboard box, sealing it shut like a coffin, struck a pathetic note of doom. Puma knew he would never have sweet little Puck back in his life. Brautigan immediately resumed his familiar bachelor habits, linking up with his drinking buddies. "I won't see her again," he lamented to Greg Keeler.

"Probably not," his friend observed.

"Why do these things happen to me?"

"I don't know."

There was no explaining fate. Richard again faced an inexorable descending curtain of despair. After Ianthe left for New York, he began eating dinner nearly every night over at Marian Hjortsberg's. The other regular guests at her table included sister Roz, Dick Dillof, Marian's current boyfriend, John Wonder ("a kind of wild white supremacist"), and Bob Bauer, a stonemason who was helping rebuild Marian's wood-heated sauna, which had burned down earlier in the summer.

Bauer, son of noted outdoor writer Irwin Bauer, lived by himself in an old one-room schoolhouse on Mill Creek Road. He had first met Brautigan in the summer of 1978. Bob was staying then in a cabin at the Pine Creek Lodge next to Jim Harrison, who seemed always to have a hangover in the morning. One day, Bauer bumped into Richard and Akiko in the store and they chatted casually. "I remember Brautigan looked so funny because he was wearing one of those stupid hats, comes up real high with a little ball on it. Little Elmer Fudd hat."

During the monthlong period in the fall of 1980 when they dined together almost every night at Marian's house, Bob came to know Richard a whole lot better and "really didn't enjoy him too much." Brautigan, upset over the divorce and Masako's recent departure, "was very pissed off," according to Bauer. "Into himself. Real self-centered." Richard revealed his deep despair during a dinner table conversation. Marian Hjortsberg's other guests that night included Roz, Becky Fonda, and Sean Gerrity. Sean told a story about a mistreated junkyard dog in Livingston. Everyone was shocked to hear about the abuse, formulating plans to liberate the animal. Bob volunteered to drive the dog over to Missoula and find it a good home. "Fuck," Richard interjected bitterly, "I don't even like fucking dogs!"

Throughout the summer, beautiful calligraphic postcards penned by Ward Dunham arrived from Enrico's. All the old gang missed him. "Get those tungsten carbide kneecaps on back home!" Ward implored. A folded card from Dunham, as elegantly inscribed as a college diploma, invited Brautigan to a Halloween Party "at the Fechhëimer [sic] Palace." A follow-up postcard included a note from Magnolia Thunderpussy. She looked "forward to sharing some witches brew on all Hallows Eve." Dunham added, "It will be good to have you back here," appending a footnote: "Dingman is massively fucked up!"

Two diversions took Brautigan's mind off his woman troubles. Greg Keeler had been recruited by some Bozeman writers to participate in a reading at Chico Hot Springs resort. Knowing Greg was friendly with Richard, they asked him to invite Brautigan. They read to a small but appreciative audience in the lobby. When Richard read his short poem "Two Guys Get Out of a Car," it brought down the house.

Shortly before Ianthe's departure early in October, photographer Michael Abramson came out to Livingston on assignment for *People* magazine. He hung around Paradise Valley snapping pictures of the local literary/art scene in flyover country. Russell Chatham's fall one-man show always occasioned a big party. Abramson photographed the McGuanes and the Fondas, Jeff and Sue Bridges, Guy and Terry de la Valdène, and Dan and Ginny Gerber. A double portrait of Richard and Ianthe, seated under a cottonwood with the big barn looming behind them, was not published by *People* until after the writer's suicide.

Cheryl McCall, an editor at *People*, arrived to write the accompanying article. She interviewed every writer, actor, and artist to be found, focusing mainly on Russell Chatham. She missed Gatz Hjortsberg, off on a trip to Europe with his girlfriend. The magazine wanted a group photo shoot of the Montana Gang, and word went out one afternoon by phone chain. Everybody gathered at Russ Chatham's place at the upper end of Deep Creek for an impromptu party.

Abramson posed the gang on and around Chatham's old pickup. The McGuanes and the Fondas were there, along with the Bridges, the Valdènes, and the Gerbers. Marian, Roz, John Fryer, Terry McDonell, Michael Butler, and Dr. Dennis Noteboom all turned up. Chatham stood close to the center, leaning on the open truck door. More than thirty people grouped together to say cheese. Masako had departed. Richard Brautigan brought Teddy Head instead, his substitute date. He sat cross-legged in the grass up-front, the stuffed bear perched on his lap as a forlorn love token. When the article was published, *People* did not run this group shot.

Near the end of October, Brautigan returned to San Francisco and took a room at the Kyoto Inn at the corner of Sutter and Buchanan streets in Japantown. His legal troubles preoccupied him. Richard had spent many hours on the phone. His Mountain Bell bill for October totaled $771.33. On the thirtieth, an interlocutory judgment of dissolution of marriage was filed in the county courthouse. All the bitter wrangling was over. What remained was pro forma, a done deal. The final terms were sealed and fixed. The same day, more good news arrived in a telegram from Seymour Lawrence. A second printing of *Tokyo–Montana* had just been ordered. "You are my sunshine," Sam crooned via Western Union.

David Fechheimer's fabled Halloween bash turned out to be a fortieth birthday party for Magnolia Thunderpussy. The festivities took place at Mrs. Robert Louis Stevenson's mansion on the corner of Lombard and Hyde, designed by Willis Polk and completed in 1900. Fechheimer owned the palatial home in partnership with a woman he met when they once accidentally shared a ride. She lived at one end. David occupied the other. Fechheimer's splendid home provided the ultimate party pad.

Thunderpussy (real name Patricia Mallon) was a third-generation San Franciscan. After working in burlesque and radio, she opened a restaurant in the Haight serving erotically inspired ice cream concoctions (the Montana Banana replicated a hard-on). Late-night delivery, rapier wit, and a flamboyant style endeared her to legions of local rock bands. Ward Dunham designed the poster/invitation for the event ("carbide tungsten kneecaps will arrive by way of the Tokyo-Montana Express") and made a concoction he called Brautigan Punch, prepared in garbage cans with 151-proof rum, orange juice, and "ten or twenty cases of Calvados." According to Dunham, "it went down like Kool-Aid."

Dunham estimated six hundred people showed up for the festivities. Everybody who thought he or she was anybody in Frisco dropped by at one point or another. Governor Jerry Brown came with Richard Hongisto, former San Francisco sheriff and a city supervisor at the time. Herb Caen might have devoted his entire column to the festivities had he been there. Instead he was over at the Old Spaghetti Factory in North Beach serving as a charity auctioneer to raise money for a re-creation of Henri Lenoir's legendary bohemian studio that would keep all the original furnishings intact.

When Richard Brautigan arrived, he read "a bunch of new poems" to the milling throng. Afterward came frequent refills of his eponymous punch. Sometime in the evening, Richard needed to "bleed his lizard" and went looking for a bathroom. Finding none available in Fechheimer's half of the house, Brautigan wandered over to the neighbor's portion. He discovered the woman in the WC. When he knocked, she would not come out. Richard stuffed newspaper under the door and set it on fire. "She was out in a flash," Fechheimer recalled.

The party of the century. An epic, manic affair. "I have never seen a party like that," Ward Dunham recalled. "That was *the* party!" Brautigan returned late to the Kyoto Inn.

Near the end of the night, David Feccheimer stood at the top of the stairs, "looking down on the carnage" clad in his T-shirt and socks. "Never again," he said, shaking his head. "Never again."

The next day, *California Living,* the magazine section of the Saturday *Chronicle,* ran "Five Stops on the Tokyo–Montana Express" with accompanying photographs. The excerpts were "California Mailman," "The Beacon," "Open," "The Butcher," and "Sunday."

Richard Brautigan's book tour began on the evening of November 2, when he flew up to Seattle/Tacoma to get "a good night's sleep." The following afternoon, Richard signed copies of the book at Walden Books in the Tacoma Mall. Around thirty-five were sold, along with some paperbacks.

That evening at 8:00, Brautigan read at Tacoma's University of Puget Sound. He was paid $1,500 (plus expenses, minus Lordly & Dame's commission) for the event. After the reading, Richard was interviewed by Jim Erickson, a reporter for the *Tacoma News Tribune.* Once his tour was over, Brautigan said he planned "to just drift." He'd eventually wind up in Japan, where he hoped to spend an entire year. The next morning, Richard departed Seattle for St. Louis, the first leg of a long travel day.

After a short layover, Brautigan took off for Memphis. An hour after arrival, he was on a flight bound for the Hattiesburg-Laurel Regional Airport in Mississippi. Bill Thompson of Lordly & Dame's travel department, who handled all the arrangements, advised Richard to "get some food along the way or eat after reading." Forty-five minutes after landing, Brautigan stood on the stage of Bennett Auditorium entertaining a group of students from the honors college at the University of Southern Mississippi in Hattiesburg.

Richard was up at first light the next day to make a 6:37 flight for Atlanta, where he waited almost four hours before catching a nonstop Delta flight to Los Angeles. After a three-and-a-half-hour layover, Brautigan was off again on Hughes Airwest, bound for his hometown, Eugene, Oregon. The flight touched down at 7:43 pm. The timing was even tighter this time, only a quarter of an hour remained before his scheduled appearance.

Someone from the University of Oregon waited at the airport and raced Richard over to the campus. Long ago, he hunted night crawlers on the lawns here with Peter Webster. At eight o'clock,

Brautigan was introduced to a group of students at the EMU Cultural Forum. The attendance was lower than the Delacorte rep had predicted. Richard had a good rapport with his audience, taking his enthusiastic listeners for a ride on *The Tokyo–Montana Express.*

After the reading, Richard was signing copies of his earlier books when he felt a tap on his shoulder. He looked up. It was Ken Kesey. The two writers had not seen each other in three years. "Sixty-cent whiskies at the Eagles," Kesey said. Brautigan took this as "a literary kind of compliment." They set out together soon after for a night of drinking. This was the first time Richard had been back in Eugene since he left for good twenty-five years before. He did not call his mother on this return trip. Nor did Mary Lou make any effort to get together with the son she had not seen in a quarter century. She knew all about his reading. "He was at the university making speeches," she said.

In the late hours after midnight, Mary Lou Folston was awakened by a loud knock at the front door. Frightened, she made no move to see who was there. The insistent knocking continued. Only bad news announced itself in this fashion. When she got out of bed at last, Mary Lou still did not open the door. She pulled back a curtain and peeked out the window just in time to see "the mysterious stranger" climb into the passenger side of a car. She watched whoever it was drive away. She didn't recognize the man, but Mary Lou remained convinced her son had come home at last to say hello to mom.

No matter how late he partied the night before, Richard Brautigan was up in time for a university bookstore book signing "party" at nine the next morning. About thirty-five copies of *The Tokyo–Montana Express* were sold to his student fans. Brautigan's royalties from these sales totaled $57.49. Not a princely sum but a fair wage at the time for two hours of autographing and small talk. At 10:49 am, Richard flew back to San Francisco nonstop on United.

November 6 was the official publication date for *The Tokyo-Montana Express.* There had been problems with the advertising for the autographing party at Enrico's. Delacorte wanted to run an ad in the *Sunday Examiner & Chronicle* featuring photographs of both Banducci and Brautigan. Richard had advertising design control. Seymour Lawrence wrote at the end of August, asking him to prepare the ad. Richard provided his publisher with Enrico's phone number only in September.

On the twenty-second, Lawrence wrote that *Tokyo–Montana* had gone into a third printing, a total of thirty thousand hardback copies in print. Sam requested that Richard send his ad copy for the signing party "with cameo photos of you and Enrico." Preoccupied with Masako's impending departure, Brautigan did nothing. Over the next two weeks, Delacorte made numerous calls to Banducci and his wife, asking for a photo. A picture of the restaurant arrived on the first of October. The ad ran on the tenth with just Brautigan's photo. Four days later, a picture of Enrico came in the mail. It was published at last, along with Richard's photograph, early in November, the official start of the book tour, in the weekly *San Francisco Chronicle Review*, along with Steve Chapple's interview. Both photos were also used on the printed invitations.

The party at Enrico's began at three in the afternoon and lasted until seven. Sam Lawrence flew in from Boston. Richard and Nancy Hodge, for whom Brautigan had also dedicated the longer version of his book, were among the gathered friends and well-wishers. At one point Richard talked with Keith Abbott about the progress of his promotional tour. Keith gathered he was "dismayed at how badly his audience had shrunk." Students, always his fan base before, no longer seemed to know who he was. "They don't read," Brautigan complained to Abbott. Keith took that to mean "they no longer read [me]."

Eunice Kitagawa, a young Hawaiian woman who worked at a local Benihana, was among those who turned out to buy a book and have a drink with Richard. Although she lived just up the hill on Vallejo Street above the Kearney steps, Eunice hadn't planned on attending the event. A friend, visiting from Honolulu, was dating Tony Dingman and kept calling from the bar, urging Eunice to come down. She relented and headed for Enrico's. The moment they were introduced, Brautigan and Kitagawa felt an immediate attraction. "We became friends from there," Eunice recalled.

Richard didn't have much time to spend with his new friend. Three days later he was on an afternoon flight to Boise, Idaho, arriving in time for a committee dinner before an 8:00 reading at Boise State University. The university bookstore had not expressed any prior interest in a book signing but rounded up a number of copies through a wholesaler and sold them after Brautigan's presentation. On the morning of the tenth, Richard met with an undergraduate class. He went later to the Book Shop on Main Street for an official autographing party. Perhaps thirty books were sold. The Delacorte rep believed the university's unauthorized session the night before cut into their sales.

That afternoon Brautigan caught a flight to Denver, connecting to Newark, New Jersey. He spent the night in New York. The next afternoon he boarded a Conrail train at Grand Central Station and traveled up the Hudson to Poughkeepsie. At eight in the evening, Richard read in the Dutchess Hall Theatre at Dutchess Community College as part of its Lyceum Performing Arts Series.

Brautigan was on a commuter plane to La Guardia in the morning, flying on to Chicago that afternoon. He had every reason to be in a good mood. It was the twelfth of November, the date when the final judgment of dissolution of marriage was filed at the San Francisco courthouse. Richard was single again.

At 8:00 pm, Brautigan read in the Ironwood Room at Triton College in River Grove, Illinois (a Chicago suburb). Not only was his audience shrinking, he now appeared at much smaller schools. Triton instead of Northwestern. Not Vassar but Dutchess Community. USM in place of Ole Miss. His lecture fee was $1,500, plus expenses, so he remained well paid, no matter how small the venue or turnout.

The next day Richard signed copies of *The Tokyo–Montana Express* at Barbara's Bookstore in Oak Park (Hemingway's hometown) from noon until one. A couple hours later he was off to Lincoln, Nebraska, for five days in residence at the University of Nebraska. This was not a Lordly & Dame booking but something Brautigan had arranged on his own. Richard stayed at the Hilton Hotel on the edge of Lincoln's rough side. His room looked down on a jesus saves sign.

At 11:00 am on the fourteenth, Brautigan sat in the Nebraska Book Store for two hours, signing copies of his new novel. Several in line with books jokingly referred to him as Mr. Robbins, saying how much they enjoyed his work. Michael Zangari, a student reporter for the *Daily Nebraskan*, the university newspaper, had been assigned to write an interview. After the signing party, they went back to Richard's room at the Hilton. Brautigan talked about Japanese literature and its influence on his work. He said he might go alone to Hong Kong or Haiti (where the Hjortsbergs spent the winters of '78 and '79) to finish a novel he'd been working on for two years.

Richard washed several pairs of underwear in the bathroom sink (just like long-gone Hotel Jessie days), telling Zangari the fast pace of his book tour made laundry service impossible. A long Lincoln layover provided plenty of laundry time, but Brautigan's needs were dire. He couldn't wait a couple days for clean skivvies. Life on the road got lonely, Richard told the young reporter, assuring him that he had a pretty girl waiting in San Francisco.

When cocktail hour rolled around, Brautigan put on a down jacket and his Elmer Fudd hat (he called it his bonnet) and set off with Zangari for the Green Frog, a local bar. Young Michael had "never seen anyone drink like that before, tumbler after tumbler of Jack Daniel's and never got drunk." Richard gave the aspiring writer some sound advice. "Any success in the marketplace is luck," he said. "If you're not enjoying what you're doing, don't do it."

Zangari hosted a midnight show at the student radio station. Brautigan went along with him to the studio but declined to go on the air. Richard spent half the night banging out time on a tabletop to the rock-and-roll sides Michael played. Thirty years later, Zangari still remembered how, walking across campus, Brautigan made him look at a leaf in the snow, calling it one of the prettiest things he had ever seen.

The rigors of the book tour began again on November 16. Richard returned to Chicago from Lincoln in time to catch a 10:15 am flight to Seattle. He arrived at 12:20 and was met at the airport by the assistant director of student activities at Everett Community College, who drove him thirty-five miles north to the waterfront town on Point Gardiner Peninsula. Halfway along, they pulled off I-5 at Lynnwood, heading for the B. Dalton bookstore in the Alderwood Mall, where between 1:00 and 2:30 pm Brautigan signed forty copies of *The Tokyo–Montana Express*.

After meeting with a class in the late afternoon, Brautigan stood before a small student gathering in the Bookstore Conference Room at Everett Community College at 7:30. Richard had his presentation down pat. What to read, what went over, recycled lines that got laughs. Once finished, Richard signed copies of his novel at the college store.

Brautigan climbed back on the merry-go-round around 5:00 the next morning. He stumbled from bed and into his clothes in time for a ride back to Sea-Tac Airport. Richard caught a 7:00 Northwest flight to Missoula, arriving a little after ten. Time for settling in and a leisurely lunch before a scheduled 3:00 book signing at B. Dalton in the Southgate Mall. About thirty-five copies were sold.

This event caused a typhoon in a teapot among local independent booksellers. Their bluster blasted all the way to the Dell/Delacorte offices in New York. Bill Thompson of Lordly & Dame had inserted a clause in Brautigan's contract, giving B. Dalton an exclusive when he read at the University of Montana. Fred Rice, manager of Freddy's Feed and Read in Missoula, was outraged. Freddy's always stocked Richard's books, "since its inception in 1972," and one of the store's founders was Brautigan's good friend (and fellow Dell author) Harmon Henkin, recently killed when his pickup rolled over on I-90 sixty miles east of town in August. Sam Lawrence, trying to calm the waters, suggested "Richard return to Missoula for another book signing party" in January or February 1981.

Brautigan spoke and read at 8:00 pm in the University Center Ballroom at the University of Montana. The crowd was larger than usual this time. After the presentation, the Associated Students' Store sold about thirty-five more copies of *The Tokyo–Montana Express*, all of which Richard signed. Three dozen books seemed the average sold at Brautigan's various signing parties.

At nine the next morning, Richard was off to Denver to do the whole routine all over again. He was met at the airport and driven fifty miles north to Greeley, where he gave an 8:00 pm reading at the University of Northern Colorado, meeting informally with classes during the afternoon. Ed Dorn drove up from Boulder with some of his students to hear his friend's presentation. The next day Brautigan flew down to Little Rock, Arkansas, at noon. A representative from Hendrix College drove him thirty-five miles north to Conway for an 8:00 pm presentation in Staples Auditorium. No book signing parties were scheduled at either venue. It was the only let-up in Richard's schedule.

On Saturday, Brautigan was on a 12:55 pm American flight from Little Rock to La Guardia. Richard decided not to call Masako Kano, just across the East River on Long Island, while he was in the city. She'd been gone from his life for two months, an eternity in the realm of heartbreak. Instead Brautigan made arrangements for Eunice Kitagawa to fly out from San Francisco and meet him for the weekend. Richard booked into a suite in the Gramercy Park Hotel at the bottom end of Lexington Avenue.

Built in 1925, the hotel maintained a shabby elegance, offering spacious quarters at reasonable rates. Like the Mayflower, uptown on Central Park West, it was popular with actors, musicians, and writers. The humorist S. J. Perelman had died in his room there the previous year. Gatz Hjortsberg stayed in the hotel just the month before on his way back from Europe.

Being with Eunice Kitagawa compelled Brautigan to call Masako Kano from the sanctity of his hotel suite bedroom. Stretched on the king-sized bed with Eunice by his side, Richard dialed Professor Turgeon's number on Long Island. Masako was happy to hear from him until she detected a voice in the background. Kano knew it was another woman. The woman was laughing.

"Was she listening in our conversation from the beginning?" Masako demanded.

"Yes," Richard said. "We were listening to you. We're listening from our bedroom."

"Why did you do this to me?" Kano pleaded. "I don't want to talk to you again." Upset, she hung up the phone. Masako didn't communicate with Brautigan until after she returned to Japan.

Kitagawa flew back to San Francisco in time for work when the weekend was over. At 8:00 on Monday evening, November 24, Richard Brautigan read at the Poetry Center of the YMHA. The Y, located at Lexington Avenue and Ninety-second Street, had long enjoyed a reputation as an urban Parnassus. Dylan Thomas had read there to great acclaim during his American tours in the early 1950s. The list of other poetical heavyweights headlining at the YMHA included Robert Frost, T. S. Elliot, and e. e. cummings. In the past six months, Lillian Hellman, Margaret Mead, Allen Ginsberg, Joseph Heller, James Dickey, Ted Hughes, Norman Mailer, Stanley Kunitz, and Jules Feiffer, among many others, had stood at the podium in the Y.

Robert Creeley traveled down from Buffalo with his pregnant third wife, Penelope, to introduce Richard's reading at the YMHA. He thought of the place as "hoary with tradition." Before the reading, Richard, Bob, and Penelope "had a very pleasant meal." Brautigan seemed withdrawn. Creeley felt Richard's reception was not altogether welcome. Bob remembered the crowd as "not a pleasant audience. A very dead audience. It was there to see what [Brautigan] looked like. By no means sympathetic." Richard was tired and the reading did not go over well. Afterward, swarms of people lined up to have books signed. "Every book dealer I knew in the city was there," Creeley recalled. Brautigan dutifully scribbled his crabbed signature in each copy, all the while thinking, "Geez, I've got to get out of here."

Richard's low-key performance stemmed not from lack of enthusiasm. He was coming down with something. By morning Brautigan felt very ill. A book signing party was scheduled at Brentano's on University Place in Greenwich Village for 1:00 pm on the afternoon of the twenty-fifth. Richard felt too sick to make it. His truancy ignited a furor in the Delacorte offices. When someone phoned the hotel, Brautigan's petulant feverish attitude was interpreted as "insecurity and prima donna behavior."

Charles Taliano, the Dell trade sales manager, wrote an indignant letter to Sam Lawrence the same day. "Should another incident arise as what happened in New York this morning, and Brautigan fail to appear for one scheduled autographing, or should he not be on his best behavior," Taliano fumed, "I will recommend to the management of this company that we cancel immediately any further autographing parties at book stores for the duration of his tour."

Richard called Eunice Kitagawa in San Francisco, asking her to come to New York and spend Thanksgiving with him. After work on Wednesday night, she jumped on a plane and flew cross-country for the second time in three days. She traveled first class because all the coach seats were booked. Eunice found Brautigan not feeling well. The next day he didn't want to go out to a restaurant. Ianthe came over to the Gramercy Park Hotel with her boyfriend, Paul Swensen, who also worked at the Roundabout Theater Company, located in a converted movie theater on Twenty-third Street. Their Thanksgiving holiday dinners were ordered up from room service. "Four adults sitting on a bed having turkey," Kitagawa recalled. "How sad."

Brautigan's health improved by the weekend. Norman Mailer invited him to Brooklyn Heights for dinner on Saturday night. Excited by the prospect of meeting the literary giant he'd once used as a fictional character, Richard and Eunice took a cab at the appointed hour over the East River to 142 Columbia Heights. They climbed the stairs in the old brownstone to Mailer's fourth-floor apartment with its crow's nest, catwalks, ship ladders, and an incredible view across the Promenade. At night the lights strung along the Brooklyn Bridge cables and glittering in the dark distant towers of lower Manhattan turned the scenic skyline into an enormous carnival fairyland. Far off in the harbor, bathed in floodlights, the Statue of Liberty glowed like foxfire.

Mailer's place, with its overflowing bookshelves, mismatched furniture, and haphazard collections of mementos and memorabilia, seemed like a more magnificent version of Brautigan's shabby Museum, the sort of palatial pad Richard imagined for himself if his income magically increased one hundred fold. What Brautigan never envisioned, and what most delighted him, was Mailer's role as the happy paterfamilias. His varied brood included nine children from six marriages. They ranged in age from a college girl to his two-year-old son, John Buffalo, whom Mailer bounced happily on his lap.

In recounting the evening much later to Sherry Vetter, Richard "thought that was so incredible that the family life was so beautiful and that the kids loved each other." Little John Buffalo's mother was Mailer's sixth wife, Norris Church, a portrait painter, fashion model, and former high school art teacher, much closer in age to some of her husband's adolescent children. Born Barbara Jean Davis in Arkansas, she reinvented herself when she moved to New York in 1976 to live with Norman. He came up with the name Church. She appropriated Norris, her former spouse's last name. Norman and Norris were very recently wed. Mailer had just married his fifth wife, jazz singer Carol Stevens, in Haiti on November 9, to legitimize the birth of their daughter, divorcing her the next day.

The evening went well. Mailer was intrigued by a blue cloth wallet with Velcro fasteners that Brautigan had recently purchased. Richard gave it to him. Norman reciprocated by gifting Richard a bottle of Moët et Chandon champagne. Mailer "thought it quite heroic" that Kitagawa would fly coast-to-coast twice in a single week to be with her man. Before the couple left and returned to Manhattan, Mailer autographed the label, signing it, "To Eunice and Richard from Norman Mailer."

Kitagawa flew back to San Francisco the next day with the champagne bottle in her carry-on. Between eight and nine that night, Spencer Vibbert, a reporter from the *Boston Globe,* came to Brautigan's hotel room to interview him. Richard was flying to Boston the following evening, and Vibbert wanted a story for Tuesday's morning edition.

At 10:45 Monday morning on the first of December, Brautigan stepped off the elevator on the thirty-fourth floor into the offices of the Canadian Broadcasting Corporation at 125 Park Avenue. Fifteen minutes later, Richard sat in a CBC studio taping a telephone interview with David Cole for his "slightly surreal" radio series *Here Come the Seventies.*

After a break for lunch, Brautigan was over on the West Side at the ABC Radio studios on the fifth floor of 1926 Broadway. At 2:00 pm he taped a fifteen-minute interview with newsman Gil Fox. After 2:30, Richard was on his own. He had an open ticket on the Boston shuttle and was free to make his own reservation. Once he arrived later that evening, Brautigan checked into the historic Ritz-Carlton Hotel in the heart of the Back Bay. Winston Churchill and JFK had both been guests of the hotel overlooking Boston Public Garden.

After a late breakfast in the hotel, Richard met with Joe Fisher, a reporter for the *Toronto Sun,* for an interview at 1:00 pm. They talked in Brautigan's room. At eight that night, Richard gave a reading in the offices of the *Harvard Advocate,* the oldest continuously published college literary magazine in the nation, whose past undergraduate editors and contributors included Malcolm Cowley, Conrad Aiken, Wallace Stevens, e. e. cummings, James Agee, Leonard Bernstein, and T. S. Eliot. Brautigan's Harvard appearance was not booked by Lordly & Dame. He arranged the details himself. Consequently, he received only $80 plus the cost of his lodging.

At 8:15 the next morning, Brautigan was on an American flight to Detroit on his way to the University of Toledo in Ohio. He had been advised by his sponsor that this route was more convenient than using the Toledo Airport. Richard's 8:00 pm appearance had been arranged by the Toledo Poets Center Arts Council. Brautigan's contract specified: "Poet will be available for an afternoon informal activity, travel permitting." He received his standard $1,500 fee and was on his way back to San Francisco at 2:45 pm the next day, flying nonstop on United from Detroit.

Brautigan moved in with Eunice Kitagawa once he returned to the city. Her Vallejo Street apartment was convenient, close to both Enrico's and his new office above Vesuvio. After a grueling month on the road, alone in hotel rooms almost every night, a solitary stay at the Kyoto Inn lost its appeal. He felt exhausted. Brautigan believed his tour had been successful. That's what he told Keith Abbott in Enrico's one afternoon after getting back to Frisco. The bar provided familiar company and a place to recharge his energy. "Apropos of nothing," Richard turned to Keith and said, "You know, there are two people I wouldn't ever fight: you and Tom McGuane."

Abbott realized his old friend had been thinking about the possibilities of an altercation. "Richard had been exhibiting such contrary and contradictry behavior that I knew it was only a matter of time." Unnerved and feeling sad, Keith got up and walked out of Enrico's, the end of an eighteen-year friendship.

Cash poor after his divorce, Richard faced a year's worth of $1,400 monthly spousal support payments to Akiko. He'd earned $1,500 for each of eleven college appearances, but after Lordly & Dame's commission, the total fell short of what he needed. Healthy sales figures for *The Tokyo–Montana Express* remained Brautigan's best hope. When he picked up the bundle of mail waiting in his tiny office, batches of clipped reviews were of particular interest.

In the *Chronicle Review*, Don Carpenter called Brautigan "a great writer," going on to say, "Not since Ernest Hemingway has anyone paid so much attention to the American sentence. [. . .] 'The Tokyo–Montana Express' is Brautigan writing at the peak of his powers." In the *Santa Barbara News & Review*, Tom Clark, another old acquaintance, called *Tokyo–Montana* "a train that travels faster than the speed of light—at the speed of mind, in fact."

Other reviewers weren't quite so enthusiastic. Writing in the *New York Times Book Review*, Barry Yougrau dismissed Brautigan: "[His] instrument is the penny whistle. So either he's trilling cutely [. . .] or he's tweeting melancholically under the bedclothes. [. . .] [His] frail pipings are only random marginalia, quotes without a context." Darryl Ponicsan (*The Last Detail; Cinderella Liberty*) came down even harder in the *Los Angeles Times Book Review*. "The best that can be said for these wee snippets is that they are harmless and inoffensive, occasionally even cute," he wrote. "The worst that can be said [. . .] The writings are probably too lightweight to register on even the most aerated of consciousnesses."

By the end of the year, the first sales reports were in. *The Tokyo–Montana Express* had sold twenty-seven thousand copies in hardcover. With royalties of $44,374 (plus $5,000 from the Quality Paperback Club), Brautigan had more than earned out his Delacorte advance. To celebrate, Richard took Eunice on a trip to Mendocino over Christmas. He failed to make restaurant reservations, and after "waiting forever for a table," they ended up heating two servings of Cup O' Noodles in their motel room microwave for Christmas dinner. "Typical," Kitagawa observed.

fifty-four: shinola

SEEKING GREATER PRIVACY for his love nest on wheels, Dick Dillof asked Marian Hjortsberg if he might park the sheepherder's wagon on her property, out of sight across Pine Creek below the house. She immediately consented, liking Dick and finding him agreeable company. When Richard Brautigan learned of this arrangement, he stormed over to his neighbor's place to protest. "I don't want to smell Dobro shit all day long."

Marian assured him the wagon would be too far away for anyone to sniff out Dick's presence. Besides, Dobro would doubtless use the bathroom facilities at her house or up at the store. In the end Richard relented. Brautigan liked Dillof, and there was nothing he could do about it in any case. He thought of Dick as his younger "little buddy." Having emerged from a bitter divorce, Richard enjoyed regaling Dick with horror stories of love gone wrong. Sometimes he'd appear outside the wagon window, comically pleading, "Dobie, throw me your sexual scraps."

A confirmed practical joker, Brautigan manifested his affection for Dobro Dick by playing elaborate tricks on him. Counting coup, he called it.

"Counting pickled turkey gizzards" was Dillof's assessment, recalling an afternoon at the Eagles in Bozeman when Richard slipped a pickled turkey gizzard (a curious bar snack favored by two-fisted Montana drunks) into his glass of ginger ale when he wasn't looking. Everyone sat around waiting to see Dick drink it.

Perhaps the most *beau coup* of all occurred when Dick arranged an important date with an attractive coed from MSU that Brautigan had also been eyeing. Richard came across the pair in Martin's Café. Dillof mentioned he planned on bringing the girl to visit his wagon the next day. "How nice," Brautigan said with the straightest possible face. "Dobie's going to show you his wagon."

Dillof skillfully arranged his camp like a stage set, creating the atmosphere Richard called "quaint bait." Every detail looked straight out of a vintage L. A. Huffman photograph. A tin cowboy bathtub sat next to the campfire. Cast-iron skillets and Dutch ovens stood scoured and neatly stacked. An ax stuck at a rakish angle out of a log. Eager to create a wholesome initial impression, Dick did his laundry that morning, hanging a half dozen pairs of snow-white boxer shorts to dry on a clothesline in the bright spring sunshine, vivid proof that a guy who lived in a sheepherder's wagon need not be some musty old codger who never bathed or changed his underwear.

When Dick drove over the Bozeman Pass to pick up his date, Richard Brautigan snuck down through cottonwoods behind his house, a can of brown shoe polish in hand. Dillof's camp was deserted, not a soul in sight. With the artistic flair of a frontier Rembrandt, Brautigan dabbed a realistic stain down the backside of each pair of boxer shorts. By and by, Dick reappeared, guiding his intended by the hand through the green meadow grass toward his romantic campsite. There to greet them, flapping in the breeze like soiled flags of surrender, the besmirched undies could not be denied, dead rats rotting atop a lemon meringue pie.

The sweet young thing pretended not to notice the unsanitary display. Dick wisely herded her straight into the wagon. They sat side by side on the bed as he proceeded to show her some of his scratchboard sketches. Turning over the third or fourth drawing, he uncovered a neatly folded set of instructions for Kwell Shampoo, profusely illustrated with pictures of prancing body lice. Beneath the bold caption kills the crab louse on contact, Brautigan had carefully printed, "Directions for Mr. Dillof." The last dim hope of romance faded. "She suddenly remembered, or *pretended* to remember some chores she'd forgotten about," Dick wrote. "The date was over. Sabotaged."

Later that week, Richard invited Dick to dinner, and he discovered a can of brown Shinola on Brautigan's coffee table. No mention was made of shoe polish or the aborted date until the food was served. Years later, Dobro Dick Dillof set down their subsequent conversation in a brief unpublished memoir:

"So," he said, dumping pasta on my plate. "How was the wagon tour?"

"Splendid," I said.

"Splendid," he repeated with the faintest grin under his mandarin mustache. "I'm glad for you."

We ate, toasting our friendship. Nothing was ever said of the Shinola.

fifty-five: blowing in the wind

THE START OF 1981 found Richard Brautigan in a financial bind. His first *Tokyo–Montana Express* royalty payment wasn't due until June and big bills kept rolling in. On the first of January, Richard sent a $1,400 support check to his ex-wife. He deliberately made it out to her maiden name, "Akiko Nishizawa," emphasizing that they were no longer married, while she endorsed the back as "Akiko Brautigan," rubbing his nose in her continuing capitalization on his famous name. Along with other expenses, Brautigan wrote a $3,255 check to Joel Shawn's law firm on the twelfth. Anticipating more debt, early in the month Richard sent Helen Brann the first forty pages of his revisions of *The Pond People of America*, retitled *So the Wind Won't Blow It All Away*. Richard had written very little on the project prior to his divorce, not wanting the novel to become part of his settlement with Aki.

Brann found the opening pages "very strong" and sent them on to Sam Lawrence, asking to negotiate a new contract as soon as he read the manuscript. Lawrence wasted no time getting down to business. He thought Richard's book was both "beautiful and evocative," believing it might "prove to be one of the finest things he will ever do." Helen Brann asked for a $50,000 advance, half payable on signing.

Sam took these numbers up with the Dell hierarchy on January 15, sending Brautigan a telegram the same day. "What a beautiful childhood memoir," Lawrence enthused, "may it go on and on." Not knowing where to find his author, he wired it in care of Richard Hodge.

Negotiations with Helen Brann proceeded swiftly, and by the twenty-third they had worked out the details. The advance would be $45,000, half up front. All the other terms would be identical to the *Tokyo–Montana* contract. Richard assured his agent that he would finish a final draft "within the next two months." Brann confirmed this potential delivery date with Lawrence. The final Delacorte contract was dated February 18, 1981, and duly signed by all parties within a few days.

Brautigan never let his short-term fiscal problems interfere with his social life at Enrico's, Cho-Cho, Specs', and the Washbag. He made no move to economize aside from moving into Eunice Kitagawa's place on occasion or sleeping on a twin bed in his narrow office above Vesuvio, where he collected his mail. Feeling a bit more flush once the first half of the Dell advance arrived, he booked a room at the Kyoto Inn whenever he wanted the comforting anonymity of a hotel.

Marian Hjortsberg and her sister, Roz Mina, were in town to escape the harsh Montana winter. Richard did his best to show them a good time. This meant frequent drinks at Enrico's. One afternoon he asked the sisters to a barbecue at Nikki Arai's apartment on Windsor Place after they finished "trucking around the city." Don Carpenter had also been invited. By the time Marian and

Roz got there, "everyone was very drunk." The boisterous drinking continued into the night. At one point, Carpenter and Brautigan began arguing over "who was a better writer."

The disagreement escalated into a physical fight. Richard and Don grappled on Nikki's back balcony. It looked to Marian like Brautigan was about to push his old friend over the railing. The women "sort of galvanized" themselves and broke it up. Being most sober, Roz was delegated to drive Don Carpenter home to Mill Valley in Marian's VW Rabbit. "I was too drunk to fuck her, but I had to ask anyway because I figured she'd be insulted if I didn't," Carpenter recalled. "So I did, and she laughed and said, 'Thank you for the offer but no.'"

Richard told Eunice about his altercation with Don. He "was remorseful after the fact," she said. "Very much like him." Brautigan introduced Marian Hjortsberg to David Fechheimer not long after the incident at Nikki Arai's. The private detective and the admiral's witty daughter hit it off right from the start. One evening they went up to Kitagawa's place on Vallejo Street with Roz for a quesadilla dinner. Another night the trio started out at Cho-Cho drinking Calvados with Richard. They all got plastered. "I was just drunk enough to walk," Fechheimer remembered, "and we decided to go up to Enrico's."

Crossing Broadway, a baby blue Cadillac brushed against David. Acting with the incautious instincts of the inebriated, he banged his hand against the car and spat at the driver. "A big mistake," Fechheimer recalled. About two minutes after they had all settled in at the bar, David was pulled from his stool by four angry Chinese gang members, not pleased at being disrespected by this bearded white guy. Before coming around to face the intruders, Ward Dunham told Marian to get in the bathroom and lock the door.

Marian did as instructed. She heard a lot of scuffling outside as Ward and the other bartender sent the Chinamen "flying through the door." Within five minutes, the rest of the tong, "a hundred Chinese guys with guns, weapons, knives," lined the sidewalk in front of Enrico's. "Like in a movie," Fechheimer observed. The cook came running in from the kitchen. "They're out back too," he cried.

"I know what to do," David said. He picked up the bar phone, dialed 911, and demanded to be arrested. It took three squad cars to get the soused private eye out of the bar. They booked him into Central District Police Station a few blocks away in North Beach. While Marian, Roz, and Eunice scrambled about the neighborhood trying to raise bail money, Brautigan went down to Central Station with a book of his stories and sat outside his friend's cell all night long reading to him. "He stuck it out with me until six in the morning," Fechheimer recalled.

Attracted to dangerous characters with an edge, Marian soon became romantically involved with David. He invited her on a trip to Africa. Fechheimer wanted to retrace his youthful *Wanderjahr* across Kenya and knew from Marian's own tales of third world adventures that she was unafraid of hard travel. Preparing for the journey, Marian asked her estranged husband to take care of their two children. At the end of January, Hjortsberg, along with his girlfriend and her young son, moved back into the spacious old house at Pine Creek.

Gatz and Peter Fonda were both born on February 23, albeit a year apart. The Pine Creek place was perfect for parties, with large rooms flowing one into the other, allowing for easy circulation. It made sense to host a shared birthday celebration. About sixty people showed up on the night of Saturday the twenty-first. The impromptu guest list included the Fondas, Jeff and Sue Bridges, Tim Cahill, singer-songwriter Kostas, Dick Dillof, and Phil White Hawk, a Native American musician.

An antique upright piano stood in an alcove off the main living room. With so many musicians in attendance, it became the center of the action. Jeff and Peter uncased their guitars and got into the jam. War correspondent Philip Caputo, recovering from a wound received in Beirut, heard the commotion from his cabin at the Pine Creek Lodge—where he worked on the longhand legal-pad first draft of what would become his bestseller, *A Rumor of War*—and crashed the party. Phil was made welcome and left in the early hours with a long list of new friends.

Another set of party-crashers from the lodge wasn't quite so welcome. The new owners had a pair of wild teenage daughters. Away for a short vacation, the owners left the girls in the care of their easygoing grandmother. Not long after dark, the sisters showed up with a group of high school kids. Gatz told them it was an adults-only party and no minors would be served. They left, but not before stealing a case of beer cooling on the porch.

The next morning, the mother of one of the town kids phoned to thank Hjortsberg for giving her son such a wonderful house present. He didn't know what she was talking about. "You know, that lovely silver tray," she said. "You told him he could go down to your big red barn and take anything he wanted." Puzzled, Gatz hung up and went to his barn to check things out, thinking the teens might have used the place for an orgy of their own. Everything looked just the same, without any sign of disturbance.

The bit about the silver tray troubled him, nagging through the fuzzy hangover fog. It dawned on Hjortsberg that his neighbor Richard had an even bigger red barn than he did. Nursing his third cup of black coffee, Gatz trudged down the frozen road to Brautigan's place. He slid the barn door open on its overhead trolley and stepped into the dim cavernous space. Hjortsberg's worst fears were confirmed. The place had been vandalized.

Discarded beer cans and empty bottles lay scattered across the wide-planked floor. Old tools and farm equipment, not used by Richard but much treasured by him, had been abused and tossed about like junk. Worst of all, White Acre, Brautigan's beloved Plymouth Fury, backed inside for the winter, had graffiti spray-painted across its roof and sides. A six-foot length of two-inch pipe had been thrust through the hood like a spear. Looking in at the engine, Gatz found all the spark-plug wires ripped free, the carburetor and distributor missing.

Wandering about the trashed barn in numb disbelief, Hjortsberg came across a stack of cardboard shipping cartons in the far corner. Most had been torn open, disemboweled of their contents. Tom and Cindy Olson were selling their log home in the subdivision behind Brautigan's spread, and he had let them store their things in his barn until they found a new place. Gatz had discovered the mother lode that yielded the purloined silver tray.

Not knowing where to find Richard and assuming he might be off in Japan, Gatz's first furious instinct was to call the sheriff. But because the girls' parents were friends and neighbors, he phoned the grandmother. When Hjortsberg told her he planned to get the law involved, she begged him to wait. She would have her granddaughters contact all the kids involved and convene a meeting at the Pine Creek Lodge. Gatz gave her twenty-four hours.

The next evening, Hjortsberg stood in a small living room crowded with sullen seated delinquents. He excoriated his unhappy audience, telling the teenagers they all belonged in jail, assuring them that was exactly where they'd find themselves should Richard Brautigan ever learn of their crime. The only way to avoid the clink, Gatz said, was to clean up the barn, restore Brautigan's car to its original condition, and return the stolen items. All the kids agreed to cooperate.

A day later, Hjortsberg met with Tom and Cindy Olson in Richard's barn to inspect the pile of returned loot. After checking things over, they agreed everything was there, deciding to move all their stuff to a safer location. Gatz had a quick look around after the Olsens left. Things were off to a fast start. Cans, bottles, and trash had been cleaned up. The old tools all hung back in place. Best of all, the Plymouth Fury had been scrubbed clean of graffiti, and the impaling pipe had been removed. The teen contingent swore that among their peers were skilled mechanics who would have the car running like new in no time. Hjorstberg said that was fine as long as it got done before Richard returned.

Brautigan was not all that far away at the time, traveling back to Boulder on Friday the thirteenth for a couple weeks in February. He stayed once again at the Hotel Boulderado, getting together with Ed and Jenny Dorn, hanging out in their kitchen like always. Dick Dillof was also in town, visiting the Dorns and performing. Afternoons, Dick played on Pearl Street to a small pedestrian crowd. He looked up and saw "a tall, gangly stork-like man" weave through the gathering with a bag of peanuts. No one knew who he was. Dillof didn't let on it was Brautigan.

Deadpan, Richard unzipped Dick's fly, placing an unshelled peanut in his crotch. He closed the zipper so that the peanut protruded from his pants. Next, Brautigan stuck peanuts into Dillof's right nostril, one of his ears, and the hole in his hat. To finish things off, a peanut was inserted into the dobro's resonator. "Sir," Richard said archly, drifting back into the sidewalk audience without another word.

Later they got together, "happy to see each other," and spent the evening "roaming around town and carousing." A book of short stories about Dick's adventures hopping freights and riding the rails was soon to be published. A paperback original, *Hobo* was released by Tower Books in 1981, with the author listed as Richard Dillof, "known on the road as Rattlesnake Dick." Dillof hoped that Brautigan, in spite of his stunts, would be enthusiastic and encouraging about the project.

Seated in a café discussing literature, Richard called "good and loud so everyone can hear" to a pretty waitress passing their table, "A drink for my friend." The waitress paused. "One Shirley Temple for my friend," Brautigan ordered, ending any chance for further lit talk with Dillof. "Strong with the Shirley. Hold the Temple."

Richard checked out of the Boulderado on February 24. On his way back to San Francisco, he detoured to Bozeman for a few days and hung out with Greg Keeler. He made no attempt to contact Gatz Hjortsberg during his brief Montana stopover. Keeler invited Brautigan to take over his evening contemporary poetry class for a one-time guest appearance. Greg had never seen his friend teach before. Scanning the room for pretty women, Richard spoke of the influences on his poetry and "talked about how he saw various movements in American writing," themes honed to perfection on his recent book tour. Greg thought "he was good. [. . .] The class hung on every word." Keeler knew he had never held his students' attention like that, a fact perhaps not lost on the acting head of the English Department, who sat in on Brautigan's lecture and "loved it."

Around the same time, in the beginning of March, Marian Hjortsberg came back to Montana from Africa. Gatz packed up his familiar third-floor Pine Creek studio for the last time, hauling his typewriter and works in progress to his office in exile, rented rooms on a hill above the Livingston railroad yard. Adrift again in Frisco, Brautigan experienced a similar displacement. Home was where he hung his hat, some nights at Eunice Kitagawa's apartment, others in his cramped rented office on Broadway. By the middle of April, Richard had moved into the Kyoto Inn for an extended stay.

The energy generated by Brautigan's recent book tour attracted the attention of *People* magazine. They assigned writer Cheryl McCall, who had written the story on the Montana lit/art scene a few months before, to put together a piece on Richard. Roger Ressmeyer, a San Francisco photographer since his graduation from Yale in 1975, known for his work with celebrities (rock stars, politician, musicians, writers), was the editors' choice to handle the camera work. From conversations with Richard, McCall became fascinated with his eccentric inability to drive a car. She decided to build the story around Brautigan's distaste for automobiles, piecing together bits of their extended tape-recorded interviews into an as-told-to mini–memoir.

The day of the vernal equinox, following a formal portrait session, mostly head-and-shoulder shots, Ressmeyer took a number of impromptu pictures on the autophobia theme. Several involved Richard being hauled around Frisco in a rickshaw by his sturdy friend Dwain Cox, cable cars, Alcatraz, and the Golden Gate Bridge variously in the background. An abandoned railroad siding provided another location, Brautigan wandering like a hobo with his knapsack. In a lighthearted moment, Richard executed a jumping jack of joy in an automobile graveyard.

Another idea was to stage a literary gathering and invite a bunch of Brautigan's old writer buddies. City Lights wasn't interested, so Enrico's became the obvious choice. *People* put the word out, hoping to draw about two hundred people. Curt Gentry figured he couldn't make it, as something else had come up. Don Carpenter called his home from the bar at the last minute. "You've got to get down here," Don pleaded. "No one showed up."

"Richard was having problems," Gentry observed. "Michael McClure didn't want to have anything to do with [him]." Curt headed loyally down to the Broadway café, where he sat at a sidewalk table drinking and swapping stories with Brautigan, Don Carpenter, and last-minute stand-in Enrico Banducci while Ressmeyer snapped pictures. A quality of artificially induced merriment pervaded these images. Out of all Richard's purported friends through the decades, only two took the trouble to help out when he needed them.

Ressmeyer also shot a roll of film in Brautigan's narrow studio above Vesuvio, capturing him in a black Hotel Boulderado T-shirt, lobbing crumpled paper hook shots at a distant wicker wastebasket, and working at his electric typewriter by the tall lone window. The project occupying Richard's creative time was *So the Wind Won't Blow It All Away*, the melancholy novel about his youth in the Pacific Northwest.

With a central theme focused on the accidental shooting death of his ninth-grade classmate Donald Husband, Brautigan threw all the other ingredients from his hardscrabble childhood into the mix: poverty, an indifferent mother, living above a mortuary, fishing the neighborhood logging ponds, jigging for frogs, early entrepreneurial efforts: collecting discarded beer bottles with his wicker baby buggy and selling night crawlers to gas stations. Everything from his past that Richard had long refused to discuss, even with his closest friends, he now resurrected as fiction.

Sometime around the middle of April, the grandmother looking after things at the Pine Creek Lodge phoned Gatz Hjortsberg to say all was well: the teenage mechanics had Brautigan's car running like new. Pleased, Gatz nonetheless thought it best to drive to Paradise Valley for a firsthand look. The moment he stepped inside Richard's barn, Hjortsberg knew that even if White Acre's engine revved up like a drag racer at the starting line, it wouldn't do the trick. The kids had replaced the punctured Plymouth Fury hood with one they found at an auto junkyard. The secondhand part came from the appropriate year. It fit perfectly. Just one problem remained. The hood was blue.

The next night, Gatz convened another teen culprit meeting at the lodge. He told them they'd done a great job and had nearly wiped the slate clean of all wrongdoing, but he warned that the replacement hood would never fly. Brautigan wasn't color-blind. If his car didn't start, it was no big deal. Junkers don't do well sitting idle through long Montana winters. But there was no denying a hood of a different color. Hjortsberg cautioned that Richard would be back by summer, no telling just when. If they didn't get the Plymouth repainted white before his arrival, the jig was up. All their hard work would mean nothing. An outraged Brautigan might even call the cops. The teenagers promised to take care of the problem.

Around the same time, Richard Brautigan worked with his ballpoint pen in his North Beach office, worrying various drafts of a brief précis of his growing novel on torn scraps of paper. He came up with: "So the Wind Won't Blow It All Away is an American tragedy that takes place in the 1940's. It remembers the independence and dignity of a small group of people whose life-style was already doomed, even as they lived it, thinking that it would go on forever. The first television antenna on an American house was their tombstone." He sent a copy to Helen Brann. She mailed it to Seymour Lawrence at the end of April.

On April 23 Brautigan settled his tab at Enrico's with a check for $500. He paid the Kyoto Inn $439.51 on Friday, May 8, squaring his account in preparation to depart for Montana. Richard changed his mind at the last minute and stayed on at the hotel through Saturday night. He arrived back in Montana that Sunday, stocking up his larder the next day with $70 worth of groceries at the Livingston Safeway.

With a book to finish, Brautigan didn't wait long before heading to his studio in the barn. The surprise sight of a blue hood on his white Plymouth struck with the force of one of his own disjointed metaphors. Richard wasted no time getting in touch with Gatz to demand an explanation. When Hjortsberg told him what happened, Brautigan flew into a furious sputtering rage.

"Why didn't you call me?" Richard fumed. Gatz said he didn't know where to find him. He could have been anywhere. The whole idea had been to simplify the situation. It was all about neighbors. Pine Creek Lodge being part of the local community, Hjortsberg hoped to take care of the whole mess without getting Brautigan involved. Richard had returned to find the cleanup completed and all the Olsons' stolen property returned. Repainting White Acre was in the works. Brautigan had nothing to worry about.

Gatz felt he had handled the incident well and perhaps deserved some faint praise. He'd devoted hours of his own time to orchestrating the project. Instead, Richard grew more and more strident, lecturing his friend like an insane school principal. "There are two kinds of delinquents," he ranted, beginning a long tedious reprimand, "juvenile delinquents and adult delinquents. Juvenile delinquents vandalize private property. Adult delinquents shirk their responsibilities."

And so it went, on and on, Brautigan tracking on the subject of "adult delinquency." Hjortsberg swallowed his pride and took the whole onslaught without further protest. When Richard sputtered to a conclusion, Gatz apologized profusely, hoping he'd heard the end of it. He never imagined what was still to come.

Over the next several weeks, Hjortsberg was awakened repeatedly by late-night calls from a raving, drunken Brautigan. The inebriated message remained the same, delivered in an almost incomprehensible stutter. "Ad-d-d-dult . . . d-d-d-delinq-q-q-quency," Richard stammered into the phone, repeating his boozy mantra again and again. Four in the morning became Brautigan's hour of choice to deliver his carbon-copy message. Finally Gatz had enough. "Richard," he yelled, "don't ever call me anymore! I never want to hear your voice again as long as I live!" He slammed down the receiver for emphasis.

Hjortsberg wasn't the only one hearing about delinquency that summer. Greg Keeler wrote of sitting with Richard on his back porch listening to "long painful discussions" about "the teenagers who had 'vandalized' his barn." Marian Hjortsberg got an earful when she drank wine with Brautigan in the evenings. He also griped about his divorce. Agriculture provided a diversion. Richard announced that he planned to put in a garden over at his place.

Marian said she'd gladly help get things started. She already tended a big garden of her own and told him, "I can't come over and weed."

"I don't want you to," Brautigan said. "I want to get it in and have a stand. I want to have a vegetable stand right on the road in August."

"What're you going to plant?" Marian asked.

"I'm going to plant onions and potatoes."

"How come nothing else?"

"Because, I just want spuds," Richard told her. "And the sign is going to read richard's alimony spuds, and I'm going to go out there and sell spuds to passersby."

"We used to talk about alimony spuds all summer," Marian recalled. "He never weeded the garden, of course. The grasshoppers came, and they ate the tops off even the onions." David Fechheimer got most of the crop. He kept the gift potatoes in a burlap sack in the freezer of his San Francisco home. On an attached tag, Brautigan wrote, "Richard Brautigan's Montana Spuds." To commemorate David's recent adventure with Marian, Richard added these words: "They've gone to Africa and traveled together and traveled in style."

One Saturday in early June, Richard went out on the town, starting at the Wrangler, where he drank up $50 before moving on to the Sport for dinner and more booze. Another $100 later, he felt no pain, his handwriting reduced to a wavering sprawl. On such nights, being not willing to drive became Brautigan's greatest gift to the world.

The article in *People*, "A Happy but Footsore Writer Celebrates His Driver's Block," appeared in the "Coping" section on the eighth of June. The byline read, "By Richard Brautigan." A short introduction mentioned that the story stemmed from a "conversation with" senior editor Cheryl McCall and referred to Brautigan's monthlong book tour as "four months of campus-hopping," perpetuating another of Richard's elaborations.

As late spring moved into the full dazzle of summer, Brautigan kept busy working on his novel. He'd missed his deadline by three months but was not bothered by being late. Richard cared more about seeking perfection than the tantalizing second half of his advance. He wanted to get this painful quasi memoir of his youth just right and worried over every word and sentence. His social life continued as always: bingeing in town, barbecues at the homes of friends, hanging out with Greg Keeler. Ianthe had gotten engaged to Paul Swensen. For reasons he never explained, Brautigan didn't care for the young man.

One afternoon, talking with Ianthe's fiancé on the phone, Richard motioned Greg Keeler over. "Here's a big local bruiser," he said. "Tell this guy what you're going to do to him if he doesn't treat my daughter right." Brautigan handed the receiver to Keeler, who "gave the poor kid some sort of macho bullshit." On reflection, Greg felt happy that Ianthe and Paul "both seemed to be good sports about antics like that."

Eunice Kitagawa came out to Montana for a two-week visit in July. Brautigan introduced her to Keeler and the Donovans. She and Greg hit it off right away and maintained a casual correspondence after Richard's death. Greg found Eunice, "of all of Richard's female companions [. . .] the easiest to get along with." Brad and Georgia also "liked her a lot." Greg thought Eunice "was so kind and considerate," a good thing for Richard.

Richard taught Eunice to fly-fish during her short stay. He and Kitagawa also drove down to Yellowstone Park (she did the driving), looping around through Old Faithful and the West Entrance to return by way of Gallatin Canyon, with a dinner stop in Bozeman. Other than this excursion and a couple fishing trips, Eunice remembered they "basically did nothing." According to a mutual friend, "Richard liked [Eunice] but he wasn't sexually attracted to her, so he wanted her to do the housework and have Masako come be the fuck thang."

Brautigan's fantasies of an Asian harem tending his every physical and emotional need remained a remote pipe dream. The immediate reality of everyday life contradicted his wild imaginings. Brautigan cooked his meals and did his own housecleaning. Most nights he was home alone, slumped on the couch in front of his TV. Richard spent his days by himself as well, forging his art in solitude, as all writers do. For company there was always Greg Keeler, usually available for the price of a phone call. And the bars of Livingston were only a cab ride away. In mid-August Sam Lawrence stopped off in Montana. On the night of the thirteenth, Russell Chatham hosted a dinner party at his place at the upper end of Deep Creek Road. Gatz Hjortsberg came, bearing a bottle of wine. He and Brautigan maintained a cordial, if distant, formality.

Unexpected phone calls offered an enticing change of pace. On a morning at the end of August, Mike Art phoned Brautigan from Chico Hot Springs. He said Rip Torn was staying at the resort with his twin sons and wanted to get together. Richard hadn't seen Rip in a decade, not since the weekend in Westport with its surfeit of middle-class suburban comfort. Troubled by the long estrangement, Torn asked Art to serve as his go-between. Rip had just finished filming *Jinxed!* for director Don Siegel.

Richard said he'd be there for drinks and dinner. He promptly called Greg Keeler, asking him to come on over and "bring Dickel." To sweeten the deal, Brautigan told Keeler they'd be going to Chico in the evening to meet Rip Torn. Four hours later, after Dickel was gone, Richard and Greg "stumbled" to Keeler's car and drove south down the valley to the hot springs. Rip and his boys waited for them in the dining room. Brautigan had last seen Tony and Jon when they were little kids. He was "tickled" to encounter them again as teenagers, beefed up from a summer of hard work on Joe Sedgwick's Big Elk Creek Ranch north of Two Dot, Montana. "I like these boys," Richard said. "I liked them when they were tykes, and I like 'em now."

Keeler observed an initial friction between Rip and Richard. They were like duelists, with cognac selected as the weapon of choice. "Two or three fifths" were consumed, the teens drinking right along with the adults and "the old hackles settled." Without quite meaning to, Greg got stuck "buying most of the drinks." He complemented Torn on his role in *Heartland* (1979), a well-received film about a homesteader and his mail-order bride, made in Montana for under a million dollars. Rip appeared "appropriately modest," telling a long story about the false teeth he had to wear to play Richard Nixon in a TV drama. He also said that Robert Redford was "maybe going to start a playhouse in Paradise Valley," a subject of profound interest to the actor.

At some point during the drink-a-thon dinner, Torn and Brautigan traded hats. Rip exchanged the black cap with a cat logo on the front that he'd worn in *Jinxed!* for Richard's blue Elmer Fudd lid. After the swap, Tony Torn got sick. The boy retreated to Rip's rental station wagon to sleep it off. Richard suggested a walk in the cool night air might clear their heads. Strolling down the gravel road, Brautigan called out to the surviving twin, "Hey, Jon, can you catch?"

Jon, famous as the family fumbler, replied, "Okay, sure," and Brautigan spiraled a brandy bottle across the road. Jon caught it one-handed, hugging the precious cognac to his chest. Everybody cheered. Driving Richard home at 2:30 am, Greg Keeler realized it was his wedding anniversary. In a deep funk, he careened "screaming" over Trail Creek Road to Bozeman and made his feeble apologies to his wife. It was the last time Greg ever drove home drunk from Richard's place.

Ten days later, the "Poets and Other Strangers" group from Bozeman staged another reading at Chico Hot Springs. Richard had originally agreed to participate, but when they printed his name on a bunch of posters without permission, Brautigan "went ape shit." He blamed it all on Greg Keeler. Reprimanded, Keeler phoned the reading's organizers, asking them to print a retraction in the *Bozeman Chronicle,* per Richard's request. One of the other poets called Greg "a spineless sack of pus." Nevertheless, he read with the rest on the thirtieth. Brautigan did not join them at Chico.

Around the same time, Richard got word from Eunice Kitagawa that she was returning home to Honolulu to work in her mother's restaurant. She didn't want this to end their friendship and hoped they might still get together occasionally in spite of the distance. Eunice was not adverse to long plane rides, reminding Brautigan of her two trips to New York during Thanksgiving week the year before.

Soon after, Ianthe called to say she planned to marry Paul Swensen, hoping for her father's blessing. Richard disapproved of their union and told her so. He also said he wanted her to be happy. After hanging up, Brautigan felt "squeezed dry," like "he had crossed one of the saddest bridges" in his life. A week later, up in his barn studio, Richard wrote a story about his feelings. His first title, "The Death of My Name," was crossed out. After another false try, he came up with "My Name Forgotten in the Grass."

Brautigan's typescript consisted of a single brief paragraph. "She is my only daughter," he wrote, "and the end of my family name. [. . .] My name became the shadow of an old deer bone cast among the green grass that once knew its name." Richard struck out the end of the last sentence, rewriting in pencil: "the green grass that doesn't know its name." When Ianthe phoned her father back, inviting him to the ceremony, set for Saturday, September 5, in New York, Brautigan said, "I'll come to your next wedding." They didn't speak again for eight months.

The Monday after his daughter got married, Richard mailed a finished copy of *So the Wind Won't Blow It All Away* to his agent in New York. Before submitting it, he gave a copy of the manuscript to Marian Hjortsberg for proofreading. Brautigan wanted her to "check the spelling." At that time, he "formally" told Marian that he planned to dedicate the novel to her and Becky Fonda. That Wednesday, Helen Brann shipped the book to Seymour Lawrence in Boston, calling it "a superlative example of Brautigan at his best." In a PS, Helen wrote that Richard preferred to wait a year before the publication date.

In spite of his enthusiasm for the first forty pages, Sam took his time reading the novel, not informing the Dell hierarchy until near the end of the month that Brautigan had "delivered a complete and acceptable ms." and was now due the balance of his advance. The same day, he sent Richard a telegram care of his attorney, Joel Shawn. This took a lighter tone: "My adviser Pisov Sheet says your new book pure dynamo and will make a million lire."

Brautigan kept busy closing down his Pine Creek house for the winter, having Bob Gorsuch drain his pipes, hauling his Chatham paintings, TV set, fishing rods, and firearms over to Marian's place for safe storage. He paid his outstanding bills, writing numerous checks, including one to Mountain Bell for $564.08. In moments of solitude, Richard racked up a lot of long-distance time.

Brautigan left Montana for San Francisco on September 27. Four months later, he wrote about this day: "I felt as if a period in my life had come to an end and I was now embarking on the next stage of my life." He again took up residence at the Kyoto Inn. For the next two weeks, Richard resumed his Frisco routine, slaving away in the room above Vesuvio ("a period of intense income tax activity"), picking up mail at Joel Shawn's law office, and hanging out at Specs', Cho-Cho, and Enrico's. He felt exhausted, both in energy and spirit, from a long summer working on his novel. Prior to leaving on a trip back east, Brautigan wrote Mountain Bell another check, in the amount of $370.33, to cover the remainder of his late-night Montana phone calls. Along with booze and bar tabs, the telephone remained his major expense.

On Saturday afternoon, October 10, Richard flew to Buffalo, New York, booking a room at the venerable Lenox Hotel. Built originally as an upscale residential apartment building in 1896, the Lenox had been home to F. Scott Fitzgerald for ten months in 1898–1899 when his father had worked as a salesman for Procter & Gamble. The Lenox Apartments were converted into a hotel in 1900. Eighty-one years later, it was a bit down at the heels, in spite of a respectable North Street address and three surrounding McKim, Mead and White–designed mansions.

Brautigan phoned Robert Creeley the next morning. Bob invited him over. One advantage of the Lenox was its location, an easy walk from where the Creeleys lived. Richard like the city of Buffalo. He found the architecture "very charming" and enjoyed strolling past the "huge brick houses" built back in a time when they were still affordable. "A time that will never come again," Brautigan noted.

Creeley and his wife, Penelope, lived with their baby in one of three cottages on a small quiet lane that reminded Richard of Hampstead in London. At 2:00 pm that Sunday, Richard gave a reading "from personal poetry" at the Albright-Knox Art Gallery, a beautiful beaux arts building in Delaware Park. Begun in 1890 and intended as the Fine Arts Pavilion for the 1901 Pan-American Exposition, the gallery wasn't completed until 1905, when it became part of the Buffalo Fine Arts Academy. Brautigan's reading was sponsored by the Black Mountain II poetry series, a name adopted by the SUNY Buffalo Department of English because so many former Black Mountain College faculty members (Creeley, Charles Olson, Erik Bentley) taught there. The department also published a journal called *Black Mountain II*.

Once Brautigan's presentation concluded, he returned with the Creeleys to their cottage, and the serious whiskey drinking began, continuing into the evening. The more Richard drank, the more he complained about his divorce from Akiko, claiming she took even the doorknobs and the toilet paper when she left. By the time they all went out to dinner, Penelope Creeley was sick of hearing Brautigan's misogynistic comments. His sexist attitude drove her crazy. Seeking a bit of peace, she dropped her husband and Richard off at the home of Bruce Jackson, a fellow faculty member at SUNY Buffalo.

Creeley and Brautigan staggered in just as Jackson and his wife, Diane, an ex-nun who also taught at the university, sat down to dinner with a houseguest. Edmund Shea had originally been introduced to Jackson by Herb Gold and had come back east to visit his mother, who was dying in Boston. Steeped in grief, Edmund traveled up to Buffalo to get away for a few days and to visit Bruce, another gifted photographer. Much of Jackson's work had been done in prisons. He had also published *Get Your Ass in the Water and Swim Like Me*, a book of "toasts," a form of "the dozens" that was a precursor to rap music. Bruce had just uncorked a treasured bottle of chablis, not the cheap swill popular with pot smokers but the real deal, an *appellation contrôlée* from the Chablis district in France.

Edmund Shea had never tasted a true chablis and looked forward to savoring his first swallow. He tried steering Brautigan toward hard liquor in hopes of preserving the good stuff for more refined palates. Already "three sheets to the wind," Richard said, "No, I'll just have some white wine," proceeding to guzzle the precious imported chablis. Brautigan wasn't talking to Shea. He'd been mad at him for several years over some silly dispute about borrowed money. That night was the last time Edmund ever saw Richard.

Monday morning, when Brautigan phoned Creeley from his hotel room, Bob "sounded tired and distracted." A young woman who lived alone in the cottage next door had been raped during the night. Richard walked over and sat in the kitchen "where the atmosphere was very slow and formal with shock." He drank cup after cup of coffee with Bob until two police detectives arrived. They asked "thoughtful and serious" questions. Brautigan felt "the shadow of the young woman's ordeal" had darkened the atmosphere for him in Buffalo.

Scheduled to give a lecture at one of Creeley's university classes, Richard fulfilled his obligation with the pall of the previous night's rape hanging over him like a poison cloud. A sense of foreboding followed him for the remainder of the day. The next morning, Brautigan phoned the Creeleys and found Bob sounding "very shakened." His wife had been awakened by an intruder wandering around their bedroom in the middle of the night. Penelope saw a man she presumed to be the rapist and alerted Bob. The stranger fled, grabbing Bob's pants on the way out.

With some consternation, Richard walked over to the Creeleys' cottage and "listened to a story of horror" from Bob. The intruder had broken in through a "heavily secured" window in the bathroom. He had not bothered to take the tape recorder or the stereo. Why the man had stolen only Creeley's trousers remained a mystery. Perhaps he reasoned a man without any pants was less likely to pursue him. The Buffalo police detectives had come and gone that morning, as clueless as everyone else. Coffee no longer seemed like the appropriate beverage. Bob Creeley poured them all some whiskey.

While Richard and Penelope "numbly" sipped their drinks, Bob went outside. He returned looking grim and led them around behind the cottage. Creeley pointed to the spot where he'd just found a large butcher knife lying on the ground. It had not been there the day before. Richard thought it looked like something used in horror movies. The police again were summoned. The two dour detectives returned, not saying much, collecting the butcher knife in an evidence bag.

The Creeleys decided they didn't want to spend another night in their cottage on the little storybook lane. Brautigan had planned to go next to Canada and visit Mina and Rosalyn Mina, who had opened a delicatessen in Toronto. Bob and Penelope offered to drive him there. The odds of getting a good night's sleep without being awakened by knife-wielding rapists seemed a lot better up in Canada.

Richard checked out of the Lenox Hotel, paying $20 for his four-night stay. Economy remained a primary concern. As of mid-October, the balance in Brautigan's main checking account stood at $131.85. Four days later Joel Shawn deposited $20,313.89 in the First Security Bank of Livingston, Montana, the proceeds from the second half of Richard's book advance, plus some additional foreign royalty money. Brautigan did all his banking in Montana, maintaining two accounts, one intended only for the expenses of his three rental properties, although he frequently used it to pay for meals at Cho-Cho or an evening's drinking at Enrico's.

The drive from Buffalo to Toronto was a little over one hundred miles but took more than two hours due to occasional delays at the border. The Creeleys crossed the Niagara River to Fort Erie, Ontario, on the Peace Bridge, about twelve miles upstream from the falls. Richard always enjoyed his role as designated passenger. It got no better than this trip, full of sparkling conversation and views of Lake Ontario. Arriving in Toronto, they checked into an old hotel popular with the local bohemian crowd and went out to dinner.

In the morning, Richard set off with Bob and Penelope to search for Roz and Mina. They found them at Slices West, the Minas' new deli on Queen Street West in a neighborhood two blocks east of Parkdale, a "hub of drugs, alcohol and crime." Mina thought the Creeleys were "two of the most kind and wonderful people" he'd ever met. They didn't stay long, leaving early to head back to Buffalo. Brautigan located his *querencia*, a tall stool off to one side of the shop, away from the customer flow, where he sat and peacefully watched the Minas slice meat and cheese, making sandwiches to go.

Like most actors, Mina E. Mina often had to look for other work to supplement his sporadic income. He'd been a college drama professor and a chef at a large Canadian resort. The delicatessen was the latest in a string of ventures guaranteeing the bills got paid. To make sure he always had a part to play, Mina assembled a one-man show, *How to Be a Great Writer,* putting together various pieces written by Charles Bukowski. He played Henry Chinaski, Bukowski's manic imagined alter ego. Because the set was a table and chair, and his only props a typewriter, a battered suitcase, and a six-pack, Mina could put the show on almost anywhere and performed the piece in venues as varied as Chico Hot Springs and the Odyssey Theater in Santa Monica.

Mina showed Brautigan his Chinaski script, hoping for some constructive input. "Garbage! Garbage!" Richard cried, hurling the manuscript out the second-floor window of Roz and Mina's apartment, his violent criticism aimed more at Bukowski's work than Mina's adaptation. The next day Brautigan went shopping. Browsing through Toronto's bookstores, he felt dismayed to find so few copies of his own books. Having sold out their initial orders, the Canadian booksellers neglected to reorder Brautigan's titles.

Richard returned to Slices West after buying two volumes of C. P. Cavafy's poetry. The esteemed Greek poet had lived most of his adult life after the age of twenty-two in the ancient Hellenistic port city of Alexandria, Egypt. Cavafy had been born in Alexandria in 1863 and died there on his birthday, seventy years later. Knowing Mina was a Coptic Egyptian, Richard gave him the books, telling him he should write a new play about Constantine Cavafy.

Mina considered Brautigan "a born storyteller." While they worked at the deli, Roz and Mina enjoyed the tales Richard spun as he sipped from his ever-present bottle. They frequently went out with him to buy wine and liquor. At one point during Brautigan's weeklong visit, Mina and Roz tried to organize an evening when he would read from his work, "but the alcohol started early and it did not happen."

What occurred instead was a brief and "bitter" love affair. The Minas introduced Richard to Barbara Gordon, an "early friend" from when they first moved back to Canada from the States and settled in Toronto. Barb was an aspiring actor, sharing her hopes and dreams with Mina Mina, further along in his quest for that same impossible goal. Brautigan remembered waking up with Gordon in her apartment the first morning after spending the night. "It's a beautiful day here in Toronto," Barb said, "and you're with a nice Canadian girl." Richard agreed on both counts.

Gordon wanted everything to be "pleasant." Brautigan prevented that from happening. "I fucked it up," he wrote a year later. "It ended abruptly and badly, which was totally my fault." Richard blamed the sudden breakup on an act of "outrageous stupidity" on his part, wishing he could "redesign the past." His stay in Toronto came to an unhappy end. In need of traveling cash, Brautigan wrote Mina E. Mina a check for $1,000 on October 19.

Richard checked out of his hotel the next morning. He had a couple hours to kill before catching his flight back to San Francisco and went to the movies. It was a cold day in Toronto. Brautigan chose a cheap theater catering to derelicts to see *Tarzan, the Ape Man*, a film made in a tropic jungle. The movie starred Bo Derek and was directed by her husband, John. Its main attraction was watching the voluptuous star take off her clothes. Even that wasn't sufficient to warm the "sparse [. . .] misbegotten audience of transients." The management elected not to turn up the heat, and "it was just as cold in the theater as outside on the street."

On his return to Frisco, Brautigan registered once again at the Kyoto Inn. His favorite hotel in Japantown remained as close to the Land of the Rising Sun as Richard would get that year. He ventured to more accessible pleasure spots: Enrico's, Cho-Cho, Specs', and the Albatross. Richard had no regular old lady in town. Nikki Arai had a boyfriend. Sherry Vetter was married. Eunice Kitagawa was back home in Hawaii. Missing her, Brautigan phoned Kitagawa in Honolulu. She missed him too, inviting Richard to come and spend Christmas.

After three weeks in town, "dwindling finances" compelled Brautigan to seek new lodging. He could no longer afford the Kyoto Inn. Tony Dingman had a friend in Berkeley, a lawyer whose wife had hanged herself from a large wooden beam in the living room of their home on 17 Eucalyptus Road the previous Christmas. After the tragedy, the man had no desire to live there anymore but didn't want to sell the place. At the attorney's invitation, Dingman moved in, rent free.

Richard Hodge, stuck in the middle of a divorce, also needed someplace to live. He had been sworn in as a superior court judge in March 1981. Governor Jerry Brown had appointed him more than six months earlier, but because he was in the middle of defending a big federal case against the Hells Angels, Hodge had to postpone his appointment. At the time, he moved from one borrowed apartment to the next, all his worldly possessions in twelve paper bags. Tony's invitation to join him on Eucalyptus Road seemed the perfect solution. Hodge recalled this period of his life as a time when he poured vodka into his cornflakes for breakfast.

Built in 1907, the house on Eucalyptus Road was a two-story, four-bedroom carpenter gothic structure brooding under the trees on a street curving into the hills above Claremont Avenue. Once Richard Brautigan learned of a free place to live with a couple old pals, he packed his few belongings and moved over to Berkeley. The morbid house fascinated Richard. After the lawyer's wife committed suicide, he left everything untouched. Christmas cards from 1980 lined the mantel in the living room, where huge wooden ceiling beams held Brautigan's attention. The fatal noose had dangled from one of them.

It was a somber house filled with shadows. Wood paneling added to the pervasive darkness. High ceilings gave the shadows a place to linger. The downstairs consisted of a small office/den with a much larger living room off the front entry vestibule. A formal dining room with doors leading to the kitchen adjoined the living room. Shadow-shrouded antiques lurked against the walls. Plenty of gloomy space for lonely guys to wander around.

Last to arrive, Brautigan slept by default in the dead woman's bed upstairs. Dingman and Hodge had both avoided bunking there when making their sleeping arrangements. As soon as he settled in, Richard picked up the professional threads of his career. He phoned Sam Lawrence in mid-November, urging him to consider publishing Don Carpenter and complaining about the dearth of his books available for sale in Toronto. His publisher wrote back the next day (care of Joel Shawn), saying he'd "taken steps to remedy the situation." Lawrence also promised to have a look at Don Carpenter's work. *So the Wind* had gone into production. Sam reminded Richard that if he wanted a dedication page, it was time to send one.

To simplify the telephone situation on Eucalyptus Road, Brautigan made all his calls using his Montana number. The Mountain Bell bill for November totaled $409.88. Hoping to cut down on expenses and maybe make an extra buck or two, Richard wrote to Helen Brann, questioning why she had taken a commission on the deal that moved *Confederate General* from Grove Press to Seymour Lawrence's imprint. Brann was furious. "I find it incredible that I have to defend my taking a commission on any work I have done for you," she wrote, reminding Brautigan of all of the effort she'd made on his behalf getting Grove to sell the rights to Lawrence. Helen rubbed salt in the wound, pointing out that the last royalty S&S statement for *Willard* "showed an unearned balance of $40,189.42.

Earlier in the month, Sam Lawrence was out of town when a letter postmarked Paris arrived at his Boston office from Marc Chénetier, "the leading French authority on RB," a professor of American literature at both the Sorbonne and the Université de Orléans. A deconstructionist critic, Chénetier had first gotten in touch with Helen Brann in 1975, after he'd been approached by Boise State University about writing a "longish piece" (forty-eight pages) on Brautigan for its Western Writers Series. This project didn't pan out for Chénetier, although Boise State eventually included Richard in the series (no. 79, written by Jay Boyer) three years after his death.

This time around, Professor Chénetier requested a meeting with Richard "sometime between now and early January." Chénetier had written six articles on Brautigan, translated *Dreaming of Babylon* into French, and recently been asked by the British publisher Methuen to write a short book (to be released simultaneously in the United States) on Richard's work. Seymour Lawrence's office forwarded Chénetier's letter to Helen Brann, suggesting she arrange a meeting with Brautigan.

Richard had made several friends in the Hells Angels over the years. He enjoyed talking with Judge Hodge about his final case as a defense attorney, which resulted in the acquittal of twenty-six members in the motorcycle club. The feds had indicted the Angels under the RICO statute. Unable to nail them on drug dealing, the prosecution hoped to gain a conspiracy conviction. Hodge's client was Jim Brandes, an enforcer for the outlaw bikers, charged with conspiring to sell meth and six counts of conspiracy to commit murder. At one point during jury selection, a prospective juror was asked what he knew about the Hells Angels. The man could only recall that they hosted an annual blood drive. Brandes leaned over to Hodge and whispered, "Give a little, take a little."

Sharing a house with a couple bachelor buddies brought back Beaver Street memories, a simpler time in Brautigan's life, when he was always broke and didn't worry about money because he had none. As a man who enjoyed visiting cemeteries and wrote about living above a funeral parlor in his youth, Richard derived perverse pleasure from living in a house haunted by a hanged woman, but when an invitation came from the Ketchikan Humanities Series to give a pair of readings, he booked an immediate flight to Alaska. The very name, Ketchikan, had long held potent magic for Brautigan. When his daughter was a newborn infant, he had written a poem, "The Silver Stairs of Ketchikan," about her 2:00 am feeding. Brautigan sat aboard a plane flying north the first week in December.

Brautigan found Ketchikan among the loveliest villages he'd ever seen. A month and a half later he wrote, "Ketchikan flows like a dream of wooden houses and buildings around the base of Deer Mountain, whose heavily wooded slopes come right down to the town, beautifully nudging it with spruce trees." Richard didn't enjoy this view of the "First City" for long after his plane touched down on Gravina Island airport, half a mile across the Tongass Narrows (future proposed location of "the bridge to nowhere") from Ketchikan, a community of seven thousand spread along the shoreline of Revilla Island. Brautigan's presentations were sponsored by KRBD-FM (assisted by a grant from the Alaska Humanities Forum). He was met by a representative from the radio station, who proposed a local scenic tour.

After Richard checked into the Gilmore Hotel on Front Street, the fellow took him to see some totem poles. Brautigan had observed lots of totem poles in a museum on a trip to Vancouver the previous year. Ketchikan boasted the world's largest collection of freestanding totem poles beneath the towering spruce forest. These totem poles were exposed to the weather (average annual Ketchikan rainfall: 137 inches), the real deal, not a bunch of hothouse museum-enclosed totem poles. Some of them were replicas carved by Native Americans employed by the CCC during the Roosevelt administration. Richard referred to them as "fake totem poles."

As they drove to see the CCC totem poles, Brautigan's host complained about his "complicated love life." Richard had no interest in these amorous details. The names of the local flora the man described meant even less as they walked through the woods toward a group of totem poles that Brautigan considered "very, very fake."

Driving back to Ketchikan, a cold December rain pelting down on the car, the one-way conversation returned to the many complications of love. Brautigan had his own disastrous love life to worry about and paid scant attention to the man's rambling discourse, watching the reciprocating sweep of the windshield wipers as he retreated within, feeling himself growing smaller and smaller, "almost childlike."

At 7:30 pm on Saturday, December 5, Richard presented "An Evening's Discussion with Richard Brautigan" in the humanities area of the Ketchikan High School. The next night, at the same time and location, he read selections from his poetry. A distinguished member of the state legislature was among Brautigan's scattered audience on the second evening. Terry Gardiner had been born in Ketchikan in 1950. He started working as a commercial fisherman at fifteen, the perfect summer job. He went off to Western Washington University in Bellingham. He first read Richard Brautigan in college. He continued fishing professionally after he was elected to the Alaska House of Representatives at age twenty-two. The state government also conducted its business in the wintertime.

Gardiner served as speaker of the house from 1979 to 1980. He planned to retire from politics after completing the last of five successive terms at the end of the coming winter session. He had recently started Silver Lining Seafood, a fish processing company. At Brautigan's reading, Gardiner and a couple of his friends thought it might be fun to "invite him out for a beer. Show him the town."

They set off together on a bar crawl of "Ketchitown," settling in for serious drinking at the Fireside Lounge. Richard drank whiskey. Terry Gardiner preferred tequila. The two "hit it off," their time together short and intense. Gardiner had just ended a passionate relationship with a Japanese woman from Chicago who felt Alaska was "too hard." Brautigan commiserated, knowing a great deal about Japanese women. He told his newfound friend that he "looked forward to arriving at a period of grace in [his] life." Richard's aim was to be "more realistic" and perhaps find some "tranquility."

During the course of their single high-powered evening, Brautigan started calling Terry the "wild legislator." When closing time rolled around, they bought a bottle to go. Richard opted for tequila, his new friend's beverage of choice. They staggered out into the falling snow. "Here, catch, wild legislator," Brautigan called, tossing the tequila bottle across the street to Terry, who snagged it out of the frozen air "effortlessly." Looking back, Richard remembered, "it was a wonderful drunken night in Alaska."

The next morning, Brautigan awoke with an enormous hangover. He lurched from his fifty-four-year-old hotel, bought a hot dog with mustard and relish for breakfast, and found his way across the street to the boat dock. Richard sat, staring up at a moored Panamanian freighter, surrounded by a small murder of crows. Halfway into his tube steak, a wave of nausea overcame him. Brautigan threw the remainder of his fast food to the crows. Richard had an appointment for an interview with Bill Green, a reporter from the *Ketchikan Daily News,* a couple hours before departing for Anchorage. He didn't want to begin their discussion by vomiting.

Brautigan met the reporter at a nearby restaurant. Benumbed by his hangover, Richard felt an unaccustomed loss for words. Wanting "to break the ice, loosen up, and put the interview on a casual footing," he launched into the story of feeding his leftover hot dog and bun to the dockside crows. Brautigan became "very animated" telling this pointless tale, getting up from the table and waving his arms in an insane crow-like manner.

Waiting to board his plane at the Gravina Island airport, Richard had time to befriend Pedro, a fat, friendly resident cat, who had free run of the terminal. On his flight up to Anchorage, which seemed to take forever, Brautigan wondered what the Ketchikan reporter would write about him. As it turned out, not a single word. Green had already assembled a file piece the previous Friday for the *Daily News* weekly art section (incorrectly claiming Richard had no phone in Montana). He had learned nothing new from Brautigan's incoherent interview.

Richard took off for Hawaii early on December 8, after spending the night in Anchorage. He made no new friends in the hotel bar and went to bed sober. Brautigan called flying with a hangover one of the "Top 40 of terrible things to do in my life." Eunice Kitagawa met Richard at the Honolulu International Airport and drove him to her home through the snarl of Honolulu traffic, "the worst case of 'Los Angeles' automobile cultural damage" he'd ever seen. A singular object caught Brautigan's attention. It was a brand-new man's brown shoe lying alone at the center of an intersection remarkable for its quietness. There was no sign of an accident. The solitary brogue did not appear to be part of a pair. Richard thought the lone shoe seemed "almost haunting," exactly the sort of odd urban detritus he always found fascinating.

In many ways, Richard Brautigan was better suited for a vacation in Ketchikan than Oahu. His fair skin didn't tolerate the sun. He preferred a cool, rainy Alaskan climate to the heat and beaches of Hawaii. Richard didn't drive. A small seaport town had everything within walking distance. In Honolulu, an automobile was a necessity. One rainy day, weather suiting Brautigan's sensitivities, he ventured out to a downtown restaurant with Kitagawa. The place had a sidewalk café, deserted due to the rain. As a devoted pedestrian watcher, Richard noted it would be a good place to sit and observe people in fair weather.

"You used the wrong word," Eunice said.

Brautigan asked what she meant.

"Cars," Kitagawa told him. "You watch cars, not people."

Mostly, Richard watched TV. "He got into this sluggish mood," Eunice recalled. "He just didn't want to move." Wanting to pick up Brautigan's spirits, Kitagawa gave him a silk-screened T-shirt made by a friend. It depicted a rooster riding in the turret of a tank above the words "Fighting chickens." Richard wanted his picture taken with a chicken while wearing it. Eunice had to work at the Pottery Steak House but asked her friend George Bennett to handle the photo session.

A big storm blew in that night, and it rained "on and off" all morning. It looked like the photo shoot might be off. When the weather cleared, Bennett phoned to say he'd located a chicken. They set off into the mountains above the city. Brautigan found the change of scenery "lush and provocative like an airplane ad." Richard and George encountered numbers of free-ranging chickens at the farm. A docile rooster was quickly captured. Brautigan knelt before the camera, holding the bewildered bird. Bennett took several snapshots. Richard thought he might have the picture framed and hung in his Montana home. This never happened. Later, Brautigan convinced Greg Keeler that the photograph showed him with a genuine "fighting cock."

Staying home alone at Eunice's place meant Richard spent hours on the phone (charging the calls to his Mountain Bell account). Back in November, Sam Lawrence had told Brautigan to get in touch with Tom Condon, assistant managing editor of Delacorte Press, if he wanted a dedication page for *So the Wind*. In mid-December, Richard sent him his dedication: "This Book is for Portia Crockett and Marian Renken." Brautigan coyly used his friends' maiden names for the printed inscription. Portia was Becky Forida's actual given name.

Money problems nagged at the edges of Richard's mind. He called Greg Keeler at 1:00 am (Montana time), asking if there was any possibility of getting a teaching job at MSU the next spring. Brautigan's employment chances were enhanced by the recent appointment of Paul Ferlazzo, bright, young, and optimistic, as the new English Department head. After a number of late-night strategy sessions with Keeler, Brautigan called Ferlazzo with some trepidation and the "wheels started turning." If things worked out, Brautigan would be appointed a visiting professor for the spring term of 1982. He needed the work. Helen Brann sent a Form 1099 listing 1981 miscellaneous income of $58,275.67, but at the end of December, the balance remaining in Richard's checking account totaled $600.17.

Brautigan and Kitagawa left Oahu only once during his monthlong visit. They flew over to Maui on a day trip. Eunice remembered finding a now-defunct airline that charged only $13 each way. "Richard's kind of deal," she said. Kitagawa, born and raised on Maui, knew every corner of the beautiful island. Brautigan had no interest in visiting the old whaling port of Lahaina, or exploring the Hana coast, or driving to the crest of Haleakalâ, Maui's dormant volcano. A self-confessed fan of cemeteries, Richard most wanted to see a graveyard, so Eunice took him to the churchyard where several of her relatives were buried. A Buddhist shrine with peeling paint stood beside the cemetery.

Brautigan and Kitagawa went separate ways inside the graveyard. She paid her respects to deceased family members, wondering why her boyfriend would rather be here instead of enjoying one of Maui's beautiful beaches. Richard wandered around on his own, observing the mundane details that always fascinated him. He stared at a pile of discarded tombstones and rows of fallen light poles entwined in rotting electrical wire. This seemed logical. Who needs lights in a boneyard?

Spotting an old Japanese couple fussing about the untended graves, Brautigan pointed them out to Kitagawa, and she went over to ask why they were there. "They are very unhappy with the condition of this cemetery," Eunice reported back. Richard felt sympathetic with their impossible task. He wondered about the pile of abandoned tombstones. Kitagawa explained that they were all from graves that surviving family members didn't want to maintain. The remains were disinterred and cremated, and the ashes stored away in the shrine. This made no sense to Brautigan. Why bother to bury the dead in the first place if their graves would not be their final resting place?

Eunice didn't really care. She wanted to catch the 2:00 pm flight to Honolulu so she'd get back in time for a nap before going to work that night. If they left right away they could drive to her mother's restaurant, Tokyo Tei, for lunch before departing. "My mother makes good tempura," Kitagawa told him. Richard thought the Japanese graveyard was the most interesting thing he had seen on Maui. He knew he'd never return. Brautigan "had used [Maui] up."

Richard didn't realize it at the time, but he'd used up the entire Hawaiian archipelago. After returning to San Francisco in mid-January, Brautigan never went back to the Aloha State. Eunice Kitagawa's next Bay Area visitors were Nikki Arai and her black boyfriend, George Bowles. Richard moved again into the dead woman's room at 17 Eucalyptus Road. He had enjoyed a rent-free month in Honolulu and his current finances demanded more of the same.

A letter from Dennis Lynch, who had chaired the MLA "Zen and Poetry" panel discussion a couple years before, brightened Brautigan's financial prospects. Lynch, a graduate student and English instructor at Northern Illinois University, invited Richard to give a presentation there in February. This was not a promissory note. Lynch's invitation came authorized by James M. Mellard, chairman of the English Department, and Jerome Klinkowitz, a rising lit/crit star.

Accustomed to living with a ghost in his gloomy Bolinas house, Richard felt no trepidation at sharing a bed with the spirit of a woman who had hanged herself downstairs. What he did feel was curiosity. Brautigan explored the spacious Berkeley home, roaming from one shadowed room to the next, trying to imagine the details of the tragedy. He wondered if the phone rang at the moment the woman hanged herself. Perhaps, barely alive, her last breath choking from her dangling body, she heard the telephone's insistent *briiing . . . briiing . . . briiing.* Maybe it was good news. She would never know. Whoever called got no answer. No one home anymore.

Brautigan knew he wanted to write about this. He decided to give himself a birthday present, an uninterrupted week at the Kyoto Inn. On Saturday morning, January 30, Richard rode the BART train under the Bay to the City, fighting an urge to tell the stranger sitting next to him, "Today is my birthday. I'm forty-seven." Before checking into his favorite San Francisco hotel, Brautigan paid $2.50 for a 160-page notebook at the Kinokuniya bookstore, a branch of an international Japanese book and stationery chain, in Japantown.

Later in the day, armed with a brand-new Pilot ballpoint pen, Richard began work in the notebook on his next novel. Financial circumstances demanded prudence, playing it safe once again in familiar Brautigan territory, but artistic impulses ran too deep, and Richard set out to explore the outer uncharted edges of experimental fiction. He arbitrarily decided that his novel would run no longer than the notebook in which he composed it. Once Brautigan reached page 160, the book was over. He also resolved not to reread any of his work until he finished the novel. No going back to revise along the way. Richard planned on flying blind into the vast unknown emptiness of the blank page.

"I saw a brand-new man's shoe lying in the middle of a quiet Honolulu intersection," Brautigan wrote on the first line of the first page in his Japanese notebook. "It was a brown shoe that sparkled like a leather diamond." Richard set out on a circuitous examination of the impact that staying in a house where a woman had hanged herself made on his life, retracing his travels over the past three months, weaving in and out of 17 Eucalyptus Road. Because he determined not to reread his material as he went along, the lone shoe spotted in Hawaii remained masculine until Glenise Sibbern typed Brautigan's handwritten manuscript. Richard altered the opening line and changed the gender of the abandoned footwear to better fit his theme. The shoe became a woman's. Deliberately haphazard, Brautigan did very little revising when he edited the typescript. Like a jazz solo, the novel flowed from him in a fluid improvisation.

By the end of a long day of writing, Richard had completed a dozen or more pages in his new notebook. He dated each day's entry, adding the word "Finished" when he was done. It had been Brautigan's intention to stay at the Kyoto Inn until he'd completed his short novel. After a week, when the plum trees in Japantown (just budding when he moved in) were in full bloom, Richard's funds ran low again. He went back to Berkeley the next day. Over the previous seven days, Brautigan had filled eighty pages, half of his notebook, with writing. He stood at the midpoint of his journey, the literary peregrinations meandering through Buffalo, Toronto, Ketchikan, and Honolulu, including a 1964 stopover in Mendocino.

Richard returned to 17 Eucalyptus Road on February 6. He had planned on staying in the Kyoto Inn to finish his book before going to Illinois for the university gig. He never wanted to return to the house on Eucalyptus. "It would no longer be a part of my life." Once he was back, sleeping again in the dead woman's bed, Brautigan felt he needed more time to experience "the atmosphere of the house."

Richard did no further work on his novel for nine days. In mid-February, he sat in the small den off the living room and began writing in the notebook again. He datelined this section "February 6, 1982," nine days earlier. A cold rain fell outside. The lurking shadows in the room grew darker.

Imbued with morbidity, Brautigan spent the next several pages describing the interior of 17 Eucalyptus Road.

Two days later, Richard Brautigan sat in a San Francisco coffee shop, writing the next segment of his novel. He would fly to Chicago in the morning. Brautigan's spring term teaching appointment at Montana State had been approved. His brief stint at Northern Illinois University would serve as a dress rehearsal for the real thing. Richard wrote about having no love life during his return to Berkeley. He was awakened each morning at dawn by the "soft animal moaning" of a woman enjoying sex. The sounds came from a house nearby. Upon reflection, Brautigan guessed they were "pretty loud." Loud enough to wake him up. For reasons of his own, Richard dated this passage February 15, 1982, off by forty-eight hours.

On the eighteenth, Dennis Lynch met Brautigan at O'Hare International Airport in Chicago. The weather was very cold, and dirty snow covered ground. They drove about fifty miles northwest to DeKalb. Richard was hungry. They stopped along the way at a McDonald's so he could eat a fish sandwich and drink a cup of coffee. Lynch took them to his one-bedroom apartment in what Brautigan described as "a student ghetto." They stayed up until 4:00 am, drinking and shooting the shit. When Dennis gave Richard his bedroom, offering to sleep on the couch, Brautigan was too tired to refuse, a decision he later regretted when Lynch's cuckoo clock sang its mechanical song every fifteen minutes through the night.

The next afternoon Richard taught Dennis Lynch's English 105 class. When it ended, Brautigan scribbled signatures at an autograph party "that lasted almost three hours." Later in the evening, Brautigan gave a formal reading at the NIU English Department. Afterward, James Mellard, chairman of the department, hosted a reception for Richard at his home. Mellard's book *The Exploded Form: The Modernist Novel in America* (1980) included a chapter on *Trout Fishing*. He was a fan and welcomed Brautigan along with a crowd of student and faculty admirers. "They drank up all the beer and wine," he recalled, "then proceeded on to our modest supply of liquor, leaving not a drop undrunk."

Mellard remembered Richard sitting on the living room floor, telling stories. Discussing his critics, Brautigan said "he would like to line [them] up and shoot them." Richard made a gesture of raising his hand like a gun "and shooting each one, complete with sound effects." It grew late. Mellard and his wife needed to get some sleep and headed upstairs, telling the rowdy group, "Y'all stay here; we're going to bed." After the Mellards' "modest" booze stash was consumed, the crowd didn't stick around much longer. They headed over to Dennis Lynch's apartment, where the party roared on until 4:00 am.

That should have been the end of it. During his book tour, Brautigan would have been on the morning flight out of town. This time he didn't leave, hanging around DeKalb for another ten days, enduring the nocturnal mechanical call of Lynch's cuckoo clock while his host tossed on the couch in the other room. For two straight days, Richard and Dennis ate nothing but franchise takeout, what Brautigan called "sub-generic" food. Slovenly bachelors, they tossed their Styrofoam containers, wax paper wrappers, and cardboard cups onto the floor, turning the small apartment into the aftermath of "a confused picnic." The final straw came when one of Lynch's students "nonchalantly" threw the packaging from his to-go hamburger onto the surrounding trash heap.

Richard and Dennis cleaned up the mess and aired the apartment, hauling the trash away. It felt like an exorcism. After their garbage epiphany, they ate out, accepting occasional invitations and seeking restaurants more gastronomically inclined than fast-food joints. One establishment offered Trout á la Brautigan on its menu. On another night, a student took Richard home to his parents' house for some "real" home cooking. At a faculty dinner party, Brautigan sat next to a young woman who sold Tupperware, a product Richard had never heard of before.

Brautigan attended many of Lynch's classes. Mainly he enjoyed horsing around with Dennis and the "stewbums," Lynch's gang of "wacky" faculty pals. The most outrageous of the bunch was a guy known as Danimal. One afternoon Dennis drove Richard past the DeKalb home of Joseph F. Glidden, a man who got rich in the 1870s as one of the inventors of barbed wire. They did not go inside. It was Brautigan's only "sight-seeing" trip while in Illinois. Richard proved a perfect fit with Lynch's bar-hopping mob. He greatly enjoyed his ten-day stay in the Midwest, finding its people "surrealistically fascinating."

Brautigan flew back to San Francisco on February 27, arriving late that Saturday night. He checked into the Kyoto Inn, spending all day Sunday in bed recovering from jet lag. Even the two-hour time difference between Chicago and California upset Richard's internal time clock. The morning of March 1 found Brautigan seated at a small wooden table outside a café in an enclosed mall within the Japanese Trade Center, at work once again on his notebook novel. Richard thought it was "a quiet place to work." He dated the current entry February 16, 1982, calling his narrative "chronologically mischievous." Brautigan had planned to end the little book when he left for Chicago but started back by writing about the trip to Illinois.

The next day, seated at the same café table, Richard described his time in DeKalb without mentioning any names. Having established the creative dictum of never rereading what he had written previously, Brautigan moved on with the narrative he called "a calendar map," seemingly unaware of time lapses and apparently pointless digressions.

Like life itself, the little novel was filled with contradiction and uncertainty. It functioned like memory, in disconnected bits and pieces, where trivial moments take on the same emotional importance as powerful events. The photograph of a Hawaiian chicken and a suicide by hanging, annoyance with Dennis Lynch's cuckoo clock (Richard spelled it "coocoo" in his manuscript), watching a crow eat a hot dog bun, an unknown rapist and a broken heart: all were given equal weight. The "Rosebud syndrome" became Orson Welles's gift to the world. Much as we pretend this is not so, seeking dignity and drama in otherwise mundane lives, in the end it all comes out the same, the memories of a philosopher count no higher than those of a fool.

Brautigan had gone to Enrico's the night before, walking through Chinatown after leaving the bar to catch a bus on California Street back to his hotel. Along the way, Richard paused to look at the lobby cards outside a Chinese movie theater. This too went into the novel, digressing from DeKalb to describing an old woman standing beside him, frightened by the image of a ghost on a movie poster. After a passage about gorging on junk food with Dennis Lynch, Brautigan put another total stranger into the "story," a Japanese man eating pastry at a nearby table. The literary diversion was completely unintentional, part of his compositional method in the little notebook. The second of March was the last day Richard worked on his novel for more than three months.

Brautigan and photographer Roger Ressmeyer had formed "a very close relationship" since meeting almost exactly a year earlier for the *People* magazine shoot. Richard asked Roger to take the photograph for the cover of *So the Wind Won't Blow It All Away*. They got together and Roger bounced some ideas off Richard, who wanted a picture evoking the life of the "pond people" he'd described in the novel. He also requested a new author photo, one showing water in the background. Their creative energies meshed perfectly. Brautigan okayed the project.

About this time, French publisher Christian Bourgois purchased the rights to *So the Wind* and hired Marc Chénetier as the translator. He also approached Helen Brann about bringing Richard to Paris to promote the book's publication. The first week of March, Brautigan met with Ressmeyer and his assistant at the marina waterfront. Roger snapped head-and-shoulder shots of Brautigan posed beside the water. They moved on to the fountain pools in the Presidio for more portraits with an aquatic backdrop. From his earliest sessions with Erik Weber, Richard always micromanaged the photography for his book covers. This time around, Brautigan trusted Ressmeyer to get things right, giving him "total control" over the project.

Roger and his employee drove across the Golden Gate Bridge to the Novato reservoir in northern Marin County, towing a U-Haul full of used furniture. In the afternoon, they arranged the secondhand furnishings on a narrow peninsula. When everything looked right, they waited for dusk, and once darkness enveloped them, Roger started the generator and lit a small fire in his prop cookstove. The lamps in his impromptu stage set burned ordinary lightbulbs. Ressmeyer, experienced in celestial photography galaxies away from his celebrity mug shots, set the camera for a long exposure, "probably a second or two," and took several pictures. The bridge lamp gleamed like a star gone nova. Once the images were developed, Roger picked the best and worked up the layout for a wraparound cover photograph, including textual elements, and presented the finished product to Delacorte Press/Seymour Lawrence. Ressmeyer did all the work, but the publisher credited Susan Lee Weiss, an in-house designer, with the jacket design.

Brautigan had plenty to occupy his time once he set his novel aside. Students wishing to participate in his upcoming writing class had been asked to submit samples of their work to the MSU English Department. Faculty members picked the best of the crop. Paul Ferlazzo sent these off to Richard for final selection. Busy days didn't mean lonely nights for Richard in Japantown. He had his last sheet-tearing rendezvous with Sherry Vetter. Eunice Kitagawa "flew up to SFO a few times while he was at the Kyoto Inn." Specific dates are lost in the fog of ancient memories. Eunice found these visits "disturbing." Richard clearly seemed to be "spiraling down." Back in Hawaii, Kitagawa called some guys she'd gotten to know at the front desk to check on Brautigan when he wouldn't answer his phone for long stretches. She worried about him. "Richard was already threatening to hurt himself."

Nights when he lacked a female companion, Brautigan set off for North Beach in search of adventure. There was always chance of a casual pickup at Enrico's, but most often Richard rode home alone on the bus after closing time. One evening he ran into Allen Moline, a stranger in town enjoying "a wild night out." They drank together and talked for three hours. "During the course of our conversation, Brautigan plopped a bullet in my glass of white wine," Moline recalled. Richard's gesture added dramatic emphasis to his drunken talk of "contemplating taking his own life."

Moline was shocked. He hated bullets. "With more and more wine," he pleaded with Richard "to think it over." They parted a little before 2:00 am, planning to meet at Tosca. Like many boozy late-night promises, it was all empty talk. Allen Moline never saw Brautigan again.

On March 14 Brautigan got up from the couch to change the channel on his TV and tripped over a coffee table in his hotel room, breaking his right leg at the ankle in two places. At first

Richard thought he'd only sprained it. After a day, the swelling didn't go down, nor did his pain diminish. Brautigan phoned Dr. Burstein, his regular physician, who referred him to Felton and Klausenstock, MDS, Inc., specialists in the sort of fracture he described. Richard made an appointment for the sixteenth, taking a cab in the morning. X-rays revealed clean breaks. No cast was necessary. Brautigan's leg was bound. He was advised to use a cane and take it easy for six weeks or so. Felton and Klausenstock billed Richard $56 for their services.

Brautigan flew to Bozeman, Montana, on April Fools' Day. Greg Keeler met him at the airport as he limped off the plane with his new cane. In addition to his Montana State University salary of $1,500 a month, a faculty apartment had been reserved for Richard at the Peter Koch Towers on campus. He went to stay at Greg's place instead. A long-standing friction between Brautigan and Judy Keeler was exacerbated by his unexpected visit. A few days later Richard wandered into the living room carrying an armload of laundry. He was "fresh from the bath," clad only in a towel. "Where should I put these dirty clothes?" Brautigan asked Judy.

"Up in the washing machines at faculty housing," Mrs. Keeler answered.

Brautigan took the hint and moved to his new apartment: a bedroom with a living room and kitchen divided by a Formica-topped counter, furnished in standard dorm-room modular. The place reeked of "industrial strength sanitizing agents." Long accustomed to the anonymity of hotel rooms, Richard felt comfortable there. He told Greg Keeler he especially liked the toilet paper. Suffering from a recent herpes outbreak, Brautigan stuffed wads of tissue around his genitals to keep from chaffing. Little bits of toilet paper started "falling out of his jean cuffs." Keeler found it funny. "He walked around with toilet paper all over the place."

Brautigan never went to college and had not been a diligent scholar, but he taught Creative Writing 202 like a pro. A wise-guy student, handpicked by Keeler, challenged Richard on his first day. "I don't like your work," he sneered. "You call this teaching?" Brautigan thought the kid's writing was "a fucking pile of pig shit." Susy Roesgen was another story. A talented writer, she also started the course with a negative attitude, telling Richard she disliked his books. Richard "didn't want to mess things up" and went to Paul Ferlazzo for advice. The department head clued him in on how to handle the situation. Roesgen ended the semester liking Brautigan's class "a lot." Richard wrote, "Dear Susy, A very good piece of writing. RB," on one of her weekly assignments.

Greg Keeler noted that Richard played favorites, "but that was based on whether he liked their work." Brautigan followed a traditional classroom approach. He gave weekly assignments, suggesting varied topics, "lightning, fishing, or death." Richard never made line-by-line criticism on his students' work, instead writing insightful comments at the top of each first page. On occasion Brautigan dashed off a quick story of his own, offering it to the class for their evaluation. One afternoon on his way to teach, Richard stopped at a small, private campus park surrounding a sundial to examine his "raging" herpes outbreak. In his ever-present notebook, Brautigan jotted down a quick tale "about an alien race of sores on another planet who had to trudge to a dark gloomy place called The Grotto to be drained." His students never guessed it to be a parable based on their instructor's private suffering.

Richard wrote this story in the warm month of June, close to the end of the term. Back in April, with the weather gripped by "a winter-like spring," the little sundial park felt as hospitable as ice-bound Point Barrow. Greg Keeler observed Brautigan, alone and depressed, hobbling "drunk with his cane and broken leg from bar to bar around the freezing icy streets of Bozeman, getting a lift back to his room, bouncing around in the back of some cowboy's pickup." An evening at the theater provided an excellent excuse for getting in out of the cold.

Montana-raised Pamela Jamruska, a young actress who had received an MFA from the University of Wisconsin the previous year, was performing in the ballroom above the lobby of the Baxter Hotel in *The Belle of Amherst* by William Luce, a one-woman play about Emily Dickinson. Long an admirer of Dickinson's poetry, Brautigan went to see the show. Jamruska portrayed fifteen different characters, roles originated six years before on Broadway by Julie Harris.

Enchanted by the play and the diminutive white-gowned actress alone in the spotlight at center stage, the audience felt they'd gotten to know a woman who had been dead almost one hundred years. One of the last lines, spoken in the voice of Emily Dickinson, struck a chord in Richard: "These are my letters I wrote to the world that never wrote to me." Brautigan had received his share of vacuous fan letters over the years and understood the poet's eternal dilemma: Is anyone out there listening?

A week or so after he started teaching, Richard went out for drinks with friends. One suggested he meet a woman they knew, someone equally "far out." When they phoned, she said she couldn't make it to the bar before closing time but suggested they get together later at the Four B's restaurant for breakfast and coffee. Shortly after 2:00 am, Brautigan's friends drove him west along Main Street toward his assignation. Richard had "never had any luck on blind dates" and didn't know what to expect.

Four B's was one of a chain of restaurants scattered about Montana serving breakfast twenty-four hours a day. When they pulled into the parking lot out front, Brautigan spotted the woman waiting alone in a booth. It was Pam Jamruska, but Richard didn't recognize her without her stage makeup. Using his cane, Brautigan "hobbled over to the window," waving his free hand "like a clown." She wore loose-fitting clothing that camouflaged her "very good tight body." Richard pressed his face to the glass, making a variety of funny expressions. "She was instantly delighted and started laughing."

Brautigan and Jamruska talked until nearly dawn. It wasn't long before Pam moved into his apartment in Peter Koch Tower. Greg Keeler remembered dropping by Richard's place one morning, "and here comes Pamela Jamruska to the door," obviously having spent the night. "Pamela was already in control," Keeler recalled. "That was a funny experience."

One evening Brautigan escorted Jamruska to the Robin Bar, just off the lobby at the Baxter Hotel. Small and dark, with a huge art deco back-bar mirror, the place was known among its regulars as the Melancholy. It was supposedly a "meat market," but no one ever made a pickup at the Robin. Renowned as a graveyard for the romantic fantasies of total losers, the little cocktail bar had gained its nickname because all those who failed to connect on Saturday night gathered there to drown their sorrows on Sunday.

One evening Brautigan came into the Melancholy with Jamruska. Pam spotted her good friend Sean Cassaday at a table with three or four others, and they joined the group. L.A.-born Cassaday, then in his mid-thirties, had moved to Montana after graduating from art university in Toronto. He earned his living as a carpenter but along the way had created several successful businesses on Main Street in Bozeman. Cassaday's most recent venture at the time was the Union Hall, a restaurant where Jamruska worked as a waitress. Sean had seen Richard at a couple parties over the years, but aside from casual conversation, they'd never talked much.

"It was a strange meeting," Cassaday recalled. Brautigan sat directly behind him and "started talking to the back of my head." Richard incorrectly assumed Sean and Pam were lovers. "There seemed to be some competition," Cassaday said. "I don't think I liked him at all at that moment." Brautigan became confrontational in a passive-aggressive manner, directing his remarks to the others at the table. Sean didn't respond "because he was being relatively negative about it, and she was there." No one cared what he had to say. Richard left, hauling Pam along with him.

Brautigan didn't like the Robin. His favorite joint in town was the Eagles, housed in the FOE Lodge far down Main Street at the eastern end of Bozeman. The polar opposite of the Robin in every way, including location, the Eagles was a workingman's bar, inexpensive and rough around the edges. George Dickel sold for fifty cents a shot during happy hour. Dave Schrieber was the manager, working both the day and night shifts according to his schedule. When he tended bar, Schrieber was known for his generous pour. Greg Keeler had introduced Richard to the Eagles. They met for burgers (no drinks) at lunchtime before Brautigan's class. After school got out, it was party time.

Friday Burger Night at the Eagles became "extra special." Brautigan held court at his favorite table, searching for what he called the Great American Good Time. Sourdough Creek flowed past along the outside wall of the bar before it was tunneled under Main Street. During spring runoff, Richard enjoyed hearing the rush of water during occasional rare moments of quiet. The regulars at Brautigan's table included Keeler, Dick Dillof, Brad and Georgia Donovan, and Georgia's sister, Mary. The Donovans had purchased a trailer (number 66) at a place called Forest Park on the Gallatin River west of Bozeman. Mary bought the single-wide next door, creating a little family compound.

Over time the core group at Richard's table expanded. Karen Datko, a young reporter at the *Bozeman Chronicle,* was among the first additions. Carol Schmidt, a colleague at the paper had arranged through Greg Keeler to interview Brautigan. The only condition stipulated that the conversation take place at the Eagles. Datko was invited to go along. She came into the office early that day, knowing she wanted to take off first thing in the afternoon.

After the interview, Schmidt returned to the *Chronicle* to write her story. Karen hung around, knocking back Dickel shots with Richard in the middle of the afternoon. "What the hell," she thought, "I don't have to go back to work." After a while Keeler left too, and Datko was alone with Brautigan, "yacking, yacking, yacking." They hit it off.

The two never became lovers, forming a close friendship instead. Karen had been born in a hardscrabble coal mining town in southwestern Pennsylvania. They formed a bond based on similar backgrounds, with single-parent working-class childhoods lived on the bitter edge of poverty. "We both knew what it was like to do without having money," Datko recalled. "Without having a lot of food, without having clothes that you wanted to have, without having the kind of love in your home that you wished you would have had, without having two parents." Richard started calling her Scoop. Everyone had a nickname at the Eagles. Karen dubbed Brautigan Old Uncle Richard. One night he told off-color stories, and she changed it to Dirty Unc. Brautigan thought this was great. Scoop always referred to him as Unc. "I never called him Richard to his face," she said.

Carol Schmidt's article on Brautigan appeared in the *Chronicle* on April 26, 1982. Along with bits of misinformation (Richard told Schmidt he'd "twice flunked first grade in Tacoma"),

Brautigan had divulged a number of personal revelations. "I don't know where my home is," he said. "I'm trying to figure that out. My life would be easier if I knew where I really lived." He admitted to being puzzled by his designation as a hippie writer. "There were tremendous changes going on in America then," he said. "It was impossible not to be involved in those changes." Summing things up, Richard observed, "There are those who say 'Richard Brautigan sits down in an hour and a half and writes his annual best seller.' I'm not quite that quick, although I am prolific. I work very, very hard to make things appear very, very simple."

One night toward the end of Brautigan's teaching stint at MSU, he reconnected with Sean Cassaday at the Melancholy. Richard's brief springtime relationship with Pam Jamruska had ended. Sean had taken her show on the road in his car, touring *The Belle of Amherst* to Missoula; Rock Springs, Wyoming; and Billings. Jamruska had since moved out of their lives. The bartender at the Robin refused to serve Brautigan, saying he was under orders from the management: "He can get crazy when he gets drunk. If he leaves here drunk and gets in an accident, we'll be held responsible."

Sean went to bat for Richard, explaining to the bartender that his friend didn't drive. They got their drinks, knocked them back, and moved down the street to the Eagles. After that night, Cassaday always had a seat at Brautigan's special table.

Brautigan met every day with his writing class. Margaret Roiter, one of Richard's students, recalled that "he talked about death a great deal" in class. A Brautigan assignment had the class bring in favorite examples from the *Billings Gazette* obituary column. Later in the spring, Richard volunteered to give a reading as part of his of his teaching residency. Greg Keeler felt nervous about this. "Few of the faculty seemed to care much about Richard's poetry," he observed. The larger Bozeman community had zero interest in poetry. Greg's doubts escalated shortly before Brautigan's scheduled reading when Richard asked about publicity.

There was no publicity, not even printed posters. "What the fuck kind of place is this?" Brautigan demanded.

"It's a state university in Montana," Keeler feebly replied.

At the last moment they made up a bunch of crude hand-lettered fliers and scurried about town, taping them in shop windows, tacking them to power poles, trees, and bulletin boards. Greg did not feel optimistic. Infrequent previous poetry readings had garnered only a collective community yawn. On the appointed hour, Keeler and Brautigan arrived outside Gaines Hall, home of the Chemistry Department. Richard rubbed snow on his face. Greg anticipated the worst.

The main lecture hall was packed. Three hundred seats filled. People standing in the aisles and along the walls. The noisy chatter subsided. A hush filled the auditorium as Brautigan "lumbered to the podium." Keeler noted even the "conservative and religious" dean of Letters and Sciences was in attendance, shocked when Richard led off his reading with the poem "Fuck Me Like Fried Potatoes."

The Montana springtime weather vacillated between warm sunny days and raging blizzards. Brautigan started spending nights at the Range Hotel, a few doors west down Main Street, past the Eagles and the Union Hall, only three blocks from Greg Keeler's house. Dick Dillof, a connoisseur of such establishments, took a cheap room there from time to time and tipped Richard off to the peculiar amenities of the place. One of the last of the early twentieth-century downtown Western hotels, the Range housed an eccentric collection of retired cowboys, railroad workers, and loggers, who sat in the lobby on the ancient sagging furniture, leaning on their canes and dipping snoose. Brautigan liked the hotel for the same reason he enjoyed drinking at the Eagles and eating breakfast at the Western Café among weathered ranchers and construction workers. These establishments retained the essence of an America that Richard knew was fast disappearing into memory.

Brautigan fit right in with the codger crowd in the lobby. He no longer used his cane. One afternoon Richard gave it away to the troubled son of faculty colleagues when he and Keeler took the boy fishing on the Yellowstone. His sparsely furnished room at the Range provided an echo of living in the Hotel Jessie a quarter century before. Those memories triggered recollections of other overnight stops at anonymous lodging places on book tours. The more Richard recalled cheap rented rooms, a fancy suite at the Ritz, and family-style California motels, an idea took shape in his imagination.

Dick Dillof had a room one floor down, directly below Brautigan's cubicle. Dick recalled sitting with Richard and a girl he'd brought, when the author waxed nostalgic about old small-town main street hotels. "When they are gone," Richard said, "America will have lost her heart. It will be like the death of hitchhiking. The transient life is the nation's heartbeat."

Dobro mentioned he'd heard a rumor that the Range might soon be closing.

"I may be checking out before then," Brautigan said.

"Out of the hotel?" the girl asked.

"Out of the Big Hotel," Richard replied.

Back at Pine Creek, Brautigan started working longhand in a clean lined notebook. He called this project "American Hotels." Sitting on his back porch after breakfast, he wrote: "Waking at dawn, then a cantaloupe and some coffee, with time to watch a feeding grey thrush in the backyard and a skunk lurching just a few feet away [from] the kitchen looking for grubs I guess or whatever they eat, I am summoned to American hotels as a ghost is called upon to haunt a house." On page 5, Richard digressed from his title and launched into a description of his posh thirtieth-floor room at the Keio Plaza in Tokyo. The words flowed fast and freely. It felt good to write about better times long ago and far away. Nine pages later, Richard took a break from his new project and returned to work in the notebook novel he had started on his birthday. His working title was "Investigating Moods."

Brautigan needed diversions to take his mind off life's harsh, insistent realities. His friend Nikki Arai was terminally ill. Troubled by unrelenting pain, she called Alan Copeland, who drove her to a San Francisco hospital. She was diagnosed with cervical cancer. Arai contacted Richard to tell him about her disease, sounding "very frightened." Brautigan always thought of Nikki as "a very strong, purposeful woman with a very dynamic and aggressive personality. Cancer had reduced her to a frightened crying little girl."

Brautigan's writing seminar drew to a close in the first two weeks of June. Grading his students presented a dilemma. "I don't want to discourage anybody," he told Brad Donovan, "so I'll just give them all A's." When Richard turned in his grades to the English Department, he was horrified to learn that MSU undergraduates evaluated their teachers at the end of the quarter. "When did this happen?" Brautigan complained to Greg Keeler. It was like "Zen students grading the masters." He didn't have to worry. Paul Ferlazzo agreed to exempt Richard from the class evaluations. As a visiting scholar, Richard was "a one shot deal."

John F. Barber (who had graduated from Boston University in 1974) was one student who would have given Brautigan high marks. Older than the others in the class, Barber had seen a bit of life, working in Yellowstone Park for several years before entering a graduate program in history at MSU in 1981. He withdrew after a year, maintaining his friendship with some of his professors. Knowing his ambition to be a writer, they told him about the upcoming Brautigan residency.

Barber's job, driving buses for the Karst Stage Company, provided a flexible schedule, allowing time to attend Richard's seminar and hang out at the Eagles with him after class. Again Brautigan compartmentalized, never introducing John Barber to his other friends or extending an invitation to the Friday night burger roundtable. Barber's final writing project for Richard was a narrative about his experience working as the purser aboard the paddlewheel steamboat hotel *Mississippi Queen* during her 1976 maiden voyage between Cincinnati and New Orleans. Brautigan liked his piece very much, phoning Barber to praise it. He told John he'd show it to Helen Brann but never did.

The next week found Richard back home in Pine Creek. The long cold wet spring had turned bright and sunny by mid-June. Snow still crowned the jagged peaks of the Absarokas, but the surrounding foothills were green, lively with wildflowers. Too late for a get-well card, Brautigan sent a telegram to Nikki Arai in her hospital room. "WORDS ARE FLOWERS OF NOTHING," he wired. "I LOVE YOU." Richard hoped "it would make her feel peaceful."

On Father's Day, Ianthe phoned Richard from New York. He had not spoken to her since the previous November. There had been no communication between them at Christmas or on either of their birthdays. "It was not a pleasant conversation," Brautigan recalled. He blathered on for fifteen minutes about his teaching experience while she listened patiently, "probably bored." More succinctly, Ianthe told her father about her own recent life. Richard confessed to definite boredom.

"Well, I guess we've spent enough time talking on your dime," Brautigan said, hoping to bring their conversation to an end without offering any invitation that might include her husband.

"I guess so," Ianthe replied. After a long, uncomfortable pause, she said, "We'll have to have lunch sometime."

Richard awkwardly replied that he might be in New York "sometime in December or later next year, maybe in the spring." He'd been invited to France. Maybe they could get together either on his way over or upon his return. When they hung up, Brautigan "felt very disturbed and wished she had never called."

Late in June, Brautigan typed a letter to his agent. In his barn rafter office, he crafted a book proposal to the Dell Publishing Company, complying with the option clause in his *So the Wind Won't Blow It All Away* contract. Brautigan had shown his work in progress to Becky Fonda. She didn't like the title "Investigating Moods," making some "appropriate suggestions." Richard listened to her advice. When he wrote Helen Brann, the working title for his proposed new work had become "An Unfortunate Woman." The book would contain "four long sections." The first, his unfinished novella, would "examine the varieties of human existence revolving around a tragedy."

The second section, "Japanese UFO," would contain stories "about contemporary Japan" written during his last trip to Tokyo, ranging "from humor to tragedy." The third part was to be "American Hotels." Rounding out the quartet, Richard proposed a final section of short stories set in Montana, none of them yet written. He proposed calling these tales "Waiting for the Deer."

The same afternoon, Brautigan sat on his back porch, watching a distant thunderstorm gather as he started writing again in his *Unfortunate Woman* notebook. Richard did not pick up where he left off. He itemized all the calendar days he'd missed ("MARCH 3, 4, 5, 6, 7, 8"—all the way through to "19, 20, 21" of "JUNE") and followed this odd countdown with a long digression about breaking his leg. After a brief attempt to get back on track regarding the tragedy of the unfortunate woman who hanged herself in Berkeley, Brautigan remarked that at the beginning of his "journey," he counted all the words on every page after each day's writing "because [he] wanted to have a feeling of continuity," a practice abandoned after twenty-two pages.

Following a three-day break, Richard returned to work on Friday the twenty-fifth, filling twenty more pages in his Japanese notebook. That night, after a long phone conversation with a depressed drunken friend, Brautigan called Nikki Arai. He had only recently learned she had a private telephone in her hospital room. Nikki's sedated voice sounded "very delicate." Richard heard "a gentleness" that had never been there before. She said she was feeling better and didn't mention her cancer. Arai told Brautigan "how much she liked the telegram," asking him to keep in contact. "It made me feel good," Nikki said. "It was beautiful. Please write me more." Richard thought she was "getting used to the idea of dying."

Too much tragedy and solitude took a toll on Brautigan. He headed back to Bozeman on Saturday in a futile search for the Great American Good Time. As usual, he "did a lot of drinking" and failed to find a willing female partner before the bars closed. The Range had nothing available at that hour. Richard, without the aid of his abandoned cane, limped almost a mile east of town to the Alpine Motel ("very modest and clean"), where he rented a room for $9.95.

The next morning, hangover throbbing, Brautigan phoned John Barber for help. "Meet me for breakfast," he said. "I'll buy and then you can give me a ride home." Barber was driving a Karst bus over the hill that afternoon to pick up a group of kids who'd spent a week at Luccock Park, a United Methodist Church camp directly above Richard's place at the head of the Pine Creek Trail. Richard had never been the only passenger on an old-fashioned yellow school bus before. He traveled in one of his own short stories. Barber stopped at the Safeway in Livingston while Brautigan bought a week's worth of groceries.

On June 28, 1982, Richard Brautigan came to the end of his 160-page Japanese notebook. His little excursion into experimental fiction was over. Brautigan left the last line blank. "I'll leave it to somebody else's life," he wrote, having filled the little book with "so many inconclusive fragments, sophomoric humor, cheap tricks, endless detail." Richard promised his future audience, "You have read the book. I have not." After stating, "writers are notorious liars," Brautigan emphasized that he had only reread his book to see where he'd left off during his many lapses. "Iphigenia, your daddy's home from Troy!" he wrote in conclusion.

Richard closed the cardboard covers, "like a door," on the most extraordinary literary adventure he'd ever embarked upon. Brautigan, a poet who reworked each word and line over and over until he got it right, abandoned his precision, returning to the old beat mantra "first word, best word." He promptly gave his handwritten manuscript to a professional typist and sent the fair copy off to his agent in New York.

Brautigan wanted to celebrate finishing another book and finagled a ride into Livingston. He wandered from bar to bar, hoping to luck out and get laid. At closing time, Richard was dead drunk and alone. Instead of calling a cab, he took a cheap room at the Murray Hotel. At the time, the establishment was a bit down at its heels. The turn-of-the-century lobby had been divided in half, with a short-order grill occupying the Park Street side. There was no one available to operate the ancient elevator. Brautigan limped up the stairs and collapsed on a narrow bed in a drab cubicle with no toilet or TV. He checked out early the next morning.

Just before the Fourth of July weekend, Dennis Lynch descended on Rancho Brautigan with his pal Danimal "like a plague of drunken, farting locusts." Richard made them welcome. They proceeded to drink him "out of house and home" as promised. Brautigan arranged for rodeo tickets at the Livingston Roundup for Friday, July 2, calling the Donovans to come over and join the fun. Lynch wore an Arab burnoose into the fairground temple of ten-gallon headgear. Upping the ante, during the intermission show, when the featured performer with a trained bison pretended to sleep while his enormous shaggy animal bent over him, Dennis shouted, "Make it good for the buffalo too!"

Rip Torn also came out to Montana over the Fourth of July weekend to visit his three children, all working at Chico Hot Springs. After visiting Joe Sedgwick, his cowboy rancher pal, Rip gave the kids a lesson in stick-shift driving in the rental car on the way back from Two Dot. They lurched and bumped down East River Road, stopping at Richard's house. Finding no one home, Rip left a brief note saying he was at Chico.

Brautigan phoned the resort, inviting Rip and his kids for dinner on the third. Dennis and Danimal were off on their own. Richard launched back into "American Hotels," digressing into a long reminiscence about his relationship with Sherry Vetter a decade earlier. He fit this to his theme by describing all the motels with swimming pools in northern California where they had stayed together.

Rip Torn and his three children drove down to Pine Creek from Chico. When they arrived, Brautigan descended from his nest in the barn, blinking "like an owl" in the sunlight. "Your dad's timing is still good," Richard told Rip's kids with a grin. "Let's jump in your car and get some groceries. [. . .] I was finishing my novel. It's done. I've turned into a hermit, but I want to celebrate."

After a quick trip to Safeway, Brautigan told Torn he didn't fish anymore. "I've given my gear away." Rip went out alone on the river and caught a couple nice trout for dinner. Richard came up with champagne and a can of mushroom soup. "Let's poach these beauties in this soup," he said. "And how about a dash of champagne?" They had a feast. Brautigan also produced a couple bottles of "hootch—Daniels or Dant." They drank until dawn. Richard's "excitement made him a kid again."

"Brautigan took his parties seriously," Brad Donovan observed. When Richard phoned to say he was throwing a wang-dang-doodle for Rip Torn, and "bring some food," the Donovans headed straight for the supermarket with their food stamps. It was a big shindig. The Fondas were there, and Marian Hjortsberg. Brautigan dispatched Brad to the kitchen to work on the spaghetti sauce with Dennis Lynch. Donovan thought Lynch was "typical of Richard's friends: fun loving, witty, tactful."

While Brad chopped onions, Dennis pulled a slip of paper from a softcover book. "Look what I found," he said. "It's a bookmark. An edible bookmark. Try it." Dennis tore the paper in half, eating one piece. He gave Donovan the other half. It was stamped with a purple dragon. Brad chewed it down and rode the dragon into fantasy land for the rest of the night.

The party raged on until dawn. Richard, not tripping on acid, told a long story about Baron von Richthofen. After a long day dueling it out in the skies over France, the Red Baron liked to head into the Black Forest alone at night, hunting wild boar with a knife to relax from the rigors of being an ace. Dennis Lynch greeted the sunrise on the roof of the chicken coop, shouting, "I'm a morning person." Rip Torn had left long before, heading back to Chico with his sleeping kids. It was the last time he ever saw Richard Brautigan, who drove back over to Forest Park with Brad and Georgia Donovan.

Ed and Jenny Dorn had been out of touch with Brautigan. Dick Dillof had recently moved an antique railroad caboose onto Marian Hjortsberg's property, parking it not far from his sheep-herder's wagon. He invited the Dorns to come and stay in it. They drove up from Boulder with their kids for the Fourth of July weekend, stopping off first to visit the Donovans. When they pulled into Forest Park in their station wagon, the Dorns were "surprised and delighted" to see Richard sitting on the trailer steps at number 66, working his way through a quart of Dickel early in the afternoon.

Kidd, the Dorns' son, wanted to go fishing. Brad rigged a fly rod with a streamer and walked the boy over to the river behind the mobile homes. Before long Kidd's younger sister, Maya, ran back to announce that he'd hooked a big one. Everybody hurried to the riverbank to watch him play his fish. Richard laughed as Kidd eased a beautiful two-pound trout out of the Gallatin. Georgia Donovan's snapshot captured the young angler holding his trophy. Everyone grinned with delight.

Over in Pine Creek that night, Dillof settled Ed and Jenny into the caboose, setting up a small tent for the kids. The next day the whole gang, including Brautigan, went to the Sunday rodeo in Livingston. Richard was "pissed at Dobro Dick." Learning of the Dorns' impending arrival, Brautigan stormed over to the Hjortsberg place, raging, "I want *no* house guests. *NO* house guests!" Even though Ed and Jenny were his friends, Richard considered Dillof's invitation an unacceptable intrusion into what he considered his territory.

Bud Swearingen was up from Texas. After a day's fishing he stopped by Rancho Brautigan late in the evening with a "bunch of trout" as a gift offering. The Fourth of July had been overcast. By rodeo time it poured rain. Delighting at the discomfort of his friends camping down at Dillof's compound, Brautigan stood on his back porch "guffawing at them" through the stormy night. Before long he blasted away into the darkness with his powerful .44 Magnum. Swearingen beat a hasty retreat over to the Hjortsbergs'.

Marian "could see it coming, like a tornado building in the Midwest." She turned off all the lights, hoping "to stay completely out of this situation." When Bud knocked on her door, she went downstairs to face the music. "It's just crazy over there," Bud said. "I thought I'd come over and say hi." They decided the best course of action would be to head into town for a drink. Marian hurried to get dressed as distant gunshots boomed like thunder in the storm.

Paradise Valley and Livingston were famous for the howling wind funneling down off Yellowstone Park plateau. On the night of the fourth, it raged at gale force. As the shooting started, a violent gust demolished the tent where the terrified Dorn children huddled, unable to sleep. Ed, Jenny, and the kids took refuge in the creek bottom, weaving between the dark trees as bullets crashed through the storm-tossed branches overhead, heading for shelter at Marian's.

Brautigan got to the Hjortsberg house before them. Marian and Bud were about to clear out when Richard came through the kitchen door. "Damn that Dobro!" he fumed. "Damn that Dobro."

"Come on in and sit down," Marian said.

Looking bedraggled, the Dorns and their kids straggled in from the tempest, followed in short order by Dick Dillof and his girlfriend. Pandemonium ensued. The decibel level escalated. "Richard and Ed were having this fight," Marian remembered, "and everyone was down on Dobro." Tempers calmed. "They hashed it all out and made up." Brautigan invited the Dorns to spend the night at his place. After a quick nightcap, they all trooped out into the night.

The next morning, chagrined by his nocturnal fusillade, Richard showed the Dorn children his guns, carefully explaining firearm etiquette and safety rules. After lunch, he took the kids down to the dump below his barn and "set them up for the afternoon," plinking away at beer cans. Brautigan rejoined the adults on the back porch and resumed drinking, "laughing with that high-pitched sequence of hoots and howls." Jenny thought "life was a very simple progression for Richard." She and Ed returned to Colorado the following morning.

Fourth of July weekend was the last time Richard ever saw Bud Swearingen. The Texan left his mark on the grounds of Rancho Brautigan. A couple years before, Bud's two sons had abandoned a 1956 Ford Victoria by the fence off to the side of Richard's barn after a futile effort at getting it running again. The derelict car became a useful platform for viewing the night sky. The hood remained warm after sunset and was wide enough to accommodate two Brautigan-sized adults reclining along its length, their backs resting against the windshield. Richard stargazed with Masako from this vantage point. Greg Keeler spent many evenings perched on the junker Ford, staring at the heavens and bullshitting the night away with Brautigan.

A letter from Masako Kano arrived from Tokyo. Richard had written her from Bozeman during his teaching stint at MSU. Masako wrote to say her father was in the hospital, dying after surgery for intestinal cancer. She told Richard he'd known of the illness when he came to America in the fall of 1980. "I don't know the reason why, but there are only two adult men I can talk [to] like a true child of nature in this world," she concluded. "I'll lose one of them within three months (at most). Dear Puma, How could I lose you, too?"

Brautigan wrote back the same day, thanking her for her sensitive letter. "I'm very sorry that your father is ill," he scrawled. "Words often fail me, so I do not know what else to say." He changed the painful subject by writing about the weather ("Storm follows storm"), signing off "Richard," without any affectionate valediction.

Nikki Arai died on July 8. She was thirty-eight years old. Brautigan didn't get the news until a couple days later, when a mutual friend called from San Francisco. He felt "deeply shocked" and sat staring at the telephone in stunned silence. Not wanting to be alone, Richard dialed Marian Hjortsberg. He had a watermelon he'd bought when Rip Torn took him shopping a few days before. It hadn't been eaten at the party. Brautigan asked Marian if she'd like some watermelon. She said okay. "Bring it in half an hour and have dinner with me and my friend Todd."

Richard said he'd be right over. He carried the watermelon down the road to the Hjortsbergs'. Gatz had moved with Sharon to the Big Island of Hawaii in January, and his kids were visiting him for the summer. Marian seemed strangely agitated when she greeted Brautigan in her kitchen. He'd interrupted a romantic moment with her new boyfriend. She'd been too embarrassed to say anything about it on the phone. He wanted to tell her about Nikki Arai's death but felt uncomfortable. The watermelon had been "just some kind of funny excuse to talk about my grief." Brautigan apologized and went back to his place.

To avoid solitude, Richard started calling his friends. Nobody was home. He got lucky when John Barber picked up. "My friend just died," Brautigan said. "Why don't you come over. Bring a bottle of whiskey."

Barber knew about Richard's sick friend. He thought the woman was dying of cancer in Japan. He got to Pine Creek an hour later, Dickel in hand, and found Brautigan sitting alone in the coal shed he'd converted into his sleeping room. Richard proudly pointed out a metallic plastic roller blind he'd bought for the only window. Those inside could look out while remaining invisible to prying eyes. "You can lie here in bed with people all around in the backyard and make love," he said. "No one can see in, no one knows what you are doing."

Brautigan and Barber drank whiskey on the back porch. Richard sat in his favorite spot, legs stretched along the porch rail, facing south, his back supported by a pillar. John occupied "a spindly wooden lawn chair." No one spoke. They watched the cottonwood fluff drift past like summertime snow as thunderheads massed over the Bridger Mountains to the west. Twilight enhanced their silence as "ghost deer" wandered at the edge of darkness.

"She's gone now," Richard said, breaking their long meditation. "It's all done."

"She's gone but not forgotten." Barber felt stupid for mouthing an easy banality.

"I have no pictures of her, none of her letters, nothing. She's gone."

"But you have memories," John said, "and you can write them down and preserve them."

"I don't write for therapy, or to eulogize," Brautigan replied, getting up and going inside the house. When he returned he showed Barber a poem he'd written on a scrap of paper.

Rendezvous

Where you are now
I will join you.

Richard set his ephemeral poetry on the green wooden table. It fluttered among puffs of drifting cottonwood snow. "Come inside," he said. "Hunger has visited us. Let's eat."

They prepared noodles with smoked oysters, peas, and green onions gathered from the weed-choked garden. Eating with chopsticks, Brautigan taught Barber how to properly *slurp* his noodles in the Japanese manner. After their meal, they talked until the whiskey was gone and drove to Livingston for another bottle. They drank half of it on the way back to Rancho Brautigan.

"My friend was Japanese," Richard said after they returned. "She was a Buddhist. The Buddhists believed that one can send things to the dead by burning them. I have two books of hers and the poem. I will burn them and you can help if you don't think it's too heavy."

They gathered the items, along with lighter fluid and kitchen matches. "She loved white wine," Brautigan said, pouring a "delicate tulip-shaped glass" full to the brim. "We will burn this also."

They wove through waist-high backyard grass and placed the offerings on a pile of rocks. Richard gathered a handful of wildflowers, adding them to the impromptu bier. Barber soaked the offerings in lighter fluid and struck a match. "She always had great style," Brautigan said as the little shrine burst into flames.

Richard and John stood, arms over each other's shoulders, watching everything burn. The stem of the wine glass snapped and the shattered glass fell into the ashes. "She's gone," Brautigan whispered. "It's done."

Greg Keeler remembered how Arai's death "devastated [Richard], and he became drawn and gaunt, staring off his back porch for hours." Five days after she died, Brautigan wrote a letter to Nikki Arai (he called her N). He described getting the telephone call about her death and bringing a watermelon over to his "close neighbor M [. . .] when I interrupted her lovemaking." Richard wanted to phone N and tell her what had occurred "because you have the perfect sense of humor to understand. It's just the kind of story you would have enjoyed." Brautigan signed off, "Love, R." He later used this fictional correspondence as the introduction to *An Unfortunate Woman.*

The next day, after completing nearly thirty-five pages, Richard Brautigan stopped working on "American Hotels." He concluded with a description of Sherry Vetter telling him years later how bored she had been during their many fishing trips to northern California. "'Then why did you go along with it?' I said.

"'Because I liked the fucking part of it,' she said." At this point, Brautigan put down his pen. Memories of happier times nagged him like ghosts from the past.

Marian Hjortsberg's boyfriend, Todd, "a berserko alcoholic," ran amok in Bozeman. Richard came over with the dire news. "This looks really bad," he told her. "He's just gone berserk in Bozeman, and there's no telling if he's coming over here. I'm sleeping in the guestroom tonight." Brautigan arrived in the evening with "his Magnum-type handgun." He went to Marian's barn and brought in all the mallets, mauls, axes, and steel wedges, every conceivable weapon, hiding them under the guest room bed. After locking all the doors, Richard slept with his loaded pistol beneath the pillow.

Todd's rage ended in Brad Donovan's trailer. Word arrived in the morning. Brautigan had Marian drive them over to Forest Park. Richard liked Todd and his "zany sense of humor" but told Marian she had to break things off with him. "You have to meet with Todd," he instructed on the trip over the Bozeman Pass. "You have to tell him you never want to see him again because that's the way it works." She found it "very painful," telling Todd she never wanted to speak to him or see him again, just as Brautigan had outlined it for her. "It was just awful," Marian recalled. Richard waited in Brad's trailer until their private meeting was over.

Heading back over the hill, Brautigan observed that Marian had a "tendency to get involved with men who aren't altogether sound." After their brief romance in 1980, they had "just sort of been having parallel lives ever since," he explained, laying out some instructions regarding matters of the heart. "I don't necessarily follow them myself," Richard said, "but I'm going to give you some rules about your future boyfriends. First of all, you have to check their apartments. If they have one!"

Marian expressed an interest. Brautigan asked, "Did you look at Todd's apartment when you first met him?

"Yes?"

"Was it neat?"

"No."

"Was it a total pigsty?"

"Yes."

Richard smiled. "Well, that should have told you right from the start that you didn't want to get involved with this person."

At 9:48 am Tokyo time on July 16, Masako Kano wrote Richard Brautigan a one-line note: "Aujourd'hui Papa est mort." Masamichi Kano was only fifty-six at the time of his death. Brautigan wasn't home to receive her letter. Unable to tolerate being alone, he moved back over to Bozeman before it arrived. Richard did not take a room the Range. Georgia Donovan's sister, Mary, was away for the summer, and her trailer at Forest Park sat unoccupied. Brad invited Brautigan to use it whenever he needed a place to stay. He moved right in. A trailer park was familiar territory. Richard had grown up in sleazy motor courts. Forest Park seemed like the Ritz. Greg Keeler enjoyed visiting Brautigan there because the trailers sat right beside the Gallatin River. He could rig a baited rod on the bank and keep an eye on it while they drank and shot the shit inside. Richard was delighted. He considered this sort of angling "a typical tawdry example" of Keeler's Okie upbringing.

Late-night gunplay during the Dorns' visit was but one ricocheting episode in a long summer of back porch shooting at Rancho Brautigan. One summer Sunday morning, suffering from a massive hangover after a hard night's partying, Marian Hjortsberg got a phone call from Richard. Dave Schrieber had arrived from Bozeman with his firearm collection. "I want you to come over, and I want you to try some of Schrieber's guns."

"Richard, I just can't come over," she said, "I have this terrible hangover. The last thing in the world I want to do is shoot guns."

"But, my dear," Brautigan said, "you must understand, it's the best thing in the world for a hangover."

Marian walked down the road and joined the firing squad. They shot all through the morning. "It was so much fun," she recalled. "I actually shot really well." At one point Richard dragged out a pachinko machine that had been a Christmas gift from Aki. They shot it to smithereens. Schrieber hauled the bullet-punctured remnants home with him to Bozeman as a souvenir. The next time they shot together, a television set became the target.

When Richard read Masako's note about her father's death, he sent her a telegram on July 30 ("TODAY SOMEBODY IS BORN"), before moving back to Forest Park. After an afternoon at the Eagles, Brad Donovan and Brautigan went to see *Cat People*, playing a couple blocks up the street at the Ellen Theater. Released early in April, the movie had only then reached Bozeman. Directed by Paul Schrader (Siew-Hwa Beh's old grad school nemesis) and starring Nastassja Kinski, known as Nasty to her intimate friends, the picture was a remake of the classic Jacques Tourneur 1942 horror film.

When the show was over, Richard and Brad sat in the lobby of the Baxter Hotel with drinks from the Robin, "talking about all the ways the movie had fallen short." They both found it "grotesque" and agreed "it should have been done as a comedy." This led to inventing mock comic scenes for *Cat People* and a discussion of "slapstick comedy in general." The more they talked, the more Brautigan and Donovan kept returning to the Marx Brothers movies. They were attracted to anarchy.

A couple days later, Richard and Brad wandered around Forest Park. "Life here is really weird," Brautigan observed. "Once you move to a trailer park, you have no more illusions about your life." Richard was captivated by the absurd reality of people living in metal boxes. They hit upon a notion of writing a comic script about the "different silly little things" in a trailer park. Brautigan called their screenplay "a goofy blueprint for a house that will probably never be built."

"Why don't we just have fun with this one?" Richard told Donovan. They planned on putting anything and everything in at random, "and then [they'd] worry about it later." Greg Keeler came by Forest Park at the start of the project. Keeler noted that Brautigan "tended to let himself go" when he stayed out at the trailer settlement. Richard "smelled pretty funky" and hadn't shaved for several days.

In a story called "The Nightly Rounds," Brautigan confessed, "I don't bathe as often as I should here in Montana, but I never really liked to bathe anyway. I don't like the feeling of water on my body, and frankly, I don't understand people who do." Richard confessed that only women kept him clean. "They don't like to sleep with you when you smell like something that Boris Karloff just dragged in after making his nightly rounds of all the local cemeteries."

"You look just like a Bowery bum," Greg said.

"I'm on vacation," Brautigan replied.

"No you're not," Brad interjected. "You're working. I'm working."

"Yes, I can tell." Keeler suppressed a smile. "The whole trailer is atremble with the bustle of industry."

"Tell him about the screenplay," Georgia Donovan said.

Richard and Brad sat Greg down at the kitchen table and described their work in progress, at that point still in the bullshitting stage. They had a working title, "Trailer," an homage to/rip-off of the film *Airplane*, along with an assortment of goofy characters, including a dwarf bird trainer, a Vietnam vet with a bowl of mechanical fish, a Nazi landlady driving a bulldozer painted with a swastika, the Borrower (a guy who always borrows things), and an old couple wrapped in tinfoil waiting for aliens. Keeler thought it sounded a lot like life in Forest Park.

After the initial sessions in the Donovans' trailer, work shifted to Brautigan's Pine Creek place. There was no implied hierarchy. Richard didn't pull rank on Brad. Both men worked as equal collaborators. "The rule was that anything we wrote was okay," Donovan recalled. Brad came over to Rancho Brautigan for two- or three-day sprints. Brautigan wrote in his barn loft office. Donovan had the use of Richard's separate outside bedroom ("the little guest house") for his studio. Brautigan now slept in a bedroom inside his home.

Shooting the breeze, the two men sat around for a couple hours in the morning, coming up with ten new scenes. After that they divided the scenes ("You want to write this one?") before heading for separate work quarters. At the end of the day, they swapped drafts, adding "lines or description or layers of detail to what the other person did." They both worked in longhand, Brautigan scribbling on yellow legal pads; Donovan on scraps of blank paper. They cobbled together "a thirty-page kind of treatment and showed it to Jeff Bridges and Peter Fonda, who both offered encouragement.

Proud of his ability to "crank it up," Brautigan never failed to deliver his daily quota in spite of drinking and hangovers. In less than a month, three weeks at most, Brad and Richard produced a rough one-hundred-page first draft. "Just going over the top," Donovan recalled. Greg Keeler remembered them working frantically. The project "seemed to have a life and death urgency about it." At the same time, Brautigan dealt with the ongoing business details for his forthcoming novel, reviewing jacket and ad copy, scrutinizing the contracts for Jonathan Cape's British edition.

As Brad and Richard wrapped up their gonzo screenplay, an offer of a $15,000 advance arrived from Seymour Lawrence for Brautigan's new book proposal. Richard was stunned. It was $30,000 below his previous advance, and he immediately declined. Helen Brann wrote Lawrence on the first day of September, turning down the Delacorte offer. Sam was severing his own connection with

Dell, forming a new imprint (Dutton/Seymour Lawrence) with E. P. Dutton & Co. Lawrence made an identical offer for Brautigan's book on behalf of his new publishing house, which Richard also turned down flat.

This was a depressing turn of events. Publishers vote with their wallets. Having his last advance reduced by two-thirds was not a vote of confidence. Richard took it in stride, searching for fun at the Eagles with Greg, Scoop, Brad, and the usual suspects. One weekend Brautigan and Keeler sat drinking the night away. A band in the dance hall above cranked out two-steps, and elderly lodge members escorted their white-haired wives up the stairs to trip the light fantastic. The more they drank, the better these old ladies started looking to Richard and Greg. "Boy, wouldn't you like that?" they remarked. "Yeah, get a load of that one."

"I've got an idea," Brautigan said. "Why don't we just go into the women's room and hang our tongues over the toilet paper roll?"

The bartender overheard this remark. The next day, when Richard and Greg came into the Eagles for some hair of the dog, a sign had been posted. It stated that the management would now charge a patron twenty-five cents every time he used a swear word. Brautigan promptly marched up to the bar and dropped a sawbuck into the collection jar. "I'll buy a few," he said. "Give me ten bucks' worth."

Summertime meant frequent picnics, barbecues, and parties in Montana. At a gathering in the Bozeman home of MSU art professor Fran Noel, Richard was accosted by an obnoxious fan. "Are you really Brautigan," he demanded.

"Yes."

"Are you really him?"

"Do you want to see my ID?" Richard asked, turning around and dropping his pants to moon the persistent stranger.

Mooning became a favorite gesture of Brautigan's. When Greg Keeler drove with him to the airport on his final departure from Montana a year later, Richard handed Greg a snapshot of him baring his ass for the camera. "Something to remember me by," he said.

Not all nervous strangers got the same treatment as the pushy fan at Fran Noel's. At a dinner party in the Livingston home of Dennis Noteboom, Brautigan stood listening to David Stein, son of author and state senator Ben Stein, play the piano. By Stein's own admission, he was "pretty good at noodling out a tune." Richard sat down beside him on the piano bench, saying he thought his playing was "very good."

Stein replied that it made him nervous to perform next to "a famous person."

"Don't worry," Brautigan assured him, "famous people are just like everyone else."

Toward the end of summer, the Bozeman poets staged another group reading at Chico Hot Springs. Greg Keeler remained in the lineup. Once again he invited Richard to participate. This time around, Brautigan agreed. At the reading, Richard got into a snit when he saw Greg sitting with Paul Ferlazzo, his department head. "I guess you know which side your bread's buttered on," he jibed. After Brautigan read, the place erupted into an enthusiastic ovation.

Keeler's reading drew only "a polite scattering of applause." Greg, just back from a summer in England, read a poem "about a British trash fish called a tench." Brautigan leaned toward Keeler. "That was pretty pre-tench-ous," he said. "You need a muse injection, big boy."

So the Wind Won't Blow It All Away was published in hardcover by Delacorte Press/Seymour Lawrence on September 10, 1982. One of the 17,500 copies printed was hand delivered to Richard in Pine Creek by Dink Bruce at the personal request of the publisher. Sam Lawrence also sent along a quart of George Dickel sour mash and a short, hand-printed note: "You're the tops / You're the Eiffel Tower / You outshine General Eisenhower." Finding no one home, Dink left a brief note of his own. The whiskey got delivered a couple days later.

Brautigan's reviews comprised his usual mixed bag of scornful denunciation and fawning praise. The detractors included the *Los Angeles Times Book Review*, *Publishers Weekly*, the *San Francisco Chronicle* (Richard told Greg Keeler that its reviewer "was a hatchet-person brought in from the outside"), and the *New York Times Book Review*. On the positive side, *Playboy*, *Booklist*, the *Oakland Tribune*, and the *Christian Science Monitor* all celebrated the novel. *So the Wind* almost always found favor with other writers. Rick DeMarinis, the only true novelist amid the honking gaggle of newspaper hacks, called Brautigan's book "a lyrical meditation told in a warm personal voice" in the *Chicago Tribune Book World*.

Sam Lawrence wrote to Richard on the twenty-fourth, sending along two favorable reviews and the news that thirteen thousand copies had been shipped. "Which ain't bad in these recession times." Brautigan was back in San Francisco at Japantown's Kyoto Inn. While he was away, another film crew from Pioneer stereo showed up in Montana. Finding Richard not at home, they sought out his sidekick, Greg Keeler, interviewing him about "how their products might function in the Montana wilderness." Greg wrote a little humorous jingle and got paid $150 in cash.

Brautigan had gone down to San Francisco for business meetings with Joel Shawn, his attorney. The Bolinas property topped the list. Richard's primary asset, paid for in full, remained a potential income producer, either through a sale or rental. The place stood in a sorry state of disrepair. Brautigan lacked the capital required to get things back into shape. He and Shawn discussed the options open to him. Getting an estimate on repairs remained item number one. Paying for the work presented another problem. The lawyer suggested a "FannyMac" loan to cover expenses.

These discussions depressed Brautigan, each mundane detail a further reminder of his declining financial status. Debts kept piling up. Prospects for future income seemed few and far between. One bright spot came in an August letter forwarded to Shawn by Simon & Schuster from the Speakers Bureau at Stanford University, extending a "warm invitation for a winter visit to sunny California." This meant a paycheck. Richard instructed Joel to turn the matter over to Lordly & Dame in Boston, his booking agent for the *Tokyo–Montana* tour.

Dick Dillof and Ed Dorn were also in Frisco at the same time. They had been invited to be part of a presentation with Tom Clark at the Intersection for the Arts. The performance space now was located at St. John's Methodist Church at 756 Union Street in North Beach, which had closed as a place of worship due to a lack of parishioners. Over the years, the Intersection had become a showcase for music, comedy, dance, theater, and the spoken word. Its current director was Jim Hartz, a poet and friend of Thomas Merton. He had studied with Chögyam Trungpa Rinpoche and was a practicing Vajrayana Buddhist.

During the program, Hartz tried to engage Clark and Dorn in a discussion about "the Naropa Poetry Wars," but they resisted, preferring to read their poems instead. When Dillof's turn came, he read a story from his book *Hobo* about a runaway kid hopping a freight train. Dobro followed this by getting out his banjo and singing a railroad song. He was dressed for the occasion in his "rambling clothes": soiled cowboy hat, colorful neckerchief, vest, and watch chain. Dick augmented his music with train sounds from a hidden tape recorder, acting surprised every time that lonesome whistle blew.

Richard Brautigan stumbled into the Intersection in the middle of Dillof's performance, dead drunk and waving a whiskey bottle, accompanied by a number of street urchins. They pushed their way to the stage, and the kids starting tugging at Dick's shirttails and pulling on his watch chain. "Making a shambles of me," he recalled.

Brautigan took a big swing at Dillof's belly and missed. Thinking it was all fun, Dick grabbed hold of Richard's cowboy boot and they hopped wildly around the stage, crashing with a wild clatter into a stack of folded chairs. Watching from the back of the house, Simone Ellis thought the fight was for real and that she had witnessed the end of a long friendship. Jim Hartz, upstairs cleaning and putting things away, didn't see a thing.

Dillof believed he and Richard were just horsing around, but later, outside on the street, Jenny Dorn felt scared. "Richard was out of his mind drunk," she said. He swung his whiskey bottle "aggressively" at Dick. Jenny thought that Brautigan resented Dobro hanging out with her and Ed, always treating Dillof in a mean and cruel fashion. When Dick and Richard took off together into the night, the Dorns went in another direction. They never saw Brautigan again.

Richard and Dick ended up at Enrico's, where they ordered drinks and some calamari. As they sat talking, Brautigan took a chair and placed it on the table between them. The manager approached. "Sir, if you don't mind," he said, removing the chair. Brautigan said it was Dillof who wanted it up there and immediately put two chairs on the table. Again the manager took them down. "Troublemaker Richard at work," Dick observed as Brautigan, utterly deadpan, stacked three chairs on the table, a re-creation of enclosing Erik Weber in furniture at the McGuanes' place ten years before. "He liked the old one-two-three," Dillof said.

They continued their conversation through the chair legs when the manager approached for a third time. As he sternly unstacked the chairs, Brautigan sighed in sympathy, apologizing for the way Dillof had been behaving. Later Richard stretched out on the floor, pretending to go to sleep under the coat rack. The manager ignored him. After a bit, Richard told Dick, "I'll be right back" and walked out onto Broadway, never to return that night.

Back in Montana by early October, Brautigan took a room at the Baxter Hotel. The Range had closed earlier that year, and the Baxter was the last of the old downtown hotels. It was also cheap. When the Baxter opened in 1929, the seven-story art deco building was a grand place, the pride of the town. Now its five-buck-a-night rooms sported bare lightbulbs dangling from cracked and flaking ceilings. Ken Nagano, one of the producers of the 1980 Pioneer stereo shoot, who Greg Keeler thought "looked like a Hollywood mover and shaker," came looking for Richard but couldn't find him in his cheap hideaway.

Nagano went to see Keeler. His company, Maxy Incorporated, wanted to use Brautigan in a commercial for Japanese Jim Beam. He asked Greg to contact Richard, and Keeler "stupidly agreed."

Brautigan wasn't pleased. "Ah, so now you're my Japanese agent?" he taunted on the phone. When Keeler hemmed and hawed, looking for a way out of an uncomfortable situation, Richard told him what to say to Ken Nagano and the others at Maxy. "I want you to tell them to get fucked."

"I don't think . . ." Greg stammered.

"That's right. You don't think. You just tell them to get fucked." With that, Brautigan hung up.

In a handwritten letter, Ken Nagano pleaded with Richard, "Since the crew is in the U.S., and all the plans have been made, my only recourse is to commit SEPPUKU." To sweeten the deal, Ken promised Brautigan an interview with Japanese *Playboy*. Nagano called Keeler and made the same half-joking suicide threat. Greg felt awful.

"It's his decision," Richard said when Keeler told him. A few months later Brautigan reconsidered and accused Keeler "of losing him a huge contract and a lot of money."

The second week in October, Richard started work again on "American Hotels." Sitting in the lobby or up in his shabby room, he wrote very quickly, launching into memories of Fallon, Nevada, and his 1958 trip to Mexico. The Baxter had been sold to a developer, who planned to close the place and convert it into condominiums. Brautigan worked steadily, knowing the world he described was coming to an end. He filled forty-seven pages of his notebook over the next two weeks, chronicling his observations of "Muhamid [*sic*] Ali" at the Keio Plaza in 1976.

Just before Halloween, Richard sat with his manuscript in the lobby of the Baxter. "There have always been hotels in this town," he wrote in the notebook. "At the end of the month the last one will close and there will be no more hotels in this town. There will be plenty of motels but you can't easily live in a motel room. I'm staying at that last closing hotel now, and it will figure off and on in this book." Brautigan worked straight through the morning.

After completing four more paragraphs, he penned an enigmatic final line: "A sequence of miss matched [*sic*] little options and realities can set me too [*sic*] howling at the moon, but I can easily accept large panoramic disruptional continuity." Richard stared at his last sentence, jotted the word "Examples" beneath it, and scrawled three more paragraphs describing his experiences during a typhoon in Tokyo. How boring it was shut up in his hotel room during the storm. About nearly being decapitated by windblown sheet metal when he finally went out to see a porno movie. Brautigan closed his notebook at this point and never wrote another word in the manuscript he called "American Hotels."

A final irony awaited him. Not wanting to be alone at Pine Creek, Richard rented a room at the Imperial 400 Motel just across Main Street from the Baxter. *So the Wind* described an innocent time in the 1950s, gone forever, along with black-and-white television and segregation. His unfinished manuscript about small-town hotels recorded the demise of another cherished American institution. Brautigan's politics always lay just beneath the surface. He sympathized with the little guy and the oppressed but was a conservative at heart, lamenting the inevitable loss of a world he cherished but knew was gone forever.

THE APPEARANCE OF *So the Wind Won't Blow It All Away* in September of 1982 marked the end of Richard Brautigan's career as a published writer. He continued working on various projects for the rest of his life, but aside from foreign editions of earlier books and a single poem and short story published together in an obscure Washington, D.C., art review the year he died, Brautigan never saw another word he wrote appear in print. Richard did not foresee this fate. That fall, he continued to hope his new novel would be a hit. Brautigan had long harbored premonitions of doom. Death had walked by his side since childhood, kept at bay first by ambition and later by success. These props no longer supported him. Without knowing it, Brautigan had begun a long spiral into the vortex of oblivion.

Good and bad news came in equal doses through the remainder of the fall. On the plus side, Lordly & Dame sent Richard the Stanford reading contract on October 20. Two weeks later the Boston booking firm followed up with another speaking engagement. The Sophomore Literary Festival Council at the University of Notre Dame invited Brautigan to read on February 23. It offered his standard fee of $1,500, the same as two months in an MSU classroom.

More welcome news arrived from Helen Brann in October. The eponymous French publishing firm Christian Bourgois made an offer to bring out a translation of *So the Wind* by Marc Chénetier in April. It planned a simultaneous French edition of *Revenge of the Lawn*. Christian Bourgois invited Brautigan to come to Paris in April "for about a week" on an expense-paid trip. Richard accepted, letting his agent take care of the details.

On the negative side of the equation, a notice from the IRS at the end of November claimed Brautigan owed $6,767.94 (including penalties and interest) on his 1981 income tax. Richard missed the first payment ($501.86) due on his 1982–1983 property taxes for the Bolinas house. Cash poor, he'd also miss the next one, due in May.

Jonathan Dolger left his job as an editor at Simon & Schuster and set up shop as a literary agent in his East Side Manhattan apartment. Brad Donovan needed professional representation for a novel he'd written. Dolger was searching for clients. Early in October Richard sent Brad's manuscript to the Jonathan Dolger Agency. Dolger liked Donovan's work and agreed to "try and place it."

Greg Keeler "barely got tenure" at MSU. He asked Richard for a supporting letter. Brautigan said anything from him was "the kiss of death" and declined. Paul Ferlazzo encouraged Keeler to write an article for the *Dictionary of Literary Biography*. "Pretty huffy about the whole idea," Greg fumed over drinks at the Eagles. "William Saroyan," Brautigan exclaimed on hearing the name of the subject, "what a wonderful writer. This should be fun."

Keeler felt dubious. Richard had once told him that fun was "an odd concept." Brautigan put in a lot of time loaning Greg books, giving him insights and a lecture about "Saroyan's early years and his relationship with Martha Foley at *Story* magazine." Keeler's essay became Richard's project by proxy. Greg suspected Brautigan had an underlying motive. Someday "he would want someone to do a good job on his own entry."

Richard also offered Marian Hjortsberg his literary expertise. She had returned to school, entering an MA program at MSU that fall. Twenty-five years away from term papers, Marian felt overwhelmed by her first assignment, an essay on *The Epic of Gilgamesh*. One of the earliest works of world literature, a compilation of epic Sumerian legends on twelve ancient clay tablets, *Gilgamesh* had survived since the seventh century bc. "I was sure I couldn't do it," Marian remembered.

"You can do it," Richard said, sitting down at her kitchen table. "Get me the book."

Marian brought the text. Brautigan opened it and set to work. "Okay," Richard explained, "this is your introduction." Underlining as he turned the pages, Brautigan outlined Marian's paper.

"He was a natural," she recalled. "So patient and kind."

Not everyone saw Richard's generous side. Toward the end of summer, John Barber and Brautigan "had a disagreement." Richard told him "to go away and never speak to [me] again." Brautigan struck Barber as "someone incapable of upholding an enduring relationship with anyone." They met on a Bozeman street not long afterward. John said he was sorry, asking to talk it through and save their friendship.

"I don't know," Richard said. "We'll see. I'll let you know." Barber never saw Brautigan again.

Richard spent much of the fall in Bozeman, staying in room 214 at the Imperial 400 Motel. Every weekend during football season, Brautigan camped at Karen Datko's house. Scoop ended up doing the camping. She gave Unc her "big-ass queen-size bed" upstairs and slept on the couch. Before bedtime, Richard stretched out on the couch in front of Scoop's "big old thirty-buck color TV." Don Carpenter maintained that Brautigan didn't like football. Richard enjoyed Datko's company. While she got into the game, he "lay on the couch and didn't move for goddamn hours," all the while regaling Scoop with tales of the old days.

Datko was not sexually attracted to Brautigan. "He was always a horny guy," she remembered. Karen liked Richard, so she never told him. "He was like Unc," she said. "He was like this big, tall, kind of dumb, potbellied, older guy." Every so often, Brautigan couldn't resist, suggesting to Scoop that they go to bed together. Getting no reply, he'd smile and say, "But why ruin a wonderful friendship?"

"You're right," Datko always replied.

Whenever Richard couldn't score a ride from Pine Creek to Bozeman, he'd hitchhike into Livingston and take a bus over the hill. "I'm just a bunch of road meat" was his description of thumbing down a ride. Once when Brautigan made it to the Bozone bus station, he phoned Karen Datko. "Scoopie," he announced, "I'm in Bozeman and you shall have the pleasure of buying me a drink. After a couple rounds, Richard pulled out a monthly rent check from one of his three Livingston properties, cashed it at the Eagles bar, and "picked up the tab for the rest of the night."

Dirty Unc spent most of Thanksgiving with Scoop. He awoke at her place on Turkey Day morning. Datko had no breakfast sausage. She said she'd run to the store and get some. Richard wanted to go along. Scoop planned a simple trip to the corner 7-Eleven. Thick snow covered the ground. The streets were icy. Brautigan climbed into her car. "Let's go to the IGA," he said.

"I don't think they're open," she protested.

"No, let's go there. I'd rather go there and get sausage."

"God knows, we drove all over the goddamn town," Scoop recalled. They went from one supermarket to the next, skidding on the ice. The IGA was closed. So were Albertsons and Safeway. "Can we go home now?" Datko pleaded.

"No. We have to try another store."

They discovered Buttrey's was the only Bozeman supermarket open on Thanksgiving Day. Inside, Scoop realized that Richard was after much more than sausage. His provisions had run low at Pine Creek, and Brautigan "went on this big shopping expedition." As they roamed the aisles stocking up, the truth dawned on Datko. "Oh no!" she thought, "I've been Unced again."

Brautigan was "really drinking hard that day." By the time they got his groceries back to Scoop's, it was too late for her to prepare Thanksgiving dinner. Richard went down to the Eagles, eating a miserable turkey meal with Dick Dillof and Sean Cassaday, teasing Dobro without mercy. Back at Datko's, he accompanied Scoop to her friend's house for "leftover stuffing and gravy." To top it all off, Richard phoned Marian Hjortsberg. She braved the frozen pass, driving him and his load of groceries home to Pine Creek.

On Friday, December 10, Brautigan arranged for a revolving line-of-credit commercial note at the First Security Bank in Livingston. His cash flow dried to a trickle. Richard needed funds to pay the monthly bills. The bank loaned him $105,000 over a two-year period, 16.5 percent annual interest to be paid quarterly. In the past, this kind of money came from book advances. Brautigan had grown used to the lifestyle of success. He wasn't about to give it up. Only now he had to borrow the cash to bankroll a lit star's extravagant behavior.

Gatz Hjortsberg came back to Montana over the Christmas holidays. After his divorce was final, he and Sharon married that summer in a Buddhist ceremony at their rented house in Kapoho, Hawaii. In the fall, *Legend of Darkness,* a film he wrote for Ridley Scott in 1980, kicked back into life. Hjortsberg flew to London to continue working on the project, living alone in the Hotel Lancaster. His new bride moved back to her parents' home in Billings. The Christmas trip was an effort to resurrect an already troubled marriage. Aside from his children, Gatz saw no one from Livingston before returning to England early in 1983.

Boxing Day, the day afer Christmas, was Lorca Hjortsberg's sixteenth birthday. She qualified for a learner's permit and Richard gave her a silver-green '62 Chevy II. It had been Greg Keeler's grandmother's car. Keeler had driven it up from Oklahoma earlier in the year and had sold it to Brautigan "for around $200." The old car had sat unused in Richard's barn.

After New Year's Day, snowbound in Pine Creek, Brautigan wrote to Masako Kano. She had sent Richard a recent photograph. Reminders of lost love didn't prompt a romantic response. Brautigan's letter talked of missing a broom when he needed to sweep his floor. He mentioned "a solitary existence," ending with no expression of affection, wishing Kano "Happy 1983."

Sam Lawrence gave Brautigan a leather-bound copy of *So the Wind* for Christmas. One night, after turning his inner rage on Greg Keeler, Richard inscribed it for him. Greg was headed for his car. His friend rushed out after him. "I have something for you," he called. "It's a book."

"Just what I need," Keeler said, "another book."

Brautigan explained that this copy was special, one of a kind. Greg asked why he wanted to give it to him. "Because I am drunk," Richard replied, "and I have just insulted my friend."

Richard flew down to San Francisco in mid-January. He took a room at the Kyoto Inn. Having a hundred grand in recently acquired credit made Brautigan feel he had real jack in his jeans again. Feeling flush, he decided to make a quick trip to Tokyo. On the nineteenth, the day of his scheduled reading at Stanford, Richard went to the Japanese Consul-General and obtained a ninety-day visa. His university contract provided for transportation from the airport and back. He arranged to be picked up at his hotel instead. At 8:00 pm, Brautigan stood before an audience in Palo Alto, singing for his supper. It was no different than standing on the balcony at The Place a quarter century before. Richard had first read at Stanford fifteen years earlier. His audience shrunk noticeably in reverse proportion to the size of his paycheck.

Having only a week to spend in Frisco, Brautigan was out for a good time, determined to pack as much fun as possible into a few days. He hooked back up with Richard Breen, his old comrade in larceny. Breen was staying with a friend, attorney Sam McCullough, who had a house up on Telegraph Hill. Richard had observed the former parking valet making a dinner engagement at Enrico's with a beautiful woman a couple nights before and on the afternoon of the big date, Brautigan dropped by McCullough's place. Breen bought a new shirt for his assignation and was taking a shower while Richard and Sam enjoyed brandy and coffee in the front room. Brautigan took note of Breen's glad rags carefully laid-out for the night ahead.

Later, at Enrico's, Richard sat at one end of the bar while Breen enjoyed a cocktail at the other with his lovely date. "I was running shit on this broad," Breen recalled, when his conversation was interrupted by one of the night waiters, who'd been sent over by Brautigan. "Richard wants to know if you have *so and so's* business card."

Breen looked down the bar to see Richard staring at him "with this weird grin on his face." He told the waiter, "Yeah. OK," and pulled out his wallet, opening it to reveal a large foil-wrapped condom sitting front and center. The young woman took one look and got up and left, her cigarette still smoldering on an ashtray, her perfume lingering in the air. "The fucker had slipped a rubber into my wallet while I was in the shower," Breen fumed.

Brautigan walked over grinning. "You were going to buy somebody dinner," he said. "It might as well be me." They took a table on the terrace and ate swordfish. "$11.50 a pop." Years later, Breen still remembered the tab he picked up that night. "And, of course, [Richard] was ordering snifters of Calvados. They look like flower vases."

On his way to Japan, Brautigan phoned Klyde Young from the airport. He was worried about the Bolinas house. Richard told Klyde the porch railing was weak. "Someone could lean against it and fall over the side." He asked Young to "please go out and fix it immediately." Richard was thinking of renting the house and wanted it to be safe. It bothered him. He was leaving the country and didn't want to think about it.

Brautigan wheedled and pleaded. Young promised to go to Bolinas the next day and take care of things, but he was busy with his own projects and ended up hiring a carpenter he knew to do the job. Klyde paid him $100 out of his own pocket for the work. "Then, he didn't rent the house," Young said, "and nobody walked on the porch for a year and a half after that, but it had to be done the next day because in his mind it was something that was bothering him."

On January 22, Richard landed at Haneda Airport and had his passport stamped, entering

Japan for the fifth time. Brautigan checked into the Keio Plaza Hotel on his shortest stay in Tokyo, slightly less than four weeks. Richard had no pressing business in Japan. His impromptu winter trip was fueled by a romantic desire to see Masako Kano. As soon as he arrived, Puma got in touch with Puck. Masako still lived at home with her mother. She had received her MA in June 1981 and had been accepted into the PhD program at Columbia University. Her hopes of returning to the States had been delayed by tight finances after her father's death. He'd been a scholar, but his primary income came from a translation agency he owned. He was the brains behind the whole outfit, and his passing marked the end of the business.

Masako had a day job as a financial systems analyst for Nippon Motorola, Inc., in Tokyo. When Brautigan called, she agreed to meet him after work. It was a cold winter afternoon. Masako wore her mother's black mink coat as she stood outside, waiting for Richard to pick her up. He arrived by taxi. Noticing the expensive coat, he nodded with displeasure as she got in. "You changed," Brautigan said. "Look at you. You're wearing fur. You've changed so much."

In truth, Kano had matured considerably since Richard had last seen her more than two years before. She'd had an affair with a journalist, spending time with him in Saigon and Phnom Penh, and was no longer an innocent virginal schoolgirl. Brautigan assumed the mink coat had been a gift from some rich paramour. Masako let him stew in his jealousy for a bit before telling him the mink belonged to her mother. Richard didn't believe her, so she took off the coat and let him smell the mothballs. Masako never forgot Brautigan's "relieved smile."

They went straight to The Cradle, which was not yet open for its evening business. Takako had arranged to unlock the place for Richard. He led Masako inside and they sat down "in the corner padded seat together," totally alone. They talked and talked, catching up on lost time. Masako felt "perhaps disappointed that he looked older and a bit overweight." He wasn't the man she remembered from Boulder, but he was her first man and the chemistry still boiled.

Kano and Brautigan started meeting after her work "to stroll around the town." Richard knew of "amazing authentic Japanese restaurants," where they stopped for refreshment before it grew dark and it was time for Masako to head for home on the Keio Line. One evening she took him to an *okonomiyaki* place for the inexpensive savory pancakes, known as Japanese pizza. Topped with meat, fish, or shredded vegetables, *okonomiyaki* had originated in Osaka and was popular with students and others on limited budgets. They went to a restaurant crowded with junior high school boys, who all wanted to practice their English with Richard. "He liked it" and "repeated some phrases from his poems," Masako recalled. "And he just laughed so much. Being called Lichard."

Business followed Brautigan to Tokyo. Helen Brann forwarded a letter from Günter Ohnemus, Richard's German translator. He had news. *Transatlantik* (Germany's *New Yorker*) planned to publish some stories from *Tokyo–Montana Express* in "their February or March issue" under the generic title "News from Tokyo." The magazine also wanted to "print something" new by Brautigan. Also, Radio Bavaria hoped to present a dramatization of *Dreaming of Babylon*. "One more step to Fame in Germany," Ohnemus enthused.

On the twenty-fourth, Brann sent a "machine copy" of a letter from Richard's French publisher, officially inviting him to spend a week in Paris (beginning April 11) for the publication of the French edition of *So the Wind*. Brautigan had asked for his return ticket to go via Tokyo instead of New York. Brann wrote to Michelle Lapautre, his French agent, forwarding the request. An answer came before the end of the month. Helen informed Richard that Bourgois would buy his ticket to Japan.

With a return to Tokyo assured, Brautigan felt confident he'd see Masako Kano again not long after his imminent departure. "I kind of tormented him for a while," Masako recalled. No longer "naive," she delayed going to bed with him right away. Richard's horny approach was "too straightforward" for Kano's new, more sophisticated tastes, but they instinctively knew one another's mischievous side. "We were kind of T. S. Eliot cats to each other," Masako said. Playful and adventurous, they found many amusing things to do together aside from lovemaking.

One cold Friday evening, Kano took Brautigan to Hanayashiki, the oldest amusement park in Japan, riding the subway to Tokyo's Asakusa District. Founded as a "flower park" in 1853, the year Commodore Matthew Perry and his fleet of four steam frigates arrived in Japan, Hanayashiki was, in Masako's description, "the funny Coney Island place with haunting castle and shabby merry-go-round." Crammed with corny carnival rides encircled by a dinky roller-coaster, the minuscule park also boasted a Ferris wheel. Richard and Masako saw only a few teenagers hanging around, "petting" outside in spite of the winter weather. The place appealed to their "Fellini-esque" sensibilities. "Kind of suited for Mountain Cat and Puck the Liar in cold Asakusa," Masako recalled.

After a painfully abrupt parting in a snowstorm ("Why did everybody in Japan want a cab at that place, at that time?" Richard wrote Masako six days later), Brautigan flew back to San Francisco on February 18. Surprised to discover the innocent grad student he had seduced two years before wasn't as young as she'd claimed to be (Masako confessed she had lied about her age during his visit), Richard felt much more distress upon learning that his poetic Yeats scholar had transformed into a sophisticated businesswoman.

Brautigan had only four days to frolic in Frisco. On the twenty-third, he was back on a plane, off to South Bend, Indiana, where a representative from the University of Notre Dame du Lac met him at the airport and drove him north of town to the campus. At 7:00 pm, Richard stood on the stage of the Memorial Library Auditorium, reading his frequently blasphemous and often ribald poetry to an audience of presumably devout Catholic students. At the reception following his presentation, two lovely young coeds came on to Brautigan. Richard was hot to trot, but an outbreak of his persistent STD foreclosed on any sexual adventuring. "If it weren't for these damned herpes we could have done a tricycle!" he remarked to Greg Keeler when he returned to Montana.

The next day, after an informal morning Q&A session at Notre Dame and several airport connections, Brautigan was back rambling around his forty-acre "Rancho." In so many ways, it was the end of the line. Nobody wanted *An Unfortunate Woman*. He lived on borrowed money. His sex life had festered to a leprous end. Europe offered a chance for salvation. They loved him in France. Possibilities were opening up in Germany. Richard had a chance to put it all back together. Like a heavyweight training for the main event, he made a determined effort to get back into top form.

Brautigan quit drinking "for about six weeks" and went on a diet, eating mostly carrots. Tom McGuane remembered "a refrigerator full of carrots." Marian Hjortsberg believed he "felt committed to cleaning up his act." Richard came over to her house "two or three times a week" to "pedal furiously" on her Exercycle for forty minutes at a stretch. "The effects were miraculous," McGuane said. "The greatest I've ever seen abstinence produce. He became a machine of energy. He lost one-quarter of his body weight. He became more creative than he'd been since he was in his twenties."

"He was trying to get into shape," Marian recalled, but "he got squirrellier and squirrellier and squirrellier." One evening they had a discussion. Brautigan told Marian, "You see, every day I get worse. I get more and more irascible and peckish and I start finding fault with everyone. I become one of those little kind of perfectionists, and drinking makes me human. That's why I do it."

Richard understood the root of his problem. He also knew the only path to salvation meant staying sober. He worked at it, day by day, a one-man twelve-step program. Sobriety did little to alleviate his irascible peckishness, and he brooded on the unfavorable reactions to *An Unfortunate Woman* from trusted professional advisers. Early in March, Brautigan had a long phone conversation with Helen Brann about his most recent novel. The matter had simmered between them, ticking away like a time bomb ever since Brautigan had sent his agent the manuscript back in September.

Brann read it immediately but waited "three or four days" before calling Richard. Priding herself "on being honest with her clients," she broke the bad news to Brautigan as gently as she could. Helen felt the new book was "very much related to that god-awful time with Akiko." It struck her as more "autobiographical" than fiction. She had offered it to Sam Lawrence. Richard had declined both his identical lowball offers. After that, the issue lay dormant for almost six months, a winter snake, venomous and waiting to strike.

"I had to tell him it simply was not going to work," Helen Brann recalled. "There was no revising it. There was nothing to do with it in my opinion except put it to one side and go on with the next work." This was not what Brautigan wanted to hear. Always loyal to his friends, Richard demanded unflinching loyalty in return and severed all contact with anyone (such as Gatz Hjortsberg) he perceived as having crossed him. Brann skated on extremely thin ice. "I knew if I told him that he would probably leave me," she said.

Hoping to forestall this possibility, Helen sent Brautigan a telegram the next morning. "I want you to know that whatever you decide to do in sending the new novel, I will follow through despite my misgivings about this work," she wired. "Believe me I am very unhappy at having this reaction to the novel and hope you know that I continue to think of you as one of the best and most important writers writing today." Brann's message came too late. Richard's "irascible nature" took control. He had already mailed her his final word on the matter, ending their thirteen-year business relationship in two terse sentences.

"Dear Helen Brann," Brautigan began (instead of the usual "Dear Helen"). "After our last conversation about my new novel <u>An Unfortunate Woman</u>, I realized that our views on this work are so vastly different that it would be very difficult to continue our working relationship because this novel is one of the main directions of my future writing.

"So I am terminating my relationship with the Helen Brann Agency effective as of March 11, 1983." He signed off with his full name (not his customary "Love, Richard"), "Regretfully, Richard Brautigan." A carbon copy was mailed to Joel Shawn.

Even as he severed one long-standing connection, Richard reestablished another troubled friendship. At Marian Hjortsberg's house one night, Brautigan expressed regret over the schism between him and Tom McGuane. He decided to make amends and phoned McGuane. "I want you to come over here," he said. "I think it's time we let bygones be bygones."

"Tom came racing over," Marian recalled.

Brautigan asked her to stay. "I want you to be the arbiter," he said.

Marian hung around downstairs, ready "to ameliorate in case anything went wrong." In short order, "they had sort of a pas de deux around each other" in Hjortsberg's living room, "hugging and kissing and weeping." Marian remembered it as "a very special moment," recalling the two men "both professing undying love and telling me I was the most wonderful woman in the world and quack, quack, quack, and it was very touching."

To cement their renewed friendship, McGuane invited Brautigan to dinner a week later at his new ranch on Barney Creek. Barry Hannah, a forty-year-old Mississippi novelist, currently writer-in-residence at the University of Montana, was a houseguest. Tom thought he and Richard should meet. Hannah's first novel, *Geronimo Rex,* had won the William Faulkner Prize in 1972. In the following decade he published two more novels and *Airships*, a book of short stories (1978) that McGuane liked very much. A new novel, *The Tennis Handsome*, was about to be published by Alfred A. Knopf. Brautigan greatly enjoyed his conversation with the younger writer. They exchanged addresses. Upon parting, Hannah gave Richard an advance copy of his new book.

Brautigan's travel plans ran into an unexpected snag. His cultural visa to Japan, issued on January 19, had been stamped "VOID" when he departed the country on February 18. Applying for another visa after such a short time presented problems. Richard needed to jump through various diplomatic hoops. The Japanese Consul in Seattle demanded signed letters from his Tokyo publisher. In a panic, he phoned Takako Shiina, and she agreed to help. It would be easy, he told her. Only four lines, he said.

A control-freak nitpicker, Brautigan proved overly demanding in his detailed instructions. Their conversations grew heated. Richard hung up on Takako twice. She thought he was "just impossible." Brautigan "upset [her] terribly," making her "so angry," but Shiina went to the Ministry of Foreign Affairs for the necessary information. Afterward she "spent all [her] precious evening" writing two long documents: an "affidavit of support" and a letter of invitation from Shobun-sha, detailing Richard's relationship with the Japanese publisher and how his visit would "contribute to Japanese culture."

The next afternoon, after Mr. Zuno of Shobun-sha said he had no time to see her, Takako tracked him down at a Shinjuku coffee shop, interrupting a meeting. She begged him to type the two letters and affix the Shobun-sha seal. The publishing company didn't have a typewriter, further complicating matters. Shiina still managed to get everything done. She sent the signed, typed letters and copies of Shobun-sha's company registration and corporate history off to Brautigan by registered express mail.

Takako posted a separate indignant letter to "My nasty brother, Richard." She signed off, "Your mad, mad, mad, sister." Brautigan received the documents and sent them, along with his passport, to the Japanese Consul in Seattle. Shiina's dogged hard work paid off. Richard was approved for a stay of six months. The consulate stamped the visa (valid entry for ninety days) in his passport on March, 24, 1983.

Aside from letters, Brautigan did no writing in March. He wrote Masako Kano four times, emphasizing how busy he was ("Work! Work! Work!"), but what exactly occupied his time remained a mystery. Richard revised the typescript of *An Unfortunate Woman* in a minimal fashion. He changed the gender of the shoe in the opening sentence. Aside from a couple other minor adjustments, his biggest alteration involved erasing the words "short novel" throughout his text and penning "journey" in their place. Brautigan finished these slight modifications in the first week of April.

Richard seemed anxious to see Masako again, his regimen of exercise and diet an effort to spruce up his image. He also consulted Becky Fonda about wardrobe improvements. She took him shopping over in Bozeman. Becky bought Brautigan a new sweater and a formal Western jacket, telling him, "You have to dress up sometimes."

A thin paperback copy of *Richard Brautigan* by Marc Chénetier, part of the Contemporary Writers series published by Methuen & Co. of London and New York, arrived in Montana before the end of the month. Richard expected to be disappointed, as he had been with Terence Malley's similarly titled book back in 1972. Chénetier lauded Brautigan with praise, maintaining that critics dismissed him unfairly because Richard's work fell outside the boundaries of traditional American literary criticism. "Mapping out a territory is as important as settling it," Chénetier wrote, "and one may prefer census-taking to sense-making: the actual weighing of the nuggets will be left to others."

"The frog got it right," Richard told all his friends.

Lorca Hjortsberg had an accident driving home from school one afternoon early in April. She totaled the old Chevy Brautigan had given her, ending up in the hospital. Richard went with Marian to visit her. "We're so glad you're all right," he said, holding her hand. He never said a single word about the wrecked car.

Brautigan left for Paris in the middle of the second week of April 1983. He flew first to San Francisco for a farewell night at Enrico's. Christian Bourgois arranged for his ticket to originate at SFO. The next day Richard was en route to New York. According to Helen Brann, he checked into "a perfectly god-awful place, some fleabag over in the Times Square area." His days at the Plaza and the Waldorf on his own dime were over. While economizing, Brautigan still found the means to take Ianthe, who was living in Brooklyn with Paul, out for a big Friday night lobster dinner at The Palm. His daughter's husband had to work and couldn't come.

Ianthe worked nights at the Roundabout Theater, so her days were free to spend with her father. For a couple years, she thought he only came to New York to see his agent, realizing now "that he wanted to see me as well." Richard spent much of his time in the city with his daughter. They went together to various museum shows and to "movies that weren't playing in San Francisco." Ianthe's half sister, Ellen, was also living in the Big Apple and often joined them on their afternoon excursions.

On Saturday morning, April 9, Richard phoned Helen Brann, asking her to join him for breakfast. She pulled on a pair of jeans and headed over from Sutton Place to a side street in the West Forties, where she met Brautigan in his shabby hotel coffee shop. They talked "about everything for about three hours." It was just like old times, as if nothing had changed between them. "He was in terrific shape," Brann recalled. "He hadn't been drinking for a couple months. He'd lost weight. Had a haircut."

This final breakfast felt important for Helen. She feared Richard harbored hurt feelings. "But he was so sweet to me," she said. "We were as close as we'd ever been." Brautigan told her about Chénetier's recent study of his work, saying he was "fed up" with the American critics. Brann recalled how articulate Brautigan sounded as he "put his entire writing career into focus."

"Helen," he said, "in another two or three years, the whole thing is going to turn around and they'll rediscover me. I'm just not going to do any new writing. If I publish anything, I'll publish it in Europe." This didn't seem off-the-wall to Brann. She thought Brautigan "sounded so bright and so acute about the way things work in this country."

Before they parted, Richard invited Helen up to his "horrible" room. "Eight by twelve, including the john," she remembered. "A little cot-like bed. A window that looked out on nothing. Had a dirty sort of curtain across it." Brautigan wanted to give her some documents. "Not a manuscript, but papers." Helen noted that he was traveling with only a duffle bag. "And that was it." They said goodbye and she left his tiny room. It was the last time Helen Brann ever saw Richard Brautigan.

That same evening Brautigan departed one hour late from JFK to Paris on TWA flight 806. On the long transatlantic passage, Richard read from a pocket copy of the *Guinness Book of World Records*. Christian Bourgois and his second wife, Dominique, awaited their author's arrival at Roissy Airport the next morning, along with Marc Chénetier and a reporter and photographer from *L'Express*. Not knowing Richard's plane had been delayed, they played a guessing game, trying to pick their mysterious author out of the swarm of arriving passengers. After a while, they wondered if Brautigan hadn't "poser un lapin." In French, "arranging a rabbit" was the colloquialism for standing someone up.

At last they spotted Richard approaching. Long-limbed, awkward, wearing bell-bottom jeans, hair in disorder, the distinctive mustache—the group recognized Brautigan right away and introduced themselves. He greeted them kindly, displaying "the exquisite politeness of a schizo." Something about Richard, at once "anonymous" and a "famous figurehead," reminded the reporter, Gérard Lefort, of a "posthumous" Boris Vian, a French bohemian poet, novelist, and jazz musician who died in 1959. Waiting by the baggage carousel, Brautigan reinforced this perception, pulling a small alarm clock from his pocket and telling his new companions it was set on Montana time.

After passing through customs, Richard bought a bottle of whiskey at the duty-free store and they set off for Paris along l'autoroute du Nord in the Bourgoises' car. Brautigan frowned out the window, sizing up the nondescript suburbs on the horizon. "So, then, this is France!' he said scornfully. Caught in a traffic jam in the Faubourg Saint-Denis, Richard's superior attitude relaxed a bit. Now everything looked just like in the movies, he thought. As they moved closer to the center of the city, Brautigan studied the shop signs and the names painted on the windows of the boutiques they passed. *Hot Dog. Pressing. Restaurant. Café.* Flashing back to his early childhood studying the labels on canned goods, Richard announced that he'd discovered a fast way to learn French.

Christian Bourgois drove Brautigan to the Hôtel d'Isly at 49 Rue Jacob in the heart of Saint-Germain-des-Prés on the Left Bank. Two things waited at the front desk. A letter from Michelle Lapautre, his French literary agent, welcomed him to Paris. She hoped to meet Richard soon, suggesting he phone her Tuesday morning once his schedule had been arranged. The other item was a copy of *Livres-Hebdo*, a weekly magazine about books published mainly for librarians and booksellers. A feature article, "Richard Brautigan à Paris" by Christine Ferrand, was illustrated with John Fryer's photo of Brautigan leaning against his Pine Creek mailbox.

Richard asked Marc Chénetier for a quick translation. The subhead, "Cousin de Boris Vian et d'Émile Ajar cet ecrivan californien rencontre pour la premier fois son editeur et ses lecteurs

francois," said it all. (Cousin to Boris Vian and Émile Ajar, this California writer meets his publisher and his French readers for the first time.) Ferrand explicated this thesis in her piece. "Il mani-
feste tantôt de côté doux et rêveur du hippy californien," she wrote, "tantôt un goût du canular et
du loufoque à la Boris Vian." Chénetier read this to Brautigan in English: "Sometimes he manifests
the sweet and dreamy side of a hippie Californian, sometimes the taste of the practical joke and the
crackpot in the manner of Boris Vian."

The reference to Ajar came after Ferrand called Brautigan a "mysterious person" who "refused
interviews on principle," quoting Jean-François Fogel, a journalist and essayist who referred to
Richard as "a sort of Émile Ajar who wrote his books himself." Richard had never heard of Vian
and Ajar. Marc explained the connection had to do with pseudonyms. Polymath Boris Vian, who
played the trumpet, sang, acted, and also worked as an engineer and inventor, had written five
hard-boiled noir novels under the pen name Vernon Sullivan. (Vian died of sudden cardiac arrest at
a screening of the film version of *J'irai Cracher sur vos Tombes* (*I Shall Spit on Your Graves*) after
shouting, "These guys are supposed to be American? My ass!")

Émile Ajar had been the pseudonym of Romain Gary, a name Brautigan recognized. Gary, who
had died a suicide from a self-inflicted gunshot wound two years before, had been an internationally famous war hero, diplomat, novelist, and film director. He'd been married to the American
actress Jean Seberg. Winning the Prix Goncourt twice immortalized him in France. The prestigious
prize for French language literature was supposed to be awarded to a living author only once in his
life. Gary won it the first time in 1956 for his novel *Les Racines du Ciel* (*The Roots of Heaven*). The
second time around, he took the prize in 1975 as Émile Ajar for the pseudonymous *La vie devant
soi*. The hoax was not revealed until after Gary's death.

Brautigan didn't get it. He'd never written under a pseudonym. Richard was unfamiliar with
the French intellectuals' love for labyrinthine word play and symbolic gesture. Failing to understand that Gary and Vian had been self-invented men much like himself, Brautigan looked bemused
by it all as J. M. Bartel, the photographer from *L'Express* took several pictures. The published
photo portrayed a healthy, exhausted man.

After Richard dropped off his duffel and deposited his traveler's checks for safekeeping with the
management, they left the small hotel and drove to the restaurant "mode," close by the Bourgois
house. They were joined by a celebrated actress and a former television director, gathering about
a round table decorated with a vase of tulips. During their luncheon, the group resembled a small
salon, everyone trying to outdo each other in a play of wits. Brautigan's conversation jumped randomly from topic to topic, what the French called *toujour du coq à l'âne*, (always from the rooster
to the lamb). When Richard was asked where he wanted to go in Paris, he replied, "To where there
is energy!"

Groaning inwardly, the distinguished group cast panicked looks at one another. Could the
visiting author be just another loutish American wanting to take in the same old boring sights.
Christian Bourgois suggested the Eiffel Tower. Marc Chénetier offered Versailles. The reporter
Gérard Lefort came up with the Folies Bergères. Brautigan was not interested in any of these places.
Richard wanted to visit "cemeteries and supermarkets."

At the end of the meal, after several glasses of plum *eaux de vie*, the group left the restaurant
and dispersed. The reporter shook Brautigan's hand, departing to write his story. Richard veered
off with Christian and Dominique Bourgois for more drinks at their home. A little more than a

year older than his author, Christian had worked in publishing since 1959, setting up his own eponymous company in 1966. Noted for publishing translations of J. R. R. Tolkien's *The Lord of the Rings* and the first book of short stories by Gabriel Garciá Márquez in France, Bourgois also introduced the American Beat writers (Ginsberg in 1967; Burroughs in 1968) to French readers.

Bourgois spoke only French fluently but knew enough English to communicate with Brautigan, who had zero knowledge of the Gallic tongue. Christian asked Richard if there was anyone he'd like to meet in Paris. "Jean-Jacques Beineix," Brautigan replied. The director's film *Diva* had received a lukewarm reception when it opened in France in 1981. It had been an art house success the next year in the United States. Richard was a big fan of the movie and had arranged through Marc Chénetier to have the Bourgois publishing house send three copies of *Mémoirs sauvés du vent* (*So the Wind*) to Beineix. Brautigan thought *Diva* "a wonderful film." Christian Bourgois said he'd try and arrange a meeting.

Jet lag and alcohol took their toll on the exhausted traveler. Before Richard left, Dominique Bourgois jotted a quick itinerary with her fountain pen on a personalized beige slip from her desk notepad. She wrote with Parisian flair in purple ink. Five appointments were scheduled—two the next day, three on Wednesday. After writing "Thursday," Dominique left the space beside it blank. Michelle Lapautre had been working to arrange for interviews on that day. The Paris Book Fair was set to open on the fifteenth. Brautigan was expected to put in an appearance at the Bourgois booth. He had a reading scheduled for Friday night, so she also left that day open, asking him to come on Saturday. Richard folded the paper and stuck it in the pocket of his denim work shirt.

Christian Bourgois brought Richard back to the Hôtel d'Isly, where he collapsed onto a luxurious bed in room H6. When Brautigan awoke the next morning, he looked at the handwritten schedule Dominique had given him. His first appointment was lunch with Jean-Baptiste Baronian, a French-language Belgian writer of Armenian descent. Born in Antwerp, thirty-nine-year-old Baronian was known as a novelist, critic, essayist, and author of children's books. At present he was on assignment for *Le Magazine Littéraire*, a monthly literary publication founded in 1966.

When Brautigan and Baronian sat down to lunch at a Left Bank restaurant, their conversation soon turned into an interview. The initial question concerned Richard's career as a poet. "My first book was a collection of poems," Brautigan answered. "I published it at the age of twenty-three. I was then very influenced by the French poets, principally Baudelaire. And there's no denying I owe a great debt to Rimbaud, Laforgue, Breton, and Michaux. They also gave me the urge to read French prose. I have been hit hard by Gide's *The Immoralist* and Sartre's *Nausea*. Then there's *Night Flight* by Saint-Exupéry, which I consider one of the most perfect novels ever written."

Richard went on to mention those American writers who'd influenced him: Stephen Crane, Mark Twain, Ambrose Bierce, Emily Dickinson. He gave no nod to Hemingway but said *Gatsby* and Faulkner's *As I Lay Dying* were among the novels that really knocked him out. When Baronian noted that he cited only classic authors, Brautigan retorted, "But I am a classic!"

"In spite of your taste for parody?" countered Baronian.

"There is no parody in my books," Richard said. "I don't believe in parody. On the other hand, I love games. I love to play. What I write is playful and when one is playful, one is inevitably attracted by humor. Besides, I love life, all of life. I love to drink, I love to eat, I love to fish, I love to make love and all of this I say in my books. Why would you speak of parody?"

Baronian replied that the passage in *So the Wind* where Brautigan comically described hamburgers struck him as parody.

"You found?" Richard retorted. "There is no such thing in my books: fiction. All is fiction. It's in the fiction—and only in the fiction—that one realizes and accomplishes the greatest human experiences. Yes, my fictions are sometimes minimalist, but they always remain fiction."

"Even when you take on the American myth?"

"That's your vision, it's not mine. Me, I don't understand your expression. We also, when we look at France, we think of and find myths, but I am persuaded it is a question of a view of the spirit. Myth, if it exists, is part of language, of literature, of the history of literature."

Brautigan had had enough of Gallic intellectual nitpicking. Baronian pressed on, insisting it was not possible to understand *Dreaming of Babylon* other than through the myths that drive the narrative.

Richard dodged the issue, telling the Belgian journalist, "It is a book I wrote after seeing numerous film noir. But, for me, it is not a black novel. I prefer to call it a gothic novel. The gothic is my passion because it is a domain where the fiction is total." Brautigan digressed into a discussion of gothic fiction, mentioning Mary Shelley's *Frankenstein* and the short stories of Poe, declaring Conan Doyle's *The Hound of the Baskervilles* "a novel that I adore."

Richard said he tried to work every day. When Baronian asked if he ever thought of his future readers, Brautigan answered emphatically, "Never." He ended the interview by declaring, "A writer is an agent of emotion. In my work, I give them emotion."

After lunch, Richard had a couple free hours before a 5:00 pm meeting with Gabrielle Rollin. He had been mostly indoors since arriving in Paris and had seen nothing of the city, so he went for a walk. Brautigan wandered through the narrow streets of the Sixth Arrondissement. Within a few blocks, he found himself on the quay along the Seine. Richard encountered two things close to his heart, fishing and books. Numbers of *pêcheurs* stood along the concrete bank, patiently holding their rods, waiting for a strike. On the street above them, *les bouquinistes* were open for business, the fronts of the wooden book stalls unfolded to reveal shelves of used books.

As Brautigan strolled along, enjoying himself, he came to a bend in the river. There, looming before him, a distinctive iron skeleton tapered into the sky. Richard stared up at it as a young man approached along the *quai*. "Excuse me. Excuse me," Brautigan said, stopping the Parisian pedestrian. "Is that the Eiffel Tower?"

"I guarantee it," the fellow said, continuing on his way. This became Richard's favorite story about his first trip to Paris.

That evening, Brautigan got together with Marc Chénetier for a nightcap. All Brautigan's good intentions declared in Montana were drowning in an ocean of French alcohol. Marc wanted to confirm a dinner invitation that he'd extended to Richard by letter in March. He also needed to establish a schedule for Friday. Brautigan dug the folded itinerary written by Dominique Bourgois out of his pocket and slid it across to Chénetier. Marc quickly filled in the blanks with his ballpoint.

"19:30. Dinner Marc," he wrote in the last open space for Wednesday. Leaving Thursday's space blank, Chénetier penned "Friday" below it, adding three appointments ("10. TV in room. 12. Lunch? - Marc. 17. Lecture"), shorthand for a busy day. Chénetier planned to bring a television crew to Brautigan's hotel room at 10:00 am on Friday morning to tape an interview. The "lecture" at 5:00 pm was a scheduled reading previously arranged by mail.

Richard's Wednesday in Paris began with a hangover. If he had a bottle in his room, he probably took a couple quick palliative drinks. He'd most likely emptied the last one the night before. At 10:30 am, Brautigan met with Michel Braudeau, a novelist and literary critic who had published his first novel, *The Amazon*, at the age of twenty. Braudeau covered film and literature for *L'Express*. He got only an hour of Richard's time. Near brain-dead, the grouchy author behaved rudely, responding to his inquiries in a curt manner.

At 11:30, F. Dumont, a reporter for *Elle* magazine, arrived to spend another hour probing into Brautigan's headache. He again behaved impolitely, and she received only discourteous answers to her questions. Lunch and the opportunity for drink couldn't come soon enough for Richard. At the end of Mlle. Dumont's "interview," Jean-François Fogel arrived to guide Brautigan to his first glass of Calvados.

Fogel, an essayist and journalist, worked for *Le Point*, a weekly news magazine founded in 1972 and modeled on *Time* and *Newsweek*. Christine Ferrand had quoted his comparison of Richard to Boris Vian in her *Livres-Hebdo* article. Brautigan took an umbrella when he left the hotel. It had rained hard in Paris before Richard's arrival, but not a drop fell during his stay. It paid to be prepared.

Fogel escorted the author to a neighborhood restaurant, *pour le dejéuner*. Brautigan didn't have much of an appetite but drank numerous full glasses of Calvados. They discussed French literature and Richard's own writing. Fogel observed that Brautigan had used the word "death" 114 times in *So the Wind*. Richard asked for someone to take him to Père-Lachaise Cemetery, saying he "wanted to breathe the air there."

Surprised that "our necropolis is known even in Montana," Fogel agreed to be his guide. "One can't refuse a stranger who has read Jules Laforgue," he thought. When they left the restaurant, Brautigan bought a bottle of apple brandy to go.

At more than 118 acres, Père-Lachaise was the largest cemetery in Paris. Named for the father-confessor to King Louis XIV, the graveyard was too distant from the city to be considered fashionable when it opened in 1804. As a publicity stunt, the administrators arranged, with much hoopla, to have the bodies of Molière and La Fontaine moved to Père-Lachaise. Sealing the deal, they reinterred the "purported remains" of fabled medieval lovers Héloïse and Abélard in their exclusive boneyard in 1817.

Since then, Père-Lachaise had been the burial ground for the illustrious. Unlike Forest Lawn and Hollywood Memorial Park Cemetery, where the famous corpses are mainly show biz greats, the tombs at Père-Lachaise contain a wide spectrum of notables, everyone from Chopin, Modigliani, Marcel Proust, Balzac, and the executed Marshal Michel Ney (unless he escaped to America and is really buried in Cleveland) to Gertrude Stein, Isadora Duncan, Rossini, Sarah Bernhardt, Oscar Wilde, and Edith Piaf (the much-beloved Parisian "little sparrow").

When a taxi dropped Brautigan and Fogel off at the gate to Père-Lachaise, the cemetery caretaker took one look at the long-haired forty-eight-year-old wearing bell-bottom jeans. Assuming him to be "a retarded hippie," he said, "You come for Jim Morrison?"

Richard climbed onto his high horse with the exaggerated dignity of the very drunk. "I don't want to see where my friend is buried. I seek the grave of Apollinaire," he replied with regal hauteur.

After getting lost under the tree-shaded avenues of Père-Lachaise, Brautigan amused himself poking through the cemetery's garbage bins with the tip of his hotel umbrella. Richard had "always been fascinated with what a society throws away." The next year he wrote, "Garbage and trash are pages of history just as valid in their own way as generals and kings." After examining the trash in Père-Lachaise, Brautigan observed, "The future of death is unlimited." Richard walked between the graves, picking up dried flowers, plastic bottles, and discarded newspapers. Fogel watched in amusement when Brautigan abandoned sanitation and started chasing stray cats, "wishing them good afternoon in Japanese." Other visitors looked on with disapproval as an inebriated American ran shouting through the sanctuary.

Richard ignored them. He spoke loudly about French poet Robert Desnos and about Maiakovsky, the Soviet "futurist" whose disillusionment with Stalin had led to sympathy with the Russian exile community in Paris before he shot himself to death in 1930. When Fogel suggested he tone it down, Brautigan complained of jet lag, saying, "I haven't completely arrived yet. My kidneys are still in the Rockies. My skin in Kansas City and my hair is in the Atlantic Ocean."

As they found their way to Apollinaire's monument, Richard took note of the many graves covered by only a simple embossed metal covering. Guillaume Apollinaire, who died in the influenza pandemic of 1918 after suffering a serious head wound on the front in World War I, lay under a rough-hewn menhir designed by Picasso. Stanzas from the poet's work (he invented the word "*surrealism*" to describe his 1917 play *Les Mamelles de Tirésias*) were carved onto the granite slab sealing his tomb. Fogel provided an impromptu translation.

On their way out of Père-Lachaise, Brautigan rapped his knuckles on a metal grave covering and said, "I was wrong. The future of death is *le zinc*." Richard knew almost no French, but in his brief stay in Paris he'd already learned the colloquial term for a bar top.

Brautigan showed up dead drunk for dinner at Marc Chénetier's apartment. Things went downhill from there. Everyone on the small guest list, all friends of Marc, was offended by Richard. The next morning things only got worse. Brautigan couldn't face another interview. Bernard Le Saux from *Les Nouvelles littéraires* arrived at the Hôtel d'Isly for his 11:00 am Thursday morning appointment. Richard refused to answer the phone when he called from the lobby.

The interview had been arranged by Brautigan's French agent. Bernard Le Saux was a distinguished journalist, and the *Literary News,* founded by Larousse in 1922, remained an influential publication sixty years later. Offended, Le Saux left a note on a page torn from a notebook of graph paper. He hoped "to be able to see you for the interview either this afternoon at what ever hour you like or, if you prefer, saturday." He left two phone numbers. Richard never responded.

While Richard hid in his room, far off in San Francisco, Bruce Conner stopped at Vesuvio and asked Henri Lenoir to let him into Brautigan's office upstairs. Conner wanted to borrow a couple pieces of art he'd given Richard, planning to include them in an upcoming MOCA "prosthetic exhibition." Brautigan had failed to inform Lenoir about this as promised. Henri knew Bruce and trusted him enough to unlock the office door. Conner signed a handwritten receipt for the drawing and collage he took.

Across the pond, Brautigan remained in terrible shape. All his physical training, hours pedaling on Marian Hjortsberg's Exercycle, gone to waste. Four days of nonstop drinking flushed weeks of sobriety down the drain in a torrent of Calvados. Richard didn't emerge from his hotel room that day, hunkering down with a couple bottles and refusing to answer the phone. Messages piled up down at the front desk. Michelle Lapautre was furious. She felt responsible. Christian Bourgois had financed Brautigan's entire trip, and her client's bad behavior was like a slap in his face. Lapautre expected to do business with the publisher in the future and was angry that Richard had tainted the relationship.

Friday went a little better. Marc Chénetier arrived at the Hôtel d'Isly at ten in the morning with a TV film crew. They set up in room H6, getting shots of Richard and close-ups of French editions of his recently published books. This was not complicated work, taking less than an hour. Chénetier had planned to meet Brautigan for lunch at noon. Marc had mentioned a manuscript he wanted Richard to read but neglected to bring it. He said he'd have it with him when he returned in an hour. Brautigan asked him to also bring a bottle of vinegar.

At 12:00 pm, when Chénetier returned to the hotel, Richard was nowhere to be found. If he was still in his room, he refused to open the door or answer the phone. Marc left the manuscript and the vinegar at the front desk, scribbling a quick note on d'Isly stationery, saying, "May see you tonight at the reception." Brautigan's whereabouts during the afternoon remained a mystery. Wherever he went, Calvados stayed close at hand. The Luxembourg Garden was within walking distance of Richard's hotel, and he went there to escape the demands of his fame.

The second largest park in Paris, le Jardin du Luxembourg was built in 1612 by Marie de Médicis, widow of Henry IV, as a private playground for her new home, le Palais du Luxembourg. She planted two thousand elm trees in the park. Spring came late to Paris in 1983, and the elms had only started to bud when Brautigan wandered beneath them. He brought along the borrowed umbrella, using it "to prod and turn about fresh garbage." Lost in his imagination, Richard amused himself in solitude.

Somehow, Brautigan made it to the Maison des Sciences de l'Homme on the Boulevard Raspail by 7:00 pm Friday in time for his reading. Afterward, at the reception following Richard's presentation, his wish came true. He was introduced to the film director Jean-Jacques Beineix. Like Brautigan, Beineix was known as something of a recluse who allowed few interviews. Their conversation didn't last long. A private moment, two artists exchanging ideas and observations. This brief moment provided the high point of Richard's visit to Paris.

On Saturday, Brautigan's last day in France, he found his way to the Grand Palais de Champs-Elysées, where the third annual *Salon du livres* took place. Built for the Universal Exposition of 1900, an era before electricity was sufficient to illuminate such large spaces, the Grand Palais was the last of the vast glass-roofed exhibition halls modeled on London's Crystal Palace. The *beaux arts* structure provided a splendid temporary temple for the world of literature.

Booksellers from France and around the world had erected a vast maze of booths, displaying their latest publications along miles of shelving arranged under the arching glass ceiling. Numerous authors sat in their publishers' booths, waiting to sign books and chat with readers. For Brautigan the place felt like a sepulcher. A week of steady drinking had taken a severe toll. The Bourgoises were not pleased with his appearance. This was no way to publicize a new book.

Photographer Louis Monier stopped by the Christian Bourgois éditeur booth while making his rounds as a freelance. The ghoulish pictures he took of Richard portray a cadaver recently clawed up out of a grave in search of human flesh. Unless he had packed several identical blue denim work shirts, the zombie author appeared not to have changed clothes since arriving in Paris. Monier's photos appeared in both *Le Point* and *Le Magazine Littéraire*. Jean-Baptiste

Baronian headed his article/interview in the latter publication "Loufoque Brautigan?" (Crackpot Brautigan?). It told the whole story. The accompanying photograph spoke a thousand times louder than any words.

Richard left France the next day, Sunday, April 17, departing for Japan from Paris-Orly on Korean Airlines after a quick farewell drink at an airport bar. It was a grueling ten-thousand-mile trip with long stops in Frankfurt, Cairo, and Aden. Brautigan suffered a twelve-hour layover in Karachi, Pakistan, and two more three-hour stops in Bangkok and Manila before the final eighteen-hundred-mile leg to Tokyo. Richard arrived in Japan four days after the grand opening ceremony for Tokyo Disneyland, an attraction Brautigan, despite his appetite for the mundane, would never visit.

Richard had planned a detour to Munich to see Günter Ohnemus, his German translator. Ohnemus had contacted Brautigan previously with an offer from West German *Playboy* to write an article on the plight of young German models living in Tokyo. Thin attractive European women deemed not beautiful enough for successful modeling careers at home were shipped off to sashay down Japanese runways. Ohnemus sent a letter of introduction to Montana, but it got lost in the mail. A second letter was on its way to Tokyo.

Boiling over with frustration after Brautigan's departure, Michelle Lapautre phoned Helen Brann in New York. "You didn't tell me Richard Brautigan was crazy," she fumed.

"What do you mean?" Helen sounded confused.

"He is the most paranoid person I've ever met in my life. He never took a sober breath the entire time he was here."

"Michelle, you're kidding," Brann said, "because he was fine when he was here."

Lapautre remained outraged. "I have to tell you, he offended the press, he offended his publisher. He behaved like a madman. And he drank brandy morning, noon, and night." The French agent caught her breath. "I'm just telling you this because I thought you should know." Helen Brann had no reply.

The day after Brautigan returned to Japan, an ocean away in L.A., the Ridley Scott production (now called *Legend* and housed in offices at the 20th Century Fox lot) fell apart due to internal bickering among the principal players. Unexpectedly out of a job, Gatz Hjortsberg started arranging studio pitch meetings. Six days later, he was offered work by Thom Mount, head of production at Universal. Gatz had his choice of two projects, a David Giler film consisting of only the title "Spartacus in Space" or a rewrite of *The Hawkline Monster*, now slated to be directed by Mike Haller. Greed encouraged him to do both at once. Common sense prevailed, and he signed on for the *Hawkline* rewrite.

In Japan, back at the Keio Plaza, it took Brautigan ten days to recover from the jet lag he suffered after the long flight from Paris. He went to bed every night at 10:30 pm and woke up again three hours later, unable to fall back to sleep. To kill time during the dark hours before dawn, Richard wrote what he called "long senseless endless" letters. He not yet rented a typewriter, so these midnight missives were all handwritten. Early in the morning of April 21, overlooking the Tokyo night from the thirty-seventh floor, Brautigan scratched out a letter to Helen Brann in response to a telegram she'd sent about further delays in Hal Ashby's *Hawkline* film project. He mentioned how good it was to see her in New York. "That extra parting hug you gave me meant so much to me. I will always remember it."

In his exhausted state, Richard "thought a lot about emptiness." Sitting at the bar in The Cradle on his second night in town, Brautigan told two Japanese friends "about arriving at complete emptiness. To become the void yet still be alive." Time had started running out for Richard and he knew it. Even at a discount, the bill for his expensive suite at the Keio Plaza was paid with borrowed money. Brautigan had no real income. No one wanted his most recent book. Only his art sustained him. He stared into total emptiness.

Jet lag didn't stop Richard from getting back to work. He liked to write at a sidewalk café. Brautigan had a favorite stationery store in Tokyo, "dark and comfortable [. . .] like a tidy warm shadow." He bought a green notebook and a few pens before heading to a table at the café. Twilight remained Richard's "favorite part of the day." Even at midday, twilight haunted his mind. A title nagged the back corners of his imagination: "The Complete Absence of Twilight." Brautigan wrote it down in his new notebook and started in. "I just bought this green notebook at a little stationary [sic] store that I always buy my writing material here in Tokyo."

Richard stopped after the first sentence. He didn't know where to go next, so he left off and began a new story, "American Airports and Tokyo Escalators." Brautigan had no concept of writer's block, a favorite cop-out of the second-rate. When the immediate well of inspiration ran dry, he drilled a new shaft deeper into his subconscious. Marriages failed, friends disappointed, money ran out, love turned sour, but Richard's art never deserted him. Alone, exhausted, running out of time and capital, Brautigan still found space to write. When all else was lost, writing became his final salvation.

At 4:00 am on the morning of the twenty-third, Richard, the jet-lagged insomniac, sat waiting for the Tokyo dawn ("I like this time of day") and started a letter to Barry Hannah on tissue-paper-thin sheets of Keio Plaza stationery, first writing the recipient's name and address on an envelope as always. Brautigan had begun reading *A Tennis Handsome* while his plane to Tokyo sat on the tarmac in Bangkok for three hours. Richard's only other recorded memory of this trip was watching a young soldier at the Karachi airport affectionately rub the barrel of his submachine gun against his cheek.

Brautigan considered this a symbol, "a premonition of where I have been led step to step to this place." The place he referred to was the void. Richard wasn't afraid of peering over the edge into the abyss. "My god-damned personal life is not important," he wrote in his notebook. "It will always be around until I'm dead. I don't believe in afterwards so I think death will pretty much close down my personal life. Bring an end to it. And the pleasures will even out like a placid stillness suddenly settling over a wind-ruffled pond."

Brautigan mentioned none of this in his letter to Barry Hannah. He detailed his morning schedule, drinking coffee at 4:00 am, going down for a "little breakfast" when the sun came up at 5:00. After eating, Richard liked to wander about the Keio Plaza, a hotel so huge that he compared it to a city-state. "It's fun to watch the hotel wake up." At 6:00 am, an English-language newspaper slid under the door of room 3705. After reading it and checking the yen/dollar exchange rate, Brautigan went grocery shopping for "milk and juice and snacks." Richard had a refrigerator and a hot plate in his room, so preparing simple meals was no problem.

After a page and a half, Brautigan set the letter aside and went to his favorite sidewalk café to write in his notebook. At 7:30 pm he closed up shop and headed for The Cradle. Nobody was there at that early hour. Richard sat at the bar, sipping brandy as he continued writing. Around nine, he had something to eat. By 10:30 the joint was jumping. Interesting people began to arrive. Brautigan gulped his brandy as the conversation grew more interesting. Brautigan didn't get to sleep until eight on Sunday morning.

Aside from a "two hour get-up," Richard slept for seventeen and a half hours. He climbed out of bed at 3:30 am on the twenty-fifth. By four in the morning, he was drinking coffee, watching the rosy fingers of dawn and completing his letter to Barry Hannah. He didn't have much to say aside from describing the mundane details of life in Tokyo. At four handwritten pages, it became one of the longest letters he'd ever written. Brautigan never mailed it. He kept the letter among his papers for the rest of his life.

Richard got back in touch with Masako Kano. Because of her job at Motorola, she could only see him in the evenings after work or on weekends. Brautigan told Kano about his assignment for German *Playboy*, a project he called "Fate of West German Models in Tokyo." He worried how the research needed to be done. Without being asked, Masako volunteered to help, offering to be his research assistant. She told Richard the *Japan Times* advertised "all the time" for Japanese women to act as "managers" for foreign models and suggested answering such an ad and interviewing for the job. Kano explained that she'd go undercover and "find out all she could about managing the models and what this entailed."

Masako was twenty-seven but could pass for seventeen, "a pretty, innocent-looking and clever girl." She would make a perfect spy. Delighted by the idea, Brautigan thought of her as his personal ninja, one of those legendary covert mercenaries of feudal Japan specializing in espionage, sabotage, and assassination. Kano never performed any cloak-and-dagger work. Her day job didn't allow the time, but Richard cherished the image of her as a ninja.

On the fourth of May, Shūji Terayama, the avant-garde Japanese poet, writer, dramatist, filmmaker, and photographer, died from cirrhosis of the liver at the age of forty-seven. He had met Brautigan in San Francisco during the spring of 1976. Later that year they reconnected at The Cradle, spending many nights there together, drinking and talking. Terayama had founded Tenjō Sajiki, an experimental theater troupe, in 1967. He named it for the 1945 Marcel Carné film, *Les Enfants du Paradis*, a title with a double meaning. {"Children of heaven" was a slang term for the audience sitting "the gods," the cheapest section in a theater's highest balcony.)

In 1979, Shūji introduced Richard to composer, Michiko "Michi" Tanaka, who worked as the secretary of Tenjō Sajiki and was also an executive producer for Terayama's 1971 film, *Emperor Tomato Ketchup*. Earlier in 1983, Michi wrote to Brautigan ("Dear Richard with cow-boy hat,) asking him to participate in "Questions," a one-hour video about writers she was directing and producing as personal project, "not a commercial one." All she requested was that Richard answer a number of questions on tape and send her "about ten photos." Many years later, Tanaka made *Questions*, a seven-minute film which did not include recorded answers from authors.

Terayama's death struck a chord in his American counterpart. Shūji was almost a year younger than Richard and shared his fondness for booze, dying from a lifetime of alcohol abuse. Terayama had published close to two hundred literary works and made more than twenty films. Now he was dead. Brautigan could only wonder if he'd be next.

Drunk in his hotel room, Richard tried to jot down memories of Shūji Terayama on a Keio Plaza notepad kept by his bedside. "Unfortunately, memory is never accurate," Brautigan wrote, enumerating a short list of his earliest recollections of his friend. They ate breakfast in a restaurant in Chinatown and had coffee afterward at a North Beach Italian sidewalk café. Terayama drew Brautigan a map of Tokyo on a paper napkin, telling him the city was actually "five major cities and ten thousand villages." Richard kept this crude map and followed Shūji's instructions during his first trip to Japan.

Terayama's funeral was held at the Aoyama Funeral Hall in the vast Aoyama Cemetery, about a kilometer's walk from The Cradle. Takako Shiina insisted that Richard go to the memorial. He wore the gray Western jacket given to him by Becky Fonda. Takako fitted his right sleeve with a black armband and drew a simple map, marking the route in red from The Cradle down Stars and Stripes Avenue and around the corner to Aoyama Saijo. Brautigan thought he wasn't properly dressed. "This is perfectly all right," Shiina told him.

"But I don't want to offend anyone," Richard replied.

"You won't offend anyone. This is all right."

"But I'm a foreigner."

"It's all right." Takako gave him a white chrysanthemum to leave in tribute.

Brautigan followed Takako's precisely sketched directions, walking in the hot afternoon to the first funeral he'd ever attended in his life. Long fond of visiting cemeteries, Richard had never been to a burial service before. As he turned the corner onto the street bordering the Aoyama Cemetery, Brautigan saw thousands of people dressed in black, waiting in line to enter the funeral hall and pay their last respects to Shūji Terayama. Richard joined the end of the queue under the broiling sun, moving slowly forward with the other mourners. During the long wait, Brautigan observed an ant crawling under the black shoe of the man ahead of him on line. A poem started taking form in his mind.

Over two pages long, "Night Flowing River" became one of Richard's most expansive poems, a rare example of his narrative poetry. Brautigan rented a typewriter and prepared a clean fair copy, which he gave to the Tuttle-Mori Agency, his literary representatives in Japan. He also gave a copy to his friend, poet Shuntarō Tanikawa, for him to translate into Japanese. When Shuntarō's work was done, Richard asked Masako to read it before he submitted the poem for publication. Tanikawa invited Kano to his hotel room. She felt embarrassed, a "nobody" giving her opinion "to this wonderful poet." After reading the poem, Masako said she thought it was more than a perfect translation. Shuntarō smiled and they bowed to each other.

When Masako learned Richard had met previously with Tanikawa, "his quiet poet friend," about her working for Motorola, she was furious. Brautigan had little interest in the world of business and couldn't understand why Kano had to work for money when he believed her family was still well-off financially. Masako adored Tanikawa and felt Richard had no right to expose her personal matters to him. She worked to reimburse her mother for all the tuition fees sent to pay for her American degree, making monthly payments to her "mum." Kano understood that Brautigan "respected and trusted Tanikawa San so much he wanted to share. Hopefully, he was not chatting to everybody who sat at the stools at The Cradle."

Richard's mind brimmed with the images and experiences of Paris. He obtained a videocassette of *Diva* with English subtitles. Brautigan and Masako watched the Beineix film "again and again" in his hotel room when she came over after work. Kano was familiar with the novel by Delacorta (a pseudonym of Swiss author, poet, and screenwriter Daniel Odier) on which the movie was based. Richard loved the scenes of Paris in the rain and the relationship between Alba, a young Asian woman, and her older, platonic lover Serge Gorodish.

One scene, where Alba roller-skates in Gorodish's empty studio, delighted them both so much that Brautigan brought a pair of roller skates to his room. He wanted Masako to put them on and skate around his bed. She tried to please him, but the skates were too big and the thickly carpeted floor made skating impossible. "Anyway, we laughed our heads off," Kano recalled.

Richard also "forced" Masako to read Marc Chénetier's book, which she felt "highly praised his style." Brautigan brought several copies of the French scholar's favorable critical study along with him to Japan and often had Kano read aloud from it to him at night, "as his bedtime story." She suspected this was to "nourish his ego."

One evening, Masako lured Richard far from The Cradle to Bunkyō-ku in the north of Tokyo, a district antipodal to foreigner-infested Roppongi. She brought him to Totoya (literally "fish eatery"), a classic Japanese seafood restaurant. "We were eating in the hidden heart of Japan," Brautigan observed, "a place concealed from the Western world." Masako said, "No blond guy has ever come until I took Richard." During the course of their formal dinner, an argument ensued, leading to "outrage after outrage."

To cap things off, Brautigan insulted Kano's family. She slapped his face. "A hard samurai slap. Whack!" Masako did this in front of the restaurant's owner, his cook, and their customers. This sort of thing might happen unnoticed every night of the week in the gin joints of Frisco. In the formal seclusion of Old World Japan, it was tantamount to the roar of a gunshot. Richard and Masako "decided to make it an early evening." They agreed not to see each other for a week or longer. "Let things cool off."

After Kano went home, Brautigan headed straight to The Cradle. At the bar, he talked with an attractive American model about West German models. The American said she'd help Brautigan with his quest and they agreed to meet again. When Richard returned to The Cradle with Masako the following weekend, he found a note from the American model saying she'd get in touch with him at the Keio Plaza. They returned to the hotel, and "there was no message from the American model."

After making love, Richard and Masako got into "a language misunderstanding" just as the phone rang. It was Takako calling to say that Francis Ford Coppola was at The Cradle and he should return. Brautigan said he'd call back. He walked Kano to the Shinjuku Station. Along the way, another language mishap occurred. Richard tried "to illustrate a point, a complicated but very sincere point of affection for her."

Brautigan said, "I'm interested in your mind and talking to you. I don't want to make you into my whore."

Kano heard, "Whore!"

Masako took off running "like a sleek horse." Richard lumbered after her "like a ponderous turtle." He caught up with her at the train turnstile and did his best "to turn the tide" of animosity. They parted when Kano promised to call during her lunch hour the next day.

Brautigan walked back to the Keio Plaza though a gentle rain, pondering the intricacies of language barriers. Up in his room, Richard phoned The Cradle. Takako put Coppola on the line and Brautigan welcomed him to Tokyo. Francis had just arrived. Jet lag loomed. Richard said he had to get to bed early and couldn't see him that night. He mentioned he "was writing a long article for a German magazine and had to get some sleep." Coppola said he would be in Japan for a few days but also wanted to go to bed early. "We left it at that," Brautigan recalled. They never got together on this particular trip to the Land of the Rising Sun.

Sometime early in May, Judge Richard Hodge arrived in Tokyo for a three week visit. He remembered the approximate date because it was during the biannual World Table Tennis Championships, held that year in Tokyo between April 28 and May 9. Brautigan told Hodge to go to the duty free shop on his way through customs and buy a bottle of Napoleon brandy for the manager of the Keio Palza. The judge did as instructed and received a forty percent discount on his hotel room in return. Hodge wanted to see a lot of Japan, takinig trips to Kyoto and "down that famous peninsula." Brautigan had no interest in leaving Tokyo.

Their relationship had become "almost completely social." Hodge was a Superior Court judge and no longer really represented Brautigan. "The way it turned out," Hodge recalled, "was that he and I would go out in the evening and we would dine wonderfully and drink a lot and round about midnight, I'd come home. And at seven in the morning, Richard would be knocking at my door. He'd be coming home at seven in the morning and we would have breakfast. That was the time Richard would go to bed and then I'd go out and get on the bullet train. I did all my traveling, and then I'd come back and we'd have dinner and go out."

Going out meant evenings at The Cradle. Brautigan introduced Judge Hodge to Takako and they struck up a warm friendship. One night, in his element among a group of editors and writers, Richard talked about looking for West German models in Tokyo and showed off the notebook which recorded his search. Hodge went home early, as usual. The next morning, Brautigan appeared outside his door at the Keio Plaza in a complete panic. He'd lost his manuscript. Richard thought he'd put it safely behind the bar. When he looked, the notebook was gone.

"He was quite desolate about it," Hodge remembered. "Kicking himself for that being his only copy." The judge was shocked and "feeling this great sense of loss." Everything turned out okay in the end. One of Brautigan's drinking companions in The Cradle had been an editor at Japanese *Playboy*. During the course of their conversation, he'd opened his portfolio, spreading papers and manuscripts across the bar. Richard's notebook got shuffled together with the other stuff and packed away. When the editor discovered it a day later, he returned Brautigan's work-in-progress to The Cradle.

On another occasion, Takako brought Hodge and Brautigan to a film set to see a Japanese movie in production. The director was a friend of hers. They spent the entire day watching take after take of the same scene. For anyone not involved, watching a film shoot ranks just below observing paint dry as an interesting pastime. When the actors speak a strange language, the boredom factor dials up several notches.

Their fun began when the day's work ended. The director invited Brautigan and Hodge to his home for something to eat. "He was pretty famous, I guess," the judge recalled. The director had an apartment in the Tokyo suburbs and on the way, they stopped off at a supermarket and bought a load of "Japanese goodies" and several bottles of Philippine sake "that everyone was very proud of." The director's party consisted of his lead actor and actress, the composer of the film's score and the two Americans.

They prepared sukiyaki, sitting around the cooking pot on tatami mats in the traditional manner. "Richard got drunk," Hodge recalled. "Boy, everybody was drunk." Gathered about the low table, the Japanese began singing. They favored opera and the songs of Stephen Foster, harmonizing on "Old Black Joe" and "Camptown Races." This became one of Richard Hodge's most enduring memories of Japan. "Every one of those people," he said, "particularly the music director, knew all the words."

Later in the evening, Brautigan made a drunken pass at the leading lady. "Ticked off," the film director asked his American guests to leave. Out on the street, drunk in the middle of the night, the two Richards had no idea in hell where they were. Hodge and Brautigan started walking, singing together off-key to keep up their spirits. "Doo-da . . . Doo-da . . ." They felt lucky to be in Tokyo where there was no chance of getting mugged at three in the morning. Sometime before dawn, they found a taxi and were safely delivered to the Keio Plaza.

Richard Hodge felt troubled by the changes he observed in his old friend in Tokyo, "My relationship with [Brautigan] was one of gravity," he said, remembering the years he'd been Richard's lawyer, "so I probably saw him at his best, when he was really being intense and productive and careful and intelligent; a businessman. I never thought of him as an alcoholic." There had been plenty of drinking together over the years but Hodge considered it fun, two guys socializing. What he "perceived in Japan was a change of mood about the drinking. It was every night. And there was a real sadness to it that I hadn't seen before."

Around the end of May, a week or so after Richard Hodge returned to California, Brautigan received a letter from an assistant program development director for the United States Information Agency at the U.S. Embassy in Tokyo. Having received a cable from the USIA informing them of Richard's visit, the Program Development office contacted American Centers all across Japan and received numerous enthusiastic replies regarding a Brautigan presentation. Kyoto, Osaka, Nagayo, Tokyo and Fukuoka all extended invitations to Richard. Travel expenses would be paid, along with a $113 per diem payment and a $75 honorarium.

Brautigan got in touch with the USIA people at the embassy, accepting their offer. He would travel to Kyoto on June 20th as requested, but wanted the Osaka date in July changed to June 21st, so he could do them both on a single trip. Tokyo in July was fine with Richard. Nagoya and Kukuoka both wanted him to come in September. Brautigan said that was too far into the future for him to make a commitment at the moment.

Not long afterward, Richard prowled the interior city of the Keio Plaza one morning and came across an American television crew filming an episode of *Love Boat* outside the lobby entrance. He recognized Ted Knight and an actress whose name he couldn't recall. Brautigan stood and watched them prepare to shoot another scene. Ted Knight waited next to the camera, getting ready. The actress who looked familiar walked past Richard to join Ted Knight. On her way outside, she said, "It's freezing out there."

Looking on, Brautigan noticed John Ritter, a popular American television actor, having a conversation about stage makeup with a young Japanese woman ten feet away. Richard approached him from behind. "Excuse me, Mr. Ritter," he said.

The actor turned, "slightly surprised" at encountering Brautigan. "I evoke that sort of response in people," Richard wrote later. "I'm kind of a strange-looking man, awkward, obviously uncomfortable in this world, not good-looking. I wear western clothes, Levis, cowboy boots, and a cap that I got at Notre Dame in South Bend, Indiana, in the winter that says on the brim 'Fighting Irish, Notre Dame.'" John Ritter regarded him curiously.

"Is that actress," Brautigan nodded his head at the scene underway outside, "Rita Moreno?"

"Yes, sir," Ritter replied, oddly charming and formal. "She certainly is."

"Thank you," Richard said, and they walked away into their separate lives.

Back in his room, well past the noon hour, Brautigan's phone rang. It was Masako. She hadn't been able to call during her lunch break and suggested they get together again that evening. Richard's sense "of ominous foreboding," lingering since the incident at the train station the previous night, evaporated like ground fog in the heat of the rising sun. Around 7:15 pm after work, Masako arrived at room 3705. Brautigan ordered takeout Chinese food. After eating they made love.

Kano had to catch an early train. She wanted a nap first. Richard set his alarm clock, and "she fell asleep instantly." Brautigan held Masako in his arms, listening to her gentle, relaxed breathing. Unable to sleep, Richard was "almost envious." When the alarm went off, Kano got up and took a shower. After she dressed, Masako kissed Brautigan and left around 10:15, "quite contented." Richard went back to bed and fell into a deep sleep, "only to be pursued by nightmares too terrible to remember."

In his search for West German models, Brautigan spent an evening with "a beautiful Japanese porno star" at The Cradle. Earlier, he'd attended the premiere of her latest "soft core" film, watching her naked as she performed simulated sex on the big screen. "She was so beautiful." Richard was a fan of this kind of movie. In person, he found the star shy and demure. Brautigan spent half an hour teaching her to pronounce three words with sounds difficult for the Japanese. Staring at her lovely lips, he made her say words hundreds of times until she pronounced them perfectly. Richard thought of her inaccessible beauty, watching the delicate star repeat over and over and over: "Already . . . I love you . . . River . . ."

This all went into the handwritten manuscript Brautigan now called "The Fate of a West German Model in Tokyo." Eventually it filled two complete notebooks, 179 manuscript pages, nearly the length of one of his novels. Little of the text involved modeling or models. West German women turned out to be in short supply in Tokyo. The narrative became a quasi journal about his relationship with Masako Kano, whom he referred to only as "the Ninji" throughout his meandering discourse. Whole paragraphs described his arousal upon seeing her take off her watch before getting into bed (no mention made of Marcia Pacaud, the girl who never took off her watch) and when showering together, the pleasure of soaping down with a beautiful unselfconscious young Japanese woman.

Brautigan continued this project until the end of July. What he didn't mention proved of greater interest than his meticulously recorded amorous details. He didn't include the many trips and local excursions made with Masako or Shūji Terayama's funeral or an uncomfortable meeting with Masako's mother ("the Japanese Sophia Loren") when she backed him into a corner or the night he and the Ninji stargazed from the roof of the Keio Plaza, sneaking up the back service stairs. Due to Richard's "rather big tummy, he could not catch me easily running up the stairs," Kano recalled. "I think I was too much for him physically." On their next attempt at rooftop astronomy, they were caught by the hotel staff and "shooed away." This episode never made it into the manuscript.

Brautigan finally made contact with a genuine West German model in Tokyo. He spent an evening talking to her and taking notes. What he gleaned from their interview became a six-page piece, also called "The Fate of a West German Model in Tokyo." Never published in English, it was one of his most powerful short stories. Like "The World War I Los Angeles Airplane," written more than twenty years earlier, it took the form of an enumerated list of quotes, all in the voice of the expatriate model.

Richard used nothing from the two notebooks he spent months compiling. It was all art and instinct now. What made the piece potent and poignant was the unknown model's repeated, enumerated assertion, "I am not a prostitute." Using his long-standing habit of list making, Brautigan keyed into the emotional heart of the story. A lonely young woman adrift in a foreign capital where she can't speak the language, sleeping with men who aren't attractive to her in a desperate attempt to bolster an already faltering second-rate career: "I am not a prostitute."

Masako Kano had her day job. Richard Brautigan had his nightlife. Often, after she left his hotel room, he headed out to The Cradle for a long night of the unknown. One early morning after the bar closed, Richard and Takako found their way to the Golden Triangle, a section of narrow lanes and ramshackle two-story buildings in Shinjuku, where "thousands of little tiny bars [were] beautifully tucked next to each other." A final remnant of the old Tokyo now lost forever in the wake of Japan's postwar "economic miracle," the Golden Gai provided a popular meeting place for artists, writers, musicians, and actors.

Brautigan and Shiina went into "a small but very elegant bar." Although dark and disreputable in appearance, the Golden Triangle was not a cheap area to find a drink. Certain establishments catered to celebrities and welcomed only regular customers. Takako proved the perfect ambassador, guiding Richard into unfamiliar territory. A stranger sat talking with a woman at the back of the pocket-sized bar. He was Kōbō Abe. Brautigan had long admired Abe's novel *The Woman in the Dunes* and was a big fan of the movie based upon it. The two internationally known authors were quickly introduced. Neither knew the other's language. Abe's companion volunteered as a translator.

Richard wanted to tell Abe a story. It took place in the Colorado summer of 1980, when Brautigan first met Masako Kano. She was not in the story. Richard rode in a Jeep with two other men, driving up a steep, remote dirt road to visit a ranch. From out of nowhere, around a narrow bend came "an extraordinarily beautiful young Indian girl" mounted bareback on a galloping horse, her black hair "streaming in the wind." She was barefoot and wore fringed buckskin, a look of ecstasy on her face as she galloped toward them.

It was a perfect Richard Brautigan story. No characters or plot, only a sudden moment of unexpected beauty. It took Richard "an unusually long time" to tell his story because he wanted to communicate it exactly, to "get the feeling of what happened." Brautigan and Abe parted company around 5 AM. Takako headed for home. Richard returned to his room on the thirty-seventh floor of the Keio Plaza.

Throughout his four-month stay in Japan, Brautigan depended primarily on the mail for conducting business. Long-distance phone calls were too expensive, and the time difference didn't align with office hours. Joel Shawn wrote to Richard, explaining the high cost of sending correspondence ($29 per mailing) to Tokyo by express mail. Shawn proposed sending Brautigan's accumulated letters via air mail on a weekly basis.

Helen Brann sent Shawn copies of recent translation rights contracts. In a curt, businesslike way, she pointed out to the attorney that, over the years, she had mailed Richard copies of all his contracts. It was unnecessary now for her to send duplicate copies to him. It was Brautigan's responsibility to keep a complete record of his publishing career. Helen insisted it was Richard who had left her, not the other way around. She offered to be cooperative, suggesting Shawn "tactfully" point out to Brautigan his own responsibilities in the matter.

Helen made no mention of any of this when she wrote to Richard on the same day, sending along a contract for the Greek edition of *Trout Fishing* for him to sign. Becky Fonda wrote to Brautigan on the eleventh of May, mostly local news seasoned with a dash of Hollywood gossip. She reported that Nicholson and Ashby had asked for fifteen to twenty million to make *Hawkline*. Their take would total seven to eight mil in salary. Universal declined, budgeting eight million with Michael Haller in the director's chair. "No star cast as of now," Becky wrote. "Gatz (regardless of personal diffs.) who is so capable will be working on the screenplay."

Brautigan returned the signed Greek contracts on "a beautiful spring day in Tokyo." A couple days later he wrote Brann again. This letter was more concerned with finances. He asked about his English *Trout Fishing* royalties and if Helen had heard anything about the *Hawkline* film project. Richard mentioned that Becky told him "Universal Pictures had allotted $80 million for a production," a gross exaggeration of what Fonda had actually written and wishful thinking of the most desperate sort.

The June 6 evening edition of *Asahi Shimbun* published Shuntarō Tanikawa's translation of "Night Flowing River" (Yoru ni nagareru kawa) on page 5. Brautigan sent a copy to Jim Sakata in San Francisco, along with a request to help him work out a deal for a one-way ticket back from Japan. When Sakata wrote back to Richard, he promised to get the best possible price on China Airlines. Jim concluded with the news that Tony Dingman had just left for New York to work on Coppola's production of *The Cotton Club*.

On the eighth of June, Richard had lunch with Donald Richie, a noted expatriate author described by Tom Wolfe as "the Lafcadio Hearn of our time." Ten years older than Brautigan, Richie had lived in Tokyo since 1947, returning to the States only occasionally over the years. Fluent in Japanese, he had published fourteen books by the time he met Richard Brautigan, including two classic works on Japanese cinema, treatises on the film work of George Stevens and Yasujirō Ozu, along with studies of ikebana (the art of floral arrangement) and *The Japanese Tattoo*.

They drank sangria and ate seafood soup. With his love of the movies and all things Japanese, Richard was fascinated by this erudite polymath. Their conversation focused on literature. Learning Brautigan had been in Paris six weeks earlier, Richie discussed French writers. Both men esteemed the work of André Gide, talking at length about *The Immoralist*. Richie mentioned a recent translation of *Corydon*, a series of Socratic dialogues on homosexuality published earlier that year, saying they "offered new insights into that admirable novel." Shortly after winning the Nobel Prize and just before his death, Gide had called *Corydon* the most important of his books. The next day Richie sent Brautigan a polite letter of thanks signed "Donald," along with a copy of Richard Howard's new translation of *Corydon*.

Early in June, after the attorney mailed a current financial report, Brautigan wrote back to Joe Swindlehurst. Richard worried about past-due rent owed on one of his Livingston properties, amounting to a couple hundred dollars at best. He also wondered about a plan to rent his Montana "ranch," guessing "nothing has happened." Brautigan asked Swindlehurst to send a monthly $115 payment to Army Street Mini-Storage in Frisco. "Japan continues to be Japan and I'm getting a lot done here," he concluded, adding a mention of his upcoming lectures in Osaka and Kyoto.

Richard's "lectures," consisting mainly of questions from the audience and his answers, were called "A Conversation with Richard Brautigan." He traveled down to Kyoto on June 20, appearing at Doshita University, and continued on to Osaka the next day. Brautigan was not happy with his performances, sensing in advance that they weren't going to go well. "Sometimes one cannot always be on," he observed. "I did the best I could." Almost all the questions from the audience concerned his early work, written two decades before. Richard hadn't read the stuff himself in years. He floundered. The audiences in Kyoto and Osaka knew more about his books than he did. "I'm not interested in reading my own writing once it's done," was his candid assessment. "I was sort of bored."

Brautigan was back in Tokyo on June 22. His lectures had been recorded. Richard planned to listen to the tapes and see if he was right about his lackluster performance. He probably never did, not being fond of revisiting past work. The day after his return to the city, Brautigan typed a letter to Helen Brann in his hotel room, pressing her to organize his foreign contracts and send copies to Joel Shawn. "There seems to be some confusion among subagents about your still representing my work," he wrote. "For instance, Mohrbooks agency in Zurich still thinks you are acting as the agent for my books that have been published so far, and Tom Mori here in Tokyo has never heard directly from you about our parting." Richard wanted "the subagents to be aware of our new situation."

Brautigan didn't understand he was the one who was confused. All commissions for the deals Brann had negotiated for him continued to be paid to her agency and remained part of their ongoing mutual business. This included all of Richard's books that were still in print. Only *An Unfortunate Woman* and any future work would become the responsibility of Joel Shawn. Helen had explained all this to Brautigan when she sent him the Greek *Trout Fishing* contract a month earlier. As usual, Richard interpreted events to suit himself.

A more pressing problem confronted Brautigan. He feared his teeth were falling out. He had not had a proper dental cleaning in quite a while. Every time he brushed his teeth, his gums started bleeding. Richard became preoccupied with aging. When he wrote about his relationship with Masako, he said he was fifty years old, adding a year and a half to his actual age. Brautigan's worries had a lot to do with Kano. As a proper, traditional Japanese woman, at twenty-six going on twenty-seven, Masako was supposed to be married. In bed with his Ninji, Richard didn't "feel 50 years old." Brautigan once discussed with Greg Keeler "the question of whether or not to marry Masako and have a hit squad of Japanese-American kids." Putting fantasy aside, he knew this was an impossible dream.

To distract himself, Richard "followed so many different drummers into the glories of the abyss." It rained all through June. "Not a pleasant month [. . .] either too cold or too mucky." Brautigan distracted himself with "a couple brief love affairs that led to nowhere" and watching "a lot of stupid television." He couldn't sleep and felt "tired all the time." Richard knew Masako wanted a permanent place in his life that he was "not willing or able to give her." Brautigan daydreamed about this possibility and found himself "drowning in ambiguity, temptation and collapsing fate."

The cold rainy Tokyo spring burst at last into full-blown glorious summer. Richard and Masako took full advantage of the good weather, heading out for sunny adventures like lovers the world over. One afternoon they went to visit the Hanazono-Jinja, an early Edo-period shrine just west of Shinjuku's Golden Triangle. Prayers offered at the shrine supposedly brought prosperity in business.

It's more likely Brautigan sought absolution in his favorite tiny bar, Shinya + 1 (Midnight + 1), hidden on a narrow cobbled lane in the Golden Gai.

Named for *Midnight Plus One*, the 1965 British thriller by Gavin Lyall, the cramped little taproom was decorated with model war planes, tattered movie posters and assorted memorabilia. Chin Naito, a 43-year-old actor, writer and comedian, whose work appeared in Japanese *Playboy*, owned Midnight + 1 which served only cold beer and bourtbon. Richard liked sitting at one of the seven stools crowding the dilapidated bar, getting drunk on whiskey while scrawling poetry on cocktail napkins. Naito sealed his friendship with Brautigan late one night at the end of May by giving him a signed copy of *Yomazunishineruka!* (Can't Die Before I Read [Those Books]!), an anthology of his *Playboy* essays, adding a manga-styled personal caricature to the inscription.

Masako and Richard both enjoyed people watching, finding "a lot of tiny incidents" to amuse themselves while wandering the streets of central Tokyo. They always discovered "something funny" to look at. Kano later acknowledged that others "probably did not get [the joke]." Searching for a larger comedic public stage, Richard and Masako found their way one afternoon to Shinjuku Gyoen, at 150 acres one of the largest public gardens in Tokyo. Formerly the Edo-period estate of the Naitō daimyō family, the gardens were only opened to the public after World War II. The lovers enjoyed observing "young people practicing mountaineering" on a climbing wall and the antics of a foreign mime ("perhaps a drug addict") performing and begging around family groups cooking rice in the park for their alfresco meals.

Enchanted by the notion of a similar picnic, Richard and Masako returned to Shinjuku Gyoen, planning on cooking a meal of their own. They brought vacuum pouches of curry paste, two hundred grams of Japanese rice, and her brother's aluminum cooker and camping stove. Just as Brautigan lit the fire, they were spotted by a park security guard, who "chased [them] down to the gate." They planned to try again on a rainy day, when the guard would be off-duty. Richard said he'd borrow a large umbrella from Takako. Like so many well-intentioned schemes, it went astray and they never came back to the park.

In mid-June, Brautigan gave a reading at the Tokyo American Center ("Literature as a Living Process"), followed by an informal reception. Around the same time, Richard and Masako traveled by train out to Kichijoji, a suburb of Mitaka City, itself part of greater Tokyo. Their destination was Inokashira Park, famous for its cherry blossoms. The park and its extensive walking paths surrounded a small lake, where paddleboats, some shaped like swans, were available for rent. Brautigan took Kano for a leisurely cruise around the pond, perhaps not knowing this was a famous way to tell your lover of an impending breakup.

A longer weekend train trip took Richard and Masako to Azumino in the Nagano Prefecture. Situated between the Hido and Kiso ranges of the Japanese Alps, this tranquil mountain plain provided an Asian echo of Montana. Brautigan wanted to go to Ajiro on the Izu Peninsula, where he'd previously spent time with Takako Shiina. Kano vetoed that plan. She insisted they go somewhere "farther away from Tokyo." Azumino was "smaller and quieter." To fortify himself against the unfamiliar, Richard drank beer all the way down on the train. Nevertheless, he "liked the place," Masako recalled, delighted by the crystalline blue sky framing the snowcapped mountains.

The best time Brautigan and Kano shared together that summer started with a search for the perfect soup. On a Friday late in June, they went to Harajuku, a district northwest of Roppongi centered around the Tōgō Jinja Shrine, looking for Eiichi Yamaguchi, the "soup king." Richard and Masako found the modest restaurant and indulged in bowls of his wondrous concoctions while discussing Stephen Hawking's black hole theory. Brautigan wrote two poems about soup before they left. The first, "If Spring Were a Bowl of Soup," he signed, "Wishing Mr. Yamaguchi a beautiful spring." "Cucumber Paradise," the second poem, began by listing various vegetables, meats, and seafood, concluding, "ingredients but a dream, it is the cook that makes / the soup." Before they left, the soup master gave them each a copy of his soup recipe cookbook.

Around seven in the evening, Richard and Masako set off on a hastily planned adventure, traveling by the Keio Line and later by bus out to Tama City on the outskirts of Tokyo. On the trip they talked about Yamaguchi San and his dedication to soup. Brautigan explained how Mr. Yamaguchi had been a chef at the embassy. As a joke, Kano teased him about writing two poems for the soup master while he'd never written a single line for her.

Richard and Masako's destination was Tama Dōbutsukōen, a 128.5-acre zoological park at the foot of Mount Takao. When it had opened in 1958, as a branch of the much smaller Uneo Zoo near central Tokyo, Tama was intended to display wild animals in a more natural setting, running free behind moats separating them from the spectators. Brautigan had wanted to go to the more local zoo in Uneo Park, but it was much too small for what they planned.

Tama Zoo closed to the general public at 5:00 pm. Richard and Masako arrived sometime after eight. They came prepared for their clandestine expedition with a flashlight. Giggling with exhilaration, they climbed the chain-link fence near the entrance some distance from the *kosha* (guard building). The two lovers felt like mischievous children. Kano went first. Brautigan boosted her up, and her tiny feet fit easily into the wire mesh. Richard followed, climbing without too much effort. Masako worried his weight might "shake down" the gate.

Laughing all the while, they ran into the darkness. Brautigan didn't want to follow the well-lit path toward the lion park. Like kids playing hide-and-seek, "pretending to hide behind the bushes," they made it to the insectarium, where bugs and butterflies of every exotic sort were housed. Along the way, they stopped to buy juice from a coin-operated machine but found they had spent all their pocket change on the bus. The insectarium was locked. Richard and Masako sat on a bench outside, staring up at the stars and constellations spangling the blue-black sky overhead. In the distance, they heard the flapping wings of hawks and eagles flying under the giant dome of the raptor enclosure.

Stargazing brought poetry to mind. Kano had always liked the "sky and star images" in Brautigan's poems. Richard pulled out his pocket notebook. He asked Masako to hold the flashlight while he wrote. When he finished, Brautigan tore out the page and handed it to her.

When the Star Stops Counting the Sky

In all the space between nothing
Where a kingdom could have existed

> *a thing bird*
> > *flies around*
> > > *the moment*
> > > > *of her wings*
> > > > > *In the beginning of oblivion.*

Kano read the poem over and over, learning it by heart on the spot. Brautigan took it back and signed the page, returning it to Masako. "You keep this," Richard said in a distant voice, the Puma nodding like a mountain cat, "and you will make a lot of money someday."

Masako was furious. She tore the poem into pieces and recited it back to Brautigan from memory. "Now, this poem is only for me," she said. "Nobody else. This is only for me to remember."

In truth, Masako saved the torn pieces, throwing them away only after she returned home that night and typed a copy of the poem. She had no interest in selling it. Richard's words were private. Masako kept them in her heart ever after. He told her that the "thing bird" was meant to be her, evoked by the flapping wings of a falcon in the distant darkness. "A beautiful poem," Kano recalled. "Perhaps a hint of sadness." She could not imagine how preoccupied her beloved Puma had become with thoughts of his own impending death.

Mr. Yamaguchi's soup seemed to breathe life back into Brautigan. He became obsessed with the subject, scribbling many poems about soup on his Keio Plaza notepad over the next couple weeks. "Soup Mountain Sunrise" went through several drafts and began, "I almost remember in dreams / soup, / the size and image of mountains / with slopes of fresh vegetables." Richard wrote "Chasing Soup," in twin columns, one mirroring the other: "This morning / I have been chasing / soup to catch / and put it / in a poem, but / the soup soon ran / away from my words." Another poem, "Strawberry Gratitude," said the strawberry "gently shows its gratitude / when in the company / of the soup." Of all his never-published soup poetry, Brautigan liked one well enough that he wrote out several copies. Mr. Yamaguchi received one. He gave another to Masako Kano.

Waiting Potatoes

Potatoes wait like edible shadows
under the ground. They wait in
their darkness for the light of
*   the soup.*

These simple lines held a hidden image of Richard's despair. He felt he dwelled in darkness like the lowly potato. In Mr. Yamaguchi's soup restaurant, Brautigan had tasted the vitality of life once again. Haunted by the downward turn his career had taken and burdened by growing debt, Richard made the nourishment of soup into a metaphor embracing hope and renewal.

Yet even soup enhancement didn't keep Brautigan away from morbid thoughts for long during his final weeks in Japan. Most nights found him at the bar in The Cradle. One evening early in July, he scratched out a poem as he sat drinking with Takako.

The Accidental, Unintentional Color of Your Death

Nobody knows how
they will die.

Their color will find
*   them.*

At the bottom of the page, Richard added, "P.S. For Shiina Takako. Everything I write is for you. My sister in this journey to oblivion."

A continuing search for West German models often led Richard far from his soul sister's watering hole. One evening Richard found his way to a place called Key West. Everything in the joint was white. Walls, floor and ceiling, tables, chairs, countertops, even the bar itself was painted white. A huge white model of a Zeppelin airship hung from the ceiling. Brautigan didn't see the humor inherent in the situation. This miniature dirigible was the closest thing to a German model he could find. Richard took note of the shining black hair of the Japanese women in the Key West, standing out dramatically against the white background like ermine tail tips on a snowfield.

The only fault Brautigan could find with Masako Kano was that she was always late. Being a punctual person, and not understanding the demands of an executive position at a high-powered firm like Motorola, Richard had no patience with those who didn't show up at the appointed hour. Masako always assumed she could make a seven o'clock date and be there on time. Sometimes things came up, business matters incomprehensible to a poet like Brautigan, and she'd have to work overtime. Richard hated "all that electrical waiting that made eternity seem like a drop in the bucket."

One July night, Masako had arranged to meet Richard at 7:00 pm at a favorite sidewalk café before going on for dinner. The original plan had been to get together at the place at eight, but Kano assured Brautigan she'd make it earlier. When she didn't show up, Richard sat seething at the café for more than an hour, "emotionally wrung out like a dish rag." Masako was "very, very embarrassed" when she finally arrived, not attempting to make excuses for her lateness.

Much later, after dinner and lovemaking, Brautigan sat naked on the couch, "blank with frustration," watching Kano dress prior to catching her homebound train. He told her that they shouldn't see each other on the coming weekend, "not until the end of next week." His words hit her hard. An expression "of great weariness and sadness" masked her pretty young face.

"Are you sure?" Masako asked in a low and painful whisper.

"Yes," Richard said, using the word like a knife.

"All right." Deeply wounded, her reply was almost inaudible.

When Kano finished dressing, she "walked like a very old woman to the door." Brautigan watched her dispassionately.

"Please lock it," he said.

While Kano "disappeared ghost-like . . . into the Tokyo night," Richard reached for the notepad and pencil on the table, scratching down a quick poem in a cold fury.

Spare Me

I want day to become night,
and night to become day, so that I
will never love again.

BRAUTIGAN DREW A circle around his title, stared at it for several minutes, and crossed it out.

Richard believed Masako Kano used "every pleasure possible" in an effort "to bring about a permanent union" between them. It spooked him. "Maybe I was in love," Brautigan reflected. "But it can't be. Somewhere in all the pressure in maze-like kisses we lost the future." From his mother to Linda Webster to Ginny and Akiko, Brautigan had learned to turn away from love. "I've been married twice and divorced twice," Richard observed. "I don't want to depress [Masako] and all the delights of being married." Brautigan felt his West German model project, with its connection to Kano, led him "into emptiness." He wrote these words at twilight while stone-cold sober.

A couple days later, "a very nice French artist" Richard had met at The Cradle phoned with an invitation to a gallery opening for a show of his work later in the week. The artist told him the French embassy was donating "some good wine" for the event. Sunk in depression, Brautigan felt in no mood for art gallery crowds. When the afternoon in question rolled around, he decided to go. "Maybe a couple of glasses of French wine would be of some help in this fucking nightmare I find myself in," he wrote in his notebook.

During his final weeks in Tokyo, Richard received a couple invitations to visit Europe. The first came from the sponsors of the One World Poetry Festival, asking him to travel to Amsterdam in October. The other, from the United States Information Service, arrived about the same time, inviting Brautigan to give a series of programs in Germany that coming December. This came as really good news. Paychecks were forthcoming. Brautigan summed up his thoughts in his notebook. "Why did I seek such an exotic gothic idea to interview a West German model in Tokyo?" he wrote. "The logical place to interview a German model would be in Germany. I'll be there in three months. I'm going to Amsterdam in the middle of October and from there take a hop over to Munich."

The first week in August, Richard went to a Japanese theater festival he called Twilight in the Mountains. His notes provided minimalist descriptions—"buildings with ancient straw roof illuminating ancient growth"—like haiku snapshots. He got into a discussion with a young American writer about the nature of the color blue. Brautigan made no comment on any of the plays being performed, all in Japanese and meaningless to him. Before leaving for the night, the young writer gave him several pages torn from a tan memo pad, containing a brief discourse about blue: "Blue is the color of my shirt. Blue is the color of my shorts when I wash them in hot water with my shirt [. . . Etc. Etc.]" It wasn't much help to Richard, but he saved the pages, another bit of found art.

The next night Brautigan returned to the theater festival. "I'm still trying to describe something that remembers the color blue," he wrote in his notebook. After watching the first of the evening's plays, Richard wrote, "Is the basis of Japanese theater fazism [sic]!" As the night wore on, he became less interested in the productions and more focused on the audience. "I think some of these people are 'American,'" he wrote, "and I am totally disgusted and will leave Japan very soon because the Americans are not like these assholes. I do not want to be thought of as an American in Japan. We, the Americans, also have dignity."

It was "a very complicated day" for Richard. He felt the Americans in the audience never stopped being humiliated. Disgusted by them, Brautigan left the theater festival. "I ain't perfect," he noted, "but I ain't them."

Brautigan's final couple days in Tokyo verged into the surreal. He wrote in his notebook about a return visit to Café Endless, after describing his first visit in 1979 following a trip to the Sea of Japan. He and Takako had caught a cab at the train station and were soon snared in a massive bumper-to-bumper traffic jam. Both badly wanting a drink, they had gotten out and walked. Along the way, they had passed a place called Café Endless. "Perhaps we should have stopped there and had something to drink," Richard noted after two meandering pages about being stuck in Tokyo traffic.

Brautigan and Shiina never had that drink in 1979. They parted company and went their separate ways. Four years later, Richard wrote about his next-to-last day in Tokyo and mentioned going to a "second Café Endless." This turned out not to be the mysterious place he and Takako had walked past in their search for a drink but his favorite café with the brick waterfall in Mitsui Plaza. Japan had always been a fantasy for Richard. Now even the fantastic Shangri-la of his imagination folded in upon itself, a dream turned inside out.

Brautigan suspected his return to America would provide nothing "to be certain of," but he had no doubts about what he had accomplished in Tokyo. "This four-month trip to Japan is either in the top ten disasters of my life," Richard wrote, "or it has been an adventure of ultimate worth allowing me to arrive at nothing."

Brautigan stopped only briefly in San Francisco when he returned from Tokyo. Financial considerations remained a primary concern. Needing to cut down on expenses, Richard should have left his little office above Vesuvio Café. Over the past year, he'd often been behind on his rent. Henri Lenoir sent several postcards reminding Brautigan about his late payments. One suggested he was "paying rent for what amounts to no more than storage." This had become an expensive proposition. The rent for the single room had risen to $150 per month. Loath to admit his dwindling literary status (and subsequent decrease in income), Richard made no move to economize. His office looking out at City Lights was his last tangible connection to North Beach and he was not about to give it up.

Brautigan maintained a long-established schedule while in the city, arriving early at Enrico's to greet the day. "It was the unwritten rule. I'd meet Richard here at ten o'clock," Richard Breen recalled. "Then would start the day off by making enemies." Brautigan usually got there first, waiting at the bar, "staring out of those marvelous, know-nothing eyes of his, just like a blind child," until Breen showed up. Their favorite victim in the search for potential enemies was a close friend. "I have to fuck over Tony," Brautigan muttered, looking around for Dingman.

"What are you going to do to him today?" Breen asked.

"I don't know but I will."

Breen reasoned that if Brautigan didn't have Tony Dingman around "to rat-fuck" he'd "have no reason to live."

Dingman, who always playfully referred to Brautigan as "the field marshal" or "the German drinking machine," was off in New York working on *The Cotton Club*. Richard scanned the bar for another scapegoat when Breen walked in one morning wearing a cap from The Arctic Bar in Ketchikan, Alaska. The logo featured "two bears fucking" and offended everyone not in on the joke. A DJ visiting Sam McCullough from Alaska had given him the cap.

"Ketchikan!" Brautigan shouted, spotting the amorous ursine logo. Assuming Breen had been to the First City, he asked, "Have you seen the cat?"

"What are you talking about, Richard?"

"The cat in the airport at Ketchikan."

"I've never been to Ketchikan," Breen said.

"Then why are you wearing that hat?"

Breen told him it came from McCullough and Brautigan related his tale of Pedro, the feline "that runs the airport." It suddenly became a matter of the utmost importance to go and see the cat. Brautigan borrowed a credit card from Bob the bartender. "Come on," he insisted, dragging Breen out of Enrico's and hailing a cab to SFO.

Breen and Brautigan flew to Ketchikan early in the afternoon. It was still daylight when they touched down at Gravina Island airport. "Richard couldn't find this cat," Breen recalled. They walked over to the ticket counter in the terminal.

"Where is the cat?" Brautigan demanded.

"Oh, Pedro?" replied the woman behind the counter. "Pedro took the day off."

Brautigan looked at Breen. "Bad idea," he said.

An hour later, the two Richards were back on the same plane on a return flight to San Francisco. They went straight from the airport to Enrico's. It was late and they were the only ones at the bar. "The place was dead empty," Breen remembered, except for a woman sitting in a side booth stroking a cat. "Wait a minute," Brautigan said as Bob set up their drinks. He walked over to the strange woman's table, speaking not to her but the cat.

"What did you say?" Breen asked, once Brautigan returned and sat down on his stool.

"I told Pedro he was a bad boy."

Back in Montana early in September, Richard reunited with his Bozeman pals at the Eagles. Keeler, Cassaday, Donovan, Scoop, and Schrieber all welcomed him home, not knowing Brautigan could no longer comprehend such a happy thought. Home had always been an illusive concept for the kid who had grown up in cheap motels, unaware when the next unexpected move might come. Neither of his houses in Bolinas and Montana was homelike in any way. At some essential level, they remained little more than crash pads.

The place in Pine Creek, purged of any residual domestic touches remaining from Akiko or Masako, no longer felt like home. The moment he arrived, Brautigan longed to leave. Whatever magic Montana once possessed had vanished. Worst of all, Richard felt he couldn't work there. Across the creek, his friend Marian Hjortsberg was living with Dan Manyluk, a sometime cartoonist Brautigan despised. This animosity went back a year to when both had lived at the Range Hotel in Bozeman. Richard referred to Manyluk as Captain Topanga. Marian hadn't followed his advice about checking out the living quarters of potential boyfriends.

Financial problems continued nipping at Richard's heels like a disobedient mongrel who'd once licked his hand. Joel Shawn did his best to calm the rabid beast. He arranged for a $100 monthly payment plan to settle Richard's debt with Sandra Musser and looked for financing to cover needed repairs on the Bolinas house. Shawn also fielded lowball offers for the film rights to *In Watermelon Sugar*. Having a lawyer as a literary agent wasn't good business. Shawn charged by the hour instead of taking a commission on the final sale.

Helen Brann helped resolve this difficulty, proposing Richard get together with Jonathan Dolger. "I suggested that he call Jonathan," she said, "which he did." By way of thanks, Brautigan sent Brann a signed copy of Marc Chénetier's book-length critical study. She was happy to receive it. "All praise richly deserved," Helen wrote to Richard. "I'm proud of our professional association and of you—and so glad to call you one of my dearest friends."

Brautigan told Dolger about "American Hotels" and his West German model project but had no work ready for submission. Jonathan convinced Richard that shelving *An Unfortunate Woman* for the moment would be their best marketing ploy. Dolger felt it was "a very downbeat, very depressed, very self-pitying book." He suggested they "try and think of different ways." Publish something more cheerful first. "If he needed money," Dolger said, "we should try and work the movie side of it." *Hawkline* was still in development at Universal, and there was word of film interest in *Babylon* and other Brautigan titles, all cause for hope.

Hope doesn't pay the bills. Brautigan's only income at the time came from his three rental properties in Livingston, barely enough to cover expenses. Richard's line of credit at the First Security Bank was nearly maxed out. He decided to list Rancho Brautigan on the real estate market. His asking price was $500,000 at a time when forty acres in Pine Creek was worth barely half that much. When his friends pointed this out to Richard, he retorted, "The Japs will buy it. They'll pay anything for it."

Another pipe dream, like the pot of Hollywood gold waiting at the end of an ephemeral rainbow. Richard already had another option, the ultimate solution, a final way out of all his problems. Brautigan often spoke obliquely about suicide with his friends. Brad Donovan remembered hearing several times about how when Jack London decided to end it all, "next to his bed was a notepad where he worked out the morphine prescription that put him under." Richard emphasized London "didn't want to get it wrong."

Greg Keeler recalled how Brautigan "knew when, how, why and with what kind of weapon Hemingway killed himself." Brautigan had also spoken to Tom McGuane about suicide. "He told me there had been a lot of cancer in his family," Tom remembered. "He said he would get it and when he was told he would kill himself. No evidence somebody told him that he had cancer, and no evidence that anyone in his family had it. Given Richard's mind, speculatively, maybe he confected this context for suicide in case he should find it handy."

Trying to sum things up, Sean Cassaday referred to an idea expressed by Doris Lessing, "People who want to commit suicide rehearse in their minds constantly how they will do it." In Japan harakiri was considered an honorable act, even a noble one. Richard believed this. Miracles might happen and solve all his problems, but if things continued to get worse, death always remained an option. This decision eased Brautigan's mind and gave him an approximation of peace. Knowing the end in advance provided a measure of consolation. Whenever the time seemed appropriate, Richard was ready to die.

At times Greg Keeler needed "a break from the alcohol and death talk," leaving Brautigan "to stew on his own." Keeler felt guilty about this. He knew if Richard couldn't find other company, "he'd spiral into a physical and psychological oblivion." By mid-September, alone in his Pine Creek house, Brautigan had grown "hugely depressed." He moved into the Murray Hotel in Livingston. At the far end of a long narrow hallway, room 211 was a dreary ten-by-twelve corner cell with drab yellow walls and no toilet. The single window with a pull-string shade looked down past the hall fire escape onto a collection of garbage cans in the back alley. There was a plain wooden chair and a one-drawer desk supporting a tiny black-and-white TV "full of fuzz and static." The iron bedstead had been painted orange, its cot-like mattress covered with an orange chenille spread. Like his sad lodgings at the Hotel Jessie, number 211 was a room where a man could easily go mad.

One evening at the hotel, Brautigan encountered film director Sam Peckinpah, who rented a suite on the third floor. They knew one another casually from brief encounters at parties hosted by the Fondas and the McGuanes. Richard invited Sam to drop by his room the following night for a drink. A lifelong fan of Westerns (with one of his own in development), Brautigan had a lot to talk about with the man who made *Ride the High Country* and *The Wild Bunch*. Knowing Sam to be a brandy drinker, Richard bought a bottle from the Murray Bar downstairs the next evening, putting the price on his tab and asking for a couple clean glasses.

When Peckinpah arrived at room 211, Brautigan's .357 Magnum handgun sat on the desktop next to the Courvoisier. Richard poured them both a drink. Sam asked him about the heavy artillery. "Protection," Brautigan replied.

Peckinpah understood, familiar with Brautigan's personal paranoia. He offered to fetch his own pistol and "liven the place up." Sam returned in a couple minutes with his .38 Colt. Looking out Brautigan's open window, Peckinpah spotted an alley cat sitting on top of a garbage can and fired a shot. He missed the cat. The pistol's report echoed among the surrounding buildings.

"My turn," Richard said, firing two loud rounds. The twice-punctured garbage can rang like a gong.

"What in the hell do you two think you're doing?" Ralph White, the hotel's crusty manager, glowered in the doorway, wearing striped pajamas and carrying the office club reserved for troublemakers. This was a lengthy speech for White, notoriously taciturn, a "yup and nope" guy at heart. He lived in room 212, right next door, and had appeared instantly, as if by magic.

"Target practice," Brautigan said.

Sam, the permanent resident, sounded more apologetic. Like Richard at Rancho Brautigan, Peckinpah had also gained a dubious reputation for shooting off weapons inside his rooms upstairs. Not wanting any trouble, Sam promised Ralph he'd "hang it up for tonight." White nodded and wandered grumbling back to his room. Peckinpah and Brautigan put their firearms away. What they did next, if anything, was anybody's guess.

Richard rented room 211 by the month. It was worth $100 to know a cheap room awaited him in town whenever the solitude out in Pine Creek grew unbearable. Brautigan fought his depression by having friends over in the afternoon to drink and shoot guns off the back porch. Dave Schrieber, Scoop, Greg Keeler, and Sean Cassaday all took turns blasting away on various occasions. Keeler remembered one time when Richard hauled a wooden chair, part of a set of expensive furniture Akiko had purchased, out into the firing line. "Take things that bother you and shoot them," Greg said.

Marian Hjortsberg was no longer included among the shooters at Brautigan's place. Richard's animosity toward her current boyfriend foreclosed on any possible invitation. "The guy was a total jackass," Karen Datko observed. "He purported to be a great artist. There's no question that Richard could not stand Dan Manyluk." The death of a pony brought all of Brautigan's bad feelings out into the open.

King didn't even belong to Marian. She'd pastured the feisty pony for years at no cost as a favor to elderly neighbors who'd once owned a Wyoming ranch but no longer had any room for livestock. King's loss was not mourned by anyone in the Hjortsberg family. He'd been quick to bite, impossible for a child to ride, and too small for an adult. Like Dan Manyluk, King was the classic freeloader, growing fat and sassy off the land without ever having to provide any work in return.

Brautigan felt offended because Marian chose not to bury the dead pony. Perhaps the odor of decay drifting up from the woods became too powerful a reminder of his death option. The carcass lay down under the trees, out of sight and far away. Marian explained to Richard that she couldn't afford to hire a backhoe to dig a hole big enough. Let the coyotes, ravens, and maggots do their work. By spring King would be a small pile of bleached bones. If Brautigan still wished some sort of ceremony, they could gather on the banks of Pine Creek and toss the pony's remains into the rushing snowmelt runoff.

This proposal didn't satisfy Richard. He started harping on the subject, repeatedly "tracking" over and over again about the immorality of leaving King unburied. Brautigan's behavior struck Marian as particularly curious. At a party at her house shortly before the pony died, Richard got very drunk and grew nostalgic, "tracking" in a different vein. "I wish we could have been able to make it together," he told her again and again. "I wish we could have been able to make it together." Once an idea became fixed in Brautigan's mind, whether about love or death, he was unable to let it go. Scoop saw things differently. "All that had to happen," she said, "was that Dan Manyluk had to drop his beer can and get off his ass and go out with a shovel and cover up the pony with some dirt."

This may have been the case, but Brautigan never confronted Manyluk directly. King still lay moldering in the woods when Toby Thompson arrived back in Montana early in October on assignment to write a magazine piece about Peter Fonda. As soon as Thompson checked into the Murray Hotel, he phoned Brautigan in Pine Creek. They hadn't spoken in over three years. Richard said he'd like to get together, but they didn't see each other until a couple nights later when Brautigan came back on the bus from a quick trip to Bozeman.

Toby sat at the Livingston Bar and Grill with Dink Bruce, Tim Cahill, and Jeff Bridges. Richard came in "staggering drunk." Brautigan "did the number of kissing [everybody] on the lips" and pulled up a stool at the bar. Thompson thought he looked "like somebody who was completely and totally vulnerable." As if to contradict this impression, Richard turned to Cahill and said, "You know, Tim, Toby is really a much better writer than you are."

"Now Richard," Tim replied in a good-natured way, "don't start these wide-awake fights at one o'clock in the morning."

No one reacted further. Thompson thought "it was the sort of remark that a senile person in a nursing home might say when they've got nothing left to lose."

Oblivious to his own rude behavior, Brautigan soon asked who'd give him a ride home. Dink volunteered, as he was heading up the valley. Toby didn't have a real conversation with Richard until a few days later when he came back to the Murray after an afternoon hike and found Brautigan sitting in the lobby. Thompson wasn't sure if he had been waiting for him or if their meeting was a coincidence.

Toby and Richard had a long talk, laying to rest any residual animosity from 1980. Thompson again felt Brautigan was "extraordinarily vulnerable" as they spoke openly about their feelings. Toby decided to accompany Richard on an evening's round of bar hopping. "I just felt like getting drunk," he recalled. An easy task with a man who "didn't want to be seen in the Livingston Bar and Grill knocking down seven or eight shots of Dickel by himself."

Brautigan and Thompson ended their pub crawl at the B&G that night. Richard began tracking about Marian Hjortsberg's dead pony. "How it was so uncivilized, and you did not leave something that you loved to decompose without proper burial." Toby drove Brautigan back to Pine Creek. Richard ranted about King rotting in the woods all the way home. He persuaded Thompson to take him to a neighbor's house. Brautigan pounded on the front door. Toby had no idea who lived there. Richard wanted to borrow a shovel, to wake the guy up and have him help bury the dead pony. Nobody was home. Thompson feared he would "have to go out and bury this damned horse in the middle of this cold October night," but Brautigan let him off the hook and went to bed. "Clearly at this point he had become obsessed with death," Toby recalled.

On another occasion, riding a motorcycle with Peter Fonda at dusk, Thompson observed Richard trudging home from the Pine Creek store with a sack of groceries. They waved as they sped past. Toby thought of Brautigan "going to spend the night alone in his isolated house." It was completely dark when Fonda and Thompson rode back along East River Road. Toby glanced in through Richard's window as they drove by his house and saw Brautigan sitting all by himself at his dining room table. "I was struck by his solitude," Thompson recalled.

Years before, the Hjortsbergs had made the same observation when they walked past Richard's house one moonlit night during the first summer he lived in Pine Creek. They saw him alone in front of his TV set. Gatz and Marian assumed their new neighbor must be very lonely. Not being loners at heart, they made the same mistake Toby did years later, equating solitude with loneliness. Brautigan often felt depressed but probably never felt lonely. Long familiar with a writer's solitary isolation, Richard had immunized himself to loneliness.

Brautigan did no new writing during his final weeks in Montana. He and Brad Donovan compiled a formal "working draft" of their screenplay "Trailer," a process closer to the mechanical than the creative. Once again they divided up the scenes, separately typing the handwritten pages. Three different typewriters (possibly more) were used in this procedure. The typefaces and formatting styles vary considerably. All the finished pages (a total of sixty-six) were hand numbered as the completed screenplay was assembled. Seven scenes near the end existed only as brief outlines. Richard and Brad planned further work on the script and needed a clean copy from which to coordinate their efforts. They dated this draft "10/83."

Richard used the rest of the time he spent alone trying to plan for what little future he had left. Brautigan made notes and drafted business letters. One was to Joe Swindlehurst. "To save money on long distance calls," he wrote, "have secretary say if you are in, 'Mr. Swindlehurst has gone fishing and will call me back.' If you are not in have secretary tell operator when you will be in." Richard mentioned that he'd give the attorney a German address in Europe and will stay at "the Keio Plaza Hotel for at least a month while I am in Japan. And then take a small apartment. Future plans for Montana: Rent an apartment or buy a house in town in Bozeman."

Brautigan outlined a letter to Lee Schultz, his new accountant in San Francisco, an itemized wish list for possible salvation. "I could make some money this year by selling book to Sam," began item one. "I have tons of deductions." Richard continued, "I could make a lot of money next year, can I transfer losses of this year to next year?" The third item on his list of impossible dreams stated, "I'm going to sell the ranch, asking $500,000, may take a long time to get it but will need structure. I'll let you know when it happens." Brautigan wondered about making quarterly tax payments. "Too late this year." He ended with a mix of pipe dreams and desperation. "Will get $25,000 upon starting a film, maybe in January. What about quarterly payments? Do I have to make any next year because my income was so low this year? I'm borrowing $50,000. Hodge got it. $10,500 for interest."

Compiling such a dismal tally would put anyone in a bad mood. Brautigan stormed over to the Hjortsberg place, drunkenly invaded Marian's kitchen, raving about the "millenniums of civilization involved" and how burying the decaying pony was the "civilized thing to do." He left

Marian and the children in tears. She phoned Tim Cahill in town, asking him to "come out and please, please keep Richard away from the kids." Tim's wife, Maureen, a good friend of Marian's, dispatched Cahill to Pine Creek. She went with him as they had an invitation to the McGuanes' later that evening.

When Tim and Maureen arrived at Richard's place, not a word was said about King. They found Scoop, Schreiber, and "two or three others" hanging out and having a good time shooting handguns off the back porch. Everybody had another drink. Brautigan did not shoot. Being most sober, Cahill shot the best and "got lots of pats on the back" as he actually hit the target, unlike the others in the crowd.

That evening, Tom and Laurie McGuane hosted a large gathering for singer-songwriter Warren Zevon ("Excitable Boy," "Carmalita," "Werewolves of London"), with whom Tom had been collaborating on song lyrics. Zevon flew in from L.A. with mystery writer Jim Crumley (*The Last Good Kiss*). Zevon and Crumley put a new spin on the concept of the "mile-high club," getting stoned out of their gourds in the airliner's restroom. They met up at the Livingston Bar and Grill with a couple other Missoula writers, Bill Kittredge, who at this stage of his career had published only a single volume of short stories (*The Van Gogh Field and Other Stories*), and Mike Köepf, whose first novel (*Save the Whale*) had come out in 1978. After a couple drinks, they headed up the valley to the McGuanes' spread.

Gatz Hjortsberg had first encountered Crumley, a burly affable Texan, the previous April at a Los Angeles book-signing party for *Dancing Bear*, Crumley's most recent Milo Milodragovich mystery. Gatz wasn't around for the Warren Zevon festivities, exiled by remarriage in Billings, where he worked on the final revisions for *The Hawkline Monster* script, a project on which Brautigan pinned much of his dwindling capacity for hope.

Karen Datko came over from Bozeman to Rancho Brautigan in the afternoon, joining Dirty Unc and several of his former MSU students, busy tying one on and blasting sixguns off the porch. The Cahills drove Richard to the party. Scoop followed, hauling the other uninvited drunks to the McGuanes' place on Barney Creek. Tom and Laurie's official guest list included Jeff and Sue Bridges, the Cahills, and the Fondas. McGuane was triply pissed when he saw Brautigan and his entourage arrive. "One, he brought uninvited guests. Two, he was already drunk. Three, he had a .357 magnum with him."

Tim Cahill had no idea Richard was packing. Tom took the big pistol from Richard, saying, "You can come, and these other people, but the gun has to go." McGuane put the magnum in his garage. "Not a good idea to have a drunk with a gun and kids in the house."

Karen Datko made a fuss over the incident. "She insisted it was some kind of competitiveness or upstaging on my part," Tom recalled. "Just because Richard was a great writer, I had no right to take it away from him. I didn't make it an issue. The gun thing is a motif in the life of Richard Brautigan."

By the time Peter and Becky Fonda showed up with Toby Thompson, most of the guests slumping in the living room were stuporous with drink and drugs. On the wagon, Tom McGuane greeted the Fondas affably and led them toward the livelier kitchen crowd. "There're some people out there who're having trouble speaking English," Tom said.

Jeff Bridges chatted with Warren Zevon in a far corner. Peter Fonda went downstairs to play the piano with the McGuanes' three-year-old daughter, Annie. The music soon attracted Zevon, who took over at the keyboard, pounding out "The Overdraft," a song he had cowritten with McGuane. About twenty people crowded in to sing along. "No one sleeps on the yellow line / No one's that alone." Zevon was plastered, barely able to speak let alone play the piano, yet still going full blast. "That was his style," Tom observed, "everything cranked up to ten." At one point McGuane advised his friend, "Take off your hat and let your brain cool down."

William Kittredge first ran into Richard Brautigan at the Washbag around 1980. He was at the bar, talking about Montana with Mike Köepf, when Richard came in with two little guys wearing dark suits and ties. Overhearing conversation about home, Brautigan gravitated toward the other writers. "Hey, Richard," one of the suits called out, "we're going to dinner now."

"Good idea," Brautigan replied, having no intention of joining them.

Richard remained atypically demure throughout the Zevon party. He sat on the living room floor, "curled up" in front of the coffee table. "He was like a little old lady that night," Thompson observed. "Just an exhausted, drunk, little old woman." This didn't prevent him from getting into an altercation with Jim Crumley, a former oil field roustabout. "You could probably beat me in fighting," Brautigan declared, "but I might be able to kill you."

Toby thought things looked bad. "I had to get over there through the haze of drugs," Thompson recalled, "to keep Richard from getting the crap pounded out of him by a bunch of writers who weren't going to take him as a role model."

The party broke up early. Almost everyone except Brautigan headed down to the bar at Chico Hot Springs, where Warren Zevon insisted on sitting in with Players, the band on deck that night. Unable to sing, play, or even remember the words to his own songs, Zevon nevertheless loudly demanded the management pay him $1,000 for his fifteen-minute "performance." Later he was hauled to the Livingston hospital for stitches after cutting his hand when he snapped the neck off a beer bottle, attempting to uncap it without an opener.

Staggering back to her car outside the McGuanes' place after Brautigan retrieved his .357 Magnum from the garage, Scoop confessed to Richard that she was drunk on her ass. "Really shit faced." Driving him back home was not even close to the realm of possibility. This turned out not to be a problem. Brautigan climbed in behind the wheel of her little manual transmission car, switched on the engine, shifted into gear, and drove the two miles or so to his house as if he'd been doing it all his life.

Karen Datko "felt honored." She knew he never drove a car, insisting friends go out of their way to provide him with transportation. Richard told Scoop an involved story about the reason for his aversion to automobiles, swearing her to eternal secrecy. "I'll never tell," Datko said. She never did. Scoop also kept mum about Unc's driving skills for as long as he lived.

Because of King, Brautigan's friendship with Marian Hjortsberg seemed irrevocably broken. Eventually a neighboring rancher offered to cart the horse away and bury it. Why waste a good stinking rotten carcass? King got hauled into the foothills and dumped as bear bait. The rancher shot a trophy black off him when the bear came to feed. Marian knew this but never told Richard. She saw no point in getting in the last word.

The day after the McGuanes' party, Brautigan phoned Sean Cassaday in Bozeman and said, "I'd like you to do me a favor."

Sean thought, "Well, here it comes," knowing Richard often made outrageous demands on his friends. "What is it?" he asked.

"I'd like you to come over and spend a couple days with me. I want to get some things packed up and get some things in order and pack my house," Brautigan told him. "I want to make some plans when I leave, because I'm going to be gone for a while, and I want to get all this straightened out. I'd like you to come over and give me a hand doing that."

"I'm not doing anything right now," Cassaday said. "That would be fine."

"And, I'll pay you for it," Richard added.

"Well, great! Fine." Sean would have done it for free. He liked Brautigan and thought spending time with him sounded like a lot of fun. Cassaday drove over to Pine Creek the next morning. "We had a great time those two days," he recalled.

They started in Richard's one-room outside sleeping house, packing the personal items in boxes. If his property sold while he was away, Brautigan instructed Cassaday to make sure the Russell Chatham painting, originally commissioned to fill in a window and take the place of the view, was not included in the sale. Richard wanted to keep it, along with the weathered found-art tailgate he called the Harry Dean Stanton Coffee Table. He made Sean promise to guard them for him. After locking the little sleeping chamber, they headed inside the main house for a drink.

A lot of drinking fueled the conversation during Cassaday's stay. Their next task involved a trip into town. Along the way Richard pointed up Suce Creek canyon at a narrow gorge filled by an aspen grove with leaves turned gold by fall. "I wrote about that small grove of trees," Brautigan said. "See how it looks almost like a waterfall of color among the evergreens?" He referred to "Kyoto, Montana," a story in *The Tokyo–Montana Express*.

Their main destination in Livingston was Western Drug, where Richard filled a prescription for the sleeping medication he took to combat his insomnia. This was of vital importance for his upcoming trip. "Now, don't take these all at once," the pharmacist quipped as he pushed several large pill bottles across the counter. Brautigan and Cassaday both got a kick out of this sort of deadpan cowboy humor. They repeated the druggist's remark throughout the day.

"Enjoying a small moment over and over was certainly something Richard did often," Sean recalled. "It seldom mattered if it was a good or bad moment. Such moments would become part of his amazing memory for detail." Ianthe once told her father that his mind was "like a stainless-steel spiderweb."

Back at Rancho Brautigan, companionship, conversation, and continued drinking took precedence over the more physical demands of packing things up. Brautigan tracked on and on about Marian Hjortsberg's dead pony. He knew he'd made her children cry, realizing perhaps that he'd gone too far. Richard wanted to apologize but said he couldn't do it in person. He asked Sean to do it for him after he left. Cassaday was to approach Marian and tell her, "Richard says he's sorry he did that." Brautigan felt concerned about tying up certain loose ends. His apology was one of the things he wanted taken care of.

Richard also had Sean make a couple phone calls. The first, to Jonathan Dolger in New York, was to inform the agent that Brautigan would be coming to town soon for a few days before leaving on an extended trip, several months at least, and would not be readily available while away in Europe and Japan. The second was an overseas call to the Netherlands. Richard's first European stop was Amsterdam. He wanted Cassaday to ask the operator the correct local time. Brautigan had been given a pen with a little inset digital clock. Once Sean learned the correct Dutch time, Richard had him enter it into the pen. "Now I know what time it is in Amsterdam," Brautigan said. "When I get there, I won't have to ask anyone. I'll have this thing."

Later in the evening, Richard told Sean he was leaving because he could no longer write in Montana. Tokyo, on the other hand, proved conducive to writing well. Illustrating his point, Brautigan got out a recent Japanese notebook and read sections of "The Fate of a West German Model in Tokyo" to Cassaday. Sean remembered a section about "sitting in a restaurant and looking at a beautiful woman, and he was imagining how he might have had an affair with this woman."

The next morning after coffee, Richard and Sean got back to work, packing things in boxes. It began to look as if someone was really moving out. They worked at a leisurely pace, conversation preferable to backbreaking labor. Brautigan talked about wanting to have another child. He hoped to do a better job this time around than he thought he had with Ianthe. When she was a baby, Brautigan had almost no money. He got rich almost overnight. Richard believed his sudden fame got in the way of being a proper parent.

Later, they talked about ghosts. Brautigan told Cassaday the Pine Creek house was haunted by an Asian poltergeist. He'd never made such a claim before; owning a haunted house in Bolinas was sufficiently supernatural. Richard spoke metaphorically. The spirits of Akiko, Masako, Siew-Hwa, and Eunice lingered at Rancho Brautigan. He deserved "to be haunted."

At one point, Richard claimed he hadn't published anything recently because of his divorce. He told Sean his settlement was structured in a way that permitted Aki to take his future earnings. This was a deliberate falsehood. Brautigan and his lawyers had worked very hard to separate his copyrights from any division of property. Richard was not publishing because no one was buying.

Around 7:00 pm, Toby Thompson stopped in to say goodbye. He'd been put off by Brautigan's drinking and "was afraid of getting roped into a really bad scene." Toby found Richard "in a reflective mood," a major move clearly under way. Thompson asked Brautigan why he was leaving the ranch.

"Its time has passed," Richard said.

They talked about Brautigan's plans to sell the place. Richard offered Toby 15 percent of "whatever he could get for it." Knowing Tom Brokaw was looking for a home in Montana, Thompson gave this notion some thought.

Because of his dead pony dispute with Marian Hjortsberg, Brautigan could no longer bring his treasured sporting equipment to her house for winter storage. The McGuanes were recruited as replacements. Richard called Tom to say he was bringing his stuff by. "He saw life in moments," McGuane recalled. "The moment when I leave—when I leave my things—when I relinquish my pistol. The moment when I first walked into your kitchen. These things are all very charged." Tom told Richard he'd be busy for awhile, working his colts out in the riding arena but he could come up later once he'd finished. Brautigan was unhappy at having to wait but had no choice.

Sean and Richard gathered up Brautigan's firearms (McGuane remembered it as a 30-30 rifle, a couple handguns, the treasured pump-action .22) and fishing equipment, along with his blue Smith Corona electric typewriter. Toby offered to prepare dinner, watching as Richard tied his tubed fly rods together with a black ribbon, binding in a bouquet of dead flowers to finish the arrangement. Along with the rods, a couple rifles, and the .44 Magnum, Thompson noticed a small plywood box ceremoniously wrapped in layers of tissue paper.

Toby asked what it was. Brautigan watched with a bemused expression as Thompson peeled back the tissue and opened the lid. Inside lay an austere glazed clay urn.

"I'll be in there someday," Richard whispered.

Toby shrugged it off as Brautigan and Cassaday hauled the stuff up to Barney Creek. It was late, and they found Tom McGuane working one of his cutting horses in a covered arena off to the side of his house. Sean hung back as Tom dismounted and walked with Richard out of the arena, across a little bridge into the front yard. McGuane found Brautigan "aloof, wounded that I didn't stop immediately, and I sort of charmed him out of it." Tom remembered thinking "he was carrying something really big around in his head."

Richard gave Tom a big kiss. "Don't worry, "he said. "I'm not really trying to kill myself." Cassaday didn't take part in the conversation as they lifted Brautigan's typewriter, guns, and rods from the car, but he heard some of what they said. "It was just goodbye between two good friends."

McGuane said something to Brautigan about his drinking. "Be careful," he warned.

Richard promised to try, saying "he wanted to go back to Japan and was thinking very seriously about getting married again and having children." He mentioned "a young girl that he had an affair with the year before. Perhaps marrying and having a child."

Sean knew he wasn't a part of this, standing back as Brautigan handed McGuane the small wooden box. "I'll send for this when I need it," Richard said.

They kissed farewell like brothers, and Cassaday drove Brautigan back to the home he was about to leave forever. Tom and Richard never saw each other again.

Down in Pine Creek, Toby Thompson found almost no food in Brautigan's kitchen. He threw together an improvised meal, "scrambled eggs, sautéed hot dogs, some peppers, and a can of Dinty Moore beef stew." When Richard and Sean returned, they gathered for this simple fare, washed down with tumblers of George Dickel. "It was a real sacramental kind of meal." Brautigan seemed "tremendously touched" that Thompson had cooked his dinner. He kept saying thank you, glancing over at Toby, who thought he looked "so ethereal." Thompson felt deep sympathy for Richard "because the phone didn't ring that night. Nobody came to see him that night—his last night in Montana."

After rinsing their dishes in the sink, the trio headed through the darkness to Brautigan's studio out in the barn. They climbed the bare wooden stairs angling from landing to landing up to the rafters, a single bare bulb lighting their way from above. Toby asked Brautigan how many books he'd written. Richard thought for a second or two. "Ten," he answered.

They set to work in Brautigan's small boxlike writing studio, the spectacular mountain view shrouded by night. Richard sorted through his papers, making stacks of thirty or forty pages at a time on the simple white wooden slab desk. "Taxes," he'd say, separating the documents he wanted to save into a new file folder and tossing the discards onto the floor. Brautigan reorganized all his files in this manner, putting what he wanted to keep into boxes (correspondence, legal matters, manuscripts), throwing the rest onto the growing trash heap at his feet.

A man who previously had preserved every scrap of paper however insignificant, Richard now ruthlessly discarded everything he once would have treasured. Letters from Masako and

Takako Shiina, early drafts of unpublished poetry, fan notes, correspondence with other writers, Mr. Yamaguchi's autographed soup recipe book—all went onto the floor, along with financial statements, tax returns, canceled checks, uncorrected galley proofs for *So the Wind Won't Blow It All Away*, assorted snapshots, birthday cards from his daughter, and an assortment of junk (foosball tournament posters, a menu from the Old Norris School House Café, a 1978 program for the District 10-C basketball tournament in Livingston, a calendar from Van's IGA, numerous contracting and plumbing receipts, and the operating instructions for a Maytag Model DE407 washing machine).

Toby Thompson stood back watching. Behind him a soft cloth sculpture of several three-foot-long trout hung on the wall. In a way, it felt like witnessing a man destroy every trace of his recent emotional past. "[Richard] was talking about death," Toby recalled. "Death was in the air." Like a potlatch, Brautigan gave Thompson his personal things throughout the night: a pen from the Wrangler ("The Most Literary Bar in the USA"), copies of his work (a second edition of *Galilee Hitchhiker*, foreign translations of his novels), inscribing each in an evolving narrative of letting go.

Richard came across copies of recent work. "Here's one for Montana," he said and read "The Lost Tree," a story of vanished love, about revisiting the tree where he and Masako had so often consummated their passion.

"This one's for Japan," Brautigan said, reading the poem "Night Flowing River." Proud of the work, he mentioned it had been printed in Japanese and posted on newspaper kiosks all over Tokyo.

"Has that ever been published?" Toby asked.

"Well, no. Not in English," Brautigan said. "This is the only English version of it."

"Can I have those?"

"Sure."

Thompson told Richard he was connected to the *Washington Review of the Arts* in D.C. He thought he might be able to get the two pieces published. After finishing in the studio, Brautigan, Cassaday, and Thompson returned to the main house for another drink. Once again, just like five months earlier in Tokyo, Richard had misplaced the manuscript of "The Fate of a West German Model in Tokyo." He started poking around among the packing boxes.

"Look for a little green notebook," he calmly instructed Toby. "Kind of important."

"What's in it?"

"The new novel."

Thompson was shocked. Holy shit! he thought. The house was full of junk. Richard didn't seem all that concerned. Toby knew he'd be going out of his mind if his book had been lost. After a search, they found the notebook under the sofa around 1:00 pm. Toby was heading back to Livingston. He planned on staying another week in Montana to finish the Peter Fonda story. Brautigan told him he'd rented a room at the Murray for the month. Thompson was welcome to use it and save some money. They embraced at the door. "It was quite touching," Toby thought, heading back toward town.

Richard and Sean got little if any sleep that night. Early the next morning, Cassaday drove Brautigan into Livingston. Their first stop was the Mint Bar, where Richard bought a pint of whiskey. After a couple snorts, Brautigan felt ready to conduct his business. A visit to his real estate agent topped the agenda. For inexplicable reasons, Richard brought his telephone into town and left it with the Realtor. Next they headed for the First Security Bank. Sean waited outside in the car while Richard went in to finesse the rough edges of his dwindling line-of-credit loan.

Brautigan went to see Bruce Erickson, the bank's president, who had signed off on his loan. Bruce liked Richard, having had long experience with his eccentricities. Once, Brautigan came to see him and said, "I've really got to show you something." He led Erickson out of the bank's back door into the alley and they turned right, walking half a block to Callender Street. Another right turn and a half-block stroll took them to the corner of Second Street, where they turned right again and walked to the front entrance of First Security. Nothing happened. No interesting new sights were seen. Just another ordinary day in Livingston. Brautigan wanted to share his fascination with the mundane.

Another time, Richard phoned Bruce from Japan on Erickson's dime. (Even if the call wasn't collect, most of Brautigan's money had been borrowed from the bank.) He called Bruce frequently, often at ungodly hours of the night. "I've got a great idea," Richard said this time.

"What's that?"

"Land yachts."

"Huh . . . ?"

"Motor homes," Brautigan repeated emphatically. "Why don't they call them 'land yachts'?"

No one remembered what the writer and the banker discussed on the morning of Brautigan's last day in Livingston, but once Richard attended to the last-minute details, he and Cassaday drove over the pass to Bozeman, where Dave Schrieber, Brad Donovan, and Greg Keeler waited for them at the Western Café. Brautigan preferred simple American food. The Western, where ranchers and cowhands ate, was one of his favorites. Sean and Richard were running late. Everyone ordered big breakfasts. After ten minutes, when the food arrived, Brautigan said, "Well, we have to go now." Their meals sat untouched on the table.

"I don't think Richard paid for anything," Cassaday recalled. On the road to the airport, Brautigan issued orders to everyone. He needed Clorets. He wanted a copy of the newest *Enquirer*. "Sort of a guerrilla action." Everyone fanned out across the terminal while Richard checked in at the counter. They all planned to meet up at the bar. Sean got change, feeding quarters into the poker machine. He immediately had "two incredible hands" and won $13. Cassaday bought everybody a round while they waited for the plane to arrive.

Brautigan went to the men's room. Sean suggested they page Richard, hoping to catch him "while he was taking a piss." Schrieber went and placed the call. When Brautigan returned he was totally flustered. "I can't understand it," he said. "They called for me and there was nobody on the phone."

Laughing, his buddies told Richard they were behind the prank, pushing a drink his way to make amends. Before long Brautigan's flight was announced over the PA system. Richard handed Greg the mooning photo and dug into his pockets, pulling out a handful of Japanese coins. He gave them to Sean without any explanation. Keeler, Schrieber, and Cassaday watched Brautigan walk on board. They stood waving by the plate-glass window as Richard's plane lifted off into the Big Sky above Montana. Richard never came back.

ONE MORNING AFTER returning from his last trip to Japan, Richard Brautigan showed up on Bobbie Louise Hawkins's doorstep. He fidgeted and stammered. "Does everyone in Bolinas have this crotch itch?"

"I don't think so, Richard," she said. Bobbie's years of nurturing Richard as a friend/fellow writer/mentor gave her a unique perspective on his personality. ("You know how you can look at a person and almost see the shape of another person inside?") To Bobbie, Richard was forever younger and smaller. She saw him always as no more than thirteen or fourteen; 120 pounds dripping wet. She addressed the waif within, asking, "What do you mean?"

More fidgeting. Bit by bit Richard disclosed that he had contracted something in Japan. He was miserable with it. The rash was "breaking out" and "incredibly itchy."

"Well," Bobbie said. "It sounds more like some kind of infection. You should use some medication. Have you been to a doctor?"

"I went to a doctor once in Japan."

Bobbie Louise had the sudden sense of being in a conversation with her mother, who suffered from Alzheimer's. "And what did the doctor say, Richard?"

"The doctor said I should use this salve."

"Do you have this salve?"

"Well, yes, I have the salve."

"And are you using it?"

"When I remember, I use it."

"When you use it, does it help?"

"Yes. When I use it, it helps."

"Well, then, I think, Richard, you should use this salve."

"Yes. I should use it."

Recalling this long-ago off-kilter moment, Bobbie Louise Hawkins lost her equilibrium all over again, the memory made even more distant by persistent disbelief. "This would qualify as a conversation," she said, shaking her head at the dizziness of it all. "I would just be feeling bemused, like *woooo!*"

fifty-eight: the pitch

During the last summer of Richard Brautigan's life, Donald Guravich, Joanne Kyger's partner, spent a July night drinking with him in Bolinas. Guravich had met Brautigan only once before, years earlier at a party at Margot and John Doss's place. What follows is a piece of found art, an exact transcription of the story as told by Donald Guravich.

"WE WERE WORKING on what Richard had decided was going to be his best-selling TV series. So we were working up a pilot for that. There was a dinner here, and Richard came just briefly. He didn't seem to like being around a lot of people at that point, so we sort of bailed after about an hour. He wanted to leave. We ended up going down to Smiley's Saloon to pick up some beer, and we'd had some beer up here. Dos Equis and double shots of bourbon, Jack Daniel's, and then on to the Bolinas Cemetery and the plot so far for this TV series set in Alaska: postcard shots of picturesque countryside, token glaciers, etc. Long shot, zoom in on Anchorage, the poshest building there, 'Call of the Wild Firm.'

"This is the name of the series: 'Timber Lawyers,' starring unknown lead actor, black, unknown Hispanic sidekick, unknown Wasp tits 'n' ass secretary. Big posh office, quiet and rich. Phone rings. This is the pilot movie. Follow tits 'n' ass secretary to Rolls Royce and at least four minutes of Anchorage and then zoom to second commercial. It's just totally visual at that point. That's fifteen minutes of TV with no plot whatsoever. Then, back to following footsteps in deep snow. We see legs moving, no face. Who is that familiar mystery voice talking to his trusty dog somewhere behind him? Timberwolf.

"Then sounds of pickup truck rolling off the rim of the Grand Canyon. Camera follows legs to the face of disgusted Reggie Jackson. So he's starring in the series—that was a brilliant hit by Richard, to get Reggie Jackson in on this. We'll get lots of people watching it.

"Then we're in the cemetery, and there's this branch that breaks in the trees, off to the left of the truck as we finish the bourbon in the dark. 'What do you think that is?' Richard says knowingly. 'Deer, at eleven-thirty,' he says.

"And I say, 'No, Richard, that's wrong. You can have deer at eleven o'clock or deer at ten o'clock. There's no such thing as deer at eleven-thirty. That gives you two directions.'

"And Richard says, 'Smart deer.'

"Then we go back to Smiley's for more beer. God, this goes on and on. More beer and bourbon to go, and we drive up the winding road to the Little Mesa. We drove up there and across, and we looked for a parking space and there's none, so we start to descend and then Richard says, 'This looks like a good spot.' Which is the middle of the road, and we just stopped there. I think it's around twelve at night at that point. So we stop in the middle of the road and turn off lights and engine. Then it's back to the series.

"After Rolls Royce, fade, and commercial break, disgusted Reggie Jackson, who turns and says, 'Again, Timberwolf? Again?' So the camera zooms in on Timberwolf, a Chihuahua, as he falls over the lip of the footprint, this is in deep snow, and into its depths. Sound of pickup truck hitting bottom of canyon.

"'Dynamite,' says Richard. 'Terrific.' Headlights coming around the curve. On with our lights, engine. Down Mesa and then back to the same spot after a quick stop at Smiley's for more beer and bourbon to go. 'Millions,' says Richard. 'It's worth millions.' Discussion of Hollywood politics and protocol ensues, whether MTM will take it. Who's in charge after the divorce. Realization that Japanese market should be tapped, hence, twenty-three-year-old hot Japanese singer zooms into series casting. She speaks only Japanese, is very beautiful, and there are no English subtitles for her. Cameo role with only three or four lines. She is a computer technician, has all the data, big monitors.

"Guy with flashlight turned off walks past pickup in middle of road. Switches on flashlight only after getting fifty feet away from us. Car headlights. Down we go. Smiley's for more beer and bourbon and down more road to lagoon mouth. 'I think we got it,' says Richard. I agree. 'The thing is, you don't need a plot. Plots are nothing. It's all visuals until you hit the commercials. The people who watch this stuff can't read. Don't confuse them.'

"And then back to Smiley's, and we decide to stay there. I play pool and leave after an hour or so, and Richard stays on talking to Jim Hartz, I think, who was down there at that point. Richard would just go on. He must have known there was a certain point you just didn't have the stamina to keep up with this."

RICHARD BRAUTIGAN'S PLANE touched down at JFK, beginning the first leg of his final journey around the world. Living on borrowed time encouraged the rethinking of established life patterns. He wanted to rectify old wrongs. Instead of heading straight for Manhattan, Brautigan went to stay with his daughter in the apartment she shared with her husband in the Greenpoint neighborhood of Brooklyn. Ianthe found his behavior "very sweet." Richard made an effort to reconcile with Paul Swensen, who helped his father-in-law find the rare Western videos he enjoyed watching.

Richard did not call Helen Brann during his brief stay in the city. He'd made his peace with her. Future publishing deals were Jonathan Dolger's job. Richard never got together with Dolger either. Unlike his long friendship with Brann, there was nothing social in his connection to Dolger. The two men met in person on only a few occasions, several times in New York, twice more in Frisco; always strictly business.

Brautigan's trips into Manhattan were all in search of fun. On his last day, Richard visited Tony Dingman on the set of *The Cotton Club*. The picture was over budget and behind schedule. Mario Puzo's original screenplay was rewritten as a rehearsal script by William Kennedy (*Legs; Ironweed*) in eight days. Gregory Hines, one of the cast, claimed "a three-hour film was shot during rehearsals." Director Francis Ford Coppola took all the budget and script trouble in stride, making no mention of his problems as he chatted amiably with Brautigan between takes. Three lovely dancers walked past them. "Francis, do you have fire insurance?" Richard asked out of nowhere.

"What are you talking about?" Coppola didn't have a clue.

"Well, you're going to need it," Richard said, "because these girls are going to set this place on fire."

"Reel 'em in," Tony Dingman thought, listening on the sidelines. "A real fisherman!"

Brautigan started drinking early that day. Feeling no pain, he walked with Dingman down a hallway behind the soundstage and encountered Gwen Verdon, who played Richard Gere's sister in the film. "Gwen, I'd like you to meet Richard Brautigan," Tony said, introducing them. "And Richard, this is Gwen Verdon."

A long pause followed. Brautigan stood looking at her. A second passed, two, three, four seconds . . . five seconds. "Damn Yankees!" Richard said at last.

Dingman loved it. "The master of delay."

Inspired by watching make-believe Hollywood evocations of Harlem in the 1920s, Brautigan headed uptown. Back when Duke Ellington's orchestra was the house band at the actual Cotton Club, a fancy speakeasy where black entertainers performed for all-white audiences, the Harlem

Renaissance had already begun, providing a national audience for gifted writers such as Langston Hughes, Zora Neale Hurston, Countee Cullen, and W. E. B. Du Bois. Richard knew this intriguing literary history and wanted to see firsthand where it had all actually happened.

By the time Brautigan got to Harlem on that chill October evening, he'd had a couple more drinks and felt no pain strolling north along Lenox Avenue, conspicuous in his absurd woolen cap with the little pompon on top. He caught the notice of two passing black men looking for a good time on a Friday night. "Hey, you in the Elmer Fudd hat!" one called in a threatening manner. Gripped by fear, Richard smiled, a goofy gesture of friendship.

"Man, leave the dude alone," the angry fellow's companion said. "Anyone who wears an Elmer Fudd hat is all right with me."

The two black men walked away, laughing at their unexpected encounter with the tall stranger capped by a cartoon character's sky piece. How Brautigan spent the rest of his only night in Harlem became lost in the boozy fog of long-forgotten benders. The next evening, nursing a killer hangover, Richard boarded a transatlantic flight to Amsterdam. He arrived on a Sunday morning and dragged his sorry ass to the Hotel Jan Luyken, housed in three converted mansions on Luykenstraat, named, like the hotel, for a seventeenth-century Dutch engraver.

Jack Kerouac's thirty-one-year-old daughter, Jan, sat in the hotel's breakfast room with her companion, Milo, when Brautigan came lurching in, wearing jeans and a red T-shirt emblazoned with a Montana logo. Suffering from jet lag, Richard slumped at a nearby table, burying his head in his hands, "muttering something about a bottle of whiskey." Jan and Milo started a conversation with the disheveled stranger. Brautigan told them about his close encounter in Harlem. When finished, he pulled his funny hat from his back pocket. "So, you see," Richard said, "this hat saved my life."

Kerouac left Milo alone with their new friend. Brautigan wasted no time before buying a bottle of whiskey and getting Milo "thoroughly plastered." When Jan returned early in the afternoon, she found them both unconscious on her hotel room floor. Richard, Milo, and Jan started hanging out together. She made no mention in her memoir, *Trainsong*, of the time Brautigan encountered her father passed out under a urinal in a Big Sur bar. Perhaps he never told Jan that story. When Richard related the episode to Greg Keeler, "he seemed to light up—as if passing out under a urinal was . . . one of the top things a guy could do." Jan Kerouac estimated that Brautigan consumed at least six quarts of whiskey over the next three days before his scheduled poetry reading. In the end, she thought Richard had drunk himself sober.

Robert Creeley and Gregory Corso were among the poets gathered in Amsterdam for the One World Poetry Festival. Bob and his wife, Penelope, had been living in Berlin on a Dodd Foundation grant with their young son, Will. The Creeleys had not seen Brautigan in two years, since their trip with him to Toronto. Bob found Richard in bad shape, "drinking more than brandy, having all the bleak aftermath of a very sad relationship." The Creeleys considered Brautigan "very affectionate and very dear," believing all his problems stemmed from his divorce. "She took the toilet paper, she took the doorknobs," Bob recalled. "I mean, hell hath no fury."

The readings were held at the Melkweg (Milky Way) club, a nonprofit organization founded in 1970 in an abandoned dairy on the bank of the Lijnbaansgracht, a "dingy canal street," in Jan Kerouac's opinion. The Creeleys, along with Jan and Milo, accompanied Richard to his reading. They had a hard time finding the place, not all that far from the Hotel Jan Luyken.

The Melkweg audience comprised a mixed bag of European youth, "Dutch, Germans, Italians, French, Danish." Jan Kerouac called them "punks and generic bohemians." She thought Brautigan looked "terrified" when he came on stage, "hangdog, terminally sad." Richard read "Night Flowing River." The crowd listened in rapt silence to Brautigan's elegy of an ant crawling under a mourner's shoe. "You could hear a safety pin snap in a punk's ear," Kerouac wrote in her memoir.

After ending his poem, Brautigan fell silent. "More!" the audience shouted. Richard shrugged and said "he didn't have any more." The outraged crowd chanted, "Brautigan! Brautigan!" Richard waited for silence. "Shūji Terayama would be insulted if I read any more," he said. "The Japanese like things simple—short and sweet, like haiku." Then Brautigan left the stage with the audience shouting in outrage. The promoters thought he "was just trying to cut short his responsibility to the festival." Robert Creeley saw things differently. "He wasn't kidding," Bob recalled. "It was true." Brautigan had no more to give.

When the weeklong One World Poetry Festival ended on Sunday the twenty-third, Richard stuck them with an "incredible" phone bill. Jan Kerouac and Milo drifted off into the rest of their lives. Robert Creeley returned with his family to Berlin. When Creeley said goodbye to Richard in Amsterdam, it was for the very last time.

Brautigan's hotel stood just across from the Van Gogh Museum and the world-renowned Rijksmuseum. Richard visited both places. His first trip to Amsterdam lasted only another three days after the poetry festival ended. He met a thirty-five-year-old half-Spanish/half-Korean woman in a grocery store. She'd traveled up to the Netherlands from Majorca, largest of the Balearic Islands, to get an abortion and "score some dope." The woman recognized Brautigan. Smitten as always by anyone tuned into his celebrity, Richard followed the woman back to Spain, flying down to Palma, Majorca on the twenty-sixth.

Richard never revealed the name of this mystery woman. He didn't identify her in his notebook journals or in conversations with friends when he talked about his travels. Brautigan wrote no poetry for his mixed-race femme fatale. Richard's poems in the final months of his life concerned death, not love. The trip to Majorca launched a three-month meandering hegira that Brautigan described in a letter to his daughter as "bumm[ing] around Europe [. . .] sort of free-fall style." He said he should have done it twenty-five years ago.

The same Wednesday Brautigan departed for Spain, half a world away in Billings, Montana, one of his most cherished dreams began unraveling. Gatz Hjortsberg, leaving soon for London where *Legend* had resumed production, finished his draft of the *Hawkline* screenplay and sent two copies express mail to Universal. They arrived in Universal City on Friday. Mike Haller and Michael Chinich, the studio exec assigned to the project, worked late into the night in the Black Tower's copy center, printing scripts. Several were left on Thom Mount's desk before the two men took off for the weekend.

When Mount drove into the Tower's underground garage Monday morning, he found his parking space stacked with carton boxes full of family photos, souvenirs, personal mementos, and various bits of office decor. Mount stormed upstairs to the lobby, where the security guard told him he was not allowed to enter the building. He'd been fired, Hollywood style. Frank Price, the new head of production, swept Mount's desk clean of every project his predecessor had green-lighted. The *Hawkline* project died at Universal before anyone in power ever read the script.

Brautigan departed Palma, Majorca on November 19, returning briefly to Amsterdam. He left no record of where he stayed on his second brief trip to the Netherlands. Next to the Singelgracht, Brautigan discovered a wooden food shack selling hot takeaway mussel sandwiches soaked in Thousand Island dressing. The place was run by "a real working-class hero," a burly fellow with a thick black mustache. Richard enjoyed the food and went to the little place by the canal often during his short stopover.

Brautigan soon was on his way to Switzerland. He'd been invited to lecture at the University of Zurich, where Albert Einstein had earned a degree in 1900. Richard spent several days in the city, strolling around, looking at the Limmat River. In his aimless wandering along the river, he met a Swiss man interested in fishing who'd never cast a line for trout. He and Brautigan walked all over town, talking about the sport. Richard pointed out spots in the water where fish might be holding. The Limmat was no trout stream, but he enjoyed talking about angling. Brautigan thought Zurich was "all right" but felt an itch to get back to Tokyo. "After only a few hours in Zurich," he wrote, "you would not confuse it for Tokyo."

Richard left Switzerland, flying to Majorca for a few days. On the fifth of December, he took off for Frankfurt, starting the German lecture tour arranged by the U.S. Information Service. Brautigan flew from Frankfurt to Munich on Lufthansa, arriving a little after five in the afternoon. He was met by Günter Ohnemus, his German translator, and Edwin Pancoast, the director of the America House. Ohnemus thought Richard "was out of control." Brautigan claimed that a computer at the Keio Plaza Hotel in Tokyo now handled all his future literary business.

They drove Richard to the America Institute at the University of Munich, where he spoke and read to an audience of students and faculty. After a reception, Brautigan spent the night at the Hotel Alexandria. Worried about his connections, Richard called Jakob Köllhofer, his contact in Heidelberg. "Listen, could you be there at the station to get me?" he pleaded. "Because I'm dyslexic and I can't read the signs."

Köllhofer assured Brautigan he'd be there. Richard boarded a train in Munich just before nine, arriving at the Heidelberg station at a quarter past noon. Jakob Köllhofer waited on the platform as promised, looking for a fragile, lost man. To his surprise, Brautigan bounced off the train with a bottle of Pernod in his hand. Köllhofer took Richard to his 2:30 program at the English Department of the University of Mannheim. After his informal activities with students and faculty came to an end, Richard went home with Jakob. "Do you have anything to drink?" he asked. Köllhofer had some schnapps. Brautigan drank that down and "ended up drinking every bottle of everything in the house." His host considered it "an amazing performance." Richard spent most of the evening on the floor, painting with Köllhofer's kids. Jakob said he'd "never seen anything like it."

Brautigan spent the night at the Hotel Schrieder. At 8:30 the next morning, he was on a train heading to Frankfurt, where he made a connection to Siegen, arriving there in less than two hours. Two members of the "Cologne program" staff met Richard at the station and whisked him off to the University of Siegen in time for his noon program at the Department of English, hosted by author and translator Glen Burns. Brautigan read to an audience of students and faculty.

After Richard's presentation, the Köln staffers drove him to Bonn, provisional capital of the Federal Republic of Germany, situated on the Rhine, twenty-five kilometers south of Köln. They took him to the American Embassy guest house on Martin-Luther-King Strasse. Günter Ohnemus reported to Keith Abbott that Brautigan "had skipped or trashed readings" on his German tour, the only evidence of any unprofessional conduct.

On the seventh of December, an informal reception at the American Center allowed Richard to mingle with his fans and get drunk on his ass. In the morning, a representative from the Bonn program office took Brautigan to Bonn University in time for an 11:00 am appearance at the English Department, where he read to an audience of students in Dr. Eberhard Kreutzer's modern American literature course. In the afternoon, an embassy staff car drove Richard to the Köln/Bonn airport at Wahn in time to catch a 2:50 flight to the city-state of Berlin, an isolated island of Western democracy surrounded by the Communist Democratic German Republic.

An hour later, Brautigan's flight touched down at the Tegel Berliner Flughäfen, located in a borough northwest of the city center. He was met at the airport by someone from the Amerika Haus Berlin, who drove him to the Hotel Astoria, a charming boutique establishment in a restored 1800s town house on tree-lined Fasanenstrasse. At eight in the evening, Richard stood before an audience of the general public at the Amerika Haus, a two-story International-style structure built in 1956 on the Hardenbergplatz. The Amerika Haus had its origins as a library of English-language books donated by American troops at the end of the war. Brautigan's reading was the culmination of his German United States Information Service tour.

The next day Richard met with several "Berlin literati," their identities erased from memory by the corrosive winds of time. Robert Creeley was not among their number. Brautigan did not get together with Bob and Penelope during his three-day stay in Berlin but found time on the ninth for a trip into East Berlin. Richard told friends he visited a concentration camp on his German reading tour. If so, it had to have been Sachsenhausen, located thirty-five kilometers north of Berlin in the DDR (Deutsche Democratische Republik), the only camp in the immediate vicinity. Later Brautigan suggested that his work in progress, *The Complete Absence of Twilight*, was based on this visit to a Holocaust death camp. Like a map of nineteenth-century Africa, most interior details of Richard's eleven months in Europe remained a blank. Only his itinerary, a detailed peripheral outline of his journey, provided any clarity.

Richard Brautigan did not write a single letter between mid-October and the end of the year. He did no work in his ever-present notebooks. Not one poem, not a line of new fiction. This prolific author became mysteriously silent, as if in free fall in outer space. On December 10, Brautigan's last full day in Berlin, he attended a 5:00 pm book signing event at Autorenbuchhandlung (the Author's Bookstore) on Carmerstrasse in Charlottenburg, a section of West Berlin considered the heart of the city's cultural life from the end of World War II until reunification.

The Author's Bookstore was a shop close to Richard's heart. Founded in 1976 by a group of writers dissatisfied when they couldn't find their work for sale at other venues, the place opened with an inaugural reading by Günter Grass, followed by an impromptu performance a few weeks later by Allen Ginsberg. It's not known if the "literati" Brautigan met the day before were in attendance. Günter Ohnemus claimed "Richard botched deals and had lost the chance to make a considerable amount of money while in Europe."

Ohnemus didn't have the whole story. While in West Berlin, Brautigan met with the editors of *Transatlantik*, the magazine that had published sections of *Tokyo–Montana Express* the year before. They were interested in using more of his work, and Richard sold them first German serial rights to "The Fate of a West German Model in Tokyo." He later described it as an "article" in a letter to his new agent. There was never a typescript of the longer notebook version; this can only have been the six-page short story.

The next day Brautigan flew out of Berlin en route back to Spain. He cleared customs, getting his passport stamped "ENTRADA" in Palma, Majorca. Seven years after Franco's death, elements of El Caudillo's security apparatus remained. A traveler entered West Berlin with less scrutiny than he did the Kingdom of Spain. Richard spent the rest of December on the island of Majorca, probably never leaving Palma. His drinking spiraled into alcoholic oblivion. After returning to the United States, Brautigan told Greg Keeler he'd once fallen down drunk in an alley behind a bodega, sleeping beside homeless mongrel dogs. People passing by tripped over him in the darkness, not giving a damn. Richard "said he liked Spain in that respect," Keeler recalled.

Richard told a similar story to Klyde Young during the summer of 1984. In this version, Brautigan rented a room in Palma down a little street from a tiny bar where he like hanging out. It was not a tourist bar. All the other customers spoke Spanish. Richard was fond of a little dog living in the bar. Word got out that Brautigan was a famous millionaire American writer. One of the local newspapers sent a reporter to interview him. Richard said he was an American writer but denied being a millionaire. "I'm a writer and that's it," he said. "I'm just here visiting."

The next day the newspaper devoted an entire page to a story about the American millionaire writer. Brautigan got totally drunk in his favorite bar. Unable to stagger back to his room, Richard lay down in the gutter to sleep it off. The little tavern dog came out and lay down on top of him. The same newspaper reported this event: American millionaire writer found drunk in the gutter sleeping with a dog. Richard "loved that story," according to Young.

Fed up with his boozing and freeloading, the mysterious half-Korean/half-Spanish woman tossed Brautigan out on his drunken ass. The final schism likely came because of epic misbehavior on New Year's Eve. Richard flew from Majorca to Barcelona on the first of January. His destination was Amsterdam, where he had "business to do," wanting "to gather some breathing space" before journeying on to Japan. Brautigan could easily have flown nonstop from Majorca. A poster advertising European train travel, seen earlier in the window of a Palma travel agency, inspired him to alter his plans.

Richard landed in Barcelona around noon on New Year's Day. He saw a 1:15 flight for Amsterdam listed on the departure board and knew he could be in the Netherlands that same afternoon. "With what little that is left of my life," he wrote, reflecting on the moment later that month, "I am where I am supposed to be and often very bored. [. . .] I thought, no, I'll never have the chance again to take the train from Barcelona to Amsterdam because I'm never returning to Europe. [. . .] I've got the time and I'm never coming back." These lines, scrawled in a four-by-six ring-bound notebook in January 1984, were as close to a suicide note as anything Brautigan ever composed. "It's one's own business why one chooses to be one place or another and how one arrives at that decision is an individual matter like staring into a mirror too long until you are not totally aware whose image is being reflected."

Richard made his way to the Barcelona train station and bought a second-class ticket to Paris. It was a long trip. At one point Brautigan found himself discussing Buddhism with a fellow passenger in his compartment, an American classical musician on his way to a week's engagement in Rotterdam. An older couple, "sophisticated and worldly," joined their company. The woman wore a sparkling array of costume jewelry. Richard's American companion spoke to them in French.

"They're gypsies," he said. "They would like to tell our fortunes."

"I'm having too much trouble with my present," Brautigan told him. "I think the future would be too hard for me to handle."

After more than twelve hours, Richard's train rolled into le Gare d'Austerlitz early in the morning. Without any knowledge of the language, Brautigan made his way to le Gare du Nord, either on the Metro or by taxi. He caught an early morning connection to Amsterdam, arriving at Central Station in time for breakfast. From *Amsterdam Hotels*, a 1982 compilation of local hostelries, he selected the Owl Hotel ("three stars, very comfortable [. . .] 61 beds/34 baths"), situated on a quiet street close by the Leidseplein and Vondelpark, quite lovely in the summertime but a frozen wasteland in January.

Utterly exhausted, Richard checked into room 47 on the top floor of the Owl, a charming boutique hotel composed of two formerly private nineteenth-century residences. The little blue-decorated chamber had everything he required: a built-in desk, a telephone, and a green-tiled bathtub, where he soaked his travel-weary bones. Brautigan felt safe here in spite of his "totally mad" start to 1984. "I could not bypass the Orwell novel at this time," he wrote soon after his arrival in Amsterdam. "His vision of a totalitarian anti-human society for the year 1984 was certainly far different from the actuality of my just-beginning 1984."

Brautigan's first purchases on his third trip to Amsterdam were several spiral-bound notebooks at a stationery store. Back in his room, Richard began writing again after three months of ricocheting back and forth across Europe, setting to work in a four-by-six notebook on "Owl Days," a long narrative prose piece chronicling the details of his train trip from Barcelona and a series of misadventures during the next five and a half weeks in Amsterdam.

In another pocket notebook, Brautigan compiled his most curious list in a lifetime of compulsive enumeration. Richard listed every item in the hotel, a long column of mundane objects, starting with "lobby: 1 elevator / 1 large color photograph of a snowy owl / 1 telex machine / 1 bell on the front desk / to ring for the clerk if nobody is on / the desk / 1 cash register, etc. etc." Richard even detailed the contents of his bathroom. His tally had a curious precision. "1 holder of paper bags on the wall. They are for sanitary napkins. 1 white round metal container to put used sanitary napkins in with a foot lever to raise and lower the lid with. 1 small metal hook on the wall to hang clothes from." A sense of solitude pervades this singular list, each item isolated by empty space. Scratching away in his notebook, Brautigan created an unintentional poem about loneliness.

On January 5, Richard resumed his interrupted correspondence, writing longhand on Owl Hotel stationery to Masako Kano, his first letter in months. He was not entirely candid about his recent travels, which he called "a remarkable time." Brautigan described his itinerary accurately but made it all sound like a business trip, "lecturing, on the move, meeting, meeting, meeting people and like that." He signed himself, "E.T. in Europe," referring to a peculiar ritual Richard concocted with Masako. Based on his affection for the Steven Spielberg film, Brautigan and Kano would touch their forefingers together in public places, replicating the movie scene, both simultaneously saying "E.T."

"Can you believe?" Years later, Masako remained incredulous at the memory of this "childish gesture." Brautigan enjoyed enacting his extraterrestrial finger touching with "real little boys" in Japanese restaurants and public places. "Everybody just stared at us," Kano recalled. "Richard sometimes became oblivious that he looked so different from the general public in Tokyo."

Brautigan lived mostly a sober life during his final stay in Amsterdam. He went early to bed and arose early. After shaving and brushing his teeth, Richard headed down to the dining room, which opened onto a garden and looked "pleasant, clean, attractive." He called it the Owl Room. Breakfast was served at 7:30 by a motherly, cheerful woman. It was always the same. Coffee, a slice of Swiss cheese and a piece of ham on one plate; four slices of bread on another; two cubes of butter and a small pot of jam on a third; and a soft-boiled brown egg perched in an egg cup. Brautigan had never eaten soft-boiled eggs before. Richard liked his eggs fried sunny-side up, scrambled, or hard-boiled but served hot. He ate them soft-boiled in the Owl Room because the hotel served eggs no other way, and he thought it was "a nutritionally sound idea [. . .] to eat an egg for breakfast."

After his morning meal, Brautigan returned to room 47, opened the curtains, and wrote for several hours. In the afternoons, he walked about the city. The first full blast of winter had not yet arrived, although the sky remained dark and overcast. Richard returned to his favorite hot mussel sandwich shack next to the Singelgracht. The owner recognized him. "Back in Amsterdam again?" he said.

"Yes," Brautigan replied. "It's my third trip."

The man looked up from preparing his sandwich. "You come for the mussels."

"Yes." Richard thought this was as good a reason as any to explain his return to the city. He wrote a story about the moment and called it "Mussels."

Other afternoon strolls took Brautigan to the Rijksmuseum, a short walk from the Owl. He went to see Rembrandt's *The Night Watch*, the Dutch master's enormous (eleven feet plus by fourteen feet plus) 1642 group portrait of Frans Banning Cocq's company of arquebusiers. At some point in 1715, the painting was cut down on all four sides to fit between two columns in the Amsterdam Town Hall. Brautigan spent an hour looking at Rembrandt's huge masterpiece. He knew "a section of the painting had been chopped off" and looked at "the section of [the painting] that was missing." The largest excised segment was a couple feet lopped off the left-hand side, eliminating two members of the illustrious military company. "A lot of people came and went and looked at the painting that was there," Richard wrote later in the year. "They were satisfied with what they saw while I was looking at what was gone."

Hungry after his hour-long excursion into conceptual art, Brautigan found his way back to the real world and the little wooden shack by the canal for another hot mussel sandwich under the oppressive leaden sky. "Often during the day I wished I was in Japan," Richard wrote around this time. "Things would be better there. The streets are lively with people."

Hoping to make his wish come true, Brautigan rented a typewriter and set to work on his Japanese entrance visa application. On the standard form, Richard stated that he was self-employed, listing his "principal former positions" as "Lecturer. University of Notre Dame, Stanford University." He asked to stay for a period of six months, saying he planned to enter Japan in "January 1984."

On a separate statement of "Personal History," Richard compiled a list of the American universities where he'd lectured over the years. He made no mention of his recent appearances in Amsterdam, Zurich, and Germany, suggesting that he suspected any inquiry would yield an unsatisfactory assessment. Brautigan mentioned that he was profiled in *Who's Who in America* and concluded, "At the age of seventeen, I came in contact with Japanese culture and it has had a profound influence on my life. Japan has been my teacher. I wish to continue my education."

Richard dated his application January 9, 1984, mailing it off, along with his passport, to the Japanese Consulate in The Hague. Approved by the ambassador's office, Brautigan was granted a six-month visa "for cultural activities," valid within three months of the date of his application. The day after submitting the paperwork, Richard sat in his hotel room, outlining a plan of action in one of his little notebooks. He was in his element, making lists, yet desperation haunted every word. His prospects in February looked bleak. This time around, Brautigan tallied a wishful compendium of dream options.

"1984," Richard wrote at the top of the page. "Plans to make $." In descending order he listed: "Screenplay: Trailer / Finish: The Complete Absence of Twilight / Sell property / Write articles (very little money) / Can I borrow more money? doubtful / Perhaps making of Hawkline Monster?" Looking at his immediate future, Brautigan contemplated his planned trip to Japan and compiled pluses and minuses. On the plus side: "I'm writing again: love book with Takako / Soup book / I'm happier / Masako?" The minus column included "It's very expensive and where am I going to get the fucking money / How do I live in Japan / Ask Takako of [illegible]."

Richard asked Brad Donovan to send a copy of *Trailer* so they could get to work and finish the project. He'd made inquiries at Dutch *Playboy,* and they expressed interest in his work. The future looked bleak, but Richard held onto a dreamer's impossible hope that somehow his writing would provide some salvation. If not, he already knew how to solve all his problems.

Addressing his present needs, Brautigan prepared a third catalog of "ifs," headed "A Plan of Action—Amsterdam." Richard decided to stay in Amsterdam at least until the end of the month, and his designated "ifs" included "Assignment from Playboy / Transatlantic Tokyo piece / Perhaps Tokyo / Money from Hodge / Reading / Screenplay arrives and I finish it / If I get a Japanese Visa." He ended the if list with the pluses of living in Amsterdam: "I can get a lot of work done," and "I can live cheaper here than in Japan." Brautigan didn't need his accountant to remind him of this.

During his first weeks at the Owl, Richard had no trouble sleeping through many nighttime storms. The rain became his "Amsterdam babysitter." When the white noise of rainfall gave way to the haunting silence of snow, Brautigan's insomnia returned, and he lay awake, his brain wandering "all over the place without duration or plot." Richard didn't like sleeping in the dark, leaving a light on in the bathroom with the door partway open to allow muted penumbral shadows to permeate his bedchamber. His difficulty falling back to sleep arose out of a fear of the "horrible nightmares" he knew awaited him.

In the daylight, everything looked different. A working copy of "Trailer" arrived from Montana and Brautigan went straight to work. He phoned Brad Donovan half a dozen times to collaborate on the project. Once, Donovan's phone rang at three o'clock in the morning. "Will you accept a collect call from Amsterdam?" the operator asked. There was something odd in her voice. Brad had no idea what she and Richard had been talking about.

"Sure," Donovan said.

"You will?" The operator sounded incredulous.

"Yeah," he said. "I really will."

Richard and Brad hashed out the details of the final unwritten scenes in the screenplay, and Brautigan set to work typing a clean reading copy. Richard had previously farmed this sort of secretarial work out to professionals. Economic considerations now demanded that he undertake the task himself. A skilled typist, Brautigan spent hours every day laboring on the script. His busy work schedule did not prevent him from further exploring Amsterdam. Long walks became Richard's only recreation. He took a break every afternoon, searching for "different things to look at." Brautigan found his way into bookstores and outdoor markets, buying "some fruit, a passport holder, two candy bars."

His leisurely strolls led him to new fiction. The few stories Richard wrote in Amsterdam (as well as ideas saved for later fiction) all arose from wandering around bleak unexplored side streets. "Real winter" raged into Holland at the end of the third week in January. Full-blown snowstorms replaced the insistent cold rain. The streets were "either icy or slushy." Every time Brautigan ventured out he found himself involved in a snowball fight. "One look at me," he wrote, "and kids want to start throwing snowballs."

Soon after the weather turned frigid, Richard changed his room at the Owl, moving to number 15 on the bottom floor near the stairs leading to the dining room, where he ate breakfast and wrote in his notebooks. He made no detailed compilation of this room's contents. With the first winter snowstorm, Brautigan was surprised to see citizens of Amsterdam break out their umbrellas. "It had a dreamlike, almost musical quality," he wrote in a story called "Umbrellas in the Snow." Richard had written about umbrellas before. They seemed to fascinate him. He featured "Umbrellas," one of the stories in *The Tokyo–Montana Express*, on the book's rear inside dust jacket flap. Three other umbrella stories, "Walking Mushrooms," "The Umbrella Photograph," and "Last Words About What Came and Went Yesterday" (about piles of shattered umbrellas in the aftermath of a typhoon), all from his 1979 Japanese notebooks, remain unpublished.

The umbrella story was one of four pieces of new fiction Brautigan took with him on his birthday to a meeting with an editor of Dutch *Playboy*. (The others included "Mussels," "The Habitue," a story about getting his shoes repaired in Amsterdam, and "Sandwalker," a fantasy of wanting to reach through the wall of the Owl and kill a young boy in the next room who was keeping him awake.) Three days before, Richard had mailed Jonathan Dolger a fair copy of "Trailer," asking his agent to make additional copies and send one to Brad Donovan in Montana.

Brautigan's passport stamped with a Japanese cultural visa arrived back from the consulate in The Hague. His plan had been to leave Amsterdam at the end of January. After trudging around the slushy streets, he came down with what he called "a very bad flucold" and decided to stay until he got better.

Richard Brautigan spent much of his forty-ninth birthday sick in bed. After meeting with the editor at *Playboy* earlier in the day, he mailed his agent a copy of "The Fate of a West German Model in Tokyo." In spite of coughing and sneezing, Richard got his work done. Ill and alone in a strange city, low on funds, he had neither the means nor the energy to go out and party. Back home, his friends might have planned a celebration. Adrift in Amsterdam, he was on his own.

The two primary local pleasure providers, coffeehouses selling pot and streets lined with prostitutes displayed in shop windows like frosted cakes for sale in patisseries, held little appeal for Richard, who didn't smoke and had no interest in whores. Brautigan made at least one excursion into Amsterdam's red-light district, riding there in a taxi with a new friend whose "huge black dog" hulked in his lap. Richard went to a brothel for a drink at the bar. His companion wanted to get laid and had his eye on a blond working in the establishment, but he had forgotten his wallet and had no money. The whorehouse accepted MasterCard. Richard's new friend only had Visa. He asked Brautigan to pick up the tab. "I don't have a credit card," Richard said.

"I thought all Americans had credit cards."

"I don't."

Wracked by fever sweats in his hotel bed, Richard gave little thought to brothels, credit cards, partying with friends, or even drinking whiskey. Nothing seemed like fun. A passport-sized photograph taken a few days before (perhaps for his Japanese visa) portrayed Brautigan as a doleful owl, mustaches frowning downward, hair parted to expose a head going bald, his mournful stare burning into the camera lens. "Yes, Europe has been good to me," Richard wrote Greg Keeler when he sent him a print of the picture. Brautigan's final birthday held little joy.

During his last week in Amsterdam, Richard climbed from his sickbed and returned to work. He'd labored hard all his life. Ever since picking beans as a kid in the fields outside Eugene, Brautigan never stopped believing hard work would see him through. Even as the curtains of doom drew darkly about him, he peered into the shadows for a gleam of hope. *Avenue* magazine, one of the biggest publications in the Netherlands, had reprinted sections from *Tokyo–Montana* in three issues the previous year. Richard made an appointment with an editor at *Avenue*. The magazine agreed to publish the German model article later in the year.

All his European business concluded, Brautigan departed for Japan, flying KAL on the eighth of February. He left no record of his long, arduous journey, no notebook sniveling about jet lag and lengthy layovers. Richard had passed beyond such petty complaints. He looked deep into the well of nothingness, and mere trials of the flesh no longer seemed so important. Teetering with empty pockets at the edge of the abyss, Brautigan acted as if nothing had changed.

Richard checked back into the Keio Plaza as always. Money he expected to be wired to the hotel had not arrived. Unable to afford a room, he called Takako Shiina, who had first arranged his reduced rate back in 1976. She agreed to pay for Brautigan's lodging, considering it a loan. Takako believed in her soul brother's talent and had not the slightest doubt that he would pay her back. As a measure of her trust, Shiina borrowed the money needed to cover Brautigan's Keio Plaza bills.

Richard did not rent a typewriter during his last stay in Tokyo, an economy move equivalent to skipping breakfast. He wrote all his letters by hand. Recovering from jet lag, Brautigan suffered a weary depression. His first creative efforts were several bleak poems written on Keio Plaza stationery. The day after his arrival, Richard penned "Reflections," nearly as brief as a haiku, in which he speculated about "all the shit" that would be written about him after his death.

Two days later, Brautigan wrote several drafts of "Death Growth," a grim meditation on mortality revealing the bleak nihilism of his innermost thoughts:

> *There was a darkness*
> *upon the darkness,*
> *and only the death*
> > *growth*
> *was growing. It*
> *grew like*
> *the darkness upon darkness*
> > *growing.*

Richard followed this stark lyric with another somber poem called "Death My Answering Service" and worked his way through four drafts of "Hopeless Candles." ("The light of hopeless candles / illuminate the vocabulary of dying roots / under freshly-burned trees.") Brautigan had come to the end of a long road stretching back to the playfulness of "Xerox Candy Bar." A poet delves deep inside for inspiration, and the Toonerville Trolley energy infusing much of Richard's early poetry gave way to a long mournful midnight dirge. Brautigan rode on the death train now.

Only writing new fiction provided solace from his morbid thoughts. Working in a notebook, Richard sketched out a piece about his friend, painter Russell Chatham, incorporating off-kilter thoughts on Rembrandt's *The Night Watch*. A few pages later, he began "The Same Story Twice," an odd sequel to *Dreaming of Babylon* narrated by C. Card's son. "My chief character flaws have been alcoholism, insomnia and eternal (illegible) desire." After five short pages, Brautigan ran out of steam and abandoned the story.

In the same notebook, Richard recycled a line about Amsterdam having the best light in the world for looking at diamonds. He liked the image, having used it first a couple times in "Wear Out and Die," a screenplay treatment he began in the Owl Hotel but never finished, giving up after only four pages. Brautigan got less done this time around, quitting after the next sentence, "Diamonds to me are like very cold flowers that only grow in winter."

Shortly after Richard's arrival in Tokyo, something odd provided a momentary distraction from darkness. Two weeks before Brautigan checked into the Keio Plaza, Alcatrazz, an American heavy metal band founded the previous year, gave a concert in Nagoya. The lead guitar player was twenty-year-old Swedish virtuoso Yngwie Malmsteen. Only moderately successful in the States, Alcatrazz gained an enormous following in Japan. For reasons forever unexplained, Richard received two fan letters from young Japanese women written to Malmsteen. Both were in English. One was dated the day after the Nagoya performance. The other, composed on Keio Plaza stationery, suggested the impassioned fan, who'd spent the night with Yngwie in Nagoya, wrote it in the hotel lobby, believing the rock star was a guest.

The rocker never got the letters. The hotel manager gave the impassioned correspondence to Richard as a curiosity after Malmsteen's departure. Brautigan was a connoisseur of such cultural detritus, saving everything from an uncashed 10¢ check from Pacific Bell to a poster advertising a Denver foosball tournament. Brautigan had never heard of Yngwie Malmsteen but held onto the imploring, undelivered fan notes for the rest of his life.

Always a creature of careful habits, Richard resumed his familiar life in Tokyo after sleeping off his jet lag. Mornings were spent writing in his room. In the afternoons, Brautigan explored the city's obscure back streets. Nighttime after dinner meant drinking and literary conversation at The Cradle. Knowing Richard's financial situation, Takako picked up his bar tab as well as his hotel bill.

To increase his nearly nonexistent income, Brautigan phoned the USIS office at the American Embassy soon after his arrival, informing them of his return to Japan. A letter from the assistant program development officer arrived at the Keio Plaza before the end of February. Both Nagoya and Fukuoka had expressed interest in having Richard present programs. Nagoya was looking at late March, while Fukuoka preferred late May. In both instances, the USIS offered to pay all transportation costs, plus a $117 per diem and a $100 honorarium for each program.

Earning money on his mind, Brautigan turned his creative attention to new screenplay ideas. "Cliché," intended as "an imitation B-movie," was inspired by the mediocrity of the 1950s. Working on loose sheets of Keio Plaza stationery, Richard envisioned "a horror-murder comedy that could be cheaply made like 'Trailer,'" with a "very strong role for a woman and a good solid role for a man to play opposite her." At the same time, Richard sketched out another screenplay notion on his hotel writing paper. He called this one "The Killer." Brautigan described his lead character, Barbara Frederick, "a sort of attractive, very worried looking woman in her early thirties," pushing a supermarket shopping cart and wondering if she should kill a total stranger, a Chinese woman in the next aisle. "Cliché" and "The Killer" were likely variations of the same idea.

Brautigan always found unexpected objects of interest on his long walks through remote Tokyo neighborhoods. When he first came to Japan, Richard was fascinated by the new: pachinko parlors, acres of neon, plastic food displays in restaurant windows. By his seventh trip, he'd come to appreciate the older aspects of the city. He wandered the back lanes looking at old handmade wooden shop signs. Brautigan recorded them in a Japanese notebook, filling several pages with annotated drawings. Many of the signs bore carved images of the products sold in the shop (red peppers, fans, knives) or of symbols representing the store's name (crane, tiger, temple). Other weathered signboards bore only old painted *kanji* characters. Brautigan had someone translate these unfamiliar ideograms (sake, vinegar, wasabi).

Early in March, the Tokyo weather turned wet and nasty. Richard caught a bad cold tramping about the narrow cobbled lanes in search of interesting shop signs. His phlegm-filled head felt like a swamp. *Washington Review* published the two Brautigan pieces brought to them by Toby Thompson in its February/March issue. Toby mailed Richard a copy. Brautigan liked the layout, looking the magazine over in his hotel room. He had no idea this was the last time he would ever see his work published in English.

One thing troubled Brautigan. He'd asked Thompson to make sure the publication assigned the copyright for the material in his name. This had not been done. Richard wrote back to Toby at the end of the first week in March. "No big deal," he said in his letter, "but please take care of it." It was a far bigger deal for Brautigan than he let on. As much as he needed the money, Richard decided not to cash the *Washington Review* check until he cleared up the copyright problem.

The details of Brautigan's last three months in Japan, like much of his time in Europe, remain obscured. He wrote very few letters and only a handful of short stories. In the past, these provided an unintended journal of his life. Without "specific information," Richard's day-to-day movements were lost. Like most lives, Brautigan's remained primarily one of habit, each new day an echo of the past. Richard followed his usual routine, repeating yesterday again and again, another life measured out in coffee spoons.

Early in April, Brautigan received a letter from Jonathan Dolger. Richard had been feeling out of touch, not knowing his last letter to his agent had been misdirected to Jakarta, Indonesia. He responded in the middle of the month with a cramped handwritten six-page reply, one of the longest letters he ever wrote. Along with discussing current publishing strategies and his screenwriting ideas, Richard launched into an extended lament about his current status in the publishing world. "My last royalty statement from Dell for A Confederate General from Big Sur showed that it did not sell a single copy in the previous 6-month royalty period."

Brautigan expressed concern that "at this point in my 'career' I've been pretty much written off." He quoted from Chénetier's book that he'd been "systematically refused recognition as a major novelist." When they spoke on the phone in January, Dolger repeated his conviction that *An Unfortunate Woman* was not the right book for Brautigan to publish next, suggesting another omnibus edition of his earlier work. Richard agreed with him, even though he'd fired Helen Brann for expressing the same opinion. Brautigan liked the omnibus notion but didn't think he had "enough coin in the marketplace to pull it off," suggesting instead, "I want to publish a hard, lean piece of machinery."

Unlike most of his terse, humorous correspondence, Richard's lengthy letter to his agent became curiously confessional. This most private and guarded of individuals opened up his innermost thoughts and feelings as honestly as a man reclining on a therapist's couch. "Book sales are not paying the rent," he wrote. "It's sort of sad to publish a book that is overpriced and looks like a piece of shit and is doomed from the beginning. [. . .] The publication of So the Wind Won't Blow It All Away was a fucking nightmare." Brautigan called himself "a youthful 49" and concluded on an optimistic note. "Anyway, there are eight months left in this year, and I want to take good writing advantage of them."

Richard expressed his doubts to Jonathan Dolger about "The Complete Absence of Twilight," saying it had a major flaw. Brautigan felt the ending was much more interesting than the beginning or the middle, claiming this was why he had not sent his agent more material. Richard was not being completely candid about what he insisted on calling a book. The eleven pages he'd mailed to Dolger from Amsterdam were not an excerpt. They were all he'd written and all he would ever write.

After a period of intense work in Amsterdam in January, when Brautigan finished "Trailer" and wrote a number of new stories (including "Twilight"), aside from recording observations in his notebooks, Richard did very little new writing during February and March in Tokyo. That all changed by the end of April. On the twenty-third, he wrote seven new poems. The twenty-ninth was Emperor Hirohito's birthday, a national holiday in Japan. Thinking the imperial birthday fell on April 30, Richard began a long story with the incorrect date. "Added Days" had nothing to do with Hirohito or the holiday celebrating his birth. It concerned a distant vague memory of whiteness from Brautigan's childhood.

After several pages, the narrator had a breakthrough, remembering a white two-story wooden apartment building in Salem, Oregon, on a summer afternoon in 1944. Perhaps unconsciously, Brautigan repeated an image from Trout Fishing in America. In the third chapter of his first novel ("Knock on Wood [Part Two]"), Richard had described seeing a waterfall in Portland as a child. Wanting to catch a trout, he rigged up a safety pin on a length of string, with bread balls as bait, setting off toward a mirage on his first angling adventure. "The waterfall was just a flight of white wooden stairs leading up to a house in the trees." Near the end of his life, Brautigan had come full circle, recycling the poignant images of his youth.

A few days later, Richard watched a man vacuuming crumbs fallen from a large gingerbread house set up in the Keio Plaza lobby. The cottage made of cake was big enough for children to play inside. Its exterior walls were covered with cookies. Earlier in the week, Brautigan observed two Japanese women in kimonos posing for photographs in front of the gingerbread house. "They gave the word exotic a new definition." Richard put it all into a short story he called "The Ad."

Despite declarations to his Montana friends that he wanted to marry Masako and father a passel of kids, Brautigan saw much less of her this time than on his previous two trips to Tokyo. Kano had become involved with another man. Since she'd last seen Richard, an attractive French computer engineer had come to work at Motorola, and Masako spent more and more time with him. Kano did not feel "truly in love" with Brautigan anymore. Too much time had passed. No

longer the innocent schoolgirl Richard had seduced four years earlier, Masako now had a successful career in a world where Brautigan would forever be a stranger.

Kano spent time with Richard, but only on her own terms. When Tamio Kageyama, a former
television scriptwriter and essayist, approached Brautigan about interviewing him for *Brutus* magazine, Richard called Masako for advice and help. He worried about what Akiyuki Nosaka might
have said about him in his 1979 I-novel describing their drink-fueled train trip together. Brautigan
feared Kageyama had read Nosaka's little book and asked Kano to translate it for him. She came
to Richard's room at the Keio Plaza, remembering him dressed in jeans, "anxiously touching his
mustache" as she read Nosaka's short novel to him in English. Masako toned down some of the
nastier descriptions to spare Richard's feelings.

Nosaka called Brautigan "Q.J." and invented most of the details and background information
in his book. Richard relaxed. Nosaka's unflattering portrait was sufficiently fictionalized to disguise his identity, and Brautigan agreed to the interview with Kageyama. They met one night early
in May at The Cradle. Tamio was fluent in English, having traveled to the States in 1968 as a hippie
troubadour with his guitar. Kageyama ended up in Big Sur. He attended a folk concert featuring
Joan Baez at Esalen, where Price Dunn duked it out with Michael Murphy.

Richard's Big Sur memories were also a quarter century in the past. He recalled camping and
hitchhiking, eating abalone pried from the rocks along the beach at low tide, and fishing for trout
in Limekiln Creek. In those days, the bohemian community had no concept of beatniks or hippies,
paying scant attention to media terminology, Brautigan said. Kageyama's Big Sur trip in the sixties
had been inspired by reading Brautigan. Tamio returned to Japan after wandering around America
for a year and a half.

The men talked late into the night, emptying two bottles of bourbon. Brautigan described his
hunting and fishing experiences. Kageyama talked about giving concerts when he played in a pop
band before becoming a writer. They never saw each other again after going their separate ways
from The Cradle. Richard returned to California soon afterward. Tamio went on to a distinguished
career as an award-winning novelist and served for a time as a judge on the TV cooking series *Iron
Chef* before dying in a suspicious 1998 house fire at the age of fifty.

All during Brautigan's final weeks in Tokyo, his financial woes provided a continual reminder of
his diminishing literary reputation. None of his recent projects was selling in America, and despite
his lifelong study of the movies, Richard found it difficult getting started on his new screenplays.
Improving his income seemed increasingly remote. Takako Shiina paid his hotel tab. Brautigan's
debt to her grew larger every day.

Richard's decision to leave Japan seemed abrupt. His cultural visa still had three months to
run, and he was scheduled to appear in Fukuoka at the end of the month. The $100 honorarium
provided little temptation when his daily bill at the Keio Plaza ran double that amount. Five days
before his departure, Brautigan scrawled a quick note to Greg Keeler on hotel stationery, announcing the possibility of "pulling up stakes" and heading back to the States. "Alert the boys to wake
up their livers," he cautioned.

Richard phoned Masako at Motorola to say he was leaving. She was working in the computer room in her capacity as a systems analyst when his call came through. The place was noisy
with the clatter of printers, and Kano moved away from her fellow workers so she could hear

"his mumbling long comments." The other technicians looked on with disapproval. "Again that Richard," their expressions declared.

Brautigan said an urgent matter had come up, and he had to fly immediately to San Francisco. He did not explain the nature of this emergency. Masako tried cajoling him into staying longer, suggesting she wanted to see him again and change her work hell into "his poetic cybernetic ecology to become mammal brothers and sisters," their code for lovemaking. Masako heard Richard chuckle on the other end, but he turned down her invitation, saying if he saw her again he would not be able to leave. This was the last time Kano ever heard Brautigan's voice.

Before leaving, Brautigan went to see Takako Shiina at The Cradle. "In case something happens, should I write you an IOU?" he asked. Takako told him there was no need, nothing would happen. Besides, weren't they eternally brother and sister? After Richard's return to California, they never talked about money. Takako strongly felt that he worried about her borrowing the money to pay his bills. She knew Brautigan wanted to repay his debt to her as soon as he was able. "I think there would be no possibility that he committed suicide without returning the money to me," Shiina wrote in a brief memoir after Richard's death. In spite of what Takako believed, he never paid her back before he died.

Brautigan flew back to San Francisco on the eleventh of March. He spent several days in the city, staying at the Kyoto Inn, where his discount rate provided affordable lodging. While in town, he got together with Tony Dingman and Richard Breen, his regular Enrico's drinking buddies. In a "rat-fuck" reversal, Dingman introduced his friends to Grasslands, a dingy Korean dive on Kearny Street near Jackson. According to Breen, it was a dangerous joint. "I wouldn't dare walk in there without Tony," he recalled. The doors opened at 6:00 am and didn't exactly close at closing time "if you knew some people."

Another regular described Grasslands as "the mother of all shitholes." A Formica-topped bar highlighted the minimal decor; tables along the far wall, empty boxes and giant bags of rice stacked everywhere. Dingman's drink of choice was a Stolichnaya gimlet. "The last of the Barbary Coast," Tony enthused about the establishment's seedy charms. The three men chatted with the Korean hostess and drank "about four or five vodka gimlets so that they would remember us."

Dingman had entrée to Grasslands. Pretty soon, Brautigan did as well. One night Richard sat at the corner of the bar beside Breen, who was seated next to "this crazy Oriental fellow." The stranger talked "a line of blood and guts bullshit" and took an "intense dislike" to Breen, pulling a knife and threatening him. "The bartender didn't give a shit," he recalled. The guy wanted to cut Breen's throat.

Brautigan got up, walked over, and sat on the other side of the knife-wielding Asian, staring hard at him. "What the fuck are you looking at?" the menacing stranger growled. Richard didn't reply. He started making weird facial and hand gestures, "like one of those people who talk deaf language on television but behind a hit of acid. Everything was exaggerated."

Brautigan freaked out the Korean. "Are you crazy?" the guy with the shiv demanded. "Are you nuts?" Richard continued his bizarre gesturing, "like arthritic karate." Finally the tough guy had enough, folding his knife. "I'm getting the fuck out of here," he said, and he split.

Richard returned to his seat. Picking up his brandy snifter, he swirled the amber liquid beneath his nose. "It always works," Brautigan said with satisfaction. "It always works."

For the next several days, Richard told anyone who would listen how he saved his friend's life at Grasslands. "Macho Brautigan and his weirdo apoplexy," according to Richard Breen.

Brautigan stopped by Cho-Cho soon after he got back. Talking with Jim Sakata, Richard mentioned he was moving out to his empty house in Bolinas. He said he didn't have any firearms in the place and "just wanted one around." Said he'd feel "more secure if he had a gun." Sakata owned a big pistol he much admired, a Smith & Wesson .44 Magnum on a custom Model 28 frame, made up specially for him by Lieutenant Bill Traynor, late a member of the SFPD's tactical squad. Jim's name was engraved on the butt. "This is big enough to scare anybody," Sakata told Richard when he loaned him the revolver. "Just show it to somebody and they'll bug out." In return, Brautigan gave Jim a brick. Sakata had no idea what it meant, but he placed it on the bar in the corner where Richard always sat. After Brautigan's death, the brick remained at his spot as a private memorial.

The house at 6 Terrace Avenue in Bolinas had been unoccupied for almost four years. Brautigan had "just closed the door and walked away." When Richard arrived back, the place was a mess. He got busy, cleaning out an area on the second floor where he could live and write. He had no one to help. It was "a hell-of-a-lot of work." Eating downtown in the little town's limited selection of greasy spoon restaurants exceeded his meager budget. Brautigan's kitchen was still disorganized, but he knew it was time to start dining at home.

On a rain-soaked day early in June, he wrangled a ride to Mill Valley and returned with six big bags of groceries, cursing himself for forgetting to buy sugar. Richard spent the afternoon sweeping and mopping the floors. Afterward, he worked on his various writing projects. That night, finished with dinner, Brautigan cleaned his kitchen. He felt he had "so many things to do" and thought his home in Bolinas was "a good place to do them."

Brutus magazine published "Story of Brautigan and Big Sur," Tamio Kageyama's article about Richard Brautigan, in its July 1 issue. It appeared only in Japanese. When Masako Kano read the magazine in Tokyo, she found it a "nice easy interview, recalling the times in their lives as a real young hippie from Japan and the young [American] writer." Richard had asked her about the *Brutus* article in a letter written two weeks earlier. Kano enjoyed the piece very much and wished she had sent a translation to Brautigan in Bolinas. "It might have boosted his ego a bit."

Richard had no telephone for most of the summer. When he needed to make a call, Brautigan went next door to the Zenos and used their phone. He did this sparingly, not wanting to become a pest. When Richard gave out the Zenos' number to a selected few he felt should have it, he was careful to ask that they not "spread it all over." He began writing letters again. Having his IBM Selectric handy, Brautigan typed many of them. Just as often, he wrote by hand. There was no order to this process, just whatever struck his fancy. Either way, Richard always typed the recipient's name and address on the envelope first before starting the letter.

At the end of the first week in June, Brautigan wrote to Marian Hjortsberg. He'd written her an amiable one-line note from Tokyo three months earlier. Richard clearly wanted to make amends. His tone was chatty, mentioning he planned on returning to Montana "in the autumn." In a PS, Brautigan asked Marian to give his address to Gatz "and tell him that I would like to get in touch with him." Gatz still lived in London at the time, alone, starting work on a new screenplay, his brief second marriage already unraveling.

Soon after his return, Richard visited Simone Ellis, who had moved to Bolinas a year before and married the artist Arthur Okamura. Simone's father was ill, and she asked Brautigan to return

Teddy Head. Richard refused. Teddy Head belonged in Montana. "It's his home." An argument ensued. Simone had seen a snapshot of the stuffed grizzly hanging on the exterior wall of Brautigan's barn. "You had him outside!" she raged. "If he's bleached, I'll kill you." Worse, she threatened to sue him.

In spite of taxidermic disagreements, Richard and Simone resumed a platonic friendship. Brautigan now regarded screenwriting as the surest way out of his financial woes. The new Mrs. Okamura was an experienced filmmaker, and he asked if she'd like to collaborate on a script based on *Trout Fishing*. They met often at the house on Terrace Avenue, acting out sections of the book, searching for dramatic structure. Both got "high as kites." Richard guzzled wine. Simone snorted coke, working late into the night almost every time. "Stay until dawn," Brautigan pleaded.

Simone felt there had long been an attraction between them. She was married now, and Richard let her know she was safe with him. Stoned, they sat side by side on Brautigan's black Naugahyde couch. Richard gently sifted through her hair, one strand at a time. Not much work got done. On another night, Brautigan and Simone both wrote to Bob Gorsuch on the back of one of Arthur Okamura's Bank of America deposit slips. They asked him to carefully pack Teddy Head and ship it COD to the address printed on the other side. Richard set the deposit slip aside and did nothing more about it until a couple of weeks later. Near the end of June, he typed a letter to Gorsuch, instructing him to take the stuffed bear from the attic and follow the instructions on the handwritten note he enclosed.

Brautigan complained often to Simone about his life. He told her he had three deals pending but worried he couldn't do the work even if everything worked out according to plan. "I'm fucked if they come through," he said. "I'm fucked if they don't come through. I'm going to kill myself."

"Oh, Richard, don't be morbid," Simone said.

Ianthe and her husband, Paul Swensen, had moved back to California and were living in Santa Rosa, about an hour's drive north of Bolinas. She phoned Brautigan at the Zenos' number on Father's Day, filling him in as best she could on everything that had happened in her life since she saw him last. Telephones provide a poor substitute for intimacy, so Ianthe made plans to come down to Bolinas for a visit.

Even as Brautigan's increasingly eccentric behavior began alienating him from his old poet pals in Bolinas, he forged closer ties with long-standing companions living across the lagoon in Stinson Beach. Kendrick Rand owned the Sand Dollar on Shoreline Highway, a restaurant built originally in 1921 from the amalgamation of three beached barges. Bob Junsch lived with his wife, Shallen, and baby son in a house with an ocean view in the hills above town. Andy Cole, another poet friend from the early North Beach days and Michaela Blake-Grand's boyfriend before she took up with Richard, had moved to Bolinas after many years in Stinson Beach. Brautigan visited them often. All three knew one another, Stinson Beach being a small, tightknit community. Richard never introduced them, keeping each in a tidy compartment. None ever realized the others were friends of Brautigan's until after his death.

When his first attempted collaboration bore no fruit, Richard hooked up with Richard Breen, who'd written for television, cajoling him into coming out to Bolinas to work on a script. "Got any ideas?" Brautigan asked.

"No," Breen said.

"Then let's do one of mine."

"Terrific." Breen suggested *Hawkline*. Richard told him they couldn't because Hal Ashby still had an option on the novel, suggesting *Confederate General* instead.

"Working with him was pretty much what I expected it to be," Breen recalled. "I listened to him ramble and he listened to me."

They took frequent breaks. When things got repetitive and boring, Brautigan said, "Let's walk downtown and ruin a couple of lives." One Saturday morning around ten, they knocked off work in just this spirit and walked to Smiley's. Breen had dropped a quarter tab of acid just to get him through the day. "Bolinas is a motherfucker to deal with," he reminisced. "All those dogs sleeping in the street and them welfare bitches and shit. You need some extrasensory perception."

Breen had only been in Smiley's bar twice, the last time ten years earlier, and he didn't like the place. "Richard, this is a bad vibe joint," he said.

"Bullshit!" Brautigan retorted. "It's American. It's a great fucking place." He persuaded Breen everything would be okay. Seated at the bar, Breen started feeling uncomfortable. Even at ten in the morning, the place was fairly crowded. "Richard, I'm getting bad vibes again," Breen said.

"Nonsense, nonsense," Brautigan replied.

He stood beside Breen, staring at a young woman shooting a solo game of pool. Without a word, she put down her cue stick, walked over to Richard, and slugged him in the mouth. "Stop looking at me!" she barked.

Brautigan asked the bartender for a napkin. "Who is that chick?" he inquired, patting the blood from his mouth before downing his drink. "You're right," Richard said to Breen. "Bad vibes." And they walked out into the sunshine.

Another time, when they ran out of steam around midnight, what Breen called "a common stupor," and had nothing more to say about their project, they took a break and walked to the Bolinas Cemetery, several miles out of town on Horseshoe Hill Road. "This was Richard's idea of a mission," Breen recalled. "He loved the cemetery."

Brautigan "toughed it out," taking a long walk on a dark night on pure "cowboy ethic." Breen took some LSD. Founded in 1853, the Bolinas Cemetery was the oldest in Marin County. Like a frontier Boot Hill, the old graves clustered under the trees in a haphazard fashion. Brautigan quietly perused the tombstones, staring at each one, soaking in the histories of the buried dead. Reading an epitaph, Brautigan mused, "I often wonder why they say what they say."

Richard Breen had no answer. "What do you want on your gravestone?" Brautigan asked him.

Breen thought it over for a while. "1946–1984. Richard Breen. Finally," he said. Brautigan chuckled. "What do you want on yours?" Breen asked.

Without hesitation, he answered: "Such and such to such and such. Richard Brautigan. Wish you were here."

Breen stayed in Bolinas at an old house owned by his attorney friend Sam McCullough, close to the ocean near Agate Beach. Built of sandstone carried up from the shingle by "some old lady" years before, the place epitomized "all that Bolinas horseshit," according to Breen. The ceilings and alcove were very low because its builder had been a small person. Anyone close to six feet tall was always ducking to avoid cracking his skull. When Brautigan came to visit, he seemed to duck naturally. Breen assumed it was because of all the time spent in Japan, whose citizens' small stature made ducking a constant for someone six foot four.

"What do you think of this place?" Breen asked Brautigan.

"Terrific," Richard said. "I think it's a charmer."

McCullough told Brautigan he "was thinking of building up the ceilings a little."

This proposed home improvement was lost on Richard, who gave Sam his own remodeling advice. "What I'd do is move that painting to the left."

Soon after, tired of inviting concussion, McCullough set to work, cutting through a skylight to raise the ceiling by several feet. When Brautigan returned, the work was done. "Richard, do you notice anything different about the place?" Sam inquired.

After a twenty-minute survey, Brautigan said, "I don't see anything."

"Don't you see what's changed?"

"Aha, I do," Richard replied at last. "You moved the painting."

One morning Brautigan phoned Breen at McCullough's from his neighbor's house to let him know he was postponing the start of their workday. Ianthe had gotten in touch again and arranged to come for a visit. They planned on having lunch together. "My daughter is supposed to be here at eleven," he said. "I'll be at Sam's at two."

"Okay."

At 11:05, Brautigan called Richard back. "Come pick me up," he said.

Breen borrowed McCullough's car and drove down to 6 Terrace Avenue. Richard stood waiting outside his house. "Where's Ianthe?" Breen asked.

"She's late," Brautigan said. "I'm not going to wait for her."

Breen said nothing, even though he thought it odd that a father wouldn't wait more than five minutes to see his daughter when she'd driven all the way from Santa Rosa for their reunion. When Breen brought Brautigan back home at midnight, he saw his friend had left a note on the door for Ianthe. It read, "Just because you haven't seen me in eight months doesn't mean you can be late. My time is important." The note was signed "Richard Brautigan." Breen was flabbergasted. He didn't regard Brautigan as punctual. "You have never been on time in your fucking life, you asshole," he snarled, "and you're pulling this shit."

Ianthe never got to see her father alive again.

After working on *Confederate General* until the end of July, the two Richards managed to come up with ten pages of "informal script" and an eight-page outline. From time to time, Andy Cole dropped in to see Brautigan during this period. Cole walked with a limp, having broken his left leg three years before. As an indigent, Cole relied on Medi-Cal and Medicare for his medical insurance. He had been taken by ambulance to Marin General Hospital in the middle of the night. The orthopedic surgeon roused out of bed to treat him had not been very happy, calling Cole an alcoholic, along with other "abusive and threatening comments." Because of the surgeon's rage, Cole believed he had maliciously received rough and incorrect treatment, resulting in permanent disability.

In May 1984, Andrew Cole filed suit against the offending orthopedic surgeon and the Marin General Hospital, asking for one million dollars in damages and another two mil in punitive damages. Knowing Richard was a stickler for detail in contracts, Andy gave him a copy of his negligence suit, stopping by often to discuss his case. Brautigan thought highly of Cole's intelligence and was very proud that his old friend had graduated from Georgetown University.

"God, the Jesuits," Richard exulted in his living room to Breen after one of Andy's visits.

Breen exploded. "I had sixteen years of formal education by the Jesuits, so I wasn't buying that act." Breen unloaded on Richard while they worked their way through a couple bottles of brandy.

He believed Brautigan "kind of had a monastic mentality" that provided the root of his admiration for the Jesuits and all things military. Learning Richard respected Ignatius of Loyola, Breen told him the Jesuits were "just overeducated whoremongers." Brautigan had "never had an experience with them [Jesuits] other than some horseshit philosophy crap." Before it was over, Breen was yelling. "Richard finally realized that I knew more about the Jesuits than he did," Breen recalled, "so he better keep his fucking thoughts to himself on the subject."

Righteous brandy-fueled anger never impaired their friendship. Brautigan and Breen remained pals even after the aborted script project sputtered to a premature conclusion. Alone in his house on July 28, watching the opening ceremonies of the XXIII Olympics in Los Angeles on his "dismal little black and white TV," Richard was moved to tears by seeing decathlon champion Rafer Johnson run around the L.A. Coliseum carrying a torch ignited in Olympia with fire from the sun.

Around this time, Greg and Judy Keeler and their two boys arrived in Berkeley to visit Greg's brother. Starting early in June, Brautigan had teased Keeler with tempting offers of salmon fishing on Bob Junsch's boat. Richard implied the fishing was great. "Excuse me while I have this delightful young girl place another bite of freshly-caught salmon in my jaws," he wrote in a letter headed "Dear Loser (formerly known as Greggie)," implying that he had just enjoyed sex with the woman. Neither claim was true. Brautigan had not had sex since Japan, nor had he been fishing. In fact, Junsch's boat was not "docked a few hundred yards away" but moored in Morro Bay, two hundred miles south from Stinson Beach. Keeler knew none of Richard's claims was serious and that Brautigan had been "rat fucking" him through the mail.

The Keelers' car broke down in San Francisco and was towed to a very expensive shop for repairs. Greg got in touch with Brautigan, saying he was in town. Richard immediately invited him over, suggesting they meet at the phone booth at the bottom of his hill. Brautigan had been making some calls there to take the heat off the Zenos. Keeler borrowed his brother's car and drove to Bolinas. Not wanting to spend the day trapped in her brother-in-law's apartment, Judy put aside her distaste for Brautigan and came along with her sons. When Richard greeted them by the phone booth, Greg reported that "his mouth literally dropped open."

Richard quickly recovered his composure and became the perfect host, leading his guests up to his old redwood house on the hill. Keeler thought "the interior was as depressing as hell." Brautigan offered some "California hospitality," which involved going down to the general store and buying Dutch treat cantaloupe and the makings for tuna fish sandwiches, which they ate out on the deck. After lunch, Richard asked the boys if they were Trekkies and sat them down in front of his miserable TV to watch a Captain Kirk rerun. "What grade are you in?" he asked Max and Chris.

"Sixth," Max replied.

"That's a shitty grade," Brautigan said.

While the kids watched an old episode about "where no man has gone before," Richard launched into a discourse on the current state of television with their parents. He told the Keelers of his fascination with the Olympics and, "always proud to be an American," exclaimed "USA, USA" several times for emphasis. Brautigan also lectured them about the quality of current American television. He cited *The A-Team, Scarecrow and Mrs. King,* and *Remington Steele* as prime-time examples of the new heights the boob tube had achieved. Never mentioned, "Timber Lawyers" must have rattled around the outer reaches of Richard's mind.

After the show, Judy and the boys went for a walk, leaving Richard and Greg alone to drink and chat. Brautigan talked about his youth, usually a forbidden topic, telling Keeler of his delinquent teenage years. He said he'd just figured out from Japanese friends that he was probably dyslexic as a kid, and he pondered how different life might have been had he learned this sooner. Greg thought there might be some truth in this, remembering Richard's "cramped and wiggly" handwriting. "But maybe if you had been cured, we wouldn't have gotten all your books," he said.

"Or maybe they would have been better," Brautigan replied.

Richard told Greg he planned on staying in Bolinas and almost in the same breath asked him "to start the wheels rolling on another teaching stint at Montana State." Keeler thought the odds were good. Paul Ferlazzo, the English Department head, liked Richard. Greg suggested he write Ferlazzo and ask for a full-time job.

Brautigan went into his house, returning with simple gifts for his friends in Bozeman. There was a single corncob holder for Brad Donovan, a request for Sean Cassaday to give him a call, and photo booth portraits of Richard for Schrieber and Scoop. In retrospect, Keeler thought Richard was maybe saying goodbye. When Judy and the kids came back, Brautigan took everyone on a guided tour of Bolinas, leading them down the steep stone steps to the beach, seagulls gliding in the pellucid air overhead. "Look how beautiful it is," he exulted. The Keelers agreed. The coastline, surrounding eucalyptus groves, and a view of the Marin headlands across the bay provided only part of the beauty of Bolinas on a sunny day. "I'm so happy," Richard said.

Later that evening they bought a couple pizzas (Dutch treat again) from a place downtown. "What kind to you want?" Brautigan asked Max and Chris.

"Anything but anchovies."

Richard ordered two anchovy pizzas to go. Without calling first, they took the pies over to the Junsches' place in Stinson Beach. Greg drove them around the lagoon, where Brautigan promptly got lost in the little beachfront town. It took an hour to find the Junsches' house. Bob and Shallen were preoccupied with their baby and watching the Olympics. Around 10:30, it was time to go. The Junsches were anxious for everyone to leave. Greg offered to take Richard home to Bolinas, as he had to drive back to Berkeley by way of Olema and Samuel Taylor Park.

"Don't worry," Brautigan told them, oblivious and glassy eyed. "You know me. I'll always find my way home." The Keelers left him at the Junsches and never saw their friend again.

The day the Olympics ended, Richard typed a letter to Masako. She had told him she was coming to Arizona in September. A postcard arrived from her the next day, saying her plans had changed. Brautigan scrawled a quick PS at the post office before mailing his letter, telling her he planned on returning to Japan in the fall. After walking back up the hill, Richard sat down and wrote a lengthy poem about his emotional response to the Olympic opening ceremony. "The Full-Moon LA Olympics" spanned seven typewritten pages in its final draft. Unlike the ironic, off-kilter humor of Brautigan's early poetry, his longest effort throbbed with ardent patriotism and near-mawkish emotion.

A couple days later, Richard phoned Don Carpenter in Mill Valley and arranged to meet him for lunch at the Sweet Water. Brautigan arrived in the middle of the afternoon and proceeded to drink five martinis "in like twenty minutes." Don was newly sober, having given up booze a few months before. "Let's go," Brautigan said before they'd ordered any food.

Richard and Don headed to the Mill Valley Market, where Brautigan bought a banana and ate it. He'd brought along his long poem about the Los Angeles Olympics and wanted to get some duplicates made. Richard told Don he thought *Newsweek* was going to publish it. After a search, they couldn't find a Xerox place in Mill Valley that could get the work done fast enough. Brautigan decided to go into San Francisco to have his copies made.

Don walked him to the depot and sat with him on the bench outside while Richard waited for his city-bound bus. "I'm seeing our friendship dissolve right before my eyes," Carpenter remembered, "because I don't drink no more, and he's stoned drunk in the middle of the afternoon. Yammering and babbling. When you first quit drinking, you go through a period where you don't like drinkers. They piss you off. So we were kind of cool." When the San Francisco bus arrived, Don watched Richard weave on board. The doors hissed shut. It was the last Carpenter ever saw of Brautigan.

A day or so later, Richard mailed a copy of "The Full-Moon LA Olympics" to Jonathan Dolger in New York. "If it is very good," he wrote his agent, "I would like to place it where it can be read. If it is a piece of shit, then that's the way it goes." The poem has never been published.

Sometime in the middle of August, Richard decided at last to close down his office above Vesuvio. He asked David Fechheimer to assist with the move. The private detective arrived in North Beach and gave Brautigan a hand packing it all up in cartons. When the last lid was sealed, Brautigan surveyed the stacked boxes and announced, "This is the total career of an American writer."

Richard and David loaded all the stuff into Fechheimer's car. David drove them to Army Street Mini-Storage, where they packed everything temporarily into unit A-32. Brautigan had also decided to terminate his connection with the warehousing facility as well. The many cartons stored there and those formerly in his office had to go somewhere else. The logical solution would have been to truck it all out to Bolinas. Brautigan had a different idea. He wanted his archive shipped someplace with no rent, where he knew it would be forever safe. Running into Keith Abbott at Enrico's in the middle of his moving project, Richard said, "This stuff is going into storage and it won't be found for years."

Brautigan went to his favorite bar to enlist Ward Dunham's help. Ward had an old pal, a six-foot-three, 250-pound professional wrestler named Mike York, who fought under the sobriquet "The Alaskan." Friends for thirty years, Ward and Mike had worked together as bounty hunters and occasionally still moonlighted in the debt collection racket. "The Alaskan" always dressed in black. When there was money to collect, they had a method that never failed. Ward arranged to meet their "client" at a bar. If he didn't pay up on the spot, Ward steered him back to the men's room, where a stall door swung slowly open to reveal Mike York hulking inside, pulling on a pair of black leather gloves. "The Alaskan" enjoyed amusing himself in other bizarre ways as well. When Enrico's was packed with customers, really hopping and the waiters distracted, York would saunter back into the busy kitchen and piss in the ice-making machine

Mike owned a tangerine-colored hot rod, a car customized into a truck. He loaded all Richard's boxes, stuffed with manuscripts, letters, contracts, Digger handouts, galley proofs, old receipts, canceled checks, passports, batches of photographs—his "total career," into the back and drove it to Colorado. Where "The Alaskan" deposited Richard's archive remained a mystery.

It lay undiscovered for years until 1996, when Ted Latty, a prominent L.A. attorney and avid Brautigan collector, saw the trove advertised for sale on the Internet. Latty was in Colorado Springs on business. In mid-March, he drove his rental car several hundred miles to the old uranium mining town of Nucla, northwest of Telluride near the Utah border. The place sat a mile above sea level, boasting a population of about five hundred.

Ted located the archive's current owner, who worked in the town's only grocery store. The guy took him next door to a boarded-up drinking establishment, where all the cartons sat stacked on the bar. Latty spent hours examining the stuff, carrying boxes one at a time out to the sidewalk, where he could look through their contents in the cold winter daylight. The attorney negotiated a price, driving away with the treasure stash, which found a permanent home in an unused office at his law firm.

Tony Dingman reflected on Brautigan's final move from Montana. "I never really believed that until he said 'The place is up for sale.' All of a sudden he was bivouacked out at Bolinas, the last place in the world you'd think he'd hang out." Dingman knew the jig was up. "When he moved out of that office, I knew something. The game was afoot." For a time, Tony thought he might go out to Bolinas and stay with his old pal, but he worried about space when Richard decided to live on the main floor, "and he'd just need the whole house." A film job came through and Dingman took it, solving the problem by default. "Then I just didn't see him much," Tony said, "because he'd only come to town here and there and get drunk. I never went out there when I was working."

Having Dingman around would have been good for Brautigan. He was running out of his longtime Bolinas friends. He'd temporarily been eighty-sixed from Smiley's for grabbing a guy by the balls and grope-walking him to the bar. "Mickey Cummings was a great big motherfucker," Bill Brown recalled. Brautigan was drunk and wanted to fight, "trying to assume the role of a bruiser a little bit," according to Brown. Richard got lucky when Cummings laughed the whole thing off.

Both Joanne Kyger and Bobby Louise Hawkins lost patience with Brautigan during his final summer, tired of his rudeness and drunken behavior. "Richard was starting to feel pretty stale to me," Kyger said. "There was very little playfulness in him. It was like he'd used himself up."

All sorts of stories circulated about Brautigan's presumed misdeeds. An anecdote about him picking up a young woman bartender at Smiley's became a tale of bondage that evolved into a lurid rumor concerning attempted murder. Magda Cregg claimed she'd heard Richard "made some chick give him head in front of the jukebox" in Smiley's. Unpleasant gossip proliferated. Don Carpenter recalled Kyger and Hawkins bad-mouthing Brautigan. "Those two old whores would sit down at Smiley's and insult Richard constantly. Talk about what a bastard he was." Simone Ellis–Okamura remembered Bobby Louise Hawkins making a point of going around to people and telling them to stay away from Brautigan.

Amid the swirling scuttlebutt, Richard's inherent paranoia kicked into high gear. He'd had a misunderstanding with a man named Russ Trevira, a Vietnam vet who worked in the tree-trimming business. An old-timer in the Bolinas area, Trevira charged Richard $300 for taking down a dead tree on his property. Brautigan didn't have the funds to pay him, offering writing lessons instead or editing a manuscript Russ had written. Trevira demanded his money. "No, this is barter," Richard insisted.

Their misunderstanding escalated into verbal threats. Brautigan already had Jim Sakata's gun in his house but sought additional firepower and borrowed a 9 mm automatic from Bob Junsch. "My wife didn't want it in the house," Junsch said.

Klyde Young told of an episode involving gunplay one time when Bob Junsch visited Richard's house in Bolinas. "They both had pistols," Young reported, "and got drunk and fired them a few times in that same room where he killed himself." A couple days later, Andy Cole limped in from the kitchen and saw the bullet holes. "Hey, buddy," he said, "what's all this?"

Brautigan just laughed. "Oh, sometimes it gets kind of exciting around here," he replied with a suppressed giggle.

Richard and Andy often had nostalgic discussions about the old days in North Beach. Brautigan kept referring to the halcyon days of the past. He pronounced it "hal-i-con." After several repeats, Cole said, "Richard, don't take offense. We're old friends. I've known you for twenty-five years. However, there's a certain word you've mispronounced constantly in the last three days, and I want to call it to your attention."

Before Andy got any further, Richard grew angry. "Did I misuse the word?" he demanded.

"No."

"Was there anything in the context that indicated I didn't understand how the words were used?"

"No."

"Is there any possible way that anyone could have interpreted this word any other way than I meant it?"

"No."

"Well," Brautigan had worked himself into full imperial mode. "Then who are you to tell me about it?"

Soon after their indoor shooting spree, Junsch asked Richard to return his 9 mm. Bob phoned Brautigan one day and said, "I don't think you need that thing. I wouldn't mind getting it back." Richard told him to come and get it. Around this time, Brautigan started packing Jim Sakata's .44 Mag wherever he went, even on trips into the city.

Enrico Banducci remembered one night about 2:00 am when Richard carried the gun into his restaurant. "He was drunk," Enrico recalled, "and he scared the shit out of me. He pulled this fucking cannon out of his pocket and said, 'I'll put this to my head and I'll blow my head off. Don't you want to see?'"

"Don't do that," Banducci said, pushing the revolver aside. Enrico remembered exactly where they'd been sitting. "He had a big gun and he had it at his head, about a month or so before the accident."

Sometime around the middle of August, Brautigan finally had a telephone installed in his Bolinas house. He'd become obsessed with the notion that writing screenplays might provide the yellow brick road to financial salvation. Knowing everyone in the movie business spent his life glued to a phone, Richard figured he'd better have one if he wanted to be a player.

Brautigan called Brad Donovan in Bozeman, asking if he wanted to come down to California and work on the *Trout Fishing* screenplay. Brad's son, Joe, had just been born, so he said no. "I'll see you up here in the fall."

Next Richard called Gatz Hjortsberg, who had returned to Montana from London in mid-July. His troubled marriage to Sharon collapsed within days of his return, and he moved to a three-room log cabin without running water on a hill overlooking the Boulder River in Sweet Grass County. Working on two contracted screenplays at the same time, Hjortsberg made sure he had a phone line hooked up before his plumbing was connected to the new well. When Brautigan called, all previous difficulties dissolved in the onrush of conversation.

Richard wanted to collaborate with Gatz on a screenplay. The idea he pitched was about an average midwestern housewife and mother, married to the local sheriff and normal in every way except she happened to be a serial killer. Gatz didn't know it at the time, but it was a retelling of "Cliché" and "The Killer," a notion Brautigan had been toying with for most of the year. Film ideas either hold a kernel of something that will work or they are duds. This one caught Hjortsberg's fancy, and he agreed to join the team. Over the course of several phone calls, the two men sketched out an outline for the opening scenes. Gatz suggested a new title, "Skeletons in the Closet," which Richard liked. It seemed they were on to something. And then the phone calls stopped forever.

During this period, Klyde Young became Brautigan's most dependable designated driver. One of the tasks Richard assigned Klyde was hauling away his garbage. Brautigan became paranoid about his trash. He didn't want people poking through it for souvenirs as someone had done to Bob Dylan, but he wouldn't pay for professional rubbish removal either. Security and economy combined in the same neurosis. After removing anything from the garbage with his name on it, scraps and letters that might identify him, Richard had Klyde take the trash away in the dead of night and dispose of the bags in dumpsters behind supermarkets and fast-food joints on the other side of the hill.

Young often went to Bolinas on a Saturday or Sunday and spent the day with Richard, laughing, drinking, and telling stories. They'd always have dinner together. Klyde thought Brautigan's ironic tales were very funny. At one point Young said, "Richard, there's enough material here to put into a book," indicating that he'd lose the energy "if you keep telling stories about yourself like this."

Brautigan's voice grew deep and decisive. "Not in my lifetime," he said forcefully. "Not while I'm alive."

Klyde took this to mean "that he at least considered the possibility that he might not be alive that much longer. Otherwise, he wouldn't be divulging these things."

Richard seemed preoccupied with death during his last weeks. A large dead sea lion had washed up on the Bolinas beach. The rotting corpse stank, keeping sunbathers at bay. Brautigan strolled down the path from his house almost every day and stared for hours into the seal's deliquescent eyes, watching them decay into vacant sockets. He took long solitary walks along the beach toward Duxbury Reef. On one of these lonely excursions, Richard came across the bleached rib of a long-dead whale. Hoisting it over his shoulder, he staggered back toward town.

Bill Brown spotted Brautigan coming up the path to his house "with that whale rib on his back." To Brown, "he looked like a comical crucifixion, carrying a cross to Gethsemane."

"Where do you want this?" Richard asked Bill.

"Put it in the whale rib locker," Brown said, pointing to a corner of his garden. Brautigan carefully propped the arched bone against an ivy-covered hedge. It remained there, a curving white grave marker, long after his death.

On another reclusive beach walk, Richard paused at the mouth of the Bolinas Lagoon as the tide swept in, bringing with it a huge school of herring. Millions and millions of fish poured in from the ocean "like a solid stream of silver," Brautigan told Klyde Young. When the tide went out, the fish were trapped in the lagoon. There wasn't enough oxygen in the water to sustain them, and they suffocated.

About a week after this event, Klyde spent the day with Richard and gave him a ride over to Stinson Beach in the afternoon, along the narrow two-lane road winding around the lagoon. The stench of dead fish was overwhelming. "There was no way to get out of it," Young recalled. They reached a spot where the receding tide had left millions of dead fish on the mudflats. Brautigan insisted they stop for a look. "Richard," Klyde said, "let's just keep driving and get out of this fucking stink. You can look at it another time."

"No," Brautigan insisted. "I want to look at it now."

Young pulled over. Richard got out of the car and stood at the edge of the lagoon, staring at acres and acres of dead fish. When Brautigan returned, he said, "Klyde, we're seeing something that neither of us has ever seen before . . . total war."

They were on their way to Bob Junsch's house, where Klyde planned to drop Richard before continuing over the hill to Mill Valley. The plan included stopping at the Sand Dollar to have a beer and chat with Kendrick Rand. They pulled in by the firehouse, looking for a place to park, and Richard spotted a toddler, a little girl maybe a year and a half old, just barely able to walk, all by herself in the middle of the street. No adults were in sight. "Wait a minute. Slow down," Brautigan said. "Drive very carefully. Something's going on."

Klyde parked the car and Richard stepped out. "You might have to talk to the little girl," he told Young, "because sometimes children are afraid of me."

Approaching the child, Richard spoke softly to her, reaching forward to pick her up. She appeared very comfortable in his arms. "Well," Brautigan said, "now we have to find out where this child came from."

They opened the nearest gate and walked into the yard, hearing a party going on in the house. "Now I know what's happening," Richard said. "These people are all inside the house snorting cocaine, and they're too fucking stupid to take care of their children. I'm going to talk to this child's parents."

Klyde rang the bell, and the owner of the house came to the door. Seeing the little girl, he immediately realized what had happened and thanked the stranger for saving the toddler. Brautigan accepted the man's gratitude but refused to relinquish the child until he had words with her parents, wanting to "heat their asses for being careless." The householder didn't care to make any more of it, and they started arguing. "They got into a pretty good argument," Young remembered.

All the while, Richard did not let go of the little girl. Finally the man convinced him that the baby would be safe and that he wasn't going to bring the parents out for a lecture. That was the end of it. Brautigan surrendered the child, and he and Young walked to the Sand Dollar. Seated over beers, Klyde told Richard, "I know that guy. I've seen him around."

"Who is he?"

"I don't know," Young said. "He seemed like some kind of a goon character."

Brautigan became alarmed. "Is he in the mob? Is there any chance that he might be violent?"

"It's a possibility," Klyde admitted. "I don't think that the guy, if he was going to, I mean, he would have been. . . . It's over with, but I don't think you should push that guy."

"I don't want this to go any further," Richard said. "Would you please go back and straighten it out?"

"What can I straighten out? I can't—"

"Just go back and tell him something," Brautigan instructed. "Smooth it over."

According to Young, "it couldn't wait a minute longer," and he went back to the man's house to explain that Richard was okay. He didn't mean any harm but was only looking out for the kid's welfare. He didn't mean anything personally. The stranger wasn't angry and held no grudge against Brautigan. "I had to go back and report that it was all taken care of," Klyde said.

Brautigan's final two weeks became a sequence of unintended farewells. The last time Simone Okamura ever saw Richard was just before she flew to Grand Junction, Colorado, to visit her father on his deathbed. Simone was downtown in Bolinas and spotted Brautigan sitting on the curb in front of the Gibson House restaurant, half-drunk with a gallon of wine by his side. He waved her over, and they wrapped their arms around each other. Richard told Simone he'd sent for Teddy Head. "Promise me one thing," Brautigan asked, sounding very dramatic. "Promise me. Promise me." Simone agreed.

"Anything I ask?"

"Anything, Richard."

"From this day forth, he shall always be called Teddy Head."

Simone gave her word, and they parted. When she returned from Colorado after her father's death, Brautigan had also died. Simone found Teddy Head waiting for her at home.

Dr. John Doss remembered seeing Richard in the Bolinas post office. Brautigan had "picked up a lot of stuff off the counter."

"From my publisher," he told Dr. Doss.

"Is it good news?"

"Yes," Richard said. "She's going to publish something." And they went their separate ways.

The last time he saw Brautigan, John was walking along Wharf Road with his wife, Margot. Fishing boats moored here in the lagoon. At the time, before Fish and Game regulations changed the practice, it was possible to buy fresh salmon off the boats. They ran into Richard, walking with a tall European stranger, a Dutch reporter in town to interview Brautigan for his newspaper in Amsterdam. Klyde Young had picked Richard up at the bus stop in Stinson Beach, bringing him back to Bolinas in time to make his press appointment.

Dr. Doss told Brautigan about having "discovered the joys of a Macintosh computer." Knowing that Richard had trouble with spelling, John bragged how his new machine checked his spelling and grammar. Brautigan said he planned on waiting for the computer's next generation, sauntering off with the Dutch reporter.

Richard continued working on the IBM typewriter during his last two weeks. He continued revising his long piece on Russell Chatham and composed a rough draft of a letter to Paul Ferlazzo at MSU. Even asking for a job, Brautigan dictated his own terms. "I would like to teach one class of fifteen students each term in writing prose." The letter was riddled with misspellings and awkward construction. A Macintosh might have come in handy.

Richard worked in the margins with his pen, adding words, altering words, attempting different spelling variations. It was at best a haphazard effort. In the end, he never finished or mailed his letter to Ferlazzo. Did Hemingway become a second-rate professor? At the deepest level, Brautigan believed in his lasting fame. A great writer didn't drop everything to go teach at some rube cow college. "Richard was never, ever, ever going to come down off his high horse," Don Carpenter observed.

Jim and Karly Zeno, knowing Brautigan to be alone and nearly friendless, invited him over to their house next door for dinner one night. While attempting to remain perfect neighbors, the Zenos were "a little bit frightened of Richard." According to Klyde Young, "he was like a monster to them" because of his strange behavior. Brautigan lived up to their worst fears, rewarding the Zenos' hospitality with a taste of monstrosity at the end of the meal. Having consumed a great deal of wine, Richard got on the phone and called Klyde. "Gee, I'm just over here at the Zenos, and they're so nice to me," he told Young. "They cooked me this fabulous, delicious meal, and they've given me so much of their wonderful wine, and after dinner Jim Zeno just made the most gracious offer because he offered his wife to me. It was quite sweet of him, and he really just wanted to watch. It was a totally wonderful experience. In fact, Karly Zeno got three of her fingers up my rectum, and she did it so beautifully and joyfully. I always thought this would not be something I'd like, but when I saw what love she did it with, I can't think of any greater happiness than to have Karly's hand up my butt."

Mr. and Mrs. Zeno looked on in disbelief, listening with utter horror as their esteemed dinner guest insulted them in their own home, spewing vile slander with a wicked smile on his face.

Richard Brautigan spent much of his free time with Bob Junsch during his last two weeks of life. On the eighth of September, he was over at the Junsches' house in Stinson and gave Bob and Shallen a number of signed books. He included a copy of *The Galilee Hitch-Hiker*, among the rarest of Brautigan's early books. He inscribed it: "'wishing and concerned one more week. Let's see what happens. Why not?' (happiness + happiness)." Richard signed his name in full, his tiny signature pinched and cramped like engraving on the head of a pin.

"These are going to be worth a lot of money someday," Richard said when he gave the couple his books. Brautigan had never played the role of a literary big shot around Bob, but Junsch thought it an "awfully pompous thing to say."

A week later, the Junsches gave Richard a ride into the city in Shallen's new Peugeot. "He called for some reason," Bob recalled. "He had to go over." Junsch was on his way to the airport to fly down to Morro Bay. On the drive, Brautigan talked a lot about Japan. He also asked about Kevin Clancy, a bartender at the Washbag that he liked. Clancy was a friend of Bob's. Junsch told Richard that Clancy was a good guy, "but you have to watch him if you're out and about. He kind of likes his fisticuffs."

The Junsches dropped Brautigan off at Kearny and Broadway, in front of Enrico's. They were in a hurry and didn't have time to stop for a cup of coffee. The next time Bob saw his friend, Richard had been dead for six weeks.

On a previous trip to San Francisco, Brautigan had stopped by City Lights. The bookshop featured a window display of Walt Whitman's books along with dried grass from the poet's grave. Lawrence Ferlinghetti spotted his old acquaintance and went outside to ask what Richard thought of the little exhibit.

"That sure gives a good argument for cremation," Brautigan said.

Richard did not go to City Lights on his last visit to Frisco, heading straight into Enrico's for a drink. He had no way of knowing that his ex-wife Akiko was also in town for the day. She had come up from Los Angeles to work on an assignment with a photographer. When the job was finished, they had plenty of time before their return flight and stopped for coffee at a North Beach café. Afterward, the photographer wanted to buy a pack of cigarettes. They went into an adult bookstore on Broadway to look for some smokes.

Inside Enrico's, Brautigan polished off the last of several drinks. He'd struck up a conversation with a strange woman and invited her to get something to eat with him next door at Vanessi's. They stepped out onto Broadway at the same moment Aki and the photographer left the adult bookstore down the block. Even from the rear and at some distance, Akiko recognized her former husband immediately. "That's Richard Brautigan," she told her companion, following after the familiar form.

Richard and the woman went inside Vanessi's. Two glass doors, one on either side of a small vestibule, separated the restaurant's interior from the street. Aki entered the first door and through the second watched Brautigan talk with the familiar maître d'. Richard turned and looked straight at Akiko, seeing her for the first time in four years. He grew pale "like he saw a ghost." Without saying a word, Brautigan walked away, toward the bar.

Aki knew in her heart she should not have attempted this surprise encounter with Richard. Feeling "so sad," she hurried back down Broadway, "crying all the way to Los Angeles in the airplane."

Richard lost his appetite but still ordered something to eat. Afterward, Brautigan parted company with the woman he'd just met and returned to Enrico's alone. In a coincidence like something invented in Hollywood, Marcia Clay decided to look for Richard, whom she'd also not seen in four years. Loading her baby into his carriage, she wheeled him over to Enrico's, hoping to find Brautigan there. Disappointed at not seeing him, she asked the bartender when Richard had last been in. "Oh, he's here now," he told her. "He just went to the bathroom."

Marcia waited for him. When he came out of the men's room, "he looked like he'd seen a spook."

"What are you doing here?" he asked, sounding startled.

"I'm looking for you, Richard."

"I don't believe this," Brautigan said. "My whole life has just happened in one day."

Marcia thought Richard was "already drunk," but she sat down to have a cocktail with him. Brautigan said, "I want to come to your house, and I want you to cook for me. I want to spend the night at your house."

Clay felt her friend didn't understand reality. "I have a husband," she said.

"All right." Richard steepled his hands together and did his little formal trademark bow. Their conversation continued, and Brautigan told her about the book he was writing. He asked Marcia to read it.

"Richard, I don't know if I should read your book," Marcia said. "What if I don't like it? I may say things that are honest."

Brautigan accepted this. He told her his new book was "a place I've been to and that nobody's ever been to." He said "it was about all the horrible things he'd seen in all of his travels. His visit in Germany, the camps. Seeing things that were devastating to him about the dark side of nature." Richard leaned over and whispered the title in Marcia's ear, swearing her to secrecy. "Don't ever tell anyone," he said.

The book's title was "The Complete Absence of Twilight." In telling Clay about it, Brautigan made things up as he went along, inventing the novel he hoped to write, not the few typewritten pages lying at home on his worktable in Bolinas. Very gently, Richard placed his hand on Marcia's leg. "I love you," he said. Clay thought it was strange. He'd never said anything like that to her before, staring deeply at her with "kind of sick eyes."

Soon it was time to go. Marcia had a baby son and a husband at home. Her days of hanging out in bars with Richard at all hours had long passed. "I want you to call me," Brautigan said. Clay thought he sounded "almost like a surgeon." Brautigan wrote something on a piece of paper and handed it to her. "This is my number," he said. "Be sure to call me."

She took his phone number. "Yes, I'll call you," she said. Marcia kissed Richard on the cheek and left, wheeling her carriage off down Broadway. Not wanting to hang out at Enrico's with no friends around, Brautigan stalked out into the early evening. He headed down to Cho-Cho. Jim Sakata stood behind the bar. He also thought Richard looked like a ghost. "You know who I just met?" Brautigan stammered. "I just saw Akiko on Broadway. She smiled at me and wanted to talk." Over several more drinks, Brautigan repeated the story again and again, telling Sakata "he just walked away."

Richard lurched out into the night, searching for friends, all the while knowing no one alive on earth could erase his terrible enduring pain. From time to time since returning from Japan, Brautigan had hung out with Lou Marcelli, his bar owner pal from the sixties. Lou tended to avoid Richard when he was drunk. "But if he was in a good humor, then he'd be the greatest guy to talk to. He had more stories! We'd laugh and talk . . . but when he was drunk, I had nothing to do with him."

That night, sitting at a North Beach coffee shop on Columbus, Marcelli spotted Brautigan "walking by with some guy." Lou didn't like what he saw. Richard "was so drunk he was glowing. I mean, he was polluted! I kind of just sat there. He walked by me." Marcelli watched Brautigan stagger past and go into Gino & Carlo's. "That was the last time I saw him," he said.

Richard's companion became just another boozing buddy lost forever in time. Brautigan was alone when he stepped into the seedy saloon on Green Street. Curt Gentry sat at the bar in Gino & Carlo's, talking to a young woman named Mary Jane. Richard put his hand on Curt's shoulder. "He obviously wanted to tell me something," Gentry recalled, "and I couldn't understand him. Nothing made sense, he was so drunk." Curt wanted to hear the end of Mary Jane's story. Brautigan squeezed his shoulder affectionately. "Just a minute," Gentry said to Richard, "and she'll be finished." When he turned around, his old friend was gone.

No telling how many bars Richard hit after leaving Gino & Carlo's, but somehow he found his way to the Washbag. Kevin Clancy drove Brautigan home to Bolinas that night after his shift ended. Clancy dropped Brautigan off on Terrace Avenue around 10:30. He declined an invitation to come in for a nightcap and headed back for the city. Richard staggered down to Smiley's and found Andy Cole at the bar. Cole listened to Brautigan's story about running into Akiko earlier in the day. Richard claimed she said she wanted to remain friends, but he acted "totally cold towards her." This was another drunken fabrication, as there had been no interaction between Brautigan and his former wife. Andy thought his old friend seemed very depressed. He advised Richard to go home and sleep it off.

Back in his gloomy house, Brautigan wandered about, inconsolable in the darkness. Sleep seemed impossible. He determined to kill himself, washing down handfuls of pills with whiskey and collapsing onto his unmade bed. In the morning Richard woke up with an all-too-familiar hangover, made even more miserable by finding himself still alive. The weather was cold and foggy. Around one in the afternoon, Brautigan wandered over to Andy Cole's house, repeating his tale of woe, tracking on the agony of seeing Akiko unexpectedly at Vanessi's, confessing his inept failed suicide attempt. Andy told him it was only depression and advised some rest. "You have to get off the booze," he told Richard.

Brautigan headed back toward Terrace Avenue, stopping in the general store to buy a steak for dinner. Turning the corner at Wharf Road, Richard encountered Margot Patterson Doss, getting her house at 9 Brighton Avenue ready for new tenants. Someone had knocked her gate off its hinges, and she struggled to set it right. "Margot, can I help you with that?" Richard wrestled the gate back into place.

"You want to have dinner with us?" Margot asked.

"I've got my dinner here in my pocket," Brautigan replied, pulling the wrapped meat out of his peacoat.

"The latchkey is always out, Richard. We're here for the weekend. If you want to come and have dinner with us, just let us know."

"Thank you, Margot," he said, "but I have to go back to Montana tomorrow."

"Well, we'll miss you," she told him. Brautigan walked away down the street.

Ironically, at almost the same time, Marcia Clay was across the lagoon at Stinson Beach, playing in the waves with her husband and baby son. Later that night, around 11:00, when Sasha was asleep, Marcia kept her promise and dialed Richard's number in Bolinas. "Oh, you're calling," he said when he heard her voice.

"How are you?" Clay asked. She thought he sounded drunk.

"Fucked up." Brautigan paused. "Marcia, I want to read you some of my new work."

"Okay."

"Just a minute," Richard said, "I have to go get it. Call me back in ten minutes."

Marcia said she would and hung up. "I'll call back because we are friends," she wrote in her diary, "and considering the many things that don't work and never will, something with us does work and always will." Clay waited twelve minutes and called Brautigan again. No answer. Marcia got Richard's recorded message. "He was so crazy," she said later. "I thought maybe I missed it by one minute and he put me on the answering machine."

Richard Brautigan woke up late on the morning of Sunday, September 16, suffering from the last hangover of his life. It was nearly noon. He'd slept in his shorts and socks. After pulling on yesterday's corduroy trousers and a T-shirt, he brewed a pot of coffee. The java was dark and bitter. There was a darkness growing, eating away inside him. The corrosion of pain and disappointment consumed the very last of Richard's dwindling supply of hope. He neatly arranged the stacks of poems and stories on his worktable. There would be no writing today. Brautigan had a more important task awaiting him.

Richard padded around in his stocking feet, double-checking the timer controlling his lights, making sure it was set to switch on and off at the proper times. He felt calm and at peace. All his rage and anger seemed very far away, like some stranger shouting at him from the bottom of a mine shaft. Brautigan enjoyed a profound sense of satisfaction. He'd set out to become a great American writer and believed he had achieved his goal. Having controlled every aspect of his career and public image, Richard knew he'd made the right decision. Almost as an afterthought, he set down his coffee cup, picked up the telephone receiver, and dialed Don Carpenter's number over in Mill Valley.

In the middle of watching a football game on television, Don felt pissed at being interrupted by Brautigan. Richard had an uncanny ability to call at inconvenient moments. Expecting the usually litany of vindictive complaint, Carpenter was surprised to hear his friend talking without rancor in a general, amiable way. Brautigan called him "honey," which he did all the time but only when drunk. At the end of their short conversation, Richard said two things Don had never heard him utter before. "I love you," he said. Then, before Carpenter had time to reply, he said "goodbye" and hung up.

Brautigan walked soundlessly into his kitchen and turned up the volume on the radio. Returning to the living area, he picked Jim Sakata's heavy nickel-plated revolver off the table and checked the cylinder. Every chamber was loaded. Richard snapped it shut and stepped to the window. The pistol felt comfortable, fitting easily into his right hand. He stared out at the trees blocking his view of the vast Pacific Ocean. Japan lay somewhere far beyond the horizon he couldn't see. Loud music echoed from another planet. Brautigan thumbed back the hammer, cocking the big Smith & Wesson. No one will ever know his final thoughts. Raising the .44 Magnum and placing the cold steel barrel in his mouth, Richard Brautigan tasted the peculiar sweetness of gun oil.

MAYONNAISE

bibliography

Note: All works consulted were First Editions.

seven handwritten notebooks by richard brautigan

Portions of these notebooks were published in *Richard Brautigan/The Edna Webster Collection of Undiscovered Writings,* Houghton Mifflin, Boston/New York, 1999. This edition did not follow the author's intentions regarding layout and chapter breaks, matters of supreme creative importance to Brautigan. Richard gave these notebooks to Edna Webster when he left Eugene, Oregon in 1956. She kept them in a safe deposit box. By 1991, the key had been lost. I paid for a locksmith to open the box and the material saw the light of day for the first time in years. Edna Webster gave me permission to photocopy the original notebooks.

i love You, Unpublished, Eugene, Oregon, 1955.

There's Always Somebody Who Is Enchanted, Eugene, Oregon, 1956.

A Love Letter From State Insane Asylum, Eugene, Oregon, 1956.

Rock Around the Clock, Eugene, Oregon 1956.

Would You Like to Saddle Up a Couple of Goldfish and Swim to Alaska?, Eugene, Oregon. 1956

I Watched the World Glide Effortlessly Bye, Eugene, Oregon, 1956.

Poems for Edna, Eugene, Oregon, internal evidence suggests this was work done at the Bartons in the Spring of 1956.

published prose by richard brautigan

The Return of the Rivers, Inferno Press, n.p. San Francisco, 1957.

Four New Poets, Inferno Press, San Francisco, 1957.

The Galilee Hitchhiker, White Rabbit Press, San Francisco, 1958.

Lay the Marble Tea, Carp Press, San Francisco, 1959.

The Octopus Frontier, Carp Press, San Francisco, 1960.

A Confederate General from Big Sur, Grove Press, New York, 1964.

All Watched Over by Machines of Loving Grace, Communication Company, San Francisco, 1967.

Trout Fishing in America, Four Seasons Foundation, San Francisco, 1967.

Please Plant This Book, Graham Mackintosh, San Francisco or Santa Barbara, 1968.

The Pill Versus the Springhill Mine Disaster, Four Seasons Foundation, San Francisco, 1968.

The San Francisco Public Library: A Publishing House, Created by Victor Moscoso, Jack Thibeau and Richard Brautigan, San Francisco, December 5, 1968.

Trout Fishing in America, The Pill Versus the Springhill Mine Disaster, and In Watermelon Sugar, (Three books in the manner of their original editions.), Delacorte Press/Seymour Lawrence, New York, 1969.

Rommel Drives on Deep into Egypt, Delacorte Press, New York, 1970.

The Abortion: An Historical Romance 1966, Simon and Schuster, New York, 1971.

Revenge of the Lawn, Simon and Schuster, New York, 1971.

The Hawkline Monster, Simon and Schuster, New York, 1974.

Willard and His Bowling Trophies, Simon and Schuster, New York, 1975.

Loading Mercury with a Pitchfork, Simon and Schuster, New York, 1976.

Sombrero Fallout, Simon and Schuster, New York, 1976.

Dreaming of Babylon: A Private Eye Novel 1942, Delacorte Press/Seymour Lawrence, n.p. New York, 1977.

June 30, June 30, Delacorte Press/Seymour Lawrence, New York, 1978.

The Tokyo-Montana Express, Targ Editions, New York, 1979.

So the Wind Won't Blow It All Away, Delacorte Press/Seymour Lawrence, New York, 1982.

Richard Brautigan/The Edna Webster Collection of Undiscovered Writings, Houghton Mifflin Company, Boston/New York, 1999.

An Unfortunate Woman/A Journey, St. Martins Press, New York, 2000.

published broadsides by richard brautigan

September California, San Francisco Arts Festival Commission, San Francisco, 1964.

Karma Repair Kit, Communication Company, San Francisco, 1967.

All Watched Over by Machines of Loving Grace, Communication Company, San Francisco, 1967.

Flowers for Those You Love, Communication Company, San Francisco, 1967.

Love Poem, Communication Company, San Francisco, 1967.

The Beautiful Poem, Communication Company, San Francisco, 1967.

Spinning Like a Ghost on the Bottom of a Top, I'm Haunted by All the Space That I Will Live Without You, Communication Company, San Francisco, October 1967.

The San Francisco Weather Report, Graham Mackintosh, San Francisco, 1968.

Five Poems, Serendipity Books, Berkeley, 1971.

Knock on Wood [Part 2], Tideline Press, 1979.

magazine and periodical publications by richard brautigan

Five Stops on the Tokyo-Montana Express, "California Living," The Magazine of the San Francisco Sunday Examiner & Chronicle, November 2, 1980.

A Happy But Footsore Writer Celebrates His Driver's Block, "People Weekly," in conversation with Cheryl McCall, June 8, 1981.

Richard Brautigan: Tokyo and Montana, "Washington Review," Cover title: Two New Works by Richard Brautigan, Vol. 9, No. 5, Washington, D.C., February/March 1984.

poetry

Another World/A Second Anthology of Works from the St. Mark's Poetry Project, 1971.

Beatitude, No. 1, May 9, 1959; No. 4, May 30, 1959.

Beatitude Anthology, 1960.

Big Venus, 1969.

Blue Suede Shoes, 424, 1973.

California Living, May 16, 1971.

Epos, Vol. 8 No. 2, Winter 1956; Vol. 9 No. 3, Spring 1958;

Existaria, No. 7, September-October 1957.

Flame, Vol. II No. 3, Autumn 1955.

Foot, No. 1, September 1959.

Green Flag Journal for the Protection of All Beings, No. 3, 1969.

Hearse, 1958, 1961.

Heliotrope, Summer 1969.

Hollow Orange, No. 4, 1967.

J, No. 4, November 1959; No. 5, December, 1959.

Mainstream, Vol. II No. II, Summer-Autumn 1957.

Man in the Poetic Mode, No. 3, 1970; No. 4, 1970.

Mark in Time Portraits & Poetry, 1971.

O'er, # 2, December 1966.

One Lord, One Faith, One Cornbread, 1973.

Rolling Stone, Vol. 32, May 3, 1969

San Francisco Review, Vol. 1 No. 2, Spring 1959.

Sum, No. 3, May 1964.

Sun, No. 9, August 7, 1968.

The American Literary Anthology/2, 1969.

The Berkeley Review, Vol. 1 No. 3, Berkeley, 1957.

The Digger Papers, August 1968.

The Free You, Vol. 3 No. 6, May 1969.

The Paris Review, No. 45, Winter 1968.

The San Francisco Keeper's Voice, Vol. 1 No. 4, April 1965.

The San Francisco Poets, August, 1971.

The World, No. 21, January 1971.

Tri-Quarterly, No. 11, Winter 1968.

Wild Dog, 18, July 17, 1965.

prose

California Living, January 14, 1979.

Change, 1963.

City Lights Journal, No. 1, 1963.

Coyote's Journal, No. 5-6, 1966.

Earth, Vol. 2 No. 1, January 1971.

Esquire, October 1970; March 1975.

Evergreen Review, No. 31, October/November 1963; No. 33, August/September 1964; No. 42, August 1966; No. 61, December 1968; No. 76, March 1970; No. 84, November 1970;

Grosseteste Review, Vol. 1 No. 3, Winter 1968.

Kulchur, Vol. 4 No. 13, Spring 1964.

Mademoiselle, July 1970.

New American Review, No. 12, 1971.

Nice, Vol. 1 No. 1, 1966.

Now Now, 1965.

Playboy, December 1970.

R. C. Lion, #2, 1966.

Ramparts, December 1967.

Rolling Stone, No. 24, December 21, 1968; No. 25, January 4, 1969; No. 26, February 1, 1969; No. 27, February 16, 1969; No. 28, March 1, 1969; No. 29, March 15, 1969; No. 30, April 5, 1969; No. 31, April 19, 1969; No. 33, May 17, 1969; No. 34, May 31, 1969; No. 36, June 29, 1969; No. 37, July 12, 1969; No. 39, August 9, 1969; No. 41, September 6, 1969; No. 42, September 20, 1969; No. 48 December 13, 1969; No. 63, July 23, 1970.

San Francisco Stories, 1979.

The Beatles Lyrics Illustrated, November 1975.

The Co-Evolution Quarterly, No. 9, March 20, 1976; No. 21, Spring 1979.

The Dutton Review, No. 1, 1970.

The Overland Journey of Joseph Francl, 1968.

The Pacific Nation, No. 1, Summer 1967.

The Stone Wall Book of Short Fictions, 1973.

Tri-Quarterly, No. 1, Fall 1964; No. 5, Winter 1966; No. 35, Winter 1976.

Vogue, July 1971.

books about richard brautigan

Abbott, Keith, *Downstream From "Trout Fishing in America", A Memoir of Richard Brautigan,* Capra Press, Santa Barbara, 1989.

Allen, Beverly, *My Days With Richard,* Serendipity Books, Berkeley, 2002.

Barber, John F., *Richard Brautigan: An Annotated Bibliography,* McFarland & Co., Jefferson, NC, 1990.

Barber, John F., *Richard Brautigan: Essays on the Writings and Life,* McFarland & Co., Jefferson, NC 2007.

Boyer, Jay, *Richard Brautigan*, Boise State University, Boise, 1987.

Brautigan, Ianthe, *You Can't Catch Death, A Daughter's Memoir*, St. Martins Press, New York, 2000.

Chénetier, Marc, *Richard Brautigan*, Methuen, London, 1983.

Fujimoto, Kazuko, *Richard Brautigan*, Shinchosa, Tokyo, 2002.

Keeler, Greg, *Waltzing with the Captain: Remembering Richard Brautigan*, Limberlost Press, Boise, 2004.

Meltzer, David, ed., *The San Francisco Poets, Ferlinghetti, Rexroth, Welch, McClure, Brautigan, Everson, talk about their lives and their work*, Ballatine Books, New York, 1971.

Showalter, Craig V., *Collecting Richard Brautigan*, Kumquat Pressworks, Pine Island, MN 2001

Weber, Erik, *Richard Brautigan Photographs 1962-1978*, Erik Weber Photography, San Francisco, 1991.

other books consulted

Alvarez, A., *The Savage God, A Study of Suicide*, Random House, New York, 1970, 1971, 1972.

Amburn, Ellis, *Subterranean Kerouac, The Hidden Life of Jack Kerouac*, St. Martin's Press, New York, 1998.

Anthony, Gene, Foreword by Michael McClure, *The Summer of Love, Haight-Ashbury At Its Highest*, Celestial Arts, Millbrae, CA, 1980.

Arons, Stephan, *Compelling Belief: The Culture of American Schooling*, University of Massachusetts Press, Amherst, 1986.

Baedeker's AA, *Tokyo, The Complete Illustrated City Guide*, The Automobile Association, UK and Ireland, 1983.

Biasotti, David, *Mad River*, Shagrat, United Kingdom, 2011.

Cassady, Carolyn, *Off the Road, My Years with Cassady, Kerouac, and Ginsberg*, William Morrow and Company, Inc., New York, 1990.

Chapple, Steve, *Don't Mind Dying, A Novel of Country Lust & Urban Decay*, Doubleday, 1980.

Charters, Ann, Foreword by John Clellon Holmes, *Beats & Company, Portrait of a Literary Generation*, Doubleday & Company, New York, 1986.

Cifelli, Edward M., ed., *The Selected Letters of JOHN CIARDI*, The University of Arkansas Press, Fayetteville, 1991.

Clark, Tom, *Edward Dorn, A World of Difference*, North Atlantic Books, Berkeley, 2002.

Connor, Judith and Yoshida, Mayumi, *Tokyo City Guide*, Ryuko Tsushin Co., Ltd., Tokyo, 1984.

Cook, Bruce, *The Beat Generation, The tumultuous '50s movement and its impact on today*, Charles Scribner's Sons, New York, 1971.

Coyote, Peter, *sleeping where I fall, (a chronicle)*, Counterpoint, Washington, D.C., 1998.

Creeley, Robert, *The Collected Poems of Robert Creeley 1945-1975*, University of California Press, Berkeley, 1982.

Cregg, Magda, ed., *Hey Lew, homage to Lew Welch*, Magda Cregg, Bolinas, CA 1997.

Davis, James E. and Hawke, Sharryl Davis, *Tokyo*, Raintree Publishers, Milwaukee, 1990.

Delattre, Pierre, *Episodes,* Allen Ginsberg, Charles de Gaulle, Richard Brautigan, and the Dalai Lama Meet in the Pages of this Wild and Magical Zen Distillation of Bohemian Life, GrayWolf Press, 1993.

Dorn, Edward, *Selected Poems,* (Preface by Robert Creeley, edited by Donald Allen), Grey Fox Press, Bolinas, 1965.

Downs, Tom, *San Francisco, The liveliest guide to the USA's most exuberant city*, Lonely Planet Publications, Melbourne, 1999.

Drabble, Margaret, ed., *The Oxford Companion to English Literature, Fifth Edition*, Oxford University Press, Oxford, 1985.

Draper, Robert, *Rolling Stone Magazine, The Uncensored History*, Harper Perennial, New York, 1991.

Ellingham, Lewis, and Killian, Kevin, *Poet Be Like God, Jack Spicer and the San Francisco Renaissance*, Wesleyan University Press, Hanover, NH, 1998.

Ferlinghetti, Lawrence, and Peters, Nancy J., *Literary San Francisco, A Pictorial History from Its Beginnings to the Present Day*, City Lights Books and Harper & Row Publishers, San Francisco, 1980.

Ferlinghetti, Lawrence, *Pictures of the gone world*, City Lights Books, San Francisco, 1955.

Fleischmann, Christa, Photographer; Johnson, Robert E., Coordinator; Harvey, Nick, Editor, *Mark In Time, Portraits & Poetry/San Francisco*, Glide Publications, San Francisco, 1971.

Fodor's, *Tokyo 1987*, Fodor's Travel Publications, Inc., New York & London, 1987.

Foster, Edward Halsey, *Jack Spicer*, Boise State University, Boise, ID, 1991.

Gilliam, Harold, *Island in Time: The Point Reyes Peninsula*, Sierra Club, San Francisco, 1962.

Gifford, Barry & Lee, Lawrence, *Jack's Book, An Oral Biography of Jack Kerouac*, With the Voices of the Men and Women Who Populate the Kerouac Novels, Including: William Burroughs, Carolyn Cassady, Malcolm Cowley, Allen Ginsberg, John Clellon Holmes, Gore Vidal, & others, St. Martin's Press, New York, 1978.

Ginsberg, Allen, Introduction by William Carlos Williams, *Howl, And Other Poems*, City Lights Books, San Francisco, 1956.

Ginsberg, Allen, edited by Barry Miles, *Howl, Original Draft Facsimile, Transcript & Variant Versions, Fully Annotated by Author, with Contemporaneous Correspondence, Account of First Public Reading, Legal Skirmishes, Precursor Texts and Bibliography*, Harper & Row Publishers, New York, 1986.

Gordon, Roxy, *Some Things I Did*, The Encino Press, Austin, 1971.

Gray, Francine du Plessix, *Lovers and Tyrants*, Simon & Schuster, New York, 1976

Grogan, Emmett, Introduction by Peter Coyote, *Ringolevio, A Life Played for Keeps*, Citadel Press, Carol Publishing, New York, 1990.

Herron, Don, *The Literary World of San Francisco & its Environs, A Guidebook,* (Edited by Nancy J. Peters), City Lights Books, San Francisco, 1985.

Hine, M. Louise, *This Is Eugene, The Culture Center of Oregon*, M. Louise Hine, Eugene, OR, 1970.

Hoyem, Andrew, *What If, Poems: 1969-1987*, Arion Press, San Francisco, 1987.

Johnson, Thomas H., ed., *The Complete Poems of Emily Dickinson*, Little, Brown and Company, Boston, 1960.

Kerouac, Jack, *The Dharma Bums*, Penguin Books, 1976.

Kerouac, Jan, *Trainsong*, Henry Holt & Company, New York, 1988.

Knight, Brenda, *Women of the Beat Generation, The Writers, Artists and Muses at the Heart of Revolution*, Foreword by Anne Waldman, (Afterword by Ann Charters), Conari Press, Berkeley, 1996.

Koller, James, *Like It Was*, Blackberry Books, Nobleboro, 1999.

Krikorian, Leo, *The Beatniks and "The Place": The Golden Age of North Beach in San Francisco* (unpublished)

Kyger, Joanne, *All This Every Day*, Big Sky, Serendipity Books, Berkeley, 1975.

Kyger, Joanne, *The Japan and India Journals 1960-1964,* Tombouctou Books, Bolinas, 1981.

Lamantia, Philip, *Selected Poems 1943-1966,* City Lights Books, San Francisco, 1967.

Law, Lisa, Foreword by Ram Dass, *Flashing On The Sixties,* Chronicle Books, San Francisco, 1987.

Leary, Timothy, Foreword by William S. Burroughs, *Flashbacks, A Personal and Cultural History of an Era, An Autobiography,* Jeremy P. Tarcher, Inc., Los Angeles, 1983.

McClanahan, Ed, *My Vita, If You Will,* Counterpoint, Washington, D.C., 1998.

McClure, Michael, Introduction by Robert Creeley, *Huge Dreams, San Francisco and Beat Poems,* Penguin Books, 1999.

McClure, Michael, *Lighting the Corners, On Art, Nature, and the Visionary, Essays and Interviews,* An American Poetry Book, University of New Mexico Press, Albuquerque, 1993.

McClure, Michael, *Selected Poems,* New Directions Books, New York, 1956.

McDarrah, Fred W., *Kerouac & Friends, A Beat Generation Album,* William Morrow and Company, New York, 1985.

McPheron, William, *Edward Dorn,* Boise State University, Boise, ID, 1988.

Meltzer, David, *Arrow, Selected Poetry 1957-1992,* Black Sparrow Press, Santa Rosa, 1994.

Miles, Barry, *Ginsberg, A Biography,* Simon and Schuster, New York, 1989.

Miles, Barry, *In the Sixties,* Jonathan Cape, London, 2002.

Miles, Barry, *Jack Kerouac, A Portrait, King of the Beats,* Virgin, London, 1998.

Miles, Barry, *Paul McCartney, Many Years from Now,* With a new epilogue, featuring Paul's final tribute to Linda, An Owl Book, Henry Holt and Company, New York, 1997.

Miller, Pat, *Gatherings,* unproduced screenplay.

O'Brien, Robert, *This Is San Francisco,* Whittlesey House, New York, 1948.

Parr, Barry; James, Kerrick and Yamashita, Michael, photo., *San Francisco,* Fodor's Travel Publications, Inc., Oakland, CA, 1999.

Perry, Charles, *The Haight-Ashbury, A History,* Vintage Books, Random House, New York, 1985.

Phelan, Deborah, *Bolinas: A Tour Through Its History,* Bolinas Museum, Bolina, California, 1990.

Phillips, Lisa, *Beat Culture and the New America: 1950-1965,* Whitney Museum of American Art, Flammarion, New York, 1995.

Richie, Donald, *Introducing Japan,* Kodansha International, Tokyo, 1989.

Rosset, Barney, and Allen, Donald, eds., *Evergreen Review, San Francisco Scene, Miller, Rexroth, Ginsberg, Kerouac, Duncan, Ferlinghetti, Miles, Rumaker,* Grove Press, New York, 1957.

Rosset, Barney, and Allen, Donald, eds., *Evergreen Review, Olson, Ginsberg, Trocchi, Dodds, Jonesco, Keourac, Adamov, Ferlinghetti, And Others,* Grove Press, New York, 1957.

Seybold, David, ed., *Seasons of the Angler,* Weidenfeld & Nicholson, New York, 1988.

Silesky, Barry, *Ferlinghetti, the artist in his time, a biography,* Warner Books, 1990.

Solnit, Rebecca, *Secret Exhibition, Six California Artists of the Cold War Era,* City Lights Books, San Francisco, 1990.

Suzuki, Tomi, *Narrating the Self: Fictions of Japanese Modernity,* Stanford University Press, 1996.

Tokyo, A Bilingual Atlas, Iris Co. Ltd, Tokyo, 1990.

Waldman, Anne, ed., *The Beat Book, poems & fiction from the beat generation,* Foreword by Allen Ginsberg, Shambhala, Boston, 1996.

Watson, Steven, *The Birth of the Beat Generation, visionaries, rebels, and hipsters, 1944-1960, Circles of the Twentieth Century*, Pantheon Books, New York, 1995.

Welch, Lew, *I, Leo, An Unfinished Novel*, (Edited by Donald Allen), Grey Fox Press, Bolinas, 1977.

Welch, Lew, *I Remain, The Letters of Lew Welch & The Correspondence of His Friends, Volume One: 1949-1960,* (Edited by Donald Allen), Grey Fox Press, Bolinas, 1980.

Welch, Lew, *I Remain, The Letters of Lew Welch & The Correspondence of His Friends, Volume Two: 1960-1971,* (Edited by Donald Allen), Grey Fox Press, Bolinas, 1980.

Welch, Lew, *Ring of Bone, Collected Poems 1950-1971*, (Edited by Donald Allen), Grey Fox Press, San Francisco, 1960, 1964, 1965, 1969, 1970, 1973, 1979, by Donald Allen, Fourth Printing, 1994.

Welch, Lew, *Selected Poems,* Preface by Gary Snyder, (Edited by Donald Allen), 1973, 1976 by Donald Allen, Second printing 1982.

interviews by tim cahill

Bauer, Bob, 11/18/1986

Blank, Karla, 12/14/1991

Brann, Helen, 11/25/1986

Breen, Richard, 10/23/1986

Breen, Richard, and Banclucci, Enrico, 10/23/1986

Breen, Richard, and Dingman, Tony, 10/23/1986, at Enrico's, with Patrick Dawson

Briggs, Robert, 10/18/1986

Carpenter, Don, 10/18/1986; 10/20/1986

Cassaday, Sean, 10/14/1986

Clay, Marcia, 10/21/1986

Coleman, Desmond, 10/22/1986

Diloff, Dick, 12/8/1986

Dolger, Jonathan, 11/24/1986

Donovan, Brad and Keeler, Greg, Summer 1985 (June or July)

Dunham, Ward, 10/21/1986

Fechheimer, David, 10/17/1986

Feigir, Michael

Fonda, Becky, 10/8/1986

Gentry, Curt, 10/22/1986

Gerber, Dan, and Harrison, Jim, 11/21/1986

Hjortsberg, Marian, 10/3/1986

Hodge, Richard, 10/17/1986

Kyger, Joanne, and Brown, Bill, 10/21/1986

Lawrence, Seymour (Sam), 11/21/1986

McGuane, Tom, 10/31/1985

Sakata, James (Jimmy), interviewed by Patrick Dawson

Shea, Edmund, 10/18/1986

Thompson, Toby, 8/11/1985

Valdene, Guy de la, 9/22/1985

interviews by ken kelley

Members of the Anderson Union High School Board, Frank Robertson, Albert Davis, various students at Anderson Union High School and residents of Shasta County, Leonard Neutze and V. I Wexner, January, 1979

interviews by william hjortsberg

Abbott, Keith & Lani, 11/27/1991; 11/28/1991 (with Price Dunn)

Abbott, Keith, 12/7/1991; 9/28/2002; 11/17/2002; 9/10/2006; 1/26/2008; 6/30/2011

Allen, Beverly, 3/7/1999

Aste, Virginia, 1/23/1999; 10/10/1999; 11/14/1999; 12/7/2000; 12/12/2000; 12/14/2000; 12/19/2000; 1/16/2001; 1/19/2001; 1/21/2001; 2/1/2001; 2/9/2001; 2/16/2001; 2/18/2001; 2/23/2001; 2/25/2001; 3/23/2001; 3/24/2001; 4/20/2001; 5/4/2001; 6/1/2001; 9/1/2001; 10/5/2001; 5/26/2003

Atkins, Sandra, 1/24/1999; 1/30/1999; 10/4/1999; 2/27/1999; 4/16/2000

Barber, Dr. John F., 7/7/2011; 7/9/2011

Barton, Hal & Lois, 8/31/1994

Beh, Siew-Hwa, 11/6/1997; 8/22/2006; 6/25/2011

Bell, Charles, 12/6/2003

Bittner, Warren, Phone Message 2001

Blaser, Robin, two letters: 11/19/2001; 12/10/2001

Board of Directors, 8/1/2000

Boericke, Art, 6/11/1992

Bolinas Museum Staff, 1/23/2002

Botto, Ken, 4/5/2002; 4/17/2002

Brach, Bill, 3/15/2003

Brann, Helen, 11/30/2003

Brautigan, Bernard, 9/10/1993

Brautigan, Ianthe, 12/12/1991; 6/19/1999; 9/9/1999; 9/22/1999; 10/12/1999; 12/1999; 1/5/2000; 1/11/2000; 1/14/2000; 1/28/2000; 2/17/2000; 3/2/2000; 5/9/2000; 5/31/2000; 6/21/2000; 7/2/2000; 9/17/2000; 12/28/2000; 1/16/2001; 2/3/2001; 2/27/2001; 10/12/2001; 8/5/2002; 9/25/2002; 9/30/2002; 12/29/2002; 7/1/2003; 7/9/2003; 10/4/2004; 11/29/2004; 2/25/2005; 3/10/2005; 7/27/2005; 11/30/2005; 1/15/2006; 6/10/2006; 1/3/2007; 1/14/2007; 2/13/2007; 7/30/2007; 7/27/2008

Brown, Bill, 6/20/1991

Bruce, Benjamin "Dink", 9/24/2005; 11/8/2008

Burns, Sherry, 8/26/2004

Cahill, Tim, 3/11/1992

Caldwell, Nancy (Hodge), 11/25/1991; 2/26/2005; 1/3/2008

Camardi, Ben, 5/20/2002

Carpenter, Don, 11/23/1991; 11/24/1991

Cassaday, Sean, 8/4/1992; 9/8/2011

Charters, Ann, 7/8/1994

Clay, Marcia, 3/14/2008; 3/20/2008

Coelho, Art, 3/3/2005

Copeland, Alan, 5/29/2011

Conlon, Bunny, 10/23/2003; 11/23/2003

Conner, Bruce, 11/27/1991;11/30/1991; 10/31/2002

Corbin, Melvin, 8/21/1993

Coyote, Peter, 11/7/1997

Creeley, Robert, 7/8/1994; 8/4/2000

Cregg, Magda, 12/5/1991; 12/15/1991 (with John and Margot Doss)

Crockett, Kent, 11/14/1997

Datilla, Bob, 9/14/2000

Davis, Kenn, 4/23/2002

Deemer, Bill, 8/25/1993

Delattre, Pierre, 2/7/2001; 2/13/2001; 2/25/2001; 10/27/2001

Dill, Sue, 2/2/2005

Dillof, Dick, 7/22/2000; 1/2/2001; 5/30/2008; 10/1/2011

Dolger, Jonathan, 11/6/1998; 1/4/2001

Donovan, Brad, 9/3/1991

Dorn, Jennifer, 1/2/2001; 6/30/2011; 7/1/2011; 10/13/11

Doss, John, 12/5/1991; 12/15/1991

Doss, Margot Patterson, 12/5/1991; 12/15/1991; 3/5/2002

Douglass, Becky, 11/22/1999

Dunham, Ward, 10/11/1994; 12/3/1997; 7/19/2011

Dunn, Price, 11/26/1991; 11/27/1991; 11/28/1991; 12/26/1991

Ellingham, Lewis, 10/28/1997; 1/17/2001

Ellis, Simone, 7/31/2011; 9/29/2011

Erickson, Bruce, 10/5/2011

Estes, Valerie, 11/30/1997; 12/14/1997; 8/6/2003; 10/4/2003; 10/25/2003; 11/9/2003; 11/23/2003; 11/30/2003; 1/23/2004

Eugene High, Class of 1953, 40th Reunion, 8/21/1993

Ferlinghetti, Lawrence, 7/7/1994

Fechheimer, David, 3/24/2001; 2/27/2011; 4/19/2011; 5/21/2011; 11/20/2011

Fick, Jorge, 11/30/2003; 12/1/2003

Fitzhugh, Barbara, 6/23/1991; 9/2/1993; 9/3/1993; 9/4/1994; 1/23/1999

Folston, Mary Lou, 6/22/1991; 6/23/1991; 8/19/1993; 8/23/1993; 8/26/1993; 8/30/1994; 5/18/1997

Fonda, Becky, 1/15/2000; 12/19/2000

Fry, Earl, 8/21/1993

Fullerton, Stanley, 5/9/2003; 5/19/2003/; 5/21/2003; 5/22/2003; 5/23/2003; 5/24/2003; 5/26/2004;

Gardner, Terry, 6/7/2008

Gerrity, Sean, 12/14/2008

Gilderbloom, Mary Ann, 1/31/2006; 2/7/2006

Gold, Herb, 11/1/2005

Goodheart, Keith, 10/7/2002

Goodman, Kazuko Fujimoto, 3/7/2007; 11/3/2007

Gordon, Judy, 10/21/2004; 10/25/2004

Grzanka, Len, 1/15/1999; 2/3/2007

Guravich, Don, 10/6/1994

Haller, Brett, 1/18/2007

Haller, G., 8/26/1991; 2/7/2001; 2/13/2005

Halprin, Anna, 12/3/1997; 3/14/2001

Hargraves, Michael, 6/19/1999

Harrison, Jim, 9/19/2000

Hawkins, Bobby Louise, 7/6/1994

Hayward, Claude, 3/14/2003

Hedley, Leslie Woolf, 2/23/2001

Hitchcock, George, 8/25/1993

Hiebert, Donald, 12/8/1998

Hjortsberg, Lorca, 12/29/2006

Hjortsberg, Marian, 7/30/1992; 1/16/2000; 7/20/2000; 4/24/2011; 4/28/2011; 6/7/2011

Hodge, Richard, 11/25/1997; 11/7/1998; 8/6/2002; 11/1/2003; 2/26/2005; 5/27/2006; 6/4/2006; 10/12/2007; 3/15/2008; 1/18/2009; 1/21/2009; 3/31/2011; 4/11/2011; 6/6/2011

Holmes, Ken, 12/3/1997; 5/12/1998

Houston, Jim and Jeanne, 9/19/1994

Hoyem, Andrew, 10/16/2002; 12/2/2002; 6/4/2003

Huffman, Lynne, 1/24/1999; 7/17/2000

Hughes, Kitty, 12/1/1991

Jersey, William, 3/14/2003; 3/17/2003 (Faulty Tape)

Junsch, Bob, 12/21/1997

Kandell, Lenore, 1/24/1999

Kano, Masako, 2/24/1991; 3/3/1991; 6/8/2011; 6/10/2011; 7/21/2011; 7/23/2011; 7/26/2011; 7/27/2011; 7/28/2011; 7/29/2011; 7/30/2011; 9/18/2011; 9/20/2011; 9/23/2011; 9/25/2011; 9/27/2011; 9/28/2011; 9/29/2011

Keeler, Greg, 8/4/1992; 2/24/1999; 9/27/2008; 6/14/2011; 8/1/2011

Kelley, Ken, 12/9/1991

Killian, Kevin, 7/29/2000

Kirkorian, Leo, 7/15/2000

Kitagawa, Eunice, 3/8/2008; 4/17/2008; 4/23/2008; 4/27/2011; 4/28/2011; 6/29/2011; 7/1/2011; 7/22/2011

Kittredge, William, 9/11/2011

Koller, Jim, 3/26/2003; 3/27/2003

Krassner, Paul, 12/5/1997

Kyger, Joanne, 10/6/1994; 11/18/2001; 1/26/2002; 2/12/2002

LaMaster, Sarah; 8/25/1993

Latty, Ted, 10/30/2000; 1/21/2001; 1/6/2002; 2/28/2002; 1/22/2006

Lebra, Dr. Joyce C., 4/22/2011

Lewis, Peter, 9/8/1993; 9/18/1993

Little, Ron, 9/11/1993

LoCoco, Anita, 11/22/1991

Loewinsohn, Ron, 12/4/1991; 9/2/2001; 3/3/2002; 7/28/2002; 10/5/2002

McClanahan, Ed, 11/14/1997

McClure, Joanna, 12/3/1997

McClure, Michael, 7/8/1994; 12/13/1997; 11/1/1998; 5/4/2002

McGovern, Terry, 5/28/2003

McGuane, Thomas, Phone Messages; 2001; 9/4/2011

Marcelli, Lou, 10/22/1997

Meltzer, David, 11/8/1997

Mergan, Barney, 10/24/1997; 11/9/1999

Miller, Peter, 9/8/1993

Mina, Mina E., 6/21/2011

Mina, Rosalyn, 1/16/2000

Moscoso, Victor, 1/22/2001; 1/30/2001; 8/22/2002

Murphy, Cindy, 2/11/1999

Murphy, Dick, 2/27/2001

Musser, Sandra Whitman, 1/26/2001

Najarian, Peter, 9/25/1991

Perry, Ginger, 4/19/2011

Peterson, Eileen, 8/30/1994

Quarnstrom, Lee, 9/16/2000

Rand, Chris, 3/15/1998

Rand, Kendrick, 12/12/1991; 3/12/1998; 2/12/2004; 3/1/2008; 3/20/2008

Reed, Ishmael, 12/14/1991

Resnikoff, H'Lane (Hayward), 3/27/2003

Ressmeyer, Roger, 7/6/2011; 7/8/2011; 7/9/2011

Rosenkrantz, Loie, 12/13/1991; 10/27/2001

Rowland, Jada, 11/30/2004

Sakagami, Akiko, 4/29/1991

Schaff, David, 12/4/2003

Shea, Edmund, 7/1/2000; 10/27/2001; 10/31/2002; 11/13/2003; 6/17/2004

Sherman, Jory, 1/20/2001

Shoemaker, Jack, 1/10/2003; 1/24/2003; 5/23/2003; 6/11/2004; 5/25/2008

Showalter, Craig, 1/11/2001; 3/1/2001; 3/4/2001

Sibbern, Glenise (Butcher), 6/14/1999

Silverberg, Lenny, 9/29/1991

Stein, David, 7/28/2002

Stewart, Dr. Gary, 9/3/1994; 11/6/1999

Takako, Shiina, 4/27/2008; 4/29/2008; 5/7/2008; 10/8/2009

Thibeau, Jack, 4/20/1991; 2/3/1999; 3/6/1999; 1/26/2002; 1/23/2007; 2/5/2007; 10/12/2007; 10/13/2007; 5/31/2008

Thompson, Toby, 8/16/1991; 12/29/2000; 1/2/2001; 6/3/2008

Torrey, Gregory Kent "Beef", 7/3/1992

Turner, Ron, 1/30/2001

Vetter, Sherry, 11/15/1997; 11/16/1997; 11/19/1997

Victor, Ed, 9/27/1993

Walker, Jayne, 11/21/1991

Weber, Erik, 12/3/1991; 8/29/2001; 11/13/2001; 2/12/2002; 3/2/2002; 5/9/2002; 9/24/2003; 9/19/2004

Webster, Edna, 6/17/1991; 8/26/1993

Webster, John, 8/26/1993

Webster, Linda, 6/24/1991; 9/1/1999; 9/2/1999; 9/14/2000; 10/12/2000

Webster, Lorna, 9/10/1993

Webster, Peter, 6/25/1991; 9/7/1993

Wenders, Wim, 5/18/2011; 5/20/2011

Wesker, Sir Arnold, 2/7/2007

Whalen, Philip, 10/11/1994

Wical, Charles and Arthur, 8/21/1993

Winslow, Jane, 11/4/1997

Young, Klyde, 11/24/1991

Zeno, Jim and Karly, 12/12/1991

magazine and newspaper articles

Abbott, Keith, *When Fame Puts Its Feathery Crowbar Under Your Rock, Reflections on the life and times of Richard Brautigan,* "California," California, April, 1985.

Abbott, Keith, *Garfish, Chili Dogs and the Human Torch: Memories of Richard Brautigan and San Francisco, 1966,* "Clinton St. Quarterly," Vol. 7, No. 1, Out of the Ashes Press, Portland/Seattle, Spring 1985.

Baronian, Jean-Baptiste, "Loufoque Brautigan," *Le Magazine Littéraire,* May, 1963.

Chapple, Steve, Cover Title: *Further Adventures (including Trout Fishing) of Richard Brautigan;* Inside Title: *Brautigan in Montana, Whimsy and Middle-Age Along the River,* "Review," San Francisco Chronicle, November 2, 1980.

Creeley, Robert, *The Gentle on the Mind Number,* "Rolling Stock" #9, Cover title: Richard Brautigan Remembered: Robert Creeley, Brad Donovan, Greg Keeler pp.4-6, Boulder, 1985.

Donovan, Brad, *Brautigan & The Eagles,* "Rolling Stock" #9, Cover title: Richard Brautigan Remembered: Robert Creeley, Brad Donovan, Greg Keeler pp.4-6, Boulder, 1985.

Ferrand, Christine, "Richard Brautigan à Paris," *Livres-Hebdo, Vol. V, No. 15,* April 11, 1983.

Fogel, Jean François, "Une Somme de riens et de sourires," *Le Point, No. 544,* May 2, 1963.

Gold, Herbert, *When San Francisco Was Cool,* San Francisco Examiner Image, June 2, 1991.

Gregor, David, *Collecting Richard Brautigan,* "Firsts," The Book Collector's Magazine, Vol. 6, No. 3, Tucson, March, 1996.

Huth, Tom, *Their Town: We're Bolinas and You're Not,* San Francisco Examiner Image, March 23, 1986.

Keeler, Greg, *Fishing the Tenses With Captain Richard,* "Rolling Stock" #9, Cover title: Richard Brautigan Remembered: Robert Creeley, Brad Donovan, Greg Keeler pp.4-6, Boulder, 1985.

Kelley, Ken, *Death-wishing in America, A Reminiscence of Richard Brautigan,* "Express: The East Bay's Free Weekly," Vol. 7, No. 5, Berkeley, Friday, November 9, 1984.

Kesey, Ken, *Skid-Row Santa,* The New Yorker, December 22 & 29, 1997.

Klindt, Robert S., *Oregon's Bridges Uncover Simpler Times,* San Jose Mercury News, December 3, 1989.

Lefort, Gérard, "Montana-Paris Express," *L'Express,* April 11, 1963.

Lorberer, Eric, *Richard Brautigan, a millennium paper airplane,* "Rain Taxi," review of books, Vol. 5, No. 3, Minneapolis, Fall 2000.

Manso, Peter and McClure, Michael, *Brautigan's Wake,* "Vanity Fair," New York, May, 1985.

McCall, Cheryl, *Bloomsbury Comes to Big Sky, and the New Rocky Mountain High is Art,* "People weekly," November 3, 1980.

Mergen, Barney, *A Strange Boy,* "San Francisco Examiner This World," January 20, 1985.

Seymore, James, *Author Richard Brautigan Apparently Takes His Own Life, But He Leaves a Rich Legacy,* reported by Maria Wilhelm, "People weekly," November 12, 1984.

Silberman, Steve, *How Beat Happened,* San Francisco Weekly, January 25, 1995.

Smith, Joan, *The Beats,* San Francisco Examiner, February 9, 1992.

Stahler, Steven W., *An Attempt to Clarify What Exactly It Is That Richard Brautigan Says About Trout,* "The Crimson Supplement," Cambridge, Mass, Tuesday, December 17, 1968.

Stickney, John, *Gentle Poet of the Young,* "Life", Vol. 69, No. 7, August 14, 1970.

Thompson, Toby, *Richard Brautigan,* "Washington Review," Vol. 9, No. 5, Washington, D.C., February/March 1984.

Thompson, Toby, *The Disappearance of Peter Fonda,* Esquire, Volume 101 No. 3, March, 1984.

Wright, Lawrence, *The Life and Death of Richard Brautigan,* "Rolling Stone," Issue No. 445, New York, April 11, 1985.

unpublished prose by richard brautigan

From the very beginnings of his career, before leaving Eugene, Oregon, to seek fame and fortune, Richard Brautigan worked in inexpensive student notebooks. Much of this work remains unpublished and is housed in the Brautigan Archive at the Bancroft Library at UC Berkeley. Brautigan regarded this work as early drafts of potential fiction. He didn't intend them to be read as personal journals and memoir but in fact that is what they are. I've read all of Brautigan's prose. The unpublished pieces used in this biography are cited below:

A Few Days Ago I Was Thinking About Russ, Unpublished, 1984.

A Gun for Big Fish, Unpublished, 1973.

A San Francisco Snake Story, Unpublished, 1976.

Added Days, Unpublished, 1984.

America the Beautiful, Unpublished, Undated.

American Hotels, Unpublished, 1982.

An Apartment on Telegraph Hill, Unpublished, 1968.

An Eye for Good Produce, Unpublished, Undated.

An Unfortunate Woman, Unpublished, 1982.

An Unfortunate Woman, Unpublished, 1983.

Another Short Story About Contemporary Life in California, Unpublished, 1963.

Another Texas Short Story, Unpublished, Undated.

Banners of My Own Choosing, Unpublished, 1964.

Beowulf Umbrella, Unpublished, 1964.

Cat Cantaloupe, Unpublished, 1978.

Coffee, Unpublished, 1962.

Come Back, Salmon, Unpublished, Undated.

Contemporary Life in California, Unpublished, 1963.

Cracker Jacks, Unpublished, Undated.

Going Home to the Locust, Unpublished, 1960.

Gone Since Then, Unpublished, 1957.

Hay on the Water, Unpublished, 1971.

In the Talisman, Looking Out, Unpublished, 1964.

Kalasbel, Unpublished, 1979.

Key to the Frogs of South-Western Australia, Unpublished, 1968.

Kitty Genovese-by-the-Sea, Unpublished, 1966.

Last Words About What Came and Went Yesterday, Unpublished, 1979.

Life Goes on in a Pornographic Theater in Tokyo, Unpublished, 1979.

Mark, Unpublished, 1963.

Missing Like Youth, Unpublished, 1979.

Moose: an American Pastoral, Unpublished, 1964.

Mussels, Unpublished, 1984.

My Name Forgotten in the [Grass], Unpublished, 1981.

One Third, One Third, One Third, Unpublished, 1965.

Owl Days, Unpublished, 1984.

Pillow Talk, Unpublished, 1981.

Poet's Easter, Unpublished, 1960.

Railroading: a Sketch for Michael McClure, Unpublished, 1964.

Russel Chatham: a Portrait of an Artist in His Own Time, Unpublished, 1984.

Seven Things, Unpublished, 1979.

The Ad, Unpublished, 1984.

The American Experience, Unpublished, 1964.

The Bed Salesman, Unpublished, Undated.

The Complete Absence of Twilight, Unpublished, 1984.

The Deserted Imagination, Unpublished, 1963.

The Elevator Down to the Hemingway Stories, Unpublished, 1960.

The Fate of a West German Model in Tokyo: a Journalistic Dream from Japan, Unpublished, 1983.

The Great Golden Telescope, Unpublished, Undated.

The Haight-Ashbury Crawdad, 1966.

The Island Café, Unpublished, 1962.

The Last of My Armstrong Spring Creek Mosquito Bites, Unpublished, 1972.

The Lost Tree, Unpublished, 1983.

The Man Who Took Out the Plumbing in His House and Replaced it With Poetry, Unpublished, 1963.

The Manderfield Tomb, Unpublished, 1970.

The Names of the Characters in This Novel, Unpublished, 1964.

The Necklace, Unpublished, 1979.

The New Apartment Thing, Unpublished, 1968.

The Nightly Rounds, Unpublished, 1981.

The Obvious Charm of Lee Mellon, Unpublished, 1958.

The Pond People, Unpublished, 1979.

The Post Offices of Eastern Oregon, Unpublished, 1962.

The Revenge of the Lawn, Unpublished, 1967.

The Why Questions, Unpublished, 1965.

Those Great American Dogs, Unpublished, 1965.

To Love a Child in California the Way Love Should Be, Unpublished, 1963.

Umbrellas in the Snow, Unpublished, 1984.

Walking Mushrooms, Unpublished, 1979.

What the Mad Scientist Left Behind, Unpublished, 1979.

Woman in a Snake Skin Coat, Unpublished, 1979.

unproduced screenplays by richard brautigan

The Hawkline Monster, (For Hal Ashby), 1975.

Trailer, with Brad Donovan, working draft, October, 1983

other sources

Listening to Richard Brautigan, Hollywood: Capitol Records release on the Harvest Label, 1970.

Tarpon, a film directed by Guy de la Valdene & Christian Odasso, Key West, 1973 (remastered for DVD, 2008)

Welcome to Hardtimes, Richard Brautigan episode, FM Tokyo, recorded 1980.

index

A

Abbott, Keith, 4, 18, 33, 38, 100, 148, 204, 208, 257–260, 265–267, 272, 275, 278, 283, 295–300, 303, 311, 319, 349, 355, 392, 395, 405, 423, 435, 447, 464, 479, 495, 503, 505, 519, 521, 537–542, 553–555, 557, 559, 620, 657, 683, 684, 687, 688, 689, 784, 802
Abbott, Lani, 394, 426
Abbott, Persephone, 559
Abe, Kōbō, 498, 756
Abramson, Michael, 681
Ace of Cups, 366
Acers, Jude, 576
Adam, Helen, 120, 215, 275
Adam, Pat, 275
Adams, Robert, 427
Adams, Verna A., 655, 657, 658
Addams, Charles, 257
Adler, Lou, 317
Agee, James, 688
Aiken, Conrad, 688
Ajar, Émile. *See* Gary, Romain
Alaskan, The. *See* York, Mike
Albee, Edward, 218
Alcatrazz, 791
Alder, Grover Cleveland, 161, 167–168
Alder, Virginia (Ginny), 13, 122–126, 130, 134–137, 140–153, 155–156, 159, 160, 161–165, 167–168, 170–181, 187–189, 191–193, 196–197, 198, 200, 203, 242, 323, 348, 357, 382, 429, 478, 495, 497, 530, 762
Alexander, Paul, 234
Alexander's Timeless Blooz band, 317
Algren, Nelson, 175, 663
Ali, Muhammad, 572–573, 731
Alioto, Joseph, 523
Alison, Barley, 250
All Night Apothecary, 304
Allen, Arch, 676
Allen, Beverly, 383–385, 401, 436
Allen, Donald (Don), 18, 122, 128, 155, 163, 183–185, 190–191, 195, 199–200, 202–205, 203, 204, 205, 209–210, 211, 215–216, 220–221, 223, 228, 230, 234, 241, 244, 248, 250, 275, 294, 301, 302, 304, 306, 327, 329, 332, 343,

344, 345, 346, 347–348, 350, 352, 356, 358, 364, 371, 374, 377, 428, 460, 552, 598
Allen, Peg, 676
Allen, Woody, 558
Alpert, Richard, 236, 269, 271, 272
Altman, Katherine, 432
Altman, Robert, 432, 433
Ama, 341
Ammons, A.R., 90
Anacreon, 498
Anderson, Chester, 290–291, 292, 294, 295, 296, 299, 306, 322
Anderson, Jack, 116
Anderson, Sherwood, 229, 266, 406, 454
Angell, Olav, 478–479
Anger, Kenneth, 328
Angulo, Gui de, 165, 190, 203
Angulo, Jaime de, 165
Annette, 316
Ann-Margret, 231
Ansado, John, 389, 503
Aoyama, Saburou, 564
Apollinaire, Guillaume, 745, 746
Arai, Nikki, 521, 679, 692–693, 704, 709, 718–720, 723, 725
Arbus, Diane, 507
Ardery, Peter, 347
Armstrong, John, 209
Armstrong, Neil, 371
Arnold, Stanleigh, 228
Art, Mike, 699
Artaud, Antonin, 118, 250
Arthur, Chester A., 138
Arthur, Gavin, 138, 232, 285
Asai, Shimpei, 610
Ashby, Hal, 492, 493, 494, 495, 496, 524, 659, 748, 757, 798
Asher, Peter, 379
Ashley, Elizabeth, 480
Ashlock, Edith, 29
Ashlock, Elizabeth Cordelia (Bessie). *See* Dixon, Bessie
Ashlock, Madora Lenora, 26, 29
Ashlock, William, 26
Aste, Ellen. *See* Spring, Ellen Valentine

Aste, Tony, 187–189, 191, 193, 200–201
Auden, W.H., 106
Aurora Glory Alice, 316
Austin, Mary, 102
Auw, Ivan von, Jr., 202, 204, 205, 206, 209

B

Baba Ram Dass. *See* Alpert, Richard
Babel, Isaak, 135, 250, 266
Bacall, Lauren, 37
Badtalking Charlie, 112, 140
Baez, Joan, 153, 385, 794
Baker, Richard, 215
Baldwin, Deirdre, 672, 676, 677
Baldwin, James, 429
Balin, Marty, 243, 322, 399
Balzac, Honoré de, 745
Banducci, Enrico, 18, 322, 403–404, 437, 523, 660, 683, 696, 804
Bankhead, Tallulah, 245
Bannon, Barbara A., 504
Bara, Theda, 229
Baraka, Amiri. *See* Jones, LeRoi
Barber, John F., 719, 720, 724, 733
Barber, John L., Jr., 83–84
Barletta, Joel, 113
Barnes, Julian, 492, 500
Baronian, Jean-Baptiste, 743–744, 748
Barrow, Helen, 424, 491
Barrow, Rosalie (Roz), 367, 368, 369, 370, 373, 392, 395, 397–398, 404, 412, 424, 425
Barth, John, 393, 398, 663
Barthelme, Donald, 202, 205, 429, 663
Barton, Hal, 83–84, 88–91, 93–94, 116
Barton, Lois, 83–84, 88–91, 93–94, 116
Bashō, 67, 124, 498, 573
Bateson, Gregory, 154
Baudelaire, Charles, 134, 137, 142, 144, 151, 262, 406, 420, 743
Bauer, Bob, 680
Bauer, Irwin, 680
Beach, Mary, 362, 363
Beach, Scott, 523
Beach, Sylvia, 363
Beach Boys, 342
Beagle, Peter, 424
Beatles, 210–211, 221, 243, 253, 315, 353, 368, 378, 379, 380, 499, 610, 617
Beausoleil, Bobby, 283
Beckett, Samuel, 93, 200, 209, 579
Beh, Siew-Hwa, 446, 494–495, 499, 501–502, 518, 521–522, 524–539, 541, 547–548, 555, 558, 591, 656, 657, 726, 773
Behan, Brendan, 361
Beineix, Jean-Jacques, 743, 747, 751
Belch, David, 376
Bell, Charles G., 357, 359, 367
Bell, Pat, 524

Belli, Melvin, 158, 435
Bellow, Saul, 99
Bennett, George, 708
Bensky, Lawrence, 273
Benson, George, 675
Bentley, Erik, 701
Bentley, James Abner, 231
Berg, Judy, 293
Berg, Peter (Hun), 18, 264–265, 269, 271, 274, 292, 293, 296, 304, 307, 318, 328–330, 341, 349, 356, 378, 398, 447
Berger, Thomas, 503
Bergman, Ray, 174
Bergsma, Judy, 532, 582
Bergsma, Stuart, 532, 582
Berlin, Lucia, 359
Berman, Wallace, 127, 160, 213
Bernhardt, Sarah, 361, 745
Bernstein, Leonard, 188, 585, 688
Berriault, Gina, 435
Berry, Chuck, 318
Besher, Alexander (Sasha), 656
Bess, Donovan, 270
Bierce, Ambrose, 102, 103, 262, 743
Big Brother and the Holding Company, 248, 267, 270, 283, 286, 296, 315, 318, 321, 348, 354
Big T, 122–123
Bill Hayley and His Comets, 90
Birnbaum, Stuart, 529
Bischer, Deane Cowan, 533, 534, 536, 539, 545, 582, 583
Bischer, Ralph, 534
Bischoff, Elmer, 104
Bishop, Elizabeth, 303
Black, Shirley Temple, 322
Blackburn, Sara, 434
Bladen, Ronald (Ronnie), 131, 132
Blake, William, 417, 634
Blake-Grand, Michaela (Mickey), 283–284, 286, 287, 299, 301, 304, 356, 377, 382, 383
Blanding, Don, 62
Blaser, Robin, 104, 109, 116–117, 128, 130, 150, 160–161, 163, 173, 188, 194, 222, 239–240, 301
Blavatsky, Madame, 107
Bloomgarden, Kermit, 474
Blue Cheer, 285, 354
Bluett, Ron, 23, 24, 32–33
Bly, Robert, 651
Bockner, Rick, 302, 326, 328, 341
Bodenheim, Maxwell, 107
Boericke, Art, 293, 328
Bogart, Humphrey, 37, 266
Bogdanovich, Peter, 474, 478
Bone, Donna, 490
Bonney, William H., 247
Booker T. and the MGs, 317
Boone, Daniel, 676
Boone, Dr. Daniel, 458

Borges, Jorge Luis, 200, 209
Boring Boris, 112
Borregaard, Ebbe, 120, 127, 130, 144, 150, 159, 161, 163, 173
Borregaard, Joy, 161
Bosch, Hieronymus, 674, 675
Botstein, Leon, 613
Botto, Ken, 238
Boucher, Sheila Williams, 105, 106
Boulez, Pierre, 585
Bourgois, Christian, 713, 732, 737, 740, 741, 742, 743, 746, 747
Bourgois, Dominique, 741, 742, 743, 744
Bow, Clara, 229
Bowen, Michael, 269, 270, 271, 284, 285
Bowles, George, 709
Boyce, Jack, 221, 229, 234, 237, 238, 244, 249, 370, 374
Boyd, Madge, 133, 148
Boyd, Pat, 133, 135, 142
Boyle, Kay, 236, 303, 347, 350, 351, 372, 393
Brach, Bill, 305, 306, 344, 378
Bradbury, Ray, 90
Braeme, Charlotte, 460
Brainard, Nellie Leah, 58
Brakhage, Stan, 238, 665
Brand, Stewart, 249, 270, 429, 629
Brandes, Jim, 706
Brando, Marlon, 526, 527
Brann, Helen, 353, 354, 356, 357–359, 364, 365, 367, 368, 371, 389, 393, 397, 400, 401, 404–405, 409–410, 412, 413, 414, 418, 419, 421, 423–424, 430, 431, 433, 439, 460, 463, 465, 468–469, 473–475, 491, 493, 495–496, 499, 502, 505–507, 518, 521, 526, 532, 534–535, 543, 553, 562, 573, 574, 588, 590, 595–596, 597, 602, 605, 608–610, 615, 620, 630–631, 639, 649, 655, 657, 692, 697, 700, 705, 709, 713, 719, 727, 732, 736, 738, 740–741, 748, 756–758, 765, 780, 792
Braudeau, Michel, 743
Brautigam, Frederic (Fritz), 21–22
Brautigan, Akiko. See Sakagami, Akiko (Aki)
Brautigan, Bernard F. (Ben), 15–16, 21–23, 28–30, 32, 98, 149–150, 231, 420, 746
Brautigan, Frederic (Fritz). See Brautigam, Frederic (Fritz)
Brautigan, Ianthe, 7–8, 13–14, 16, 19, 21, 95–96, 162–163, 165, 168, 171–172, 176, 179–181, 187, 191–193, 197–198, 199, 200–201, 203, 210, 229, 230, 250, 256–259, 273, 275, 311, 319, 323, 356, 370, 378, 382, 419–420, 429–431, 446, 455–458, 460–462, 472–473, 475–477, 478, 484, 494–496, 513–514, 516–517, 519, 522, 525–527, 529–530, 532–534, 536, 539–540, 542, 543, 545–546, 548, 557–558, 579–581, 596, 597, 626–627, 648, 650, 657, 673, 677–681, 687, 698–700, 719, 740, 772, 773, 780, 797, 799

Brautigan, Rebecca, 22
Bray, Ronald Milton, 58
Breen, Richard, 7, 118, 661–662, 663, 735, 764–765, 795–800
Breton, André, 74, 105, 743
Brick, Ann, 617
Bridges, Harry, 218
Bridges, Jeff, 480, 485, 487, 672, 675, 677, 681, 693, 727, 768, 770
Bridges, Sue, 677, 681, 693, 770
Brigden, Madeline Tracy, 204, 215, 216, 233
Briggs, Robert, 124, 140, 413, 414, 422, 627, 655
Bright, Richard, 246, 322, 480
Brissie, Carol, 405, 418–419, 473
Brodecky, Bill, 234, 240
Broder, Sam, 163, 180
Brokaw, Tom, 773
Bromige, David, 254, 299, 574
Brooks, Louise, 389
Brother Antoninus, 366, 374, 422
Brotherson, Robert, 160
Broughton, James, 127, 163, 164, 197, 238, 285, 308
Brown, H. Rap, 353
Brown, Jerry, 574, 651, 682, 704
Brown, Joan, 301
Brown, Maggie, 250
Brown, William (Bill), 17, 71–72, 75–78, 80, 111–112, 120, 121, 210, 216, 242, 250, 275, 304, 308, 316, 354, 355, 364, 365, 799, 801, 803, 805
Brown, Willie, 265, 312
Brown, Zoe, 304, 307, 327
Broyard, Anatole, 434
Bruce, Benjamin (Dink), 452, 453, 454, 476, 477, 478, 525, 672, 729, 768
Bruce, Lenny, 139, 140, 153, 256, 324, 462, 575
Bryan, William Jennings, 666
Bryant, Anita, 15
Buchwald, Martin. See Balin, Marty
Buckley, Lord, 139, 153
Bufano, Benjamin, 251
Buffalo Springfield, 575
Buffett, Jimmy, 448, 451, 452, 454, 466, 467, 468, 478, 480, 484, 485, 486, 637–638
Bugliosi, Vincent, 9, 526
Bukowski, Charles, 77, 129, 379–380, 438, 674, 703
Bull, Sandy, 246
Bunting, Basil, 289, 306
Bunting, Sima Maria, 289
Burgess, Gelett, 103, 262
Burke, Clifford, 278, 428
Burks, John, 399
Burns, Bob, 489
Burns, Glen, 783
Burns, Mary, 489
Burroughs, Billy, 402
Burroughs, Joan Vollmer Adams, 105

Burroughs, William S., 105, 174, 197, 322, 361, 379, 402, 406, 743
Burstein, Dr., 714
Burton, Phillip, 347
Butcher, Brooks, 274, 292
Butcher, Glenise. *See* Sibbern, Glenise
Butler, George, 616
Butler, Michael, 681
Byrds, 317, 575
Byrem, John, 225
Byron, George Gordon, 287, 634

C

Caen, Herb, 16, 18, 103, 158, 240, 313, 340, 356, 374, 402, 435, 438–439, 523, 576, 593, 682
Cahill, Maureen, 770
Cahill, Thomas, 291
Cahill, Tim, 693, 768, 770
Cairnie, Gordon, 395
Callagy, Bob, 216
Camões, Luis de, 115
Campana, Frank, 27, 28, 29, 30, 32, 235
Camus, Albert, 193
Canned Heat, 366
Cannon, Howard, 351
Capote, Truman, 99, 127, 616, 663
Captain Topanga. *See* Manyluk, Dan
Caputo, Phillip, 694
Carey, Harry, Jr., 288
Carey, Steve, 278
Carpenter, Don, 4, 6, 12, 140, 163, 167, 195–198, 205, 209, 218–220, 234, 249, 253–254, 257, 266, 268, 273, 278, 292, 308, 319, 322, 331, 343, 371, 372–373, 377, 381–382, 428, 433, 436–438, 446, 452, 465, 478, 493, 494, 498–500, 507, 519, 520, 521, 530–531, 535, 537, 542, 553, 570, 574–576, 588, 592, 603, 604, 613, 614, 621, 661, 677, 678, 688, 689, 692–693, 695, 696, 704, 705, 733, 801, 807–808, 812
Carradine, David, 495
Carroll, Lewis, 672
Carson, Johnny, 438, 522
Carter, Jimmy, 629
Carter, John (Shob), 321
Carter, Mama Maybelle, 617
Cartwright, Donna, 617
Casey, Charles, 504
Cassaday, Sean, 715–717, 734, 765–767, 771–776, 801
Cassady, Carolyn, 105, 186
Cassady, Neal, 105, 106, 108, 137, 139, 186, 188, 353
Castaneda, Carlos, 634
Castro, Fidel, 250
Catfish Black, 396
Cavafy, C.P., 703, 704
Cerf, Christopher, 367, 430

Cernan, Eugene, 462
Chamberlain, John, 417
Chandler, Charlotte, 610
Chandler, Raymond, 628
Chapple, Steve, 679, 680, 683
Charlatans, 243, 244
Chatham, Mary, 514
Chatham, Russell, 5, 11, 15, 451, 470, 498, 514–515, 522, 523, 528, 530, 544, 551, 603, 681, 699, 772, 791, 807
Cheech & Chong, 575
Cheever, John, 189
Chénetier, Marc, 705, 713, 732, 740, 741, 742, 743, 744, 746, 747, 752, 765
Chin, Frank, 354
Chinich, Michael (Mike), 782
Chopin, Frédéric, 745
Christagau, Robert, 504
Christie, Agatha, 253
Christo, 361
Chugg, Gail, 195
Church, Frank, 499
Church, Norris, 687
Churchill, Winston, 688
Ciardi, John, 223, 241, 242, 330, 341, 372, 392, 393
Clancy, Kevin, 808, 810
Clark, Bob, 265
Clark, Tom, 5, 268–269, 270, 273–274, 342, 668, 689, 728, 729
Clark, Walter Van Tilburg, 97, 126
Clarke, Arthur C., 361
Clay, Marcia, 6, 17–18, 576–578, 593–594, 609, 614–615, 621, 628–629, 643, 655–656, 809–811
Cleaver, Eldridge, 345, 421
Clemens, Samuel (Sam). *See* Twain, Mark
Cleveland Wrecking Company, 285, 348
Cloud, 396
Cocq, Frans Banning, 787
Coelho, Art, 466, 467
Coelho, Eli, 466
Coelho, Suzy, 466
Cogswell, Henry D., 171, 262
Cohen, Allen, 269, 270, 271, 274, 284, 299, 321
Cohen, Leonard, 244, 319, 349, 350, 362
Cohon, Peter. *See* Coyote, Peter
Cole, Andy, 6, 17–18, 200, 284, 797, 799, 804, 810, 811
Cole, David, 688
Cole, Lester, 308
Coleman, Esmond H., 343, 440, 464, 659
Coleman, John, 406
Collier, Peter, 331
Collins, Burgess Franklin. *See* Jess
Collins, Judy, 385
Colonel Sanders, 402
Columbini, George, 27
Commander Cody and His Lost Planet Airmen, 318, 432

Commins, Saxe, 654
Condon, Tom, 708
Conlon, Bunny, 351, 357, 359, 360, 361, 362, 364
Conlon, John, 351
Conlon, John Francis (Jack), 357, 361
Connell, Evan, 523
Connelly, Michael, 30, 31
Conner, Bruce, 18, 104, 160, 212–213, 238, 258–301, 324, 328–329, 342, 356, 442, 456, 557, 575, 598–599, 639–644, 659–660, 746
Conner, Jean, 659
Conrad, Barnaby, 523, 593
Cook, Bruce, 411
Cooper, Alice, 380
Copeland, Alan, 521, 718
Coppola, Eleanor, 525, 574, 614
Coppola, Francis Ford, 18, 311, 525, 537, 539, 574, 614–615, 621, 626, 629, 632, 659, 752, 780
Corbin, Melvin, 43, 44, 45
Corbitt, Jerry, 371
Corman, Cid, 562
Cornell, Katherine, 462
Corso, Gregory, 108, 115, 157, 163, 216, 504, 665, 781
Corso, Lisa, 665
Country Joe and the Fish, 236, 286, 303, 304, 315, 317, 403
Cousins, Terry, 544, 545
Cowan, Lexi, 516–517, 533–534, 536
Cowley, Malcolm, 108, 183, 189–190, 197, 306, 326, 688
Cowley, Robert, 320
Cox, Dwain, 8, 609, 696
Coyote, Peter, 263, 265, 269, 277, 285, 290, 292, 294–295, 305, 349, 378, 398
Crabtree, Lotta, 627
Crane, Hart, 61
Crane, Stephen, 743
Crawford, John F., 278, 286, 287
Creedence Clearwater Revival, 285
Creeley, Bobbie, 141, 373–374, 397, 414, 416–418, 435, 440, 443, 575
Creeley, Kate, 417
Creeley, Penelope, 686, 701–703, 781, 784
Creeley, Robert (Bob), 4, 5, 107, 114, 140–141, 161, 163, 191, 193–194, 198, 221, 234, 239, 244, 258, 357–358, 360, 372–374, 393, 397–398, 414, 416–420, 431, 435, 439–440, 443–444, 456, 460, 463–464, 503–504, 575, 686, 701–703, 781–782, 784
Creeley, Sarah, 417
Creeley, Will, 781
Cregg, Maria Magdalena (Magda), 219, 266, 319, 348, 354, 370, 374, 399, 402, 420, 428, 803
Crews, Judson, 129, 141
Crockett, Davy, 644
Crockett, Kent, 365, 366
Cronkite, Walter, 370–371, 663

Crosby, Margaret (Maggie), 617, 622
Crosby, Stills and Nash, 399
Crowley, Aleister, 328
Crumb, Robert (R.), 299, 342, 348
Crumley, Jim, 11, 770–771
Cugat, Xavier, 466
Cullen, Countee, 781
Cummings, e.e., 686, 688
Cummings, Mickey, 803
Cunningham, Imogen, 356
Curtin, Frank, 124, 148–149, 154, 166, 197, 256
Custer, George Armstrong, 323, 467, 633, 653

D

Dahlstrom, Eric Frank, 321–322
Daley, Sandy, 362
Daniel, John, 336
Danimal, 712, 721
Darin, Bobby, 342
Datko, Karen (Scoop), 716, 733, 767, 770–771
Dattila, Andrew, 469
Dattila, Bob, 11, 450, 452, 462, 469–470, 473, 518, 520, 528, 529, 548
Davenport, Guy, 406
Davis, Albert, 622, 623
Davis, Barbara Jean. See Church, Norris
Davis, Kenn, 124–126, 141, 142, 143, 148–153, 155–156, 173, 176, 179, 257, 278, 304
Davis, Miles, 577
Davis, R.G. (Ronnie), 264
Dawson, Eileen, 62, 63, 64
Dawson, Fielding, 196
Dawson, Robert (Bob), 345
Dean, James, 92
Dee, Ann, 139, 140
DeFeo, Jay, 113, 301
Delacorta. See Odier, Daniel
Delattre, Lois, 144
Delattre, Pierre, 144, 153–158, 160, 161, 184–185, 203, 206
Delon, Alain, 231
DeMarinis, Rick, 729
Demme, Jonathan, 528
Dempsey, Jack, 621
Dentoni, Joseph, 10
Denver, John, 589
Derek, Bo, 704
Derek, John, 704
Dermer, John, 512, 550
Desbarats, Peter, 253, 268
Desmond, Kitty, 523
Desnos, Robert, 134, 214, 746
Dewey, Greg, 302, 303, 326, 327, 343, 371, 403
DeWilton, R.L., 93
Dickerson, Vera, 119
Dickey, James, 686
Dickinson, Emily, 151, 715, 743
Dienstag, Allen, 278, 299

Diggers, 18, 263, 264, 271–274, 276–279,
    283–284, 286, 291–295, 297–299, 302, 304,
    306–308, 315–322, 326–327, 329, 335, 349,
    354, 375, 378, 398–400
Dill, Dave, 464, 468, 469, 480, 532
Dill, Sue, 464, 468, 469, 480
Dillof, Richard (Dobro Dick), 673–674, 680, 690–
    691, 693, 695, 716–718, 722–723, 729–730,
    734
Dine, Jim, 361
Dingman, Tony, 6–9, 18–19, 259, 311, 494, 502,
    519, 525–528, 530–531, 533, 537, 539, 555,
    562, 567, 572–573, 592–593, 597–598, 602,
    605, 607, 609, 618, 632, 635, 637, 648, 659–
    662, 684, 704, 757, 764, 780, 795, 803
Dionne, Virginia. *See* Alder, Virginia
Disch, Thomas M., 508
Discords, 544
Dixon, Bessie, 26–29, 34–35, 52
Dixon, Billie, 246, 322
Dixon, Edward Martin, 27, 29–30, 32–34, 35, 645
Dixon, Jesse George, 26, 27, 28
Dixon, Jesse Woodrow, 26, 29
Doda, Carol, 256
Dolger, Jonathan, 5, 6, 8, 418, 419, 427, 430–431,
    433, 491–492, 504–505, 732, 772, 780, 789,
    792–793, 802
Domagalski, Victoria, 385–387
Donahue, Tom (Big Daddy), 243, 328
Donleavy, J.P., 358, 503, 523
Donne, John, 151, 226, 634
Donovan, 244, 316
Donovan, Brad, 668, 675–677, 699, 716, 718, 721–
    722, 725–728, 732, 766, 769, 776, 788–789,
    801, 804
Donovan, Georgia, 668, 676, 677, 699, 716, 722,
    726, 727
Donovan, Joe, 804
Doors, 317, 372, 398
Dorn, Edward (Ed), 140, 163, 196–198, 238–239,
    372–374, 379, 502, 542, 594, 660, 665–669,
    671, 673, 686, 695, 722–723, 726, 729–730
Dorn, Jenny, 373, 379, 542, 594, 665–666, 668–
    669, 671, 673, 695, 722–723, 730
Dorn, Kidd, 373, 665, 722
Dorn, Maya, 665, 722
Dorroh, Fritzi, 370
Dorroh, Michael, 370
Doss, Dr. John, 3, 215, 247, 249, 266, 306, 319,
    355, 402, 440, 458, 520, 575, 592–593, 598,
    603, 606, 778, 807
Doss, Jock, 458
Doss, Margot Patterson, 206, 215, 229, 244, 249,
    257, 266, 317, 355–356, 401–402, 440, 458,
    498, 519–520, 575, 592, 598, 603, 606, 648,
    778, 807, 811
Doss, Rick, 249
Douglass, Becky, 514, 582, 583
Douglass, Kent, 514

Dowie, Ann, 444
Dowie, Mark, 444, 459
Doyle, Arthur Conan, 744
Doyle, Kirby, 318, 319, 349
Dr. Che, 576
Dry Paint, 316
Du Bois, W.E.B., 781
Duberstein, Larry, 434
Dubiner, Dr. Bennett, 12
Duerden, Richard, 117, 159, 163, 165, 190,
    195–196
Dufy, Raoul, 363
Dull, Harold, 238
Dumont, F., 745
Dunbar, Jennifer. *See* Dorn, Jenny
Dunbar, John, 379
Duncan, Isadora, 745
Duncan, Robert, 104, 105, 109, 114, 116, 118,
    120, 127–129, 148, 153, 159–160, 163, 173,
    185, 194, 215, 239–240, 275, 303, 341, 344,
    347, 424–425, 428, 463
Dunham, Marian, 609, 649
Dunham, Ward, 523–524, 593, 609, 649, 658–659,
    680–682, 693, 802
Dunn, Bruce, 310, 394, 395, 407, 408, 409
Dunn, Carolyn, 127, 128
Dunn, Joe, 120, 127, 128, 129, 143, 150, 160
Dunn, Price, 131–137, 142, 148, 150, 165, 172,
    176, 180–182, 186–189, 194, 203–204, 211,
    214, 220, 232, 241, 242, 265–266, 273, 279–
    280, 309–312, 325, 353, 354–356, 394–395,
    407, 426, 436, 442, 460, 511–512, 517, 519–
    521, 543–547, 794
Durbin, Deanna, 181
Duskin, Alvin, 281, 307, 326
Dylan, Bob, 244, 247, 248, 267, 361, 384, 436,
    663, 805

E

Earle, Roy, 194
Earp, Wyatt, 633
Eastlake, William, 241, 338, 359
Eastwood, Clint, 394
Eberhart, Richard, 99, 114
Eco-Hawk, Roger, 668
Ehrlich, Jake, 126
Eichele, Bill, 113
Einstein, Albert, 783
Eisenhower, Dwight D., 231, 729
Eliot, T.S., 120, 352, 372, 634, 673, 688, 737
Ellingham, Lewis, 117, 188, 195, 243
Ellington, Duke, 665, 780
Ellis, Simone, 665–667, 669–671, 730, 796–797,
    803, 807
Ellison, Harlan, 90
Ellsworth, Sallie, 244, 253
Elsner, Gisela, 221
Embree, Lou, 158–159, 179, 181

Emergency Crew, 248
Emerson, Ralph Waldo, 362
Emperor Norton. *See* Norton, Joshua A.
Erickson, Bruce, 776
Erickson, Jim, 682
Escher, M.C., 125
Estes, Dave, 10
Estes, Valerie, 259, 344–348, 351–371, 374–376,
    379–382, 393, 396, 398–399, 402, 410–412,
    414–415, 431, 468, 593
Everard, William, 264
Everson, William. *See* Brother Antoninus
Eylar, Al, 357

F

Fagin, Larry, 195, 234, 247
Faithfull, Marianne, 379
Fariña, Mimi, 153
Farrell, James T., 218
Faulkner, William, 189, 429, 434, 454, 530, 551,
    654, 739, 743
Featherstone, Joanna, 424
Fechheimer, David, 8, 10–11, 14, 17–18, 186–187,
    415–416, 505, 524, 609, 631–632, 681–682,
    693, 802
Feiffer, Jules, 686
Felts, James, 116
Fenu, John, 482, 488
Fenu, Justine, 482
Ferlazzo, Paul, 708, 713, 714, 718, 728, 732, 801,
    807
Ferling, Larry. *See* Ferlinghetti, Lawrence (Larry)
Ferlinghetti, Kirby, 108
Ferlinghetti, Lawrence (Larry), 103, 108, 110,
    126–128, 131–132, 157, 163, 186, 195, 197,
    208, 235–236, 246–247, 265, 285, 300, 303,
    331, 344–345, 347, 363, 366, 379–380, 422,
    428, 443, 808
Ferrand, Christine, 741–742, 745
Feynman, Richard, 287–288
Fick, Jorge, 431, 445
Fiddling Red, 673
Field, Tom, 234
Fields, Arthur, 292
Finkle, Dr. Alex, 226
Finley, Cassandra, 307–308, 319
Fisher, Eddie, 54
Fisher, Joe, 688
Fitzgerald, F. Scott, 99, 127, 202–203, 253, 634,
    701
FitzGerald, Russell, 126, 148, 150
Fitzhugh, Jim, 49
Fitzsimmons, Thomas, 612
Fixel, Lawrence, 308
Fjetland, Eveline. *See* Kehoe, Eveline Elaine
Flaherty, Joe, 508
Flaubert, Gustave, 432, 619
Flores, Gene, 148

Flying Burrito Brothers, 399
Flying Circus, 322
Flynt, Larry, 540
Fogel, Jean-François, 742, 745–746
Foley, Martha, 458, 733
Folston, David, 15, 49
Folston, Larry, 53
Folston, Mary Lou, 15–16, 21–24, 26–34, 36–41,
    43–45, 47–53, 55–59, 66–67, 84–87, 93–96, 419,
    683
Folston, William (Bill), 48–53, 55, 57, 59–60, 71,
    85, 93
Fonda, Becky. *See* McGuane, Becky
Fonda, Jane, 495
Fonda, Peter, 8, 525, 528, 539, 543–544, 546, 681,
    721, 727, 766, 768–770, 775
Foodym, Doralyn, 392
Ford, Ford Madox, 289
Forman, Milos, 84
Forrest, Frederick, 526, 527
Foster, Stephen, 754
Four Aces, 90
Fox, Gil, 688
Francl, Joseph, 344, 654, 660
Franco, Francisco, 785
Frank, Robert, 140
Frankenthaler, Helen, 119
Freud, Sigmund, 193
Friedman, Bruce Jay, 418
Fritsch, William (Bill), 265, 269, 278, 284, 292,
    303, 307, 308, 316, 322, 326, 341, 399, 400
Frost, Emily (Nemi), 120, 127, 148, 150, 200, 210,
    234, 239, 244, 247
Frost, Robert, 352, 665, 686
Frumkin, Gene, 160
Fryer, John, 11, 454, 467, 491, 504, 530, 534, 675,
    681, 741
Fugs, 245, 246, 363, 379
Fujimoto, Kazuko, 464, 465, 475, 504, 519, 535,
    536, 563–564, 569–570, 586, 588
Full Tilt Boogie, 354
Fuller, Blair, 331, 351, 523
Fuller, Ethel Romig, 66, 68
Fullerton, Stanley, 152–153, 162, 176, 180, 196,
    309–310, 312

G

Gaines, Charles, 468–469, 616
Gaines, Virginia, 469
Galey, Brenda, 617
Galloway, Donna, 609
Gannon, Francis X., 620
Garcia, Andrew, 448
Garcia, Jerome (Jerry), 248, 308
Gardiner, Terry, 707
Gardner, Leonard, 435
Garfield, John, 673
Garrett, George, 90

Gary, Romain, 742
Gatten, Joan, 192
Geissler, Dora, 188
Gelber, Jack, 216
Gene the Scrounge, 140
Genet, Jean, 93
Gentry, Curt, 6, 8–10, 18–19, 311, 436, 437, 439,
    478, 502, 518–519, 523, 526–527, 531–532,
    535, 537, 555, 562–563, 565–566, 568–570,
    572–574, 576, 614, 654, 659, 696, 810
Gentry, Gail. *See* Stevens, Gail
George, Henry, 440
Gerber, Dan, 450, 469, 471, 476, 517, 547, 559,
    588–591, 600–601, 681
Gerber, Frank, 559
Gerber, Ginny, 547, 559, 600, 681
Gere, Richard, 780
Gernreich, Rudi, 233
Gerrity, Sean, 632, 636, 680
Gershwin, George, 420
Gibson, Juliette Claire, 62–64, 72, 91
Gide, André, 550, 743, 757
Giesecke, Morton, 620, 622–623
Gilbert, Jack, 106, 120
Gilderbloom, Mary Ann, 444, 459–460, 478–479,
    486, 515–516, 518
Giler, David, 748
Gilliam, Bernard, 231
Gilmore, Gary, 167
Gingrich, Arnold, 234
Ginsberg, Allen, 105–110, 114–116, 126–128, 132,
    140, 154, 163, 185, 190, 195, 197, 236, 239,
    242, 244, 246–247, 256, 265, 272, 281, 284–
    286, 344, 349, 355–356, 363–364, 379, 428,
    439, 443–444, 665, 668, 686, 743, 784
Girard, Victor, 181
Glass, Philip, 375
Gleason, Ralph, 246, 265, 278, 284, 290, 294, 296,
    330, 354
Glidden, Joseph F., 712
Godare, Gene, 325
Godfrey, Arthur, 66
Gold, Herbert, 197, 308, 331, 350, 372, 523, 702
Goldhaft, Judy, 293
Goldman, William, 258
Goodman, David, 464, 563, 570
Goodman, Kazuko Fujimoto. *See* Fujimoto, Kazuko
Goodrow, Gary, 247, 265
Goodwin, Jack, 106–107, 109–110, 117
Gordon, Barbara, 704
Gordon, J.C. (John Calvin), 403, 466
Gordon, Judy, 374, 402–403, 414, 419, 420, 424,
    431, 445, 466, 467
Gordon, Roxy, 258, 374, 402–403, 414, 419, 424,
    431, 466–467
Gores, Joe, 632
Gorsuch, Bob, 664, 701, 797
Gottlieb, Robert, 418
Gould, Lois, 505

Goya, Sue, 122
Grabhorn, Robert, 254, 256
Graham, Bill, 245, 246, 248, 267, 274, 304, 321,
    324, 443
Graham, John, 164, 185
Grant, Ulysses S., 34, 362
Grass, Günter, 784
Grateful Dead, 248, 270, 283, 286, 303, 308, 315,
    317, 318, 321, 398, 399
Gray, Francine du Plessis, 616
Great Society, 244, 248
Green, Bill, 707
Green, Sue, 250–251
Greene, A.C. (Alvin Carl), 419
Greene, Bob, 305
Greene, Graham, 418
Greer, Maretta, 284, 285
Grey, Zane, 174, 406
Grgich, Rose Marie, 331
Griffin, Rick, 285, 342
Griffith, E.V., 141, 159, 175
Grissam, John, 553–554
Grogan, Emmett, 265, 269, 271–272, 273, 274,
    276, 277, 283, 284, 285, 286, 290, 291, 292,
    293, 294, 295, 296, 297, 298, 299, 315, 317,
    319, 322, 326, 349, 354, 355, 398, 399, 400,
    607
Grzanka, Len, 562–563, 580, 586–587
Gunn, Thom, 303
Guravich, Donald, 778
Guthrie, A.B., 510
Guthrie, Woody, 343, 495

H

Haig-Brown, Roderick L., 174
Haley Street Snack Factory, 317
Halleck, Henry W. (Old Brains), 102
Haller, Bret, 480, 494, 495, 560, 561
Haller, Eric, 480, 485, 494, 495, 560
Haller, G., 480, 481, 483, 485, 487, 494, 495, 560
Haller, Michael, 480, 492, 494, 495, 496, 560, 748,
    757, 782
Hallinan, Terrence (Kayo), 341
Halprin, Anna (Ann), 163–164, 172, 185, 225
Halprin, Lawrence, 163, 164
Ham, Bill, 243, 244, 321
Hamilton, Alexander, 461
Hamilton, William (Bill), 19, 604
Hammett, Dashiell, 632
Hammond, Lawrence, 302, 304, 326, 327, 341,
    343, 383
Hamsun, Knut, 550
Hannah, Barry, 739, 749, 750
Hanrahan, William, 126
Hansen, Steve, 405
Hara, Mia, 389
Harcourt-Smith, Joanna, 463
Harlow, Jean, 247

Harmon, Beverly, 131, 132
Harmon, James (Jim), 115, 131, 132
Harnaka, Vale. *See* Vale, V. (Valhalla)
Harper, Walter, 607
Harris, Julie, 715
Harrison, George, 211
Harrison, Jim, 11, 341, 450–454, 469–473, 475–477, 489, 503, 517–520, 522, 527–529, 553, 574, 605, 635, 637–638, 680
Harrison, Linda, 469, 517, 527
Hart, James D., 425
Hart, Kelly, 341
Harte, Bret, 102
Hartnett, John, 502, 573–574, 602, 608, 620
Hartz, Jim, 729, 730, 779
Harvey, Laurence, 152
Harwood, Lee, 418
Hasegawa, Kazuhiko, 591
Hasegawa, Shiro, 569
Haselwood, David, 215, 222, 254, 420
Hatch, Lorraine, 366, 367
Hatfield, Mark O., 58
Hawkes, John, 221
Hawking, Stephen, 760
Hawkins, Bobbie Louise, 4, 212, 306, 360, 435, 777, 803
Hayes, Gabby, 654
Hayes, Hanorah, 22
Hayward, Claude, 290–291, 292, 295, 298, 305, 306, 319, 322, 328
Hearn, Lafcadio, 757
Hearst, Patty, 542
Hedley, Leslie Woolf, 119–120, 125, 143, 157
Hedrick, Wally, 104, 105, 113, 301
Heflin, Van, 231
Hefner, Hugh, 377, 426, 427
Heller, Joseph, 418, 686
Hellman, Lillian, 632, 686
Hells Angels, 236, 258, 265, 270, 274, 276, 277, 283, 285, 290, 298, 303, 306, 307, 322, 326, 338, 348, 398, 399, 400, 704, 705, 706
Helms, Chet, 243–244, 248, 304, 322
Hemingway, Ernest, 17, 61–62, 68, 72, 74, 77, 79, 93, 99, 119, 123, 127, 130, 170, 179–181, 183, 241, 253, 262, 266, 406, 412, 429, 434, 452, 454, 476, 478, 484, 485, 496, 551, 597, 634, 684, 689, 743, 766, 807
Hemingway, Pat, 602
Hendricks, George (Chocolate George), 277, 283, 322
Hendrix, Jimi, 262, 317
Henkin, Harmon, 471, 511, 531, 532, 685
Henry, O., 359, 361
Henry IV, 747
Herms, George, 160, 301
Herndon, Fran, 160, 189, 234, 239
Herndon, Jim, 188
Herron, Patricia, 599
Hesse, Hermann, 279

Hiebert, Donald, 44–45, 46, 54
Hiebert, Johnnie, 45, 172
Hiebert, Ronald, 44–45, 46
Hill, Fred, 187, 219
Hills, L. Rust, 197
Hinckle, Warren, III, 15, 290, 294, 299
Hine, Daryl, 352, 354
Hines, Charlie (Grandpa), 51
Hines, Gregory, 780
Hirohito, 793
Hitchcock, Alfred, 253
Hitchcock, Billy, 236
Hitchcock, George, 155, 308
Hjortsberg, Ida, 637
Hjortsberg, Lorca, 461, 462, 559–560, 734, 740
Hjortsberg, Marian, 462, 464, 467, 469, 471, 487, 514, 528, 529, 534, 540, 544, 545, 546, 547, 552, 582, 597, 598, 600, 601, 603, 613, 636, 648, 652, 653, 663, 664, 671, 672, 673, 674, 675, 677, 680–681, 690, 692–693, 695, 698, 700–701, 708, 721–723, 725–726, 733–734, 737–739, 740, 746, 765, 767–773, 796
Hjortsberg, Max, 559, 637
Hjortsberg, William (Gatz), 5, 11, 21, 400, 446, 450, 460–462, 464, 467, 469–471, 483–485, 487, 491, 493, 496, 501, 510, 514, 515, 520, 528, 533–535, 544, 545, 546, 552, 559, 565, 590, 597–598, 600, 601, 613, 633, 636–637, 648, 663–664, 665, 672, 681, 686, 693–699, 723, 734, 738, 748, 757, 769–770, 782, 796, 804–805
Hoberman, Martin, 129
Hochberg, Dottie, 325
Hodge, Aaron, 635, 636
Hodge, Nancy, 387, 432, 445, 456, 465, 469–470, 478, 516, 519, 520, 521, 599, 605, 621, 631, 635, 636–637, 648, 683
Hodge, Richard (Dick), 8, 13, 14, 18, 318, 347, 348, 357, 361, 387, 432–433, 435, 445, 456, 465, 469–470, 478, 493, 495, 516, 519, 541, 575, 579, 594, 597, 599, 605, 606, 618, 621, 631, 635, 636–637, 648, 683, 692, 704, 705, 706, 753–754, 769, 788
Hodgson, Moira, 528, 529
Hoffman, Abbie, 272, 349, 393
Hoffman, Anita, 393
Hoffman, Dustin, 496
Hoffman, Hilda, 378
Hoffman, John, 109
Hogan, William, 198, 215, 228, 230
Hollingsworth, Ambrose, 285
Holmes, John Clellon, 103, 154, 216
Holmes, Sherlock, 622
Holy Modal Rounders, 245
Hongisto, Richard, 682
Hooker, Joseph (Fighting Joe), 362
Hooton, Harry, 111
Hoover, J. Edgar, 270
Hope, Mary, 508

Hoppe, Art, 341
Hopper, Dennis, 259, 626–627
Horn, Clayton, 126
Houston, James, 433, 435, 628
Houston, Jeanne, 435, 628
Howard, Peter, 427
Howard, Richard, 757
Hoyem, Andrew, 215, 222, 229, 240, 244, 247,
    251, 253, 254, 256, 265, 268, 278, 285, 286,
    287, 288, 289, 303, 306, 308, 401, 423–424
Hoyem, Sally, 256
Hube the Cube, 112, 140, 154
Huffman, L.A., 690
Huffman, Lynne, 653, 672
Hughes, Kitty. See Loewinsohn, Kitty
Hughes, Langston, 781
Hughes, Ted, 686
Hull, Dr. William D., II, 666, 678, 679, 680
Humphrey, Hubert H., 341
Hunt, Mie, 389
Hunter, Meredith, 400
Hurston, Nora Zeale, 781
Husband, Donald, 48, 53, 541, 696
Huston, Angelica, 537
Huston, John, 523
Hutter, Donald, 202, 204, 205, 238, 244, 246, 268,
    270
Huxley, Aldous, 147

I

Ignatius of Loyola, 800
Ikezawa, Natsuki, 535, 536
Inman, Will. See Thorne, Evelyn
Inoki, Antonio, 572, 573
Ionesco, Eugène, 93
Irving, John, 243
Isohachi, Mr., 644
Issa, 498, 573
Ito, Eiko, 612

J

Jackson, Bruce, 702
Jackson, Diane, 702
Jackson, Joseph Henry, 436
Jackson, Reggie, 778, 779
Jackson, Thomas Jonathan (Stonewall), 362
Jacobus, Harry, 104, 234
Jaffe, Rona, 505
Jaffe, Sherril, 574
Jagger, Mick, 400
Jahrmarkt, Billy (Batman), 301, 307, 318–319, 378
Jahrmarkt, Caledonia, 319, 378
Jahrmarkt, Digger, 319, 349
Jahrmarkt, Hassan, 319
Jahrmarkt, Jade, 319
Jahrmarkt, Joan, 318, 378
James, Clifton, 480

James, Henry, 634
James, Joni, 54
Jamruska, Pamela, 715, 717
Jefferson Airplane, 243, 244, 246, 248, 286, 317,
    399, 407, 456
Jennings, Waylon, 431, 575
Jensen, Edna Webster. See Webster, Edna
Jersey, William, 320, 321, 324
Jess, 107, 109, 116, 129, 160, 185, 194, 234, 240
Jindrich, Dr. Ervin J., 12
John, Elton, 575
John Coltrane Quartet, 244
John Handy Jazz Ensemble, 283
John Handy Quintet, 248
Johnson, J.J., 577
Johnson, Lyndon, 236, 304
Johnson, Rafer, 800
Johnson, Robert, 303
Johnson, Samuel, 436
Jonas, Steve, 129
Jones, Elvin, 244
Jones, James, 128–129
Jones, LeRoi, 198, 210, 239, 402, 663
Joplin, Janis, 244, 248, 258, 283, 305, 315, 317,
    321, 342, 348, 349, 353, 354, 355, 424
Jordan, Larry, 104, 132, 238
Joy of Cooking, 318
Joyce, James, 138, 363
Judge, Tom, 652
Junsch, Bob, 9–10, 14, 451, 452, 455, 538, 797,
    800, 801, 803, 804, 806, 808
Junsch, Shallen, 797, 801, 808
Just, Ward, 458

K

Kafka, Franz, 151, 172, 192, 226, 502
Kageyama, Tamio, 794, 796
Kahlo, Frida, 103
Kallianiotes, Helen, 554
Kanai, Mieko, 630
Kandel, Lenore, 158, 186, 190, 265, 274, 284, 285,
    295, 297, 300, 303, 306, 307, 308, 316, 322, 326
Kano, Masako, 666–681, 683, 686, 699, 723,
    725–726, 734, 736–737, 739–740, 750–752,
    755–756, 759–762, 765, 773–775, 786, 788,
    793–796, 801
Kano, Masamichi, 666, 671, 678, 725
Kantner, Paul, 5, 407
Karloff, Boris, 727
Karsh, Yousuf, 179
Kastner, Elliott, 525
Kaufman, Bob, 117, 143, 148, 154, 157, 159,
    438–439, 537–538
Kaufman, Eileen, 148, 157
Kaufman, Phil, 18
Kawabata, Yasunari, 498, 500
Kawarazaki, Choichiro, 612
Kearney, Larry, 200, 240

Keating, Edward, 230
Keats, John, 634
Keeler, Chris, 800, 801
Keeler, Greg, 6, 618–620, 628–629, 632, 637–638, 652, 654, 664, 670, 673, 675–680, 695, 698–700, 708, 714–718, 723, 725–735, 737, 758, 766–767, 776, 781, 785, 790, 794, 800–801
Keeler, Judy, 619–620, 637–638, 714, 800–801
Keeler, Max, 800, 801
Keenan, Larry, 247
Kees, Weldon, 108, 115
Kehoe, Eveline Elaine, 15, 26–29, 31–32, 34
Kehoe, Lula Mary. *See* Folston, Mary Lou
Kehoe, Michael Joseph, 26
Kelley, Ken, 15, 615–617, 622–623, 632–637, 648
Kelly, John, 154
Kennedy, Jacqueline (Jackie), 202
Kennedy, John F., Jr. (John-John), 202
Kennedy, John Fitzgerald, 207, 439
Kennedy, Robert, 353, 499
Kennedy, Roger, 375
Kennedy, William, 780
Kenner, Hugh, 120
Kerouac, Jack, 103, 105–110, 112, 114, 116, 118, 127–129, 132, 139–140, 144, 148, 154, 158, 163, 167, 186, 197, 200, 221, 242, 291, 353, 358, 359, 394, 406, 412, 428, 628, 668, 781
Kerouac, Jan, 781–782
Kesey, Ken, 20, 47, 84, 236–237, 249, 262, 270, 274, 276–277, 289, 294, 306, 434–435, 463, 628, 683
Khayyam, Omar, 34
Kherdian, David, 209
Kiamatsu, Soji, 580
Kidder, Margot, 525, 526, 527, 528, 529, 534, 546
Kienholz, Edward, 127
Kincaid, Ann, 237, 376
Kincaid, James, 666
King, Dr. Terence, 38
King, Hayward, 104
King, Martin Luther, Jr., 353, 364
Kingston, George, 22
Kingston, Rebecca. *See* Brautigan, Rebecca
Kinnison, Joanna. *See* McClure, Joanna
Kinski, Nastassja, 726
Kipling, Rudyard, 34, 510
Kirkendall, Betty, 346, 356
Kitagawa, Eunice, 684, 686–689, 692–693, 695, 699–700, 704, 708–709, 713, 773
Kitt, Eartha, 49
Kittridge, William (Bill), 770, 771
Kizer, Caroline, 393
Kleinsinger, George, 361
Klinkowitz, Jerome, 709
Knell, Pete, 277, 283
Knight, Ted, 754
Köepf, Mike, 770, 771
Koller, James (Jim), 249, 250, 275, 303, 423
Köllhofer, Jacob, 783

Koppel, Ted, 18
Korda, Michael, 630
Kornfield, Anita Clay, 577
Kornspan, Harvey, 318, 322
Kostas, 693
Kot, Hairy Henry, 276–277
Kovach, Jonas, 443
Kovacs, John. *See* Kovach, Jonas
Kovaly, Andrew, 192
Kovic, Ron, 626, 649
Kozmic Blues Band, 354
Krassner, Paul, 272, 349, 378, 393
Krementz, Jill, 499–500
Kreutzer, Dr. Eberhard, 784
Krikorian, Leo, 112–113, 114, 116, 139–140
Krim, Seymour, 197, 216, 250, 253, 508
Kroll, Steven, 427
Krug, Peter, 294
Kunitz, Stanley, 686
Kuniyuki, Anne, 465, 466, 468, 469, 475, 478, 481, 501
Kupferberg, Tuli, 245
Kyger, Joanne, 14, 117, 120–121, 127, 128, 144, 145, 147–148, 158, 161, 163, 190, 196, 210–211, 216, 220–221, 224, 229, 234, 238, 240–241, 244–245, 249–250, 268, 275, 303, 306, 316, 325, 330, 370, 374, 402, 420, 435, 455–456, 519, 521, 778, 803
Kyle, Tom, 482, 483, 485

L

La Fontaine, Jean de, 745
La Mortadella. *See* La Morticella, Robert
La Morticella, Robert, 274, 276
Ladd, Alan, 47
Laforgue, Jules, 743, 745
Laing, E. William (Bill), 63
Lamantia, Philip, 105 , 108–110, 163, 165
Lambert, Doretha, 528, 547
Lambert, Wilbur, 528, 547
L'Amour, Louis, 292
Landon, Jack, 116
Langton, Daniel J., 129, 186, 247
Lapautre, Michelle, 736, 741, 743, 746–748
Lardner, Ring W., 90
Larner, Jeremy, 18
Larousse, Pierre, 746
Larsen, Carl, 129, 141
Larsen, Marthe, 114, 193
Latty, Ted, 802–803
Laughlin, James, 190, 199
Laverine, Dr. J. Robert, 12, 16, 19
LaVey, Anton Szandor, 230
LaVigne, Robert, 106, 113, 132, 139, 246, 247
Lawrence, D.H., 322, 359
Lawrence, Merloyd, 358
Lawrence, Seymour (Sam), 11–12, 15, 19, 358, 359, 364, 365, 367, 371, 372, 381, 382, 392, 393,

395, 397, 401, 404, 406–407, 412–414, 433,
439, 446, 459, 463, 502, 506–507, 508, 592,
595, 596, 604, 605, 609, 610, 615, 617, 620,
630, 631, 650, 655, 657, 660, 663–664, 669,
681, 683, 685, 687, 692, 697, 699, 700, 705,
708, 713, 727, 729, 734, 738
Laws, Judy, 306
Le Saux, Bernard, 746
Leary, Rosemary, 399, 421, 463, 540
Leary, Timothy, 236, 271, 272, 279–280, 291, 302,
350, 399, 401, 420–421, 463, 540
Leath, A.A., 164, 185
Lebra, Dr. Joyce, 666–667, 669, 671–672, 678
Lederle, Del, 144
Lee, Paul, 350
Lee, Robert E., 362
Lee, Sandi, 544, 551, 552
Lefort, Gérard, 741, 742
Leibovitz, Annie, 616
Leitaker, J.D., 604
Lennon, Cynthia, 379
Lennon, John, 211, 315, 322, 353, 379, 499, 615,
617
Lenoir, Henri, 593, 658, 682, 746, 764
Leroy, Sharon, 672, 723, 734, 804
Leslie, Albert, 140
Leslie, Hubert. *See* Hube the Cube
Lessing, Doris, 766
Lester, Richard, 253
Levertov, Denise, 303
Levin, Ira, 474
Levin, Martin, 230
Lewis, Clayton, 201, 202, 301
Lewis, Huey, 219
Lewis, Peter, 483, 547–552
Lewis, Sinclair, 241
Liddy, G. Gordon, 269, 540
Lind, Carol, 123
Link, Terry, 409
Lipset, Hal, 8
Lipsett, Cadence, 162, 168, 542, 545, 558
Lipsett, Shirley, 150, 162, 168, 174, 185
Lipsett, Tom, 150, 162, 168, 185
Lish, Gordon, 423
Little, Ron, 482, 483, 484, 486–487
Loading Zone, 286
Lockwood, Todd, 252
LoCoco, Anita, 643
Loewinsohn, Joan, 195
Loewinsohn, Joe, 168
Loewinsohn, Kitty, 300, 362, 446, 456, 519, 574,
578, 579, 595, 596, 613, 614, 656
Loewinsohn, Ron, 101, 114–117, 120, 122–126,
128, 130, 138, 140, 143, 145, 153–154, 161,
163, 168, 174, 179–180, 182–185, 187–188,
191–192, 194–199, 215, 216, 238, 254, 278,
284, 299–300, 303, 329, 362, 372, 395, 405,
407, 428, 446, 456, 513, 530, 547, 574, 578,
596–597, 603, 613–614, 656

Loewinsohn, Sue, 168
Loggins, Kenny, 318
London, Jack, 61, 90, 103, 118, 123, 262, 634, 766
Lopez, Ray, 176, 180
Lorca, Federico García, 118, 218
Lord Byron. *See* Byron, George Gordon
Loren, Sophia, 755
Lorraine, Lilith, 71, 87, 88, 90, 141
Lorre, Peter, 47
Louis XIV, 745
Lovecraft, H.P., 90
Lovin' Spoonful, 243, 288
Lowe, Ernest, 323, 324
Lowell, Robert, 197
Lowinsky, Simon, 521
Lucas, George, 525
Luce, William, 715
Lynch, Dennis, 651, 709–712, 721–722
Lynn, Loretta, 663

M

Mabou Mines, 375
MacDermott, Patricia, 383
Macdonald, Ross, 253
Mackintosh, Graham, 150, 200, 222, 234, 239,
240, 328, 341, 342, 668
Maclaine, Christopher, 166, 238
Mad Marie, 140
Mad River, 303, 304, 317, 318, 326, 327, 328,
341–343, 342, 355, 371, 403, 424
Magee, David, 285
Magee, Dorothy, 285
Magnolia Thunderpussy. *See* Mallon, Patricia
Magritte, Rene, 379
Maiakovski, Vladimir, 746
Mailer, John Buffalo, 687
Mailer, Norman, 19, 167, 245, 363, 502, 508,
686–688
Major, Clarence, 129
Malamud, Bernard, 663
Malley, Terence, 458, 740
Mallman, Jerome, 127
Mallon, Patricia, 18, 680–681
Malmsteen, Yngwie, 791
Mamas and Papas, 315
Mandel, William, 579, 596, 597
Manerude, Mrs., 55–56, 65–66, 466
Manning, Thomas, 302, 326
Manso, Peter, 19
Manson, Charles, 9, 283, 318, 463, 526
Manyluk, Dan, 765, 767–768
Mapplethorpe, Robert, 362
Marcelli, Lou, 284, 285, 347, 348, 810
Marcus, Greil, 399
Margolis, William J. (Bill), 154, 157
Marisol, 663
Marko, Zekial, 107, 116, 122, 124, 231, 253
Marley, Bob, 526, 646

Marquette, Richard Lawrence, 174
Márquez, Gabriel García, 634, 743
Marsh, Don, 520
Marsh, Joan, 520
Marshall, John, 479, 481, 482
Martin, Peter, 103
Marx, Groucho, 610
Marx, Harpo, 151
Marx Brothers, 726
Maschler, Tom, 371, 415
Masekela, Hugh, 317
Masters, Edgar Lee, 150, 361
Mathis, Johnny, 139
Mathison, Melissa, 574, 614
Matisse, Henri, 363
Matson, Peter, 245
Matthiessen, F.O., 11
Matthiessen, Peter, 663
Maupassant, Guy de, 266
Maybeck, Bernard, 149, 150
Mayerson, Charlotte, 270, 275
Maysle, Albert, 400
Maysle, David, 400
Maytag, Fritz, 344
Maytag, Ken, 343
Maytag, Missy, 356
McCabe, Charles, 436, 523
McCall, Cheryl, 681, 696, 698
McCartney, Paul, 355, 378–379, 617
McClanahan, Ed, 336, 365–366, 407, 434–435
McClure, Jane, 213, 214
McClure, Joanna, 104, 105, 106, 131–132, 186,
    211–214, 244, 306, 373–374
McClure, Michael, 6, 18–19, 102, 104–105, 106,
    107, 108–110, 112, 115, 117–118, 127, 131,
    132, 152, 158, 160, 163–165, 186, 196, 211–
    214, 216, 218, 220, 222, 238, 241, 244, 246,
    247, 262–263, 265, 267–268, 274–277, 281–
    282, 285, 297–298, 300–301, 303, 319, 320,
    322, 323, 324, 338, 340, 342–343, 344, 348,
    356, 372–374, 377, 380, 386, 406, 412, 420,
    439, 440, 445–447, 480, 501, 503, 508, 696
McCullough, Ken, 551
McCullough, Sam, 764, 798–799
McDonald, Joe, 236
McDonell, Terry, 15, 681
McGill, Frank A., 28
McGovern, Molly, 312
McGovern, Terry, 311–312
McGuane, Annie, 771
McGuane, Becky, 8, 11, 14, 17, 450, 452–456, 471,
    472, 476–477, 487, 525, 528, 529, 532, 539,
    544, 582, 600, 635, 653, 679, 680, 700, 708,
    719, 740, 751, 757, 770
McGuane, Laurie, 603, 770
McGuane, Thomas (Tom), 5, 11, 13, 15–16, 34,
    335, 356, 364–365, 406, 432–433, 449–456,
    459, 460, 466–473, 476–480, 485–487, 489,
    512, 525–529, 531, 540, 544, 546, 549–552,
    603, 681, 688, 730, 737–739, 766, 770–774

McKee, Elizabeth, 243, 245
McKenzie, Scott, 315
McKibbon, Mike, 307
McKuen, Rod, 411, 503
McLellan, Joseph, 503
McLuhan, Marshall, 291
McMurtry, Larry, 431
McNeill, Bill, 234, 238, 275
McPherson, Aimee Semple, 142
McQueen, Steve, 320
Mead, Margaret, 686
Medel, Ronald, 54
Médicis, Marie de, 747
Meissner, Janice, 219, 224–227, 229, 232, 234,
    237–238, 240, 242, 244–245, 247–249, 251–
    254, 268, 274, 371
Meleager, 498
Mellard, James M., 709, 711
Melnick, Norman, 13
Meltzer, David, 117, 127–128, 153, 163, 165, 188,
    247, 284, 294, 303, 343–344, 366, 422, 423,
    441, 442, 445, 446
Meltzer, Tina, 441, 442, 445
Melville, Herman, 461
Mercer, Johnny, 360
Mergen, Barney, 97–99, 100, 101, 345
Merrick, Doug, 480
Merritt, Vernon, 411
Merry Pranksters, 236, 248, 249, 262, 270, 274,
    289, 629
Merton, Thomas, 729
Merwin, W.S., 668
Meyer, Helen, 620
Meyers, Marsha, 57
Michaels, Lorne, 528
Michaux, Henri, 743
Micheline, Jack, 438, 439
Mifune, Toshiro, 210
Miles, Barry, 351, 354–355, 356, 367, 368, 378,
    379, 380, 381
Miles, Josephine, 116, 127, 347, 350, 372, 393
Milford, Penelope (Penny), 462, 495
Millay, Edna St. Vincent, 93
Miller, Aaron, 112
Miller, Arthur, 218, 361
Miller, Bob, 167, 196, 201
Miller, Chuck, 330
Miller, Cincinnatus Hiner. See Miller, Joaquin
Miller, Henry, 127, 131, 165, 186, 322, 379
Miller, Joaquin, 103, 262
Miller, Peter, 138, 395–397, 404, 406–407, 466,
    467, 468, 473, 479, 481–482, 483, 484–485,
    487
Miller, Stanley (Mouse), 270, 285, 290, 294, 295
Miller, Steve, 299, 317, 318
Mills, Robert P., 273, 275, 276, 277, 278, 292,
    320, 329, 330, 331, 340, 381–382
Milo, 781, 782
Milton, John, 634
Min, 494, 495

Mina, Mina, 674, 703, 704
Mina, Rosalyn (Roz), 672–674, 680, 681, 692–693,
    701, 702, 703, 704
Minault, Kent, 269, 274
Minor, Wendell, 491, 499, 507
Mishima, Yukio, 498, 568–569, 671
Mitchell, Joni, 385, 575
Mitchum, Robert, 641
Mitford, Jessica, 432
Modigliani, Amedeo, 745
Moebius, 304
Molière, 745
Moline, Allen, 713
Mondale, Joan, 663
Monier, Louis, 747
Montaigne, Michel Eyquem de, 436
Montgomery, John, 158
Montgomery, Stuart, 418
Mooney, Tom, 436
Moonshine Bess. See Dixon, Bessie
Moore, Wayne, 668
Morgan, Althea Susan, 288, 289, 298, 299, 300,
    301, 304, 316
Morgan, Dennis, 38
Mori, Tom, 606, 629, 758
Morisette, William, 22
Morning Glory, 304, 378
Morrill, Bob, 345
Morrison, Jim, 372, 745
Moscoso, Dana, 348
Moscoso, Gail, 267
Moscoso, Victor, 267–268, 295, 342, 348, 375,
    376
Mother McCree's Uptown Jug Stompers, 248
Mount, Thom, 496, 748, 782
Mountain Girl, 249
Mouse. See Miller, Stanley (Mouse)
Muggeridge, Malcolm, 230
Muir, Kenneth, 358
Mulholland, Kate, 240
Mungo, Raymond, 466, 542
Murakami, Ryū, 574, 575, 587, 591
Murao, Shigeyoshi, 126, 132, 158, 247, 443, 444,
    648
Murcott, Billy, 269, 271–272, 291
Murphy, Cindy, 489, 490
Murphy, Dennis, 132, 133
Murphy, Dick, 489, 490
Murphy, Michael, 794
Musser, Sandra G., 654, 655, 657, 658, 659, 660,
    765
Mystery Trend, 248

N

Nagano, Ken, 730–731
Najarian, Peter, 535
Nakai, Keisuke, 611
Nakamura, Katsuya, 563
Nash, John, 418

Nathan, Mike, 121, 124, 229
Natural Suzanne, 349
Neal, Duane, 450
Neiss, Roger, 151
Nelson, Alix, 370
Nelson, Craig, 507
Nelson, Willie, 663
Nerval, Gérard de, 254
Neutze, Leonard, 622
New Age, 304
Newman, Barnett, 416–417
Newman, Charles, 215, 216, 218, 221, 222, 223,
    224, 225, 226, 229, 230, 237, 238, 268, 326
Newton, Huey P., 615
Ney, Michel, 745
Nichols, Luther, 126, 183, 189, 190, 223, 327, 331,
    340, 350–351
Nicholson, Jack, 492, 493, 496, 526, 537, 554,
    555, 757
Nicol, Duncan, 103
Nijinsky, Vasily, 138
Nishiyama, Yuri, 387, 389, 592
Nishizawa, Akiko. See Sakagami, Akiko (Aki)
Nishizawa, Fusako, 596, 608, 609, 610, 629, 641
Nixon, Richard M., 155, 172, 353, 400, 700
Noel, Fran, 728
Nord, Eric (Big Daddy), 18, 158
Norman, Geoffrey (Geoff), 517
Norman, Gurney, 365, 434, 435
Norris, Charles, 103
Norris, Frank, 103
Norris, Kathleen, 103
Norse, Harold, 197
Norton, Joshua A., 261, 263
Nosaka, Akiyuki (Claude), 644–645, 794
Noteboom, Dr. Dennis, 467, 470, 485, 681, 728
Nugent, Jack, 106
Nyro, Laura, 317

O

Oates, Warren, 480, 528, 544, 607, 664
Ochs, Phil, 380
O'Connor, Flannery, 243, 434, 634
Odasso, Christian, 475
Odier, Daniel, 751
Oe, Hikari, 611
Oe, Kenzaburo, 610, 611–612
O'Faolain, Sean, 358
Oh, Sadaharu, 595
O'Hara, J.D., 406
O'Hara, John, 253
Ohnemus, Günter, 736, 748, 783, 784
Okamura, Arthur, 5, 796–797, 803, 807
Okamura, Simone. See Ellis, Simone
O'Keeffe, Georgia, 359, 360
Oldenberg, Claes, 361
Olsen, Tillie, 628, 650
Olson, Charles, 118, 127, 128, 150, 198, 200, 239,
    357, 364, 374, 379, 463, 701

Olson, Cindy, 632, 677, 694, 695
Olson, Tom, 632, 694, 695
Ondaatje, Michael, 663
O'Neill, Jim, 9
Ono, Yoko, 353, 379, 615
Orkustra, 283, 296, 299, 328
Orlovsky, Lafcadio, 106, 247
Orlovsky, Peter, 106, 108, 115, 127, 132, 154, 163, 244, 247, 284–285
Orwell, George, 786
Osaki, George, 360, 368
Osborn, Robert, 382
Osterday, Mary, 617
O'Sullivan, Paddy, 112
Oswald, Lee Harvey, 202
Oswald, Stan, 54, 65
Otogawa, Kobun Chino, 588, 589, 590
Ozick, Cynthia, 458
Ozu, Yasujiro, 757

P

Pacaud, Marcia, 259, 319, 320, 321, 323, 324, 325, 330, 342, 345, 350, 356, 362, 363, 377
Pacino, Al, 537
Page, Geraldine, 394, 433
Page, Patti, 54
Page, Tim, 626
Painter, Charlotte, 335
Palance, Jack, 47, 231
Palladino, Jayne, 407, 413, 428, 442, 444, 463–465, 470–471, 474–475, 478, 481, 515
Palmer, Scott, 452, 477, 485, 486
Pancoast, Edwin, 783
Park, David, 104
Park, James, 230, 231
Parker, Dorothy, 558
Parker, Pam (Flame), 292
Parkinson, Ariel, 190, 229
Parkinson, Thomas (Tom), 190, 197, 198, 229, 230, 234, 241, 285, 330, 338, 372, 463
Parkman, Francis, 292
Parsons, Alfred B., 441, 442, 445
Parsons, Mary Elizabeth, 6, 441, 442, 457
Partch, Harry, 164
Parton, Dolly, 522, 641
Passaro, Al, 400
Patchen, Kenneth, 124, 218, 344, 379, 406, 593
Patchen, Miriam, 124
Paterson, Paul, 66
Peace, 396
Pearl. See Joplin, Janis
Peckinpah, Deneen, 240
Peckinpah, Sam, 240, 478, 544, 767
Pelieu, Claude, 362, 363
Penn, Arthur, 478, 526
Pennebaker, Donn, 317
Pepiot, Vida, 76
Percy, Walker, 357, 429
Perelman, S.J., 686

Perry, Charles, 270, 295
Perry, Frank, 480
Perry, Ginger, 666, 673
Perry, Matthew, 735
Persky, Stan, 122, 188, 194–195, 240, 247
Peter and Gordon, 379
Peterson, Clarence, 427
Phelps, William H., 623
Phillips, John, 315, 317
Piaf, Edith, 745
Picasso, Pablo, 744
Pickins, Slim, 480
Pig Pen, 296
Pink Lady, 628
Pinter, Harold, 218
Pisanni, George, 27, 28
Pisanni, Johnny, 27, 28, 32
Plath, Sylvia, 651
Platt, John, 304
Plimpton, George, 347, 351
Plymell, Charles, 238, 342, 363
Poco, 366
Poe, Edgar Allan, 744
Poindexter, Norwood (Pony), 139
Pointer Sisters, 575
Poirier, Richard, 244
Polk, Willis, 681
Ponicsan, Darryl, 689
Pope, Alexader, 287
Porter, Arabel, 204
Porter, Katherine Anne, 358
Porterfield, Barbara. See Titland, Barbara Jo
Porterfield, Robert Geoffry (Tex), 36, 37, 38, 39–40, 181, 538, 608
Porterfield, Sandra Jean (Sandi), 37, 39, 43, 48–49, 50–51, 55, 56, 84, 91, 413, 544, 552
Pound, Ezra, 165, 289, 352
Powers, Allen, 416, 417
Powers, Gary Francis, 436
Preminger, Otto, 343
Price, Frank, 496, 782
Primack, Ron, 194
Proust, Marcel, 745
Puzo, Mario, 630, 780

Q

Quaid, Randy, 526
Quicksilver Messenger Service, 267, 285, 286, 303, 318

R

Rades, Jane, 254
Rafelson, Bob, 616
Ragne, Gerome, 362
Rago, Henry, 218
Rahv, Philip, 230
Rand, Annie, 393
Rand, Christopher, 281–282

Rand, Kendrick, 281, 282, 325, 326, 332, 341, 348, 350, 356, 393, 409, 410, 426, 621, 797, 806
Rattlesnake Dick. *See* Dillof, Richard (Dobro Dick)
Raw Violet, 317
Ray, Gordon, 347
Ray, Johnnie, 54
Reagan, Ronald, 274, 276
Rechy, John, 216
Red Baron. *See* Von Richthofen, Baron
Red Fred, 112, 140
Redding, Otis, 317
Redford, Robert, 700
Reed, Ishmael, 327, 372, 424, 472, 628
Reed, J.D., 363, 364, 450, 473
Reich, Steve, 424
Remington, Deborah, 104, 113
Resnikoff, H'lane, 290, 298
Ressmeyer, Roger, 696, 712–713
Rexroth, Kenneth, 103–110, 114–115, 126–127, 132, 193, 197, 216, 422
Reynolds, Frank (Freewheelin' Frank), 274, 276, 277, 285, 297, 300, 303, 348
Rice, Anne, 308
Rice, Fred, 685
Rice, Stan, 308
Richards, Charles, 108
Richards, Dave, 354
Richie, Donald, 757
Rijn, Rembrandt van, 690, 787, 791
Rimbaud, Arthur, 123, 144, 176, 743
Ritter, John, 754, 755
Rivera, Diego, 103
Rivers, Larry, 223, 345, 361
Robbins, Tom, 350, 351, 628, 684
Roberts, Flora, 474, 478, 493, 495
Robertson, Frank, 622
Robillard, Alexander, 231
Robinson, David, 302, 326, 341, 343
Robinson, Grace, 101
Rodgers, W.R. (Bertie), 286
Roeg, Nicholas, 554, 555, 574
Roesgen, Susy, 714
Rogers, Cathy, 481
Rogers, Michael, 500
Rogers, Roxie, 452
Roiter, Margaret, 717
Rollin, Gabrielle, 744
Rolling Stones, 398, 400
Ronstadt, Linda, 342, 574, 651
Rose, Stefanie, 604
Rosen, Sue. *See* Loewinsohn, Sue
Rosenberg, Carl, 305
Rosenberg, Harold, 202
Rosenthal, Irving, 344
Rosenthal, Lester, 122, 123, 124, 179
Rosset, Barney, 204, 205, 242, 268, 322, 620
Rossini, Gioachino Antonio, 745
Rothberg, Gerald, 234
Rothko, Mark, 104
Rowland, Jada, 462

Ruby, Jack, 202
Rukeyser, Muriel, 303
Rumi, 351
Ruska, Willem, 573
Russell, Theresa, 554
Russo, Anthony (Tony), 10, 13, 14, 16–17
Ryan, John Allen, 104, 109, 113, 114, 115, 129
Ryan, Patricia, 473

S

Sabol, Audrey, 370
Saijo, Albert, 157–158, 285, 302
Saint-Exupéry, Antoine de, 743
Sakagami, Akiko (Aki), 17, 95, 260, 581–589, 591, 593–600, 602–603, 605–611, 613–615, 618–619, 621–622, 624, 626–627, 629–633, 635–639, 641–643, 646–649, 654–663, 670–671, 676–678, 680, 689, 692, 701, 738, 762, 765, 767, 773, 808–811
Sakata, James (Jimmy), 16–19, 647, 658, 757, 796, 803–804, 810, 812
Sale, Roger, 492
Sales, Grover, 209, 215
Sales, Tommy, 209, 229
Salinger, J.D., 576, 606
Saltoon, Donna, 627
San Francisco Mime Troupe, 245, 246, 248, 263, 264–265, 269, 271, 274, 276, 293–294, 299, 305, 375
Sanchez, Thomas, 308, 628
Sandberg, David, 273, 278, 283
Sanders, Ed, 245, 363, 668
Santana, 399
Santana, Carlos, 410
Sappho, 124, 420
Saroyan, Aram, 363
Saroyan, William, 118, 119, 123, 229, 275, 363, 663, 732
Sartre, Jean-Paul, 743
Savitt, Beverly, 658, 663
Savoca, Anna, 198–199, 200, 201–202, 301
Scaggs, Boz, 432
Schaff, David, 254, 284, 356, 374
Schlage, Walter, 224
Schmidt, Carol, 716
Schmitt, Harrison, 462
Schneck, Stephen, 250, 308, 331, 350, 353, 372, 374, 380
Schoenfeld, Dr. Eugene (Dr. Hip), 553
Schorer, Mark, 126
Schrader, Leonard, 591
Schrader, Paul, 494, 591, 726
Schrieber, David, 628, 637, 716, 726, 765, 767, 776, 801
Schroeder, Barbet, 631
Schultz, Charles, 427, 612
Schultz, Lee, 769
Schwarzenegger, Arnold, 616
Schwiebert, Ernest G., Jr., 174

Scorsese, Martin, 591

Scott, Ridley, 734, 748

Sears, Loren, 324

Seastone, Leonard, 631, 649

Seaver, Richard (Dick), 191, 196, 200, 202, 204, 205, 209, 210, 223

Seberg, Jean, 742

Sedgwick, Joe, 699, 721

Sellers, Peter, 496

Serkin, Wendy, 666

Service, Robert W., 34

Sexton, Anne, 347

Sexton, Woody, 451

Shahn, Ben, 121

Shakespeare, William, 93, 606, 627, 634, 667

Shankar, Ravi, 317

Shaw, Irwin, 351

Shawn, Joel, 8, 14, 660, 663, 692, 701, 703, 705, 729, 738, 756–758, 765

Shea, Edmund, 257, 324–325, 329, 340, 344, 360, 371–373, 375–378, 380–382, 384–386, 389, 392, 395, 398, 401, 424–425, 428, 443, 701, 702

Sheen, Martin, 376

Sheets, Kermit, 164

Shelley, Harriet, 162

Shelley, John, 265

Shelley, Mary, 744

Shelley, Percy Bysshe, 162, 634

Sheppard, Jeffrey (Jeff), 278, 283, 303, 316

Sherman, Jory, 158, 163, 185, 186, 242

Sherman, Leander, 627

Sherman, Ori, 256, 266

Sherrill, Robert, 230, 232, 233, 234, 241, 242, 244, 274, 276

Sherrod, Tony, 195

Shields, Frances, 41

Shiina, Takako, 390, 548, 549, 564, 565, 568–571, 573–576, 579, 581, 586, 589, 591, 611–612, 641–643, 650, 736, 739, 751–753, 756, 759, 761, 763–764, 775, 788, 790–791, 794–795

Shoemaker, Jack, 288–289, 316, 317, 321, 328, 330, 340, 341, 356, 410–411, 422, 425, 427–428

Shoemaker, Vicki, 288–289, 316, 321, 328

Shorthill, David, 484

Shorty, 174

Shostakovich, Dmitri, 194

Shrimpton, Jean, 416

Shuster, Rosie, 528–529

Sibbern, Glenise, 493, 614, 649, 710

Siegel, Don, 394, 699

Signoret, Simone, 152

Silver, Joel, 370

Silverstein, Shel, 493

Simmons, Kathy, 657

Simpson, David, 104, 318

Simpson, Louis, 347

Sinatra, Frank, 508

Singer, James M., 129

Siodmak, Curt, 47

Skinner, Eugene, 38

Slade, Bob, 349

Slattery, Pat, 370

Slick, Grace, 248

Slovick, Eddie, 40

Smith, Alice, 78

Smith, Burton W., 36

Smith, Clark Ashton, 90

Smith, Claude E., 100, 101

Smith, D. Vincent, 87, 111

Smith, Dr. David, 299

Smith, Dr. James E., 12, 16, 677

Smith, Lorna, 52

Smith, Lydia, 69

Smith, Margarita G., 68

Smith, Patti, 362

Smith, William, 82, 83

Snodgrass, W.D., 218

Snyder, Gary, 107–110, 114, 127, 138, 144, 147–148, 150, 158, 161, 163, 167, 190, 195, 197, 210, 218, 229, 238–239, 282, 284–286, 302, 343, 349, 357, 366, 402–403, 410, 420, 424, 428, 562, 573, 600–601, 618, 651

Snyder, Kai, 282

Snyder, Richard, 418, 491

Socrates, 117, 757

Solomon, Carl, 106, 108, 109

Sondheim, Stephen, 474

Sons of Champlin, 317

Sopwith Camel, 265, 322

Sorenson, Rex, 54, 425

Sorrentino, Gilbert, 196, 238, 344, 345

Spaceman. *See* Fenu, John

Spectorsky, A.C., 292

Spender, Stephen, 218

Spicer, Jack, 104, 109, 112, 116–118, 120, 126–130, 138, 140, 143–144, 148, 150, 153, 155, 159–161, 163, 165, 170, 173, 183–185, 188, 190, 193–195, 200, 203, 211, 218, 222, 228, 234, 237, 239–241, 266, 329, 340, 436, 472

Spielberg, Steven, 786

Spike, Robert W., 144

Spillane, Mickey, 68

Spock, Dr. Benjamin, 303

Spring, Ellen Valentine, 323, 324

Sōseki, Natsume, 500

St. James, Margo, 18, 322

St. Jim, Jim, 196

Stafford, Jean, 406

Stafford, William, 218, 393, 619

Stair, Sandra J. *See* Porterfield, Sandra Jean (Sandi)

Stalin, Joseph, 633

Stanley, Augustus Owsley, III, 243, 248, 267, 286, 291, 399

Stanley, George, 117, 127, 128, 144, 147, 148, 161, 163, 194, 195, 234, 284

Stanley Mouse. *See* Miller, Stanley (Mouse)

Stanton, Harry Dean, 480, 485, 486, 487, 492, 496, 520, 526–527, 537, 548, 552, 575, 605, 772

Stanwood, Susan, 215, 218, 221, 223, 234
Stark, Pete, 432
Starkweather, Charlie, 139
Starr, Ringo, 211
Steger, Pat, 655
Stegner, Wallace, 335, 336, 337, 364, 535, 628
Steig, Walter, 382
Steiger, Rod, 132
Stein, Ben, 448–449, 728
Stein, David, 728
Stein, Gertrude, 229, 291, 745
Steinbeck, John, 189, 628
Sterling, George, 90, 102, 103, 262
Stermer, Dugald, 444
Stern, Isaac, 585
Steve Miller Blues Band, 299, 317, 318
Stevenot, Barden (Bart), 347
Stevens, Carol, 687
Stevens, Gail, 311, 502, 526, 527, 531, 532, 555,
    562, 563, 570, 572, 573
Stevens, George, 757
Stevens, Roger L., 347
Stevens, Wallace, 99, 287, 688
Stevenson, Mrs. Robert Louis, 681
Stevenson, Robert Louis, 102, 103
Stewart, Gary, 42, 44–46, 48, 53, 61, 74, 77–81,
    89, 91
Stewart, Milo, 42, 94, 97
Stickney, John, 396, 397, 411
Stiles, Knute, 112–113, 234
Still, Clyfford, 104
Stock, Robert, 115, 116, 129
Stoddard, Charles Warren, 103
Stone, Alan, 356
Stone Poneys, 342
Storrs, Anthony (Antonio), 356
Story, Eileen, 582
Story, Polly, 559
Stravinsky, Igor, 104
Streisand, Barbra, 580
Stroud, Joe, 283
Stryk, Lucien, 651
Styron, William, 243
Sugiyama, Yoko, 569
Sukenick, Ron, 665
Sullivan, Sir Arthur, 106
Sullivan, Vernon. See Vian, Boris
Sumac, Yma, 49
Sunday, Billy, 666
Super Spade, 299, 322
Sutherland, Jack, 129
Suzuki, Shunryu, 285, 588
Suzuki, Tomi, 500
Swaim, Bob, 11
Swami Bhaktivedanta, 291
Swanson, H.N. (Swanee), 253, 287
Swearingen, Bud, 542, 722, 723
Sweet William. See Fritsch, William (Bill)
Sweet Willie Tumbleweed. See Fritsch,
    William (Bill)

Swensen, Ianthe. See Brautigan, Ianthe
Swensen, Paul, 13, 687, 698–700, 780, 797
Swigart, Rob, 508
Swindlehurst, Carolyn, 467
Swindlehurst, Joseph (Joe), 8, 14, 467, 512, 541,
    757, 769

T
Tagawa, Tadusu, 569, 570
Taliano, Charles, 687
Tallman, Ellen, 240, 374
Tallman, Warren, 221, 240, 374
Tanikawa, Shuntarō, 612, 629, 642–643, 751, 757
Tanizaki, Jun'chirō, 498, 588
Tanner, Tony, 406
Targ, William, 630, 631, 639, 649, 655, 657
Tate, Myrtle, 375, 376
Tate, Yancey S., 375
Tayama, Katai, 500
Taylor, Elizabeth, 416
Taylor, Harry, 88
Terayama, Shōji, 750–751, 755, 782
Thelin, Jay, 265, 286, 294, 307, 321, 330
Thelin, Ron, 265, 269, 286, 294, 307, 321, 330
Thibeau, Jack, 200, 237–239, 273, 284, 375–376,
    391, 515, 554, 555, 567–568, 592–593, 603,
    650, 651
Thomas, Agnes, 125
Thomas, Dylan, 99, 115, 193, 361, 686
Thomas, John, 663
Thomas, Stephen C., 125
Thomas, William, 10, 11
Thompson, Bill, 682, 685
Thompson, Toby, 6, 544–546, 550–553, 672,
    676–677, 768–771, 773–775, 792
Thomson, Virgil, 361
Thoreau, Henry David, 176, 362, 396, 406
Thorne, Evelyn, 77, 87
Time, 348
Tiny Tim, 262
Titland, Arthur Martin, 32
Titland, Barbara Jo, 32, 34, 36, 37, 39, 41, 42, 43,
    47, 52, 53, 55
Toad the Mime, 432
Tolkien, J.R.R., 253, 743
Torme, Mel, 523
Torn, Jon, 699, 700
Torn, Rip, 322, 323, 326, 394–395, 404, 407–409,
    433, 493, 608, 699–700, 721–723
Torn, Tony, 699, 700
Tourneur, Jacques, 726
Toyotomi, Hideyoshi, 569
Tracy, Spencer, 178
Travis, Weldon, 10
Traynor, Bill, 796
Tree, Alicia, 142
Treloar, Raymond Forrest, 231
Tresca, Carlos, 103
Trevira, Russ, 803

Truman, Harry S., 341
Trungpa, Chögyam, 665, 668, 729
Tsuno, Kaitaro, 563, 564
Turgeon, Edgar Lynn, 679, 686
Turner, Florence, 362
Turner, J.M.W., 417
Turner, Ron, 443, 444
Tuttle, Lyle, 300
Twain, Mark, 19, 52, 61, 102–103, 186, 201, 323, 361, 373, 454, 508, 552, 743

U

Udall, Mo, 663
Ueno, Hidesaburō, 589
Ulerick, Sarah, 396–397
Ultra Violet, 404
Underground Railroad, 317
Updike, John, 663
Urayama, Kirio, 612

V

Valdène, Guy de la, 451, 452, 454, 469, 470, 471, 472, 473, 475, 476, 477, 478, 479, 503, 517–518, 522, 527–530, 548–549, 553, 681
Valdène, Terry de la, 452, 475, 527, 528, 529, 530, 548, 681
Vale, V. (Valhalla), 354
Van Aelstyn, Ed, 250
Van Meter, Ben, 283, 321, 328
Van Ronk, Dave, 153
Vega, Janine Pommy, 308
Venet, Nik, 342, 343
Verdon, Gwen, 780
Vetter, Blaine, 421
Vetter, Sherry, 212, 257, 385–388, 389, 402, 419–421, 425–427, 429–432, 434, 435, 439–446, 452, 454–458, 460, 497–498, 517, 536–537, 592, 687, 704, 713, 721, 725
Vian, Boris, 741, 742, 745
Vibbert, Spencer, 688
Victor, Ed, 371, 415
Victoria. *See* Domagalski, Victoria
Viva Superstar, 404
Voigt, Jon, 495
Von Richthofen, Baron, 721–722
Vonnegut, Kurt, Jr., 358–359, 422, 484, 499, 503

W

Wada, Fumio, 598, 603, 635, 636, 637, 648
Wada, Mieko, 598, 603, 635, 636, 637, 648
Wagner, Durrett, 543
Waits, Tom, 575
Wakefield, Dan, 406, 503
Wakoski, Diane, 197
Waldman, Anne, 361, 372, 665, 668
Walker, Jayne. *See* Palladino, Jayne
Walker, Madge, 582

Wallace, Tom, 200
Walsh, Jim, 322
Wang, Arthur, 250
Warhol, Andy, 324, 361, 404, 416
Warlocks, 247, 248
Warren, Robert Penn, 458
Warsh, Lewis, 238, 239, 361
Washington, Horace W., 93
Waterston, Sam, 480, 485, 487
Watkins, Bob, 480, 588, 589, 600
Wavy Gravy, 262
Wax, Mel, 216
Wayne, John, 511
Weaver, Ken, 379
Webb, Charles, 243
Weber, Avril, 244, 352, 440
Weber, Erik, 200–204, 206–208, 228–229, 232–233, 237, 244, 246, 256, 259, 262, 266, 268, 273, 278–279, 299–302, 305, 320, 323–324, 327, 329, 332, 352–353, 382, 385, 388–389, 395, 400, 404–405, 422–424, 440, 446, 448, 451–455, 499, 503, 506, 507, 542, 592, 595–596, 607, 621–622, 654, 713, 730
Weber, Lois (Loie), 200, 201, 232, 244, 246, 256, 257, 258, 262, 266, 283, 284, 301, 320, 323, 353, 385, 404–405, 406, 413, 422–424, 431, 440, 459, 463, 468, 499, 504–505, 542–543
Weber, Selina, 424
Webster, Edna, 22, 69–95, 111, 323, 453, 543
Webster, Linda, 69, 70, 71, 73–74, 76–80, 82, 83–84, 88, 90, 251, 313, 314, 762
Webster, Lorna, 69, 70, 313
Webster, Peter, 46, 47, 51, 55, 57, 61, 65–69, 71–72, 82–83, 91, 682
Wedekind, Frank, 237
Weir, Tom, 305
Weiss, Susan Lee, 713
Welch, Lew, 23, 107, 116–117, 139, 148, 155, 158, 163, 186, 190, 196, 199, 215, 218–220, 238, 247, 258, 266, 281, 284, 302–303, 306, 319, 322, 344, 348–349, 354, 366, 370–372, 374, 399, 401–403, 411, 420–423, 428–429, 525
Welles, Orson, 310, 712
Welty, Eudora, 123, 197
Wenders, Wim, 632, 659
Wenner, Jann, 290, 294, 330, 353, 369, 393, 423, 616
Wernham, Guy, 106
Wertmüller, Lina, 524
Wesker, Arnold, 564
West, Jessamyn, 393
Weston, Doug, 575
Wexler, Haskell, 341
Wexner, V.I., 604, 605–606, 617, 622
Whalen, Philip, 107–110, 114, 116, 127, 138–139, 148, 152, 158–159, 161, 163, 167, 186, 196, 209, 218–220, 222, 224, 232, 250, 275, 303, 343, 344, 411, 420, 504, 573, 651
Whistler, James Abbott McNeill, 417
White, Emil, 131

White, Ralph, 767
White Hawk, Phil, 693
Whitman, Walt, 98, 117, 129, 176, 354, 420, 630, 808
Who, 317
Wical, Art, 46, 51, 54, 59–60
Wical, Charles, 46, 51, 54, 59–60
Wickenden, Dan, 278
Wicks, Jerry, 46
Wicks, John, 46
Wieners, John, 117, 128, 163, 165, 344
Wilbur, Richard, 197
Wilde, Oscar, 745
Wildflower, 270
William, Cole, 500
Williams, Ace W., 125
Williams, Cecil, 293
Williams, Hank, 466, 493, 616
Williams, Jonathan, 411
Williams, Lucinda, 143
Williams, Miller, 143
Williams, Tennessee, 361, 616
Williams, William Carlos, 98, 107, 406, 481, 634
Willner, Phyllis, 277
Wilson, Adrian, 164
Wilson, Joe, 668
Wilson, Lawrence, 231
Wilson, S. Clay, 342
Wilson, Wes, 294, 304
Winstanley, Gerrard, 264, 269
Witt-Diamant, Ruth, 104, 108, 110
Wittliff, Bill, 419, 420, 424, 431
Wittliff, Sally, 424
Wizard, 328
Wohl, Barbara, 265
Wolf, Leonard, 190
Wolfe, Thomas, 361
Wolfe, Tom, 289–290, 757
Wolman, Baron, 331, 399
Wonder, John, 680
Wood, Caroline, 61
Woods, William, 617

Wreden, William P., 344
Wright, Charles, 424
Wright, Frank Lloyd, 563
Wright, Lawrence, 19, 498, 608
Wroth, Will, 250
Wurlitzer, Rudolph, 431

Y

Yamaguchi, Eiichi, 759–761, 775
Yanger, Frank, 606
Yanoff, Lenore, 122
Yardley, Jonathan, 427
Yasuhara, Akiro, 630
Yates, Richard, 358
Ydra, 133, 134, 194
Yeats, William Butler, 289, 668, 670, 678, 679, 737
Yee, Men, 524
York, Mike, 802
Yoshimura, Akiko. *See* Sakagami, Akiko (Aki)
Yoshimura, Hiroshi, 610, 613, 629
Yoshimura, Yoko, 613, 629
Yoshiyuki, Eisuki, 587
Yoshiyuki, Junnosuke, 587, 588
Yougrau, Barry, 689
Young, Al, 335
Young, Klyde, 7–8, 538, 562, 735, 785, 803, 805–808
Young, Neil, 575
Youngbloods, 371

Z

Zangari, Michael, 684–685
Zappa, Frank, 256, 380
Zapruder, Abraham, 202
Zeno, Jim, 3, 7, 10–11, 796–797, 800, 808
Zeno, Karly, 3, 7, 9, 10–11, 796–797, 800, 808
Zevon, Warren, 770–771
Zimmerman, Robert, 244
Zuno, Mr., 739

acknowledgments

TWO DECADES IS a long time to spend on a single project. At the end of the journey, I want to thank all those who shared their memories with me. I'm in debt to everyone who agreed to be interviewed. It's sad to tally how many have been lost along the way. The list is twenty-years long, and many who generously gave their time are no longer here to receive my appreciation. In my heart, I'll be forever grateful to them all.

Special thanks are due to those without whose help this book would never have been finished.

Ted Latty's archive of original Brautigan material filled many of the gaps in Richard's life story. Almost everything not housed in the Bancroft Library at U.C. Berkeley can be found in Latty's collection. While making this material available, Ted welcomed me as a guest in his home, let me use his office copying machine, and expedited much of the transcription that the project required. Words aren't sufficient for the thanks I owe him.

Tim Cahill, a friend and fellow writer who lives about two blocks away in Livingston, Montana, began researching his own Brautigan biography soon after Richard died. By the time Tim decided life was too short for such a project, he'd conducted more than two dozen interviews and very generously turned his tapes and transcriptions, along with copies of Seymour Lawrence's and Helen Brann's office files, over to me. Without this material I would have been lost. Several of Cahill's subjects had second thoughts about talking on the record by the time I became involved. Thanks, Tim.

Dr. John F. Barber has maintained an interest in Richard Brautigan since being his student at Montana State University in 1982. Barber published the first unique Brautigan bibliography in 1990. He spent years creating the www.brautigan.net website, a true labor of love. John has long been an enthusiastic supporter of this biography, and we've traded information about Richard for more than a decade. His help has been invaluable.

Anthony Bliss, Curator of Rare Books and Literary Manuscripts at the Bancroft Library, always provided expert guidance and kind assistance during my many long hours of archival research, an endeavor spanning almost a decade. Close to the end, I needed to verify certain exact quotes, and a trip from Livingston to Berkeley wasn't feasible. Tony rolled up his sleeves and did the work for me. I'm forever grateful.

Greg Keeler and Keith Abbott are friends and fellow writers who have both published memoirs about Richard Brautigan. They have been very generous with their time, always willing to answer my questions and supply useful information. Greg additionally has allowed me to use several photographs and images from his personal collection. A thousand thanks, guys.

Valerie Estes and Masako Kano, two of the many women in Brautigan's life that I interviewed, became friends and constant correspondents. Masako provided translations from the Japanese whenever needed. I'm indebted to both for their candor and insightful observation. If gratitude were flowers, I'd be sending them each a huge bouquet.

Greg Miller is another passionate Richard Brautigan fan and collector. We've never met, yet he generously copied material from his archive for my use and supplied a previously unpublished photograph of Richard, which is reproduced in this book. Thanks, Greg.

Samantha Childs was still in high school when I asked her to photocopy Donald Allen's correspondence (regarding Richard Brautigan) archived at the University of California San Diego. She's working on her master's degree thesis now. Thanks, Sam, for saving me a trip to SoCal.

Valerie Chazot earned my lasting appreciation for translating articles about Brautigan in the French media when my limited knowledge of her native tongue proved inadequate for the task. *Merci beaucoup*, Valerie.

Barbara Fitzhugh (Brautigan's sister) and her husband, Jim, not only granted numerous interviews but also fed me several times at their home. Thanks for the delicious meals and the gift of a railroad lantern, which has been a handy tool up at my cabin.

Ianthe Brautigan and her filmmaker husband, Paul Swensen, provided encouragement and advice from the moment I started writing the book. Ianthe's memoir about her father offered a view of Richard from a child's perspective, which proved very useful to me. I hope this biography lives up to their expectations.

Also, I'm extremely grateful to Erik Weber for both agreeing to be interviewed and permitting the use of eleven of his fine photographs in my biography. For almost two decades, Weber chronicled Brautigan's life on film, a powerful visual record of the writer's spectacular rise and inevitable fall. Thanks for your vision, Erik.

Some of the work needed for this book was done for hire. Nevertheless, excellence should be rewarded with something more than a paycheck, and I'd like to thank Warren Bittner of Ancestors Lost and Found in Centerville, Utah, for all the fine genealogical research, Gloria Thiede for her skilled transcription typing, and Gil Stober of Peak Recordings in Bozeman, Montana, for re-mastering a number of defective, inaudible interview tapes. Kudos also to Kelly Winton at Counterpoint for undertaking the thousands of nameless tasks involved in book production and Kirsten Janene-Nelson for a superlative job of freelance copyediting.

Finally, thanks must go out to two men without whose efforts and encouragement this biography might never have made it into print. My agent, Ben Camardi, never ceased believing in the project, even when everything seemed hopeless. Jack Shoemaker not only was a friend of Richard Brautigan and agreed to several interviews, but he is also the publisher of this book. I am deeply indebted to both of them for keeping the faith over all these years.

6/19/13 - STAINS ALONG EDGE NOTED (LB)